A COMPANION
TO
ANCIENT EPIC

BLACKWELL COMPANIONS TO THE ANCIENT WORLD

This series provides sophisticated and authoritative overviews of periods of ancient history, genres of classical literature, and the most important themes in ancient culture. Each volume comprises between twenty-five and forty concise essays written by individual scholars within their area of specialization. The essays are written in a clear, provocative, and lively manner, designed for an international audience of scholars, students, and general readers.

ANCIENT HISTORY

Published

A Companion to the Roman Army
Edited by Paul Erdkamp

A Companion to the Roman Republic
*Edited by Nathan Rosenstein and
Robert Morstein-Marx*

A Companion to the Roman Empire
Edited by David S. Potter

A Companion to the Classical Greek World
Edited by Konrad H. Kinzl

A Companion to the Ancient Near East
Edited by Daniel C. Snell

A Companion to the Hellenistic World
Edited by Andrew Erskine

A Companion to Late Antiquity
Edited by Philip Rousseau

In preparation

A Companion to Ancient History
Edited by Andrew Erskine

A Companion to Archaic Greece
Edited by Kurt A. Raaflaub and Hans van Wees

A Companion to Julius Caesar
Edited by Miriam Griffin

A Companion to Byzantium
Edited by Elizabeth James

A Companion to Ancient Macedonia
Edited by Ian Worthington and Joseph Roisman

A Companion to the Punic Wars
Edited by Dexter Hoyos

A Companion to Ancient Egypt
Edited by Alan Lloyd

A Companion to Sparta
Edidted by Anton Powell

LITERATURE AND CULTURE

Published

A Companion to Classical Receptions
Edited by Lorna Hardwick and Christopher Stray

A Companion to Greek and Roman Historiography
Edited by John Marincola

A Companion to Catullus
Edited by Marilyn B. Skinner

A Companion to Roman Religion
Edited by Jörg Rüpke

A Companion to Greek Religion
Edited by Daniel Ogden

A Companion to the Classical Tradition
Edited by Craig W. Kallendorf

A Companion to Roman Rhetoric
Edited by William Dominik and Jon Hall

A Companion to Greek Rhetoric
Edited by Ian Worthington

A Companion to Ancient Epic
Edited by John Miles Foley

A Companion to Greek Tragedy
Edited by Justina Gregory

A Companion to Latin Literature
Edited by Stephen Harrison

A Companion to Classical Studies
Edited by Kai Brodersen

In preparation

A Companion to Ancient Political Thought
Edited by Ryan K. Balot

A Companion to the Ancient Greek Language
Edited by Egbert Bakker

A Companion to Hellenistic Literature
Edited by Martine Cuypers and James J. Clauss

A Companion to Ovid
Edited by Peter Knox

A Companion to Horace
Edited by N. Gregson Davis

A Companion to Food in the Ancient World
Edited by John Wilkins

A Companion to the Latin Language
Edited by James Clackson

A Companion to Classical Mythology
Edited by Ken Dowden and Niall Livingstone

A Companion to Sophocles
Edited by Kirk Ormand

A Companion to Aeschylus
Edited by Peter Burian

A Companion to Vergil and the Vergilian Tradition
Edited by Michael Putnam and Joseph Farrell

A Companion to Greek Art
Edited by Tyler Jo Smith and Dimitris Plantzos

A Companion to Families in the Greek and Roman World
Edited by Beryl Rawson

A Companion to Tacitus
Edited by Victoria Pagán

A Companion to the Archaeology of the Ancient Near East
Edited by Daniel Potts

A COMPANION TO ANCIENT EPIC

Edited by

John Miles Foley

WILEY-BLACKWELL

A John Wiley & Sons, Ltd., Publication

This paperback edition first published 2009
© 2009 Blackwell Publishing Ltd
Edition history: Blackwell Publishing Ltd (hardback, 2005)

Blackwell Publishing was acquired by John Wiley & Sons in February 2007. Blackwell's publishing program has been merged with Wiley's global Scientific, Technical, and Medical business to form Wiley-Blackwell.

Registered Office
John Wiley & Sons Ltd, The Atrium, Southern Gate, Chichester, West Sussex, PO19 8SQ, United Kingdom

Editorial Offices
350 Main Street, Malden, MA 02148-5020, USA
9600 Garsington Road, Oxford, OX4 2DQ, UK
The Atrium, Southern Gate, Chichester, West Sussex, PO19 8SQ, UK

For details of our global editorial offices, for customer services, and for information about how to apply for permission to reuse the copyright material in this book please see our website at www.wiley.com/wiley-blackwell.

The right of John Miles Foley to be identified as the author of the editorial material in this work has been asserted in accordance with the Copyright, Designs and Patents Act 1988.

Wiley also publishes its books in a variety of electronic formats. Some content that appears in print may not be available in electronic books.

Designations used by companies to distinguish their products are often claimed as trademarks. All brand names and product names used in this book are trade names, service marks, trademarks or registered trademarks of their respective owners. The publisher is not associated with any product or vendor mentioned in this book. This publication is designed to provide accurate and authoritative information in regard to the subject matter covered. It is sold on the understanding that the publisher is not engaged in rendering professional services. If professional advice or other expert assistance is required, the services of a competent professional should be sought.

Library of Congress Cataloging-in-Publication Data

A companion to ancient epic/edited by John Miles Foley.
      p. cm. — (Blackwell companions to the ancient world. Literature and culture)
   Includes bibliographical references and index.
   ISBN 978-1-4051-0524-8 (alk. paper), ISBN 978-1-4051-8838-8 (pbk. : alk. Paper)
1. Epic poetry—History and criticism. 2. Epic literature—History and criticism.
3. Epic poetry, Classical—History and criticism. I. Foley, John Miles. II. Series.

PN1317.C66 2005
809.1′32—dc22

                                        2004018322

A catalogue record for this title is available from the British Library.

Set in 9.5 on 11pt Galliard
by SPi Publisher Services, Pondicherry, India
Printed in Singapore by C.O.S. Printers Pte Ltd

02   2009

Contents

Figures

Notes on Contributors

Richard Hamilton Armstrong is Associate Professor of Classical Studies at the University of Houston. He studied literary theory, classical and medieval literature at Yale University (MPhil., PhD), and his main interests lie in the reception of classical culture, the history of psychoanalysis, and translation studies. He is author of *Compulsion for Antiquity: Freud and the Ancient World* and is currently co-editing a volume of essays on the translation of classical poetry.

Michael H. Barnes is currently Visiting Assistant Professor of Classics at the University of Missouri, Columbia. He has held a postdoctoral fellowship at the Honors College of the University of Houston, and has contributed articles to *Oral Tradition* and the *Enzyklopädie des Märchens* in addition to serving as assistant editor of this *Companion to Ancient Epic*. His research interests include comparative epic poetry, particularly ancient Greek, and Hellenistic literature.

Shadi Bartsch is Professor in the Department of Classics and the Committee on the History of Culture at the University of Chicago. Her publications include *Decoding the Ancient Novel*; *Actors in the Audience*; *Ideology in Cold Blood*; and *The Mirror of the Self: Specularity, Sexuality, and Self-Knowledge in the Roman Empire* (forthcoming). She is also co-editor of the *Oxford Encyclopedia of Rhetoric* and *Erotikon: Essays on Eros, Ancient and Modern*.

Gary Beckman is Professor of Hittite and Mesopotamian Studies and Chair of Near Eastern Studies at the University of Michigan. He is author of *Hittite Birth Rituals* and *Hittite Diplomatic Texts* as well as co-editor of the Norton *Epic of Gilgamesh*, and is currently completing an edition of Gilgamesh texts found at the Hittite capital. He also serves as an editor of the *Journal of Cuneiform Studies* and the *Journal of the American Oriental Society*.

Jonathan S. Burgess is an associate professor in the Department of Classics at the University of Toronto whose research focuses on early Greek epic and myth. His major book is *The Tradition of the Trojan War in Homer and the Epic Cycle*, and he has published articles in *Classical Philology*, the *American Journal of Philology*, and *Transactions of the American Philological Association*. He is currently working on a project about the death and afterlife of Achilles.

Walter Burkert studied classics, history, and philosophy at Erlangen and Munich and has taught classics as professor at Berlin (1966–9) and Zurich (1969–96), and as visiting professor at Harvard University, the University of California, Berkeley, and other institutions in the United States. His research and publications concentrate on ancient Greek philosophy and religion, including oriental contacts and perspectives from anthropology. Among his publications are *Homo Necans*, *Greek Religion*, and *The Orientalizing Revolution*.

Olga M. Davidson is currently Associate Professor of Women's Studies at Brandeis University. Her teaching interests center on Persian and Arabic languages and literatures. She is author of *Poet and Hero in the Persian Book of Kings*, and *Comparative Literature and Classical Persian Poetry*. Her articles include "Formulaic analysis of samples taken from the *Shâhnâma* of Ferdowsi," in *Oral Tradition*, as well as papers in the *Journal of the American Oriental Society* and *Arethusa*.

William J. Dominik is Professor of Classics at the University of Otago and has taught widely in classics and the humanities at a number of universities. He is the author and editor of numerous books and other publications on such topics as Statius, Flavian Rome, Roman rhetoric, and Roman verse satire, including *Speech and Rhetoric in Statius' Thebaid* and *The Mythic Voice of Statius*. He is also the founding editor of the classical journal *Scholia*.

Casey Dué serves as an assistant professor of Classical Studies in the Department of Modern and Classical Languages at the University of Houston. She holds an MA and PhD in Classical Philology from Harvard University, and her teaching and research interests include ancient Greek oral traditions, Homeric poetry, and Greek tragedy. Among her publications are *Homeric Variations on a Lament by Briseis* and *The Captive Woman's Lament in Greek Tragedy*.

Lowell Edmunds is Professor of Classics at Rutgers University. Among his publications are *Myth in Homer: A Handbook*, *Theatrical Space and Historical Place in Sophocles' Oedipus at Colonus*, and an edited volume entitled *Approaches to Greek Myth*. His most recent book is *Intertextuality and the Reading of Roman Poetry*, and he is at work on a volume on Oedipus for the Routledge series, "Gods and Heroes of the Ancient World."

Mark W. Edwards is Emeritus Professor of Classics at Stanford University. He is the author of *Sound, Sense, and Rhythm: Listening to Greek and Latin Poetry*, *Homer: Poet of the* Iliad, and Volume 5 (Books 17–20) of the six-volume Cambridge Commentary on the *Iliad*, as well as a series of three articles on formulaic phraseology and narrative patterning in the Homeric poems, published in *Oral Tradition*.

Joseph Farrell is Professor of Classical Studies and Edmund J. and Louise W. Kahn Endowed Term Chair in Humanities at the University of Pennsylvania. He is author of *Vergil's Georgics and the Traditions of Ancient Epic*, *Latin Language and Latin Culture*, and "The Vergilian intertext" in the *Cambridge Companion to Vergil*, as well as numerous articles in such journals as *Classical Quarterly*, *Classical World*, the *American Journal of Philology*, and *Harvard Studies in Classical Philology*.

Helene P. Foley is Professor and Chair of Classics, Barnard College, Columbia University. She holds MA degrees in Classics and English from Yale University and a PhD in Classics from Harvard University. She is the author of numerous publications on Greek epic and drama, on women and gender in antiquity, and on modern performance and adaptation of Greek drama. Her books include *Ritual Irony: Poetry and Sacrifice in Euripides*, *The Homeric Hymn to Demeter*, and *Female Acts in Greek Tragedy*.

John Miles Foley is W. H. Byler Endowed Chair in the Humanities, Curators' Professor of Classical Studies and English, and Director of the Center for Studies in Oral Tradition at the University of Missouri, Columbia. His research interests include ancient Greek, medieval English, and South Slavic oral traditions. Recent publications include *Homer's Traditional Art*, *How to Read an Oral Poem*, and an experimental edition-translation of a South Slavic oral epic, *The Wedding of Mustajbey's Son Bećirbey as Performed by Halil Bajgorić*.

Monica R. Gale is a Senior Lecturer in Classics at Trinity College, Dublin. Her research interests include the poetry of the late Roman Republic and the Augustan period; she is the author of *Myth and Poetry in Lucretius*, *Virgil on the Nature of Things*, and *Lucretius and the Didactic Epic*, as well as editor of *Latin Epic and Didactic Poetry: Genre, Tradition and Individuality*. She is currently working on a commentary on the poems of Catullus.

R. Scott Garner received his PhD from Princeton University and is currently an assistant professor in the Department of the Classics at the University of Illinois at Urbana, Champaign. In addition to his primary research, which focuses on traditional oral techniques of composition within non-epic archaic Greek poetry, he has also written on the ancient novel as well as features of oral-formulaic performance within the South Slavic oral epic tradition.

Sander M. Goldberg is Professor of Classics at the University of California, Los Angeles. He is the author of *The Making of Menander's Comedy*, *Understanding Terence*, *Epic in Republican Rome*, and other studies of Greek and Roman literature. His current research centers on the developing idea of literature in the Roman Republic and, with Professor Tom Beghin, the relationship of classical rhetorical theory to eighteenth-century music.

Michael W. Haslam is Professor of Classics at the University of California, Los Angeles. Special areas of interest include archaic Greek lyric, Homer, tragedy, and Hellenistic poetry; also textual transmission as well as literary criticism and exegesis both ancient and modern. He has edited Greek papyri in the Oxyrhynchus Papyri series and elsewhere, and contributed "Homeric Papyri and the transmission of the text" to *A New Companion to Homer*.

Alan James received his PhD from King's College, Cambridge. He has served as Fellow and Lecturer in Classics, Selwyn College, Cambridge University; and as Senior Lecturer in Classics at the University of Sydney. His research specialties are early and later Greek epic poetry and didactic poetry, poetry of the Hellenistic period, and translation of the *Iliad*, and his major publications include two books on Oppian, a translation of Malalas, and a commentary on Quintus Book 5.

Richard Jenkyns is Professor of the Classical Tradition in the University of Oxford and a Fellow of Lady Margaret Hall. He also serves as Public Orator at Oxford. His most recent books are *Dignity and Decadence: Victorian Art and the Classical Inheritance*; *Virgil's Experience: Nature and History: Times, Names, and Places*; *Westminster Abbey*; and *A Fine Brush on Ivory: An Appreciation of Jane Austen*.

Minna Skafte Jensen is Professor Emerita of Greek and Latin at the University of Southern Denmark, having also taught at the University of Copenhagen. Among her major publications are *The Homeric Question and the Oral-Formulaic Theory* and *A History of Nordic Neo-Latin Literature*. She has also contributed to collective volumes such as *Translators and Translations* and *The Kalevala and the World's Traditional Epics*, as well as to the *Symbolae Osloenses* debate over the divisions in the Homeric epics.

Craig Kallendorf is Professor of Classics and English at Texas A&M University. He is the author of eleven books and several dozen articles, mostly on the reception of Virgil in early modern Europe. His latest books are *Virgil and the Myth of Venice: Books and Readers in the Italian Renaissance*, *Humanist Educational Treatises*, and *In Praise of Aeneas: Virgil and Epideictic Rhetoric in the Early Italian Renaissance*.

Joshua T. Katz is a linguist by training, a classicist by profession, and a comparative philologist at heart. An assistant professor of Classics, the John Witherspoon Bicentennial Preceptor, and a member of the Program in Linguistics at Princeton University, he is widely published in Indo-European studies and has a particular interest in the languages, literatures, and cultures of Greece and the Ancient Near East.

Robert Lamberton received his PhD from Yale University and currently serves as Professor and Chair in the Department of Classics at Washington University in St. Louis. Among his publications are *Homer the Theologian: Neoplatonist Allegorical Reading and the Growth of the Epic Tradition*, *Hesiod*, and "Homer in antiquity," which appeared in *A New Companion to Homer*. Together with J. Keaney, he has also edited *Homer's Ancient Readers: The Hermeneutics of Greek Epic's Earliest Exegetes*.

Bruce Louden received his PhD from the University of California at Berkeley and has written widely on Homeric epic, including a book entitled *The Odyssey: Structure, Narration, and Meaning*. He has also published on Indo-European myth and poetics, Bacchylides, Roman drama, *Beowulf*, Shakespeare, and Milton. He is currently finishing a book on the *Iliad*, as well as pursuing parallels between Greek myth and the Old Testament.

Raymond D. Marks received his PhD in Classics from Brown University and is currently an assistant professor of Classical Studies at the University of Missouri, Columbia. His research interests include post-Augustan epic poetry and literature of the Flavian period; the latter will be the subject of his next research project, supported by a Loeb Fellowship. He is presently preparing a book tentatively entitled *In Defense of Empire: Scipio Africanus in the* Punica *of Silius Italicus*.

Richard P. Martin holds the Antony and Isabelle Raubitschek Chair in Classics at Stanford University. He received his PhD in Classical Philology from Harvard University, and is the author of *Healing, Sacrifice, and Battle: Amechania and Related Concepts in Early Greek Poetry*, *The Language of Heroes: Speech and Performance in the* Iliad, and *Myths of the Ancient Greeks*. His research interests include ancient and modern poetics, Irish language and literature, modern Greek culture, and oral epic traditions worldwide.

Gregory Nagy is the author of *The Best of the Achaeans: Concepts of the Hero in Archaic Greek Poetry* and *Pindar's Homer: The Lyric Possession of an Epic Past*, among many other books. Since 2000, he has been the Director of the Harvard Center for Hellenic Studies in Washington, DC, while continuing to teach at the Harvard campus in Cambridge as the Francis Jones Professor of Classical Greek Literature and Professor of Comparative Literature.

D. P. Nelis is Professor of Latin in Trinity College Dublin. His central research interest is the influence of Hellenistic Greek poetry at Rome. He is the author of *Vergil's Aeneid and the Argonautica of Apollonius Rhodius*, editor (with D. S. Levene) of *Clio and the Poets: Augustan Poetry and the Traditions of Ancient Historiography*, and author of a number of articles on Apollonius Rhodius.

Stephanie Nelson received her MA and PhD from the University of Chicago and presently serves as an assistant professor in the Department of Classical Studies at Boston University. She has published *God and the Land: The Metaphysics of Farming in Hesiod and Vergil* and a wide range of articles on Homer, James Joyce, and other subjects. Her most recent book is *Aristophanes' Tragic Muse: Tragedy, Comedy, and the Polis in Classical Athens.*

Carole E. Newlands is Professor of Classics at the University of Wisconsin, Madison. She is the author of *Playing with Time: Ovid and the Fasti* and of *Statius' Silvae and the Poetics of Empire*, and has also written articles on Roman poetry and early Roman literature as well as on the reception of Ovid. She currently serves as an associate editor of the *American Journal of Philology.*

Susan Niditch, who specializes in the traditions of ancient Israel, is the Samuel Green Professor of Religion at Amherst College, where she has taught since 1978. Her books include *War in the Hebrew Bible: A Study in the Ethics of Violence*, *Ancient Israelite Religion*, and *Oral World and Written Word: Ancient Israelite Literature*. Current projects are a new translation/commentary for the biblical Book of Judges and a study of "Hair in ancient Israel."

Scott B. Noegel is Associate Professor of Ancient Near Eastern Languages and Civilizations at the University of Washington. His recent works include *Nocturnal Ciphers: The Allusive Language of Dreams in the Ancient Near East*, *A Historical Dictionary of Prophets in Islam and Judaism*, and *Prayer, Magic, and the Stars in the Ancient and Late Antique World*. He is currently co-editing *The Linguistic Cycle: Selected Writings of Carleton T. Hodge* and writing a monograph on magic and the Bible.

Michael C. J. Putnam is MacMillan Professor of Classics and Professor of Comparative Literature at Brown University. His books, including *Virgil's Epic Designs* and *The Poetry of the Aeneid*, have been largely concerned with Latin literature of the Republican and Augustan periods, especially with the poetry of Virgil, Horace, and Tibullus. A former president of the American Philological Association, he is a trustee of the American Academy in Rome and Fellow of the American Academy of Arts and Sciences.

Kurt A. Raaflaub is David Herlihy University Professor and Professor of Classics and History at Brown University. His main research interests include archaic and classical Greek and Roman Republican political, social, and intellectual history, war and society, the cultural interaction between Egypt, the Near East, and Greece, and the comparative history of ancient civilizations. He recently published *The Discovery of Freedom in Ancient Greece* and is working on a history of early Greek political thought.

Jack M. Sasson is the Mary Jane Werthan Professor of Judaic Studies and Hebrew Bible, Professor of Classics, and Director of the Program in Jewish Studies at Vanderbilt University. He writes on the archives from Mari in the early second millennium BCE and has produced commentaries on the biblical books of Ruth and Jonah. He is past editor of the *Journal of the American Oriental Society* and editor-in-chief of *Civilizations of the Ancient Near East.*

Susan Sherratt is Honorary Research Associate, Department of Antiquities, Ashmolean Museum, University of Oxford. She is author of *Arthur Evans, Knossos, and the Priest-king* and the *Catalogue of Cycladic Antiquities in the Ashmolean Museum: The Captive Spirit*, as well as " 'Reading the texts': archaeology and the Homeric question," published in *Antiquity.* She is also editor of the three-volume collection, *The Wall Paintings of Thera.*

Robert Shorrock read classics at University College, Durham and Christ's College, Cambridge, where he obtained his PhD. He is the author of *The Challenge of Epic: Allusive Engagement in the Dionysiaca of Nonnus* and of a number of articles on ancient literature and the classical tradition. He teaches at Eton College, Windsor.

Laura M. Slatkin teaches classical studies at New York University (Gallatin School) and the University of Chicago. Her research interests include ancient Greek and Roman poetry, especially epic and drama; wisdom traditions in classical and Near Eastern antiquity; comparative mythology; gender studies; anthropological approaches to the literature of the ancient Mediterranean world; and cultural poetics. Among her publications is *The Power of Thetis: Allusion and Interpretation in the* Iliad.

Dennis E. Trout is an associate professor of Classical Studies at the University of Missouri, Columbia. He is the author of *Paulinus of Nola: Life, Letters, and Poems* and, most recently, "Damasus and the invention of early Christian Rome" in *The Cultural Turn in Late Ancient Studies*. At present he is working on Latin epigraphic poetry of the fourth and fifth centuries, giving special attention to the poems of Damasus, bishop of Rome from 366 to 384.

Nicholas Wyatt has a personal chair in ancient Near Eastern religions in the University of Edinburgh. He is the author of *Myths of Power: A Study of Royal Myth and Ideology in Ugaritic and Biblical Tradition, Religious Texts from Ugarit: The Works of Ilimilku and his Colleagues,* and *Space and Time in the Religious Life of the Near East.* He has also written numerous articles on Old Testament, Ugaritic, Indian, and comparative topics.

Andrew Zissos received his PhD from Princeton University and was Fellow of the American Academy in Rome in 2000–1. He presently serves as an assistant professor of Latin Literature and Graduate Director in the Department of Classics, University of California, Irvine. He has published numerous articles on Latin epic, primarily on Valerius Flaccus' *Argonautica* and Ovid's *Metamorphoses*, and is currently completing a commentary on Book 1 of the *Argonautica*.

Acknowledgments

Over the three years and more that the *Blackwell Companion to Ancient Epic* has been in preparation, I have incurred myriad debts and profited enormously from the generosity of many people and institutions. Chief among heroic colleagues deserving thanks for their epic efforts is Michael Barnes, assistant editor for the volume, who has brought considerable philological and editorial talents as well as admirable energy to his role as *wilgesith*. We have been fortunate to labor alongside forty specialists from widely diverse fields within Near Eastern, ancient Greek, and Roman epic studies; from initial discussions through the formulation of their chapters and on to the inevitable last-minute modifications, it has been a pleasure as well as an education to collaborate with all of them. Nor should I forget the expert advice of Peter Machinist and Scott Noegel, who helped so much with the initial shaping of the Near Eastern section.

Thanks are certainly due to my home institution, the University of Missouri, Columbia, and to other advisers of various sorts. Deans Richard Schwartz and Ted Tarkow authorized three years of research assistance that proved crucial for contending with the many tasks associated with creating the *Companion*. Colleagues in the Department of Classical Studies have typically shown remarkable patience and good will in answering questions and making valuable suggestions as the planning and editing proceeded. Given the traditional nature of the genre that is this volume's *raison d'être*, let me also remember my earlier and later teachers of epic: Robert Payson Creed, Anne Lebeck, Barbara Kerewsky-Halpern, George Dimock, Albert Bates Lord, Nada Milošević-Djordjević, Svetozar Koljević, Svetozar Petrović, and especially Lauri Honko.

At Blackwell Publishing, Al Bertrand, Commissioning Editor, has provided dependable guidance and responsive advice from the very beginning stages of the project, and Angela Cohen, Editorial Controller, has made the end-game much easier to plan and carry out through her careful administration of copy-editing and production.

Finally, I thank my family – Anne-Marie, Isaac, Liz, Joshua, John (*in memoriam*), my foster mother Frances (*in memoriam*), and now Jessica and little Grace – who have been steadfastly encouraging even when the goal of this epic quest was so far in the distance as to appear unreachable.

Abbreviations of Ancient Authors and Works

Ael.	Aelian
NA	*De natura animalium* ("On the Characteristics of Animals")
VH	*Varia historia* ("Historical Miscellany")
Aen.	*Aeneid*
Agath.	Agathias (Scholasticus)
Hist.	*Histories*
Amos	Book of Amos
AP	*Anthologia Palatina* (Palatine Anthology)
Apollod.	Apollodorus
Bibl.	*Bibliotheca* ("The Library")
Epit.	*Epitome*
Ap. Rhod.	Apollonius Rhodius
Arg.	*Argonautica*
Ar.	Aristophanes
Ach.	*Acharnians*
Archil.	Archilochus
Arist.	Aristotle
Anal. Post.	*Analytica posteriora* ("Posterior Analytics")
De An.	*De anima* ("On the Soul")
Met.	*Metaphysics*
Poet.	*Poetics*
Arr.	Arrian
Anab.	*Anabasis of Alexander*
Athen.	Athenaeus
Deip.	*The Deipnosophists*

Aug.   Augustine
  Conf.   *Confessions*
  De civ. Dei   *De civitate Dei* ("The City of God")

Call.   Callimachus
  Aet.   *Aetia*
  Ap.   *Hymn to Apollo*
  Epigr.   *Epigrams*

1 Chron.   First Book of Chronicles

Cic.   Cicero
  Arch.   *On Behalf of Archias*
  Att.   *Epistulae ad Atticum* ("Letters to Atticus")
  Brut.   *Brutus*
  Fin.   *De finibus* ("On Moral Ends")
  Flac.   *On Behalf of Flaccus*
  Leg.   *De legibus* ("On the Laws")
  Off.   *De officiis* ("On Obligations")
  Pis.   *Against Piso*
  Q. fr.   *Epistulae ad Quintum fratrem* ("Letters to his brother Quintus")
  Tusc.   *Tusculan Disputations*

Cl.   Claudian
  Get.   *De bello Getico* ("The Gothic War")
  Get. praef.   Preface to the *De bello Getico*
  Stil.   *De consulatu Stilichonis* ("The Consulship of Stilicho")
  III Cons.   *Panegyricus dictus Honorio Augusto tertium consuli* ("Panegyric on the Emperor Honorius' Third Time as Consul")

Deut.   Book of Deuteronomy

Diod. Sic.   Diodorus Siculus, *Library of History*

Diog. Laert.   Diogenes Laertius, *Lives of Illustrious Philosophers*

Dion. Hal.   Dionysius of Halicarnassus
  Ant. Rom.   *Roman Antiquities*

Donat.   Donatus
  Vit. Verg.   *Life of Virgil*

Enn.   Ennius
  Ann.   *Annales*

Enu. El.   *Enuma Elish*

Epicurus   Epicurus
  Ep. Hdt.   *Epistola ad Herodotum* ("Letter to Herodotus")

Esther   Book of Esther

Eur.   Euripides
  El.   *Electra*
  Hel.   *Helen*
  Phoen.   *The Phoenician Women*

Exod.	Book of Exodus
Ezek.	Book of Ezekiel
Fr.	Fronto
Ep.	*Epistles*
fr.	fragment
frr.	fragments
Gell.	Aulus Gellius
NA	*Noctes Atticae* ("Attic Nights")
Gen.	Book of Genesis
Gilg.	*Epic of Gilgamesh*
Hab.	Book of Habakkuk
Hdt.	Herodotus, *Histories*
Hes.	Hesiod
Th.	*Theogony*
WD	*Works and Days*
[Hes.]	Hesiod, *fragmenta dubia*
Hom.	Homer
Il.	*Iliad*
Od.	*Odyssey*
Hom. Hymn	*Homeric Hymn*
Hom. Hymn to Ap.	*Homeric Hymn to Apollo*
Hom. Hymn to Dem.	*Homeric Hymn to Demeter*
Hor.	Horace
Ars. P.	*Ars Poetica*
Carm.	*Odes*
Ep.	*Epistles*
Epod.	*Epodes*
Sat.	*Satires*
Isa.	Book of Isaiah
Isid.	Isidore of Seville
Etym.	*Etymologiae*
Jerome	Jerome
Adv. Ruf.	*Against Rufinus*
Ep.	*Epistles*
Jer.	Book of Jeremiah
John	The Gospel of John
Josh.	Book of Joshua
Judg.	Book of Judges
Juv.	Juvenal
Sat.	*Satires*

Juvenc.   Juvencus
  Evang.   *Evangeliorum libri quattuor* ("Four Books of the Evangelists")

1 Kgs.   First Book of the Kings
2 Kgs.   Second Book of the Kings

Liv.   Livy, *History of Rome*

Liv. And.   Livius Andronicus, *Odusia*

[Long.]   pseudo-Longinus
  Subl.   *On the Sublime*

Luc.   Lucan
  BC   *Bellum civile* ("The Civil War")

Lucr.   Lucretius
  DRN   *De rerum natura* ("On the Nature of the Universe")

Luke   The Gospel of Luke

Lycoph.   Lycophron
  Alex.   *Alexandra*

Mart.   Martial, *Epigrams*

Naev.   Naevius
  BP   *Bellum Poenicum* ("The Punic War")

Neh.   Book of Nehemiah

Non.   Nonnus
  Dion.   *Dionysiaca*

Num.   Book of Numbers

OGR   *Origo gentis Romanae* ("The Origin of the Roman Race")

Or.   Paulus Orosius
  Adv. Pag.   *Historiarum adversum paganos libri VII* ("Seven Books of History
                             against the Pagans")

Ov.   Ovid
  AA   *Ars amatoria* ("The Art of Love")
  Am.   *Amores*
  Fast.   *Fasti*
  Met.   *Metamorphoses*
  Pont.   *Epistulae ex Ponto* ("Letters from the Black Sea")
  Tr.   *Tristia*

P   papyrus

Paul.   Paulinus of Nola
  Carm.   *Carmina*

Paus.   Pausanias, *Description of Greece*

Pers.   Persius, *Satires*

Petr.   Petronius, *Satyricon*

Pind.   Pindar

Isth.	*Isthmian Odes*
Nem.	*Nemean Odes*
Ol.	*Olympian Odes*
Pyth.	*Pythian Odes*
Pl.	Plato
Leg.	*Laws*
Rep.	*Republic*
Tht.	*Theaetetus*
Plaut.	Plautus
Asin.	*Asinaria*
Trin.	*Trinummus*
Plin.	Pliny the Younger
Ep.	*Epistles*
Plut.	Plutarch
Alex.	*Life of Alexander*
de Hom.	pseudo-Plutarch, *On Homer*
Thes.	*Life of Theseus*
Mor.	*Moralia*
Polyb.	Polybius, *The Histories*
praef.	preface
Prop.	Propertius, *Elegies*
Ps.	Book of Psalms
Quint.	Quintilian
Inst.	*Institutio oratoria* ("The Education of the Orator")
Quint. Smyrn.	Quintus of Smyrna, *The Trojan Epic*
Sall.	Sallust
Cat.	*The War Against Catiline*
1 Sam.	First Book of Samuel
2 Sam.	Second Book of Samuel
schol.	scholia to
sed. inc.	*sedes incerta* ("location uncertain")
Semon.	Semonides
Sen.	Seneca the Younger
Const. Sap.	*De constantia sapientis* ("On the Firmness of the Wise Man")
Ep.	*Epistles*
Serv.	Servius
ad Aen.	Commentary on the *Aeneid*
Serv. auct.	Servius auctus
Sil.	Silius Italicus
Pun.	*Punica*

SN	*Shâhnâma*
Soph.	Sophocles
Aj.	*Ajax*
Ant.	*Antigone*
Stat.	Statius
Achil.	*Achilleid*
Sil.	*Silvae*
Theb.	*Thebaid*
Stes.	Stesichorus
Strabo	Strabo, *Geographica*
Suet.	Suetonius
Aug.	*The Divine Augustus*
Claud.	*The Divine Claudius*
Dom.	*Domitian*
Gram.	*De grammaticis et rhetoribus* ("On Grammarians and Rhetoricians")
Tit.	*The Divine Titus*
[Suet.] *Vit. Luc.*	pseudo-Suetonius, *Life of Lucan*
Tac.	Tacitus
Ann.	*Annales*
Dial.	*Dialogus de oratoribus*
Hist.	*Histories*
Thuc.	Thucydides, *History of the Peloponnesian War*
Tib.	Tibullus
V	Venetus A (Manuscript of Homer)
Vac.	Vacca
Vit. Luc.	*Life of Lucan*
Val. Fl.	Valerius Flaccus
Arg.	*Argonautica*
Val. Max.	Valerius Maximus
Mem.	*Facta et dicta memorabilia*
Var.	Varro
Antiq.	*Antiquitates rerum divinarum* ("Antiquities of Things Divine")
Ling.	*De lingua Latina* ("On the Latin Language")
Rust.	*De re rustica* ("On Agriculture")
Ven. Fort.	Venantius Fortunatus
VM	*Vita Martini* ("Life of Martin")
Virg.	Virgil
Aen.	*Aeneid*
Ecl.	*Eclogues*
Geo.	*Georgics*
Zech.	Book of Zechariah

Abbreviations of Modern Reference Works

ACW   *Ancient Christian Writers*. Series.

ANET   *Ancient Near Eastern Texts Relating to the Old Testament*, 3rd edn., ed. J. B. Pritchard. Princeton, NJ: Princeton University Press. 1969. 4th edn. 1974.

B-W   *Die frühen römischen Historiker*, vol. 1 (Von Fabius Pictor bis Cn. Gellius), ed. H. Beck and U. Walter. Texte zur Forschung, 76. Darmstadt: Wissenschaftliche Buchgesellschaft, 2001.

CAH   *The Cambridge Ancient History*, 3rd edn. Cambridge: Cambridge University Press, 1970–.

CANE   *Civilizations of the Ancient Near East*, ed. J. Sasson et al. New York: Scribners, 1995.

CCSL   *Corpus Christianorum Series Latina*. Latin texts.

CIL   *Corpus Inscriptionum Latinarum*. Latin inscriptions.

CPL   *Clavis Patrum Latinorum*. 3rd edn., ed. E. Dekkers.

CS 1, 2   *The Context of Scripture*, vols 1 and 2, ed. W. W. Hallo and K. L. Younger. Leiden: Brill, 1997–2002.

CSEL   *Corpus Scriptorum Ecclesiasticorum Latinorum*. Latin texts.

D-K   *Die Fragmente der Vorsokratiker*, ed. H. Diels and W. Kranz, 6th edn. Berlin, 1952.

FGrH   *Die Fragmente der griechischen Historiker*, ed. F. Jacoby. Berlin, 1923–.

GMAW   *Greek Manuscripts of the Ancient World*. ed. E. G. Turner. Oxford: Clarendon Press, 1971. 2nd edn. 1987.

KTU   *Die Keilalphabetischen Texte aus Ugarit*, ed. M. Dietrich, O. Loretz, and J. Sanmartín. Alter Orient und Altes Testament, 24/1. Neukirchen-Vluyn: Neukirchener Verlag; Kevelaer: Verlag Butzon und Bercker, 1976. 2nd edn.:

The Cuneiform Alphabetic Texts from Ugarit, Ras Ibn Hani and Other Places. Abhandlungen zur Literatur Alt-Syrien-Palästinas, 8. Münster: Ugarit-Verlag, 1995.

MGH AA   *Monumenta Germaniae Historica: Auctores Antiquissimi*. Latin texts.

M-W   *Fragmenta Hesiodea*, ed. M. L. West and R. Merkelbach. Oxford: Clarendon Press, 1967.

OCD   *Oxford Classical Dictionary*, ed. S. Hornblower and A. Spawforth, 3rd edn. Oxford: Oxford University Press, 1996.

OLD   *Oxford Latin Dictionary*, ed. P. G. W. Glare. Oxford: Oxford University Press, 1982.

P   *Historicorum Romanorum Fragmenta*, vol. 1, 2nd edn., ed. H. Peter [1914]. Leipzig: Teubner, 1993.

PMG   *Poetae Melici Graeci*, ed. D. Page. Oxford: Clarendon Press, 1962.

RE   *Real-Encyclopädie der klassischen Altertumswissenschaft*, ed. A. G. Pauly, G. Wissowa, and W. Kroll. Stuttgart: Metzler. 1893–.

SC   *Sources Chrétiennes*. Latin texts and French translations.

TUAT   *Texte aus der Umwelt des Alten Testaments*, ed. O. Kaiser. Gütersloh: Gütersloher Verlagshaus Gerd Mohn, 1982–2001.

W   *Remains of Old Latin*, 2 vols, ed. E. H. Warmington. Loeb Classical Library. Cambridge, MA: Harvard University Press, 1961. 1st edn. 1936.

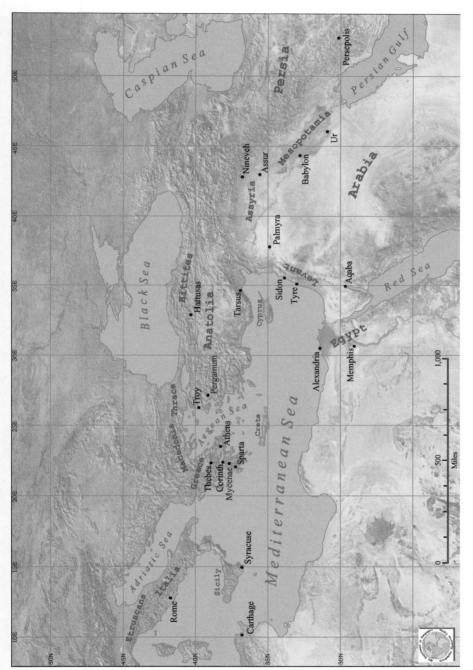

The ancient epic territories.
Source: James Harlan, Geographic Resources Center, University of Missouri.

Introduction

John Miles Foley

Epic is the master-genre of the ancient world. Wherever and whenever one looks, epics had major roles to play in ancient societies, functions that ranged from historical and political to cultural and didactic and beyond. As charters for group identity, ancient epics seem always to have been at the center of things. The mere ubiquity of *Gilgamesh* fragments from Nineveh, Assur, Nimrod, Uruk, and Babylon argues the widespread and longstanding importance of a gripping saga that some have called the world's oldest story. Plato's preoccupation with Homer and the myriad reflections of the *Iliad* and *Odyssey* in the plastic art of vase-painting bear witness to a similar depth of concern and awareness through many centuries of Greek culture. Always closely allied with Roman history, real or constructed, Roman epic reached a new stage of political reflexivity in the hands of Virgil, who in his *Aeneid* forged a powerful ancestral link between his hero Aeneas and his regent Augustus. But as instrumental as epic demonstrably is in the ancient world, it is hardly a monolith. At once both the composite of many other genres and an important influence on nearly all of them, ancient epic presents real challenges to conventional literary history: not only do we discover panegyric and catalogue in the *Iliad*; we also see the influence of drama on Apollonius, of pastoral on the *Aeneid*, of rhetoric on Lucan, and of Christian scripture on late Latin epic. From every perspective epic is an integral partner in a many-sided synergy.

This *Companion to Ancient Epic* addresses these and many other complex, engaging realities in what we contributors hope is a comprehensive and useful way: by providing a broadly inclusive reference work on the three traditions of Near Eastern, Greek, and Roman epic. Indeed, there are at least two pressing reasons why we have collectively created this resource aimed at a wide, interdisciplinary audience of advanced undergraduates, graduate students, and scholars in adjacent fields.

First, the second half of the twentieth century, and particularly its last few decades, have seen major shifts in the ways that we conceive of and explain ancient epic. Modern topics such as the role of women, the history of reception, Indo-European backgrounds, comparative archaeological contexts, epic and myth, epic and history, the media employed to preserve and transmit epic texts, bardic performance, and living analogues from oral epic traditions have come prominently to the fore. Additionally, the traditions we once found it convenient to segregate are starting to reveal interesting genetic relationships. Of course, Greek and Roman epic have long been recognized as intimately connected in fascinating and important ways, but in recent times the deep influence of Near Eastern traditions on ancient Greek epic has become much clearer. Nor should we forget the riddling practice of translation: since the mid-1980s or so there has been a rash of new translations from all three ancient areas, renderings on which many students and scholars (whose experience of the epics will often be wholly dependent on such liaisons) could profit from an expert perspective. In fact, enough new and different topics and approaches have emerged that the need for a compendium of contextual information – plainly presented without bias toward any single viewpoint – is more compelling than ever before.

A second and complementary reason for formulating this *Companion* is simply that at present nothing remotely like it exists. At one end of the spectrum lie author-based collections focused on single major figures; here one finds such volumes as the *Cambridge Companion to Homer* (ed. R. Fowler, 2004) and *Cambridge Companion to Virgil* (ed. C. Martindale, 1997), as well as *A New Companion to Homer* (ed. I. Morris and B. Powell; Brill, 1997) and *A Companion to the Study of Virgil* (ed. N. Horsfall; Brill, 1995). At the opposite end we find more general books, such as *Roman Epic* (ed. A. J. Boyle; Rout-ledge, 1993), which treats ancient Roman writers and their Renaissance inheritors; or *Reading Epic: An Introduction to the Ancient Narratives* (ed. P. Toohey; Routledge, 1992), focused on the principal authors of Greek and Roman works. In short, there is no single, comprehensive source that aspires to aid its readership – whether students or scholars in adjacent fields – in navigating the huge and complex territory of all three ancient epic traditions: Near Eastern, Greek, and Roman. This *Companion to Ancient Epic* attempts to fill that gap.

Overall Organization

The organization as well as the content of the volume reflects the current state of the involved fields as well as the needs of the projected audience. In addition to being as up-to-date, multidisciplinary, and exhaustive as the format permits, the *Companion* uses a tiered structure to present its information, moving from general to particular and from cross-traditional to single-discipline and single-author chapters over the course of Parts I–IV. We trust that this strategy will optimize the usefulness of the book as an introduction to various kinds of inquiries, whether comparative or more focused.

Part I: Issues and perspectives

The opening section consists of thirteen broad-based topics that prove significant throughout the world of ancient epic, even as they demand markedly different kinds of investigation and explanation within each more limited arena. Logically enough, then, Richard Martin opens this first section and the volume-long discussion with the funda-mental problem of the *epic genre* itself: the challenge of determining what an epic consists of and what qualifies as "epic," not solely in ancient Greece (which gave us the term) but also cross-culturally. For the record, the authors in this volume do not espouse a single boilerplate definition for "epic," which remains – as Martin emphasizes – a heuristic tool for comparative evaluation rather than an inviolate, archetypal reality. Joshua Katz provides a complementary perspective by considering the place of ancient epic in the overall *Indo-European* family of languages and traditions. Not only genetically related words but phrases and narrative patterns shared across wide expanses of space and time suggest, if dimly as yet, a possible Proto-Indo-European prototype for various stories. Such partial stories in turn raise the question of the relationship between *myth and epic*, the subject of the next chapter by Lowell Edmunds. In addition to offering a welcome treatment of the terminology surrounding myth and epic, he surveys the story-context, especially folktales, behind and within *Gilgamesh*, Homer's *Iliad* and *Odyssey*, and Virgil's *Aeneid*.

Another general concern over all three traditions is the set of perspectives offered by history, archaeology, and the physical media. Kurt Raaflaub concerns himself primarily with the vexed question of the correspondence between *epic and history*, that is, the portrayal of reality with which we are presented in ancient epic as compared with what we can piece together from independent contemporary and comparative evidence. In this respect he differentiates between "historical" and "heroic" epics, understanding the former as much closer to our notion of history than the politically and culturally augmented tales of heroes. As Susan Sherratt points out, *archaeology and epic* have been natural partners from the start, both committed to the unearthing and analysis of artifacts that happen to have survived to us. Showing how archaeology has evolved radically from its Eurocentric origins to its present forms, she considers what light the material culture of the ancient world can shed on its epic epitomes, especially the Homeric poems. No aspect of history or archaeology is more fundamental than the actual *physical media* in which epics reach us, and Michael Haslam's chapter on tablet, scroll, and codex provides a fascinating glimpse of the development of writing materials that encoded epics in the Near East, ancient Greece, and Rome, authoritatively probing the technological, linguistic, and cultural aspects of media use and evolution.

How were these ancient epics composed, presented, and transmitted? Of course, a vital part of the answer to this line of inquiry rests with the archaeological record and the history of media, but in recent years a great deal of research on the origins of ancient epic in oral tradition has emerged. Beginning with a brief overview of the twentieth-century research that inspired investigation into the unwritten roots of ancient poetry, Minna Skafte Jensen considers both external and internal evidence for *oral performance* in the three epic traditions, with special attention to Homer and Hesiod. Issues such as Plato's attitudes, the role of the *aoidos* (bard), rhapsodic contests, and the Panathenaic rule are among her topics, as is the coexistence of performance and written texts in the Near East and Rome. My own contribution to this volume focuses on *modern oral epics* as analogues for ancient works. Areas covered include terminology and comparative "epic"; bards or singers; performance and audience; epic language; transmission; "new" epics; the role of literacy and texts; collection, textualization, and edition; and epic as one species of verbal art within the larger ecology of oral poetry in a given culture. Understanding the pretextual roots of ancient epics, however partially and indirectly, can help us grasp how deeply they are embedded in and reflective of ancient cultures.

Whether within a single epic or across all three ancient traditions, no concerns loom larger than the roles of women, heroes, and gods. As Helene Foley points out, the assumption that epic is always a primarily male genre is belied by the rich variety and vital significance of the *roles of women* across Near Eastern, Greek, and Roman epics. Proceeding thematically, she looks at categories such as blockers and helpers, mothers and sons, women and war, and women as narrators, pointing out congruencies among different epics and revealing the significance of female characters and their actions. Generic, cross-cultural, and traditional patterns of action also underlie the portrayal of *epic heroes*, as Gregory Nagy illustrates in careful detail. Concentrating on Achilles and Odysseus in a comparative context that also includes Gilgamesh and Enkidu, Aeneas, and Arjuna from the Indic *Mahâbhârata*, he explains both the Indo-European background shared by these poetic traditions and the irreducible differences among various heroes. Correspondingly, Bruce Louden shows how the identity of the *gods in epic* is linked to the core actions of heroes, with emphasis on how the gods shape Homer's *Iliad* and *Odyssey*, Virgil's *Aeneid*, the Ugaritic *Aqhat*, and Apollonius of Rhodes' *Argonautica* as characters within the narrative.

Interpretation of these and other aspects of ancient epic is always a contingent process, mediated in the end by the singularities of the interpreter's time and place and by the forms in which the epics are encountered. In considering the *ancient reception* of the three traditions, Robert Lamberton reviews, among other topics, what we can decipher about transmission, possible paths of influence between Near Eastern and Greek epics, the advent of commentaries, the place of the *Iliad* and *Odyssey* in school curricula, the recycling of Homeric epic into other genres and media, the canonization of the *Aeneid*, and the influence of Virgil on contemporary and subsequent Latin poetry. Finally, Richard Armstrong rounds out the "Issues and Perspectives" section with a chapter on the crucial problem of *translation of the ancient epics* from their languages of origin into modern English. Starting from the premise that translation mandates cultural reinvention rather than simple rote conversion, he highlights some of the fundamental attitudes and challenges that have accompanied the theory and practice of translating these works: the uncertain status of the source-text, the role of oral tradition and transmission, the idea of epics as sacred texts deserving authoritative renderings, and the role of creativity in the process of translation.

Part II: Near Eastern epic

The second section of this *Companion* attempts to provide an introduction to the vast and heterogeneous body of Near Eastern epic. In order to assist in orienting readers to a collection of traditions and works that span many centuries across an enormous geographical expanse, Jack Sasson opens this section with a *comparative overview*. His chapter includes discussions of the inherent diversity of languages, scripts, media, levels and kinds of literacy, orality and aurality, and genre; a roster of Near Eastern works with handy references to English translations; and general treatments of process (inspiration, transmission, and presentation), literary issues (motifs, themes, structure, modes), and modern literary reflexes of ancient epics.

Against this background the next five chapters treat more localized traditions and works. Scott Noegel's unit on *Mesopotamian epic* divides a complex collection of works into two main groups: Sumerian (the Enmerkar traditions, Lugalbanda traditions, *Epic of Shulgi*, Gilgamesh traditions, and *Epic of Sargon*) and Akkadian (the Gilgamesh traditions, *Atrahasis Epic*, and *Epics of Sargon*). He also includes a section on interpreting Mesopotamian epic and a listing of available introductions, translations, and analyses. After surveying various opinions on what constitutes *Ugaritic epic*, Nicholas Wyatt discusses the *Baal* cycle, *Keret*, and *Aqhat*, providing story summaries and thematic analysis. Gary Beckman's chapter on *Hittite and Hurrian epic* looks at "fantastic" stories, including the famous *Song of Ullikummi*, according to three categories: narratives in which humans interact with deities, narratives involving the gods alone, and narratives combining the historical and the fantastic. Olga Davidson's chief focus in her chapter on *Persian/Iranian epic* is the *Shâhnâma* attributed to Ferdowsi; among the topics she addresses are its historical backgrounds, its origin in a pre-Islamic oral tradition, and parallels to ancient Greek epic and Indo-European mythic patterns. In her discussion of *Israelite epic*, Susan Niditch moves from querying the viability of the term "epic" within the corpus of Biblical materials to affirming their epic character through analysis of the role of heroes, war and epic, war and women, the divine warrior, oral and written, possible Hebrew terms for "epic," political dimensions, and other features that she notes are shared across many international epic traditions.

Part III: Ancient Greek epic

The third section of the *Companion* proceeds in a roughly chronological sequence through what most readers will find a more familiar (because more often canonized) group of authors and works. As a bridge from the preceding section, Walter Burkert's chapter on *Near Eastern connections* lays bare some of the fascinating linkages between Greece and its neighboring cultures and epic traditions, many of which were not recognized until about the 1970s and 1980s. The monumental poems of Homer, the model for so much in the ancient world and well beyond, merit two chapters: Mark Edwards on the *Iliad* and Laura Slatkin on the *Odyssey*. Stephanie Nelson's chapter on the poems of Hesiod, chiefly the *Theogony* and *Works and Days*, illustrates that, although very different from Homer's in thematic content, they are epic in their own right. Nor were the poems attributed to these two celebrated bards the sole pertinent productions from the earliest era in ancient Greece; the chapter on the *Epic Cycle* by Jonathan Burgess explains how numerous additional epics, known to us from fragments and summaries as well as references in other authors, filled out a much larger tradition. Three latter-day epic poets, artistically descended from Homer but each with his own vision and agenda, are the subjects of chapters by Damien Nelis (the *Argonautica* of Apollonius of Rhodes), Alan James (the *Posthomerica* or *The Trojan Epic* by Quintus of Smyrna), and Robert Shorrock (the *Dionysiaca* of Nonnus). The section on ancient Greek epic closes with R. Scott Garner's wide-ranging discussion of *Epic and other genres* and Casey Dué's chapter on *Homer's post-classical legacy* in various media from the medieval period to the present.

Part IV: Roman epic

Like the ancient Greek section, this fourth group of twelve chapters follows a more familiar, largely self-explanatory path from the earliest remnants of Roman epic through all of the major authors and works and on to the apotheosis of the tradition in more modern creations across various media. Thus Joseph Farrell opens the series with a discussion of the *origins and essence of Roman epic*, tracing various opinions on its evolution and relationship to Greek literary culture via analysis of both ideological and historical issues. Sander Goldberg's subsequent chapter on *Early Republican epic* focuses on Livius Andronicus' retelling of the *Odyssey*, Naevius' *Bellum Poenicum*, Ennius' *Annales*, and multiple epics from the late Republic and early empire. From this point Part IV continues with Monica Gale on Lucretius' *De rerum natura*, Michael Putnam on Virgil's *Aeneid*, Carole Newlands on Ovid's *Metamorphoses*, Shadi Bartsch on Lucan's *Pharsalia* or *Bellum civile*, Andrew Zissos on Valerius Flaccus' *Argonautica*, William Dominik on Statius' *Thebaid* and fragmentary *Achilleid*, Raymond Marks on Silius Italicus' *Punica*, Michael Barnes on Claudian's *De Bello Gildonico*, and Dennis Trout on the *Latin Christian epics of late antiquity*, including such authors as Juvencus, Proba, Paulinus of Nola, Prudentius, and the biblical and hagiographic epicists. The Roman epic section concludes with Richard Jenkyns's treatment of *Epic and other genres* and Craig Kallendorf's chapter on *Virgil's post-classical legacy*.

Other Features

Several additional features have been incorporated with the broad spectrum of the *Companion*'s projected readership in mind. First, each chapter ends with suggestions for "Further Reading," so that the interested scholar or student can pursue particular themes, authors, and works beyond the necessarily limited scope of this single volume. Second, both those suggestions and the chapters themselves are keyed to a master bibliography that provides full citations for the telegraphic (author-date) in-text references. Third, in order to facilitate connections across traditions, topics, and individual authors and works, each chapter has been fully cross-referenced with other chapters in the volume. Fourth, I have fashioned a comprehensive and detailed index of poets, poems, salient historical and mythic figures and events, important terminology, and the like. In seeking materials on a particular theme, author, or work, then, readers can consult any or all of three complementary resources: the table of contents, the introduction, or the index.

Transliteration of names, titles, words, and phrases from ancient languages varies a great deal from one discipline and publication to the next, with many different solutions both available and viable. This volume presents a special challenge in that regard, ranging as widely as it does over ancient Near Eastern, Greek, and Roman epic. In general, I have tried to impose a limited, practical uniformity in two respects. First, vowels are rendered by using circumflex accents instead of macra (long marks) to indicate length; thus *mimêsis* instead of *mimēsis* and *Mahâbhârata* instead of *Mahābhārata*). Second, ancient Greek is transliterated phonetically (e.g., Patroklos instead of Patroclus) except when the Latinized form has become so familiar that it must take precedence on grounds of simple recognizability (e.g., Telemachus instead of Telemakhos). Within this overall system individual authors have been permitted some idiosyncratic spellings, but I do not anticipate that any of the allowed variations will prove a genuine hindrance to the broad-spectrum readership of this Companion.

It is the collective hope of the 42-person *comitatus* assembled to create the *Companion to Ancient Epic* that it may faithfully serve the constituency for which it was intended: advanced undergraduate students, graduate students, and scholars in adjacent fields. As a single volume it of course cannot provide the last word, but it can aspire to help readers gain an initial acquaintance with ancient epic as well as chart the next few steps toward deepening the relationship. If it fulfills that mandate, then the undeniably epic efforts that went into its making these last few years will have been rewarded. And that will be *kleos* enough.

near Makana, Kauai
July, 2004

PART I

Issues and Perspectives

CHAPTER ONE

Epic as Genre

Richard P. Martin

1 Introduction

If "epic," ancient or modern, represents a "genre" in any meaningful sense, our first task should be not to enumerate the characteristics of a classification, but to ask what might be the ultimate usefulness, whether to literary criticism or cultural studies, of such categorizing. What do we gain from calling something an epic? Should the category therefore be as wide as possible or bounded and narrow? To answer fully, we need to look at the historical roots of our own taxonomy of genres in classical Greek sources (section 2, below), as well as at a broad range of contemporary comparative evidence from non-western societies in which traditions seemingly comparable with classical "epic" exist (section 3).

The circularity in the latter procedure will be immediately apparent. If the first rule of the comparative method is to know what to compare, there will always be the chance that we do not know *enough*: that our initial selection of epic-like material from India, Africa, the Middle East, and Central Asia somehow omits highly important poetry or prose that a Eurocentric mindset, raised on classical epic, cannot grasp as relevant. Even to divide verbal art into "poetry" and "prose" might turn out to be misleading, from the standpoint of non-western traditions (as Dennis Tedlock and others have argued, focusing on Native American works). But since every investigation needs to start somewhere, the critic's hope is that the "hermeneutic circle" morphs into a spiral: that the initial selection prompts re-thinking of old classifications, and even leads to productive reactions by others working in different fields. Although this volume is concerned primarily with ancient epic, from regions near the Mediterranean, it might lead to fresh analyses of compositions from many periods and places.

To enable this dialogue, and to prevent a premature canonization of "genre" that only impedes further understanding, we should begin with the assumption that "epic" is a contingent and culture-bound category. It may be "poetry" or "prose" or some *tertium quid*, by our reckoning. It may even look like what we would call "drama" or "lyric." Despite such *formal* differences, many societies may share a *functionally* similar category. What this chapter will argue is that "epic," applied to similar categories across cultures, plays a necessary role that *transcends* genre (thus making fruitless the attempt to pin it down as any single genre). In other words, "epic" stands out precisely by presenting itself, time after time, as the "natural" state of speech, the pre-existent mode, the word-before-genre, the matrix of other forms. And this consistent tendency can in turn best explain the semantic development and assumptions that have given us the very term which we are undertaking to analyze.

Ultimately, any concept of genre that underwrites the specific classification of "epic" should stress, above all, two *communicative* functions. First, as a means of channeling and clarifying communication between authors and readers (or performers and audiences), a shared genre acts as an agreement concerning the horizon of expectation, whether about the language, motifs, characterizations, themes, or even length of a given work. (We do not expect a "novella" to be 700 pages long. One might expect an "epic" performance to last at least an evening.) It is an implicit signaling device for senders and recipients of verbal art. Second, for those, like ourselves, removed in time from the immediate experience, genre forms an essential piece of cultural information. Knowing a culture's genre system, and its network of associations, is as significant as learning about its history, geography, economy, or languages. Once the native system is elicited, we can compare it with those of other societies, just as we can compare languages. And as with any such anthropological explorations, the knowledge thereby gained only counts when taken further, as a means of fostering human communication. To put it negatively, we should not define "genre" or "epic" simply as an ideal Platonic form for static contemplation. Definitions need to be dynamic aids to learning and social integration.

Modern handbooks of literary terms, in defining "epic," inevitably mention features of content, such as a cosmic scale; a serious purpose; a setting in the distant past; the presence of heroic and supernatural characters; and plots pivoting on wars or quests. The presence or absence of any such features should not be decisive, however, in defining a genre. Nor because they happen to be common to both oral and written (or "primary" and "secondary"epic), can these features be seen as proof that a natural or universal "epic" form exists, since "secondary" epics are of course explicitly modeled on the former. More recent scholarship, by contrast, has deconstructed the wall between written and oral modes and all but abandoned notions (going back to the early twentieth century) of "primary" epic (supposedly, Homeric poetry, *Beowulf*, and most non-western poems) as opposed to "secondary" epic (Apollonius of Rhodes' *Argonautica*, Virgil's *Aeneid*, the works of Milton, Spenser, Tasso, etc.; see further Chapters 25, 33, and 13, by Nelis, Putnam, and J. Foley). The match between "primary" and "oral" was never satisfactory, anyway, since most of the compositions available to readers had long been texts, whatever their performance history. A better solution has been the recognition of "transitional texts" in the formulaic style typical of composition-in-performance. In addition, modern ethnographers can attest to the fluidity of the very idea of "text" in many cultures that are most productive of "epic." Finally, the distinction between "primary" and "secondary" has been seen to encode more insidious contrasts between "primitive" song produced by underdeveloped, often tribal groups and "cultivated" writing done by elite males, usually in the service of a developing nation-state. At its worst, the contrastive pair was just a polite substitute for the chauvinistic opposition of "pre-art" versus "high art."

What has led handbook writers to associate as "epics" such disparate compositions as *Beowulf* and *Paradise Lost*, over and above the features of content just mentioned, are roughly comparable formal features including the length of a poem; the very fact of poetic form ("heroic" verse lines); musical accompaniment or song style; highly rhetorical speeches by heroic figures; invocations or self-conscious poetic proems; similes; and "typical" or recurrent scenes and motifs. These formal features are usually treated rather clinically as isolated textual markers, rather than as intertwined relics of possible performances. For instance, length of composition is often considered an absolute, apart from possibly variable contexts of audience interaction. Was *Beowulf* ever longer or shorter and still, for medieval English hearers, the "same" poem? Does performance length depend on where the "epic" was shared (during work or festivals, in royal hall or tavern)? Could a 50-line version still be "*Beowulf*"? Does cosmic scale demand extreme length? By the same token, can the Old English *Seafarer* be "epic" (and if not, what genre is it?). Such questions arise especially with ancient texts for which we have multiple versions, such as *Gilgamesh*. They can be approached, if not positively answered, by examining such Indic traditions as *Ramcaritmanas*, of which even a brief song session by women at local shrines is still regarded as "epic" recitation. To take another example, long similes – seemingly the stock-in-trade of "epic" composition – turn out in many cultures to be poetic interludes consciously imported from companion traditions (what one might call "lyric"). In these cases, as in many others, contemporary performances force us to question traditional handbook definitions. "Epic" emerges as a notional instead of normative term.

2 Defining "Epic" in Ancient Greece

Thematic and formal features are inevitably joined in the handbook "epic" definitions by reference to the *Poetics* of Aristotle (384–322 BCE). As a wide-ranging scholar with access to written sources later lost, as well as to living traditions of composition and commentary, Aristotle must have first place in any discussion of ancient literary criticism. But one problem in treating him as an authority on ancient "epic" is that he is relentlessly literary. By his era, the tradition of Homeric poems had most likely passed through two if not three stages of crystallization, in oral and textual phases, with relative degrees of fixity and vastly different conditions of audience reception. Thus a fourth-century Athenian intellectual's perception of "epic" gives no guarantee of resembling an eighth-century Ionian perform-er's sense of his or her poetic repertoire. Paradoxically, performers of Homeric epic even in Athens, two centuries before Aristotle, may not have known that they were singing or reciting "epic." That is to say, we can no more posit a cohesive and unchanged "Greek" notion of epic than we can a universal definition.

From the surviving early texts in hexameter meter (Homer, Hesiod, Homeric Hymns, Epic Cycle; see Chapters 21–4 and 28, by Edwards, Slatkin, Nelson, Burgess, and Garner), it is clear that the word for the production of entertaining tales of heroes or gods, to the accompaniment of a stringed instrument (*phorminx*) is called "song" (*aoidê*) and the performers are "singers" (*aoidoi*): see for example the descriptions of the Ithacan bard Phemius (*Od.* 1.325–52) and the Phaeacian singer Demodocus (*Od.* 8.43–6, 469–521). But a synonym for long narrated stories can be *mûthos* (plural *mûthoi*; in Homer, the word usually denotes "authoritative utterances"). For example, the heroes Nestor and Machaon "took delight in tales (*muthoisi*) speaking in detail (*enepontes*) to one another" (*Il.* 11.643). A minor variation of the same poetic verse introduces the night-long narrative session shared by Odysseus and Penelope upon his return (*Od.* 23.301; note that the concluding portion of the hero's tale is called *epos*, *Od.* 23.342). The main distinction between *aoidê* and *mûthoi* seems to be whether music is involved, and whether the performer is a professional. Both Odysseus and Achilles straddle the line by being expert at *mûthos*-speech and also like bards (Achilles when he plays the *phorminx* at *Il.* 9.186–91, Odysseus when compared to an enchanting singer at *Od.* 17.518–21). In fact, as we shall see, "epic" is most comparable to "myth" (the word derived ultimately from *mûthos*) both in archaic Greek terms and in the contemporary non-Eurocentric world.

For Aristotle in the *Poetics*, *mûthos* has what appears to be a completely different meaning than our word "myth." He uses it to mean something like "plot" or more broadly "narrative" (see *Poetics* 1449b5–8). As we shall see below (section 4), this development is not unexpected given the earlier semantic range of *mûthos* before the fifth century BCE. The further reach of the concept, as we see it in the *Poetics*, actually accords well with a similarly broad reach of "epic" both in classical sources and later. Yet despite the extensive cultural spread of both myth and epic in Greece, Aristotle significantly chooses as his centerpiece for an all-inclusive poetics the Athenian genre of tragedy. This has several implications. First, it means that he nowhere tries to define "epic" as a closed category distinct from other genres. Instead, because Aristotle always seeks to articulate the larger components in the construction of verbal art, he comments on features that usually overlap epic and tragedy, such as plot-structure, recognition, diction, and reversals of fortune (see e.g. *Poetics* 1455b16). For Aristotle, drama is as self-evident and singular an experience as film is for us; opposing it to *epopoiia* (his word for "epic-verse-making" or "epic") is more akin to contrasting film and "the novel" taken as a whole – without regard to particular sub-genres like romance, western, techno-thriller, mystery, or other. The smaller-scale features that might be used to separate out sub-categories of poetry are, for Aristotle, less important than the matter of imitation (*mimêsis*, his overarching concern in the *Poetics*). *Epopoiia* is one of six named types of performance: a mixed group we would consider untidy in its inclusion of musical arts such as pipe-playing and concert lyre-playing with tragedy, comedy, and dithyrambic poetry. All are supposed by him to be forms of "imitation" but differing in their means, manners, or objects of representation (1447a). What distinguishes "epic" in this connection is its representation of characters who are "noble" or "people of quality" (*spoudaios*: see *Poetics* 1449b10), a point to which we shall return. The *mimêsis* is done by means of a particular meter ("heroic" verse, i.e. dactylic hexameter); at considerable length; with many episodes; through a combination of narrative and character speeches and using elevated vocabulary and unusual words (1459b9–18). But these features are only noted by way of making the contrast with tragic drama, not in order to capture the essence of "epic."

A second important implication of choosing tragedy as his model is that the spirit of competitive dramatic production in Athens infiltrates Aristotle's own analysis. The habit of making value judgments must have been normal for Athenians of several generations, accustomed as they were to see one playwright each year awarded first place at the Dionysiac festival, by the decision of a citizen panel. Thus, though starting with a purely descriptive examination of the aspects of poetic mimesis, Aristotle in the *Poetics* shifts into a prescriptive and critical stance. He describes only partially "tragedy" or "epic" before taking up the *best* way of making both. For the latter, this means that Homeric poetry eclipses any discussion of the genre as a whole, for Homer is judged best, by Aristotle, given his use of diction and "thought" (*dianoia*), of focused plots, and of plausible fictions (see *Poetics* 1459a17–1460a19). In short, Homeric poetry is best because it most closely approaches tragic drama.

We have dwelt on Aristotle's treatise because, consciously or not, every writer and critic of western epic since the fourth century BCE has been influenced by its choices and assumptions. Although the elevation of Homeric epic to a place of primary importance, overriding numerous other hexameter poems in Greek, began most likely at a specific socio-political stage in sixth-century Athens, the reasoned approval of Aristotle ensured this canonization. When we peer around this brilliant spotlight of attention, trying to see within the shadows it has created, even the *Poetics* can provide tantalizing glimpses of a lost world of poetic art. That world, had it survived, might have radically altered later and modern notions of "epic" as a genre. A starting point for imagining this rich and varied archaic verbal tapestry comes from Aristotle's own notion that Homer was not the composer of the *Iliad* and *Odyssey* exclusively; he also authored the *Margites*, a poem (now almost entirely lost) using a mixture of hexameter and iambic meter to narrate the ridiculous adventures of a numbskull, the title figure. Aristotle places this composition within the category of "blame" or "lampoon" (*psogos*) and speculates that there must have been many such poems before Homer, although the *Margites* was the earliest to survive to his own day. As with his general elevation of Homeric art, he finds the *Margites* to be far beyond the personal invective characteristic of *psogos*, and as much a model for later dramatic comedy as the Homeric epics were for tragedy (1448b38). The fourth-century philosopher clearly distinguishes this comic piece from the more serious compositions, mostly on the basis of its tone and object of *mimêsis*. Whether the same generic distinction would occur to a performer or audience two or three centuries earlier is an open question.

Another way into the lost world of "epic"-like works, that may help us extract a definition of "epic" from Aristotle, is via meter. He himself uses the term *hêrôikon* to denote the meter of Homeric epic, but indirectly shows awareness that others (whom he does not name) call the same verse-form *epos* or *epê* (plural of *epos*); this much we can extrapolate from his corrective words (1447b15–18) chiding those who talk of *epopoioi* ("*epos*-verse-makers") while referring only to the meter they use, not to the sort of imitation they pursue. In Aristotle's view, this approach leads to absurdities, such as putting Homeric poetry into the same category as the verses of the philosopher Empedocles, although "there is nothing common to Homer and Empedocles except the meter" and the latter in his opinion should be called "scientist" (*phusiologos*) rather than poet. Reading this comment together with his further remarks on *mimêsis*, one can see, first, that Aristotle intends to use the term *epopoiia* more circumspectly, bringing it closer to what "epic" has meant since his time. Essentially, he defines it in terms of an attitude and style: high-language praise of the "serious." But the second observation to be made – an interesting corollary – is that *some* of his contemporaries or predecessors were willing to elide such differences among poems as lay in content or attitude. For these anonymous others, *epopoiia*, inasmuch as it signified the body of work in hexameters, composed by *epopoioi*, would have extended far beyond the circumference of Homeric or Aristotelian "epic." It would most likely have included those poets (again, lost to us) whom Aristotle distinguishes from Homer on the basis of how they represented characters, whether like the norm (as did Cleophon) or worse (as did Hegemon of Thasos, the first to compose "parodies") (1448a13). Only in smug retrospect, however, can we say that these un-named, all-embracing non-Aristotelians, embedded in their own historical periods and performance cultures, were wrong and Aristotle right.

As it turns out, we may have an interesting reference to such a broader sweep in the work of the historian Herodotus, who flourished a century before Aristotle. On one hand, Herodotus seems to share Aristotle's view that *epopoiiê* ("epic-verse-making," in his Ionic dialect form) demands a certain selectivity and seriousness. Significantly, Herodotus retrojects this view onto Homer himself (whom he believes lived around the ninth century BCE). Speaking of a version of the Trojan saga in which Helen with her paramour Paris visits Egypt on her way to Troy, the historian concludes (2.116.1): "And, in my opinion, Homer knew this story, too; but seeing that it was not so well suited (*euprepês*) to epic poetry (*epopoiiê*) as the tale of which he made use, he rejected it, showing that he knew it" (trans. Godley). After citing verses that he claims show Homer's knowledge of the alternate version (*Il.* 6.289–92, *Od.* 4.227–30, 351–2), Herodotus remarks on an inconsistency with yet another version to argue that "the Cyprian verses (*Kupria epea*) are not the work of Homer but of someone else" (2.117.2).

The poem he alludes to – now known as the *Cypria* and surviving only in a few quotations – was clearly "epic" in having thematic and formal features found in the *Iliad* and *Odyssey*. Yet the historian's phrase can denote either "epic poetry" or "hexameter verses." This ambiguity, frequent in the classical period, on the other hand makes it possible that a poem decidedly *non*-Homeric in its themes might also have been "epic" to Herodotus and his audiences. The composition in question, cited for its ethnographic details, is referred to as "the epic/hexameter verses (*epea*) now called by the Greeks

Arimaspea" (4.14.3) and attributed to one Aristeas of Proconessus, a Greek town in Asia Minor. "This Aristeas, possessed by Phoebus, visited the Issedones; beyond these (he said) live the one-eyed Arimaspians, beyond whom are the griffins that guard gold, and beyond these again the Hyperboreans, whose territory reaches to the sea" (trans. Godley). The mention of divine possession by Apollo and mythical wonders already marks a great gulf between this archaic poem and the generally more realistic Homeric epic, although Herodotus does say that Aristeas got his stories of one-eyed men and griffins as hearsay from the Issedones (4.16.1). More astounding is the biography of the poet: according to tales Herodotus has heard, Aristeas dropped dead in a fuller's shop, vanished before burial, and reappeared alive seven years later, at which point he composed the poem about his wanderings. He vanished again, turning up 240 years later in a Greek settlement of southern Italy, where he announced (before his final disappearance) that Apollo had blessed the townspeople with a divine visit and that he himself had followed the god in the form of a crow.

Scholars have rightly seen in this weird tale a memory of age-old shamanistic practices, involving out-of-body experiences and animal transformation. How could such a poem, though *epea* (i.e. hexameter verses), be "epic"? Before we too quickly eliminate it from the category or narrow our definition, it is worth recognizing the strong family resemblances between the *Arimaspea* and another travel narrative, the *Odyssey*. We might especially be reminded of the first-person wonder-tales of Odysseus in Books 9–12 of the *Odyssey*. Those adventures, in turn, resemble what we know of at least one hexameter poem attributed to the mythical Orpheus, telling of his descent to the Underworld. Orpheus, the magical singer, able to move trees and animals with his song, bears more than a passing resemblance to a shaman, as many have seen; his association with the initiatory-quest epic, the *Argonautica*, draws us closer to more familiar "epic" territory. Finally, the stories of the shaman-like adventures of the philosopher-priest Pythagoras, to whom hexameter verses were also attributed, fit into this expanded "wonder epic" category.

The usefulness of such a broadened class, within Greek tradition, becomes clear when we look once again at the Homeric *Iliad* and *Odyssey*. The audiences for both epics surely obtained additional meanings from the way in which these poems drew on material with an oblique connection to their more obvious "heroic" themes. Just as the *Odyssey* can be seen as expanding itself by way of the poetry of shamanic quest, the *Iliad* can be observed complicating its plot through the inclusion of a quest and trickster figure, Odysseus. Such a lateral, relational approach might even lead us at this point to formulate a further definition of genre: a set of allowable intertexts (oral or written), embracing all those compositions that communicate through consistent mutual allusivity. (It should be noted that the set also allows for "null allusion" – that is, for producing a point precisely by refusing to make overt reference to one or another contemporary and related tale or poem-type.) If the *Iliad* cannot be fully appreciated without the figures, themes, or diction of other Trojan War sagas, in whatever form these existed, these others qualify for inclusion in the genre. The Epic Cycle, a series of poems in hexameter that gained shape in the eighth through fifth centuries BCE, would for example fit this definition. So would the *Theogony*, the *Shield of Herakles*, and the *Catalogue of Women* attributed to Hesiod. The *Theogony*, a poem of about 1,000 lines telling of Zeus' rise to power, has even been read as the heroic biography of the chief god, although the story is framed by the first-person introduction of the poet himself, singing of his initiatory encounter with the Muses on Mt Helicon. As Jenny Strauss Clay (1989) and Leonard Muellner (1996) have shown, the long narrative "Homeric Hymns" also form a close bond with the fore-mentioned compositions. Both these and the shorter hymns in the collection seem to have functioned, at some stage, as preludes to longer "epic" compositions.

If we continue to open the field, to admit such verses, how then does one prevent a notional "genre" of epic, even within Greek, from becoming too unwieldy a tool? More bluntly, what is *not* epic? How, for instance, would we account for another long hexameter poem, the *Works and Days*, which includes a narrative of conflict (Hesiod and his brother Perses, apparently feuding over an inheritance), but also includes proverbs and maxims, fables with a political point and advice on farming and ritual? What of those diverse (now fragmentary) compositions that seem to have been swept together and placed under the name of the Boeotian "peasant" poet: the *Instructions of Cheiron, Bird-Prophecy, Marriage of Ceyx, Descent of Theseus to the Underworld, Astronomy,* etc.? Such apparently non-"epic" verse can have a mutually allusive interconnection with what became, in time, mainstream Homeric epic. For example, the Hesiodic *Works and Days* in its lengthy meditation on "right" justice (*dikê*) makes an indispensable poetic counterpart to the central themes of both the *Iliad* (the disputes between Agamemnon and Achilles, Achaeans and Trojans) and the *Odyssey* (the vengeance on the hubris of the suitors). By the same token, the *Theogony* puts in dogmatic form the key points, in similar formulaic phrases, that Odysseus uses to instruct the Phaeacian nobility in Book 8 of the *Odyssey*. Again, the *Odyssey* features an extended "catalogue" of heroic women in the Underworld scene of Book 11, which even in antiquity was matched with the Hesiodic *Catalogue*. Clearly, generic interplay and expansion, allusion and multiformity, were essential to the art of *epopoiia* in archaic Greek. It does not make sense to isolate only some of the resultant multilayered compositions as "epic."

A straightforward assumption can account for the tight bonds among all these hexameter poems: namely, the existence, from at least the sixth century BCE, of travelling reciters or singers, called "rhapsodes" ("song-stitchers"), at least some of whom traced their ancestry to the master singer Homer himself. These shapers of the canon in any given generation could define "epic" simply as the substance of their repertoire. They could also explicitly cross-reference, and explain to audiences, the complex ways in which the mythological, heroic, and "folk" lore of their poems fit together. We know, from depictions in Plato's *Ion, Republic,* and *Laws* (among other sources) that the rhapsodic repertoire included poetry attributed to Homer and Hesiod, as also Orpheus, Musaeus, and other shadowy earlier poets. In sum, the genre inhered in its performers. Neither formal nor thematic boundaries prevented rhapsodic cross-pollinization. Our notion of "epic" will not be too large if it expands to fit the performance repertoire of these important figures, and by extension, the cognitive and aesthetic capabilities of their audiences.

3 "Epic" Cross-culturally

"Epic" – or any other literary genre – cannot be classified apart from the performers who transmit it. One can even argue, as Gregory Nagy does, that the invention of "genre" as a system of categories in Greek literary history only occurs when the oral-traditional performances of the archaic period are reduced to writing, mostly during the fifth century BCE, and the originating events lost or forgotten. "Genre," in this regard, is a tool for scholars and librarians. This is not to say that poets themselves never had an awareness of technical and thematic distinctions among, for example, verses to honor gods, tell of heroic deeds, mock social offenders, or accompany religious processions. But this was a matter of implicit poetics, both performers and audiences following what tradition suggested.

A review of contemporary verbal art in sub-Saharan Africa, India, and Egypt will show that the fluidity of early Greek modes – and, as far as we can tell, that of Near Eastern ancient epic – is the norm in traditional societies. At the same time, we shall see:

- that while something resembling "epic" *can* be distinguished *from* other forms, it is even more significant to see it *in relation to* its accompanying genres in performance;
- that the specifics of textual or performance style cannot be used to determine whether or not a performance is "epic";
- that the epic "genre" has symbiotic ties with folktale, myth, and especially praise-poetry;
- that, above all, epic stands out as the most pervasive, "unmarked" genre, in terms of when and where it can be performed, while at the same time it is the culturally most significant and "marked" form in terms of its ambitions and attitudes.

These observations, brief as they are, can help us to rethink the classical and western notion of "epic" while leading us to a deeper sense of the limits and possibilities of genre definitions.

Let us begin with the issue of boundaries. Daniel Biebuyck places the Mwindo narrative from the Congo within an array of other distinct verbal art forms practiced by the Nyanga people (Biebuyck and Mateene 1969). Significantly, the sequenced singing and recitation of long narratives (*kárisi*) incorporates these other genres of discourse: proverbs, riddles, and prayers in poetic form, eulogistic recitations, formulas used by diviners and medicine men, personal songs, animal tales, instructions and political advice, all find a place within *Mwindo*. Such generic inclusiveness is common throughout African epic narrative. A crucial further point can be adduced from the work of Dwight Reynolds on the *Sirat Bani Hilal* as performed in northern Egypt (1995). Reynolds points out that the urge to treat as the "epic" the pure story-line of one Bedouin tribe's exploits must be resisted, if one is to appreciate the full impact of the performance. The Egyptian bard always dovetails his singing with two other equally important and formally different components, the praise of Mohammad (*madih*) and proverbial advice in lyric form (*mawwal*). More surprisingly, even when *within* the epic a character is about to speak, the same canonical sequence of genres occurs. In short, the "epic" must be taken as total social event including audience interaction, instrumental music, and these framing genres, not just the "text" we might want to cull from it.

We know that epic recitation was preceded by proems resembling the Homeric Hymns (see Thuc. 3.104). As mentioned above, Homeric and Hesiodic poems could be recited by the same rhapsodic performers. The Hesiodic corpus encompasses proverbial lore in diction and structures that have been compared to Greek lyric. In short, one can imagine an ancient Greek performer sequencing exactly the same functionally similar genres as the Egyptian bards: praise (*humnoi*), wisdom (*gnômai*), and "epic" (narrowly conceived). Furthemore, it can be argued that Greek epic not only can be *framed by* but itself consciously *embeds* such subgenres as praise and blame poetry, maxims, and lyric similes (see further section 4).

Such fluid genre boundaries relate to the wide range of "epic" performance styles, both in the course of one composition and across regions. Mande hunters' epics comprise three genres – narrative, song, and praise proverbs – and hence three performance styles. In Central African epic traditions it is common for the main reciter to be accompanied by backup singers performing melodic portions organic to the tale (often the character's "speech" as song). The Nyanga bard dances and dramatically mimes parts of *Mwindo*, even taking on the hero's role, while select respondents repeat his verses (compare the narrative and dance event described at *Od.* 8.255–369). In contrast to Central African multimedia productions, West African performances such as the widespread *Sunjata* epic often feature a solitary reciting *griot*. (There are many local indigenous names for this role, which combines historian, praise-poet, herald, and arbitrator.) One such, the Maninka *jeli*, recites the epic at high speed, accompanying himself on a small four-string instrument.

Joyce Flueckiger's research in northern and central India shows not only that "epic" can be done in widely different styles, but that even the same long, heroic narrative, like the Dhola-Maru tradition, sung in communities a few hundred miles apart, qualifies as "epic" in one but not the other (1999). Community self-identification, caste ambitions, and local religious cult all determine whether a people views the epic as its own defining narrative.

If content or consistent style fail to demarcate contemporary "epic," neither do the Eurocentric contrasts with "folktale" or "myth." For example, the *mvet* narrations of the Fang (southern Cameroon, Gabon) recount episodic struggles between two clans, a mortal and immortal. There is no central protagonist; magical elements abound, along with romance or folktale motifs. Yet the night-long narrations function like other Central African epics to address the society's abiding concerns. Their human quest stories are simply a strand in a much larger tapestry of cosmic issues: how plants, animals, and social hierarchies came to be. In Greek, we might at first perceive fewer cosmic issues in the martial or adventure epics. But the Hesiodic corpus, especially the *Catalogue of Women*, is clearly related to local concerns, rites and tales; the *Theogony* embodies an entire cosmology. The investigations of Georges Dumézil have been especially useful in illustrating how "epic" in Greece, and even more so in the related languages of Iceland, Ireland, India and Rome, is often a matter of cosmic myths, historicized and secularized (1968, 1971, 1973).

Myth and folktale might be considered the deeper roots of epic, yet they can just as easily be synchronic and interactive with epic. It is perhaps best to think of them along a spectrum, with audience interest the determining factor in how unspecified, as to time and place, a story can be, and what belief it engenders. A different dynamic exists between epic and praise poetry. As described by Africanists, praise-poetry is an allusive, highly compressed, and non-narrative evocation of the genealogies and successes of chieftains. Marked by often obscure, riddling names, brief references to events, and a repetitive, incantatory style, this genre is more widespread than epic, especially in southern and eastern Africa. Instead of a range on a spectrum, the praise-poem is a telescope: what is compressed in a style that imitates the instantaneous exultation of a client before his patron, in epic is expanded to fill out chronology, cause, and characterization. While praise (often in second-person address) is more direct and more lucrative, epic (usually third-person) is more lucid. The dynamic interaction of praise and epic should make us think of such poetic forms as ancient Greek *epinikia* and *enkômia*, as preserved mainly in the work of Pindar (*ca.* 518–438 BCE), often noted for the same features – allusive, elliptical, gnomic, and narrative only in a kernel form. Medieval Irish bardic verse and prose sagas exhibit a similar kernel-and-expansion relationship. Whether or not we construct a diachronic development from praise poetry to epic, the synchronic reality of their interdependence must be kept in mind,

In brief, contemporary "epic" stands in at least three typological relationships to other types of verbal art. It can (1) incorporate *smaller* forms (proverbs, songs, etc.). It can (2) embody an entire *deep* form, providing epic skin for the bones of myth or folktale concerns; and it can (3) expand a socially functional *kernel* form, praise-poetry. Furthermore, all three relations can occur simultaneously, as in *Sunjata*. The many versions available (1) feature songs of *griots* and wise sayings; (2) embody a folktale type of the boy's success story, about a marginalized mother–son dyad and its rise to power; and (3) contain frequent formulaic praises of the hero as founder of the kingdom of Mali (and of his *griot* as ancestor of modern singers). Perhaps, indeed, we should define epic as that form that consistently represents all three of the above relations.

The *expansiveness* of epic as "super-genre" brings us, finally, to observe a matching *pervasiveness* on the level of performance. From the accounts of numerous ethnographers, it is clear that "epic" events are unconfined in contrast to most other stylized verbal art, and not pinned to authorized occasions, rituals, or audiences, such as initiatory groups. Epic can be sung in almost every setting, by professionals or amateurs. Just as epic as *actual* performance functions as a soundstage, an environment for setting off all sorts of smaller genres, so epic as *possible* peformance is equivalent to the cultural environment itself, ready to be instantiated and evoked at any moment. As dozens of field studies show, the total "epic" is in fact never performed unless elicited by an outsider, such as the folklorist. Yet even when it is brought forth, as usually, in shorter episodic form, the performance depends on an audience and performer's unspoken awareness of the *totality* of a story and its conceivable permutations. In potential size, epic is hugely ambitious, undertaking to articulate the most essential aspects of a culture, from its origin stories to its ideals of social behavior, social structure, relationship to the natural world and to the supernatural. The scope of epic is matched by its attitude: as Aristotle noted, it dwells on the serious. (Even its meter, says Aristotle, is "most stately and weightiest": *stasimôtaton kai onkôdestaton, Poetics* 1459b34–5.) Epic, the ultimate metonymic art form from the perspective of its *pars pro toto* performance, is on the level of ideology a metonymy for culture itself.

4   Concluding Coda

At this point we might return to a significant conundrum within ancient Greek semantics, one already alluded to above. *Mûthos*, the word that gives us "myth," denotes in Homeric epic an authoritative utterance. It usually marks a long and detailed speech most often performed before a critical audience, expecting assent, and in the sub-genre mode of a command, an insult, or a detailed act of memory-recitation. This might sound like a good synonym for "epic" itself, which, as we have seen, in scope and ambition is homologous with "myth" in the societies where it flourishes. Oddly enough, the word that gives us "epic" is in fact *contrasted*, within our oldest Greek poetry, with *mûthos*. It can be described, within the synchronic system of Homeric diction, as unmarked. *Epos* usually refers to short utterances; non-public "sayings"; brief ordinary remarks; or intimate communication as between husband and wife or hero and companion. Later, the plural *epea*, as we have seen, comes to mean "hexameter verses" or "epic" whereas within Homer this plural (but not the singular) can be a synonym for *mûthos*. How does this transformation occur? Are we dealing with a historical development or something deeper, embedded in the very nature of an art form? In the light of the Greek evidence above, particularly about the status of *epos* as both *marked* (in literary history) and *unmarked* (in Homeric diction) we might notice that "epic" as a genre, as seen from a non-western stance, illustrates exactly this paradoxical bifocal relationship. On the one hand, it is as pervasive as everyday speech: intimate, simple, potential in any utterance. It can happen at any time; it can embody any matter and make it significant. On the other, "epic" – like the plural *epea* and especially its most famous occurrence, in the formulaic phrase describing speech as *epea pteroenta* "winged words" – is a mode of total communication, undertaking nothing less than the ideal expression of a culture. If the usefulness of "genre" is to provide a heuristic tool for honing inter-cultural communication, the good of "epic" lies in its power to craft, through generations of performers and audiences, larger harmonies, in which the discrete pieces of the individual's life fit and make sense.

FURTHER READING

1 Introduction

bibliography on world oral tradition: Foley 1985 with updates at www.oraltradition.org.
contemporary epic, introductory surveys and analyses with further reading: Oinas 1978; Hatto and Hainsworth 1980, 1989; Okpewho 1992; Reichl 1992; Beissinger et al. 1999.
genre and ancient texts: Depew and Obbink 2000b.
genre in practice: Bynum 1976; Bauman 1992.
handbook definition and discussion: Revard and Newman 1993.
Indic traditions: Blackburn et al. 1989; Flueckiger and Sears 1991; Lutgendorf 1991.
native genre categories: Bauman and Sherzer 1989.
poetry/prose distinction: Tedlock 1983; Fine 1984.
"primitive" epic: Bowra 1952; critique in Farrell 1999b.
transitional texts: Foley 1990, 1991; Lord 1995.

2 Defining "epic" in ancient Greece

Aristotle: Halliwell 1986; Richardson 1992.
Epic Cycle: Burgess 2001.
Greek definitions: Ford 1997; Nagy 1999b.
Hesiod: West 1985; Lamberton 1988; Nagy 1990b.
Homeric depiction of song: Nagy 1989; Ford 1992; Segal 1994.
Homeric Hymns: Clay 1989; Muellner 1996; Martin 2000.
intertextuality in epic: Martin 1984, 2001.
mûthoi as "tales": Edmunds 1997.
Orphic poetry: West 1983; Martin 2001.
other Greek epics: Huxley 1969.
rhapsodes, text fixation: Nagy 1996b, 1996c, 2002.
semantics of mûthos and epos: Martin 1989.
shamanism: Dodds 1951.

3 "Epic" cross-culturally

African traditions: Stone 1988; Belcher 1999.
Egyptian epic: Slyomovics 1987; Reynolds 1995, 1999.
epic and myth: Dumézil 1968, 1971, 1973.
genres of discourse: Martin 1984; Todorov 1990.
genres within epic: Martin 1984, 1989; Davidson 1998a.
Indic performance: Flueckiger 1989, 1999.
Irish bardic poetry: Bergin 1970.
Mwindo epic of Nyanga: Biebuyck and Mateene 1969.
relationship between lyric and epic traditions: Nagy 1990c.
shifts in performance style and genres: Phillips 1981.
similes and lyric: R. P. Martin 1997.
Sunjata: Austen 1999.

4 Concluding coda

mûthos and epos; markedness: Martin 1989; Nagy 1999b.

CHAPTER TWO

The Indo-European Context

Joshua T. Katz

> The *Sanscrit* language, whatever be its antiquity, is of a wonderful structure; more perfect than the *Greek*, more copious than the *Latin*, and more exquisitely refined than either, yet bearing to both of them a stronger affinity, both in the roots of verbs and in the forms of grammar, than could possibly have been produced by accident; so strong indeed, that no philologer could examine them all three, without believing them to have sprung from some common source, which, perhaps, no longer exists. (Jones 1993 [1807]: III.34)

With these famous words, spoken by the great Anglo-Welsh Orientalist and jurist Sir William Jones in the middle of his "Third Anniversary Discourse, on the Hindus" before the Asiatick (as it was then spelled) Society in Calcutta on February 2, 1786, began the scientific study of linguistic relationships in general and of what would come to be known as Indo-European in particular (see, e.g., Cannon 1990: esp. pp. 241–70, and for an overview of the development of nineteenth-century linguistics, Morpurgo Davies 1998). The Sanskrit (as it is now spelled) language is indeed of a wonderful structure, though linguists now understand that the formal architecture of each and every tongue is entirely suited to expressing all that needs to be expressed. There can, in other words, be no yardstick for measuring perfection or copiousness or exquisite refinement, for all human languages are manifestations of a single very real, but biologically still very mysterious, underlying Human Language. From this point of view, which took hold only toward the end of the twentieth century, Sanskrit is certainly like Greek and like Latin but also, for that matter, like Swahili and Xhosa and Chinese: all are forms of one and the same thing, Language (with a capital L), arguably the principal characteristic that separates humans from all other species. There is, however, another perspective, and it is here that Jones and, in his footsteps, many nineteenth-century scholars we would now call historical/comparative linguists left a mark that remains very much with us still today: when inspected comparatively, certain languages – but, crucially, not others – bear such strong and pervasive affinities, ones that cannot be explained by accident or massive borrowing, that they simply have to have sprung – that is to say, arisen historically – from some common source. Sanskrit, Greek, and Latin are, as Jones noted, remarkably similar to one another; Swahili and Xhosa, too, are remarkably similar, as we now know, though not to Sanskrit, Greek, or Latin; and Chinese is not similar to any of these other languages. To sum up: if we are concerned with the idea and ideal of Language in the brain, then all six languages are somehow the same; but if we are concerned instead with data from real languages, then the first three have sprung from one common source, the next two from a different source, and the last from yet another. (There are numerous introductory textbooks on linguistics: reliable ones include Fromkin 2000 and Akmajian et al. 2001 and, specifically for historical/comparative matters, Anttila 1989, Hock and Joseph 1996, and Campbell 1999.)

The source of the Indic language Sanskrit and the two European languages Greek and Latin is what is now known as Proto-Indo-European. (By contrast, Swahili and Xhosa come from Proto-Bantu, itself a daughter of the much larger Niger-Congo family, and Chinese goes back to Proto-Sino-Tibetan.) The prefix "proto-" (Greek "first") conveys the fact that the language in question – the source, which does indeed no longer exist – is not actually attested in any documents but has rather to be inferred from the existence of its children (conventionally "daughters"). These so-called Indo-European languages, among which is numbered English, have a tremendous geographical and temporal range: even before the recent spread of English to the United States, Australia, and virtually every corner of the globe, Indo-European languages spanned the northern half of the Indian subcontinent and all the way to Ireland and Iceland in westernmost Europe; our earliest records date to the middle of the second millennium BCE, and there are, of course, numerous Indo-European languages alive and well today, including all those modern languages of India (such as Hindi) that have developed from Sanskrit, modern Greek, and the Romance languages, which are Latin's legacy. (Watkins 2000a provides a splendid introduction to Proto-Indo-European based on the vocabulary of modern English.)

The Indo-European language family comprises twelve principal branches, or sub-families, listed here roughly in the order in which they are first attested: Anatolian, Indic, Iranian, Hellenic, Italic, Celtic, Germanic, Armenian, Tocharian, Slavic, Baltic, and Albanian. (A few other branches, such as Illyrian and Phrygian, are also known, but too poorly to be mentioned except parenthetically.) Some of these sub-families are fairly simple (Hellenic, for example, consists solely of the various dialects of ancient and modern Greek), others more complicated (Germanic encompasses Old, Middle, and modern English, as well as German, Dutch, Swedish, Danish, Gothic, and a host of other languages). But in all cases, it is on the basis of whatever actual documentation we are lucky enough to possess of the languages in question that we are able to draw a picture of the family's earliest reconstructible "mother," Proto-Indo-European, and, in the process, numerous intermediary stages, such as Proto-Germanic (itself the mother of Proto-West-Germanic, whence English, German, and Dutch; Proto-East-Germanic, whence Gothic; and Proto-North-Germanic, whence Swedish and Danish). (The clearest general account of the Indo-European languages is Fortson 2004; for a technical survey, see Meier-Brügger 2003.) The location in time and especially space of the last speakers of an as-yet-unbroken Proto-Indo-European tongue remains a scholarly hot potato, but assuming a homeland somewhere around (and more north than south of) the Black Sea around 3500 BCE will not raise too many eyebrows (for a sober overview, see Mallory 1989 and 1997).

All reputable linguists who reconstruct proto-languages rely first and foremost on a technique known as the Comparative Method (the classic exposition is Meillet 1925/ 1967). This simple procedure for determining linguistic relatedness remains, after nearly two centuries, the most consistently validated theory of language ever put forward. It relies on the startling (and – it is embarrassing to say – still far from understood) fact that phonological change is fundamentally regular: if someone makes a speech error, substi-tuting a [t] for the very similar sound [d] in the word *drape*, say, and if that mispronun-ciation is for some reason subsequently taken up by the wider speech community (so that everyone starts to say *trape*), then *all* forms in which the initial error could have occurred (e.g., *drain*, *drake*, and *drill*) come to be uttered in the new, and newly correct, way. The critical word here is "all": if it is true that certain basic changes apply in all cases, across the board, then we have a scientific method for determining whether two or more languages are related, that is to say, go back to a common source. Put in as simple a fashion as possible, given language X, with the words *drape*, *drain*, *drake*, and *drill*, and language Y, with the words *trape*, *train*, *trake*, and *trill* with (more or less) the same meanings, the comparison of X and Y *proves* that these two languages are related to each other and go back to Proto-Z, for there is no other possible explanation for why [d] in X should invariably be correlated to [t] in Y.

To take an actual and more or less unadulterated example (which necessarily introduces complexities that cannot be dealt with here), consider the following words in language E(nglish): *two*, *foot*, *father*, *mother*, *three*, and *thee*. Compare the semantically identical forms *deux*, *pied*, *père*, *mère*, *trois*, and *toi* in language F(rench), the semantically identical forms *duo*, *pod-*, *patêr*, *mêtêr*, *treis*, and (dialectal) *te* in language G(reek), and the semantically identical forms *duo*, *ped-*, *pater*, *mater*, *tres*, and *te* in language L(atin). Inspection makes it clear that there are regular correspondences among the words: [t], [f], [m], [ð/θ] (i.e., "th"), and [r] in E correspond regularly to [d], [p], [m], [t], and [r] in G and L; as for F, here, too, we see most of these same sounds, only there is no consonant at all in both instances where we might have expected to find something like a [t] or [ð/θ] between vowels (*père* and *mère*). It is thus clear that E, F, G, and L are related: each of these sets of corresponding words, or cognates, has arisen, via a series of regularly chartable successful speech errors, from a distinct form in Proto-Indo-European. (Further data would establish that F arises out of L and that L and G are not as closely linked as the few examples given above might lead us to believe.) The words for "two," all of which begin with the sound [d] except the English, can be shown to go back to something like **dwoH* (the asterisk has the same function as the prefix "proto-"; **H* is a so-called laryngeal, probably in this case the third). As a cautionary note, it needs to be pointed out that changes are by no means always so easy to see or hear: the Armenian word for "two" is *erku*, which happens to be the regular (!) development of **dwoH* (Proto-Indo-European **dw-* yields *erk-* in Armenian).

Now, phonological change is just one part of linguistic development, but it is, of course, basic: only once we know how sounds have changed can we think about morphemes; only once we understand morphemes can we think about words; and only once we understand words can we think about phrases, clauses, sentences, and larger narrative structures. The bigger and more unusual the units of analysis, the harder they are to deal with, and so there is a clear reason why most historical/comparative linguists concentrate on phonology and morphology rather than on syntax, discourse, or – in some ways hardest of all – the artful devices of poetry. Nevertheless, there is an obvious appeal to going beyond simple sounds, and one of the most exciting ways that linguists can bridge language and culture is by considering forms that have special and obvious societal importance. There is nothing remarkable about the referents of such words as *two*, *foot*, and *father*: all languages have conventional ways to speak of low numbers, basic body parts, and close kin. But one does not need to be a linguist to know that there are some words that carry special semantic or pragmatic weight.

Consider, for example, the name of the highest god in the Roman pantheon, the most revered figure for speakers of Latin: *Iupiter* (Jupiter). For the Romans, *Iupiter* was a culturally special word, but, in the end, it was, linguistically speaking, a word like any other. Modern linguists, however, can tell a more interesting story: *Iupiter* has an exact cognate in Greek, *Zeu patêr* – a phrase, not merely a single word, and a phrase, moreover, that has a clear synchronic meaning and analysis, "O Father Zeus!" Greek *patêr* is, of course, the word for "father" that we have just looked at, and so, too, is the Latin form *-piter*, a fossil in the second half of a synchronically opaque old compound. As for *Zeu* and *Iu-*, close attention to religious language across the Indo-European world demonstrates that this name originally meant "(Bright) Sky." In other words, a historical analysis of the comparative evidence leads us to the conclusion that the highest god in the

Proto-Indo-European pantheon is a personification of the sky and that speakers very often invoked him as a father figure. The Proto-Indo-European reconstruction *$dyew$ ph_2ter* is thus a much grander thing than a mere asterisked preform on a dusty page. (There is a vast literature on these words: see, e.g., Strunk 1982).

This brings me, finally, to my subject: the Indo-European context of ancient epic. To say that languages are related is to say that there are identifiable linguistic correspondences among them and that these correspondences reflect the fact that the languages in question were once upon a time – before speakers went their different ways – one and the same proto-language. Linguists usually deal with, and reconstruct, ordinary language, but humans will always tell tales, compose poetry, engage in what we may broadly term "verbal art," and there is good reason to believe that if we take care to start small and not use too broad a brush, we can legitimately consider what a leading scholar has termed "genetic intertextuality" (C. Watkins 1995: 11; see also Matasović 1996). We can, in other words, aspire to reconstruct not just language, but poetic language, and thus recover features of a common Indo-European artistic tradition. Poetic language – it is usually referred to by its German name, *Dichtersprache* – has been a major topic of Indo-European research for some decades now, and it seems best simply to make reference here to the two most influential works, Schmitt 1967 and C. Watkins 1995, as well as to a few other books that everyone who is interested in the subject should study with special care: Schmitt 1968; Durante 1976; Campanile 1977, 1990; Meid 1978; Bader 1989; Watkins 1994 (esp. vol. II); Matasović 1996; Janda 1997, 2000; and Jackson 1999, 2002. (In general I am trying in this chapter to cite principally Anglo-American scholarship, but here I have chosen to mention authors of different nationalities so as to present Indo-European studies as the international subject it truly is.)

Since epic poetry, a specific – if very hard-to-define – form of verbal art, plays an important role throughout the Indo-European family, it is reasonable to suppose that at least some of the individual instances of the genre reflect a shared tradition (see Chapter 1, by Martin). In what follows, I will trace some manifestations of this tradition among speakers of the older languages. My emphasis will be on Greece, for two reasons: first, we know more about Greek epic material than about early epic poetry in any other branch aside from Indic (see Chapters 21 and 22, by Edwards and Slatkin); and second, most contributors to and readers of this volume are classicists. As for secondary emphases, there are two plausible candidates, India and the Indo-European Near East: India because there is an abundance of primary sources and also because the Hellenic and Indo-Iranian branches are (along with Armenian) generally considered to form a loose dialectal grouping within the Indo-European family; the Near East because it is geographically adjacent and culturally very closely tied to the Greek mainland, islands, and colonies in Asia Minor and because there are few topics as hot in classics at the beginning of the twenty-first century as the interactions, whether they are linguistic, literary, or artistic, between Greece and the East (Anatolia, Mesopotamia, and the Levant) in both historical and prehistoric times (notable contributions include Burkert 1992; Morris 1992, 1997; Penglase 1994; and West 1997b). I will focus more on India because this book has no chapter on South Asian epic, whereas there is an entire section on the Near East (see Chapters 14–19, by Sasson, Noegel, Wyatt, Beckman, Davidson, and Niditch), and also because discerning the *echt*-Indo-European elements in the society of the Hittites (to name the most prominent Indo-European people of Anatolia) amidst all the Hurrian and Semitic influences is a job of its own.

In order to be able to consider its tradition, we first have to come to some sort of understanding of what epic is as a genre, a notoriously contentious matter (see Chapter 1, by Martin; Revard and Newman 1993 give a concise, wide-ranging, and unpolemical account; the best treatments from the point of view of archaic Greece are

Ford 1992: esp. pp. 13–56, and 1997). Both for better and for worse, the word "epic" itself inevitably invites us to begin with the Greek tradition, for the word is a borrowing from Greek, in which ἔπος, ἔπη, literally "word(s)," is a standard classical (though not archaic) term for the sort of poetry exemplified by the (roughly eighth-century BCE) *Iliad* and *Odyssey* (see, e.g., Koster 1970). Cross-culturally, the most usual way to define epic is in terms of (to put it crudely) heroic length; witness, for example, the opening sentence of the entry "Epic" in *The New Princeton Encyclopedia of Poetry and Poetics*: "An e[pic] is a long narrative poem…that treats a single heroic figure or a group of such figures and concerns an historical event, such as a war or conquest, or an heroic quest or some other significant mythic or legendary achievement that is central to the traditions and belief of its culture" (Revard and Newman 1993: 361; compare Bowra 1952). Certainly the two Greek poems just mentioned are epics in this sense, but many scholars, especially classicists, follow up on one or another of the various visions held by ancient authorities themselves and characterize epic additionally in terms of meter (dactylic hexameter) or its dependence on the very tradition that Homer founded; compare the testimony of the Roman poet Horace (*Ars Poetica* 73–4): "res gestae regumque ducumque et tristia bella/quo scribi possent numero, monstrauit Homerus" "Homer showed in what meter the deeds of kings and generals and grim wars could be written."

While the three characteristics of epic just cited (Homer as *primus inuentor*; narrative themes and unusual length; and the hexameter) make sense from a classicist's point of view, they are of only partial utility when we try to extrapolate from archaic Greece back to Proto-Indo-European and the Indo-European tradition. While there is no doubt that Homer stands at the head of an extraordinary body of classical and classicizing heroic poetry that extends from Virgil to Derek Walcott via such towering figures as Dante and Milton (see now the essays in Beissinger et al. 1999), viewing him before an Indo-European background is at some level to take away his status as founder of a genre and instead place him in the middle of a much deeper, as well as wider, tradition. Just as there were kings before Agamemnon, so too were there bards (an Old Irish word that goes back to a compound in Proto-Indo-European that literally means "praise-maker": see in the first place Campanile 1980) before Homer, and from an Indo-European perspective, defining epic as the genre that Homer founded simply is too restrictive. But if we cast our nets more widely and consider any lengthy narrative poem to be epic, then we end up with a quasi-universal genre (Do any poetic traditions lack stories of heroes, quests, and monsters?) and fail to isolate those particular features that have "the Indo-European touch" (C. Watkins 1995: 297). (Studies that compare archaic Indo-European and non-western epic poetry are legion: for Bantu, see Opland 1983: esp. pp. 152–93, and many other publications; for Chinese, see, e.g., Wang 1988: esp. pp. 73–114, on what he calls the *Weniad*. Generally on oral traditions, see the works of John Miles Foley, esp. Foley 2002.)

This leaves the criterion of meter. Obviously, the dactylic hexameter is not a characteristic of epic the world over, but on most accounts a striking Greek innovation, one that Roman poets (in the first place Ennius) latched on to and borrowed as an elegant way of rising above the "cruder" native Italic verse and one, furthermore, that in more recent times has been adapted by classically inspired traditions (even the English iambic pentameter ultimately goes back to it). However, no other branch of Indo-European has epics in dactylic hexameter that are free of Greek influence. How, then, can Homeric epic be intimately tied in this respect to anything else? Is the hexameter in the end really a Greek touch rather than a more deeply traditional (Proto-)Indo-European one?

Consider the fact, just mentioned, that the English iambic pentameter is generally regarded as having developed out of our Greek hexameter. (On the evolution of European meters in general, see Gasparov 1996.) This example suffices to show that unity can lie beneath apparent difference (even extreme disparity, as in the case of English *two* and Armenian *erku*), and it follows from this both that there could be other verse-forms in early Indo-European languages that are genetically connected to the dactylic hexameter and that the Greek form itself need not have arisen fully formed. In fact, scholars since Meillet (1923) have slowly begun to acknowledge that early Greek lyric (N.b. not epic) meters are cognate with meters in other Indo-European branches, certainly in Indic, Slavic, and Celtic, and very likely in others besides (see Matasović 1996: 97–114 for an appropriately cautious overview). Much work remains to be done on meter and metrical development in non-Indo-European languages before we can confidently isolate specifically Indo-European features from the mass of cross-cultural metrical tendencies (see Matasović 1996: 113–14). Still, it appears to be the case that the Greek dactylic hexameter, the defining meter of epic, has indeed arisen out of a lyric form of the type that Meillet and others view as having a cognate in Sanskrit: the most closely worked-out exposition of this opinion is Nagy 1974, who sees the "Aeolic" archetype of the dactylic hexameter in a 16-syllable internally expanded pherecratean, which is itself a catalectic version of another lyric metrical base, the octosyllabic glyconic. If this or something like it is correct, the consequences are stunning for the study of Greek poetry (it greatly complicates the relationship between epic and lyric, two verse-forms that have synchronically rather different characters) and strikingly alter how we might understand the Indo-European context of epic. For one thing, the standard poetic unit of the classical Sanskrit genre of epic, the *śloka*, likewise has 16 syllables, and it, in turn, is based on an older octosyllabic type in Vedic that is comparable to the glyconic and pherecratean of Greek lyric. That the deep connection between lyric and epic poetry extends beyond meter to poetic language is clear from Nagy's extended study, which takes as its point of departure the simultaneously metrical and formulaic relationship of the Greek poetic phrase κλέος ἄφθιτον "imperishable fame," found in lyric (Sappho fr. 44.4) and, most famously, epic (*Il.* 9.413: Achilles' great speech), and the exactly cognate collocation in Vedic Sanskrit, *śrávas . . . ákṣitam* (*Rigveda* 1.9.7).

The collocation – some have said "formula" – κλέος ἄφθιτον (from Proto-Indo-European *$\hat{k}lewos\ \underset{.}{n}dhg^whitom$) expresses a concept that may well be common outside the Indo-European world, but it is definitely not just any old poetic phrase. It is *the* poetic phrase. Indeed, from the Greek point of view, it is *the* epic phrase, for in the words of one critic, the standard view of the type of poetry exemplified by the *Iliad* is precisely that "it recounts 'a heroic quest for fame and immortality' " (Haubold 2002a: 4). And to go one step further, from the Indo-Europeanist's point of view, it is *the* poetic phrase of phrases, for it was with the recognition of the equivalence between κλέος ἄφθιτον in our oldest Greek poem and *śrávas . . . ákṣitam* in our oldest Indic one (the core of the *Rigveda* is datable to roughly the second half of the second millennium BCE) that the now-burgeoning study of comparative poetics was born – in 1853, in a passing remark by one of the leading linguists of his time, Adalbert Kuhn. (The literature on this equation and its significance is enormous: see Volk 2002a and Katz forthcoming.) If undying (ἄφθιτον) fame (κλέος) is what the Greek epic hero seeks above all (*communis opinio*); if the congener of κλέος, namely *śrávas*, and the congener of ἄφθιτον, namely *ákṣitam*, are likewise put together in a cognate tradition, Sanskrit (countless scholars since Kuhn); and if, furthermore, the metrical forms of the Greek and Sanskrit phrases can be reconciled in Proto-Indo-European (Nagy) – if all these things, then it is from here, surely, that the meaty part of a discussion of ancient epic's Indo-European context must begin. And yet there is the problem of genre: *Rigveda* 1.9 is a hymn to the god Indra and thus, like the other 1,027 poems in the collection, a small-scale instance of ritual praise poetry, not an example of epic.

Does this mean that the Proto-Indo-European context of what we conventionally refer to as "epic" might be something other than epic? The answer, in short, is that we do not know, though it may be possible soon to give a more satisfying response since there has begun to be a proliferation of work (an example is Watkins 2002a) on the Indo-European background of the most arcane of Greek lyric poets, Pindar (early fifth century BCE), whose odes are in both content and form the closest Greek equivalent to the *Rigveda*. (Pindar, it seems, is the new Homer.) But rather than dwell further on what we do not know, let us turn for the remainder of this chapter to a few more of the positive features of Greek epic that have plausibly been seen as inherited.

Beyond meter, the most concrete work on what we may as well call Indo-European epic diction (even if we do not know what exactly "epic" means in this phrase) concerns formulae, a controversial term that essentially refers to set phrases like "imperishable fame," "swift horses," and "rosy-fingered dawn." (For an account of the sorts of things that interest an Indo-Europeanist about Homeric formulae, see Katz forthcoming.) Since linguists are in the habit of comparing words – using the Comparative Method to make sure that the sounds and morphemes match up – and since formulae are typically made up of just a couple of words (most usually a combination of noun and adjectival epithet), the idea behind the Indo-European-based investigation of formulae is clear enough, as we have seen in the equation of κλέος ἄφθιτον and *śrávas... ákṣitam*. However, poetry consists of more than words and phrases, and the reconstructive enterprise would ideally move beyond these small building blocks of verse to larger units. But how can we responsibly reconstruct scenes and entire plots?

As is well known, if one gets away from the fine points of diction, then what appear to be much the same stories show up again and again the world over. This very interesting fact tells us a great deal about what it means to be human (that is to say, humans compose stories about men who unknowingly sleep with their mothers and fish that find rings at the bottom of the sea), and there is a large and important scholarly industry devoted to cataloguing so-called folk motifs (see most prominently Thompson 1955–8). But this is obviously troublesome for anyone who wishes to find the Indo-European (or Bantu or Chinese) touch in a given story, and there is, simply put, only one way to do it, at least in the first instance – and that is precisely *not* to get away from the fine points of diction.

Diction matters because it is only by paying attention to what Meillet (1925) famously calls *détails singuliers* that we can have any hope of tracing the tradition in traditional narrative rather than merely ticking off lists of narrative types. At the very beginning of his justly famous monograph on the Comparative Method, Meillet mentions the work of "a young French scholar" – Dumézil – who has studied "the Indo-European myths pertaining to the drink of immortality" and explains how we know that it truly does have the Indo-European touch:

> The idea that there was a drink capable of conferring immortality is too natural to be characteristic. But when one finds in a more or less complete way among the various Indo-European peoples the legend of a beverage of immortality made in a gigantic vat, and when to this legend is joined the story of an untrue fiancée and the account of a struggle between gods and demoniacal beings, there is therein a set of singular facts which do not in themselves have any connection with each other and whose convergence cannot consequently be fortuitous. (Meillet 1967: 13–14 (1925: 1–2))

A more immediate demonstration that diction matters comes from what I call the "Goldilocks Principle," picking up on an observation by the Indologist and Indo-Europeanist Stephanie Jamison on the importance of recognizing that marked language can be very subtle:

The word "porridge" is a fairly rare one for American English speakers, and for most of us – however long removed from childhood – it has one semantic association. This single word, no matter what context we hear it in, can instantly evoke the whole narrative complex of Goldilocks and the Three Bears, the bowls of steaming porridge, the messy beds. The word "oatmeal" on the other hand does not. Alertness to the different associational ranges of two apparent synonyms can give a window on the cultural knowledge of the speakers who have these unconscious distinctions. But marginal vocabulary is not the only source of this knowledge. The same instant access to the same narrative is given by the perfectly well-formed, syntactically uninteresting English sentence, "Who's been sleeping in my bed?" Formulaic language of this sort binds a speech community with invisible semantic fetters that close attention to language will bring to light. (Jamison 1996: 11)

My point in citing this is not of course to claim an Indo-European pedigree for this children's story (for what we do know about its history, see Opie and Opie 1974: 199–200); rather, I note that in order to compare stories meaningfully across cultures with an eye to reconstructing a prototype, we need first to pay very close attention to exactly how each individual tale is told and, whenever it is somehow possible to gain access to this, to the societal resonances of the choice of words and narrative devices. It is no accident that one of the fathers of the Comparative Method was Jacob Grimm, best known to the general public as a collector of fairy tales.

There is plenty of secondary literature on Homer that compares Sanskrit epic and talks in general terms about the Indo-Europeans (see, e.g., Baldick 1994, a book-length Dumézilian account), but no one has treated the Greek epic material better than Jamison herself, who in a series of articles (Jamison 1994, 1997, and 1999) casts light on curious scenes in the *Iliad* and *Odyssey* by reading them as though they were part of the Sanskrit tradition. As she has repeatedly pointed out, certain peculiarities in the Greek narratives disappear, or at least start to fade, when we look at them comparatively, imagining that the stories are in fact taking place in the world of the two great classical Sanskrit epics, the *Mahâbhârata* and the *Râmâyaṇa*. These works, though considerably younger in their canonical form than the *Rigveda* (they date very roughly to the millennium between 500 BCE and 500 CE), nevertheless contain a great deal of very old linguistic material (and are anyway, as we have seen, metrical descendants of Vedic octosyllabic verse). Also, they are indubitably epic in scope, with the somewhat older *Mahâbhârata*, the longest epic in existence, roughly eight times the length of the *Iliad* and *Odyssey* combined, containing commentary on virtually every aspect of Indic life and lore in the course of describing the struggle between two branches of the Bhârata clan, the Pâṇḍavas and the Kauravas. The conclusion we must draw from such successful comparisons is, of course, that Homer and Sanskrit epic have sprung from a common source, Proto-Indo-European.

Jamison's principal contribution to Hellenic studies has been to show how traditional (i.e., Indo-European-based) Greek poetry comments on the traditional (again, Indo-European-based) legal status of three of epic's most interesting female characters: the abducted Helen in the *Iliad* (Jamison 1994) and the virginal Nausicaa and abandoned Penelope in the *Odyssey* (Jamison 1997 and 1999: 227–58, respectively). For example, in her extraordinary paper of 1994, Jamison considers the Teichoscopia (*Il.* 3.161–244), in which Priam, the father of Paris, Helen's second/improper (?) husband, stands with Helen on the walls of Troy, questioning her – seemingly quite bizarrely – about the identity of the Greek warriors and kinsmen who have come to reclaim her, among them her previous/proper (?) husband, Menelaos. The *Iliad* and the *Râmâyaṇa* are both "essentially stories about the repercussions of an illegal abduction" (Jamison 1994: 9), but it is on a single story in the third book of the sprawling *Mahâbhârata* that Jamison concentrates: the kidnapping of the heroine Draupadî (~ Helen) by King Jayadratha (~ Paris) and her subsequently successful and, from the Indic point of view, legally binding re-abduction by her husbands, the five Pâṇḍava brothers (~ Menelaos and the Greeks), a re-abduction that takes place only once Draupadî, questioned by Jayadratha, has carefully identified by name each of her husbands, who are in swift pursuit. The question-and-answer exchange is crucial since it makes Draupadî's re-abduction legal in a way that her original seizure by Jayadratha was not, for in ancient India (and by extension in some place at a prehistoric time when Sanskrit and Greek were still one and the same) there was a type of union known as Râkṣasa ("demonic") marriage – low in the hierarchy, but recognized by Indian law – whereby one could in fact kidnap a girl legitimately, provided certain formal requirements had first been met. (On the various kinds of Indic marriage and a woman's legal rights, see in greatest detail Jamison 1996: 205–50.) The "set of singular facts" (*ensemble de faits singuliers*) makes it clear that these two epic stories have a common prototype. An Indo-European perspective on narrative is thus especially useful when it explains something that makes little synchronic sense, as in the case of the Teichoscopia, whose elements we may assume remained part of the traditional repertoire into which Homer dipped even once the Greek laws of marriage were no longer what they once had been.

If Jamison tells us something about law and the role of women in (Proto-)Indo-European society and literature, there is, of course, also much to be said about more typically epic themes: manly exploits involving heroes and adversity that can be overcome only by force. The subjects that have received the most attention are cattle-raiding (see, e.g., Lincoln 1981b) and dragon-slaying, the latter thanks to a number of articles and a seminal book by Calvert Watkins, *How to Kill a Dragon: Aspects of Indo-European Poetics* (1995: esp. pp. 293–544). Dragons are by no means confined to the Indo-European world, needless to say, but it is possible to employ linguistic methods to determine some of the characteristics of specifically Indo-European monsters and above all, as Watkins shows, how to vanquish them. Starting with a simple schema that involves a hero, a serpent (in the first place $*h_1og^whi$- and $*ang^who$-, as in Greek ὄφις and Latin *anguis*, respectively), and a verb that means "smite, slay" (in the first place $*g^when$-, as in Greek πεφνέμεν, Latin *(of-/de-)fendere*, and also English *bane*), Watkins charts the manifold developments of this "formula" throughout Indo-European: the Greek tale of Bellerophon and the Chimera (e.g., in the Glaucus and Diomedes episode in *Iliad* 6), the Sanskrit myth of Indra and the serpentine Vṛtra (e.g., in *Rigveda* 1.32), the Hittite "Myth of Illuyankas" (a convenient version is to be found in Hoffner 1998a: 10–14 and 93), etc., in each case elucidating the changes rung on the diction and taking care to explain what is traceably and specifically Indo-European. Particularly impressive and of evidently wide interest are comparisons of phrasal collections and whole stories, for these bespeak a Proto-Indo-European narrative prototype. Take, for example, the second-millennium BCE "Myth of Illuyankas", best known to classicists as the source of the Greek story of Zeus' defeat of the monster Typhon (see, e. g., C. Watkins 1995: 448–59). In the Hittite story, the storm god, after many trials and tribulations, finally vanquishes the fearsome *illuyankaš* (the word means literally "eel-snake" and is closely connected to the Greek name *Bellerophon*, etymologically "Bane of the 'Eel(-Snake)' ": see Katz 1998). This tale, which is told as part of the Hittite New Year's ritual, is narratologically astonishingly similar, as Watkins shows, to an old story preserved in a sixteenth-century CE manuscript halfway across the world, the Irish "Saga of Fergus mac Léti," in which the hero Fergus defeats the *muirdris* "mere-dragon" (see C. Watkins 1995: 441–7). Similar stories about snaky creatures associated with watery depths are found in many other Indo-European traditions as well, including Greek (the names *Typhon* and *Python* are cognate with the English words *deep* and *bottom*, respectively), Indic, Germanic, and Slavic (see C. Watkins 1995: esp. pp. 460–3, with special reference to V. N. Toporov; see also Katz 1998); the Slavic tale in question, like the Hittite one, is associated with the end of one year and the birth of the next, which suggests that we have here evidence of not just Proto-Indo-European heroic narrative, but – remarkably – the very context in which the epic struggle between hero (∼ man) and dragon (∼ universal forces of darkness) was properly narrated or performed.

It is worth making explicit at this point that invoking a Hittite myth in a chapter such as this inevitably makes it necessary to comment on both how it got into Hittite in the first place and whether it was then borrowed into Greek from Hittite rather than making its way independently into the two languages from a common source. On the one hand, most scholars believe that few Hittite tales are of good Indo-European stock, being mostly either clear borrowings from (non-Indo-European) Hurrian or – as in the case of the Myth of Illuyankas (see, e.g., Hoffner 1998a: 9) – of presumed (and likewise non-Indo-European) Hattic origin; on the other, classicists are mining Near Eastern material more and more for sources of Greek stories, and no piece of Hittite literature has received as much attention from this point of view as the Myth of Illuyankas. As always, the best way to distinguish inheritance from borrowing from quasi-universal feature is to pay close attention to language (for some case studies of cultural diffusion from the Near East to Greece, see Watkins 1998, 2000b, 2000c, and 2002b); largely undiscussed lists of vague similarities between Greek and "oriental" material, as in West 1997b, establish beyond any doubt a shared intellectual environment but do not much help us understand who learned what from whom, and how (see further Chapter 20, by Burkert). In the case of Illuyankas/Typhon, for example, many features of each story are or may be borrowed, but some are obviously inherited; it is important to know which are which. Or, to take a different sort of example, Puhvel (1991: 21–9) calls attention to the fact that elaborate "Homeric" similes are found also in Hittite and enjoins scholars to spend more time comparing Greek and Anatolian; but lengthy similes seem to be cross-culturally common in epic (see Bowra 1952: 266–80 and Revard and Newman 1993: 362), and I for one would not wish to speculate on just what conclusions we would draw if we were to engage (as I hope someone will) in a detailed study of formal poetic devices in Greece and the ancient Near East. Watkins (1994: II.700–17 and 1995: 144–51), who has suggested that the Trojans may have spoken Luvian (an Indo-European language of Anatolia closely related to Hittite), has made the strong claim that we possess the first line of a "Luvian epic lay" about the city of Wilusa (∼ Ἴλιος, i.e. Troy): *aḫḫ=ata=ta alati awienta Wiluśati*, which he translates as "When they came from steep Wilusa." The idea that this clearly poetic line is the incipit of an otherwise unknown Anatolian analogue to the *Iliad* (a *Wilusiad*, as it were) has, unsurprisingly, given rise to considerable skepticism (Neumann 1999: esp. pp. 20–1, weighs the evidence carefully). Right or wrong, it is a rare example of an idea about not just Indo-European poetry, but Indo-European poetic genre. The title of a nuanced recent discussion of this genre, Johannes Haubold's "Greek epic: a Near Eastern genre?" (2002a), gives away that the author, like so many Hellenists today, is interested in finding (non-Indo-European) Near Eastern analogues (specifically from the Akkadian *Epic of Gilgamesh*) in Homer and Hesiod. This is very important, but we must not forget that Greek epic has an Indo-European context as well, and it behooves us to try to learn as much as we can about it.

So, then, what in the end do we know about the Indo-European context of ancient epic? Not as much as we would like, it is true, but work is continuing apace, and I hope to have encouraged others to work on the sorts of problems I have posed in this chapter, including venturing into languages that have received short shrift here. (See, e.g., Fenik 1986, who compares Homer and the Middle High German *Nibelungenlied*, and both Chapter 18, by Davidson and Davidson 1994 on the Middle Persian *Shâhnâma*; the account of the Indo-European background of Armenian epic in Petrosyan 2002 is seriously flawed.) My goal has been less to show what has already been done and more to explain how we need to proceed in order to know more. There is a striking amount of prejudice in

academia against Indo-European linguistics, notably on the part of those who are repelled
by its name (and its German equivalent, *Indogermanisch*), by certain scholarly personages
of unsavory character, and by theories tinged with ethnic and racial isms (Lincoln 1999 is
especially aggressive). The fact remains, however, that the careful assessment of the
historical and comparative background of languages and cultures has led to important
and sometimes brilliant revelations of both a scientific and a humanistic kind. When it
is done right, the reconstruction of Proto-Indo-European (as, indeed, of any proto-
language) is, to put it in epic diction, θαῦμα ἰδέσθαι "a wonder to behold."

NOTE

I am grateful to Jay Fisher for intellectual stimulation, to Martin Kern for sparking my interest in the
relationship between Greek and Chinese epic, to John Miles Foley for forbearance and unusual good
will, and to the Director and faculty of the Institute for Advanced Study for the luxury of membership during the year in which this chapter was conceived.

FURTHER READING

Not surprisingly, the best way to learn about the Indo-European context of ancient epic is to read
and think about texts from as many Indo-European traditions as possible. In this chapter I have
concentrated for practical reasons on Homeric Greek, while comparing in some detail phrases and
stories from the Indic *Rigveda* and *Mahâbhârata* and casting more than just a passing glance at
Anatolian. Both classicists and those who do not know Greek will find useful the revised bilingual
Loeb Classical Library editions of the *Iliad* (Murray 1999) and *Odyssey* (Murray 1995). Unfortunately, there is no complete and reliable rendering into English of the major Sanskrit works: until Joel
Brereton and Stephanie Jamison come out with their long-awaited translation of the entire *Rigveda*,
Wendy Doniger O'Flaherty's 1981 Penguin edition of some of the major hymns is the place to start;
as for the *Mahâbhârata*, the fourth fat installment in a projected ten-volume edition has appeared
(Buitenen 1973, 1975, and 1978 and now Fitzgerald 2004). For a good introduction to Hittite
literature, see Hoffner 1998a.

   The next best way to find out about the subject is to peruse the finest scholarship there is on Indo-
European poetics and try to learn by example what sorts of questions interest linguists and what
techniques they use to arrive at answers. The clearest exposition of the fundamental principle known
as the Comparative Method remains Meillet 1925/1967; reliable textbooks on historical/compara-
tive linguistics in general include Anttila 1989, Hock and Joseph 1996, and Campbell 1999; and
Fortson 2004 examines the Indo-European languages specifically. The leading practitioner of Indo-
European "genetic intertextuality" broadly conceived is Calvert Watkins, whose oeuvre is worth
reading cover to cover: note especially C. Watkins 1995 and the papers collected in vol. II of Watkins
1994.

CHAPTER THREE

Epic and Myth

Lowell Edmunds

Scholars discussing the ancient Near East, Greece, and Rome use concepts and terms for those concepts that would not have been immediately, if at all, comprehensible to ancient persons: "ideology," "imbedded economy," "intertextuality," "metatheater," and the like. They use other terms, like "history," "irony," "aesthetic," and "metaphysics," that, while taken directly from Greek words, mean something in English different from what their originals meant. "Myth" and "epic" are among these other terms. They refer to modern analytic ("etic") categories, which are necessary when ancient native ("emic") categories are either lacking or, if available, not useful for cross-cultural comparisons.

The word "myth" can be taken to refer generally, in relation to epic, to the background of traditional oral storytelling, available to the poet in written versions in some cases, from which epic derives (Edmunds 1997: 416–18). None of the ancient peoples whose epics are considered in this chapter abstracted a general concept of traditional oral story from the traditional stories they used, nor did they establish genres for different kinds of stories (see Hansen 1983: 108). The definition of "myth" as traditional oral storytelling looks not to a concept nor to genre but to a social custom or practice.

Scholars of myth now, however, often separate traditional oral stories into categories based on narrative content – myth, legend, and folktale – and these categories will be employed in this chapter. Myths are about gods, legends about heroes, and folktales about ordinary people (for further elements of the definitions, see Hansen 1997: 444–5). Legends are distinct from the other two categories in that they purport to be historical. All of the epics to be discussed here – the Gilgamesh epic, the *Iliad*, the *Odyssey*, and the *Aeneid* – are about legendary heroes. (The meaning of "epic" is dealt with in Chapter 1, by Martin.) The most obvious difference between myth and epic is the latter's metrical and other formal qualities (see Burkert 1985: 120–1).

The topic "myth and epic" raises, then, the question of epic's relation to its ultimate origin in oral stories concerning legendary heroes. In order to refine this question, a description of oral storytelling is required.

Analysis of storytelling by characters in Homer has shown that, while the stories told by characters in Homer are traditional, in the sense that the internal addressee's and the external audience's prior knowledge of the story is assumed (cf. Moran 1995 for the storyteller's appeal to memory), each telling of the same story, because it has a particular motivation, has a new focus. So, against the reification of myth as a collective expression of society's beliefs (Burkert 1979: 29, 1992: 9–24) must be set the consideration that a traditional story can survive only if it can be retold, and it can be retold only if it can be applied to new circumstances. A story is therefore, in retrospect, a set of variants on a fundamental pattern, while, on the occasion of any retelling, the present, individualist version is the authoritative one (Edmunds 1997: 416–20). The Gilgamesh epic corroborates this finding. Utanapishtim's retelling of the flood story to Gilgamesh is a good example (Tablet 11). Whatever larger purposes this story may have had in other versions, in this first-person retelling by the sole survivor of the flood, the figure on whom Enlil conferred immortality, it has a single, ad hoc point: because the flood and Enlil's dispensation were a unique and unrepeatable set of circumstances, Gilgamesh cannot expect to win immortality.

The topic "myth and epic" thus also leads to a question or questions about the emergence of epic from a background of variant narrative traditions. To what extent does epic reflect the variation that it presumably must overcome in pursuit of its aesthetic goals (see again Burkert 1985: 120–1)? This general question can be posed in three different ways. First, can an epic as a whole be understood as a variant of a tradition, whether written or oral? Can an epic be regarded as a retelling, in its own way, of a traditional story? Second, in myths or legends subordinate to the main story of the epic as a whole, does an epic reflect synchronic variation? Third, does an epic adapt heterogeneous, or non-legendary, stories that can be assumed to be known to its audience and therefore perceptible as variants? Folktales are the stories that this third question concerns.

For two reasons, these questions might seem somewhat strange or inappropriate as applied to the epics named above, which come to us as written texts. First, writing ought, someone might argue, to have retarded the process of variation, and it would have to be conceded that, even within the oral phase of the *Iliad* and the *Odyssey*, some degree of textual fixation would have begun (see Nagy 1996c: 107–9, 1990c: 77–81). In the form in which we have them, they are not exactly oral but oral-derived (for this concept as applied to Homer, see Foley 1997: 163). So the point concerning writing applies even to the most "oral" of the epics considered here. Further, as highly sophisticated poems ranking with the acknowledged masterworks of world literature, all of the epics discussed here might seem to have rendered superfluous the precursors of the legends they narrate. From this point of view, they are more appropriately approached by the methods of literary history and literary criticism, and indeed the intertextual relations between these epics themselves, especially the *Aeneid* and Homer but also Homer and the Gilgamesh epic, have provided rich material for discussion (see Chapters 20 and 33, by Burkert and Putnam).

Second, it might be argued that, in keeping with this literary perspective, variation within the works of authors of great genius should be studied only for the purpose of removing or reducing it. This strictly negative view of variation has a background in textual criticism. The papyri and manuscripts of classical texts present variants, and it is the job of the modern editor to "to establish what the author originally wrote," which is the same as "what the author intended to say" (West 1973b: 48). Presumably the author intended a single version, and so one textual variant must be chosen as correct and the others must be relegated to the apparatus criticus or forgotten about. The notion of an original is all-important. As Richard Tarrant observes (1995: 98), the "tendency to idealize the lost original" is characteristic of the editors of Greek and Latin texts. The text-critical model of the text is thus the original version, which expresses a single intention and can therefore ideally be shorn of later variation. Judged by this model, internal *narrative* variation is as bad as textual variation. This same model tends to govern the numerous studies of the "origin and development" of legends, especially the legend of the Trojan founding of Rome, in which a single, uniform "good" tradition is sought. The model of textual criticism is even expressly invoked (Poucet 1985: 237–8).

The objection to the model of textual criticism and to study of "origin and development" is that there is no author of a traditional oral story, even if, logically, someone had to tell the story for the first time. For practical purposes, authorship disappears in proportion as the story succeeds. This disappearance has two consequences: no unique originary intention to which one can link the story; and no original story, only a tradition with variation. It can be shown, for each of the epics discussed in this chapter, that it contains irreducible variation, a symptom of a dynamic relation to antecedent and synchronic traditions.

Gilgamesh

The Gilgamesh epic seems to present the most difficult challenge to the thesis of this chapter. It is attested in writing already at the end of the third millennium BCE. It seems to be "literary" from the beginning and to be composed for the elite of its day (Foster 2001: xiv; see also xxi for sophisticated intertextuality in this epic; on the epic generally see Chapter 15, by Noegel). A supposed "evolution" can be traced down to the text of the Standard Version (hereafter SV) found in the excavation of the library of Ashurbanipal (668–627 BCE). In this teleological view, the earliest Sumerian sources are linked to the first Akkadian sources (*ca.* 1800 BCE), and these in turn to the formation of the SV at the end of the second millennium. To describe what motivates development conceived in this way, standard literary-historical explanations present themselves: social and political changes external to, and absorbed by, the epic; and changes internal to the text driven by authorial and editorial taste or by literary climate. Even a scholar taking this approach to the SV has to reckon, however, with "elements...borrowed from literary or even nonliterary sources which originally had nothing to do with Gilgamesh" (Tigay 1982: 21; cf. 247–8). Further, with increasing awareness of the comparative evidence of other oral literatures, it has become necessary to conceive of the interaction of oral and written traditions (Cooper 1992: 109; Alster 1995: 2318–19) and also of non-literate spheres of audience (Liverani 1995: 2354–5). In short, "the mind of the author and [of] subsequent editors of the epic" (Tigay 1982: 22) ceases to be the single driving force in the creation of the Gilgamesh epic, and a more complex model, taking account of divergent traditions, written or not, emerges.

In the flood story, different elements in the story are attested in different sources: the Old Babylonian *Atrahasis*, the Middle Babylonian fragment from Ras Shamra in Syria, and also later versions (Tigay 1982: 217). Although the recasting of the flood story as a first-person narrative on the part of Utanapishtim makes aesthetic sense, the author or editor of the SV did not bother to reconcile his sources with the rest of his narrative. A glaring example is the name Atrahasis in Tablet 11 for the person elsewhere called Utanapishtim. It is, then, more difficult to imagine the author or editor of the SV as attempting a redaction of various texts on the desk in front of him, as it were, than it is to hypothesize the same kind of inconsistent response on his part to variant synchronic traditions to be observed in the *Iliad* and the *Odyssey* and even in the *Aeneid*. Further, it is unnecessary to assume that these traditions were all derived from the Atrahasis epic. It would be more appropriate, given the diffusion of the flood story in ancient western Asia, to speak of parallel, interdependent traditions (Schmidt 1995: 2348–9; see also Chapter 20, by Burkert).

The flood story in Tablet 11 also contains a notable heterogeneous element: the plant of rejuvenation. It is a folktale motif (Thompson 1955–8: D1346.5, H1333.2.1), attested in a somewhat different form in *Etana*, a poem about one of the rulers of Kish who, because he was childless, flew to heaven on an eagle's back to find the plant of life or of birth (texts in *ANET* 114–18). When this motif became part of the Gilgamesh epic is unknown; it appears in the story of Gilgamesh for the first time in the SV. The author or editor has skillfully adapted the motif: it is now the plant of rejuvenation and, as such, a second-best acquisition after Gilgamesh has failed in his quest for immortality. (He shows his ineligibility immediately by failing the test of wakefulness, another folktale motif: Thompson 1955–8: C735.1.2, H1247.) In fact, the plant is no longer the object of a quest but comes to the hero as a parting gift from Utanapishtim, who tells him where to find it. Though heroic effort is required (he has to dive into the depths of the sea in order to get possession of it), the gift is assured. The careless loss of the plant to a snake overdetermines the futility of Gilgamesh's hopes: no immortality and now no rejuvenation, either. No matter how skillful the adaptation, the fact remains that it is a non-essential element that has come, at whatever date, from outside a specifically literary tradition of the Gilgamesh story. (In another folktale, which Sir James G. Frazer called "The story of the cast skin," the power to cast the skin, which humans once had but lost to certain animals, in particular the snake, stood for immortality; see Frazer 1923: 26–31.)

The best evidence for the SV as a whole as the variant of a tradition is Tablet 12. The author or editor has tacked it onto a poem that was thematically and formally complete at the end of Tablet 11. Further, from all the texts presumably at his disposal, he has chosen an Akkadian translation of lines 172–301 of the Sumerian poem "Bilgames and the Netherworld" ("In those days, in those far-off days"). From the aesthetic or literary-critical point of view, the anomaly is obvious (cf. Tigay 1982: 27, 105–7, 138). From another point of view, the one taken by the present writer, Tablet 12 illustrates the interference, typical even of epics that have achieved a monumental status in their own time, of synchronic tradition. In this case, while it is a tradition that demonstrably, because textual, goes back to the third millennium, it was still compelling to the mind of whoever added Tablet 12, who believed that the story should end with the death of Gilgamesh. A story concerning the birth of Gilgamesh must also have been part of the Gilgamesh legend. This story, a multiform of the one about the birth of Sargon (*ANET* 119) but not preserved in any Sumerian or Akkadian text, somehow made its way into Aelian (165/70–230/5 CE; *NA* 12.21).

By the end of the second millennium, the Gilgamesh epic had been translated into Hurrian and Hittite (a prose abridgement). If its undoubted influence on the *Iliad* and the *Odyssey* also occurred in this period, when various kinds of Near Eastern influence on Greece can be demonstrated, the transmission would have to have been oral. (For East–West influence, see West 1997b: ch. 1; for the influence of the Gilgamesh epic on Homer, chs. 7–8.) If the influence took place, or took place again, later, in the early archaic period (*ca.* 750–650 BCE), when the Greek alphabet was in use and, some would say, written texts of Homer were in existence, then it could have been in the mode of reading and writing (Burkert 1983: 51–3; 1992: 93–6; Chapter 20). The mode of transmission is a difficult problem that cannot be solved here and may be insoluble. The kinds of reflexes of the Gilgamesh epic in the *Iliad* seem, with few exceptions, sufficiently inexact not to require a Greek bard's consultation of Akkadian cuneiform texts. Audition of the Gilgamesh poem would have sufficed – in Akkadian, if he knew Akkadian, or in a Greek translation. (The same points can be made concerning the transmission of the Gilgamesh poem into Hurrian and Hittite.)

Homer's *Iliad* and *Odyssey*

Both the *Iliad* and the *Odyssey* can be seen in their entirety as variants of the traditional stories they narrate. The *Odyssey* is the easier to explain in these terms. Its story appears as a variant both within a specifically Greek perspective and also against a larger comparative background. As for the former, one of the poems of the Epic Cycle (on which see

Chapter 24, by Burgess, and West 1996) tells how Odysseus, having finally reached home after ten years' wandering, leaves for further adventures, a new marriage, and eventually death at the hands of his son by Circe, a development unknown to the *Odyssey* (cf. Edmunds 1997: 423–4). In the prophecy of Teiresias, however, the *Odyssey* acknowledges this variant (*Od.* 11.119–37; cf. Hansen 1990).

Against a comparative background, the story of the *Odyssey* corresponds to the folktale called "The homecoming husband." This folktale, defined in the Aarne–Thompson index of types by a single motif ("Husband [lover] arrives home just as wife [mistress] is to marry another") has been found across a vast area of the globe, from Iceland to Indonesia, and has received literary treatment many times (Aarne and Thompson 1981: Type 974; see also Holzapel 1990; Hansen 1997: 446–9, 2002: 201–11). A primary comparandum for classicists is the South Slavic version (cf. Foley 1990, 1999b; Lord 1991: 216–19, 1960: ch. 8).

As might be expected, the telling of the story tends to include more than one motif. In the following synopsis, cross-references to Thompson 1955–8 (capital letter plus number) and to the *Odyssey* are given in parentheses. (Note that not every motif is in the Motif-Index and not every motif is in the *Odyssey*.) The story begins with contests among suitors (H331), which may include archery (H331.4). The hero leaves home after his marriage (Odysseus goes to fight in the Trojan War). He sets a period for his wife to wait, after which she may remarry (18.259–70). He is imprisoned or tarries in a strange land (Odysseus is at Troy for ten years; then spends ten years in returning to Ithaca). Sometimes the hero goes to the Underworld (Book 11). There are false reports of the hero's death (14.89–90). His wife is forced to remarry (15.16–17, 19.158–9). The hero learns that his wife is about to remarry (cf. 11.115–17). He then returns home; it is a magic journey (D2121; 13.81–95). Sometimes the hero is asleep during the journey (13.79–80). He presents himself in disguise (cf. K1816.0.3.1; Odysseus is dressed as a beggar). He is recognized by an animal – a dog, a horse, etc. – before he is recognized by his own relatives. He returns just as his wife is about to marry another (N681) – this is the motif that defines the type in Aarne and Thompson 1981. (Cf. the sham wedding at 23.129–52). The hero is identified by tokens (H80; 19.392–502 (scar), 21.217–21 (scar), 23.183–204 (bed)). Often the hero identifies himself by a ring or half of a ring (his wife has the other half) dropped in glass of wine (H94.4). In this way he is recognized by his wife. Either the new marriage is peacefully cancelled or the impostor is punished (Q262; 22 (the slaughter of the suitors)).

This type divides into two subtypes, which can be called compound and simple. The compound subtype has the suitor contests at the beginning: the hero must win the bride whom he soon leaves to go on the journey that will separate them for many years. The simple subtype, of which the story of the *Odyssey* is an example, lacks this motif and begins with the hero already absent or with the departure of the hero. And yet there is some ancient evidence that Odysseus had to compete for the hand of Penelope (Apollod. *Bibl.* 3.10.9; Paus. 3.12.2); thus the story may once have been compound. The story as told in the *Odyssey* might, then, be regarded as a choice among alternate traditions.

The simple subtype tends to be western or European and the compound tends to be eastern. The most notable representative of the compound subtype is the story of Alpamysh, which is found in the forms of folktale and epic song (*dastan*) over the whole territory of the Turkic peoples (the Uzbeks, Kazakhs, Karakalpaks, Kirghiz, and Turkmens), from the Altai Mountains and the Urals in the East to the Volga and down through the Central Asian republics of the former Soviet Union to Turkey. It was still told as a folktale in the Altai as late as the 1960s. The best-known form of the story is the version (of about 14,000 lines) recorded from Fazil Yuldashev, an Uzbek singer (see Zhirmunsky

1967; Reichl 2001). Special attention is called to "Alpamysh" because it has been strangely neglected in the comparative study of the *Odyssey*.

The *Iliad* begins, "Sing, goddess [the Muse], the anger of Achilles son of Peleus." The main story of the *Iliad*, which is the story of this anger, is an episode in the life of Achilles and as such seems to lack a folktale analogue. The life of Achilles as a whole, however, corresponds to the story of Meleager (Aarne and Thompson 1981: Type 1187), a version of which is recounted by Phoenix in his attempt to persuade Achilles to re-enter the fighting (9.524–605). Phoenix' version, which is of course shaped by his immediate rhetorical purpose, ironically invites reflections on the tacit similarity between Achilles and Meleager: their inevitable death in battle (Edmunds 1997: 425–32). The *Iliad* also presents itself as a variant of the Trojan War myth as a whole. This variant concerns Helen. In the *Iliad*, Helen is at Troy; she is a character in the poem. According to another tradition, first attested in the poet Stesichorus (7th–6th c. BCE; *PMG*: fr. 15), Helen and Paris went from Lacedaemon to Egypt, where Helen stayed, while her phantom went on with Paris to Troy (cf. [Hes.] fr. 358 M-W; Eur. *Hel.* 31–55, *El.* 1280–3; Pl. *Rep.* 586c). The Trojan War was thus fought over a phantom. The historian Herodotus (fifth century BCE) has a rationalized version that omits the phantom: Helen was detained in Egypt as a runaway adulteress; Paris returned to Troy; when the Achaeans arrived at Troy, they refused to believe that Helen was not there. Thus, according to this version, the Trojan War was fought for nothing (Hdt. 2.113 ff.). In both versions, Menelaos eventually finds Helen in Egypt and returns to Lacedaemon with her. The *Odyssey* seems obliquely to recognize the variant with its references to Menelaos and Helen in Egypt (3.299–312, 4.81–9, etc.).

Both the *Iliad* and the *Odyssey* show variation in myths and legends subordinate to the main story of the epic as a whole. The most prominent example is the two versions of the throwing of Hephaestus in the *Iliad*. In Book 1, Zeus had seized him by the foot and thrown him from Olympus (586–94). It is likely, but not explicit, that the lameness of Hephaestus is the result of his fall. In Book 18, Hera, his mother, had thrown him from Olympus because she was ashamed of his lameness (394–7). Here Charis is his wife, whereas in *Odyssey* 8.266–369 it is Aphrodite. While there is no other contradiction of this magnitude within either the *Iliad* or the *Odyssey*, further examples of variation are hardly lacking. In Book 7 of the *Iliad*, Poseidon says that he and Apollo built a wall for Laomedon, the Trojan king (451–2), and in 12.13–33 the poet tells how Poseidon and Apollo will destroy the wall after Troy is captured. In 21.441–57, however, it is Poseidon alone who built the wall, while Apollo tended Laomedon's cattle. Another wall, one built by Athena and the Trojans and not mentioned elsewhere, is referred to at 20.145–8 (cf. Apollod. *Bibl.* 2.5.9). The purpose of this wall was to afford protection for Herakles when he retired from fighting the sea monster that had been sent by Poseidon when Laomedon defrauded him and Apollo for payment for their services (which included the building of a wall!).

The *Odyssey* provides an example comparable with the variable wall. Neleus, king in Pylos, would give his daughter Pero in marriage only to the one who could drive the cattle of Iphiclus out of Phylacê in Thessaly. A prophet, Melampus, volunteered, but was imprisoned for a year. He was released after he had given prophecies to Iphiclus. So ends the legend as summarized in 11.281–97. The legend is recapitulated again in 15.228–38: Melampus does not volunteer; his assets having been frozen by Neleus, he is coerced into seeking the cattle; he is imprisoned, as in the previous version; he then drives off the cattle; in this way he secures the marriage of his brother to Pero. In this second version, the Thessalian king, who was Iphiclus in the first, is Phylacus. Both versions are told in a highly allusive manner that presupposes the audience's knowledge of the legend (Heubeck and Hoekstra 1989: 246–7).

Both the *Iliad* and the *Odyssey*, like the Gilgamesh epic, adapt folktales, a point that has not been lost on classical scholars. From their literary-critical perspective, however, it appears that, once a folktale was transmuted into epic poetry, its oral existence ceased, or at least ceased to matter (cf. Page 1973). It can be shown, on the contrary, that the continued existence of the folktale is assumed by the epic poet and subtends its adaptation in epic poetry. In particular, the epic poet assumes his audience's knowledge of his adaptation as a new variant. In this way, the folktales in epic again reflect epic's dynamic relation to variant, synchronic tradition.

Besides the Meleager story, the *Iliad* contains only one other story, about Bellerophon and Anteia (6.152–70), that has an international folktale analogue (Thompson 1955–8: K2111, "Potiphar's wife"). The *Odyssey*, however, offers a richer trove with, besides "The homecoming husband," nine others. The best-known of these is the "The ogre blinded" (Aarne and Thompson 1981: Type 1137), the basis of the Polyphemos story (9.105–542). This was in fact the story that, in Wilhelm Grimm's study, launched the comparative folkloristic approach to Homer (Grimm 1857; see more recently Hansen 2002: 289–301).

The Polyphemos story is the most fully narrated of the adventures that Odysseus recounts to the Phaeacians in Books 9–12. (The following discussion of the Polyphemos episode is taken from Edmunds 1993, which is out of print.) Odysseus begins with a general description of the lawless Cyclopes (plural; the singular is "Cyclops") and of the beautiful island opposite their land, where Odysseus' fleet puts in (9.105–41). Odysseus then crosses over from the island with his own ship and companions to the Cyclopes' land; they see a cave and a pen for sheep and goats, which will prove to belong to a monster man who is now absent (142–92). Odysseus has come with a particular question: he wants to find out if the Cyclopes are savage or if they are hospitable to strangers (174–6). Odysseus and twelve of his men go to the cave, taking with them a goatskin of very strong wine (193–230). Inside, they find lambs, kids, and cheeses. Odysseus' companions urge him to steal some of these things and return to the ship. But Odysseus wants to find out if the Cyclops will give him gifts of hospitality (229–30). The Cyclops, whose name is Polyphemos (403), returns, drives his flocks into the cave, and blocks the entrance with a huge boulder. Odysseus presents himself as a suppliant and a guest, asking for gifts (267–71). The Cyclops replies scornfully; he eats two of Odysseus' men for supper and two more for breakfast (231–316). Odysseus would have killed him during the night while he was asleep but he and his men would not have been able to remove the boulder. When the Cyclops goes out to herd his flock in the morning, he replaces the boulder, imprisoning Odysseus and his remaining men in the cave.

Odysseus devises a plan: he and his men sharpen a stake (317–35). When Polyphemos returns, he eats two more of Odysseus' men; he drinks the wine Odysseus offers him, and asks Odysseus' name. Odysseus says: "No Man." Polyphemos falls into a drunken sleep; Odysseus and his men heat the point of the stake in the fire and drive it into Polyphemos' eye (336–94). (Homer never says that Polyphemos has only one eye, but the narrative presupposes it.) Polyphemos wakes up screaming and calls his fellow Cyclopes, who come to the rescue. From outside the cave, they ask: who is hurting you? He answers: "No Man," and they go away (395–414). In the morning, Polyphemos has to let his sheep out, and Odysseus and his men escape by clinging to the bellies of the sheep. They take some sheep on board their ship and sail away. From what he thinks is a safe distance, Odysseus taunts Polyphemos. Polyphemos throws a rock that almost sinks the ship. Odysseus again taunts Polyphemos, this time declaring his real name. Polyphemos now recalls a prophecy he had once received: he would lose his sight at the hands of someone named Odysseus. Then Polyphemos calls upon his father, Poseidon, cursing Odysseus (415–535). (Poseidon hears his son, and the anger of the sea-god against Odysseus determines the future difficulties of Odysseus' return to Ithaca.) Polyphemos throws another rock, again nearly sinking the ship; the wave produced by the rock drives the ship back to the island whence Odysseus had started out on his visit to the land of the Cyclopes (536–42).

The Polyphemos story is widely attested in folklore. The earliest version after antiquity is in *Dolopathos*, a collection of tales written down *ca.*1184 CE by a monk named John of the Cistercian Abbey of Haute-Seille in Lorraine. Following up on Grimm 1857, in 1904 Oskar Hackman published a collection of 221 versions; more have come to light since then. They come from a geographical area stretching from England to Russia, down to Turkey and the Near East and also to northern Africa. In the *Dolopathos* version, the story is told by a retired robber. He and one hundred men tried to steal gold from a giant. They were captured by the giant and nine other giants and divided up among them. The robber and nine of his men fell to the lot of the giant who had been robbed. They were imprisoned in his cave, where the giant ate all the men but the robber. The robber offered to heal the giant's eyes, which were ailing (this giant has two eyes). Instead, the robber blinded him. The robber escaped by clinging to the underside of a ram. He taunted the giant, who threw him a ring as a gift. The ring was magical. It kept saying, "Here I am," so that the giant could pursue the robber. The robber could not remove the ring. Just as the giant was about to catch him, the robber cut his finger off, threw it away, and thus he escaped.

Fifty-two versions can be found in the second volume of the Loeb Library edition of the mythographer Apollodorus (Frazer 1921). The motifs that constitute the type are as follows (references are to Thompson 1955–8). It begins with the attempt by a thief or thieves to steal from a giant (G100: Giant ogre). Or the protagonist, who is not a thief, seeks shelter with the giant. The protagonist is caught and imprisoned. The door is immovable. The giant is cannibalistic and blear-eyed or one-eyed. The protagonist offers to cure the giant's eyes (K1011: Eye-remedy). Under this pretense, the trickster blinds the giant, often with a glowing mass thrust into the eye. When the giant lets his sheep out of the cave (or other enclosure), the protagonist escapes dressed in the skin of one of the animals (K521.1: Escape by dressing in an animal (bird, human) skin) or by clinging to the underside of a ram (K603: Escape under ram's belly). Often the giant addresses his favorite ram or buck goat, the one underneath which the protagonist is hidden. Having escaped, the protagonist taunts the giant, who gives the protagonist a magic ring. The ring has a voice, which enables the giant to pursue the protagonist. The ring cannot be removed. To avoid capture, the protagonist cuts off his finger.

The No Man ruse does not belong to this folktale type. In all the hundreds of folktale versions of "The ogre blinded," only two examples of the No Man ruse have been found. On the other hand, Hackman (1904) has 50 examples of the No Man ruse as a separate tale: the hero injures the devil or a fairy; then avoids retaliation by giving a false name, "Myself" or "Nobody." The devil or fairy goes looking for the hero and says, "I'm looking for Myself" or "I'm looking for Nobody." Thus he cannot catch the hero (cf. K602, 602.1). Hackman also has 47 examples of the No Man ruse and blinding motifs together but without the rest of the story of the Blinded Ogre.

The necessary conclusion is that Homer has combined two separate folktales. One is the No Man ruse, which often goes together with the blinding of an adversary. The other is Type 1137 (Aarne and Thompson 1981), which also has the blinding of the adversary and entails the other ruse, the escape from the giant's den.

Homer follows Type 1137 rather closely. His main divergence is in (1) the incorporation of the No Man motif and (2) his omission of the magic ring and of the hero's self-mutilation. These two variations on the type work together. An epic hero could not be presented as cutting off his own finger, and therefore there could not be any magic ring to guide the blind giant's pursuit of the hero. How then could Polyphemos complete the requirements of the folktale type, pursue Odysseus, and nearly destroy him? (Note that Polyphemos tries in vain to lure Odysseus back with the offer of a gift: 517–19.) Odysseus himself orchestrates the pursuit. Having used the No Man ruse as part of the escape from the cave, Odysseus' desire to taunt the giant finally causes him to reveal his own name and thus to locate himself as a target for the giant's second missile. Further, having learned Odysseus' name, Polyphemos can pray to his father, Poseidon, for vengeance. The anger of Poseidon against Odysseus replaces the punishment of the hero through self-mutilation.

As mentioned above, the adaptation of a folktale or folktale type in the Polyphemos episode has long since been recognized by classical scholars (but denied by Fehling 1984; cf. on this matter Edmunds 1990: 240–1 and Hansen 2002: 293–4). Generally, they understand this adaptation on a model such as the following: Homer took a folktale, rationalized it, leaving out fantastic elements like the magical ring, and transformed it into poetry; as for the original folktale, either it is assumed to have disappeared or its continued existence has no relevance. Homer's narrative replaces the original story.

But an alternative model can be proposed. The folktale or folktales would have persisted in the larger oral culture in which the oral epic tradition developed and of which Homer's epic was the culmination. Part of the experience of Homer's audience was, then, the difference between the folktale(s) and Homer's adaptation. But how did the audience perceive the difference, or what difference(s) did they perceive? Whereas the standard model presented above calls attention to Homer's rationalizing away of the fantastic elements and to the poetic or artistic superiority of the transformation over the original, Homer's audience might have been equally or more aware of the ways in which the Homeric version of the folktale projects both a past (the prophecy concerning Odysseus that Polyphemos recalls) and a future (the anger of Poseidon), so that Odysseus' role as the protagonist of this story becomes continuous with the narrative of the *Odyssey* as a whole. Whereas the folktale was an independent story that could be told by itself and for itself, the Homeric adaptation works it into a larger whole. A second aspect of the alternative model, then, is the adaptation of the shorter story to the larger one. The adaptation shows the audience how the hero of the folktale can become Odysseus (or vice versa). Again, the audience experiences the difference between the independent folktale and the larger narrative.

Virgil's *Aeneid*

The last of the epics to be discussed is the *Aeneid*, the composition of which probably began in the early twenties of the first century BCE and continued until Virgil's death in 19 BCE. Its opening lines, in asserting an epic theme, also implicitly make two assertions about the origin of Rome: that it goes back to the Trojan Aeneas, and that it was preceded by a particular sequence of events in Italy (1.1–7). The first, concerning Aeneas, reflects an old view, held especially in Etruria, but not for that reason the majority one. In Republican literature, Romulus is the founder of Rome. The Trojan origin of Rome, ultimately a Greek tradition, was useful as a way for Greeks to think about Rome and also for Romans to think about Greece (Ogilvie 1965: 33; Erskine 2001: 36–43). Greeks could believe that Aeneas was a Greek, as Dionysius of Halicarnassus argued in his *Roman Antiquities*, written at about the same time as the *Aeneid*. Even the Aborigines whom Aeneas encountered were Greeks (Dion. Hal. *Ant. Rom.* 1.11.1 cites Sempronius Tuditanus F 1 P = F 1 B-W and M. Porcius Cato (hereafter Cato) F 6 P = F 1.4 B-W). Romans, for their part, could believe that they, the descendants of Trojans and now conquerors of Greece, had avenged their ancestors. The *Aeneid* takes this view of the matter (1.283–5), though it may also offer the hope of reconciliation (see Momigliano 1984).

As for the sequence of events following Aeneas' arrival in Italy, the first is implicit in the phrase "Lavinian shores," in which the adjective is proleptic (*Aen.* 1.2–3): the shores will become "Lavinian" because of the city, Lavinium, to be founded by Aeneas. It will be named after his wife, Lavinia, the daughter of the Italian king, Latinus (cf. Liv. (59 BCE–17 CE) 1.1.10; Var. (116–27 BCE) *Ling.* 5.144). The marriage – again, it is implicit – will begin a *genus Latinum*, a "Latin race" (1.6). The "Alban fathers," i.e. the Alban kings, will be the rulers of this race. Virgil's concision here omits their beginning, their succession, and the birth of the twins Romulus and Remus from the daughter of Numitor, the last of the Alban kings in the period before the "walls of Rome" (1.7).

Virgil's recognition of the chronological gap between Aeneas' arrival in Italy and the founding of Rome reflects a choice among variant traditions. Dionysius says that both the founder and the time of the founding are in great dispute; he finds a welter of variants in Greek historians (*Ant. Rom.* 1.72). The founder is either Aeneas or one of his sons or his grandson. For example, in the Greek historian Alcimus (fourth century BCE), Aeneas was the father of Romulus, he of Alba, and she the mother of Rhomus, who founded Rome (*FGrH* 560 F 4). (For further references, see *FGrH*, 3rd part, b (Notes), p. 331 nn. 309–11.) The Roman historian Sallust, writing only a few years before Virgil began work on the *Aeneid*, has a coalition of Aborigines and Trojans led by Aeneas as the founders of Rome (Sall. *Cat.* 6.1). As for the earlier Roman epic poets, Naevius and Ennius (on whom see Chapter 31, by Goldberg), in them Virgil read that Romulus was the grandson of Aeneas and founder of Rome (see Serv. auct. on *Aen.* 1.273; cf. Hor. *Carm.* 3.3.31–2; see also Norden 1966: 390).

Within his chosen chronological framework, Virgil had further choices to make, especially as concerned the son of Aeneas as the first of the Alban kings. Was Ascanius the son of Aeneas and Lavinia and thus half-Italian (Liv. 1.1.11)? Or was he the son of Aeneas and Creusa, born in Troy and of pure Trojan blood (Liv. 1.3.1–3)? The double tradition was already troublesome to Cato. In his *Origines* (begun in 168 BCE), he wrote that, after the war with the Italians and the deaths of Latinus and Aeneas, Ascanius held Laurolavinium (another name for Lavinium). Fearing him, Lavinia fled to the hut of a shepherd, and there she bore Silvius. Ascanius then conceded Laurolavinium to her and founded Alba. He died without children and left his rule to his half-brother Silvius, after whom all the subsequent Alban kings were called Silvii. Cato adds that Silvius is also called Ascanius, in this way trying to reconcile the purely Trojan and the half-Italian origin of the Alban kings (Serv. *ad Aen.* 6.760 = Cato F 11 P = F 1.11 B-W; the authenticity of this fragment is debated: see Schröder 1971: 131–2). The late and anonymous *Origo Gentis Romanae* (*Origin of the Roman Race*, hereafter *OGR*) moves the problem into the next generation: the son of Ascanius, called Iulus (i.e., the grandson of Aeneas), and the son of Lavinia, Silvius (i.e., the son of Aeneas), quarreled over the kingship, and Silvius was declared king, "as is written in the fourth book of the annals of the pontifexes" (18.5).

Virgil's solution was to give different versions in different places. In Jupiter's great prophecy in Book 1, Ascanius will receive the name Iulus after Aeneas has ruled in Latium for three years (and has died, though Jupiter is silent on this point). After thirty years, Ascanius/Iulus will found Alba Longa (1.261–71). Compare Cato for the earliest attestation of the name change: Ascanius assumes the new name after his defeat of Mezentius, just at the time his first beard (Greek *ioulos*) was starting to grow (in Serv. *ad Aen.* 1.267 = F 9 P = F 1.9 B-W). At Alba Longa, the "race of Hector," i.e. the Trojan race, will reign for three hundred years, until the birth of Romulus and Remus and the founding of Rome (1.272–77). This tradition makes the Julian family, who claimed descent from Iulus (cf. Dion. Hal. *Ant. Rom.* 1.70.4 and another writer contemporary with Virgil, Livy 1.3.2), the continuators of a dynasty. In Book 6, however, among the souls awaiting rebirth whom Aeneas sees in the Underworld, it is Silvius, described as the late-born son of

Aeneas and Lavinia, with whom the succession of Alban kings will begin (760–6). The contradiction in this regard between Books 1 and 6, an old chestnut of Virgilian scholarship, reflects the existence of two equally compelling traditions.

Virgil's desire to honor Julian dynastic claims in his presentation of the early history of Rome can also be seen in his assertion of a striking variant against a demonstrable norm. What is the name of the mother of Romulus and Remus? In his prophecy in Book 1, Jupiter says that three hundred years after Iulus has transferred the seat of the kingdom to Alba Longa, Ilia (the daughter of Numitor) will bear twins (267–71). This woman was better known in Virgil's time as Rhea Silvia (Var. *Ling.* 5.144, Liv. 1.3.11, Dion. Hal. *Ant. Rom.* 1.76.3, *OGR* 19.4–5). In the Roman epic tradition, Ilia was the name of Aeneas' daughter (as in Naevius and Ennius). This name makes good sense when Aeneas is still in the picture. Three hundred and three years later, why would Numitor name his daughter Ilia, "woman of Ilium (Troy)" (Schröder 1971: 79)?

Besides the kind of variants discussed so far, which clearly honor Augustus in particular as *pulchra Troianus origine Caesar* "a Caesar who is Trojan from a noble line" (*Aen.* 1.286; see Williams 1972 on this line) and thus can be considered deliberate, there are others that seem to be simply an undigested reflex of the contemporary state of a particular story. This second kind of internal variation in the *Aeneid* would, one surmises, have been removed if Virgil had lived to finish the work. Two examples, both prophecies concerning the founding of Rome, will be discussed.

In the Aeneas legend as received by Virgil, a cryptic prophecy concerning the eating of a table or tables was traditional. Lycophron in his *Alexandra* (early 2nd c. BCE), apparently locating its fulfillment in Etruria, refers to it in fact as "ancient prophecy" (1250–2). Others say that Aeneas got the prophecy from the oracle of Zeus at Dodona (Serv. *ad Aen.* 3.256 = Var. *Antiq.* 2, Appendix l Cardauns (Cardauns commentary: 1976: vol. 2, 162); Dion. Hal. *Ant. Rom.* 1.55.4) or from a Sibyl on Mount Ida in the Troad (Dion. Hal. ibid.). Strabo (b. *ca.* 64 BCE) reports that an oracle bade Aeneas remain wherever he ate his table: "This happened in the Latin land near Lavinium, when a large loaf of bread was set out instead of the table they lacked and was consumed along with the meat upon it" (13.1.53). The story was common in Virgil's time, as Conon (36 BCE–17 CE) indicates. He refers to the story that traces the Roman race to Aeneas and makes him the founder of Alba (note the variant) and the oracle concerning the eating of the tables at a sacrifice, and calls it trite (*FGrH* 26 F 1 (45)).

In the *Aeneid* the Trojans land on an island in the Strophades, kill some cattle, and prepare a meal. They are attacked by the Harpies, whom they drive off. One of them, Celaeno, a prophetess, proclaims what she has learned from Apollo: the Trojans will reach Italy, but they will not found a city until hunger and the wrong they have done the Harpies force them to eat their tables (3.245–57). The eating of the tables is thus an atonement. The setting and source of the prophecy in Virgil are apparently an innovation, except that, as Servius says, Virgil alludes to the Dodona variant by making Celaeno cite Jupiter as her ultimate authority (Serv. ibid.).

The prophecy is fulfilled when the Trojans, having reached the mouth of the Tiber, land and prepare a meal (7.109–34; cf. Dion. Hal. *Ant. Rom.* 1.55.2–3). They heap gleanings from the countryside on flat wheat bread. Hunger drives them to eat the bread, and Iulus exclaims: "We are eating our tables, too" (7.116). Aeneas immediately perceives the fulfillment of Celaeno's prophecy: "Here is our home, this is our country" (7.122). His reaction does not seem to include any sense of atonement. Perhaps the reader is to understand that a dismissive remark by the Trojan seer Helenus has overruled Celaeno (3.394–5).

Aeneas proceeds, however, to attribute the prophecy to Anchises, whom he quotes (7.124–27). Celaeno is forgotten. Traces of the version in which Anchises is the source of the prophecy remain in *OGR* 11.1. Anchises (who in this version, unlike Virgil's, is still alive when the Trojans reach Latium) perceives the eating of the flat bread as the fulfillment of a prophecy he had received from Venus: when, having landed on a foreign shore, the Trojans are driven by hunger to eat consecrated bread, that will be the fated place for founding a city. Forthwith, the sow, to be discussed below, leads Aeneas to the exact location of the prospective city. In this version, then, the sow is closely linked to the eating of the tables, as also in Dionysius (*Ant. Rom.* 1.55.4). *OGR* cites L. Julius Caesar (cf. Weinstock 1971: 4, 17) and Lutatius Catulus (probably the one described at *OCD* (1) and *RE* 7) for this story.

Explanations for the contradiction between Celaeno and Anchises as the source of the prophecy continue to occupy philologists and literary critics (see, for example, Horsfall 2000: 112–13). In the perspective of synchronic variation, it appears that Virgil has left his innovation (Celaeno) awkwardly juxtaposed with current tradition (Anchises).

Another portent, which concerns the sow that Aeneas encounters soon after he reaches the Tiber, shows the same kind of narrative inconsistency. The sow is the protagonist in what was in Virgil's time one of the best-known episodes in the early history of Rome. The sow could be seen in bas relief on Augustan monuments, the Belvedere Altar (Taylor 1931: 187–90) and the Ara Pacis (Canciani 1981: items 163–5). (These monuments postdate the death of Virgil, and thus the *Aeneid*, but the thousands who saw them would not have needed this text or any other in order to understand the iconography.) Bronze images of the sow and the piglets stood in Lavinium, where the sow's body was preserved in brine (Var. *Rust.* 2.4.18; for the images cf. Lycoph. *Alex.* 1253–60 quoted above). The variation in her story is in proportion to its great popularity. In most versions, the sow has to do with the founding of Lavinium, though even these vary considerably among themselves. A well-attested version (cf. Dion. Hal. and *OGR* cited above), and one certainly known to Virgil, is reported as follows in Diodorus Siculus, whose source is Fabius Pictor, the first Roman historian (third to second century BCE): "An oracle came to Aeneas that a four-footed animal would lead him to the founding of a city. When he was about to sacrifice a pregnant sow, white in color, it fled from his hands, and was pursued to a certain hill, having reached which it gave birth to thirty piglets. Aeneas, astonished at the unexpected event and remembering the oracle, tried to settle the place but seeing in his sleep a vision that clearly forbade him and counseled him to found a city after thirty years, such as the number of the litter was, he desisted from his plan" (Diod. Sic. 7.5.4–5 = Fabius Pictor F 4 P = *FGrH* F 2 = F 5 B-W; cf. Var. *Ling.* 5.144).

The animal that leads the founder to the site of the new city is a folktale motif (Thompson 1955–8: B155.1, B155.2.1–4). An example in Greek myth is the cow that leads Cadmus to the site of Thebes (Eur. *Phoen.* 638–44, Hellanicus *FGrH* 4 F 51, Apollod. *Bibl.* 3.4.1). On the Roman side, a bull (Latin *bos, bovis*), escaping from an altar on the Alban hill where it is about to be sacrificed, is captured at a place eponymously named Bovillae, the city to which the Julian family traced its roots (schol. Pers. 6.55; cf. Weinstock 1971: 6). This story can perhaps be discerned in Cato (Serv. auct. on *Aen.* 10.541 = Cato F 55 P = 2.25 B-W). A minor variant of the sow in the Aeneas legend has a cow as protagonist. Conon reports that, when Aeneas reaches the Brousiad (*sic*) land, the mooing of a cow that he had brought from Mount Ida causes him to sacrifice the cow and found a city. The city is at first called Aeneia and later Aenos. Conon recognizes the tale as a type of foundation story (*FGrH* 26 F 1 [45]).

An essential component of the story about the sow is her litter of thirty piglets. Different sources assign different meanings to the number thirty. Lycophron wrote:

> And he shall found a territory in places of the Boreigonoi [i.e., Aborigines: cf. Strabo 5.3.2 and Liv. 1.1.5], a settled territory beyond the Latins and the Daunians – thirty cities, having

numbered the offspring of a dark sow that he shall transport from the hills of Ida and Dardanian places, rearer of this number of pigs in her litter. Of this sow and her milk-fed young he will also, in one city, set up an image, having it moulded in bronze. (*Alex.* 1253–60)

In an alternate tradition, thirty stands for the number of years before the city of Alba Longa will be founded; that is, it signifies, in effect, that Aeneas will not be the founder of this city, despite the implication of Diodorus Siculus (quoted above). Varro writes:

Thirty years hereafter the city Alba is founded; it is named from a white sow; this sow, when it had escaped to Lavinium from the ship of Aeneas, bears thirty young; from this prodigy thirty years after the founding of Lavinium this city is founded called Alba Longa after the color of the sow and the nature of the place. (Var. *Ling.* 5.144; the prodigy seems to be assumed by Cato F 13 P = F 1.14b B-W, who says that Ascanius founded Alba after thirty years; cf. Schröder 1971: 140–7).

A Greek analogue from the *Iliad* is Calchas' numerological interpretation of the portent of the sparrows and the snake witnessed by the Achaeans at Aulis: the eight chicks and the mother sparrow devoured by the snake make a total of nine, which means that in the tenth year the Achaeans will capture Troy (*Il.* 2.295–330).

How does Virgil accommodate the story about the sow, which was an essential element in accounts of the founding of Rome? In Book 8, Aeneas is encamped at the mouth of the Tiber. He has a vision of the river god Tiberinus, who tells him of a portent that will confirm his vision (8.43–5) and sends him up the Tiber to Pallanteum, to seek its king, Evander, as an ally. The portent will be a white sow lying beneath the holm-oaks on the bank of the river with thirty newborn piglets. Tiberinus also explains the meaning of the portent: after thirty years Ascanius, or Iulus, will found Alba (47–8; cf. the prophecy of Jupiter at 1.267–71). Soon after he awakens, Aeneas finds the sow, which he sacrifices to Juno (81–5). As observed above, Virgil breaks the link between the eating of the tables and the sow. In so doing, he is able drastically to reduce the role of the sow: she only confirms Aeneas' vision, and the truth of what Tiberinus has said.

Tiberinus' description of the sow (8.43–6) repeats verbatim the prophecy given to Aeneas by Helenus in Buthrotum (a port on the coast of Epirus in northwest Greece) in Book 3.390–2; Helenus, however, gives the sow a different meaning. He says that it will mark the end of Aeneas' journey: "This will be the site of a city, this is sure rest from your toils" (393). Here "a city" must mean Lavinium, as in the tradition followed by Varro. The prophecy of Helenus, then, is in accordance with the folktale motif (the animal guides the founder of a city), whereas Tiberinus' prophecy follows the numerological variant, which places significance on the offspring of the sow and, paradoxically, disallows the founding of a city, Alba Longa, by Aeneas.

As in the case of the eating of the tables, this contradiction has given rise to much discussion among scholars of Virgil. From the perspective of synchronic variation, it can be observed again that Virgil has neglected to reconcile an innovative use of the tradition (Book 8) with a more conservative one (Book 3). The innovation is marked, by the way, by Aeneas' sacrifice of the sow to Juno, which accommodates the motif to the plot of the *Aeneid* (8.81–5). On the Ara Pacis, Aeneas is sacrificing the sow to the Penates (Dion. Hal. *Ant. Rom.* 1.57.1; cf. Zanker 1988: 203–5), and the setting is probably to be understood as Lavinium, where there were images of the Penates (Dion. Hal. *Ant. Rom.* 1.67.4 = Timaeus *FGrH* 566 F 59), which Roman consuls and praetors were required to visit every year (Var. *Ling.* 5.144). It is thought that the seated figure of a woman on the Belvedere Altar is Juno; if so, this conception of the sacrifice would correspond to Virgil's (again Taylor 1931: 187–90), though any viewer would have been able to perceive the legend of the sow without grasping a possible allusion to Virgil.

Of the epics discussed in this chapter, the *Aeneid* might have seemed least susceptible to analysis in terms of a dynamic relation to synchronic variation in narrative traditions. It became an instant classic and school text. Despite its lack of a final revision (cf. Donat. *Vit. Verg.* 35), it has a high polish line by line, and, as a whole, a formal perfection. For the legend of the founding of Rome, it is the last word. And yet clear traces of its response to synchronic narrative traditions have appeared. A symptom of this response is internal contradiction, observed also in the SV of the Gilgamesh epic in Tablet 12 and at various points in the *Iliad* and the *Odyssey.* It is also the case that, in relation to a welter of contemporary traditions, both Greek and Latin, Trojan Aeneas as the ancestor on Italian soil of the founders of Rome is the affirmation of the truth of a single variant, and, as such, repeats the stance of the oral storyteller, who always, explicitly or implicitly, denies the truth of others' versions of the same story in order to assert the truth of his own (Edmunds 1990: 14–15; Nagy 1990c: 60–1). Finally, even the *Aeneid*, like the other epics discussed in this chapter, admits folktales and sets its version against those current among its audience. Virgil's sow is sacrificed near the mouth of the Tiber. Others' sows reached Lavinium, and in that city some of Virgil's readers had seen the supposed remains pickled in brine.

FURTHER READING

Myth and epic tend to be studied independently of each other. "Epic and myth," which is not an established category of scholarship, has a small bibliography. If, as I have argued, the topic "epic and myth" is about the emergence of epic from a background of variant narrative traditions (myths, legends, folktales), comparative folklore provides the clearest view of the process (see Hansen 1990, 1997, 2002). The plasticity of an oral epic tradition (Foley 1990, 1997) allows the incorporation even of other cultures' myths (Burkert 1984/1992; West 1997b). For a study of the interaction of myth and epic in a single ancient tradition, see Edmunds 1997.

CHAPTER FOUR

Performance

Minna Skafte Jensen

Right through antiquity literature was oral. Poems were sung, speeches delivered, and stories told, and even reading and writing in private could normally be heard: you read aloud to yourself or had a slave reading to you, authors dictated their works to scribes, and also for relatively informal writings such as letters to friends, slaves were regularly used for doing the actual job. Going to the marketplace you were able not only to buy goods, but also to attend lawsuits, participate in philosophical dialogues, or listen to the odd performance, for instance of epics. Public festivals for the gods included solemn processions, sacrificing animals, dining in common, and attending all kinds of entertainment. Literature was an integral part of life, performed officially at public and private occasions or informally to accompany work or sweeten leisure hours. Women sang or told stories at the loom, harvesters were entertained by musicians, rowers kept the rhythm by singing sea-shanties, and gentlemen sang or made speeches at drinking parties.

However, ancient literature has reached us in written form, either via unbroken transmission during the Middle Ages, or dug out by archaeologists and deciphered by philologists. Our access to the texts is in silent reading, often slowly with patient consultation of grammar and lexicon. If we want to get an impression of how the same texts were experienced by their contemporary audiences, we have to reconstruct the original settings in our minds. The sources for this are the literary texts themselves and other written or material sources. But in order to interpret them in a congenial way, interest has focused on the way oral literature works in our own times.

Interest in the performance of epic began in Homeric studies, with the oral-formulaic theory of Milman Parry and A. B. Lord. Their understanding of the formulas and themes of Homeric poetry linked these characteristics to the conditions under which the poet created his work: he was not sitting splendidly isolated at his table writing poetry, but composed as he performed, face to face with his audience. Accordingly, to understand this special kind of poetry, studies of the context of performing became of paramount importance.

Parry and Lord were concerned with the epic genre, but their theory claimed relevance for oral poetry as such since it was concentrated on how oral composition works. So for a start it is important to underline that oral poetry includes a broad spectrum of genres, and that these differ from one community to another. They are all traditional in the sense that poets rely on the experience of their craft, and memory always has an important role to play. Some texts or parts of them are more easily memorized than others: poetry is remembered better than prose, brief poems better than long ones, and in rhymed verse the end of a line is more stable than the beginning. Formulas may be retained even after poets and audiences have forgotten what they meant.

It makes a fundamental difference whether texts are supposed to be true or not. Variation may be appreciated in lyrics, but is considered erroneous in genres that have as their purpose to give reliable information of events in the past or other kinds of useful knowledge. Singers or storytellers who handle such material invariably claim that they are able to repeat exactly what they have been taught, and both they and their audiences feel confident that oral transmission may be precise and reliable. Variation is frowned upon as a sign that the performer is no expert in his field. This respect for correctness of data stands in a paradoxical relation to the fact that poems actually change, and not only in matters of detail. This was a main experience of Parry and Lord's fieldwork, and it has been massively documented in fieldwork since then.

The present chapter is about epic, and based on the following definition of the genre: epic is a long narrative poem describing historical events. By "long" I mean: longer than other forms in a community's spectrum of genres. "Narrative" means: mainly concerned with action, but allowing for both description and reflection. It is not always easy to define a "poem"; it has for instance been contested that epic existed in Africa because scholars did not agree on what was poetry, what prose (Finnegan 1970: 108–9 vs. Biebuyck 1976: 5; Seydou 1990: 403). I take for poetry whatever is performed in a style distinguished from daily speech, whether by rhythm, rhyme, music, choice of words, pitch of voice, or whatever. By "historical events" I mean: events that both singer and audience consider to have actually taken place once upon a time, including such that scholars might call myth or legend. (Definitions of folklore genres: Ben-Amos 1976; definitions of epic: Blackburn and Flueckiger 1989: 2–5; Honko 1998b: 20–9; Beissinger et al. 1999: 16.)

Oral epic belongs to the wonders of humanity (see Chapter 13, by J. Foley). Singers are reported to be in command of huge traditional stories and ready to perform for hours on end. The Kirghiz bard Jusup Mamay performed his version of the Manas epic in 1979; it amounted to almost 200,000 lines and was published in 18 volumes 1984–95. Besides, he knew eleven other epics (Ying 2001). The Tibetan Gesar epic was sung by "Old Man Thrapa" in a version of 600,000 lines (Gyaltsho 2001: 281). The Mongolian Jangar epic was published in twelve volumes 1985–96; in this case more than a hundred singers contributed (Chao 2001b: 404). In northern Africa, Sirat Bani Hilal, an Arabic tradition taking its stories from the immigration of the Hilal tribe during the tenth to twelfth centuries, has been studied by several scholars since the last few decades of the twentieth century. A Tunisian singer, Mohammed Hsini, recited a 20-hour version during sessions between 1974 and 1980, and the recording ran to over 1000 manuscript pages (Saada 1985: 24). In lower Egypt, Shaykh Biyali Abu Fahmi sang a 32-hour version over eleven nights (Reynolds 1995: 42). In Andhra Pradesh in India a Telugu bard recited a version of the Palnadu epic, the recording of which took place during two weeks in October 1974 and lasted about 30 hours (Roghair 1982: vii). And an epic of similar length sung by Gopala Naika during six days, 26 hours' singing time net, has been published (Honko 1998a). These long texts, telling the story from beginning to end, were mostly produced at the request of scholars, while the normal performance was of single episodes. It is remarkable that in the two best described cases both singers were immediately able to conform to the scholar's wish and during performance give form and structure to a poem of an unfamiliar kind (Reynolds 1995: 42 and Honko 1998a).

Analyzed as communication, oral epic differs from written first and foremost in the way contact is established (Jakobson 1960: 353–9). It is direct; addresser and addressee are face to face. They can see, hear, smell, and touch each other, and they mutually influence each other as the performance proceeds. The experience is shared, and joy, melancholy, fear, or aggression is contagious among the participants. The success of a singer depends on his ability to catch the interest of his audience and keep it. He is intent on meeting their demands and is all the time attentive to their reactions. If they show signs of being bored, he introduces something exciting or, on the contrary, abbreviates his narrative and hastens to the end. The more often he performs the same narrative, the better he knows what will make people laugh or cry, and the experienced singer is skilled at manipulating the feelings of his audience. But when asked, listeners say that they have been moved by the truth of the tale.

There are many variations from one tradition to another in the way songs are presented. Often singers accompany themselves on a stringed instrument, and there may be other musicians involved; the music is considered very important (Seydou 1983: 43–4; Saada 1985: 24; Reynolds 1995: 12–13). There may be extra singers, and parts of the narrative may be dramatically performed (Biebuyck 1972: 262–4). But there are also singers who use no other instrument than their voice (Honko 1998a). Perhaps the audience takes part; for instance, they may repeat lines or refrains (Honko 1998b: 548–57). Even the singer who performs alone may establish a dramatic effect by means of mimicry, gesture, and variation of voice. Some scholars talk of the epic text as a libretto, to remind us that the words we read are only part of the event (Foley 1998c: 80–5). The style varies with differences in aesthetic, but it is everywhere characterized by repeated phrases, parallelisms, adding style, type scenes, and patterned narrative.

The linguistic form tends to be solemn and characterized by archaisms (Quain 1942: 16; Biebuyck 1976: 28–30; Reynolds 1995: 44–6; Chao 2001b: 420). But little seems to have been done in the way of precise study. Epic traditions in the modern world typically exist in communities peripheral to the centers of wealth and power, and express themselves in languages that often do not even have an orthography. It is doubtful if the language and style of any living tradition will ever be analyzed in a way remotely similar to how Homeric language has been studied.

Occasions may be of many kinds, and in most communities who have an epic tradition they vary from big, formal events to private entertainment. Parry's and Lord's informants had their most important function during Ramadan, when many innkeepers hired a singer to entertain their customers at night (Lord 1960: 15). The singer Awadallah Abd aj-Jalil Ali, living near Aswan in Egypt, stated that he used to perform during pilgrimages, in cafés, and at private parties arranged by a patron, such as at the end of Ramadan, at weddings, or at the annual workers' feast at the local sugar factory (Slyomovics 1987: 10). In communities where the interest in epic is sufficiently widespread to offer a basis for industrialization of performance, singers become good at delivering versions that fit precisely into a radio program or a tape (Wadley 1998: 155). Tulu epic makes an integral part of the cult at certain religious festivals, which may last 10–14 hours per night during two to four nights (Honko 1998b: 389–499, 2000a: 13). The Palnadu epic is regularly recited at the annual festival for the heroes of the narrative. The festival is formally called, sacrifice given, and during the week's festivities epic is recited the first evening and the following four days. Certain episodes are prescribed for certain occasions, not following a chronological order of the narrative. On the fourth day there is a procession in which the protagonists of epic and festival are represented dramatically (Roghair 1982: 26–31). What is of paramount importance is that the occasion must offer a sufficient period of time for an audience to attend a rounded, harmonious performance.

As a rule, epic singers are male. Their social status varies from one community to another, and so does their education. They may learn just simply by attending other singers, as described by Lord (1960: 13–29), and often their teacher is their father or grandfather (Slyomovics 1987: 6–7; Harvilahti 2000: 218–19). There are communities in which epic singing is highly specialized and runs in certain families, as among the Bambara in the central parts of Africa. Here one and the same family recruits musicians, counsellors, negotiators, and epic singers, and small boys are under constant supervision so that the most gifted can already begin training as young children; apprenticeship lasts 10–15 years (Bird 1972: 278–80; Biebuyck 1976: 20). To learn the epic properly, they must make a tour from master to master and end at a recognized center at Krina in Mali. Here a special ritual takes place every seventh year at the sanctuary of the ancestors; the established bards participate in secret rituals and recite to each other, and young singers pass a kind of exam (Seydou 1990: 414). Sometimes singers state that they have been taught supernaturally, in a dream or a trance (Gyaltsho 2001: 280–6), and one tells of his grandfather that he had a book given in a dream and was immediately able to read it (Slyomovics 1987: 11–12). The above-mentioned Kirghiz singer was taught by his brother and by reading, but nevertheless maintained that he had been instructed by the heroes of the epic who had met him in a dream (Ying 2001: 223–8). Since the text is flexible, each performance is a recomposition of the narrative. Accordingly, in oral epic the terms "singer," "bard," and "poet" are synonymous.

The audience can be mixed or only male, but is seldom narrowly restricted. One instance is reported of an epic being regularly performed to a female audience, the Tulu tradition of Karnataka in India. Here one of the situations in which epic is performed is during work in the paddy-field. The singer is male, but the female workers join in as a choir, and some of them are also able to perform as main singers (Honko 1998b: 552–3).

The influence of the audience on the performance has been described as social control (Bogatyrev and Jakobson 1929: 901–3). What is not accepted by the audience will disappear from the tradition. In the case of epic, it is especially a question of truth: normally the story is known to the audience already, and they will accept only what they feel to be correct. Ancestors of persons who are powerful in the community will be important in the narrative; if their family dies out, they tend to disappear. This mechanism is called "telescoping" (Henige 1974: 5–6). In some cases performance is arranged by a patron, who as a special kind of audience exercises supreme authority over the text. This is not necessarily taking the form of open control, but may function as a self-censure on the part of the singer.

All kinds of performance to an audience have as one of their main functions to establish a feeling of group identity. But this is of special importance in epic performance, since it links participants not only to each other, but also to their ancestors. When attending the epic, the audience members feel that their own world is a continuation of theirs, and that they contribute to keeping the heroes alive by hearing of their great deeds. The performance reactivates the events of former times, and one scholar even speaks of "the intense tripartite relationship that obtains between the poets, their listeners, and the heroes" (Reynolds 1995: xiv). Often epics work as a means of legitimating affairs of the present. A narrative about how the tribe traveled until they finally reached the place where they now live, confirms their claim to be the legitimate inhabitants of the area in question (Vansina 1985: 91–3). There is also a didactic aspect of epic performance: people identify with the heroes, take them as their models, and learn from their misfortune or success. Among the Nyanga in Congo the hero even embodies features not appreciated in the community and thus tests the boundaries of good and bad (Biebuyck 1972: 272; Seydou 1990: 409). The group who is attending is inevitably led into negotiating their shared values.

In spite of this great, varied mass of examples, it is striking that a series of common traits link them all together: the special register of style and language, the respect for facts, the feeling of shared values among those present, including gods and ancestors, and of course the sheer entertainment of narrative. These characteristics are all based upon the event of performance, the face-to-face communication during which the singer recomposes his poem under the steady cooperation and control of his audience. It is his mastery of the tradition that renders his words authoritative and gains the acceptance of the listeners. This magic, creative, and potentially dangerous situation has been called an arena, in which word-power is established by means of the enabling event of performance and the enabling referent of tradition (J. Foley 1995: xiv and *passim*).

Even though each performance normally concentrates on a single episode, the full story lies behind, known in more or less detail to both singers and audiences. This has been called the "pool of tradition," which furnishes the singer with stuff for his narrative (Honko 1998b: 66–74, cf. Biebuyck 1972: 266; Aloni speaks in the same sense of a "macrotext," 1998: 25).

The word "text" is currently used in different ways by scholars. To some it means a written text as opposed to the ephemeral oral poem (e.g. Bakker 1997: 1), and a similar understanding is implied also in the new word "textualization" for the process of recording an oral poem (the idea is discussed in Honko 2000a). Others speak of text also in oral performance, and even of "mental texts," songs that exist as basic entities in the singer's repertory. When learning a new song, the singer works on it in his mind and in performance until it finds a form with which he is satisfied. However much he varies his narrative from one performance to the next, he sticks to this mental text, being able to retain it in his memory over any length of time. Such mental texts are not, however, transmitted from one singer to the next (Honko 1998b: 92–9).

One may speak of pools of tradition on more than one level. Considering the similarities that exist among Near Eastern and Greek poems (Chapter 20, by Burkert), the stories behind them might be called a common pool of tradition extending over a period of two millennia and the whole area of the eastern Mediterranean and Mesopotamia. Similar musical instruments suggest that this pool of tradition included not only stories, but also the habits of how to perform them. Next come pools of tradition that unite more limited areas linguistically or geographically, and at the other end of the scale are pools that contain single cycles of stories such as the deeds of Gilgamesh or the Trojan War.

Only in one case is the performance context of a Mesopotamian epic actually known (see Chapter 15, by Noegel). *Enûma Elish* is mentioned in a ritual text which describes in great detail the new year's festivals for Marduk (Pritchard 1955: 331–4). On the evening of the fourth day the *urigallu*-priest shall recite this poem to the god. This makes good sense with respect to the text we know since it is full of generous praise of the god. There are also passages of the poem in which orders are given about cult practice and recital (e.g. VI. 106–22), and it ends with an epilogue stating that it should be remembered and commented upon, discussed by experts, recited by father to son and heard by shepherds and herdsmen (VII. 145–8). The very last verses even state that the text has been dictated by an older man and written with the purpose of being heard by younger generations (VII. 157–8, according to West 1997b: 598). In the ritual text there is nothing to suggest that an audience should be present when the priest recites to the god, so the just mentioned passages point to other, less formal, performances. It is interesting that this written text so clearly counts upon an oral afterlife. The Hittite *Kingship in Heaven* opens with an address to various gods, a fact that suggests that this poem was meant for a similar cultic context (see further Chapter 17, by Beckman).

Mesopotamian epic shares with oral epic in the modern world the characteristic features of style, and it is composed in a special hymnic-epic dialect, different from common speech (Foster 1993: 3). Add to this the intriguing fact that there often exist more than one version of a poem. Experts do not agree, however, on the question of the relevance of the oral-formulaic theory (Vogelzang and Vanstiphout 1992). The Gilgamesh epic is impressive not the least for its great number of manuscripts in several languages from widely differing areas. The classic study analyzes the history of the epic exclusively in terms of written composition (Tigay 1982). But a more recent survey of the epic's history tells a fascinating story of Sumerian and Akkadian oral traditions existing side by side, a great Old Babylonian poem composed and transmitted in writing and eventually lost, and a new written composition, the Standard Babylonian version, which was then preserved in written copies during many centuries (U. and A. Westenholz 1997: 23–54).

Poetry from the Near East is often accompanied by information about how it is to be performed. The biblical psalms are introduced by such notes, and Sumerian poems have comments on genres and instruments. Even epic is regularly opened with the phrase "Let me sing . . . ," and the texts are interspersed with instructions about how they are to be remembered, recited, and heard. At the end the scribe often added a colophon declaring that he has copied the text carefully. From Ugarit we even know the name of a scribe, Ilimilku; he says of himself both by whom he has been taught and that he works for the king, Niqmaddu (Parker 1997: 42, 141, 164). And when at the end of the Kirta epic he states that the text was donated – presumably by the king – we have what seems to be a reason for the writing of the poem, that it should be dedicated to a god.

Since oral epic has no need to be written down and both singer and audience feel convinced that memory is reliable, it has become a difficult question why texts were written at all. In the case of Near Eastern epic it has been suggested that a reason for writing might be found in the scribal milieus, and that the poems have been written so that scribes might have classics to study and copy (Alster 1992: 26).

Compared to the vivid Homeric representations of performing singers, Near Eastern epics are fairly reticent about singers in action. In two of the Sumerian Gilgamesh versions, however, the king's singer plays a minor but crucial role ("Gilgamesh and the Bull of Heaven" 103–20 and the Gudam epic 13–24), reminding king and people of their duties. It is remarkable that in both contexts the singer does not try to please his audience, but is on the contrary teaching them moral lessons.

The poet Enheduanna has described how she composed the poem *Ninmesharra*: she bore the song during the night, recited it to herself, and when the day had come called for a singer and taught him the poem (138–40, see Alster 1992: 29; West 1997b: 598). A similar passage is in the *Poem of Erra*: Kabti-ilani-Marduk, son of Dabibi, composed the tablet. God had revealed the poem to him during the night, and in the morning he recited it without leaving out or adding a single verse. The divine hero attended the recital and accepted it (42–6).

Such passages both testify to the experience of poetic composition as a divine gift, and argue for the authority of the poem in question. Scribes insist on the reliability of their work, whether they have copied from a written text or taken it down from dictation. The Standard Babylonian version of the Gilgamesh epic opens with such a guarantee of truth: the poem goes back to a stele erected by the hero himself, and the reader may even consult a book preserved in a shrine at the foundations of the city walls of Uruk (I.1–29). In a similar way *Naram-Sin and the Enemy Hordes* is framed by references to a tablet-box and a stele, written by the protagonist (J. Westenholz 1997: 266, 279, 301).

Cooperation between poet and scribe seems to have been normal. A fascinating description of the whole process of producing a book is to be found in the Bible (see Chapter 19, by Niditch), where it is said of the prophet Jeremiah that God wanted to use him for taking the impious king Jehoiakim to task (Jer. 36). The prophet was not allowed to visit the temple, however. Therefore God commanded him to call for a scribe, and a book was produced. The scribe brought it to the temple and read it aloud to a big audience. When the king heard of this, he asked for the book, had it read aloud, and as the recitation proceeded, the king cut the book-roll in slices and threw it bit for bit into the fire. But God's words came back to the prophet, he called again for the scribe, a new book was written with the same content, only this time the prophet added more words. We may note, firstly, that the book was only needed because of the special problems the prophet had in gaining access to an audience. Next that he considered dictating to a scribe the normal way of writing. Finally that the king's attempt at annihilating the text by burning the book was of no avail: the prophet had his mental text which he could reproduce, in even a fuller form than the first one.

While Near Eastern poetry is very conscious of its being written, archaic Greek poems hardly ever mention writing. And it is significant that in the Near East truth is ultimately guaranteed by reference to written texts: Gilgamesh's monument and book, the tablet of fate that the Anzu-bird stole from the god Enlil, the ten commandments handed over in writing from God to Moses, and the book of law found by king Josiah when purifying the temple (2 Kgs. 22–3). Homer and Hesiod, on the contrary, base the authority of their poems on the Muses. This difference must have to do both with the fact that the Near Eastern poems belong to a community in which writing was much older and literacy more widespread than in archaic Greece, and with the different status of scribes: in Mesopotamia and Palestine they were respected professionals, while in Greece writing was slave work. Even in the classical period Sophocles' *Antigone* holds king Creon's written laws in contempt as something easily changed compared to the unwritten, eternal laws of the gods (453–7).

The *Iliad* and the *Odyssey* both begin with an invocation of the Muse in which she is quite directly asked for the story and told where to begin. The assumption is that she is in command of the story line and able to start at any given point in the sequence of events. The situation is parallel to a passage in the *Odyssey* in which the Phaeacian bard Demodokos is entertaining at a meal in the king's court. One of the guests asks him, to sing of the Trojan Horse from the point when Epius constructed it with the help of Athena. And when he begins, the phrasing is revealing: he began with the Muse and showed the song (*phaine d' aoidên*) (8.492–501). It is as if the story is materially there, ready to be taken forth just as you would take some precious object out of its cask and show it to your guests.

Nowhere is the Homeric poet as explicit about his relationship with the Muses as when in the *Iliad* he is beginning his long register of the warriors who participated in the campaign, the so-called "Catalogue of Ships" (2.484–93). Here he underlines that the Muses are there as his eyewitnesses. They are immortal goddesses, they were present when the war took place, and they know. But in the immediately following lines the poet's worries shift from the problem of knowing to that of performing: so many were there that I could not mention them all, even if I had a hundred tongues and lungs of steel, if the Muses were not willing to support me. The problem of knowing shifts into a problem of physical capacity. An important trend in performance studies is concerned with interpreting the rhetoric of the poems as specially designed for oral delivery (e.g. Minchin 1996 and Bakker 1997).

In discussions of when and how Homer and Hesiod were performed, scholars have of course first and foremost looked at what the various poems say. The scenes in which singers perform to an audience have been taken as a kind of self-portrait, and so has Odysseus' elaborate narration of his travels, commented upon by the Phaeacian king with the remark that he has described it all truthfully, just as if he had been a singer (*Od.* 11.368). Subtle analyses have been made of the speeches in the *Iliad* as performance: how in scene after scene performer and audience interact; how different kinds of performance are successful, or not; and how structures of power control the performance (Martin 1989, discussed and continued by Minchin 2002). It is by no means simple, however, to deduce from these texts' internal scenes how performance of the poems themselves worked. In other matters the narrator is explicit about the distance between the world of the heroes and his own: at the time of the Trojan War princes were richer and heroes bigger and stronger than those he and his audience meet. Roughly speaking it seems probable that situations and protagonists may be idealized, but that ideas of aesthetics and procedure are those that the poet himself embraces.

Meta-passages are more reliable, but they are few. The narrator of the *Theogony* describes how Hesiod was called by the Muses to become a singer (22–34), but the syntax of the passage does not make it clear whether narrator and Hesiod are one and the same person or not, and anyway, how an epiphany is to be understood is not easy for us to know. Simpler to handle is a passage of the *Works and Days* in which the narrator tells of his experience as a singer: he once participated in a contest at the funeral of a Euboean magnate, an occasion at which he won a tripod which afterwards he consecrated to the Muses (650–9). The convention of the Homeric hymns is that the narrator begins – as was the rule already in Mesopotamia – by declaring: "I will sing," and the object of his song is a god. At the end he takes leave of the god, asks for his or her support and states that he will proceed to another song. The help he asks for is often concerned with winning a prize. In a famous passage (3. 104. 4) Thucydides refers to the *Hymn to Apollo* and calls it a *prooimion*, a prelude, a terminology that suggests that such hymns have as their function to introduce epic performance, and that "the other song" mentioned at the end of the hymns is an epic narrative. The most detailed comment on the "poetic I" is a passage in the *Hymn to Apollo* in which the narrator addresses a chorus of young girls in Delos, asks them to tell everybody that the best songs are those sung by the blind bard from Chios, and promises to sing their praise wherever he comes (156–76). This is presumably where the portrait of Homer as the blind singer originated.

These passages all refer to the poet's activity as a sung performance, deeply embedded in competition. The occasions for performance are a private funeral and a public festival for a god, and the singers involved are itinerant and presumably professional. The audiences mentioned in the *Hymn to Apollo* are the god and the young women, and it is a reasonable guess that men were present too.

From many other sources – literary texts, inscriptions, and decorated vases – it is known that epic was sung by rhapsodes; a portrait of such a rhapsode is given by Plato in the dialogue *Ion*. It has been suggested that the singers who perform in the *Odyssey* were creative "singers of tales," as were those Parry and Lord met in Yugoslavia, whereas the rhapsodes learned the *Iliad* and the *Odyssey* by heart and recited them, and that such a development from creativity to memorization is expressed by the different terms, *aoidos* as against *rhapsôidos* (Sealey 1957). However, considering that even the most creative of singers maintain that they are repeating faithfully the song they have learned, it seems unlikely that singers and audiences were aware of such a distinction, and the difference in terminology is understandable instead as a difference in style, *aoidos* being poetic and *rhapsôidos* prosaic. (The meaning of the word *rhapsôidos* has been discussed in Patzer 1952; Ford 1988; Nagy 1996c: 60–6; Aloni 1998: 48–9.) In antiquity two different etymologies were given: from *rhaptein*, to stitch, or from *rhabdos*, a staff; the rhapsode is one who stitches verses or stories together, or he is one who is leaning on a staff. In modern times the *rhaptein* etymology is considered correct. Both understandings of the word are documented in Pindar's poetry (*Nem.* 2.1–3, *Isth.* 4.37–8), and when in the *Theogony* the Muses hand a staff to Hesiod as a sign of his initiation this seems also to suggest that he was considered a rhapsode (30).

Much interest has been focused on the so-called Panathenaic rule. A couple of sources mention that either Solon or Hipparchus ordered that the Homeric epics should be sung at the Panathenaic festivals "in order, so that where one stopped the next should take over." It has been argued that here we have the reason why the *Iliad* and the *Odyssey* were recorded in writing: in order to be able to perform like that the rhapsodes would need a fixed, authoritative text. Some have proposed that the purpose of the rule was to control the political message of the performance. There is also a discussion of the terms of the competition, and recently the competitive form of the Platonic dialogues has been used as a key to understand rhapsodic contests (Merkelbach 1952; Jensen 1980: 128–58; Nagy 1996c: 107–14; Bakker 1997: 31; Jensen 1999: 26–7; Collins 2001; Nagy 2002).

Oral performance of epic continued in the Greek world, as inscriptions testify; rhapsodic contests were a common element in many festivals of the city-states. However, singers hardly occur in our other sources, a fact that is probably to be explained not by disappearance, but by loss of social status. A sign of their existence is to be found in the *Biographies of Homer* and the description of the *Contest between Homer and Hesiod*, since they show that in imagining the way of life the great poet had led, the natural model was that of an itinerant bard.

However, a lot of names of epic poets have survived (Ziegler 1988). Typically they were employed by the great military commanders who dominated the Greco-Roman world after the death of Alexander. Little is known of them and their poetry. Nevertheless, there are two epic poets who have survived with a certain individuality, one historical and one fictitious, and both of them are described by Roman authors. One is the poet Archias whom Cicero defended in a case of citizenship. Among other things he had accompanied a Roman general in his campaigns. In his speech Cicero not only states that Archias is an excellent poet of written Greek epic, but also dwells on his exceptional ability to compose verses extempore (*Arch.* 8.18). The other one is a figure in Petronius' *Satyricon*, carrying the Greek name of Eumolpus, but speaking and composing in Latin. Like Archias he is able to perform on the spur of the moment, and his longest work is an iambic poem describing the fall of Troy, inspired by a series of pictures he and the narrator contemplate in a portico. His performance comes to an abrupt end when passers-by begin to throw stones at him. Later we hear of a similar incidence in a public bath. But he is so dedicated to his art that he resumes his performance at the first possible moment, and even when at a certain point he suffers shipwreck he has no time to be saved because he is just finishing a verse (Petr. 89–93, 115). Again, such a figure must have been drawn after a living model.

The epics that have been preserved are not of this type, however. In literature as in so many other matters the Hellenistic period marked a fundamental change. At the museum in Alexandria, Callimachus and his contemporaries discussed whether it was possible at all to compose epic any more, considering that the *Iliad* and the *Odyssey* were the masterpieces nobody could compete with. Nevertheless, the genre continued and even seemingly unchanged, in hexameters and with mythic content. But an epic such as the *Argonautica* by Apollonius Rhodius is careful to handle traditional myths in untraditional ways, and there is nothing to indicate that it claims to offer a true narrative. When Roman poets began to imitate Greek epic, they had basically two concepts to choose between, the encomiastic form presumably embraced by poets engaged to celebrate military achievements, and the intellectualistic form as cultivated by Apollonius; the situation is best known from Ennius (Ziegler 1988: 63–92; Goldberg 1995: 111–34).

In the field of Latin literature, performance studies have mainly concentrated on questions of rhetoric (e.g. Vogt-Spira 1990). Poetry may be oral with respect to composition, transmission and performance (Finnegan 1977: 17), and in this last sense epic continued an oral life in imperial times. Reciting poetry or reading it aloud was a well-known feature of Roman cultural life. Virgil's *Eclogues* are said to have been recited in the theater by *cantores*, singers, and the poet himself read aloud from his works to Augustus and Maecenas (Donat. *Vit. Verg.* 26–34). Horace is highbrow and speaks condescendingly of readings, and especially of such that take place in theaters or baths. He himself prefers to read only to friends, and only if they compel him to (*Sat.* 1.4.74–6). Martial envisages a great variety of places in which his book will be recited (7. 97 and 12. 2). It is clear that readings offered important means for a poet to gain publicity for his works, and also that patrons took an interest in the institution, as is demonstrated by the fact that both Nero and Domitian arranged for poetic competitions as part of their cultural policy. Of the poet Statius it is said that performance of his epic *The Thebaid* was a great success (Juv. *Sat.* 7. 82–6).

Pliny often refers to literary readings, and he sees them as a kind of pre-publication of works. By reading aloud to an audience the author has the chance of getting feedback, which is a useful stage in the finishing of a book (*Ep.* 7.17, cf. Cic. *Off.* 1.147). In such private readings the audience have presumably been polite and cooperative. But in one of the more entertaining descriptions, Pliny complains that listeners show little interest in such events. They prefer to sit chatting outside and only now and then have a slave report how far the reading has proceeded. They enter to attend only late and with hesitation, and many leave quite openly before the performance has been brought to an end (*Ep.* 1.13).

The coexistence in Rome of books, readers, and bookshops on one hand and oral performance of literature on the other has been discussed by scholars in some detail. Performance to invited friends seems to have been the most prestigious context for literature, whereas the very fact that a book left its author's control and offered itself to anybody who might take an interest in it gave it a status similar to that of a prostitute (Habinek 1998: 103–21).

Arma uirumque cano, "I sing of weapons and a man" – such are the opening words of Virgil's *Aeneid*. But Virgil was not singing. His choice of verb was a way of inscribing his epic into a tradition that was not his, but which he wished to call into life in the minds of his readers. And when a few verses later he says, *Musa mihi causas memora*, "Muse remind me of the causes," his expression is metaphorical: he was not relying on memory in order to master his story. He built on a careful reading of his forerunners, preferably with commentaries, and if he needed a Muse she was not called for to furnish him with material for a performance, but to ensure inspiration in a much vaguer way. In Virgil, the singing poet and the reminding Muse are literary convention, and as such they were to have a long afterlife in western literature.

FURTHER READING

The point of departure for the interest in performance is Lord 1960, which still makes for stimulating reading. Its second edition (2000) is accompanied by multimedia examples on CD. Interesting theoretical discussions are to be found in Finnegan 1977: 28–9, Zumthor 1983: 145–206, and J. Foley 1995: 1–28.

For accounts of how performance works in oral epic traditions of the modern world, see Chapter 13, by J. Foley; also Beck 1982: 58–88, Slyomovics 1987: 71–4, Finnegan 1995, and Reichl 2000a. Especially exciting is the work of Reynolds (1995), who was accepted as an apprentice by an Egyptian Sirat-Bani-Hilal-singer and is therefore in a position to describe performance from the singer's angle. Blackburn et al. 1989 establishes an overview of oral epic traditions in India; of special interest for the question of performance are the contributions by Claus and Wadley.

Kindred oral traditions may also be of relevance; thus Scheub 1977 is focused on the performers' body-language, and Børdahl 1996 is detailed in its description of the performance context of Chinese storytelling. Both Scheub 1977 and Børdahl and Ross 2002 contain attractive photographs of artists.

Performance of the Homeric poems is the theme of Aloni 1998, Minchin 2001, and Scodel 2002.

CHAPTER FIVE

Epic and History

Kurt A. Raaflaub

Heroic epics or *Heldensagen* have existed in many cultures from antiquity to our own days. Few attempts have been undertaken so far to compare these epics systematically and from various perspectives or even to establish a "typology" of heroic epic (notable exceptions include Bowra 1952; Hatto 1980; see also Hatto 1991; Hainsworth 1991; Ulf 2003b). Nor has anybody undertaken a systematic effort to determine to what extent heroic epics reflect history or, more generally, what kind of historical information, if any, we can retrieve from such epics, and what methodologies we can use to achieve this. Understandably: each epic is imbued with, and thus reflects, the specific conditions of the culture that produced it, and adequate interpretation is impossible without thorough familiarity with that culture. Whoever ventures into fields not his own risks censure of the kind suffered by C. M. Bowra at the pen of Klaus von See (1978: 22 n. 55): "The fat volume has deficiencies; in particular it lacks elementary knowledge of facts in the field of *Germanistik*" (my free trans.). In this chapter, I will make an effort, based on a sample of three ancient cultures, to understand the relationship between epic and history in antiquity. For this purpose, I cannot avoid using comparisons, even beyond the realm of the ancient world. I appeal to the tolerance of all specialists into whose turf I trespass.

My approach requires little justification. The evidence available in antiquity is often incapable of providing sufficient answers to many of the questions historians need to ask of it. How, for example, can we determine how well or badly oral poetic tradition preserved over many centuries the memory of events that may lie at the core of the Trojan War story and thus are perhaps reflected in the *Iliad* – if no record of these events survives outside the epic? How can we decide where in history to locate the "social background" to the epic action if, to use the same example, the *Iliad* is itself the earliest extant document offering a detailed and lively description of any Greek society? In the latter case, we can at least examine the consistency of the epic's evidence and its relation to conditions attested at other times. In the former case this method leads nowhere.

Later epics (such as the *Nibelungenlied,* the *Song of Roland*, or Serbo-Croatian songs) provide a better base for analysis. As we shall see in section 3, independent historical evidence exists both about the events at the core of these epic traditions and about the social conditions at the time of these events and at the time when the epics received their final form. Comparison between such external evidence and the epics' internal evidence permits us to perceive correspondences and differences and to establish general patterns.

Not that such patterns can simply be transferred to the ancient world. Comparison cannot provide definitive answers to our questions about ancient epic. But it can stimulate our thinking, reveal possibilities or even probabilities, and conversely help us understand what is improbable. The combination of such insights with others, reached through different approaches and methodologies, will enable us to formulate reasonably plausible answers to our questions.

As far as early Greek epic is concerned, the questions posed above continue to be hotly debated. I will analyze them in the second section of this chapter. The same questions are being asked for Near Eastern heroic epic, which seems fraught with even more uncertainty and offers a much smaller textual base. In the first section, I will briefly discuss one example, Sumerian epic.

Roman heroic epic seems an entirely different matter. The *Aeneid,* the earliest fully surviving representative of the genre, is a literary masterpiece, composed not in the early phases of an emerging civilization but at its height. It is the heir of long literary, not oral, traditions and consciously competes with earlier models, both Greek and Roman. Although elaborating on the historicized myth of Rome's earliest ancestors and beginnings, it shares with the early history of Rome by Virgil's contemporary, Livy, an abiding interest in, and critical distance from, the authors' own time. The historical questions we ask of Augustan (as of early imperial) epic are thus very different from those we wish to answer about Homer's – although, as we shall see, to some extent the historical relevance and timeless significance of these late epics are based on concerns that are similar to those of their early ancestors. More properly "historical epics" were a specialty of Rome as well. Ennius's *Annals* and Lucan's poem about Caesar's civil war (*De bello civili*) offer good examples, and the question of the treatment of history here is again very different from that in "mythical epics." I shall discuss these questions in the fourth section.

1   History and Sumerian Epic

The earliest extant poetic and narrative texts date to the Early Dynastic Period in the mid-third millennium BCE. They were written in an abbreviated, skeletal form that clearly assumed the writer's and reader's familiarity with the stories concerned. One of them mentions Lugalbanda, who is one of the heroes of old stories that were much later featured in epic poems (Michalowski 1995: 2281). According to the latter, Gilgamesh was the son of Lugalbanda and the goddess Ninsun, while Lugalbanda performed his heroic deeds under king Enmerkar and then became king himself. One of the Sumerian epics places Gilgamesh in the context of a feud with Akka, king of Kish, and is unique in dealing only with humans, avoiding divine elements and mythical elaboration. The event is usually assumed to be historical (Römer 1980; Katz 1993). Gilgamesh's name was later also connected with the magnificent walls of Uruk. Even so, only circumstantial evidence supports the historicity of these personalities (Michalowski 1983; Kuhrt 1995: 1. 29–31).

Although this too is much debated (Michalowski 1992: 227–8; Chapter 15, by Noegel), I accept here the traditional view that the form into which these stories eventually were elaborated was "epic." This apparently happened in the time of the Third Dynasty of Ur (*ca.* 2112–2004), when particularly Shulgi, the second king, enacted wide-ranging reforms that affected not least the scribal school curriculum. Shulgi and his successors were especially interested in two aspects: the use of Sumerian literature as cultural and political propaganda and the establishment of a kinship connection with Gilgamesh (whom Shulgi claimed as his "divine brother") that provided a source of legitimation and a foundation myth for the royal dynasty (Michalowski 1995: 2284; cf. 1988). This explanation is countered by another that sees entertainment as the epics' primary purpose. Rather than presenting models of an ideal king, they express an ideology typical of folktales: the cleverness and luck of an "underdog" who prevails over those superior in strength and power. If so, the stories may have been especially popular among the poor and illiterate lower classes (Alster 1995: 2322).

The texts survive mostly from the Old Babylonian period (first half of the second millennium BCE), when Sumerian may no longer have been a spoken language. The social function of these texts is much debated (Vogelzang and Vanstiphout 1992). One group of scholars argues that the extant texts and the stories told in them corresponded to and preserved a widespread oral tradition (Alster 1995). Others consider it possible that "writing provided a completely different medium of expression, and that from the very beginning the literature of the clay tablets was fundamentally different from the oral compositions that circulated in society." If so, the texts were entirely restricted to the scribal curriculum and thus isolated from a wider public. In this view, the "average man or woman probably knew nothing of the poems and stories that we have recovered from the ground of Mesopotamia, and therefore we should not identify the sentiments and values of the literature with the ideals of all members of those ancient societies" (Michalowski 1995: 2279–80, 2283; cf. 1992). A different view claims that the audible and visible aspects of literature continued to be two aspects of the same process, that students in scribal schools were trained in rhetoric as well as writing and literature, and that the art of the singer may have been the highest step in their training. "Many features suggest that Sumerian compositions were fundamentally meant to be recited before an audience." It might thus be best to think of "performance poetry" (Alster 1995: 2318–19).

What, then, were these epics about? Since they are the subject of another chapter, I need not go into details (see Chapter 15, by Noegel; for bibliog., see also Römer 1999). The two Enmerkar epics (Kramer 1952) deal with the antagonism between Enmerkar, king of Uruk, and the ruler of Aratta, a city in Iran. Both kings claim superiority, and their conflicting claims are resolved peacefully, through a series of competitions that seal Enmerkar's victory. In the Lugalbanda epics (Wilcke 1969), this competition has evolved into a war. Lugalbanda, the youngest of eight brothers, has to overcome great odds and his brothers' hostility to prove his qualities and achieve high status. He prevails through superior intelligence and cunning, even securing for himself supernatural abilities that enable him to render to the king a unique service. Having thus conquered Aratta, he eventually becomes the king's successor. The *Epic of Gilgamesh*, the best known of the series, extant in several versions and popular throughout Mesopotamian history (Moran 1995), focuses on a more universal theme: the fear of death and the quest for immortality in achieving everlasting fame.

Much has been made of the significance of these epics in illuminating historical events, relations, or institutions, but since this is virtually the only evidence we have, caution is recommended. Moreover, the historical information conveyed is unspecific, and the events merely provide the backdrop for what really matters: the hero's or king's achievement and superiority. Thus the patterns of trade between Uruk and Iran reflected in the Enmerkar and Lugalbanda epics merely confirm what we know from archaeological finds: that the "Mesopotamian cities maintained far-flung trading relations in order to acquire exotic goods." But "their specific mode of organisation is not illuminated by the Enmerkar story" (Kuhrt 1995: 1. 31). The search for historical marriage patterns in "Gilgamesh and the cedar forest" is fraught with uncertainties (Shaffer 1983).

"Gilgamesh and Akka" offers an especially interesting case. Early versions of the story probably focused on Gilgamesh's heroics in the fight to overthrow Uruk's dependence on Kish. In the extant version, the hero consults both a council of elders that advises against, and an assembly of warriors that supports the revolt from Kish. Thorkild Jacobsen (1943) based some of his (re)construction of "primitive democracy" on the juxtaposition of these institutions. Comprehensively reexamining all issues involved and identifying literary devices, Dina Katz (1987) concludes that the epic contains more fiction than fact and cannot be used for purposes of historical reconstruction; the bicameral political structure is the result of an ideologically motivated reinterpretation of the story, in which Gilgamesh's leadership, originally usurped against the wish of the elders, receives the backing of an assembly that legitimizes his rule (cf. Katz 1993; Römer 1980; Kuhrt 1995: 1.31).

Nor do the extant parts of an epic on Sargon the Great offer much historical information. Overall, then, unlike their much longer Homeric counterparts, the Sumerian epics do not throw much light even on the social or political background to heroic actions and events. Whether and to what extent some of the events themselves are historical cannot be demonstrated on the basis of evidence currently available.

2   History and Early Greek Epic

The epics that are preserved under the name of "Homer" were composed, by one or two brilliant poets, in the late eighth or early seventh century BCE. Virtually nothing can be found in them that reflects objects or conditions from later than the first half of the seventh century. Hesiod, who presents himself with a distinct persona, probably is slightly younger than Homer. In contrast to the latter's heroic and narrative epic, his is didactic, representing a different social and economic perspective. For all non-historical aspects I refer the reader to Chapters 21, 22, and 23, by Edwards, Slatkin, and Nelson. I will focus here on Homer and discuss three historical issues: the historicity of the event (the Trojan War) in which the *Iliad* is embedded, the historical nature of the society that is described in Homer's epics and forms the background to heroic action, and the poet's function as an educator and "political thinker." I should warn the reader that all these issues are intensely controversial.

Later generations criticized certain aspects of Homer's epics, most notably his portrait of the gods and their interaction with humans. But they had no doubt that the Trojan War was historical. Thucydides applied to it his argument from probability to demonstrate that it had been minor in comparison to the great war he was going to describe (1. 9–11), and eminent scholars competed in dating it correctly (Burkert 1995). This view remained prevalent even in modern scholarship (Cobet 2003). It received a boost more than a century ago when Schliemann excavated the magnificent ruins of Mycenae and Troy and found much that seemed to confirm Homer (see Chapter 9, by Sherratt). Those who disagreed were in a difficult position (Finley 1977: 10), even though the discrepancies between Homer's world and that unearthed by the archaeologists' spades seemed all too obvious. The decipherment of Linear B in the 1950s further enhanced the differences (Finley 1982: chs. 12–13). Moreover, earlier in the century Millman Parry's and Albert Lord's studies of oral epic song, conducted in then-Yugoslavia where it was still alive, made it possible to recognize that the Greek epics too stood in a long tradition of oral song composed in performance (Lord 2000; see also Chapter 13, by J. Foley). All this has great significance for how we assess the tradition about the Trojan War and the historicity of "epic society."

Homer and the Trojan War

Homer's epics presuppose a great and long war that was fought, in a distant heroic age, between a coalition of Greek leaders with their followers (variously called Achaeans, Danaans, and Argives), led by Agamemnon, lord of Mycenae, and the city of Troy or Ilion across the Aegean, which was defended by the Trojans and many eastern allies. This was virtually an ancient world war between a panhellenic coalition and a pan-eastern alliance. It broke out because Paris (or Alexandros) of Troy stole from the home of Menelaus of Sparta many valuable objects and his wife, beautiful Helen – and because the Trojans refused to return woman and treasures, when a Greek embassy demanded it. The war ended with the destruction of Troy and the sad homecoming of many of the leaders, most especially of the hero of the *Odyssey*. Most of this story was featured in other epics (see Chapter 24, by Burgess). The *Iliad* itself focuses on an episode played out during a few days in the tenth year but incorporates much of the rest through flashbacks and anticipation (see Chapter 21, by Edwards).

The main question that has fascinated laymen and scholars alike is whether this story originated in a real, historical war in which Troy was destroyed by Mycenaean Greeks. A direct answer to this question is impossible because conclusive evidence that is at least near-contemporaneous with the supposed event is lacking. Still, Manfred Korfmann, whose new excavations in and near Troy have yielded impressive results, and Joachim Latacz, an eminent Homerist collaborating with Korfmann, claim that sufficient circumstantial evidence now exists to allow a positive answer. They have presented their arguments (based on archaeological finds in Troy and elsewhere, Egyptian and Hittite sources mentioning names of persons, places, and peoples perhaps identical with those mentioned in the *Iliad*, new Linear B tablets found in Thebes, the Bronze Age origin of Greek epic, and the specific nature of hexametric song, among others) in articles (including Korfmann 1998, 2002), a book (Latacz 2001), and an exhibition (*Troia* 2001; Behr et al. 2003).

Although Korfmann and Latacz are not alone (see, e.g., Starke 1997; Niemeier 1999), some of their claims have prompted an intense, at times heated, public debate and met with serious opposition (for summaries, see Cobet and Gehrke 2002; Heimlich 2002; for detailed discussion, Ulf 2003a). Upon close inspection, the arguments supporting the historicity of the Iliadic Trojan War still prove far from conclusive (see also Raaflaub 1998b; Thebes tablets, Palaima 2004). True, Troy was destroyed several times, including twice in the final phase of the Bronze Age, but the destroyers remain unidentified. Mycenaean pottery proves trade and nothing more (Hertel 2001). Name and geographical identifications are still controversial. Egyptian inscriptions list a kingdom of *Danaya* and Hittite tablets mention one of *Ahhiyawa*, but so far no explicit record of a war between *Ahhiyawa* (whose location is still contested: Benzi 2002) and Troy survives in Hittite sources. The one conflict about *Wilusa* (Ilion?) mentioned there pitted the Hittite king against his Ahhiyawan counterpart and was apparently diplomatic rather than military.

Latacz proposes that the "straitjacket" of the hexameter uniquely enabled Greek epic song to preserve historical data over many centuries, but this suggestion too is less than compelling. All that we know about the nature of oral tradition and orally transmitted song speaks strongly against it. As A. T. Hatto observes (1980: 2.207–12), fossilized words and phrases (often not even understood anymore) survive in many epic traditions; they lend authority to the story but are unable to prevent or delay the processes of transformation typical of all oral transmission. Oral tradition that is not tied to metric song may be less relevant here but what anthropologists have to say on this should at least be noted (Vansina 1985; Ungern-Sternberg and Reinau 1988). Three points seem especially important for our present purpose.

The first concerns conclusions suggested by heroic epic in other cultures (see section 3). Oral traditions and oral song underlying great heroic epics often originate under the impression of a great historical event in the distant past and one or several remarkable individuals. Yet over time, events can be combined arbitrarily and reinterpreted so profoundly as to produce a story that bears very little, if any, resemblance to the original event(s). As a result, without independent historical evidence, the latter cannot be reconstructed, even in its most elementary outline, from the extant epic. The epic heroes are reinterpreted as well and often have vastly different origins that may or may not be related to the original story. Greek epic too functioned as a magnet, attracting and combining figures from various myths and legends (Hampl 1975). Despite subjective and short-term conservatism, over time oral epic undergoes constant change, adaptation, and reinterpretation, in order to remain timely and topical, and a leveling process from the specific and individual toward the typical and universal. The perspective of the last and extant version is that of the final poet's society, which is often marked by deep and strongly contested changes in social values and structures.

The second point is based on a completely different line of argument, presented impressively by Barbara Patzek (1992). Her observations concern the conditions of mythopoiesis, the emergence and role of historical memory, and of historical consciousness. I cannot discuss these aspects here in detail (for a summary, see Raaflaub 1998b: 398–401). On the basis of such considerations it seems perfectly possible that the Trojan War story could have emerged or at least been shaped into its extant form, in a time span of a few generations before the great poet(s) who created the epics we have.

The third point concerns the fact that the Greek world underwent two profound and comprehensive processes of transformation between the putative historical event (a Trojan War in the Bronze Age) and its Iliadic elaboration. These must have deeply influenced the subject matter (concerning both the event and epic society) and outlook of heroic song (Raaflaub 1998b: 397–8). One was the destruction of Mycenaean palace society at the end of the Bronze Age and the subsequent gradual decline of Greece into the much more modest and restricted conditions of the "Dark Ages," in which local and regional concerns and perspectives largely replaced Aegean and Mediterranean ones. The other is the chain of reverse changes that began in the tenth century, accelerated greatly in the eighth, and created the world of archaic Greece, with a widening of horizons, the emergence of *poleis* and panhellenism, widespread emigration, and massively increased social mobility. By the eighth century, close to Homer's time, a panhellenic perspective (attested in panhellenic sanctuaries, games, and poetry) became possible (again?). In many ways, the extant epics reflect the worldview of precisely this time.

Overall, then, it would not seem implausible, whatever traditions survived from the Bronze Age and however old Greek epic song may have been, that the great war celebrated by the singers became precisely a war between Troy and Greeks under Mycenaean leadership for no other reason than that the giant ruins of Troy and Mycenae were the most magnificent remains of a heroic age for which only Homer's recent ancestors had developed a fascination (Hampl 1975; Patzek 1992; Hertel 2003: 185–218). In the epics themselves, songs performed by bards consistently focus on very recent events (the end and aftermath of the Trojan War: *Od.* 1.325–7; 8.73–82, 485–520); even stories told by heroes that might have provided the subject matter for song extend no further back than one generation (*Il.* 9.529–99, 11.669–761; and think of Odysseus' own story, *Od.* Books 9–12), and we hear explicitly that audiences always want to hear the newest songs (*Od.* 1.350–2; on the dynamics of epic performance, see Chapter 4, by Jensen).

Like much of the background matter embedded in the heroic story (below), this seems to suggest the possibility of a fairly rapid turnover in epic subject matters. By contrast, the comparative evidence of German, French, and Serbo-Croatian epics supports the assumption that some distant historical event lies at the core of the Trojan War tradition. Yet, as long as we lack explicit independent evidence confirming the destruction of Troy by "Achaeans" and the latter's identity as Mycenaean Greeks, we cannot identify this core. We can certainly not reconstruct it from the epics, and current archaeological as well as textual evidence is insufficient to provide specific clues. In outlook and, as we shall see, in the social conditions they depict, the extant epics reflect the time of their creation at the beginning of the Archaic Age.

Homer and "epic society"

Homer places the society he describes in his epics in a distant, "heroic" past, in which men were stronger and more enduring and in which humans freely communicated with the gods. Precisely because the epics contain so much potentially valuable information about social and political structures, conditions, and relationships, scholars have tried repeatedly to locate this society in time and place: in the Bronze Age, the Dark Ages, and in Homer's own time. Others have resisted such temptations, focused on contradictions and inconsistencies, fantasy and exaggeration, and concluded, as Cartledge puts it, "that Homer's fictive universe remains immortal precisely because it never existed as such outside the poet's or poets' fertile imagination(s), in much the same way as Homeric language was a *Kunstsprache* never actually spoken outside the context of an epic recital" (2001: 157).

Again, the historian faces the problem that no independent contemporaneous evidence survives. Hesiod emphasizes the concerns of a farming population that needs to work hard to survive at or near the subsistence level. He is suspicious of the agora and the polis' leaders and judges, and worries about justice and good neighborhood relations rather than martial glory, status, honor, and elite interactions. The society he depicts complements Homer's rather than reduplicating it (Millett 1984; Tandy and Neale 1996). The lyric poets reflect a later stage in social and political development. Hence we cannot but rely on the epics themselves, with occasional assistence by archaeology (Raaflaub 1991). Caution and clear methodological principles are thus indispensable.

One principle is to realize that the picture does contain heterogeneous elements and to understand their function. Bronze Age, Dark Age, and non-Greek items are undeniable but scattered and easily identifiable as such. Elements of fantasy and exaggeration abound but they too are easily recognizable. Together, they all serve the purpose of "epic distancing" and creating the impression of a long-past, heroic society. A second principle is to pay attention to issues that are not emphasized but mentioned in passing or in etiological stories. Such issues throw light on what poet and audience took for granted. A third principle is to understand and respect the singer's narrative technique and to try to sense how the audience would have reacted to the story they were told. A fourth principle is to apply, with all due caution, anthropological models that may elucidate specific issues that are no longer understandable to us. Such principles help us "lift off" heroic elements that are important to the poet's concept of a heroic society but do not otherwise distort the social picture, and to reconstruct much that is crucial in and for epic society. Examples include the role of the polis or of council and assembly, the way foreign relations are conducted, or the nature of wars, fighting tactics, and even the psychological impact of battle on those fighting in it (Raaflaub 1998a, forthcoming with examples and bibliog.).

In fact, despite the *Iliad's* heroic flavor, gigantic dimensions, and panhellenic aspirations, in its practical details the poet's description of the Trojan War combines two patterns that were much more modest and thoroughly familiar to his audiences (Raaflaub 1997b). One, the retaliatory raiding expedition by sea was common throughout the Dark Ages, continued long thereafter, and recurs frequently in both epics. The other emerged in the Greek world toward the end of the eighth century: a war between neighboring *poleis* (often about the control of contested territory); this motif occurs repeatedly in the *Iliad*.

Elaborating on pathbreaking earlier work by Moses Finley (1977), several scholars have since then built a strong case supporting the view that the epic description of the social background to heroic actions and events is sufficiently consistent to be taken as reflecting either the poet's own time or, since the poet makes a noticeable effort to avoid recent innovations (such as writing), a slightly earlier period that was still fully accessible to living memory in the poet's time (Ulf 1990; van Wees 1992; Raaflaub 1997a, 1998a with bibliog.; Donlan 1999). Moreover, direct lines of development lead from the structures and institutions of epic society to those attested in the mid- to late-seventh century in many parts of Greece (Raaflaub 1993). As we shall see, these conclusions find confirmation in later epics, whose social background consistently matches conditions closely familiar to poet and audiences and thus close in time to their own.

Homer, political thought, and the poet's role as educator

Yet another aspect that illuminates the historical dimension of early Greek epic and its significance for contemporaneous society is its political and educational purpose. Even if we do not subscribe to Eric Havelock's view (1963, 1978) that the epics represent an encoded moral charter for preliterate Greek society, it is obvious that some of the conflicts dramatized in the epics (between Agamemnon and Achilles in the *Iliad*, between the suitors and Odysseus' family in the *Odyssey*) contain a marked political component. Yet political interpretation of the epics was long deemed inappropriate because the lack of formal institutions and a firmly established political sphere seemed to characterize epic society as "prepolitical." Dean Hammer (1998, 2002) now demonstrates impressively that such focus on institutions is too restrictive. Rather, epic society conducts politics differently, through performance and competition in areas and on issues that are essential for the communal well-being.

For example, the *Iliad* begins with a proem that emphasizes not heroic deeds of magnificent heroes but the quarrel between two leaders that caused great harm to their community. Agamemnon, the overall leader of the Achaean army at Troy, makes two crucial mistakes, blinded by selfishness and suspicion of a rival. He thereby exposes his entire army to divine retribution and prompts Achilles, his most important "vassal," to withdraw from the fighting. The community, lacking the means to resolve conflicts between its most powerful members, suffers grievous setbacks; its success in the war has become doubtful, its very survival is at stake. Agamemnon has violated the "heroic code," which relates high status and honors bestowed by the community to the obligation to protect its interests and needs; he suffers public humiliation, his leadership enters a severe crisis. Gradually, he realizes and admits his mistakes and offers rich compensation to Achilles, thus paving the way for reconciliation and communal reintegration. For this he is respected and recognized as "being more just."

By contrast, Hector, Agamemnon's counterpart on the Trojan side, though praised throughout as a man with an exceptionally deep commitment to his community, fails in this very respect. Rejecting good advice, he exposes his army to the vengeful fury of Achilles and terrible losses. When he realizes his mistake, he finds himself incapable of facing the criticism, shame, and humiliation he fears to encounter when returning to the city. Hence he chooses to fight Achilles, although he knows that he is likely to die – thus valuing personal honor higher than his obligation to the community. The message seems clear: although the community depends for its survival on the outstanding martial capacity of its leaders, on the long run it is better served by one who is capable of reconciling honor and responsibility. Everybody makes mistakes; what matters most is that inevitable rifts between leaders can be overcome in the interest of communal well-being (Raaflaub 2000: 27–34).

Such concerns must have been deeply and troublingly familiar to the poet's audiences. In dramatizing the clash between individual aspirations and communal needs, he emphasizes communal values and the ethos of good leadership (an aspect given highest priority in Hesiod's epics as well: Raaflaub 2000: 34–7). He guides his listeners from the outbreak to the successful resolution of a communal conflict; he makes them politically aware and educates them, not by lecturing them, but by weaving his specifically political interpretation into a heroic narrative that serves many other purposes as well. This aspect seems to me significant, and it clearly anchors the epics in their own time.

This, too, is perhaps a universal function of epic. In its preserved version, the *Nibelungenlied* is a written work, produced for aristocratic members of courts. Like other literature of the time, it was expected to reflect this society's social and moral perspectives. The poet both does and does not do this. "By a differently-angled positioning of 'key concepts' of the courtly worldview, the poet is able to hold up his creation as a critical mirror for the court to view itself and, by implication, its imperfections. For by taking what seems to be familiar, but shifting the perspective just slightly, the poet forces his audience into a dialectic confrontation with its own ideals and their inadequacies" (Gentry 1998: 66). He challenges his characters, and through them his audience, to reconsider traditional obligations, patterns of behavior, and values; he forces them into uncomfortable choices and illustrates their consequences (p. 77).

3 History and Medieval Epic: Comparative Evidence

The *Nibelungenlied*, composed around 1200 CE, offers particularly interesting insights (Ehrismann 1987; Haymes and Samples 1996: pt. 1). With few exceptions, the main characters are well attested in historical sources. They lived during a time span of some 200 years, between the late fourth and the late sixth century CE. Dietrich (Theoderic, 451–526), king of the Ostrogoths and king of Italy from 493, appears in the epic as a guest at the court of the king of the Huns, Attila, who died in 453, soon after Theoderic's birth. Theoderic's historical opponent, Odoacer, is replaced in the epic's tradition by Ermanaric, king of the Ostrogoths as well, who died in 375. Gunther (Gundaharius) and his brothers perished in 436, in a disastrous defeat of the Burgundians at the hands of the Huns, a battle in which Attila was not involved. Hagen, Rüdiger, and even Siegfried cannot reliably be connected with known historical personalities. Finally, the two heroines, Brünhild and Kriemhild, are patterned, although in somewhat reversed roles, after two Merovingian queens, Brunichildis, a Visigothic princess, and Fredegund, whose fierce and unscrupulous rivalry in the latter half of the sixth century soon became legendary. All these were strong and colorful personalities, but historically, most of them had nothing to do with each other, and it is difficult to reconcile their epic and historical portraits. The Burgundians settled on the Rhine in the early fifth century, were defeated by the Roman general Aëtius in 435 and destroyed by the Huns in 436. The epic's concluding event, the catastrophic end of the Burgundians, thus is historical as well but totally unrelated to the ways in which the epic describes it. If we knew only the epic we would never be able to reconstruct the historical event.

Virtually nothing is known about the oral transmission of the epic material over the first few centuries. Interestingly, the epic preserves a more positive assessment of Theoderic and Attila than the (clerically influenced) written sources. Finally, the epic reflects concerns and relationships, social and political conditions of the time of its composition, when aristocratic society, exposed to new ideologies and challenges and to severe power struggles, experienced profound changes and a serious clash and crisis of values (Haymes 1998). Overall, then, the tradition underlying the epic is based on personalities and events that are mostly historical but belong to different times and contexts. Over time they were combined, reinterpreted, heroicized, and placed into a dramatic story in which we can hardly recognize the historical originals. The conflicts that are dramatized in the epic are universal and typical, encouraging the audiences to identify with them and to be challenged by them.

The *Song of Roland,* composed around 1100, is probably the earliest of a large number of medieval French epics, called *chansons de geste,* accounts of heroic deeds that were based on long oral tradition and composed in performance by singers of tales (*jongleurs*), although the extant versions received their final shape by written composition (Vance 1970; Brault 1978). The underlying historical event dates to 778 and is well-known from Einhard's *Vita Caroli Magni* (28–30): upon returning from a campaign against Muslims in Spain, the rearguard and baggage train of Charlemagne's army were ambushed and destroyed at Roncevaux in the Pyrenees. Gascon treachery was blamed, Muslim involvement is debated. The space Einhard devotes to this event reflects the impression it made on contemporaries. Roland was among the noble victims mentioned by Einhard. The other characters in the epic entered the story at later stages: their origin is largely unknown. The interpretation the event receives in the epic (the rivalry between Ganelon and Roland, the former's treason in conspiring with the Saracenes, the fight at Roncevaux as a battle between Christians and Saracenes, the friendship between Roland and Oliver, and the trial of Ganelon) is far removed from the original: only the bare bones of the narrative are still recognizable as historical. Names are often anachronistic. So is the the epic's entire social setting and system of ethics and values that are strongly imbued with Christian elements and the politics of the time of its composition (Haidu 1993): "The *Song of Roland* is an exalted stylization of the realities of the feudal world" at a time when these new realities still clashed with the earlier heroic ideals of the ruling aristocracy (Vance 1970: 19, 26). Again, we find old songs and themes elaborated into a complex and multidimensional epic in a period that experienced profound changes and massive challenges.

Finally, a few brief comments on Serbo-Croatian epic, studied intensively in the nineteenth and early twentieth centuries (Coote 1978, Lord 2000; see also Chapter 13, by J. Foley). Two types of epic are of special interest in our present context. One is the "Kosovo Cycle," that is, various songs (never, it seems, elaborated into a big and complex epic) focusing on the battle of Kosovo in 1389, in which the expanding Turks clashed with the Serbs, apparently with an initially unclear result (first reports even celebrated it as a Christian victory), and both leaders, Prince Lazar and Sultan Murad, died. The historical record is very thin. Soon however, Kosovo came to symbolize the loss of Serbian greatness and freedom. Legends emerged, elaborated in later epic versions, to provide a fuller story (Emmert 1990; Malcolm 1998).

> Prince Lazar and Miloš Obilić, who assassinated the sultan, became the heroes of the legend, the one a martyr king who preferred the heavenly kingdom to an earthly kingdom, the other a perfect knight who sacrificed his life to save his honor and to display Serbian heroism. Legend also required a villain, and so made a traitor of Vuk Branković, even though the historical Vuk seems to have been loyal to Lazar... Blame for the disaster was laid upon disunity among the Serbs: a quarrel arose between Lazar's daughters, the wives of Vuk and Miloš, which set the two sons-in-law at odds and caused Vuk to slander Miloš as a traitor... thus provoking Miloš to his daring act. (Coote 1978: 263)

The other type of epic song reflects a more limited and intimate range of "heroic activities." It was produced in an area that was divided into many population groups distinguished by ethnic origin, nationality, religion, culture, and political orientation. This illustrates another "milieu" that fosters heroic song.

> Constant conflict over the boundaries of these groups created a prolonged "Heroic Age" during which the deeds and qualities of heroes were essential to the survival of society. Heroism was the business of every grown male, and a necessary concomitant of heroism were the songs that celebrated it and made it immortal. (Coote 1978: 258; Djilas 1958 illustrates this well.)

As Matthias Murko writes, each song is likely to be based on a historical experience, but the depiction remains too general and vague to allow reconstruction of a specific historical event (1978: 386, 392–3; cf. 1929; Skendi 1980: chs. 8–9). The epics focus on the actions of individuals who dominate in the hostilities against members of another state or religion. Women, duels, and larger fights, caused by women or violated honor, play a big role: abduction of girls or women, weddings and processions and their interruption, ransoming of captured heroes, often for the price of a woman, gifts to heroes, often consisting of brides, revenge for violence and injury, drinking parties ending in brawls and escalating into bloody fights: these are the usual themes.

Finally, Serbo-Croatian epic also offers an opportunity to study the nature of ongoing change and transformation. Scholars tend to be impressed by the conservatism of epic song, both subjectively and objectively. The substance of a given story is often preserved over a long period of time. Singers do not crave for originality and innovation. They are convinced that in various performances they essentially present the same song. Elaboration and condensation of episodes, expansion of ornamentation, variations in the sequence of episodes, and replacement of certain episodes by others are the main forms of change that are compatible with the "truth" of a story (Lord 2000: 99–123). Yet, as in non-poetic oral traditions, in oral song too gradual change is inevitable, not least in order to satisfy the audience's need for identification. Most songs studied by Murko refer to events that happened at most 150 or 200 years ago (1978: 391–92). Moreover, as Coote observes, by 1913 the withdrawal of the Turks created new conditions.

> The preservation of the singing tradition in new circumstances depended upon its continuing to function as a means of edification and entertainment. Eventually, as values changed and occasions both for traditional heroism and for singing heroic songs became less frequent, singing also changed its style and subject. (1978: 258)

In other words, as is to be expected, the survival and thematic constancy of oral heroic song is tied to the continuation of the social conditions that produced it in the first place. Massive changes in the latter will necessarily cause corresponding changes in the former. It seems an important desideratum to verify this principle in a broader range of epic traditions than I was able to investigate here.

4   History and Roman Epic

Historical epic

Although with his Latin *Odyssey* Livius Andronicus introduced heroic epic to Rome (on which see Chapter 31, by Goldberg), most of his successors chose topics that were closer to history or entirely historical. They had few predecessors on the Greek side. For example, Choerilus of Samos composed in the late fifth century BCE an epic about the Persian Wars (*Persika*), and various authors in the third and second centuries wrote epics on local or regional histories (Häussler 1976: 60–91). For the Romans, especially of the generations that witnessed the Punic Wars and the rapid expansion of the empire in the third and second centuries, history offered a far more exciting field to exercise their talents, and one in which they could both contribute to the rising sense of patriotic pride and compete with the equally new genre of history (Häussler 1976: chs. 2–5; Goldberg 1995).

Gnaeus Naevius (*ca.* 265–190s) had participated in the last phase of the First Punic War and wrote an epic about this war (*Bellum Poenicum* or *Carmen belli Poenici*), using the traditional Italian Saturnian verse (see, again, Chapter 31, by Goldberg). About 60 very short fragments survive (Warmington 1961: 2. 46–73). Whether or not he already knew the earliest Roman prose history by Fabius Pictor, he inserted (apparently as a digression filling about a third of the work) an extensive account of Rome's earliest history, from Aeneas' flight from Troy to the foundation of Rome by Romulus (whom Naevius considered Aeneas' grandson). This "mythical" section contained a series of prophecies that pointed forward to the historical events narrated in the second part. The transition between the two parts seems to have been very brief. Naevius' work thus already reflects two important characteristics of the Romans' dealing with their past: a strong fascination with the period of "origins," and the "hourglass" shape that is typical of early annalistic historiography (Raaflaub 1986: 1–3) and must be explained by the influence of oral tradition emphasizing the legendary period of the founders, as it was "remembered" in its mythical transformation, and the recent past that was still accessible to living memory (Ungern-Sternberg 1988). Although apparently criticized by Ennius (Cic., *Brut.* 72–6), Naevius' epic influenced subsequent poets including Ennius himself (who, as Cicero points out, paid implicit homage in his *Annals* by virtually omitting the First Punic War) and Virgil. The meager remains do not permit us to form an impression of the epic's historical qualities (Richter 1960; Häussler 1976: ch. 2; Goldberg 1993, and Chapter 31; Suerbaum 2002: 111–15).

The *Annals* of Quintus Ennius (239–169) certainly helped shape Roman patriotic sentiment. Written in dactylic hexameters, this work covered, for the first time in Latin, the entire prehistory and history of Rome from the fall of Troy to the triumph of Ennius' patron, Fulvius Nobilior, in 187 BCE and a few years beyond. About 600 fragments are preserved (Warmington 1961: 1. 2–215). The hourglass structure, though less marked, is visible here too. Presenting himself as Homer's successor or even incarnation, Ennius incorporated Homer's entire artistic apparatus, including interaction among gods and of humans with gods, speeches, similes, ekphrasis, and brilliant performances of individual leaders. Unlike Homer, he also described naval and cavalry battles and featured panegyric and autobiographical elements (see Skutsch 1972, 1985; Häussler 1976: chs. 3–4; Dominik 1993; Suerbaum 2002: 133–9; Chapter 31, by Goldberg). Despite its non-historical components, the *Annals* was broadly comparable with contemporaneous prose works but, because of its powerful poetic quality, more widely influential.

Although we know little about them, historical epics continued to be written, for example, on Caesar's Gallic wars, Octavian's expedition to Egypt after Actium, or, by the "hero" himself, Cicero's consulship (Häussler 1976: chs. 5–6; Courtney 1993). The genre reached a new climax in Lucan's *Bellum civile*, written at the time of Nero (see Chapter 35, by Bartsch). Lucan, a nephew of Seneca, initially enjoyed the emperor's friendship but soon aroused his jealousy, lost his favor, was prohibited from publishing his works, and died in the aftermath of the Pisonian conspiracy of 65 CE. The subject matter (the civil war of 49–48 BCE between Caesar and Pompey) was politically sensitive, as the emperor Claudius, himself an accomplished historian, had learned in his youth (Suet. *Claud.* 41.2); an epic on this topic thus had the potential of being read as an expression of protest against Nero's tyranny. That this was indeed Lucan's intention in the latter part of the work can hardly be doubted: in his assessment, the final battle seals the enslavement of Rome by tyranny (*BC* 7.250ff. *passim*). Whether he began the epic with the same intention or changed his mind while working on it is much debated and depends on how we interpret the notorious encomium of Nero (1.33–66) and the generally more differentiated representation of Caesar (despite the negative portrait in 1.143–57) in the first three books.

The epic is artistically and historically of great interest, not least because is is based on good sources (including Livy's lost books on the civil wars) and displays the poet's uncanny ability, enhanced by his rhetorical training, to formulate essential observations or facts in memorable epigrammatic lines. In explicit contrast to the Homeric tradition that was followed by most of his predecessors (including even Cicero), Lucan demonstratively dismissed the entire divine apparatus (even denying the existence of gods, 7.445–7) and replaced it with impersonal, though no less powerful, fate. On the level of historical action, human motivation prevails. Already his contemporaries reacted critically to this innovation. Petronius inserted in his *Satyricon* (118–24) a sample opening of a civil war epic that corrected this omission, and later critics debated whether Lucan was more of a historian than a poet (Brisset 1964; Ahl 1976; Lebek 1976; Masters 1992; Bartsch 1997).

Although Lucan's model was not imitated, the genre of historical epic continued to enjoy some prominence. Examples include Silius Italicus' *Punica* on the Second Punic War (composed before 100 CE), which attempts to revive the traditional model of heroicizing history (see Chapter 38, by Marks), and Claudian's epics, produced three hundred years later and converging with panegyric, on some of the great wars of his time (see Chapter 39, by Barnes). Much earlier, however, one of Rome's greatest poets had chosen a different solution to the challenge of dealing with history in epic.

The Aeneid

In *Georgics* (3.1–48), Virgil announces his intention to write a panegyric epic on Augustus. We know from comments of other poets that Augustus desired greatly to be celebrated in this way. None of his protégés indulged him. Instead, Virgil wrote the *Aeneid*, an epic on the mythical ancestor of Rome and the Julian clan who escaped the destruction of Troy and found his destiny in Italy, and whose descendants would build the city on the Tiber, create an empire, and culminate in the greatness of Augustus and Augustan Rome. Virgil's purpose, according to ancient critics, was to imitate Homer and celebrate Augustus. The former is obvious in many ways (see Chapter 33, by Putnam). The latter Virgil achieved by incorporating the history of Rome, from Aeneas' death to Augustus, in pronouncements and previews that are inserted at crucial moments into Aeneas' story, most prominently in Anchises' survey in the Underworld of Rome's heroes and leaders who are waiting to reach the light of life (6.703ff.), and in the ekphrasis of Aeneas' shield (8.626–731).

By focusing on Aeneas, Virgil avoided direct panegyric. As the works of some of his contemporaries, most notably Dionysius of Halicarnassus' *Roman Antiquities,* show, even the remote prehistory of the Trojans' arrival in Italy was accepted as history and subjected to learned historical discussion (Gabba 1991). Livy, writing at about the same time as Virgil, chose a more critical perspective: "Events before Rome was born, or thought of, have come to us in old tales with more of the charm of poetry than of a sound historical record" (*praef.* 6–7, trans. de Sélincourt). What matters to him is the kind of lives these ancestors lived, their virtues and vices that helped Rome reach the climax of power and then caused it to decline, morally and politically, "until the dark dawning of our modern day when we can neither endure our vices nor face the remedies needed to cure them." Writing from the perspective of a deeply troubled time, Livy finds – and elaborates – in Rome's earliest history an "infinite variety of human experience," including, for individuals and the collectivity of citizens, positive and negative examples: "fine things to take as models, base things, rotten through and through, to avoid" (*praef.* 9–10).

The earliest historians, Herodotus and Thucydides, saw the purpose of writing history not only in reconstructing and preserving the course of history, but also in remembering memorable achievements and educating audience and readers, making them politically more conscious and responsible (Raaflaub 1987, 2002). In Thucydides' famous formula, history was to serve as an "everlasting possession" (1.22.4). That is, it was to "have permanent value" and be useful (Hornblower 1991: 61), in the sense not of moral improvement but of political education. Polybius made this even more explicit: history offered a unique range of learning to the politician and statesman (Sacks 1981: ch. 4). Livy, followed by Sallust and Tacitus, placed the emphasis squarely on the moral side: in accordance with the Roman preoccupation with moral qualities and values, history (especially, but not only, that of the mythical period) provided an element that was traditionally emphasized in education: *exempla*, models. More than that: since the prehistory and earliest history of Rome were riddled with uncertainties, they offered unique opportunities to engage the reader in a dialogue with the present. And indeed, as recent scholarship makes increasingly clear (e.g. von Haehling 1989), Livy's interpretation of events and personalities in the first book, and to some extent the entire first decade, reflects the author's intense concerns with developments in his own time.

Virgil's epic shares these concerns and uses a similar approach. It is as much a poem on his own time and Augustan Rome as it is one on Aeneas and the arrival of Rome's earliest ancestors in Italy. Whatever the *communis opinio* of Aeneas was before the *Aeneid*, indications are that his image was not fixed. Virgil combined various sources and traditions, adding his interpretations and inventions, to create his own Aeneas (Horsfall 1987, 1991). Yes, there is praise of Augustus and hope that through his principate the Roman world, shaken in its foundations by decades of hatred and civil war, can find peace and prosperity (see esp. *Aen.* 1.286–96; 6.791–805; 8.671–728). The primary character trait of Aeneas is *pietas*, commitment to parents, tradition, and community. At the very beginning in burning Troy and again in Carthage, he sacrifices heroic ambition in order to save his family and people and secure a future for them. To place highest value on communal service lies at the root of the Roman value system. In overcoming resistance (in a war which is characterized as fratricidal!) with the help of Latin, Etruscan, and Greek allies, Aeneas fosters reconciliation out of war and unity out of division. Both these aspects were deeply meaningful at the end of an age of civil strife driven by excessive personal ambitions.

Yet the overall impression falls far short of the panegyric we might expect. There are dark sides, brought out especially in the troubling end of the epic that is much debated in scholarship (see, again, Chapter 33, by Putnam). Aeneas' travails are constantly linked, implicitly and explicitly, to the travails of Augustus himself and Virgil's Rome. Like Horace, Virgil is still uncertain and ambivalent. His poem thus dramatizes both the mythical past and the present. In throwing light on both the light and dark sides of its hero, it helps attentive and sensitive readers think through some of the major questions and tensions with which they find themselves confronted. For the new leader who sees himself as the new founder of Rome, it offers praise, encouragement, and warning. It is not in any meaningful sense a historic epic but in a very profound sense a political one. In this respect, too, we conclude, Virgil meets the challenge posed by Homer. At the same time, Virgil "fully assumes the legacy of the Roman historical epic: his poem is a national epic, in which a collectivity needs to reflect itself and feel itself united" (Conte 1994b: 283).

5   Tentative Conclusions

The relationship between epic and history, we have found, is complex. Historical epics, that is, epics dealing either with the history of specific events (such as the Persian Wars or Rome's civil wars) or of cities, regions, or an entire nation (such as some Hellenistic and Roman epics) are a special case. They narrate history, although in various ways heroicizing and mythologizing it. (Aeschylus' *Persians,* performed only a few years after the events, offers a comparable example.) They can thus be used, with due caution, to reconstruct history. If all our historical sources had perished and only Ennius' and Lucan's epics survived, we would still learn much about Roman republican history and Caesar's civil war – although somewhat less reliably and, of course, without being able to check the very question of reliability.

This is emphatically not the case with heroic epic and least of all with those epics that represent a great poet's final elaboration of a long tradition of oral song. Despite subjective conservatism inherent in the genre that prompts singers to improve on previous versions of a given song rather than altering it, over time a number of factors cause the original story to be reinterpreted, possibly more than once, and potentially to be distorted beyond recognition. These factors include, among others, audience pressure that forces singers to adjust to changing tastes, needs, and social conditions; deeper transformations and disruptions in the world in which the singers live that cause changes in outlook and values; new events, experiences, and outstanding personalities that capture the imagination of singers and audiences and induce them to replace old songs by new ones or to reinterpret traditional themes more radically; and an inherent tendency, common to all forms of oral tradition, to suppress the individual and specific in favor of the universal. In the cases of medieval and later epics, where independent historical evidence is available, it is clear that only a minimal historical core survives in the extant poems. To reconstruct this core from the epic is impossible because the process of transformation does not follow set rules, is different in each case, and can thus not be unraveled from the end.

The situation is different when we focus on the social background or environment in which the poet places the heroic events and actions. Wherever the epic evidence is substantial enough, the depiction of social structures, conditions, and interactions proves sufficiently consistent to reflect a historical society – despite archaisms, anachronisms, exaggerations, and occasional contradictions that help create a heroic aura and are traits or remnants of composition in performance. The society portrayed is usually the poet's own. It is usually also a society that is affected by profound changes and challenged by the transition from old structures, values, and norms of behavior to new ones. Based on the limited corpus discussed in this chapter, one might tentatively conclude that, whatever the nature of their predecessors, large and complex heroic epics thrived especially in such deeply unsettled and challenging conditions. This thesis obviously needs to be tested much more broadly, but I suggest that such epics were meaningful to their audiences precisely because the poets dramatized in them some of the major problems and ethical dilemmas that were agitating their listeners. The audience was invited, and needed to be able, to identify with these dilemmas. Heroic distancing and exaggeration were compatible with this purpose, but the basic patterns of social interaction needed to remain recognizable. Hence, theoretically, thematic constancy over a long period of time was possible as long as it permitted the elaboration of topical issues and as long as the description of the social background kept being adjusted to ever changing social conditions. In fact, the themes changed and adapted as well, and the historically authentic core of events became ever more minimal.

Although usually believed to represent history, heroic myth thus became an instrument of ethical, social, and political reflection and offered a timeless and continually valid repertoire which enabled the poets to weave contemporary concerns into the epic action, to illuminate and educate their audiences. Although varying in emphasis and execution, this function is embedded in the monumental heroic epics that survive from antiquity to the Middle Ages. Whether or not this applies less to shorter epic songs (mentioned in the *Odyssey* or recorded in modern Former Yugoslavia) needs to be explored further. Where this function of epic appears, it confirms a conclusion suggested at least in the Graeco-Roman world by other literary genres that dealt with the past (tragedy and historiography): the heroic or historical past was tied to, and remained meaningful for, the present precisely because, and as long as, it served the needs of the present. The concept of preserving the memory of a distant past (in whatever form) simply because it deserved to be remembered or was encapsulated in interesting stories – this concept was not alien to antiquity (we need only think of Herodotus) but not sufficient in itself.

FURTHER READING

Almost all the epics discussed in this chapter are easily available in modern translations with good introductions and bibliography, most of them, for example, in the Penguin/Viking series. For the *Iliad* and *Odyssey* one might also consider the vigorous versions of Stanley Lombardo (1997, 2000).

Oinas 1978 offers introductory essays on epics across the world. Bowra 1952 and Hatto 1980 discuss heroic poetry in cross-cultural comparison. Hatto 1991, Hainsworth 1991, and Ulf 2003b explore the nature and social purpose of heroic epic.

Bibliography on individual epics and epic traditions is given in the relevant sections above and detailed in the bibliography at the end of the volume.

CHAPTER SIX

The Epic Hero

Gregory Nagy

The words "epic", and "hero" both defy generalization, let alone universalizing definitions (see Chapter 1, by Martin). Even as general concepts, "epic" and "hero" do not necessarily go together (Lord 1960: 6). While recognizing these difficulties, this chapter explores the most representative examples of ancient poetic constructs generally known as "epic heroes," focusing on Achilles and Odysseus in the Homeric *Iliad* and *Odyssey* (see Chapter 21 by Edwards and Chapter 22, by Slatkin). Points of comparison include Gilgamesh and Enkidu in the Sumerian, Akkadian, and Hittite cuneiform records (see Chapters 15, 17, 14, by Noegel, Beckman, and Sasson respectively); Arjuna and the other Pâṇḍavas in the Indic *Mahâbhârata*; and Aeneas in the *Aeneid* of the Roman poet Virgil (see Chapter 33, by Putnam). These constructs – let us call them simply "characters" for the moment – are in some ways radically dissimilar from each other. Even within a single tradition like Homeric poetry, heroes like Achilles and Odysseus seem worlds apart. In other ways, however, "epic heroes" are strikingly similar to each other, sharing a number of central features. The question is, how to explain these similarities?

Two general explanations are current. Some have detected vestiges of a poetic system stemming from a prehistoric time when Indo-European languages like Greek and Indic were as yet undifferentiated from each other (see Chapter 2, by Katz, and Dumézil 1995; cf. Davidson 2000, esp. 85–7). Others have argued for patterns of cultural exchange among linguistically unrelated traditions, focusing on parallels between the ancient Greek epic and various narrative traditions stemming from the ancient Near East (see Chapter 20, by Burkert, Chapter 3, by Edmunds, and Burkert 1984).

These two general explanations can be subdivided into a wide variety of specific approaches. Some of these approaches, like the one worked out by Georges Dumézil, are more systematic than others, but none seems self-sufficient. Each has something to add to an overall picture of the "epic hero," but, taken together, most comparative approaches seem to be mutually exclusive. What is needed is an integration of comparative perspectives. In order to achieve the broadest possible formulation, I propose to integrate three comparative methods, which I describe as (1) typological, (2) genealogical, and (3) historical.

The first of these three methods is the most elusive, though it happens to be the most general. It involves comparisons of parallels between structures that are not necessarily related to each other. I describe this comparative method as *typological* – meaning that it applies to parallelisms between structures as structures pure and simple, without any presuppositions. Such a mode of comparison is especially useful in fields like linguistics: comparing parallel structures in languages – even if the given languages are unrelated to each other – is a proven way of enhancing one's overall understanding of the linguistic structures being compared (Benveniste 1966: pt III). From the very start, I emphasize the word "structure," evoking an approach generally known as "structuralism"; this approach stems ultimately from the field of linguistics, as pioneered by Ferdinand de Saussure (Benveniste 1966: 91–8).

The second method involves comparisons of parallels between structures related to each other by way of a common source. I describe this comparative method as *genealogical* because it applies to parallelisms between cognate structures – that is, structures that derive from a common source or proto-structure, as it were. In linguistics, this genealogical method was called by Antoine Meillet "la méthode comparative" – as if it were the only kind of comparative method (Meillet 1925). Whatever we call it, the *genealogical method* is fundamentally structuralist in perspective, depending on both synchronic and diachronic analysis of the cognate structures being compared. Meillet himself was a student of Saussure, and he is well known for his structuralist understanding of language as a structure or *system*: "Une langue constitue un système complexe de moyens d'expression, système où tout se tient" (Meillet 1921: 16).

The third comparative method, which I describe as *historical*, involves comparisons of parallels between structures related to each other by way of historically attested or at least reconstructed *intercultural contact*. One form of such contact is the linguistic phenomenon known as *Sprachbund* (Jakobson 1931). In terms of this concept, whatever changes take place in a language that makes contact with another language need to be seen in terms of the overall structures of both languages (Jakobson 1949). This concept of *Sprachbund* can be applied to the more general cultural phenomenon of intercultural contact, that is, to any situation where the structure of one culture is affected by a corresponding structure in another culture, whether by borrowing or by any other kind of influence. Any such contact needs to be viewed as a historical contingency, which requires historical analysis. Diachronic analysis is in this case insufficient, since it cannot predict history (Jacopin 1988: 35–6). That is why I describe as *historical* the comparative method required for the study of parallels resulting from intercultural contact. As in the case of the genealogical method, the *historical method* depends on synchronic analysis of the parallel structures being compared. But it cannot depend – or at least it cannot fully depend – on diachronic analysis, which cannot independently account for historical contingencies.

Having outlined the three kinds of comparative methodology to be applied, I now propose to fill in by surveying the actual comparanda. By "comparandum" I mean simply the evidence to be compared, and I will be referring to the comparanda in terms of the same three methodologies I have just outlined: (1) typological, (2) genealogical, and (3) historical.

In the case of typological comparanda, the comparative methodology involves, to repeat, a structuralist perspective. Earlier, I mentioned the linguistics of Saussure as the historical prototype of what we know today as structuralism. In its more recent history, however, the term has been detached from its moorings in linguistics. It is nowadays associated mostly with the study of literature. In its newer applications, "structuralism" has become an unstable and even unwieldy concept, which cannot any longer convey the essence of the methodology it once represented. My object here is not so much to advocate a reform of structuralism for future applications to the study of literature but to record an early moment in its past history when structuralism was first applied to the study of pre-literature, that is, to the study of oral traditions as the historical sources of literature as we know it.

Here I return to Meillet. It was this former student of Saussure who advised his own student, a young American in Paris named Milman Parry, to undertake a typological comparison of ancient Greek epic with modern South Slavic "heroic song," as represented by the living oral traditions of the former Yugoslavia (see Chapters 13, by J. Foley, and Chapter 4, by Jensen). The work of Parry was cut short at an early stage of his career by his violent death in 1935, but it was continued by his own student, Albert Lord, who ultimately published in 1960 the foundational work on oral poetry, *The Singer of Tales* (1960, 2000). This book, reflecting the cumulative research of Parry and Lord, is a masterpiece of scientific methodology. It is empirical to the core, combining synchronic description with typological comparison. The object of this typological comparison in *The Singer of Tales* is oral poetry, specifically the medium that we know as epic. But what is "epic"? And what, for that matter, is an "epic hero"?

In terms of this combination of words, "epic hero," we could answer that *epic* is the medium that defines the message, which is, the *hero*. Still, Lord himself had reservations. The more he learned from typological comparanda, the less certain he became about the cross-cultural applicability of either of these two terms, "epic" and "hero" (1960; cf. Nagy 1999b: 23).

Lord's most extensive typological comparisons linked the epic heroes of ancient Greek traditions, especially Achilles and Odysseus, with modern South Slavic analogues (see esp. Foley 1990, 1991, 1995, 1999b, 2002). Such modern epic comparanda are not at all irrelevant, even in the present volume, dedicated as it is to ancient epic, since typological comparison is not bound by time. The same observation holds for medieval comparanda: in *The Singer of Tales*, Lord's typological comparisons extended to such "epic heroes" as Beowulf in Old English, Roland in Old French, and the Cid in Old Spanish traditions.

It was left for others to extend the comparison to other relevant figures in other medieval traditions – as in the Old Norse *Völsunga Saga*, the Middle High German *Nibelungenlied*, and the Old Irish "Finn Cycle" (Nagy 1985; Mitchell 1991). Moreover, ever since *The Singer of Tales*, there has been an unabated stream of further comparisons centering on modern collections of living oral traditions. The comparative evidence comes from Eastern Europe (Lord 1991), Central Asia (Reichl 1992), the Indian subcontinent (Blackburn et al. 1989), Africa (Okpewho 1975), and so on. Even with all the additional new evidence, however, the basic pairing of typological comparanda remains what it was in *The Singer of Tales* – that is, the juxtaposition of ancient Greek epic with modern South Slavic "epic." The Homeric *Iliad* and *Odyssey* of ancient Greek epic traditions remains the initial point of comparison, while the original evidence of the South Slavic songs collected by Parry and Lord "still has a claim to being one of the best comparanda" (Martin 1989: 150). And the basic question dating back to the original comparanda still remains: how are we to define the terms "epic" and "hero"?

Typological comparanda cannot provide a unified definition. In his typological comparisons, Lord could go only so far as to explain "heroes" in terms of the "epics" that framed them: in other words, he analyzed the "heroic" character as a function of the "epic" plot. By "plot" here I mean *muthos*, as Aristotle uses that word in his *Poetics*. To this extent, at least, the compound term "epic hero" continues to provide an adequate point of typological comparison, even if the simplex terms "epic" and "hero" seem inadequate of and by themselves.

It made sense for Lord to choose the ancient Greek epic tradition of the Homeric *Iliad* and *Odyssey* as the first comparandum, to the extent that the concepts of "epic" and "hero" are derived from this tradition. Once we invoke the facts of derivation, however, we leave behind the methodology of *typological* comparison, shifting to *genealogical* and *historical* comparison.

Let us turn, then, to the genealogical and historical comparanda, starting with the *genealogical*. Whereas typological comparison involves only synchronic analysis of the structures being compared, genealogical comparison combines, to repeat, the synchronic and the diachronic. Moreover, the structures being compared must be cognate.

A most prominent case in point is the genealogical comparison of ancient Greek epic with its cognates in the ancient Indic, by which I mean, broadly speaking, the language that evolved into classical Sanskrit. In both form and content, ancient Indic poetry is cognate with ancient Greek poetry. Even the meters of ancient Indic hymns and "epic" are cognate with the meter of ancient Greek epic, the dactylic hexameter (Nagy 1998). The ancient Indic and Greek poetic traditions are cognate also in phraseology (Nagy 1974). Moreover, there are remarkably close parallels in both plot- and character-formation linking the monumental Indic "epics" of the *Mahâbhârata* and the *Râmâyaṇa* with the Homeric *Iliad* and *Odyssey* (Allen 1993; Baldick 1994; Vielle 1996 (cf. Nagy 1999c); cf. also Gresseth 1979). As we will see later on, some of these comparanda are relevant to the concepts of "epic" and "hero," even if the comparison fails to yield a unified answer to the question of reconstructing these concepts back to a common source.

Pursuing the question further, we look to evidence about the "epic hero" in publications of new collections of living oral traditions from modern India (Blackburn et al. 1989 is a good starting point). Some of these modern traditions are cognate with the ancient Indic traditions, though many are not – derived instead from non-Indo-European linguistic communities. While both the cognate and the non-cognate traditions contain a wealth of typological comparanda about the "epic hero," only the cognate traditions provide genealogical comparanda. As we will see later on, some of these modern comparanda, like their ancient counterparts, are relevant to the concepts of "epic" and "hero."

Also relevant is the evidence of the South Slavic oral poetic traditions themselves. Here too we find genealogical as well as typological comparanda, since these Slavic traditions are cognate with the Greek and the Indic (Jakobson 1952). Further, there are important genealogical comparanda to be found in the poetic traditions of medieval Europe; the evidence comes from a wide variety of poetic forms in a wide variety of cognate languages, such as Old Irish, Welsh, Old English, Middle High German, and Old Norse (see Schmitt 1967). Some of these poetic traditions, like the Old English, had already been compared typologically by Lord in *The Singer of Tales*, but the comparison needs to be continued – and extended to the genealogical level. The same observation applies to medieval Greek poetic traditions, as represented by the "epic" poetry about the "hero" Digenis Akritas; in *The Singer of Tales*, Lord had studied the themes and characters of this poetry from a purely typological perspective, but the added perspective of a genealogical approach can in this case help further highlight the comparandum of the "epic hero," especially since the Digenis tradition is at least in part a continuation of heroic constructs stemming from the ancient Greek poetic past – as well as extending into modern Greek oral traditions. Looking even further east, we find that the Iranian "heroic" traditions in the medieval Persian "epic" *Shâhnâma* of Ferdowsi (see Chapter 18, by Davidson) are also derived, like the corresponding Indic and the Greek traditions, from a common Indo-European poetic source (Davidson 1994, 2000). Further, there is a strong continuity between the medieval Iranian epic traditions and ancient Iranian counterparts (Skjærvø 1998a, 1998b). Relevant too are the modern Ossetic *Nart* ("hero") narratives, derived from the ancient nomadic Iranian "epic" traditions of the Scythians (Vielle 1996: 159–95).

The examples can be multiplied, but the case has already been made. In short, there is a wealth of comparanda about the "epic hero" that are genealogical (e.g. Puhvel 1987 and Watkins 1995). Still, the details of the genealogy have in many cases not yet been fully worked out.

Finally, we turn to the historical comparanda about the "epic hero." In this case, the comparative methodology involves synchronic analysis of structures in intercultural contact with each other. The most important example is ancient Roman epic, especially Virgil's *Aeneid* (see Chapter 33, by Putnam), a vast literary achievement that took shape in the social milieu of the imperial world of Augustus in the fourth quarter of the first century BCE. The actual form of this epic is not so much cognate with Greek epic as derived – or, better, appropriated – from it. I will have more to say at a later point about this all-important appropriation of ancient Greek epic – and of its "epic heroes" – by the cosmos and imperium of Rome.

In the history, as it were, of ancient Greek "epic heroes," the second most important example of intercultural contact dates from many centuries earlier, back to the first half of the first millennium BCE, especially around 750 to 650. In that era, aptly described as the "orientalizing period," the Greek-speaking world was strongly influenced by the civilizations of the Near East, as represented most prominently by the various dynasties of ancient Anatolia, Mesopotamia, the Mediterranean east coast facing Cyprus, and Egypt. In *The Orientalizing Revolution*, Walter Burkert has surveyed the most salient comparative evidence, viewing the Near Eastern comparanda from the historical standpoint of a number of linguistically diverse societies that were making contact with Greek-speaking societies, especially in the eastern Mediterranean (Burkert 1992).

Such contact between ancient Greek and Near Eastern "epic" traditions in the early first millennium BCE presupposes a cultural *lingua franca* (see Chapter 20, by Burkert). I am invoking a linguistic metaphor here because it conveys the idea of structural causes and consequences in the course of any such contact. In the sense that contact between cultures is equivalent to contact between systems of thinking – let us call them "structures" – the linguistic metaphor of *Sprachbund*, as I introduced it earlier, is apt.

In addressing the relevant Near Eastern comparanda, Burkert and others concentrate on the Mesopotamian traditions, paying special attention to the narratives about Gilgamesh. These narratives were codified over many centuries in a scribal tradition that made its way through various dynasties and various languages, from Sumerian to Akkadian to Hittite. The most canonical surviving form of the narratives is a standard Babylonian "library tablet version," composed in Akkadian and thematically formatted in twelve tablets (cf. Foster 2001: xi–xiv). An example of this version is the Gilgamesh text housed in the library of the Assyrian king Assurbanipal in Niniveh (668–627), and it is this version of the Mesopotamian "epic" that contains some of the closest parallels to what we know about the "epic hero" in the Homeric *Iliad* and *Odyssey* (see Chapter 15, by Noegel, and Chapter 14, by Sasson; also West 1997b: 587; Cook 2004).

There has been speculation about a "hot line" connecting Niniveh in the seventh century BCE with Greek-speakers who introduced the Gilgamesh themes into the Homeric *Iliad* and *Odyssey*. Such speculation seems too extreme. It is enough to say that the Gilgamesh "epic," as preserved in the "library tablet version" at Niniveh in the seventh century BCE – and most likely in other versions as well – came into contact with analogous "epic traditions" of Greek-speaking poetic craftsmen. In fact, that is what Albert Lord says in *The Singer of Tales*, on one of the rare occasions where he explains a comparandum not typologically but historically: Lord actually posits a phase of cultural contact, starting with the eighth century BCE, between the library lore of Assyrian Niniveh and the oral poetic traditions of contemporaneous Greek-speaking peoples (Lord 1960: 156, 158). Moreover, Lord actively compares the figure of Gilgamesh with the epic heroes of the Homeric *Iliad* and *Odyssey* (1960: 197, 201; see also 1991: 7, 37, 102, 142–5; 1995: 12, 104, 107).

Most revealing is Lord's analysis of the poetic themes centering on the death of Enkidu, the feral companion of Gilgamesh: "Here is our earliest example in epic of death by substitution. Enkidu dies for Gilgamesh. Gilgamesh like Achilles struggles with the horror of his own mortality and is reconciled to it" (1960: 201; cf. Sinos 1980: 58, Hendel 1987a). Curiously, the pioneering work of Lord on such relevant Near Eastern comparanda has been ignored in some quarters.

Besides the Gilgamesh "epic," Lord stresses the comparative value of other Mesopotamian traditions, including the various cosmogonies (foremost are the *Enûma Elish* and the *Atrahasis*), which he connects with West Semitic "epic" narratives to be found in the Hebrew Bible (1960: 156).

In his work on biblical comparanda, Lord notes the characteristics of the "epic hero" in such celebrated passages as chapter 32 of *Genesis*, where Jacob wrestles with the "angel"; Lord compares the passage in *Iliad* 21 where Achilles struggles with the river-god Xanthos (1960: 196–7). The parallelisms can be extended by including other Western Semitic traditions besides the Hebrew, especially the Ugaritic and the Phoenician. Discovery of the Ugaritic tablets at Ras Shamra (tablets attested from the fifteenth to the early twelfth century) has yielded a vast new reservoir of comparanda (Hendel 1987b: 73–81). There is also some fragmentary but telling comparative evidence in the Phoenician lore retold by the Greek-speaking Philo of Byblos (ibid.: 125–8).

Having noted the historical background of contacts between the Near East and the Greek-speaking world of the "orientalizing period," I stress that some of the comparanda from Near Eastern sources may be a matter of typological parallelism, not cultural contact (Nagy 1990a: 81).

Rounding out this list of Near Eastern comparanda, we come to the Indo-European languages of Anatolia, especially Hittite, Luvian, and Lycian (see Chapter 2, by Katz, and Chapter 17, by Beckman). Of these three languages, Hittite represents the dominant imperial culture of Anatolia in the second millennium BCE – until the destruction of Hattusa, the capital of the Hittite empire, around 1180 BCE. Luvian, the main language of West Anatolia, is amply attested in texts dating from the Hittite empire, and the language continued to thrive in later periods; as for Lycian, it was the dominant language of southwest Anatolia in the early first millennium BCE (Mellink 1995). Taken together, these Anatolian languages represent an important source of comparative evidence for heroic traditions that were cognate with those of Greek and other languages of Indo-European origin. Just as important, however, is the fact that these Anatolian languages were in actual contact with Greek as spoken in the East Mediterranean not only in the "orientalizing period" but even before, in the era of the Hittite empire (see Mellink 1986). Homeric poetry shows clear traces of this contact. A striking example is the Homeric usage of the ancient Greek word *therapôn*, conventionally translated as "attendant," which is evidently derived from one of the Anatolian languages; in Hittite ritual texts, *tarpanalli-* means "ritual substitute" (Van Brock 1959). Comparable is the application of the Greek word *therapôn* to Patroklos, the faithful attendant and best friend of Achilles in the Homeric *Iliad*: the word is applied to this hero in the context of narrating the ritualized death of Patroklos as a substitute – even a body double – for Achilles (Nagy 1979a: 33, 292–3).

Another example of ongoing contact between ancient Greek and Anatolian cultures is the use of the Greek word *tarkhuein*, "make a funeral for," in *Iliad* 16.456 and 674; the funeral here is for Sarpedon, hero king of the Lycians, and it takes place in his homeland of Lycia. The word is evidently a borrowing from the Lycian language: *Trqqas* in Lycian texts designates the god who smashes the world of the unrighteous, and his name is cognate with Luvian *Tarḫunt-*, the thunder-god who is head of the Luvian pantheon (Nagy 1990a: 131–2; see also West 1997b: 386). These associations, as we will see later, are relevant to the theme of the divine thunderbolt as an instrument of heroic immortalization.

Having surveyed the three kinds of comparanda for the "epic hero," I reach the primary point of comparison, ancient Greek epic. I propose to start with the characters of Achilles and Odysseus in the Homeric *Iliad* and *Odyssey*. Why these two epic heroes? Although they are by no means prototypical for defining the "epic hero," they represent an ideal point of entry for typological comparison because both embody a convergence of the concepts of "epic" and "hero" in a specific historical time and place. The time is the fourth century BCE, and the place is Athens. The convergence is most clearly visible in the works of Plato and Aristotle, which stem from that time and place. Here is where we find an apt point of departure for a systematic comparison. This particular point, I must stress, is not preordained: it is simply a historical contingency, most suitable for typological comparison.

Plato and Aristotle, as we see especially in the *Ion* and the *Poetics* respectively, both offer a grounded idea of what is "epic," what is a "hero," as we see from their use of the words *epos* (plural *epê*) and *hêrós* (plural *hêróes*).

I start with epic. At the beginning of the *Poetics* of Aristotle (1447a13–15), *epos*, "epic," is defined synchronically as a genre, and the definition operates in terms of an active comparison with the other genres listed here by Aristotle: tragedy, comedy, dithyramb, lyric accompanied by *aulos*, lyric accompanied by *kithara*. All these genres listed at the beginning of Aristotle's *Poetics* correspond to genres performed at the two major festivals of the Athenians: (1) the Panathenaia (epic, lyric accompanied by *aulos*, lyric accompanied by *kithara*) and (2) the City Dionysia (tragedy, comedy, dithyramb) (Nagy 1999b: 27). In Aristotle's listing, he ostentatiously pairs the genre of epic with the genre of tragedy (*epopoiia . . . kai hê tês tragóidias poiêsis*) (Nagy 1999b: 26–7). Elsewhere, he says that he views these two particular genres, epic and tragedy, as cognates (*Poet.* 1449a2–6) (Nagy 1979a: 253–6). In the works of Plato as well, epic is viewed as a cognate of tragedy, and Homer is represented as a proto-tragedian (*Tht.* 152e; *Rep.* 598d, 605c, 607a).

Plato's identification of tragedy with Homer – and of Homer with epic in general – can be understood in light of the history of Athenian institutions. In Athens, ever since the sixth century BCE, the genre of epic as performed at the Panathenaia and the genre of tragedy as performed at the City Dionysia were "complementary forms, evolving together and thereby undergoing a process of mutual assimilation in the course of their institutional coexistence" (Nagy 1996c: 81). By the time of Plato and Aristotle, the only epics performed at the festival of the Panathenaia were the Homeric *Iliad* and *Odyssey*, and these two epics shaped and were shaped by the genre of tragedy as performed at the festival of the City Dionysia.

Other ancient Greek epics, attributed to poets other than Homer, were less compatible with tragedy. They belong to an ensemble known as the Epic Cycle (see Chapter 24, by Burgess). For Aristotle, the Cycle was categorically non-Homeric. In his *Poetics*, where he mentions two of the Cyclic poems he knew – the *Cypria* and the *Little Iliad* – he makes clear his view that the authors of these epics were poets other than Homer, and he chooses not even to name these poets (1459a37–b16). Other sources offer specific names and provenances: for example, the author of the *Cypria* was Stasinus of Cyprus; of the *Little Iliad*, Lesches of Lesbos; of the *Aithiopis* and the *Iliou Persis*, Arctinus of Miletus (Burgess 2001).

Aristotle viewed Homer as the author of only two epics, the *Iliad* and the *Odyssey* (again, *Poetics* 1459a37–b16; cf. 1448b38–1449a1). Plato, as we see in such works as the *Ion*, evidently held the same view. In general, the verses that Plato quotes explicitly from "Homer" are taken exclusively from the *Iliad* and the *Odyssey*, not from the Epic Cycle.

In the sixth century BCE, by contrast, the epics of the Cycle were attributed to the authorship of Homer. In that earlier era, Homer could be viewed as the notional author of all epic, as represented by the idea of the Epic Cycle before it became historically differentiated from the *Iliad* and *Odyssey*. In that era, moreover, the traditions represented by what we know as the Epic Cycle were still part of the program, as it were, of the Panathenaia (Nagy 2001b). From the evidence of Athenian vase paintings dated to the sixth century BCE, we can see that the epic repertoire at the Panathenaia in that period included the heroic themes of what we know as the Epic Cycle (Lowenstam 1997). In the archaic era of the Panathenaia, the idea of the Cycle was still being equated with the idea of epic as a comprehensive totality: the term "Cycle" or *kuklos* was sustained by metaphors of artistic comprehensiveness (Nagy 1996b: 38, 89).

In the classical era of the Panathenaia, however, newer ideas of comprehensiveness had replaced the older idea. These newer ideas were now being determined by the artistic measure of tragedy. Aristotle says explicitly that only the Homeric *Iliad* and *Odyssey* are comparable to tragedy because only these epics show a comprehensive and unified structure, unlike the epics of the Cycle (again, *Poetics* 1459a37–b16). In Plato as well, as we have seen, the standards of tragedy are evident in descriptions of Homer as a proto-tragedian in his own right. For Plato and Aristotle, the Homeric *Iliad* and *Odyssey* measured up to the standards of tragedy, whereas the epics of the Cycle did not.

Thus the criteria of epic comprehensiveness vary from age to age: from the archaic notion of the Epic Cycle to the classical notion of Homer the tragedian. What remains an invariable, however, is the basic institutional context in which the very idea of epic comprehensiveness took shape: that context is the festival. In the case of epic as performed in Athens, that context remained the festival of the Panathenaia. In its archaic phase, to repeat, the Panathenaia featured the Epic Cycle, including the repertoire of what we know as the Homeric *Iliad* and *Odyssey*. In its classical phase, this same festival of the Panathenaia featured only the Homeric *Iliad* and *Odyssey*, excluding the repertoire of the Epic Cycle. Even the term "Cycle" was no longer appropriate, since the Epic Cycle no longer embodied the notion of epic as a comprehensive totality.

A typological comparandum for the notion of epic as a comprehensive totality is the case of heroic epics and dramas at festivals in latter-day India: the notion of comprehensive totality in the performing of these epics and dramas is determined by the ideologies of the festivals that serve as the historical contexts for such performances (Nagy 1999b: 28). Observers of actual performances of epics at festivals in latter-day India have found that there are various different ways of imagining and realizing such a notional totality (Flueckiger 1986: 133–4). There are even cases of differences determined by gender: when women instead of men sing the "same" epic, observers have found differences in form (meter, melody, phraseology) and even in content (Flueckiger 1989: 36–40; Nagy 1996b: 56–7). There are close parallels to be found in the songs of Sappho about epic heroes like Hektor and Andromache (Nagy 1996b: 57). Still, despite all the variables, the actual notion of epic as a totality remains a constant.

Having first considered the form of "epic," both historically and comparatively, I will now move on to consider the content. In other words, I shift from plot to character, from "epic" to "hero." Just as *epos* is "epic" in the age of Plato and Aristotle, so also *hērōs* is "hero." Moreover, the same word *hērōs* is used in the Homeric *Iliad* and *Odyssey* to refer to the characters in those epics.

The complementarity of plot and character in tragedy is comparable to the complementarity of *epos* and *hērōs* in Homer. The heroic plots of the Homeric *Iliad* and *Odyssey* are complementary to the heroic characters of Achilles and Odysseus respectively, each of whom has become streamlined as the centralized hero of each of the two epics.

The monolithic personality of Achilles, supreme epic hero of the *Iliad*, is matched against the many-sidedness of Odysseus, the commensurately supreme epic hero of the *Odyssey*. Whereas Achilles achieves his epic supremacy as a warrior, Odysseus achieves his own kind of epic supremacy in an alternative way, as a master of crafty stratagems and cunning intelligence.

There are of course many other heroes in Homeric poetry, but Achilles and Odysseus have become the two central points of reference. Just as the central heroes of the *Iliad* and *Odyssey* are complementary, so too are the epics that centralize them. The complementarity extends even further: between the two of them, these two epics give the impression of incorporating most of whatever was worth retelling about the world of heroes – at least from the standpoint of the Greek-speaking people in the age of Plato and Aristotle.

In the case of the *Iliad*, this epic not only tells the story that it says it will tell, about Achilles' anger and how it led to countless woes as the Greeks went on fighting it out with the Trojans and striving to ward off the fiery onslaught of Hektor (see Chapter 21, by Edwards). It also manages to retell or even relive, though with varying degrees of directness or fullness of narrative, the entire Tale of Troy, including from the earlier points of the story-line such memorable moments as the Judgment of Paris, the Abduction of Helen, and the Assembly of Ships. More than that: the *Iliad* foreshadows the Death of Achilles, which does not occur within the bounds of its own plot. In short, although the story of the *Iliad* directly covers only a short stretch of the whole story of Troy, thereby resembling the compressed time-frame of classical Greek tragedy (Aristotle makes this observation in his *Poetics*), it still manages to mention something about practically every-thing that happened at Troy, otherwise known as Ilion. Hence the epic's title – the Tale of Ilion, the *Iliad* (Nagy 1992: xv).

The Homeric *Odyssey* is equally comprehensive (see Chapter 22, by Slatkin). It tells the story of the hero's *nostos* "return, homecoming." This word means not only "homecom-ing" but also "song about homecoming" (Frame 1978). As such, the *Odyssey* is not only a *nostos*: it is a *nostos* to end all other *nostoi* (Nagy 1999b: xii–xiii). In other words, the *Odyssey* is the final and definitive statement about the theme of a heroic homecoming: in the process of retelling the return of the epic hero Odysseus, the narrative of the *Odyssey* achieves a sense of closure in the retelling of all feats stemming from the heroic age. The *Odyssey* provides a retrospective even on those epic moments that are missing in the *Iliad*, such as the story of the Wooden Horse (8.487–520). As we see from the wording of the Song of the Sirens in the *Odyssey* (12.189–91), the sheer pleasure of listening to the song of Troy that is the *Iliad* will be in vain if there is no *nostos*, no safe return home from the faraway world of epic heroes: in other words, the *Iliad* itself will become a Song of the Sirens without a successful narration of the *Odyssey* (Nagy 1999b: xii).

As we see from Albert Lord's far-ranging survey of typological parallels to the theme of the epic hero's return in the Homeric *Odyssey*, the idea of *nostos* is deeply ritualistic (1960: 158–85). In fact, the *nostos* of Odysseus in the *Odyssey* means not only a "return" or a "song about a return" but even a "return to light and life" (Frame 1978). This ritualistic meaning, as we will see, has to do with the epic "hidden agenda" of *returning from Hades* and the heroic theme of *immortalization after death*.

On the surface, however, the *nostos* "return" of the epic hero includes a wide variety of interactions between different characters and different plots. The following list is organ-ized in terms of these different characters and plots, all of which fit both the hero Odysseus and the epic of the *Odyssey* as analyzed by Lord:

(a)   The returning king reclaims his kingdom by becoming reintegrated with his society. The king, as king, is the embodiment of this society, of this "body politic"; thus the society, as reembodied by the king, is correspondingly reintegrated.
(b)   The pilot lost at sea finally finds his bearings and reaches home. The pilot or *kubernḗtēs* (Latin *gubernator*) is the helmsman who directs the metaphorical "ship of state" ("government").

(c)   The soldier of fortune returns home to reclaim his wife, whose faithfulness deter-
      mines his true identity.
(d)   The seer or shaman returns home from his vision quest.
(e)   The trickster retraces his incorrect and misleading steps, returning all the way back
      home, where he had started, and thus showing the correct steps for all to take.
(f)   The son goes off on a quest to find his father in order to find his own heroic identity.

The last case is particularly instructive. It is about the quest of Telemachus for the *kleos*
"glory" of his father Odysseus (*Odyssey* 3.83); his quest is also for the father's *nostos*
"homecoming" (2.360). In the *Odyssey*, as I observed earlier, *nostos* is not only a "homecoming" but a "song about homecoming"; Odysseus achieves *kleos*, "glory," by way of
successfully achieving a *nostos*, "song about homecoming." Whereas Achilles has to
choose between *nostos* "homecoming" and the *kleos* "glory" that he gets from his own
epic tradition (*Iliad* 9. 413), Odysseus must have both *kleos* and *nostos*, because for him his
nostos is the same thing as his *kleos* (Nagy 1999b: xii). Once again we see an active
complementarity between the Homeric *Iliad* and *Odyssey*.

Such complementarity between the two Homeric epics becomes a classical model for
the Roman epic of Virgil's *Aeneid* (see Chapter 33, by Putnam): the first half, Books 1–6,
re-enacts the *Odyssey*, while the second half, Books 7–12, re-enacts the *Iliad*. On the other
hand, the complementarity inherent in the contrast between Odysseus and Achilles, the
two principal epic heroes of the *Odyssey* and the *Iliad*, is not directly replicated by the single
character of Aeneas, the principal epic hero of the *Aeneid*. This character can better
be described as an amalgam of earlier epic heroes. Although the Aeneas of Virgil's *Aeneid*
shares some of the characteristics of Odysseus and Achilles, his identity is shaped by other
Homeric characters as well, including the Aeneas of the *Iliad*. Moreover, the identity of
Aeneas as an epic hero transcends Homeric poetry, incorporating aspects of generic figures
like the "founding hero" and the "love hero" developed in the Hellenistic poetry of
scholar-poets such as Callimachus and Apollonius of Rhodes (see Chapter 25, by Nelis).

Whereas the epic hero comes into focus through the lens of Homeric poetry, the picture
is blurred as we look further back in time to earlier forms of poetry that used to
be performed at the festival of the Panathenaia at Athens in the sixth century. These
forms can be described as Cyclic, Hesiodic, and Orphic. By "Cyclic" I mean the poetry of
the Epic Cycle, which represents a more general form of epic, to be contrasted with the
more differentiated form that we know as Homeric poetry (see Chapter 24, by Burgess).
As for "Hesiodic," I mean non-epic forms of poetry that can be described in general terms
as cosmogonic and anthropogonic (see Chapter 23, by Nelson, and Nagy 1990a: 74, 198;
see also Slatkin 1987 and Muellner 1996). The same description applies to "Orphic,"
except that the poetry attributed to Orpheus had become even more peripheral than
Hesiodic poetry in the democratic era of Athens, at least by the time we reach the fifth
century BCE (Nagy 2001a). In general, as Homeric poetry became ever more central in
the performance traditions of the festival of the Panathenaia in Athens, the Cyclic,
Hesiodic, and Orphic forms of poetry became ever more peripheral. Hence the blurring
of the picture they present of the epic hero. In retrospect, this blurred picture gives the
impression of a more aristocratic and more Ionic alternative to the Homeric tradition as it
existed in the classical period represented by the age of Plato and Aristotle.

A case in point is Achilles in the Cyclic *Aithiopis*, attributed to Arctinus of Miletus, to be
contrasted with Achilles in the Homeric *Iliad*. The *Aithiopis* stems from the aristocratic
local epic traditions of the Ionic city of Miletus in Asia Minor, which were in close contact
with the aristocratic local epic traditions of the Aeolic cities on the island of Lesbos and on
the facing mainland of Asia Minor. The Achilles of these elite Ionians and Aeolians is more
exoticized, more eroticized, than his Homeric counterpart. The Ionic Achilles resembles a

delicate Scythian archer in Milesian traditions (Pinney 1983; Nagy 1990a: 71 n. 96), while the Aeolic Achilles of Sappho's songs becomes the object of every young girl's erotic desires. Achilles is a passionate lover in the *Aithiopis*. Retrospectively, he resembles in many ways the love heroes of later epics, such as Jason in Book 3 of the *Argonautica* of Apollonius or even Aeneas himself in Book 4 of the *Aeneid* of Virgil. The Achilles of the *Aithiopis* falls desperately in love with the Amazon Penthesileia at the moment of killing her in battle, and then, in a fit of passion, kills Thersites for mocking that love. The Homeric Achilles is comparably passionate in expressing his love for the Aeolic girl Briseis in the Homeric *Iliad*, but the erotic aspects of his passion are understated by Homeric poetry (Dué 2002). Much the same can be said about the passion of Achilles for his best friend in the *Iliad*, Patroklos: the erotic aspect of this passion is made explicit in the version of the story as retold in the tragedy *Myrmidons*, by Aeschylus, but it is only implicit in the version as told in the epic of the *Iliad*. At least, that is what Aeschines says in his speech *Against Timarkhos* when he refers to this passion (Dué 2000, 2001). The orator goes out of his way to insist that the erotic passion of Achilles for Patroklos is implicit in the Homeric *Iliad*, restricted to the special understanding of the cognoscenti.

Besides the differences we find in the Homeric *Iliad* and in the Cyclic *Aithiopis* when we look for characterizations of the hero Achilles, there are also radical differences in plot. In the *Aithiopis*, unlike the *Iliad*, Achilles is immortalized after death. In the *Iliad*, by contrast, the theme of heroic immortalization is nowhere made explicit, though there is reason to argue that this theme is implicit throughout Homeric poetry. By contrast, heroic immortalization is a theme that is explicit in Cyclic, Hesiodic, and Orphic poetry.

In order to pursue this non-Homeric theme of heroic immortalization in the ancient Greek traditions of the epic hero, I return to the subject of cosmogonic and anthropo-gonic forms of poetry. Of special relevance is the story of the overpopulation of Earth personified, and of the solutions devised by the divine apparatus to remedy this overpopulation. According to the version of the story preserved in the Epic Cycle, specifically in the *Cypria*, the divine solution is a war to end all wars, destined to destroy the vast numbers of heroes who are overpopulating the earth. That totalizing war, according to the Cyclic *Cypria*, is the Trojan War, precipitated by the wedding of the mortal man Peleus to the immortal goddess Thetis. The scholia to the *Iliad* quote the relevant verses from the *Cypria*, where it is specified that the Trojan War resulted from the Will of Zeus (fr. 1.7). The sources report also a variant epic tradition involving a combination of the Trojan War with a preceding Theban War (the story of which was later converted into a tragedy by Aeschylus, the *Seven Against Thebes*). They also report various alternatives to the concept of a totalizing war, including (1) a cosmic conflagration by way of the fiery thunderbolts (*keraunoi*) of Zeus or (2) a cosmic cataclysm, by way of floods (*kataklusmoi*). In Ovid's *Metamorphoses* (253–9), we see a related version, derived from the Orphic tradition: Jupiter/Zeus first considers the alternative of ecpyrosis before deciding on the alternative of cataclysm (see Chapter 34, by Newlands). In the Hesiodic tradition, we find references to a composite epic version involving both the Trojan and the Theban War (Nagy 1990c: 15–16, 126), and there are also allusions to a cataclysm and other blights as alternatives to the theme of totalizing war (*WD* 156–73; fr. 204. 95–143).

There are striking parallels to be found in Near Eastern traditions (see Chapters 14, 15, 19, 20 by Sasson, Noegel, Niditch, and Burkert, respectively). In the Hebrew Bible, Gen. 6: 1–4, we find the well-known narrative of Noah's Ark and the Deluge, which is closely related to Mesopotamian traditions, especially as represented by the Babylonian *Atrahasis* and the *Enûma Elish* (Hendel 1987a: 13–17). In Tablets I and II of the *Atrahasis* and in Tablet I of the *Enûma Elish*, the story is told that Earth is suffering from overpopulation, and, here too, the divine apparatus provides a solution in the form of a deluge, a cosmic cataclysm; in the *Atrahasis*, there are other cosmic blights, such as plague and famine, that take place as preludes to the eventual cataclysm (ibid.: 17–18; cf. Burkert 1992: 101). In the Hesiodic tradition as well, we see other such references to cosmic blight, as manifested in the failure of vegetation (fr. 124–43). Presiding over the blight is a cosmic snake (*deinos ophis*: F 136). The Gilgamesh narrative in Tablet XI (182–5) refers to the cosmic flood and to various other blights catalogued as alternatives to the flood, such as a lion, a wolf, and a cosmic famine (West 1997b: 491).

There is also a most striking parallel to be found in an important example of Indo-European poetic traditions, the Indic *Mahâbhârata* (see Chapter 2, by Katz, and Nagy 1990a: 14–15). This monumental epic, comprising over 90,000 *śloka*-s in its Northern recensions, is pervaded by the theme of the war of the Pâṇḍavas. This totalizing war is precipitated by the overpopulation of the Earth personified; the gods' decision to initiate this war is correlated with their decision to initiate the incarnation of the five heroes known as the Pâṇḍavas. "In this way the major epic narratives of the Greek and Indic peoples are inaugurated with a cognate theme, and it is hard to imagine more compelling evidence for the Indo-European heritage of the epic traditions about the Trojan War" (Nagy 1990a: 16, with further references).

One observer, dismissing the comparative evidence of the *Mahâbhârata* as "coincidence," points to the existence of various historically unrelated myths about overpopulation and its divine remedies, such as war, flood, fire, famine, plague, noxious beasts, and so forth. He adduces the existence of these typological parallels in order to back up his claim that the Indic myths about overpopulation and totalizing war are not genealogically related to the corresponding Greek myths. But then he goes on to claim that the Near Eastern myths about overpopulation and a cosmic flood are indeed the actual historical source for the corresponding Greek myths, and that the Greeks borrowed these myths in a relatively late period, no earlier than the second half of the sixth century.

The worldwide attestations of myths about overpopulation and a cosmic flood can be used to make an altogether different argument, namely, that the parallelisms between the relevant Greek and Near Eastern narrative traditions are primarily typological. In making this alternative argument, however, there is no need to exclude the possibility that these Greek and Near Eastern traditions actually made contact with each other, and that such contact resulted in mutual influences between typological parallels.

As for the claim that Greek myths about a cosmic flood are relatively recent, to be dated no earlier than the sixth century BCE, it simply cannot stand. The myth of cosmic cataclysm, as well as the myth of cosmic ecpyrosis, is in fact deeply embedded in the overall structure of the oldest surviving epic of Greek literature, the Homeric *Iliad*. A signal of these myths is the theme of the Will of Zeus at the beginning of the *Iliad* (1.5), which is coextensive with the plot of the *Iliad* just as the Will of Zeus in the *Cypria* (F 1. 7) is coextensive with plot of the entire Trojan War in the Epic Cycle. As we have already seen, the Will of Zeus in the Epic Cycle translates into one of three alternative divine solutions to the overpopulation of Earth: cataclysm, ecpyrosis, and war. So also in the *Iliad*, the Will of Zeus translates into cataclysm, ecpyrosis, and war, though the theme of overpopulation is absent. In fact, the cosmic themes of cataclysm and ecpyrosis pervade the story of the war in the *Iliad*: ecpyrosis applies to both the Trojans and the Achaeans, while cataclysm applies only to the Achaeans (Rousseau 1996: 403–13, 591–2; see also Nagy 1996b: 145–6). Both ecpyrosis and cataclysm are the visible epic manifestations of the Will of Zeus (Nagy 2002: 66).

In the *Iliad*, the fire of the Achaeans that is destined to destroy the Trojans and, conversely, the fire of the Trojans that threatens to destroy the Achaeans are both pervasively compared to a cosmic fire of Zeus, which threatens to destroy the whole world. In *Iliad* 12.17–33, on the other hand, where it is prophesied that the rivers of the Trojan plain will erase all traces of the Achaean Wall at Troy, the flooding of the plain is described in language that evokes a cosmic cataclysm.

A related Homeric scene is the battle of the epic hero Achilles against the river Xanthos, where the god who embodies the waters of Xanthos is on the verge of destroying the hero in the mode of a cataclysm: at the climax of this cosmic battle, the river-god roars like a bull (21. 237); so also the cosmic river-god Akheloîos assumes the form of a bull when he battles Herakles (Archilochus F 286–7) (Nagy 1996b: 145–6). Such divine theriomorphism is paralleled in Near Eastern traditions. In Canaanite narratives, for example, the Divine Warrior Baal is conventionally pictured as a bull as he battles the forces of cosmic cataclysm (Hendel 1987b: 30, 104). Other comparanda include the theriomorphic aspects of the Canaanite god El ("Bull El") and even of the Israelite Yahweh ("the bull of Jacob").

The vision of cosmic cataclysm in the Homeric *Iliad* is signaled by the word *hêmitheoi* "demigods" (12.23), referring to the epic heroes of the *Iliad* from the retrospective standpoint of the prophecy that foretells the destruction of the Achaean Wall. Nowhere else in the Homeric *Iliad* and *Odyssey* do we find *hêmitheoi*: it is a word conventionally associated not with the poetry of epic but with the alternative poetry of cosmogonies and anthropogonies, as we see from the attestations of *hêmitheoi* in Hesiod F 204.100 and *Works and Days* 160 (Nagy 1979a: 160–1). In the latter case, the word *hêmitheoi* signals the last generation of heroes, who were obliterated in the time of the Theban and the Trojan Wars (*WD* 161–5) – but who were preserved after death and immortalized by being transported to the Islands of the Blessed (*WD* 167–73) (Koenen 1994: 5; Nagy 1996b: 126).

The scenario of obliteration followed by preservation for the *hêmitheoi* in Hesiodic poetry must be contrasted with the scenario of obliteration followed by no preservation for the *hêmitheoi* in *Iliad* 12.17–33, where Homeric poetry refers to its heroes exceptionally as the last generation of heroes. In this unique Homeric reference, as we have seen, the obliteration of these heroes in the time of the Trojan War is expressed in language appropriate to obliteration by a cosmic cataclysm. A parallel can be found in the language used by Sennacherib, king of the Assyrians, in inscriptions commemorating his destruction of Babylon in 689 BCE: after burning down the city, the king leveled it further by flooding it, and the inscription boasts that this leveling was more complete than the devastation that took place in the wake of the cosmic flood that destroyed the world. Another parallel is the language describing the Nephilim and the Rephaim in the Hebrew Bible. This generation of humans is literally destined for obliteration: they "exist in order to be wiped out" – by the flood (Gen. 6: 4), by Moses (Num. 13: 33), by David (2 Sam. 21: 18–22, 1 Chr. 20: 4–8), and others (Hendel 1987a: 21).

In sum, the myths about cataclysm and ecpyrosis that we find embedded in Homeric poetry are parallel to and evidently cognate with the myths we find in the *Cypria* and elsewhere about a totalizing war that alleviated the heroic overpopulation of Earth – myths that derive from a prehistoric Indo-European existence. Such myths, as we have seen, gravitate toward non-epic forms of poetry, which I have described as cosmogonic and anthropogonic. These forms, as we have also seen, are represented primarily in the residual Cyclic, Hesiodic, and Orphic traditions. Such non-Homeric traditions are typified by the heroic concept of the *hêmitheos* (as signaled in *Homeric Hymn* 31.19 and 32.19) (Nagy 1990a: 15–16, 54).

Even though the word *hêmitheos* is associated primarily with non-Homeric traditions, the actual theme of the *hêmitheos* is all-pervasive in Homeric poetry. The epic heroes of this poetry can be defined simply as mortals of the remote past, male or female, who are endowed with superhuman powers because they are descended from the immortal gods themselves. In the *Iliad*, for example, the primary hero Achilles is the son of Thetis, an immortal goddess with far-reaching cosmic powers whose forced marriage to the mortal man Peleus precipitated the totalizing war that is being narrated. Achilles himself, then, can be described in non-Homeric terms as a *hêmitheos*.

This word *hêmitheos* shows a "genetic" understanding of the hero. The heroic potential is "programmed" by divine genes. The component *hêmi-* "half" of *hêmitheos* refers to the starting point, as it were, of any heroic line. There has to be a god involved at the beginning of any hero's "family tree." In terms of this word *hêmitheos*, it is just as important that the other side of the immortal half of the hero's origins should be a mortal. In the case of Achilles, for example, his father Peleus is mortal, and so this greatest of heroes must therefore be mortal as well. This principle holds for all heroes in the ancient Greek traditions: even though they are all descended, however many generations removed, from a sexual union between an immortal and a mortal, heroes are all mortals. They all have to die, like ordinary mortals. No matter how many immortals you find in a heroic "family tree," the intrusion of even a single mortal will make all successive descendants mortal. Mortality, not immortality, is the dominant gene (Nagy 1992: ix).

There is a close parallel to this Greek epic concept of *hêmitheos* in the Indic *Mahâbhârata*. The five central heroes of this epic, the mortal Pâṇḍavas, are begotten by five corresponding immortal gods, and each hero inherits the divine characteristics of his divine father. For example, the hero Arjuna is born of a mortal mother and an immortal father, the god Indra, whose traits as the Divine Warrior are re-enacted by Arjuna throughout the *Mahâbhârata* (Nagy 1979a: 323–5). As we have already seen, it is the totalizing war of the Pâṇḍava-s that ultimately fulfills the divine plan of alleviating the Earth of its overpopulation. As we have also seen, the Indic theme of this divine plan is cognate with the ancient Greek theme of the Will of Zeus, who ordains the obliteration of the generation of humans known as the *hêmitheoi*.

To say that the *hêmitheoi* are mortal is not to say that heroes do not become immortal: they do, but only after they have experienced death. After death, heroes are eligible for a life of immortality.

Here I return to the case of Achilles in the Epic Cycle, specifically, in the epic known as the *Aithiopis*: after the hero is killed at Troy, his body is transported by his goddess mother to a paradisiacal realm, where he is made immortal. In this same epic, an analogous immortalization awaits Memnon, the son of the dawn-goddess Eos, after he is killed at Troy. In the *Iliad*, by contrast, there are references to the ultimate immortalization of Achilles, but these references are kept implicit and are never made explicit. So also in the *Odyssey*, the immortalization of the hero is kept implicit. Throughout this epic, the theme of immortalization is expressed metaphorically through the theme of *nostos* "return, homecoming," in the transcendent sense of "return to life and light" (Nagy 1979a, following Frame 1978).

A most explicit example of the hero as a *hêmitheos* is Herakles, conceived by a mortal and fathered by the immortal Zeus, chief of the gods and executive of the universe (Davidson 1980; Nagy 1996b: 12–15). Only after undergoing his Labors, culminating in the ultimate labor of his suffering and death on Mount Oeta, does this hero achieve immortality. (See Diod. Sic. 3.38.3–3.39.3 for the story told most explicitly.) Suffering the most excruciating pain imaginable, Herakles in his agony mounts the funeral pyre built on top of the mountain and orders the lighting of the fire of cremation. The moment the fire is lit, the hero is struck by lightning, blasted by the *coup de grâce* of a thunderbolt sent by Zeus. All goes up in flames and nothing is left of Herakles, not even the expected bones. At the same moment of his disappearance from the world of mortals, he joins the world of immortals. Herakles now finds himself in the company of the gods, and at this point the goddess Hera, who had been the ultimate cause of the labors suffered by the hero throughout his life, becomes his surrogate mother: she even goes through the motions of giving him birth (Diod. Sic. 3.39.3: *tên de teknôsin genesthai phasi toiautên: tên Hêran anabasan epi klinên kai ton Hêraklea proslabomenên pros to sôma dia tôn endumatôn apheinai pros tên gên, mimoumenên tên alêthinên genesin.* "And the birth happened this way: Hera mounted her bed and took Herakles next to her body and ejected him through her clothes to the ground, re-enacting the true birth").

Birth by Hera is the hero's rebirth, a birth into immortality. Death by lightning is the key to this rebirth; the thunderbolt of Zeus, so prominently featured in the poetry of cosmogony and anthropogony, simultaneously destroys and regenerates. "Elysium," one of many different names given to an imagined paradisiacal place of immortalization for heroes after death, is related to the word *en-élusion*, which designates a place struck by lightning – a place made sacred by contact with the thunderbolt of Zeus (Nagy 1990a: 140–2, with further bibliography). In a word, the hero can be *immortalized*, but the fundamental painful fact remains: the hero is not by nature *immortal* (Nagy 1992: x).

But the questions must go deeper. Besides engaging in the comparanda linking "epic heroes" to each other from a Panhellenic perspective, it is important to consider also the "local color" that anchors the individual hero to the locale that keeps his or her memory alive. This "local color" reveals the ritualistic nature of local acts of remembrance, and how such memorialization becomes ultimately formalized as poetry, "epic" or otherwise.

The concept of the hero transcends epic or drama or any other genre of verbal art. In the ancient Greek language, the *hérôs* is not just a character, not just a figure shaped by a genre of verbal art, whether epic or tragedy. The *hérôs* is also a figure of cult. In other words, the *hérôs* is a figure who was worshipped.

We see in this simple formula an essential historical fact about ancient Greek religion. Not only were gods worshiped. Heroes were too, but this kind of worship was formally differentiated from the worship of gods. The differentiation has to do with the ultimate derivation of the practice of worshiping heroes from older practices of worshiping ancestors (Nagy 1979a: 115; 1990a: 11, 94, 116, 129). In considering this derivation, we find a vital point of contact between the genre of epic and the genres of anthropogony and cosmogony, as represented primarily by Hesiodic and Orphic poetry.

As a most important and ancient typological parallel, I cite the case of Gilgamesh. The identity of this figure, as we trace it back to its earliest Mesopotamian cultural contexts in the Sumerian civilization of the third millennium BCE, was shaped by ideologies of the generic king and dynastic ancestor, who is worshiped as the generic embodiment of anthropogonic and cosmogonic power (Hendel 1987b: 99–100). In the ancient Egyptian traditions of the Pyramid Texts, there is a comparable envisioning of the generic Pharaoh as the fusion of the divine antagonists Horus and Seth (ibid.: 124). Also comparable is the evidence for the worship of dead dynastic ancestors in Ugaritic and other West Semitic texts.

The ritual aspect of worshipping Gilgamesh as a prototypical dynastic ancestor is parallel to the mythical aspect of envisioning him as the king of the underworld and judge of the dead (Hendel 1987b: 80–1 n. 38). In this context, the myth about the rejection of the proposal of marriage made by the immortal goddess Ishtar to the mortal man Gilgamesh can be seen as a parallel to the rejection of the nymph Calypso by the epic hero Odysseus in *Odyssey* 5.

Besides the numerous typological parallels to the ancient Greek practice of worshiping heroes there are genealogical parallels as well. A prime example is the Indic practice of worshiping heroes, which continues to this day in a wide variety of forms. A heroic figure like Arjuna, one of the Pâṇḍavas in the epic *Mahâbhârata*, is actually worshiped in the context of numerous local festivals in modern times, featuring sacrifices of animals and various re-enactments – both epic and dramatic – of the hero's life experiences (Sax 2002; on Indic hero worship see Harlan 2003 and McGrath 2004).

From a survey of the ancient Greek evidence, it is clear that the worship of heroes was a fundamentally local practice, confined to specific locales (Brelich 1958). Every locale had its own set of local heroes, who could be male or female, adult or child. There were literally thousands of local heroes being worshiped in their own respective locales throughout the ancient Greek-speaking world. Some of them are well known to us through poetry, including epic (every hero – major or minor – mentioned in the *Iliad* and *Odyssey* was potentially a local hero). Others are never mentioned in any poetry known to us.

Even if we had no epic or drama surviving from the ancient Greek world, we would still be fairly well informed, on the basis of non-poetic evidence (prosaic references, inscriptions, archaeological remains of cult sites, and so on) of the historical existence of hero worship in the period extending from (roughly) the eighth century BCE onward (Nagy 1979a: 115).

The hero was considered *dead* – from the standpoint of the place where the hero's *sôma* (body) was situated; at the same time, the hero was considered simultaneously *immortalized* – from the standpoint of the paradisiacal place that awaited all heroes after death. Such a paradisiacal place, which was considered *eschatological*, must be contrasted with Hades, which was considered *transitional*. The name and even the visualization of this otherworldly place varied from hero cult to hero cult. Some of these names are: Elysium, the Islands of the Blessed, the White Island, and, exceptionally, even Olympus. Many of these names were applied also to the actual site or sacred precinct of the hero cult.

The "marker" of the *sôma* of the cult hero was the *sêma*, which ordinarily took the physical shape of a "tomb." The "marking" of the *sôma* could also be a sign or signal or token or picture; the word for such a marking was also *sêma*.

The marking of the *sêma* could be a sacred secret. The local details of ritual and myth surrounding a given hero cult were held to be sacred in any case; as such, they tended to be considered secret as well. Or, at least, some of the sacred details were screened by the local inhabitants as secrets that must not be divulged to outsiders. The "outsiders" were not only those who were non-local: they were also those of the local inhabitants who had not yet been initiated (the word for which is *muein*) into the secrets (the word for which is *mustêria*, "mysteries") (Nagy 1990c: 31–2, 1996b: 129–30).

In both the *Iliad* and the *Odyssey*, we see "signatures" of the double meaning of *sêma*: sign and tomb-marker of a hero. In *Iliad* 23.326, *sêma* refers to (1) a sign that signals metaphorically a "turning point" of life; at 23.331, the same word refers to (2) the tomb-marker of a mystically unidentified hero (Nagy 1990a: 208–22). In *Odyssey* 11.126 *sêma* refers to (1) a sign that signals a critical point in the hero's life and (2) the tomb-marker of the place where the hero's own body is buried in the local "mother earth," contact with which will make the local people *olbioi* (11.137) (ibid.: 212–14). This word *olbioi* means "prosperous" on the surface and "blessed" underneath the surface. The meaning of "blessed" applies both to the dead, that is, the cult hero, and to the living who benefit from contact with the cult hero (ibid.: 127 n. 21).

In terms of these Homeric "signatures," the tomb-marker of the cult hero *is* the meaning of the hero cult. That is, the medium of the *sêma* or tomb-marker of the hero (or ancestor) *is* the message of the hero (or ancestor). In order to understand his own *sêma*, an epic hero like Odysseus must have *noos*, which is a special kind of mentality that enables the hero to see more than one side of reality (Nagy 1990a: 202–22). In the *Odyssey*, as we read at the very beginning of the epic (1.1–5), the hero must undertake a vision quest in order to achieve this kind of mentality or *noos* (1.3) and then he must experience a successful return or *nostos* (1.5). In other words, the epic hero must experience a "journey of a soul" (Nagy 1990c: 231–2).

The fact that ancient Greek heroes were worshiped could never be grasped on the sole basis of the everyday usage of the English word "hero," even though it was borrowed from the Greek. In ancient Greek usage, on the other hand, *hērōs* regularly conveys the sense of "cult hero," not just "hero" in the everyday sense of English hero. So we must go beyond the word's ordinary levels of meaning in casual contemporary usage. We need to defamiliarize the English word, tracing it back to the semantics of ancient Greek *hērōs*.

In its historical context, the Greek word *hērōs* integrates the concept of the cult hero with the concept of the epic hero – as well as the tragic hero – in classical Greek traditions. From such an integrated perspective, we can see three basic characteristics of the *hērōs*:

(a) He or she is unseasonal.
(b) He or she is extreme – positively (for example, "best" in whatever category) or negatively (the negative aspect can be a function of the hero's unseasonality).
(c) He or she is antagonistic toward the god who seems to be most like the hero; antagonism does not rule out an element of attraction (often a "fatal attraction"), which is played out in a variety of ways. The sacred space assigned the hero in hero cult could be coextensive with the sacred space assigned to the god who was considered the hero's divine antagonist. In other words, god–hero antagonism in myth – including the myths mediated by epic – corresponds to god–hero symbiosis in ritual.

All three characteristics converge in the figure of the hero Herakles. His name *Hēraklēs*, "he who has the glory [*kleos*] of Hera" marks both the medium and the message of the hero. Our first impression is that the name is illogical: it seems to us strange that Herakles should be named after Hera, that his poetic glory or *kleos* should depend on Hera, since he is persecuted by her throughout his heroic life span. And yet, without this unseasonality, without the disequilibrium brought about by the persecution by Hera, Herakles would never have achieved the equilibrium of immortality – and the *kleos* that makes his achievements live forever in song.

At the core of the myth of *Hēraklēs* is the meaning of *hērōs* 'hero' as a cognate of *Hērā*, the goddess of seasonality and equilibrium, and of *hōrā*, a noun that actually means "seasonality" in the context of designating hero cult (as in *Homeric Hymn to Demeter* 265) (Nagy 1990a: 136, 1990c: 140). The unseasonality of the *hērōs* in mortal life leads to the *telos* or "fulfillment" of seasonality of immortal life in the setting of hero cult; the cult-epithet of Hera as *teleia* expresses this concept of "fulfillment."

Let us consider Herakles in light of the three heroic characteristics I listed earlier:

(a) He is made unseasonal by Hera.
(b) His unseasonality makes it possible for him to perform his extraordinary Labors. He also commits some deeds that are morally questionable. For example, he destroys Iole's city and kills her brothers in order to capture her as his bride, even though he is already married to Deianeira (Diod. Sic. 4.37.5). It is essential to keep in mind that whenever heroes commit deeds that violate moral codes, such deeds are not condoned by the heroic narrative.
(c) He is antagonistic to Hera throughout his life span, but he becomes reconciled with her through death; as we have seen, the hero becomes the "son" of Hera by being

reborn from her. As the hero's name makes clear, he owes his heroic identity to his *kleos* and, ultimately, to Hera. A parallel is the antagonism of Juno, the Roman equivalent of Hera, toward the hero Aeneas in Virgil's *Aeneid*.

The involvement of the concept of *kleos* in the typifying of Herakles as a cult hero is relevant to the fact that the same concept is involved in typifying Achilles as an epic hero in the Homeric *Iliad*. In the *Iliad*, *kleos* designates not only "glory" but also, more specifically, *the glory of the hero as conferred by epic*. In the *Iliad* (9.413), Achilles chooses *kleos* over life itself, and he owes his heroic identity to this *kleos* (Nagy 2003: 39–48). In other words, Achilles achieves the major goal of the hero: his identity is put on permanent record through *kleos*.

We find in the figure of Achilles the same three heroic characteristics that we found in figure of Herakles:

(a) He is unseasonal: in *Iliad* 24.540, Achilles is explicitly described as is *pan-a-(h)ôr-ios*, "the most unseasonal of them all." His unseasonality is a major cause for his grief, which makes him "a man of constant sorrow."

(b) He is extreme, mostly in a positive sense, since he is "best" in many categories, and "best of the Achaeans" in the Homeric *Iliad*; occasionally, however, he is extreme in a negative sense, as in his moments of martial fury. In war, the warrior who is possessed by the god of war experiences this kind of fury, which is typically bestial. For example, martial fury in Greek is *lussa*, meaning "wolfish rage." Comparable is the Old Norse concept *berserkr* and the Old Irish concept of *ríastrad*, "warp spasm" or "distortion."

(c) He is antagonistic to the god Apollo, to whom he bears an uncanny resemblance. When Patroklos stands in for Achilles, he displaces Achilles as his ritual substitute in the god–hero antagonism of Apollo–Achilles. At the moment when Patroklos dies, in *Iliad* 16.786, he is called "equal to a *daimôn*," a sign of his status as ritual substitute (Nagy 1979a: 143, 293).

The death of Patroklos is analogous to the death of an animal slaughtered at a sacrifice (Lowenstam 1981). Homeric poetry, with its staggering volume of minutely detailed descriptions of the deaths of warriors, can serve as a compensation for sacrifice itself (Nagy 1992: xii). Similarly in the Indic epic of the *Mahâbhârata*, death in war is equated with sacrifice (Hiltebeitel 1976).

Whereas the epic hero is generally shown as antagonistic toward the god who most resembles him – and the antagonism is most forcefully reciprocated by the corresponding god – the cult hero becomes conventionally reconciled in the ritual context of the actual cult. Beyond the patterns of god–hero antagonism in epic and of god–hero symbiosis in cult (see Chapter 7, by Louden), we find occasional narratives where both the antagonism and the symbiosis are accommodated, as in the story of Herakles' rebirth from Hera. There are parallels in Indian traditions, as in the stories about the Indian heroes Śiśupâla and Jarâsandha in the epic *Mahâbhârata*: the identities of these heroes become absorbed into the corresponding identities of their divine antagonists.

Finally, in one exceptional instance, the identities of god and epic hero are merged in the picturing of the poet who sings the epics of heroes. In *Il.* 9.189 Achilles is pictured as singing the *klea andrôn*, "glories of heroes," and accompanying himself to the lyre (Nagy 1990c: 201–2). In this picture we see the very image of Apollo's own self-accompanied performances. The god prefigures the hero who sings the glories of epic heroes, but the hero in turn prefigures the poet. Just as the poet who "quotes" the hero becomes the medium of the hero and thus becomes identified with him, so also the hero of epic becomes identified with the poet of epic (Nagy 2001c: xxx–xxxii; cf. Martin 1989; Reynolds 1995; Foley 1996).

FURTHER READING

On epic heroes in oral poetry in general, see especially Lord 1960 and 1991. For an application of the facts of hero cults to the study of the ancient Greek epic hero, see Nagy 1979a. A most incisive work on ancient Greek hero cults is Brelich 1958. On the ancient Greek epic hero beyond the Homeric *Iliad* and *Odyssey*, see Burgess 2001. On pre-Homeric models of epic heroes, see Davidson 1980. On themes of afterlife for the ancient Greek hero, see Dué 2001.

On early Roman models of epic heroes, see Dumézil 1980. On Near Eastern examples of epic heroes, Cross 1973 remains most useful; see also Hendel 1987a and 1987b.

On Gilgamesh as an "epic" hero, a most useful introduction remains Foster 2001. On the Indic epic hero, see Dumézil 1968/1986; also Hiltebeitel 1976 and McGrath 2004.

On the medieval Persian epic hero, see Davidson 1994 and Skjærvø 1998a and 1998b. On the Byzantine epic hero, see Jeffreys and Jeffreys 1986.

On Old Norse "epic" heroes, see Mitchell 1991. On Old Irish "epic" heroes, see Nagy 1985 and Ó Cathasaigh 1977.

CHAPTER SEVEN

The Gods in Epic, or the Divine Economy

Bruce Louden

The gods serve different purposes in different kinds of myths. They can embody natural forces in the physical world – and even the universe itself – or serve as figures of destiny, fertility, prophecy, etiology, moral instruction, and more. In epic poetry, which can contain within its framework almost any kind of myth, but emphasizes the heroic kind, how the gods are depicted is partly determined by their relationships to the hero (on whom see Chapter 6, by Nagy). In a given epic a small group of key deities are closely concerned with the hero, and either interact with him directly or influence his circumstances from a distance; these gods tend to play the biggest divine roles in a given epic. Other aspects of an epic's presentation of the gods depend on specific qualities of a particular epic plot that may or may not depend upon the hero. Epics tend to have thematic plots, and consequently the thematic organization of a given epic influences its depiction of the gods. An epic focusing on war, for instance, tends to depict the gods at war. We will here focus on the divine economies (from the Greek *oikonomia*, "management, government") of *Gilgamesh*, Homer's *Iliad* (at greater length than the others because of the problems it presents) and *Odyssey*, the *Aqhat*, Virgil's *Aeneid*, and the *Argonautica* of Apollonius Rhodius. My remarks are not intended to apply equally well to all other epics. I focus on the chosen texts both to keep discussion to a reasonable length and because my argument fits these epics best. Readers are invited to consult Chapters 15, 16, 21, 22, 25, and 33, by Noegel, Wyatt, Edwards, Slatkin, Nelis, and Putnam respectively, for specific comments on the gods in these epics. My emphasis will be on how the gods shape these epics as characters within their narratives; I will not attempt to, say, interpret the gods allegorically or to situate a given epic in a historical context and so interpret that epic's gods through the prisms of history and culture (though I seek no quarrel with those who pursue such approaches).

The Epic Triangle

Amid a diverse and populous immortal contingent, three particular deities, who can be envisioned as standing in a triangular relationship with the hero, tend to dominate the divine economy of a given epic. These three gods take part in three type-scenes that embody their specific relationships with the epic hero: the divine council, theophany, and divine wrath. A sky father figure (on whom see further Chapter 2, by Katz) presides over the divine council, which typically convenes to discuss the hero's fate (cf. the divine councils at Job 1: 6–12, 2: 1–6), though they may also convene for additional purposes. The sky father serves an executive function over the rest of the gods and supports the hero, but does not personally intervene on his behalf. A second deity more actively supports the hero, serving as his mentor, appearing in person to him in a theophany, and advising and aiding him in performing heroic deeds – often resulting in a case of "overdetermination," in which both god and mortal share responsibility for an event (Janko 1992: 3). A third deity has an opposite relationship to the hero, developing a divine wrath against him. This "epic triangle" is evocative of a legal configuration: the sky father serves as a judge over the hero, while the mentor deity can be seen as the hero's advocate or defense attorney, and the wrathful deity as a prosecuting attorney seeking punishment, or even the death, of the hero.

Gilgamesh and the *Odyssey* have similar divine economies, each with three principal gods forming the epic triangle around the hero. In *Gilgamesh* Anu is the sky father who convenes and presides over divine councils that concern the fate of the hero (I. 2, VII. 1). Shamash is the hero's mentor, or advocate, who appears in a theophany to Gilgamesh (V.1, VII.1; cf. I.5, "Shamash loves Gilgamesh") and advises him on heroic acts, while Ishtar, as a result of Gilgamesh's arrogance, conceives a divine wrath against him (VI. 3). We might schematize the relationship thus:

Anu (sky father;
presides over divine councils,
acts as judge)

Ishtar (wrathful;
acts as prosecutor)
        Shamash (mentor;
appears in theophany,
acts as advocate)

Gilgamesh (hero)

We might also note that Gilgamesh has a divine parent, the female goddess Ninsun; and that Siduri, who is often compared by scholars to Calypso (and/or Circe), gives him key advice (both discussed below, with Thetis). Enlil is another god whose wrath is directed at at Gilgamesh and Enkidu (VII.1).

The *Odyssey* has Zeus, Athena, and Poseidon for its epic triangle. Zeus, of course, is the sky father presiding over divine councils (1.26–95; 5.3–42, etc.); Athena, the god who mentors the hero, serves as his advocate and appears in theophany to him (1.48–62; 3.231; 7.18–78; 13.221–439; 16.157–76; 22.205–40); and Poseidon, owing to the *Odyssey*'s surprisingly complex chronology, is already enraged by Odysseus even before the poem has begun (1.20–1, 68–79; 5.282–96, 339–41; 8.565; 13.126–60). Our schema will look just like the one above:

Zeus (sky father;
presides over divine councils,
acts as judge)

Poseidon (wrathful;
acts as prosecutor)
        Athena (mentor;
appears in theophany,
acts as advocate)

Odysseus (hero)

Poseidon's wrath evolves for the same reason that Ishtar's and Anat's does: disrespect on the part of the protagonist. The reason for his wrath is often misunderstood. As Friedrich observes (1991), Odysseus is justified in blinding Polyphemos, Poseidon's son, but not justified in then claiming that Poseidon himself will not be able to heal Polyphemos' eye (*Od.* 9.525; further discussion in Louden 1999: 83–4). This is disrespectful to the god, if less blatantly so than Gilgamesh to Ishtar, Achilles to Apollo, and Aqhat to Anat. The *Odyssey* develops Poseidon's divine wrath so deliberately that it even uses a specific verb, πλάζω (*plazó*: "to strike, drive") to denote it. The verb occurs in the active voice when a god, usually Poseidon, is its subject (as at 1.75, 24.307), but in the passive when a mortal (usually Odysseus) is the subject (as at 1.2; 5.389; 8.573; 9.81, 259; 16.64; for further discussion see Louden 1999: 71–90). We will return below to other aspects of the *Odyssey*'s divine economy.

The *Iliad* also suggests the epic triangle in its thematic references to the myth of Herakles. Several inset narratives about Herakles again feature Athena, as in the *Odyssey*, as the deity who offers aid to the hero (especially at *Il.* 8.362–5; cf. 20.146), personally intervening on his behalf, and Zeus as the sky father, ruler of the other gods; here, however, it is Hera who famously harbors a divine wrath against the hero (as at *Il.* 15.26–7). Moreover, in Herakles' case Zeus is rather less than impartial, taking a more interested, more biased, and occasionally more active role in the struggles of his special son (*Il.* 15.29–30).

But the *Iliad*'s divine economy is more complex than those of the *Odyssey* and *Gilgamesh*. The few key factors that complicate its plot are: (1) Hektor functions as a second hero who generates his own epic triangle; (2) the poem contains frequent episodes of theomachy, or divine battle (virtually absent from *Gilgamesh*, the *Odyssey*, and the *Aqhat*); (3) Thetis is prominent (she is a central deity who is *not* part of the usual epic triangle, but serves as the hero's advocate in a way that is more maternal and less concerned with heroic acts); and (4) heroic parody is used extensively in figures such as Paris. In spite of these factors, the core of the *Iliad*'s divine economy forms the usual epic triangle around its hero Achilles. Zeus is again the sky father who convenes divine councils, and supports the hero without intervening directly on his behalf; Athena is the mentor who appears in theophany and advises the hero on heroic action; and Apollo is the deity who harbors wrath against the hero. As in *Gilgamesh*, the divine wrath results in the death not of the hero, but of his dear companion Patroklos. Achilles is also disrespectful, even abusive, in a face-to-face meeting with Apollo (*Il.* 22.15–20), as is Gilgamesh with Ishtar. The chronology differs, however: Apollo has already caused Patroklos' death (*Il.* 16.787–805), whereas Ishtar instigates the Bull of Heaven (*Gilg.* VI.3–VII.6), which will lead to Enkidu's death only after Gilgamesh is disrespectful to her.

But Apollo's wrath against Achilles is less a decisive factor in the present time of the *Iliad*. Part of the difference is one of sequence or position. As noted above, Poseidon is already angry with Odysseus before the *Odyssey* begins. His divine wrath looms large up through Book 13, but has less impact for the concluding books (14–24). (Virgil follows the *Odyssey* by also having Juno's wrath operative right from the beginning.) Indeed, in Book 1 of the *Iliad* Achilles helps defuse Apollo's wrath against Agamemnon and the Greeks through his resolution of the conflict between Agamemnon and Apollo's priest, Chryses. For a deity with a wrath against the epic hero, Apollo is uniquely self-controlled when compared with Ishtar, Poseidon, Anat, and Juno. He similarly refuses to take part in the theomachy (21.461–9). Apollo has no pre-existing reason for being angry with Achilles, except his divine knowledge that Achilles will slay Hektor and thus precipitate the fall of Troy. Interestingly enough, Homer does not exploit this possibility, as Virgil does with Juno's anger at Aeneas (whose descendants will sack her favorite city, Carthage); his wrath against Achilles surfaces only briefly (*Il.* 22.7ff., 24.32–54), and its full force is postponed until after the end of the poem, as is clear in Hektor's dying prophecy to Achilles about "that day when Paris and Phoibos Apollo destroy you, brave as you are, at the Skaian Gates" (22.359–60). Apollo will help slay Achilles, the analogue to Athena having helped Achilles slay Hektor (the two climactic instances of overdetermination in the myths of the Trojan War), but not within the *Iliad*. Other gods besides Athena support Achilles: we will discuss Thetis below, but we should remember as well that it is Poseidon's and Hera's concern for Achilles that prevents Apollo from acting against him earlier.

The *Iliad* affirms the triangular relationship around Achilles by replicating it more clearly around two of his surrogates, Diomedes and Patroklos. Diomedes' rampage in Book 5 is at one point held back by Apollo (5.437–44), but he later receives a theophany and full support from Athena (5.792 ff.), who had inspired him in Achilles' absence (5.1–8). In the funeral games in Book 23 Athena again helps Diomedes and Apollo obstructs him, which episode can be seen as a miniature of the poem's epic triangle: Diomedes (who at 23.357 is again the "best of the Achaeans") winning the chariot race with Athena's aid, despite Apollo's divine anger (23.383). On the other hand, Patroklos, the other substitute for Achilles, receives the fullest force of Apollo as the deity with a divine wrath. Foreshadowing Athena's role in the death of Hektor, here the angry Apollo helps cause the death of the hero (16.788–93), even the death of one later called the "best of the Achaeans" (17.689). Apollo's wrath against Patroklos – one scholar (Janko 1992: 312) has claimed that "Apollo's final intervention against Patroklos is the most terrifying scene in the *Iliad*" – springs from his implicit disrespect of Apollo in presuming to attack Troy, and his arrogance in wearing Achilles' divine armor. Achilles warns him specifically about Apollo's likely anger on the former point (16.91–4), but not regarding the armor. Patroklos' slaying of Sarpedon, a son of Zeus, is a further act of arrogance by a mortal, though not necessarily arrogance directed at Apollo (cf. Arruns' slaying of Camilla at *Aen.* 11.759 ff.).

But, in the first complication the *Iliad* imposes on this governing triangle, Books 8–15 treat Hektor as a principal hero who enjoys the favor of Zeus. Consequently the *Iliad* also depicts an epic triangle for Hektor: the same three deities, in fact, but with the positions of Apollo and Athena reversed. Athena is now the wrathful god opposed to the hero, and Apollo is the mentor-figure who aids him. There are further significant differences, however, between Hektor's and Achilles' triangles. First, Zeus has a more active role. He does not merely preside over divine councils but personally intervenes on Hektor's behalf (8.75–7; cf. Zeus' errand for Apollo at 15.220–62). Zeus does not directly intervene to help Achilles (though his direct intervention for Hektor amounts to *indirect* intervention on Achilles' behalf), nor, for that matter, does he directly assist Odysseus in the *Odyssey*. Second, unlike Apollo's wrath against Achilles, Athena's anger has mortal consequences in the *Iliad*, leading directly to Hektor's death in Book 22. The contrast between these triangles is driven home when Apollo, who has offered Hektor significant aid from time to time (especially at 15.59–63, 220–62), deserts Hektor (22.213) when the hero needs him most.

Though a heroic figure, Hektor is an alien to the composer (tellingly, Hephaestus, the deity most like the composer, sides with the Greek cause) and to the original audience of the poem. As a member of a community who has collectively offended a number of the gods (21.441–57), including Zeus, Hektor *will* go down in defeat, unlike Achilles, Odysseus, Gilgamesh, or Aeneas. He is a defeated, not a victorious, epic hero. Athena's function prevails, and Apollo largely steps aside for Book 22. One of the reasons, at the divine level, for Hektor's failure is that Athena's function as the deity opposed to the hero is buttressed by Hera, a second wrathful deity. Hera is not so much opposed to Hektor as to the Trojans as a whole (here we look ahead to Juno's wrath in the *Aeneid*). Finally, the *Iliad*'s twice-occurring epic triangle is commemorated in a formula, αἲ γάρ, Ζεῦ τε πάτερ καὶ ᾿Αθηναίη καὶ ᾿Απολλον ("Father Zeus and Athena and Apollo": 2.371; 4.288; 7.132; 16.97; cf. *Od.* 4.341; 7.311; 17.132; 17.235; 24.376), reinforcing the idea that this is the default epic triangle, whatever the particular alignments, within Homeric epic.

Theomachy

Though common enough in myth as a whole, theomachy – the gods warring against each other – is less frequent in epic (I classify Hesiod's theomachian *Theogony* as creation myth and hymn to Zeus rather than epic, but see Chapter 23, by Nelson). Of the six epics under consideration only the *Iliad* makes significant use of theomachy, and it does so out of thematic concerns absent from the other epics. The *Iliad* is constructed around two strifes, the larger conflict between Greeks and Trojans, and the inner conflict that develops between Achilles and Agamemnon. The *Iliad*'s divine economy echoes both of these human conflicts. The quarrel of Achilles and Agamemnon finds a divine parallel in Hera's resisting and contesting Zeus' executive function, while Athena's defeat of Ares (5.793–867; 21.391–414) thematically parallels the Greeks' war against, and imminent victory over, the Trojans, particularly the Achaeans' duels with Hektor (Books 7 and 22).

There are two essentially different types of theomachy, a serious type set in the distant past, often before mortals yet exist, and while the gods are still jockeying for power; and a comic type, set in the present, with lower stakes. Both of the *Iliad*'s two sets of theomachies, Hera's rebellion against Zeus and Athena's defeat of Ares, are of the comic present-time type. But the *Iliad* also includes inset narratives that suggest the other, serious, kind of theomachy. In these retrospective incidents Zeus is presented as in danger of being defeated (1.393–412; 15.18–24; see also 15.78–149), a situation reminiscent of the divine power struggles in the *Theogony*. Most important of these for the *Iliad*'s plot is the occasion when Thetis aided him long ago (1.396–406), thus securing his present favor in the opening book of the poem. Readers of the *Iliad*, ancient and modern, have often confused the two types, and mistakenly assume Zeus is in real danger of being defeated by other gods in the present time of the *Iliad*, ignoring Poseidon's declaration that Zeus' power is now unchallenged (*Il.* 8.210–11).

It is worth observing that the *Iliad* imposes theomachian relationships on many of the gods that they probably do not have outside of the poem. (The Homeric Hymns offer glimpses of their more typical relationships, in which they usually get along with each other.) Within the *Iliad* the full present-time theomachies are confined to Books 5 and 20–1. Unexpectedly, the inverted modality of the middle books (8–16, in which the Trojans achieve temporary advantage over the Greeks) removes some of the theomachian elements (other than the friction between Zeus and Hera) and allows a more typical view of the gods' relations with each other. Athena's apparent sisterly concern for Ares (15.113–42) parallels Anat's concern for Baal in Ugaritic myth, and Aphrodite and Hera also get along (14.188–224) better than in the early or late books.

Hera's rebellion against Zeus requires further comment. At various times in the *Iliad* she attempts to replace Zeus atop Achilles' epic triangle. The strife between the king and queen of the gods lacks the violence that characterizes Athena's defeat of Ares, Hephaestus' of the river-god Xanthos (which, as an elemental conflict, reverts to the serious, retrospective type of theomachy, and is evocative of a creation myth or hymn), or the catfights between Athena and Aphrodite (21.417–34) and Hera and Artemis (21.470–96). Rather, Hera employs deception, a theme that characterizes much of the middle books of the *Iliad* (e.g. the spy missions in Book 10, Patroklos' wearing Achilles' armor in Book 16). In spite of the sex comedy, the stakes are higher here than in the violent confrontations between the other gods, because unlike those other gods, Hera contests Zeus' executive function and temporarily usurps it. Moreover, her predilection for authority is revealed elsewhere by how frequently she delegates other deities to perform her will.

The *Iliad* employs this dynamic as a theme early on (1.195) when it is Hera, not Zeus, who sends Athena to contain Achilles' anger at Agamemnon, and who again dispatches Athena to prevent the Greek flight (2.155–6) after Agamemnon tests the troops. In fact, Zeus' very first words in the poem point to Hera's potential to resist his decrees (1.518–19). Hera goes on to suborn Iris without Zeus' knowledge (18.168), and, during the poem's main theomachy, orders Hephaestus to attack Xanthos (21.328ff.). In Book 14, she usurps Zeus' executive function outright. As a prelude to seizing power she again serves an executive function by sending Hypnos to incapacitate Zeus. Hera's seizing power thus results both in temporarily turning the battle in the Greeks' favor and in the temporary incapacitation of Hektor (parallel thematically to Hera's incapacitation of Herakles at 15.26–8). Hera also takes the leading role in the divine consultation at 16.431–61, where she, not Zeus, makes the dominant suggestion regarding how to act, and Zeus follows her (16.458). This is a complete reversal of most divine councils in Homeric and other epic. However, her own approach to the executive function is portrayed as too partisan and extreme to be stable. The executive function usually arbitrates and seeks a balance between opposed divine forces (as Zeus achieves at *Il.* 24.65–76; cf. *Od.* 12.377–88; 13.128–45), and does not itself occupy an extreme position.

Because of their diametrically opposed roles in the two triangles we might expect Athena and Apollo to confront each other in a theomachy in the *Iliad*. Athena does refer contemptuously to Apollo as groveling before Zeus (*Il.* 22.220–1), but she has no face-to-face confrontation with him. But the opposed deities, the mentor and the wrathful, do not confront each other in any of the epics under discussion in this chapter. Instead the sky father (as judge of the legal triangle) mediates and adjudicates, ensuring that each of their competing or conflicting perspectives is respected.

Athena: The Narrative Functions of the Mentor Deity

Athena is the only deity besides Zeus to appear not only in all three epic triangles in Homer (for Achilles, Odysseus, and Hektor), but in Herakles' triangle as well (cf. her close relationships with other heroes: Tydeus, alluded to at *Il.* 5.826, and Telemachus, in the opening books of the *Odyssey*). This suggests that Athena possesses a uniquely important role in ancient Greek epic and its divine economy. As noted earlier, Zeus supports the epic hero, but does not act on his behalf. Instead, Athena is the divine actor or agent, expressing and embodying his will, while Zeus, almost like the Ugaritic El, rarely acts or intervenes himself, except to thunder and hurl lightning once in each epic (*Il.* 8.75–7; *Od.* 12.415; this is also Yahweh's favorite heroic deed; cf., e.g., 1 Sam. 7: 10; Ps. 46: 6). He does, however, act in ways that harm those around the hero, for instance when he slays the crew who profane Helios' cattle in the *Odyssey* (12.415). Zeus – again, like El – prefers to allow the younger generation of gods to execute the plot. Of this younger generation of divine actors, Athena is the one Zeus seems to admire and trust the most.

Athena mediates between Zeus and the epic protagonist, embodying (and expressing) the divine will toward the hero. Partly as a result of her acting in place of Zeus, Athena serves as a divine version of the epic protagonist in each poem, having Achillean characteristics in the *Iliad*, but Odyssean qualities in the *Odyssey*. Thus in the *Iliad* she defeats Ares by a neck wound (21.406), just as Achilles will slay Hektor by wounding him in the neck (22.324–6). In the *Odyssey*, on the other hand, she is more likely to use disguise and spin lengthy narratives (as at 1.105–318; 13.221–99). Each epic has her working closely in tandem with the protagonist, a relationship occasionally signaled grammatically by the use of the dual number to describe her teamwork with Achilles and Odysseus (*Il.* 22.216–8, 446; *Od.* 13.372–3). Furthermore, the climax of each epic is an instance of overdetermination, accomplished by Athena and the respective protagonist: Achilles' slaying of Hektor in *Iliad* 22, Odysseus' slaying of the suitors, which is jointly planned (*Od.* 13.375ff.) and jointly executed (22.233–309). Athena briefly (and grimly) parodies these functions when she deceives Hektor as he is about to face Achilles, encouraging Hektor to take a joint stand with "her," as she pretends to be his brother, Deiphobos (*Il.* 22.231). Below, in a comparison with the Ugaritic goddess, Anat, we will reconsider Athena's deception of Hektor, and of Pandaros (at *Il.* 4.88–104), in the comparative light of Anat's treatment of Aqhat.

Thetis and Ninsun, Calypso and Circe

Though not part of the *Iliad*'s epic triangle, Thetis plays a key role as Achilles' divine parent, confidante, and source of prophecy. In much of this she looks back, to Ninsun in *Gilgamesh*, and ahead, to Venus in the *Aeneid*. In the single most distinctive feature of the *Aeneid*'s divine economy, Virgil essentially makes Venus part of the epic triangle and dispenses with Minerva; we will consider this below. First, Ninsun: all of Thetis' central functions are predicted by Ninsun's role in *Gilgamesh*. Gilgamesh's divine mother, the goddess Ninsun, meets with him (I.5–6, III.1–4), discusses his impending encounters with Enkidu and Humbaba, and worries about his risking his life (III.2–5). As a goddess, she also interprets his dreams, a counterpart to Thetis' relaying prophecies to Achilles and warning him about the implications of his duel with Hektor. Thetis' prominence, a further Iliadic complication beyond the traditional triangle, partly obscures Athena's more typical epic role as Achilles' mentor. There is some overlap in Thetis and Athena's dual roles as Achilles' confidante (though even Hera and Poseidon briefly have this function), but the poem carefully signals Athena's primary role as mentor by giving her the first theophany (1.194), and employing a climactic instance of the same when she oversees Achilles' slaying of Hektor (22.214). (On the role of divine mothers in epic poetry, see Chapter 8, by H. Foley.)

Thetis' functions in the *Iliad* suggest broad structural parallels with Calypso and Circe in the *Odyssey*. All are goddesses outside the Olympic pantheon who have intimate interactions with the hero, but are less involved with his actions as a warrior than is typical of deities such as Athena or Apollo. But in the thematic way of epic the *Odyssey*'s presentation of Circe and Calypso is affected by plot concerns specific to the *Odyssey*. The poem has a thrice-repeated sequence of Odysseus landing on an island and carefully approaching and negotiating with a powerful female figure who holds power over his access to the next stage of his homecoming (for fuller discussion see Louden 1999: 4–14, 104–29; see also Chapter 8, by H. Foley on women in epic generally). The *Odyssey*'s presentation of Circe is largely shaped by this overriding concern. She is one of a series of females (including his wife, Penelope, and the Phaeacian queen Arete), who impose tests on Odysseus, and, when he passes their tests, help him advance ever closer to his *nostos*, or homecoming. Calypso, on the other hand, though readers often lump her together with Circe, is presented as a deliberate antitype to Circe (and to Penelope and Arete), a female who desires Odysseus without imposing tests upon him, who does not want to help him leave. Odysseus has sex with both Calypso and Circe, but again, with almost opposite effect. The *Odyssey* alludes to a lengthy sexual relationship between Odysseus and Calypso, but to only one occasion when Odysseus and Circe have sex. When Odysseus wishes to leave Calypso attempts to detain him, but Circe immediately tells him how to leave. Thetis' sexuality, meanwhile, is treated very differently, but does indirectly affect the protagonist, Achilles. The *Iliad* merely alludes to Thetis' sexual desirability to Zeus, instead presenting his acquiesence to her request as dependent upon her role in an earlier, serious, theomachy (1.396–406). Calypso and Thetis share an additional feature: both have an important blocking effect on the overall plot; each helps to remove the protagonist from the main storyline, thus stalling its progression in his absence. When Thetis gets Zeus to accede to Achilles' request, it results in his being essentially missing from action in Books 2–17. Calypso likewise keeps Odysseus on her remote isle for seven years.

Parody in Aphrodite and Ares

In the *Iliad*, Aphrodite's relations with Aeneas replicate Thetis' role as the goddess mother of the special hero. Although the relationship of Aphrodite and Aeneas is never depicted as intimately as Thetis' with Achilles, Aphrodite's rescue of Aeneas (5.312), together with that hero's special destiny (discussed below), establish Aphrodite as the same basic type. But in her relations with Paris, which the *Iliad* prefers to develop at greater length and in much greater detail than her relations with Aeneas, Aphrodite functions as a parody of Athena's mentor role. Aphrodite's relationship with Paris, himself a highly ironic and parodic figure, is essentially a parody of Athena's relationship with Achilles; she gives him divine aid to help him succeed in his endeavors, as Athena does Achilles. All four of Aphrodite's appearances in the *Iliad* have a parodic modality. When she rescues Paris in Book 3 and deposits him in his fragrant bedroom (3.382) instead of elsewhere on the battlefield (as Poseidon does with Aeneas at 20.328), the implicit meaning is hard to miss: Paris is a champion in the bedroom, not on the battlefield. Similarly (in the *Iliad*, at least), Aphrodite is a goddess of the bedroom, not of the battlefield. When Aphrodite then disguises herself as a maid to bring Helen to Paris, the couple have sex, while everyone else wonders where Paris is and what has become of his duel with Menelaos. In Books 5 and 21 Aphrodite is twice defeated: by Diomedes, a mortal, in the former, and by Athena, in a one-sided theomachy, in the latter. While her defeats thematically parallel the overall Trojan defeat, they also underscore her irrelevance to those heroic acts with which the *Iliad* is primarily concerned. Finally, Hera's visit to Aphrodite to borrow some allure (14.198) may allude to the Judgment of Paris (Janko 1992: 169, 185). Immediately before visiting Aphrodite, Hera dons a robe made by Athena (14.178–81). The episode thus involves, if indirectly, the same three goddesses who came before Paris.

The *Odyssey* maintains Aphrodite's association with parody, though using satire of a different sort. The Phaeacian bard Demodokos' song about Hephaestus, Aphrodite, and Ares (*Od.* 8.266–366) is patterned on the *Odyssey*'s plot, and parodies Odysseus' relationship with Penelope, casting Odysseus as Hephaestus (more on this below) and Ares as the suitors. So far the parallels work well, but Aphrodite, instead of serving as a parallel for Penelope, is instead an outrageous parody of Penelopean fidelity. Virgil, however, completely rehabilitates her, replacing her highly active sexuality with her role as *genetrix*, or foundress (anticipating Christianity's treatment of Mary, mother of the hero who is to found a new empire).

Much like Aphrodite, Ares is treated in Homeric epics with considerable parody. In general he embodies the chaos and fury of war, but not strategy or victory, which Homeric epic consistently associates with Athena; she is "the concomitant of success" (Hainsworth 1993: 229). Divine conflicts that parallel the heroic duels of mortal warriors are, in the *Iliad*, the climactic type of theomachy, reserved for the awesome *aristeiai* of Diomedes and Achilles. Athena's defeat of Ares is the central such encounter, foreshadowing and embodying the outcome of the war itself. In both poems, in fact, Ares is the thematic divine loser. In the *Iliad* he is soundly defeated not only by Athena (21.391–414), but by a mortal, Diomedes (5.792–867), and, in a retrospective account, by the giants Ephialtes and Otos (5.385–91). In the *Odyssey*, in Demodokos' second song, he is defeated by Hephaestus (who is hardly a heroic figure) and publicly humiliated before the other gods (8.296ff.). In the *Iliad* he is closely identified with the Trojans, and embodies their more negative characteristics. Zeus proclaims him the most hateful of all the Oympian gods (*Il.* 5.890). In the *Odyssey* he is associated with the suitors by virtue of his adulterous role in Demodokos' song. Some of Ares' association with defeat suggests intriguing parallels with Baal, the Ugaritic war and storm god, whom Anat rescues. We earlier noted that Athena's concern for Ares, including her counseling of him at *Iliad* 15.113–42, is very close to Anat's sisterly concern for Baal in the *Baal Cycle*. Though not the figure of parody that Ares is, Baal, the vigorous storm god, is nonetheless temporarily defeated more than once by his brothers, Yamm (Ocean) and Mot (Death), and would not survive without the intervention of Anat. It is intriguing, then, that in one of his key moments of defeat, Ares is compared in a simile to a storm (*Il.* 5.864–7), thus combining two of Baal's key characteristics.

Epic Boundaries

Heroic myths delineate mortality by reference to the three planes of existence: the earth's surface, the proper sphere of mortals; the heavens, associated with the gods and eternity; and the underworld, the place of death. An epic plot typically visits or invokes, directly or indirectly, all three planes, and the epic hero partakes of each plane of existence. Hades appears briefly in each Homeric epic as an instantiation of the underworld, and as part of an ancient motif also present in *Gilgamesh*: the threatened inversion of the proper relations between the living and the dead. When he lends *gravitas* to the start of the theomachies at *Il.* 20.61–6, the episode articulates an ancient motif: a god concerned that the nether regions will be visible to all, and thus potentially invert the positions of the living and the dead. As the gods prepare to fight each other, Hades fears that Poseidon will break open the earth and reveal the underworld for all to see, making even the gods shiver. In the *Odyssey*, the sun-god Helios, enraged when Odysseus' crew profane his cattle, threatens to go down and shine in Hades (*Od.* 12.383). In *Gilgamesh*, an angry Ishtar threatens to turn her face to the infernal regions and raise up the dead, so that they may eat the living (VI.3; Dalley 1989: 129, n. 62 notes that the same formulaic threat occurs in both the *Descent of Ishtar* and *Nergal and Ereshkigal*). Each episode threatens the order of the cosmos with a rupturing of the usual boundaries between the three planes of existence: the heavenly gods, earth-bound mortals, and the subterranean dead. In the *Odyssey* and *Gilgamesh* scenes the heavenly fathers, Zeus and Anu, explicitly mediate the threat, acting in a conciliatory manner to placate the angry deity. In the *Iliad*, Zeus implicitly supervises the goings-on and thus contains the threat (20.22–3). In much the same way that he rehabilitates Homer's weak Aphrodite into the *Aeneid*'s more assertive Venus, so Virgil will also rehabilitate the realm of Hades in his presentation of Elysium (*Aen.* 6.637ff.), and again present the ancient inversion of the proper relations between the living and the dead.

Hermes is the ultimate boundary-crosser. He has the distinction of being the only god to visit all three planes of existence. In both Homeric epics he is present at the heavenly councils with Zeus. In the *Odyssey* he not only descends to the underworld as psychopomp ("escort of souls;" 24.1ff.), but retrospectively is present both on Circe's island Aiaia – which itself has underworld associations – and on Calypso's island, Ogygia, which has paradisiacal associations. Hermes is not a heroic figure, which probably accounts for his not having larger roles in the Homeric epics. In Ugaritic myth, too, the herald gods are at a lower level in the divine hierarchy, and this rank is implicit in the Homeric Hermes, especially when compared to, say, Athena or Apollo.

Hermes is further distinguished as the Olympian who most enjoys the company of mortals (see *Il.* 24.334–45), which reflects both his status as the god of heralds and his secondary status among the gods themselves. Homeric epic particularly associates him with ironic charm and deceit; two examples are his encounter with Priam (*Il.* 24.352ff.) and his intervention with Odysseus (*Od.* 10.277ff.). In addition to Hephaestus (discussed below), a number of supernatural beings complete the Homeric divine economy: second-ary helper-figures, such as Iris, Dione, Kharis, Eidothea, and Leukothea; earlier gods, such as Okeanos and Tethys; immortal monsters such as Scylla and Charybdis; negative ab-stractions, such as Ate ("Ruin") and Eris ("Strife"); and the rivers, both those summoned to the great divine council in *Iliad* 20 and the Phaeacian river god to whom Odysseus prays (*Od.* 5.445–50).

Hephaestus, Mediating between Composer and Hero

Much as Athena can be seen to mediate between Zeus and the hero in Homeric epic, so Hephaestus serves a significant function, mediating between the *composer* and the Hom-eric protagonist. Let us begin with the protagonist. Like Athena, Hephaestus is portrayed as possessing qualities that associate him with Odysseus in the *Odyssey*, but that also associate him with Achilles in the *Iliad*. In Demodokos' song, Hephaestus triumphs over his opponent, Ares, by means of trickery and deception in his fashioning of a bed (*Od.* 8.275–81); Odysseus, in the poem's crucial reunion scene, is also depicted as having fashioned a bed (*Od.* 23.184–201). In a similar vein, the poor shape of Odysseus' legs (*Od.* 8.231–33) is a point of emphasis suggestive of Hephaestus' crippled limbs (*Od.* 8.300, 349, 357). In the *Iliad* Hephaestus, while fashioning Achilles' new armor, wishes that it may keep the hero safe from death (*Il.* 18.464–7). The participle used at *Il.* 18.479 to describe Hephaestus at work (δαιδάλλων, "intricately working") recurs elsewhere in Homeric epic only of Odysseus fashioning his bed (*Od.* 23.200). As Richardson (1993: 82) notes, the epithet πολύμητις ("cunning") is used exclusively of Odysseus in Homeric epic, except once of Hephaestus (*Il.* 21.355). An underexplored figure, Hephaestus may once have occupied a position of greater importance than he does in our version of the Homeric epic, much as Slatkin (1991) has suggested appears to be the case with Thetis.

Hephaestus has much in common with the bard in Homeric epic. The epithet περικλυτός ("renowned") is used almost exclusively of Hephaestus (e.g., *Il.* 1.607; 18.383) and of bards (e.g., *Od.* 1.325; 8.83). Many of the Odyssean parallels between Hephaestus and Odysseus occur within the song of Demodokos, who is not only a bard but also the figure in Homeric epic traditionally associated with Homer by ancient biographical criticism. Like Hermes, Hephaestus is a god of lesser status, a contractor, if you will, who mainly does work for other gods. In some respects, his position of fashion-ing elaborately structured works of art for the gods is analogous to the position of the epic singer fashioning elaborate narratives for heroes and kings, patrons and audiences. When Hephaestus creates a new shield for Achilles (*Il.* 18.478–608), he also, like a bard, creates a well wrought narrative. The *Iliad*'s detailed portrait of a divine craftsman at work on an intricately fashioned shield has as its final image "a divine singer, playing the lyre" (18.604–5). Though these lines have often been suspected as a later addition to the poem, Edwards (1991: 231) notes that other scholars, including Schadewalt and Rein-hardt, regarded them as authentic, and as a representation of Homer. Thus the epic poet may have himself identified with Hephaestus.

The Ugaritic *Aqhat*

Aqhat, a Ugaritic epic, also makes use of an epic triangle, positioning the gods El and Baal and the goddess Anat around the titular hero. In Ugaritic, as in much Old Testament myth, El is the sky father, judge, and creator of gods and mortals. From a Greek perspective he combines aspects of Zeus and Kronos (Zeus' father, imprisoned by him in the Underworld). Baal, a younger male deity, is that typically Near Eastern combination of storm and war god, combining some of Ares' and some of Zeus' functions in Homeric epic. Anat, an impetuous young warrior goddess, displays particularly close parallels with the Homeric Athena. As the myth begins, Aqhat is not yet born. Danel, his father, asks the gods to pity him by granting him a son. Baal then intervenes with El on Danel's behalf, asking that his wish be granted, much as Athena intervenes for Odysseus at *Odyssey* 1.48ff., and as Venus does for Aeneas in the *Aeneid*. Later, in a telescoping of time uncharacteristic of Homeric epic, Danel's wish having long ago been granted, his son, Aqhat, is now a man, and has received a special bow, made and given by Kothar, the Ugaritic equivalent of Hephaestus (see Morris 1992: 79–101). The goddess Anat desires the bow and approaches Aqhat, offering him first wealth, and then, when he rejects that, eternal life. While commentators have long noted parallels with Gilgamesh's rejection of Ishtar (*Gilg.* VI.1–3), other Homeric and Old Testament parallels are also suggestive (on epic elements in the Old Testament see Chapter 19, by Niditch). A mortal offered valuable choices over his life suggests the Judgment of Paris, and especially Solomon's dream, in which he is offered two of the same things Anat offers Aqhat (1 Kgs. 3: 4–15).

Aqhat rejects her offers, both times disrespectfully. He first suggests that Anat herself take the wood and other ingredients to Kothar for him to make her a bow. To her offer of eternal life he arrogantly responds that women have no place with archery (cf. Diomedes' vaunt to Aphrodite at *Il.* 5.348–9, and Zeus' remark at 5.428) – a face-to-face insult to a powerful goddess. An enraged Anat first consults with El, much as Ishtar does with Anu (*Gilg.* VI.3–4), and as both Helios and Poseidon do with Zeus (*Od.* 12.375–88, 13.127–59; cf. Athena with Zeus at *Od.* 24.473–6). For the *Aqhat*, then, we have the following triangle:

El (sky father,
presides over divine councils,
judge)

Anat   Baal
(wrathful, prosecutor)   (mentor, advocate)
Aqhat (hero)

Baal intervenes originally to help Danel, and his support clearly extends to Aqhat, for he helps recover the body after Anat causes Danel's death. Athena's tendency to help Telemachus and Diomedes, sons of fathers she also champions, perhaps helps to bring Baal's helping Danel and his son Aqhat into focus.

Anat's role in engineering the death of Aqhat, as well as a unique episode in the *Baal Cycle*, suggest a bloodthirsty nature that commentators tend to find troubling in a deity. In the *Baal Cycle*, Anat is depicted as striding knee-deep in the blood of warriors she has slain, and wearing their heads in a belt around her waist (KTU 1.3 II). But the Homeric Athena is similarly depicted. A repeated setpiece attributes comparable, if less graphic, violence to Athena:

She ascended the gleaming chariot, and seized her spear, heavy, great, and stout, with which she subdues the ranks of heroes, those at whom her mighty father is angry.

(Il. 5.745–7 = 8.389–91; cf. Od. 1.99–101)

Prior to these lines Athena is described as donning her aegis, about which she arranges Phobos ("Fear"), Eris ("Battle-strife"), Alkê ("Battle Prowess"), Iôkê ("Rout"), and the terrifying Gorgon's head (5.739–42). When Athena tells Odysseus how to proceed against the suitors, she declares that she "expects his boundless floor to be splattered with [the suitors'] blood and brains" (*Od.* 13.395). Commentators have found Anat cruel in luring Aqhat to his death, but Athena does the same thing to both Hektor and Pandaros. Anat's divine wrath against and deception of Aqhat are in fact particularly close to Athena's deceptive treatment of Hektor (*Il.* 22.227–300), in which she poses as his brother (Anat makes a similar claim to Aqhat), and, to a lesser extent, her instigation of Pandaros (who, like Aqhat, is an archer) to break the truce at *Iliad* 4.86–104. The poet earlier notes (2.827) that Apollo gave Pandaros his bow, which suggests an epic triangle around Pandaros, with Athena occupying the divine-wrath position, and Apollo serving as his mentor. After Pandaros is successful in breaking the truce, Athena herself guides the spear that slays him in the violence that shortly follows (5.290–6), much as she oversees Achilles' slaying of Hektor.

The *Aeneid*

Though firmly rooted in the tendencies we have thus far explored, in its use of the divine economy the *Aeneid* demonstrates considerable innovation on Virgil's part. In the scope of its plot (the founding of an empire hundreds of years in the future) and astonishing sweep of its prophecies (covering some 1200 years since the fall of Troy), the *Aeneid* uses some mythical elements more in the way that the Bible does than in the manner of the epics we have so far considered. Indeed, if the subgenres of myth at the heart of the *Aeneid* seem very biblical, that is because they are essentially the same as some of those occurring in the Old Testament from Exodus through the depiction of David. But at its core, the *Aeneid* still makes use of the epic triangle, marking thereby the influence of both the *Odyssey* and the *Iliad*. Three deities are central to the plot, Jupiter, Venus, and Juno, and they operate, for the most part, in the same three slots we have earlier observed.

Jupiter is the sky father, serving the executive function, largely supportive of Aeneas' endeavors, and able, at the slightest prodding, to launch into lengthy, detailed prophecies, both about Aeneas' own accomplishments and those of his myriad descendants. But as with Zeus and El, Jupiter refrains from personally intervening on Aeneas' behalf. Venus is the deity who personally intervenes on the hero's behalf, but she does so in a way that little suggests the heroic link that binds Shamash to Gilgamesh, and Athena to Achilles and Odysseus. Rather, Venus combines the functions of Athena and of Thetis in the *Iliad*. Juno, though again with some key differences, particularly in the cause and scope of her wrath, serves as the deity with a divine wrath against the hero. These three thus constitute a typical epic triangle at the heart of the *Aeneid*'s divine economy.

Venus represents the greatest innovation, in a number of respects. Gone is the Homeric Aphrodite's unbridled sexuality, and its attendant parodic modality. Also entirely absent is a heroic connection between Venus and Aeneas of the kind that exists in all four of the other epics we have considered. We have dropped our other two descriptors for the position she occupies in the triangle because she really does not appear in theophany to Aeneas, nor is she his mentor. She is his advocate, suggesting that the judicial dimension of the epic triangle is the strongest for the *Aeneid*'s divine economy. When she appears to her son at *Aen.* 1.314ff., she is disguised, just as Athena is disguised as Mentes before Telemachus (*Od.* 1.105–319) and as a girl drawing water on Skheria (*Od.* 7.19–78). These disguised appearances are not, strictly speaking, theophanies. The mortal is unaware that he is in the presence of a deity. The particular information Venus gives Aeneas is closest to that which Athena gives Odysseus on Skheria, for in the Phoenician Dido, Aeneas must carefully approach a foreign queen, much as Odysseus began his careful negotiations to persuade the Phaeacian queen Arete to help him return home. Though these are the closest Homeric analogues to Venus' appearance to Aeneas, we should recall that in the *Iliad* both Athena and Thetis appear to Achilles. Virgil would also seem to have in mind the larger structural parallel of Thetis' meeting with her son in the first book of the *Iliad*. But unlike Thetis, Venus here suppresses her larger knowledge of the future and prophecy, and instead shares with Aeneas knowledge of a much more immediate nature, as Athena does with Odysseus at *Od.* 7.19–78.

It is in the divine councils that Venus' larger functions become clear, as well as her parallels with Thetis and Ninsun. As goddess mothers, Thetis and Ninsun are privy to greater divine knowledge and use this information to advise their heroic sons, the former through prophecy, the latter by interpreting dreams. Venus does this at a distance, less for her son's benefit than for the reader's. In her councils with Jupiter she brings out the larger consequences of Aeneas' actions and thus gives shape to the uniquely historical dimension of the *Aeneid*, which, again, resembles Old Testament myth more than previous epic. In pre-Virgilian epic, the hero may or may not have a notably heroic son, but in either case that is about as far as the epic is concerned with his progeny. The *Aeneid*, by contrast, combines myths of patriarchs, such as are common in Old Testament myth (cf. Euripides' *Ion*), so that the hero will now be the father of a nation. Behind all of Aeneas' numberless progeny is the divine spark of Venus *genetrix*.

While Juno occupies the expected slot of the deity whose wrath the hero incurs, much as Poseidon does in the *Odyssey*, her animosity is directed not so much at Aeneas, personally, as at what she sees him as embodying or representing. Unlike Gilgamesh, Aqhat, or Odysseus, Aeneas has not given a deity any direct offense. Though contemporary readers may be less attuned to its implications, since we are not taught to seek moral instruction in such works, Aeneas is established as a moral man as far back as the *Iliad*. Poseidon, a Greek partisan, singles Aeneas out (20.297–9) as not sharing in the collective guilt that Troy has incurred from Laomedon's abuse of the gods (21.441–57) and Paris' violation of the sanctity of hospitality (3.351–4). Aeneas, in the *Iliad*, is a common mythic type we might designate as "the one just man," destined to survive a god-sent calamity, a type frequent in Old Testament myth (cf. Enoch at Gen. 5: 18–24, Noah at Gen. 5: 29–9. 29, Lot at Gen. 19, and Daniel at Ezek. 14: 14). Because of his morality, Aeneas is destined to survive the war (*Il.* 20.302–5) and the divine destruction of Troy and have numerous descendants, not unlike an Old Testament patriarch such as Abraham or Joseph.

More so than Poseidon in the *Odyssey*, the *Aeneid*'s Juno is a blocking figure, always ready to hurl obstacles in Aeneas' path. Her wrath seems based on a deliberately petty foundation, the Judgment of Paris and the eventual sack of Carthage – the latter to be performed by Aeneas' descendants, to be sure, but not for a millennium. Divine hostility of this sort is much closer to that which the New Testament and subsequent Christian myth locates in the Devil. In fact, Juno's methods in the *Aeneid* suggest strong parallels with powers and techniques commonly assigned to Satan. The second half of the *Aeneid* closely associates Juno with the underworld, and with the frightening powers thought to reside there. Juno herself opens the second half of the poem by asserting that "if I am unable to bend the will of the gods above, then I will put Acheron into motion" (7.312). Juno's tendency to have lesser divinities perform her bidding recalls Hera's theomachian tendencies in the *Iliad*. Juno goes on to summon the Furies to do her will. The dynamics here are quite similar to the New Testament notion of demons under the direction of Satan. In two of the Gospels, Satan enters into Judas as he is about to betray Christ (Luke 22: 3; John 13: 27). In Virgil's *Aeneid*, Allecto essentially enters into Amata (7.344ff.) with the result that the queen becomes the biggest blocking character in the *Aeneid*. Though traces of this behavior are found in the *Iliad*, in Hera's association with Ate (*Il.* 19.91–133), here too Virgil has considerably expanded the latent Homeric possibilities.

The *Argonautica*

We close with a brief consideration of the gods in Apollonius' *Argonautica*, which, though it antedates the *Aeneid*, is more innovative, and therefore "newer," particularly in its divine economy. The *Argonautica* begins by suggesting the epic triangle, for it quickly casts Hera in the slot of the hero's champion, a role the poem repeatedly assigns her. Thus it is Hera whom Phineus singles out as having aided the Argonauts (2.216–17), who makes Jason appear more attractive when he first meets Medea (3.922), sends helpful winds (4.241–2), and the like. In waiting over halfway through his epic to delineate Hera's reasons for supporting Jason (3.66–8), Apollonius may follow the *Odyssey*, which waits until Book 13 to articulate Athena's reasons for serving as Odysseus' mentor (13.296–310). The *Argonautica* departs from the other epics, however, in its treatment of the other two positions of the epic triangle.

Our previous epics generally make the gods' motivations obvious, whereas Apollonius tends to obscure, or at least postpone stating, their motivations, those of Zeus in particular. Apollonius presents us with a Zeus who never presides over a divine council and does not, in fact, occupy the executive position. Though there is occasional reference to "Zeus' plan," it is oblique by comparison with the god's designs in Homeric epic. We learn one fourth of the way through the poem, for instance – and through the sea-god Glaukos, not Zeus himself – that he does not want Herakles to accompany the Argonauts (1.1315ff.). In Book 2 we learn that Zeus blinded Phineus for revealing too much through his prophecies, which suggests a parallel in Apollonius' own technique (Feeney 1991: 60–1). Halfway through the poem (2.1194–5; cf. 3.337) we finally learn that Zeus is angry with the descendants of Aeolus over the attempted sacrifice of Phrixus, and that Jason's retrieval of the fleece will atone for this. But we do not learn any of this from Zeus himself, who remains remote throughout the poem.

It is Hera who also occupies the executive position, evident not only in her presiding over the divine council (3.7ff.), but in her tendency to dispatch other gods to perform her behests. But there is no suggestion that she is usurping Zeus' position and power, as in the *Iliad*'s theomachian presentation. Rather, it is Zeus' own remoteness that allows Hera to act so assertively. In Apollonius' treatment, Hera's own concerns have a larger impact on the myth's trajectory. Because of her anger with Pelias, she will see to it, if indirectly, that Medea travels to Greece to slay him. It is Zeus, on the other hand, who develops a hostility to Jason (4.558–61) over his role in the murder of Apsyrtus, whereas never in Homer, nor in *Gilgamesh*, the *Aqhat*, or the *Aeneid*, does the sky father become angry with the protagonist. Hera will cause storms in response (4.578), acting to direct or channel Zeus' wrath, much as Zeus does for Poseidon and Helios in the *Odyssey*.

An epic's divine economy parallels events on the mortal plane. Zeus tends to be figured in the *Argonautica* largely in ways that connect him to some of the poem's darker themes: sexual liaisons outside of marriage, for instance, and the violent means through which kings sometimes attain their position. The organizing allusion in this divine economy is to Hera's deception of Zeus in *Iliad* 14, the consummate episode of divine unfaithfulness.

Widespread allusion to Hera's deception allows Apollonius to comment obliquely on the problematic morality of Jason's relationship with Medea.

In a Zeus remote and finally wrathful, a Hera concerned with making Pelias pay, and an Eros with dominion over the world, Apollonius suggests a greater gulf between gods and mortals than is found in Homer. In this world mortals are less able to recognize the workings of the gods, and Hera's greater involvement conveys a fear that capricious gods may be using mortals to accomplish their own agendas.

FURTHER READING

In my view, acquaintance with the Ugaritic myths is invaluable for gaining a larger perspective and context for understanding a typical epic divine economy. Ugaritic myth has a full polytheistic conception that roughly parallels most of the central gods of Greek and Roman myth, and was the backdrop out of which later Israelite monotheism evolved. To this end, then, see first Chapter 16, by Nicolas Wyatt in this volume. Mark S. Smith's *The Origins of Biblical Monotheism* (2001) is invaluable, as is basic familiarity with the main Ugaritic myths, *The Baal Cycle* and *Aqhat*. Together, these provide the reader with larger contexts for analyzing the gods in the Homeric epics, *Gilgamesh*, the *Aeneid*, and Old Testament myth, in particular.

Robert Mondi's essay, "Greek mythic thought in the light of the Near East" (1990), is one of the most original and useful attempts to provide a Near Eastern context for Greek myth, bringing in Ugaritic and other Near Eastern myths and formulating original arguments about them. Martin West's *The East Face of Helicon* (1997b) pursues similar connections between Greek and Near Eastern myth on an even larger scale.

Other works also useful for exploring connections between various divine pantheons include Sarah Morris 1992; see also her article "The sacrifice of Astyanax" in Carter and Morris 1995: 221–45. Also recommended are Patrick D. Miller's *The Divine Warrior in Early Israel* (1973), Frank Moore Cross's *Canaanite Myth and Hebrew Epic* (1973), E. Theodore Mullen's *The Divine Council in Canaanite and Early Hebrew Literature* (1980), and Peggy Day's entry on "Anat" in the *Dictionary of Deities and Demons in the Bible* (van der Toorn et al. 1995).

CHAPTER EIGHT

Women in Ancient Epic

Helene P. Foley

In the first lines of the *Aeneid*, Virgil brings his Greek models, the *Iliad* and *Odyssey*, together by defining the parameters of heroic epic as *arma virumque cano*, "I sing of arms and the man." If the real subject of heroic epic is "kings and battles" (Virg., *Ecl.* 6.3) and more generally how to face life and death as a man and member of a community (army, band of heroes, city-state, republic, or empire) defined and dominated by men, where do women fit in? Roman poetry often creates an explicit contradiction between women and epic by insisting on the masculinity of epic as a genre in contrast to the focus on erotic and feminine matters in elegy, and then including these very erotic topics (especially women in love and male conflicts over women) in epic itself.

Yet ancient epics in fact contain a much broader range of important female figures, even if they must often act and speak from the margins of the male community. Women are both the passive and, in the case of Roman epic, increasingly the active cause of wars as well as its carefully delineated, sometimes explicitly sacrificial victims. Women play a critical role as objects of exchange between men for the purpose of procreation, pleasure, and alliance; at the same time, a woman imported from another household or country can prove unfaithful or untrustworthy. As keepers of men's households who can make decisions in their absence, wives in particular wield a dangerous power over men if they do not serve their husbands' interests or if they step out of designated female roles. Mothers, on the other hand, are often powerful supporters of their sons, serving as prophets, mediators, and sources of wisdom. As prominent mourners of the dead, women can mark the losses that men's heroic actions inflict on the community and provide a form of closure; indeed, although women tend to speak back to heroic values above all in this particular role as mourners, epic can endow them with other sorts of resisting or supporting voices as well. When a hero travels into the wider world beyond his community on a journey or quest, female figures play a major role as dangerous sexual predators and blockers, but also as necessary helpers, prophets, workers of magic, and forces of civilization. Goddesses are ubiquitous in similar roles within the male community as well. Unusual women warriors such as the barbarian Amazons actually make brilliant if short-lived forays into the battlefield itself. Occasionally women serve as significant leaders or even epic narrators.

This essay will select from a limited number of epics in order to delineate briefly some of the major roles of women in heroic epic and how they evolved over time, including

Gilgamesh, the Homeric *Iliad* and *Odyssey*, Apollonius Rhodius' Hellenistic *Argonautica*, Virgil's *Aeneid*, and its successors under the Roman empire, Lucan's *On the Civil War*, Valerius Flaccus' *Argonautica*, Statius' *Thebaid* and *Achilleid*, and Silius Italicus' *Punica*. These Greek and Roman epics, whether myth- or history-based, represent a continuous tradition focusing on the feats of kings and heroes. Given limits of space, I omit a large body of works in hexameter verse that the ancients would regard as epic poetry, such as the "Homeric" and other Hymns, the didactic and cosmological poems of Hesiod or Lucretius, or Ovid's mixed-genre *Metamorphoses*.

Blockers and Helpers

Ancient epics are full of goddesses, lesser divinities, and mortal females who facilitate heroic action, impede it, or both. The Gilgamesh epic is the first to establish the full range of female roles in this category (see Chapter 15, by Noegel). In *Gilgamesh*, the gods create a wild hairy man, Enkidu, as a companion to distract the unruly king Gilgamesh, who is abusing his citizens. The prostitute Shamhat is sent to seduce Enkidu, initiate him into the ways of sexuality and civilization, and lead him to the city. Although the dying Enkidu later turns angrily on Shamhat for separating him from nature and his life in the wilderness and for initiating him into mortality and complexity, the poem appears to present the kindly, maternal prostitute in positive terms, even if she cannot offer an entry into the higher levels of civilized life. Gilgamesh's mother, the goddess Ninsun, interprets her son's dreams and assists his quests. Later in the poem, other female figures play a facilitating role on Gilgamesh's journey to find the secret of immortality. The wise tavernkeeper Siduri helps Gilgamesh on his journey but advises him to accept mortality, give up his quest, and be content with wife and child and domestic life; the wife of the Scorpion man apparently persuades her husband to admit Gilgamesh to critical mountain passes; the immortal Utnapishtim's wife urges her husband to make sure that Gilgamesh does not depart empty-handed from the world beyond. These figures indirectly help Gilgamesh accept his mortality. After his return from the underworld, he resigns himself to mortal achievements: progeny and city-building.

Traditionally the goddess Ishtar, who mixed the erotic powers of Greek Aphrodite with the warrior skills of Greek Athena, became a symbolic bride to early Babylonian kings and offered them blessings, prosperity, and a link to the divine. Ishtar approaches Gilgamesh after his first heroic endeavor with Enkidu and offers to make him her consort. In contrast with earlier tradition, Gilgamesh rudely rejects her offer, citing her untrustworthy, uncivilized behavior, and her promiscuity with earlier consorts. The poem's perspective on Ishtar, who can indeed be a destructive goddess (she sends the Bull of Heaven to threaten the heroes), seems to reflect a shift from using her to support dynastic claims to divinity to an historically later view of the king as paradigm of humanity. Some scholars perceive a devaluing of the authority of goddesses and royal women in this narrative shift (Frymer-Kensky 1992: 77–9), as well as in the foregrounding of the partially eroticized male bonds between Gilgamesh and Enkidu over those between goddess and consort (Foster 1987). This episode anticipates the prominent role in Greek and Roman epic of complex and often ambivalent goddesses, lesser female divinities, and mortal women in alternatively seducing, threatening, or delaying heroes, and or in making their heroic success possible.

In the *Iliad* (see Chapter 21, by Edwards), the assertive alignment of the goddesses Hera and Athena with the Achaeans develops to the point that Hera even seduces her husband Zeus in order to distract him temporarily from the battlefield (14.188–223), while the warrior goddess Athena frequently fights at the side of her favorites. Athena plays a similar role in the *Odyssey* (see Chapter 22, by Slatkin), where she not only backs Odysseus in his battle against the suitors, but makes clear that her favorite's distinguishing characteristics – tricky intelligence, civilized diplomacy, even craftsmanship (exercised on his special bed) – are her own and thus explain her special support for him. Aphrodite (Roman Venus), goddess of erotic love, anticipates her later support of her Trojan son Aeneas in the *Aeneid* (see Chapter 33, by Putnam) by rescuing various Trojans, including Aeneas and Paris (whom she rewards because he pronounced her victorious in the beauty contest with Hera and Athena) on the *Iliad*'s field of battle. She forces Helen, who incarnates her erotic powers on earth, to return to Paris' bed in *Iliad* 3. Similarly, the powerful sea goddess Thetis actively intervenes at Troy to enhance the honor and glory of her all-too-mortal son Achilles. In epics about the voyage of the "Argo," all three Olympian goddesses offer active support to Jason and his companions in their quest for the golden fleece.

In the *Iliad*, Hera, motivated above all by the judgment of Paris against her, expresses the most relentless divine rage against the Trojans: she has the capacity to eat her enemies raw (4.31–6); she fiercely opposes the burial of Hektor; she is even willing to subject her favorite cities to future punishment from Zeus in order to defeat Troy (4.51–61). In Apollonius Rhodius (see Chapter 25, by Nelis), her desire to avenge herself on Jason's uncle and enemy Pelias motivates her persistent support of Jason (3.1134–6, 4.241–3). Juno (the Roman Hera) develops an even more insistent link with place and peoples – Carthage and native Italians (*Aeneid*), Argos (*Thebaid*) – and with the forces of terrifying and ultimately fruitless irrationality and historical resistance that threaten the building of the Roman empire. Hera's constant tensions with the king of the gods Zeus (often over his adultery with other females) may arise in Homer because of a loss of the prehistoric powers that once made her the central deity in various locations in Greece (O'Brien 1993); similarly, Juno was a goddess initially linked more heavily with Etruscans and native Italians than Romans (Feeney 1991: 149–51). In Valerius Flaccus (see Chapter 36, by Zissos), however, Juno is less vengeful (since she is ignorant of the future, she has no grand designs, 7.192), and her concern for Jason is more altruistic than in Apollonius. In Statius (see Chapter 37, by Dominik), she displays no malevolence and even actively helps the female relatives of the dead after the war between the Theban brothers Eteocles and Polynices in their quest to bury sons or husbands. Why these last two imperial epics domesticate Juno remains as yet an open question.

Lesser divine figures also play major roles, especially in Greek epic. During his journey home from Troy to Ithaca, Odysseus encounters numerous female figures: the Sirens who tempt him by offering all the knowledge embedded in epic poetry; the whirlpool Charybdis, who sucks boats into her vortex; the monstrous Scylla, who snatches sailors from ships to devour; the sea nymph Leucothea, who rescues Odysseus from drowning with a magic veil in *Odyssey* 5; and above all the nymphs Circe and Calypso, who hold Odysseus on their remote islands, locked in obscurity, through seductive care and sexuality, but in the end facilitate his journey. The more human of these figures, such as Circe and Calypso, possess a combination of physical allure and knowledge already embodied in a more powerful form in Ishtar. With the help of the god Hermes Odysseus can counter Circe's magic and her threat to unman him, but requires divine intervention to escape from Calypso's promise of immortal anonymity (her name means "the concealer"). Their islands embody the allure of a female world outside history and replete with physical pleasure that subordinates the eventually unwilling male to the female (Calypso) and threatens to reduce him to bestiality, as Circe does to all visitors to her island but Odysseus. For an epic hero to be excluded from history and poetic fame is a form of symbolic death.

Many of these figures reappear in later epics based on related Greek myths; Circe and her magic play a prominent role in both *Argonauticas* as a powerful and still dangerous aunt to her similar but more vulnerable niece Medea; in Apollonius she purifies Jason and Medea after their killing of Medea's brother at the offended Zeus's behest, but refuses further help and will not approve Medea's actions. Jason's men drown out the Sirens with the male poet Orpheus' music, whereas in the *Aeneid* Aeneas' men pass by both Circe and the Sirens, and thus the temptations and threats experienced by Odysseus, before arriving in Italy. Later epics include various other female threats such as the Harpies, winged females who continually pollute the banquets of Phineus on Thynea and are defeated by the Argonauts; forces of rage and vengeance often linked to the underworld such as the fury Allecto, who stirs up the native Italians against the Trojans at Juno's behest in *Aeneid* 7; and the furies Tisiphone and her sister in Statius, who rouse both sides in the war between the Theban brothers until they are outdone in ferocity by Polynices and Eteocles themselves (*Theb.* 11.537–8). These Roman furies are forces of pure disorder, unlike their Greek counterparts, who avenge crimes and the overstepping of human limits as part of a normative order.

At the same time, not all female figures on epic journeys, whether mortal or immortal, are as threatening or ambivalent. Odysseus' encounter with Phaeacian women literally reintroduces him to civilization. Princess Nausikaa accepts the naked and shipwrecked hero as a suppliant on the beach, reclothes him, and sends him off to a second suppliancy of her mother, queen Arete. After questioning the hero and apparently accepting that he is no threat to her daughter, Arete plays a role in insuring that Odysseus returns home with gifts. In Apollonius, both the Nereids and the nymphs of Libya rescue the "Argo" from disaster. In Virgil, the nymph Kymodokea (formerly a Trojan ship) warns Aeneas of attacks on his first camp in Italy (*Aen.* 10.219–48). Female figures also serve epic heroes as interpreters of the future. In addition to the goddesses Ninsun and Thetis, examples include: various Delphic priestesses from Homer to Lucan; the Roman matron in Lucan who under Apollo's influence envisions the future, replete with Pompey's headless corpse lying on the sands of Egypt, in Bacchic mode (*BC* 1.673–95); and a woman made prophetic by the god Bacchus and the Greek seer Tiresias' daughter Manto in Statius (*Theb.* 4.377–405, 463, 518–73).

Finally, many critical male–female encounters during epic journeys have mixed results. In the *Odyssey*, an encounter at the court of Sparta with the beautiful and intelligent Helen sends Odysseus' son Telemachus home with fears that his mother might be about to remarry; at the same time, he receives gifts and recognition, as well as gaining experience from this visit. In both *Argonauticas*, Medea and her magic are critical to Jason's winning of the fleece, but her help comes at a price. In Apollonius' version the helpless hero, whose skills run more to verbal persuasion than physical prowess, depends on Medea to give him the power to harness fire-breathing bulls with whom he must plow the soil and to sow the dragon's teeth that spring up as armed men. Medea enables Jason to turn the warriors' violence against each other and then tames the dragon that guards the fleece so that he can acquire it. In Valerius Flaccus' version Jason relies more on his own eagerness and physical prowess (he initially proves himself on the battlefield fighting in a civil war for Aeetes and takes a more active role in his trials), but remains beholden to Medea's magic and craft. Later Apollonius' Medea devises a stratagem to escape the pursuing Colchians (notably by killing her brother by trickery) and to rescue the Argonauts from the bronze Cretan monster Talos. As both epics hint, Medea's combined magical capacity and intelligence and her untamed barbarian character thwart all Jason's attempts to escape his unfortunate destiny both within the epics and in the future. Some of the Argonauts are reluctant in principle to accept a woman's help (Ap. Rhod. *Arg.* 3.556–63) and even before the voyage began Jason rejected the company of the famed huntress and warrior Atalanta for fear that her female presence would be disruptive (1.773). Yet the opening of Apollonius 4 (1–5) asks the Muse to interpret Medea's ambivalent labor, wiles, and motives, not Jason's, as the central heroic theme. In this final book of the epic, Medea ominously begins to take on language associated with both male warriors and immoral women (Hunter 1987: 136). Although hints of gender inversion (Jason is compared to a young girl at 4.167–71) and the use of deception during Jason's feats to win the fleece can be interpreted as a part of heroic initiation in myth (Hunter 1987: 448–52), his audience's knowledge of his unfortunate future continues to raise questions about every aspect of the gender relations explored in this story.

Female magic in Roman epic can provoke even more perversions of the norm. The witch Erichtho in Lucan, Book 6 (413–830) undertakes necromancy for Pompey's son Sextus by resuscitating a corpse, who indicates that civil war has even invaded the underworld. Sextus' desire to be assured that he will not die at Pharsalia seems to be yet another indication of the degree to which civil war has driven the entire universe into a state of ghastly imbalance. In short, women in ancient epic increasingly retain a link with the supernatural and an ability to mediate among worlds that can be used for good or ill. Goddesses, on the other hand, prove ferocious and persistent as patrons of heroes and historical causes or places important to them.

Mothers and Sons

Gilgamesh's goddess mother Ninsun, Achilles' mother Thetis, and Aeneas' mother Aphrodite/Venus powerfully support their half-divine sons through their knowledge of and access to the divine world and the future. Enkidu dies for Gilgamesh, who survives with his mother's help to become a great king. Thetis wins honor for her son from Zeus by insuring that the Greek army will be devastated by the angry Achilles' withdrawal from battle in *Iliad* 1; when he returns to battle she provides him with divine armor. Yet Thetis' knowledge of her son's future – his choice between a long peaceful life and a short glorious one – spurs Achilles to question the mores of heroic life before he chooses to return to battle knowing that he will die. Statius' *Achilleid* depicts the equally hopeless attempt of Thetis to hide the young Achilles on Scyros in female disguise so that he will not go on to die in Troy. Thetis' painful brush with mortality is an example of a situation more frequent in epics for female than for male deities (other examples include the goddess Demeter in the Homeric *Hymn to Demeter*, the Latin prince Turnus' immortal sister Juturna in the *Aeneid*). Neither Thetis nor Demeter can immortalize young males whom they bore or nursed, whereas Zeus can do so with the beautiful Trojan youth Ganymede. Thetis serves as a divine example of a female sacrificed to dynastic concerns in being forced to submit to a mortal husband, Peleus, lest Zeus sire on her a son destined to replace him. In the *Aeneid*, Venus also burdens her son with a difficult historical mission, a painful abandoned love affair with the Carthaginian Dido, and a divine shield with a depiction of the Roman future that awes Aeneas, although he cannot comprehend it. Nevertheless, her erotic and persuasive powers that seemed so irrelevant on the battlefield of the *Iliad* (she is even wounded by the mortal Diomedes in *Iliad* 5) ultimately prove successful in defending her son's and grandson's glorious destiny in Italy.

In the *Odyssey* Penelope feels forced to remarry in order to protect the status and life of her only son from the increasingly angry suitors; the poem develops Telemachus' adolescent tensions with his mother as he grows into an adult role as his father's son. In Statius the Lemnian princess Hypsipyle is finally rescued from slavery by the sons that she was forced to leave behind in Lemnos. Maternal lamentation for dead sons will be discussed below. Heroic epic generally both privileges and celebrates relations between mothers and sons, even if the mothers tend to resist their sons' entry into battle and danger. The mother–daughter relationship, such as that of Arete and Nausikaa in Phaeacia or the Latin Amata and Lavinia in the *Aeneid*, generally remains at the margins of the predominantly public world of epic. Exceptions include the goddess Demeter's devotion to rescuing her daughter Persephone from the underworld in the Homeric *Hymn to Demeter* and the relations between the Theban Jocasta and her loyal daughters Antigone and Ismene in Statius.

Women and War

The world of heroic epic is predicated on the exchange of women and gifts among men. When women such as the famous Helen of Troy or Medea (with the golden fleece) are abducted, the act disrupts fundamental bonds between men and justifies violent action. The opening of Homer's *Iliad* reprises the disastrous quarrel over Helen within the Greek community itself, when Agamemnon takes Briseis, the war prize of his best warrior Achilles, because he has had to surrender his own captive woman Chryseis to her father. His act disrupts the hierarchies of the Greek camp and opens questions about status, leadership, and service among his followers. Similarly, in Virgil's *Aeneid* war erupts between the native Latins and the Trojan newcomers to Italy over the marriage of Lavinia, daughter of King Latinus. Her mother and her native suitor Turnus do not accept the Latin king's decision to establish through Lavinia's marriage to Aeneas peaceful dynastic bonds with the powerful and sophisticated future founders of Rome and its empire. In the *Odyssey*, Penelope's suitors disrupt the hero's household and the Ithacan community in their effort to woo the absent king's wife, and Odysseus must reject the opportunity to marry the Phaeacian princess Nausikaa in order to return home and win back his kingdom.

While both Helen and Penelope are capable of manipulating their role to a limited extent, archaic Greek epic largely treats exchanged women as passive. Later epic, on the other hand, recreates from myth women who are increasingly active and dangerous players in the game of marriage and war. In his *Argonautica*, the Hellenistic poet Apollonius' Medea essentially initiates her own increasingly disastrous marriage when she chooses – under overwhelming pressure from the goddesses Hera and Aphrodite – to help Jason win the golden fleece. Medea's betrayal of her father Aeetes for Jason leads to a dangerous return journey, the killing of her brother Apsyrtus, and ultimately, even if this conclusion is only hinted at, to her killing of her children because of Jason's marital betrayal. In Virgil the active and hysterical interference of Lavinia's mother Amata initiates war in Italy, while the curse of the Carthaginian queen Dido, after her desertion by Aeneas, results in Rome's Punic Wars with Carthage, a point that resurfaces in Silicus Italicus' later epic about Hannibal, *Punica* (e.g. 1.99–119; see Chapter 38, by Marks). Both Lavinia and Dido are associated with the founding of cities (Lavinium and Carthage respectively), and Virgil develops a link between land claims and the exchange of women that becomes pervasive in Roman epic (Keith 2000).

In Lucan's *Bellum civile* about Republican Rome's civil wars (see Chapter 35, by Bartsch), the struggle between Pompey and Caesar features active and often explicitly disastrous roles for Marcia, the wife of Cato, the two wives of Pompey (Julius Caesar's daughter Julia, who remains active in the poem as a ghost, and Pompey's current wife Cornelia), as well as the Egyptian queen Cleopatra. Lucan's women clearly reflect the role taken in political matters by Roman wives, for both good and bad, during this unsettled period, whereas Apollonius explores the transgression of proper female (and male) roles in a more hypothetical mode through Medea, an exotic, barbarian foreigner endowed with magical powers. Statius' first century CE *Thebaid* develops the character of Polynices' wife Argia, who persuades her reluctant father to favor the unfortunate war between the Theban brothers after they could not share their kingdom (3.687–710) and gives away the fatal necklace of Harmonia, which leads to the death of innocent seer Amphiareus (4.187–213). Once again, the role of influential imperial women in the Julio-Claudian dynasty may lurk behind the poet's inventions.

At the same time, however, women also star as epic's quintessential victims of war. The *Iliad*'s Trojan women are in the process of losing husbands, sons, and fathers on their way to becoming, if they survive, slaves without a homeland, like Briseis and Chryseis and the female captives of the Greek camp. Hektor's wife Andromache, who has lost her entire family of origin to war and death, defines him as a replacement for every close relative (*Il.* 6.429–30), even as she also knows that she will soon mourn for his death and fears for her son. Hektor's mother Hecuba exposes her maternal breast as she pleads with her son to return within the city just before his final duel with Achilles (*Il.* 22.79–89). The sacrifices of the innocent virgins Iphigeneia or Polyxena frame the Trojan conflict in the lost post-Homeric Epic Cycle poems *Cypria* and *Iliou Persis* (see Chapter 24, by Burgess). Penelope has struggled for twenty years to preserve a kingdom for the long-delayed Odysseus and is on the verge of being forced to marry against her will.

Wives

War and adventure repeatedly call epic warriors from home, thus leaving the survival of a man's household in the hands of the aged, the young, or the hero's wife. As Hektor makes clear to his beloved wife Andromache, the Homeric warrior's chaste wife is to stay at home weaving, caring for the goods of the household, and producing and nurturing children. His reminder comes at the moment when Andromache has taken the liberty of giving advice on masculine matters; she wants Hektor to take a defensive role in the war in order to insure the survival of himself and Troy (*Il.* 6.431–8). Hektor's adviser Polydamas later gives him similar advice (18.273–9), and the hero dies because he has foolishly taken an overly aggressive stance in battle. But Hektor's role as masculine warrior prevents him from taking his wife's suggestion seriously and silences Andromache's resisting female voice except in her later role as mourner.

The *Odyssey*'s women, and above all the extraordinary faithful wife Penelope, are given a chance to play their traditional spousal roles more actively. Here the ideal wife has the same mind and capacity for virtue as her husband, even if she cannot exercise her talents as fully (H. Foley 1995: 95). Penelope wins *kleos* or fame, the goal of every Homeric warrior, for devising her trick of constantly unweaving her web to delay her suitors and for remembering Odysseus and everything he stood for (*Od.* 2.125, 24.196–7). We see her struggle to make the virtuous choice about her marriage, despite pressures from her suitors, her son's endangered situation, and her own uncertainty about Odysseus' survival. Her like-minded intelligence emerges in her final test of Odysseus concerning the secret of their immovable bed and in her exclusive sharing of stories with her husband after their reunion in Book 23. Like the Phaeacian queen Arete, whose husband trusts her to enact a public role in adjudicating quarrels among men (7.73–4), we expect Penelope to take on a public role in the court of her returned husband; after all, even Helen, whose questionable past is still a bone of contention with her husband Menelaos, actively does so. As wife, Penelope has an assertive role and voice in the *Odyssey* that the poem celebrates, however cautiously, given the behavior of the adulterous wives Clytemnestra and Helen.

Such paradigms of wifely virtue play a smaller role in later Greek or Latin epic, however. Exogamous liaisons and marriages create partnerships between strangers and so may endanger masculine goals. In order to achieve his mission, Apollonius' Jason must abandon his liaison with the Lemnian queen Hypsipyle to continue on his journey to win the golden fleece; to protect the "Argo" and its men he later threatens to abandon his promises to marry and defend a Medea who has sacrificed everything for him. Without the intervention of the Phaeacian wife Arete with her husband Alkinouos in Book 4, Medea would have been given up to her pursuing countrymen for punishment. In the *Aeneid*, Aeneas loses his loyal wife Creusa in Troy and goes on, after her ghost restores his courage and the urge for survival in Book 2, to desert Dido in Carthage (Book 4) and nearly all of the Trojan women who voyaged with him in Sicily (Book 5). He is destined instead to make a dynastic marriage in Italy with the virginal Lavinia, who may or may not be in love with her former suitor Turnus (Lyne 1983). Indeed, whereas the *Odyssey* makes home and Penelope a goal for which the hero gives up immortality with the nymph Calypso, the *Aeneid* entails a process of abandoning beloved wives or women for the masculine goal of empire and heroic self-control.

In *Bellum civile* Lucan depicts Pompey's wife Cornelia as a passionately devoted spouse, who suffers visibly over every separation from and failure of her husband and blames herself (or is blamed by others) for his misfortunes (2.348–9, 3.21–2, 8.88–105, and 639–50). Cato's wife Marcia promises to devote herself to her husband's cause in the civil wars (2.347–9), but their remarriage immediately after the death of her second husband (to whom she had been married at the stoic Cato's behest) is represented as an abnormal ritual that will establish a union in name only. The angry dead Julia, once a mediating link between Caesar and Pompey who helped defer conflict (1.111–20), harasses her husband in his dreams as a ghost (3.10–34). In Silius Italicus' *Punica*, Hannibal's devoted wife Imilce expresses both fear for her spouse and an equal willingness to follow her husband into battle; she stays to care for their son, who is soon under threat of being sacrificed by Hannibal's rival Hanno (3.97–157 and 4.770–807); their situation echoes the pathos of the *Iliad*'s Hektor and Andromache. Only Argia in Statius' *Thebaid* 12 rivals Penelope's wifely devotion in that she travels from Argos to Thebes in order to bury Polynices' body, where she is later joined by other mourning wives and mothers. The *Odyssey*'s climactic celebration of family and private life often gives way in later epic to an Iliadic concern with more public goals, to which wives are less relevant and more dangerous, even when they attempt to serve their husbands' interests, because of their pointedly less rational and weaker natures or their divided allegiances.

Mourners

All ancient epics endow women with an important role as mourners of the dead, but this role becomes increasingly ambivalent over time. The *Iliad* gives Achilles' captive consort Briseis a supportive role in the hero's own extravagant mourning for his dead companion Patroklos; Andromache mourns Hektor with her women even while he is still alive (6.500–2); and the poem closes by putting three female mourners of Hektor, Andromache, his mother Hecuba, and his sister-in-law Helen, on center stage to lament the dead hero. In this final scene, Andromache anticipates the death of her child, the destruction of Troy, and the enslavement of its women; Hecuba mourns all her lost sons; and Helen laments her own fate and the loss of Hektor's unique kindness to herself. Since the *Iliad* repeatedly confronts the price paid by heroes for engaging in war and other dangerous enterprises, these mourning women help to ritualize its major themes. Similarly, the continual mourning of the *Odyssey*'s Penelope for the absent Odysseus is a sign of her chastity and of her role as a bearer of civilized cultural memory.

In later epic, however, mourning women can become much more ambivalent figures, especially when not engaged in the formal mourning of public figures or destroyed communities or in enhancing the glory of heroic achievement with their fearful anticipation and regrets. This may well reflect historical reality, in that as early as the sixth century BCE legislation began to be passed in Greece that restricted female mourning, either by privatizing it or by giving it a carefully defined and limited role in public funerals (Alexiou 1974; on epic and history generally, see Chapter 5, by Raaflaub). Women mourners were thought prone to foment vendetta, to consolidate aristocratic political rivalries, or to undermine public rhetoric promoting war and other service to the state. Lament foments vendetta in Roman epic in instances where the social order is breaking down under the stress of civil war or familial disaster, as in the angry call for vengeance in Statius' *Thebaid* against Hypsipyle by the mourning mother of the baby Opheltes, whose accidental death occurred under Hypsipyle's care (6.135–83). The women mourning the hero Anchises in *Aeneid* 5 end up setting fire to the Trojan ships to prevent a continued journey. In *Aeneid* 9 (473–502) the mother of the young Trojan Euryalus, who had insisted on continuing the voyage to Italy, is abruptly silenced when her wild mourning for her dead son drains courage from the Trojans whom Aeneas has left to guard his first encampment. Women's mourning becomes a sign of their less controlled and less rational nature in contrast to epic men of military age, who increasingly resist despair and lament even if they can give way to them (older men such as Evander in *Aeneid* 11 give way to grief more extensively).

Statius' *Thebaid*, however, offers a complex representation of female mourners that pervades the whole poem and dominates the ending. Lament marks the death of the Thebans killed in their treacherous ambush of Tydeus, the death of Creon's son Menoeceus, and numerous other casualties. As in earlier versions of the myth, Creon, who has replaced Eteocles as king of Thebes after the death of the warring brothers, forbids the burial of Polynices and of the remaining warriors who supported the Argive attack on Thebes. The female relatives and wives of these warriors gather to seek burial for them; most go to ask for the help of Athens and its king Theseus. In Book 12 Polynices' wife Argia sets off on a solo night and day pilgrimage to bury her much-loved lord herself. She meets his sister Antigone on the battlefield and the two prepare the corpse for burial and put it on the glowing embers of the pyre of another warrior. The smoldering pyre belonged to Eteocles, and the flames divide, expressing fraternal hostility even in death. This recurring hostility of the brothers now begins to infect the two women with a loss of proper *reverentia* (12.461). After Argia and Antigone are arrested and brought before Creon, each is depicted as so in love with death that they compete to accept responsibility for their action.

Their punishment is interrupted by the arrival of Theseus and his army. After Theseus kills Creon, the Thebans welcome him into the city. The poem threatens to end with an echo of the concluding lament for Hektor in the *Iliad*, when the female relatives of the warriors, like Thyads maddened by Bacchus, take pleasure in lamenting their dead. Yet the poet declares himself incapable of recounting the mourning fully, and abruptly concludes the poem with a brief mention of Evadne's suicide, the laments of Tydeus' wife, Deipyle, Argia's story, and Atalanta's sorrow for her boyish son Parthenopaius.

How do we evaluate the *Thebaid*'s unusual representation of women and mourning? The poem links the heroism of the devoted Argia and Antigone, which first unites representatives of the two warring sides, with *fides*, *pietas*, and *virtus* (fidelity, pious devotion, and masculine courage) as well as *clementia* (mercy); despite their heroic devotion, Argia, Antigone, and her sister Ismene are at their introduction all models of chastity and virginal modesty. Moreover, as mediator figures, Antigone and her mother Jocasta have earlier in the epic attempted several times, and failed, to resolve the brothers' quarrel and defer the war (7.470–534, 11.315–82). Here the poet notes that the lesser sex has remarkably become the better one (7.479). Elsewhere, Atalanta is also viewed as a peacemaker (4.249–50), and even the suicidal Evadne eloquently persuades Theseus to respect the women's cause at Athens (12.545–86). At the same time, the burial of Polynices has brought not resolution but further dissension; early in the poem the lamentation of Ide, the mother of Theban twins killed by Tydeus, is compared to the behavior of a Thessalian witch (3.140); Jocasta is compared to the most ancient of the Eumenides (7.477, perhaps a more legitimate fury than Tisiphone).

On the one hand, Statius may be imitating Euripides' play on the battle of the heroes, *Phoenissae*, in representing women and those not of military age as sources of sanity in a fruitless war (12.442). Indeed, Elaine Fantham (1999: 232) argues that in this poem the female mourning of the victims serves to represent the lack of glory and of closure inherent in civil war. On the other hand, Statius certainly flirts with offering a positive role to uncharacteristically assertive female behavior in this complex and overdetermined conclusion. Perhaps the poet acknowledges the unusually central role he gives women when in the final lines he characterizes his own poem as following from afar and venerating Virgil's *Aeneid* (12.816–17). The image suggests Virgil's devoted Creusa following her husband at a distance as they leave Troy, yet failing to adhere to Aeneas' path.

Warriors and Leaders

From their earliest mention, women warriors provoke a variety of irresolvable questions in epic. Amazon warriors, especially those who came to the aid of the Trojans, are mentioned in Homer, but since their most important incursion in the war occurs after the *Iliad*'s conclusion, their brief moment of glory (*aristeia*) is reserved for a later (lost) Epic Cycle poem, the *Aethiopis*. Only the first book of Quintus of Smyrna's third-century CE *Post-homerica* preserves the *aristeia* of the Amazon Penthesileia, who in this poem foolishly believes that she will rival Hektor, kill Achilles, and set fire to the Greek ships (on this poem see Chapter 26, by James). Her *aristeia* is distinct from those of other overconfident young warriors in its repeated emphasis on her beauty, which stirs Achilles to an erotic response as he views her dead body. This moment was popular in early Greek art, which sometimes depicts a compelling glance between Achilles and the dying Amazon. In archaic Greek epic Amazons are viewed as inevitably to be defeated by Greek warriors, but compellingly attractive and admirable for their prowess. Over time, the monstrosity of the armed female begins to dominate her representation more heavily. Amazons and their monuments naturally lurk menacingly at the margins of the voyage of the "Argo" to the Black Sea; both Apollonius' and Valerius Flaccus' Argonauts come close to encountering them. Penthesileia's *aristeia* significantly appears in a mural on Dido's temple to Juno in Carthage (*Aen.* 1.490–3). Statius' *Thebaid* makes a point of establishing the Attic hero Theseus' credentials as a creator of order by noting his recent return from a successful expedition against the Amazons; his new consort, the Amazon Hippolyte, cannot join the battle at Thebes, despite her eagerness to do so, because she is pregnant. For both post-Homeric Greeks and for Romans, the defeat of the Amazons plays a role in envisioning their relation to, and conquest of, barbarians outside epic and colors their portrait within it.

Camilla, Virgil's native Italian warrior, is, like her Amazon predecessors (to whom she is compared at *Aen.* 11.648), beautiful and skilled on the battlefield. But the text emphasizes the unnaturalness of a female presence there, and this heroine is as vulnerable to wealth and beauty as she is herself beautiful. She dies in pursuit of extravagantly attractive armor, feminized by a wound in her exposed breast (11.803). As in Quintus, the female warrior has a disturbing effect on ordinary matrons, who are temporarily inspired to step out of their traditional roles and take to action on the city walls (*Aen.* 11.891–5) or even to begin to arm themselves (Quint. Smyn. 1.403–76). At the same time, Camilla's story evokes sympathy and becomes part of the poem's stress on the loss of talented youths caused by the Trojan incursion into the rural innocence of Italy. Silius Italicus' nomadic horsewoman Asbyte, who is modeled on Penthesileia and Camilla, falls a heroic victim to a Cretan priest of Hercules, and is avenged by Hannibal (*Pun.* 2.56–269) without the stress on her femininity found in Virgil and Quintus; the focus on Carthage and its exotic allies perhaps explains this difference.

Women's political leadership or professional roles provoke even stronger doubts. Medea, priestess of Hecate, has already symbolically stepped beyond virginal modesty in Apollonius because the path she has chosen habitually takes her outside the confines of her palace (*Arg.*3.250–2). The *Aeneid* evokes admiration for Dido's courage in founding

Carthage, building a city, and dispensing law and justice. But once in love, Dido neglects her duties, betrays her first husband by entering into a liaison with Aeneas, incurs the wrath of native African suitors, and ends by fomenting future enmity between Carthage and Rome with her curse. The ancient commentator Servius insists that the curt opening description of Dido's leadership, *dux femina facti* (the leader of the expedition was a woman, 1.364), should evoke astonishment in the hearer. Lurking behind Virgil's queen is the historical figure of Cleopatra, who in the Roman view feminized and orientalized the Roman general Anthony even if she ended with a courageous suicide. The monstrous Cleopatra appears in the battle of Actium represented on Aeneas' shield in *Aeneid* 8 and reappears in Lucan's *Civil War* as seducer of Julius Caesar. The only woman mentioned in the vision that Anchises presents to Aeneas of the public future of Rome in the underworld of *Aeneid* 6 is Ilia. She was the mother of Romulus and Remus who was raped by the god Mars and sent to her death (the fragmentary early Roman epic Ennius' *Annales* preserves bits of her story; see Chapter 31, by Goldberg). The *Aeneid*'s women generally remain more oriented than its men to the past. As noted above, the aggressive wives of Cato and Pompey in Lucan's poem may reflect the active participation of aristocratic women in politics and even on the battlefield after Julius Caesar's death. Anthony's first wife Fulvia, for example, was pilloried for involving herself directly in battles.

Both *Argonauticas* and Statius' *Thebaid* feature the story of the Amazon-like (Statius 5.144) Lemnian women, who kill their husbands and male children because they have been sexually neglected by their spouses; they establish their own government, and then mate with the Argonauts to repopulate their island. Hypsipyle, the daughter of the former King Thoas, is established as a just leader of this all-female society; unlike the other women, she maintained reason and piety and rescued her father from death. Yet without the advantage of deceit the Lemnian women are no match for men and readily give way to the erotic attractions of the Argonauts (Statius' Hypsipyle, however, is raped by Jason), thus confirming that an all-female society is both given to monstrous and irrational behavior and inevitably short-lived, like that of the Amazons.

Women in Love

Early Greek poetry is less self-conscious about the proper content of heroic epic than is the case in Rome. Yet as the tension develops between poetry that addresses erotic themes and the higher realms of epic, which ideally addresses public themes and martial deeds, romance begins to play an increasingly larger role in the poems themselves. Erotic dalliance with Circe and Calypso takes on an important role in the *Odyssey*, and Calypso in particular is deeply regretful over Odysseus' departure. The attractive virginal Nausikaa becomes the prototype of later epic virgins who fall in love like Apollonius' Medea. Although the encounter with Odysseus stirs the imagination of the marriage-minded princess, his tacit rejection of her father Alkinoos' matchmaking soon leaves this possibility behind. Nausikaa is left with a brief farewell to her potential suitor, but the poem does not develop her response to Odysseus. Under the influence of early Greek love poetry (especially Sappho) and tragedy (especially Euripidean tragedy), female victims of desire begin to play an increasing role in epics based on Greek myth if not, as in Lucan or Silius Italicus, in epics based on history (see Chapter 28, by Garner). Virgil's underworld in the *Aeneid* even provides a separate space, the Mourning Fields, for mythic women who died for love, including his own Dido.

From Apollonius on, Medea and to a lesser extent Hypsipyle play a central role in or become the models for erotic heroines in Roman epic. As noted earlier, Medea is compelled to fall in love with Jason by Hera and Aphrodite in order to facilitate his quest to Colchis for the Golden Fleece. While Homer lets us briefly into the mind of Nausikaa, as a divinely-sent dream urges her to wash the family linens as a prelude to marriage, Apollonius describes in detail Medea's hopeless struggles to resist betraying her family for Jason. He records every shiver of passion, every move from paralysis to action, her fear and panic once she has helped Jason yoke the bulls and sow the dragon's teeth with her magic. Valerius Flaccus expands on his predecessor's portrait, redoubling Medea's resistance to betraying her family. Juno's first attempt to make her give way to love fails, and the goddess is forced to turn to Venus for help. The love goddess herself then disguises herself as Medea's aunt Circe, whose authority proves to be overpowering – more so than that of Medea's merely mortal sister Chalciope, who in Apollonius' version asks Medea for help in protecting her sons.

Medea and the divided and doomed heroes and heroines of tragedy then serve as the model for Virgil's Dido. Once again, the heroine is the victim of the goddesses Juno and Venus, who want a favorable reception for Aeneas at Carthage. Yet the poem is far more ambivalent about Dido's fall into a typically female and dangerous irrationality than in Apollonius' treatment of Medea. Apollonius certainly relies on and hints at Medea's future crimes and highlights her betrayal of her father and her complicity in the killing of her brother, but Valerius Flaccus' heavier emphasis on the dark future of the couple makes clear how delicate the treatment of Medea's terrifying aspects are in the Hellenistic epic, especially since Jason's willingness to deceive and betray the heroine is already playing an active part in the narrative. In Apollonius, Jason raises suspicions about his fidelity from the start, when he reminds Medea of the example of the Cretan Ariadne, who was left behind by Theseus after she helped him kill the Minotaur and escaped with him (*Arg.* 3.997–1007). The more mature Dido is propelled in betraying her dead husband by divinely-inspired feelings and dynastic incentives. She deceives herself into treating her liaison with Aeneas, begun without witnesses in a cave, as marriage, and her shift to destructive anger against the departing Aeneas is rapid. In Apollonius, the wedding of Jason and Medea also takes place in a cave, rather than, as they would have preferred, in Greece. In this case, the marriage is genuine despite the unusual setting, as are Jason's sworn oaths to the heroine, and hence Medea's anger at Jason for toying with abandoning her is pointedly justified. By contrast, Aeneas' bonds with Dido can and must be more easily broken, and his resistance to the heroine in favor of the Trojan destiny in Rome is also the result of explicit divine command. Both heroines in love rescue their lovers, but Dido is from the beginning also blocking Aeneas' fated path, whereas Medea's destiny becomes inextricable from Jason's.

Hypsipyle serves as a prototype of a female leader for whom erotic attachment plays a critical role. However, in contrast to Dido, Hypsipyle does not surrender to the murderous passion that sweeps over her fellow Lemnian women; she allies her women to the Argonauts to produce children, accepts Jason's destined departure on his quest, and, unlike Dido, she does produce male children by her lover who, in Statius' *Thebaid*, eventually seek out their enslaved mother and are re-united with her. The Hypsipyle episode in both *Argonauticas* prefigures and contrasts with the far more complex and ambivalent Medea episode, although as a whole it stands as a kind of paradigm for the dangers for men of erotically rejecting women. Statius' portrait of the beautiful Deidamia on Skyros in his *Achilleid*, for whose sake the young Achilles temporarily accepts female disguise, seems inspired by Hypsipyle as well; she too reluctantly accepts Achilles' departure for the Trojan War, in part because of the noble male child he has given her, Neoptolemus.

Overall, later epic portraits of lovesick women confirm the famous Virgilian remark about Dido that *varium et mutabile semper / femina* (a fickle and ever-changing thing is woman, *Aen.* 4.569–70); at the same time these women often facilitate the heroic achievements of men who are themselves also capable of passion, fear, deceit, betrayal, and despair. From the beginning, heroic epics about journeys tend to address all humanity and its place in the cosmos. Hence they include even the most irrational or exotic women in the human race and evoke sympathy for their difficulties.

Women as Narrators

Many epic women speak at length on their own behalf, but rarely (despite the example of female Muses) narrate their own stories. Statius' Hypsipyle, however, becomes, like Odysseus in the *Odyssey*, the perhaps unreliable narrator at length of her own story (*Theb.* 5.48–498), even if this tale remains dominated by relations between fathers and sons (Nugent 1996). Helen in *Iliad* 3 (125–8) also weaves the stories of the battle fought for her into her web and is highly conscious of her future role in epic poetry (6.357–8). In *Odyssey* 4 she tells the story of Odysseus' foray into Troy in disguise as a beggar and her own role in bathing, recognizing, and keeping silent about his presence; Menelaos' subsequent story indirectly questions her claims for devotion to the Greek cause, however. As daughter of Zeus and a future goddess, Helen can adopt a role that places her both mentally and physically beyond ordinary human consequences. By contrast, we do not hear the story that the virtuous Penelope tells to her returned spouse in bed or learn of the subject that she weaves on the web that she constantly unravels in order to delay her marriage to the suitors, even if we do hear her speak of her difficult dilemma. Homeric women seem to acquire more potency as members of an audience, preferring certain themes (Penelope does not want to hear the story of the returning warriors from Troy at *Od.* 1.325–44) and rewarding storytellers, as the Phaeacian Arete does at *Od.* 11.335–41. Arete appears immediately charmed by Odysseus' dwelling on the mothers of famous heroes that he encountered in the underworld. Both Dido and Valerius Flaccus' Hypsipyle fall in love hearing Aeneas and Jason tell their stories. Statius, however, makes a point of having Argia and Antigone narrate their own experiences to each other and Argia's story is mentioned once again as she tells it to her sister in the closing lamentations by the women discussed earlier. Although Statius does not include their full stories in the text, his epic seems particularly sensitive to the power and importance of a female voice and perspective in a context where transgressive male violence is proliferating. Argia, for example, tells Antigone that Polynices wanted to return to Thebes above all to see his sister (12.392–7). The poem had earlier offered standard heroic motives for the war.

Conclusion

Ancient epic, especially by Homer and Virgil, was important in educating the young. Homeric epic, for example, deliberately avoided many myths concerning intrafamilial crime and conflict favored by later epic and drama, and gave a central role to a heroically faithful wife such as Penelope, who represents the ideal partner for a long-suffering hero. Although over time the influence of tragedy and elegy, and historical shifts in the role of women, broadened the scope and tone of epic's representation of women, it remained in many respects a genre more restrained and self-conscious about its role and tradition than other literary genres. In epics primarily devoted to "kings and battles," women, the rare female warrior excepted, largely serve as causes and victims of conflict, occasional mediators among warring men, and sometimes heroic mourners of the dead. In contrast to Homer, Virgil's women more actively impede heroic destiny and foment conflict among men more inclined to make peace. Imperial Roman epic, despite its obvious debt to Virgil, seems to complicate its representation of the female to include mediators for peace like Jocasta and Antigone powerful enough to be a threat to the fury Tisiphone herself (*Theb.* 11.102–5), fanatically devoted wives, and defenders of children (Imilce) or the dead

(*Thebaid*). Even the traditionally ferocious goddess Hera/Juno becomes a more benign and effective historical force in Silius Italicus and Statius.

Epics depicting heroic journeys are less constrained by historical realities and more experimental in their treatment of gender roles. Medea's or Circe's magical powers or the Lemnian women's revenge for their erotic rejection offer examples of the female capacity to enslave men to their appetites or condemn them to an unheroic destiny or disaster. When these epics focus on domestic life, they occasionally include significant roles for non-aristocratic women such as the *Odyssey*'s unfaithful servant Melantho and the devoted slave and nurse Eurykleia. Although all ancient epics can play on standard cultural clichés about female irrationality, infidelity, uncontrolled passion, vengefulness, and incapacity for public life, women and female divinities in these epics can play the role of helper and civilizer, especially in brutal foreign or exotic environments.

FURTHER READING

women, goddesses, and gender in Gilgamesh: Foster 1987; Harris 1990; Frymer-Kensky 1992; Abusch 1999; Cooper 2002.
women in Homer: H. Foley 1978 and 1995; Arthur 1981; Katz 1991; Felson-Rubin 1993; Cohen 1995; Doherty 1995; Holmberg 1995; Louden 1999.
goddesses in Homer: Slatkin 1991; O'Brien 1993.
women and gender in Apollonius: Hunter 1987 and 1993b, with further bibliography.
women and gender in Virgil: Perkell 1981; Lyne 1983; Muecke 1983; Rabel 1985; Starr 1991; Nugent 1992; Oliensis 1999.
women and gender in Lucan: introduction to Braund 1999.
women and gender in Statius: Vessey 1973; Dominik 1994a; Braund 1996; Nugent 1996; Lovatt 1999; Pagán 2000.
women and gender in Valerius Flaccus: Hershkowitz 1998b.
women in Roman epic: Keith 2000.
female lament in Roman epic: Fantham 1999.
goddesses in post-classical epic: Feeney 1991.
gender and genre in Roman epic: Hinds 2000.

CHAPTER NINE

Archaeological Contexts

Susan Sherratt

Archaeology and ancient epic have been natural companions in several different ways from antiquity onwards. This is quite apart from the obvious point that, were it not for archaeology, we would know little or nothing about some ancient epics at all, since in the last two centuries the recovery and decipherment of physical texts in the form of inscribed clay tablets have played a crucial part in our knowledge of the variety, longevity, and capacity for travel of Near Eastern epics such as *Gilgamesh* and *Atrahasis* (see Chapters 10, 14–17, by Haslam, Sasson, Noegel, Wyatt, and Beckman respectively). Thanks to archaeology, we can trace the history of the Akkadian *Epic of Gilgamesh*, for instance, backwards from its Standard Babylonian version recorded on cuneiform tablets in Ashurbanipal's Library at Nineveh and other first millennium Mesopotamian sites to older versions current in the Old Babylonian period of the early second millennium, and back beyond that to shorter heroic tales composed in Sumerian probably initially during the reign of Shulgi of the Third Dynasty of Ur in the late third millennium (Figure 9.1). Moreover, other texts have provided circumstantial evidence for thinking that Gilgamesh was a real king of Uruk in the earlier third millennium, and yet others give grounds for believing that heroic tales about him were probably already being written down within a few generations of his reign (see Chapter 5, by Raaflaub).

The other thing that the archaeological discovery of clay tablets has made clear about ancient Near Eastern epic, and the *Epic of Gilgamesh* in particular, is that it had no trouble transferring from one language to another. There are not only Sumerian and Akkadian versions of Gilgamesh, but also second-millennium Hurrian and Hittite versions among the preserved texts from the Hittite capital at Boğhazköy, while during the first millennium it almost certainly also became familiar in Aramaic (Dalley 1989; 1998, esp. chs. 3–8). This often comes as a surprise to students of Greek epic in particular, who, steeped in a long-lived Romantic view of epic traditions as language- (and "people"-) specific, consider that the history of epics such as those associated with Homer can be projected backwards only unilineally within a single linguistic line of descent – through early and proto-Greek and possibly back to some form of proto-Indo-European, but not laterally, to other non-Greek (and particularly not Semitic) languages.

Yet there are sufficient reflections of *Gilgamesh* and other Near Eastern epics, tales, and literary motifs within Homeric epic to make quite clear that Near Eastern epic was probably quite familiar in the Aegean area, and not only at the time (roughly around 700 BCE) when

the Homeric epics themselves are believed to have been composed (see Chapter 20, by
Burkert). Indeed, there is some reason for thinking that the version or versions of *Gilgamesh*
reflected in the *Odyssey* may already have reached the Aegean in the early second millennium.
In this case, like other Near Eastern elements eventually incorporated in the Homeric epics,
and like the numerous Near Eastern motifs that also entered Aegean art before 1500 BCE, it
almost certainly made its Aegean debut in a language or languages (such as those spoken in
pre-Greek-speaking Crete and the Cyclades) other than Greek.

   One of the defining features of what is commonly classed by modern western scholars as
epic (both ancient and more modern) is its unifying thrust – its significance to collective
groups of people who seek to identify themselves along tribal, ethnic, religious, or national
lines (see Chapter 1, by Martin). This immediately brings it into a political arena which

reflects, not only on the contexts in which epics were originally compiled or created and subsequently adopted and reshaped in a variety of new circumstances, but also on the modern ideological and intellectual contexts that formulated this definition in the first place. While its close relationship to politics and history (in the sense of the creation or shaping of a "past") have meant that archaeology, in some sense or another, has probably always been an adjunct of epic, it is only really in the last two hundred years or so that modern archaeology was developed, side by side with philology and this perception of the significance of epic, as parallel handmaidens in the quest for the earliest origins and history of nation-states and their peoples. As such, it is a peculiarly European (and more generally western) phenomenon.

The Eurocentric origins of modern archaeology have had some interesting effects on its relationship with ancient Near Eastern epic. Biblical archaeology (specifically the archaeology of the biblical "epics"; see Chapter 19, by Niditch), which was first initiated in the days of Constantine and carried on throughout the Crusades of the Middle Ages, was transformed relatively seamlessly into modern archaeology at around the beginning of the nineteenth century, because of the fundamental importance of biblical tradition to European identity and history. In other parts of the Near East, however, the relationship between archaeology and epic has generally been rather more low-key. True, various attempts were made by early archaeologists to pinpoint the Flood, recorded on a Sumerian King List of the late third millennium (as well as in the *Epic of Atrahasis*) as having taken place in the remote past, long before Gilgamesh reigned at Uruk (Mallowan 1964; Lloyd 1978: 91–93). But even this was at least partly driven by its biblical implications and the interest these aroused in a western public. However, although we have reason to believe that a character like Gilgamesh was probably originally a real person, there has been little interest in using archaeology (in the spirit of either a literal or rationalizing approach) to demonstrate the existence of some essential historical core underlying his epic adventures, as has been the case with the Bible or certain forms of European (including Homeric) epic. This is partly because in much of the ancient Near East for much of the time we have a wealth of written history and literature, which has relieved scholars of the need to create "history" out of the non-textual archaeological record as they have sometimes been tempted to do in other areas. More importantly, it is also because of the lack of emotional and ideological involvement on the part of Europeans with the deep history of an East conceived as the permanent "other" with which the West habitually contrasted itself. Even modern Middle Eastern states, which have in general not hesitated to use archaeology in the service of political agendas, have seen little need to develop an archaeology specifically devoted to epic, since there is plenty of scope in the documented historical record to harness archaeology in this way. Instead, archaeologists have tended to confine themselves to identifying artistic representations of epic characters or episodes, which provide a subsidiary medium in which to track their currency and spread (Figure 9.2). Where epics such as that of Gilgamesh have been looked at more recently through archaeological eyes, it is in the matter of the reconstruction, with the help of archaeology, of more general contexts which provide the ideological or social matrix for the development of such tales.

In areas to the west, however, where history (even in the classical world) is comparatively short, and where written texts go back a few millennia at most, the scope for modern archaeology to forge a close relationship with epic "histories" has traditionally been much greater, as has the motivation to harness archaeology in this way. There is no doubt that epics of all sorts and all ages have probably had a long relationship to archaeology in a loose sense, in that accidentally found "relics," or ancient ruins or peculiarities in the landscape, will prompt stories which then live on to be incorporated in grander epics, or will be related to personae or events already familiar from widely circulated epic or quasi-epic accounts, whether written or oral (see Chapter 13, by J. Foley and Chapter 4, by Jensen). Thus it is possible for characters such as King Arthur or St Patrick to have several

Figure 9.2 Gilgamesh and Enkidu slaying Humbaba, from a moulded clay plaque of the Old Babylonian period. British Museum, London. Drawing by T. Rickards.

different seats or birthplaces or for figures such as Robin Hood to have frequented an impossible range of habitats – which did not matter as long as travel was generally difficult and restricted (or at least as long as those who cared most did not travel).

To some extent, however, the invention of modern archaeology in the nineteenth century imported a new seriousness into this relationship, turning it into a quasi-scientific endeavor to establish (among other things) the "truth" between rival claims, particularly where nationally or ethnically significant epics were concerned. The seriousness and continued longevity of this relationship varied according to the nature and content of the epics concerned and the nature of the societies which wished to relate to them. Within the small and self-contained island of Iceland, for instance, first settled (according to historical sources) by Norsemen in the ninth century CE, archaeology and the sagas developed an intimate relationship, which encouraged the population to identify the initial homesteads of their ancestors by means of archaeology illuminated by the saga literature (fantastic though much of this was) – a relationship that continued well into the twentieth century. In many other cases, however – such as the epic *Beowulf* – where the content was either so fantastic, or the need for continued historical self-definition on the part of the interested parties (in this case the Anglo-Saxon English) so attenuated, the relationship was neither so committed nor so long-lived. In the case of most of the epics of the ancient classical world, their self-consciously contrived literary nature, their evidently derivative status, or their lack of direct relevance to modern political concerns also seemed to place them beyond the bounds or interest of archaeological investigation. There was, though, some antiquarian enthusiasm for tracing, through ancient iconography, the earliest date at which the legend of the suckling of Romulus and Remus by the she-wolf might have existed in recognizable form (Figure 9.3). The exceptions to this were the Homeric epics – the *Iliad* and *Odyssey* – the earliest, most intriguing and most monumental of all ancient European epics, and from which the very notion of epic was largely seen to derive (see Chapters 11, 21, 22, and 29, by Lamberton, Edwards, Slatkin, and Dué respectively).

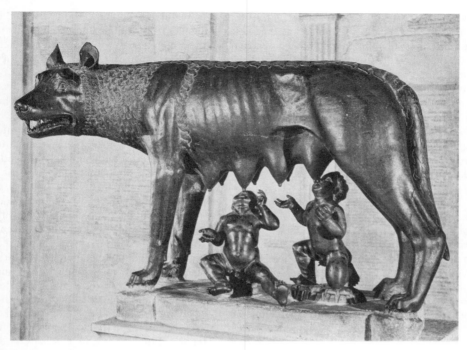

Figure 9.3 Bronze figure of a she-wolf. The wolf is probably of Etruscan workmanship dating to around 500 BCE. The figures of the children were added during the Renaissance, but there is reason to think that some such figures formed part of the original. If so, it shows that the legend of the suckling of Romulus and Remus by a she-wolf already existed by the end of the sixth century. Museo Capitolino, Rome. Archivo Fotografico.

Of all relationships between archaeology and epic, that between archaeology and the Homeric epics is, if not the longest, at least the longest traceable and almost certainly the most complex, and has probably existed in some form or another as long as the epics themselves. This relationship has an interesting history of its own, which not only reflects the unique status these epics enjoyed in the ancient world, but also encapsulates much of modern European intellectual history, including the history of archaeology and its relations with ancient historical and literary scholarship, over the last 150 years or so. In what follows, I shall attempt to outline a few of the main stages in this history, suggest why it took the course it did, and offer some thoughts about where a relationship between archaeology and ancient (above all, Homeric) epic can now most usefully lead us.

Epic "Relics"

As suggested above, the practice of relating topographical features and ancient remains visible in the landscape to the heroes and events which figure in folklore, legends, epic, or popular history is probably as old and widespread as humanity itself. So, no doubt, is the practice of creating the latter on the basis of the former. By the dawn of archaic Greece the landscape inhabited by the Greek-speaking world was marked with the sometimes impressive ruins of earlier centers of settlement and littered with the tombs and funeral mounds of past millennia. At Mycenae, for instance, the monuments seen by Pausanias in the second century CE were almost certainly still more impressive a millennium earlier in the eighth century BCE. At that time, at the place probably already known as Ilion close to the shores of the Hellespont, a small local shrine sat amidst the ruins of the late second-millennium citadel walls, while a handful of deserted tells and perhaps burial mounds were even then visible in the surrounding terrain. It is impossible to know, at that point, what stories surrounded locations such as these, but stories there undoubtedly were. The "tombs" of Myrine and Aisyetes near Ilion, both mentioned in the *Iliad*, may already have had these names, the more so since neither Myrine nor Aisyetes figure in any other capacity in the the epic. But what the supposed tombs really were, and when they acquired their names, is something we shall almost certainly never know (see Cook 1973; Luce 2003). Mycenae and Agamemnon may well have been names that went together, at least locally, long before the creation and widespread dissemination of Homeric epic, but whether the character and deeds of an earlier Agamemnon bore any very coherent and detailed resemblance to those attributed to him in the *Iliad* and *Odyssey* is perhaps a different matter.

The importance of much ancient epic (and Homeric epic in particular) as a representation of the shared "history" with which a very wide group of people could identify themselves meant that its exploitation by means of what might loosely be called ancient archaeology was almost inevitable. In the case of Homeric epic, this is particularly marked in the Hellenistic and, especially, the Roman periods, following Alexander the Great's deliberate manipulation of an ideology based on Homeric military glory and especially following Virgil's imperial Roman twist on the Trojan hero Aeneas. Epic "relics" or tales of "relics," for instance, had similar ideological, political, and commercial roles in the Graeco-Roman world to those of Christian "relics" in the Middle Ages. Pausanias (2.18.3), for instance, saw the shield which Menelaos was said to have taken from Euphorbos (cf. *Il.* 17.60) hanging in the Argive Heraion; Plutarch tells us that Alexander was offered a sight of Paris' lyre during his visit to Ilion in 334 BCE (*Alex.* 15.4); while Arrian says that, on the same occasion, he removed from the temple of Athena Ilias the arms that had been preserved there since the Trojan War (*Anab.* 1.12). While we can probably regard Paris' lyre and the Trojan War arms as a figment of the Alexander mythology, and doubt that the shield seen by Pausanias was of any great antiquity, in a few cases it seems likely that "relics" were acquired by means of some form of archaeology, whether accidental or deliberate. The "scepter of Agamemnon," which according to Pausanias (9.40.11–12) enhanced the fame (and no doubt the tourist income) of Chaeroneia in the second century CE, was apparently discovered in the ground along with some gold. Pausanias' observation that the Chaeroneians gave it the curious name "spear" (δόρυ) suggests that it may have been some antique form of spearhead, perhaps from a third or early second millennium grave. In the archaic and classical periods we also have literary hints of the kind of active archaeology for blatantly political purposes which, for instance, led to the opening of "Arthur's tomb" at Glastonbury by the English King Edward I in 1278. The story of the sustained search by Spartan special agents for the tomb of Orestes in order to ensure Sparta's alliance with Tegea in the sixth century BCE is one such example (Hdt. 1.67–8). Another, if Plutarch's account (*Thes.* 26.1–2) is to be believed, is Cimon's hunt in the early fifth century for the bones of Theseus on Skyros, which were eventually found in a burial mound along with a bronze spear and sword and "repatriated" to Athens. In the latter case, this "archaeological" activity was motivated by the need for a plausible excuse to legitimize the Athenian seizure of Skyros in 475 BCE.

Such active "archaeological" ploys can only have had some point if enough people believed that the bones of Orestes or Theseus really existed to be found; and, generally speaking, the ancients (like the legendary St Helena in her quest for the true Cross) never publicly or explicitly doubted the basic historicity of their epics and other "historical" accounts, and did not need archaeology to "prove" it. The visible monuments were there around them, and when they wanted "relics" for political or commercial purposes all they had to do was "find" or manufacture them. The presence or absence of such "relics" (or indeed the matter of their authenticity) did not affect belief in the "history" in any way. Historical epic, whether composed orally or in writing, worked by telling people what they already "knew," or by refashioning this disparate "knowledge" into new synthetic narratives which made eminent sense in the ideological or political context of their own contemporary world. They were conditioned to accept it as historical "truth," and needed no independent confirmation. The historicity of heroes and their various deeds was largely taken for granted by literary commentators and popular masses alike. And even if we can assume some cynicism on the part of those who manipulated their tales for political or ideological purposes, including the original creators of ancient epic and their patrons, this rarely betrays its presence in the literature. Insofar as there is dissent, it tends to be of a minor nature and to concern anomalies or contradictions within epic texts, between epic and other accounts, or between these and monuments believed by contemporary populations to relate to them, rather than the historical basis of epic itself. Thus, in the fifth century BCE Herodotus could argue that Helen never actually reached Troy (2.112–20), and in the first century Strabo, following Demetrius of Scepsis, could produce various reasons (including the recognition of changes in the coastline) why the Hellenistic and Roman city of Ilion could not have been Homer's Troy (Strabo 13.1). None of these, however, questioned the historical reality of either Homer's Trojan War or Troy itself.

Archaeology and Homeric Epic in the Nineteenth and Early Twentieth Centuries: Schliemann and the "Fundamentalist" Diversion

A completely new use for archaeology in relation to Homeric epic was introduced with loud fanfares in the later nineteenth century in the form of Heinrich Schliemann's highly self-publicized and self-dramatized quest to prove the historical truth of the Iliad by uncovering Priam's Ilion and Agamemnon's Mycenae (see Chapter 29, by Dué). Several factors contributed to this development, among them the gradual transformation of archaeology from an antiquarian pastime to a historical discipline of a scientific or quasi-scientific nature, and the harnessing of it to push back the boundaries of the earliest European history beyond the limits of strictly historical records in a Romantic quest for the origins of national roots (see Schnapp 1993, esp. ch. 5).

As mentioned above, other European epics were already being linked with archaeological findings in a relatively productive but unsystematic and often more or less fanciful manner (see Frank 1992: 49–50), but for many of these historicity as such was not a central issue. In many cases, historical records existed to demonstrate the historical nature of a few isolated characters and events that figured in them – enough, indeed, to show that, although these epics themselves had a history, as a whole they were not "history" – a fact often abundantly clear from their fantastic content. It was a thrill to discover, for instance, that helmets like Beowulf's boar-crested one really existed in Anglo-Saxon England in the sixth to seventh centuries, at a time more or less contemporary with a Scandinavian leader mentioned by Gregory of Tours who might be identified with the Geatish king Hygelac. However, while it encouraged a belief that the epic was several centuries older than its first (tenth-century) manuscript version and might contain some important historical allusions (Ker 1897), nobody could possibly believe that its central theme of Beowulf's adventures with a series of monsters was anything other than fantasy.

The Homeric epics, on the other hand, were very much older than any known European epics, and belonged to a time long before any historical records. Since history could not shed light on them, archaeology was therefore the only possible means of investigating their nature and context. In addition to that, there was the peculiar authority and respect accorded to classical literature generally, and the Homeric epics in particular, since the

Renaissance. The ancients themselves believed that the epics represented their earliest history, and, while Enlightenment thinking may have brought some skepticism in its train, more Romantic admirers of the ancient world were not disposed to dismiss this belief lightly. Indeed, as a result of the nineteenth-century Romantic movement, the Homeric epics (often in translation) had acquired a new form of naturalized significance. Not only were they of national importance to the newly emerged modern Greek nation, but they were seen as having a broader significance for the roots of a distinctively European civilization. They stood at the beginning, not only of classical and more generally European literature, but also of European history.

It is almost certainly not coincidental that Schliemann, whose excavations at Hissarlik/Troy (the site of ancient Ilion) began in 1870, was a German. In 1870 Germany was just on the point of being formally unified into a single state under the leadership of Prussia and was in need of popular foundation heroes, all the more so since the realpolitik of Wilhelm I and his Chancellor Bismarck was based on a political pragmatism which made little concession to popular self-expression or nationalist sentiment. This is not to suggest that Schliemann's activities at Troy provided a classically-derived foundation myth for the new Germany of the sort that Geoffrey of Monmouth provided for twelfth-century Englishmen when he traced their origin back to the Trojan Brutus, or indeed that Virgil provided for Augustus' Romans. Nonetheless, in a way, the success of Schliemann in unearthing Homer's Troy and Mycenae precisely when he did, created in him a nineteenth-century German national foundation hero, whose exploits at Troy in particular are still deeply embedded in German national consciousness and entrenched in popular education. His search for Homer's Priam and other Trojan War heroes took place in the context of a particularly potent mix of popular currents in Germany that contributed by the late nineteenth century to a peculiarly German sense of national and European identity in which the cultural heritage of ancient Greece had been thoroughly internalized. On the one hand, was the precocious growth in the German states from the mid-eighteenth century onwards of a Romantic particularism, which itself encompassed several separate but intertwined strands; these (often simplified) strands were, by the late nineteenth century, disseminated widely in German popular thinking. Central to this was an essentialist concept of *Volk* and *Volkskultur*, expressed and defined most purely through its language, whose earliest roots (*Urgeschichte*) could thus be sought through a combination of historical philology, folktale, and saga; and this, from the later eighteenth century, was progressively bound up with a developing anthropological notion of a vigorous Indo-European race with unique cultural and spiritual traits. A related strand was the Romantic Hellenism of classical scholars and historians of ancient art such as Johann Winckelmann (1764), which saw in the culture of ancient Greece the fount, not only of truth and beauty, but of all personal and political freedom, both the model and origin of all that was most desirable in modern European nation-states.

A particularly pertinent conjunction of these two came about as a result of the long-term effects on German popular education of the work of Friedrich Wolf (1795), who first suggested in the introduction to a school-text of Homer that the Homeric epics were edited compilations of transmitted oral folk-lays first composed by a much earlier "Homer," long before the Greeks had learnt how to write. While in strictly academic circles, Wolf marked the beginning of the increasingly introverted "Analyst" school of German literary criticism of Homer, one result of his ideas on popular views of Homer's epics (by then as widely consumed in translation as imbibed by rote in the original) was the implication that they thus belonged to the very infancy of the Greek and, by extension, the European race. In addition to this, another source of popular pride was the parallel growth in Germany of a commitment to the natural and physical sciences, including physical anthropology and archaeology, firmly founded in a belief in scientific progress; this led to a strongly empiricist strand in German thought and along with it the conviction that everything was susceptible to scientific proof. By 1870, all these sometimes inherently contradictory strands had permeated well into the German intellectual environment, forming at certain levels a kind of distilled blend of by then largely intuitive beliefs, and setting the scene for a specifically German attempt by an academic outsider to find the scientific evidence that would prove that the earliest accounts of Greek (and therefore also European) history were indeed true.

Schliemann may not have thought of himself as molded by any of these currents, nor may he have thought of his desire to prove the veracity of Homer's epics as having any bearing on German national identity. According to his own account, he had a burning desire to vindicate Homer and confound (by means of the science of archaeology) the skepticism of those professional literary scholars, including the increasingly rarefied and inaccessible "Analyst" school in Germany, which had long lost any interest in whether the Homeric epics contained anything of genuine historical value. Nevertheless, in his highly romanticized autobiography Schliemann (1880: 1–66) seems almost consciously to set himself up as a classic and simply understood folk-hero for the new, and defensively insecure, Germany: the motherless son of an impoverished clergyman, deeply inspired by the folk-history of the landscape around him, whose early education was cut short by financial considerations, but who nonetheless, by dint of unremittingly hard work combined with incessant study, steadily amassed a fortune which eventually allowed him, at the age of almost 50, to pursue the vision for which he had maintained a single-minded passion since an early age. Not only that, but he achieved his goal in the face of ridicule and downright hostility from the learned (and often apparently jealous) experts whom he was to prove wrong by his contributions to the science of antiquity.

The story of Schliemann's archaeological explorations, not only at Hissarlik (Ilion/Troy) and Mycenae, but also on Ithaca, at Orchomenos, Tiryns, Marathon, Kythera and Sphacteria, are well known. He was convinced that he had found Priam's Troy in the remains of what subsequently became known as Troy II (but by the end of his life he was forced to recognize that it belonged to a much earlier period than the traditional Greek dates for the Trojan War), and the graves of Agamemnon and his companions within the walls of Mycenae, in a grave circle constructed and used in the mid-second millennium. Despite such initial chronological hiccups and uncertainties (which were soon smoothed out by his contemporaries or successors), his work had a profound and lasting effect.

Schliemann is often credited (not entirely justly) with having discovered Aegean prehistory and inaugurating its archaeology. What he certainly did was to bring the prehistory of the Aegean area as uncovered by archaeology to the attention of a very wide public throughout Europe and America. To a large extent he shaped its form and preoccupations for a good many decades to come, and in the field of what rapidly came to be called "Homeric archaeology" for almost a century. This was partly because of the difficulty the archaeology of the prehistoric Aegean continued to have in finding an independent role for itself. Classical archaeology was still largely a matter of art and architectural history, for which there was seen to be limited scope in the cultural remains of periods before *ca.* 700 BCE, and its ability to shed light on history was regarded as very much secondary to the work of ancient historians whose historical constructions were pieced together from fragments of literary and epigraphical texts. In 1855, for instance, Athanasios Rhousopoulos, Professor of Archaeology at the University of Athens, had published his *Manual of Greek Archaeology*, which was concerned far more with the ancient literature than with archaeology itself. As a result, and particularly under the influence of Schliemann, archaeologists dealing with an earlier era turned themselves, literally, into prehistorians, turning fragments of later (including Homeric) legends into a coherent "prehistory," using much the same modus operandi as ancient historians, and squeezing the archaeological record into conformity with its predominantly narrative form. This "fundamentalist," text-based approach to the archaeology of remotest antiquity, wholly in accord with the spirit of Schliemann, had contemporary analogies in nineteenth- and early twentieth-century biblical archaeology, to which the archaeology of Homeric epic can be seen as directly parallel. Like biblical archaeology, it had a prolonged life, developing out of belief in the written word into an orthodoxy whose tenets became increasingly hard to challenge as they penetrated deep into popular literature and school textbooks, and attracting funding from those for whom it had become an article of faith.

During and after Schliemann's lifetime, the archaeology of the Greek (or "Mycenaean") Late Bronze Age in the later second millennium BCE quickly became synonymous with the archaeology of the "Age of Homer" or the "Age of Heroes." The presence of boar's tusk helmets (cf. *Il.* 10.261–5) and representations of figure-of-eight and tower-like body shields (cf. e.g. *Il.* 6.117, 7.219) in the Mycenae shaft graves and other Late Bronze Age contexts, was taken to have demonstrated that the world portrayed by Homer was essentially a Late Bronze Age one; and reconstructions of Odysseus' palace, based ostensibly on Homeric descriptions, instead of resembling classical houses (as they had before 1880), came regularly to look like the Mycenaean palaces unearthed by Schliemann at Tiryns or later by Carl Blegen at Pylos and grandiosely reconstructed by contemporary artists. It was agreed that the Trojan War, which antiquity (from Herodotus in the fifth century to Eratosthenes in the later third century) concurred in dating variously between 1250 and 1183, must have taken place at a time when these Mycenaean palaces still flourished, probably under a Mycenaean empire headed by the king of Mycenae, and before the Dorian invaders arrived to destroy this first flowering of continental European civilization and drive its creators eastwards as refugees to the shores of Asia Minor and the East Mediterranean. For a fairly representative summary of this conventional composite picture, which has as its starting point a belief in the basic historicity of Homer's Trojan War, and which is still reproduced in the early chapters of school textbooks on Greek history and not infrequently in television programs, see e.g. Page 1964b: 18–19. Most of its elements can also be found in varying combinations in works such as Nilsson 1933, Schachermeyr 1935; Page 1959; Blegen 1962; Wace and Stubbings 1962; Mylonas 1966. See also the bibliographical essay "Homer and history" by Finley (1962: 157–9). Further representative works are listed in the chapter bibliographies of McDonald and Thomas 1990, esp. chs. 3–7.

The sixth city of Troy (Troy VI), which flourished between the nineteenth and thirteenth centuries BCE, was recognized by Dörpfeld shortly after Schliemann's death as the one which Homer's Achaeans destroyed. After 1924, when Emil Forrer pointed out apparently suggestive similarities between Homeric names and names found in thirteenth-century historical texts at the Hittite capital of Boğhazköy, there was a growing sense in some quarters that the historical reality of the Trojan War was on the verge of being confirmed beyond all doubt. Wilusa in the Hittite texts was (probably rightly) equated with Greek Ilios/Ilion, and the land of Ahhiyawa (almost certainly wrongly) with an entity conceptualized by archaeologists from Schliemann on as Mycenaean Greece, the inhabitants of the latter assumed (as a matter of unthinking faith) to be one and the same as Homer's Achaeans who, under the leadership of the king of Mycenae, mounted a united expedition against Troy. This particular development, by introducing the whiff of "real" history into the equation, possibly did more than anything else to prolong the aberrant belief, initiated against the academic odds by Schliemann, that Homer's *Iliad* and *Odyssey*, uniquely of all known epics, faithfully preserved a coherent historical core that could be pinned down in time and space through archaeology. One is reminded of an apt story recounted by Roberta Frank (1992) in discussing the sensational effect that the unearthing of the Sutton Hoo ship burial in 1939 had on perceptions of the historical background to *Beowulf*; the story is of a stranger who, late one night, saw a man on hands and knees beneath a streetlight searching for something and offered assistance. "Are you sure this is the spot?" he asked. "No," came the answer, "but this is where the light is."

Against the background of the view, by then widely regaining acceptance, of the coherent literary unity of Homer's epics, one effect of the notion of a historical Late Bronze Age Homeric world contributed to by archaeology in this way was to hypothesize a shadowy Homer himself in the Bronze Age. There were, for instance, theories that whole chunks of the extant epics, such as the Greek "Catalogue of Ships" (*Il.* 2.484–759), preserved virtually intact original thirteenth-century compositions which survived down to later centuries (Allen 1921; Wace and Stubbings 1962: 285). As late as 1970, R. Hope Simpson and J. F. Lazenby felt able to "illustrate" the thirteenth-century nature of the Catalogue by the largely circular method of giving Homeric names to otherwise anonymous Late Bronze Age sites in what were assumed to be roughly the right areas. A glance at the numbers of fourteenth-to thirteenth-century sites then known from excavation or survey shows that this was hardly a difficult exercise.

What the mechanisms were by which such compositions straddled the half-millennium or so between the events which they recounted and the traditional date of Homer himself, when many supposed the epics were first written down, is often not clear, but these compositions seem to have been envisaged as having been transmitted faithfully down through the centuries, gaining later accretions (sometimes described as "anachronistic") along the way. Even after Milman Parry, in the late 1920s and early 1930s, successfully documented the fundamentally oral nature of the epics and demonstrated the ways in which a tradition of oral-composition-in-performance actually operated (see Chapter 4, by Jensen), the effect, if anything, seems merely to have been to bolster the view that the epics preserved a historical core going right back to the time of the Trojan War in the Late Bronze Age, and that this was the period in which even an eighth-century Homer somehow strove unconsciously (or perhaps even consciously) to "set" them. At around the same time as Parry was publishing his studies in the epic technique of oral verse-making, Carl Blegen was embarking on renewed excavations at Troy (1932–8). Following these, in 1939 he turned his attention to the site of Ano Englianos in Messenia, which he identified as a possible site for the hitherto elusive Palace of Nestor at Pylos.

Blegen was a serious, scientifically-minded prehistoric archaeologist and (unlike Schliemann) an excellent excavator. He had already excavated numerous prehistoric sites on the Greek mainland, ranging in date from the Early to Late Bronze Age, without feeling the need to make much reference to Homer. Nevertheless, when it came to the sites of Troy and Ano Englianos, Blegen showed himself to be just as much a Homeric "fundamentalist" as Schliemann had been. His excavations at Troy convinced him that the stratum labelled Troy VIIa, rather than VI as had previously been thought, must be the city besieged by Homer's Achaeans. In a small area beside the citadel wall, which had escaped levelling in Hellenistic and Roman times as well as Schliemann's destructive attentions, he found a number of patched together small-roomed houses packed full of storage jars. The vivid picture he conjured out of this was of the inhabitants hastily crowding into the citadel in the face of some sustained threat from outside and making preparations for a long siege. Above the houses the level was covered by a mass of stones and mudbrick along with burned and blackened debris, indicating that Troy VIIa was destroyed by fire, undoubtedly the result of hostile action. The discovery of human bones amongst the wreckage put the finishing touches to the conclusion that this was the city destroyed by the Achaeans.

The effects of Blegen's fundamental conviction that a Trojan War was there for the finding can be seen particularly clearly in his attitude to the date of the destruction of Troy VIIa. To all intents and purposes, this date was based on the latest Mycenaean (Late Helladic) pottery found in levels associated with this city, and should therefore have been arrived at by a reasonably objective route: by using the latest identifiable pottery (and its accepted date range) as a guide to the chronological span within or after which the levels were deposited. On the basis of the Mycenaean pottery, Blegen concluded that Troy VIIa fell during the course of Mycenaean (Late Helladic) IIIB, before the transition to the Mycenaean IIIC style. So far, so good. By the late 1950s, when Blegen published the detailed results of his excavations, the state of knowledge of Mycenaean pottery chronology would have suggested that this meant that Troy VIIa was destroyed during the course of the thirteenth century. Blegen, however, was surprisingly precise. In *Troy IV* (published in 1958), he dated the fall of Troy VIIa to around 1240 BCE. Shortly afterwards, in a fascicle of the revised edition of the *Cambridge Ancient History* first published in 1962, he updated it by around ten years to around 1250 BCE, which accorded well with Herodotus's date for the Trojan War. Finally, later in 1962, in *The Mycenaean Age*, he moved it another ten or twenty years further back to *ca.* 1270–60 BCE.

Contrary to what one might suppose, Blegen had not changed his mind about the stylistic classification of the latest Mycenaean pottery from Troy VIIa; nor had anything happened meanwhile to allow a more precise dating of Mycenaean IIIB pottery. Both 1240 and 1270 BCE are well within the date range usually assigned to Mycenaean IIIB even down to the present day. What seems to have happened is that he felt an increasing need to reconcile the date given to his (and Homer's) Troy with at least some of the later Greek traditions, above all with the one, first found in the *Odyssey*, which suggests that the Greek heroes returned to trouble at home, and with that which associated the return of the Heraclidae, eighty years after the Trojan War, with a Dorian conquest of the Peloponnese (Thuc. 1.12). Since at that time a Dorian invasion was the most favored explanation for the destructions which hit palatial centers such as Mycenae, Tiryns, and Pylos after the end of the Mycenaean IIIB period, which in turn had been set by Arne Furumark (1941) at around 1230 BCE, a date of not much later than 1270 was needed in order to give the returning heroes and their descendants eighty years' grace. It also reflected Blegen's belief that Troy VIIa was a relatively short-lived settlement, consistent with its nature as the direct result of a siege. This series of curiously precise adjustments in date, unjustified in purely archaeological terms, was produced for no other reason than to make the ostensibly objective evidence for dating Troy VIIa fit Blegen's (and others') historicizing rationalization of literary legends. It was a question of supposedly independent evidence for the authenticity of a synthetic myth being determined by faith in the myth itself.

The Anti-historical Reaction

Slowly, however, attitudes were changing. Already by the 1950s, among those who devoted most attention to the details of the relationship between the archaeological record and the Homeric epics, Hilda Lorimer and Dorothea Gray were consistently stressing the extent to which Late Bronze Age material cultural references were closely interwoven with (and actually outnumbered by) those belonging to later periods, especially to the Early Iron Age of the tenth to ninth centuries. It became increasingly difficult to regard these as mere inadvertent "anachronisms," introduced into an original "core" by later bards, and instead the epics had to be seen as effectively composite products of several periods.

From around this time, too, a more general anti-fundamentalist backlash gradually began to make itself felt. To some extent, this was led by classical literary scholars and ancient historians, many of whom had always been skeptical of Schliemann's credulous approach (and who, it might be added, often harbored grave doubts about archaeology as a serious academic subject). In 1954, the ancient historian Moses Finley published *The World of Odysseus*, in which he argued that it was necessary to take the implications of the oral nature of Homeric epic seriously (see Chapter 13, by J. Foley). Emphasizing one of the characteristics of the techniques of oral-composition-in-performance – the propensity to create something new and different on every occasion – and using comparative epic analogies, such as the *Chanson de Roland*, he argued that, while there might be some vague historical reminiscences behind some of the stories and characters recounted by Homer, the contents of the epics as such were essentially creations of a period no earlier than the tenth to ninth centuries, no more than a century or so before the time conventionally assigned to Homer. Any vague echoes of much earlier historical events or characters, like the *Chanson*'s account of Roland and the skirmish at Roncevaux, were bound to be so distorted as to be unrecognizable. Drawing on comparative anthropology (though with little archaeological argument), he further argued that the society and values portrayed in the epics were consistent ones, entirely in accord with the fragmented world of the Greek "Dark Age," which lay between the civilization of the Mycenaean palaces and the beginning of literate, historical Greece. The decipherment of Linear B by Michael Ventris in 1952, which revealed the palaces as administrative bureaucracies with complex hierarchies of officials and land-holdings and characterized by obsessive record-keeping, for him provided further conclusive evidence that Homer's epics preserved no trace of memory of Late Bronze Age Greece.

Finley returned to this theme in the early 1960s with a full frontal attack, on both archaeological and comparative grounds, on the whole idea of the historicity of Homer's Trojan War, which, he argued, "had best be removed in toto from the realm of history and returned to the realm of myth and poetry"(Finley 1964: 9). The comparative examples he cited, which included the *Chanson de Roland*, the *Niebelungenlied* and the still-living South Slavic traditional songs about the Battle of Kosovo, made clear that, while such epics could contain the names of historical characters or be centered nominally around historical events, they were essentially ahistorical, in that characters who lived centuries apart and in quite different regions could be mingled together, and events transported in time and space or distorted beyond all possible recognition. This was a point of view which, in the case of the Homeric epics, few would have disputed before Schliemann's powerful appeal to a popular willingness to believe in the Greeks' own belief in their earliest history, and before the tangible evidence for an Ilion much older than Homer coaxed them into a faith in the apparently magical powers of archaeology. Since then, at least among English-speaking classicists, historicity in the case of the Homeric epics has not been an issue, and much more effort has gone into analyzing the social, ideological, and philosophical contents of the epics in their own terms, with little reference to archaeology.

Among archaeologists, too, a more determined backlash arose from the later 1960s onwards, partly as a result of the influence of processual archaeology, invented in the New World but increasingly also practiced in the Old. An important component of this was not only the bid to establish archaeology as an independent, entirely free-standing discipline, with its own coherent Problematik, but also a rejection of the view that it was a poor relation of ancient history, compelled, in the absence of contemporary historical records, to create forms of pseudo-politico-military narrative out of the remains of walls, potsherds, and anonymous graves. In the Aegean the creation of such pseudo-history, with (or indeed without) the aid of legendary material recorded in literature many centuries later, came to be seen as entirely illegitimate, the product of an unhealthy and uncritical privileging of the written word and of a traditional ancient historians' mindset. Archaeology could show that important centers existed at Mycenae and Troy many centuries before the conventional date of Homer, and that Troy suffered destruction or damage many times in its long history, but it could not possibly tell who (or often even what) caused destruction in any given instance, or in what circumstances. It was also quite clear that a chronology dependent on pottery could never provide the kind of resolution that would allow interpretation in terms of this kind of narrative history, and that might have given weight to Blegen's otherwise meaningless juggling with the dates of Troy VIIa. Archaeology could give us a clue to long-term processes of an economic, social or ideological nature, but unless it also produced contemporary historical records which could be specifically tied to a particular context, it could not give us event-centered history, let alone the personae behind such events. The result was that, increasingly, any attempt to relate the archaeological record to the Homeric epics began to be seen as, at best, a waste of time and, at worst, downright misleading. The role of "Homeric" archaeology, insofar as it continued to exist, was thus reduced to providing "illustrations" for epic texts, in the form of boar's tusk helmets, different types of weapons and the like; or in the words of Peter Levi in his preface to the 1984 edition of Leonard Cottrell's *The Bull of Minos* (1984: 13), it became merely "the strange subject . . . which attempts to relate Homer to physical monuments, and which is used, at least at Oxford, as an excuse to introduce young classical scholars to archaeology and to open their minds to the tradition of Schliemann and Evans." "Today," Levi adds, "most archaeologists set little store by the Homeric poems as evidence for the material culture of Mycenaean Greece."

Only in Germany has the idea that archaeology has the ability to shed light on real historical events of the Mycenaean palatial period as a basis for Homer's epics really survived, as much for reasons to do with German national and political psyche as anything else. The results of renewed German excavations at Troy and identifications of names in Hittite texts have been used in an attempt to give Homer's Trojan War some real thirteenth-century basis. It was probably no coincidence that the publication of this argument occurred at about the time of the emotive return to Berlin, as a temporary exhibition, of Schliemann's long lost Early Bronze Age Trojan treasures, which had been discovered in the stores of the Pushkin Museum in Moscow. The principles and methods behind this attempt differ little from those used by Schliemann and his fundamentalist followers. The argument is that, because a city known to the first-millennium Greeks as Ilion and to the late second-millennium Hittites as Wilusa actually existed from 3000 BCE to sometime around the end of the second millennium, because it was destroyed or damaged several times during its long history, and because between the late fifteenth and thirteenth centuries successive kings of a land called Ahhiyawa operated on or near the Anatolian coast in a manner more or less irritating to the Hittite rulers, Homer's account of the Trojan War must therefore have some real and recognizable historical basis. Equally, however, as Finley pointed out, we know that there were battles at Roncevaux and Kosovo in the eighth and fourteenth centuries CE respectively, and we know that Gunther was king of the Burgundians in the fifth century. Nevertheless, these facts do not provide any basis for believing that there is genuine "history" in the twelfth-century *Chanson de Roland*, the thirteenth-century *Nibelungenlied*, or twentieth-century Serbian epics, any more than digging up Carthage or recognizing in Dido the Elissa who figures in that city's Tyrian foundation legend proves the historicity of Virgil's *Aeneid*.

From the Archaeology of "History" to an Archaeology of Epic

The fixation on a historical Trojan War introduced by the impact of Schliemann's discoveries was almost wholly responsible for the archaeology of Homer becoming synonymous with the archaeology of the Aegean Bronze Age and vice versa. With hindsight, it can be seen that this wholehearted diversion of Aegean prehistoric archaeology into what many would now regard as the cul de sac of Homeric historicity, was in many ways also an aberration in the history of the relationship between archaeology and epic generally. This, before Schliemann, and in the case of most later epics, had rapidly settled down to focus mainly on uncovering general chronological and cultural contexts rather than narrative history. And it is arguably in further development of the exploration of different types of contexts that archaeology has been, and could be, most useful in illuminating and aiding appreciation of epic and its subject matter. Since both epic and the archaeological record are cultural artifacts it is self-evident that there has to be some sort of relationship between them. Indeed it is the nature of this relationship that is potentially especially fascinating, and in order to understand this we need to be able in some sense to compare and combine them. Both, however, need their own appropriate source criticisms before we can do so, and in particular we need to investigate the social, cultural, and ideological contexts which formed each of them. In the case of orally created epics, such as the *Iliad* and *Odyssey*, therefore, among the most important questions are: When were they created in the form in which we know them, what was the context in which they were created, and what sort of bardic "prehistory" (if any) lay behind them? To all of these questions archaeology can contribute something more positive than just physical illustrations of the material cultural elements which epic from time to time describes. If we are lucky, it can begin to give us something approaching a true archaeology of epic, a means of gaining insight into an oral cultural equivalent of the material cultural record provided by archaeology.

When were they created in the form we know them?

Although the ancients' own traditional dates for Homer are notoriously vague, for at least the last century there has been a consensus among classicists and archaeologists which places the creation or emergence of the *Iliad* and *Odyssey* in more or less the form we know them at around 700 BCE, give or take a few decades on either side. It seems clear from various scraps of literary evidence that they were already familiar in the seventh century, and the archaeological record appears to bear this out, since a number of scenes of specific narrative recognizable from the epics (for example the Trojan horse on a pithos from Mykonos, or the blinding of Polyphemus on pots from Athens, Argos, western Greece and Etruria) first begin to appear in various regions of Greece from around 700 BCE, following the anonymous, generic scenes of warfare and funerals which characterize the preceding century (Figure 9.4). The epics themselves include a few references which it is difficult to date any earlier than the later eighth century, while on the other hand they contain nothing which can clearly be pinned down to the seventh century. A date of around the end of the eighth century, from which time we see a new interest in the representation of specific narrative in art generally, therefore seems about right.

What was the context in which they were created?

Given that Homer's epics, particularly the *Iliad*, came quickly to be regarded by the historical Greeks as the basis of their own earliest "history," it is inconceivable that their most prominent characters and their deeds, or indeed the Trojan War theme, which forms the essential background of both epics, could have been invented entirely out of nothing in the eighth century. Indeed, it is a feature crucial to the success of all such epic "histories" that they contain what people "know" intuitively to be "true." This is not to say, however, that we should take any of it, including Homer's Trojan War, at face value as a transmitted memory (let alone a record) of any specific person who actually lived or any specific event which actually took place several hundred years earlier, or that we should believe we can find the evidence (direct or circumstantial) of such historical personages or events in the ground. To do so would quite certainly be to perpetuate a uniquely simplistic view, both of the potential of the archaeological record and of the nature and historical role of epic, which grew up specifically around Homeric epic against the background of a particular convergence of modern historical circumstances. The epics undoubtedly represent "history", but "history" is largely what people believe to have happened, rather than necessarily what actually happened; and just because stories exist need not mean that they are in any sense objectively true. Though the Homeric epics, like most "historical" epics,

Figure 9.4   Representation of the Trojan Horse on a pithos from Mykonos, seventh century BCE. ©
Hellenic Republic, Ministry of Culture, Mykonos Museum.

had a deep prehistory which contributed to their formation, they were products of their
own time (Morris 1986). If we are to understand them we have to begin by looking at the
internal structure of their contents, and the context of this in the wider archaeological
context of the period in which they emerged.

Various aspects of the Homeric epics encourage us to see them as having a consciously
integrative function with an unmistakable (if embryonic) panhellenic force. These include
the theme of a collective war against Troy, led by Agamemnon as *primus inter pares*, which
is the essential background against which both *Iliad* and *Odyssey* are set; the setting of the
Iliad at Troy, on the eastern edge of the historical Greek "homeland," and the *Odyssey* on
Ithaca, at its far western edge; the series of dualities or sometimes even triplicities (the
highly artificial combination of Ionic and Aeolic dialects, the three names – Achaeans,
Danaans and sometimes also Argives – used interchangeably to mean "all Greeks," two
interchangeable names for Troy, Paris etc.), all of which look like the deliberate and self-
conscious merging, or reconciling, of more than one regional tradition; the striking
appearance of regional comprehensiveness in terms of early historical Greece, especially
in the Catalogues in *Iliad* 2; and the distinction between Greek and other (particularly
eastern) languages, embodied in the epithets "barbarophonoi" and "allothrooi," together with the linguistic unity which gives the Greeks a military advantage over the
Trojans and their allies. Similarly, various aspects of the archaeological record of the later
eighth century, taken together and in parallel, suggest a strong sense of ethnogenesis – of
Greek-speakers in the process of discovering and defining their own collective identity,
particularly in relation to an eastern "other," in which the discovery and definition of a
collective past plays an important part. On the one hand, the evidence for the growing
importance of supra-regional sanctuaries as a focus for wider identity above and beyond
the purely local or regional, the formal establishment of overtly political colonies at
crucial points on maritime routes in the central Mediterranean, and even perhaps the

introduction of the Greek alphabet can all be linked with a growing sense of specifically Greek identity, created in response to increasing encounters in the Aegean and the west with Phoenician commercial competitors and (in the case of colonization) their similar tactics (Sherratt and Sherratt 1993; Sherratt 1996, 2003). On the other hand, the evidence for cult activity at Mycenaean chamber tombs, the probable beginnings of hero shrines and the development of representational art of a clearly specific narrative nature are signs of an interest in identifying and relating in various ways to a past, probably conceived in terms of linear history, which could form a common focus for a shared identity.

Together, these have some clear implications for the particular form that Homer's "history" takes. To take the most obvious example, the theme of a collective Achaean/Danaan expedition against Troy under the consensual leadership of Agamemnon – which could hardly have happened in real life at any period in Greek history – makes perfect sense in this ideological context, whereas it seems thoroughly anachronistic when measured against what we know (once the rose-tinted spectacles of Homeric faith are removed) of the social, political, and ideological environment of Late Bronze Age Greece when there is not a shred of evidence to support the idea of a united "Mycenaean" (or "Ahhiyawan") empire based at Mycenae or any other palatial center in Greece. The "Mycenaeans" are our concept, invented in the late nineteenth century as a retrojection back into prehistory of the idea of modern (or classical) Greece, with its territorially-based concepts of political or ideological unity. We have absolutely no reason to think that what we call "Mycenaeans," whose scattered palatial centers appear much more like the small-scale historical emirates of the Persian Gulf or Indonesia than the national blocks envisaged as the norm in modern European thought, thought of themselves as a collective unity, either politically or in any other way.

Do they have a "prehistory"?

For reasons to do with their effective "authenticity" (as mentioned above), it is impossible to escape the conclusion that behind most epics, whether oral or literary, lies a long "prehistory" of subject matter which feeds directly into them, and which itself – regardless of any actual historical reality – forms much of the recognized "history" they contain. In the case of the orally created Homeric epics, there is good reason to suppose that much of this "prehistory" consists of bodies of hexameter heroic songs and cycles of songs; the ultimate origins of some at least of them could almost certainly reach as far back as the mid-second millennium BCE and possibly, in certain instances, even further. We can deduce this partly on linguistic grounds (Ruijgh 1957; Watkins 1987; West 1988), but also, more concretely, on archaeological grounds – from datable early material cultural references which are quite often (though not invariably) embedded at various structural levels in the epics – in certain noun-epithet combinations, for example, certain repeated lines or line-endings, certain types of formulaic scenes, or certain story-patterns – which give a clue to the kinds of mechanisms which may have helped preserve them over a long period. Thus, the "tower-like" shield of Aias, a description particularly appropriate to the types of very large body-shield last seen in military use around 1400 BCE, is contained exclusively in a thrice-repeated line which ties Aias and his shield indissolubly together (*Il.* 7.219; 11.485; 17.128); Penelope's shining upper chambers in Odysseus' palace, and the implied staircase which leads to them, both of which seem infinitely more in keeping with Late Bronze Age dwellings than with even the grandest structure of the Early Iron Age, are mentioned mainly (though not exclusively) in a repeated pattern of line-endings (*Od.* 18.200; 19.600; 22.428; cf. also 1.330; 21.356; and 23.85); the massive single spears with which heroes and gods like Achilles, Hektor, and Athena arm themselves, and which gave way to smaller paired throwing spears around the beginning of the twelfth century, often appear in arming scenes, which are among the most formulaic in the *Iliad* in that the equipment is invariably taken up in the same order and in very similar language; the confused (and confusing) impression of "palatial" architectural complexity in Odysseus' palace on Ithaca arises most graphically from the details of the fight with the suitors in *Od.* 22.105–46 (Gray 1955: 11). In this way, it seems clear that an eighth-century Homer knew about such things only because they were an integral part of the inherited bardic (and therefore "historical") traditions with which he had to work. Indeed, nobody has ever explained entirely satisfactorily how an eighth-century bard could know about them by any other means.

Elements of material culture which archaeology suggests are of greatest antiquity usually appear relatively infrequently in the texts, and are often inconsistent or contradictory in character. It thus seems most improbable that they were consciously introduced in the eighth century as deliberate "archaizing" devices to create what Ian Morris (1986) has called epic distancing effects, since if this were the case one might expect them to be much more frequent and consistent. As it is, it is highly unlikely that an epic audience, given the relatively slow pace of performance in which lines of song were probably interspersed with bars of lyre-playing, would have noticed these contradictions and anomalies in the same way that a modern reader can. Heroes can arm themselves with huge single spears with shafts several meters in length (comparable to the very large spearheads with long shafts known from the early Late Bronze Age), and yet throw them repeatedly in battle as though they carried a number of smaller spears in the much more mobile style of fighting characteristic of the period after 1200 BCE. A shield which extends from its bearer's neck to his ankles can morph into a completely circular shield within the confines of a single battle, or a tower-like shield made of several layers of oxhide acquire a bronze face and a bronze boss within the space of a few lines. One of the most striking instances of such anomalies arises with the unworked lump of iron which is both thrown as a discus and offered as a prize during Patroklos' funeral games (*Il.* 23.826–35). Having been the highly prized possession of two proud owners, to whom it never occurred to convert it into anything more useful, suddenly and almost bathetically, at the end of the passage describing its illustrious pedigree and its value in its unchanged state as a prize, its desirability is seen as an afterthought in terms of the number of agricultural and pastoral tools it will furnish. In this case, what we have is the clear juxtaposition of two chronologically quite different attitudes to iron: one, characteristic of the period before 1200 BCE, when iron was regarded as a precious metal immensely valuable in its own right; and the other, characteristic of a full Iron Age (probably no earlier than the ninth century BCE), when iron had become a fully utilitarian material with minimal prestige value, used only for those tools and implements for which its practical properties were advantageous. The four-line addition at the end of the passage would seem to have had the purpose of explaining to an Iron Age audience the apparent idiosyncrasy of the prize's pedigree, which we might therefore conclude itself was the product of a long bardic history stretching back to a time when a lump of unworked iron would have been valued in its own right in this way.

Patterns of archaeological context

Archaeologically datable elements of material culture contained within the epics also produce some interesting patterns in that they seem to cluster in certain chronological periods more than others. As O. T. P. K. Dickinson (1986) has shown by means of a simple totting-up method, the great majority of these can be seen to fall within the approximate limits of the twelfth and ninth centuries BCE. Nevertheless, there are a few elements that are difficult to place any earlier than the eighth century, and an irreducible minimum of others for which the material correlations are best provided by a much earlier period, in most cases preceding the Mycenaean palatial period of the later fourteenth and thirteenth centuries. This is a curious pattern, which needs some explanation. What it implies is that the prehistory of bardic activity that contributed ultimately to the epics was a complex one, determined not only by straightforward passage of time but by different modes of creation and use of heroic song in different social or political contexts. The fact that some periods seem to have contributed more material cultural elements than others suggests that these may have been periods in which a great deal of active bardic creation or reinterpretation was primarily concerned with contemporary image and life-style and perhaps aimed at defining and projecting the deeds and ideals of individuals or small groups with social or political aspirations within their particular communities. Alternating with these were periods in which "possession" of a commonly agreed past, inherited by the community as a whole, may have been more important, and in which the main concern of bards and their patrons was to preserve the general themes and forms (and already antique setting) of inherited heroic songs.

We can perhaps detect the sorts of principles underlying this kind of pattern from some examples of imagery taken from the twentieth century, specifically from a study of the changing political role of street murals in Loyalist areas of Belfast carried out by Bill Royston (1991). Typical of the murals which could be found in such areas from the 1920s down to the start of the troubles at the end of the 1960s was the image of William of Orange on his white horse, crossing the River Boyne in 1690; it was an icon of the far distant past, and a symbol of enormous historical significance to the Loyalist community as a whole. If one were to look closely at this image one could probably find small details which were anachronistic, but the image as a whole was without doubt archaic, firmly set in the late seventeenth century. It was an image with which – because of its chronological distance – the entire Protestant-Loyalist community could identify to a greater or lesser extent, despite its own internal political differences, and even though for some (particularly outside the Orange Lodges) it was essentially a passive symbol of the shared long-term inheritance of a British Protestant Ulster rather than a focus of contemporary ideological activity.

During the 1970s and 1980s images of William of Orange in the Loyalist areas were largely supplanted by new images: the foundation of Sir Edward Carson's Ulster Volunteer Force at the time of Herbert Asquith's Home Rule Bill in 1912, and the paramilitary image and activities of its equally murky reincarnation during the early 1970s. The latter images were sometimes juxtaposed to scenes of the legitimate and wholly patriotic part the Ulster Volunteer Force played in the fighting of the First World War; and the juxtaposition of these two contemporary, or near-contemporary, images (one strictly contemporary, and the other set within the three generations or so which bound historical memory) served the purpose, by association, of legitimizing the contemporary UVF and similar Loyalist paramilitary organizations and their activities. At the same time, these were images with which only a section of the Loyalist community as a whole could identify unambiguously – above all those who were members or supporters of the contemporary paramilitary organizations and their activities and ideology.

Also particularly prominent in the murals of the 1970s and 1980s was the representation of contemporary paramilitary weaponry: often a gun on its own, perhaps with just a single slogan. And, in fact, the ability to produce accurate representations of such things as Armalites and Kalashnikovs was an acknowledged source of pride among the young, predominantly male, mural artists. A further contrast perhaps worth noting between these images and the William of Orange ones of the 1960s is that, whereas the latter were of an identifiable individual and referred to a specific historical narrative (William's victory at the battle of the Boyne), the former were overwhelmingly generic in character. On the whole, they did not represent identifiable individuals, or specific, identifiable events or episodes, only anonymous gun-toting paramilitaries, stylized encounters with Republican paramilitaries, or emblematic weapons.

To return to the Homeric epics, it is particularly interesting that the chronological patterns of material cultural input preserved in these also appear to parallel more general patterns visible in the archaeological record of mainland Greece from the mid-second millennium onwards, including patterns in representational art. What we might see as phases of active generation correspond to periods of social fluidity and instability (for instance the formative, pre-palatial and proto-palatial periods, and again the post-palatial period), during which competing groups of elites seek to define their image and life-style through such devices as ostentatious burial with emphasis on the individual at the time of funeral, and generic representations of military and other prowess, complete with the latest, most prestigious equipment. Alternating with these is a period (the Mycenaean palatial period) of more institutionalized power structures, in which the long-term visual effect of architectural elaboration above ground takes the place of the short-term individual display involved in richly equipped burials, and in which representational art often takes on what appears to be a specific narrative aspect in which "antique" elements can sometimes be detected. This is a period in which the heritage and stability of the "history" represented by bardic song may have been more important, and it might well explain why any trace of the material culture of the Mycenaean palaces and their society is (as Finley (1957) pointed out) apparently much more elusive in the epics than that of the period which preceded it. The same principle might explain the surprising rarity of clear eighth century reflections. This led Finley to conclude that the epics were essentially products of the tenth to ninth centuries, since, when they emerge in the form we know them, it is in a context in which they are clearly regarded as "possessions" of a very much wider Greece. At any rate, these alternating patterns suggest that we cannot talk about Homer's epics either as representing the end of a straightforward line of transmission which started sometime in the Bronze Age and gradually changed as time went on, leaving a "core" (historical or otherwise) intact at its center, or as something that has no continuous bardic traditions behind it but was effectively created out of amorphous snippets of folktales in the later eighth century.

Archaeological contexts of ideology

As with aspects of material culture, certain ideological and symbolic elements of the Homeric epics can also be shown to have a "prehistory" which almost certainly contributed to the "thick" history which made the eighth-century epics so effective as representations of a shared history. Likewise, some of these elements can be traced back archaeologically well beyond any supposed date for an historical Trojan War (Vermeule 1986; Morris 1989). For example, the artistic motif of the siege of a walled city appears in a variety of forms in representational art in the Aegean around the middle of the second millennium. It is a motif, however, which has a very long history in Egypt and the Near East, going back as far as the third millennium, and there are elements of the iconography which suggest that the motif itself was adopted in the Aegean from the East, probably initially through Crete. What it implies is the adoption and adaptation by Aegean elites, as part of their own ideology, of a theme of great importance to the self-image of eastern rulers: the idea that anyone who was anyone had to have carried out (or claimed to have carried out) the successful siege and capture of a city. Later Greek legends, including Homeric epic, preserve various verbal versions of the same motif: not just, most obviously, the Homeric Trojan War, but also the Seven Against Thebes, the exploits of Herakles at Orchomenos and his pre-Trojan War sack of Troy, and the frequent Homeric use of the epithet πτολίπορθος ("sacker of cities") to describe Odysseus, Herakles, and other heroes as well as gods. This is a generic ideological motif of eastern origin borrowed by Aegean elites as an integral part of their image and life-style aspirations, not an item arising from some single specific historical event. It existed as an ideology independent of individuals and individual cities, and as such has some interesting implications for our attitude to the historicity of Homer's Trojan War theme. Sieges – and the idea of sieges as part of the required agenda of elite heroic exploits – existed quite independently of Troy, and long before the thirteenth century. They could almost certainly attach themselves to any character and any city, probably regardless of any real "history."

This is just one verbal and visual motif of eastern origin which archaeology shows was adopted by Aegean elites no later than the mid-second millennium BCE. But there are numerous other elements in Homeric epic which clearly betray their eastern or non-Greek linguistic or cultural origins and their antiquity. In addition to purely linguistic and literary borrowings (see Chapter 20, by Burkert), these include characters such as Odysseus – who may well have started life as a Cretan hero, to be transplanted to Ithaca, the westernmost boundary of a territorially discrete Greek "homeland," only in the eighth century – and other elements of epic imagery which can be traced as visual imagery in the archaeological record of more than one geographical region. For example, the images of lions used by oriental and Egyptian rulers to symbolize their power in battle was adopted into the Aegean Late Bronze Age visual repertoire and almost certainly also into the Late Bronze Age heroic lays which formed part of the deep "prehistory" of Homeric epic (Marinatos 1990). Other eastern borrowings, apart from those derived from *Gilgamesh* and *Atrahasis*, reveal themselves in Homeric story patterns, one such being the story of the competition between Odysseus and the suitors to shoot an arrow through a line of twelve axes (*Od.* 21), which makes little sense if one thinks of the design of Aegean axes (which were never used in battle) but a great deal of sense in terms of the fenestrated, lunate or exaggeratedly curve-butted shapes of eastern battle axes. This story, moreover, has strong echoes of a regular type of iconography and rhetoric emanating from New Kingdom Egypt, which is likely to have reached the Aegean during that time, ready for adaptation and absorption into a succession of local contexts. The implications for the question of the historicity of Homer's Trojan War of what Calvert Watkins (1986) has suggested may be a sixteenth- or fifteenth-century Luvian "Wilusiad" among the catalogue of cultic songs from the city of Istanuwa preserved on texts at Boğhazköy are potentially equally revealing. Preserving the first line of a song which begins "When they came from steep Wilusa . . ." (cf. Ἴλιος αἰπεινή, – "steep Ilion", *Il.* 13.773, also 9.419, 686; 15.71, 215, 558; 17.328), these texts hint at the possibility of a Luvian sacred song perhaps recounting some famous tale about Ilion which probably had nothing to do with any Greek-speakers and was certainly sung about long before the end of either Troy VI or VIIa. It offers another reason for eschewing the archaeological search for specific history in favor of a cumulative internalization of polymorphic material with origins in a variety of different regions, periods, and languages which eventually provided the ready-made ingredients for an ideological bricolage in the eighth century BCE.

Conclusion

In general, save in very exceptional and limited circumstances involving a direct and intimate relationship with contemporary historical documents, archaeology's greatest strengths lie not in furnishing traditional event- or personality-centered history, but in uncovering wider contexts of an economic, social, cultural and ideological nature (see Chapter 5, by Raaflaub). Where some ancient epic (particularly literary Greek and Roman epic, and to some extent also Near Eastern epic) is concerned, much of this context can be provided by other contemporary and earlier literature, including literature of a historical nature, and the role of archaeology is therefore mainly a subsidiary one. When it comes to the Homeric epics, however, such contemporary literary contexts are lacking, and this is why, ever since the 1870s or so, archaeology has often been regarded as a particularly crucial key to their elucidation, and why (in conjunction with their own ideological heritage, including a powerful ideological inheritance from the Greeks themselves) archaeologists have been tempted, aberrantly and for so long, to batter their heads against the brick wall of Homeric historicity. However, although we can excavate Troy, Mycenae, and Pylos, we cannot excavate Homer's Trojan War, or his Odysseus, Achilles, or Agamemnon, any more than we can excavate Virgil's Aeneas or the relics of his adventures. The most we can do is excavate the heterogeneous elements which formed the cumulative "history" out of which Homer's epics were fashioned. These are to be sought not in the archaeology of specific epic history but in the history of epic glimpsed through the archaeology of contexts.

This question of archaeological contexts for the Homeric or indeed other oral epics can be approached in different ways and at different levels. At a mechanical level, archaeology, by documenting the latest datable material cultural references, can help confirm an approximate date for their creation. At a more fundamental level, aspects of the archaeological record of the period in which the epics can thus be shown to have emerged in recognizable form can shed light on the wider social and ideological contexts which produced them, and (in conjunction with ideological aspects of the texts themselves) why they may have done so and the purpose they served. In other ways, by tracking datable elements of material culture in their content, and the contexts in which they occur, archaeology can both demonstrate the existence and hint at the nature of a deep bardic "prehistory" which contributed to the material out of which they were created and without which they would have lacked the "authenticity" necessary to serve this purpose (see Chapter 13, by J. Foley and Chapter 4, by Jensen). In addition, it can detect material (including visual) correlates of elements of epic symbolism and ideology, and can trace these diachronically and across cultural and linguistic boundaries, thus shedding light on the kinds of originally disparate material which finally converged in the creation of the epics. Finally, by revealing alternating patterns in the ways in which such social practices as funerary display are used, or how representative art of a generic, emblematic nature gives way to art of a specific narrative form, the archaeological record may also give us some insight into the differing social and socio-ideological contexts in which differing forms of earlier bardic output may have been created, transmitted, or re-interpreted over a prolonged period.

FURTHER READING

Heinrich Schliemann's own highly dramatized account of his life's mission to uncover the archaeological contexts which lay behind Homeric epic (and thus demonstrate the essential historical veracity of Homer's tales) can be found in Schliemann 1880. A more sober, if somewhat astringent, modern biography of Schliemann in English is Traill 1995. Cottrell 1984 provides an enduringly readable introduction to Schliemann's excavations at Troy and Mycenae, which still have the power to inspire the imagination. Fitton 1995 puts Schliemann's work firmly in context from the point of view of the development of Greek prehistoric archaeology and its changing preoccupations over the last 150 years or so.

The history of changing views of the relationship between Homeric epic and archaeology, from the earlier twentieth century to the present, can be traced through a series of "companion" volumes: Myres 1958; Wace and Stubbings 1962; and Morris and Powell 1997. While works such as Page 1959 and Blegen 1962 continued to cling to the belief that archaeology had demonstrated that the epic world was essentially that of Late Bronze Age Greece, in the 1950s and early 1960s Finley produced a series of influential attacks on this notion (see Finley 1962 and espec. 1964). To some extent, particularly insofar as the use of archaeology was concerned, these built on the quieter skepticism of earlier archaeologically based commentaries, such as Lorimer 1950 (see also Gray 1968). Although more recent books, including Luce 1975, Wood 1985, and Latacz 2001, continue to display something of a hankering for a Late Bronze Age historical basis to the epics, a wide range of articles written since the 1970s demonstrates some of the potentially diverse ways in which the epics can be approached through archaeology and the question of archaeological contexts. Among these are Snodgrass 1974; Dickinson 1986; Morris 1986; Vermeule 1987; Morris 1989; Sherratt 1990; and Manning 1992.

Suggestions for further reading for Near Eastern and Roman epic (including archaeological approaches and the history of these traditions) are best sought in the relevant chapters elsewhere in this volume. However, I would draw attention to Silberman 1982, esp. chs. 12–18, and Lambert 1997.

CHAPTER TEN

The Physical Media: Tablet, Scroll, Codex

Michael W. Haslam

There were brave men before Agamemnon, and epics were sung before they were written – at least, some were. But written they were, and in written form they traveled through time and space, outlasting or deferring any performance beyond scribe's and reader's. This chapter explores the ways in which they did so, focusing not directly on the dynamics of transmission or even on the conditions of readership but on the physical media themselves, the media of poems recurrently instantiated in concretely textualized form, where the eye takes precedence over the ear as the organ of reception.

The principal media may be said to be three: clay tablet, papyrus scroll, and parchment codex. That will mundanely determine the organization of this chapter. Underlying the physical forms is the intersection of writing systems and materials. Cuneiform script ("wedge"-writing) is correlated with clay, while alphabetic Greek came into the Egyptian tradition of papyrus and ink. That is a mini-set of data with implications and ramifications that go far beyond the scope of this chapter. Another important factor is the cultural function performed by textualization. Written epic is typically not put on public display, does not take the monumental form of incised stone. Rather than memorializing, it preserves and transmits itself, in the more dynamic form of what may broadly be called books. Only at Helicon would Hesiod's *Works and Days* (see Chapter 23, by Nelson) be perpetuated in lead.

A stripped-down narrative account would go like this. The standard textual vehicle throughout the Near East (Egypt apart), for some three thousand years, was the clay tablet. It died not with the advent of papyrus but with the death of cuneiform, killed off by Aramaic. Sumerian and Akkadian epic went with it, as did Ugaritic (see Chapter 16, by Wyatt). Greek and Latin literature was carried on papyrus scrolls. Later the codex form superseded the scroll, and papyrus was displaced by parchment. That account embeds more than facts, and certainly needs refining and contextualizing, but it is usable. The main divide, unmistakably, is between Near Eastern on the one hand, in cuneiform, and Greek and Latin on the other, in pen and ink; the interface between the Ancient Near East and early Greece (see Chapter 20, by Burkert) did not extend to the written medium. The papyrus scroll, for its part, has as long a history as the cuneiform clay tablet, but within the Greek-Latin continuum something remarkable occurs: a shift of medium, as the scroll gave way to the codex.

Each of the three, clay tablet, papyrus (or parchment) scroll, and parchment (or papyrus) codex, makes a very different kind of book, and a reader experiences each in a correspondingly different way. The Akkadian Gilgamesh epic (see Chapter 15, by Noegel) consists of a set of separate tablets. A reader takes the first, reads the text on the front, flips the tablet vertically to read the text on the back, then moves on to the next tablet. The *Iliad*, up to the time of the Roman empire, is a set of papyrus scrolls, the text written in a series of columns. A reader works his way laterally through each scroll, ending up each time with a scroll that needs to be rewound. The codex, by contrast, has pages. On reaching the end of a right-hand page, you turn it over and continue – or not, of course; these idealized vignettes, in outlining what actual reading entails in the respective media, presume a user whose interest is in reading the text. Cultural leveling apart, that is to respect the function that text-carrying objects ostensibly serve, but in fact they tend to make their presence felt as the artifacts that they are. In mediating the contact between text and user, the artifact sets the terms under which both its featured text and its contextualizing self are viewed.

These three, each in approximate turn the culturally dominant medium, claim primary status; no matter that the parchment codex is genetically a bastard form. But other media too come into play, which fit less neatly into this already over-tidy schema. Sometimes used for high-class library texts in Mesopotamia, alongside clay tablets but far less visible in the archaeological record (see Chapter 9, by Sherratt), were wax-surfaced boards (or tablets) of wood or ivory. Two things give wax tablets special interest. They bridge the cuneiform/alphabet divide. And unlike clay tablets they can be joined together; the most familiar form is the diptych, a joined pair, but they were often multiple. And then there is skin. For ink-written scripts in the Near East and other regions where papyrus was not available (it was an Egyptian product), and sometimes even where it was, suitably prepared animal skins were used; they could be cut to shape and stitched together. Preparation techniques are complex, but skin and papyrus make comparable writing materials. Unfortunately, the history of writing-skins prior to the emergence of the parchment codex early in the Roman empire is exceptionally hard to track, and their use for epic is quite uncertain. These matters will receive more attention below, as will the well-attested but relatively short-lived papyrus codex, a second-generation bastard.

"Book," "epic" – we are dealing in terms and concepts far more at home in Greek and Latin context than in ancient Near Eastern, where the continuities of discourse with our own culture are less direct, the category systems less transparent, the goal of a truly historicized account further beyond reach (see Chapter 14, by Sasson). It is rightly harder to think of a clay tablet as a book than to think of a papyrus scroll as one, and it is highly questionable whether any Near Eastern civilization had any notion of epic (see Chapter 1, by Martin). Cultural distortion is built in. But the problems of relativization can here be skirted without too much intellectual discomfort, at least in one important respect; for however we may choose to define it, epic has no medium peculiar to itself. Greco-Roman epic is one literary genre among others, the most prestige-laden to be sure, but not mediumistically distinct from other kinds of literature. In the Near East the category itself is more dubious, but it is on the basis of textual form and content, not of medium, that modern scholarship affixes or withholds the label. "Literature" has various ways of distinguishing itself from other kinds of document – calligraphy, dedicated storage areas (libraries) – but otherwise shares its media with much else. In the cuneiform world formal communications and records of all kinds were committed to clay, and archived. In the Greco-Roman world, where writing had greater social penetration, papyrus scrolls served an even more extensive range of purposes; the codex, a more elaborate and custom-made product, is less multi-purpose, but still quite versatile. To say that the media of epic are not genre-specific is not to say that epic manuscripts are entirely without distinctiveness as a class. If epic is defined formalistically – as composition in dactylic hexameter in Greek and Latin, less straightforwardly in Akkadian – the look of the text as laid out on (so to speak) the page enables a Greek or Latin epic text to be recognized as such at a distance, practically at a glance, without reading a word. That may not be quite the case with tablet texts, but experienced eyes have little difficulty identifying the nature of a text by appearance alone.

Something all the media have in common is materiality, and a text which in consequence is artificially broken up. Until the codex becomes sufficiently capacious to accommodate epics in their entirety, the text has to be parceled out over more than a single carrier object. That makes for practical problems of continuity and sequentiality, and may have less obvious effects on poems' stability and identity, as well as conditioning their internal articulation. Size matters. A banal but related point is that as textual vehicles get roomier, epics get bigger. The rule is valid only in the most general terms, and the capacity of the medium is not the only factor, but even so, it is no accident that the shortest epics (if they may be called that) are Sumerian, the longest Nonnus. And whether or not a text can be contained within the compass of a single manuscript, it still has to be interrupted at frequent (ideally regular) intervals, turned into a succession of blocks of text, whether sides or columns or both. Each of the various media organizes the text in its own manner, and acquires its own aesthetic proprieties.

It is worth bearing in mind that an ancient book, being a manuscript (a thoroughly anachronistic concept, if we discount cylinder seals), has a uniqueness that its modern printed counterpart does not. A written text is a less fleeting performance than an oral-aural one (see Chapter 13, by J. Foley and Chapter 4, by Jensen) – the thing is still palpably there when a song is but a memory – but a poem in writing depends no less on replication (never exact) for its continued existence, and institutional praxis variously addresses or evades the issue of textual instability. Greek and Latin epics unvaryingly sustain their given identity, and while variants may sometimes be registered, evidencing collation of one text against another, it is rare to find individuation of manuscript or of edition, or notice of transmissional lineage; the austerity is eventually broken at Rome with subscriptions to texts of the *Aeneid*. Akkadian epics can be transmitted in no less faithfully fossilized form, but tend to be ontologically more labile. Scholars talk of different "versions" or the like, but the point at which a poem evolves into a different one is not readily fixed. The opening words serve as a poem's identifier, however, and subscriptions ("colophons") define a particular tablet-set's place in the world.

Clay tablets may get chipped, or crack and break, but can last practically forever. Portable but bulky, they tend not to move far from home, except when carried off as booty. Tablet-texts from one place may be copied onto new tablets at another, and a copy may record points at which the exemplar was damaged. Tablets are local products, whereas papyrus as a writing material is a commodity imported from Egypt in the form of made-up scrolls ready for use; it is the written scroll that is the local product, easily transportable in turn, and with a shelf-life comparable to that of modern books. Scrolls were liable to suffer wear and tear at the edges and especially at the beginning; a cedar-oil preservative was sometimes applied to protect them from insect and worm damage; if torn, they could be repaired.

With all that by way of preliminary, we can take a closer look at the individual media.

Tablet

"Mud sometimes gives the illusion of depth."
(Marshall McLuhan)

Cuneiform originates in clay, and the two make naturally good partners. Already well established in the third millennium not only in Sumer, where it is generally reckoned to have originated, but in Elam to the east and at Ebla to the west, the clay tablet was a textual medium shared by many different languages and cultures. The materials, unlike the scribal skills needed to use them, were not hard to acquire. Rivers provided the clay, marshes the reeds from which styli were cut. The production process was technologically simple. The soft clay was shaped and smoothed, the "wedges" (or "nails") that comprised the characters were imprinted with the stylus, to form those mysterious signs that somehow represented language: "The Lord of Aratta scrutinized the clay. But the spoken word was a nail" (*Enmerkar and the Lord of Aratta*). Whether or not clay merits the title of "the best writing material yet devised by man" by virtue of its unmatched cheapness and durability (Oppenheim 1964: 229), the nature of the material goes a long way towards explaining the range and persistence of cuneiform writing systems in the Near East.

With papyrus scrolls, manufacture of the writing material does not need to be coordinated with the actual writing, but the production of written clay tablets is a single integrated process, which must have been thoroughly organized in the temple and palace centers. Clay quality, geographically variable, will have been a matter of consistency of composition, plasticity, both wet and dry strength, possibly color. The finished product, the written tablet, was air-dried; it could be oven-baked, but it seems fewer tablets were accorded this treatment than was once thought, for many of today's tablets were baked only in fires of conquest or accident, or upon excavation as a conservation measure. Most of the technical as well as institutional aspects of manufacture and manuscripture still await proper investigation, but the simple point that bears stressing here is that with clay tablets the preparation of the writing material goes hand in hand with the writing itself. Once the clay is dry, further writing is not altogether impossible (some of Assurbanipal's acquisitions have their new ownership scratched or ink-written in imitation cuneiform), but the primary text is final; the making of a clay tablet text is a from-start-to-finish business. Text has to fit tablet, but tablet may be made with textual fit in view. The mutual accommodation of tablet and text is another subject in need of more investigation than it has so far received.

Tablet size and shape vary considerably, as also do size and spacing of the writing, which can be quite astonishingly small and compact. The one consistency, for "epic" texts at least, is that the tablets are approximate rectangles, the writing linear. They are sometimes exaggeratedly tall and narrow, sometimes more nearly square, sometimes broader than tall, not often exceeding 30 cm on the longer axis; thickness and curvatures are likewise variable. The writing is on both sides of the tablet (a point of affinity with the codex as opposed to the scroll), and it habitually starts at the very top and occupies the full width of the tablet, any empty area coming only at the end of the tablet's text. The text may be disposed in a series of columns, two or three or more per side, close-set; the wall-to-wall furrows present a very different appearance from the parade of columns through the length of a papyrus scroll, black blocks of text set in lavish white surroundings. Columns are routinely taller than they are wide, often about twice as tall or more, but the relative as well as the absolute dimensions show considerable variation. Both single-column (per side) and multi-column tablets were in coexistent use in many different eras and places, with correspondingly different shapes. In some cases it is possible to discern formats which may have been more or less standard: tall narrow tablets for *Enuma Elish*, large broad multi-column ones for *Gilgamesh* (whether or not in its first-millennium "Standard Babylonian" form, Sha naqba imuru), but such constancies may not extend very far. The tendency overall is for tablets to get bigger, texts to get longer, columns of writing to get broader, but such sweeping generalizations are subject to many qualifications. An Old Babylonian text of the Atrahasis epic found at Sippar, dating from *ca.* 1700 BCE, was written on large tablets (25 cm high × 19.5 cm broad) with four columns per side; a text of the "Standard Babylonian" version of the same epic, also from Sippar but produced about a thousand years later, occupied narrow tablets (17 × 7 cm) with only one column per side.

Such variations aside, the medium is very stable. The texts copied for the palace collections at Nineveh under Ashurbanipal show the ultimate state of the art, palpably inviting admiration while at the same time being wholly conventional: large, very well made tablets with straight edges, squared corners, and smooth plane surfaces, not square but variously oblong, the writing calligraphically executed in ruled columns with very narrow gutters. The unprodigal use of space, which contrasts with the spaciousness of de-luxe Greek and Latin manuscripts and is only accentuated by the occasional intrastichic gaps, is here an item of refined showmanship. As thoroughly aestheticized products they do their job, or much of it, without needing to be read. The inscribed cylinders and other such artifacts in the palace show the same or analogous features, contrived perfection rendered in the economy of fit between the writing and the recipient object.

However big the tablet and small the writing, few tablets carry more than three or four hundred lines. And unlike a scroll, which can always have more added to it if it turns out not to be long enough for its assigned text, a tablet is not extensible. It has been suggested that the commonest size of tablet in the Old Babylonian period, *ca.* 13 × *ca.* 9 cm, carrying about 30–5 lines on each side, is responsible for articulation of Sumerian poetic compositions in multiples of around 60–70 lines (Vanstiphout 1995: 2184). There is room for skepticism here, for Sumerian poems may not show sufficient consistency in either length or structuring, but it is undeniable that there is interdependence between tablet and text, and there clearly has to be some form of negotiation between the size and shape of the one and the size and shape of the other. It could be that the text is controlled by the medium not only in the form of its presentation but also in a more constitutive sense. At all events, the question of their interaction is much more significant than is the case with scrolls.

Whatever the inhibitions, a text can be split up and divided between two tablets, or more than two. Once text and tablet cease to be physically coextensive, limits on length are removed. At the same time, once a text is split up, its integrity is lost, or at least jeopardized; each tablet is a literally independent entity. Methods of repairing the loss of physical unity were in fact much the same as with modern multi-volume works: the constituent tablets could be of the same size, and match in appearance; there could be labels, on pieces of clay attached by string; and a set or group of tablets could be kept in a container, itself labelled, or in the same "pigeonhole" (this sort of storage system is preserved at Khorsabad and Sippar, the walls lined with tiers of niches or minicubicles), or simply adjacent on the same shelf. Internally, correct sequence is facilitated by catch-lines, i.e. by including the first line of the next tablet at the end of the current tablet's text, ruled off from it or not. Most significantly of all, there was what may be termed metatext, in the form of the colophon, a subscription appended at the end of the main text. Its first and most indispensable item is the tablet's self-identification: "tab. 3, Enuma elish" (the poem's first words serving in effect as title). By these means a text's sundered members could be united. A reader (scribe/librarian/priest/scholar/functionary) would know what tablet came next in the series (as well as what came first), whether or not he could find it.

The organization of multi-column multi-tablet texts must have required quite careful planning. The Old Babylonian *Atrahasis* mentioned above, for example, has 1,245 lines, distributed over three tablets each with four columns per side: the arrangement had to be worked out in advance, so as to ensure that each tablet's text would end in its eighth column, with enough room left for the colophon. This particular set of tablets, like many others, registers the line-count of its text, tablet by tablet: every tenth line is marked (line-initial wedge for "10"), and the colophon of each tablet, after identifying its membership of the set, records its line-count (416 lines for tab. 1,439 for tab. 2,390 for tab. 3 and then "total 1,245, 3 tablets"). The primary function of the line-count was no doubt as a control on textual integrity, but it may have incidentally assisted the distribution into columns and tablets. Things did not always go well: sometimes a tablet turned out to be not quite big enough for the text it was assigned to hold, forcing the scribe to compress the layout and use the tablet edges in order to get it all in. Worse miscalculation would be ruinous. Such exigencies do not apply to scrolls, but return with the codex.

The columns of text on either side of the tablet are arranged in a way that may seem odd to us, and would certainly have seemed odd to Greeks and Romans. On the front of the tablet (the "obverse") everything proceeds in familiar fashion: the direction of writing is from left to right (a third-millennium innovation), the sequence of columns likewise. But on the other side (the "reverse"), while the direction of writing is still from left to right, the sequence of columns is from right to left; and the text is upside-down relative to the text on the front. The upper lefthand corner of the obverse, the beginning, will be the lower lefthand corner of the reverse, the end. It all seems less odd once the implied procedure is recaptured. On arriving at the end of the last column of the front, the scribe – or the reader – turns the tablet over, from top to bottom, and as it were continues the column; the remaining columns then proceed leftwards. It is a standing convention of the medium.

A composition's poetic form is normally given recognition by the layout of the text, indeed is virtually constituted by it. In the main Mesopotamian tradition, Sumerian and Akkadian, the written text consists of stichoi, lines of verse, each of which is at the same time a sentence or something like it, sense-units and verse-units being coextensive. In the absence of a self-defining metrical form such as the dactylic hexameter, analyses have trouble avoiding circularity, but each line of text is what is conventionally termed a verse. Lines are right-justified as well as left-justified (that is to say, they not only begin but also end in vertical alignment), intensifying a visual effect further enhanced by the columns' being set very close to one another and often marked off by vertical rulings to left and right. This contrasts with the practice in Greek and Latin poetic manuscripts, which conspicuously make no attempt to regularize the line-length of metrically equal lines. Within the line, too, the practice differs. Whereas in Greek and Latin manuscripts the verse is written uniformly letter by letter from beginning to end, in Mesopotamian there is intrastichic articulation. The verses often fall into two halves (hemistichs), and the written tradition often indicates the medial segmentation (caesura); in some manuscripts the second halves are set in vertical alignment, just as the line-beginnings are; there is little inhibition against resultant gaps within the line. In short, there is correlation between the formal layout of the lines on the one hand and their poetic structure in terms of syntax and sense on the other, both at the level of the verse (with the privilege of a line to itself) and also within the verse (the medial articulation). This is how the song is scribally actualized. Equivalent oral rendition can be imagined (substituting temporal actualization for spatial, vocal for visual). The written poem is self-standing.

The Ugaritic "epics" (see Chapter 16, by Wyatt), curiously, do not observe this tradition of stichic layout. Though internally they appear to show comparable verse-forms, and were written on multi-column tablets, they are written simply as continuous text, not in lines that correspond to the verses, or only intermittently so. They are not acknowledged as poems at all. The same is true of Hittite texts (see Chapter 17, by Beckman). There may be special factors at work in each case. The Ugaritic texts are single-copy specimens, most if not all of them the product of a single scribe (the colophons identify him), and there is no way of judging their typicality. The Hittite texts, for their part, are versions of Hurrian originals, and their status as verse seems open to question. Texts of Akkadian epic at Hattusas follow the same system of layout as elsewhere.

Justified verse layout calls for lines far from equal in the number and form of their constituent characters to occupy the same extent of horizontal space. In practice it is not feasible, and the system not rigorously sustained. Often a long line cannot be accommodated within the alloted space and spills over, or when columns are narrow verses may be divided over two lines; conversely, verses are sometimes doubled up (especially when the scribe realizes he will otherwise run out of space on the tablet), or inconsistently lineated. But scribes do have means of achieving the requisite equalization, by elongating the component signs of the shorter verses, by leaving gaps between their character-groups; such leveling can be done unobtrusively, masking the inequalities, but preferred practice is to leave pronounced gaps. In ostentatiously calligraphic manuscripts it appears to be something of an affectation, these intermittent blanks on an otherwise fully inscribed surface standing out like bursts of sudden silence.

The verse is normally the largest poetic unit accorded textual recognition, but horizontal rulings sometimes mark off larger structures. They sometimes mark speech termini (as paragraphi sometimes do in Greek manuscripts), sometimes effect other, less organic demarcations; sometimes they occur at points in the text where other manuscripts pass from one tablet to another, and in such cases that is perhaps just what they are indicating.

Soft clay is not the only substance that will take and hold an impression, and so be suitable for cuneiform. There is also wax. The waxed writing-board – sometimes referred to as a stylus tablet, to distinguish it from the hard-surfaced pen-and-ink tablet – in fact outlasted the clay tablet, for it successfully made the transition from the cuneiform world of the Near East to the non-cuneiform world of Greece and Rome. It is true that non-cuneiform scripts can be written with a stylus in clay as well as in wax, and clay tablets were routinely used for Greek in the Mycenaean age, as the thousands of Linear B tablets testify. But once Greek had its alphabet, there was little further place for clay, except in the very different form of the ostrakon, broken pottery. The wax tablet, however, retained its utility. In the Greco-Roman world it was not used as a medium of literature in other than draft or exercise form; its great advantage is that it can easily be used over and over again. But in the Near East it was employed not only for day-to-day purposes but also for library texts. Actual survivals are next to none, but colophons of surviving clay-tablet copies of texts sometimes attest writing-board exemplars, and inventories of accessions to the royal libraries at Nineveh under Assurbanipal catalogue writing-boards along with clay tablets.

The board was ordinarily of wood, one or both sides shallowly recessed for the writing area, which was filled with a thin layer of wax. The wax itself was actually a mixture of beeswax and orpiment (trisulphide of arsenic), a mixture which is more workable and gives a more plastic writing surface than wax alone and has a more attractive yellow color; in the Greco-Roman sphere pigments of other colors were used. The orpiment and in some regions the wood would have to be imported, but widespread use is attested from the second millennium on, in a variety of woods.

Boards can be used singly. But it is the simple fact that they can be joined together that in terms of mediumistic potential crucially distinguishes tablets of wood (whether wax-surface or hard-surface) from tablets of clay. The diptych (to use the Greek term) is a pair of boards attached in such a way that it can be opened and closed. The writing was on the two facing sides, exposed to view when the diptych was opened, concealed and protected when it was folded shut. The "folded board" with its "lethal signs" that Bellerophon took with him from Greece to Lycia in *Iliad* 6, the only mention of writing in Homer, shows at least indirect acquaintance with the medium. What must be an exceptionally fine example was recovered from the fourteenth-century Uluburun shipwreck off the Lycian coast. Less than 10 cm in height, with a correspondingly small writing area of *ca.* 7.5 × *ca.* 4.5 cm, this pair of boxwood boards had ivory hinges (three hinges, at least two of them ivory), equipped with hidden wooden dowels and attached to the grooved edges of the boards by hidden wooden nails; rotation through 180° enabled the boards to lie flat when open, a loop-and-hook mechanism fastened them closed. All in all it is a fairly elaborate piece of carpentry. Normally, one may imagine, the construction would be simpler, the boards linked by cords passing through bored holes, as later at Rome; but it could be that the diptych had a status that called for less crude styles of manufacture.

The number of boards is not limited to two. Several of the writing-board accessions itemized in the Nineveh catalogues consisted of more than four. The distinction between "diptych" and "polyptych" used in modern discussions does not correspond exactly to Akkadian classification, where the (waxed) writing-board medium is generally designated *le'u*, sometimes specified as wood (the kind of wood sometimes also specified; other materials are ivory and lapis lazuli), and an individual board is referred to as a *daltu* or "door" (the word comes into Greek as *deltos*, carrying the writing-board signification); a writing-board set consists of a given number of "doors." In the context of the codex – to shift again to later terminology – these are "leaves" (Lat. *folia*), a term more apt for parchment than for unpliable wood. The assumption might be that the multi-board sets were constructed in the familiar form whereby the boards are linked all at one side, as in a codex. But a remarkable survival suggests otherwise. A late eighth-century polyptych discovered at Kalhu, made not of wood but of ivory and consisting of no fewer than sixteen boards, was put together by hinging the boards one to the other concertina-style, "like the separate leaves of a Japanese screen" (Howard 1955). Admittedly this was no ordinary book; the level of craftsmanship is phenomenal, especially in the sophistication of its hinging, and no ordinary book was ever made of ivory. In fact, as its cover-title proclaims, it was made for the king of the world, Sargon II, destined (or rather intended, for it never got there, or if it did was promptly purloined) for his new palace at Dur-Sarrukin. Even so, it would be surprising if there is anything new about its basic make-up, and it is best taken as a maximally luxurious rendering of a conventional form. It seems quite possible, then, that this concertina method of construction of multi-board sets was standard. The boards would both unfold and fold very neatly, and it is certainly no less "natural" a way of extending a diptych than the alternative codex method, which is without Near Eastern attestation. Indeed, if the first stage of development is thought of in terms of joining two diptychs together, the concertina arrangement is the only way of having the written sides directly succeed one another. This kind of construction is known in other cultures (China, most notably), and it is interesting to find it independently resorted to in the case of a set of thin folded wooden leaves used by Roman military personnel in Britain around the end of the first century CE (Bowman and Thomas 1983: 40, 83–4). This concertina form of book has no established name; it could be called a "ptych."

The Sargon ptych is a book that can be judged by its cover, which grandly displays a centered and boxed four-line inscription incised in the ivory, identifying the thing:

"Palace of Sargon, king of the world, / king of Assyria. The text series (beginning) Enuma Anu Enlil / he had written on an ivory writing-tablet and / deposited it in his palace at Dur-Sarrukin" (trans. Wiseman 1955). The very existence of covers, and potentially of cover-titles, is a feature of the medium inherently alien to the clay tablet. A clay tablet has only two sides, which is to say it consists only of front and back (and edges), and the text always begins at the very top. A ptych, like a codex, has not only front and back, which are now exterior sides, but interior sides too, and the exterior ones can serve as covers to protect the text written on the interior. Wooden diptychs, such as the Uluburun specimen mentioned above, had only the inner sides recessed to receive the wax and the writing, and Sargon's polyptych follows suit. How usual it was to utilize the otherwise vacant front cover for identification is impossible to say, but the medium certainly lends itself to that. This stands in sharp contrast with clay-tablet practice, where all such metatextual data are deferred to the end, in the colophon.

The layout of the text on writing-boards may be assumed to have followed the model of the clay tablet, but the Sargon ptych is the only surviving specimen on which it can be observed. This particular ptych, perhaps unusually large (though wooden boards found in the same cache were somewhat larger), was about twice as tall as it was wide (*ca.* 34 × *ca.* 15.5 cm), a common shape for clay tablets, and the impression of height was enhanced by the text's being laid out in two long narrow columns per board-side, about 125 lines to the column, the writing small. The whole book, if it did indeed comprise the sixteen boards as reconstructed, would have accommodated around 7,500 lines. That is more than epic length. The text, however, is a well-known astronomical omen series; copies of such texts, embodying the forms of Babylonian scientific prognostication, hugely outnumber copies of epics. The fact remains that in the ptych we meet a high-prestige medium with the capacity to contain whole epics.

It was on clay that Enmerkar had invented writing, and one might have imagined that the venerable clay tablet was always the more authoritative medium, immutable and ideologically pre-eminent. Whether such a view can survive the challenge posed by the Sargon ptych seems to be an open question.

Scroll

In Egypt grew papyrus, from which papyrus scrolls were made. ("Roll" not "scroll" is the usual term among classicists, after German "Rolle," but no one speaks of the Dead Sea Rolls, and "scroll" has the advantage of suggesting affinity with the process of "scrolling" on a computer screen, though a papyrus roll was scrolled through not vertically but laterally.) The process of manufacture was again fairly simple, the technique already perfected by the end of the fourth millennium. A sheet of papyrus was made from two sets of pith strips from sections of the freshly cut stem, one set laid across the other; under compression they bonded. Sheets were then pasted together together one next to the other, and the resultant length, tough but very supple, could be rolled up. The sheets were arranged in such a way that on the inside of the scroll the papyrus fibers ran horizontally, interrupted only by the sheet-joins. This was the side written on (the "front," therefore: the term "recto" is not properly applied to the scroll, only to the codex), in a succession of columns through the length of the scroll. The outside (or back) was normally left blank. The actual writing, a wholly separate operation from the two-stage manufacture of the papyrus roll itself, was done in ink, in Egyptian tradition both black and red, applied with a rush pen, in "hieratic" script, the difference between hieroglyphic and hieratic being determined by their respective media, the one incised in stone, the other ink-written on papyrus. Texts could be long; scrolls of over 30 meters in length are found. But Egypt had no epic (unless the tale of Sinuhe qualifies). As far as epic is concerned, the papyrus scroll was a medium in waiting.

It had a long time to wait. There is no clear evidence for use of the papyrus scroll outside of Egypt before the first millennium. Papyrus could probably have been acquired through trade by the Minoans and the Mycenean Greeks if they had wanted it, but apparently they did not. In those societies writing was confined to the administrative centers and served exclusively bureaucratic purposes, for which their incised tablets sufficed. If there was Mycenean epic, it was not written. Within Mesopotamian and Anatolian orbits, the dominance of clay and cuneiform was slow to yield. The case of Ugarit is telling: a city with trade access to Egypt, and with a proto-alphabetic script, yet rendered in cuneiform. In between northern Syria and Egypt, however, peoples emerged who did not write their texts in clay. The Phoenician script and its congeners, Aramaic and Hebrew, and alphabetic Greek, were non-cuneiform, suited to writing with pen and ink. If there was Phoenician epic, and it took written form, it was written on scrolls. The same is true of Hebrew epic. None of the poetic books of the Bible can be called epic (see Chapter 19, by Niditch), but some scholars have envisioned epic poems lying behind some of the transmitted prose narratives, and the excerpt quoted at Josh. 10: 13 is suggestive. Greek epic we have, Homer and Hesiod its defining foundational figures, and it must have been written on scrolls from the outset.

Whether such scrolls were of papyrus or rather of skin, as some prefer to assume, the point of primary importance is the mediumistic divide between cuneiform and non-cuneiform writing systems. This is neatly epitomized by Assyrian reliefs of the eighth and seventh centuries depicting a pair of standing scribes, officials or clerks, identical except for their equipment. One (the one to the front, significantly) holds either a clay tablet or a hinged diptych – on some representations it is unambiguously a diptych, the spine clearly marked, on others it looks more like a tablet. The other holds a scroll – whether papyrus or parchment, or sometimes one and sometimes the other, is disputed, and it may be wrong to think of the question as resolvable even in principle, when both materials were in use (a letter of the time of Sargon II acknowledges receipt of papyrus scrolls). There is no ambiguity about the basic differentiation. The kings of Nimrud and Nineveh kept records both in cuneiform Akkadian and in pen-and-ink Aramaic. But Akkadian literature was stuck on the older side of the divide, and its classic medium was the clay tablet. Its tenaciousness persisted – *Gilgamesh* was still being copied in Babylon around the end of the second century BCE – but the literature and the medium diminished and died together.

As between skin and papyrus, uncertainties are inevitable when the material evidence is so sparse, and the textual so uninformative. Specific data are few, most of them much-rehearsed. The most salient item in regard to the Greek-speaking world is the statement appended to Herodotus' account of Ionian Greeks' adoption of Phoenician script: the Ionians had from of old called (papyrus-)books "skins" (*diphtherai*) because when (papyrus-)books were scarce they used to use sheep and goat skins, which in his day many of the barbarians (i.e. non-Greeks) still did. This reflects a fifth-century Greek perspective. Papyrus – the material of contemporary Greek books – is viewed as the more modern and advanced medium; the very word for "book," *biblos* or *byblos*, means papyrus. The statement gives no ground for thinking that Greek literature was ever actually written on skins whether in Ionia or elsewhere. Certainly the use of skins as a writing material was current, the most telling testimony being the reported and perfectly credible claim by Herodotus' contemporary Ctesias that he had consulted "the royal skins," i.e. palace archival sources, for his Persian history. Even in Egypt there was a place for leather scrolls, from very early times, in special ritual contexts.

Though little is known of patterns of production or usage, writing-skins were unquestionably in use before Herodotus' time not only in Ionia but in Syria and Palestine, in Mesopotamia, and in regions further east, written in ink in Aramaic and related scripts, alphabetic Greek quite possibly among them. But in some parts papyrus too was present. The earliest actual survival is an eighth-century Hebrew letter found in Judaea; this should not surprise, given contemporary attestation of papyrus use in Assyria. The most tantalizing traces come in the form of bullae, or sealings. Papyrus documents, like others, were sealed with clay; nothing remains of the papyrus except for a few fibres caught by the clay, or the impression left by them. This form of evidence has been found in Phoenician, Hebrew, and Assyrian contexts in the earlier centuries of the first millennium, and continues to come to light. There is hope of further progress here, and a comprehensive study would be welcome. Caution is required, for there may be confusion as between papyrus and other materials and as between real and illusory impressions; evidence may have been missed, for attention generally focuses more on a sealing's front, the seal impression itself, than on its back. One very nice conjunction is between the discovery of a bulla inscribed with the name of Baruch son of Neriah, with papyrus traces on the back, and the lively account in Jeremiah of scrolls written by Baruch – evidently on papyrus. On the basis of later practice leather rather than papyrus has sometimes been unwarrantably assumed for Hebrew texts in pre-exilic times. Papyrus was probably the principal writing material in Phoenicia and neighbouring regions, and in any event Phoenicia is likely to have played a key role in the Greeks' acquisition of papyrus and the writing practices associated with it, quite apart from the matter of the alphabet itself. There is no need to wait for direct Egyptian-Greek commerce, when there were such entrepots as Byblos.

Often adduced in this connection is the tale of Wen Amun, a report written around 1100 BCE by an Egyptian temple official sent to Byblos to procure timber for the sacred barge of Amun Re. One of the Egyptian goods traded in exchange was once taken to be 500 papyrus scrolls, and this continues to feature in the scholarly literature, but it turns out that the 500 items in question are not papyrus but something else, perhaps "a kind of undergarment" (Goedicke 1975: 96f., 155). Egyptian export of papyrus is thus not attested by this document (except perhaps insofar that the records consulted by the ruler of Byblos may be assumed to have been of papyrus). Nor does the Greek *byblos*/ Byblos homonymy have the evidential value sometimes claimed for it, for rather than imagining that Greek adopted the port-name Byblos as the word for papyrus it is better to think that it assimilated the name of Gbl to the pre-existing word. But there is no question of the existence of the trade relationship, and what reached Phoenicia will have reached other places in the Mediterranean. Whatever view is taken of the time and place of the first writing of the Homeric and Hesiodic epics, the probability is that papyrus was the material used – scrolls made in Egypt.

Putting the *Iliad* into writing was no casual event, and its circumstances are highly contested (see Chapters 13, 4, 6, by J. Foley, Jensen, and Nagy respectively). It is not just a matter of when and where but of how and why, and of what difference writing made to the composition of the poem itself. Given that the poem as it was written down was generated under extraordinary conditions, its very constitution is at issue. In particular the phenomenal length of the Homeric poems, each much too long for continuous one-man performance yet signaling no intermissions, seems best accounted for by reference to the specialness of the occasion of their first writing. For the Homeric as also for the Hesiodic poems (see Chapter 23, by Nelson) the indications are that there was just one formative writing down of each poem, which controlled subsequent transmission; only writing can be responsible for the early arrest of the poems' linguistic development. The written poems culminate an oral tradition, and oral performance continued to be the principal medium until at least the fourth century, but once written, they were fixed, more or less;

the crucial event in the poems' history was their first writing, and that seems to have been certainly before the end of the seventh century, quite possibly before the end of the eighth. Thereafter there is a written transmission as well as an oral one, with various kinds of mostly unfathomable interplay between the two. Competitive performances by rhapsodes, firmly attested for Sicyon early in the sixth century, may or may not be taken as implying the existence of book-texts underlying them, and competing stories about who first introduced Homer to such-and-such a place (Lycurgus to the Peloponnese, Hipparchus to Athens) are similarly equivocal. Though the textual tradition is basically unitary, a certain amount of apparently rhapsodic improvisation was still feeding back into written texts of the Homeric epics in the third century BCE.

Whether written in Ionia or in Boeotia or elsewhere, whether in the seventh century or earlier or later, there is no reason to think that the first manuscripts will have differed greatly from the Homeric papyri that survive in Egypt in considerable numbers from the third century onwards. Nor is it of much consequence whether the poems were written first on skins or from the outset on papyrus. They were written on scrolls in pen and ink, and the text took the form of a succession of lines of verse written column by column through the length of each scroll. Reed pen, carbon-based ink, black, neither mordant nor fading, perfect for papyrus, less so for parchment.

Greek epic verse intrinsically consists of a succession of hexameters, and the written layout reflects this by giving each hexameter a line to itself. It has been suggested that the Greek practice is informed by indirect familiarity with the Akkadian cuneiform tradition (Wendel 1949; West 1997b: 26), but no precedent is needed for stichic verse to be written as stichic verse. More notable perhaps are the ways in which Greek practice differs from Mesopotamian. When verses take written form they are of unequal lengths, despite their metrical equality, and in the Greek tradition no attempt is made to equalize them or even to mitigate the unevenness of their appearance; each verse is allowed to occupy whatever length its constituent letters give it, long or short. This results in columns with one straight edge (the left) and one very jagged one (the right). And with papyri it is the custom not to fill the entire area from top to bottom with writing but to leave upper and lower margins, often quite wide ones, and to set the columns well apart from one another, and without the rulings often found in clay-tablet texts. It is of course only sensible to leave margins as a precaution against the sort of damage to which papyrus scrolls are liable, but in calligraphic manuscripts the area of papyrus left unoccupied by writing can be greater than the area taken up by the text, and the overall aesthetics of the formatting are very different.

In its purest form the written text is presented as having two and only two constituents: the stichos (simultaneously the line and the verse) and the letters. Division into an indefinite number of columns, and of scrolls, interrupts without compromising the continuity of the stichoi which constitute the poem. The letters when read are converted into syllables, words, metrical phrases, sentences. If the eighth-century Nestor's cup inscription from Ischia is anything to go by, there may at first have been interpuncts placed between word-units or phrases, but if so this was soon dropped in favor of a cleaner style of presentation, each line consisting of an unbroken string of letters:

ΜΗΝΙΝΑΕΙΔΕΘΕΑΠΗΛΗΙΑΔΕΩΑΧΙΛΗΟΣ
ΟΥΛΟΜΕΝΗΝΗΜΥΡΙΑΧΑΙΟΥΣΑΛΓΕΕΘΗΚΕΝ

The earliest texts will have used less fully differentiated spelling conventions (perhaps only five vowel signs, as in Latin), leaving a little more for the reader to disambiguate; and the very earliest were probably written not left-to-right but right-to-left (as in the Nestor's cup inscription), or in the continuous "ox-plowing" or boustrophedon style, in which scribe's hand and reader's eye reverse direction rather than jerking back to the line-beginning for each verse. But left-to-right was standard by the time that circulation can have been anything more than extremely small and specialized. Panhellenic alphabetic uniformity followed Athenian reforms at the end of the fifth century, and orthographic stabilization was consolidated at Alexandria.

Modern readers are habituated to seeing gaps inserted between words, and find the practice of *scriptio continua* disconcerting. But it presented no difficulty to ancient readers. There are two points to bear in mind here. First, the alphabet gave Greek (and subsequently Latin) a uniquely high level of correspondence between the language's phonemic constitution and its written representation. In a language with such poor consistency of correlation between letter and sound as English the system would be less feasible, and in the Mesopotamian languages the relationship between written verse and its oral rendition can scarcely be discussed in these terms at all, given that the Sumerian and Akkadian signs only partially represent sounds; in these and other cuneiform societies both writing and reading were highly specialized skills. Second, there is the matter of cultural conditioning, both ours and theirs. The ancient Greek educational system, an institution as conservative in its methods as in its syllabus, taught children first the alphabet, its signs and sounds, then to read and write syllables; Homer followed. What a reader of epic reads is a verse-by-verse stream of letters and syllables, subject to cognitive processing in the act of reading. Reading a text presented in this way implies vocalization, actualizing the sounds represented and making them meaningful in the process, the spelt-out text triggering a sort of one-man simulation of the oral-aural experience of live communication. Silent reading is not impossible in principle, for the sounding-out process may be interiorized, but it is no surprise to discover that in practice it was not usual; and constraints against speed-reading are built in.

While it was the letters alone that constituted the text proper, over time it became more common for scribes or readers to add a certain amount of lectional apparatus in the form of the various extra-alphabetic signs designed to supplement or clarify the information given by the letters themselves. We may distinguish (i) prosodic specification, by means of diacritics (accents, breathings, quantity-marks, diaeresis), and (ii) textual articulation and punctuation. (i) Accents were as a rule not written until later antiquity; earlier they would have been for the most part supererogatory, and probably viewed as indecorous (imagine stress-marks in English). Practice remained very variable, with some fifth-century CE manuscripts having almost as many accents as our modern printed texts, others very few or none. Lyric texts, where there could be dialect problems, called for more generous provision of prosodic data than did epic. (ii) The word-defining function, insofar as that needs performing, is effectively performed by the accentual system; accents serve better than the modern system of interposing gaps between "words" both in linguistic principle (what of particles, prepositional prefixes, enclitics, what of phrase units?) and at least arguably as a means of facilitating fluent reading. A word-separator could be used if needed, which it rarely was. Its opposite, the "hyphen," a sublinear curve linking components of a single word, could be used in the case of compounds or words whose recognition would be helped by such clarification. The scribe of a high-quality second-century CE manuscript of *Il.* 2 presents the sequence οτριχαϲοιετεαϲ (i.e. ὅτριχαϲ οἱέτεαϲ) as ὁτριχαϲοιέτεαϲ plus a hyphen linking οι and ετεαϲ, thereby obviating even momentary puzzlement (τρίχαϲ, οἱ, ὁίετε, ἐτεάϲ); but most manuscripts presuppose more capable readership. Elision in Greek verse is normally effected but use of the apostrophe to signal it is dispensed with more often than not. Distinction between upper and lower case is modern. Punctuation is sometimes present in post-hellenistic manuscripts but is always sparse. While the articulation of the Homeric text was studied by ancient scholars in great detail and with fine precision (Nicanor in the first century devised an eight-grade punctuation system specifically for Homer), the punctuation applied in manuscripts is always very simple. It normally took the form of a single dot in middle or high position at the end of sentences, in places where modern texts might put a full stop, high stop, comma, or what passes for a question mark. Greek texts tend to be self-articulating, thanks largely to the use of particles, and not to depend upon punctuation, and this is especially true of epic. But certainly ancient readers had to do more work for themselves than modern ones do.

Both punctuation and accentuation, then, are ancillary features, varying from manuscript to manuscript, introduced to ease understanding of the given text as the distance between the epic language and the contemporary language grew ever greater. Sometimes added by students, they exercise control over the text and its interpretation. Calligraphic manuscripts usually have a modicum of punctuation but little more, until late antiquity when accents become more plentiful. Such lectional aids as are provided tend to be applied unsystematically, with discrimination. A pair of lines taken at random from the second-century manuscript of *Il.* 2 just mentioned will illustrate the sort of discreet help that a reader might sometimes be offered:

ιπποιμενγαραριϲταιέϲανφηρητιαδαο
ταϲέμηλοϲέλαυνεποδωκεαϲορνιθαϲῶϲ (plate 13 in Turner 1971).

The treatment of somewhat more challenging texts, such as Apollonius' *Argonautica*, was not appreciably different. Latin scribal practice essentially followed suit. Latin, though, had no written accents at all; and elision, understandably, was not scribally effected. Interpuncts between words are found in a first-century CE manuscript of Gallus' elegiacs, but this may be exceptional, like other features of the layout; given the Greek-Latin continuity of epic versification, it is reasonable to assume identical conventions of textual presentation.

A text as long as the *Iliad* or the *Odyssey* (see Chapter 21, by Edwards and Chapter 22, by Slatkin) required quite a number of scrolls. But the strangely inorganic subdividing of each poem into 24 books – or rather "rhapsodies," as they were designated – did not come about because of the exigencies of the medium, as is sometimes asserted, but in spite of them: the individual books are much shorter than the normal length of a papyrus scroll. The partitioning has been much discussed, and it is generally agreed that it is not original, though there should be no doubt that it is pre-Alexandrian: some texts carry book line-counts in Attic stichometry. Something that has gone underappreciated is the fact that A–Ω is not a numerical system but an alphabetical one. "Why 24?" (e.g. West 2001: 19) is the wrong question. "Why A–Ω?" on the other hand practically answers itself: Homer is the alpha and the omega, and everything in between, the A–Z of Hellenic culture. The symbolism was powerful enough for it to be universally adopted, the unique system of reference encoding the unique status of the Homeric poems. The books of all other epics, as of prose works too, are simply numbered. The *Aeneid*'s 12 books and Nonnus' 48 place themselves in relation to the Homeric 24, to be sure, but Book 24 of any work other than Homer's would be just that, KΔ (*xxiiii*), not omega.

The unquestionably authorial division of Apollonius' *Argonautica* (see Chapter 25, by Nelis) into four books of between 1,200 and 1,800 lines apiece reflects bibliographic norms, and belongs in the context of the thoroughgoing systematization of Greek literature undertaken in the Alexandrian Library. Books – in the sense of papyrus scrolls – could be long or short, but Greek tragedies and comedies, each occupying one scroll, may have helped fix ideas of appropriate book-length. A "book" of a multi-book work is coterminous with the physical book, the papyrus scroll; it is only the distinction between book and rhapsody that saves the Homeric poems from bibliographical self-contradiction.

Eventually the correspondence breaks down – Nonnus' *Dionysiaca* (see Chapter 27, by Shorrock) never took the physical form of 48 books – and division of a work into "books" no longer has to entail bibliographic actualization but may be viewed as more of a generic convention or structuring device, in epic as in history; but not until the codex does it become normal for more than one "book" to be housed within the confines of a single actual book. Homeric scrolls may routinely have contained two rhapsodies or more, but there seem to have been no standard groupings; one first-century BCE scroll comprised *Il.* 19–22, a four-rhapsody chunk of the poem all the odder if this scroll was one of a complete set. It is curious that while Lucretius' book-lengths (see Chapter 32, by Gale) are comparable with Apollonius' though somewhat shorter (between 1,000 and 1,500 lines), the *Aeneid*'s and the *Metamorphoses*' (see Chapter 33, by Putnam and Chapter 34, by Newlands) are shorter again (between 600 and 1,000): book-length is brought progressively closer to Homeric rhapsody-length. While the physical fragmentation of the Homeric and other long epics did not compromise their integrity as poems, it naturally made it easier for parts to be read separately, and for some parts to be read more than others. There are significantly more surviving fragments of *Od.* 11, for instance, Odysseus' trip to the Underworld, than of most of the other *Odyssey* books. The situation is essentially the same as with clay-tablet texts, except that the Greek and Latin epics have, as it were, built-in divisions (Book 1, 2, etc.) to serve both as articulation points and as a reference system, whereas Near Eastern epics have only tablets, whose contents may shift.

The main text is followed by a notice giving formal identification of the text whose end has now been reached: "Eratosthenes' Hermes," "Homer's Iliad Z," or whatever. No other information is given: no date, no scribe, no provenance, nothing, in fact, that acknowledges any particularity or even any identity *as a manuscript*. Papyrus manuscripts represent themselves not as text-carriers but as text-instantiations. This Greek practice contrasts with the self-labeling of cuneiform texts, according to which each tablet-text is an entity with a distinct and defined place in the scribal-textual universe. The fact that the title comes at the end rather than at the beginning has sometimes been seen as a carry-over from Near Eastern practice, illogical on a papyrus scroll since if the scroll has been properly rewound the reader would not arrive at it before getting to the end. But the function of the notice is not to inform the reader what the text is but more to ratify its completion. Its actual end may be signalled by a coronis, the conventional marker of the end of any text or major textual unit. For identification purposes scrolls had a protruding tag pasted on, and the title could be written on the back of the scroll where it would be visible prior to opening; and a set of scrolls could be kept together in a labeled container. Sometimes the title was also written at the head of the text. But the only components of a literary papyrus scroll treated as indispensable are the letters constituting the stichoi constituting the text, and the end-notice.

Other paratextual elements are often present but cannot claim such status. In professionally made copies stichometry is routine: each hundredth line is attended by a letter-numeral in the left margin. Such copies were also checked against their exemplars and corrected accordingly, though usually it seems in rather desultory fashion. In some manuscripts variant readings are recorded, whether from the exemplar or subsequently by collation with a different manuscript. Corrections and variants are entered above the line, or in the right margin, the place for all sorts of notation. One advantage that the papyrus scroll has over the clay tablet is the potential for secondary text. In scrolls of epic, however, the room afforded by the margins is normally made little use of, and scholarly annotation when present at all tends to be sparse and abbreviated. Homer and Apollonius accumulated much learned commentary, but it took bibliographically independent form, with little transferred to the margins of the manuscripts of the epics themselves. There are exceptions: a second-century CE scroll of the *Argonautica* has notes so copious that they spill over on to the back; a first-century one is elaborately equipped with a threefold apparatus of variant readings, interlinear glosses, and marginal notes – a manuscript of precisely such form has been postulated as underlying the medieval tradition. But whole-sale transfer of commentary into the margins of the main text comes only with the later development of the codex.

Variables of the papyrus scroll itself, the before-use factory product, include its height, its length, the breadth of its constituent sheets, and its quality of manufacture. Add writing, and more complex questions come to the fore, questions of *mise-en-page*, of relation between scroll length and text length, of size and kind of script, and more. The thousands of fragmentary Greek literary papyri reveal the actualities of the medium; nothing distinguishes scrolls of epic from other kinds of literature except the textual content itself, with its wider-than-average ragged-edged columns. Change over the centuries is practically confined to gradual change in styles of handwriting; certain more or less standard types of book-script develop. But there is considerable variability, both in the manufactured product and in the manuscripted one. Scroll height may fall anywhere between 16 and 35 cm (and occasionally outside this range), and the number of lines to the column is even more variable, according to column height and writing size and spacing. Length is indefinite, since the factory product, normally consisting of 20 sheets, can be shortened by cutting or lengthened by pasting on more, but a manuscript would not be expected to contain more than around 2,000 lines of verse, or to exceed 12 or so meters. Little is known of the organization of production and trade, but less standardization is in evidence than might have been expected; an account of papyrus in Pliny's *Natural History* includes details of quality and size classifications in first-century Rome (Lewis 1974). Criteria of papyrus quality according to Pliny are sheet-breadth (broader is better: fewer joins to cross), fineness (*tenuitas*), firmness (*densitas*), whiteness (*candor*), and smoothness (*levor*). Papyrus darkened somewhat with age, and unscrupulous book-sellers, capitalizing on gullible scholars' lust for old manuscripts, could artificially age book-scrolls by dipping them in wheat.

Latin books follow the form of Greek; another *Odyssey* begins (see Chapter 30, by Farrell and Chapter 31, by Goldberg). Livius Andronicus' saturnianization of the Homeric poem was presumably written on papyrus scrolls no differently from contemporary copies of its hexametric Greek counterpart: the medium is untouched by switch of language and meter. The only questions concern length and book-organization. Naevius' *Punic War* (still in saturnians) was put into seven books by Octavius Lampado in the following century; before that, who knows? There was no need to organize Ennius, the composer of Latin's first hexameter epic, the *Heduphagetica*. The structuring of the eighteen books of the *Annales* as six triads is a textually achieved manipulation of the external realities (for each book was physically independent of each of the others: there could be no question of separate circulation of any three books), and points the way to the architecture of the twelve-book *Aeneid*.

Codex

The papyrus scroll was eventually displaced by the parchment codex, seemingly a Roman invention, and it is at Rome that epic in codex form makes its first appearance. The Saturnalia gifts epigrammed by Martial towards the end of the first century CE include books: heading the list, Homer's *Battle of Frogs and Mice*, book-form unspecified and hence to be imagined as a papyrus scroll; but others are spectacularly miniaturized parchments (*membranae*) – Homer, Virgil, and Ovid's *Metamorphoses* among them. More than a century earlier Cicero recorded a parchment *Iliad* enclosed in a nut-shell, a still more remarkable feat of miniaturization; that is thought more likely to have been in scroll form, but Martial's Homer (*Iliad* and *Odyssey* in one) is expressly *in pugillaribus membranis*, and that unequivocally implies codex form. *Pugillares* ("fistfuls") had hitherto been wooden notebooks. The parchment codex in fact represents the fusion of two separate media, and proceeds more from the reapplication of pre-existing technologies than from the invention of new ones. The original codex (or caudex), composed of wooden boards, has little place in an account of the media of epic; the diptych and related forms were looked at above in the context of cuneiform literature, but in the Greco-Roman world the literary use of such tablets is confined to informal verse, first drafts, or school exercises.

Parchment is another matter. Skins (Gk. *diphtherai*, Lat. *membranae*), as we also saw above, were in use in western Asia around the middle of the first millennium and no doubt earlier, and Cicero's *Iliad* in a nutshell, however much of a freak (and anecdotally reported), is a significant item of evidence for the literary use of parchment prior to the end of the Roman Republic, when (as still in Martial's day) books were ordinarily papyrus scrolls. A strong line of continuity from Asia to Rome is provided by Pergamum, which gave its name to parchment and which Roman tradition associated with its invention. Development of parchment at Pergamum, perhaps spurred by disruption of Egyptian supplies of papyrus during the internecine turmoils of the Hellenistic kingdoms (R. Johnson 1970), will have led to its introduction to Rome in the earlier second century BCE; maybe Crates brought parchment along with Homeric scholarship. The processing of animal skins is both complex and varied (Reed 1972), and the lines of development from the earlier *diphtherai* to parchment scrolls, whether in technology or in usage, are impossible to chart or even to define; the distinction between leather and parchment is inadequate, and there is little material evidence before the Dead Sea Scrolls. It is quite conceivable that the Pergamene Library, in contrast with the Alexandrian, held not only papyrus-scroll books but also parchment-scroll ones; here if anywhere there is reason to query the assumption that because Alexandria set the bibliographic norms books in Egypt may be taken as representative of books elsewhere. But the Roman evidence suggests that parchment did not come into regular use for (non-biblical) literary texts until the new codex form had established itself.

Martial's parchment miniatures were ahead of their time (a proposition inviting deconstruction, however). The papyrus scroll continues to be the proper medium for highbrow literature until at least the end of the second century, while the codex upgrades its respectability. The intersections are multiple, the dynamics complex: parchment challenges papyrus, codex challenges scroll. The switch from papyrus to parchment seems at Rome to have accompanied the primary transition of scroll to codex, but in Egypt (papyrus-land) was very gradual, and of limited success: even in late antiquity a Homer codex is still much more likely to be of papyrus than of parchment. The more significant development – for in the end it does not make so very much difference whether a book is made of papyrus or of parchment, or of paper – is the switch from scroll to codex, the form of book we still use today. It constitutes a radical change in the reading experience; and as a textual vehicle the codex has certain advantages. What in time proved to be the most important of these is precisely the distinction claimed by Martial for his Saturnalia curiosities: compendiousness. *Quam brevis immensum cepit membrana Maronem*: "How short a parchment has captured boundless Virgil!" A codex could conveniently accommodate vastly more than a scroll. In this sense the codex realized its potential at its inception, a most unusual phenomenon in the history of a new medium. But how large a part this practical consideration played in determining the codex's early trajectory is hard to tell. Christian predilection for the codex markedly antedates widespread adoption of it for pagan literature (epic is thus shifted from center-stage), suggesting socio-religious factors over against purely pragmatic ones; and some early codexes do not seem to have contained more text than contemporary scrolls. But some certainly do, and recognition of the codex's capaciousness must go far towards accounting for the unstoppability of the upstart's success in overcoming the resistance of the traditional medium. Other advantages will have become apparent too. With a codex it is easy to flip through and find a particular passage; in one third-to-fourth-century *Odyssey* codex (it contained the entire poem, something no papyrus scroll ever did) such reference is facilitated by the relevant book-number being repeated at the top of each right-hand page. In fact the practical advantages lie wholly with the codex, at least from a user's point of view, and the scroll had little with which to withstand the new form except its deep entrenchment – potent, but not potent enough. The scroll's displacement is far from instantaneous. The codex does not overtake it until around the end of the third century CE (at any rate in Egypt: perhaps a little sooner at Rome and elsewhere?), and Homer scrolls were still being produced in the fifth, and probably beyond.

A codex consists of a number of folded sheets, stitched together at the fold. By virtue of the fold each sheet has two leaves (*folia*, sing. *folium*); each leaf has two pages, front and back, a.k.a. recto and verso (recto the right-hand side, verso the side you reach when you turn the page; the terminology presupposes left-to-right progression). A simple four-sheet (8-leaf, 16-page) codex could be constructed in either of two ways: (1) fold each sheet, then place the folded sheets on top of each other; or (2) place the (unfolded) sheets on top of each other, then fold; you then have a four-sheet "quire" or gathering. Method 1 replicates the construction of wooden tablet sets, but it was method 2 that dominated: a simple enough assembly method, but attended by two practical problems. One is physical: with a large number of sheets, the construction is put under strain, and the book becomes awkward to use. The solution lay in the multiple-quire codex, with quires of around four or five sheets apiece. But standardization took centuries, and most early codexes are composed of a single quire, even when the number of sheets is large. A fourth-century papyrus codex of *Iliad* 11–16 (!?) consisted of a single gathering of 31 sheets (62 folia, 124 pages), and there are still larger single-quire Christian codexes of the third century. The other problem concerns the organization of the text. In a quire the sequence of leaves will be consecutive only in the case of the innermost sheet; in a four-sheet quire (a quaternio), the innermost sheet will be pp. 7–10 (fol. 4r to fol. 5v), while the outermost one will be pp. 1–2 and 15–16 (fol. 1rv and fol. 8rv). Whether or not the writing of the text is done before the codex is stitched together, there is an appreciable amount of preplanning required to achieve the correct match between the text and the pages; this is another feature that gives the codex affinity with the clay tablet, over against the simplicity of the papyrus scroll, but the complexities of the codex are that much greater. In medieval scriptoria the whole process was thoroughly systematized, but in the early centuries control of the medium can be less than fully assured. A third-century papyrus codex of *Iliad* 1–6 (omitting the "Catalogue of Ships" from Book 2) was for some reason written only on the recto pages. By the fourth century the standard conventions are securely in place, and technically wondrous products such as the great biblical codexes are created.

Tradition and simplicity, and perhaps cost, sustained the viability of the papyrus scroll in the face of the codex's annexation of its territory. At the same time, and not without success, papyrus adapted itself to codex form. A papyrus codex's sheets were cut from ready-made papyrus rolls. (Thus the leaves of a papyrus codex may have sheet-joins, since its sheets do not coincide with the original sheets of the roll.) Though there is some debate about priority, the papyrus codex is clearly to be recognized as genetically secondary to the parchment codex, and papyrus is in fact fundamentally ill-suited to codex use: it does not take at all well to folding. Nonetheless, in this deracinated form papyrus continued to maintain a strong hold on books of the higher literature, at any rate in Egypt; in other areas no doubt the parchment codex dominated earlier, or from the outset, eventually to be challenged in turn by paper, introduced to Byzantium before the twelfth century. The parchment scroll, for its part, mimicking the conventions of the papyrus scroll, had (except in Jewish religious contexts) more rapidly given way to the codex.

From a technological point of view, the parchment codex does not represent much of a breakthrough; it is hardly comparable with the invention of paper, for instance, or of movable type. Nor does it quite have the significance sometimes claimed for it in the survival of Greek and Latin literature. Texts were intermittently transferred from scroll to codex (and then from codex to codex), as earlier they had been transferred from scroll to scroll. Codexes held more than scrolls, to be sure, but transference from scroll to codex was certainly no guarantee of successful passage through to the Middle Ages, as Menander and other non-survivors can attest. In that process sheer luck was a large factor but not the only one: the surviving epics are those which were most favored throughout their history. None of this detracts from the fact that the codex's ousting of the venerable papyrus scroll is a momentous occurrence in the history of media.

The codex redefined the nature of the book and transformed the experience of reading, scarcely less than the computer screen and hypertext are in the process of doing in our own day. For all that, the new form of vehicle made little impact upon epic itself, too grand and stolid a genre to be seriously impinged on by its medium. Whether the Flavian epics (see Chapters 37, 38, 36, by Dominik, Marks, and Zissos respectively) first circulated on scrolls or in codexes hardly matters; the poets did not write for one or the other form, they wrote epics, whose conventions, numbered "books" and all, were securely in place. But it was the codex that enabled Virgil to be a single tangible corpus (complete with appendix), and it was the codex that allowed the material of Homeric commentaries to be lassoed into the margins of the mother text. One does not have to be a technological determinist to see the codex's capaciousness as taking on an active role in conditioning the reception of the transmitted poems. While the paradigm of the papyrus scroll carried over into the new form (sometimes to extremes: was no absurdity perceived in the four-column-per-page layout of the *codex Sinaiticus*?), the mold-breaking role of the codex is clear enough. The self-sufficiency of the poetic text is increasingly given up, as the classic austerity of the papyrus scroll is pushed aside by more colorful and variegated styles of presentation. Martial's Saturnalia Virgil had anticipated modern practice in including an image of the poet's face (advertised in the second of the two lines of the attendant epigram), and "coffee-table" books of Homer and of Virgil from later antiquity feature illustrations of the action. More generally, with the codex we get numbered pages, enlarged and decorated initials, all sorts of prefatory and ancillary material. Not all these features originate in the codex, but the coming of the codex heralds a sea-change in exploitation of potentialities. Differences of function and aspiration display themselves much more prominently in the codex than they ever did in the scroll, and repackaging options are taken advantage of. The book itself can now be a prestige object, a thing of tremendous beauty and value, the codex lending itself to far greater mediumistic variation than the papyrus scroll: pocket-sized or too heavy to lift. The emperor Maximinus' Homer is said to have been a codex of purple vellum written in letters of gold; Alexander's had been a papyrus scroll with no claim to distinction except that it was corrected by Aristotle.

In the precarious passage from antiquity to the Middle Ages the invention of minuscule script and the revival of Hellenism in ninth-century Constantinople mark a fresh beginning of sorts, as old uncial codexes were replaced by new minuscule ones. On the Latin side there was greater continuity, however tenuous: the Carolingian revival involved less change in the medium, and codexes produced in the fourth and fifth centuries, some sumptuous Virgils among them, survived to find a haven in European libraries. Such texts might be pedigreed by their subscriptions; signing and dating explicitly confers individual identity on a manuscript. Paper came into increasing use as a cheap but inferior alternative to parchment, and the later decades of the fifteenth century saw the arrival of print, a mechanism finally enabling genuine textual identicality in multiple copies. The new technologies left the medium otherwise intact: early printed codexes are simulacra of handwritten ones. The codex remained unchallenged until the advent of electronic media.

FURTHER READING

The following bibliography is organized roughly according to the sequence of this chapter's text, and thematically rather than alphabetically or chronologically. It is far from comprehensive, and excludes much important earlier work; the works listed all contain further bibliography. An asterisk (*) marks items featuring plates of the media concerned, but tablets and codexes must be seen (and can sometimes be handled) in museums and libraries; digitized images of papyrus fragments are plentiful online. Repetition of items given in other chapters is largely avoided.

*J. T. Hooker (ed.) *Reading the Past: Ancient Writing from Cuneiform to the Alphabet* (1990).
H.-J. Martin, *Histoire et pouvoirs de l'écrit* (1988).
C. Wendel, *Die griechisch-römische Buchbeschreibung verglichen mit der Vorderen Orients* (1949).
M. L. West, *The East Face of Helicon: West Asiatic Elements in Greek Poetry and Myth* (1997).
G. Kopcke and I. Tokumaru (eds.) *Greece Between East and West: 10th–8th Centuries BC* (1992).
W. Burkert, *The Orientalizing Revolution: Near Eastern Influence on Greek Culture in the Early Archaic Age* (1992).
M. E. Vogelzang and H. L. J. Vanstiphout (eds.) *Mesopotamian Epic Literature: Oral or Aural?* (1992).
J. Rüpke (ed.) *Von Göttern und Menschen erzählen: Formkonstanzen und Funktionswandel vormoderner Epik* (2001).
*R. Reed, *Ancient Skins Parchments and Leathers* (1972).

Tablet

*C. B. F. Walker, *Cuneiform* (1987; repr. in Hooker 1990: 15–73).
D. O. Edzard, "Keilschrift," *Reallexikon der Assyriologie* 5 (1976–80).
A. Kuhrt, *The Ancient Near East c.3000–300 BC* (1995).
S. M. Dalley (ed.) *The Legacy of Mesopotamia* (1998).
G. Pettinato, *The Archives of Ebla: An Empire Inscribed in Clay* (1981).
A. L. Oppenheim, *Ancient Mesopotamia: Portrait of a Dead Civilization* (1964; 2nd edn. 1977).
E. M. Meyers (ed.) *Oxford Encyclopedia of Archaeology in the Near East* (1997).
J. M. Sasson (ed.) *Civilizations of the Ancient Near East* (1995).
J. Bottéro, *Mesopotamia: Writing, Reasoning and the Gods* (1992).
W. Röllig (ed.) *Altorientalische Literaturen* (1978).
J. A. Black, *Reading Sumerian Poetry* (1998).
B. R. Foster, *Before the Muses* (1993).
A. George, *The Epic of Gilgamesh* (1999).
J. H. Tigay, *The Evolution of the Gilgamesh Epic* (1982).
S. M. Dalley, *Myths from Mesopotamia* (1989).
*A. R. George and F. N. H. Al-Rawi, "Tablets from the Sippar library VI, Atra-Hasis," *Iraq* 58 (1996).
W. G. Lambert and A. R. Millard, *Atra-Hasis. The Babylonian Story of the Flood* (1969).
O. Pedersén, *Archives and Libraries in the Ancient Near East 1500–300 BC* (1998).
R. Veenhof (ed.) *Cuneiform Archives and Libraries* (1986).

*F. N. H. Al-Rawi and A. R. George, "Tablets from the Sippar library II," *Iraq* 52 (1990).
*F. N. H. Al-Rawi, "Tablets from the Sippar library IV," *Iraq* 57 (1995).

W. G. Lambert, "Ancestors, authors, and canonicity," *Journal of Cuneiform Studies* 11 (1957).
F. Rochberg-Halton, "Canonicity in cuneiform texts," *Journal of Cuneiform Studies* 36 (1984).
S. Lieberman, "Canonical official cuneiform texts: towards an understanding of Assurbanipal's personal tablet collection," in I. T. Abusch et al. (eds.) *Lingering over Words: Studies in Ancient Near Eastern Literature in honor of William L. Moran* (1990).
W. von Soden, "Das Problem der zeitlichen Einordnung akkadischer Literaturwerke," *Mitteilungen der Deutschen Orient-Gesellschaft* 85 (1953).
J. Bottéro, "Les Noms de Marduk, l'écriture et la 'logique' en Mésopotamie ancienne," in M. de J. Ellis (ed.) *Essays in honor of J. J. Finkelstein* (1977).
P. Michalowski, *The Lamentation over the Destruction of Sumer and Ur* (1989).
H. Donner and W. Röllig (eds.) *Kanaanäische und Aramäische Inschriften* (1964).
C. Wilcke, "Formale Gesichtspunkte in der sumerischen Literatur," in S. J. Lieberman (ed.) *Sumerological Studies in Honor of Thorkild Jacobsen* (1975).
K. Hecker, "Untersuchungen zur akkadischen Epik," *Altes Orient und Altes Testament* 8 (1974).
M. L. West, "Akkadian poetry: metre and performance," *Iraq* 59 (1997).
M. Koitabiashi, "Music in the texts from Ugarit," *Ugarit-Forschungen* 30 (1998).

D. J. Wiseman, "Assyrian writing-boards," *Iraq* 17 (1955).
M. Howard, "Technical description of the ivory writing-boards from Nimrud," *Iraq* 17 (1955).
S. Parpola, "Assyrian library records," *Journal of Near Eastern Studies* 42 (1983).
R. Payton, "The Ulu Burun writing-board set," *Anatolian Studies* 41 (1991).
*D. Symington, "Late Bronze Age writing-boards and their uses: textual evidence from Anatolia and Syria," *Anatolian Studies* 41 (1991).
*A. K. Bowman and J. D. Thomas, *Vindolanda: The Latin Writing-tablets* (1983).

Scroll

N. Lewis, *Papyrus in Classical Antiquity* (1974)
N. Lewis, *Papyrus in Classical Antiquity, A Supplement* (1989).
*E. G. Turner, *Greek Papyri* (1968; 2nd edn. 1980).
*E. G. Turner, *Greek Manuscripts of the Ancient World* (1971; 2nd edn. 1987).
W. A. Johnson, "Pliny the Elder and standardized roll heights in the manufacture of papyrus," *Classical Philology* 88 (1993).

*J. F. Healey, *The Early Alphabet* (in Hooker 1990).
A. Heubeck, *Schrift* (1979).
C. J. Ruijgh, "La date de la création de l'alphabet grec et celle de l'épopée homérique," *Bibliotheca Orientalis* 54 (1997).
F. M. Cross, *Canaanite Myth and Hebrew Epic* (1973).
M. E. Aubet, *The Phoenicians and the West* (2nd edn. 2001).
G. Markoe, *Phoenicians* (2000).
H. Goedicke, *The Report of Wenamun* (1975).
R. P. Dougherty, "Writing upon parchment and papyrus among the Babylonians and the Assyrians," *Journal of the American Oriental Society* 48 (1928).

B. B. Powell, *Writing and the Origins of Greek Literature* (2002).
R. D. Woodard, *Greek Writing from Knossos to Homer* (1997).
M. L. West, *Studies in the Text and Transmission of the Iliad* (2001).
M. W. Haslam, "Homeric papyri and the transmission of the text," in I. Morris and B. Powell (eds.) *A New Companion to Homer* (1997).
T. J. Morgan, *Literate Education in the Hellenistic and Roman Worlds* (1998).

R. Cribiore, *Gymnastics of the Mind: Greek Education in Hellenistic and Roman Egypt* (2001).
M. B. Parkes, *Pause and Effect* (1992).

P. Saenger, *Space between Words: The Origins of Silent Reading* (1997).

Codex

See also under "Scroll" above.

C. H. Roberts and T. C. Skeat, *The Birth of the Codex* (1983).

*E. G. Turner, *The Typology of the Early Codex* (1997).

*C. de Hamel, *Scribes and Illuminators* (1992).

*L. D. Reynolds and N. G. Wilson, *Scribes and Scholars: A Guide to the Transmission of Greek and Latin Literature*, 3rd edn. (1991).

B. Bischoff, *Latin Palaeography, Antiquity and the Middle Ages* (1990).

L. Glenisson (ed.) *Le Livre au Moyen Âge* (1988).

C. F. Bühler, *The Fifteenth-Century Book: The Scribes, the Printers, the Decorators* (1960).

G. G. Harpham, *The Ascetic Imperative in Culture and Criticism* (1987).

R. McKitterick, *The Carolingians and the Written Word* (1989).

M. T. Clanchy, *From Memory to Written Record* (1993).

B. Stock, *The Implications of Literacy* (1983).

L. Febvre and H.-J. Martin, *The Coming of the Book: The Impact of Printing, 1450–1800* (1976).

E. Eisenstein, *The Printing Press as an Agent of Change* (1979).

M. Giesecke, *Der Buchdruck in der frühen Neuzeit* (1991).

J. J. O'Donnell, *Avatars of the Word: From Papyrus to Cyberspace* (1998).

CHAPTER ELEVEN

Ancient Reception

Robert Lamberton

The interaction of epic text and audience over time is a matter destined to remain most obscure at precisely those points where we would most like to know more. Epic seems to surface in the written record in Mesopotamia, shortly before 2000 BCE (Black 1998: 23 and n. 57) but as a genre that again and again has been shown to straddle the line between preliterate narrative and literature as such, it may be assumed to have a much deeper, unrecoverable history.

If the stories of Gilgamesh, Lugalbanda, and the other early Sumerian kings can in fact be said to have taken on a form resembling what we have during the third dynasty of Ur (2112–2004), then the tales they tell are, by the most conservative recent estimates, projected back more than half a millennium into the past (*CAH*: vol. I, 235–6). The dissemination and reception of the written text are hardly less obscure than those of its oral antecedents. That the poems were copied tells us little more than that they were the valued property of the scribal elite (Black 1998: 26; Visicato 2000) and that they had currency among the elite generally. These texts are remarkably uninformative concerning their audience, providing us little basis for designating or defining their narratee.

Closely bound up with the issue of reception is that of transmission. Given that the Gilgamesh stories, as poetry praising the exploits of heroes and demigods of the remote past, do in some sense participate in the same genre as the *Iliad* and *Odyssey*, are we to imagine some historical link between the two poetic traditions? Greek epics found expression in writing about a millennium and a half after the Sumerian ones. No documentation of a tangible path of transmission is likely, though we can point to two intriguing possibilities.

First of all, the library of the Hittites at Boğazköy offers a bridge between the two cultures. These earliest documented Indo-European speakers had their own epic tales (Güterbock 1946, 1961), in a tradition linked to the fertile crescent by the intermediary of the Hurrians of northern Mesopotamia. And they knew about the Greeks to the west; indeed, to an outsider, the lion gate of Mycenae might well have evoked the regal lions of Hittite Alacahöyük in central Anatolia, and the arts and symbols of Hittites and contemporary middle and late Bronze Age Greeks may have had more in common than we can document. "Anatolianisms" have been detected in Homeric language, and Hittite and Luwian poets may even have told tales of Troy (Güterbock 1986; Puhvel 1991; Watkins 1986, 1995, 1998). Sumerian/Semitic epic, or some notion of such heroic song, may well have reached the ears of Greek speakers as early as the first half of the second millennium, through Anatolia.

Another possible path can be found in the Syro-Palestinian heroic poetry of Ugarit (Ras Shamra), dating from the fourteenth and thirteenth centuries (Parker 1997). The major spokesman for Ugaritic studies in the mid-twentieth century, Cyrus Gordon, seems in retrospect to have badly overstated his case when he asserted (on the evidence of this poetry and of his decipherment of Minoan) that "until sometime after 1500 BCE, Greece, Ugarit, and Israel all belonged to the same cultural sphere" (Gordon 1966: 7; cf. Gordon 1949). Still, the continuity between the earliest Sumerian epic, adapted into the Semitic languages, and the Ugaritic epic of Kirta (or Krt) is indisputable, as is the currency of the Ugaritic poems among the highly mobile northwest Semitic traders of the Late Bronze Age. No one doubts that centuries later the Greeks learned alphabetic literacy from the successors of those same traders, whom we call the Phoenicians. They may well have learned something of heroic song from similar, much earlier contacts.

Such tantalizing traces are all that remain of any Greek "reception" of *Gilgamesh* and related Near Eastern epic. Of Gilgamesh himself, nothing survived in the Greco-Roman world beyond a fabulous story of his birth, reported explicitly as a parallel for the story of Danae and Perseus (Ael. *NA* 12. 21).

The reception of the *Iliad* and *Odyssey* in the Greco-Roman world is, by comparison, exceptionally well documented, but we would still like to know a great deal more than we do about the earliest phases. Here, we are limited to the fascinating, but inevitably self-serving, information provided by the poems themselves (Segal 1992). If the *Iliad* is to be believed, the tradition of heroic song – of performing *klea andron* ("the glorious deeds of heroes") – can be traced to the Bronze Age warriors themselves, who between battles might transform themselves into bards (*Il.* 9.186–91), alternately generating the matter of song and participating in its transmission. The *Odyssey* even contains an aborted performance of its narrative antecedent in the Epic Cycle, the *Nostoi* or "Returns" (*Od.* 1.325–7) – though perhaps we should read this as an anticipatory gesture on the part of the performing *Odyssey* bard toward a prequel to come. In *Od.* 9–12, when the protagonist becomes the narrator (though explicitly not the bard, since he plays no instrument and "tells tales" [*Od.* 11.345, 376; 12.451, 453] rather than sings them) we are given the most elaborate and perhaps most wishful dramatization of audience response in the poems: the wages of the teller of tales are so vast that a special taxation will be required to balance the royal accounts (*Od.* 13.7–15).

On the whole, the audiences represented in the *Odyssey*, from the disorderly suitors in Ithaca to the gullible Phaeacians, reinforce the poem's self-representation as elegant, elite entertainment whose strengths are vivid representation and the successful manipulation of the emotions and the imagination. The expectation is that these audiences listen attentively, abandon themselves to the bard's performance, believe him and, most of all, reward him generously.

Commentary, along with the documented reception of the poems, begins when that belief is suspended or withdrawn. The earliest recorded comments are negative and address issues of veracity. Xenophanes of Colophon gets credit for first having called attention, around 550 BCE, to some of the all-too-evident contradictions and inadequacies of Homeric theology.

> Homer and Hesiod attributed to the gods
> everything that in men brings shame and reproach:
> thieving, screwing around, and mutual deceit. (fr. 11 D-K)

It is clear here and in other fragments of Xenophanes that in late archaic Greece "Homer and Hesiod" constituted a convenient designation for a traditional worldview, widely disseminated and already associated with elementary education (fr. 10 D-K), that was vulnerable to philosophical attack, perhaps most notably in the area of theology. The most striking fact to emerge here is that an issue could be made of the veracity of poetry that frequently dramatizes deception, while representing itself primarily as entertainment. Equally important is the fact that Xenophanes challenges Homeric theology as a rival poet, expressing himself in elegiac couplets as well as Homeric hexameters, and advocating a rival theology that emerges out of the debunking of the competition. Xenophanes' contemporary, the lyric poet Stesichoros, seems to have challenged and revised Homer's account of the Troy tale, and it is in the context of such rivalries that Xenophanes' challenge should be situated.

The fact that we see these "rivals" as individual challengers of a monolithic Homeric orthodoxy is to be traced to pedagogy and to the schoolroom. A substantial amount of oblique or anecdotal evidence, ranging in date from Xenophanes early in the sixth century to Plato in the fourth, reinforces the notion that throughout this period education in Greek letters and literature started from Homer and returned repeatedly to Homer. The *Iliad* and *Odyssey* were thus established as the common cultural property of literate Greeks. In Athens, where as usual the documentation is richest, the educational practice of sixth-century aristocrats was democratized in the fifth century, with the result that a substantially increased literate public shared in this cultural property. What happened in the classroms seems to have had as precedent the sixth-century canonization of the Homeric poems in the framework of the greatest of Athenian festivals, the Panathenaia. With this dramatic gesture (which we may see as the work of the tyrant Pisistratos), Athens took possession of the poems and marked them as Athenian for the subsequent tradition (see e.g. [Plut.] *de Hom.* 2.12). The education of the polis moved from the collective exercises of the festivals to the formal education of the classroom, but Homer and the Troy tale retained a privileged position in both.

The earliest preserved commentary we possess on specific Homeric difficulties takes the form of "problems" (*problemata*) and "solutions" (*luseis*), a collection of which was attributed to Aristotle. This attribution in itself means little more than that Aristotle was given a privileged position in the long succession of educators who expounded the meaning of the epic texts and explained away at least some of their thorny contradictions and other difficulties. Of the roughly forty Aristotelian "solutions" that reach us through the scholia (the marginal notes of medieval manuscripts) and a handful of other sources (Aristotle frr. 366–404, 3 Gigon), most are hermeneutically modest and – in the context of ancient commentary – relatively plausible. Their importance for our purposes, though, is that they bring us close to the mundane, pedagogical foundations of Homer commentary. "Why did Achilles drag Hector around the tomb of Patroclos? . . . Aristotle points out that there is a solution by reference to the customs of the time" and goes on to indicate the existence of similar customs today (fr. 389 Gigon).

In the larger classification of such solutions, this particular example would fall in the category of solutions "from custom," alongside which were distinguished solutions "from the diction" (*lexis*), including the decipherment of such potentially misleading tropes as allegory and irony, and "from history," a mode in which certain Homeric problems can be seen to arise from differences between Homer's time and the present (Schol B ad *Il.* 20.67; Dindorf IV, 231–2).

The theological muddle of the Homeric poems has the longest and perhaps the most interesting history in the interpretive literature, and in that area interpretations based on Homer's rhetorical allegory – his saying one thing to designate another, veiled meaning – was long the dominant one. The famous Socratic assault on Homeric theology dramatized in Book 3 of Plato's *Republic* – one that results in Socrates banning Homer, as pedagogically inappropriate, from his fantasy of an optimally just state – is essentially the concluding skirmish in the battle opened by Xenophanes. Homer's inconsistent, manipulative, sometimes malicious deities (on whom see the chapter by Louden) had no place in the training of bold, confident guardians of Socrates' utopian community. Furthermore, Homer's portrayal of death and the heroes' attitudes toward death were poorly equipped to render those guardians fearless in the face of mortal combat.

Socrates' ejection of Homer from what was precisely his stronghold – the core of the curriculum – was based on an odd combination of pragmatism and willful aesthetic obtuseness. The two are quite separable within the *Republic*, though Plato refuses to make the separation. Socrates demands simultaneously that the stories told the young guardians be effectual, in producing the desired character traits, and true in representing the gods and the fate of souls as they are. The first demand is entirely a function of the idiosyncratic social engineering of the *Republic*, and as such may be assumed to have no implications beyond that interesting, hypothetical construct. The second demand is far odder and more problematic. That Xenophanes might choose to challenge the truth of poetic theology can perhaps be explained as a combination of archaic naiveté and willingness to compete on Homer's own terms. That Socrates should be troubled by the same issues hardly seems plausible. The proverbial mendacity of the poets – *polla pseudontai aoidoi*, "The poets tell a lot of lies" – is said to have been part of the traditional wisdom of Solon (fr. 26 West) and was certainly received opinion for Plato and Aristotle (*Met.* 1.2). How could Socrates' indignant rejection of Homer – for doing just what was expected of poets – be credible? If we are the victims of irony (Platonic or Socratic) here, then we are in good company. As we shall see, the issue of defending Homer against Socrates' attack was to have an interesting future, after a long hiatus.

There is in any case a fourth-century watershed, falling between the *Republic* and Aristotle, who had little use for irony (or metaphor) in serious inquiry. The *Poetics* as reaction against Plato's simplistic and oddly moralizing aesthetics of imitation, along with his perverse "monkey see, monkey do" account of aesthetic response, cleared the way for a serious analysis of poems, plays, and other examples of verbal art on an aesthetic and rhetorical basis. Issues of the truth of poetry seem at a sweep of the hand to disappear from critical discourse, to surface again only centuries later in a radically altered cultural context. The Athenians did not follow the *Republic*'s advice and displace Homer from the core of the curriculum any more than they started educating girls or abandoned the nuclear family. Indeed the absurdity of any of these constructs expressed as actual social change should help us to contextualize the thought experiment that forms the core of the *Republic*. In the early fourth century, it was still possible, in the tradition of Xenophanes, to imagine what it would be like to take Homer's theology seriously (or rather, literally), but it was probably already impossible for an educated person actually to do so.

On the other hand, one could certainly ask why Homer might have told those particular lies, and the literature of commentary was constantly being enriched with more and better answers to that question. It would be a considerable accomplishment and a major step forward in our understanding of the evolving role of the Homeric epics in Greco-Roman culture if we could credibly formulate a normative, pedagogical account of Homeric theology as taught in the classrooms of the Hellenistic and Roman world. The closest we are likely to get is the window opened by a synthetic introduction to Homer attributed to Plutarch, and probably to be dated to the high Roman Empire (Keaney and Lamberton 1996). Its author explains Homer's anthropomorphic, visible, intrusive gods as a poetic fiction: Homer's own creation and his way of communicating first, that the gods exist, and secondly, that they have a providential concern for mankind (*de Hom.* 2, 112, 115). It is not difficult to imagine Aristotle saying much the same to his student Alexander, and the classroom explanations of Homer's theology must have sounded much like this as long as, and wherever, Homer was taught in a polytheist context. The answer to the troublesome question how the Greeks could both carry on the cults of their gods and enjoy and retell the poets' endlessly contradictory, often disreputable and obscene, stories about those same gods, lies here. They knew the distance and the complex relationship between poetry and truth.

This, in fact, is an explanation entirely compatible with the views of the later polytheist Platonists who, from the third to the seventh century repeatedly asserted the truth of Homeric theology behind the screen of Homeric fiction. The enemy, from their perspective, was the literalists – most obviously, the hostile and largely simple-minded Christians – who saw only the inconsistencies and the obscenities, and therefore, confusing the representation with the reality, denied what Homer's fiction most profoundly asserted: the existence in the universe of providential deities. This is the context where, at least for the dwindling community of polytheists, Socrates and Homer had to be reconciled (as Proclus set out to do in his Commentary on the *Republic*). It was, indeed, only in that late Roman context that the issue of Homer's veracity returned one final time, before a new Christian pedagogical establishment learned to teach the poems on its own terms. From that point on, stripped entirely of theological authority and appreciated exclusively for its rhetorical and aesthetic qualities, Homeric poety crossed another hermeneutic threshold, which took it beyond our present concerns. Its transformation into a purely aesthetic object had, however, been begun by Aristotle, and the fact that this poetry could finally be divorced from its odd and archaic theology should be traced to the Greek enlightenment rather than to the Christian usurpation.

If this broad outline has indicated something of the rich and complex history of the Greco-Roman world's intellectual and pedagogical interaction with the *Iliad* and *Odyssey*, it nevertheless has left aside an important aspect of the reception of the poems: imitation.

As the latest in the succession of genres in which the Greeks re-enacted their traditional stories in a truly collective, community art form, fifth-century Attic drama was in an obvious sense the heir of epic, but it was neither the first-born nor the direct heir. The history of the differentiation of poetic genres in archaic Greece is complex, but just as individual voices espousing intellectual positions, like that of Xenophanes, define themselves against the background of "Homer and Hesiod," so subsequent poetic genres appear to define themselves against the same foil.

The earliest evidence for the currency of some of the tales we know from the *Iliad* and *Odyssey* belongs to the seventh century, when individualized scenes begin to appear on figured pottery (Fittschen 1969; Snodgrass 1998). It is, of course, seldom indisputable that a given scene is derivative from, much less illustrative of, a specific passage in one of the epics as we have them. Twentieth-century scholarship in this area began (in the spirit of Schliemann) looking for, and so finding, artifacts to illustrate the texts – in this instance, pots to illustrate passages of Homer. The ways in which the vase painters represented Homeric scenes seemed initially far more striking than the divergences. By the century's end, however, scholars were in doubt whether in fact any such illustrations of actual known texts exist or ever did exist.

The seventh- and sixth-century pots do tell us that the Troy tale had cultural currency, that customers would buy pots decorated with anecdotal scenes evoking episodes in that tale as well as a range of other identifiable material from saga and myth. Very seldom, however, would these images constitute appropriate illustrations of the texts we actually possess (even if we could imagine such an anachronism as an archaic manuscript with illustrations). To take only one of the most famous examples, a notorious and striking calyx crater in the Metropolitan Museum, signed by Euphronios as painter and datable to about 510 BCE, explicitly represents Sleep and Death removing the dead hero Sarpedon from the battlefield, a scene memorably narrated in *Iliad* 16. But even at this relatively late date, when most scholars would assume that some sort of "Homeric" text existed, Euphronios gives us a version of the story that is not Homer's. The sequence is wrong: the body has not been washed, Hermes, not Apollo, is directing the proceedings, and wherever Euphronios got the attendants labeled Leodamas and Hippolytos, it was not from our *Iliad*. More important than the anecdotal differences, however, is the striking difference in tone, and the grim physicality of the decidedly dead hero (Shapiro 1994: 24–5).

What this comparison illustrates vividly is that right down to the beginning of the fifth century – and beyond – the Troy tale in its details and in its message was up for grabs. The closer one looks, the less monolithic the backdrop of "Homer and Hesiod" appears. There are important differences between the two, to begin with, and rival poets, as well as painters, clearly appropriated and reworked Homer's (and Hesiod's) material from an early date.

And when, finally, can we even speak confidently of our *Iliad* and *Odyssey* as discrete and complete poems? Cogent and persuasive arguments have been mustered for the eighth century, the sixth, and even the second. This last argument rests on the fact that the earliest papyri have a significantly high percentage of "extra" lines, as do citations of Homer in the literature of the fifth and fourth centuries. From the second century BCE on, by contrast, the manuscript tradition is remarkably uniform, but before this normalization (which must have stemmed from the work of Alexandrian scholars, though the details remain obscure), "long" or "wild" texts clearly were in circulation. This in turn may be interpreted as evidence that down through the third century, texts of Homeric passages (which demonstrably existed and were used in classrooms) represented specific performances and might vary substantially one from another. It may well be that we owe the standardization and canonization of the conservative, relatively short versions of the two poems that form the basis of the "vulgate" of medieval manuscripts to the increased demand for uniform texts created by the burgeoning educational establishment, as demand for teachers of Greek mushroomed in Egypt, Syria, and most of all in the Roman western Mediterranean.

Wherever they came from, the normalized *Iliad* and *Odyssey* of the classrooms of the Roman empire – which are essentially the versions of the epics we read today – may reasonably be taken to be the first versions we would recognize as our Homer. If so, our Homeric epics are the fruit of Hellenistic scholarship: the best attempt of learned, well-informed, conservative scholars in third- and second-century Alexandria to give a definitive literary form to a tradition of performance poetry that had existed for more than five centuries and had circulated in at least partial written texts for more than three, but had not previously undergone real standardization.

If we accept, at lest provisionally, a model such as this, then the interaction of a Xenophanes, a Stesichoros, or even a Plato, with Homer must be re-thought. The Troy tale, the story of Achilles, and the story of Odysseus were fundamental and widely disseminated cultural property for all three, but our *Iliad* and *Odyssey* were not. The stories in question were, for centuries, Homer's stories, but how Homer told them depended on the intervening performer, whether as audience they listened to that performer or read a transcription of his rendering. "Homer and Hesiod" designated a foil of traditional cultural material against which new ideas and new modes of performance might be acted out, but it was a shifting foil, a self-transforming backdrop not fully disengaged from its roots in preliterate, oral performance.

The competing material in the epic genre fared badly by comparison, and the vast bulk of it is lost to us. Although its history can be reduced to what appears to be a straightforward, linear narrative (Huxley 1969), this reduction involves the same sort of anachronistic imposition of dubiously relevant models of the generation of texts that gave birth to the biographies of Homer and the other mythic poets in the first place. The fact is that the lost cyclical epics, completing the Troy tale and patching in the Theban sagas, contained very old, undatable, traditional material, just as did the stories of Achilles and Odysseus (see Chapter 24, by Burgess). For whatever reasons, the literary versions of those stories failed to establish themselves in the pedagogical canon. Some of this material, notably the poetry of Orpheus (in competition with Hesiod, perhaps, rather than Homer) seems to have had a very substantial but also very sharply defined audience, a jealous one that used ritual and perhaps initiation to keep the texts from the attention of the profane. Like many ancient secrets, this one was well kept, and we know that poetry only from shreds, some of them accidentally exposed to the eyes of posterity (West 1983). Deliber-ately sequestered texts of this sort were clearly not in competition for status in festivals or canonization within the curriculum, but much other epic decidedly was, some of it closely bound up with and advertising local traditions, and some Panhellenic in the manner of Homer. It is not impossible that the major factor in the survival, entrenchment, and endurance of the *Iliad* and *Odyssey* was their appropriation by the Athenians and their subsequent participation in the odd process by which Athenian literature came to be so disproportionately dominant in the Greek literary canon. If, for instance, Corinth and not Athens had managed to emerge victorious in the competition for cultural dominance, would we be reading Eumelos' *Corinthiaca* (even the title is uncertain) as the foundation of European literature while a few interested scholars picked over scant remains of the *Iliad* and *Odyssey*?

The epic competition in any case, fell by the wayside, and throughout the seventh century (from which more than fifty "Homeric" vases have been identified), the lyric poets seem not to have paid much attention to the Troy tale or to other Homeric material. It is only with Stesichoros in the sixth that we find lyric invading Homer's turf, and the intent is clearly revisionist and its impact substantial (see Burkert 1987; on lyric and epic see Chapter 28, by Garner). Stesichoros produced a version of the Troy tale that explicitly rehabilitated Helen (by keeping her in Egypt for the duration of the war, rather than cohabiting with Paris) and it was this odd version of the tale that Euripides would follow in one of his incursions into Homeric material (the *Helen*). The surviving sample of Attic tragedy (33 plays out of many hundreds produced) might suggest that the dramatists avoided content marked as Homeric in favor of traditional tales selected from the un-Homeric margins of the Troy tale or the traditions of Thebes, Corinth, or other cities. Sorting through the attested titles and fagments of lost plays somewhat alters the picture, but it remains the case that the most conservative and bombastic of the tragedians, Aeschylus, trespassed fairly freely on Homeric material, while Sophocles and Euripides, for reasons that may have had more to do with aesthetics than humility, tended more consistently to look elsewhere (see, again, Chapter 28, by Garner).

As Attic tragedy dried up in the fourth century, so did the recycling of epic material into new modes of poetic performance. What remained to influence subsequent genres – for the most part genres intended for solitary reading or reading aloud in small groups – were pervasive Homeric patterns and paradigms. The language of Homer and the stories of the *Iliad* and *Odyssey*, as the child's introduction to literary language, remained a constant point of reference for all literate Greeks. A Homeric word or turn of phrase was constantly available to add resonance to poetry or prose, increasingly so as classical Attic's rigorous, spare partitioning of vocabulary into prose words and poetry words broke down. The Greek prose of the high Roman empire – Plutarch is the exemplary figure – is larded with poetic, and particularly Homeric, words, serving a range of functions from pure ornament to allusion to citation. The paradigms, however, are more striking than the Homeric language itself. One could say that the process starts with Aristotle and the identification of the *Odyssey* as paradigm for at least one sort of comic plot (*Poet.* 1453a30–6). As prose fiction developed in the Greek world, the *Odyssey* became its most frequently invoked, quoted, and imitated model. Its shaping influence has been found even in early lives of saints.

Once again, the key to all these developments is the position of the *Iliad* and *Odyssey* in the curriculum, ensuring their availability both as models of literary language and narrative, and as points of reference for all literate Greeks. Their pervasive authority was both cultural and aesthetic, and endured down into the Byzantine world and beyond. Indeed, it is in Christian contexts (including that of the apostate emperor Julian) that Homeric echoes, tags, and citations are most pervasive in Greek prose. It has been claimed, mistakenly, that Julian's Homeric language was used piously, that the emperor cited Homer as contemporary Christians cited scripture; but in fact, those Christians came to lard their own prose with Homerisms as richly as Julian did, and they certainly did not confuse the epics with scripture. The authority both sought to appropriate in this way was cultural. Whether the Christians liked it or not, Homer was the fount of Greek eloquence, and they quickly learned to like it. Epic had, as we have seen, been conveniently divorced from truth claims long before this issue arose.

The history of the reception of Virgil is in part a fast-action replay of the reception of Homer (Horsfall 1995b, followed here). Inevitably the poor cousin of Greek education, Latin education reached the Augustan period with an epic-sized hole in it, waiting to be filled. Within Virgil's lifetime, his poetry was taught to the young, first, it seems by an innovative *grammaticus* named Quintus Caecilius Epirota (Suet. *Gram.* 16; Horsfall 1995b: 250). The evidence for Latin curricula in the early empire is only slightly more satisfactory and less anecdotal than that for earlier and contemporary Greek curricula, but there can be little doubt that the *Aeneid* was quickly patched into the Latin curriculum right at the point long occupied by the *Iliad* and *Odyssey* in the teaching of Greek. Nicholas Horsfall, whose two studies of the impact (as opposed to the literary influence, imitations, etc.) of Virgil (1984, 1995b) assemble evidence from a dozen categories, ranging from reported conversational quotation to graffiti, inscriptions, coins, and the visual arts, amply documents the pervasive knowledge of Virgil in Roman life down through the empire and beyond. As he emphasizes (Horsfall 1995b: 250–2), public theatrical recitation of the *Aeneid*, for which we have substantial evidence, must be credited with an important role in the dissemination of the poem throughout Roman society. As with Homer centuries earlier, knowledge of Virgil in the Roman empire extended beyond those privileged to receive an education in letters.

Almost as remarkable as the speed with which Virgil's poem was canonized as the foundation of education in Latin is the speed with which the *Aeneid* came to be credited with the ability to answer questions ranging far beyond the Troy tale and the prehistory of the Romans. Virgil the *vates*, the initiate, the privileged speaker tapping superhuman knowledge, is of course present in the epic itself. This voice of limitless pretense and self-proclaimed authority is created out of the Homeric voice and demands deference, awe, and credence on the part of its audience. But the Homeric narrator was lost in the mists of time and spoke through many generations of intervening voices. That the *Iliad* and *Odyssey*, by virtue of the interrogations of many generations of teachers, thinkers, and scholars, could have been endowed with the ability to yield truths about cosmology, the gods, and the fate of souls, is perhaps explicable on these grounds. Certainly there were those who subscribed to the notion that Homer tapped (and both revealed and, where appropriate, encoded) a primitive revelation of such truths (Lamberton 1986). But Virgil? Virgil, whose biography was by comparison unproblematical, however untrustworthy most of the givens might seem today? Virgil's ancient readers knew that he lived in the time of Augustus, and that he committed himself to writing an epic that would in a fundamental way serve to glorify Augustus, his program, and his accomplishments. He participated in the economy of the arts of Augustan Rome. He could not be lightly transmogrified into a blind, visionary poet of the remote past. If we can, with some effort, imagine how the mythical Homer might be assimilated to his Tiresias, it is far more difficult to conceive of the process that resulted in the assimilation of the very historical P. Virgilius Maro to his Sibyl or his Laocoon.

Nevertheless, the Servian commentary on the *Aeneid*, at less than 400 years' distance from the composition of the poem, demonstrates very clearly that Virgil scholarship (and therefore Virgil pedagogy) had assimilated all the traditional techniques of Homer scholarship. Questions Virgil did not answer on a literal level might yet be answered somewhere behind the screen of the fiction, and it is on this level that Virgilian theology yields its true messages and that Virgil's profound knowledge of Roman rite is revealed (Jones 1961). Many of these interpretive claims seem to go back at least to Aelius Donatus, a Virgil commentator half a century before Servius, and may well go back much further still.

Does this mean that the *Aeneid* was scripturalized? Again, the issue is inseparable from its Homeric analog. There were moments, particularly in the period when Christians were most aggressively tearing down the institutions of polytheism and either destroying or appropriating polytheist texts, when some polytheists looked to epic for an authoritative account of theology. For the *Aeneid*, this process is vividly dramatized in Macrobius' *Saturnalia* where the parallelism of Homer and Virgil is pervasive and the theological authority of Virgil a central tenet (cf. Lamberton 1986, 261–72). This does not, however, change the fact that Virgil's authority, like Homer's, was fundamentally aesthetic at all periods, rooted as it was in the authority of the grammaticus, the schoolteacher, rather than that of the priest.

The history of the influence of Virgil on contemporary and subsequent Latin poetry is the proof of this picture. Much of the history of scholarship on later Augustan poetry, Silver Latin poetry, and the Latin poets of late antiquity has taken the form of identifying Virgilian citations, references, and adaptations (Barnes 1995, for a selection). This exercise is tedious but essential, serving as a substitute for the fundamental baggage all of these poets' audiences brought to their work. Just as Virgil is shallow and bombastic – or at the very least loses much of his complexity – if the reader is unable to see through his language to Homeric prototypes, so the ideal readers of subsequent Latin poetry were engaged in an enterprise of recognition, behind the screen of the poem before them, of a whole tradition of poetry, all of it dominated by the language and poetics of Virgil.

The burst of polytheist Homer and Virgil scholarship of the fourth and fifth centuries defined the terms on which the epic tradition was handed on to the monotheists. That story is beyond the scope of this survey, but a single example may serve to characterize both the rupture and the continuity that resulted. For Augustine, around the year 400, epic poetry with its demonic deities and capacity to seduce the imagination was a hazard and a threat. We owe to one Fulgentius, very likely himself (like Augustine) a North African bishop, who lived a century later, a rich allegorical elaboration on the *Aeneid*. The pedagogic tradition, it seems, was one of the very few strong enough to survive the impact of the rage of the monotheists to reshape and exorcize their world. The *Aeneid*, the *Iliad*, and the *Odyssey* were so entrenched in their respective pedagogic niches that Christians simply had to learn to read them in ways that did not threaten their own theology and values; they had, in any case, no alternative to learning Latin from Virgil and Greek from Homer.

FURTHER READING

The reception of Homer and Virgil is a field of evident importance in European literary history and one that has been richly worked. Modern reception of Homer attracted attention earlier than ancient reception, and the only comprehensive survey of the field is still Georg Finsler, *Homer in der Neuzeit von Dante bis Goethe* (1912, repr. 1973). For an overview of ancient interpretive strategies, see the essays in Lamberton and Keaney 1992, with bibliography. An oddly attractive, learned study by Howard Clarke, *Homer's Readers: A Historical Introduction to the* Iliad *and* Odyssey (1981) reads Homer over the shoulders of interpreters from Dares and Dictys to the twentieth century.

The most concise, just-the-facts account of the evidence for the immediate impact and early influence of Virgil will be found in the concluding essays of Horsfall 1995a. These are complemented by the six essays on "translation and reception" in *The Cambridge Companion to Virgil* (Martindale 1997). Virtually all studies of "silver epic" are in fact studies of the use of Virgil: one that covers the issue from a Virgilian perspective is Philip Hardie's *The Epic Successors of Virgil* (1993). Two others that follow the story beyond the Middle Ages are Thomas M. Greene's classic *The Descent from Heaven: A Study in Epic Continuity* (1963) and Richard Thomas's *Virgil and the Augustan Reception* (2001).

Gilgamesh is another story, as Chapter 15, by Noegel indicates. The scriptural parallels are catalogued in Heidel 1946. Those parallels and elusive indirect influence aside, the true history of the reception of the Gilgamesh epic in the European tradition of literature begins in the twentieth century, and remains to be written.

CHAPTER TWELVE

Translating Ancient Epic

Richard Hamilton Armstrong

The translation of ancient epic poetry is a very complex topic since it is an activity that is at least four millennia old and comprises thousands of works in more languages than any individual scholar could hope to survey. The enormous prestige of epic within the hierarchy of texts and genres has fueled an unprecedented amount of translating activity over the centuries, which in turn makes translation one of the best indices to critical thought on the genre itself. In addition, the high-stakes game of translating epic has also occasioned some of the most revealing discussions of literary translation in general, such that the very history of translation can be traced through epic examples. Lastly, since the majority of ancient epic's readers have encountered the poems almost exclusively in translation for some time now, our reception and conceptualization of epic as a whole are deeply indebted to the work of translators, who forge the links between *traductio* and *traditio* that have kept epic viable in modern culture. The first words of John Dryden's introduction to his translation of the *Aeneid* show the awesome significance of the endeavor for him: "A heroic poem, truly such, is undoubtedly the greatest work which the soul of man is capable to perform. The design of it is to form the mind to heroic virtue by example" (1944: ix). The genre itself thus clearly raises the stakes for the translator's task; only biblical translation can rival that of epic in cultural importance.

Given the vast scope of the subject, this chapter will best serve its purpose by providing a taste of the issues with reference to particular types of translation, but without any pretense to either chronological or topical comprehensiveness. My examples will be taken largely from Homeric and Virgilian translation simply because these traditions show the greatest variety and chronological range (see the survey of Homeric translation in Young 2003); however, the concepts under discussion will be easily exported by the reader to other epics in translation. In what follows we shall focus on issues that show the interplay between the *source text* (or "original") and the *target text* (or "translation") and its *target culture* (the culture that creates and receives the translation).

Translation is not a simple act like pouring water from one bucket into another. It is a term that covers a broad spectrum of transference activities, ranging from the lowly student trot (the proverbial "word for word" translation) to the free adaptation across media (e.g., from epic poem to prose novel, drama, opera, or film). The criteria for success vary greatly according to the medium, era, and expectations surrounding both original and translation. This wide variation renders impossible the quest for a "definitive" translation, since there is no agreement as to what *defines* "definitive." What the new field of Translation Studies can add to this discussion is mostly a deeper historical awareness of translational practices and a more refined descriptive apparatus (as explored especially by Gideon Toury, 1995; for Translation Studies in general, see Baker 1998; Venuti 2000; Munday 2001). Any *prescriptive* apparatus at this point would be a matter of taste or particular circumstances and needs, but not of academic authority. However, the prescriptive approach, when it is well articulated, is very helpful for the descriptive project, as in the case of Matthew Arnold's famous essay, "On translating Homer" (1861), which brings to life the controversial positions on translation for English culture. While that essay remains a classic of translation criticism, its approach would be out of place here, though its observations will serve us below in dissecting *how* the task of translation is framed within the nineteenth-century English horizon.

1   Status of the Source Text

One problem common to the translation of ancient and medieval epic is that the status of the source text itself is not always clear and may even change drastically over time. In the cases of the *Epic of Gilgamesh* and the Homeric poems, the concept of the source text remains in a state of flux as new evidence arises and new theories of textual crystallization and transmission alter the conceptual horizon. This being the case, a scholarly translation may well have to dispense entirely with the notion of a unitary source text, as is done for example in Andrew George's translation of the Gilgamesh material, which might be described as a translated textual *repertory* rather than a rendering of a single "original text" (1999). His inclusive approach effectively dispenses with the notion that there is a single definitive form which we must posit, construct, assume, or select before translating, and in this regard his work is very different from the scholarly rendering of only the "standard version" of the epic (the so-called Sîn-leqi-unninnî version), as was done by Gardner and Maier (1984), Kovacs (1989), and a great many others. He includes along with the standard version the remains of the earlier Old Babylonian version as well as the Sumerian tales of "Bilgames" which form the nucleus of the legend. George's approach thus refuses to synthesize the disparate pieces into a single whole for the modern reader, as in modern retellings like the "verse narrative" version by Herbert Mason (2003) or the Penguin edition by Nancy Sandars (1972). In his introduction to the paperback edition, George reminds us dramatically of the instability of his source: "New pieces of Gilgamesh continue to appear. This paperback edition differs from its hardback predecessor in being able to use on p. 90 a fragment of Tablet XI that came to light only in June 1999" (1999: xi).

A similar problem faced the translator/editor of the Greek medieval epic, *Digenis Akritis*, which exists in two linguistically and stylistically distinct forms. The Grottaferrata Version is in a higher linguistic register and was championed as "the original" by modern adherents to *katharevousa* (the "purified" version of Modern Greek, only officially abandoned in 1974), while proponents of the demotic upheld instead the Escorial Version, a less polished piece of poetry couched in a markedly more popular idiom. The translator/editor Elizabeth Jeffreys, convinced that both versions are drawn from a common but missing source and refusing to take sides on the language issue, had no choice but to translate both versions and present them *seriatim* as traces of a missing ancestor (1998). We are thus not presented with an "original" and a translation, but with two witnesses to an hypothesized original. Even in the comparatively simpler case of Virgil's *Aeneid*, the translator must address the problem of a text that was reportedly left unfinished, includes seemingly unfinished verses, and whose very beginning lines vary in the textual tradition. The Virgilian translator thus faces the task of in a sense *completing* the text (see section 4), and still must grapple with the matter of textual variation, even if it is on a smaller scale.

The problem of the source can be greatly complicated by the idea that an epic text may represent the residue of an oral tradition; indeed, the most radical view of oral epic challenges *all* assumptions about the singularity and originality of *any* "text" (on these issues, see especially Nagy 1996b and 1996c). A team of scholars at the Center for Hellenic Studies in Washington, DC is undertaking a translation of the Homeric textual repertory in conjunction with their development of a Greek multitext, which will include "plus verses" from the papyri not represented in the medieval manuscripts and as many textual variants as the technology will allow. This would represent a decisive change in Homeric translation, one which in conceptual terms moves well beyond even the most literal translations of the past by leaving the source text *open* to different philological interpretations. The age of hypertext, which can facilitate such complex and layered approaches to a fluid textual tradition, may well permanently alter the possibilities and parameters of translation as we know it at the same time it moves us beyond the Platonic idea of a fixed recension (i.e., a singular "reconstructed original").

We might also say that the notion of the source as a "naked text" encountered without mediation is a widespread myth, quite often propagated by translators themselves, who may be quick to deny their reliance upon others. Besides the crucial interventions of copyists and editors on the source, we must consider the influence of scholia, commentaries, dictionaries, and other ancillary works on the translator's understanding. It is also rare in the case of ancient epic that a translator is truly the first to render the source text, which leads us to ask: Did the translator work via an intermediary translation or translations? Did these influence the target text's style or approach, either as models to follow or as bad examples to be avoided? Was the intermediary translation in the target language, or in another (e.g., a Latin translation of Homer used by an English translator)? One must seriously consider the possibility that the "source text" is not in fact the "original" at all, but rather that the source comprises a whole *series* of previous translations with perhaps only *some* input from the "original," or even none at all. In sum, the hieratic primacy of the "original" is itself an ideology or position to be taken, and it has *not* always been the position taken in practice by every translator for a variety of reasons. A tenuous connection to the source often has no effect on the success of the translation in its target environment. Indeed, we know from the Ossianic "translations" of James Macpherson (1736–96) that a highly successful target text can even lack an identifiable source (see Chapter 29, by Dué). There are also known literary texts that trade on the outright *fiction* of their translation, like the *History of the Destruction of Troy* attributed to Dares the Phrygian. This Latin work sports a bogus letter of introduction supposedly from the Roman historian Cornelius Nepos to his colleague Sallust, which attests to the scrupulous translation of a Greek original Nepos found in Athens. While the Latin *may* in fact be a translation of a Greek original, the point is: the story of *its translation by Cornelius Nepos* is definitely a fiction used to authenticate it for the target audience.

Considerations stemming from the source text go well beyond the basic outlay of the textual tradition – i.e., its manuscripts, tablets, or papyri (on which media see Chapter 10, by Haslam) – and its intermediaries. How one will translate a text in point of style, diction, and even narrative approach will differ according to the *kind* of text one assumes the source to be. For example, if one assumes that the epic to be translated reflects the poetics of an oral tradition, then features like formulaic diction, repeated verses and epithets take on a new importance (see Chapter 4, by Jensen). If one assumes rather that the poem was composed by a court poet in a high and solemn style, then this will condition the style and language of the target text accordingly. If one assumes the ancient poem is just one version of a tale available for retelling, then the translator feels understandably freer to render the plot with significant lexical, stylistic, and even narrative divergence according to the tastes of the target culture. If one assumes instead that the poet's *ipsissima verba* contain arcane wisdom of great importance, the tendency to take a word for word approach (perhaps with exegetical digressions) is more likely. In each of these cases, then, we can see that *the assumptions that frame the source text for the translator are the point of departure* for the target text which will emerge. Since assumptions about the source text are rooted in the target culture, there is understandably a certain hermeneutical circularity at work. By way of illustration, we shall now examine more closely the four sets of assumptions mentioned in the scenarios above.

2   Orality, Folklore, and Homeric Translation

In the case of translating the "orality" of a source text, the most illustrious examples we have to hand concern the Homeric poems, which were conceived of as "oral poems" in a rigorous sense (i.e., products of composition-in-performance, or at least somehow derived from such a technique) only in the twentieth century, after the Parry–Lord investigations established the empirical reality of oral composition-in-performance for the scholarly world (for a brief overview, see Foley 1997 and Chapter 4, by Jensen and Chapter 29, by Dué). Previous to this change in paradigm, the oral features of Homeric verse were dealt with variously by translators who did not have to take a stand on their inherently compositional/functional nature. As such, the vast majority of translations suppress repetitive oral features as inconcinnities of style without much soul-searching about the mutilation of the Homeric fabric. Exceptions to this explicitly reflect the scholarly shift in horizon, such as the translations of Richmond Lattimore, a classics professor well aware of the new views of the Homeric text (see his introduction to the *Iliad*: 1961: 39). But to this day, viable translations of Homer are made which ignore large amounts of the formulaic diction and epithets, such as Stanley Lombardo's very American *Iliad* (1997) and *Odyssey* (2000). The assumption behind such translations is that oral features of style are "embellishments that were meant only to please the ear – stock epithets and recurring phrases where the meaning is of no account" (Rouse 1966: 7). At present, the most rigorous approach to rendering the formularity of Homeric verse in English translation is in the above-mentioned project at the Center for Hellenic Studies, which will attempt as far as possible to render identical phrasings identically in the translation – something which even Lattimore shied away from doing mechanically.

However, not even "orality" is a stable, unitary concept, and here again different assumptions can lead to very different target texts. The nineteenth century saw orality in terms of the European traditions of folk balladry, and some translators sought to render Homer in line with living folk song traditions; these traditions, however, represented more oral *performance* and *propagation* than oral *composition* (for this reason the ballad is sometimes referred to as an instance of "aurality"). The concept of a "ballad Homer" had been first raised seriously in F. A. Wolf's textual criticism on the original Greek texts, but the idea had a profound impact on the nineteenth-century imagination. One of its extraordinary by-products was Thomas Macaulay's rendering of the historian Livy's first books into the *Lays of Ancient Rome*, with the belief that such was the original form of the Roman historical narratives (1842). Matthew Arnold in his essay "On translating Homer" combats at length the ballad-style translation of Homer, which was clearly a vogue he thought unworthy of the source: "To apply that manner and that rhythm to Homer's incidents, is not to imitate Homer, but to travesty him" (1960: 132). But translators such as William Gladstone, Francis W. Newman, and William Maginn found in the English ballad and Spenserian stanzas both a meter and a diction they thought rendered Homer well *as song* in a register comparable to the source. Maginn found that there was no contradiction in believing in both a unitary Homeric corpus *written* by a single author and the oral propagation (and corruption) of his texts "sung in scraps" and later only recollected in Athens by Pisistratus (1850: 12–13). Thus his *Homeric Ballads* (1850) comprise twelve unconnected "songs" from the *Iliad* and *Odyssey* (with facing Greek text!) presented *not* as an image of their true form *qua* epic, but rather as he imagined one would encounter them in Greek performance.

The concept of oral culture implies more than just a style and has implications for how one conceives the entire *cultural situation* of the epic. Proponents of a "folkloric" Homer seen more as a vital part of a popular culture will render their Homer accordingly. This was at the heart of the debate between Francis Newman and Matthew Arnold, since Arnold chided Newman for failing to observe Homer's *nobility* – a term with clear sociological as well as stylistic implications (1960: 127). Newman replied that Arnold, in insisting that Homeric quantitative hexameters be rendered in English accentual hexameters, failed to understand the implications of their one point of agreement:

> "Homer is popular," is one of the very few matters of fact in this controversy on which Mr. Arnold and I are agreed. "English hexameters are not popular," is a truth so obvious, that I do not yet believe he will deny it. Therefore, "Hexameters are not the metre for translating Homer." Q.E.D. (Newman 1905: 124)

Newman relates his earlier eagerness to see "how unlearned women and children would accept my verses," and his pleasure to hear "how greedily a working man has inquired for them, without knowing who was the translator," all of which shows that his criterion for success was based on the assumption that Homer was widely accessible in style and *must* be so in English (1905: 124).

In more recent times, Georgios Psychoundakis has rendered both Homeric epics into Cretan 15-syllable couplets, the verse form of Cretan folk song (1995, 1996). It is also the form of the Renaissance courtly epic *Erotokritos*, by Vitsentzos Kornaros (*ca.* 1553–1613), which retained wide popularity in Greek culture through cheap editions and even oral propagation into the twentieth century. In this respect, the Cretan translator can advantageously span *both* the folkloric and epic categories with one popular form. Psychoundakis was not a learned man, but a World War II Resistance veteran well versed in Cretan folklore and modern warfare. In his old age he turned popular "bard" and re-stitched Homer (working from previous modern Greek translations) in a very local idiom; but the translations were not *performed* by him, and were eventually published by the University of Crete Press, thus showing the assistance of the academy in the construction of a national "popular" culture in modern Europe. Nor is folk *poetry* the only option for a folksy Homer. In the 1930s, W. H. D. Rouse was convinced that Homer's language was not an effete poetical construct, but was composed largely of words "taken directly from the common man's lips, the vivid images which he uses naturally to describe what he sees" (1937: 285). Thus reacting against other English translations which he found "filled with affectations and attempts at poetic language which Homer himself is quite free from," Rouse proclaimed "Homer speaks naturally, and we must do the same" (p. vii). His *Story of Odysseus* is thus couched in a storyteller's prose: "This is the story of a man, one who was never at a loss," it begins (p. 11). "At the time when I begin, all the others who had not been killed in war were at home," he continues; "Well then, the seasons went rolling by..." (p. 11). While both of these translations strive to make Homer vital and accessible to their target audiences, neither addresses vigorously the problem that the poems are composed in a hybrid *Kunstsprache* that presented a greater linguistic alterity to the average ancient Greek audience than the translators convey (something the English "ballad" Homers did address with their archaic diction). Psychoundakis and Rouse assumed that "Homer" was the common possession of "his people," and any translation ought to be the same for the target culture.

These last examples show us that *even apparently radical divergences from the original's form are still often rooted in assumptions about the source text and its culture*. In other words, the ballad Homers and Rouse's prose version make clear concessions to target-culture norms and forms, but do so under the conviction that they are *better* representing some essential aspect of the source. Therefore, a fair assessment of a translation can only be made when the full assumptions of the translator are disclosed, which is why the mini-genre known as the "translator's preface" is of inestimable value (though one must read such texts with due caution!).

3 Courtly Bards and Kingly Subjects

At the opposite end of the spectrum from the "folkloric" Homer, we have the assumption that the epic poet is essentially like Virgil or Ovid; i.e., an author who *writes* for a well defined aristocratic audience, or at least performs for one, and in whose works "may alle valyaunt princes and other nobles see many valorous faytes [feats] of armes" (Caxton 1962: 10). Encouragement for such a view is rooted in the Homeric texts, where the *aoidoi* such as Demodocus seem to cut just such a figure (*Odyssey* 8), and in the historical situation of the Roman Augustan poets. In epochs when court cultures and their patronage are *the* reality for the translator, it is not surprising that these features of the source sway the translation a good deal more, since they reflect the power relations that often stand behind the act of translation. Indeed, one often finds such courtly values inscribed in the dedications, such as in George Sandys' *extension* of Ovid's dedication to Germanicus (*Fasti* 1.3–6; 17–20) to King Charles I of England (1970: 23). The early English translator George Chapman (1559?–1634) treated the Homeric poems as something like a mirror for princes: "Only kings and princes have been Homer's Patrones, amongst whom Ptolomie would say, he that had sleight handes to entertayne Homer had as sleight braines to rule his common wealth" (1967: 546). In florid verses he dedicated his "English Homer" to Prince Henry, son of King James I, offering him "Princely presidents [precedents]" in Homer's works, "in which Humanitie to her height is raisde [raised]" (pp. 3–4). Given his sensitivity to court etiquette, Chapman could not contain his courtly interjection over the upstart Thersites, who rails against King Agamemnon in the Achaean assembly in *Iliad* 2. The *Iliad* says Thersites was a man:

> ὃς ἔπεα φρεσὶ ᾗσιν ἄκοσμά τε πολλά τε ᾔδη,
> μάψ, ἀτὰρ οὐ κατὰ κόσμον, ἐριζέμεναι βασιλεῦσιν,
> ἀλλ' ὅ τι οἱ εἴσαιτο γελοίϊον 'Αργείοισιν
> ἔμμεναι.
>
> (2.213–16)
>
> who knew words in his mind, disorderly and many,
> all amiss and not in due order, just to wrangle with princes
> with whatever seemed to be funny to him in the eyes of the Argives.

This Chapman renders:

> ...A most disordered store
> of words he foolishly powrd [poured] out, of which his mind held more
> Than it could manage – anything with which he could procure
> Laughter he never could containe. *He should have yet bene sure*
> *To touch no kings. T'oppose their states becomes not jesters' parts.*
>
> (2.181–5; my emphasis)

Such a divergence in the translation might seem simply an unpardonable liberty, but it stems from Chapman's conviction that Homer's world reflects the courtly values of Jacobean England and its views of monarchy. Thus he has Odysseus call Agamemnon not "Atreides" but "our king," and warn Thersites: "do not take into that mouth of thine / The names of kings, much less revile the dignities that shine / In their supreme states" (2.217–19). After Thersites' drubbing by Odysseus, members of the Achaean host comment "I think his sawcie spirit / Hereafter will not let his tongue abuse the soveraigne merit" (2.239–40). These examples show not only Chapman's use of an inventive and ornate poetic diction (complete with conceits and circumlocutions of the kind expected of poetry in Elizabethan and Jacobean times), but a whole exalted attitude toward kingship which he assumes Homer would find natural and appropriate. The assumption is that the source text reveals a world of royalty that is based on timeless truths of regal sovereignty, truths which an "English Homer" can easily express.

Though Alexander Pope (1688–1744) was of a very different temperament from Chapman, he nonetheless shows a great affinity with him precisely on the nature of royalty, which as we said, is a feature of the *source* text that resonates with elements in the target culture. Writing during what is often called the "Augustan Age" of British literature, Pope worked under a neoclassical poetics that asserted values of control and natural hierarchy in ways which shaped his interpretation and rendering of Homer. One can see his linkage of natural order and monarchy in his other poems, such as *Windsor Forest* (1713): "Rich industry sits smiling on the plains / and peace and plenty tell, a *Stuart* reigns" (lines 41–2; original emphasis). In the same scene from *Iliad* 2 discussed above, Pope has the Achaean host move even further toward the language of English politics:

> "Ye gods! what wonders has Ulysses wrought!
> What fruits his conduct and his courage yield!
> Great in the council, glorious in the field.
> Generous *he rises in the crown's defence,*
> *To curb the factious tongue of insolence,*
> Such just examples on offenders shown,
> *Sedition silence, and assert the throne.*"

(Pope 1943: 29; my emphasis)

It is clear that, like Chapman, Pope assumes the political crisis of *Iliad* 2 takes the form of a threat to the individual royal sovereignty and dignity of Agamemnon, and that Homer frames the Thersites episode in these terms. They both infuse their translations with overtones of feudal monarchy, even though the loose confederation of Greeks under Agamemnon is in fact more *ad hoc* and much less hierarchical. Contrast Pope's rendition with that of Richmond Lattimore, whose understated tone is closer to the *Iliad*:

> "Come now: Odysseus has done excellent things by thousands,
> bringing forward good counsels and ordering armed encounters;
> but now this is far the best thing he ever has accomplished
> among the Argives, to keep this thrower of words, this braggart
> out of assembly. Never again will his proud heart stir him
> up, to wrangle with the princes [*basilêas*] in words of revilement."

(1961, 2.272–7)

In *Iliad* 2, there is an explicit sensitivity about how one speaks to *aristocrats* (Homeric *basileus* is quite often more accurately rendered "prince, chief, or noble" than simply "king" because of the feudal associations of the English word), but there is no "rising to the crown's defense" and "assertion of the throne" as in Pope's version. Lattimore's "assembly" emphasizes (following the Homeric *agoraón*) the *collective* nature of Greek politics, and this is even further accentuated in Lombardo's unabashedly American version:

> "Oh man! You can't count how many good things
> Odysseus has done for the Greeks, a real leader
> In council and in battle, but this tops them all,
> The way he took that loudmouth out of commission.
> I don't think he'll ever be man enough again
> to rile the commanders with all his insults."

> (2.294–9)

With "commanders" Lombardo has so softened the socio-political implications of the Achaean host's hierarchy that we could imagine this scene occurring in a democratic army of fifth-century Athenians or twentieth-century Americans (so much is overtly suggested by the D-Day photograph used on the book's cover).

These examples show how inherent features of the source text resonate differently to different audiences and generate varying responses in the target text accordingly. To simplify, we might say *the translator shapes the target text as a set of responses to perceived virtues and vices of the source*, where the terms "virtue" and "vice" can be both moral and aesthetic. The translator is thus inherently a mediator between sets of values, working between the (often extreme) alterity of ancient cultures and the urgency of presenting the source text to a contemporary audience. In this regard it is often revealing of the translator's strategies to locate just where the source text generates a *maximal* tension with the values of the target culture (for a study of translations of Penelope's immodest proposal to the suitors at *Od.* 21.68–79, see Armstrong 2000a). For example, in the Thersites episode, Odysseus threatens to strip off Thersites' clothing and expose his genitals (*ta t' aidô*, "shameful parts, naughty bits"), and then beat him out of the assembly (*Il.* 2.261–4). This is clearly an act of shaming intended for a social inferior (cf. the genital and facial mutilation of Melanthios at *Od.* 22.473–7), and seems to some readers problematic for such a "noble" hero to threaten. Chapman had no difficulty in having his Ulysses promise to "take and strip" Thersites to his "nakednesse" (2.228), but Pope's Augustan decorum expurgated the hero's words quite utterly, having him threaten instead "to strip those arms thou ill deserv'st to wear" (1943: 29). Even Lattimore reverts to Chapman's vaguer "nakedness," softening the genital reference in the original which increases Thersites' vulnerability to shameful and emasculating violence (1961: 2.262). Here Lombardo's American diction has the virtue of bringing home the threat with idiomatic vigor, even though it foregoes the exact words:

> "[. . .] I guarantee
> That if I ever catch you running on at the mouth again
> As you were just now, my name isn't Odysseus
> And may I never again be called Telemachus' father
> *If I don't lay hold of you, strip your ass naked,*
> *And run you out of the assembly and through the ships,*
> *Crying at all the ugly licks I land on you."*

> (2.279–85; my emphasis)

Lombardo's is clearly a time when ass-kicking heroes are easier to imagine than in the age of the periwig. Though he too diverges from the letter of the text, he does seem to capture the level of threat in a balance between the source and the target audience (this is known as *communicative* instead of *semantic* translation). Such a balancing act between source and target norms constitutes the *art* of translation; keeping it up for several thousand lines constitutes the perennial challenge of translating epic.

4   A Tale for the Telling

Translation, as was said at the beginning, represents a complex spectrum of activities that extends at one end into what are often qualified as acts of "imitation, adaptation, redaction, reworking, homage," rather than what is commonly called "translation" (see "Adaptation" in Baker 1998: 5–8; Lefevere prefers the general term "rewriting" which includes translation and much more; Lefevere 1992). Indeed, in many cultures and eras, a narrative text has to acquire an unusual status in order to be "translated" at all in our normative sense. It was far more common in previous eras for a narrative to be *retold* in another tongue rather than translated; thus we are looking – at least at one extreme of the translational spectrum – at a dynamics of *recomposition*. A relevant example would be the Arthurian tales of medieval Europe, which took various forms in numerous languages. In the *Lays* of Marie de France, for example, it is clear that Celtic, French, and English language barriers are involved, but it does *not* seem her lays are translations. The Gilgamesh epic, to take another example, was gradually shaped out of a group of unrelated Sumerian tales which were retold/rewritten in Akkadian – perhaps via some intermediary Akkadian paraphrases or maybe just an oral tradition – in relation to a larger narrative structure forged by Babylonian redactors (Tigay 1982; see Chapter 14, by Sasson and Chapter 15, by Noegel). When a version of the epic became internationally current, it was in turn translated into Hittite and Hurrian, though there too some changes and abridgements were made to fit the narrative into the target culture (Tigay 1982: 110–19; see Chapter 17, by Beckman). Here we must ask the crucial question: in the minds of adapters and translators, the source text is the source *of what*, exactly? In the case of Gilgamesh, we might say it was not the source *of a style or of a genre*, so much as of the narrative elements.

Medieval versions of the *Aeneid* and other Latin works make an interesting study in this regard, since they exhibit a common feature of textual transfer which often differs markedly from post-Renaissance translation: namely, what is called *volgarizzamento* in Italian, or "vernacularization" (Segre 1953). Latin was the language of high literary culture in the Middle Ages, thus Virgil's Latin text was not an ancient relic, but a high-cultural artifact of perennial influence and importance in the ongoing Latin literary milieu. To translate it into a contemporary romance language was thus in a sense to *degrade* it to the level of the vernacular, whose literary norms were still under development. This implies, however, a certain *freedom* from the source text and its established norms, which by appearing vastly superior become accordingly *inapplicable* to the target culture. There may be a degree of doublethink behind vernacularization, which allows for the rich creativity of the target text *in spite of* the well-established authority of the source and its norms, yet this is very often the situation in vigorous examples. The widely disseminated *volgarizzamento* of the *Aeneid* by the Florentine notary Andrea Lancia (*ca.*1280–1360) reflects the birth of a vibrant rhetorical culture among the bourgeoisie of the Italian communes, at times markedly at odds with the Latin culture of the Church (text in Fanfani 1851; for the manuscript diffusion, see Folena 1956: 234–44). Lancia's work is in prose (translated from a lost Latin prosification of Virgil), and it is clear from extant manuscripts that a form of vernacular classicism serving the political and cultural context of the Trecento was nurtured via such translations from ancient texts. Lancia's *Virgilio* *volgare* lived on in printed editions well into the sixteenth century (Folena 1956: 244–6). This shows how the prestige of the source epic can contribute *beyond* its genre into the formation of a prose culture serving very different textual ends – in this case, the civic culture of the medieval Italian city-states and their emergent forms of lay literacy.

A classic case of poetic vernacularization is the Norman French verse romance *Eneas* (*ca.* 1150), which is an artful reworking of the *Aeneid* that nowhere even mentions Virgil's name, though the French poet could hardly believe medieval clerics would not know it. The *Eneas* dispenses with the temporal complexity of Virgil's work, which moves the reader back and forth in time from the fall of Troy to the Augustan age and beyond. Instead, it narrates the events in their "natural" historical order and dispenses with material not directly germane to the story of Aeneas. There is much removed, such as the funeral games for Anchises, and a certain amount added, such as an Ovidian love scene between Eneas and Lavine (unlike the Virgilian treatment of Lavinia, who represents merely an important dynastic alliance for Aeneas). One could say that the poet was moved to *complete* the *Aeneid* by adding a betrothal, wedding (which lasted a month, we are told at line 10123), and a long earthly reign granted to Virgil's short-lived hero (Aeneas, we know from the *Aeneid*, will be raised to heaven three years after the poem ends – 1.259–66). However, the *Aeneid* is only domesticated up to a point in the *Eneas*, which remains a pagan poem, though the role of the gods is reduced, and which retains in basic outline Virgil's version of events, even with its liberal changes. A simple comparison with the more drastic reworking of Statius' *Thebaid* in the contemporary *Roman de Thèbes* will show the *relative* narrative fidelity of the *Eneas*.

Just as the source text might be deemed simply a source of narrative, so too it might be deemed a source of "information" or "truth." Erich Poppe has suggested that a medieval Irish version of the *Aeneid*, the *Imtheachta Æniasa* (before 1400 CE), "was perceived as a historical narrative rather than as a literary epic or mere entertainment," and as such was rendered in a prose that had more in common with the historical works of Irish tradition than with Virgilian epic technique (1995: 1). Here it may be the idea of the historical truth of the source that works *against* the maintenance of its poetic form. The Irish example is not at all isolated, since parts of the Virgilian narrative find their way into vernacular historical works in Spanish, French, and Italian during the medieval period. The blurry line between historiography and fictional narrative is clearly shown in the way that the *Aeneid* is used as a source of information in the massive work of universal history known under the modern title *L'Histoire ancienne jusqu'à César* (composed by an anonymous northern French writer between 1208 and 1230, and extant in numerous deluxe manuscripts; see Singerman 1986: ch. 3). This text purports to be a work "of history, without any fables" (cited on p. 154), and displays a critical attitude toward the medieval romances of antiquity. Yet it relates as historical events whole episodes taken directly from Virgil, some of which even the *Eneas* chose to omit, like the burning of the ships by the Trojan women and the death of Palinurus.

Though historically prose translation has usually been thought of as more faithful than poetic attempts (see the next section), the medieval situation shows us that there is no reason to assume this *must* be so. Prose was the medium of history, but also of the prose romance, a precursor to the modern novel with its own distinct notions of style. A colorful example of the *Aeneid* reworked as a prose romance is *Le Liure des Eneydes*, done by a Frenchman in the fifteenth century (printed at Lyons, 1483). William Caxton (*ca.*1422–91) turned this French text into English, in which guise it appeared as one of the very first books printed in England (*Eneydos*, 1490). This work rearranges the Virgilian narrative as it sees fit, even interspersing sections from Boccaccio's *De casibus virorum illustrium* that describe a very different end to Dido. Instead of killing herself as Aeneas' jilted lover, she kills herself to preserve her chastity and avoid marriage to a barbarian king. This account is followed by Virgil's contradictory version without any concern for resolution. The Scottish bishop Gavin Douglas (?1475–1522) claimed to have "spittit for dispyte" to see Virgil's text so mangled, and he was moved by Caxton's bad example to give Britain its first whole English *Aeneid* – in broad Scots! – which he completed in 1513 (on Douglas's nationalist agenda in using Scots, see Canitz 1996).

We still tend to assume, like Gavin Douglas, that what makes a translation *truly authoritative* is its fidelity to the *author* and his/her creation; though it might vary somewhat in words, a translation should capture the "spirit" and intention of its originator. But the author can be upheld as a source of authoritative truth and still find his text greatly altered, as we find in Heinrich von Veldeke's Middle High German version of the *Eneas* (which Heinrich may have compared to the *Aeneid* in the process). At the end of his tale, the poet identifies himself as

> Heinrich/ who read [the story] in French books / where it was expressed in poetry [*getihtet*]/ all according to the truth./ The books were called *Eneide* / which Virgilius wrote concerning this / and from him the tale [*diu rede*] has come down to us, / [though] he died a long time ago. / *If he did not lie, then what Heinrich has made of it afterward is true.* / He [sc. Heinrich] was not so quick with his words / that he, to his own fault, / wanted to destroy the sense / once he undertook the task. / [. . .] If [the original] did not lie, then [Heinrich] will be innocent: / as it is in French and Latin / [here it is too] without deviation. (13506–13527; my emphasis)

Clearly Virgil is an important link in *authorizing* the translation with reference to the truth of its events; but nowhere is there a concern for the author's style and diction as a *part* of that truth (Heinrich even signals his own omissions from "Virgilius" at one point: 357–61). Here we see how even as the source text falls from view, it retains a mythical importance, and how the original author continues to *authorize* the tradition of the text even as it undergoes considerable metamorphosis.

Speaking of metamorphosis, one can also see how the source text's purported truth value can compromise its own integrity from another angle in the case of the medieval French *Ovide moralisé*. This is a 72,000-line compendium in verse that both translates/ retells Ovid's tales of transformation and offers allegorical interpretations of them (De Boer 1966). The source text in this instance is clearly crystallized within the refractions of its medieval reception, for the process of translation is simultaneously a process of exposition. The author of the French text is even capable of scrupulously rendering the source and then openly *criticizing* it, as when he translates Ovid's opening appeal to the gods (*di*, i.e., in the plural; *Met.*1.2–4) and quickly adds the verses: "Although the pagans believed / that there were many gods / we must firmly hold / that there is but one single God," and there follows a veritable Trinitarian credo that ends with the assertion, "Who does not believe this is doomed!" (pp. 107–18). As bizarre as this French text might seem, it represents a horizon on Ovid's *Metamorphoses* that persisted for many centuries and can be found still at work in the translation with allegorical commentary by George Sandys (1578–1644), one of the very first works of literature produced in North America (Sandys was resident treasurer of the Jamestown colony).

It would be very wrong to assume that these types of medieval translation are simply quaint and unsophisticated. We can find modern instances where the source is treated simply as a narrative matrix, or even as history (think especially of Homer in the immediate wake of Schliemann's archaeological research (see Chapter 29, by Dué)). We can see in many modern translations that a sense of human truth and urgency about the text can still lead the translator to dispense entirely with the source text's norms of style or even its narrative economy. Herbert Mason's highly existential *Gilgamesh* (1970), Christopher Logue's "account" of *Iliad* 16–19 in *War Music* (1981), Ted Hughes's *Tales from Ovid*

(1997), Rouse's storytelling *Odyssey*, and Lombardo's robust vernacularizations of Homer show us clearly that many medieval strategies have modern analogues – just as we still allegorize ancient myth, but now into psychology *à la* Freud, Jung, or Lacan. To exclude such practices from consideration by invoking a normative concept of translation would be a mere victory by definition. It is more profitable to think of them as part of the *spectrum* of translation.

To illustrate the historical continuity of this tradition, I cite here a passage from R. L. Eickhoff's 2001 translation, *The Odyssey*, which styles itself "a modern translation of Homer's classic tale." Like his medieval forebears, Eickhoff freely supplements the source text according to his own sense of prose style, which has been shaped by his long experience as a novelist. In the sample below, which is taken from Penelope's challenge to the suitors in book 21 (based on lines 21.57–67), parts for which no basis in Homer can be found are italicized.

> Then she wiped her tears and, resolute, stood and carried the supple bow in her hands with the quiver full of its death-dealing darts over her shoulder back to the great hall where the suitors feasted. Behind her came her handmaidens bearing the great axheads in baskets.
>
> She *paused behind* a pillar and adjusted a shimmering veil over her beautiful face *and took a deep breath. Then, summoning her handmaidens, she stepped out from behind the pillar and faced the suitors in the great hall.*
>
> *Immediately a hush fell over the room as all looked up a the strange sight of Penelope with the great bow of destruction in her hands. She looked with loathing around the hall until her eyes lit upon the beggar, and then they softened. But then she remembered her purpose and a hard light shone from her eyes as she spoke.* (2001: 330)

For Eickhoff, it is entirely "modern" to render eleven verses of Homer as three short paragraphs of psychologically nuanced prose. The *modus operandi* here is clearly not the transfer of verses, but the logic of narrative itself.

5   The Paradox of the Sacred Text

Matthew Arnold declared to his Oxford audience that the translator of Homer must have his work judged by scholars "who possess, at the same time with knowledge of Greek, adequate poetical taste and feeling" (1960: 99). He rooted his criteria, in other words, clearly on the side of the source text and its principal interpreters, like "the Provost of Eton, or Professor Thompson at Cambridge, or Professor Jowett here in Oxford." His assumption was that this was the only "competent tribunal" that could judge "whether the translation produces more or less the same effect upon them as the original" (1960: 99). This is to say, lacking a "native audience" on which to gauge the effect of Homer, one has recourse to *professors* to test the validity of the translation. Here, then, is the opposite extreme of our vernacularization phenomenon: the hieratic cult of epic as a kind of sacred text, to be dispensed in "authoritative" translation with the source text always closely in mind. What truly distinguishes Virgil and Homer (and other poets on their model) – particularly at the birth of printing – is the scholarly attitude toward them that worked against the dissolution of their works into mere narrative elements and that made a fetish of their integrity, both in the careful preparation of their original texts and in the strategies of translation.

Though Homer had long been deemed the sovereign poet by reputation in the Latin West, no extensive Homeric text survived in Latin translation until the Italian humanists Francesco Petrarca ("Petrarch," 1304–74) and Giovanni Boccaccio (1313–75) sponsored an interlinear translation by a highly disagreeable Calabrian Greek, Leonzio Pilato, who later died after being struck by lightning (the precedent did not inhibit later translators).

Looking at this glorified crib, which was composed between 1358 and 1362, it is hard to imagine the thrill that broke through the early humanist circles at hearing "Homer" for the first time. But there was no doubt that they really *had* Homer, word for word, as we can still see in the autograph manuscript of the translation:

> *Virum mihi pande Musa multimodum qui valde multum*
> ἄνδρα μοι ἔννεπε Μοῦσα πολύτροπον ὃς μάλα πολλὰ
> *erravit ex quo Troie sacram civitatem depredatus fuit*
> πλάγχθη, ἐπεὶ Τροίης ἱερὸν πτολίεθρον ἔπερσε

(texts and plates in Pertusi 1964: 169–219)

In his literary epistle to Homer, Petrarch mentioned this translation project and said, "By Jove, your Penelope did not wait for her Ulysses any longer or more anxiously than I have for you" (*Rerum familiarum libri* 24.12; 342). He even claimed to enjoy the quirky translation in Latin prose, though he knew very well the observation of St Jerome: "If someone doesn't think a language's charm (*gratia*) is altered by translation, just let him translate Homer word for word into Latin, or better yet, translate Homer into prose in his own language. He'll see the order is laughable and that this most eloquent poet can barely speak!" (*Chronicon*, praefatio). All the same, Pilato's translation was eagerly disseminated and formed the basis for later Latin versions, which sought to put the rhetorical colors back in Homer (for a list of Latin translations, see Pertusi 1964: 522–9). Pier Candido Decembrio's rendition of *Iliad* 1–4 and 10 in the next century (*ca.*1441) was still indebted to Pilato's version, and it in turn made its way to Spain and was eagerly translated into Castilian for the lay learned clustered around Juan II of Castile (Serés 1997). It is hard to imagine such a literal approach being taken for another poetical text at the time. As Pertusi observes, "literal" or close translation becomes in effect the *dominant* mode of Latin translation for Homer from 1551 to 1764, and in the recycled Latin translations still printed for schools in the nineteenth century (1964: 521–2).

It is important not to underestimate the significance of this fact: the persistent "literal" or close translation of epic represents a very unusual phenomenon, but one that reveals the hieratic quality of the epic source text within the receiving cultures. One might compare this to translations of a less exalted genre, like the ancient novel, for which such a strategy would be unthinkable. Part of what the cult of the literal points to in the age of printing is the gradual elevation of these texts within a power and educational hierarchy that posited knowledge of them as necessary cultural capital for entry into the elite. The *necessity* of the source text for social advancement is what understandably underwrites the *necessity* of this style of translation. As an English translator put it in defending his own literal English rendering, a student may lack a good tutor:

> In many cases the youth is perhaps poor, and cannot afford to pay for private tuition. His future prospects in life may depend upon his being able to scrape together as much knowledge of Greek and Latin as will enable him to take a degree; and is a translation to be condemned because it has been useful in the attainment of this object? ("H.P." 1847: vi)

In this case, then, the production of translations of a very particular kind is an index of the *source* text's enduring primacy, not the translation's success or popularity. The imposing presence of the source text in a side-by-side edition, like those in the Loeb Classical Library or the French Budé collection, exerts a considerable influence on the style of the translation, whose norms shift precisely because of the possibility of constant cross-referencing with the original. This situation is highly anomalous and frames the act of translation in an unusually source-dominated way. Therefore, we must realize that such subservient forms of translation are *just a particular genre* of translation, since without the proximity of the original, the lowly companion will most likely fail *as a text*, since subservience is its *raison d'être*. Herein lies the paradox of treating the source as a "sacred text" whose very word order is a mystery to be respected. To paraphrase Jerome: when mirrored in every possible feature, Homer can barely speak in the target language; to translate Homer's poetry so faithfully is to slaughter it with good intentions. In other words, one can bring Homer's *language* piecemeal across the linguistic barrier, but that does not mean one has thereby created an identifiable literary *text*.

We will see in the future who, besides cyber-cribbing students of the source text, will actually read the translation of Homer being made by the diligent scholars of the Center for Hellenic Studies. They are working along lines of source-dominated translation quite similar in spirit to Leonzio Pilato (though with a very different conception of the source), rendering faithfully verse for verse and phrase for phrase with as much syntactical mirroring as possible. But they are operating in an environment thick with competition from a half dozen or more English Homers that remain vigorously in print – a situation which did not trouble Leonzio, whose pristine horizon we shall *never* be able to recover. The source text is constantly allowed to intrude in the CHS version through parenthetical appearances of key Greek terms:

> The anger [*mênis*] of Peleus' son Achilles, goddess, perform its song –
> disastrous anger that made countless sufferings [*algos* pl.] for the Achaeans,
> and many steadfast lives [*psukhê* pl.] it drove down to Hades,
> heroes' lives, but their selves it made prizes for dogs
> and for all birds; the will of Zeus was being fulfilled.
>
> (1.1–5)

This translation, once divorced from its role as intermediary to the accompanying source, will have to compete with Lombardo's vigorous vernacularization, among many other versions going all the way back to Chapman that are still kept in print:

> Rage:
>   Sing, Goddess, Achilles' rage,
> Black and murderous, that cost the Greeks
> Incalculable pain, pitched countless souls
> Of heroes into Hades' dark
> And left their bodies to rot as feasts
> For dogs and birds, as Zeus' will was done.
>
> (1.1–6)

In a sense, then, the CHS translation's greatest challenge will be found not in wrapping English around Homer's winged words, but in holding its own as a voice within the chorus of English Homers.

Close translation can operate as more than a crutch for the limping student of the source text, as we know from the case of biblical translation. The first close translation of Virgil's *Aeneid*, made by the Spaniard Enrique de Villena in 1428, was not meant to teach idle boys Latin, but rather to serve as the means for expounding the deep wisdom of Virgil to a lay audience. As Don Enrique says in his letter to King Juan II of Navarre, only he who can penetrate into the most hidden recesses of the text will know its true benefits, and so the King should take up this reading

> since it has pleased God to so bless the Castilian tongue that such a glorious history [*istoria*]
> has been translated into it, and that, thus preserved in that tongue, such a fruitful doctrine can

live on among the lay learned [*los romançistas* – i.e., those who only know the romance vernacular] who have no knowledge of Latin, in which it originated and remains among the learned [*los entendidos*], where its most delectable sweetness is better savored. (1994: 27)

De Villena openly broke with the tradition of *volgarizzamento* even as he clearly supported the emergent culture of vernacular learning. He was highly conscious of the special nature of his approach:

[. . .] in Italy some vernacularized [*vulgarizaron*] this *Aeneid*, but only in reduced or abridged form, leaving out many of the poetic fictions contained in it, caring only for the most part for the simple story; this is especially true regarding the material from the fifth book concerning the games Aeneas held in Sicily. And others translated the Italian into French and Catalan just as abridged as they found it in the Italian version; but never until now has anyone taken it from the Latin itself without diminishing anything from it. (1994: 54).

De Villena characterized his translation *not* as word-for-word, but rather as "word for word according to the sense and in the order which sounds or seems best in the vernacular" (1994: 28). The result is a target text that signals in its halting reformulations the numinous influence of the source, but also the source's multivalent openness; and yet this Spanish text is *not* meant to be a mere handmaid to the nearby original, but rather a kind of working mine for the laity. I hazard here my own translation of his translation of *Aeneid* 1.8–11:

O Muse – or Science – recall to me the causes – or occasion – through which the divinity was offended – or rather, which deity was offended [*quo numine laeso*]. What compelled you – or moved you in a painful way – Juno, Queen of the gods, to drag or trundle through so many adventures that man of notable piety, and to thrust so many labors upon him? And can the celestial intelligences – or heavenly dwellers – conceive such anger? (see de Villena 1994: 54)

In addition to this "exegetical translation," de Villena planned a lengthy commentary (which he did not complete beyond Book 3) that filters a great deal of medieval-style information, such as the factoid that Juno represents humidity which comes from the air, and that she is said to be the wife of Jupiter in order to express that the heat of fire exerts its generative power in the humidity of the air (1994: 70).

De Villena's text shows us, among other things, that one can have a devoutly faithful attitude toward the articulations of the text while holding a very peculiar conception of its function and meaning. His example and that of Gavin Douglas mentioned earlier (see section 4) remind us also that even the practice of "faithful" or literal translation is not *simply* a matter of the source text/target text relation, but rather a situation that might appear instead like this:

> source text
> previous translation 1
> previous translation 2
> previous translation 3
> . . .
> ↓ target text *n*.

This is to say: the target text's current horizon is *always already* informed by the previous translations, which may not only predetermine the horizon for stylistic and lexical choices (even what would be "new and different" in a translation can only be understood against the backdrop of what has been tried before), but also condition how the source text itself is understood, and consequently how the new translation is likely to be received. The choice for "close" over "loose" translation is itself *most often* mediated by previous translations, closer translations being – as in the case of Douglas and De Villena – patently motivated by the wanton outrages of the looser ones.

In fact, we might even say that in a language with a high number of translations of ancient epic, such as English or German, all subsequent translations are the result of *both* the continued urgency and importance of the source text *and* the ongoing dynamics of the target-text series. For if truly adequate and acceptable translations have already been achieved, what would necessitate further translations at all? At this point, we can say in the case of English that the changing literary dynamics which have an impact on the target text are *largely* what make new translations of Homer or Virgil necessary (though, as stated in section 1, changes in the status of the source text may also play a role, as in the case of the Gilgamesh epic). Underestimating the importance of shifting target-culture norms can lead one to misunderstand dramatically the nature of translation; such miscalculation has been responsible for a lot of flops in translation history.

I will conclude this section by considering the *target* norms influencing Richmond Lattimore's translation of the *Iliad*, one highly praised by classicists for its apparent fidelity to Homeric style and diction. Lattimore, a professor of Greek and a poet in his own right, would seem the ideal Arnoldian translator. But rather than emphasizing Lattimore's ballyhooed fidelity, I will argue instead that his Homer is successful for the *middle* course it steers, distancing itself from well-worn grooves in English translation as well as some of the consequences of slavish fidelity. First of all, since he wrote in the 1940s and early 1950s when the canon of verse form had loosened up greatly and allowed for less regular lines, Lattimore was free to adopt a loose six-beat line that was dactyloid without being pure dactylic hexameter. His translation is thus *less* close to Homer's form, but also farther away from the English hexameter translations that had shown the enormous difficulty of such metrical mimesis in our tongue, in spite of Arnold's fervent pleading for it (for painful examples, see Way 1904; Cotterill 1911; on the "hexameter mania" in general, see Prins forthcoming). In fact, an *Iliad* rendered in accentual dactylic hexameter had only just appeared seven years before Lattimore published his own version, and it reads like a relic of the nineteenth century, utterly uninformed about the state of English poetry (Smith and Miller 1944). With its vague dactylic feel, Lattimore's verse *alludes* to Homeric hexameter, yet does not attempt to replicate it, thus dodging the lapse into jigging doggerel that is the curse of the English hexameter.

Even more important was Lattimore's divergence in point of poetic diction, where he tried to fulfill three of Arnold's four criteria for translating Homer: that the target diction be rapid; plain and direct in thought and expression; and plain and direct in substance. Lattimore balked, however at Arnold's fourth criterion: nobility.

> I do not think *nobility* is a quality to be directly striven for; you must write as well as you can, and then see, or let others see, whether or not the result is noble. *I have used the plainest language I could find which might be adequate, and mostly this is the language of contemporary prose.* This is not "Homeric." Arnold points out that Homer used a poetic dialect, but I do not draw from this the conclusion, which Arnold draws, that we should translate him into a poetical dialect of English. In 1951, we do not have a poetic dialect, and if I used the language of Spenser or the King James Version I should feel as if I were working in Apollonius of Rhodes, or at best Arktinos, rather than Homer. (1961: 55; my emphasis)

Lattimore's decision in point of diction reveals the dense corpus of Homeric translation that informs his horizon *negatively*; Butcher and Lang's prose rendering of the *Odyssey* was in fact in "biblical English" (1879) and the ballad Homers were often couched in an archaizing dialect redolent of Spenser. But his avoidance of an artificial dialect is *not* a matter of fidelity to Homer; it is very much tied up with the seismic changes in

English-language poetry ushered in with the poetics of modernism (cf. T. S. Eliot's notorious critique of Gilbert Murray for being a belatedly pre-Raphaelite translator of Euripides; Eliot 1967). So Lattimore's *Iliad* oddly occupies a place between poetic and prose translation: loose poetry in the plain language of prose. On occasion one glimpses an encroaching banality brought about by this compromise, as when he renders Odysseus' threat to Thersites as:

> ...let me nevermore be called Telemachos' father,
> if I do not take you and strip away your *personal clothing*
> your mantle and your tunic that cover over your *nakedness*,
> and send you thus bare and howling back to the fast ships,
> whipping you out of the assembly place with the *strokes of indignity.*

> (2.261–4; my emphasis)

The prosy phrase "personal clothing" seems quite bathetic in the context of this powerful threat; indeed, we might ask: "personal" clothing as opposed to *what*, exactly? "Nakedness," as I pointed out above (section 3), is a compromise that suppresses the unnerving specificity of Thersites' genitalia. "Strokes of indignity" (for the Homeric *aeikessi plēgēisin*, "disgraceful blows") in addition, seems rather abstract, given the concrete nature of the threat. But the choice of such diction is conditioned by the dactyloid feel of the line, since it generates hard-to-find dactyl-spondee combinations at line's end (*pérsonal clóthíng* – the latter word is really a trochee; *báck to the fást shíps*) and two good dactyls (which should *not* fall at the end in dactylic hexameter!): *óver your nákedness, strókes of indígnity.* How close this language is to contemporary prose we can see by simply comparing Rouse's prose version of the same passage from thirteen years before:

> ...may I no longer be called the father of Telemachos, if I don't strip the clothes from your body, strip off the cloak and shirt that cover your nakedness, and send you off to the ships roaring with pain after a good sound drubbing! (1966: 27)

Now contrast these two versions with the hexameter translation of Smith and Miller, keeping in mind that this latter fulfils Arnold's criteria in form and diction perfectly, and appeared around the same time as Lattimore was working on his translation:

> ...nor again let me ever be called Telemachus' father,
> If I shall fail to take thee and strip thee of thy precious raiment,
> Mantle and tunic and all that thy nakedness hides, and in such wise
> Back to the swift-keeled galleys in loud lamentation expel thee,
> Beaten and driven with blows of dishonor from out the assembly.

> (1944: 38)

Smith and Miller's version is the last gasp of the Arnoldian Homer, delivered some eighty-three years after Arnold laid out the desiderata for translation. Lattimore's version, in contrast, shows us poetry's peculiar convergence with prose by the mid-twentieth century, a convergence that remains in force even in the latest English hexameter translations, which have clearly benefited from the poetics of Lattimore's dactyloid prose (Kemball-Cook 1993; Merrill 2002).

6 Conclusion: Creativity, Innovation, Tradition

Having addressed the problems of the literal approach in the previous section, I end with the question: What is the role of creativity in translation? At first blush, creativity in translation might seem as undesirable as creativity in basic arithmetic; and yet, there are different ways to frame the creativity of translation beyond the simple scenario of poetic "liberties" taken at the expense of the ravished source text. A first way of framing creativity is with regard to the nature of the translation as a *poetic* text given in place of another (a "metapoem"); the second way of framing it is with reference to the influence of the activity of translation on the *whole* target literary milieu (the "leavening" effect).

To take the first approach, we can begin with the view put forward by Walter Benjamin, which asserts that the life of the original poem attains in its translations to "its ever-renewed latest and most abundant flowering" (1969: 72). Rather than seeing the translation as a parasite living off a host text, the Benjaminian scenario would have us see the translation as the "afterlife" of the text, a kind of creative descendant. Here we might benefit from a shift in paradigm, away from the original/copy model toward an essentially dramatic model of script/performance. There are in fact translators of epic who prefer to "get inside" the scenarios and characters of the source and then translate according to their feel for the dramatic situation, instead of according to the word or verse as it stands on the page (see the example of Eickhoff in section 4). Given the performance background for some forms of epic, this would be even more appropriate than a bookish literalism. The original in this model establishes a script that can be variously "performed" or actualized by later translators. Seeing the source/target relation as one of script/performance is one way of framing translation as a creative response without condemning it to the role of being a jejune or inferior copy. Like the performer who interprets a script, the translator must know the target audience and gauge its expectations against his own ambitions *vis-à-vis* the material. Hence it is useful to recall James Holmes's characterization of poetic translation as interpretation not by analysis but by *enactment* (1988: 11). This dictum nicely links the derivative nature of the content ("interpretation" based on a script by another author) with the performative element inherent in encoding the target text.

Besides the script/performance model, there is also the model of "poem for poem"; that is, that the translator produces not a copy but a "metapoem" with its own poetic integrity. To be "equivalent" to its source in fully literary terms, a translation must be a *whole* poem, and therefore, it must be coherent and creative in some sense, and must generate genuine poetic effects. This means that the translation of an original poem must have something new that gives the metapoem its ontological independence (the functional equivalent of the source's "originality"), and this newness can only be articulated with respect to target-culture norms. Indeed, according to this logic, if the source text is itself effecting some rupture or transformation of the genre, should not the target text as well signal this in some way? Lucretius, for example, worked hard to fashion an Epicurean jargon in Latin that would function in hexameter epic, and a poetic translation should reflect the risky nature of his linguistic innovation. So Rolfe Humphries rose to the task, when translating Lucretius' attempt to find a language for the material basis of reality:

> *quae nos materiem et genitalia corpora rebus*
> *reddunda in ratione vocare et semina rerum*
> *appellare suemus et haec eadem usurpare*
> *corpora prima, quod ex illis sunt omnia primis.*
> (Lucr. *DRN* 1.58–61)

Humphries framed this in terms that highlighted the provisional and transgressive nature of Lucretius' new poetic language:

> ... These things we call
> Matter, the life-motes, or the seeds of things,
> (If we must find, in schools, a name for them),
> Firstlings, we well might say, since every thing
> Follows from these beginnings.
>
> (1969: 21)

The novelty and provisionality of the vocabulary, however, is *not* mirrored in the regularity of Humphries's vigorous iambic pentameter, which helps the translator's metapoem to mirror the Lucretian synthesis of new content (Epicurean philosophy) delivered in a standard form (dactylic hexameter).

When one attempts to translate a poet like Ovid, whose formal mastery is so exuberant as to be exasperating, one might also consider to what extent the translation can *productively* transgress the source. The language of the *Metamorphoses* constantly bristles with brilliant and gratuitous effects of rhythm, word order, and narrative surprise, effects which cannot literally come over into English with the same force. And yet, a translator with the proper Ovidian panache might show his kinship to the ancient poet in the very nature of his playful divergences from the letter of the text. See for example the skillful wordplay, assonance and sudden rhymes tossed out by Allen Mandelbaum, whose metapoem might with justice be termed a truly Ovidian translation:

> The earth, more dense, attracted elements
> more gross; its own mass made it sink below.
> And flowing water filled the final space;
> it held the solid world in its embrace.
> When he – whichever god it was – arrayed
> that swarm, aligned, designed, allotted, made
> each part into a portion of a whole,
> then he, that earth might be symmetrical,
> first shaped its sides into a giant ball.
> He then commanded seas to stretch beneath
> high winds, to swell, to coil, to reach and ring
> shorelines and inlets. And he added springs
> and lakes and endless marshes and confined
> descending streams in banks that slope and twine:
> these rivers flow across their own terrains;
> their waters sink into the ground or gain
> the sea and are received by that wide plain
> of freer waters – there, they beat no more
> against their banks, but pound the shoals and shores.
>
> (1993: 4)

These nineteen lines render fourteen from Ovid's *Metamorphoses* (1.29–42). Someone unaccustomed to the fireworks of Ovid's verse might well accuse Mandelbaum of encoding excessive poetic effects, like the end-rhymes that appear and disappear, the rich English alliterations, assonances, and internal rhymes, or the heaping up of words in overwhelming ensembles ("to swell, to coil, to reach and ring"). While Mandelbaum's techniques are very English – as is the feel of his skillful iambic verse – the overall effect reproduces quite well the creative verve behind Ovid's account of the very *act of creation* itself. We arrive then at the conclusion that an Ovidian translation ought never to be a literal translation of

Ovid; for how can one perform with justice a highly original work in a *derivative* fashion? This leads us toward the concept of an "abusive fidelity" that prevents the dynamic source text from becoming an all-too-tame and domesticated target text by deploying strategies of creative divergence (see Lewis 2000).

One might object, however, that this kind of metapoetic model only works for source texts that are themselves striving to be "original" in the modern creative sense of the term. It works well for Ovid, who used conventional means to unconventional ends. But does such a notion apply at all to the Homeric texts? Was "originality" even a desirable concept among the singers of tales in archaic Greek antiquity? Would an *avant-garde* Homer be a complete mistake in conceptualization? Would a "King James" or "ballad" Homer be more appropriate as to register and performance context? Whenever we examine further the issue of "equivalent effects," we will inevitably run up against the basic problem that the source and target literary horizons are incommensurable. Indeed, the very fact that an epic work is *still* being translated after so many centuries shows that this cannot be modeled on any ordinary target-culture situation of success, like the latest best-selling novel. In cases like Homer and Virgil especially, we must realize that a *foundational* text is in play, such that translating it may reflect upon the whole previous configuration of literature.

Here the second way of framing creativity in translation can come into our discussion: the "leavening" effect that translation has on the whole target culture "poly-system" of literary texts and values (on polysystem theory, see Baker 1998: 176–9). Translation reclaims and repositions epic within the new game of the target culture, not only by (re-) situating the ancient text within the pantheon of contemporary genres and styles, but also by inscribing the target culture onto the epic. In this way, both the source and target textual systems are locked in a creative *pas de deux*. When an author undertakes to make a "modern" Homer – a Homer couched in the idiom and style of the modern novel, say, in direct contradiction to the previous strategy of archaizing verse – she not only makes Homer accessible to the target audience, who may be put off by older translations that cannot "speak to them" in a voice of their generation; she also in effect creates a foundation for the modern poetics she deploys, by recasting the alpha of western literature in an omega form, i.e., the latest literary dress. This is one way to understand Ezra Pound's dictum that "A great age of literature is perhaps always a great age of translation, or follows it" (1954: 232).

Indeed, though such moments are historically unique, we can definitely say that the translation of epic has been a foundational act for certain target cultures, as in the case of Livius Andronicus' early Latin translation of Homer's *Odyssey* into Saturnian verse (third century BCE), or Alexandros Pallis's translation of the *Iliad* into demotic Greek (1904) in an age when the very choice of demotic was highly controversial. Thus part of the "originality" in translating epic is not just a matter of linguistic creativity, but also a matter of providing *origins* and strategies of legitimation for the current literary culture. We might look at the case of Livius Andronicus as the "primal scene" of western epic translation (see Chapter 31, by Goldberg, and Goldberg 1993). What is significant in terms of Roman culture is not simply that he kick-started Roman literature by introducing the story of Odysseus in Roman dress, i.e., in the Saturnian meter that was of general use at the time. It is equally significant that he introduced the *poetics* of Homeric epic, which the Romans would cannibalize and digest more fully than any other culture, eventually making the dactylic hexameter meter *their* epic form and founding a chain of epics longer and more varied in style and content than the Greeks' own tradition: Naevius, Ennius, Lucretius, Virgil, Ovid, Lucan, Statius, Valerius Flaccus, Silius Italicus and onward to Petrarch's *Africa* and the *Christiad* (1535) of Marco Girolamo Vida. Only the Germans, through the influential Homeric translations of Johann Heinrich Voss (*Odyssey*, 1781;

Iliad, 1793), have come anywhere near the Romans in the total appropriation of a foreign epic form.

It is also very telling that after Ennius effectively established dactylic hexameter as the definitive meter of Latin epic, Livius' Saturnian *Odussia* was *rewritten* into dactylic hexameters – perhaps the first clear instance we have of how shifting target-culture norms alter the horizon of translation (see *Livius refictus*, Courtney 1993: 45–6). Cicero's hexameter translations of Homer in the first century BCE further show this standardization under the influence of Ennius' successful propagation of the Greek metrical form (Blänsdorf 1995: 161–6). We might take the passage from the Saturnian *Odussia* to the *Livius refictus* as a paradigm instance of the *symbiosis* of epic translation and epic emulation: as a target-culture notion of epic emerges and finds its own voice, this emergent form in turn shapes the translation of the very texts that spawned the native epic to begin with. Virgil's *Aeneid* in many ways definitively fixed the epic voice of Latin literature for many centuries (see Chapter 42, by Kallendorf), so much so that by the time the Renaissance humanist Angelo Poliziano came to translate Homer into Latin verse, the Virgilian voice resounded so loudly that Poliziano's translations read at times more like a Virgilian *cento* or patchwork than a rendering of Homer (Poliziano 1976: 431–523). There is perhaps no greater way to gauge Homer's *creative* influence than to see how the Homeric text itself becomes translated into the language of one of its greatest imitators.

Such symbiotic relationships recur throughout the history of epic translation, and give the appearance of a carnivalization of literary tradition; for one can genuinely speak of "Milton's influence on Homer" in the translations of William Cowper (1731–1800) – highly criticized by Matthew Arnold – which twist Homeric poetry into the sinewy, Latinate blank verse of *Paradise Lost*. One can also speak quite seriously about "Dante's influence on Virgil," not only because the *Divine Comedy* stimulated a renewed interest in Virgil in the late Middle Ages (in fact, it was through reading Dante that Juan II of Navarre came to commission Enrique de Villena's translation of the *Aeneid*, done at the same time as he translated the *Divine Comedy*), but also because some of the first Italian verse translations of the *Aeneid* are in *terza rima*, Dante's trinitarian epic form (see Cambiatore 1532). One could equally speak of Ariosto's influence on Virgil in the case of Lodovico Dolce (1508–68), who rendered the great Roman epic into *ottava rima*, the stanzaic form of *Orlando Furioso* (1568, see the study by Borsetto 1989). It would be a grave error to dismiss this kind of formal anachronism as naive projection or unreflective "domestication," for this process crystallizes the imitative/emulative dynamic of epic tradition by *refounding* the target-language epic through finding it in the *Urtext*. This shows along a broader arc how the original text *originates* in a transitive sense, i.e., how it releases creative energies in the target culture that come home to roost in translation. Even in the case of Voss, who more than any modern European appeared to forge a seamless hexameter Homer, we find that his first translation came only *after* the hexameter masterpiece *The Messiah* by Friedrich Klopstock (1724–1803) had grounded German epic in a viable form. Once again, creative emulation preceded and influenced translation, such that we cannot sunder the target-culture dynamics of the epic genre from the horizon on the epic source text.

Perhaps every translator would like to believe he is the first to find the "true voice" of the original in his native tongue, or that he is the faithful vessel through which the ancient poet speaks as did the muses of antiquity. But it would be truer at this stage to assert that what the epic translator provides is an *archival performance*, one which not only mediates the archive of the ancient source text, but also reflects both upon the history of that text in his own culture and the history of the culture itself. As Rodney Merrill observes, to use an English phrase like "wine-dark sea" for *oinopa ponton* is to invoke a *traditional* English translation of a Homeric epithet, revealing the kinship between the bard's traditional wordhoard and the translator's native resources (2002: 71). But, although he or she writes from a given cultural perspective, the translator remains an individual making very particular and often very difficult choices in finding a new voice for old song. This personal trajectory is movingly illustrated in the poet Seamus Heaney's translation of *Beowulf* (2000), through which he came to recover not only the Anglo-Saxon text, but the particular voice of the "big-voiced Scullions" that were his father's rural Irish relatives. By claiming *Beowulf* as part of his "voice-right," Heaney inserts it in the canon of his own poetic tradition; and by translating *Beowulf* in the voices of his Irish upbringing, he inscribes it within the arc of his experience. This is the truest dynamic of literary tradition, which must betray the text in order to bestow life upon it (Latin *traditio* encompasses, after all, both "handing down" and "betrayal"); and this explains why translation will remain the perennial means of keeping ancient epic a vital part of modern culture.

FURTHER READING

Translation Studies as a field has grown considerably since the early 1970s, though more slowly in the United States than in the United Kingdom, Israel, Latin America, and the European continent. The *Routledge Encyclopedia of Translation Studies* (Baker 1998) is a solid general guide, while Munday 2001 is one of the best brief introductions to the various theoretical approaches. Venuti 2000 is a useful anthology of twentieth-century texts on translation, though Hardwick 2000 will appeal more directly to the classicist; ancient translation practices are discussed by Seele 1995 and García Yebra 1994.

Those who prefer a more cultural or reception-oriented approach will do well to read the work of André Lefevere (1992 especially) or other works by Venuti (1992, 1995, 1998). His *Scandals of Translation* (1998) is an impassioned plea for dispensing with the arid abstractions imposed by linguistic approaches, and it presents a strong case for making Translation Studies more a part of the arsenal of reception studies in general (how Classical Studies would make a vital contribution to this is discussed in my review; see Armstrong 2000c).

For epic in particular, most studies tend to be tightly focused on a given translator (e.g., Canitz 1996) or an era (e.g., Borsetto 1989), and broad surveys prove difficult to write given the huge array of texts.

Reference works such as Young 2003 (a large catalogue of Homer translations) and Kallendorf 1994 (a bibliography of Renaissance Italian translations of Virgil) are essential for educating the reader about the vast and largely uncharted territory of epic translation. The best advice to the student is simply to read several different translations at some length after familiarizing himself/herself with a passage in the original. All translation is a study in difference, and this exercise will immediately bring fresh issues to light.

CHAPTER THIRTEEN

Analogues: Modern Oral Epics

John Miles Foley

Perspectives on a Method

Ancient epics survive to our time as tablet, scroll, papyrus, and vellum, but some of them – in particular, the earliest Greek and Near Eastern epics – emerged in various ways from oral traditions (see the Chapter 10, by Haslam, and Chapter 4, by Jensen; also Chapters 21–23, 14–19 by Edwards, Slatkin, Nelson, Sasson, Noegel, Wyatt, Beckman, Davidson, and Niditch respectively). Just how did that evolution from performance to encoding and the various stages of transmission take place? Can we piece together our few shards of once-thriving traditions to yield some idea of the now-lost larger whole? Most fundamentally of all, what difference does it make that an oral tradition informed the *Iliad*, *Odyssey*, *Gilgamesh*, *Shâhnâma*, and perhaps other works that our text- and print-centered ideology has taught us to understand merely as books? These and many related and equally tantalizing questions have presented themselves in recent years, as scholars have begun to address the unwritten origins of some ancient epic texts. The modern rediscovery of ancient oral traditions has given new shape to the Homeric Question, and, we might say, the Near Eastern Question as well.

Of course, such questions (and Questions) cannot always be easily and forthrightly answered. In most cases we lack the critical information – the very documentation on which conventional literary history is characteristically based – to pronounce with absolute confidence on the origins, evolution, and interpretation of oral-derived works from the ancient world. Indeed, the ebb and flow of scholarship has shown just how dangerous overreaching can prove: to assume too much, to oversimplify, or to extrapolate too enthusiastically from fragmentary evidence, is to invite refutation. Too parochial or positivistic an opinion is quickly challenged and discarded, and many times the potentially important perspective from oral tradition dies with that overstatement.

It is precisely at this point that modern oral epic traditions can offer help by providing an analogy – or better, a group of diverse analogies. Consulting epic traditions that have been or in some cases still can be experienced on a firsthand basis can prompt possible answers to the questions (and Questions) posed above, potential answers that can be glimpsed in no other way. In this respect the results of present-day fieldwork on living oral epic traditions can inform our understanding of the fragmentary remains of long-vanished epic traditions, potentially helping to fill in some of the blanks that have necessarily been left unaddressed. The gains made by philology, history, archaeology, and comparative mythology have obviously been enormous (see the Chapters 5, 9, 3, by Raaflaub, Sherratt, and Edmunds respectively), but there are some areas that these document- and item-based approaches simply cannot effectively or completely treat. For such areas, comparative studies in oral tradition – in this case, the analogy with modern oral epics – are the most promising option. (See Honko 1998b: 169–217 for far the most complete survey of contemporary oral epic traditions and the fieldwork and textualization that has brought them to prominence; the traditions treated therein are the Finnish *Kalevala*, the central Asian *Manas*, the Native American Mohave epic, the South Slavic *epske pjesme*, the *Sunjiata* or *Son-Jara* epic from Mali, the West Sumatran epic of Anggun Nan Tungga, the Tamil *Annanmaar Epic*, the *Epic of Palnaadu* from Andhra Pradesh, the Bani Hilal cycle from Egypt, and the *Pabuji Epic* from Rajasthan. Cf. also Oinas 1978, Hatto and Hainsworth 1980, 1989; Clover 1986; Foley 1998d, Beissinger et al. 1999; Chao 2001a; and McCarthy 2001.)

But with opportunities come sobering responsibilities, so let me immediately add two caveats to calibrate this initiative and the remarks made below. First, analogy is never the same thing as proof. No matter how suggestive this or that observation made on the basis of living oral epic may seem, it will always remain at the level of a heuristic. That is, comparative work along these lines (almost always non-genetic) will prompt us to construct certain kinds of responses to ancient works, but cannot by its very nature constitute the same sort of evidence that direct experience of the ancient epics would yield. Second, and correspondingly, investigation by analogy will work best when we involve as large and diverse a selection of comparisons as possible. Focusing exclusively on one or two selected parallels will unfairly bias the procedure by limiting the possibilities for understanding oral-derived ancient texts; only by surveying (at least to some degree) the vast horizon of modern oral epics, performed today on six of seven continents in hundreds of languages, can we be confident that our analogy is suitably flexible and multifaceted.

With these observations in mind, then, I propose to examine modern analogues to ancient oral-derived epics by considering a series of nine linked topics: (1) terminology and comparative "epic," (2) bards or singers, (3) performance and audience, (4) epic language, (5) transmission, (6) "new" epics, (7) the role of literacy and texts, (8) collection, textualization, and edition, and (9) epic within the ecology of oral poetry. None of these topics can be exhaustively treated in the present format, and throughout this chapter I will be citing supplemental resources to which readers can turn for more extended and in-depth discussion. Nevertheless, some attention to the international genre of oral epic – in all of its remarkable diversity – may assist us in coming to terms with the inevitably partial picture we have inherited of the emergence and context of oral-derived epics in the ancient world.

Terminology and Comparative "Epic"

One of the most challenging problems in confronting oral epic is to fully and straightforwardly grasp just what constitutes this much-described but often quite parochially conceived genre (on defining epic, see Chapter 1, by Martin; also Ford 1997; Honko 1998b: 20–9; Foley 2004a). If, whether intentionally, ideologically, or simply by force of cultural habit, we search the world only for *Iliad*-like analogues, we will have relatively little to show for our efforts and what we do discover will only further reinforce the narrowness of our original conception of the genre. We will be indulging in an exercise in tautology and foreshortening the investigation from the start. A dramatic case in point was the initial proclamation that the entire continent of Africa lacked oral epic, a radical misapprehension that stemmed from limiting the search to *Homeric*-style epic (for a corrective, see Johnson 1980). Thanks to more recent work, we now know that Africa teems with oral epics of all sorts, with a large array of heroic figures, nationalistic connections, musical and instrumental dimensions, and the like (see especially Okpewho 1975; Johnson et al. 1997; Hale 1998; Belcher 1999; Johnson 2003; and, as background, Okpewho 1992).

Or consider the case of South Slavic oral epic, which since the fieldwork of Milman Parry and Albert Lord has become a touchstone for comparative studies (see Parry 1971; Lord 1960, 2000; Foley 1988; also *SCHS*; Kay 1995; Foley 2004c). Native scholars in Croatia, Bosnia, and Serbia have applied the term *epska pjesma* ("epic song") to everything from Muslim songs many thousands of lines in length to Christian oral poetry that can be as short as less than one hundred lines. For these investigators, what makes a poem "epic" is its historical and sociopolitical significance in the formulation of ethnic identity. Subjects may range from epochal conflicts (like the original Battle of Kosovo in 1389 or the massive martial projects undertaken by Ottoman beys as early as the fourteenth century) to biographical episodes chronicling the adventures of favorite, often politically iconic heroes (as with the redoubtable Prince Marko, recalcitrant Serbian mercenary of the Turkish tsar) to *Odyssey*-like stories of hard-won return from faraway, multi-year exile (on Muslim versus Christian epics, see Coote 1978; Foley 1991: 61–134; Alexander 1998; English translations of Muslim epic available in *SCHS* (vols. 1, 3) and Foley 2004c, of Christian epic in Holton and Mihailovich 1997).

Linked to these considerations is the basic question of length. How long must a narrative be in order to qualify as an epic? Many classicists may be surprised that against the background of international epic the *Iliad* at about 16,000 lines and the *Odyssey* at about 12,000 are only middling in size. Performances from Central Asia commonly run to five and even ten times their combined length (Foley 2004a: 175), while other traditions, such as the South Slavic, have produced some shorter as well as equivalent-length epics. Cognate with the crude measurement of number of verses is the challenging problem of the so-called "cycle", the putative agglomeration of "separate" epics into a larger "whole" either within one bard's repertoire or across a tradition, as instanced in the ancient Greek Epic Cycle (see Chapter 24, by Burgess). However we decide to interpret the fragments and summaries that are our only surviving evidence of the larger epic tradition that once surrounded the *Iliad* and *Odyssey*, we should be aware that living oral epics are never discretely organized into a well-anthologized series but exist as complementary and overlapping stories loosely associated with various heroes, events, and the like (see Foley 1999a; cf. Holmberg 1998). The model of an ordered whole with neatly demarcated, interlocking pieces is a textual imposition on the immanent, emergent nature of oral tradition. A more apposite model for oral epics is the very one to which Homer alludes when he cites the Muses' gift to singers not as items but as "pathways" (*oimas*, *Od.* 8.481; see further Foley 1998a).

Divergence between the customary, usually unexamined notion of Homeric-style epic and what we actually find across the spectrum of modern analogues also foregrounds two additional principles of comparative study. First and more obviously, perhaps, we need to recognize the often overlooked difference between "emic" and "etic" analysis and terminology, that is, between how the singers and audiences construe verbal art from within the culture and how outside investigators apply their own external sets of assumptions to the process (see Ben-Amos 1976; Honko 1998b: 117–31). Much impassioned rhetoric has accompanied contributions from both sides of this discussion, but it seems best to conclude that both perspectives have something unique to offer and that each can be pressed into service appropriately. It is certainly useful to understand how singers and audiences themselves perceive what they are doing, and it is likewise valuable to widen the perspective and bring other possibilities into play. In a sense, this chapter amounts to an argument for etic analysis, with the caveat that the external models summoned for comparative investigation be as wide-ranging and diverse as possible.

A second principle warns that we must be extremely careful in evaluating "evidence" on oral tradition from within the epics themselves (see Segal 1992). In short, epic description and ethnography are not the same thing. Research on modern traditions has made it clear that comparison of idealized, fictional portraits of bardic practice with reports from actual fieldwork must be tempered with a clear awareness of what each mode of description represents. This is not to say that episodes such as those involving Phemios and Demodokos in *Odyssey* 1 and 8, respectively, cannot be mined for clues on the performance of *aoidoi* in the "real world" of ancient Greek epic praxis. It simply cautions – and this is a fundamental theme of all dimensions of comparative studies – that we take full account of the nature of each type of source.

Under such conditions any too-specific definition of oral epic will naturally be difficult or impossible to maintain, and yet some sort of touchstone to rationalize the obvious heterogeneity is desirable. For this practical purpose I cite Lauri Honko's generic profile, based as it is on a wider and more diverse sample of oral epic than any other definition of which I am aware:

> Epics are great narratives about exemplars, originally performed by specialised singers as superstories which excel in length, power of expression and significance of content over other narratives and function as a source of identity representations in the traditional community or group receiving the epic (1998b: 28).

This view has the advantage of not deferring to the *Iliad* and *Odyssey* as the archetypes (the "original sin" of comparative epic studies) while still highlighting oral epic's function as a charter for group identity and leaving room for observed variations in style, subject, characters, singer(s), mode(s) of performance, religious or secular content, poetry versus prose (and their combination: see Harris and Reichl 1997), and other parameters.

Bards or Singers

Collectively, modern analogues present us with a complex conception of the bard or singer most directly responsible for oral epics. Although there can be little doubt that both tradition and individual are crucial to each performance (just as both a language and a speaker are crucial to any discourse event), we find wide variation in the particular activity of the individual. Among the Mande peoples of western Africa (Johnson 2003: 22–9), for example, the *griot* is a professional bard who plays many roles: chronicler of family, local, and national history; provider of entertainment; preserver of social customs; and mediator. Indeed, not only does the Mande bard arbitrate between the divine and earthly realms through divination, but he also mediates everyday rifts between lineages or other disputing parties. Reaching such an important status, with its array of social responsibilities, requires years of formal apprenticeship (though there are no bardic schools as such), and even then some aspiring singers never become masters themselves.

The exceptionally well-documented singer of the Tulu *Siri Epic* (Honko 1998a) from southern India, Gopala Naika, on the other hand, is an agriculturalist and a possession priest who attends to a cult group of about 80 women involved in the religious rituals surrounding the goddess Siri. Through interviewing the bard, the fieldwork team was able to determine that, despite not earning his living from performing the epic, he was committed to its signal importance for the Tulu people: "the epic clearly functions as a myth, a charter for ritual behavior concerned with central human values and the sacred origins of institutions" (Honko 1998b: 12). Gopala Naika underwent no apprenticeship as such, formal or informal, in learning his repertoire of six epics; some came from individuals, while the *Siri Epic* was apparently an amalgamation of stories from multiple sources (p. 133).

Even more fundamental than the expectable phenomenon of natural heterogeneity among bards from around the world is the question of just how "real" the reputed master-singers of ancient and modern epics truly are. In other words, while there can be no ambiguity about the real-life existence of contemporary bards whom fieldworkers have interviewed and recorded, we should be wary of automatically extending this same level of concreteness to the figures who seem to stand behind certain of the ancient oral-derived epics. Conventional literary history abhors a vacuum of authorship, of course, preferring to impute a supremely gifted individual as the ultimate source of each of the works that constitute a tradition, but that desperate search for an author-like figure may well obscure the process behind the product. The troublesome quandary of Homer's authorship is the most famous instance of this dilemma. Within a few centuries after his supposed lifetime, Homer has already attracted multiple and contradictory biographical accounts, and any fair-minded modern evaluation of ancient attestations as a whole must choose among irreconcilable reports on his geographical origins, parentage, repertoire, and so forth.

As analogous figures from modern oral epic traditions reveal, however, this multiformity is characteristic of a widespread legendary figure we might call the "Greatest Singer" (see Foley 1998b, 1999b: 49–63; with Mongolian and medieval English parallels). Such paragons exist on the periphery of singers' and audiences' actual experience: perhaps a generation removed in time or located in another district and, in any event, never personally encountered by any of those who cite him or her as their most admired forebear and ultimate source of all of their best songs. The tradition of South Slavic oral epic offers a dramatic and well-attested "Greatest Singer," who is identified by different names (Isak, Huso, Ćor Huso, and Mujo within just one region), assigned different parents, accorded unrealistically large and variant repertoires, and credited with diverse, larger-than-life accomplishments and adventures. Nor is this fictive multiformity merely a distortion of historical fact. Rather, the legendary bard's flexibility as a character-type – with a malleable biography molded to fit the specifics of the real-life's singer's personal situation – functions as a ready means of certifying his bardic progeny's pedigree and excellence. Anyone who can trace his lineage to the Greatest Singer must, in other words, be credited with a virtually idiomatic respect. From an external point of view, then, such figures as Homer stand as personified embodiments of the epic tradition, anthropomorphizations of oral and oral-derived epic.

Performance and Audience

Oral epic performances simply don't exist without audiences (see Chapter 4, by Jensen), even if, as in many modern fieldwork situations, performances are staged chiefly for teams of outsiders. Most if not all oral epic performances that reach textual form (as printed, audio, or video "text") are in fact stimulated by external forces (see the section entitled "Collection, Textualization, and Edition," below), so the goal of capturing an event in its "natural context" without the "distortion" induced by a group of strangers or without influence by an amanuensis or mechanical recording apparatus proves a romantic ideal without much application in reality. In conceiving of the relationship between the bard and audience, it is therefore helpful to invoke the principle of the "performance arena", the virtual space where singer and auditors meet in order to carry on the specialized communication that is oral epic (J. Foley 1995: 47–9, 79–82). Rhetorically speaking, the bard assumes a certain kind of audience with a certain level of fluency, a programmatic assumption that has important implications for the structure and meaning of his epic language (see the next section). This is certainly not to deny the palpable influence of a real and present audience, but simply to observe that shifts in audience make-up do not cause singers to code-switch out of the traditional language into what amounts to a foreign tongue. Whatever the particular nature of performance in a given tradition – and the possibilities are many and varied – the channel of communication is prescribed by the framing and yet flexible rules that govern the event.

Central Asian oral epic traditions offer a glimpse of one such set of flexible rules governing performance, guiding composition and reception both from one area or ethnic group to another and over time within a single epic tradition (see Reichl 1992: especially 93–117; also 2000b). The performance arenas for epic storytelling among Tatar and Siberian peoples, for example, are often ritualistic, linked to a feast, wedding, religious festival, coffeehouse gathering, or some other communal event. In the central Asian republics epic performance frequently takes place at night and can last many nights, with the length and shape of the bard's poem directly dependent on the interest generated by the audience, who in some traditions prescribe the particular episode to be performed. In fact, Reichl reports Kazakh situations in which members of the audience actually challenge the bard to a singing contest. Another widespread practice bearing on singer–audience interaction is the composing of what the Uzbeks call a *terma* or lyric poem that acts as an introduction to the epic. Some *termas* praise the bard's accompanying instrument, while others extol the virtues of historical personages or political movements. Kazakh singers start with short poems detailing their own singer-biographies, including an account of their masters and repertories, before proceeding with *termas* and then with the epic itself, in much the same way as some scholars (following Pindar and Plutarch) have described the Homeric Hymns' hypothetical function as *prooimia* for the main event of epic. As for the evolution of performance arenas in central Asia, both the court setting and preference for Ramadan, the Muslim holy month of fasting, have now generally given way to unofficial, more secular settings. These changes entail shifts in audience makeup as well.

Nor should our exclusively textual record of epics from the ancient world obscure the fact that, as Homer makes clear enough in his (admittedly poetic) description of singers' performances, in many cases music and dancing once accompanied the narration. As Thomas Hale has explained in some detail (1998: 146–71), the performances of *griots* and *griottes* across Niger, Mali, Senegal, and Gambia show that music is an integral facet of their epic presentations. Among the different sorts of lutes played by performers, the *kora* and *balafon* are men's instruments while the *ardin* and *karinya* are exclusively used by women. Vocal singing styles are diverse, as are the often complex tunings of bards' instruments. As with many oral epics around the globe, the relationship of words and music within these African traditions is reported to be very close and mutually sustaining, although the exact nature of the correspondence remains elusive here and elsewhere (a welcome exception to that truism is H. Wakefield Foster's research (2004) on the vocal melodies employed by the South Slavic epic *guslar*, which establishes that melodic shifts act as cues for new developments in the narrative). In some Central African traditions the chief performer is supported by one or more auxiliary instrumentalists and backup vocal singers; he may act out the dramatic content mimetically, and the audience may join in dancing and singing. Overall, the spectrum of possibilities in this region stretches from a nearly exclusive focus on the single performer to a deeply communal event in which "the distance between performer and subject collapses; the performer becomes the hero (or his antagonists); and the audience is given an integral role in the event" (Belcher 1999: 29).

Epic Language

It is a truism that many of our ancient epics resonate with a kind of language that has been labeled "elevated," "austere," "formal," and the like. Here again modern-day oral epics offer the opportunity to understand the origin and function of such stylistic convention. By looking at analogues from the contemporary world we can gain an appreciation of both the structure and the meaning of epic registers (types or subsets of language) in the *Iliad*, *Gilgamesh*, and even such deeply literary works as the *Aeneid* (see Sale 1999).

Research has established salient differences between what we may for the sake of convenience term the "standard" and poetic registers employed in oral traditions (see J. Foley 1995: especially 49–53, 82–92). Whereas an everyday language, that brand of discourse glossed in most desktop dictionaries, follows certain rules of order, flexibility, and implication, epic registers tend to diverge from the standard set of rules (on ancient Greek, medieval English, and South Slavic, see Foley 1990, 1991, 1999b). Often an epic language will mix dialect forms from various geographical regions, as well as preserve archaic words and forms that long ago dropped out of the quotidian register used outside the performance arena. Word order will often be more dependent on the meter and music that partner phraseology than on the usual rules for everyday speech.

The basis for the creation and maintenance of these features may be traced to the oral poet's special lexicon. As the South Slavic singers attest, they think and compose not in terms of our words (typographically or linguistically defined) but rather in terms of "large words" – in the case of the *guslari* no smaller than a metrical verse-part in length and as large as a narrative pattern or even a whole epic (Foley 2002: 11–21). Thus bytes of phraseology are frequently recurrent, as bards deploy a vocabulary of phrases that have been called "formulas." At the level of narrative structure, many oral epic traditions employ recurrent "typical scenes," multiform units that recur in the same and different songs, varying within limits. At the top level, "story-patterns" present structural pathways for the action of entire epics; the dramatis personae and all other details are subject to change, but the flexible framework of the story as a whole governs the bard's composition and the audience's reception (Lord 1960; Foley 1999b). Of course, modern-day epic registers are distinctly unalike one from the next, but, while each shows its individuality, most such registers are alike in the fact of their conventional structure, and thus in their divergence from what linguists might refer to as the "unmarked standard."

Consider a few examples of this epic language from South Slavic oral tradition. At the level of the entire story, hundreds of epics recorded from various parts of Bosnia and Croatia follow the same basic narrative sequence as Homer's *Odyssey* (see Chapter 22, by Slatkin). Interestingly, the morphology of this pattern in South Slavic and everywhere else the so-called Return Song has been thoroughly collected is binary: alongside the "faithful wife" outcome stands the "unfaithful wife" possibility, in what amounts to approximately an equal distribution among well-collected traditions (see Foley 1999b: 135–67; also Reichl 1992: 160–70 on the Turkic *Alpamïs*; Badalkhan 2004 on Balochi oral epic). Just this much information about the structure of the epic language in an analogous tradition suggests a great deal about the anachronistic texture of the *Odyssey*, the obstinate indeterminacy of Penelope, and the climax of the story in a riddle known only to wife and husband (all well-established, indeed defining conventions of the Return Song). Similarly, the South Slavic tradition contains numerous examples of typical scenes, from the arming of heroes to caparisoning of horses, preparing of feasts, testing of subordinates and family members, verbal combats, and beyond. These story-patterns and typical scenes, both of them examples of "larger words" (which the *guslari* emically call *reči* (literally, "words")), are flexible conventions that both vary within limits and convey idiomatic meaning from instance to instance, song to song, and bard to bard. Such is the multiform and echoic nature of the epic register as a dedicated language.

Nor should we leave the analogy of the South Slavic register without examining the simplest, most obvious feature of epic language: its highly patterned, recurrent phraseology. Through the performances of the *guslari* we find dozens of equivalents to Homer's "swift-footed Achilles," "prudent Penelope," "sweet sleep," and "green fear." Like their Homeric equivalents, these South Slavic phrases are metrically defined in extent and internal organization, and in that respect the meter–phraseology symbiosis helps to preserve them over time. Once realized as part of "larger words," the variant dialect forms and anachronisms that can distinguish constituent elements tend to persist because they are parts of integral wholes, shielded from linguistic change by having become "syllables" within the larger units. But an understanding of structure is not the only yield of the analogy. Phrases like *kukavica crna* ("black cuckoo") and *suzanj nevoljnice* ("miserable captive") are far more than metrical accommodations or ready-made fillers. Bards use the "black cuckoo" phrase to indicate that the woman so designated is now or soon will be a widow; it thus has a traditional, sometimes proleptic force idiomatically greater than the sum of its parts. Likewise, a "miserable captive" names by convention not just any captive but quite specifically the imprisoned hero of a Return Song; fluency in the epic language provides characterization far beyond anything available in even the most detailed lexicon of the standard language. Thinking comparatively, then, we will not be surprised to learn that "swift-footed Achilles" and "prudent Penelope" can serve as cues that summon complex characterizations by convention, that "sweet sleep" marks a narrative fork in the road, or that "green fear" has little to do with its literal denotation but carries the traditional sense of "supernatural fear" (numerous additional examples at Foley 1999b: 201–37). Oral epic language is conventional in idiom as well as structure; at every level, both its systematic morphology and its connotative power are simply special cases of the general theorem of human language. As I have suggested elsewhere by formulating a pseudo-proverb (2002: 127–8), "Oral tradition works like language, only more so."

Transmission

Within oral epic traditions stories travel easily from one individual to another, both within local or linguistically defined groups and, perhaps surprisingly, across such perceived barriers. Person-to-person contact is, however, often mythologized, just as the identity of the Greatest Singer is characteristically more legend than verifiable biographical fact. Thus the narrator of the *Mwindo Epic* from the Banyanga, Shé-Kárisi Candi Rureke, tells of learning his tale from an unnamed member of the Babúyá people, while he indicates that his colleague Kanyangara received the story from a certain Bishusha whose identity remains indistinct (Biebuyck and Mateene 1969: 15–18). In the case of Gopala Naika, the bard who performed the *Siri Epic*, the question of transmission proved subjective enough that Lauri Honko rephrased it as a process not of attribution to an individual but of the bard's authorization of his performance by reference to respected resources. Thus the Tulu epic singer invokes not only Mallanna Shetty, a leading ritualist in the region, but also his teacher Soomayya Naika, several female Siri acolytes who sang him various parts of the mythology, and divine intervention. The South Slavic *guslari* characteristically provide unstable accounts of the sources of their epics, in one interview attributing a given tale to a certain relative or colleague and in a second interview claiming to have heard it elsewhere. Honko effectively speaks of many modern oral epic traditions when he observes (1998b: 527) that "the secret of Gopala Naika's learning the Siri epic is that he never acquired it as a whole from anyone. Instead, the sources were multiple and the process of composition and mental editing long." Seeing the ancient epics only as singular, always fossilized artifacts or items may lead us to expect prior transmission processes that, while comfortably familiar in the modern western world of fixity and print, amount to untenable impositions. Single-item transmission from one individual to another may be as much a mythology as the Greatest Singer.

The analogy with modern-day oral epics also illuminates the thorny problems of transmission across languages and of the individual versus the tradition. Regarding the former, we have the incontrovertible evidence of Salih Ugljanin, a *guslar* who sang heroic songs in both South Slavic and Albanian although he was literate in neither tongue (Kolsti 1990; cf. Skendi 1954). What Ugljanin seems to have been able to do was to compose fluently in either of these specialized epic registers – wholly unrelated branches of the Indo-European family tree – in an act not of direct translation but of bardic bilingualism. This model should suggest a great deal about the transmissibility of ancient epic stories from one tradition to another (see Chapter 20, by Burkert; also Rinchindorji 2001 on Mongolian and Turkic epic interchange). Likewise, the reality of a flexible language rather than a fixed item goes a long way toward explaining the joint importance of individual bard and epic tradition without diminishing either side of the equation. Time and again scholars have struggled with the terms improvisation, creativity, tradition, innovation, and the like because they raise the question of whether the composer or the inheritance is the more determinative factor in any given oral or oral-derived work. But such quandaries emerge only if we reduce a long-term, multiform process to a fixed, singular product. What the analogy from living oral epics suggests is that bards operate creatively within a set of compositional rules, just as any speaker of any language deploys a grammar and a lexicon idiolectally. Reports from central Asia (Reichl 1992: 219–61), the Altay (Harvilahti 2003: 95–6), India (Honko 1998b: 506–13), and many other areas reflect the same interdependence of bard and tradition.

One final aspect of transmission is the basic question of what exactly gets transmitted. Internationally, the common practice in oral epic is for bards to perform "part" of what we would consider the "whole" tale. That is, whether the people involved construe their tradition as a series of linked but freestanding stories or as a composite cycle (on which, more below), the usual situation is that described by Biebuyck in reference to the typical practice among the Banyanga (Biebuyck and Mateene 1969: 14):

> the narrator would never recite the entire story in immediate sequence, but would intermittently perform various select passages of it. Mr. Rureke, whose [*Mwindo epic*] is presented here, repeatedly asserted that never before had he performed the whole story within a continuous span of days.

Similarly, as John D. Smith (1977: 144f., 1979: 349f., 1991: 17–18) has demonstrated for the Pabuji epic in rural Rajasthan, the *bhopa* will sing and dance only one section of the epic story at a time, aided by a helper who points to a visual representation of that action in a panel on the tapestry hung behind them. John William Johnson explains that Mandekan-speaking bards customarily perform what we would call excerpts of the *Son-Jara* epic "according to the specific needs of the moment" (2000: 245). Correspondingly, the Kpelle of Liberia attest that the bard can begin and end at any point, and that this non-linearity "underscores the very continuity of the event" (Stone 1988: 6). In these and so many other cases, the bard performs *pars pro toto*, the part implying the whole, without rehearsing the entire linear compass of the implied traditional context. Thus "traditional referentiality," as I have called it elsewhere (1991, 1995; see Bradbury 1998), affects transmission as well as composition, two aspects of a larger process that are after all not neatly separable in oral epic. Both the idiomatic meaning of the epic language and the notional, part-for-the-whole texture of performance make considerable demands on the audience's as well as the singer's fluency. We would do well to remember this analogy when we seek to understand the interrelationships among ancient epics.

"New" Epics

One of the most puzzling questions raised by the analogy of modern-day oral epic concerns the possibility of "new" epics, that is, of whether bards and traditions are capable of generating performed works outside their usual constellations of subjects, events, and characters. The same question comes into focus in the *Odyssey* (Book 1, line 352) when Telemachus responds to his mother's disquiet over the bard Phemios' account of the heroes' returns from Troy by stating that audiences always value the newest (*neôtatê*) song most highly. Can an epic tradition, whose strength is usually perceived as adherence to a stock set of stories via a recurrent tale-telling idiom, also license and yield something unprecedented? Let us consider a few examples; once we give some thought to how they may be explained, we may see that "new" is anything but the antonym of "traditional."

The panoply of central Asian traditions, to take a very broad sample, offers a spectrum of bards from "reproductive" to "improvising." New epic poems were assuredly within the ability of the improvising Kirghiz singer Džüsüp Mamay, for example, since he could fashion epics from stories with which he was not formerly acquainted as well as convert prose accounts into poetic performances of epic (Reichl 1992: 223; also Lang 2001). Within the South Slavic tradition, epic story-patterns and other tale-telling stratagems have been pressed into service to chronicle a long series of modern-era events; these include the "partisan songs" that celebrate the heroic achievements of the resistance movement (often picturing the quite historical General Tito) during World War II and the epic dirge on John F. Kennedy's assassination (*Smrt u Dallasu*, or *Death in Dallas*) (see J. Foley 1995: 103 n. 15). From medieval times we have the case of *Andreas*, a long narrative on the apocryphal story of Andrew among the cannibalistic Mermedonians that was transferred into the Anglo-Saxon epic register, a tale that even features an excursus by the composing poet as he contemplates his own capability of carrying on with his performance (see J. Foley 1995: especially 201–7). From my own fieldwork I can report the case of the Serbian *guslar* Milutin Milojević from the village of Velika Ivanča, who fluently harnessed the epic idiom to describe what he had never before experienced – his photograph being taken (2002: 213–15).

What do these four examples have in common? We can start by recalling what the analogy of modern-day oral epics has suggested about the rule-governed pliability of epic language, and in particular about how "Oral tradition works like language, only more so." Each of the instances cited above puts the lie to the text-based presumption that singers simply learn self-contained works, and that they would therefore struggle to create anything outside the purview of the tradition as a whole (if indeed they ever considered trying to do so). If we understand that oral epics persist because of their pattern-based flexibility, then the assumption of fixed, fossilized wholes – reproduced more or less "accurately" via rote memorization – will be shown to be inapposite. Each of the four examples features a bard who has mastered a tale-telling idiom, who is fluent in the specialized epic language from the level of the entire story-sequence through the "large words" of narrative action and phraseology, and who can therefore adapt the traditional medium to a new message. With this ability to "speak the register," as it were, comes the opportunity to interpret recent or contemporary events and people by invoking an implied frame of reference. Thus the "new" figure joins the pantheon of traditional heroes, and the "new" event is inserted in the identity charter that epic so typically provides a culture.

In a real sense, these and other examples show that not only are "new" epics possible; to keep pace with a traditional but ever-changing cultural perspective, they must prove necessary. In other words, no matter how unprecedented the topic, tales told via the traditional idiom are never wholly unprecedented.

The Role of Literacy and Texts

In the early days of studies in oral tradition, it seemed crucial to draw a hard and fast line between well-defined and mutually exclusive categories of orality and literacy in order to make a place for the (re)discovery of textless and non-literate phenomena. That era saw the establishment of the so-called Great Divide between oral and written, according to which general thesis investigators, working principally from the model of the illiterate South Slavic *guslar*, sought to determine whether ancient and medieval epics – the mute artifacts that have survived to our time – were in fact "oral" or "literate." Without doubt, more heat than light resulted from the often acrimonious exchange between adherents from one camp or another, but with the advent of fieldwork on a wide variety of oral epic traditions the simplistic binary of orality versus literacy has receded into the background and more nuanced theories have arisen (see Finnegan 1977, 1988). We now know that not only a given culture but even a single individual can manage an extensive repertoire of expressive styles and media, so that a person who uses literacy and texts for other social activities may also harness the idiom of oral tradition. The relationships and interactions between oral performances and texts are myriad and fascinating, and currently represent one of the primary challenges to – and opportunities for growth in – the ongoing articulation of this comparative field (for a pluralistic model, see Foley 2002: 29–57).

Since generalization across the rich diversity of case studies would be misleading (a continuing theme of this chapter), I will cite a few samples of interactions between oral epics and texts in order to mark the overall territory with a few signposts. Parbu Bhopo, the literate singer of the *Pabuji Epic* from Rajasthan, describes the genesis of his epic as taking place among the high-caste poets known as Carans; after being written down in a book entitled *Pabuprakasa*, it eventually was learned by the Nayaks and from that point passed on orally by them (Smith 1991: 18–19). Of course, the ideology of ultimate textual origins may seem to contradict the fact of oral provenance, and not only here; witness the Tibetan tradition of "excavating" an actual manuscript book as a talismanic cue for oral performance (Zhambei 2001: 285–6), or the text of Mexican folk-drama that lies ready to hand on the stage during rehearsal but is never consulted (Bauman and Ritch 1994). Complementarily, consider the much-discussed Persian national epic called the *Shâhnâma*, which apparently reached its present canonical form through the work of a poet named Ferdowsi but which certainly owes an enormous debt to prior and contemporary oral traditions (see Chapter 18, by Davidson). As Ulrich Marzolph observes,

> the relationship between written and oral tradition is further complicated by the fact that the oral performers of the *Shâhnâma*-recitations often employed as a written medium small booklets or rolls of paper (*tumâr*). These *tumârs* did not contain a text to be recited verbatim but rather supplied a comprehensive outline to be memorized. (2002: 282)

Both the Rajasthani and the Persian instances illustrate that literate singers may be involved with both oral epics and texts, and the examples multiply as one searches through the tremendous diversity of the world's traditions (cf. Blackburn and Flueckiger 1989: 10–11 on oral and written epics across the traditions of India; of particular interest is the account of how the South Sumatran oral epic, the *guritan* of Radin Suane, made the journey from performance to transcription and translation (Collins 1998: especially 9–16)).

However, two additional cases must suffice for our present purposes, one involving an oral epic that is also a literary construction and the other illustrating how the "two worlds" of oral epic composition and the making of texts can merge in the very same person. The former case involves the intriguing and much-debated phenomenon of the Finnish national epic, the *Kalevala*, stitched together and augmented by its collector-editor, Elias Lönnrot. For some scholars Lönnrot's gathering of parts into a postulated but hypothetical whole (3 percent of which was wholly of his own composition) amounts to falsification of a tradition, or at least interference. To others, however, the collector-editor was in effect "singing on the page," using his earned fluency in the poetic idiom to continue (and perhaps to epitomize) the Karelian oral epic tradition (see Branch 1994; DuBois 1995; Honko 2002b). Our final example concerns Nikola Vujnović, Milman Parry and Albert Lord's field assistant and translator in the 1930s who later came to Cambridge, Massachusetts to transcribe many of the same acoustic recordings of South Slavic epic he had helped to collect. But the other side of Vujnović's expertise – the fact that he was himself a practicing *guslar* – has not yet been fully appreciated. During the process of re-auditing Halil Bajgorić's performance of *The Wedding of Mustajbey's Son Bećirbey*, I discovered that the transcriber-singer Vujnović had in fact modified what I heard on the audio record of Bajgorić's performance. In effect, he re-made the song as he wrote it down. Variant words, inflections, lines, and other features point to something very different from mere verbatim transcription; as a *guslar* himself, the amanuensis-bard had harnessed the epic language idiolectally to create his own page-bound performance (Foley 2004c: 145–91).

Collection, Textualization, and Edition

Trajectories from performance to edition are multiple and uncertain even in the most well-documented and transparent of modern-day oral epic traditions. Thus it can come as no surprise that the fragmentary evidence from the ancient world has led to the formulation of radically divergent theories of how the *Iliad*, *Odyssey*, and several Near Eastern epics might have reached the form in which they have survived to us (see Chapter 10, by Haslam and Chapter 4, by Jensen). Three of these theories have been especially prominent in recent years: oral dictation, crystallization, and coevolution with the Greek alphabet. The first builds on Albert Lord's original hypothesis of an oral-dictated Homeric text (Lord 1953; also Janko 1990, 1992: 37–8), which was based on the Parry–Lord fieldwork experience with the South Slavic *guslari* and the ability of some of these preliterate singers, especially Avdo Medjedović, to use the slower method of composition to achieve longer, more elaborate poems (but see Foley 1990: 50–1 for counterexamples). The second approach envisions a Panhellenic narrowing or focusing of variant local traditions into a single, master version before literal textualization enters the picture; according to this view, crystallization is part of the oral stage of an epic's media-ontogeny (see Nagy 1990c: 52–84, 1996b: 65–112). The third hypothesis posits the development of the Greek alphabet specifically for the writing down of the Homeric poems (see Powell 1991, 2002). Like oral dictation, this approach locates the fixation of some of the ancient epics in their actual graphic fossilization. From a realistic perspective, the few hints we have about the evolution from performances to texts are sufficiently scattered – as well as different enough among themselves across the gamut of ancient Greek and Near Eastern epics (see Chapter 10, by Haslam) – that unqualified advocacy of one or another of these three approaches can in my opinion only amount to positivism. Let us adduce what can be gleaned from an overview of actual, verifiable case studies involving parallel trajectories of modern-day oral epics.

As a volume entitled *Textualization of Oral Epics* (Honko 2000b) reveals in some depth, the conversion of an orally performed epic to a text of some sort is hardly a natural or inevitable process. Contributions treating areas from Turkic central Asia and Siberia to India, Africa, North America, and Oceania resonate with a recurring theme: it is most often an outsider, a member of another culture or another stratum of the same culture, who hatches the idea and fosters the process of recording an oral epic. One need only read the accounts of scholarly "salvage operations" over many decades in Siberia and beyond (Hatto 2000); or of the incremental, academically meticulous progression of collecting and editing the Arabic Bani Hilal epic(s) (Reynolds 2000; also Reynolds 1995 and Connelly 1986); or the building of a superstory in the Cook Islands (Siikala 2000) in order to glimpse this self-evident truth. While curiosity about the written preservation of oral epic has manifested itself in rare cases – the Tulu bard Gopala Naika expressed such an interest in recording the *Siri Epic* (Honko 1998b: 13–14) – in none of those instances, as far as I am aware, did that curiosity lead directly to an intracultural project to produce a text. While singers, and indeed their oral epics, regularly celebrate the craft of writing that the bards themselves may or may not personally use, they do not themselves seek to translate their performances to what is *for this particular purpose* a foreign, unnatural medium. In the terms developed above in the section on epic language, no written vehicle can contain and re-present the full reality of the oral epic register.

Of course, if we lay aside our own ingrained media bias in favor of the printed page, what amounts to an aversion to intersemiotic translation only makes sense. In fact, from this point of view we undervalue the performance-to-text process if we see it as merely the riddle of how oral epics are converted into books. The extremely well-collected South Slavic oral epic tradition offers a helpful analogy here, the more so because we can learn from two distinct fieldwork-to-edition projects within the same larger tradition (see further Foley 2004b). First, consider the so-called Christian poems collected, edited, and published by the nineteenth-century linguist and ethnographer Vuk Stefanović Karadžić, who elicited epic songs from a wide variety of bards both personally and via a country-wide network of intermediaries. He then selected what he believed to be the best poetry, often concentrating on stories surrounding the famous hero Prince Marko or the epochal Battle of Kosovo (1389), and published them in anthologies internally organized by subject, character, or event. His editing was light in comparison with the usual practice of the time, but he did intervene to "correct" inflections and to substitute phrases. Karadžić's volumes of *Srpske narodne pjesme* (*Serbian Folk Songs*) reflected a contemporary generation's awareness of the overall body of epic as traditionally implied in each song, and provided later generations with a textual reflection of that tradition that is still rehearsed in the schools as well as appreciated as a heritage outside the academic setting. We note in passing that although Karadžić spent his childhood experience as part of the "epic culture," his interventions in instigating the collection project, as well as the editing and publishing that followed, were made from the perspective of a professional scholar seeking to translate folk art into an academic medium. In other words, he too was an outsider.

The other major fieldwork and publication enterprise in South Slavic epic studies was the ground-breaking research of Milman Parry and Albert Lord. Here the quarry was Muslim epic, the longer, more elaborate subgenre of oral epic from the former Yugoslavia that more closely matched the Homeric poems, and the investigators were (in every way but one) clearly outsiders. Parry and Lord thus preselected the sample of oral epic to be collected, edited, and published, concentrating chiefly on illiterate bards from Bosnia and encoding actual performances on aluminum records for later transcription and analysis. Part of their vision for the presentation of the South Slavic songs was to report as precisely as possible what the *guslari* actually sang, complete with "infelicities," and to reflect in publication the regional organization they had encountered. Thus their interviewer Nikola Vujnović – a partial exception to the rule of insiders not being directly involved in textualization (but see the description of his bardic transcribing in the previous section) – was engaged to transcribe the acoustically recorded performances. In order to provide readers a sense of the tiered organization typical of South Slavic epic, which has elsewhere been described as pan-traditional, dialectal, and idiolectal (Foley 1990: 178–99, 288–328), Parry and Lord committed to publication by geographical area (the dialectal level of the epic tradition) divided into multiple performances by representative bards (the idiolectal level). The entire *Serbo-Croatian Heroic Songs* series (*SCHS*) is collectively meant to image the pan-traditional level of oral epic across the regions they surveyed (for Russian oral epic, see Bailey and Ivanova 1998).

The analogy of modern-day oral epic thus offers a number of insights on the performance-to-text evolution. First, the impulse to collect, textualize, edit, and publish derives almost exclusively from outsiders who seek to translate the indigenous experience of oral epic tradition into the colonializing medium of fixity and print. Second, the process that we too easily reduce to a simple song-to-book trajectory actually begins with fieldworkers' predispositions and selections, continues with the idiosyncratic conditions of the performances they attend and engender along with the editorial decisions they make, and results in necessarily partial reflections of much larger, variously contextualized, multimedia events. On this basis one would have to posit that the textual fixation of Homer and the Gilgamesh story, for example, must have had as much to do with an external stimulus (historical? social? political?) as with any other incentive, and further that we need to consider not only the availability of a written medium and task-focused craft literacy but also the question of who within contemporary society had the learning, the expertise, and the desire to actually use these unwieldy products of textualization.

Epic within the Ecology of Oral Poetry

Oral epic does not stand alone in any culture. It occupies a major place, but only one place among many, in a composite ecology or ecosystem of living, interactive oral genres. Among such species fieldworkers have regularly tended to privilege the epic, along with such other widespread forms as lyric, panegyric, and, as a rule, all those genres that have won cultural validation as literary forms in the contemporary West. In other words, they have tended to look for and then to record, analyze, and publish what canonically qualifies as poetry for us, in turn applying such derogatory terms as "minor genres" to riddles, charms, proverbs, and the host of other more menial, functional types of oral poetry that for the most part fall below the collector's scholarly radar. This textually induced myopia is unfortunate for at least two reasons. First, the practice effectively blinds us to the forest for the sake of a few privileged trees; concentrating on just a few of the existing species leaves us unaware of the overall environment. Second, in many milieus there is an active interplay between the grand charter of identity that is epic and the smaller genres, with more modest but still significant individual roles, that one often finds both as freestanding forms and as parts embedded in the larger epic matrix. Cross-culturally, the epic is often an "omnibus" genre (see Foley 2004a: 181–2). In order to show how such ecologies work, and further to suggest that oral-derived ancient epics may well have participated in just such verbal ecosystems, I will briefly summon two instances to illustrate the interactive dynamics of oral epic in its macro-environment.

Beginning with the *Iliad*-length *Siri Epic* sung by the Tulu possession priest Gopala Naika, we note that the epic proper is preceded by three substantial invocations (563 lines in all) to gods, lesser deities, chieftains, and epic personages (see Honko 1998a; Foley

1999c). The bard felt these invocations to be crucial enough to the religious context of his narrative that he offered to complete an existing oral-dictated transcription of an earlier epic performance after the fact by singing these preliminaries for the Finnish–Tulu research team (Honko 1998b: 271). In addition to this ritually preparatory subgenre, however, the team also uncovered both a wider variety of five non-epic categories in Tulu verbal art as a whole (long, multi-episode and short, single-episode narrative poems, work songs, ritual songs, and dance songs) and, yet more interestingly, a constellation of generic species that directly participate in the Siri mythology. Along with place-names, Honko identifies "belief legends, aetiological narratives, historical legends, prayers and incantations, proverbs and phrases, omens and taboos, rituals and customs" (1998b: 322) as part of the epic universe or ecology. We understand the *Siri Epic* most faithfully, field reports and analyses show, when we realize that it is caught in and supported by a web of other traditional oral activities. To forcibly remove it from this web of meaning may bring it more comfortably into our text-centered orbit, but by doing so we compromise its ecology and (unavoidably) misread it.

South Slavic epic provides us another model for epic's place within an ecosystem populated by various oral traditional species. In the same region where our fieldwork team discovered and recorded Christian epic through the early 1980s, we also found a larger ecology that included genealogy (emically called *pričanje* or "telling, declaring"), magical charms (*bajanje*), funeral laments (*tužbalice*), women's songs (*ženske pjesme*), folktales (*bajke*), and other genres. (Audio and textual examples of many of these various genres, with English translations, are available at www.oraltradition.org/hrop/eighth_word.asp.) That is, along with, for instance, the epic story of "The Widow Jana" as performed by Aleksandr Jakovljević, the team was able to collect a cross-section of the oral traditions that typified Serbian culture in that place and time: spells that cured skin disease and other ailments, thirteen-generation accounts of lineage histories, dirges that aimed at healing the community after the loss of a loved one, and various other kinds of functions including, of course, instruction and entertainment. Some genres were the exclusive province of women and were composed in octosyllables (charms, laments, women's songs) while others were performed by men in decasyllable format (epic, genealogy); folktales were told by men in prose, with occasional interspersed verse-lines. Within the boundaries of prosodic structure and subject to the uniqueness of the performance arena in which each speech-act takes place, some traditional phraseology apparently does "leak" among genres, though minimally (see Foley 2003). Overall, what this situation exemplifies is an economical division of verbal labor between genders and among individuals, as well as what amounts to the semi-independence of oral epic within the Serbian village ecology. Nonetheless, even the endemic singularity of the supporting but mostly non-cognate species helps to highlight the position of epic in the larger ecological sphere.

Conclusion

Over the course of this chapter we have shown that the category of oral epic must be conceived very broadly lest we fall victim to a textual brand of "Homer-centrism." Cross-culturally, a few defining characteristics seem to recur – the genre's function as a charter for group identity, its omnibus nature, its specialized language – but many other supposedly universal features fall away as the comparative sample increases in size and variety. Nor do bards fit an archetypal mold; they may dance or play instruments as well as sing, they may have assistants, and they may be involved in ritualistic contexts. In order to accomplish their epic exchange, bards and audiences alike enter a performance arena, a virtual space where the epic language or register, something quite distinct from everyday speech, serves as the designated *lingua franca*. Although different traditions prescribe different sorts of arenas, the transactions that take place within them are parallel in their communicative dynamics. On another subject, bards' claims about their sources (a textual idea at any rate) are not to be taken any more literally than their insistence on a certain Greatest Singer as their most celebrated real-life forebear.

Modern-day oral epics also illustrate how patterned and idiomatic their specialized languages are, and how their structure and implications provide a ready frame of reference for every epic performance. "Words" of various sizes – as small as a phrase and as large as an entire narrative – stand *pars pro toto*, the part for the whole, invoking idiomatic meaning with great expressive economy. Additionally, "new" epics, long a point of contention among scholars, were shown to be "new" only in subject; since they are (and must be) composed in the bardic register, they automatically engage a ready context for the fluent audience as well as the singer. Likewise, bilingual bards can transfer oral epics from one language base to another simply by composing in the alternate register. The key to understanding these qualities of oral epic is to resist the model of a fossilized, discrete item in favor of a rule-governed, pliable *language*.

As for the interaction of literacy and oral epic, recent research has shown that not only cultures but even single individuals can manage a range of expressive technologies or media. And while we will never know with certainty precisely how the ancient epics were fixed in writing, modern-day oral epics teach us that the instigation for doing so almost always comes from outside the tradition itself. Textualization begins with the fieldworker's predispositions, reflects the idiosyncratic nature of the performance, and proceeds in accordance with the particular goal(s) of the editor as the performance evolves toward book form. After the once-living performance has been enshrined in textual format, it may be difficult or impossible for any readership to credit the reality that oral epic is always embedded within an overall ecology of oral traditions, one species among many that populate the ecosystem.

In the end the analogy of modern-day oral epics proves most valuable not by pinpointing singular solutions to nagging problems in ancient epic, but by suggesting the natural plurality of parallels. The very diversity of scenarios around the world cautions against one-to-one comparisons and instead urges the consultation of living witnesses across as wide a spectrum as possible. Although we must never confuse analogy with proof, modern oral epics can suggest insights that would otherwise remain hidden behind the veil of conventional assumption. Most importantly, they can alert us to perspectives outside the usual program of textual studies, perspectives that may well be crucial for the interpretation of the *Iliad*, the *Odyssey*, *Gilgamesh*, the *Shâhnâma*, and other ancient works.

FURTHER READING

Comparison between ancient epics, which have of course reached us only as texts, and modern oral epics began in earnest with the textual analyses undertaken by Milman Parry from 1925 forward (repr. in Parry 1971) and with his and Albert Lord's fieldwork in the former Yugoslavia (see especially Lord 1960; Foley 1988). Transcriptions and English translations of the heroic epics that Parry and Lord collected from the South Slavic tradition, mostly in the 1930s, are available in the *SCHS* series.

In later years fieldwork from oral epic traditions around the world has shed light on the structure and meaning of ancient epics by suggesting possible parallels and analogies. For a magisterial summary of most of the major fieldwork projects on oral epic to date, see Honko 1998b: 169–217; on the question of how oral epics become textual artifacts, see Honko 2000b. Other useful sources of information about multiple oral epic traditions include Foley 1998c; Hatto and Hainsworth 1980, 1989; and Oinas 1978; on individual or grouped traditions, see, for example, Chao

2001a (minority traditions of China); Connelly 1986 (Arabic); Hale 1998 (multiple African traditions); Harvilahti 2003 (Altay epic); Honko 1998a (the *Siri Epic* from the Tulu people); Johnson 2003 (the Mande *Son-Jara*); Reichl 1992 and 2000b (Turkic epic from central Asia); and Smith 1991 (the *Pabuji Epic* from Rajasthan).

For specific comparisons and contrasts among ancient Greek, medieval English, and modern South Slavic oral epic, see Foley 1990, 1991, 1995, and especially 1999b; for a brief summary of the theoretical backgrounds and implications of "oral poetry," see Foley 2002. Important discussions of Homer and modern-day traditions of epic are available in Lord 1991, 1995, and Nagy 1996b, 1996c. Readers can actually experience a South Slavic oral epic, *The Wedding of Mustajbey's Son Bećirbey*, as performed by the *guslar* Halil Bajgorić in 1935, by visiting www.oraltradition.org; the streaming audio, transcription, and English translation to be found at that site are meant as an E-companion to Foley 2004c.

PART II

Near Eastern Epic

CHAPTER FOURTEEN

Comparative Observations on the Near Eastern Epic Traditions

Jack M. Sasson

We must not doubt that stories were told and enjoyed long before humans learned how to transpose what the ear hears into what the eye sees. Whether brief or developed, transmitted verbatim or embellished, these tales were likely sung, chanted, intoned, or declaimed, with or without bodily accompaniments. Neither must we doubt that long before what we call writing (characters with visual codes) developed just over 5,000 years ago, people had found many ways to stimulate their memory of words they have heard: through distinctly shaped tokens, via paintings or artifacts, evocative music, or the dance. We may imagine, too, that at the dawn of history the literature that we want to call "epic" had been evolving for millennia. People gathered around fires and made their world more human by telling and hearing stories about worthy deeds, gained or lost. Therefore, when in this chapter we focus on the ancient Near East's manifestation of the epic tradition, we have already lost the thread of its earliest development.

The "Ancient Near East" (henceforth ANE) is a vast and unwieldy setting from which to draw the material for our discussion. The label itself is of relatively recent coinage and has no equivalent in ancient documents. Beyond a unity of time and space and a participation in technological developments, the cultures were regionally distinct, in the languages they spoke, in the religions they professed, in the governments they shaped, in their art, in their architecture and, as we shall see, in their literature. Let us arbitrarily but reasonably limit the time span to the two and half millennia before the Christian era and the area to those in Mesopotamia, Anatolia, Canaan, Israel, and Egypt. The comments will address selected issues about diversity of contexts, process in the development of epic literature, and literary features.

Diversity

Languages

We are told by linguists that each century witnesses regressively the extinction of many more languages than are generated. This is true of the ANE as well, where names of places and of individuals often betray unknown linguistic families. Some of the languages we know from recovery of documents resist attachment to families (Sumerian, Hurrian, Hattic, Elamite). Others represent the earliest written representatives of Indo-European (Hittite, Luwian). Most belonged to branches of Semitic that have not survived the times:

Akkadian, Ugaritic, Phoenician, biblical Hebrew. One, Egyptian, evolved into Coptic, and now barely survives.

With their capacities and idiosyncrasies, these languages play a major role in shaping thought patterns (perhaps also vice versa), and although we want to believe that story lines, themes, and motifs can survive crossing language barriers, the evidence is not encouraging. We debate the very few tales that betray their importation from other cultures. For example, *Elkunirsha and Ashertu* and *Astarte and the Sea*, both containing Canaanite themes and motifs, have been found respectively in Hatti (Anatolia) and Egypt, but not yet in their own homeland. For the Gilgamesh epic, there are Hurrian and Hittite renderings, the latter even containing motifs probably not available either to the Old Babylonian original or the contemporaneous Middle Babylonian version of the epic (Beckman 2003). Yet it remains a fact that before the Hellenistic period literary works that are simply translated (rather than, say, adapted or recast) for foreign audiences are scarce.

This is not to say that fluency in more than one language was abnormal in the ANE. In fact, trade and diplomacy depended on such capacity, and armies brought their own tongues into occupied territories. Bilingualism (even multilingualism) could not have been rare; but the available documents written in more than one language had limited goals. Aside from dictionary compilations destined for scribes, bilingual documents come from multiethnic communities, and they preserve mostly cultic materials, such as prayers, omens, rituals, and mythic etiologies. To claim the prestige of a dominant tradition or to mollify suzerains, such rulers as the Hittite Hattusili I, the Elamite Puzur-Inšušinak, the Etruscan Thefaries Velianas, the Syrians Azatiwada of Karatepe and Hadad-Izri of Sikanu, commissioned official pronouncements in two languages, their own as well as in the prestige one then current. A good number of bilinguals from Mesopotamia, including fawning letters or poems in praise of gods and kings, were written both in Akkadian and Sumerian, the latter a language that had lost native fluency late in the third millennium BCE.

The ANE languages we know most about (Sumerian, Akkadian, Egyptian, Ugaritic, Hittite, Hebrew) come to us with complications. The Bible's Hebrew has been manipulated by generations of scribes; the recording of its consonants occurred much earlier than its vowels, resulting in a composite language that barely approximates how it originally sounded. Despite the homogenizing influence of scribal schooling, the languages of Mesopotamia are rich in dialects (even two that are major: Assyrian and Babylonian). But they also include arrangements (not dialects) that are peculiar to learned compositions: Sumerian breaks into Emesal (etymology disputed, but once thought to be a woman's language), while Akkadian displays a "hymnic-epic" mode that exaggerates poetics. Such manifestations limit successful exportation of narratives, if only because they challenge understanding by the non-initiated.

Languages control the way narratives are shaped. Semitic languages in all their dialects are poor in abstraction, relatively ambiguous syntactically, and fond of circumlocutions. How such idiosyncrasies affected the production of literature is hard to say; but it is observable that Semitic narratives avoided physical descriptions, whether of people or places, rarely made the age of protagonists crucial to a story, and seldom attributed introspection to characters. The same can be said about Egyptian storytelling. Yet languages and their eccentricities are not alone in controlling the forms narratives take. Script and writing media are no less crucial.

Scripts

What is striking about the scripts of the ANE is their deficiency. Not one of the scripts used before the first millennium CE conveys accurately what was heard. Many of them give us consonants (not a complete set of phonemes at that) but not vowels – for example Egyptian, Ugaritic, Hebrew, Aramaic, and Phoenician. (Egyptian scribes compensated through an elaborate scheme of complements and determinatives, eventually even devising, but not successfully applying, a syllabic series of signs.) We know from the history of biblical interpretation that the limitations of such scripts generated interpretive problems in antiquity; the more so for us. Ugaritic narratives, for example, are not for the faint, and determining what they say is more of a scholarly convention than is admitted. Sumerian is still difficult to assess and there are almost as many grammars for it as there are Sumerologists. Akkadian and Hittite adapted the scripts of other languages; but in doing so they lost a capacity to fully deploy it phonologically. The only Aramaic candidate for inclusion in our category, *The Two Princes*, is preserved in Egyptian demotic script, so compounding our problem in establishing its basic meaning. (See below.) The consequence of script complications is twofold: in antiquity, the transfer of narratives *across languages* might have not have fared well if it depended on the written rather than the spoken word; in our own days, translations from some ancient languages may not be as secure as we might like them to be.

Media

Stone, wood, skins, and bones were among the writing materials in the ANE. In all regions, stone (of all varieties) was preferred for monumental inscriptions. Clay was the choice writing medium in Mesopotamia and Khatti, papyrus in Egypt, a combination of both in Canaan. Chalked or waxed wooden boards were often used but few have survived. Sumerians shaped compositions to fit on single tablets and so avoided the elaborate storage and retrieval systems for narratives requiring more than one tablet. Not uncommon, however, were single-tablet stories that shared the same protagonist (for example, five so far for the Sumerian *Gilgamesh*). Such single-tablet tales average 500 lines (for example, the size of four Sumerian narratives about *Enmerkar* and *Lugalbanda*). Unusual are the two 60 cms high clay cylinders with 1,360 "lines" that recounted Gudea's building of a temple in Lagash.

Akkadian compositions, however, could stretch over a number of tablets. The longest "heroic" narrative in Akkadian is a version of the Gilgamesh epic that required twelve tablets. The whole is estimated to be about 3,000 lines (20 percent of which is still missing), so a fraction of the *Iliad* (15,600 lines) or the *Odyssey* (12,000 lines). The Old Babylonian version of *Atrahasis* is shorter: 1,245 lines over three tablets, according to the precise count of Nur-Aya, a scribe of King Ammisaduqa of Babylon (seventeenth century BCE). The longest composition in Ugaritic cuneiform, *Baal and Anat*, stretches over six multi-column tablets that might have contained a total of 3,000 lines; but it is not yet certain that the whole was a single unit. Other narratives (*Keret* and *Aqhat*) are much more modest, three tablets each, with anywhere between 250 and 350 lines per tablet. Narratives in Hittite literature tend to be even briefer; the longest, the *Song of Ullikumi*, covers three tablets.

In Egypt and Israel scribes had a broad selection of writing materials, but they wrote and copied sacred literature on papyrus scrolls. Egyptian papyri can reach 40 meters, but narratives occupied much smaller dimensions. Sporadically Egyptian scribes also used leather, its technology having been perfected late in the third millennium BCE. Israel probably adopted leather rather late; but as scrolls could attain 10 meters and still retain their integrity, the potential for threading a single subject over a full roll (if not also in a series of rolls, such as the Five Books of Moses) gave narratives a density and complexity far beyond their deployment in other media. Israel could, therefore, unfold its story over millennia and across a vast canvas, filling it with themes that repeat, characters that prove paradigmatic, and events that are verisimilar. Because they are embedded within a single story, even its laws, regulations, and moral exhortations become part of a narrative with a single lesson: the only God that ever was is committed to the welfare of a single, albeit unpromising, people.

Literacy

Literacy has many levels. Between the illiterate (no ability to read or write) and the learned (creative reader and writer), there are people who can recognize symbols but not read, read but not write, or do both but within specific genres. Those who could record original, esoteric, and abstract thought were probably rare. (We have notices from Old Babylonian Mari, a relatively literate age, that kings scoured their empires for the few scribes who could work in literary languages.) What is striking, however, is that the level and range of literacy do not seem tied to the complexity of a script. It is very likely, therefore, that illiteracy went deeper (or at least just as deep) in urban medieval Europe, where the alphabet reigned, than in urban Babylon with its cumbersome cuneiform. It might also be noted that antiquity esteemed varieties of literacy that are scarcely acknow-ledged among us, for example the capacity to read omens in the sky or to decipher markings on the innards of animals, both of which required the assimilation of much traditional lore only a fraction of which was written in our sense.

Many scholars have offered estimates of the percentage of literates in given populations; these estimates are all speculative and obey the swings of the scholarly pendulum, although currently the trend is to find it wider than previously allowed. (Overview in Vanstiphout 1995. For the Levant, see Parpola 1997: 320–1; Wilcke 2000; Charpin 2003: 502–3; for Egypt, see Lesko 1990 and Wente 1995.) Within individual communities, the number of literates may have been affected by taste and political institutions. From mid-third mil-lennium Ebla (near Aleppo in Syria) comes a repertoire of texts that betrays heavy dependence on Sumerian literary taste. Whether this condition reflects folk, elite, expatri-ate, or a merely scribal interest is not easy to tell; but it must certainly have required expansion of school facilities. Centuries later, as Mesopotamia became home to multi-national empires, the centers of literary knowledge moved from the scribal schools, associated with private quarters, to those within temples and palaces. There remains continuity in copying the inherited documents; but creativity begins to gravitate toward the production of omens and ritual texts, while heroic narratives (*Etana, Atraḫasis, Adapa*) are folded within incantations (Michalowski 1992: 233–40).

Orality/Aurality

The above observation is of import to a debate on the composition, reception, and transmission of literature deemed heroic or even mythic that has claimed attention ever since Milman Parry and Albert Lord first investigated the relationship of oral tradition to Homeric studies. Parry's basic premise is that our received Greek epics betray evidence that illiterate bards crafted and orally delivered heroic and mythic literature by improvising on absorbed folklore and by using a formulaic yet poetic language. The earliest audiences marveled at what these bards told, but they also delighted in finding a correspondence between their own worldview and that of the past. The premise here is that unlike written literature, which can lie dormant for centuries, orally forged literature cannot ever be antiquarian or historically distant from its presentation.

Over the years, these tenets have been critiqued and denied by classicists, with defenders offering modifications galore on such issues as premeditation, memorization, dictation, presentation, and performance. The same debate has made a universal impact on the study of literature, including that of the ANE. Parry and Lord could offer their hypothesis because all the Homeric manuscripts were appreciably later than the date of their presumed composition (generally eighth century BCE), let alone of their inspiration (sometimes claimed to be Mycenaean). However, except for the biblical material, which parallels the Homeric epic in its complex transmission history and in its lack of chronological anchoring, the literatures from Mesopotamia, Ugarit, Hatti, and Egypt are excavated from well-defined contexts, even if one cannot always pinpoint the process of transmission before they were committed to writing. Many compositions occur in critical recensions or even multiple versions, and they betray active scribal (thus, written) reshaping. It is not surprising, therefore, that the sharpest conviction about the orality/aurality of Hebrew literature originated at Harvard, where Lord was spreading the gospel.

Other ANE specialists have been ambivalent about the matter, most often ignoring the issue as it pertains to the creation of texts, but delivering diverse opinions as it applies to the presentation of compositions. Sumerian compositions tend toward economy of words and location, attachment to doxological formulation, and narrative pivots at regular intervals, hence easing aural absorption (Vanstiphout 1995). Yet a significant portion of this literature was crafted when Sumerian was no longer a living language, so unlikely to be based on living transmission, dispensed by illiterate bards, or appreciated by multilingual audiences. (One notable exception is the imperfectly understood *Lugalbanda and Ninsun* from the Early Dynastic period when Sumerian was still spoken. It may have told the birth of Gilgamesh, traditionally Lugalbanda's son!) Moreover, Sumerian literature, while full of word-pairing and fond of strophic repetition, is not particularly formulaic. It is dense in imagery (for us, much of it far-fetched) that impacted emotionally but was hardly easy on the ears. It was also full of the long repetitions that would have put an insomniac to sleep but easy on the reader who might simply skip them.

Genre

There is also the problem of determining what kind of literature is "epic". The best scribes of antiquity were multilingual and were fond of categorizing and classifying objects known to them, from animals to the zodiac. They certainly could have crafted a theoretical language to discuss literature or developed labels by which to discriminate among compositions. The mystery is that they hardly bothered. (Contrast Black 1998: 25 and Parkinson 2002: 32–6, 108–12.) Each ANE culture attached a rudimentary roster of labels to some of its compositions. Yet for us these rubrics (often given as subscriptions or in colophons) are maddeningly imprecise or ubiquitous, drawing haphazard scholarly allegiance. No ANE composition was assigned a label that is anything like the terminology we use. This lack of classifying categories is matched by the absence of any argued theory of literature, its goals, and its many channels of interpretation.

Our own classifiers, however, have not been as reluctant to fix markers. Long ago, the works of Homer acquired the term "epic" (earlier: Epick, Epos); but only in the recent past began the accumulation of labels (many imported from distinct traditions) for narratives with heroic or historical characters. To begin with, there came to be subdivisions within "epic" (Assyriologists distinguish between "royal" and "historical" epic, featuring the heroics (however imagined) of actual kings and those dealing with all other heroes respectively; see Westenholz 1997: 16–24). But other labels are also used, among them "geste" (unfolding exploits, often assonantic), "legend" (fabulous story with historicizing touches), "saga" (family histories, occasionally heroic, often in multiple episodes), "folktale" (traditional, anonymous, and placeless narrative), and "romance" (not unlike legend, but accentuating intimate goals). Myths, said to rehearse cosmogonic themes involving supernatural characters, were set apart from epics, which were thought to enhance solidarity through paradigmatic human deeds. While myths were mined to explain theology and worldviews, epics delivered on ancient mores and informed on national aspirations. In fact, for no decent reason, when the Romantic Age was at its ripest, mythopoeism (the crafting of myths) was linked to folk speculation, while the production of epics was associated with elite, "nationalistic" drives. Yet, narratologically speaking, ANE myths and epics hardly differ, in form or structure, and even less so in the character-roles of protagonists. Both were regarded as equally historical (or not) and both equally challenge our capacity to disbelief. In some myths gods die and in some epics heroes are translated to heaven. It is not surprising to find Mesopotamian no less than Egyptian scribes as equally dedicated to praising the kingly acts of gods as the supernatural acts of heroes (Beaulieu 1993). Moreover, they shuttled at will motifs, themes, even globs of material between what we label myths and epics.

This unwillingness on the part of the ancients to concretize boundaries has spilled into our own scholarship. We now find "maximalists," for whom an epic must have breadth, a noble vision, and national or ethnic symbolism, and "minimalists," for whom the genre applies whenever two characters are tracked beyond a thousand words. Some specialists label a composition a myth and others an epic (Pongratz-Leisten 2001). Others, including such sophisticated literary analysts as Wasserman (2003) simply treat both as matched vehicles for fantasy. Still, discrimination between the two categories seems to be field specific: Egyptologists hardly recognize the epic in their literature; if at all, comparativists (like me) force it on them. Sumerologists apply the label on a distinct set of compositions (see list below), but not without protest (Michalowski 1992: 243–5; Edzard 1994). Specialists in Akkadian, Ugaritic, and to a lesser extant Hittite, readily assign compositions to one or the other category; but they are also likely to find "epic qualities" in both categories. Thus, Assyriologists do not find it anomalous to speak of the "Creation *Epic*" or the "Erra *Epic*" for compositions that are manifestly mythical. Biblicists who locate (fragments of) myths in the Bible blame Canaanite influence, denying Yahwists a capacity to forge their own fantasies. Likewise, those that find epic elements in scripture are inspired by analogies with Ugaritic narratives, thus prompting the suggestion that the saga of the patriarchs (and matriarchs) developed from a pre-biblical oral epic churned out during the Late Bronze Age. (For a range of opinions, see Conroy 1980; Talmon 1981; and Hendel 1987b.)

Roster of Works

In this *Companion*'s ANE pages, you are likely to find those who construct the epic genre very strictly and so work with a very spare list. Yet in the literature one is apt also to meet with more elastic definitions and so with a broader list of applicable compositions. The following roster is of texts likely to be discussed in the literature (albeit not all in these pages), with at least one reference for each to readily accessible *complete* translations. An asterisk indicates those within the looser definition.

SUMER (Internet translations: www-etcsl.orient.ox.ac.uk/catalogue/catalogue1.htm)
Lugalbanda and Enmerkar (from Vanstiphout 2003):
  Enmerkar and the Lord of Aratta
  Enmerkar and Ensuḫgirana
  Lugalbanda in the mountain cave
  Lugalbanda and Enmerkar (Lugalbanda and the Imdugud-bird)
  Lugalbanda and Ninsun (from Jacobsen 1989)
Gilgamesh (from George 1999: 141–208):
  Gilgamesh and Aga

Gilgamesh and the Bull of Heaven
The Death of Gilgamesh
Gilgamesh, Enkidu, and the Nether World
Gilgamesh and Huwawa (in two versions)

AKKAD (Babylon and Assyria)
Etana (*CS* 1: 453–7)
Gilgamesh epics (all versions, from George 1999: 1–140; 2003)
Sargon narratives (from Westenholz 1997: 33–169):
   Birth of Sargon (*CS* 1: 461)
   Sargon, King of Battle (from Westenholz 1997: 102–39)
   Sargon, the Conqueror (from van der Mieroop 2000).
Naram-Sin narratives (from Westenholz 1996: 173–332):
   Naram-Sin and Erra
   Great Revolt against Naram-Sin (many versions; see also Tinney 1995, Charpin 1997)
   Cuthean legend of Naram-Sin, or Naram-Sin and the enemy horde (many editions)
"Historical" royal epics (select examples, mostly fragmentary; see full listing in Röllig 1978–90):
   Zimri-Lim (not yet fully published)
   Tukulti-Ninurta (from Foster 1993: 211–230)
   Nebuchadnezzar and Marduk (from Foster 1996: 299)
   Adad-shum-uṣur (from Grayson 1975: 56–77)
   Nabopolassar (from Grayson 1975: 78–86).
*Adapa (*CS* 1: 449–50)
*Atraḫasis (Foster 1995: 52–77)
*Nergal and Ereshkigal (2 versions, *CS* 1, 384–90)
**"Epic" of creation (from Foster 1995: 9–51)
*Erra "Epic" (*CS* 1: 404–16)
*Anzu (from Foster 1995: 115–31)
*Ishtar and Ṣaltu ("Agushaya"; from Foster 1993: 81–91)

SYRIA (Ugarit)
Keret (Kirta) (*CS* 1: 333–343)
Aqhat (Aqhatu) (*CS* 1: 343–58)
*Ba'al and Anat (Ba'lu myth) (*CS* 1, 241–74)

ARAM
*The two princes (from Steiner and Nims 1985 = "The revolt of Babylon," Vleming and Wesselius 1985)

EGYPT
Sinuhe (*CS* 1: 77–82; see Parkinson 1997)
Battle of Qadesh (*CS* 2: 32–8; see also pp. 38–40).
*Astarte and the Sea (*CS* 1: 35–6; see Collombert and Coulon 2000)
*The Destruction of Mankind (*CS* 1: 36–7)
*The Two Brothers (*CS* 1: 85–9; see Hollis 1990)
*The Foredoomed Prince (from Lichtheim 1976: 200–3)
*Setne Khamwas tales (from Lichtheim 1984: 125–38 and 142–51)
*Wen-Amun and Tale of Woe (from Lichtheim 1976: 224–30; Caminos 1977)

HATTI (Anatolia)
The Queen of Kanesh and the Tale of Zalpa (*CS* 1: 181–2)
The Siege of Urshu (in Akkadian!; from Beckman 1995b)
*Gurparanzakh (from Güterbock 1938: 84–90; Daddi 2003)
*The Hunter Kessi (from Hoffner 1991: 67–8; Salvini 1988; possibly rehearsed in tablet EA 341 in the Amarna archives www.tau.ac.il/humanities/semitic/ast.html
*The Song of Ullikumi (from Hoffner 1991: 52–61)
*The Song of Silver (from Hoffner 1991: 45–8)

Process

In discussing the process by which ANE literature developed meaning, it is convenient to distinguish among three steps: *inspiration* (generally conceived as recording literature), *transmission* (copying, but possibly also dictating from prototypes), and *presentation*.

Inspiration

ANE authors of narratives (in contrast to many writers of wisdom) did not acquire immortality for their work. As recovered in palaces and temples, several compositions are said to be inspired by inscriptions left behind by their hero, and this was deemed enough of a motivation for followers and emulators to keep their stories alive. (No one in antiquity would credit such material to folk derivation.) The attribution of personal authorship, however, operates on many levels: Sinuhe's adventures are claimed to be autobiographical, *tout court*. Gilgamesh is said (in one version) to have left behind a lapis lazuli tablet that may have inspired the carving of his *narû* (from Sumerian for "inscribed stone"; later also *musarû*, "inscribed name"). In turn, the *narû* ostensibly provoked the bard into telling his story. The same for cursed Naram-Sin (the Cuthean Legend), who is cited as condemning an ancestor for failing to write his own *narû* as a potential guide. In a further twist, the bard quotes Naram-Sin's (fictitious) inscription as inspiring readers to write down their biographies.

Occasionally, however, we are treated to something more. The *Erra* "epic," which circulated in more copies than did *Gilgamesh*, tells of divine violence unleashed and sheathed, with consequences for deities and humans. The story is told from multiple angles, occasionally also from the first person (Erra himself); yet, in an attribution that is nicely woven into the narrative itself, just one person is credited with keeping it alive:

> For innumerable number of years, praise of the great lord Nergal [Erra, a chtonic deity] and of heroic Ishum (will tell) that an angered Erra had planned to level the earth and to eradicate mankind, (but that) his adviser Ishum had cajoled him into leaving a remnant. Kabti-ilī-Marduk, son of Dabibi, is the compiler of his composition (*kâṣir kammišu*). In just one night (God) revealed it to him, so that when he recited it on awaking, he skipped nothing from it, nor did he add a single line to it. Listening to it, Erra was satisfied with it; what his herald Ishum (said/did) pleased him, and, along with him, the gods in assembly are praising it.

Kabti-ilī-Marduk's effort was compensated, for the fifth and final tablet of his composition was often shaped into a talisman because it promised absolution and redemption. This sort of application is not at all uncommon in Mesopotamia, for some of the versions of such works as *Adapa*, *Etana*, and *Atraḫasis* served as prophylactic incantations before they reached us.

Transmission

Yet attributing *Erra* to inspiration is deceptive. Although the Dabibi family is historical, Kabti-ilī-Marduk is likely not. (Elsewhere, he is implausibly associated with Ibbi-Sin, a king of Ur from around 2050.) Attributing a composition to a specific figure was by no means unknown – Enḫeduanna, daughter of Sargon of Agade (2300) is the earliest named "author" on record – but we are dealing here with a phenomenon increasingly favored in the first millennium BCE, in which pseudanonymity is conferred on compositions, even those allegedly dependent on *narús*. Scribes (themselves anonymous) attributed important works to personalities in the past, fictive or legendary. They did not do so because they wished to give due credit; rather, like us, they had powerful attachment to historicity. By matching epics to authors, scribes and scholars attach narrative flesh to annalistic bones and make paradigms out of barely recalled lives. For this reason, despite the intimation that Gilgamesh's own story inspired his epic, a first millennium BCE catalogue of works (Lambert 1962) claimed that it was written "on the instruction of Sin-leqi-unninni, the lamentation specialist." Whatever his historicity (scholars would place him in the Kassite period, so around 1300 BCE), Sin-leqi-unninni himself got retrojected into the distant past until, in a document from the Seleucid period, he was made a scholar in Gilgamesh's court, hence privy to Gilgamesh's own story (Beaulieu 2000): a neat solution all around. Conferring pseudanonymity on inherited lore also tightens membership around the scribal guild. This is obvious in Mesopotamia where the shift from scribal schools to bureaucratized temple and palace services brought with it an increasingly proprietary attitude to texts and the production of texts, and the heroes of history became the keepers of that history. Somewhat similar is what occurred in Jewish lore. Despite ready acceptance of a divinely inspired literature, talmudic rabbis nevertheless assigned writers to individual books of the Bible (Babylonian Talmud *baba bathra* 14a–14b). The gist of all this is that, unlike the scribes of antiquity, we cannot confidently match any of the works listed above (with the possible exception of the Ugaritic material) to a specific individual.

We often find names of scribes in colophons (scribal subscription), but cannot always agree on their role. For example, a colophon to the Ugaritic *Baal and Anat* states: "Ilimalku of Shuban is the *spr* (scribe?; writer?), *lmd* (disciple?) of Attanu, the diviner, Head Priest, Head Shepherd (a military title), *t'y* (of Tha'i?). . . ." The vocabulary in italics is slippery. Does *spr* tell that Ilimalku is its creator, its editor, or its copyist? What does *lmd* say about his connection with Attanu? Is the last his teacher, his (oral) source, or merely his sponsor? Each answer, alas, is plausible. Tantalizing is the fact that the Ugaritic narratives, though recovered from different locations, are so far without duplicates, even when recovered from different "archival" rooms; so they were possibly created just then rather than copied. Yet a number of them seem scripted by the same hand, presumably Ilimalku's. If so, the two observations would encourage us to credit Ilimalku (if not Attanu) with imagining this literature, albeit inspired by native lore.

More interesting is the issue as raised by the many versions of the *Battle of Qadesh*, which report Ramses II's alleged triumph, in his fifth regnal year, over a potentially devastating defeat. The event is known to us from many sources: carvings on the walls of several temples with lively captioned scenes, an overall commentary on what they depict, and a parallel lyrical version of the same. Later (how much is disputed) the lyrical version was rehearsed at least twice on papyrus, the better preserved of which [P. Sallier 3] containing the following colophon, "This text (was written) in Year 9 . . . of/ for . . . Ramesses [II]. It was successfully completed. [This copy is] For the *ka* [spirit] of Amenemone, the Chief Archivist of the royal treasury, and of Amenemwia, the Scribe of the royal. Made by Pentaweret, Scribe for . . ." Research into the period (Spalinger 2002) has shown that much leeway was taken by Pentaweret in modifying the narrative.

From his works on other compositions, it is even possible to credit Pentaweret (perhaps also his sponsors) with a stake in the welfare of pharaohs who were challenged by enemies.

Presentation

How to imagine the presentation of composition has been especially challenging to scholarship, for we can find hints in each composition to suggest that it was read, with eyes or mouth, quietly or aloud, recited or chanted, accompanied or not by musical instruments. Yet the evidence we draw from inspecting the documents themselves is but a fragment of what may have occurred during a presentation. We cannot recover the tonal inflections, the pacing, the gestures, and the body language that added meaning to a particular phrase or pumped emotion into a presentation. Morever, if chanting (*a capella* or not) or miming rather than just declamation was involved, the performer will have had many opportunities to expand effectiveness.

Occasionally, one reads that all narrative poetry was performed. This is said about Sumerian compositions even when there is doubt about the language's living status; see Black 1992, where performance of compositions is taken for granted. It is likewise attributed to some Egyptian texts, even when their archaism or formalism is likely to have impeded their comprehension. Sometimes staging (of some sort) is presumed, as for example regarding the Semitic *Gilgamesh*, because a relatively small cast is assigned a great number of dialogues over a large composition. In some of the Ugaritic texts, we find rubrics instructing a return to a specific segment of the story, suggesting a manipulation of a presentation, perhaps implying declamation if not staging. There are hints that some works were chanted, and may have been written for singing. Enḫeduanna is inspired to praise her goddess in the middle of the night, her words repeated by a singer the following noon (*Exaltation of Inana*, 138–40). King Shulgi of Ur (2100) claims to be "a composer of songs and a composer of words," so, hendiadycally, a "composer of sung words" (Shulgi B: 363–365, see: www-etcsl.orient.ox. ac.uk/cgi-bin/etcslmac.cgi?text=t.2.4. 2.02#).

No less challenging is deciding who sponsored presentations and whom they addressed. What does it mean, we ask, when colophons give the name of scribes and place them at a temple or at the court of a ruler (as is the case of Ilimalku or his mentor)? Were they set there because their creativity was appreciated? Or was it because they dependably produced what their sponsors required? Were they expected to deliver functional works that steered people towards communal identity? Or were they appreciated for crafting mimetic products that stimulated personal emotion? In the case of the Ramses' *Qadesh* poem if, as it has been shown, Penteweret did not always understand the original (or its copy) from which he worked, he may have been fulfilling an obligation or a specific request rather than responding to a creative urge. We might draw a similar conclusion whenever we meet with versions of the same tale. Segments of *Etana, Atraḫasis, Gilgamesh*, and of some Naram-Sin tales can differ appreciably from each other when repeated in different versions, and it is tempting to believe that the differences are there because they are addressing different audiences. (Compare how the Tristan narratives adapted to a changing audience.) We have hints of the process when Old Babylonian scribes dealt with Sumerian stories about Gilgamesh, normally each complete in itself. For example, *Gilgamesh, Enkidu, and the Nether World* normally features a bleak account of life after death. In their version of the story, however, the scribes of Meturan (a town) added an appendix that tied this tale to another, *Gilgamesh and Huwawa*, in which Gilgamesh searches for the meaning of life; see Cavigneaux 1999: 256–7. Was it taste of the time that made them resist the stifling of hope?

While the many versions of the Semitic Gilgamesh epic share characters and central episodes, they differ in how they begin and end, in their development of character, and in allocation of episodes (Tigay 1982 and Abusch 2001a.) In particular, the first-millennium version is endowed with a psychological dimension hardly discernible in the older version, recorded two-thirds of a millennium earlier. For example, the seduction of the feral Enkidu unfolds pedagogically in the older version as the prostitute and shepherds patiently bring him into adulthood. In the later version, however, maturation occurs to Enkidu when his previous world rejects him and he has no choice but to accept human companionship. Moreover, an ironic link between Gilgamesh and his audience is totally new in the later version. It is forged when the bard opens by alerting his audience to Gilgamesh's flaws no less than his virtues, so inviting an audience to be judgmental as he makes choices (Sasson 1992).

Some scholars believe, however, that many of these texts pleased a very specialized audience, whether it was the circle of scribes who took pleasure in their own creations or of the elite at the royal court. In particular, the deeds of kings of Early Dynastic Uruk were deemed paradigmatic by rulers of Ur half a millennium later. There, King Shulgi took credit for guiding bards towards authenticity: "I swear no one has ever put anything mendacious about me in my hymns; no one has embellished my prayers with achievements that I have not matched; I, Shulgi, have never allowed exaggerated praise of power to be put in a song" (Shulgi E, 40–6, at: www-etcsl.orient.ox.ac.uk/cgi-bin/etcslmac.cgi? text=t.2.4.2.05#). We can imagine court poets testing their mettle when singing the heroics of their nearly contemporaneous patrons Pharaoh Ramses II, Tukulti-Ninurta of Assur, or Nebuchadnezzar I of Babylon (see list above). The royal epic genre, in fact, was established centuries earlier, in Egypt since the Middle Kingdom, and in Mesopotamia at least since the eighteenth century BCE, for we have an as yet unpublished example wherein a minor ruler of Mari (Zimri-Lim) is lionized within a few years of usurping the throne. Bards, it seems, found inspiration even when depending on dole.

Literary Issues

We argue circularly whenever we address the nature of an ANE "epic." We justify the existence of the genre and assign narratives to it because we locate in the target examples literary characteristics – motifs, themes, structures, and modes – that were charted in classical and medieval literature long before ANE literature was seriously studied. The application therefore can be ungainly. Nonetheless, it might be useful in this survey to lightly comment on some of these features with minimal illustrations.

Motifs

Motifs are essential components in narratives. Sequences of actions (by animates or not) coagulate into a motif, a coherent tale-unit that achieves individual integrity, often becoming crucial in moving the plot. Scholarly awareness of such an element anteceded the birth of folklore as a discipline; but more precise cataloguing of the repertoire was due to Antti Aarne in 1964 (see Aarne and Thompson 1981) and to Stith Thompson (1955–8). Since then ANE specialists (for example, Gaster 1969; Irvin 1978; Hollis 1990) have isolated motifs within ANE literature for comparison, across and within literature. Here, the issue of artistic resiliency and the capacity to adapt arise, as writers of antiquity (no less than today's) can poach phraseology and motifs that cut across a number of genres. Thus, the intimately autobiographical *Apology of Hattusilis III*, king of Hatti (thirteenth century) is so steeped in the language of the heroic, including the motif of combat through champions, that its historicity is compromised (van den Hout 1995). The same can be said about the "autobiography" of Idrimi, from Late Bronze Age Alalah in Syria (Oppenheim 1969: 557–8). Its storehouse of literary vignettes, such as the triumphing youngest child and the questing hero, has almost convinced me to place it among Canaanite (or Syrian) literature. Egyptian autobiographies are thick in motifs for virtue (care for the poor, obedience to superiors, foolish bravery during combat, etc.) that often coincide with what is assigned to the heroic. While we can cite few motifs that were *knowingly* shuttled across linguistic borders (across Sumerian and Akkadian is an obvious exception), some compositions such as the *Epic of Gilgamesh* are repository for globs of narrative units that were transferred across genres.

One can find images that evoke the heroic in material that is not normally treated as literature. In the letters from Mari (admittedly more loquacious than others), there is a dossier on the marriage of King Zimri-Lim that can easily be placed alongside *Keret* or the biblical Isaac saga. In them we meet anxious *schadchans*, complicated voyages to distant lands, presentation of gifts, veiling the bride, anxious parents, trekking back, and preparing the bridal chamber. We may never know how much of Gilgamesh's story was known to a vassal who allowed that because of his lord's sensitivity and strength, "my gray hair turned black and I found youth. My heart was rejuvenated beyond compare and my reputation spread all over Idamaras" (Kupper 1998: no. 145). And when diplomats report on their experiences, they can be omniscient in their knowledge of events or of motivation and can fill their canvas with characters that are nearly stock, including dense rulers, dark-hearted courtiers, and scheming enemies. Their rhetoric can emulate the best found in heroic tales, with people "shaping their mouth" to speak, repeating acts a set number of times (seven is a good one), and indulging in the bold repartee or the *bon mot* (Sasson 2001).

With such adaptability in mind, it is not surprising that even the briefest composition in our roster has proven to be a storehouse of motifs. What to do with them then becomes an issue. While no researcher today would approve of Peter Jensen's deriving of practically all of human literature from *Gilgamesh* antecedents (1906–29), it remains obvious that accumulating individual motifs for comparison rarely deepens our sense of how compositions mean or evolve. (How useful is it to know that, throughout the globe, heroes of literature are said to survive the murder of their parents, that they confront evil, that they display courage or cleverness, or that they win the hearts of their destined?) Ex-cathedra methodological formulations have sought to sharpen the comparison of motifs, among them that there should be a unity of time and space with the material in which they are embedded or that there should suggest a correspondence of contexts (social, cultural, political, or the like) in their derivation or application. Such considerations often force the affinity among motifs to remain within ANE confines. More interesting, because they allow breaking away from time or place constraints, are those studies (influenced by the work of Vladimir Propp) that establish comparison only when *strings* of motifs bead into in a logical sequence, a series of which form distinct tale genres, depending on the syntax with which they connect. (See below, under "Modes".)

Themes

It is not always possible to uncover the themes of ancient epic, not just because many gaps mar the examples at hand, but because we cannot be certain that our judgment about them corresponds with that of its original hearers. Nonetheless, some prominent themes can be mentioned.

Continuity of a family line is certain to be one of them, albeit displayed in a broad variety. In *Keret*, it is frontal: the story opens on a king's line facing extinction. This is resolved when the king's hard-earned bride produces a potential heir who, alas, proves so wanting that Keret curses him, hence again compromising the future. This exposition of the theme is purposely unsatisfying because it is made subservient to another theme that develops an object lesson for *Keret*: a distressed king makes a vow that he neglects to fulfill when times get better, with the expected consequences. Continuity is also a major theme in another Ugaritic tale, *Aqhat*. King Danel's plea for a son is answered, but dynastic continuity is endangered when the son impudently angers a goddess. Whether in Ugarit such unhappy endings were favored by audiences or parabolically reflected historical events is beyond us to easily recover. The continuity theme gives ample occasion for transmutation: the threat of extinction because of infertility, a wife's sterility (heavily invested in biblical lore), or simply on facing death, might prompt heroes to alter human fate, by storming heaven (*Etana*), by arresting aging (Utnapishtim in *Gilgamesh*), by partaking divine fare (*Adapa*), by regaining youth (potential in *Gilgamesh*), or by reincarnating (Bata in *The Two Brothers*, Ahwere in the *Setne Khamwas* tales). Immortality, resurrection, and metempsychosis are other exploited alternatives.

Linked to this theme is that of *Reputation* or *Name*. In ANE lore, reputation is hardly limited to a single lifetime; rather, it reflects on past and future generations and must not be halted by one person through ignoble deeds or sloth. Preserving or expanding a reputation effectively neutralizes the limitations of human life. In this sense, *Gilgamesh* is less about longing for objects of desire or about halting death than about extending prestige, initially as the reward for courageous deeds through personal efforts, but eventually as the permanence of communal achievement through thoughtful leadership. This heightening of status can be acquired by testing the limits of human endurance, as in the materials concerning the Sumerian Gilgamesh and Lugalbanda, and the Egyptian Sinuhe. It can also be achieved by display of indomitable will when disorder threatens, as in the stories involving Sargon of Agade and Hattushili of Hatti (*Siege of Urshu*). This resolve can be displayed agonistically, as in the Naram-Sin sagas: despite his name ("Beloved of the god Sin") Naram-Sin slights the gods and pays for his hubris by losing political prestige (unhistorically, his kingdom is said to collapse); but he also gains immortality as a fine example of an *Unheilsherrscher*, a misfortune-prone elect of the gods. A variant vein, the *taming of chaos*, comes to be a major theme in what is labeled the "historical" or "royal" epic, involving kings and pharaohs who marshal and deploy their forces against barbarian hordes no less cosmically, symbolically, and triumphantly than do the gods of theogonies.

Structure

How a narrative unfurls a plot over a number of sequences without sacrificing literary cohesion owes much to the discrete use of structural devices. In most examples, the matter is about form, how material is organized to achieve a derived effect. However, in a few cases, such as the Semitic *Gilgamesh* and some of the Naram-Sin material, such devices give coherence to a broad canvas. (This is especially true if a work is orally communicated.) Among the storehouse of available devices to realize narrative integration is the periodic renewal of scenes, such as those around a banquet, or the recurrent repetition of a situation or an idea, such as those that are experienced during travel.

The banquet

In real life, banquets give a special rhythm to affairs of state or of family, creating bonds and solidifying loyalty. (For agreeable essays on *Banquets et fêtes au Proche-Orient ancien*, see the Dossiers d'archéologie 280, February 2003.) In ancient lore, however, banquets serve to focus on a critical juncture of a story (as when gods banquet at the crowning of Marduk in *Enuma Elish*, or when Keret is assured progeny by banqueting deities). Often they offer an ironic setting for violent acts against guests (frequent in the Bible, as in the murder of Amnon, 2 Sam. 13: 28–30, but also elsewhere as in the Hittite *Gurparanzakh*). Banquets also serve to punctuate different moments of an unfolding drama (as when Keret's nobles set a destiny for his throne). They can also be used as brackets for reversal of fortune, as in the Lugalbanda tales when, left to die, the hero uses food to attract divine goodwill. In some narratives (for example, the biblical Esther and the Demotic tales of *Setne Khamwas*), banquets can be displayed virtuosically, punctuating major moments of a tale. Banquets, too, can be veritable storehouse of motifs: crowning (or uncrowning) of kings, clothing (or unclothing) of guests, wining friends, inebriating foes, challenging enemies, empowering kin, and altering the status of individuals (but always as thresholds for major unfolding of plots (Grottanelli 1989)).

The journey

In lore as in monumental inscriptions, the activities of kings that are most often deemed heroic and worthy of emulation are those that recount many voyages of conquest termed unique or never previously attempted. Here is what Sargon boasts (*Birth of Sargon*):

> [For x] years I reigned as king. I ruled and governed the black-headed folk. With copper tools, I traversed rugged mountains. I ascended high mountains and cut through low mountains. Thrice I circled the Sealands; Dilmun surrendered ... Any king that comes after me [and compares to me] should rule for [x years], should rule the black-headed folk, should traverse rugged mountains with copper tools ... (after Westenholz 1997: 42–5).

The most elaborate narratives can be built around a simple notion: someone goes far from home and then comes back. So, we might consider grist for our mill any imaginative narrative (prose, lyrical, or poetic) in which someone (or some folk) undertake distant journeys though which they acquire status, wisdom, or insight. Naturally, we must enter qualifications: the journeys must be demanding physically but possibly also psychologically (though not necessarily spiritually), with all the complications and unexpected challenges that such experiences entail. When told, it should partake something of the grand gesture and of the ceremonial. From this perspective, it is noticeable that a good number of the compositions in our list divide neatly on how pronounced or integrated is the journey as a plot structure. In some myths, the travel of gods furnishes etiologies for festival rituals ("Nanna-Suen's Journey to Nippur") or delivers theological or cosmological explanations ("Nergal and Ereshkigal"). Journeys are intrinsically interesting as they convey (imaginatively or not) information about distant places. They are nicely evoked in tales (Egypt's *Sinuhe* and *The Foredoomed Prince*) and in pseudo-autobiographies (Egypt's *Travel of Wen-Amun* and *Tale of Woe*), where they establish a remarkable carving of foreign space as imaginatively antithetical to native topography (Loprieno 2003); but they can also serve as vehicle for the heroic where they invariably also acquire a psychological dimension.

The journey is an essential component of the Sumerian tales, ostensibly about Uruk and its chief deity, Inanna, but really about its heroic rulers. However, none of our tales plots the journey conventionally. In two about Lugalbanda (*Enmerkar and the Lord of Aratta*, *Enmerkar and Ensuhgirana*) that are likely to belong to a single cycle, crossing space to arrive at a destination (the city of Aratta) is itself the locus of significant developments (see Vanstiphout 2002). In one (*Lugalbanda in the mountain cave*), abandoned by his troops to die Lugalbanda makes discoveries about his capacity to survive. In a dream sequence that itself is another journey, he learns how to deal properly with the god. (Dreams often occur bunched repetitively in narratives, among them *Kessi*, *Gilgamesh*, and frequently in the Hebrew Bible, raising the stakes for a hero who rarely interprets correctly.) In another (*Lugalbanda and Enmerkar*), once again left behind, Lugalbanda accepts the power of speed after showing proper respect to the great Anzu (or Imdugud, a pre-anthropomorphized urge). Later, he uses that gift to personally achieve victory over Aratta. In the two tales about Enmerkar, however, the hero does not journey between his city and Aratta, but his henchmen, messengers and magicians, do.

While not all the Sumerian Gilgamesh tales are plotted around travel, one, *Gilgamesh and Agga*, brings foes to the gate of Uruk while two others rehearse a line that will be featured in the Semitic version. *Gilgamesh and Huwawa* takes Gilgamesh to the "land of the living" where he ends Huwawa's life, for which he earns the god Enlil's hatred. (Although the language is Sumerian, this composition is open-ended, replaying themes and motifs developed in the Semitic *Gilgamesh* from which it may have been adapted, rather than the other way around.) Another tale, *Gilgamesh, Enkidu, and the Nether World*, grafts an epic segment to a mythological introduction. Here Enkidu is the traveler, becoming the eyes and ears of Gilgamesh as he reports on the Nether World. Similarly attached to a mythic initial situation is the story of Etana whose journeys to heaven and back are background to a favored theme, the immortality of the human species (but not of individuals), a theme that is at the core of the Hebrew Eden narrative (Sasson 2000). *Adapa* explores a somewhat similar theme, when its hero crosses boundaries and appears before the gods in heaven.

The journey is heavily invested as a plot structure in other compositions as well. Israel brackets its entire story between voyages from Babylon to the promised land: one brings Abram from Ur of the Chaldeans, the other the exiles from Babylon. Within this huge canvas, many voyages (of Jacob, of Joseph, of David) are replayed, with different import on the narratives in which they are embedded. Most ambitious among these are the trips into and out of Egypt that not only illustrate God's saving grace, but also occasion the delivery of all the laws that Israel will ever need. In Canaanite lore, Keret launches an expedition to retrieve a destined bride and makes a vow along the way that he fails to fulfill, thus initiating reversal of his fortune. Disguised as an autobiography of confession, *Sinuhe* is epic in goal and proportion, centering on exploits of survival and attachment to the homeland. Fearing implication in a crime against pharaoh, Sinuhe escapes Egypt and finds status among Asiatics. Welcomed back by pharaoh, Sinuhe returns home where alone his destiny can unfold. (Such events are realistic enough to be replayed in the life of the composer John Dowland.) Interestingly, the journeys from Egypt and back contribute to the plot by embedding within their unfolding five different explanations – from at least three differing perspectives – for Sinuhe's initial flight, and thus they permit endless speculation on his motivation.

In all its versions, the Semitic *Gilgamesh* is built around voyages, but most sharply so in a series where it exhibits an exceptional accent. In the first half of the epic (tablets I–VI), voyages are either generated by the plot (Enkidu's arrival at Uruk) or heroic (journey to the cedar forest), the last stretching over a number of tablets. They are reversed in the return to Uruk and in the death of Enkidu. From that point, the voyages take on a surrealistic dimension paralleling the distraught mind of the hero. Disheveled and wasting away, Gilgamesh embodies his friend's unpromising beginnings and for almost a third of the epic is in perpetual roaming. At the outset he begs for a dream, but in a cryptic scene whose ambiguity and centrality evoke Jacob's Jabbok struggle, Gilgamesh rises to battle unknown enemies (his own fears?). It is conceivable that the epic's remaining travels, to the end of the earth and beyond, are but one night's hallucinations.

Modes

As it concerns the deeds of heroes, real or imagined, some epics find it convenient to depict their adventures as pages (single or multiple) from their "biographies." As narrated, the events carry the hero beyond specific hurdles. Ramses II, Tukulti-Ninurta, and Hattusili I (in *The siege of Urshu*) are among many who must surmount deceit and villainy, staples in sagas that concern kings. But protagonists must also counteract manifest lack (Sinuhe's distance from home, Lugalbanda's hunger and abandonment) or fulfill a need (most often, a desire for an heir, as in *Keret*, *Aqhat*, *The Queen of Kanesh*, and the *Tale of Zalpa*). Despite their potential for failure (which of course hardly ever materializes), the subjects of such biographic pages replay themes that can be paradigmatic, archetypal, or simply conventional, all meant to multiply potential linkage with their audience.

The biographies themselves can be emblematic, episodic, or melodramatic (Sasson 1984). The first, the emblematic biography, is rarest in that one specific event in the hero's life is exposed for its parabolic potential. It is also the most contested, for such narratives skirt the epic genre and so may cogently be placed among other categories. This is the case of *Adapa*, wherein the hero's personal gain (a successful appeasement of the gods) is his species' loss (mortality assigned to human beings). In ANE literature, however, most commonly we meet with the episodic mode in which a single hero is the subject of a series of self-contained, integral tales. Characters, even plot lines, may resurface in a number of them; but no detail from one is necessary to the denouement of another. Because of its clay tablet medium, episodic narratives are perfect for Mesopotamia, so we have the Sumerian Enmerkar, Lugalbanda, and Gilgamesh tales as well as the Akkadian stories centering on the kings of Agade. But this mode can occur also in Egypt as in the demotic stories regarding Setne Khamwas, a son of Ramses II, who acquired folk status as a seeker of secrets better left to the gods.

In biblical lore, the story of Abraham is a perfect example of the episodic biography. Between Genesis 12 and 24, we have series of tableaus that are barely dependent on a chronological sequence and oblivious to cogent transitions. But each has a specific goal, delivering diverse manifestations of the heroic character: resourceful, cunning, martial, generous, magnanimous, and argumentative, but also indecisive, duped, and henpecked.

More appealing to us is the melodramatic biography. Rather than conveying specific behavior, it explores the inner world of a hero, progressively and deliberately, achieving a portrait that is unique and non-transferable. To this mode belong such exceptional works as the standard *Epic of Gilgamesh* and the biblical stories of Jacob and of David. This portraiture is achieved not through authorial intent but through the sophisticated editing of inherited or adapted tales. Early on, the destiny of the hero is presented (by the bard in *Gilgamesh*, through an oracle for Jacob, and by divine selection for David), setting a clear path toward its fulfillment. There is a tendency to shape into the narrative an emotional fault-line, with the hero undergoing major psychological transformation just as he triumphs against all odds. No sooner does Gilgamesh vanquish Humbaba than his world is jolted by the death of his companion, Enkidu. The epic shifts course at this point, moving from the realistic (battle against a foe, in an earthly setting) to the surrealistic (battle against fear, at the edges of consciousness). The same can be said about Jacob and David who have it all before their children wreck their hopes and aspirations.

Epic: Theirs into Ours

But for the stories of Israel, ANE literature died two millennia ago, largely disappearing from public knowledge, victimized by the suppression of polytheistic creeds and a casualty of scripts no longer decipherable. When this literature returned to public attention, ironically enough it was largely because it was linked it to the Bible. Some of this linkage was well motivated, for example Hermann Gunkel's recovery of the Bible's pre-literate stage though comparison with Near Eastern literature. Others had sinister goals, for example Friedrich Delitzsch's distortion of Assyriology to prove the Bible (in fact, Judaism) "a great deception" (Larsen 1995). However misguided, P. Jensen's drive to center the *Epic of Gilgamesh* within world literature did bring it to wide notice (1906, 1929). At first intrigued mostly by the Epic's flood segment, the public eventually took it to heart, resonating to its humanism, its existentialism, and its manifold transfigurations of desire. (It might not have fared as well had it surfaced a century earlier, when sensibility differed.) Segments of *Gilgamesh* are now featured readings in secondary school and oodles of *Gilgamesh* for kiddies can now be purchased. Aside from countless translations (see Chapter 12, by Armstrong), some more faithful or poetic than others, in dozens of languages, the epic has spawned: novels (Robert Silverberg, *Gilgamesh the King*, 1984), retellings (Stephan Grundy, *Gilgamesh*, 2000; Stephen Mitchell, *Gilgamesh*, 2004), avatars (Joan London, *Gilgamesh, a Novel*, 2001; Eduardo Garriques, *West of Babylon*, 2002), poetry (Charles Olson; see Maier 1983), operas (Per Nørgard, *Gilgamesh, Voyages into the Golden Screen*, 1974; Stephen Dickman, *Gilgamesh, an Operatic Ritual*, 2002), oratorio (Bohuslav Martinů, *Epic of Gilgamesh*, 1955), ballet (Augustyn Bloch, *Gilgamesz*, 1968), pantomime/dance (numerous, including one by Teresa Ludovico, *Gilgamesh*, 2003), and videos, DVDs (Scott Noegel, *Gilgamesh XI: An All Digital Film*, 2000). A Hollywood dressing cannot be too distant in the future.

In itself this contemporary absorption in Gilgameshiana is interesting. The epic that has inspired us was far from the Mesopotamian scribe's most copied composition (omens were) and hardly was the national epic that our great scholars want it to be. Moreover, for a substantial period of time, the epic was a composite that never existed in any single version, so was a vessel for compacted material with resulting contradictions and tensions that now strike us as appealingly contemporary. Nonetheless, *Gilgamesh* remains the sole example in our list of ANE compositions to have reached a discerning audience or to have provoked sustained comparison with classical parallels (Abusch 2001b). The Creation "epic" similarly serves biblical comparison, but not always for the best reasons; *Sinuhe* has inspired a novel that was turned into a movie and the "Birth of Sargon" is dragged into every Exodus commentary.

How will this literature, which scholars have so lovingly resurrected, fare in our cultural future? My sense about its prospects is not encouraging. To begin with, its fragmentary nature (tablets and papyri are full of inopportune breaks) and its grammatical density (Sumerian and Ugaritic are not yet exact sciences) compromise a full appreciation. But we also generate the hurdles against its acceptance. We are trained to focus on authors as vessels for genius and are unnerved by a literature that is anonymous even when assigned composers. We applaud narratives with a taut pace, minimal repetitions, a rich vocabulary, and scintillating dialogue, but often meet with opposite manifestations. We want literature to be a window to the ambitions and the anxieties of the past, and are annoyed when it is anchored in punctual or local context. As a result, beyond academia we analyze this literature's repertoire of plots and characters with detachment, resist understanding its aims or point of view, and feel little urgency to incorporate its examples into the streams of modern culture. It seems to me that for a while longer this literature will remain alien to our larger public.

FURTHER READING

In a reference set (such as this) that focuses on a single subject, you are likely to find multiple reference to the same resources. With apologies for any duplication, I offer the following suggestions. (For fuller version of each entry, see the bibliography.)

For overviews and background, you cannot do better than read the chapters in the multi-volume reference set *Civilizations of the Ancient Near East* (Sasson 1995). It contains many chapters on the history, literature, art, sociology, and economy of the cultures that are of most interest to us. The contributors are all distinguished specialists and write a clear prose that is not compromised by footnotes. In English there are two collections of ANE texts in translations: Pritchard's *Ancient Near Eastern Texts Relating to the Old Testament* (*ANET*, 1969) and Hallo and Younger's *The Context of Scripture* (1997, 2002). But there are also volumes that collect translations by individual cultures, such as Foster 1993 (repr. 1996); Hoffner 1991; Lichtheim 1976, 1984; and Vanstiphout 2003.

Specialized studies on literature (not to say epic literature) are relatively few. Those who believe there is a biblical epic are served by Hendel's *The Epic of the Patriarch* (1987b). For Sumer there is Black's *Reading Sumerian Poetry* (1998). For Mesopotamia, see Westenholz 1997, and Grayson 1975. For Ugarit, see Parker 1997.

Older notions of the epic were often fixated on collecting and comparing motifs that allegedly traveled from one culture to another; good examples are Gaster 1969 and Irvin 1978. Unfortunately, we mostly have collections of articles on newer perspectives regarding the epic, not all their contents of equal merit: see Parker 1989; Loprieno 1996; and two collections by Vogelzang and Vanstiphout (1992 and 1996). Worth exploring is Spalinger 2002.

CHAPTER FIFTEEN

Mesopotamian Epic

Scott B. Noegel

It is difficult to find a consistent definition of epic in the scholarly works on Mesopotamian literature (see Chapter 1, by Martin). Some scholars define Mesopotamian epics rather broadly (Hecker 1974), often including texts that others might label "legends" or "myths" (Kirk 1970; Hallo and Younger 1997). Others define epic less broadly, but include the boastful first-person royal narratives known as *narû*-inscriptions or "pseudo-autobiographies" (Westenholz 1983, 1997). Still others prefer even narrower definitions based on methodological considerations derived from anthropology (Jason 1969) or the study of world folklore (Alster 1974, 1976, 1995; Berlin 1983), themselves fields with differing, indeed changing, definitions of the term (Bowra 1952, cf. Lord 1960).

Reasons for this inconsistency are not hard to find. Mesopotamian languages, after all, do not possess any words that we might readily translate as "epic." Though the Mesopotamian bards produced many diverse literary texts, they typically labeled them according to the names of musical instruments to which their recitations were set (Michalowski 1995), or sometimes titled them according to the first line of the composition (Bottéro 1995).

Mesopotamian poems also are not composed in meters, as one finds in later Greek epics, nor do they contain rhymes, but depend instead upon other rhythmic patterns, especially syntactic parallelism. They tend to make wide stylistic use of repetition and variation, stereotyped word pairs and idioms, formulaic epithets, chiasm, elevated diction, similes, metaphors, paronomasia, polysemy, and subtle developments in plot. Their vocabulary is often highly erudite, deriving from a long tradition of compiling complex lexical lists.

The length of poems also does not prove useful for classifying Mesopotamian epics since, unlike Greek epics, Mesopotamian poems, especially the earlier ones, are typically short. The Sumerian poems that are often called epics, for example, range from about one hundred to a little more than six hundred lines in length, a fact that has led some scholars to question the validity of the term when discussing them (Moran 1995).

In this essay, I adopt a definition for epic based upon content, one that I believe will facilitate comparisons with other essays in this volume. Specifically I treat as epic all poetic narratives that praise the accomplishments of a heroic figure of history or tradition. I do not include poetic narratives about gods, which I leave to the category of "myth" nor do I include the so-called pseudo-autobiographical texts, building inscriptions, or hymns, though reference to them has been necessary at times.

I have divided the Mesopotamian epics into two sections on the basis of the language in which the texts are composed, Sumerian or Akkadian, and have grouped related epics together under single rubrics (see Chapter 14, by Sasson). For each of the epics I have provided a brief description of its plot, its relationship to other Mesopotamian epics, and, if known, the text's historical context. The two sections on Sumerian and Akkadian epics are followed by two brief discussions. The first comments on the changes that take place in Akkadian epics of later periods. The second looks at the various ways that Mesopotamian epics have been interpreted.

Sumerian Epics

The world's earliest epic literature appears in Mesopotamia in the form of several cunei-form texts composed in the Sumerian language. Most scholars date them to the Third Dynasty of Ur (*ca.* 2112–2004 BCE) even though most of the texts detail the heroic exploits of much earlier kings and come from archives that date to a slightly later time (i.e., the Old Babylonian period, *ca.* 2003–1595 BCE). These dates notwithstanding, we know that the genesis for Mesopotamian epic traditions is far more ancient because of several textual fragments from Abu Salabikh and Fara that relate to these epic traditions and date to the twenty-sixth century BCE (Biggs 1974; Bing 1977).

The kings of the Ur III period, however, appear to have been the first to promote epic traditions widely. They probably did so because the glorification of previous heroes (each of whom was a "Lugal," a Sumerian term for a military leader and king or "En," a king with close ties to the cult) created a precedent for the glorification and support of their current regimes. They also legitimated their kingship at Ur by claiming ties to Uruk, a city that Sumerian tradition considered the seat of the first kings (Jacobsen 1939; Klein 1976). Moreover, two of the Ur III kings, Ur-Nammu (*ca.* 2112–2095 BCE) and his son Shulgi (*ca.* 2094–2047 BCE), were deified, and both claimed the epic hero Lugalbanda as their father and the goddess Ninsun as their mother, thus making the famed Gilgamesh their brother. Such claims provide additional evidence that the epics served ideological and propagandistic purposes (Michalowski 1988).

Early Sumerian epics, therefore, must be read on at least two levels: one that praises the heroic accomplishments of the ancient kings they name, and one that uses this hero paradigmatically in a "supra-historical role" to echo or justify the exploits of the reigning monarch (Alster 1974; Berlin 1983, but cf. Cooper 2001). A lack of sufficient information makes it impossible to ascertain to what degree any of the epics were adapted to meet the ideological needs of the kings under whom they were produced.

Enmerkar traditions

Two of the Sumerian epics probably date specifically to the reign of king Shulgi, even though they glorify an earlier deified king named Enmerkar (*ca.* 2800 BCE) from Uruk and his war against the king of Aratta, a city near Hamadan in modern Iran (Majidzadeh 1976). It remains a matter of dispute whether the two Enmerkar epics should be read together as one poem or as two related, but separate poems (Wilcke 1969) analogous to Homer's *Iliad* and *Odyssey* (Alster 1990, cf. Vanstiphout 2002, 2003).

The first of these epics, "Enmerkar and the Lord of Aratta," tells of how Enmerkar outwitted the king of Aratta in an effort to obtain tribute from him. After wooing to his side the king's spouse, the goddess Inanna, Enmerkar is advised by the goddess to send a courier to Aratta to instruct its king to send luxury goods and ore to refurbish the temples of Uruk, Kullab, and Eridu. If he does not obey, Enmerkar warns, Aratta will be destroyed. The king of Aratta, realizing that Inanna is no longer protecting him from military threat, responds by saying that he will obey, but only if Enmerkar accepts a challenge of wits. Enmerkar is to send the king grain, not in tightly woven sacks, but in open nets. Enmerkar outwits the king in this seemingly impossible task by sending grain that has germinated. It thus holds together and does not slip through the mesh. The king then requests that Enmerkar send a scepter made of no known wood or ore. Enmerkar grows an exotic plant that yields him the needed scepter. Finally, the king asks him to send a champion to duel with an athlete from Aratta. The king stipulates that the champion must wear clothes decorated in a color unknown to humankind. Enmerkar's champion is sent dressed in undyed cloth. Having outwitted the king at every turn, Enmerkar then threatens to annihilate Aratta by sending a written missive to the king. Since we are told that Enmerkar invented writing just for this purpose, we must again see this act as a demonstration of his superior intelligence. Having lost the battle of wits, the king then sends Enmerkar the tribute he desired.

The epic contains three features that remind us of the later rule of king Shulgi. The first is that of Aratta. Like Enmerkar, Shulgi's long reign was marked by a huge territorial expansion, much of it into ancient Iran. The second is the goddess Inanna's special relationship with Enmerkar. During the Ur III period the kings represented the god Dumuzi when performing the sacred marriage rite, and thus were regarded the husbands of Inanna. The third feature is the invention of writing, a detail that echoes Shulgi's later and unique claim of mastery of the written arts.

The second tale belonging to this cycle of traditions, "Enmerkar and Ensukhesh-danna," opens with a demand by Ensukheshdanna, the king of Aratta, that Enmerkar acknowledge him as the goddess Inanna's preferred ruler of the land. When Enmerkar disobeys, Ensukheshdanna seeks the advice of his counselors. One of the counselors proposes that a magician from Aratta perform a spell that causes the milk-giving animals of Eresh to withhold their produce. When this is successful, two shepherd twins step in and request the aid of Utu, the sun-god. Utu responds, and it is decided that a fishing contest will be held to settle the issue of which king is superior, Enmerkar or Ensukheshdanna. Pitted in the contest are the magician, representing Aratta, and an old woman, representing Uruk. Though the magician is able to catch five creatures from the river, the woman catches larger ones, each of which devours the magician's smaller catch. Enmerkar is recognized as superior, and therefore the favorite of Inanna, and the magician is drowned in the river.

Lugalbanda traditions

Two Sumerian epic poems involve a hero named Lugalbanda, the successor of Enmerkar. Though both Ur-Nammu and Shulgi claimed Lugalbanda as their father, the historical evidence for Lugalbanda, and it is meager, suggests that he reigned some time around 2800–2700 BCE. Like the Enmerkar tales, the plots of these two epics are so inter-connected that many read one against the other as two parts of a longer epic tradition, even though they are the work of two different authors.

In the first, "Lugalbanda in Hurrumkura," Aratta once again takes center stage, this time in a war waged by Enmerkar. Eight brothers are selected to lead the war, the youngest of them being the future king Lugalbanda. When Lugalbanda falls ill while en route to Aratta, his brothers leave him in a cave along with some food; the story goes into great length to describe the food. When he recovers, he receives divine favor after showing his great piety through prayer and food offerings (here again the food is described in detail). He then leaves the cave and makes his way back to his brothers and the war, overcoming a number of other obstacles along the way.

The second related epic, "Lugalbanda and Enmerkar" (also referred to as "Enmerkar and the Imdugud [or Thunder] Bird"), was perhaps used as political propaganda to flatter envoys from ancient Iran when visiting the court of Ur (Jacobsen 1987). It tells of Lugalbanda's encounter with the mythical Anzu bird, a giant raptor with special powers whose very flight frightens wild oxen and mountain goats. Upon finding the bird's nest while the bird is hunting, Lugalbanda feeds its young and straightens its nest. When the bird returns he is so taken with Lugalbanda's deeds and smooth talking that he offers him a number of special gifts, including wealth and strength in battle, all of which Lugalbanda refuses, with one exception – the ability to run quickly. The bird grants him this gift but tells him that he must tell no one how he received it. Lugalbanda then speeds to Aratta, where his brothers have been waging an unsuccessful year of siege. When king Enmerkar requests that someone embark alone on a dangerous journey to Uruk and obtain advice on how to proceed from the goddess Inanna, Lugalbanda steps up to the challenge. He races off and, in one day, arrives at Uruk where Inanna reveals to him how to defeat Aratta. Through a ritual act of what appears to be sympathetic magic, she advises Enmerkar and his troops to catch and eat a certain fish associated with Aratta. They eventually do so and Aratta is defeated. Its precious stones and raw materials are transported back to Uruk.

Epic of Shulgi

A more straightforward epic in honor of King Shulgi appears in the form of another poem sometimes classified separately as a "hymn" because of the hymns it contains. It is roughly six hundred lines long and referred to by scholars as "Shulgi the Avenger" (Westenholz 1983). In this text, which opens with a hymn in honor of King Shulgi and an account of Shulgi's miraculous birth and ascension to the throne, the king decides to avenge the death of his father, Ur-Nammu, by annihilating the Gutians who had killed him while waging a raid against Sumer. Before launching his campaign, Shulgi receives a dream from the god of dreams, Zaqar, in which the gods of Sumer promise to aid him in a battle. After the successful battle, Shulgi travels to Sumer's major sanctuaries, sharing with them some of the items obtained from the war. There then follows a long hymn placed in the mouth of the goddess Inanna praising Shulgi as a lover. The epic then closes with another hymn, again in praise of Shulgi. Though often not classified as epic because it praises a contemporary ruler, "Shulgi the Avenger" underscores how blurry the boundaries of ancient literary genres can be, and anticipates an important direction that Mesopotamian epics will take at a later date (see below).

Gilgamesh epic traditions

Gilgamesh (originally Bilgamesh), the famed king of Uruk and subject of a much later and longer series of epics written in the Akkadian language, appears first in a number of Sumerian epics. Though we cannot place the Sumerian epics in a certain chronological order, their transmission, if not also their compositions, probably also date to the reigns of Ur-Nammu and Shulgi since it is they who made the widest use of Gilgamesh in their royal ideologies (Falkenstein 1951; Klein 1976). Recall that both Ur-Nammu and Shulgi claimed Gilgamesh as their brother. Such a claim, however, does not fit well with what we know about Gilgamesh as a historical figure, since Gilgamesh appears to have been king of Uruk around 2700 BCE, roughly six hundred years before the Ur III kings. Moreover, about one hundred years later his name appears in a cuneiform list of gods. Thus, even though Ur-Nammu and Shulgi certainly helped to popularize the heroic stories of Gilgamesh, and possibly may be credited with composing some or all of these epics, his fame certainly preceded them by several centuries.

Ironically, his fame also surpassed and long outlived them, and indeed all of Sumerian civilization, since epics about Gilgamesh continued to be written, copied, and even translated into other languages until the second century BCE (Tigay 1982). The enormous popularity and longevity of the Gilgamesh tradition are probably related to its tragic vision (Jacobsen 1990), its themes of mortality and the overcoming of the fear of death which all of the Gilgamesh traditions have in common – themes that hold a universal and timeless significance (Mills 2002).

The first of the Gilgamesh Sumerian epics, "Gilgamesh and Agga," relates the story of a siege upon Uruk by Agga the king of Kish that Gilgamesh brought about when refusing to acknowledge Agga's lordship over Uruk. Though the elders of Uruk advise Gilgamesh not to rebel against Agga, the younger men of the city support him, and so Gilgamesh asserts his political independence from Kish. This incites Agga's ire, and he and his army quickly come downstream in boats and lay siege to Uruk. After one of Gilgamesh's contingents fails to break up the siege, Gilgamesh sends his servant Enkidu to the front lines. Enkidu is successful and drives Agga's soldiers back to their boats. It is there that Enkidu captures Agga. Gilgamesh has Agga released, however, as an act of political kindness, and in repayment for a kind act Agga once did.

In "Gilgamesh and the land of the living" (also known as "Gilgamesh and Huwawa"), the king sets out to establish his name for all eternity by searching out and destroying Huwawa (known later as Humbamba), a monstrous semi-divine guardian of the cedar forests. With the help of seven constellations shown to Gilgamesh by the sun-god Utu, he and his army navigate their way to the cedar forest, crossing seven mountain ranges along the way. When he arrives at the forest, his men begin logging its lofty cedars while he naps. The logging disturbs Huwawa, who comes to the camp hurling his frightening auras upon the men. This wakes Enkidu, who in turn wakes Gilgamesh, who quickly attempts to flatter Huwawa. After disarming the monster, Gilgamesh eventually enters Huwawa's home, and through a ruse suggested to him by the god Enki, tricks Huwawa out of his auras of power by persuading him to exchange them for a marital alliance with his sisters, and for a number of luxury items. Once he is stripped of his powerful auras, Gilgamesh takes him captive. When Huwawa calls to the god Utu for help, Gilgamesh shows clemency and releases him. This does not sit well with Enkidu, however, who in a moment of anger and fear cuts off Huwawa's head. The two then bring the head in a leather sack back to the god Enlil, thinking that it will please him. Enlil is enraged, however, and promptly removes the auras of power from Gilgamesh and bestows them upon a number of places and things (e.g., field, river, lion, woods, etc.). The remaining auras he keeps for himself.

The Sumerian epic "Gilgamesh, Enkidu, and the Nether World," tells the story of the goddess Inanna's request that someone craft her a bed from a *huluppu* tree. Apparently, she has planted the tree in the hope of some day making the bed, but it has since become home to a serpent, thunderbird, and female demon. She calls upon Gilgamesh to help her, which he does by killing the creatures and felling the tree. With some of the extra wood he makes two playthings, a *pukku* and *mekku* (both of which defy precise interpretation). One day, while he is playing with his friends, the two items accidentally fall into the Underworld through a hole in the ground. When his friend Enkidu offers to retrieve them, Gilgamesh warns him not to associate with the dead. Enkidu fails in this endeavor, and hence becomes trapped in the Underworld forever. The gods then help Gilgamesh to raise Enkidu's ghost, who then describes for him the bleak Underworld. He tells him, for example, that those who have died in fire do not enter the Underworld, and thus cannot receive offerings, and that Amorite tribes harass the shades of the people of Sumer and Akkad. He also instructs Gilgamesh to make statues of his ancestors, and remarks upon the importance of providing grave offerings for one's deceased parents, since those who die childless never receive offerings. This news, in turn, informs Gilgamesh how to prepare for his own death, and thus serves to remind him of his own mortality. If this text was composed, as some have suggested (George 1999), after the Ur III Dynasty fell to Amorite invaders, Enkidu's message would have been an especially powerful means of registering resentment against the new regime and of underscoring the importance of connecting to one's ancestors through proper ritual.

There also are a number of fragments that appear to belong to other epic traditions involving Gilgamesh. The fragments of the texts "The death of Gilgamesh" and "The dream of Gilgamesh" are believed to belong to a single epic and concern the death and burial of the famed king of Uruk. The combined tale opens with a lament for Gilgamesh who is lying on his deathbed. While awaiting death, he receives a dream in which he sees the divine assembly debating whether Gilgamesh will become immortal or descend into the Underworld (he is after all semi-divine, the son of a goddess). They decide in the end that he should die like a mortal, but that for his heroic achievements he will become judge over the shades in the Underworld. They also decree that his death will be memorialized in an annual festival of ghosts in which torches are lit and wrestling matches occur. After a break in the text, we next find Gilgamesh diverting the Euphrates river from its natural course in order to build his tomb at a divinely selected location on the riverbed. A macabre passage then follows which describes how his wives, musician, steward, servants, barber, and others of his retinue were laid to rest in the tomb to accompany their king to the Underworld. When Gilgamesh is placed in the tomb, the river is again diverted so as to conceal its location forever, and the people of Uruk mourn. The text then concludes by underscoring the importance of making statues in honor of the dead and of pronouncing their names, both of which allow the dead to live on in the memory of others.

The third epic exists only in poorly preserved fragments and its meaning is unclear. Typically entitled "Gilgamesh and the Bull of Heaven" it is apparently a precursor to the sixth tablet of the later Akkadian Gilgamesh epic (see below). In it, and in a passage that reminds the reader of the sacred marriage rite, Inanna makes a series of sexual advances toward Gilgamesh, inviting him to become her husband. When he refuses she convinces the sky god An to unleash the colossal Bull of Heaven against Gilgamesh. With Enkidu's help, however, he kills the bull and distributes its meat to Uruk's poor.

Epic of Sargon

A final example of the Sumerian epic tradition that dates to the Old Babylonian period concerns the first king of the Akkadian dynasty, Sargon "the Great" (*ca.* 2334–2279 BCE). According to this epic, Sargon has a dream while serving in the court of Ur-Zababa at Kish. In his dream he sees Ur-Zababa drown in a river of blood, an act that in essence ensures that Sargon would become king. Upon hearing about the dream Ur-Zababa secretly prepares to have Sargon burned alive in a furnace. When this is unsuccessful Ur-Zababa places a secret missive in a clay envelope and sends it by the hand of Sargon himself to Lugalzagesi, king of Uruk. The message instructs the king to kill Sargon. Sargon, however, is able to read the cuneiform document and thus escapes his intended fate. Some have seen the episode involving the letter as a subtle allusion to the invention of cuneiform referenced in the Sumerian epic "Enmerkar and the Lord of Aratta" (Alster 1995). The end of the story is unfortunately missing, but most scholars assume it related the ascension of Sargon to the throne. The epic shares features with a number of other ancient Near Eastern stories including the biblical stories of Joseph (Gen. 39–41) and of Uriah (2 Sam. 11: 14–15) (Cooper and Heimpel 1983; Alster 1987). The latter account tells how King David sent Uriah to his death by his own hand, a motif that appears also in the *Iliad*'s account of Bellerophontes and Shakespeare's *Hamlet*.

Akkadian Epics

After the Ur III period the Akkadian language gradually replaced Sumerian as the lingua franca of Mesopotamia, and consequently epic poems began to appear in Babylonian and Assyrian (both dialects of Akkadian).

Gilgamesh traditions

Of the more famous Akkadian epic traditions are those concerning the hero Gilgamesh, the earliest of which dates to the Old Babylonian period (*ca.* 2003–1595 BCE). Though they are fragmentary, we know that the Old Babylonian version of *Gilgamesh* contained more than one thousand lines of poetry. Its collation of diverse earlier textual traditions is fluid and complex, and as a unified epic, it constitutes a remarkably original composition (Kramer 1946; Komoróczy 1975; Tigay 1982).

The Old Babylonian version of Gilgamesh opens by characterizing Gilgamesh as an oppressive king, placing onerous demands on the people of Uruk, though just what these demands were remains a matter of debate (Tigay 1982; Klein 2002). Following a well-known ancient Near Eastern literary motif, his oppressed subjects call to their gods for help. The gods respond by creating the figure Enkidu, who is intended as an equal match for Gilgamesh. Enkidu, we are told, is a hairy savage, more beast than human, walking on all fours and eating with the animals of the steppe. After he has caused problems for trappers and hunters, a prostitute is sent to "civilize" him. After seven nights of love-making, Enkidu finds himself bathing, dressing in human clothes, drinking beer, and even singing; he is thus now completely humanized. He enters Uruk and acknowledges Gilgamesh as king. After they become close friends, and perhaps lovers (Cooper 2002), in an effort to make his name immortal, Gilgamesh launches an expedition with Enkidu to the cedar forests to kill its primordial guardian Huwawa. Their campaign is successful, but in punishment for their slaying of the monster, the gods cause Enkidu's death, which forces Gilgamesh to confront his own mortality. The latter two episodes thus depart significantly from the earlier Sumerian tale "Gilgamesh and the land of the living."

Gilgamesh's desire for immortality compels him to journey beyond the periphery of the known world to find Utnapishtim (Sumerian Ziasudra), the Mesopotamian counterpart to the biblical Noah (Heidel 1946), the only mortal known to have achieved immortality. At this point, the story becomes fragmentary, and we are at a loss to know how the epic ends (though some scholars reconstruct it on the basis of a still later version of the epic). Nevertheless, it is clear that Utnapishtim issues Gilgamesh a test; he must stay awake for seven days. Gilgamesh fails the test and after sleeping for seven days again is reminded of his own mortality.

Evidence for the ancient appeal of the Gilgamesh story (in broad outline more than details) appears in the fourteenth and thirteenth centuries BCE throughout the Levant where fragments of the epic have been found composed not only in Babylonian, but in the Hittite, Hurrian, and Elamite languages (see Chapter 17, by Beckman; also Wilhelm 1988; Diakonoff and Jankowska 1990). It is not until the seventh century BCE, however, that we find our most complete copies of the Gilgamesh epic at Nineveh in the libraries of King Assurbanipal (*ca.* 669–627 BCE). Owing to the general uniformity of these copies, which probably reflects the epic's gradual "canonization" under the auspices of a scholar named Sin-leqi-unninni, scholars have dubbed this exemplar the Standard Version (Tigay 1982). It consists of more than three thousand lines composed on twelve tablets, though about a thousand of these lines are lost or fragmentary (tablet XII is often understood as a later appendage, but see Vulpe 1994).

The Standard Version opens by informing us that Gilgamesh committed all of his experiences to writing and placed them in a chest on a tablet made of lapis lazuli called a *narú*. The author further encourages readers to open this chest and read the *narú* for themselves. Typically the word *narú* signifies a genre of Mesopotamian texts inscribed on stelae that are often called pseudo-autobiographies (Gurney 1955; Longman 1990; Noegel 1993) because of their heavily didactic and fictitious first-person accounts of contemporary kings. This has encouraged some scholars to include *narú* texts in discussions of Mesopotamian epic (George 1999; Westenholz 1983, 1997). Others have seen the reference in the Gilgamesh epic as the author's clue on how to interpret the text, namely to read it didactically and see the life of Gilgamesh as providing lessons on how to live life wisely (Foster 1987; Moran 1991, 1995, cf. Jacobsen 1990). The author's invitation to read the *narú* also demonstrates the self-referential nature of many Mesopotamian texts; the very story that Gilgamesh recorded is, in fact, the tablet that the reader is holding (Foster 1991).

The Standard Version of the Gilgamesh epic also differs considerably from the earlier traditions in a number of ways. First, it characterizes the hero differently: Gilgamesh is now far more human than divine, though he is now gigantic in stature, and his achievements, once based on his personal strength and aura, are attributed to his knowledge and wisdom. The Standard Version also assigns a greater role to the sun-god Shamash in instigating the slaying of the forest guardian (now Humbamba).

In addition, this version adds a new episode in which the goddess Ishtar (Sumerian Inanna) makes a series of sexual advances toward Gilgamesh, an addition related in part to the earlier Sumerian epic "Gilgamesh and the Bull of Heaven." Gilgamesh, unimpressed by her charms, insults her with remarks that characterize her wedding invitation as an invitation to death (Abusch 1986). Ishtar responds by having her father, the sky god Anu (Sumerian An), send the Bull of Heaven to attack him. In turn, Gilgamesh and Enkidu respond by killing the Bull, thus bringing upon them the wrath of the gods. After a celebration of their victory, Enkidu falls ill and dies twelve days later.

As in the Old Babylonian version, Enkidu's death forces Gilgamesh to face his own mortality, and he embarks on a distant journey to meet the immortal Utnapishtim. Here details differ again: in the Standard Version Gilgamesh encounters a being who is part human and part scorpion who warns him not to continue. He goes on, however, and finds himself under the earth in complete darkness. This trek takes him to a garden whose trees are bedecked with precious stones. Shortly thereafter he meets a tavern keeper named Siduri who reluctantly directs him to a boatman named Urshanabi. It is Urshanabi who ferries him across the waters of death and brings him to Utnapishtim, who in turn tells Gilgamesh of how he escaped a cosmic deluge by constructing a boat into which he placed his family and a number of animals. Utnapishtim informs him that after surviving the cataclysm, the gods bestowed immortality upon him and his wife and relocated them on the distant island. Upon hearing this Gilgamesh realizes that he can never obtain immortality.

Though the Old Babylonian version of the epic contains an encounter with Utnapishtim, it is unclear how much of the flood story it once related. Most scholars, therefore, see this section (the eleventh tablet) as the work of the seventh-century editor who based the addition upon an earlier source known as the "Atrahasis Epic" (see below).

Like the earlier Old Babylonian version, the Standard Version includes the account of Gilgamesh's attempt to overcome his humanity by avoiding sleep for seven nights. Unlike the earlier account, however, Utnapishtim afterwards directs Gilgamesh to the bottom of the sea to obtain a plant that will restore his youth. After much effort, Gilgamesh seizes the plant, but while bathing himself afterwards, sets it down, only to have it devoured by a serpent, a detail that provides an etiology for why serpents shed their skins.

The twelfth tablet of the Standard Version contains a partial translation of the earlier Sumerian epic "Gilgamesh, Enkidu, and the Nether World," and the reasons for its inclusion are not altogether clear (but see Vulpe 1994). It is possible that it intended to lead into and explain Gilgamesh's later role as king of the Underworld, but this remains speculation.

Of all of the ancient Mesopotamian epics, *Gilgamesh* was clearly the most widespread. Not only have fragments of the epic been discovered beyond Mesopotamia proper (e.g., at Boğazköy, Amarna, Ugarit, Emar, and Megiddo; see Chapters 14 and 16, by Sasson and Wyatt), but the epic continued to be copied as late as the second century BCE. Moreover, the epic's influence was remarkably pervasive after this period since we find it in refracted forms in a number of later literary works. Thus, we find Gilgamesh appearing with Humbaba (=Humbamba) and described as a giant in the Enochic text known as "The Book of the Watchers" found among the Dead Sea scrolls (this description matches an earlier Hittite version in which he stands 11 cubits tall). Humbamba also appears as Hobabish in a later Manichaean work known as the "Book of the Giants" (a book that survives only in late medieval fragments). Aelian, a Greek rhetorician writing in the second century CE, makes reference to a king of Babylon named Gilgamos in his *On the Characteristics of Animals* (*NA*, vii, 21). Gilgamesh also appears in the eighth century CE as Gmigmos in the Syriac writings of the Nestorian writer Theodore bar Konai. Whether or not the Gilgamesh epic played an influential role in Homer's *Odyssey* (Lord 1990; Burkert 1982, 1992; Abusch 2001b), the *Alexander Romance*, or the tales of the *Arabian Nights* remains an ongoing discussion (Tigay 1982; Dalley 1991).

Atrahasis epic

The *Atrahasis* epic, which provided the source material for the eleventh tablet of the Gilgamesh epic, was composed sometime in the first half of the second millennium BCE (Lambert and Millard 1969; George and Al-Rawi 1996). The tale provides the mythic origins and primordial history of humankind, and details the account of one man's survival (i.e., Atrahasis) from a cosmic flood, a story that appears in a number of forms in the ancient Near East (Schmidt 1995; Greenstein 1998). It opens with a number of younger gods staging a coup against the older divinities because of the onerous tasks they imposed upon them. The older gods put down the revolt and kill its leader. With his blood and some clay they fashion the first human beings, seven pairs in total, and command them to perform their manual labors. However, the humans reproduce at such a fast rate and create such a noise that they anger the sleeping god Enlil. Enlil thus tries to wipe them out by sending plagues, drought, and famine, but is outsmarted at every turn by the god Enki, whose interest in saving humankind is unexplained. Eventually, Enlil and the assembly of gods decide to send a devastating flood, and so Enki leaks the news to a man named Atrahasis (Utnapishtim is called Atrahasis also in the Gilgamesh epic) through a series of elaborate word plays (Hoffner 1976; Noegel 1991, 1994, 1995, 1997). Enki further instructs Atrahasis to build a boat that will save his family and a great deal of animal life. For his wisdom and ability to understand Enki's secret message (the name "Atrahasis" means "exceedingly wise"), he is spared. The flood lasts seven days and nights and concludes with Atrahasis leaving the ark and performing sacrifices to the gods. The assembly of gods is then moved to a compromise position; instead of completely annihilating humanity, they decree that sterility, infant mortality, and other forms of childlessness will forever trouble humankind.

Epics of Sargon

We also possess several fragments of Akkadian epics that concern King Sargon (*ca.* 2334–2279 BCE). Two of these epics, "Sargon the conquering hero" and "Sargon in the lands beyond the cedar forest," date to the Old Babylonian period (*ca.* 2003–1595 BCE). The first of these is so fragmentary that it defies easy translation, though it is clear that it glorifies nine of Sargon's military victories, one of which, in a way reminiscent of the *Epic of Gilgamesh*, required that he traverse a land of deep darkness. The second Sargon epic, also reminiscent of some passages in the *Epic of Gilgamesh*, tells of Sargon's quest to the cedar forests beyond the Amanus mountains. There he apparently requests a divine omen, to which the goddess Irnina responds by encouraging him to destroy the land of Maldaban.

Among the cuneiform texts discovered at Amarna in central Egypt that date to the fourteenth century BCE is a copy of another short epic which scholars refer to as "Sargon and the Lord of Purushkhanda" (its ancient title was "King of Battle"). It tells the story of how the merchants of Purushkhanda, a city in central Anatolia, called upon Sargon of Akkad to save them from the oppression of their own king Nur-Daggal. Despite the concerns of his own officers, Sargon launches on the distant trek, a motif the story perhaps borrows from the Gilgamesh epic (Franke 1995). Sargon arrives at the city, and while Nur-Daggal and his army are feasting and becoming drunk, he storms the city, tears down its walls, and kills its mighty men. Nur-Daggal capitulates and so Sargon retains him as a puppet king, returning home three years later (see also Chapter 17, by Beckman).

The transformation of Akkadian epic traditions

Beginning in the eighteenth century BCE we begin to see some important changes in the way some Mesopotamian poets composed their Akkadian epics. In a marked departure from earlier traditions, save for the Sumerian Shulgi epic (see above), these new epics extol the heroic exploits of living kings, not past heroes. Moreover, they constitute literary hybrids in which elements of royal inscriptions are interwoven with sophisticated literary tropes and genres found in the more ancient epics. The mixture of the ancient and the contemporary has led scholars to label them as "historical epics."

Three such texts exist, the first of which, the *Epic of Zimri-Lim*, details the military deeds of Zimri Lim (*ca.* 1776–1761 BCE) king of Mari, a city located on the central Euphrates river (Charpin and Durand 1985), and therefore on the periphery of Mesopotamia. The second, the *Epic of Adad-Nirari*, lauds the military accomplishments of the Assyrian monarch Adad-Nirari I (*ca.* 1307–1275 BCE). The third, the *Epic of Tukulti-Ninurta I*, praises the Assyrian monarch Tukulti-Ninurta I (*ca.* 1244–1208 BCE) for his victory over Babylon in 1235 BCE (Weidner 1939/41; Machinist 1978). The tradition of composing historical epics continues into the following centuries and is exemplified perhaps best by a poem praising the Assyrian monarch Shalmanezer III (*ca.* 858–824 BCE) and his conquest of Urartu in eastern Anatolia.

Interpreting Mesopotamian Epic

Mesopotamian epic as folklore

It has for some time been common practice in scholarship to interpret Mesopotamian epics in accordance with advances derived from the study of world folklore (e.g., Limet 1972; Komoróczy 1974; Alster 1974, 1976, 1995; Berlin 1983; Edzard 1994). Such an approach seeks to identify universal, or nearly universal, narrative techniques, structures, and themes (Thompson 1955–8), sometimes called "mythic patterns" (Lord 1990; see also Chapters 14 and 3, by Sasson and Edmunds). A number of these patterns have been identified and represent "firsts" in world literature. One often finds, for example, a special relationship between the goddess and the hero (e.g., Enmerkar and Inanna, Gilgamesh and Ishtar) who is frequently semi-divine (see Chapters 6 and 7, by Nagy and Louden). Often this hero has miraculous origins (e.g., the births of Shulgi) or is saved from grave danger while still an infant (e.g., Sargon). Sometimes he is even an unlikely choice for a hero (e.g., Lugalbanda is the youngest of eight sons). An adversary often demands the surrender of the hero's community, which leads to the summoning of a messenger (e.g., Lugalbanda), and causes the hero to prepare for a threatening encounter (e.g., Lord of Aratta and Enmerkar). The encounter frequently requires that the hero undertake quests to distant and dangerous places (e.g., Lugalbanda to Uruk, Gilgamesh to the Underworld, Sargon to Purushkhanda) which distinguish him from ordinary men. These travels are filled with exotic things and fabulous creatures (e.g., Gilgamesh visits the Scorpionman and a garden of jeweled trees). The return and reintegration of the hero often marks a transformation of character (e.g., Gilgamesh's new understanding of humanity (Afanasjeva 1974)) and often confers upon him a special status (Lugalbanda obtains "saintly" status (Vanstiphout 2002)). While on their journeys one also finds heroes performing miraculous feats that force their adversaries to admit defeat (e.g., Enmerkar's contests with the Lord of Aratta). The hero also demonstrates superior wisdom and cunning at critical moments in the story (Enmerkar beguiles the Lord of Aratta, Lugalbanda outwits his jealous brothers), but nevertheless shows unexpected kindness toward his adversaries (e.g., Gilgamesh does not kill Agga, Sargon does not kill Nur-Daggal).

Scholars often use such themes to demonstrate how Mesopotamian epic draws upon popular oral traditions (see Chapter 13, by J. Foley) and interpret them as serving didactic purposes, especially to demonstrate the superiority of knowledge and wisdom over physical might. Thus, some epics have been read as didactic tools for teaching important lessons in life, an assessment that finds support from a close reading of the literary development of heroes' characters (Afanasjeva 1974; Moran 1995).

Mesopotamian epics as propaganda

Scholars also have long examined Mesopotamian epics as propaganda since they appear to function as paradigms for justifying the military campaigns of later rulers (Alster 1974; Klein 1976; Renger 1978). Indeed, there can be little doubt that the increasingly powerful institution of kingship played a significant role in the creation and promulgation of the earliest epic poems (e.g., Sumerian epics and the Shulgi epic). As propaganda they would have served to promote a sort of nationalism (Landsberger 1960; Berlin 1983), and would have been disseminated through the royal court, possibly in the form of entertainment, and through the scribal academies, in the form of textual models for emulation and education. It is possible that the royal house encouraged some epics to circulate orally in the general populace as well, though we cannot know this for certain (Laessøe 1953).

Be this as it may, Mesopotamian epics were probably not written simply to justify the military efforts of contemporary kings, for the military exploits extolled in these texts often say less about a particular royal ideology than about competition for land, water, and labor, and about access to natural resources (Liverani 1995). Moreover, the heroic achievements of the kings whose names these poems celebrate often are predicated upon their obedience to the gods and their omens, and in some cases the hero in question is an En, a "priestly king." Thus, we also must understand these epics as serving the theological and political ideologies of Mesopotamian ritual experts (Moran 1995; Parpola 1998; Vanstiphout 2002). It is probable that Mesopotamian epics enjoyed multiple audiences and thus served many different purposes (Alster 1992; Cooper 2001). Some of these epics might even contain elements of political opposition (Michalowski 2003).

Mesopotamian epics and literary criticism

The pervasive influence of literary criticism has also shaped the way scholars approach Mesopotamian epics by shedding light on their sophisticated literary forms and devices (e.g., Abusch 1993a, 1993b; Moran 1987; Hallo 1990; Kilmer 1996; Maier 1997; Noegel, 1991, 1994, 1995, 1997). These changes in perspective have been accompanied by a concomitant change in the way we understand the historical contexts of these texts (e.g., Klein 1976; Frahm 1999; Abusch 2001a, cf. Berlin 1983). They also have led to, and have been influenced by, a more thorough knowledge of the close interaction between written and oral modes of textual transmission in Mesopotamia (Vanstiphout 1992; Vogelzang and Vanstiphout 1992; Alster 1992, 1995). These changes in perspective, coupled with a greater appreciation for the interdisciplinarity of the ancient scribal profession (see Chapter 10, by Haslam), as well as an increased knowledge of changing literary tastes, have led scholars to question the often rigid (and almost always western) classificatory schemes that distinguish one literary genre from another.

As a result scholars have begun to see the generic boundaries of Mesopotamian epic, indeed of much of Mesopotamian literature, as far more fluid. It is now seems likely that when composing their epics, Mesopotamian bards utilized a stock repertoire of literary expressions and features common to other genres as well (e.g., hymns, prayers, proverbs, love songs, letters, didactic literature, historical annals, and myths (see, e.g., Hallo 1990)). Depending on the historical period in question, therefore, one or more of these genres had a greater impact upon, or were impacted by, the epic traditions. Thus, while monumental building accounts and autobiographical inscriptions, in particular, may have provided some of the literary influences on early epic (Alster 1995), in later periods, epics appear to have influenced historical annals and hymns (Liverani 1995), as well as *narû* inscriptions (Renger 1978; Westenholz, 1983). This rather fluid state of exchange between genres makes some texts difficult to categorize (see, e.g., Volk 1995).

Mesopotamian epic and other modes of interpretation

Changes in the interpretation of Mesopotamian epic also have come about under the influence of feminist criticism and ritual theory. The former has given scholars a clearer understanding of the cultural stereotypes and the literary roles that women play in Mesopotamian epic (Harris 1990; Frymer-Kensky 1992). The latter has allowed them to read the epics as representing rites of passage (Falkowitz 1983; Vanstiphout 2002; Mills 2002, but cf. Alster 1990) and to see them as confirming cultural values concerning the sacred (Capomacchia 2001).

As new methods of analysis are brought to bear upon Mesopotamian epics (e.g., discourse analysis, see Buccellati 1990, and poetics, see Michalowski 1996), they undoubtedly will yield additional insights into the cultural values and literary tastes of the ancient Mesopotamians. New methods of interpretation, however, can only confirm what scholars of Mesopotamian literature and the ancient Mesopotamian scribes themselves have always known: that Mesopotamian epic traditions are as rich in meaning as they are timeless.

FURTHER READING

Good general introductions to Mesopotamian epic
Alster 1995; Bottéro 1995; Jacobsen 1976, 1987; Komoróczy 1975; Limet 1972; Michalowski 1995; Renger 1978; Schmidt 1995; Westenholz 1997; Wilcke 1971.

Translations and textual analyses of Sumerian epics
Alster 1973, 1990; Berlin 1979; Bing 1997; Cohen 1973; Cooper and Heimpel 1983; Edzard 1991; Ellis 1982; Falkowitz 1983; George 1999; Hallo 1983; Hallo and Younger 1997; Hruška 1974; Jacobsen 1976, 1987; Katz 1993; Klein 1983; Kramer 1938, 1944a, 1944b, 1946, 1949, 1952; Kramer and Jacobsen 1954; Römer 1980; Shaffer 1983; Vanstiphout 1992, 1998, 2002; Vogelzang and Vanstiphout 1992; Volk 1995; Wilcke 1969, 1971.

Translations and textual analyses of Akkadian epics
Abusch 1986, 1993a, 1993b, 2001a; Bottéro 1992a; Campbell-Thompson 1930; Cavigneaux and Renger 2000; Charpin and Durand 1985; Dalley 1989; Ferry 1992; Foster 1993, 1995; Gadd 1966; Gardiner and Maier 1984; George 1999; George and Al-Rawi 1996; Hallo and Younger 1997; Hecker 1974; Heidel 1946; Kovacs 1989; Lambert and Millard 1969; Landsberger 1960, 1968; Lord 1990; Machinist 1978; Maier 1997; Mason 2003; Moran 1987, 1995; Parpola 1997b; Sandars 1960; Speiser 1950; Tigay 1982; Vogelzang and Vanstiphout 1992; Vulpe 1994; Weidner 1939/41; von Weiher 1980, 1983; Westenholz 1983, 1997; Wilcke 1977.

CHAPTER SIXTEEN

Epic in Ugaritic Literature

N. Wyatt

Introduction

A survey of general discussions on ancient West Semitic (Ugaritic language) literature reveals a considerable imprecision about the nature of genre, particularly with regard to the appropriateness of this or that definition of a given composition. Not only is one man's myth another man's history, but "epic," "legend," "saga," and "folktale" can all be (or if they cannot, or should not be, they *are*) used to denote the same texts. Some scholars even use two or three of these terms for the same composition in the same discussion. In the following essay I am not going to try to solve this problem, if only because it is a futile exercise, except perhaps insofar as it illustrates the inherent impossibility of confining any real literature within various designs of theoretical taxonomic straitjacket. But I am going to discuss three bodies of literature, which are linked by one important feature: they are all associated with the name of one author, redactor, or editor.

The most general approach would tend to distinguish the *Baal* narratives from Ugarit as myths, while conceding to *Keret* and *Aqhat* epic characteristics, but this generalization disguises a wide range of conflicting views among scholars, as noted. Smith (2001: 23) wrote that "if there is one text that all scholars can agree is a myth, it is the Baal cycle." In a footnote to this sentence (p. 208 n. 159) he noted that Jason (1977: 32), and Milne (1988: 169–70), classified the *Baal* cycle as a "mythic epic." Note also his own useful observations on the problem of myth in *Baal* (Smith 1994: 27–8). Albright (1942: 227) called all three compositions under consideration "epics," while Watts (1989: 443) called them all "myths." The briefest survey of the critical literature reveals that when it comes down to details, scholars are at sixes and sevens over their strategy.

Having recently claimed that myth is not really a literary genre at all (Wyatt 2001), but rather a mind-set appropriate to religious experience, discourse, and literary composition, I tend to regard all three compositions as mythic (that is, as exhibiting the workings and perceptions of what I call "the mythic mind"), since each moves in a world peopled either exclusively by gods (*Baal*) or has gods and men interacting in a matter-of-fact fashion such as we see in other "epic" literatures such as the *Iliad* or *Gilgamesh* (*Keret* and *Aqhat*). They are composed from an emic perspective.

I am also content to treat all the material discussed here as epic, on the basis of a minimalist view of epic as heroic and ideological narrative, generally poetic in form, which seeks to promote the identity, values, and concerns of a culture, and perhaps specifically of the ruling classes within a community (see Chapter 1, by Martin). The theme of *Baal*, though it has exclusively divine characters (thus constituting "myth" as "stories about gods," according to the common, if inadequate view) fits into this ideological and hierarchical framework. Epic is definitely *not* proletarian in its concerns! It may even be quite heterogeneous with regard to genre in its constituent parts (Hendel 1987b: 26–7).

As regards the issue of historical reference in epic literature (on which generally see Chapter 5, by Raaflaub), I think that this must be regarded as an accidental rather than intrinsic element. The broad significance of epic is surely that however trivial and even factual its origins, such as warfare at Troy (*Iliad* and *Odyssey* and even, by a leap of faith, the *Aeneid*!), a monarch out of control (*Gilgamesh*) or an ambush in the Pyrenees (*Chanson de Roland* and the *Orlando* tradition), or in the case of *Keret* perhaps a dynastic crisis in Ugarit, occasioning reflection on the problem of dissonance between an institution and its incumbent, and conceivably echoing ancient lore about the ancestral king Didanu/Ditanu (Schmidt 1994: 72–82, 89–91; Wyatt 2002b: 433 n. 12), the final "epic" product is a raising of the trivial or merely fanciful to a heroic and cosmic level, exploring the deepest human problems of life and death, social affiliation, and above all of the wielding of power. By its nature, this would entail an element of ideology, serving the interests of the social group to whom the *poetes* belonged. By such a token, the three compositions treated below are all epic. They are also all in verse, the techniques of Semitic prosody such as regular parallelism, extensive assonance, and wholesale use of chiasmus pointing to a long oral tradition, though it would be premature to claim that the present texts are necessarily the end products of an oral process. *Baal* and *Keret* in particular betray evidence of the conflation of diverse elements (on *Keret* see Parker 1977: 1989). A case could presumably be made for the *Baal* cycle, since the *Chaoskampf* motif is exceedingly dispersed, and presumably by oral communication. However, written versions already appear in the mid-third millennium. (See Wyatt 1998 for a survey of the material, to which may be added Annus 2001 and Wyatt 2004.)

Poems concerning Baal

A number of narrative texts, in varying degrees of preservation and legibility, feature the West Semitic storm-god Baal, the patron deity of Ugarit (Tell Ras Shamra). These are KTU 1.1–1.6, the so-called "*Baal* cycle," which will form the basis of the following discussion; 1.7–1.9 (fragments of school exercises, excerpts from the main text); 1.10, 1.11, and 1.13, which deal with the erotic encounters of Baal and Anat; 1.12, apparently a myth relating to atonement and redemption rites, and featuring Baal; and 1.92, which narrates an attempted seduction by Baal of the virgin goddess Athtart (Astarte). KTU 1.133 is a fragment paralleling an episode in KTU 1.5. KTU 1.10 may in fact be part of the "cycle" of 1.1–1.6 (I now consider it to be perhaps the end of Ilimilku's composition), and KTU 1.13 has been interpreted as a fragment of the third column of 1.10. (For this numbering system see Dietrich et al. 1976, 1995; for convenient recent translations see Pardee 1997a, 1997b, 1997c; Parker 1997; Wyatt 2002b.)

KTU 1.1–1.6 constitute by broad consensus the main body of *Baal*. Something in the order of 50 percent of the text on these tablets is missing, though a certain amount of minimal reconstruction is possible, thanks to the use of reiterated poetic formulae. There is also a broad consensus on the order in which the tablets are to be read, in the sequence of numbering, though KTU 1.2 appears to contain parts of two distinct tablets (Meier 1986; Wyatt 2002b: 37), thus perhaps representing a parallel version; there are also some sequence dissonances elsewhere. Most interpreters take it as a working hypothesis that there is a rough unity of composition in the main body of material.

Tablet KTU 1.6 ends (col. vi 54–8) with a colophon listing the titles of Ilimilku, the scribe, to whose significance we shall return. A broken colophon may have identified him as the scribe of KTU 1.4 (col. viii lower edge); the other texts of the series, in addition to further ones, notably, in the present discussion, KTU 1.10, being commonly attributed to him on epigraphic grounds. (See also KTU 1.22, one of the surviving *Rpum* texts, which have been linked by some scholars with the *Aqhat* story; KTU 1.14–1.16, *Keret*: Ilimilku named as the scribe at 1.16 vi lower edge; KTU 1.17–1.19, *Aqhat*: Ilimilku may have been named in colophon at 1.17 vi lower edge). It should be conceded that there is no colophon on tablet KTU 1.10, the reverse of which is uninscribed, and this *could* be construed as evidence against its putative place as concluding *Baal*. It could similarly be argued that the full formulation at the end of KTU 1.6 vi marks it out as the end of the composition. But neither argument is conclusive.

The narrative in *Baal* runs as follows (all references in KTU 1. series). In this synopsis I list the missing materials as well, where they can be inferred, in order to indicate the precise elements of continuity and of discontinuity between various parts.

KTU 1.1 (6 columns: fragmentary): Various embassies are sent, and the sea-god Yam is enthroned as divine king.

KTU 1.2 (fragments, perhaps of 8 columns: see Wyatt 2002b: 36–7): Athtar's royal claim is rejected, and Baal is surrendered by the divine assembly... Bound beneath Yam's throne, he emerges to kill Yam with divine weapons.

KTU 1.3 (6 columns: half missing): Baal is feasted, and Anat goes to war, in a real battle, followed by a ritual one (see Lloyd 1996). On receiving messengers from Baal, she insists that she had already killed his enemies, and demands a palace for Baal from El, the high god. Baal sends Athirat's assistant to Kothar the artificer god...

KTU 1.4 (8 columns: about two column-lengths missing):... who makes gifts for Athirat. She intercedes with El, the palace is built and inaugurated. Mot is not invited.

KTU 1.5 (6 columns: about two column-lengths missing): Mot demands Baal's surrender, and he goes into the Underworld. El mourns him.

KTU 1.6 (6 columns: about two column-lengths missing): Anat mourns Baal. She and Shapsh recover his body and she buries him. Athtar is enthroned. El dreams that Baal is restored. A restored Baal fights a restored Mot, and Shapsh separates them, awarding Baal the victory.

KTU 1.10, supposed by some to belong here (3 columns: about half missing): Baal goes hunting, where Anat meets him. They watch a cow in labor, make love, and a son is born to Baal.

A wide range of interpretations has been offered for the *Baal* story, being largely variations on two main themes, which we may summarize in the briefest form here. There are several useful surveys, which may be consulted for further details (de Moor 1971; Smith 1986, 1994: 58–114; Wyatt 1996: 117–218; 1998.). Initial attempts belong to the "myth and ritual" era of scholarship; they saw two main features in the text: firstly, the deities were seen fairly simplistically as allegorical figures, personifications of every kind of natural and cultural phenomenon, and as essentially "immanent in nature," a pantheistic evaluation which now seems perverse, but which belongs largely to the polemics of biblical scholarship. Secondly, this approach, adopted from the inception of Ugaritic studies by Virolleaud and Dussaud (for references consult Smith 1994 and Wyatt 2002b), was refined into a pan-Near Eastern ritual pattern by Gaster (1950; cf. Gray 1964), and into a rigorous ritual calendar for Ugarit by de Moor (1971).

This approach is now regarded as broadly discredited, and an ideological basis is seen as a more probable motivation. The discovery of a ritual application of the motif, linked to the cultic use of "divine weapons" in Mari, published by Durand (1993), offers a far more plausible *Sitz im Leben*, which I followed up in a comparative survey (Wyatt 1998). Now the *Chaoskampf* theme is seen as part of the larger issue of royal ideology, and serves as legitimization of war, in which kings recapitulate the primordial victories of their patron deities.

The distinctive feature of *Baal*, compared with all other versions, is its incorporation into a larger composition, which is perhaps to be attributed to Ilimilku himself (Wyatt 2002a). The implicit point of the common theme of the possession and use of royal weapons is here linked to the theme of the acquisition of a royal palace (Ugaritic *hkl*, like its cognates, means both palace of a king and temple of a god). And Baal's building and inauguration of a palace constitutes a challenge to other rival royal claims; both Yam and Mot are presented as gods challenging Baal's hegemony. (This rivalry may be compared with the tension between Zeus, Poseidon, and Hades.) Finally, in a *tour de force* which skillfully echoes the structure of the *Chaoskampf* narrative (Petersen and Woodward 1977), Baal's conflict with Mot echoes that with Yam, and is resolved with a comparable setting of Baal's royal power under the aegis of that of El, the high god. (For further discussion see below.)

The Story of *Keret*

An abbreviated colophon at the end of KTU 1.16 confirms that Ilimilku is responsible at least for the writing of this text. Some suppose there to have been further tablets (e.g. Pardee 1997c: 333; Margalit 1999: 204), but the extant text is broadly coherent, and comes to a satisfying if uncomfortable solution. The narrative runs as follows.

KTU 1.14 (6 columns: about 75 percent surviving): Keret's family is destroyed (whether seven wives or seven children remains uncertain); El appears to the distraught king, offering wealth as consolation. Keret refuses, and El instructs him on how to find a new wife by seizing her from Pabil of Udum. He must reject Pabil's attempts to buy him off. En route to Pabil's kingdom, Keret turns aside to make a vow to Athirat. He besieges Udum; Pabil sues for peace . . .

KTU 1.15 (6 columns: about half surviving): Pabil reluctantly gives his daughter Hurriya. Keret feasts the gods. El blesses him, foretelling a fruitful marriage, guaranteeing the succession. The gods depart; El's promises are fulfilled. The vow to Athirat is not fulfilled, and she remembers. At a banquet for the nobility, Hurriya announces that Keret is dying. The banquet seems to turn into an anticipatory wake.

KTU 1.16 (6 columns: about a third missing): Keret's son Ilhu weeps for him; the king tells him to fetch his sister . . . She arrives, also bewailing Keret . . . A ritual fragment compares Keret's death to Baal's . . . Divine heralds are instructed to summon the gods. El asks which of them will heal Keret. When no one offers, he creates a goddess, who does so. The heir Yasib bursts in on the now cured Keret, demanding his throne, assuming that he is still ill, and is cursed by the king.

Early analysis of *Keret* (first treated *in toto* by Ginsberg 1946) fell into historicist, or myth-and-ritual, frames of understanding, as was well characterized in Margalit (1999, with references). But in the latter's evaluation of Pedersen (1941) and Merrill (1968), he went too far in dismissing an ideological dimension; and Margalit's own analysis of *Keret*, which he treated as theater (literally: a drama in three acts), a light-hearted romp and a parody of Late Bronze Age religion, and particularly its royal ideology, was wide of the mark.

The broad subject matter is self-evidently royal and ideological in nature (see, broadly, though with reservations, Gray 1964). Its interpretation as satirical (as in Margalit) or as a critique of old royal dogmas (as in Parker 1977) is dubious in my view; rather is it a fairly serious analysis of the limits of individual autonomy within a dynastic line, and of the absolute requirement of true piety in a monarch. Keret fails, and thus shows how disastrous is irreligion. Thus the old values are firmly upheld.

In the matter of historicity, we have noted the claimed link with Didanu/Ditanu. If Keret is to be identified with Kirta (perhaps = Sanskrit *kṛta*) king of Mittanni (Wilhelm 1989: 28), we may suggest a romance on some episode in the life of the king, adapted to Ugaritian concerns. Similarly, we may ask whether his capital of Bet Hubur (= Khabur) is the lost Hurrian capital of Waššukanni. But this is conjecture. The motif of the childless king is shared not only with *Aqhat*, but with Job, and is a common folklore motif.

The Story of *Aqhat*

A fragmentary colophon on the edge of KTU 1.17 vi, together with the script, suggest that this composition is from the hand on Ilimilku (Wyatt 1999a: 234–5).

KTU 1.17 (6 columns: about half surviving): Danel spends six days in the temple, trying to gain a son. Then on the seventh Baal intercedes for him with El, so that he may beget a son who will perform the appropriate filial duties on his father's behalf. Aqhat is born, Danel rejoices, offering thanks to the childbirth goddesses, and the years pass ... After two missing columns, Kothar brings a wonderful bow, which is given to Aqhat. At a sacrifice, Anat sees the bow and covets it. When she tries to persuade Aqhat to give it to her, with promises of wealth and immortality, he insults her. She goes to El ...

KTU 1.18 (4 columns: about a third surviving): ... threatening him with violence if he does not give her freedom to punish Aqhat. He gives her *carte blanche*. She comes to Aqhat, inviting him to go hunting with her ... She plots his death with her hit man Yatipan, who will swoop on him like (or in the form of) a falcon.

KTU 1.19 (4 columns: most of the text survives): The bow is smashed. The enraged Anat laments the bow and tears Aqhat to pieces. Danel, unaware of the tragedy, sits to judge his people. His daughter Pughat, intuiting his loss, rends his cloak. Danel utters a terrible curse. Still unaware of what has happened, he tours his fields, and two messengers bring the news of Aqhat's death. Danel curses the falcons, retrieves Aqhat's remains and buries them. He then curses the neighborhood of Aqhat's death, while Pughat plans her revenge. She comes to Yatipan's camp disguised as Anat, bent on revenge, and plies him with strong drink ...

If the very fragmentary *Rpum* texts (KTU 1.20–2 appear to be parallel versions of the same narrative) *are* related to this composition, a view now largely discounted (Wyatt 1999a: 235 and n. 3, 237), and relying on the circumstantial mention of the name *Danilu* in the text, then it would appear that a *kispum* feast of dead kings (the *rpum* are perhaps close in conception to the Greek heroes; cf. Wyatt 2002b: 305 n. 1) takes place at a threshing floor. We might conjecture that Danel, but hardly his son, was included in their number.

The most recent surveys of *Aqhat* scholarship are Margalit (1989) and Wyatt (1999a). Early attempts were historicist and seasonal (that is, seeing the narrative as an allegory of the flow of seasons, with ritual application) (Virolleaud 1936), or seasonal and astronomical (Gaster 1950; Astour 1967), both categories rejected by Caquot and Sznycer (Caquot et al. 1974). De Moor (1988) extended his seasonal theories concerning *Baal* to *Aqhat*. A royal ideological dimension was recognized by Ginsberg (1945a, 1945b) but rejected by Gibson (1975), who followed Driver (1956) in seeing the theme of death and resurrection in the narrative, which is emphatically absent from the surviving text, except in the offer which Aqhat rejects. Del Olmo Lete (1981) judged *Aqhat* to be epic, but "more mythical" than *Keret*, thus illustrating the problem of trying to apply genre categories. Margalit's analysis (1989) was driven by two theoretical points, the so-called Kinneret hypothesis and the non-royal nature of the story. The former has not commanded assent; the latter is rebutted in my treatment (Wyatt 1999a: 249–51). I would now go further than my comments there, to see the composition as dealing specifically with royal ideological issues, however much it is dependent on traditional and diverse literary motifs.

Ilimilku's Motives

Let us first briefly address the status of Ilimilku (cf. Wyatt 1997, to be modified by the revision of Ilimilku's date, Wyatt 2002a), to whom some ± 4,250 lines of tablet text (therefore rather more individual cola) are to be credited in the three compositions discussed here, of which a little over half survives. The only information we have concerning him appears in the colophon at the end of KTU 1.6 vi, as noted above. Lines 54–8 are in prose, and state that

> Ilimilku the Shubanite wrote (it), the student of Attanu the diviner, chief of the priests, chief of the temple herdsmen, sacrificer of Niqmaddu king of Ugarit, Lord of Yargub and Ruler of Sharruman.

Other fragments of colopha survive, but provide no further information. Our main problem is to determine which of the titles belong to which of the people named. Ilimilku is certainly the student of Attanu; but are the titles "the diviner, chief of the priests, chief of the temple herdsmen, sacrificer" those of Attanu or Ilimilku himself? To be honest, we cannot tell from this text. It will be seen from the punctuation in my translation that I have taken "diviner" to be a title of Attanu, leaving the possibility that the following ones all belong to Ilimilku, until we reach those of Niqmaddu. This is a guess, but I hope a reasonable one, and is broadly in agreement with the line taken by other scholars. In support of it can be cited the regular and mature cuneiform style of the writer. This contrasts sharply with the roughness of style of other tablets, which are agreed to be those of school-pupils, such as KTU 1.7 and 1.8 among the religious texts. Ilimilku is at least the scribe, if nothing more, and this office alone implies advanced education and high office. Moreover, as chief of the temple herdsmen (*nqdm*), he might have other remits: his position might be comparable to that of Amos (Amos 7: 14: *nôqéd* (herdsman)).

The fact that the same scribe is credited with the three main literary compositions from Ugarit (*Baal*, *Keret*, and *Aqhat*) together with at least one of the *Rpum* texts, KTU 1.22, and a further fragment (RS 92.2016, an incantation) points to a writer with considerable authority, and possibly freedom of action with regard to the handling of his materials. He certainly uses a consistent style and outlook (see Korpel 1997), with many formulations recurring through the corpus. It is the last-mentioned fragment, found in the house of Urtenu in the southern part of the city, which has forced a recalculation of the date of Ilimilku, who is now to be seen as a contemporary of Niqmaddu III or IV in the late thirteenth century BCE, rather than Niqmaddu II of the mid-fourteenth century.

The importance of the identification of the author or redactor (or both) of this poetic corpus is surely significant for our overall interpretation of the material. While it is entirely possible that the work covers a lengthy period in Ilimilku's life, we should see it as more probably fitting into the reign of his patron, and to some extent reflecting the concerns of that reign, in terms most likely of a public relations and propagandistic function (*pace* Margalit). Furthermore, if we can discern specific concerns of the reign of Niqmaddu III or IV in *Baal*, it is reasonable, in view of Ilimilku's offices, at least to ask whether the same concerns, or similar ones, do not also lie behind his composition of *Keret* and *Aqhat*. I have suggested (Wyatt 2002a) that it was the occasion of a royal wedding, that of Niqmaddu

III or IV to a Hittite princess, Eḫli-Nikkal (see Singer 1999: 701–4), that motivated Ilimilku to write an epithalamium, beginning with the traditional *Chaoskampf* story, and adding a considerable amount of extraneous material of his own devising to make the connection. *Baal* was the outcome of this process. It served the double purpose of celebrating the king's wedding and flattering the bride's father, the Hittite emperor Tudḫaliya IV, with a treatment of the old martial ideology (KTU 1.1–2), a transparent reference in the palace-building episode to the establishment of a royal house (KTU 1.3–4), which itself might allow a pun on the play between a material house (palace, temple) and a dynastic house (offspring) such as lay behind 2 Sam. 7, and according to Merrill (1968) *Keret* as well. The conflict with Mot (KTU 1.5–6) also allowed construal as the triumph of fecundity over death, appropriate to the celebration of a marriage.

At the most basic level, *Keret* is a moral tale, drawing on a traditional and ubiquitous theme, the desire for children, of particular importance when the destiny of a royal line is at stake. But this must be pursued through true piety and unquestioning obedience to the gods. Keret behaves exactly as he should, until on the third day of his journey to Udum, he turns aside to offer a vow to Athirat (KTU 1.14 iv 34–43), indicating a lack of trust in El's promise. Thus, in the name of one level of piety, he commits a greater impiety. The parallel with 1 Kgs. 13: 11–26 is patent. The episode's interruption of the seven-day sequence of Keret's journey has been noted by Cartledge (1992: 108; cf. Wyatt 2002b: 200–1.) It is Keret's subsequent failure to fulfill this impious vow which compounds his sin, and brings down on him the wrath of Athirat, which cannot be deflected even through El's healing power. With his final curse on his son and heir, Keret is back where he began, all hope dashed. The irony is that it is Yasibu who, through his rebelliousness (an equal impiety!), triggers the final cataclysm. It might be objected that this is rather heavy stuff from a court poet. But it should be remembered that Ilimilku was also a priest. Perhaps he acted as moral theologian to the king, warning him with impunity of dangers, much as Nathan could be perfectly frank in his discourse with David (2 Sam. 12: 1–15).

Keret is also about a royal marriage, of course. We may note the parallel between Keret and Hurriya and Paris and Helen, where two kingdoms, Udum and Troy, are threatened on behalf of a woman marrying out of the dynasty, though the circumstances of the two situations are rather different, and any direct link is conjectural. However, Niqmaddu's marriage to Eḫli-Nikkal was also an exogamic one, where the parallel with *Keret* may have been deliberately evoked.

A similar moral construction may be put on *Aqhat*. Again we have a tale of a sonless king, who goes to considerable lengths to remedy the situation. In this case the king is beyond reproach, but his son (just like Yasibu in *Keret*), who should perform the duties of filial piety outlined four times in the narrative, is impetuous and outspoken, insulting Anat. He thus signally fails to maintain these standards. The message of both narratives is therefore in part at least not to spare the rod. (Again, we have the biblical parallel of David's indulgence of his sons, with tragic consequences.)

A function of epic is without doubt to maintain traditional values in a changing world. Ours is not the first age to lament a lost past. Both *Keret* and *Aqhat* offer a nice example of the problem of being offered a bribe by a god. El offers Keret limitless wealth and power (expressed in the martial figure of chariots); Keret demands offspring, who will perpetuate his line and thus grant him immortality of a kind. Anat offers Aqhat limitless wealth; he then spurns the further offer of immortality. Keret subsequently exhibits levity in religion; Aqhat does so at this point. Far from exhibiting a moral bankruptcy, as claimed of Ugaritian religion by de Moor (1997: 83–4), this corpus emphatically champions the old moral certitudes which are challenged anew in every generation.

Divine kingship is a theme that is perhaps somewhat out of fashion, many treatments of Egyptian and West Semitic kingship stressing the human aspect of the institution, with a tendency to downplay, or represent as merely figurative, the divine aspect. In my estimation such modern pleading misrepresents the institutions of the ancient world, and flies in the face of clear evidence to the contrary. In a previous article (1999b) I re-examined the Ugaritian evidence, indicating the agenda of Ilimilku, and showing how the ritual texts and the iconographic convention reinforce the arguments of the present literary compositions, making comparisons between Keret and Baal that are vacuous unless the divinity of both is conceded, and suggesting that *Aqhat* takes the agenda for granted.

A recent publication is worth mentioning here, because it initiates a new dimension of study. Wright (2001) has examined the literary use of the ritual accounts in *Aqhat*. He notes that the ritual scenes in *Keret* are too fragmentary for a similar detailed study, but *mutatis mutandis*, his conclusions probably fit both narratives, the surviving text of *Aqhat* devoting the surprisingly high figure of 82 percent of the total to ritual (Wright 2001: 8). *Baal* is also well endowed with ritual sequences, including two accounts of an enthronement (KTU 1.1 iv, 1.6 i), and is thus also eminently suitable for such analysis, particularly with regard to royal ideology. This approach does not seek to reintroduce the old myth-and-ritual agenda by the back door: what it demonstrates fairly persuasively is the way in which the non-linguistic communication system of ritual parallels the role of language, thus reinforcing at every turn the literary tensions and dynamics of the text, and indeed constituting a subliminal reinforcement of any ideological agenda the text may have. This provides some confirmation, in my view, of the royal agenda I see the texts as serving.

FURTHER READING

General

S. B. Parker, *The Pre-Biblical Narrative Tradition* (1989).
W. G. E. Watson, and N. Wyatt, (eds.) *Handbook of Ugaritic Studies* (1999).
N. Wyatt, *Myths of Power: A Study of Royal Myth and Ideology in Ugaritic and Biblical Tradition* (1996).

Translations

J. C. de Moor, *An Anthology of Religious Texts from Ugarit* (1987).
G. del Olmo Lete, *Mitos y leyendas de Canaán según la tradición de Ugarit* (1981).
D. Pardee, "The 'Aqhatu legend," in Hallo (ed.) *The Context of Scripture* I (1997a).
—— "The Baʿlu myth," in Hallo (ed.) *The Context of Scripture* I (1997b).
—— "The Kirta epic", in Hallo (ed.) *The Context of Scripture* I (1997c).
S. B. Parker, (ed.) *Ugaritic Narrative Poetry* (1997).
N. Wyatt, *Religious Texts from Ugarit*, 2nd edn. (2002b).

Baal

J. Day, *God's Conflict with the Dragon and the Sea* (1985).
M. S. Smith, "Interpreting the Baal cycle," *Ugarit-Forschungen* 18 (1986).
—— *The Ugaritic Baal Cycle*, vol. 1: *Introduction with Text, Translation and Commentary of KTU 1.1–1.2* (1994).

N. Wyatt, "Killing and cosmogony in Canaanite and biblical thought," *Ugarit-Forschungen* 17 (1985).

—— "Arms and the king: the earliest allusions to the *Chaoskampf* motif and their implications for the interpretation of the Ugaritic and biblical traditions," in Dietrich and Kottsieper (eds.) "*Und Mose schrieb dieses Lied auf...*" (1998).

—— "Degrees of divinity: mythical and ritual aspects of West Semitic kingship," *Ugarit-Forschungen* 31 (1999b).

—— "Ilimilku the theologian: the ideological roles of Athtar and Baal in KTU 1.1 and 1.6," in Loretz, Metzler, and Schaudig (eds.) *Ex Mesopotamia et Syria Lux* (2002b).

Keret (Kirta)

J. C. L. Gibson, "Myth, legend and folklore in the Ugaritic Keret and Aqhat texts," *SVT* 28 (1975).

H. L. Ginsberg, *The Legend of King Keret* (1946).

J. Gray, *The KRT Text in the Literature of Ras Shamra* (1964).

B. Margalit, "The legend of Keret," in Watson and Wyatt, *Handbook of Ugaritic Studies* (1999).

Aqhat

J. C. L. Gibson, "Myth, legend and folklore in the Ugaritic Keret and Aqhat texts," *SVT* 28 (1975).

B. Margalit, *The Ugaritic Poem of Aqht* (1989).

N. Wyatt, "The Aqhat Story (KTU 1.17–19)," in Watson and Wyatt, *Handbook of Ugaritic Studies* (1999a).

CHAPTER SEVENTEEN

Hittite and Hurrian Epic

Gary Beckman

1 Introduction

"Epic" in the sense of extensive poetic narrative featuring human protagonists (see Preminger 1965, under "Epic") was not a native genre among the Hittites, but since a number of texts from the Hittite royal archives, particularly the "songs" of the Kumarbi cycle, have often been adduced in studies of Greek epic (e.g., Walcot 1966: 1–26; Watkins 1992; West 1997b: 101–6), Hittite literature deserves attention in this volume. After a brief discussion of the evidence for poetic literary form in early Anatolia, we will proceed to consider fantastic narrative, beginning with accounts in which humans interact directly with deities. Then we will examine compositions whose action is set entirely among the gods and conclude with a survey of accounts of the past in which historical elements keep company with the implausible and outlandish.

But first a few preliminary remarks about Hittite culture and the nature of the tablet collections found at the capital, Ḫattuša (the modern Turkish village of Boğazköy or Boğazkale), may be in order. Ḫatti, as the Hittites themselves referred to their polity, was a multicultural civilization, arising from the melding of an indigenous Hattic culture based on its own language (Klinger 1996) with elements introduced into Anatolia by Indo-European immigrants, probably sometime in the early third millennium BCE. The newcomers themselves contributed at least three new tongues to the mix (Melchert 1995, 2003: 10–22): Hittite, the language of administration; Luwian, which was predominant in the south and west; and the poorly attested Palaic.

As a result of the influence of Assyrian merchant settlements established in their midst during the nineteenth and eighteenth centuries BCE (Orlin 1970), and as a consequence of the campaigns of their early kings in northern Syria in the seventeenth century (Bryce 1998: 75–87, 101–5), the Hittites were drawn into the cultural orbit of Mesopotamia, adopting many aspects of Sumerian and Akkadian civilization along with the cuneiform writing system. These borrowings included the use of the Akkadian language for some prestige and educational purposes, and limited study of Sumerian in the course of scribal instruction (Beckman 1983). Further complicating the picture is the intermediary role played in the diffusion of Mesopotamian culture by the Hurrians, an ethnic group and speech community that occupied much of northern Mesopotamia and Syria in the second millennium (Hoffner 1998b; Wilhelm 1989).

Hittite cuneiform texts, the great bulk of which have been recovered from the single site of Ḫattuša (Pedersén 1998: 42–80), were composed exclusively for the use of the royal administration, in the widest sense. We find in Ḫatti none of the private records of individual families so abundant for certain periods of Babylonian history. Since the Hittite monarch exercised responsibilities as chief priest and judge, in addition to those as head of state and commander-in-chief of the armies (Beckman 1995a), hymns, prayers, and rituals were as relevant to the performance of his duties as were diplomatic and administrative correspondence and historical accounts extolling the great deeds of himself and his predecessors (van den Hout 2002). Even texts employed solely for the instruction of young scribes, as was possibly the case with some belletristic material, may be placed under this rubric, if we consider that it was the school that produced the bureaucrats to whom the king delegated many of his routine tasks (Singer 2003).

2   Ancient Anatolian Poetry

Since singing an established composition implies reproducing relatively fixed wording often coordinated to music with a rhythmic and perhaps a melodic pattern, the first place to look for poetry among the tablets of the Hittites is in those texts labeled "song" – Hittite *ishamai-*, Sumerographic SÌR (Güterbock 1978: 232–3; Hoffner 1998a: 66), and those said to be "sung" (*ishamiya-*, "to sing," Akkadographic *ZAMĀRU*; note also *ishamatalla-*, "singer"). Indeed, the etymological kinship of this family of words with *ishiya-*, "to tie, bind" (Puhvel 1984–: 2.394–5) betrays its association with "bound" language.

Songs attested in the Hittite archives (de Martino 1995: 2662–3) include the brief "Song of the war-god" (Beckman 1995b: 25, rev. lines 14–15) and "Clothes of Nesa" (Soysal 1987: 181), as well as the more substantial myths of the Kumarbi Cycle (see below, section 4.1) and the Hurro-Hittite bilingual "Song of Release" (section 4.2). Particularly intriguing is the Luwian "Wilusiad" (Watkins 1995: 146–9), which might have presented an Anatolian analogue to the Homeric *Iliad*. Unfortunately, this composition is known only from its incipit: "When they came from steep Wilusa [= Troy?]." Neither hymns and prayers (Singer 2002) nor antiphonal chants employed in worship need detain us here where we are concerned solely with "epic."

The difficulties in even recognizing, let alone analyzing, verse in the cuneiform texts of Ḫatti are substantial (Carruba 1998: 67–9): the cuneiform script was not well adapted for the precise rendering of the phonology of Indo-European languages, the scribes made liberal use of ideograms that mask underlying words, and furthermore they failed to indicate breaks between lines of poetry through punctuation or line division. Nonetheless, patient study of the Old Hittite song "Clothes of Neša" has revealed some of the basic principles of meter and stress employed in Hittite poetry (Melchert 1998; see also the pioneering work of McNeill 1963, Durnford 1971, and Eichner 1993). In this dirge, at least, each line consists of equal lines of four stresses, divisible into two cola:

> *Nesas wáspus Nesas wáspus // tíya–mu tíya*
> *nu=mu ánnas=mas kattan árnut // tíya=mu tíya*
> *nu=mu úwas=mas kattan árnut // tíya=mu tíya*
>
> Clothes of Neša, clothes of Neša – bind on me, bind!
> Bury me down with my mother – bind on me, bind!
> Bury me down with my nurse(?) – bind on me, bind!

Unfortunately, it has not been possible to detect this or any other pattern employed consistently in the longer Hittite-language songs (Güterbock 1951: 141–4). Indeed, it may be the case that verse was used only sporadically in these texts, perhaps in order to highlight dramatic moments in the exposition (Carruba 1998: 84–7). However, the songs do share certain other stylistic features (de Vries 1967), such as the use of a small number of set scenes (the departure of a messenger, the preparation of a banquet, a father's recognition of parentage and bestowal of a name upon a child (Hoffner 1968)), the verbatim repetition of messages, and the introduction of speech by a formula restricted to literary contexts (*memiskiuwan dais*, "began to speak"). Each composition also seemingly begins with a formal proemium, although this section has been badly damaged or lost in several instances.

For Luwian and Hattic verse, see Eichner 1993: section 3 and section 7, respectively, and for our scant knowledge of Hurrian verse, consult Neu 1988: 246–8.

3 Fantastic Narrative Involving Humans

With the exception of the cult stories discussed in section 3.1, the tales included under this rubric all originated outside of Ḫatti, either in Mesopotamia or in a Hurrian milieu.

3.1 The conflict of the Storm-god with the serpent Illuyanka (the Hittite common noun for "snake") is presented in two versions (Laroche 1971: no. 321; Beckman 1982; Hoffner 1998a: 10–14), which are embedded within a ritual context, namely the Hattic *purulli*-festival. The text states explicitly that the stories are to be recited by a priest in the course of the proceedings. In a classic mythological expression of the alternation of the seasons, each tale begins with the triumph of the serpent over the god upon whose rains the flourishing of nature was dependent. The Storm-god is ultimately able to defeat his rival to regain the dominant position in the world – and in one instance his physical integrity – only with the assistance of a mortal, who soon perishes as a result of his too-intimate association with the divine. Thus a basic belief of the Hittites is communicated symbolically: every deity and every human being has an essential role to play in the functioning of the universe (and in the microcosm of society), but the individual must remain in his or her proper station.

3.2 Legends of the Sargonic kings. The monarchs of the dynasty founded by Sargon of Akkad in the late twenty-fourth century BCE not only lived on in the historical imagination of Mesopotamia (Liverani 1993), but were also of great importance in the traditions of those neighboring cultures, like that of Ḫatti, that entered the cultural orbit of Babylonia and Assyria (Beckman 2001b). Sargon himself became the very model of a successful ruler and conqueror, while his grandson Narām-Sîn was (inaccurately) remembered as the exemplar of a hubristic king punished for his impiety with failure in battle and the collapse of his realm.

3.2.1 *šar tamḫari*, "King of Battle," which celebrates a fictional campaign of Sargon to the city of Purušḫanda in the heart of Anatolia, is known in an Akkadian-language version from Tell el-Amarna in Egypt, as well as from Nineveh and Aššur in Assyria (Izre'el 1997: 66–75, 87–8; Westenholz 1997: 102–39). In a fragmentary Hittite-language recension found at Boğazköy (Laroche 1971: no. 310; edition Güterbock 1969), the greater part of the preserved lines describes the occupation of Purušḫanda by the Akkadian army and the felling of trees there in order to erect monuments to the conqueror and his goddess Ištar. Over the course of events both Sargon and his opponent Nurdaḫḫi (= Nūr-Dagan) come into direct contact with deities, from whom they receive foreknowledge of the outcome of their war.

3.2.2 Traditions concerning Narām-Sîn. One of the problems that arise in the evaluation of works of cuneiform literature is that the available manuscripts are usually incomplete and quite often unique. Therefore it is frequently necessary to supplement the text under consideration with material from duplicate or parallel tablets from other sites. This is the situation in regard to the sources at Ḫattuša dealing with Narām-Sîn. Among the Hittite archives were recovered two badly damaged clay prisms bearing a variant of the Akkadian-language saga of the king's struggle against fearsome hordes, "before whom humankind fled into caves" (edition Westenholz 1997: 280–93), as well as several Hittite-language fragments of the same composition (edition Güterbock 1938: 49–65; cf. Hoffner 1970).

These enemies are so awe-inspiring that the king devises a test to determine if they are even human: do they bleed when pricked? Even though a gash indeed brings forth blood, the invaders proceed to rout several Mesopotamian armies. And no wonder: in one of the few intelligible paragraphs of the Akkadian recension the god Ea takes responsibility before his fellow deities for creating these monstrous troops. From the better-preserved first-millennium edition, reconstructed from eight scattered manuscripts (Westenholz 1997: Text 22), we find confirmation that the terrifying marauders are indeed superhuman, and learn that their raid is intended as a divine rebuke to the arrogance of Narām-Sîn.

A second composition, known at Ḫattuša only in Hittite, also features the junior Sargonic ruler, this time confronted with a revolt of many lands against his authority (Laroche 1971: no. 311; edition Güterbock 1938: 66–80). Although little beyond a fragmentary list of rebels is preserved in the Boğazköy material, an Akkadian version, probably from Sippar in Mesopotamia (Westenholz 1997: Text 17), indicates that one of the enemy was a personage "neither flesh nor blood."

3.3 The Tale of Gurparazaḫ (Laroche 1971: no. 362; edition Daddi 2003), the name of whose protagonist is formed with the Hurrian term for the Tigris River (Aranzaḫ), has thus far been attested solely in the Hittite archives, although its setting is the city of Akkad, capital of the Sargonic kings. The broken text reveals a number of folkloristic elements: Gurparazaḫ seemingly wins the hand of a princess as a result of his prowess in hunting, and then defeats "60 kings, 70 young men" in an archery contest.

3.4 Anatolian versions of the Epic of Gilgameš (Laroche 1971; no. 341; see Chapter 15, by Noegel). The story of the mighty deeds of Gilgameš, his quest for immortality, and his ultimate acceptance of the human condition was widely disseminated throughout the ancient Near East. At Boğazköy, tales of the Mesopotamian hero and his companion Enkidu have been recovered in the original Akkadian language, as well as in Hurrian and Hittite adaptations. This literary complex was probably brought to the Hittite capital as part of the scribal curriculum, but it is possible that the royal court was also treated to recitations of the Hittite version (Beckman 2003: 37–8).

3.4.1 Fragments of two Akkadian editions have been recognized (edition George 2003: 306–26). Both, to judge from their script, were probably inscribed in Anatolia, rather than imported in the baggage of some visiting Assyrian or Babylonian scribal instructor. The earlier edition (fourteenth century) is in substantial agreement with the text known from Mesopotamia in the Old Babylonian period, while the later (thirteenth century) shows greater similarities to the "canonical" Twelve-Tablet Version of the neo-Assyrian royal libraries.

3.4.2 The Hurrian adaptation of Gilgameš (Salvini 1988: 157–60) was of considerable length, as indicated by the colophon on one of the surviving fragments ("fourteenth tablet, unfinished"). Of the 3,000 or more lines of text originally present, only around 450 have been preserved. Unfortunately, our knowledge of the Hurrian language is still so rudimentary that a meaningful comparison with other realizations of the Gilgameš story is impossible.

3.4.3 The Hittite-language reworking of the Gilgameš epic (editions Otten 1958; Beckman forthcoming; translation Beckman 2001a) involves a change of emphasis from the hero's activities in and around his hometown of Uruk in southern Babylonia to the battle with Ḫumbaba (Ḫuwawa). The cedar forest guarded by this monster was of greater interest to an Anatolian audience, since by this time its location had shifted in the popular imagination from the mountains of western Iran to the Amanus range of nearby Syria. The Hittite text is of particular importance in examining the development of the Gilgameš tradition over the centuries, since it is the best-preserved witness to a crucial stage in the process, one which is but poorly represented by sources from Mesopotamia itself (Beckman 2003: 48–9).

3.5 At Boğazköy the Mesopotamian flood story featuring the culture hero Atraḫasīs, "The Most Wise" (Lambert and Millard 1969), is represented by one Akkadian fragment and two Hittite pieces (Laroche 1971: no. 347; edition Polvani 2003). Little has been preserved of this tale from Ḫattuša, but it is immediately apparent that the Hittite version has introduced a new character to the narrative, the protagonist's father, named Ḫamša, "Five" (Akkadian). Ḫamša seems to have assumed the role played by the god Ea in the Mesopotamian sources, advising Atraḫasīs on how to escape the destruction planned for humankind by Enlil (here Kumarbi).

3.6 The fragmentary Tale of Kešše (Laroche 1971: no. 361) is found among the Boğaz-köy tablets in both a Hittite (edition Friedrich 1950: 234–43; translation Hoffner 1998a: 87–9) and a Hurrian version (Salvini 1988: 160–70), and is represented as well by an Akkadian-language scrap from Tell el-Amarna in Egypt (Izre'el 1997: 17–19). The first portion of the story is lost in all sources; the available Hittite-language text begins with the marriage of the hunter Kešše to a beautiful woman, who soon claims all of his attention: "He listened only to his wife." Chided by his mother for neglecting his duties toward her and the gods, Kešše returns to the field, only to find that the angry deities have hidden his prey. He falls ill, and in his fevered slumber experiences several enigmatic dreams. Here the Hittite version breaks off. The Hurrian text remains largely unintelligible, but does feature the active participation of several deities. The Akkadian fragment is too small to contribute to our understanding.

3.7 The question of a man's legacy lies at the center of the charming *Märchen* of Appu (Laroche 1971: no. 360; editions Friedrich 1950: 214–25; Siegelová 1971: 1–34; translation Hoffner 1998a: 82–7). Appu is the wealthiest person in his community, but long remains childless. Stung by the reproaches of his wife, who blames him for this sorry state of affairs, he approaches the Sun-god, offering in hand. The deity promises the supplicant that the next time he sleeps with his wife he will sire a son. Indeed, Appu's wife gives birth to two boys in succession, who are given the programmatic names "Unjust" and "Just." When the time comes to divide their inheritance, "Unjust" attempts to cheat his brother. The matter is presented for adjudication first to the Sun-god and then to Ištar of Nineveh. Unfortunately, the resolution of the dispute has not been preserved.

3.8 The Story of the Fisherman and the Foundling (Laroche 1971: no. 363; edition Friedrich 1950: 224–33; translation Hoffner 1998a: 85–7) has a similar theme and may indeed be part of a complex narrative including the Appu tale. The anthropomorphic Sun-god impregnates a cow, who delivers and rejects a human child: "Why have I borne this two-legged creature?" Apparently guided by the divine father, a childless fisherman rescues the abandoned baby and plots to convince his neighbors that the infant is his own offspring. The story continued on a further tablet, now lost.

4 Fantastic Narrative Featuring Deities

The texts in this group are all myths of foreign origin, and unlike the native Anatolian mythological material, they are free-standing compositions (Güterbock 1961: 143–4; Beckman 1997b: 565) that most likely had no function in Hittite society beyond their use as the substance of exercises in the scribal academy. Many of these tales are cosmological; no individual human being plays a role here.

4.1 In the Kumarbi Cycle (Lebrun 1995) we find an explanation of the state of the divine hierarchy current in Hittite times. The Storm-god Teššub reigned as king of the gods, having displaced Kumarbi in that role, and having resisted successfully several attempts of the latter to regain his position. Each component of the overarching narrative is known as the "Song" (SÌR) of a particular deity.

4.1.1 The Song of Kumarbi or Kingship in Heaven (Laroche 1971: no. 344; translation Hoffner 1998a: 42–5) is attested in only a pair of mutilated manuscripts, one very small. The text relates the succession of gods at the head of the pantheon:

> Once upon a time Alalu was king in Heaven. Alalu sat upon the throne, while mighty Anu, foremost of the gods, stood before him. He bowed down at his feet and placed the drinking cups in his hand.
> For nine measured years Alalu was king in Heaven, but in the ninth year Anu gave battle to Alalu. He defeated Alalu and he fled before him and went down to the Dark Earth. While he went down to the Dark Earth, Anu took his seat upon the throne. Anu sat upon his throne, and mighty Kumarbi provided him with drink. He bowed down at his feet and placed the drinking cups in his hand.

In turn, Kumarbi rebels against Anu, driving him from the throne. Adding injury to insult, he bites off and swallows the genitals of his predecessor. But Alalu enjoys a sort of revenge: within Kumarbi his seed develops into five gods, among whom are Teššub, his brother Tašmišu, and the Tigris River. It is not entirely clear just how these deities are born from the male Kumarbi, but we do read that Teššub successfully emerges from "the good place." The parentage of the Storm-god is significant: while Alalu is his father, Kumarbi is in a sense his mother! Thus the following supplanting of Kumarbi by Teššub and the repeated efforts of the former to reverse the situation may be understood as a continuing family quarrel.

4.1.2 Although the sequence of his schemes is uncertain, it seems likely that the first of Kumarbi's machinations is related in The Song of the Tutelary Deity (^{d}LAMMA) (Laroche 1971: no. 343; translation Hoffner 1998a: 46–7). Somehow Kumarbi and his ally Ea have elevated the Tutelary Deity to universal rule, with unfortunate results. As Ea complains: "This Tutelary Deity whom we have made king in Heaven – he is hostile and has alienated the lands, so that no one any longer gives bread and drink offerings to the gods!" While the denouement of the story has been lost, there can be little doubt that the upstart is expeditiously removed from his post.

4.1.3 The Song of Silver (Laroche 1971: no. 364; edition Hoffner 1988; translation Hoffner 1998a: 48–50) is in its very fragmentary condition most unclear. A fatherless personage named Silver learns that his sire is none other than Kumarbi. In some manner he becomes king of the gods, displacing Teššub, and commanding the obedience of the Sun and the Moon. How he forfeits this position is lost along with the end of the text.

4.1.4 In the Song of Hedammu (Laroche 1971: no. 348; edition Siegelová 1971: 35–88; translation Hoffner 1998a: 50–5) the role of Kumarbi in instigating a challenge to Teššub is more apparent. He engenders the monstrous, reptilian, Ḫedammu by the daughter of the Sea-god. This creature poses a strong threat to the rule of Teššub until the latter's sister Šaušga (a variety of Ištar) takes matters in hand: she dances by the seashore until she attracts the attention of Ḫedammu. After plying the fearsome creature with strong drink and seducing him, she seemingly disposes of the challenger.

4.1.5 The Song of Ullikummi (Laroche 1971: no. 345; Güterbock 1951, 1952a; Hoffner 1998a: 55–65) is the best-preserved constituent of the Kumarbi cycle and, in three tablets, by far the longest. A Hurrian-language version has also been recovered (Giorgieri 2001). Here Kumarbi once more produces a grotesque child to challenge the Storm-god, this time through sexual intercourse with a great rock. He names his stone offspring Ullikummi, "Oppress (the city of) Kumme" (Hurrian), in reference to the home of Teššub, and conceals him in the midst of the sea. Unseen by Teššub and his allies, Ullikummi grows rapidly into a dangerous giant before he is finally spotted by the Sun-god on his daily journey through the sky. When the troubling news of the challenger's appearance is brought and her brother Teššub weeps in despair, Šaušga attempts to deal with this new agent of destruction. But as she again displays her charms by the sea, a wave asks her:

> For whom are you singing? For whom do you fill your mouth with wind? (This) male is deaf – he does not hear. His eyes are blind – he does not see. He has no mercy. Go away, Šaušga!

The unresponsive nature of Ullikummi, his stony indifference, is surely a countermeasure taken by Kumarbi after the foiling of his plans for Ḫedammu. Thus the sequence of these two songs within the cycle is certain.

Ullikummi defeats the younger gods in an initial battle. But before the final confrontation with the monster, Teššub consults with the wise Ea, who has abandoned his earlier allegiance to Kumarbi. Ea discerns that Ullikummi stands upon the shoulder of the Atlas-like figure Ubelluri and orders the fetching of the primeval saw used long ago to separate Heaven and Earth. Although the text breaks off here, there can be little doubt that once severed from his base, Ullikimmi is overcome, or that Teššub remains king in Heaven. After all, it was the Storm-god, and not Kumarbi, whom the Hurrians and Hittites honored above all other deities.

4.1.6 Only a single fragmentary Hurrian-language tablet has survived of The Song of the Sea (Rutherford 2001), in which is narrated a struggle between Teššub and the Sea-god. Although it almost certainly belongs to the Kumarbi cycle, its precise position among the tales is unclear. It has been suggested that it may be part of the Ḫedammu story.

4.1.7 Several additional fragments may also find their place within this complex (Groddek 2000–2; Archi 2002 = Laroche 1971: no. 351; cf. also Laroche 1971: nos. 346, 352–3).

4.2 The Song of Release, SÌR *parā tarnumas* (edition Neu 1996, who calls it an "Epos"; translation Hoffner 1998a: 67–77), a Hurro-Hittite bilingual preserved in a number of copies, is a tripartite composition. Following the proemium is a collection of seven parables, each characterized as a piece of "wisdom" (Hittite *hattatar*). For example, as translated from the Hittite version:

> A mountain expelled a deer from its expanse (lit. "body"), and the deer went to another mountain. He became fat and he sought a confrontation. He began to curse the mountain: "If

only fire would burn up the mountain on which I graze! If only the Storm-god would smite it (with lightning) and fire burn it up!" When the mountain heard, it became sick at heart, and in response the mountain cursed the deer: "The deer whom I fattened up now curses me in return. Let the hunters bring down the deer! Let the fowlers capture him! Let the hunters take his meat, and the fowlers take his skin!"

It is not a deer, but a human. A certain man who fled from his own town arrived in another land. When he sought confrontation, he began to undertake evil in return for the town (of his refuge), but the gods of the town have cursed him. (Neu 1996: 74–7; Beckman 1997a: 216)

The second section of the song presents the description of a feast in the palace of the goddess of the Underworld, to which the Storm-god Teššub has been invited. The text has unfortunately been truncated by a break, so that its interpretation remains uncertain. Hoffner (1998a: 73) suggests that the gathering symbolizes the reconciliation of the chthonic and celestial deities.

Concluding this complex work is an allegorical narrative in which the sufferings of Teššub as a debt-slave are parallel to those of human bondsmen held by the wealthy citizens of Ebla, a prosperous city in northern Syria. The deity announces to the ruler Megi (lit. "king" in the local Semitic language, but here understood as a proper name) that should the local council not institute a general remission of debts, he will destroy the town. Yet again the end of the story has been lost, but it is likely that the notables rejected the god's demand, for this segment of the song is apparently an aetiology for the ruin of Ebla that actually took place during Ḫatti's Syrian wars of the seventeenth century BCE.

Leaving aside the incomplete second section, the common theme linking the segments of the bilingual seems to be the reinforcement of societal norms, particularly those of gratitude, honesty, and compassion (cf. Archi 1979).

5   Texts about Early History containing Fairy-tale Elements

Such texts were composed only in the Old Hittite period (seventeenth century BCE) (Beckman 1995b: 31–3; Güterbock 1938: 101–13). In this genre we frequently encounter legends at home in particular localities, rather than "national" traditions (Uchitel 1999).

5.1   The best-known example of this type of text is a chronicle of the troubled relations between Ḫattuša and the city of Zalpa, located on the Black Sea coast near the mouth of the Maraššanta (Halys or Kızıl Irmak) River (Laroche 1971: no. 3; edition Otten 1973; partial translation Hoffner 1998a: 81–2; cf. Ünal 1986). Prefaced to an account of warfare stretching over three generations that culminated in the destruction of Zalpa is an anecdote of primordial events, set in the city of Kaneš, an early focal point of Indo-European settlement in Cappadocia:

The queen of Kaneš gave birth to thirty sons in a single year. She said: "What is this – I have produced a horde!" She caulked containers with grease, placed her sons therein, and launched them into the river. The river carried them to the sea, at the land of Zalpa. But the gods took the sons from the sea and raised them.

When years had passed, the queen once more gave birth – to thirty daughters. She raised them herself. The sons were making their way back to Kaneš . . .

A break intervenes soon thereafter, just as the boys, who have retraced their childhood journey along the river, are ignorantly preparing to marry their sisters, despite the misgivings of the youngest son. In a way now unclear, the classic *Märchen* motif of the exposed royal child (cf. Moses, Oedipus, and Sargon of Akkad) is adduced in explanation of the origins of hostility between the regions of central and coastal Anatolia. As far as the damaged text allows a judgment, the ensuing narration of the wars of Zalpa with Ḫattuša contains no further fantastic events.

5.2 The very fragmentary account of the deeds of the early Hurrian ruler Anum-Ḫirbi in southern Anatolia also seems to begin with the abandonment of a baby, who on this occasion is rescued by a herdsman and his animals (Laroche 1971: no. 2; Helck 1983: 272–5; Ünal 1986: 132–5; Uchitel 1999: 62–4).

5.3 The Puḫanu Chronicle (Laroche 1971: no. 16; edition Soysal 1987, cf. 1999: 110–37; partial translation Hoffner 1997) is a narration of Hittite campaigns in Syria and against a Hurrian foe, much of it spoken by the otherwise unattested Puḫanu. The text is, as so often with this material, fragmentary and enigmatic. Along with the reported speech of gods, the Hittite monarch, and lesser mortals (including the song "Clothes of Neša" discussed in section 2 above), we find an aetiology for the existence of a pass through the Taurus mountains between Anatolia and Syria:

> He [the Storm-god?] became a bull, and his horns were a bit cracked. I ask him (the king?) why his horns are cracked, and he says: "When I used to go on campaign, the mountains were difficult for us. But this bull was strong, and when he came along, he lifted that mountain, turning it aside, so that we conquered the sea(coast). Therefore his horns are cracked."

5.4 Also set in northern Syria is the very incomplete composition known to scholars as the "Menschenfresser (Cannibal) Text" (Laroche 1971: no. 17; edition Güterbock 1938: 104–13; cf. Soysal 1988, 1999: 137–45). Mentioned among cities and peoples well known for this region in the early second millennium (Aleppo, Ilanzura, Suteans) is a population under the leadership of a man called "Mighty Son of the Steppe." Of this group it is said: "If they spot a fat man, they kill him and eat him up!" This fate indeed befalls an unfortunate woman later on in the story. Although some writers have understood this reported cannibalism as realistic ethnographic description, there can be little doubt that we are dealing here with a folkloristic motif.

FURTHER READING

Many of the texts discussed here have been translated in Hoffner 1998a, and others may be found in volume 1 of Hallo's *The Context of Scripture* (1997). In addition, see Archi 2002; Groddek 2000–2, Polvani 2003; and Rutherford 2001. Beckman 2003 discusses the reception of the Gilgameš tradition by the Hittites.

Comprehensive introductions to Hittite mythology are Beckman 1997b and Güterbock 1961 and 1978.

On the difficult question of Hittite meter and poetic form, see Carruba 1998; Durnford 1971; Eichner 1993; McNeill 1963; and Melchert 1998.

CHAPTER EIGHTEEN

Persian/Iranian Epic

Olga M. Davidson

The poet Ferdowsi, whose name means "man of paradise" in Persian, was reportedly born in Ṭôs, a city of Khorâsân province in the eastern sector of medieval Iran. He is credited with the creation of a monumental Persian epic poem known as the *Shâhnâma*, "Book of Kings," over 50,000 couplets in length, which was reportedly completed around 1010 CE. This poem is considered the epic of Iranian civilization. (See Davidson 1994 for an overall analysis. Quotations of *Shâhnâma* follow Bertels 1960–71 in numbering vols., pp., lines.)

Although there were other Persian epics besides the *Shâhnâma* of Ferdowsi, it is this poem that is recognized in Persian culture as Iranian epic par excellence. The nearest competitor was the *Garshâspnâma* of Asadi, completed about 1056 CE. Moreover, from the standpoint of classical Persian literature, this epic defines the very concept of an Iranian empire. Linguistically, "Persian" epic is defined by "Old Persian" (the time-frame is the Achaemenid dynasty, 559 BCE to 330 BCE), "Middle Persian" (Sasanian dynasty, *ca.* 224 CE to 651 CE), and "New Persian" (Islamic period, after *ca.* 652 CE). Culturally, a more appropriate term is "Iranian," referring to the realities and the ideologies of the Iranian empire.

Persian/Iranian epic traditions basically tell the story of this Iranian empire, envisaged as a continuous succession of kings. Here we see the basis of the name *Shâhnâma*, which literally means "Book of Kings." Although Ferdowsi represents the most canonical version of the *Shâhnâma*, both the concept and the reality of a Book of Kings precedes him, as we will see.

The *Shâhnâma* of Ferdowsi reflects the notional history of the Iranian empire before Islam by telling the stories, or *dâstâns*, of a canonical number of fifty pre-Islamic kings or *shâhs*, beginning with the very first king of the world, the mythical Gayomars, who is the *shâh* at the time of creation, and ending with the last of the Sasanian *shâhs*, Yazdgerd (632–51 CE), who died only a few years after the Islamic conquest of Iran. The *Shâhnâma* divides these fifty *shâhs* into four dynasties: Pishdâdians, Keyânids, Ashkânians, and Sasanians. The first two dynasties, especially the first, are grounded in myth, but the last two are "historical" to the extent that they do coincide with the history of pre-Islamic Iran as we know it.

As we can see from an overview of the contents of the *Shâhnâma*, its story of the four dynasties is narrated as a notional totality. The Pishdâdians are traced back to primordial times and are said to last for 2,441 years. There are ten *shâhs*, the first being Gayomars, the prototype of all humankind. He incurs the jealousy of Ahriman, the exponent of Evil, who attacks him and kills his son. Gayomars is followed by Hushang, his grandson, who introduces agriculture. The next *shâh* is Tahmuras, who subdues the archfiend Ahriman and the *divs*, demonlike figures who ally themselves with Ahriman in hopes of overthrowing the social order established by Ahura Mazdâ, the exponent of Good. Tahmuras is followed by Jamshid, who organizes society into four classes: (1) priests, (2) warriors, (3) farmers, and (4) artisans. He rules in peace and prosperity, but his good fortune makes him so arrogant that he likens himself to divinity. Jamshid is punished for his excess by losing his *farr*, "luminous glory," the visible sign of kingly grace that accompanies rulers and entitles them to reign with success. With no *farr*-bearing king, Iran falls into the hands of the evil oppressor, Ẓaḥḥâk. Faridun, with the aid of a smith called Kâva, overthrows Ẓaḥḥâk and chains him inside Mount Alborz, where he must stay until the eschatological moment of reckoning.

Faridun has three sons, Salm, Tur, and Iraj, and he divides his kingdom, ostensibly the world, among the three of them. Salm gets the western realms; Tur gets the north and east, namely China and Turân, the second of which is a mythologized realm that will figure prominently in the discussion that follows; and Iraj gets Iran, which is considered the center of the world and therefore the choice territory. Jealous because Iraj inherited Iran, Salm and Tur murder him. Manuchehr, the grandson of Iraj, avenges his grandfather by killing both Salm and Tur, thus becoming the next *shâh*.

During the reign of Manuchehr, Zâl, son of Sâm, is born; he is rejected by his father because of his white hair. Exposed on a mountain, Zâl is raised by a magical bird, the Simorgh. Sâm later reclaims his son Zâl, who, after a long courtship, marries Rudâba, a descendant of the evil Ẓaḥḥâk himself; Rudâba and Zâl conceive Rostam, the primary heroic figure of the *Shâhnâma*.

The second of the four dynasties in the Book of Kings, the Keyânid, consists of ten *shâhs* and lasts for 732 years. After a period featuring no *farr*-bearing *shâh* on the throne, the hero Rostam is sent out to fetch Key Qobâd, who is said to be of princely origin. He finds Key Qobâd sitting on a throne by a stream under Mount Alborz. Seeing that Key Qobâd has the bearings of *farr*, Rostam brings him back to Iran to be the *shâh*. Key Qobâd begins the Keyânid dynasty. He is succeeded by his son Key Kâus, phlegmatic, arrogant, unpredictable. The reign of Key Kâus is marked by chaos, and many a time is Rostam compelled to come to his rescue. Though Rostam has as much difficulty in respecting Key Kâus as Achilles has with Agamemnon in the Homeric *Iliad*, he is loyal enough to sacrifice the life of his own son, Sohrâb, for the sake of the Iranian throne. During the reign of Key Kâus there is continuous warfare against Iran's archenemy, the land of Turân, led by Afrâsiyâb, king of the Turanians.

Key Kâus and Afrâsiyâb share a grandson called Key Khosrow, who becomes the next Iranian *shâh*. This *shâh* is thus of both Iranian and Turanian descent. Famed for his wisdom and nobility, Key Khosrow is the *shâh* who finally ends the fiendish Afrâsiyâb's life. Shortly after defeating Afrâsiyâb, he vanishes from public view, choosing the life of a hermit, having already left instructions that a distant relative, Lohrâsp, should succeed him as *shâh*.

The reign of Lohrâsp is followed by that of his son, Goshtâsp. This succession happens prematurely in that Goshtâsp, in his eagerness for the crown, had put pressure on his father Lohrâsp to abdicate before the fullness of time. Despite this characterization of rashness, Goshtâsp is treated with reverence in the *Shâhnâma* inasmuch as his reign marks both the coming of Zoroaster and the prophet's acceptance by both king and empire. At a later point, King Goshtâsp is in turn threatened by his son Esfandiyâr, who shows a similar impatience for the crown. Such impatience eventually leads Esfandiyâr into an inevitable confrontation with Rostam, who is faced with the awkward situation of having to abandon his conventional role of defending the crown, as is always expected of him, and being forced either to kill Prince Esfandiyâr or to lose face. Rostam does indeed kill the future *shâh* Esfandiyâr. When it finally happens, however many earlier times Rostam may have been tempted to kill any of the *shâhs* that he had served, this killing of the king by the kingmaker is conceived by the *Shâhnâma* of Ferdowsi as a fundamentally unnatural act. This deed seals Rostam's own fate: he is to die prematurely, and in the end he is murdered by his half-brother.

With the death of Rostam, the *Shâhnâma* shifts into a narrative mode that becomes ever less mythical and more historical as the tales about the kings begin to coincide more and more with what the Persian and Arab chroniclers report – and with what we ourselves interpret as historical facts. After Goshtâsp, a series of successive *shâhs* culminates with Dârâ the Second (Darius), who is overthrown by Sekandar, that is, Alexander the Great. Although the historical Alexander in fact posed a threat to the very fabric of Iranian society by overthrowing the authority of its kings, dividing the empire among feudal lords, and undermining all that is sacred to Zoroastrianism, he is nevertheless treated with sympathy in the *Shâhnâma*. Ferdowsi's poem highlights the legendary life of Alexander and portrays him as a legitimate ruler of Iran, the true son of Dârâ the First – the son that Dârâ never knew he had. Here, then, is a clear example where epic mythmaking reshapes history to serve its own purposes.

The third of the four dynasties celebrated by the *Shâhnâma* is called the Ashkânian, which is described as lasting for 200 years. In this version of dynastic succession, there is hardly any trace of the historical reality of the Seleucid dynasty, descended from Seleucus, one of Alexander's generals. Also, there are only fleeting references to the Arsacids, considered heirs to Alexander. The *Shâhnâma* merely focuses on one branch of the decentralized Arsacids, namely, the Ashkânians, inasmuch as they were the strongest of the Arsacid feudal principalities, ruling over western and central Iran and controlling Babylonia. In effect, the *Shâhnâma* collapses a succession of eleven historical Arsacid kings into one figure, King Ardavân, making him the successor of Alexander. The entirety of the Seleucid and Arsacid dynasties is attributed to him alone. This way, the narrative of the *Shâhnâma* maintains the flow of the Book of Kings as a succession of sovereignty without any interruption of centralized government. The very idea of such interruption would have been utterly alien to the Iranian social order.

The fourth and last dynasty that the *Shâhnâma* celebrates is the Sasanian, described as lasting for 501 years and comprised of a succession of twenty-nine *shâhs*. Ardavân the Ashkânian is overthrown by Ardashir Pâpagân, a vassal king from the House of Sâsân. Ardashir is the great-grandson of Shâh Goshtâsp, and he is therefore of Keyânid descent. He founds the Sasanian dynasty and is succeeded by twenty-eight *shâhs*, the last one being Yazdgerd.

With the death of Yazdgerd and the fall of the Sasanian dynasty, historically dated at 651 CE, the *Shâhnâma* comes to an end. Thus the poem stops precisely at the time of the Islamic conquest, where the history of Islamic Iran begins. This beginning inaugurates the social milieu of the poet Ferdowsi himself.

After the Islamic conquest, the historical Iran at first ceases to be an empire ruled by *shâhs*. Still, after a difficult period of Arab-centered rule by caliphs, the rudiments of empire return, albeit in strikingly different shapes and sizes. New dynasties appear, the major ones being the Buyids in the West (932–1062 CE) and the Ghaznavids in the East (977–1186 CE). Our interest centers on the Ghaznavids, a dynasty of newcomers descended from Turkic invaders, and on one particularly powerful ruler in this dynastic line, the Sultan Mahmud of Ghazna (998–1030 CE). It was under the reign of this Mahmud that Ferdowsi is said to have completed the *Shâhnâma*.

The *Shâhnâma*, as a medium meant to be performed, underwent countless transformations in the lengthy history of its transmission over the centuries. Even as late as the fifteenth century CE, in the era of Shâh Bâysonghor Mirza, we find indications that the *Shâhnâma* was still being performed in a wide variety of versions stemming from a commensurately wide variety of locales. The recension of the *Shâhnâma* commissioned by Bâysonghor and completed in 1426 BCE involved the collecting and collating of a mass of manuscripts, and the variety they revealed is vividly described in the Preface to the Bâysonghori Recension. As the narrative of the Preface makes clear, the *Shâhnâma* lived on in live performances (on which see Chapter 4, by Jensen).

Until recent times, in fact, the *Shâhnâma* has survived by way of performance in oral tradition. The medium of transmission is the professional storytelling, *naqqâli*, of the *Shâhnâma* as it is performed in the Iran of recent times (Page 1977). The word for the professional storyteller is *naqqâl*, meaning literally "transmitter".

The traditional social context for such performances was a setting of coffee- and tea-houses. A German traveler, Adam Olearius, describes such a coffee-house in his account, dated 1631–2 CE, of the main square in Iṣfahan:

> The coffee-house is an inn in which smokers of tobacco and drinkers of coffee-water are found. In such inns are also found poets and historians whom I have seen sitting inside on high stools and have heard telling all manner of legends, fables, poeticized things. While narrating they conjure up images by gestures with a little wand, much as magicians play tricks. (Olearius 1656: 558; my translation)

While the older phases of the poetry of the *Shâhnâma* reflect the era of the Sultan Mahmud of Ghazna, the signs of whose patronage are still embedded in that poetry, newer phases, when the poetry was no longer tied to this patronage, could be accommodated over the centuries through the accretion of themes that dramatize a pattern of opposition – or at least indifference – on the part of Ferdowsi toward the patronage of Mahmud. This way, the poetic legacy of Ferdowsi is legitimated *through time*, from one phase to the next in the history of its overall reception.

This pattern of legitimation works not only forwards but also backwards in time, reaching into the traditions of pre-Islamic Iran. Though the *Shâhnâma* of Ferdowsi was created in the Islamic Iran of the early part of eleventh century, both its narrative time-frame and even its orientation are pre-Islamic. This orientation reflects at least in part the Zoroastrian worldview of the old empire. As we can see from the internal evidence of the *Shâhnâma*, this poetry integrates and promotes the legitimizing of poetic traditions that we can trace back to such a Zoroastrian provenance (Davidson 1994: 42–53).

Ferdowsi describes his pre-Islamic poetic sources in terms that suit both oral and written traditions. The oral traditions are represented as stylized performances by learned men called *môbads* and *dehqâns*, while the written traditions are attributed to an archetypal *Book of Kings* written in Pahlavi, the language of the Sasanian empire.

It has been thought that the book claimed as a source by Ferdowsi actually goes back to the Pahlavi *Khwatây-nâmak*, the equivalent of the Persian *Khodâynâma*, "Book of Lords," originally commissioned by King Yazdgerd (632–51 CE).

On the surface, Ferdowsi's own references to a prototypical *Shâhnâma* as an archetypal book seem to contradict the argument that Ferdowsi's poetry is the product of an oral tradition. In terms of the cultural background of the *Shâhnâma*, however, oral poetry is basically not incompatible with literacy, as represented by the archetypal book. The cross-cultural evidence of social anthropology suggests that no universalized formulation can be made about the phenomenon of literacy: in some societies, literacy erodes the traditions of oral poetry, whereas in others, these traditions may remain unaffected (see Zumthor 1983). There is therefore no justification in assuming a priori that the poetry of Ferdowsi is not oral poetry, or that it is some kind of "semi-oral" poetry, solely on the grounds that the *Shâhnâma* refers to itself as a book in the making (see Zumthor 1983: 34 on "semi-oral" poetry). Moreover, the poetic phraseology of Ferdowsi, even in contexts where it refers to the medium of writing, reveals characteristics typical of oral poetry (Davidson 1988).

In the historical context of Ferdowsi's world of medieval Persian poetry, the idea of an archetypal book as his source is not at odds with the idea of listening to the performances of *môbads* and *dehqâns* as an alternative source. In fact, the two sources are envisioned not as alternatives but as different ways of saying the same thing. The stylized descriptions of performances by *môbads* and *dehqâns*, evoking the idea of oral poetic traditions, are matched by an equally stylized description of the genesis of the Pahlavi Book of Kings, which the poet claims as his written source. Ferdowsi's description of this genesis amounts to a myth-made stylization of oral poetry (Davidson 1994: 48, 2000: 46–58). The story is told that a noble sage, born of the *dehqâns*, assembles *môbads* from all over Iran, each possessing a "fragment" of a pre-existing ancient book. Each *môbad* recites his portion and, in this way, this ancient but once "fragmented" book is wondrously reassembled (*Shâhnâma* I 21.126–36).

It is implicit in this passage that the authority of the unified empire and of the unified Book of Kings is one. The key to this essentially Zoroastrian concept of the empire is to be found in the traditional role of the *môbad*. In a Zoroastrian document known as the *Selections of Zâtspram* (23.5), the idealized Iranian empire of the supreme god Ohrmazd is visualized as one in which every district is represented by a *mogbad*, "high priest" (Pahlavi for *môbad*), who is the guarantor of truth (see Molé 1963: 338 for the text and trans.). It appears that the "truth" of the *môbad* is a foundation for the structure of the empire just as it is a foundation for the structure of the poetry that glorifies the empire.

As for the *dehqân*, "landowner," he is the "authority" not only in a given locale but he actually validates the traditions of that given locale (Davidson 1994: 35). In fact, Nezâmi in his *Chahâr Maqâla* reports that Ferdowsi himself was a *dehqân* (Qazvini and Mo'in 1953: 74).

In short, Ferdowsi's claimed control over both oral and written traditions is an expression of authority derived primarily from oral poetic traditions. Ferdowsi's poetic tradition was an oral tradition in its own right, and his *Shâhnâma* was transmitted – even beyond his own lifetime – not only in writing but also in live performance.

The internal evidence of the *Shâhnâma* about its pre-Islamic oral origins can be supplemented by the external evidence of prose prefaces attached to the manuscripts of Ferdowsi's *Shâhnâma*. To be highlighted here are two such texts: (1) the so-called Older Preface, dated to the middle of the tenth century CE, and (2) the Bâysonghori Preface, dated to 1426 CE (see also Riyâhi 1993: 170–80). These texts serve to contextualize both the poet Ferdowsi himself and his poetry *through time*, in a variety of historicized settings. Moreover, they reveal patterns of accommodation and coexistence between older and newer traditions in the evolving poetics of the *Shâhnâma*.

Even more explicitly than the poetry of Ferdowsi's *Shâhnâma*, the various prose prefaces that introduce it go out of their way to explain the Zoroastrian background of the *Shâhnâma*, in terms of both patronage and reception. And they do so while all along enfolding this background with a foreground of Islamic worldviews.

The Older Preface (hereafter = OP) is most explicit about this background (the paragraph nos. used below are from the trans. by Minorsky 1964). In Tôs of Khorâsân province, the native city of Ferdowsi, there was a local potentate called Ibn 'Abd al-Razzâk who, in concert with his administrator, Abu Mansur al-Ma'mari, commissioned a Book of Kings (OP §6), which was finished in 957 CE (§7). The Zoroastrian cultural agenda of Ibn 'Abd ar-Razzâk and his administrator, Ma'mari, are carefully and accurately described in the narrative. The Book of Kings that they are said to assemble is notionally based on a "compilation," executed by four wise men, of older books (OP §6). This "compilation" is described in terms that are parallel to a poeticized narrative already cited in the earlier discussion: in the *Shâhnâma* Ferdowsi describes a stylized compilation of an archetypal Book of Kings, executed by a wise man who assembles the *môbads* of the Iranian empire in order to compile this book to end all books (Davidson 2000: 64–5).

The Book of Kings commissioned by Ibn 'Abd ar-Razzâk is supposedly composed in Persian prose (OP §§ 15–16). According to the story, it is only after this prose compos-ition that Ferdowsi is given the opportunity to convert the prose into poetry; his patron is specified as Mahmud of Ghazna (OP §16). In this narrative, there is no explicit time-gap between the "compilation" of the Persian prose version and its subsequent conversion into Persian poetry: "And after they had compiled it in prose, Sultan Mahmud, son of Subuk-tegin, ordered the sage Abu'l-Qâsim Mansur Ferdowsi to turn it into the *dari* [Persian] language in verse, and the circumstances of it will be mentioned at their proper place" (again, OP §16).

According to one theory, this crucial part of the narrative, this climax, is to be dismissed as an "interpolation" (Minorsky 1964: 271). Such a theory devalues the logic of the narrative as a whole. By way of editorial and interpretive excisions, the rhetoric of the Older Preface as an organic whole is thus undone, and the truncated text is then explained as having had a completely different purpose from what the Older Preface itself declares to be its own *raison d'être*, which is, to introduce the poetry of the *Shâhnâma*. According to the theory behind such excisions, the text had been meant to introduce a hypothetical "prose *Shâhnâma*," no longer attested, which supposedly corresponds to the original text commissioned by Ibn 'Abd al-Razzâk.

But the internal logic of the Older Preface requires the predecessor-text of the poetic *Shâhnâma* to be a foil: something very good but not quite so good as the final product. In terms of narrative precedents for what a foil like this should be, it is clear that the predecessor-text has to be in prose, at least in terms of the rhetoric and "poetics" of the narrative. That was the case with the prose Persian *Kalîla and Dimna* of Bal'ami, the predecessor-text for the poetic Persian *Kalîla and Dimna* of Rudaki (OP §5). We see a comparable situation in the case of the "prose" Persian *Shâhnâma*: in terms of the logic that takes shape in the narrative of the Older Preface, just as the *Kalîla and Dimna* has a prose version that is capped by a poetic version, so also the *Shâhnâma* must have a prose version as a predecessor-text of the poetic *Shâhnâma* of Ferdowsi. Such a rhetorical build-up, where a prose *Shâhnâma* commissioned by Ibn 'Abd al-Razzâk becomes a stepping stone leading to even bigger and better things, would make sense from the standpoint of a later era marked by a poetic *Shâhnâma* commissioned by Mahmud of Ghazna.

This is not to say that there never existed a prose *Shâhnâma* commissioned by Ibn 'Abd al-Razzâk as potentate of Tôs. But it is to say that the Older Preface narrative about such a commissioning of a prose *Shâhnâma* is inextricably tied to the Older Preface narrative about the conversion of this prose into poetry by Ferdowsi as poet of Tôs. Thus the narrative of the Older Preface rhetorically motivates the *Shâhnâma* of Ferdowsi, not the earlier "prose *Shâhnâma*" that serves as its foil (Davidson 2000: 64–5).

The question remains whether the "prose *Shâhnâma*" mentioned in the narrative of the Older Preface must have been Ferdowsi's actual source. It has been shown that Ferdowsi was not confined to any single textual source, and that he had free access to other "sources" as well, most notably to contemporary oral traditions of the "Book of Kings" traditions. Moreover, the historicized narrative of the Older Preface, centering on the idea of putting pieces together to reconstitute a lost totality, is as we have seen parallel to Ferdowsi's own poeticized narrative concerning the genesis of the Book of Kings.

A similar idea is recapitulated in the Bâysonghori Preface (hereafter = BP) (the para-graph numbering below follows Riyâhi 1993). According to the narrative of the Bâysonghori Preface, it was Shâh Khosrow I Anôshirvân (531–79 CE) who commissioned an archetypal collection of popular stories concerning ancient kings, emanating from all the provinces in the Iranian empire (BP pp. 368–9). The narrative goes further: the last *shâh* of the pre-Islamic Sasanian empire, Yazdgerd (632–51 CE), commissioned the *dehqân* Dâneshvar to put together the Book of Kings (BP p. 369). On the basis of such parallel versions as narrated in the Bâysonghori Preface, involving two different generations of kings commissioning two different "prototypical" Book of Kings, it can be argued that the version of the Older Preface, even if it has a historical basis, conforms to a narrative strategy that keeps revalidating the Book of Kings by way of explaining its "origins." The version of the Older Preface where the man who commissions the Book of Kings is not a king but a local potentate, counts as a variant in its own right.

To be contrasted with the "historicized" specificity of the Older Preface narrative about the genesis of the Book of Kings is the poeticized universalism of Ferdowsi's own narrative about the archetypal Book of Kings. The same kind of universalism is achieved in the narrative of the Bâysonghori Preface not by way of generalizing several different versions, as in the case of Ferdowsi's own narrative about the genesis of the Book of Kings, but rather by way of including the widest possible variety of different versions. Just as the recension commissioned by Shâh Bâysonghor is markedly inclusive in its synthesis of textual variants, the Preface of the Bâysonghori Recension is likewise inclusive in its synthesis of narratological variants. The Bâysonghori Preface synthesizes the different versions of the story about the genesis of the Book of Kings as a way of explaining the genesis of the Bâysonghori text itself.

By contrast with the Bâysonghori Preface, the Older Preface particularizes one version. Even so, there are a number of important parallels between the universalizing Bâysonghori Preface and the particularizing Older Preface. Most important is the parallelism centering on the trope of representing the art of making poetry as equivalent to the "event" of turning prose into poetry. The parallels between the tropes of the Older Preface and the Bâysonghori Preface emerge from a juxtaposition of the narratives. In what follows, we see two paragraphs presenting the raw narratological material for such a juxtaposition. The first of the two paragraphs is a paraphrase of the narrative in the Older Preface, which is brief and simple; the second paragraph paraphrases the relevant narrative in the Bâysonghori Preface, which is enormously long and complex.

1. In the Older Preface, the "event" of turning the prose of the Book of Kings into poetry can be paraphrased in a single narratological layer: the prose Book of Kings, as compiled by Abu Mansur al-Ma'mari at the behest of Abu Mansur 'Abd al-Razzâk and as translated into Persian by four distinct wise men (OP §6), is turned into poetry by Ferdowsi, as commissioned by Mahmud of Ghazna (OP §17).

2. In the Bâysonghori Preface, by contrast, this "event" can only be paraphrased in multiple layers. The prose Book of Kings is compiled by Abu Mansur al-Ma'marî at the behest of Abu Mansur 'Abd al-Razzâk b. 'Abd-Allah b. Farrokh (BP p. 370; his full name no longer matches exactly what is reported by the Older Preface), who in turn acts at the behest of Ya'qub of the Saffarid dynasty of Khorâsân. In other words, Ma'mari and 'Abd al-Razzâk do not get full credit in the narrative. It is said that this Ya'qub of the Saffarid dynasty of Khorâsân had acquired the "original" Pahlavi version *by sending an envoy to fetch it from India* (BP p. 370); this version of the Book of Kings is said to originate from the Book of Kings that had been compiled by the aforementioned *dehqân* Dâneshvar and commissioned by King Yazdgerd. That older Book of Kings had been plundered from the king's treasury at the time of the Arab conquest and was then brought to the Caliph, who rejected it (BP pp. 369–70); now it gets allotted to the

people of Abyssinia, and its fame spreads throughout Abyssinia and India (BP p. 370). So, according to the story, it is from India that the "original" Book of Kings version makes its comeback to Iran (again, BP p. 370). This version of the Book of Kings is then translated into Persian prose, at the initiative of 'Abd al-Razzâk, who as we have seen is ordered to do so by his superior, Ya'qub of the Saffarid dynasty, and to this new version is now added all that happened between the reigns of Khosrow Parviz and Yazdgerd himself, so that the Book of Kings is now updated to cover the whole line of Iranian kings (BP p. 370). This new version is combined with four other versions, emanating from the authority of four distinct wise men, and the project is finished in 970 CE (BP p. 370, as opposed to 957 CE, the date given in the Older Preface). Copies of this new version thereafter proliferate throughout Khorâsân and Iraq. The patronage of the Book of Kings then passes from the dynasty of the Saffarids to that of the Samanids, who commission the poet Daqiqi to turn the prose of the Book into poetry. But the dynasty of the Samanids is then cut short, and there is a transfer of power to Mahmud of Ghazna; correlatively, the life of the poet Daqiqi is cut short, and the turning of prose to poetry is interrupted (Daqiqi gets only as far as one or two thousand lines: BP p. 370). At the court of Mahmud, the West Iranian poet Khor Firuz from Fars takes up where the East Iranian Daqiqi left off. Like Daqiqi, Khor Firuz has his own engagements with the turning of the prose of the Book of Kings into poetry; there follows an extended narrative about this poet's adventures and poetic feats at the court of Mahmud, including interactions with the court poet of Ghazna, 'Onsori (BP pp. 370–4). Then, at long last, the narrative approaches its climax. Another East Iranian poet, Ferdowsi, enters the scene, and from here on this figure dominates the rest of the narrative and earns his poetic name, "poet of paradise," in the process (BP pp. 374–418). Before this core of the "Life of Ferdowsi" gets underway, however, the narrative pauses to offer a supplementary catalogue of further textual sources that Mahmud collects to augment the repertoire of his Book of Kings (BP p. 375). After this final narratological motivation of the poet's sources, the story of the poet's actual life can begin in earnest. This final story, once it is told, becomes of course the ultimate narratological motivation of Ferdowsi's authority as the definitive poet of the Book of Kings.

The enormity of the second of these two paragraphs is a fitting symbol for the great complexity of the Bâysonghori Preface narrative, in contrast to that of the Older Preface. Whereas the Older Preface shows the trope of turning prose into poetry as an event that takes place in a single phase, the Bâysonghori Preface shows multiple phases, involving multiple poets drawing from multiple sources.

The "Life of Ferdowsi" traditions that we see in the Prefaces of the *Shâhnâma* – as also in the self-references embedded in the actual poetry of the *Shâhnâma* – need to be seen not simply as raw data about the real life and times of the poet but as a traditional discourse that merges factual details with an ongoing mythical reinterpretation of the poem's role in society (Davidson 1994: 31–2).

Even though the prose prefaces of the *Shâhnâma* are based in part on historical facts, they conform to a mythmaking pattern that keeps revalidating the Book of Kings by way of explaining its "origins." The greater density of historical information in the Older Preface version does not take it out of consideration as a variant. Cross-cultural studies of interaction between myths and historical events that are independently known to have taken place show that myths tend to appropriate and then reorganize historical information (Davidson 2000: 62–4).

As for Ferdowsi's own version of the story, it is more versatile because it is more stylized and therefore generic. Ferdowsi's version of how the Book of Kings came about can usurp more specific versions precisely because it is so generic. His version acknowledges the variation of these stories by not identifying the persons, places, or time involved in the genesis of his own source "book" for the *Shâhnâma*. And by acknowledging this multiformity, Ferdowsi is in effect transcending it. His *Shâhnâma* does not depend on any one version for the establishment of a text. The myth gives validity to the text by making the assembly of wise and pious men in the community the collective source of the text (Davidson 1994: 52).

As we see from the Preface to the Bâysonghori Recension, the immediate predecessors of Ferdowsi include Daqiqi, whose poetry is overtly acknowledged (and competed with) by Ferdowsi (*Shâhnâma* VI 136.9–15). The New Persian *mutaqârib* meter of the epics composed by the likes of both Ferdowsi and Daqiqi is evidently derived from Middle Persian forms (Elwell-Sutton 1976: 172–3).

In fact, we know that Daqiqi's and Ferdowsi's Zoroastrian themes share the heritage of a Middle Persian epic tradition: a case in point is a Pahlavi narrative poem, *Ayâdgâr î Zarêrân*, "The Memorial of Zarêr," the themes of which converge with those of Daqiqi, which in turn are incorporated into the *Shâhnâma* of Ferdowsi (Boyce 1955).

The Iranian epic traditions as represented by Ferdowsi can be traced even further back, beyond the Sasanian dynasty, to the earlier Arsacid dynasty of the Parthians. The most striking testimony, collected by Mary Boyce, centers on the New Persian and Middle Persian contexts of the Parthian word *gôsân*, roughly translatable as "minstrel" (Boyce 1957). Boyce sums up the essence of this testimony:

> The *gôsân* played a considerable part in the life of the Parthians and their neighbours, down to late in the Sasanian epoch: entertainer of king and commoner, privileged at court and popular with the people; present at the graveside and at the feast; eulogist, satirist, storyteller, musician; recorder of past achievements, and commentator of his own times. He is sometimes an object of emulation, sometimes a despised frequenter of taverns and bawdy-houses; sometimes a solitary singer and musician, and sometimes one of a group, singing or performing on a variety of instruments. The explanation of such diversity is presumably that for the Parthians music and poetry were so closely entwined, that a man could not be professional poet without being also a musician, skilled in instrumental as well as vocal music . . . As poet-musicians, in Parthian society as in any other, the *gôsâns* presumably enjoyed reputation and esteem in proportion to their individual talents. (Boyce 1957: 17–18)

Evidence for this Parthian phase of Iranian epic traditions comes not only from the later Sasanian phase (as exemplified by the *Letter of Tansar*: Minavi 1932: 12) but also from still earlier pre-Parthian phases: we can see traces of analogues to the *gôsân* in the Iranian traditions of the Achaemenids (Xenophon *Cyropaedia* 1.2.1) and Medes (Athenaeus 633) (Boyce 1957: 20–2).

The poetic heritage of Iranian epic can be traced even further back than the Achaemenid and Mede dynasties. The earliest phases of Iranian epic can best be seen from an internal analysis of characters in Ferdowsi's Book of Kings who are pointedly not kings of the Iranian empire in their own right.

The main character of the *Shâhnâma* who corresponds to what we know as a "hero" in other epic traditions is Rostam. This character, although he is not a *shâh* of the Iranian empire, is hardly peripheral to the Book of Kings. His exploits dominate the overall narrative of Ferdowsi's *Shâhnâma* for vast stretches, and in fact the combined lifetimes of this hero and of his father Zâl overlap with the set chronology of a kingly succession that lasts beyond a millennium, covering the reigns of kings extending from Manuchehr all the way to Goshtâsp (Wikander 1950: 324). This stretch of narrative takes up practically the first six volumes of the nine-volume Moscow edition of the *Shâhnâma*. No king served by these two heroes rivals the span of roughly 500 years allotted to Zâl and Rostam each; the closest is the *shâh* Key Khosrow, whose own span is 150 years. As Georges Dumézil has observed, the parallel narratives of the kings on the one side and of these heroes on the other reveal distinctly different "rhythms" (1971: 231; see also Skjærvø 1998a, 1998b).

Always a kingmaker but never a king of the Iranian empire, Rostam has as his main task in life the continual protection of the current Iranian *shâh* and thereby of the Iranian empire itself; one of the hero's distinctive epithets is in fact *tâjbakhsh*, "crown-bestower" – always a kingmaker, never a king (SN II 96.383, II 104.533, III 189.2887, and so on). And yet Rostam is also often at odds with the kingship, and at times seems more of a menace to the *shâh* than a help. Moreover, he is an outsider to the national ways: he comes from Sistân, a region visualized in the *Shâhnâma* as a remote outpost in the eastern stretches of the empire. The culture and the very name of Sistân can be traced back, at least in part, to a Northeast Iranian population who were called the Saka: by its etymology, Sistân means "land of the Saka" (Christensen 1932: 142–3).

The Rostam tradition has now been discovered in yet another branch of the Northeast Iranian family. Fragments of a text composed in Sogdian, a language closely related to that of the Sakas, tell of the adventures of *rwstmy*, "Rostam," and his wondrous horse *rγśy*, "Rakhsh," as they confront murderous demons or *dywt*, "*divs*" (Sims-Williams 1976). These narratives correspond to those found in the *Shâhnâma* about the war of Rostam against the *divs*, "demons," of Mâzandarân (SN II 106–110.562–634), but the Persian version is clearly independent of the Sogdian (Davidson 1994: 82–8).

Rostam stories of the Sakas developed into a national Iranian epic tradition, through Parthian intermediacy. By the beginning of the seventh century CE, it is clear that this national tradition was already in effect: in Mecca itself, according to a report by Ibn Hishâm, the citizens of that city were entertained with the stories about Rostam and Esfandiyâr as narrated by one Naṣr Ibn al Ḥârith, who learned them in the course of commercial travels along the Euphrates (Wüstenfeld 1858: 191, 235; Davidson 1994: 88–9).

The anomalies in the Rostam stories of the *Shâhnâma* cannot be explained away simply by tracing them back to the regionalisms of the Saka. The Rostam stories are anomalous in the *Shâhnâma* for a more basic reason: because the "epic of heroes" and the "book of kings" represent two distinct aspects of poetic tradition.

Besides Rostam, another comparably anomalous figure in the *Shâhnâma* is the fiendish Afrâsiyâb, king of the Turanians. The life of Afrâsiyâb is long enough to span a succession of kings ranging from the generations that followed the primordial King Faridun himself, before the dynasty of the Keyânids, all the way to the reign of a Keyânid *shâh*, Key Khosrow. Throughout the *Shâhnâma*, Afrâsiyâb is primarily the enemy of the Keyânid kings, only secondarily that of the Sistanian heroes. Afrâsiyâb is clearly a mythical figure, corresponding to the Frâsiyâp of the earlier Pahlavi texts and the demonic Fraŋrasiian of the even earlier Avesta (Dumézil 1971: 231). His enmity with the national kings of Iran is a unifying theme in the "book of kings" traditions about the Keyânids, from Key Qobâd to Key Apiva to Key Kâus to Siyâvosh to Key Khosrow (Davidson 1994: 89–90).

Dumézil's comparative studies establish in detail that the story patterns concerning the Keyânids and their enemy Afrâsiyâb are a heritage of Indo-Iranian and even Indo-European mythmaking traditions. The titular Key of the Keyânid dynasty (Key Qobâd, Key Apiva, Key Kâus, Key Khosrow), attested in the earlier Avestan tradition as *kauui*, is cognate with the Indic word *kaví-*, which in the diction of the Indic Vedas designates a priestly or at least hieratic figure endowed with special supernatural knowledge bordering on the magical. The ultimate *kaví-* in the Vedas is one Kâvya (derivative of *kaví-*) Uśanas, smith of Indra's thunderbolt (with which the god kills the demonic Vṛtra/Ahi); this theme is comparable with that of the Iranian Kâva, the smith who helped Faridun smite the dragonlike usurper Ẓaḥḥâk in the aetiological story about the banner of the Keyânid dynasty (SN I 61–7.183–277) (Dumézil 1971: 137–238).

Dumézil shows that the traditions about the Indic hero Kâvya Uśanas and those about the Iranian *shâh* Key Kâus are cognate, both centering on the water of life and its magical powers in bringing the dead back to life. Dumézil's argument about the Keyânids can be taken further: it can be argued that the relationship between the Keyânid kings and the Sistanian heroes, namely, Rostam and his family, is in its own right an equally old mythical theme of Indo-European provenience, cognate with such themes as the relationship of Agamemnon and Achilles in the Greek epic tradition of the *Iliad* (Davidson 1994: 75–127). In other words, it can be argued that the combined themes of Rostam's being simultaneously an "insider" and an "outsider" with relation to the Keyânids is an aspect of an overall Indo-European mythmaking tradition about heroes and kings. Further, the theme of Rostam's being an "outsider" with relation to the Keyânids is parallel to the conceptual conflict between Turanians and Iranians in Iranian storytelling traditions (Davidson 1994: 168–9).

For a reconstruction, it is best to start with the most recent precedents. The "book of kings" tradition about the Keyânids, like the tradition about Rostam, can be traced back to early Parthian as well as Northeast Iranian mythmaking traditions, which are in many ways alien to the Zoroastrian orthodoxies prevalent in the Gâthâs of the Avesta (Wikander 1938: esp. 107–8). In the Pahlavi documents that preserve fragments of the Iranian poetic traditions in Sasanian times, we can actually witness convergences between the poetry about Rostam and the poetry about the Keyânids. In the *Draxt Asûrik*, for example, a text that has been shown to be composed in a Parthian dialect of Northwest Iran, and in verse (Benveniste 1930), there is a passing reference to the saddles upon which Rotastaxm, "Rostam," and Spendadât, "Esfandiyâr," had been seated (Unvala 1923: §41, 657–8; Davidson 1994: 92).

The story of Rostam and Esfandiyâr, which as we have seen is attested as the topic of an entertaining narrative performance in seventh-century Mecca, culminates in their mortal combat (SN VI 254–70). In the context of this combat, there is a conscious juxtaposition of the two combatants *as epic characters*: the Zoroastrian prince Esfandiyâr, a prime character in the Keyânid tradition, is being contrasted with Rostam, a prime character of the "Sistanian" or heroic tradition. As a prelude to their combat, the epic traditions surrounding these two characters are juxtaposed in the form of matching sets of seven-part narratives about their heroic exploits. These sets are known as the *Haft Kh*ᵂ*ân* 'Seven Courses'; the word *haft* means "seven," cognate with Latin *septem*, Greek *hepta*, while *kh*ᵂ*ân* means "spread cloth or board covered by a cloth, with meats on it," and, by extension, "feast, banquet-course"; but it also carries the meaning of "adventure" or "exploit," which is ostensibly being narrated at a feast (Davidson 2000: 23–4). Here we see distinct battle narratives framed by distinct banquet settings, ostensibly enjoyed by the hero and also dramatizing the context of the recitation of the narrative itself. The first *Haft Kh*ᵂ*ân* represents the "Sistanian" epic tradition of Rostam (SN II 91–110.280–6340) and the second, the Keyânid epic tradition of Esfandiyâr (SN VI 166–92.1–451).

The poetic device of fully treating two sets of seven deeds in the *Shâhnâma* establishes a large-scale opposition of the two heroes involved, and the seed for this poetic device is already evident in the small-scale juxtaposition of the two heroes in the *Draxt Asûrik*.

The Keyânid epic tradition, as reflected in the story of Esfandiyâr in the *Shâhnâma* of Ferdowsi, is reflected also in the story of his uncle Zarêr, a Keyânid prince, whose name is attested already in the *Avesta* (*Zairiwairi* in *Yašt* 5.112 and *Yašt* 13.101). He is celebrated as a heroic paragon of the Zoroastrian way: in the aforementioned Pahlavi poem known as the *Ayâdgâr î Zarêrân*, "Memorial of Zarêr," he is presented as a pious warrior who was instrumental in a key victory of the Iranians over King Arjâsp and his Turanians, and who lost his own life in that battle. This Pahlavi poem is strikingly parallel in both form and content to the later narrative about the death of Zarêr in the *Shâhnâma* that is attributed to Daqiqi (SN VI 66–119.39–787).

Let us pursue the narrative patterns juxtaposing the royal line of Keyânids with heroes or *pahlavâns* like Rostam and his father Zâl in the *Shâhnâma*. This pattern reaches further back than the poetic heritage of the Parthians and Northeast Iranians. It is inherited from Indo-European mythology, centering on the theme of the coexistence and the conflict between the king who rules and the hero who serves him. This theme has been studied in some non-Iranian contexts by Dumézil, with a focus on three different heroes in three different Indo-European traditions: Starkaðr in the Old Norse, Śiśupâla in the Indic, and Herakles in the Greek (Dumézil 1971: 17–132). Each of these heroes is not only in the service of but also in conflict with his respective king(s). A close parallel can be found in the Iranian traditions about Rostam and the *shâhs* that he defends.

In the case of the Indic Śiśupâla, the medium of narration is explicitly epic; in the case of the Old Norse, the medium is saga and Latin retellings of saga; in the case of the Greek Herakles, most of the best comparative evidence comes from late prose retellings. Despite the asymmetry of the media of narration, Dumézil shows that all three heroes can be traced back to a common epic tradition.

All three heroes are kingmakers, not kings. Although they may have kingly features that are overt or latent, they are socially inferior to others who are more kingly than they are. Though they are constantly involved in the affairs of kings, they do not achieve supreme kingship themselves. Starkaðr is in the service of several kings; Śiśupâla is the subordinate of Jarâsandha; and Herakles serves King Eurystheus throughout his labors.

There is a further relevant detail from ancient Greek myth, with reference to Eurystheus as king and Herakles as hero. The relationship between these two figures is explicitly drawn into a parallel, by the Homeric *Iliad* itself (19.95–133), with the relationship between Agamemnon as king and Achilles as hero (Davidson 1980). In the case of Agamemnon and Achilles, the theme of an opposition between king and hero is an explicitly *epic* theme.

Turning from myth in general to epic in particular, note that the crucial passage involving Herakles' being out of season is directly attested in Greek epic, *Iliad* 19.95–133. The story of Herakles as retold in this Iliadic passage highlights the theme of a superior hero in the service of an inferior king – which is a theme central to the *Iliad* itself (see Chapters 21 and 6, by Edwards and Nagy). We see it in the relationship of Achilles to Agamemnon. As Nestor says, Agamemnon has dishonored the best man in his service (9.110–11). Achilles says as much about himself, both to Agamemnon (1.244) and to his mother, Thetis (1.410–11). In the words of the hero, Agamemnon suffered from an *atê*, "aberration," in failing to give him his due honor (1.411). The importance of Achilles' use of this word *atê* becomes clear at a later point of the narrative, where Agamemnon blames the goddess Atê personified for his having dishonored Achilles (19.88, 91, 126, 129). In giving this excuse, Agamemnon cites the myth of the birth of Herakles, a story that tells how a superior hero came to serve an inferior hero, to his own dishonor (19.95–133).

The Greek model of Achilles, as an internal parallel to the model of Herakles, is especially pertinent for comparison with the Iranian model of Rostam. Just as the hero Rostam is king in his own right in his remote native region of Sistân, the hero Achilles is a king in his own right in his remote native region of Phthia. Another parallelism is equally instructive: just as Achilles is primarily a hero and secondarily a king while Agamemnon is primarily a king and secondarily a hero, so also with Rostam and the royal line of the Keyânids in the *Shâhnâma*.

What detracts from Rostam's kingliness is that he is not Keyânid but "Sistanian." We see here a hero who is genetically part *div*, "demon," and who is qualified to rule the Turanians, enemies of the Iranians, for seven years. After all, through his maternal grandfather, Mehrâb, he can trace his lineage back to the dark figure of Zaḥḥâk. And yet this same hero Rostam, despite all his quarrels with the Keyânids, is their protector and thus the mainstay of all Iran.

A sign of this role of Rostam is his association with the concept and epic reality of the *farr*, "luminous glory." This *farr* is not connected with the hero's local kingship of Sistân. Rather, it is connected with his role in protecting the national kingship of Iran. In one scene, for example, Rostam's mother, at the birth of the hero, immediately perceives that he has the *farr-e shâhanshahi*, "the luminous glory of the King of Kings" (SN I 239.1516).

The earlier traditions preserved in the sacred books of the Avesta reveal an analogous pattern: the primordial king Yima (= Persian Jamshid) himself serves as a model for the loss of $x^{v}ar\partial nah$ (= Persian *farr*) on the part of a king who has lapsed into evil ways (*Yašt* 19.34).

Since the loss of the king's *farr* is conventionally linked with national disasters, it is significant that the absence of Rostam in times of national crises is consistently pictured as a disaster for all Iran. For example, Rostam is summoned in a time of crisis as the hope of the Iranians (SN IV 143.444–5).

By virtue of being a guardian of the king's *farr*, "luminous glory," Rostam is a mainstay of Iran more consistently than the national kings themselves. It has been said that "Rostam is consistent, while the image of the king is shifty, opaque, perplexing – it emerges radiant only to submerge again; this, certainly, is one of the most interesting aspects of the *Shâhnâma*" (Hansen 1954: 147; my translation). Moreover, the Sistanian heroes not only sustain the *farr* of the national kings: they also confer it. For example, it is Zâl who assembles the *môbads* of Iran to ascertain the identity of the new national king, and the *môbads* reveal to him that it is Key Qobâd who will now have the *gorz*, "mace," and *farr* of the Keyânids (SN II 56.110–11). And it is Rostam himself who must then fetch the new king from Mount Alborz (SN II 56.112–13). In sum, the national hero Rostam seems to be thematically linked with the *farr-e shâhanshahi*.

The theme of Rostam's possession of the *farr-e shâhanshahi* appears to be attested already in the Avesta, and yet, perhaps surprisingly, the actual name and figure of Rostam are not. In other words, even though the figure of Rostam is not directly attested in the Avesta, at least the figure of a national hero who guards the *farr* is definitely there. The internal evidence of the *Shâhnâma* suggests that the figure of Rostam matches the figure of Apạm Napât in *Yašt* 19, to the extent that Rostam, like Apạm Napât, protects the $x^{v}ar\partial nah$ (= *farr*) from Fraŋrasiian = Afrâsiyâb, who seeks to possess it (Davidson 2000: 71–97).

In conclusion, the role of Rostam is not only heroic but also central to the very concept of Keyânid kingship. Although he is portrayed as an outsider to the kingship in the sense that he is disqualified from becoming an overlord himself, we see finally that he is in fact an insider to the very traditions that represent him this way. He is, after all, central not only to the Iranian heroic tradition but also to the "book of kings" tradition, both of which are incorporated in the epic we know as the *Shâhnâma* of Ferdowsi.

FURTHER READING

On classican Persian epic, see Davidson 1994. For Iranian pre-forms of Persian epic, see Wikander 1950, Molé 1960, and Puhvel 1987. For other Iranian epic traditions, see Skjærvø 1998a and 1998b.

CHAPTER NINETEEN

The Challenge of Israelite Epic

Susan Niditch

To study ancient Israelite epic is indeed a challenge. Does the term "epic" refer to an agreed-upon corpus or genre in the view of biblical scholars? While scholars of the Bible and the ancient Near East frequently use the term, they do so variously, and the history of scholarship on "biblical epic" requires some sorting out. Secondly, is there a universal or international genre one can call "epic" and if so what are its characteristics? For the answer to this question we turn to recent scholarship by scholars of folklore, comparative literature, and classics (see Chapter 1, by Martin). Finally, is there an ethnic genre within ancient Israelite literature that Israelites themselves might have recognized as "epic" in line with one of these modern scholarly constructs? Issues of texture, text, and context serve as guides in the search for an Israelite genre, epic. A first step is a brief history of scholarly engagement with the notion of Israelite epic.

Biblicists on "Epic"

Charles Conroy provides a detailed overview of the ways in which nineteenth- and twentieth-century scholars of ancient Israel have employed the term "epic" as a designation for various portions of the Hebrew Bible. He writes "the term epic has been used in a bewildering variety of ways with reference to early Hebrew literature" (1980: 14). A sampling of representative scholars cited by Conroy, in fact, reveals certain recurring interests and themes.

Cyrus Gordon referred to the Pentateuch as "the Epic of Nationhood" (see also Augusti 1827: 137–49; Conroy 1980: 2) and imagined an oral recitation or singing of this epic during the Passover festival, to "knit the segments of the nation together telling how they achieved their place in history in the course of a great event" (Gordon 1962: 293). Emphasizing the texture of language and other stylistic criteria, Hermann Gunkel wrote of an "epic style" (*epischen stil*) in passages such as Gen. 19: 30–8, Judg. 9: 8ff., and Job 1–2, characterized by "purposeful parallelism" in content, repetition in language, and a particular variety of artfulness (1910: 218). Gunkel, however, drew a distinction between biblical works such as Genesis and Homer. In his view, the former is not epic in the same sense as the ancient Greek material (1910: xcix; see also Reuss 1881: 159).

Relying on a definition of epic that emphasizes "narrative" quality and "creative treatment," R. G. Moulton pointed to epics of various subtypes in Gen. 1–11, Ruth, and Jonah (1896: 221–43; Conroy 1980: 4; for an outline of "subgenres of epic" see also Jason 1977: 30–2). Sigmund Mowinckel viewed the titles "Book of the Wars of Yahweh," mentioned in Num. 21: 14, and "Book of Jashar," mentioned in Josh. 10: 13 and 2 Sam. 1: 18, as allusions to a collection or collections of national epic material. Mowinckel translated "Yashar" as *brav* in the German, "excellent, high-born, noble" (1935: 131–2), and viewed the Sefer Yashar as having been a collection of "narratives in poetic form," linked with happenings in a *Wonderwelt* and related to *Märchen* (wondertales or folktales) (pp. 133–4). Like modern folklorists, he noted that the stuff of what he considered to be epic could be employed in both delimited and more expansive ways: a tale of a flood may be presented as an account in and of itself or as part of a larger tale or tale cycle (p. 141). Building on the work of Eissfeldt, he saw the *moshel* mentioned in Num. 21: 27 as a kind of "rhapsode," a singer of tales of the deeds of heroes (p. 143). Mowinckel was thus sensitive not only to the texture and text or content of the literature, but also to its authors' compositional orientations and the compositions' possible performance contexts.

Pfeiffer and Pollard also wrote of two epics, the sources to Samuel and the Yahwist composition, in their book *The Hebrew Iliad* (Conroy 1980: 5). As the title and subtitle of their work indicate, in contrast to Gunkel they strongly identified biblical narrative of a certain variety with Homeric epic and were quite daring, some might say fanciful, in identifying the Israelite "bard" who composed the Israelite "Iliad." Exploring matters of style and content, Umberto Cassuto found a number of epic threads and indicators in the Hebrew Bible (1955). Most important among more recent contributions to the discussion of epic is the seminal work of Frank Moore Cross, who himself has refined and developed his view of Israelite epic over a lengthy career.

In Cross's view, epic refers to a hypothesized common poetic tradition that lies behind the "so-called JE sources" (1973: 83 n. 11; 293). Included in this definition is the belief in the existence of specific, written sources that lie behind the Pentateuch, the documentary hypothesis. "Epic" becomes a means of distinguishing richly narrative materials from priestly sources which show special interest in preserving or shaping texts concerned with ritual, genealogy, purities, and other matters of relevance to priests (Cross 1973: 203, 315, 324, 343). For Cross, the plot of this quintessential epic included the exodus from Egypt, the covenant at Sinai, and the conquest of the land of Israel (p. 85). He sees the poetic epic underlying JE as similar in genre to epics from ancient Canaan and Greece, but expressing a historical orientation and worldview particular to ancient Israel. Epic events, moreover, would have been re-enacted in the festivals of pre-monarchic Israel in ancient sanctuary settings, as essential story and ritual drama combined to "renew" Israel's "life as a historical community" (p. 143). Contributing to themes in this epic tradition are a variety of biblical scenes such as the visitation to Abraham promising a son born of Sarah in Gen. 18 (p. 182) and the rebellion of Dathan and Abiram in Num. 16 (p. 205).

Cross's more recent work (1998) is influenced overtly not only by Albert B. Lord, who figured in his 1973 treatment of epic, but also by Cedric W. Whitman and contemporary scholars including Gregory Nagy and John Niles. In *From Epic to Canon*, Cross outlines more systematically the traits of Hebrew epic:

> Oral composition in formulae and themes of a traditional literature; narrative in which acts of gods and men form a double level of action; a composition describing traditional events of an age conceived as normative; a national composition, especially one recited at pilgrimage festivals. (1998: 29)

Certain themes and interests do emerge from this history of scholarship on the biblical epic: concern with poetic style and other stylistic criteria; emphasis on heroes' great deeds and the theme of national identity; comparisons to Homer; interest in a possible festival context; and discussion of the place of so-called epic material in the Bible's redaction history.

Cross's particular use of the term "epic" to describe stretches of Israelite tradition, both extant biblical portions of biblical literature and hypothesized traditions lying behind the Hebrew Bible, has been strongly criticized by Charles Conroy, who roots his own list of the criteria of epic in the classic works of H. M. Chadwick (1912) and C. M. Bowra (1952, 1972), among others. For Conroy, epics are quintessentially heroic. They "tell of men and doings greater and grander than in the poet's own generation" (Bowra 1972: 3, 79); they are poetic (Conroy 1980: 19); they are often although not always aristocratic (Conroy 1980: 19, 20); in epic, relationships are based in "personal loyalty" and are "not nationalistic in a narrow sense" (Conroy 1980: 20; Chadwick 1912: 329–32); they deal with battle, "valiant deeds on fields of battle or perilous combat with fearful monsters" (Conroy 1980: 20). Working from such a definition, one is hard-pressed to include tales of the patriarchs in the epic genre, as Conroy points out. Inclusion depends, however, on one's definition of the genre. Indeed, Bowra himself was less than certain that the Israelites ever produced what he would call "heroic poetry," a category important to Conroy's view of epic. Even while allowing that "Deborah's song," David's laments, and tales of Samson suggest qualities of the heroic, Bowra viewed biblical "chief characters" as "more life-like than ideal," the tales as more "historical than heroic" (1952: 14–16). Thus Bowra might exclude even what Conroy does include.

Additional Definitions and Criteria: Contemporary Scholarship

Later twentieth-century work on the epic by folklorists, classicists, and other students of early or oral literatures allows for much greater flexibility than does Conroy in defining epic (see Chapter 13, by J. Foley). They too are often convinced that there is some international or global genre that is the epic, but manifestations of epic, its textural, textual, and contextual qualities, depend upon the tastes and norms of the particular culture and society which frame and give life to its stories of olden times. Particular societies, in fact, may conceive as a single genre a range of traditional narrative forms that scholars may or may not recognize as epic. Ethnic genres matter, as Dan Ben-Amos's influential work insists.

As Lauri Honko notes, western scholars often view the Homeric poems as "templates" of the genre, but these too are "as idiosyncratic as those of any tradition" (1998b: 20, quoting Hatto 1980; see also Nagy 1999b: 24–5). Gregory Nagy notes how the very word *epos* undergoes a shift in meaning over time within the classical Greek tradition. He suggests that, on the one hand, "epic" is an entire tradition about this or that hero or event, and all the possibilities and associations that belong to that epic tradition; on the other hand, a specific epic is what may have been performed at any one time (1999b: 28).

In the search for a definition of epic, Honko provides a variety of other scholars' lists of traits. Like Conroy, he alludes to the work of Bowra. In Honko's presentation, the Bowra-influenced definition of epic seems rather reminiscent of Joseph Campbell's "hero of a thousand faces." The stories of epic reveal the human desire "to pass beyond the oppressive limits of human frailty to a fuller and more vivid life"; its heroes desire "to win as far as possible a self-sufficient manhood, which refuses to admit that anything is too difficult for it" (Bowra 1952: 4, quoted in Honko 1998b: 21) As presented by Honko, John William Johnson's work describes epic as: (1) poetic; (2) narrative; (3) heroic; (4) legendary; (5) of great length; (6) multigeneric; (7) multifunctional; (8) within a line of cultural and traditional transmission (1998b: 27, quoting Johnson 1986: 31)

Honko also includes the definition by Brenda Beck, who works with South Indian material. In this view, epics are created by "professional bards"; they are "extremely long" (longer than folktales); the heroes are sometimes "sacred figures"; the stories link to "wider mythological and civilizational traditions"; and audiences and tellers "both believe their epic depicts actual historical events" (1998b: 28, quoting Beck 1982: 196). Honko adds to his version of Beck's list that epics "function as a source of identity representations in the traditional community or group receiving the epic" (1998b: 28). This set of epic qualities raises many questions as well. What is a traditional community as opposed to any cultural group? As Honko himself asks, "How long is long?" While Edward Haymes sets epic length as "mostly longer than 200–300 lines," Honko sets "the lowest limit" as "one thousand lines" (1998b: 35–6, quoting Haymes 1977: 4). Influenced by Dan Ben-Amos, Honko wisely warns us that any definition of epic is "as dependent on the context and reception of the story as on its form," and urges us to think in terms of the work's "relation to its cultural function as a source of 'enlarged' human exemplars and moral codes" (p. 22). The reference to "enlarged human exemplars" would seem to bring us back to Bowra and Conroy's notions of the heroic, but lest we think so, Honko writes in the same breath that "concentration" on the "heroic ethos" of epics "must be equally qualified" (pp. 22–3). And so Conroy's exclusion of an unheroic Abraham from Israelite epic seems not so necessary, and Cross's inclusion entirely possible.

Another interesting working definition offered in an anthology edited by Beissinger, Tylus, and Wofford is more simple and inclusive and not as reliant as some of the above on "strict formal limits":

> The epic is defined here as a poetic narrative of length and complexity that centers around deeds of significance to the community. (1999: 2)

The contributors to this project attempt to bridge both contemporary and ancient epic, oral and written, with this rather inclusive definition, although one might again inquire about the meaning of "poetic," "length," and "community" in particular cultural settings.

Like many of the scholars mentioned above, Beissinger and colleagues point to qualities of the heroic in epic "narrated from within a versimilitudinous frame of reference." They also emphasize, however, the intense political capacities, even "explosiveness" of performed epic, given its "complex connection to national and local cultures." An epic often presents "an encyclopedic account of the culture that produced it" (1999: 2–3). The essays of their volume emphasize further the role of lament in epic, and the importance of word-play, punning, and "verbal performance" (p. 12). Also important is the "idea that the dynamics of epic, both oral and literary, are created and sustained through the challenging of boundaries – boundaries of genre, gender, locality, and language" (pp. 11–12). The emphases on "political explosiveness," "the challenging of boundaries," and "verbal performance" would seem to be entirely relevant to the challenge of Israelite epic. The big question, of course, is what did the Israelites think themselves? That is, did they themselves recognize a genre of epic or produce work that suits what the modern scholars suggest epic to be? A first step is to see if a certain term is applied regularly in Israelite tradition to a sort of literature that looks like one of the "global" definitions offered above. Another strategy is to explore whether key phrases or stylistic criteria introduce or frame certain narrative traditions that one might call epic.

Terms for Epic?

A possible model in approaching Israelite terminology for epic is provided by the study of the term *mashal*, which was applied by biblical writers to various literary forms that modern westerners might call sayings, parables, oracles, and so on. Analysis reveals that a certain conceptual framework does indeed encompass these various examples of what an ancient Israelite would term a *mashal*, and thus a genuine "ethnic genre" emerges (Niditch 1993a: 67–87). The case of "Israelite epic" is more difficult. One begins with a genre variously defined by modern scholars with attention to certain criteria of texture, text, and context, and attempts to discover if any recurring biblical term seems to match. As noted by S. Mowinckel, the Hebrew term *shir* (literally a "song" or "poem") seems one likely candidate, for the term is applied to songs or poems about victorious and heroic battles at Exod. 15: 1, 15: 20, and Judg. 5: 1, and is frequently the ancient "header" to psalms characterized by such content (e.g. Ps. 48: 1, 65: 1, 76: 1, 83: 1, 87: 1). As Mowinckel observes, the Septuagintal version of 1 Kgs. 8: 53 refers to "Sefer Hashir" (1935: 131–2), perhaps suggesting that at least some Israelites thought of tales of the ancient heroes as belonging to an epic-as-song tradition. And yet as Mowinckel goes on to imply, such evidence is a thin reed upon which to construct theories of an Israelite epic. He notes that the term for song is simply too general and embraces too many works in the preserved Israelite tradition for one to consider it an Israelite term for "epic."

Recurring Phrases or Markers

Like Herman Gunkel, Umberto Cassuto suggested that Israelite epic is demarcated by certain recurring phrases. He cited, for example, the phrase, "And X lifted up his eyes and saw...," found at Gen. 18: 2, 24: 63 and 64, 37: 25, etc. (1971: 36–8). Given the nature of the content and the wide distribution of the repetitions presented, however, Cassuto's case for epic language is less convincing than the case for a general, traditional-style language that characterizes much of the Israelite tradition, across genres (see Niditch 1987, 1993a, 1996). Victor Sasson suggested that one of the essential linguistic patterns of Israelite narrative, the so-called waw-consecutive, "was originally used in Old Aramaic and Biblical Hebrew in war, war-related epic, and mythic texts" (2001: 603). Again, the notion is intriguing but too sweeping to be useful in a search for an ethnic genre. Something more specific is required comparable to Frank Cross's observation that the phrase *'lh twldwt*, "these are the generations," marks the presence of a certain kind of priestly material in the Hebrew Bible (1973: 301–5). Possible candidates for such markers of epic are the phrases, *wyhy bymym hhm*, literally "And it was in those days..." or "It came to pass in those days...," the related *bymym hhm*, "in those days," *wyhy bymy...*," "And is was in the days of X," and *wyhy 'yš*, literally, "And there was a man...."

Wyhy, the so-called waw-consecutive of the imperfect form of the verb "to be," is used throughout ancient Hebrew narrative to demarcate time (see van der Merwe 1999). In an extremely common use of this term, the narrator provides a specific time frame for the scene or story that follows: e.g. "(It was) at that time" (Gen. 21: 22; 38: 1; 1 Kgs. 11: 29) or "(It was) at the end of X amount of time" (Gen. 12: 41, 41: 1; Deut. 9: 12; Judg. 11: 39; 2 Sam. 15: 7; 1 Kgs. 2: 39) or "(It was) on the next day" (Num. 17: 23; Judg. 9: 42; 21: 4; 1 Sam. 11: 11, 18: 10, 31: 8). Less common throughout the narrative portions of Hebrew Bible is the phrase literally translated "And it was in those days" and the briefer variant "In those days." These phrases are represented densely in Judg. 19: 1, 17: 6, 18: 1, 20: 27 and 28, 21: 25, and in 1 Sam. 3: 1, 28: 1; LXX 1 Sam. 4: 1. The context for all of these usages is foundation myth, often including a war or battle and reference to the career of a hero. The formulaic phrases mark tales of olden times. After such a phrase at Judg. 17: 6, 18: 1, 19: 1; 20: 27 and 28; 1 Sam. 28: 1; LXX 1 Sam. 4: 1, the story of a war or battle that took place in the significant past is soon to follow. Judg. 21: 25, an *inclusio* for 17: 6 or 19: 1, comments on the battles that have just been described. At Judg. 20: 21 and 1 Sam. 3: 1, particular heroes are introduced who are significant in a cultural history. Variation upon the phrase, "in those days," does seem to frame the sort of content scholars exploring various traditions have found in epic. And the phrase is found densely in a specific corpus of similar tales, tales from the days of the early rulers of Israel. There are relatively few uses of these phrases outside of Judges and Samuel, and five of these introduce passages that are similar in orientation to those of Judges: Gen. 6: 4 refers to the presence of the great heroes of old, the Nephilim; Exod. 2: 11 introduces the bandit career of Moses; Ezek. 38: 17 refers to old-time prophets; in Neh. 6: 17 and 13: 15 and 23, Nehemiah describes his role in his own memoir as a significant feature of the nation's past.

Two additional temporal phrases may mark epic material in the Hebrew Bible. The first phrase, "It was in the days of King X," alludes to some aspect of the career of a king. Gen. 14: 1 and Isa. 7: 1 are both preludes to battle accounts while Esther 1: 1 introduces the tale of threat to Jews in diaspora that ends in self-defense, battle, and survival. The reference in Gen. 14 is especially interesting because it places Abraham in a heroic, epic-like setting, quite in contrast to other patriarchal accounts. This mock-heroic tale may suggest that Israelites themselves recognized and adapted an epic genre (Niditch 1993b: 101–2). The second phrase, "There was a man," is found densely in Judges and 2 Samuel (Judg. 13: 2, 17: 1, 19: 1; 1 Sam. 1: 1; 9: 1; 2 Sam. 21: 20; 1 Chr. 20: 6) and introduces a figure who will be part of an important founding myth, often the hero's progenitor (Samson's father Manoah in Judg. 13: 2; Samuel's father in 1 Sam. 1: 1; Saul's father in 1 Sam. 9: 1), other times the key player in the unrolling of a series of events in the foundation tale (Judg. 17: 1, 19: 1; 2 Sam. 21: 20). A close examination of one aspect of "texture" when matched with qualities of "text" or content thus seems to reveal some linguistic markers of heroic and perhaps "epic" material and has led scholars repeatedly to Judges and 1, 2 Samuel. A closer examination of the content is in order.

The Role of Heroes: Activities and Contexts

The heroes of Judges and 1 and 2 Samuel are comparable to traditional definitions of epic heroes in the largeness and charisma of their characters and deeds, the divine favor they enjoy, at least for a time, in their roles in national founding myths, and, above all, in their battle prowess. The Israelite version of the hero, however, is culturally framed by another international type, studied so brilliantly in sociopolitical contexts by Eric Hobsbawm: the "social bandit." Hobsbawm locates social banditry "in all types of human society which lie between the evolutionary phase of tribal and kinship organization, and modern capitalist society" (1969: 14). While the rise of capitalism is not an issue in biblical material, nevertheless the tales of the judges and early kings do mark a significant transition between a socio-structural group identity that is based upon kinship and one that is based upon allegiance to a state, such as the monarchies of the ancient Near East. Admired by their communities, social bandits are "champions, fighters for justice, perhaps even leaders of liberation" (Hobsbawm 1969: 13). Bandits arise during periods of transition and flux and are young men of rural origins. They are often marginal figures in their own societies, sometimes victims of injustice, and are rebels in personality. They kill in just vengeance or self-defense and in Israelite versions are tricksters who often succeed through deception. A run-down of the judges and early kings, Saul and David, reveals such a list of criteria beautifully, although Moses as well might be seen to qualify as a social bandit in the narratives of Exodus. Gideon, Saul, and David all have agrarian or pastoral roots. Jephthah is an illegitimate son of a prostitute, denied rights by his brothers, Deborah a female leader, an unusual role in this literature about men. Ehud is a left-handed man in a symbolic world in which the "normal" preferred side is the right, and David, a youngest son, is an enemy of the Saulide establishment. All of these heroes qualify in ancient Israel for the designation "marginal." Samson is an explosive hero, a type of bandit Hobsbawm calls "the avenger" because his warring boils over into uncontrolled manifestations of violence.

He takes shelter in caves, kills with his bare hands, and is Israel's weapon against the powerful and oppressive Philistines. All the judges, Saul, and David confront Israel's political and cultural enemies in war and save their people. Tales of the heroes are war tales *par excellence*, and if there is an Israelite epic material to be found in Judges and 2 Samuel, its central component, as in so many other traditions deemed by scholars to be "epic," is battle.

War and Epic

Warring in tales of the early heroes is characterized by a specific bardic ideology, by certain roles played by women, and by the interesting juxtaposition of themes of eroticism and death. War is sport to these "men of valor," as Gideon, David, and his men are called (Judg. 6: 12; 1 Sam. 14: 52, 16: 18; 2 Sam. 17: 10, 23: 20, 24: 9). Combat is a contest in which heroes use special, sometimes unusual, weapons and skill. (See Beniah (2 Sam. 23: 20–1; 1 Chron. 11: 23); Elhanan (2 Sam. 21: 19); David and Goliath (1 Sam. 17); Ehud (Judg. 3: 12–30); Shamgar (Judg. 3: 31); and Samson (Judg. 14: 6, 15: 15).) Abner, the general of Saul, proposes to Joab, David's general, that the lads on each side "rise up and make sport before us" (2 Sam. 2: 12–16). They do so, but the contest between warriors ends in the death of all of them. Opponents frequently engage in taunting behavior before or during battle (e.g. Goliath and David) and nevertheless respect the skill of their enemies. A certain code applies whereby men of comparable experience and skill are expected to confront one another in battle. Hence Goliath's resentment of the young man David in the cameo scene in 1 Sam. 17: 41–9 and Abner's hesitation to kill Joab's younger brother, Asahel, who insists upon pursuing him in battle. Waving him away, Abner calls, "Turn aside from following me. What purpose would it serve for me to strike you to the ground? How could I face your brother Joab?" (2 Sam. 2: 22). Respect for the enemy is also evident in the conversation between Gideon and the captured Midianite kings (Judg. 8: 20). They comment on the noble demeanor of Israelites they have killed in battle and ask that Gideon be the one to kill them, for his son, an inexperienced warrior, is not up to the task.

Much of the fighting in Judges and 2 Samuel is between Israelites and non-Israelite enemies, but battle frequently erupts among Israelites over the distribution of booty, leadership rights, or perceived insults. The civil war between the forces of Saul and David is one of the lengthiest of these accounts, but also in this category are Gideon's vengeance in Judg. 8, Abimelech's rebellion in Judg. 9, Jephthah's confrontation with the men of Ephraim in Judg. 12, and the civil war in Judg. 20–1.

War and Women

Critical in the relationships between warriors are women. They frequently serve as prizes of war and as valuable items of exchange. Michal is David's reward, promised by King Saul, her father, in return for a hundred Philistine foreskins (1 Sam. 18: 17–29). Likewise Achsah is the prize meted out by Caleb to the hero Othniel (Judg. 1: 12–15). The women create relationships between the men. In the case of Saul and David, however, as in the case of Samson's marriage to the Philistine Timnite woman and the affair with Delilah, the relationship leads to or reflects enmity rather than accord. The sacrifice of Jephthah's daughter as a war vow in Judg. 11: 29–40 also reflects this theme of exchange between males, but in this case the demanding receiver of the valuable woman prize is God himself. The girl is offered as a sacrifice to the Lord in return for Jephthah's success in battle. Jael, slayer of the enemy general Sisera, is mistakenly perceived by Sisera as a helper because of his king, Jabin's, relationship to her husband (Judg. 4: 17). The characters are portrayed to assume certain kinds of bonds between men of power, bonds often mediated by women. Instead of serving as a mediator of this positive relationship, however, Jael serves the cause of the Israelites, a subversive manifestation of the folk motif of "the iron fist in the velvet glove."

Women's treatment is sometimes involved in causes of war as in the case of the rape and murder of the Levite's concubine in Judg. 19. This crime leads to civil war when the men of Benjamin side with their kinsmen in Gibeah, where the heinous incident occurred, rather than back pan-Israelite vengeance. In 1 Sam. 30, David attacks and defeats the Amalekites who had stolen his women in a raid. Women are also involved in the process of reconciliation while their voices and experiences offer a critique of men's wars. It is the stealing of women of Shiloh at the end of the war and the forced marriage of daughters of the town of Jabesh-gilead that close the hostilities in Judg. 21. The words of Sisera's mother and her ladies in waiting in Judges 5 serve as an implicit woman's critique of the phenomenon of war, which creates heroes but eliminates sons. The receivers of this exquisite tale know that Sisera, for whom the mother waits, has been killed by Jael, an Israelite woman warrior.

Finally, the Israelite war tradition that may be characterized as epic equates death on the battlefield with sex. As shown by Emily Vermeule (1979) for Homeric material (see also Shulman 1986 on Tamil tradition), the defeated warrior metaphorically is the woman who has been raped. The language and imagery of the tale of Jael and Sisera drip with the confusion between battle death and sexual conquest. Terms such as "kneel" and "lie," and the phrase, "between her legs," found in Judg. 5: 27, create the double-entendre in a traditional Israelite medium (Niditch 1989). Tales of the heroes Ehud (Judg. 3: 12–30) and Samson (Judg. 16) are similarly informed (See Niditch 1990: 116–17, 1993b: 113–19).

Laments

With death comes the lament, a sub-genre that scholars of various traditions frequently find in literature that they regard as epics. Once again the Israelite material in Judges-2 Samuel offers some excellent parallels. In 2 Sam. 1: 17–27 David intones a lament over Saul and the son of Saul, Jonathan, David's own beloved companion. The messages of the lament emphasize the heroic qualities of the warriors, their bravery (v. 22) and their prowess (v. 23). The weeping of the women is alluded to (v. 24), as is the enemies' temptation to gloat over the fallen men (v. 20). The close relationship between the two young warriors is also typical of bardic material. The briefer lament over Abner, employed to exonerate David of the rival general's death, mourns that Abner's death was not duly heroic but the result of treachery. Death through treachery, of course, is typical of epic heroes. Both laments come at critical junctures in the rise of the hero David, marking transitions in power and status.

Verbal Art and Performance

The style of the literature about heroes in Judges and 1 and 2 Samuel is fully traditional, as is much of the Hebrew Bible (see Chapter 4, by Jensen). Repetition within tales and across the biblical corpus is common, for example, as authors frequently use the same language to convey similar content. The authors of tales in Judges and 2 Samuel take special pleasure, however, in having characters use riddles, proverbs, and *meshalim*, media of oral performance. Thus Samson propounds a riddle at his wedding in traditional style (see Noy 1963; Judg. 14: 14) and responds to his riddle opponents in proverbial language (Judg. 14: 18). Gideon calms the Ephraimites, jealous for booty, with a proverb emphasizing their honor; indeed, much in these battle accounts has to do with men's shame and honor (Judg. 8: 2). Enemy kings, facing their own defeat or death, speak in proverbs (Adonibezek in Judg. 1: 7 and Zebah and Zalmunna in Judg. 8: 21; cf. 1 Kgs. 20: 11). Jotham employs a *mashal* to deliver a stinging political critique of the illegitimate ruler Abimelech, who has murdered all of his rivals for power (Judg. 9: 7–21). Finally the judge Jephthah offers a case for the justness of his cause in battle with a rhetorically rich speech that draws upon the traditional history of the exodus (Judg. 11: 4–28).

Poetry and Prose, Oral and Written

It is axiomatic to many biblical scholars in search of Israelite epics that such works were originally poetic and orally composed, even if only hints of these qualities remain visible in the corpus of the Hebrew Bible (see for example Schedl 1965: 239–41; Cross 1973). As James Kugel (1981) has noted, however, the line between "poetry" and "prose" is often blurry in Israelite literature. Aware of ethnic genres, we must allow that cultures will have their own registers of specialized language, quite apart from what we might recognize as poetry or prose in English literature. And as Honko notes, from culture to culture, the epic register will vary. Even within single epics, multiple genres and switches of linguistic style and register are possible (Honko 1998b: 27). Thus Judges 5, the Song of Deborah, is characterized by a particular kind of language. Lines are parallel in content and consistent in length while language is formulaic, densely repetitive, and refrains are common. The laments in 2 Sam. 1: 7–27 and 3: 33–4 are also formulaic and parallelistic, exhibiting language typical of the Israelite lament. And yet, large portions of the narratives of Judges, which modern readers might consider prose, are also presented in highly stylized language. Formulas abound and images are repeated in the parallelistic style seen in more obviously "poetic" works. Each thought, moreover, is complete at the end of each line so that the tale can be set up in a series of self-contained lines, a trait of traditional-style literature as described by A. B. Lord (1960: 54; see e.g., Judg. 6: 12–40, 8: 1–40). But is this traditional style indicative of oral composition? The style is indication of oral-style tastes and aesthetics and may be rooted in a tradition of extemporaneous oral composition of the kind studied by Lord and Parry whereby "singers of tales" build compositions by means of formulaic patterns in language and content; but writing was also available, at least to certain Israelites, even as the oral tradition flourished. The very existence of the various writings of the Hebrew Bible in their traditional style serves as proof of the interplay between the oral and the written, the continuum between them, as studied by Ruth Finnegan (1977) for other cultures. Certain pieces may have been orally composed whereas others may be imitative of oral style. Written works may have been performed orally while oral works may have been written down by scribes or recreated from memory. There were, no doubt, oral and written versions of the narratives of Judges and 2 Samuel and the relationship between the oral and the written is complex and not possible to unravel in the search for Israelite epic (Niditch 1996). While Honko suggests that "poetry" in our terms is not a necessary criterion of epic, Beisssinger and other modern scholars indicate that neither is oral composition. Questions of poetic style and oral composition are important considerations in exploring Israelite epic, but we need to resist the temptation to oversimplify.

Political Dimensions

Judges and 2 Samuel carry a foundational narrative that expresses and helps to create a national identity, roles often ascribed to epic. "Us" is frequently defined over against "them." The Philistines, for example, are the uncircumcised "Other," the Midianites, oppressors. As is the case with comparable material from other traditions, the tales of Israel's early heroes are not, however, ideologically monochromatic. The narratives wrestle in complex ways with defining Israelite political and cultural identity. Supportive of Davidic kingship, tales in 1 and 2 Samuel nevertheless reveal the leader's shortcomings, such failings again being typical of a cross-cultural range of so-called epic heroes. Tales of the Judges are particularly critical of monarchical, centralized leadership. While Israel has no kings in Judges, enemy kings are oppressors. The hero Gideon refuses kingship, stating that the Lord is the only king. His son Abimelech attempts to establish a monarchy by murdering his kin, other contenders for leadership. The *mashal* of the surviving brother, Jotham, compares the man who would be king to a useless bramble. Judges-2 Samuel, moreover, reveal political tensions between two models of polity, one based in kinship and the other in the state. This tension is explored in the civil war narrative of Judg. 19–21 but continues in the narratives of the monarchy in which Benjaminites and northerners chaff under the rule of a Judahite king. The subversive quality and potential "political explosiveness" of these tales are thus apparent.

Shaping the political and ideological dimension of Judges-2 Samuel, as the works now stand in the Hebrew Bible, is the guiding force of God. It is his relationship with Israel and the hero that determines the outcome of events. The deity of Israel, however, is not merely the hero's divine helper. In a set of narrative traditions that scholars frequently consider within the category of "epic," the deity is himself the protagonist, and we cannot conclude our study of the challenge of Israelite epic without some attention to such biblical material.

The Divine Warrior

In passages such as Exod. 15; Ps. 24: 1–10, 89: 8–18; Hab. 3; Zech. 9; and throughout Isa. 40–55, Yhwh is the divine warrior. His victorious battles create or recreate the world as in Marduk's defeat of Tiamat and the forces of chaos in the Mesopotamian tale of creation. Frequently, world-creation intertwines with the establishment of Zion, one of the centers of Israel's symbolic universe, and the divine warrior's victory is on behalf of Israel, his beleaguered people. He rescues them and establishes them as a very part of the cosmogonic process. The "victory-enthronement" pattern that describes the plot of these narratives is rooted in and formulaically expresses the essence of war: challenge by enemies; preparation of weapons for the hero; march to battle; victory; victory shout; march out of battle/procession; celebration (banquet); house-building. The motifs of victory-enthronement, not all of which need appear in any one account and all of which metonymically evoke the larger pattern, also describe military aspects of the narratives about human heroes, set as they are in actual patterns of war. In the pattern of battle and in their function as foundation myths, tales of human heroes and the divine hero are thus comparable. The emotions of war are manifested in each variety of epic-like material, as are the warrior's boasts, his special weapons, and his obvious power. The camaraderie between warriors, the bardic code, the mediation by women (except perhaps for the case of Jephthah's daughter, who is given to the male deity in exchange for victory) are more within the purview of the human hero's tale, but much of the content expected of epic does seems to provide Israelite authors with a means of imaging the explosive machismo of the deity as well as the aspirations of human beings.

Conclusions: Israelite Epic?

In his introduction to Felix Oinas's anthology (1978) of articles on epics of the world, folklorist Richard Dorson provides a brief but masterful overview of traits that recur in the analyses of various traditions included in the volume. He notes that so many of the works that might be considered to be epic are "stirring traditional narrative(s) of perilous adventure, daring, and manhood." They may be "sung, chanted, recited, acted out, danced," but the role of oral composition "remains an open question in each culture where folk epics have arisen" (1978: 4). He observes that heroes manifest human qualities such as bravery or physical might, that they often have divine helpers, and that they may use "guile" as well as strength to vanquish enemies. Underlying story patterns involve conquests, travels, and valor, but the relationship of these works to history varies, for "the hero of history attracts splendid legends and the hero of fiction assumes a realistic and historical dimension, so that they tend to converge over the course of the epic and saga process" (p. 4).

All of Dorson's observations apply well to materials explored in the study of "the challenge of Israelite epic." Did Israelites themselves consider the heroic tales of Judges-2 Samuel and of Yhwh, the divine warrior, to be epic? The least one can say is that the Israelites produced a literature entirely comparable to those of the many cultural traditions explored in Oinas's anthology. Such narratives appealed within ancient Israel as elsewhere, employed in culturally specific ways as a deeply expressive means of asserting and declaring national and ethnic identity.

FURTHER READING

To situate himself or herself in the culture of ancient Israel the reader might consult the *Oxford History of the Biblical World* (Coogan 1998), *Life in Biblical Israel* (King and Stager 2001), *The Religion of Ancient Israel* (Miller 2000), *Ancient Israelite Religion* (Niditch 1997), and *War in the Hebrew Bible* (Niditch 1993b). Conroy's article (1980) provides a thorough overview of earlier studies of the Bible and epic while the works by Frank Moore Cross (e.g., 1973, 1998) remain among the most seminal and influential recent treatments.

Works cited in the present article provide additional avenues for exploration and an indication of major scholarly lines of inquiry. For those who wish to learn more about Judges and 1 and 2 Samuel, biblical works frequently discussed above as providing potential examples of epic literature, see the commentaries by Boling (1975) and McCarter (1980). Three new translations of and commentaries on Judges are due to be published by Jack Sasson (Anchor Bible Commentary), JoAnn Hacket (Hermeneia Series) and myself (Old Testament Library), each of which will address in unique ways an important corpus of tales about biblical heroes.

PART III

Ancient Greek Epic

CHAPTER TWENTY

Near Eastern Connections

Walter Burkert

In the perpective of the western world, "Homer" had long been the solitary beginning of literature, nay the origin of poetry, concentrated in one person, "the original genius of Homer." With the development of scholarship, a more historical approach had to take over, owing to at least three discoveries: (1) The analysis of Homeric language proves that there have been generations of singers, of oral performance underlying the texts we have (see Chapters 13 and 4, by J. Foley and Jensen); (2) The archaeological exploration of Greece and Crete have brought to light Bronze Age civilizations vaguely remembered in "Homer," the "Mycenaean Age" (see Chapter 9, by Sherratt); (3) The recovery of Near Eastern literature of the Bronze Age and post-Bronze Age gives a comprehensive context to Greek epic in what constitutes a Near Eastern-Aegean cultural community (*koiné*).

In the following, there will be first an overview of the manifold interconnections both in the Bronze Age and after; then the transfer of oriental myths from "orient" to Greece will be in focus; finally, parallels of Eastern epic with "Homer" will be discussed, including some cases where literary borrowing seems the most likely diagnosis.

High cultures first developed in Egypt and in Iraq/Mesopotamia in the third millennium, with Syria-Palestine in between and Anatolia right to the side. These civilizations were distinguished by advanced forms of societal organization, with a power system centered on kings and temples, and with the current use of writing (see Chapters 14, 15, and 10, by Sasson, Noegel, and Haslam). Writing, used first for trade and administration, soon developed "literature" in a closer sense, works consciously formed from the resources of language. Writing existed in two strikingly different forms, "hieroglyphs" in Egypt, i.e. elaborate pictures, "cuneiform" in Mesopotamia, i.e. more abstract signs made up of "wedges" in clay tablets. Cuneiform was used for two languages from the beginning, Sumerian and Akkadian. Akkadian became an international means of communication from Anatolia through Syria to Egypt in the second millennium. As against the complications of the original writing systems with hundreds of signs in different functions, which required professional scribes, there were attempts at simplification from the second millennium onwards, first with syllabic systems requiring about 80 signs, then with the alphabet, which can do with about 26 phonetic letters. The alphabet appears in a peculiar form in Ugarit at the coast of Syria (see Chapter 16, by Wyatt), in the thirteenth century BCE; its triumphal career is under way by the first millennium.

Bronze Age civilizations had a complicated history with ups and downs that need not be recorded here. While central Syria remained exposed to Mesopotamian, Egyptian, and Anatolian influences or even attacks, civilizations of their own evolved in North Syria and Anatolia: Hurrites based in North Syria, and Hittites in central Asia Minor, with Hattusa (Turkish name: Boğhazköy) for their capital. Both Hurrites and Hittites adopted Mesopotamian cuneiform to write their own languages, using "international" Akkadian besides (see Chapter 17, by Beckman).

The Bronze Age system swept into Europe to become the first European high culture in Crete: "Minoan" culture flourished from the first half of the second millennium, with palaces such as Knossos, Phaistos, Mallia, and Kydonia (Chania); it came to use a syllabic writing system, "Linear A," which remains undeciphered. This culture reached mainland Greece by about 1600 BCE, by which point it is known as "Mycenaean." Its palaces were at Pylos, Mycenae, Tiryns, and Thebes; it used a modified linear script, "Linear B," which has been deciphered as representing an archaic form of Greek. Linear B also appears at Knossos and Kydonia, which means that Northern Crete was dominated by Mycenaean Greeks by then. Unfortunately Linear B so far seems to be confined to administrative texts.

Among connections with neighboring cultures already in the Bronze Age, those between Crete and Egypt stand out for intensity and continuity. The periodization of "Minoan" history, as established by Arthur Evans (Evans 1921–35), follows that of Egypt on account of the many findings of Egyptian objects in Crete: Early Minoan, Middle Minoan, Late Minoan corresponding to Old, Middle, and New Kingdom in Egypt. Among striking documents of the Egypian connection, there is the ship fresco in Minoan Thera, which represents a trip to Egypt or Libya (Marinatos 1973: pl. XL–XLI). Typical Minoan frescoes, dating from the sixteenth century, were found in Egypt, at Auaris-Tell Daba'a (Bietak and Marinatos 1995; Marinatos 1998). An inscription from Amenophis III, of about 1400, refers to foreign regions under two headings: "Kaftu" (Crete), with place names such as Knossos, Amnisos, Kydonia, and "Tanaju," which must be Greece, country of the "Danaoi," and with the place name Mukana (Mykene) (Edel 1966; Helck 1979: 28–33). The Greek name for Egypt, "Aigyptos," is attested in the Mycenaean language; it derives from Egyptian "Hikuptah" (Memphis).

The interrelations of Minoan/Mycenaean culture with Syria/Palestine should not be underrated either. The palace of Mari on the Euphrates is clearly similar to the palace of Knossos in the iconography of its frescos, which date from about 1800 BCE. The goddess is presenting royal insignia to the king (Amiet 1977: 146, fig. 65; cf. Marinatos 1993: 155, fig. 133). In excavations being conducted at Qatna, Syria, since 2002, Minoan frescoes are turning up, too. A linear writing system appears first at Byblos, in Syria, hence in Crete and Greece and, with three further forms, in Cyprus. Ugarit had close contacts with Cyprus, called Alasia in Ugaritic correpsondence; tablets with Cypriot linear writing have been found at Ugarit, too (Masson 1974; Woodard 1997: 5f.). More distant connections are attested by a hoard of Mesopotamian seals found at the Mycenaean palace of Thebes (Porada 1981). Distinct Mycenaean immigration seems to have reached Cyprus in the twelfth century (Karageorghis 1976). One city continuously inhabited since then is Paphos; it contains the sanctuary of Aphrodite, called "Wanassa" (the "Queen") in perfect Mycenaean language. Cypriot linear writing, used for Greek, is attested by about 1100 BCE and remained in use until the third century BCE (Masson 1983).

The third region for Mycenaean–eastern contacts was Asia Minor, dominated by the Hittite kingdom of Hattusa with its vast archives. New findings and analyses have brought some clarity to geography as seen from Hittite evidence (Starke 1997). Their power clearly extended towards the Aegean. Two rock monuments with inscriptions in Hittite hieroglyphs, between Smyrna and Sardis, had been known for a long time: the warrior reliefs at

Karabel (Hawkins 1998) and the "Niobe" at Mount Sipylos (André-Salvini 1996). In Hittite correspondence, the country "Ahhiyava" has commanded attention. This evidently is what the Greeks called "Achaia," a name which unfortunately turns up in quite different regions. Discussion centers on a city called "Wilusa" in Hittite, with a king Alaksandus about 1300 BCE. Is this Greek "Wilios" – Ilios, Troy (Starke 1997; Latacz 2001)? Has Alaksandus anything to do with Alexandros-Paris in the *Iliad* (see Chapter 21, by Edwards)? Does this bring the "Trojan War" back to real history (Latacz 2001)? There are no written documents from "Troy," but for one seal in Luwian hieroglyphs of the twelfth century (Hawkins and Easton 1996; Latacz 2001: 67–93). We know about various Minoan and Mycenaean settlements in Asia Minor by the Bronze Age, notably Miletus (Gorman 2001: 20–31). A distinctly Mycenaean sword was dedicated by King Tutchalia to his storm-god at Hattusa, as booty "from Assuwa," the inscription says (Hansen 1994); "Assuwa" will refer to some part of the Aegean coast, called "Asie" by Greeks.

Most Bronze Age civilizations around the Aegean collapsed about 1200 BCE in a strange catastrophe; it struck Greece, Crete, Hittite Anatolia, Syria, and Palestine. Palaces, large stone architecture, and even metal work practically disappeared for some centuries in Greece; writing systems fell out of use and were forgotten, such as the Ugaritic alphabet, Hittite cuneiform, and Greek Linear B. Less affected were Egypt and Mesopotamia, the islands and Cyprus. The reasons for this multiple catastrophe are obscured by the break-down of literacy. What remains is guesswork: invasions or economic failure, social upset, plague or drought? Egyptian sources speak of "people of the sea" attacking (*ANET* 262f.); the most tangible of these are the Philistines who occupied Palestine (Dothan and Dothan 1992).

The new world that gradually emerged around the eastern Mediterranean had Philistines in Palestine, flourishing coastal cities such as Tyre and Sidon in Phoenicia, small dynasties of Aramaeans and Luwians from Northern Syria to Anatolia, a major kingdom of Phrygians, probably of western immigrants, farther northwest with Gordion for their capital (Gusmani et al. 1997), and another powerful kingdom, Urartu, around the lake of Van. Urartaeans wrote cuneiform; their language is closely related to Hurrian. Luwian cities, such as Tell Halaf-Guzana, Malatya, Carchemish, and Karatepe, continued to use a form of Hittite hieroglyphs, while the Aramaean-Phoenician alphabet was on the move; it had had its greatest success in the western regions, among the Palestinians, Phoenicians, Aramaeans and soon the Greeks and the Phrygians; the Etruscans in the West followed suit. The main effect of the alphabet was to take literacy from the hands of royal or temple bureaucrats and make it available for the enterprising individual (Sommer 2000). Assyrian administration too adopted alphabetic Aramaean, besides cuneiform. A prince at Karkemish, about 800 BCE, said that he knew twelve languages and four forms of writing, which probably included cuneiform and the alphabet besides Luwian hieroglyphs (Hawkins 2000; vol. II, p. 131, nr 24) – a perfectly "international" situation at the crossing of the Euphrates.

Progress and crisis in these centuries were due to two main factors: the development of Mediterranean trade by Phoenicians and Greeks turning West, and the onslaught of Assyrian military power from the East.

Trade was the enterprise of Phoenicians, mainly from Tyre and Sidon, especially in search of metals. Their city in Cyprus, Kition, was founded by about 900 (Karageorghis 1976). The Phoenicians went on to establish their presence in Africa, Sardinia, Sicily, and Spain; their new city, Carthage, was founded in 814. The Phoenicians were followed by the Greeks, who took up connections with Syria and founded their own colonies in southern Italy and Sicily; the center of activity was at first Euboea, with Chalkis and Eretria (Boardman 1999); in the eighth century Corinth took over. One group of enterprising Greeks, in particular those of Euboea, had been called "Iawones," which became "Iones" in classical Greek, while the orientals took this name to designate Greeks in general: Hebrew "Jawan," Akkadian "Iauna," "Yunan" in modern Arabic and Turkish. In fact it was the Phoenician–Greek initiative that shifted the center of civilization from the Near East to the Mediterranean, giving a unique chance to the Greeks as the most eastern people in the Near West.

As for Assyria, the king had long held the title "Lord of the Whole, Lord of the Four Quarters of the World." But it was the kings of Assur who embarked on unlimited conquest: relying on their superior military power, they began to plunder the neighboring tribes, kingdoms, or cities, year on year; booty and devastating tributes were used to entertain the army. Building prestigious palaces in new capitals, the fine reliefs of which now fill western museums, they turned west, by the ninth century, to reach the Mediterranean. The climactic point came in the eighth and seventh centuries: Damascus was conquered about 800, Israel in 722, Cyprus about 700, Sidon was destroyed in 672; Egypt came under Assyrian domination 671–655.

The main adversary of Assyria in eastern Anatolia, Urartu, collapsed about 700 under a northern invasion by "Cimmerians" ("Gimirra" in Akkadian, "Kimmerioi" in Greek); so did Phrygia (Ivantchik 1993). In these fierce times a usurper, Gyges, became king of Lydia, with Sardis for his capital. There was flourishing gold production in that region by then, and Gyges was remembered by the Greeks for that (Archil. fr. 19,1). The Greek cities of Asia Minor succumbed to his power. Gyges also sought recognition from the East and made obeisance to Assurbanipal, king of Nineveh, who in turn considered him his vassal (Ivantchik 1993). Thus a direct road from Asia Minor to Mesopotamian Nineveh was discovered, one that remained in constant use, and was later called the "King's Road." The Greeks remembered forms of "soft living" imported from Lydia, the most characteristic of which was lying on couches, instead of using chairs for a symposium; the first visual record of this is the relief "Assurbanipal's garden party" (Amiet 1977: fig. 634; Burkert 2003a: 16).

To sum up: In the first centuries of the first millennium BCE the Eastern–Greek relations were channeled in two main currents: the Phoenician line, with Assyrians in the background and Cyprus as a meeting place, and the Lydian line, also leading to Assyria. Greek contacts with Syria existed from the ninth century; the land connection was finally established by Gyges after 700. Egypt became a dominating partner when the Assyrians retreated and Psammetichus I (twenty-sixth dynasty) gained power, bringing a large-scale influx of Greek mercenaries and Greek traders. These had installed their market-place at Naukratis in Egypt by 600; Cyprus too became dominated by Egyptian products and style.

The unique luck of Greeks, in contrast to Phoenicians, was to be touched but not to be crushed by the eastern developments. When the Assyrians had occupied Syria, Cyprus, and part of Anatolian Cilicia, the Greeks must have had contact with them. It seems that refugees from Syria came to Crete, while at the same time Greek entrepreneurs engaged in trade and piracy in Syria. Greek mercenaries, together with Carian ones from Anatolia, were to infiltrate the current wars. A cuneiform letter of about 738, from Syria, mentions invaders from "the country Iaunaia," that is, Ionians who were plundering the Syrian coast (Saggs 1963; Burkert 1992: 12). There was a naval battle between Ionians and Assyrians near Tarsos in Cilicia about 700 (Momigliano 1974: 409–13).

Closer and more persistent were the contacts with Phoenicians. Greeks and Phoenicians met at Kommos, a port of southern Crete, and at Ischia, in view of the Italian mainland; both turned up in Etruria, and both settled in Sicily, where fierce antagonism was to develop.

The decisive "Phoenician" import to Greece – be it from Phoenicians in the strict sense or from Aramaeans farther north – was the alphabet. The transfer included wax tablet, leather scroll, and text arrangements. Greeks at Cyprus went on to use their linear form of writing; the others adopted "Phoenician" signs (*Phoinikeia*). The Greek alphabet has some modernizations, especially the consistent writing of vowels; but Greeks continued to learn the immutable sequence of letters, apparently laid down by the first Bronze Age inventor, in spite of the fact that *alpha, beta, gamma* are Semitic words that do not make sense in Greek. The Greek word for writing tablet, *deltos*, and one word for the wax on the tablet, *malthê*, are Semitic, too. A bowl with Phoenician inscription had reached Crete by the ninth century (Niemeyer 1984: pl. 8). More impressive are the bronze "horse plates" in North Syrian style of Hazael, king of Damascus (ninth century), which somehow came to Greece and had been dedicated to Greek gods at Samos and Eretria by the eighth century (Kyrieleis and Röllig 1988). Did any Greek take notice of their Aramaean inscription? The first apparently Greek letters so far attested were written in Latium shortly after 800 BCE (Peruzzi 1998), and an explosion of Greek literacy occurred by the second half of the eighth century. The first hexameters written in Greek letters, of about 730 BCE, are found on the "Dipylon vase" at Athens and the "Nestor vase" at Ischia (Jeffery 1990: 76 n.1; 239 n. 1). The Athenian inscription is the only one that keeps the letter *alpha* lying on its side, as does Semitic *aleph*. At Ischia Greeks at any rate were intermingling with Phoenicians/Aramaeans, as the mixture of inscriptions shows (Bartonek 1997).

Unfortunately the modern form of writing was normally used on perishable materials: leather, wood, and – later – papyrus. As a result, there is a sudden blackout of documentation, in distinct contrast to the Bronze Age situation. This does not mean that there was less writing and reading, less literature in Syria, Cyprus, and the adjacent West. It just means that only those parcels of literature survived that became selected as "classic" in specific literary traditions, be it Greek or Hebrew (see Chapter 19, by Niditch). For the rest, tiny scraps of evidence must do.

Surely there was no divide between Akkadian, Aramaean, and Phoenician, nor between these and Greek. We have stories about Nineveh in the Hebrew book of Jonah, and in the Aramaean tale of Ahiqar (*TUAT* III, part 2: 320–47); this book was also read in Egypt and somehow got into the Greek "Life of Aesopus." The name of Gilgamesh appears once in an Aramaean text from Qumran (Milik 1976: 313), apart from a curious reference in Aelianus (*NA.* 12.21). It is less clear whether we should postulate the existence of Luwian literature that follows the great Hittite period; Lydia remains totally obscure to us. We cannot identify either the places or the exact time of literary contacts, even if the line Syria – Euboea/Athens – Ischia obtrudes itself. All that can be done is to catalogue similarities. But it should be kept in mind that we are not bringing bits and pieces together from afar: we are moving within a cultural *koinê* from Nineveh through Karkemish to Egypt, to Cyprus, to Sardis, and to Euboea.

For Greek mythology, the publication of the Hittite text "Kingship in heaven" (Güterbock 1946; *ANET* 120; *TUAT* III, part 4: 828–30) came as a fundamental shock. The text so closely resembles not only the system of Hesiod's theogony but also the scandalous detail in it that independent development seems impossible. Both texts introduce divine generations prior to the ruling storm-god, with a prominent position for the god "Heaven" (Anu/Uranos). The concept of ancient, vanquished gods is shared with Phoenician and Babylonian mythology. But the appalling detail, from Kumarbi to Hesiod, is the castration of "Heaven," effected by Kumarbi in Hittite, by Kronos in Greek; Kronos uses a sickle, whereas Kumarbi bites and swallows Anu's manhood. Nevertheless the line from Hittite to Hesiod is not without problems, especially since the motif of swallowing Heaven's phallus has recently turned up in the theogony of Orpheus (Burkert 2003a: 98–100). Kumarbi is the name of a Hurrite god, also known at Ugarit. Thus a Hurrite-Syrian-Ionian line could be constructed as well as a Luwian-Ionian one.

The other Hurrite-Hittite text which seems to point towards Hesiod is the tale about a dangerous antagonist arising to challenge the ruling storm-god, with a battle and the defeat of the usurper in the end. In Hittite this is Ullikummi, son of Kumarbi, born from a rock (Güterbock 1952b; *ANET* 121–5; *TUAT* III, part 4: 830–44); the text points to Mount Hazzi, which is "Kasion Oros" in Greek, a mountain north of Ugarit with a sanctuary of the storm-god – Teshub in Hurrite, Hadad in Syrian, and Zeus in Greek – which was still in existence in late antiquity (Burkert 2001). In Greek the usurper is Typhon; the *Iliad* has an enigmatic reference (*Il.* 2.783), where *en Arimois* might point to Aramaeans. Has Greek *Typhon/Typhoeus* anything to do with the Semitic word for the "north mountain," *har Zaphon*? Even a perfect *koiné* situation leaves uncertainties.

A more general theme is the fight between the god and a snake or dragon. It comes in numerous variants, and might be a universal theme. But there are distinctive traits to show dependencies. The dragon appears as a multi-headed monster, usually seven-headed, on Sumerian seals and in a sequence of texts, from Sumerian via Ugarit to the Hebrew Bible, and is also manifest in the multi-headed water snake *Hydra*, the antagonist of Herakles (Burkert 2003b, 56f., 239). Another variant introduces a one-headed monster snake. The tale of Illuyankas, told in two versions in Hittite (*ANET* 125f.; *TUAT* III, part 4: 808–11), finds its most striking parallel with the *Typhon* version in the library of Apollodorus (1.6.3; Burkert 1992: 103). The fight of two gods with a huge snake appears in a stone relief at Luwian Malatya (Akurgal 1976: pl. 104) – called "Illuyankas" by scholars, while the strange rays on its back point directly to much older Mesopotamian seals, and to the cuneiform sign for "snake" (MUSH). The dragon also takes the form of a monster of the sea. This is *Yam* in an Egyptian text evidently reproducing an Ugaritic tale; the attractive goddess Astarte has to cajole the monster towards his defeat (*ANET* 17). Greek myth has Perseus rescuing Andromeda from the sea monster; the tale is localized at Ioppe/Jaffa in Palestine, and the earliest vase painting illustrating this fight copies the iconography of Assyrian seals, with misunderstandings (Burkert 2003b: 72). It is hopeless to reconstruct a single line of tradition for the snake combats; coexisting variants found different applications in Greek mythology and imagery, as they had been wandering between the neigboring civilizations for some time.

One piece of Egyptian royal ideology seems to have engendered a Greek myth: The supreme god, accompanied by his servant, visits the queen in the guise of her husband in order to generate a new pharaoh, or else Herakles (West 1997b: 458 f.). Another impressive myth that seems to arise in Akkadian and Sumerian literature and spread to Israel, Greece, and India is the story of the flood (Caduff 1986; Bremmer 1998). This will be dealt with in the next section.

Greek epic as literature, against the background of Near Eastern literature, appears as narrative in an elaborate literary style, i.e. poetry about gods, sons of gods, and great men from the past (see Chapters 1 and 7, by Martin and Louden). Such epics mainly exist in Akkadian, with *Atrahasis* and *Gilgamesh* as the foremost examples and *Erra* as the latest representative. Hurrite-Hittite mythological compositions are related to the genre, as are the few texts from Ugarit.

On account of very different languages one might expect to encounter quite different principles of style and structure in the East and the West. Yet whoever cares to look at the evidence will be struck by the similarities (Burkert 1992: 114–20; Morris 1997; West 1997b). This has been known for a long time (Bowra 1952). To start with the openings of *Gilgamesh* and the *Odyssey*: attention is called to a hero who wandered wide and saw many things, while his name is intentionally withheld (Burkert 1992: 117. West 1997b: 403f.).

No less striking is the similarity of the meeting and dialogue of Gilgamesh with his dead friend Enkidu and of Achilles with the "soul" of Patroklos (Burkert 1992: 200; West 1997b: 344 f.).

But it is in the styles that the really important parallels begin: in Greek as in Akkadian, a long verse is employed, repeated indefinitely without strophic division. In this texture there recur formulaic verses, the repetition of verse groups, standard epithets, and typical scenes such as the "assembly of the gods." Epithets had always appeared to be characteristic of Homeric style, such as "cloud-gathering Zeus" or "Odysseus of many counsels," "Odysseus of many sufferings." In Akkadian and Ugaritic epic too the chief characters have their epithets (West 1997b: 220 ff.): the hero of the flood is "Utnapishtim the far-away," and the dangerous "Seven" in *Erra* are "champions without peer"; Ugaritic has "the Virgin Anat," and "father of gods and men" for a superior god. The epithets are ornamental insofar as they are not essential for the actual context nor specially modeled for it; all the same, they are extremely helpful in filling out a verse or half-verse. Besides formulaic epithets, comparisons are a popular device in Akkadian epic as in related poetry, including Hebrew psalms; lions are favorites (West 1997b: 218 ff.).

As for repetitions of verse groups, a striking feature is the exact verbal correspondence between command and performance, reporting and repetition of the report. The Mesopotamian scribes, weary of wedges, even use a "repeat" sign. In formulaic verse the complicated introduction of direct speech is especially notable. In Akkadian this reads, in a literal translation: "He set his mouth and spoke, to X. He said (the word)" (West 1997b: 196–8). This makes three synonyms, and a whole line. It is the same with the well-known Homeric formula: "Towards him/her, raising his voice, the winged words he/she spoke." It is natural for a narrative to move from day to day, but to employ stereotyped formulae for sunset and sunrise, pause and action, is a specific technique, both in *Gilgamesh* and in Homer. In *Gilgamesh*, the new day is introduced with the formula: "At the brightening of some of morning," less poetic and still equivalent to Homer's "But when early-born rosy-fingered Eos appeared."

Among typical scenes the assembly of the gods (*puhur ilani*) is prominent. This is a fixed concept in Akkadian, which recurs in Ugaritic and is elaborated also in *Ullikummi* (West 1997b: 177–80). The "assembly of gods" has even invaded the Hebrew Bible, at the beginning of Job (see Chapter 19, by Niditch). One may state that the oriental assembly of the gods is more a kind of senate, whereas Homer makes them a family, including the current quarrels between parents and scolding and blows for their offspring.

At least in *Gilgamesh* more complicated forms of narrative technique are tried out, and these also characterize Homer's *Odyssey*. The story of the flood is introduced into *Gilgamesh* in the form of direct speech, by the main participant, Utnapishtim "the far-away." The *Odyssey* too incorporates most of Odysseus' adventures in a first-person tale by Odysseus himself at the Phaeacians' palace. The double action at the beginning of *Gilgamesh*, leading to the first meeting of Enkidu and Gilgamesh, is built up in the way that the narrative first follows Enkidu's adventures and then introduces Gilgamesh, his position in the city and his preparations for the encounter through the direct speech of the prostitute addressing Enkidu. The *Odyssey* engineers a complicated double plot to bring Telemachus and Odysseus together.

Battle scenes invite comparisons, too. One notable example of combat poetry is the Egyptian text about Pharaoh Ramses II in the battle of Qadesh, when the hero finds himself alone amidst the enemies, prays to his father, the god Amun, and then sets out to kill all the enemies in his onslaught (Lichtheim 1976: 57–72). A suggestive Akkadian text, in fully "Homeric" style, is incorporated in the *Annals of Sennacherib*, referring to the battle of Halule (691 BCE): the king takes up his armor piece by piece, mounts his chariot, and finally rides victoriously through splatters of blood (Luckenbill 1927: §§ 252–4; cf. *Il.* 20.498–501; Burkert 1992: 118 f.). The genre of combat stories is also represented in the Hebrew Bible, especially by the "Song of Deborah and Barak" (Judg. 4).

Assembling motifs in such a way may still not yet be considered probative: "Parallels" may be found everywhere. Yet there are more complex structures for which sheer coincidence becomes quite unlikely: a system of major deities dividing the cosmos by lots; a decree of the ruling god to destroy mankind because it has become a burden to the earth; a family scene among gods with appropriate characters for father, mother, and daughter. It should be stressed once more that we are not bringing together distant worlds, but moving within the Near Eastern and Mediterranean *koiné*.

First, some passages from the *Iliad* which show correspondences to important passages of *Atrahasis*, *Gilgamesh*, and *Enûma Elish*, the most important Akkadian classics. There is one passage in Homer where cosmogony unexpectedly comes to the fore. Aristotle (*Met.* 983b27) found here the very beginning of natural philosophy: Hera, in her lying speech within the section called the "Deception of Zeus" by the ancients, says she is going to Oceanus, "origin of the gods," and to "Mother Tethys"; somewhat later Oceanus is even called "the origin of all" (*Il.* 14.201 = 302; 14.246 cf. 15.189). Oceanus and Tethys, the primeval couple, Hera alleges, have not fulfilled their nuptial rights for a long time, separated by "strife." This has its closest parallel in the beginning of the Babylonian epic *Enûma Elish* (I.1–5; Dalley 1989: 233): "When above," this text begins, "skies were not yet named nor earth below pronounced by name, Apsu, the first, their begetter, and Tiamat who bore them all, had mixed their waters together. . . then gods were born within them." Apsu is ground water, Tiamat is the sea; mixing together, "begetter" and "mother," they were the origin of all.

It is clear: Hera's incidental inventions correspond to the beginning of *Enûma Elish* to a surprising degree. Tethys, however, was not an active figure in Greek mythology; no one had anything further to tell about her. But note the names: *Ti-amat* is normally written in the cuneiform text, but the normal form of the Akkadian word is *tiamtu* or *tâmtu*, "sea," and the orthography *taw(a)tu* is found too. If one could proceed from "Tawtu," "Tethys" is an exact transcription (Burkert 1992: 93; but see West 1997b: 147). Eudemus, pupil of Aristotle, who evidently had at least a partial translation of *Enûma Elish*, wrote "Tauthê" (fr. 150 Wehrli). Thus right in the middle of the *Iliad*, the water cosmogony with a mysterious name for the "mother" directly stems from an Akkadian classic.

The connection of *Dios Apaté* with Akkadian literature has become more close with the publication of *Atrahasis* (Lambert and Millard 1969). The oldest version of this text is dated to the seventeenth century BCE; various Old Babylonian tablets have survived in fragmentary form; the library of Assurbanipal contained several editions with slight variants. A fragment of another recension has been found at Ugarit; this text had been in circulation, nay popular, for more than a thousand years.

"When gods were in the ways of men," the text starts; with no humans yet in existence, the gods had to do all the necessary work themselves, digging canals and building ditches. So they created men to act as robots: "They shall bear the burden." But soon, "after 600 (and?) 600 years," these creatures multiplied, to become a nuisance. The earth was crying out, the gods were disturbed; hence they decided to annihilate mankind again – and they failed. First there was a plague, then a famine, and finally the flood. Yet the cunning god of the deep, Enki, in alliance with the man "outstanding by wisdom," Atrahasis, plays off the gods one against the other, and finally Atrahasis builds his ark. The final part of the text is an older parallel to *Gilgamesh* XI, the story of the flood as it had been known since the nineteenth century.

At the beginning of the *Atrahasis* text, the Babylonian pantheon is introduced in a systematic fashion: "Anu, their father, was king; their counsellor was the warrior Enlil; their chamberlain was Ninurta; and their sheriff Ennugi." These verses are copied in the *Gilgamesh* epic, but not the following lines: "They grasped the flask of lots by the neck, they cast the lots; the gods made the division: Anu went up to heaven," a second god – gap in the text; probably Enlil – "took the earth for his subjects," and "the bolts, the bar of the sea, were set for Enki, the far-sighted." Anu, Enlil, and Enki, sky-god, weather-god, water-god, make up the usual triad of cosmic gods. The *Atrahasis* text repeatedly comes back to this threefold division.

In Homer's *Iliad*, however, there are those famous, oft-quoted verses in which the world is divided among the appropriate Homeric gods (*Il.* 15.190–3; Burkert 1992: 89f.; West 1997b: 109–11). Poseidon is speaking: "When we threw the lots I received the grey sea as my permanent abode, Hades drew the murky darkness, Zeus however drew the wide sky of brightness and clouds; the earth is common to all, and spacious Olympus." This differs from the system of *Atrahasis* insofar as the earth together with Olympus is declared to be a joint dominion. Still, the basic structure is quite similar: three distinct areas of the cosmos, heaven, the depths of the earth, and the waters, assigned to the three major gods, male gods altogether; and in both instances the division has been established by drawing lots. The three brothers and their realms do not play any further common part in Homer, nor do they make a triad in Greek cult. By contrast, in *Atrahasis* the pertinent passage is fundamental for the narrative, and is referred to repeatedly. There is hardly another passage in Homer which comes so close to being a translation of an Akkadian epic.

From *Atrahasis* we are led to notice another important connection beyond the *Iliad*. The basic idea, human overpopulation that oppresses the earth, recurs in a prominent Greek text, the very beginning of the "Trojan Cycle," the *Cypria*, an epic that was popular down to the classical epoch (see Chapter 24, by Burgess). The opening lines have been preserved as a fragment (fr. 1 Bernabé = fr. 1 Davies). This was the ultimate cause of the Trojan War: Zeus, as he noticed the oppression of the earth, "took pity and deep in his heart he decided to relieve the all-nourishing earth of men, by setting alight the great conflict of the Ilian War." As a variant, a prose narrative tells how Zeus, in order to lighten the burden of the earth, first caused the Theban War and later the Trojan one, rejecting other options, such as lightning or flood. The variants cannot be combined directly; but they come together in recalling *Atrahasis*, in the earth suffering, the decision of the ruling god. This is not to forget that the story of the flood also came to Greece, in several variants and localizations (Caduff 1986; Bremmer 1998), probably through oral communication; in its early phases it cannot be pinned down to definite literary works.

As regards the *Cypria*, there is a further hint at the East: the title *Cypria* evidently refers to the island of Cyprus. While iconography indicates that at least the "Judgment of Paris," a main episode of the *Cypria*, was known around 650 BCE (Schefold 1993: 127–9, fig. 120a), we are led to an epoch when Cyprus, though flourishing with a mixture of eastern luxury and "Homeric" life-style, was formally under Assyrian sovereignty (Karageorghis 1969); memorial steles of Assyrian kings such as Sargon had been set up there (Luckenbill 1927: 100–3, cf. 261). We do not know why it was the "Homeric" theme of the Trojan War which produced a "Cypriot epic." But it is a fact.

To come back to the *Iliad* in comparison with *Gilgamesh*: in *Gilgamesh* there is one famous encounter of divinity and man, of Ishtar and Gilgamesh (VI. 1–91). When Gilgamesh has killed Humbaba, the demon of the forest, and has cleansed himself of the grime of battle, Ishtar "raised an eye at the beauty of Gilgamesh" and proposes sexual union. But Gilgamesh scornfully rejects her, giving a catalogue of all her partners whom she once "has loved" only to destroy them in consequence; "If you would love me, you would [treat me] like them." Whereupon Ishtar, enraged, goes up to heaven: "Forth went Ishtar before Anu (Heaven), her father; before Antum, her mother, her tears were flowing"; she complains about Gilgamesh's insults. But father Anu answers with mild reproach: "Surely you have provoked (the King of Uruk)."

Compare a scene from the *Iliad* (5,330–431; Burkert 1992: 96–8; West 1997b: 361 f.): Aphrodite, trying to protect her son Aeneas, has been wounded by Diomedes, her blood is flowing. Beside herself, she goes up to Olympus, she falls into the lap of her mother, Dione, who consoles her, while sister Athena makes scornful comments. But father Zeus has a mild reproach: "You are not given to the works of war."

The two scenes are parallel to one another in structure, narrative form and "ethos" to an astonishing degree. A goddess, injured by a human, goes up to heaven to complain to her father and her mother, and she earns a mild rebuke from her father. Ishtar's meeting with Gilgamesh is firmly anchored in the structure of the Gilgamesh epic, since Ishtar, in her wrath, brings down the "Bull of Heaven" for the next exploit of Gilgamesh and Enkidu. In Homer we have a genre scene, depicted with gusto but, on the whole, irrelevant. Still, the persons involved are, in fact, identical: the sky-god, his wife, and their common daughter the goddess of love. In analogy to Ishtar's love affairs, Aphrodite has offered herself to a mortal man, Anchises the father of Aeneas, who suffered some strange fate as a result. By force of an even more special parallelism, Aphrodite has a mother in Olympus here, Dione. This name is just the feminine form of "Zeus," exactly as Antu, the mother of Ishtar in the Gilgamesh text, is the feminine form of Anu, "Heaven." Anu/Antu are a couple firmly established in cult and myth in Mesopotamia; Dione at Olympus makes her appearance solely in this scene, and nowhere else. Hera seems forgotten for a while, as is the Hesiodic account of Aphrodite's birth from the sea; later in the *Iliad* Dione is non-existent, while Hera is back again. "Homer" proves to be dependent on *Gilgamesh* even at the linguistic level, introducing Dione as a calque on Antu. This Akkadian/Greek connection is hardly less impressive than Tawtu/Tethys, though it works at the level of narrative structure and divine characters instead of cosmic agents.

The influence of *Gilgamesh* may also be detected in a scene from the *Odyssey* (4.759–67). When Penelope learns about the risky journey undertaken by Telemachus and about the suitors' plot to kill him, she first bursts into tears and complaints. Then, calming down, she washes and dresses in clean clothes; she goes up to the upper story of the house. Together with her maids, she takes barley corn in a basket, prays to Athena for safe return of Telemachus, throws out the barley and ends with an inarticulate shriek (*ololyge*). This form of prayer was found puzzling for historians of religion: was it an "abbreviation of sacrifice," or an otherwise unknown ritual? But look at *Gilgamesh* (III. 38–45): when Gilgamesh, together with Enkidu, is leaving his city to fight Humbaba, his mother Ninsun takes to ceremonial prayer.

> She cleansed herself in water [perfumed with] tamarisk and soapwort, she dressed in a fine garment, the adornment of her body…the adornment of her breast….She leapt up the staircase, she climbed on to the roof, she set up a censer before Shamash, she scattered incense before Shamash, she lifted her arms. (trans. George 2003)

In this form she prays, full of distress and sorrow, for a safe return of her son. The situation, a mother praying for an adventurous son, is not an unusual one. Yet in its details the scene from the *Odyssey* comes close to being a translation of *Gilgamesh* (Burkert 1992: 99f.; West 1997b: 421). In fact it is closer to the *Gilgamesh* text than to a comparable scene in the *Iliad* (15.189), when Achilles is praying for the safe return of Patroklos. What appears odd in the *Odyssey* is quite at home in *Gilgamesh*: burning incense on the roof.

To sum up: there is continuity, nay a *koiné* of culture from Mesopotamia via Syria/ Palestine to Anatolia and Egypt (see Chapter 14, by Sasson). There were channels reaching the Greek world from all three sides. The influence is manifest in myths about cosmogony and divine combats, in which Hittite traditions play a special role (see Chapter 17, by Beckman), and it is especially working in epic poetry, mostly in tales about the gods, both in adumbrations of cosmogony and in special scenes. Some parallels to Akkadian classics come close to translation. Literary influence is to be accepted, even if the links, possibly via Phoenician/Aramaean versions, have disappeared with the perishable writing materials on which they had been drawn.

FURTHER READING

J. B. Pritchard (ed.). *Ancient Near Eastern Texts Relating to the Old Testament*, 4th edn. (*ANET*) (1974).

John Boardman. *The Greeks Overseas*, 4th edn. (1999).

Stephanie Dalley. *Myths from Mesopotamia* (1989). Repr. 1991, 1998.

Benjamin R. Foster. *Before the Muses: An Anthology of Akkadian Literature*, 2 vols. (1993). Repr. 1996. 2nd edn.

Harry A. Hoffner (trans.). *Hittite Myths*, ed. Gary M. Beckman (1998). 2nd edn.

W. G. Lambert and A. R. Millard. *Atra-hasis: The Babylonian Story of the Flood* (1969).

Sarah Morris. "Homer and the Near East," in Morris and Powell (eds.) *A New Companion to Homer* (1997).

Charles Penglase. *Greek Myths and Mesopotamia* (1994).

Peter Walcot. *Hesiod and the Near East* (1996).

Martin L. West. *The East Face of Helicon* (1997).

R. M. Whiting. (ed.) *Mythology and Mythologies: Methodological Approaches to Intercultural Influences* (Melammu Symposia 2) (2001).

CHAPTER TWENTY-ONE

Homer's *Iliad*

Mark W. Edwards

The *Iliad* and the *Odyssey* (see Chapter 22, by Slatkin) are epics isolated by their size and their quality from their contemporaries and successors in ancient Greece, and very probably from their precursors too. They were commonly attributed to one exceptionally gifted and enormously respected man, Homer, about whom nothing that we would call historical was known, though the poems attributed to him were put together in a period about which we have a good deal of other information. Already in antiquity, however, these two poems were sometimes attributed to two different authors, on grounds we would find insufficient; and the question of authorship, like those of composition and recording in writing, remains controversial.

During the twentieth century our understanding of the historical background against which the Homeric poems were composed changed, but not very greatly. The bigger changes came as a result of discoveries in the characteristics of oral poetry and their application to Homeric studies, which brought about the abandonment of the older purposes and methods of research, which had often treated the poems as agglomerations of disparate material or as heavily-interpolated with "late" accretions. The new approach concentrated on traditional oral techniques appearing in the poems, techniques which facilitated composition and memorization, such as verbal formulae, repeated set scenes, patterns of plot, and the means of expanding or contracting a song which had no standard length, but whose features differed at every performance, even if sung by the same singer.

A product of our improved understanding of the essential nature of the Homeric songs and the techniques of oral poetry enshrined in them has been the possibility of distinguishing traditional elements in the poems, inherited by the singer from his predecessors and shared with his contemporaries and immediate successors, from the modifications and adaptations made by the outstandingly talented singer (or singers, if there were two) responsible for the *Iliad* and the *Odyssey*. Here a good deal must, of course, remain hypothetical and disputed. But certain features and examples of the great poet's creativity can be distinguished with fair precision, and will be noticed in what follows.

The Plot

In speaking of the structure and plot of the *Iliad* it is convenient to refer to the conventional book divisions, though these were almost certainly not employed by Homer himself but inserted in the Hellenistic period. First a short proem (1.1–5) invokes the name of the Muse and concentrates not (as one might have expected) on the glories of a Greek conquest or the might of their leading hero, but on Achilles' anger and the devastation it caused to the Greek forces. Then the starting point of the tale is set, "from when the quarrel began between Agamemnon and Achilles" (1.6–7), and after a few lines in anticipation of the immediate crisis (the plague imposed by the offended Apollo: 1.8–11) the narrative and direct speech begin at once. Apollo's priest attempts to ransom his daughter, Agamemnon's prize; the Lord of Men harshly refuses; in answer to the priest's prayer the god descends and inflicts the army with plague, Achilles calls an assembly to hear what the chief seer considers its cause, and the scene is set for the conflict between Agamemnon and his restive subordinate (1.12–58).

Their harsh words reveal a history of disagreement between the two, and Agamemnon compounds his folly in antagonizing a god by antagonizing his most important ally also, threatening to seize Achilles' prize captive to replace the one he must now surrender to her father, and after further angry exchanges he actually follows through on this. During the encounter, Achilles is restrained from violent action by the advice of Athena (1.188–222), and the old counselor Nestor vainly attempts mediation (1.247–84). Essentially, the cause of the strife is not the work of the gods, the Trojan enemy, or human wickedness, but unwise actions by two powerful egos in an unfortunate juxtaposition and relative rank order – a continuing and universal human problem.

The enraged Achilles withdraws from the Greek army, and in response to his goddess mother Thetis' supplication Zeus promises that in his absence the Greeks will be defeated. But before this happens (in Book 8), the poet enlarges the range of the narrative with further issues: an account of the beginning of the expedition to Troy and the forces engaged there (Book 2); a recapitulation of the cause of the war, the seduction of Menelaos' wife Helen by the Trojan prince Paris (Book 3); a further insult to the gods by the Trojans' breaking of a truce (Book 4); the battlefield exploits of Diomedes, a temporary surrogate for the absent Achilles (Book 5); the introduction of the Trojan leader Hektor and his wife and child (Book 6); and a formal duel between Hektor and Ajax (Book 7), a preview of his final encounter with Achilles (in Book 22).

Beaten back as a result of Zeus' decision (Book 8), Agamemnon and the disheartened Greeks send an embassy to Achilles and offer him an immense compensation if he will return (Book 9), but he rejects three appeals in succession and vows not to return until the Trojans reach his own ships. After an irrelevant night-time Greek patrol (Book 10, perhaps a later addition by the same poet), five books (11–15) describe the ebb and flow of battle around the newly-built Greek defensive wall, lightened by some humorous action on the divine level (14.153–353). In addition, the next part of the plot is introduced by Nestor's suggestion to Achilles' friend Patroklos that the latter don Achilles' armor and lead Achilles' troops into the battle in the brooding hero's place (11.793–802). In response, Patroklos persuades Achilles to let him do this, and he returns to the battle as his surrogate (Book 16). He is killed by Hektor, and after a long struggle his body is recovered by the Greeks (Book 17).

The grief-stricken Achilles vows to avenge him, but first his mother Thetis obtains a newly-made set of armor for him from Hephaestos (Book 18), and the gifts promised to him by Agamemnon's envoys in Book 9 must be handed over (Book 19). He then returns to the battle and kills many Trojans, survives an assault by the god of one of the rivers near Troy (Books 20–1), and eventually kills Hektor in a duel (Book 22). He then presides over Patroklos' funeral and the games which honor the dead man (Book 23).

This concludes the tales of withdrawal, return, and revenge, but the last book (24) introduces a further theme of consolation. Despite his revenge, Achilles remains inconsolable and continues to mutilate his enemy's corpse (24.1–22). Encouraged by the worried gods, old Priam journeys to Achilles' camp to ransom the corpse of his son, and Achilles consoles him; they share a meal, Achilles restores the body, and gains control over his own anger and sorrow (24.159–676). The Trojans (and Helen) lament over the body of Hektor and bury him (24.697–804). The poem thus concludes not with the fall of Troy or the death of Achilles (though both events are heavily foreshadowed throughout), but by the hero's acceptance of his mortal limits (as in *Gilgamesh*; see Chapters 15, 20, and 6, by Noegel, Burkert, and Nagy) and the universality of human suffering. Achilles finds closure not by killing the man who slew his greatest friend, but by showing compassion to the family of his victim.

Story-lines, Traditional and New

A number of the story lines (often called "themes") of the *Iliad* are found more than once in the poem, and these and others also recur in other tales of Troy (and of course in storytelling worldwide). The quarrel between the leaders Agamemnon and Achilles which begins the poem is matched by references to quarrels between Agamemnon and Menelaos, Achilles and Odysseus, Ajax and Odysseus. The central action of the plot, the withdrawal of the major hero from the battle, the devastation that results, and his eventual return and victory, is known in many cultures, and recurs in the tale of Meleager (9.529–599). Abduction of a woman is three times a cause of trouble in the poem (Helen, Chryseis, Briseis), and similar tales open the *History* of Herodotus (and were well enough known to be parodied by Aristophanes, *Acharnians* 524–9). Smaller repeated patterns are also common: a set-piece duel between major heroes (Paris and Menelaos in *Iliad* 3, Hektor and Ajax in *Iliad* 7, Achilles and Hektor in *Iliad* 22), supplication scenes (major occurrences are Zeus' supplication by Thetis in *Iliad* 1, Achilles by Odysseus, Ajax, and Phoenix in *Iliad* 9, Achilles by Patroklos in *Iliad* 16 and by Priam in *Iliad* 24); and funeral games in honor of a hero (in *Iliad* 23 for Patroklos, and those for Achilles described in *Odyssey* 24).

There are cases where one may surmise that the *Iliad* poet has adapted a traditional theme for its use in his great poem. A struggle to rescue the corpse of a downed hero occurs in brief form over the bodies of the Trojan ally Sarpedon and Hektor's charioteer Cebriones (Book 16) before the major instance in the case of Patroklos (Book 17) – and of course over the dead Achilles himself (described in *Od.* 24.36–92). But in *Iliad* 24, the "struggle" for possession of Hektor's body takes place between his old father Priam and Achilles in very different circumstances. In fact the continuation of Achilles' inordinate grief and his resumed mistreatment of Hektor's corpse after his eminently courteous behavior towards his peers at the splendid games in honor of Patroklos is unexpected, and the addition of this "consolation" theme after the ending of the "revenge" theme may well be an innovation by the poet.

Many standard themes contribute to the groundwork for the culminating battle of Achilles and Hektor (Book 22), among them revenge for the killing of a friend and the stripping of a victim's armor, and there are signs that much is taken over from the tale of Achilles' revenge on Memnon for killing Antilochos, his best friend after the death of Patroklos. This tale was included in the *Aethiopis*, and Homer must have sung of it in some form, just as he must have sung of many other episodes in the Trojan story (and perhaps the Theban and other cycles too). Memnon, like Achilles, was the son of a goddess (Eos), and it is likely that he too wore divinely-made armor for the conflict; and Homer seems to have copied this by devising that Hektor in the final duel wears Achilles' own divinely-made armor, which he had stripped from Patroklos' corpse. This armor was a wedding-present from Hephaestos to Achilles' father Peleus, passed on by him to Achilles himself. To bring this about, Homer contrives the disguise of Patroklos in Achilles' armor, an unusual motif and one which plays no actual part in the ensuing conflict; and takes great advantage of the opportunity to introduce Hephaestos' construction of the replacement set of armor, especially his decoration of the shield (18.483–607). This (probable) innovation contributes a great deal to the drama and human feeling of the episodes, including the unjustifiable arrogance of Hektor in daring to don such a panoply.

The Handling of Myth

In the *Iliad* the characters constantly refer to other tales about the adventures of Greek heroes, which of course derive from traditional oral stories. Often the tales involve the gods, and might be loosely referred to as myths (see Chapters 3 and 7, by Edmunds and Louden). Among the most prominent are Phoenix's story of Meleager (9.529–99) and Agamemnon's of the dispute between Zeus and Hera at the time of the birth of his son Herakles (19.95–133). It is noticeable that the tales are in the mouths of characters, rather than told by the poet himself.

In some instances the handling of such a story appears to be idiosyncratic and even inventive (as happens later in the case of the Athenian tragedians; see Chapter 28, by Garner). The freedom to modify or invent may appear in the tale of Thetis' aid to Zeus when he was set upon by Hera, Athena, and Poseidon (1.396–406), which is not found elsewhere. Another example occurs in a *paradeigma*, an example of conduct (good or bad) held up by a character in order to persuade another to a course of action, which is a very common use of a myth. In order to persuade Priam to take a meal, despite his grief at the loss of Hektor and his other sons, Achilles uses a *paradeigma*, the tale of Niobe (24.602–17). Niobe mourning for her slain children was famously inconsolable, her tears still flowing down the rock-face of Mount Sipylus in Asia Minor, but Achilles drastically modifies her tale, in order to make his point, by insisting that she finally consumed a meal.

Despite the constant presence of the gods, there is little of the miraculous in the *Iliad* except for their occasional removal of a hero from danger, and even less that we would associate with magic. The mighty heroes do not perform grossly superhuman feats, as happens in other epic traditions. The armor made by Hephaestos and worn by Patroklos, Achilles, and Hektor is never said to be invulnerable, though hints that it had this quality remain; Patroklos is stripped of the armor by Apollo before his fatal wound, and Hektor dies from a spear through his unprotected neck. Achilles himself, far from being invulnerable, is constantly pitied for his short life span by his immortal mother.

How the Story is Told

To our modern eyes, certain aspects of the *Iliad* (and also of the *Odyssey*) are unexpected and remarkable. First, the sheer size of the poems, which would have made continuous performance impractical (estimates of the time required vary according to the imagined circumstances, but it could hardly be less than 24 hours for either poem). Second, in order to create such massive poems, the author did not pile story upon story, or (in the case of the *Iliad*) go through the whole history of the Trojan War, but instead contracted the time-frame into a narrative covering only five days, amplified by a few summaries of the passage of periods of time at the beginning and end (in Book 1, nine days for the plague and twelve for the gods' visit to the Ethiopians; in Book 24, eleven days for Achilles' mistreatment of Hektor's body, and nine for Hektor's funeral).

Another remarkable feature is the amount of time given over to direct speech by the characters, in the *Iliad* about 45 percent. Nearly half the time, the audience is not dependent on the narrator but listens directly to a character's words and thoughts, almost as in a staged drama; and often in the most intensely emotional scenes (Hektor's farewell to his wife Andromache in Book 6, Achilles' anguished dialogue with his mother in Book 18) the change of speaker is shown only by a formulaic line lacking even an adverb, as unemotional as the bare speaker's name in the text of a drama. Book 9, the dispatch of the Greek embassy and its discourse with Achilles, is about 81 percent direct speech.

Most of the speeches fall into certain categories: persuasive (often in assemblies), messages, and battlefield challenges, vaunts, supplications, encouragement, and rebukes. Of particular note are the soliloquies, directly presenting a character's thoughts (instead of having the narrator tell us about them). There are eleven of these in the *Iliad*, all introduced by a normal verb of speaking as if they were uttered aloud (as they would be, of course, by the bard), sometimes leading to a decision, as in Hektor's moving reflections and resolve to face Achilles (22.99–130), sometimes simply giving the character's reaction to a situation (as in Zeus' meditations on the buoyant Hektor and Achilles' grieving horses, 17.441–55).

The personalities of the characters who thus reveal themselves to the listener are not only clearly drawn but often strikingly unexpected. At the very beginning of the poem, the Greek supreme commander Agamemnon betrays himself as brutal (towards a suppliant priest), coarse (in a reference to his wife), ineffective (in face of the plague), and arrogant and foolish in dealing with his disaffected ally Achilles; later, in the face of reverses in battle, he is the first to give up hope and suggest, before all the army, they give up and go home (9.17–28). The immoral wife who abandoned her decent husband to go off with a smooth-talking young foreign guest presents herself as a remorseful penitent who grieves for all the suffering she has caused, and is treated with respect by old King Priam – but still finds her seducer irresistible (Book 3); at the climax of the affliction of the Trojans in the poem, as they receive Hektor's body, the poet dares to give her a lament for him, moving but still self-absorbed (24.761–75). The warrior leader of the Greeks' deadly enemies, Hektor, is also kind to Helen, and a devoted family man (with a loving father and mother too), who goes into battle because of the responsibilities of his position (6.441–6) and is to many modern readers the most attractive man in the poem.

Among the legendary Greek heroes, we ourselves might find our ideal soldier not in Achilles, who prays for the defeat of his own allies and rejects a huge compensation for the insult he has received, but in the equally valiant and triumphant young Diomedes, tactful, respectful, and already a wise counselor. Menelaos and Patroklos, each in a subordinate position to a dominant figure (Agamemnon, Achilles), are characterized as gentle, sensitive men, loved and protected by their principals, though both are strong warriors too. There is also much to surprise us in the characters of the gods (see that section, below). Of course we cannot know how much of these conceptions of the figures in the poem is due to its author's originality, or how different the expansive amount of speech in the *Iliad* and *Odyssey* may have been from other epics of the time.

The persona of the narrator also emerges in the *Iliad*, and is likewise rather surprising to us. The proem of the work emphasizes not the glory of the Greeks and their heroes in defeating and sacking the mighty city of Troy, but the suffering and losses inflicted upon them by a quarrel between their leaders. In the battle scenes, the fighters brag of their victories, but the narrator constantly reminds us of the grief of the victim's survivors and the pathos of the death, far from home, of a young husband and father. He knows the outcome of the characters' decisions and actions, and occasionally comments upon them, mostly because of their ignorance ("Foolish man!") rather than from a moral standpoint. Together with his audience (whom he occasionally addresses directly, in "You would not have thought . . ." style) he looks back on the great days of the past: the world he shares with his audience is the world of the similes (see that section, below).

Traditional Techniques

To what extent Homer may have known of the art of writing remains uncertain; but it is beyond doubt that he was familiar with – in fact expert in – compositional techniques which were developed by singers who were ignorant of it. These traditional techniques made possible composition (to some extent at least extemporaneous) in a fairly complex meter, adaptation of the length and complexity of a song to the demands of the immediate performance, memorization of the narrative content of a song, the development of varying levels of skill in a singer, and standardization of some aspects which assisted the audience's comprehension. It is noteworthy that when rhetorical devices became a subject of study among ancient scholars they were able to draw their examples from the Homeric poems, richly endowed as they were with ornamental devices as well as basic structural forms.

Language

In the first place, the language of the poems is unlike spoken Greek of any period; it is an amalgam of forms from different dialects and different periods which (with minor modifications) is the same as that used by Hesiod and other early hexameter poets. This artificial, standardized diction was common to poets on the coast of Asia Minor, the Greek mainland, and the islands, no matter what the local dialect, and must have been understood by audiences all over the Greek world. It is thus dignified, distinct from normal speech, archaic, and very rich in vocabulary, producing something like the effect on us of the familiar archaism of the King James version of the Bible and the enormous vocabulary and metrical form of Shakespeare's plays. (For more information see Janko 1992: 8–19.)

Meter

This traditional poetic language is intimately linked to the metrical form, the dactylic hexameter. This meter has always been looked upon as a sequence of six dactyls (a heavy syllable followed by two light ones) or spondees (two heavy syllables), the fifth unit being usually a dactyl and the last composed of two syllables only. In the course of the twentieth century it became common to place importance on word-end and phrase-end, thus analyzing a verse into a series of groups or blocks of syllables divided by word-end. These units (usually four in number, often three, occasionally perhaps only two), each composed of one or more words, differ from each other in metrical shape, providing much variety of effect. Though this variety makes it hard (and perhaps unhelpful) to generalize, a common shape of verse would be heavy-light-light-heavy (word-end), light-light-heavy-light (word-end), light-heavy-light-light (word-end), heavy-light-light-heavy-heavy (verse-end). But the length of words (or word-groups) in common occurrence varies between one heavy syllable (often a single-syllable verb beginning the verse, followed by a sense-boundary) to single words filling the five-syllable final unit. (For more information see Kirk 1985: 17–37.)

Formulae

Naturally, expressions which filled the different units that make up the line, such as epithets combining with a noun or proper name, were of great convenience in composition, and a complex formulaic system developed covering a great range of frequently-occurring sense units. These traditional formulae include not only proper names and nouns of various metrical shapes (and in the different grammatical cases), combined with suitable epithets to fit them within the verse-units, but many common verbal expressions too (such as "he answered"); and in some cases the available items are very extensive. It has been shown, for instance, that there are expressions for ending a speech ("[So] he (she) said") ranging from one to many syllables, and the often pleonastic phrase "in his heart" can be added to a verse in lengths ranging from one light syllable to an expression filling the second half of the verse. There is also a rigorous "economy" in the expressions: for a given sense (e.g. "Achilles" as subject) one expression, and one only, is normally used in each metrical unit.

Such metrical units and sense-units are about the same length as the units into which ordinary speech falls, and similarly Homeric sentence-structure follows the patterns of spoken language. The essential sense becomes clear early ("Of the anger sing, goddess!"), then qualifications follow ("Achilles"), and descriptions ("destructive!") and elaboration and explanation ("which laid many sufferings upon the Greeks": 1.1–2). Such techniques make both composition and comprehension easier, and are common in oral poetry. (For more information see Hainsworth 1993: 1–31.)

Similes

Homer very often uses short similes, "like a lion", "like man-slaying Ares", similar to those occurring in other epic traditions. They add color and emphasis, as do the traditional epithets. Characteristically Homeric, however, and rare in other traditions, are the longer similes, pictures painted by the poet to illustrate the narrative and bring it vividly before the eyes of his hearers. The subjects of these similes, which may run up to nine lines in length (as 12.278–86), are drawn from the contemporary life of the poet and his audience. Though very few similes are repeated verbatim, many topics often recur – predators attacking domestic animals, wildfire, storm, and flood, and similar depictions of human-kind in a losing struggle with nature. Such frequent subjects may well be traditional.

Besides these, however, are others which occur once only, and are often the most evocative: Patroklos looks up imploringly at Achilles like a little girl tugging at her mother's skirt and begging to be picked up (16.7–10), Apollo kicks over the Greek rampart like a boy kicking over a sandcastle (15.362–4), Athena turns aside an arrow from Menelaos as a mother brushes a fly away from her sleeping child (4.130–1). It is hard not to think that these are due to the sensitivity and inventiveness of the individual poet Homer. The pictures depicted by Hephaestos on Achilles' great shield (18.483–607) are likewise drawn from the everyday life of poet and audience. (For more information see Edwards 1991: 24–41.)

Metaphors

Metaphors are common in Homer, ranging from the utterly traditional ("shepherd of the people" for the army's leaders) to vivid expressions occurring only once (Herakles "widowed" the streets of Troy, 5.642). In most of the latter cases we cannot tell if the metaphor is new. Iron, not yet in the vocabulary as the material of weapons, is nevertheless commonly used metaphorically for the "hardness" of men's hearts or the intensity of battle; the sky over the battlefield is more than once "brazen," and "trumpets" around the gods as they march to war (21.388). (For more information see Edwards 1991: 48–53.)

Sound effects

Sound effects are also very common, both for euphony (for instance, the vowel sounds for Calypso "singing in her lovely voice", *aoidiaous' opi kalêi, Od.* 5.61), harshness (*trichtha te kai tetrachtha* "three times, four times" accompanies the tearing of Odysseus' sail, *Od.* 9.71), and various effects of onomatopoeia (the sea splashes, *kumata paphlazonta polu-phlois-boi-o thalassês, Il.* 13.798; mules gallop in all directions, *polla d' ananta katanta paranta te dochmia t' élthon, Il.* 23.116). There are also many kinds of word-play and repetition, lovingly documented by the ancient commentators. (For more information see Edwards 1991: 57–8.)

Type-scenes

Human life is full of repeated routines – not just religious and legal rituals, but ordinary happenings such as getting dressed and eating a meal. In the Homeric narrative, repeated actions and scenes take standardized forms in which the sequence of events is usually unchanged but the wording used differs and the amount of description given to each element varies widely. Some of these type-scenes (sometimes called "themes") are obvious: sacrifices, meals, a warrior donning his armor, a ship being beached or launched. Equally obvious is the variation in length: Paris arms himself in nine verses (3.330–8), Patroklos in 25 (including the harnessing of his horses: 16.130–54), and Agamemnon in 31 (with descriptions of his shield and corselet: 11.17–46). Then as the climax of the poem approaches, Achilles himself puts on his shining armor in 27 lines (19.365–91), but these are amplified by the conversation with his chariot-horse which follows and the making of his armor by Hephaestos in the preceding book.

This is the essential quality of type-scenes, the patterns upon which the entire action of the Homeric poems is structured. The framework of the scene remains the same, but the elaboration, the flesh upon the bones, can be expanded or limited, depending upon the emphasis to be given to the scene, the needs of a particular performance, and the skill of the performer. Much of the quality of a poem depends upon nature and extent of the amplification. As usual with Homer, however, besides showing superb skill in choosing the nature of such amplification in his scenes (besieged citizens looking over their city wall at their attackers becomes a characterization of Helen and Priam in *Iliad* 3; a supplication scene develops into the great confrontation and conversation of Priam and Achilles in *Iliad* 24), he feels free to alter the framework for some special purpose. Hektor, seeking his wife in their home like any other Homeric visitor, does *not* find her there; and instead we have the intensely dramatic scene between them on Troy's wall (6.369ff.); a similar change appears when Thetis visits Hephaestos' home on Olympus, and their meeting is deferred by his welcoming wife until the smith-god can emerge from his workshop (18.369ff.). (For more information see Edwards 1991: 11–23.)

The Gods and the Human World

The humans

Competitiveness is the prime feature of the heroic world, as we see it in the *Iliad*. A man's aim must be "Always to be the best, pre-eminent among others" (the summary of Glaucus the Lycian, 6.208), and this means "both a speaker of good counsel and an achiever in action" (the instruction of Achilles' father to his mentor Phoenix, 9.443). This pre-eminence must be recognized by one's peers, and hence the importance of being awarded honor from others. This is made evident right at the start of the poem, when Agamemnon disgraces Achilles (in his own eyes) by removing the prize of honor he had been awarded by the army, the captive woman Briseis, and the hero reacts strongly. Similarly, Hektor justifies his leaving his wife to rejoin the battle by telling her he would be ashamed not to fight amongst the foremost of the Trojans, "winning great glory for my father and for myself" (6.446), and Sarpedon the Lycian examines the issue in detail in a superb speech of encouragement to his companion, explaining that it is their duty to lead their men into battle because they are honored by them, looked upon like gods and given wealth and pride of place (12.310–28). He adds the further point that since death for mortals is certain, the only relief from it comes from glory.

Besides claiming due honor for oneself, one must show proper consideration for the honor of others. Agamemnon violates this principle twice as the poem begins, rejecting (against the feelings of the army) the generous ransom offered by the priest for his daughter, and seizing the prize of honor awarded to Achilles. Achilles, however, behaves with proper respect towards Agamemnon's heralds (1.330–6), to Andromache's father (as she tells us, 6.416–20), the envoys sent to him (9.192ff.), and the suppliant Priam (24.512ff.); in particular, he exhibits model behavior towards his companions during the funeral games for Patroklos (Book 23), when several problems arise among the competitors.

A man also has duties towards his community. He must fight to protect his wife and children, and stand bravely beside his companions in battle. These duties are, however, lower in importance. Hektor appears to rank his personal fame, his family, and his country in that order (6.447–65). The standard of conduct is common opinion, which must be respected; neglect of it means public disapproval. Women should be treated with respect (as is shown by Hektor in particular, in Book 6), and must observe their own especial virtue by properly performing their household duties and being faithful to their husbands.

The deities

For the heroes on both sides of the battlefield, and for the audience, the gods in the *Iliad* are omnipresent (see Chapter 7, by Louden). In the heroes' world, the gods demand respect and sacrifices, and in return they may or may not give their help. Hektor's pride and confidence after he has killed Patroklos wins Zeus' pity for his ignorance of what is in store for him (17.198–208), and as his corpse is being mistreated by Achilles, Zeus, and Apollo both speak of their affection for him because of his sacrifices to them (24.31–8, 66–70); but neither of them has the will (or perhaps the power) to save him from his early death. In a famous passage Achilles declares to the grieving Priam (24.524–8):

> Nothing is achieved by wretched lamentations.
> For the gods have woven thus for unhappy mortals,
> That they live in sorrow; but they themselves have no cares.
> For on Zeus' threshold stand two urns,
> For the gifts he sends: one of evils, the other of blessings.

And he goes on to say that Zeus may give a man a mixture of both, or evils alone; but Achilles gives no indication of Zeus' thoughts or motivation. For him the deity is all-powerful, but inscrutable. Zeus' power, and his apparent irresponsibility in using it, is laid directly before us at the end of the first book of the poem, when he decides to acquiesce in Achilles' request (through Thetis) for the defeat of the Greeks in his absence; not after considering the ethical issues, but in order to get the suppliant Thetis away from his knees before his jealous wife Hera sees them together. Only once in the *Iliad*, in the untraditional situation of a simile, is Zeus said to punish humankind for passing inequitable decrees in assembly and driving away Justice, "heedless of the watchful concern of the gods" (16.385–8).

In the *Iliad*, fate (*moira* or *aisa*, not much personified) determines when a mortal will die, as Hektor says to his wife as he goes off to the battle, not knowing whether he will return (6.486–9). Both Agamemnon (4.163–5) and Hektor (6.447–96) declare that Troy must one day fall, but it is not made clear whether this is because of fate or a decision of Zeus. In fact the relationship between these two powers remains obscure, the poet seeming to refer to either according to the effect he wishes to produce rather than to theological doctrine. In a famous passage (16.431ff.), Zeus wonders whether to rescue his beloved son Sarpedon from the death-day which fate (as usual) has appointed for him, but eventually does not do so, and the question whether he actually had the power to override fate remains moot; it seems that the poet wants to elaborate even further the death of the hero at the hands of Patroklos, and so brings in both another altercation between Zeus and Hera and another vignette of the sadness of human mortality, remaining unconcerned about a possible violation of divine decorum.

Besides their importance for the lives of humans, in the *Iliad* the poet makes use of the gods in three ways: to provide a contrast – very close to comic relief – to the grimness and tragedy of the human story; to bring out the pathos of human transience by contrast with their immortality; and sometimes to enable him to handle the plot in ways which would otherwise be difficult or impossible. The divine family dwells on Olympus, living in close proximity and spending much of their time together, feasting or in assembly, and in their disagreements and alliances, their sibling squabbles and marital misadventures, they amuse us with a constant display of all-too-human follies and foibles.

Their constant involvement with what has been called their favorite spectator-sport, the heroic struggle before Troy, brings out one of the deepest human emotions in the *Iliad*, the juxtaposition of the strength of the humans in facing the troubles of their lot and their inevitable defeat in the end by death. Achilles is the prime symbol of this; the greatest fighter, the strongest character, and the one whose coming death is constantly brought before us, above all by the figure of his always-grieving and devoted goddess mother Thetis. Achilles is "short-lived" in two senses: he is to die young, and he has a mother who herself will never die.

Through much of the *Iliad* the Greeks suffer defeat, but since this is by the will of Zeus their descendants need not be ashamed of them. In similar fashion, the poet can pit Paris against Menelaos, Aeneas against Achilles, and have a friendly divinity rescue the weaker man in the nick of time without violation of human probability or loss of face – for having a deity look out for one increases, not diminishes, one's honor. The climactic meeting of Priam and Achilles over the ransoming of Hektor's corpse would be impossible to arrange without the help of the gods (in this case Hermes). But when the two antagonists confront each other no deity intervenes and the humans, as in the quarrel between Agamemnon and Achilles which begins the poem, know what the gods want but are free to obey them or not. This is characteristic of the poem: though gods may rescue and otherwise assist their favorites, the grossly supernatural is avoided; humans are not invulnerable (even when wearing armor made by the god Hephaestos), and they do not slay dozens of adversaries at a blow.

Just as ancient Greek myth is elastic and open-ended, and can constantly be retold and refashioned, so the presentation of the gods is flexible, with a certain number of basic fixed family relationships and spheres of operation but wide freedom for modification and invention for the sake of the plot and emotional effect. This appears vividly in the differences between the treatment of the gods in the *Iliad* and in the *Odyssey*. In the latter poem, Athena assists her favorite, Odysseus, but tells him (*Od.* 13.341–3) that respect for her uncle Poseidon, who has been angered by Odysseus' ill-treatment of his son the Cyclops Polyphemos, has sometimes prevented her from helping him. It is made very clear at the beginning of the *Odyssey*, both by the poet and by Zeus himself, that it is human folly and wickedness that brings troubles upon mortals, not any divine malignity. Fate is also given a rather wider scope in the *Odyssey*, since it is said more than once to be fated that Odysseus and Menelaos shall reach home – a more benign decree than those found in the *Iliad*.

The Historical and Cultural Background

In the *Iliad* Homer speaks of his heroes as men of the past, and addresses his audience as his contemporaries: several times in formulaic language he tells how some hero easily hoists a rock such as no two men could lift, "as men are now." How far does his poem represent the world of the past, and how far the world in which he and his hearers were living?

To deal with the second question first. Of the poet personally we know nothing, quite probably not even his name, since "Homer" may derive from the later "Homeridae," professional singers whose name in turn may come from an old word meaning "meeting-place." Later on, tales of his life and death proliferated. The lack of factual data is surprising, and has been variously accounted for. References and pictorial representations of Iliadic scenes are found from the last part of the eighth century BCE, and the general ancient opinion that he came from Ionia, the west coast of modern Turkey, or one of the nearby islands, is supported by internal evidence from the poem. The Greeks had been founding settlements in these areas for centuries, and these were linked by their common language, religion, and festivals. Their farming life is depicted in the similes, and especially on the shield of Achilles, which also shows their social and legal institutions and the position of the local aristocratic landowner, here called the *basileus*, the word for the leaders of the contingents at Troy.

The society depicted in the *Iliad* to a large extent matches up with that deduced from archaeological and other data for Greek society around 800 BCE, though some archaisms are evident. Most men work as farmers, herders, craftsmen, and the primary social unit is the household. Wealth is obtained by booty (cattle-raiding, warfare) or prizes, and consists of manufactured goods, valued not by coinage (not yet invented) but by its equivalent in cattle. The economy is based upon social relationships, and these goods are not for purchasing subsistence, but for giving away, to enhance prestige; laterally for guest-friends and marital alliance, downward for maintaining a following. Chiefs draw sustenance from the land they own, and demand gifts from the lower classes when necessary The system perpetuates a hierarchy and the hereditary elite.

Chieftains jealous of their independence head conglomerations of small households, but there is already a sense of a larger community to which loyalty was due, though not yet the fully-developed *polis* (city-state). The poet assumes his audience is familiar with assemblies and councils, where issues are publicly discussed even though decisions may not be democratically taken. He also presents them with the picture of a lawcourt, an institution which apparently includes a presiding officer (if that is the meaning of *istôr*) and a number of "elders," whose decisions may be swayed by a vociferous population (*Il.* 18.497–508). This seems an advance on entrusting enforcement of justice to a chief or king, and is probably more contemporary with Homer and his audience than is the basic social structure shown in the poem.

Conclusion

In an essay entitled "Existentialists and mystics," published in 1970, Iris Murdoch, a scholar of philosophy trained as a classicist, and also a distinguished novelist and literary critic, made a distinction (p. 225) between two types of modern novel: the "existentialist," which "shows us freedom and virtue as the assertion of will," and the "mystical," which "shows us freedom and virtue as understanding, or obedience to the Good." The first is

> The story of the lonely brave man, defiant without optimism, proud without pretension, always an exposer of shams, whose mode of being is a deep criticism of society. He is an adventurer. He is godless. He does not suffer from guilt. He thinks of himself as free. He may have faults, he may be self-assertive or even violent, but he has sincerity and courage, and for this we forgive him.

In this context she mentions the works of D. H. Lawrence, Hemingway, Camus, and Sartre. On the other hand, the characteristic of the "mystical" novel is that

> it keeps in being, by one means or another, the conception of God. Man is still pictured as being divided, but divided in a new way, between a fallen nature and a spiritual world. I call these novels mystical, not of course as a term of praise, but because they are attempts to express a religious consciousness without the traditional trappings of religion.

The existentialist response, she suggests, is "the first and immediate expression of a consciousness without God," and "the mystical attitude is a second response, a second thought about the matter, and reflects the uneasy suspicion that perhaps after all man is not God" (p. 226). Further, "Whereas the existentialist hero is an anxious man trying to impose or assert or find himself, the mystical hero is an anxious man trying to discipline or purge or diminish himself" (p. 227).

Though Murdoch does not mention Homer, Achilles, or Odysseus, the differences between the two types of novel she describes have much in common with those between the two Homeric poems and their respective heroes. From the beginning of the *Iliad*, Achilles becomes isolated, an outsider: robbed of the prize of honor given him by the army, he sits alone on the seashore (1.348–50, 488–92); his peers visit him only to convey the words of his enemy Agamemnon (9.308–429); he returns to fight only to avenge the loss of his friend, though he knows that will mean his own death is close (18.95–9); and at the poem's conclusion he sends home the king of the enemy city and the body of its slain leader, with a promise of a truce for the funeral, entirely as his own decision, ignoring the will of his commander-in-chief (24.650–8). When told what the gods want him to do, he decides (in a few unenthusiastic words) to follow their advice, but is hardly intimidated into the decision (1.216–18, 24.139–40, cf. 22.15–20). He is the ideal of freedom and independent judgment.

On the other hand, the first thing we hear of Odysseus (in the *Odyssey*) is that he strove to save the lives of his companions, but fails in this because of their own criminal folly (in antagonizing a god); then in his loneliness he thinks only of returning to his wife and his home (*Od.* 1.5–13). Then we hear at considerable length of the care the gods have for him, and how they set about arranging his homecoming (1.48–95). Similarly, the suitors are constantly presented as wrongdoers and violators of the laws of hospitality (as well as planning the murder of Telemachus, the son of their unwilling host and hostess). At the time of their destruction Athena provides much assistance to Odysseus and his small band (22.273, 397–8), as indeed Odysseus had predicted to his son (16.267–9). The divine world ensures that human wickedness is punished and human virtue rewarded – which is close to Murdoch's division "between a fallen nature and a spiritual world."

Both the *Iliad* and the *Odyssey* came into being at a time of rapid change in the Greek world, as prosperity and populations increased, city-states developed, and better communications fostered – and were fostered by – Panhellenic religious festivals. It is not surprising that in such circumstances different ideals, as well as a certain amount of archaizing and inconsistency in detail, appear in the two poems we still have. What is, perhaps, surprising is that the universal qualities of both should appear so clearly and should have been valued for so long.

FURTHER READING

Fairly technical accounts of all aspects of Homeric studies can be found in the thirty chapters of Morris and Powell 1997. Each of the six volumes of the Cambridge University Press *Commentary* on the *Iliad* (in sequence: Kirk 1985; Kirk 1990; Hainsworth 1993; Janko 1992; Edwards 1991; Richardson 1993) includes several introductory sections on various topics. These publications are intended primarily for readers familiar with ancient Greek, but can usually be understood by others with a keen interest.

Those approaching the *Iliad* from a general literary viewpoint will find guidance in Edwards 1987 (chapters on various topics, and commentaries on ten books of the poem), Griffin 1980 (especially on characterization, pathos, and the gods), and Taplin 1992 (a detailed study of certain episodes). For the oral aspects of the poem in particular, see Bakker 1997 (especially on language and linguistics), Foley 1999b (including analogies with South Slavic epic), Lord 1960 (the fundamental work on the oral Homer, repr. 2000), Martin 1989 (especially on performance and speeches), Nagler 1974 (on the theory behind repeated phrases and type-scenes), Nagy 1996c (on the development of the *Iliad* from oral song to written text), and Parry 1971 (the trailblazing study of traditional Homeric expressions; it requires knowledge of ancient Greek). The society appearing in the Homeric poems is studied from different angles in Donlan 1999.

Translations of the *Iliad*, both in prose and in verse, are plentiful, new versions appearing every year. Virtually all are faithful to the original, include line references to the text, and have sound introductory sections. The choice between them is best left to the reader's preference for the English style adopted by the translator.

CHAPTER TWENTY-TWO

Homer's *Odyssey*

Laura M. Slatkin

Like the *Iliad*, the *Odyssey* represents the culmination and refinement of a long antecedent tradition, and we might best approach it with at least double vision: as a central culture-poem of mid-eighth century BCE Greece, and as a poem that makes a bid to continue to be "ours." The poem survives and gets remade through its ongoing vital reception and recreation in the minds of its readers, teachers, critics, and re-inventors.

Since the late 1970s, our sense of the *Odyssey* has been enriched by new, sustained critical attention. Scholars influenced by structuralism and narratology have scrutinized the intricate architectonics of the poem, including its implicit structural divisions (e.g. Books 1–4, the Telemacheia; 5–8, Calypso and the Phaeacians; 9–12, core adventures; 12–24, the Ithacan adventure, with its prolonged, multi-phased tests and recognitions), while insights gained from the theory of oral composition yield continuing breakthroughs. Critics have elucidated the circulation of themes in the poem, its type-scenes, its complex allusions, its reworking of traditional topoi, the conditions of its performance. Anthropo-logically-minded critics have investigated the poem's preoccupation with sacrifice and cannibalism, its hints of colonization, its interest in genealogy and legitimacy, its center-piece *katabasis*, or descent to the Underworld. Issues of class have been usefully illumin-ated; and feminist scholars have persuasively argued that this *nostos* – both return and song of return – depends as much on the intelligence of its heroine as on its many-minded hero. Although it exceeds this and indeed any essay to pursue all these critical strands, the discussion that follows proposes to highlight some of their implications for reading en route, guided by the poem's narrative unfolding.

With its opening lines, the *Odyssey* ushers its audience into a world unprecedented in Greek heroic tradition and a narrative design of incomparable richness and scope. An-nouncing its subject as *andra polutropon* – a "man of many ways" (an epithet shared only with Hermes, the divine boundary-crosser) – the poem simultaneously introduces and conceals its protagonist, withholding his name until the end of its proem (1.21), a lacuna that corresponds to Odysseus' absence from the poem's first four books. When the *Odyssey* begins, its hero is missing; or to put it another way, the poem's first arena of action and interaction is where its hero is *not*. Deferring his presence, the poem creates an oppor-tunity for the emergence of a range of characters and a set of issues: identity, history, memory, the relations among family, community, social order, culture, through which the distinctive trajectory of this epic of return (and the goals of its hero) take shape. The poem traces two distinct paths, as it narrates both Odysseus' journey and the course of events on Ithaca. Under what circumstances, and with what consequences, the two will ultimately converge is a question the narrative presses with increasing urgency. But his absence also opens a space for the audience to discover, and reconsider along the way, who Odysseus is.

Who is the man of many ways? He who "saw the cities of men and knew their minds" (1.4). Before identifying the hero by name, the poem's opening highlights his perception, his experience, his suffering, his desire (1.1–6). Not sacking cities but *seeing* them will be the matter of this poem. Odysseus was no stranger to the epic's earliest audiences, of course. In choosing him as its central figure, the poem presented to its ancient listeners a familiar hero of the *Iliad*, whose role there, while not a starring one, is substantial and well delineated. As with all its heroes, the *Iliad* draws for its characterizations, both explicitly and through allusive reference, on a variety of mythological and poetic traditions, to locate Odysseus' particular contribution to its story. The *Iliad* characterizes Odysseus as a figure of not wholly positive qualities. Although commanding, verbally dexterous, and an energetic fighter, Odysseus in the *Iliad* is also portrayed as cunning – even guileful, just this side of sleazy – in episodes like the night raid on the Trojan ally Rhesus in *Iliad* 10. In the embassy to Achilles in Book 9 he seems to be the tool of Agamemnon, relaying to the alienated hero the king's grandiose, overbearing offer of material riches. In contrast to such outstanding warriors as Achilles or Ajax, who station their ships at the vulnerable edges of the Achaean fleet, Odysseus takes up a position in the more protected middle. The Epic Cycle poems too knew legends that amplify this somewhat unflattering picture of Odysseus, such as his equivocal victory over Ajax in the contest for the armor of Achilles (apparently an episode in the *Little Iliad*, and alluded to in *Od*. Book 11).

The *Odyssey*, like other oral epic poems of the archaic period, is grounded in the stories known to the *Iliad* and the Cycle and must adapt and select its narrative within those traditions (see Burgess 2001, and Chapter 24). How are the cherished Iliadic ideals of loyalty and effective leadership to be conjured in a poem centering on Odysseus, given his variegated history – especially if that history includes traditions about Odysseus as the sole survivor of his band of men, who is both unsuccessful in protecting his companions from destruction and, once he gets back (transported on someone else's ship), is responsible for the destruction of the youth of his city? (On Odysseus' loss see Haubold 2000: 100–9.) The *Odyssey* thus, against real odds, has the task of making Odysseus into a character with whom its audience sympathizes and whom it wants to see succeed, a hero whose goal of homecoming its audience is expected to value. To this end, the poem narrates his journey homeward and depicts its destination in such a way as to generate in the audience a shared stake in Odysseus' hope of return. Also implicitly valorized are Odysseus' reclaiming and reordering of his household (*oikos*) and resumption of his kingship. The poem fosters our sense that he and Ithaca belong together; and in such a way that the features that made him other than "the best of the Achaeans" (Achilles' designation in the *Iliad*; see Nagy 1979a: ch. 3) – namely, wiliness, a way with stratagems, fast-talking aplomb, an instinct for survival – become positive attributes, precisely those that enable him to overcome the obstacles to achieving his return.

The *Odyssey*'s larger challenge is to create a poem that will be an appropriate counterpart to the *Iliad*, the epic with which it evolves in a relationship of careful complementarity. So closely aware is each poem of the other's content that, although both elaborate events surrounding the Trojan War, no episode in either is duplicated in the other (see Monro 1901: 325 and Nagy 1979a: 21–2). Linguistic studies have shown that the *Odyssey*, in the form in which it has come down to us – after generations of oral composition/performance (see Lord 1960; Foley 1990) – is roughly contemporary with our *Iliad*, perhaps slightly later (see Janko 1982 on relative chronology). The premise of the *Odyssey*, however, is that it comes definitively "after" – as the song of an aftermath, conditioned by, and looking back to, the prior song that immortalizes the glory and dire toll of the battlefield – all the while moving into literally and literarily uncharted territory.

The postwar reconstruction of shattered communities and families, the varied returns of the warriors from Troy, their re-engagement with the civilized institutions they fought for (such as the institution of marriage, violated by Paris and Helen), their successful or failed reintegration, the confrontation with the meaning of home: all these become a domain of exploration for epic and later for tragedy, and all are launched as themes in this poem.

It is the *Odyssey*'s accomplishment that it asserts the secure authority of its own narrative at the same time as it pays tribute to the *Iliad*. As the *Odyssey* begins, the determining point from which all positions are plotted is Troy. The story of the Trojan War is *the* story, the ultimate reference point for human endeavor. At the outset of the poem (1.236–40), Telemachus, lamenting his father's disappearance, voices the view that it would have been preferable for Odysseus to die at Troy, thereby gaining glory (*kleos*) for himself and for his son – *kleos* denoting the imperishable fame that poetic song confers for heroic achievement. But the *Odyssey* as it unfolds corrects and enlarges that perspective, claiming its own conditions for heroic reputation, so that by the time Athena reveals Odysseus' homeland to him in Book 13, she can describe Ithaca as a place so important that its fame has gone even to Troy "which people say is very far away" (13.248–9).

The *Odyssey* represents the journey of return (*nostos*) not as a direct path between two discrete points, but as a process of shifting back and forth among recollection, recognition, projection, anticipation, in which past, present, and future dovetail, are refracted in the imagination, and become reconfigured. When we meet Odysseus on Calypso's island, he is pining for Ithaca and evoking the image of his wife (5.215–20); to the Phaeacians in Book 9 he describes his island and claims that he cannot think of any place on earth sweeter to look at (21–8). Yet when he is transported home and awakens on Ithaca, he does not recognize it.

The *Odyssey* itself introduces a developing genre of return songs. For the entertainment of Penelope's suitors feasting in the house of the absent Odysseus, the bard Phemius sings "the painful homecoming of the Achaeans," inflicted upon them by Athena (1.326–7). When Penelope intervenes to put an end to his performance – because the song calls to mind her missing husband, who cannot be included in it – Telemachus objects, reminding her (and the *Odyssey*'s audience) that "the newest songs are always the most popular" (1.351–2). The latest return song of all, although they do not know it, is the one that is forming around and about them, the still unfinished, open-ended one: the *Odyssey* itself. The poem sustains and often brilliantly foregrounds this gap, this play and tension, between the knowledge of its internal audiences (first on Ithaca, later among the Phaeacians) and that of its external audience (including ourselves) (see Pucci 1987), or, to approach it from another angle, between what *this* poem is singing versus what other poems might elsewhere sing or have sung. Beyond its thematic innovations, the *Odyssey* here invites reflection on the relations among audience, song, and singer, exploring a dimension of poetics that culminates in Odysseus' own recitation of his travels in Books 9–12. Explicitly compared by King Alkinoos to a singer's performance, the retrospective of Odysseus' adventures in his own voice constitutes not only an unconventional subject for epic but a stunning departure from the impersonal Iliadic narrative point of view and from its linear structure (see Slatkin 1996).

Phemius' song alludes to a tradition in which Athena obstructed the heroes' homecomings out of resentment at their conduct during the sack of Troy (also referred to by Nestor, 3.130–46). The *Odyssey*, however, foregrounds her sponsorship of Odysseus' success, substituting Poseidon as the divinity whose anger hinders Odysseus' passage. Here Athena, whose like-mindedness with Odysseus and shared characteristic of wily intelligence (*mêtis*) the poem emphasizes, plays an entirely facilitating role (see Cook

1995 and J. S. Clay 1983). Taking advantage of Poseidon's absence from Olympus, Athena both jump-starts Odysseus's stalled journey and at the same time sets in motion the parallel plot of Telemachus' travels in search of information about his father. Although with Telemachus she takes a more hands-on approach, accompanying as well as encouraging the young man, it is not until Odysseus arrives back on Ithaca that Athena reveals herself to him; as Odysseus notes regretfully when they finally meet, her assistance has all been invisible to him (13.311–28).

Athena's injunction to Telemachus to search out his father's whereabouts is a confusing one, combining accurate and misleading details: first she announces (1.195–9) that his father is not dead but is held captive against his will on an island (true) in the keeping of savage men (false), then shortly thereafter (1.287–92) instructs him to ascertain whether his father is still alive. As Athena explains in the council of the gods, she intends to enhance both Telemachus' confidence and his reputation; the journey she prompts him to make with this mixed message is designed to yield both more and less than factual information about the outcome of his father's travails. When the poem begins, Telemachus cannot even say with certainty, in response to an inquiry from "Mentes", who his father is; by the time he is on his way back from his travels, he responds to the fugitive Theoklymenos' questions with the words, "Friend, I will answer exactly what you ask me: Ithaca is my country and Odysseus is my father" (15.266–7) – despite the persistent mystery of his father's precise location:

Telemachus' journey, then, involves the securing of his identity, in terms of city and genealogy, as much as any quest for his father's concrete whereabouts. And it is striking that, however much the poem valorizes home, it is travel and the proto-ethnographic cultural comparison travel invites that allows the son, as well as the father, to re-think, as well as re-enter, the space of home.

Not only the residents in Odysseus' house but the gods as well are thinking about homecoming, as the poem begins. Even before Athena's intervention, Zeus invokes as a cautionary tale Agamemnon's disastrous re-entry into Argos, his murder at the hands of his wife's lover Aegisthus, and the vengeance wrought by his son, Orestes. This calamitous set of events is reported in varying degrees of detail by different speakers within the poem, including the ghost of Agamemnon, who assigns the blame to his unfaithful wife as well as to her lover. The example of the triangle of Agamemnon, Aegisthus, and Clytemnestra underscores in particular the threat of sexual infidelity, promiscuity, and its ruinous social costs, renewing the lesson of the Trojan War itself. The tale stands implicitly as a negative paradigm for Odysseus and Penelope but a positive model for Telemachus (see Katz 1991 on the Orestes story within the *Odyssey*). Athena (as Mentes) and Nestor both explicitly enjoin him to emulate the avenging Orestes. By recalling this story Zeus links the goal of return to that of revenge, bringing to the fore the ethical and political dimensions of homecoming: households and communities left behind by the warriors away at Troy, made susceptible to instability and corruption, need to be restored to proper functioning. Considerations of culpability, and larger questions of theodicy largely downplayed in the *Iliad*, are put squarely on the table in this poem. Return thus becomes more than a private objective in the *Odyssey*: it becomes an instrument of justice, sanctioned by the gods, through which the social order will be rescued.

The *Odyssey* presents a situation that has much in common with that of Agamemnon's household, but is subtler and more complex. While Clytemnestra was unmistakably adulterous, Penelope's position with regard to her suitors is more ambiguous: is Odysseus alive or not? If not, she is a widow, eligible to be courted; if he is alive, however, she is still married to him, in which case the suitors are not legitimately wooing Penelope but attempting to seduce her (see Felson-Rubin 1993 on Penelope's status). The suitors, of course, claim that they are fully entitled to court her, and blame her for delaying the resolution of their suit (2.87 ff.). At the same time, the poem puts its audience in the position of knowing that Odysseus is very much alive, thus reinforcing our sense of the suitors' behavior as inappropriate and pernicious. Penelope's expressions of longing for his return, given voice from her first appearance in the poem (1.328–64), indicate from the start that their insistent attentions, if not improper, are unwelcome.

Penelope's suitors have taken over Odysseus' house. Whatever their claims on her uncertain status, the *Odyssey* stresses the impropriety of their conduct by representing them as putting in jeopardy not only the rules of courtship, but the wider framework of social norms. Voraciously consuming the stores of Odysseus' household – eating up his "substance" (1.160) – as though it were their own, the suitors behave abusively to his servants, turning some against their master and sleeping with the servant girls at the same time as they are courting Penelope. Shameless as guests, they are equally reprehensible as hosts, ignoring (at their peril) the visitor "Mentes" who arrives at the door. Although the suitors are rivals for Penelope's favor, they behave more like a pack than like individuals hoping to distinguish themselves as worthy of her hand.

What may seem to be simple, if extreme, boorishness is in fact an egregious violation of the key institution of hospitality (*xeinia*), which the poem represents as essential to all social interactions, indeed as the core of civilized life. Indispensable especially in a world of travel and continual encounters with foreigners, but fundamental and paradigmatic in all social intercourse, the honorable treatment of guests and hosts is guaranteed under the highest authority, that of Zeus himself. The term *xeinia* – often translated "guest-friendship" – expresses the necessary reciprocity of relations between guest and host. Like "hospitality" or "friendship," it is a reciprocal term necessarily entailing two parties, denoting both what is offered and what is received. The noun *xenos* denotes both "guest" and "host," as well as their precondition, "stranger." The guest/host paradigm of *xeinia* points to social distance, a potential estrangement whose dangers are defused by hospitality: *xeinia* makes actual or potential strangers into guests and hosts, while the violation of *xeinia* creates enmity. The exchanges that constitute *xeinia* create a mutual (and hereditary) relationship in which each *xenos* (and his descendants) may in the future be the other's guest – or host – and which is governed by a strict etiquette. Proper reception of a guest entails a sequence of hospitable gestures, including offering him a bath, food, entertainment, gifts – and only after those are provided, asking his name, his origins. The guest, for his part, must treat his host's household with utmost respect. Paris' seduction of Helen, the wife of his host Menelaos, was thus an outrage against the sanctity of *xeinia* as well as that of marriage.

The suitors' breach of *xeinia* is a symptom of more deadly intentions: from disregard of Odysseus' household, the suitors easily turn to violence against it, as they plot the ambush and murder of Telemachus. Although the *Odyssey* singles out an individual suitor or two – notably Antinous and Eurymachus – as more brutal and duplicitous than the rest, none of the others speaks against the treacherous plan. The *Odyssey's* focus on the determinants of civilized relations – those arrangements fought for yet tragically undermined by the institution of war – makes it (among other things) the epic of *xeinia*.

Telemachus' sojourns on Pylos and in Sparta provide examples not only of the fitting reception of a *xenos* but of other significant cultural practices as well. On Pylos, he observes an elaborate sacrifice being carried out – a ritual the suitors in his home are never seen to perform (see Vidal–Naquet 1996). At Sparta, festivities for a sanctioned wedding are in progress, setting into relief the chaos of the situation on Ithaca. Through his encounters, as *xenos*, with Nestor on Pylos and with Menelaos and Helen in Sparta, Telemachus has direct contact with his father's history. Thus he shadows his father's journey, figuratively although not in fact: he remains far from his father's actual route, but his travels enable him, like Odysseus, to see the cities of men and know their minds. What he observes will offer him alternative models for his own city and his own house.

When Athena "Mentes" instructs Telemachus to voyage in search of the fame (*kleos*) or the homecoming (*nostos*) of his father, she signals two alternative epic themes – and indeed, two alternative epics. On Pylos and Sparta, Telemachus hears versions of each. The *Odyssey* is capacious enough to include *kleos* songs (e.g. of the fame of valiant warriors, of dead heroes) within its overarching *nostos*, such that this epic of *nostos* eventually becomes its own song of glory, announcing its own triumphant vision of *kleos*. But as Telemachus sets out, Odysseus is at a place where neither *kleos* nor *nostos* may be achieved – Calypso's island. It is here, after four books, that the poem shifts its focus from reports about Odysseus to Odysseus himself, and takes up the narrative of his adventures. Rather than recounting them in order from beginning to end, or else starting with his last adventure and working continuously back to his departure from Troy, the *Odyssey* forgoes any simple narrative and temporal sequence to introduce Odysseus at his penultimate, but most extended, sojourn. Of the ten years Odysseus spends endeavoring to reach Ithaca once the war is over, seven are passed in the limbo of the goddess' embrace. Yet the poem distills the episode into two days and a crucial conversation.

Calypso's desire for Odysseus brings with it an offer of nothing less than immortality. The ultimate temptation – to remain with Calypso, to live like a god, deathless and unaging, forever desired: what could be more irresistible? But to accept such an offer would mean the irrevocable abandonment both of home and of heroic renown; it would truly mean to vanish, without *kleos* (to be *akleiôs*). Calypso's name, derived from the verb *kaluptein*, "to conceal, cover," suggests that, from a heroic perspective, she is a hider, whose care of Odysseus obscures and suppresses his heroic potential. Heroic values presuppose risk, the need for courage and for commitment: the very challenges that living like a god would obviate. In this sense, endless life with Calypso would be, paradoxically, a kind of demise, rendering meaningless not only aspirations for achievement yet to come but also the arduous struggles of the past. By the time Odysseus confronts the choice with which Calypso presents him, he has already (as we later learn) visited the underworld and has heard Achilles' lament for the costs of mortality, his regret for his own lost future, for which no *kleos* can compensate (11.489–91). Odysseus' refusal of immortality, therefore, is not based on abstractions; he has sojourned with the dead and been warned. Nor are the terms in which his renunciation is articulated abstract: the poem expresses his choice not as an existential reckoning in favor of a mortal destiny but as a preference to return to the human lineaments of his wife.

Such a proposition as Calypso's is never contemplated in the *Iliad*; the very possibility of immortality demarcates the territory into which Odysseus voyages as a world of unforeseen horizons and alien prospects. The *Odyssey*'s debt to folktale traditions – stories with elements of magic, enchantment, and the supernatural – has been much discussed (e.g. Carpenter 1946; Page 1973; Hansen 1990); these can be discerned in a number of episodes where, for example, Polyphemos fits the pattern of the ogre in folktales, and Circe that of the sorceress; and Calypso has a prototype in the dangerously seductive nymph who abducts men and makes them disappear (Crane 1988: 15–33). Homeric epic incorporates such motifs but transforms them, such that Odysseus explores through his travels a world both exotic and existentially severe. As the stay on Calypso's Ogygia is the first of Odysseus' adventures to be narrated, we understand all those that follow (even when, from a chronological standpoint, they have preceded it) as taking place under the sign of Odysseus' consent to the conditions of his life, situating him definitively in time and space.

Odysseus' reintegration into the world bound by mortal limitations foregrounds both his age and the distance he has traveled. The shipwrecked sailor who manages to crawl ashore naked on Scheria, bereft of companions, possessions, any token of identity – of all but the bare ember of vitality (cf. 5.488–90 – a lonely spark in a pile of ashes) – meets the young Nausikaa, whose life (like that of Telemachus) is just opening to the possibilities before her. The scene in which Odysseus, awakened by sounds that evoke in him fears of hostile men, faces instead a group of teenage girls playing ball, is both comic and poignant as it measures the difference between their expectations and stages of experience. Later, as he is challenged to compete in an athletic contest, Odysseus acknowledges the toll that age and journeying inevitably take. This is not, then, the epic of the beautiful death (one way to read the *Iliad* (e.g., see Vernant 1991: 50–74)) but the epic of timeworn, embraceable life.

Odysseus' stay among the Phaeacians, the most extensively narrated of any sojourn, provides a crucial transition to Ithaca. Scheria is a charmed setting, magical in its golden-age features: its perfect climate, its spontaneously-flourishing vegetation requiring no agricultural labor, the sterling character of its women (6.111), its ships that sail as fast as thought (7.36). Yet its people are a familiar mixture of culture and incivility, who know and depend on the rules of hospitality to guide social relations. Unlike the other places Odysseus visits, moreover (as we shall see), the Trojan War is their point of orientation; like the audience on Ithaca, they listen to songs about it, without knowing that they have their part in a narrative that will incorporate and move beyond those earlier events. Nor do they realize the eventual cost to them of being in Odysseus' story: at the very least, the loss of their ship. In the absence of an anaesthetizing drug such as Helen dispenses to the audience in Sparta (4.219–26), Odysseus can only weep to hear the tale of his own sufferings. Demodocus' song about Troy ultimately creates the opportunity for Odysseus to relinquish his anonymity among the Phaeacians and to claim his own song, putting before his Scherian audience – and that of the epic itself – an unprecedented vision of the heroic.

Unlike later treatments of Odysseus, notably those of Dante and Tennyson, the Homeric figure is not a restless, willful seeker after the untried; his entry into the untried comes, in fact, as a surprise. We hear that, after the fall of Troy, Odysseus and his men sail from that city to an entirely predictable first venture, the sacking of the Ciconians' city (9.40–56) – a recapitulation of the various city-sackings referred to in the *Iliad*, even a re-enactment in miniature (however finally unsuccessful) of the assault on Troy itself, complete with Iliadic diction and an evocative Iliadic simile. Still within recognizable terrain – the geographical, institutional, and temporal coordinates of which are familiar – they continue in the kind of history-making enterprise that might be included in any singer's repertoire memorializing the exploits of the past. Familiar too, and deeply mourned, is the loss in battle here of the first of Odysseus' men, killed in the familiar way. The attrition of his companions, announced in the poem's proem, begins immediately, in this first adventure, now described in Book 9. Odysseus reiterates the proem's emphasis on their own folly as the cause of their destruction; he accentuates the contrast between their lack of judgment and restraint and his foresight and self-discipline, thus initiating the theme of their hopeless vulnerability and progressive divergence from him (see Frame 1978 on the significance of Odysseus' intelligence and his companions' lack of it; also Horkheimer and Adorno 1999 for a Marxian take on Odysseus' survival through self-discipline).

At this point in Odysseus' song, the survivors of Troy are within striking distance of home. Had they reached it, the story of their *nostos* might have been unexceptional, like that of Nestor, or those briefly summarized by Nestor in Book 3. The violent winds that carry Odysseus and his remaining companions away from the land of the Ciconians, however, propel them off their course, immeasurably beyond all that is familiar – off the map, as it were, of identifiable spatial and temporal dimensions, into a domain where time loses its accustomed meaning, where history and its mediating agent, memory, are at risk. Among the Lotus Eaters, on whose shore they first arrive after the storm, those who eat the honey-sweet fruit forget their *nostos*: they lose track of past and future. Ultimately, Odysseus will be borne to the navel of the sea, where an endless present awaits him on Calypso's island, having first sailed to the Underworld, where for the dead only the past exists, and earlier to the abode of Circe, where a year goes by without his noticing. But their landing in the country of the Lotus Eaters gives Odysseus and his companions their first introduction to the disorienting, mysterious, even dreamlike ordinance of time that the beings they encounter variously inhabit, and that subsequent adventures will variously manifest.

The poem profoundly links the predicament of temporality to the production of culture. The peaceable Lotus Eaters, oblivious to the passage of time, indifferent to history, nevertheless produce what may be understood as a kind of hospitality; it is not only deficient, however – they don't ask their guests' names because they don't care – but it undermines all future possibility of *xeinia* exchanges. In the adventures that follow, Odysseus comes to "see and know" ways of life, *mores* that disrupt or invert the norms according to which human society is organized and its members are made recognizable to each other. While the arc of Telemachus' travels takes him from the disarray on Ithaca to the more ordered communities of Pylos and Sparta, Odysseus' journey proceeds in a contrary direction, from the highly-regulated (albeit destructive) public arena of war to a world whose strangeness sets into relief the everyday social practices human society takes for granted.

Nowhere is this more dramatically illustrated than in the encounter with the Cyclops. If the Lotus Eaters effect an obliviousness to history, the Cyclops exhibits a positive disdain for the record of human achievements, the exploits that constitute the subject of epic. To Odysseus' announcement that he and his followers are the victors of the Trojan War, whose rights as suppliants are protected by the gods, Polyphemos declares his contempt for all that. For this response the poem has prepared its audience, introducing the Cyclopes by their defining feature, a complete lack of social and political organization: they have neither councils nor institutions, so that each Cyclops is a law unto himself. Not surprisingly, then, Polyphemos' reception of Odysseus and his men is a thorough perversion – even a parody – of *xeinia*, the rituals of which the Cyclops not only disregards, but derides. In a grisly mockery of the proper sequence of fundamental procedures by which one receives a guest – namely, feeding the guest and then asking his name – the Cyclops first asks Odysseus and his companions to identify themselves and then proceeds to feed *on* them; his gift of guest-friendship will be to eat the companions first and Odysseus last. The Cyclops' scorn for the rules of social conduct, culminating in his bestial voracity, disquietingly recalls the contemptuous, dissolute suitors, whose taste for "the substance of another man" turns them to plot the death of their host.

The art of disguise, which later serves Odysseus so well among the suitors, is displayed in a preliminary form here. Odysseus' ruse of giving his name as "Nobody" exposes a problem to which the Cyclopes' anti-social, anti-cultural way of life makes them vulnerable: their linguistic naiveté. When his Cyclopean neighbors, roused by the howls of the injured Polyphemos from inside his cave, inquire who is harming him, he responds "Nobody" (*Outis* or *mê tis*) – at which they throw up their hands and go away. Odysseus' pleasure in the success of his own wily intelligence – *mêtis* (a homonym of *mê tis*) – causes a catastrophe, however, both for himself and for his men. Unable to resist claiming credit for outwitting Polyphemos, Odysseus calls out his own name to taunt the Cyclops, as he and his men sail away. How else could one achieve *kleos*? But once Polyphemos knows his adversary's name, he is in a position to curse him, and from this ensues Poseidon's unrelenting, stormy retribution.

If Odysseus endangers his companions with the parting shot at the Cyclops that boomerangs against them all, it is the companions who cause a supremely disappointing outcome to the subsequent encounter, that with Aeolus. On Aeolus' island, although the parameters of geography are confounded (the island floats!) and social relations drastically rearranged (brothers are married to sisters), nevertheless the voyagers receive an altogether more promising initial welcome. In contrast to the indifference of the Lotus Eaters and the contempt of the Cyclops, here the historical record retains its value, so that the heroes of the Trojan War and their stories are duly solicited and appreciated. Aeolus' corresponding piety, however, means that when the companions foolishly mistrust Odysseus' motives and release the pent-up winds, Aeolus takes it as a sign of the gods' hatred of Odysseus and withdraws his assistance. Thus rather than landing on Ithaca – to which they had come close enough, with Aeolus' help, to see people on shore – they arrive instead in the land of the Laestrygones, to meet with a reprise of Polyphemos' savagery. This is in some ways even more dreadful because more human, since, monstrous though they are, the Laestrygones actually have political organization.

More disorienting still is the landing on Circe's island, where it is impossible to tell East from West (10.190–4), and where Odysseus and his men confront an even more complex relation to the practices of hospitality than earlier inversions of them had presented. Rather than revealing a bestial side of her own, as do the Cyclops and Laestrygones, Circe, having graciously entertained her guests, transforms them into animals (on Near Eastern parallels, see Crane 1988: 63–8). When she fails to work her magic on Odysseus, the routine inquiry from host to guest about name and origins becomes an astonished quizzing (10.325–35), to which Circe herself, realizing who her guest must be, provides the answer; and with it her summons to the pigpen turns into an invitation to her bed. Circe's erotic power is a greater threat to the homecoming of Odysseus and his men than her drugs. Once Odysseus has entered her "surpassingly beautiful bed," a year passes, as it were, before he notices; this is the unique instance in which Odysseus' men need to remind him to resume their voyage.

The temptation posed by Circe, and her consequent potential to derail the goal of return, constitute – along with Calypso and Nausikaa – the most troubling of all the byways on the route to Ithaca, because they offer alternatives to life with Penelope, willingly undertaken. Other poetic traditions, notably that followed by the Epic Cycle's *Telegony*, apparently envisioned Odysseus as pursuing those alternatives. The *Odyssey*, by contrast – as we saw in the episode with Calypso – represents Odysseus as affirming his life with Penelope in his *oikos* by declining (however belatedly, in Circe's case) the allure of other erotic possibilities. At the same time, the poem represents his own charisma as such that Circe, Calypso, and Nausikaa are converted into facilitators of Odysseus' return rather than obstacles to it, modulating from actual or potential lovers into allies who advance his, and the narrative's, progress toward Ithaca (see Felson and Slatkin 2004: 105–6). It is Circe's instructions that protect Odysseus and his companions from a perilous seduction of another sort: the Sirens' irresistible lure of infinite knowledge, anchored in their competing song of the Trojan War – a pseudo-*Iliad*, from the fatal charms of which "entertainment" no visiting audience can escape (see Doherty 1995).

At the narrative center of all the adventures is the descent to the Underworld. Understood by Odysseus and his men as an unprecedented, uniquely estranging exploit, it forms a return story within the larger frame of homecoming. The retrospective character of Odysseus' account intensifies here, as the shades, reanimated, recall their own lives and deaths. Odysseus' meeting with the shade of his mother, and his sorrow at being unable to take her in his arms, movingly convey the finality of his mortal journey, his mortal choice. Urged on by his Phaeacian audience, too enthralled to let

Odysseus interrupt his own story, he describes encounters with the shades of his fellow-warriors from Troy and the celebrated figures of an earlier generation, like Herakles. Here time has stopped; their stories are over, and all are dominated by the past, most powerfully his old competitor Ajax, who has taken his sense of injury, as it were, to the grave. Agamemnon, still rehearsing his wife's betrayal, enjoins Odysseus not to reveal himself when he arrives in Ithaca. The episode points forward as well, however; with the seer Teiresias' prophecy, it looks beyond the epic's own ending to a mysterious last voyage even after Odysseus' return to Ithaca – in which that sailor will travel inland so far that he will reach a place whose inhabitants have no knowledge of the sea – and to Odysseus' reconciliation with Poseidon and his own death (see Finley 1978: 111–16).

But Teiresias also grimly announces the hazards on the way to Ithaca, of which Circe later warns in even more detail, anticipating the fatal landing on Thrinakia, the sun-god's island. The narrative thrust toward this event calls to mind Chekhov's remark that if a playwright hangs a gun on the wall in the first act, it has to go off by the fifth act. The episode of the sun-god's island is the *Odyssey*'s equivalent of Chekhov's gun, announced in the poem's earliest lines as the occasion of the companions' downfall and anticipated ever since. The self-restraint counseled by Teiresias – to forebear to eat the cattle of the sun – is Odysseus' strong suit, but, as demonstrated on earlier occasions, it is beyond the capacities of his followers. No monstrous adversary does them in, in the end, but their own mortal frailty, their appetite; and Odysseus' mortal need for sleep keeps him from protecting them one last time. Having eluded the terrors of the deep, including the hideous Scylla and Charybdis, the companions prove to be their own worst enemies, and pay with their lives for their last meal. Odysseus survives alone.

After ten years of struggling for his *nostos*, Odysseus is smoothly transported to Ithaca overnight, in his sleep. The folktale quality of this longed-for arrival might be imagined to presage an effortless conclusion to the poem, complete with untroubled reunion with Penelope. After the drama of his travels, how can the poem render Odysseus' return not as an anticlimax but an appropriate culmination of all that has come before? By making Ithaca his final adventure, a challenge to cognitive as well as physical powers, for which all his previous trials of *mêtis*, strength, and endurance seem like preparation. His conversation with Athena, no longer working behind the scenes but finally fully revealed to him, signals a new level of collaboration, as the goddess applauds Odysseus' fluent introductory falsehood (13.287–95); his earlier strategy of self-concealment and selective self-representation will take the form, with her help, of disguise and lying tales with which to test the loyalty of his household.

The paradigms of social and natural order, of temporal constraints, and of individual identity within these, interrogated in the course of the poem, are put under heightened pressure on Ithaca. Odysseus' return is a re-entry into the world of time and its effects. The life span of the dog Argos, who has patiently awaited his master's homecoming, measures the elapsed years of Odysseus' absence. The passage of time itself creates the crisis of the plot as viewed from Ithaca: the maturation of Telemachus means that Penelope must act (she quotes Odysseus' instruction that she marry once Telemachus is bearded, i.e. grown up). Her scheme to forestall the suitors' importuning shows her fully equal to the *mêtis* – and the boldness – that Odysseus and Athena share. Penelope's stratagem of weaving and unweaving the shroud for Laertes is no less than a daring effort to reverse time's flow: for the ruse to be a successful delaying tactic, not only must she not be discovered but Laertes must not die! Yet Penelope, of all the characters in the poem, has a sense of life's stages, and not only for Telemachus: she says wistfully to Odysseus, when they reunite, that the gods begrudged them the chance to have their youth and grow old together (23.210–12).

The poem's recuperation of the figure of Odysseus, which this chapter began by discussing, and the concomitant idealization of "home" that it develops, depends on its characterization of Penelope. The audience's desire – produced by the narrative's teleological momentum – to see Odysseus reinstalled in his *oikos* can only be met if Penelope is a character of corresponding magnetism, who reciprocates his aspirations. Odysseus articulates to the young Nausikaa an ideal of marriage: that husband and wife are "likeminded." The *Odyssey* creates in Penelope, therefore, a wife not divinely beautiful, as Calypso points out, but one who is the counterpart of her husband, and of the same mind (her epithets are "intelligent," "thoughtful"). Because, unlike her husband, Penelope does not have a part in the tradition of the *Iliad*, the poem can form an identity for her without needing to take account of any residue familiar to its ancient audiences. She is thus in many senses unprecedented.

Yet while the poem constructs a plot whose linchpin is Penelope's trustworthiness, it also repeatedly raises the specter of wifely infidelity, not only in its constant iteration of the negative models of Clytemnestra and Helen, but also in Demodokos' song about the adultery of Aphrodite and the revenge of her cuckolded husband, and even through Athena-Mentes' provocative hints about Penelope (15.10–23). If some scholars have read the *Odyssey* as a triumphalist celebration of the married couple, others have drawn attention to the opaqueness of Penelope, as the poem represents her, and to the ambiguity of such elements as her dream of the geese, where she seems to lament a proleptic image of the suitors' destruction (see Katz 1991 on Penelope's indecipherability). From the standpoint of the characters within the poem, of course, the duress of Penelope's situation makes her dangerously susceptible to the suitors' pressure; an appreciation of history, in the form of the Trojan War and its triangulations, does not reassure them. The *Odyssey*, then, manages to depict Penelope as a devoted wife, while leaving open an ominous sense of her possible choices – and it is these unsettling options that endow her with agency. The poem, in other words, has it both ways: it maintains a tension between the expectations of its audience and the anxieties of its characters, prolonged by the strategy of Odysseus' disguise and gradual self-disclosure (see Murnaghan 1987).

The "man of many ways" undertakes yet another "way," in order to view a last city of men – his own – and become acquainted with their minds. In the guise of a beggar who has seen better days, Odysseus is in a position to witness at close range the suitors' brutality and shocking abridgement of *xeinia*, all too reminiscent of Polyphemos and the Laestrygones. At the opening of the poem, they display their discourtesy to guests; here their offensiveness is taken to a further extreme, as they abuse the suppliant – verbally and physically – and attempt to humiliate him by staging a mock-epic fight with a local bully. And in addition to their insatiable consumption of their host's goods, here they are shown to have corrupted members of his household. The suitors want both to eat food they are not entitled to and to sleep with women they are not entitled to. By contrast, Odysseus' disguise also allows him to witness the spontaneous hospitality of the swineherd Eumaios and other loyal servants like Eurykleia, and the unimpeachable behavior of his family.

The sign of Eumaios' integrity and piety is his respectful, welcoming treatment of the *xenos*, all the more marked because unhesitatingly offered, not to a visiting hero but to an evidently abject wanderer; even before, that is, Odysseus spins the Cretan tales that establish him as a displaced aristocrat and veteran of Troy, the swineherd receives him sympathetically (on the sociology of the *Odyssey* see Finley 1962; on class attitudes see Thalmann 1998). Eumaios' openhandedness serves as a reflection of the hospitality of the household in former years; he laments its diminished prosperity while gratefully recalling the benevolence of its absent master. As surrogate host, the swineherd makes the disguised

Odysseus a guest in his own home, such that he can perceive it at the same time as outsider and insider.

Odysseus' return, therefore, consists of a series of reciprocal, though not simultaneous "seeings": recognitions, which trace the sameness and change in his *oikos*. Odysseus controls the process – up to a point. With his convincing, fictional Cretan autobiography, he invents an effective persona – until Eurykleia inadvertently finds the scar that identifies him, the mark in the flesh that defies all dissembling. But all revelations of his identity, including Eurykleia's, build to the final recognition of him by his wife – a recognition the poem defers to a climactic moment that takes her husband himself unawares.

Odysseus advances his re-entry strategically; even so, with his solitary, pseudonymous return, the *Odyssey* puts its hero in a quandary: how, given his bare handful of supporters, will he rid his house of its numerous intruders without their recognizing and overpowering him? The poem's answer to the problem it poses is to have Odysseus' need to take action converge with Penelope's need to make a decision; it plots a simultaneous solution to both exigencies– and it gives the devising of it not to Odysseus, but to Penelope. She must determine whom she will marry; in the presence of the as yet unrecognized master archer, she sets up the test of Odysseus' bow. The *Odyssey* thus structures Odysseus' return in terms that focus on the sexual and marital order that is under siege in his household: in order to re-establish himself both as king and as lord of his estate he must win his wife once again.

The aristocratic practice of competing for a bride – and thereby a network of relatives, allies, and enemies – recurs as a motif in early Greek literature, often centering on a decisive contest among competitors. Typically, the bride's father arranges the contest and confers his daughter on the victor. In an inspired masterstroke that answers to the complexity of her uncertain marital status, Penelope will choose the man who can wield Odysseus' bow; she will give herself away (see Felson-Rubin 1993 and H. Foley 1995). By putting the bow in Odysseus' hands, Penelope lets him recapitulate the role of successful suitor of his own wife and take a just revenge on his would-be usurpers all at once.

The *Odyssey*'s virtuosity is such that it manages to make the improbable courtship of a middle-aged, motherly queen by an aging beggar into high romantic drama. It also offers its hero a chance to demonstrate his warrior prowess in an *aristeia* so brilliant – one fighter against so many adversaries – that it may even trump the *Iliad*. And in a simile that compares his handling of the bow to a singer with his lyre (21.404–9), the poem conjoins Odysseus' warrior-hero and narrator-hero roles. Odysseus' only competition in stringing the bow is from Telemachus; yet unlike the Epic Cycle's *Telegony*, this epic does not pursue the implications of such a rivalry (although it suggests them), preferring to leave Odysseus as the unchallenged head of his household. Telemachus' *kleos* is to be neither his father's avenger, as recommended by Nestor, nor his supplanter, but his father's rightful ally and eventual successor to the *oikos* he has helped to maintain. The *Odyssey*'s interest in the production of culture – e.g. in song, war, work, exchange, marriage – is also an interest in its reproduction.

The slaughter of the suitors, prefigured in an eerie scene of their hysteria at a final banquet, has been anticipated since the poem's opening, when Athena-Mentes predicts that if Odysseus returns, their wedding plans will turn into funeral arrangements (her prediction/wish is echoed by Menelaos at 4.341–6). The long-postponed "wedding," as the *Odyssey* draws to a close, does take place, but it takes place between Odysseus and Penelope; to achieve it, Odysseus – the relentless tester – must be tested himself. The competition of the bow that reveals Odysseus' identity to the suitors, proving his ownership of his possessions and his reputation, is not decisive for Penelope; she awaits further proof. The ultimately persuasive test is one that *attests*: to intimacy, to memory, to conversation, to promise, to like-mindedness – to the knowledge of their bed (on the meaning of the bed, see, e.g., Zeitlin 1996).

Ancient critics considered the *telos* (both goal and endpoint) of the *Odyssey* to be Book 23 line 296, where husband and wife go to bed together. The poem proceeds to further crucial reckonings, however, including the much-deferred meeting between Odysseus and his father (see Finley 1978: 224–33 and esp. Henderson 1997: 87–116). Odysseus identifies himself to Laertes, much as he is made known to Penelope, through privileged knowledge and shared memory. If the couple's bed embodies their history and tested loyalty, the orderly orchard materializes the patriline, making Odysseus' childhood continuous with his achieved – and now acknowledged – condition as husband and father. In each case, the touchstone of identity is one that links Odysseus to his particular locale, to its shaping and shaped terrain.

Narratively satisfying as it might have been to conclude with the reunion between Odysseus and Penelope, it is important to observe that in our *Odyssey*, the individual *oikos* has a wider context. At the beginning of Book 24, the poem returns its audience to the perspective from the Underworld; it joins the *Iliad* to the now nearly-completed *Odyssey*, as the *Iliad*'s heroes meet the shades of the suitors. Their retrospective discourse allows the *Iliad*, as it were, to interpret and endorse the *Odyssey*, praising its moral outcome and predicting its fame, and that of Penelope above all. And the conclusion of the book insists on a broad sociopolitical framework as the poem's largest scaffolding: a final consideration of what constitutes the cities of men and their ongoing tribulations. The battle with the suitors' insurgent relatives ends before it becomes a bloodbath, and oaths of friendship are exchanged – the tokens of *xeinia* – thanks to the intervention of Zeus and Athena, who close the poem, as they had opened it, reflecting on human deeds and misdeeds.

The *Odyssey*, with the *Iliad*, is often regarded as a foundation poem in western – or more precisely, European – culture. Its comic structure, its humanity, its picaresque humor, its moving scenes of family engagement (in the Underworld and in Ithaca), its preoccupations with survival, risk, travel, courage, and home: all have contributed to the poem's perpetual interest, for artists (in our century, James Joyce, Derek Walcott, Primo Levi, Louise Glück) as well as scholars, students, and diverse other readers. The complexity of the poem resists any straightforward attempt to appropriate it, or to domesticate it: for all its remarkable elaboration of the figure of the wife and queen, Penelope, and its extended focus on the journey of the son Telemachus, the poem is not only an epic family romance but a sustained, albeit episodic, inquiry into identity, paradigms of social order, the political economy of sex and the family, and civilization and its discontents.

NOTE

The author is grateful to Sara Bershtel, Celia Brickman, and especially Maureen McLane, for their stimulating comments on this essay.

FURTHER READING

Scholarship on the *Odyssey* is vast and varied, a subject for study in itself. Among numerous contributions to our understanding of the poem, the following works are easily available to an English-speaking readership; they are grouped roughly by general area of interest, but the scope of each of these studies extends beyond any single topic indicated here.

Background

G. Crane, Calypso. *Backgrounds and Conventions of the* Odyssey (1988).
J. M. Foley, *Traditional Oral Epic: The* Odyssey, Beowulf, *and the Serbo-Croatian Return Song* (1990, repr. 1993).
D. Frame, *The Myth of Return in Early Greek Epic* (1978).
G. Nagy, *The Best of the Achaeans*, chs. 1–3 (1979a).
W. G. Thalmann, *Conventions of Form and Thought in Early Greek Epic Poetry* (1984).

Narrative/poetics

A. L. T. Bergren, "Odyssean temporality: many (re)turns," in C. A. Rubino and C. W. Shelmerdine (eds.). *Approaches to Homer* (1983).
J. S. Clay, *The Wrath of Athena: Gods and Men in the* Odyssey (1983).
N. Felson-Rubin, *Regarding Penelope: From Character to Poetics* (1993).
M. A. Katz, *Penelope's Renown: Meaning and Indeterminacy in the* Odyssey (1991).
W. Hansen, *The Conference Sequence: Patterned Narration and Narrative Inconsistency in the* Odyssey (1972).
M. L. Lord, "Withdrawal and return: an epic story pattern in the Homeric Hymn to Demeter and in the Homeric poems," *Classical Journal* 62 (1967).
J. Peradotto, *Man in the Middle Voice: Name and Narration in the* Odyssey (1990).
P. Pucci, *Odysseus Polytropos: intertextual readings in the* Odyssey *and* Iliad (1987).
L. Slatkin, "Genre and generation in the Odyssey," *Métis* 2 (1987).

Society/politics

M. I. Finley, *The World of Odysseus* (1962).
J. Haubold, *Homer's People: Epic Poetry and Social Formation* (2000).
W. G. Thalmann, *The Swineherd and the Bow: Representations of Class in the* Odyssey (1998).
H. Van Wees, *Status Warriors: War, Violence and Society in Homer and History* (1992).
P. Vidal-Naquet, "Land and sacrifice in the Odyssey," in S. Schein (ed.) *Reading the* Odyssey (1996).

Gender

B. Cohen, (ed.), *The Distaff Side: Representing the Female in Homer's* Odyssey (1995).
L. E. Doherty, *Siren Songs: Gender, Audiences, and Narrators in the* Odyssey (1995).
H. Foley, "Reverse similes and sex roles in the *Odyssey*," *Arethusa* 11 (1978).
J. Winkler, "Penelope's cunning and Homer's," in *Constraints of Desire: The Anthropology of Sex and Gender in Ancient Greece* (1990).
F. Zeitlin, "Figuring fidelity," in *Playing the Other: Gender and Society in Classical Greek Literature* (1996).

Themes

S. Murnaghan, *Disguise and Recognition in the* Odyssey (1987).
C. Segal, *Singers, Heroes and Gods in the* Odyssey (1994).

Reception

W. B. Stanford, *The Ulysses Theme*, 2nd edn. (1963).
In addition, *Reading the Odyssey: Selected Interpretive Essays* (1996), edited and with an introduction by Seth Schein, is a useful collection of essays on a range of topics, including several by European

scholars (in English translation). A valuable general guide to the poem is W. G. Thalmann, *The Odyssey: An Epic of Return* (1992).

Editions

D. B. Monro and T. W. Allen, *Homeri Opera I–V.*, 3rd edn. (1920). Reprinted many times. Contains the Greek text and a critical apparatus but does not include commentary.

W. B. Stanford, *The Odyssey of Homer*, 2nd edn. (1967). (First published 1947–8, revised in 1958 and reprinted many times since, has an introduction (including a grammatical introduction to the Greek text) as well as extensive notes and commentary on the text.)

Commentaries

A. Heubeck, S. West, and J. B. Hainsworth (eds.) *A Commentary on Homer's Odyssey*, 3 vols. (1988–90).

I. DeJong, *A Narratological Commentary on the* Odyssey (2001).

Translations

The Odyssey, trans. George Chapman (1967) (First published 1614–16.)

The Odyssey of Homer, trans. Alexander Pope (1943) (First published 1725.)

Both Chapman and Pope render the Greek in rhymed couplets; these are translations of unsurpassed vitality.

The Odyssey of Homer, trans. Samuel Butler (1968) (First published 1900, a prose translation.)

Homer, The Odyssey, trans. Robert Fagles (1996, 2nd edn. 1999). Lively, highly readable; lends itself well to reading aloud.

Homer, The Odyssey, trans. Robert Fitzgerald (1962, repr. 1988). Elegant free-verse rendering.

The Odyssey of Homer, trans. Richmond Lattimore (1967, 1991). Corresponds line-for-line to the Greek hexameters; especially valuable in preserving the formulaic character of the Greek text.

Homer, Odyssey, trans. Stanley Lombardo (2000). Excellent introduction by Sheila Murnaghan.

CHAPTER TWENTY-THREE

Hesiod

Stephanie Nelson

Introduction: Hesiod and the Hesiodic Tradition

Hesiod, whether or not he ever existed, has always lived in the shadow of Homer. As early as the *Contest of Homer and Hesiod* the association of the two poets, and Hesiod's membership as the junior partner, was all but canonical. Although the extant *Contest* may go back only to the time of Hadrian, it appears to be based upon an original which may date to around 400 BCE. Herodotus refers to "Homer and Hesiod" as the poets who taught Greece about the gods (Hdt. 2.53), and goes on to engage in a spirited dialogue with Homer (2.112–20). Aeschylus' alleged remark about taking crumbs from the table of Homer is not paralleled by any similar remark about Hesiod, and it may be worth noting that the one surviving tragedy whose basis is Hesiodic, the *Prometheus Bound*, is often considered unworthy of Aeschylean authorship. Plato, of course, although he regularly cites both poets (*Rep.* 377d, etc.), picks out Homer as "the first and greatest of the tragedians" (*Rep.* 607a) and, perhaps deadliest of all, appears to prefer the work of Hesiod (see favorable mentions of Hesiod in *Rep.* 466b, 468e, 546e). We have seen this before (see Chapter 28, by Garner). In the *Contest* the people choose Homer, but the king gives the prize to Hesiod as the more educational poet. Hesiod may have won the battle; Homer was quite clearly set to win the war.

Hesiod's debt to Homer (if that is the term) goes back even as far as his identity. Commonly accepted by the classical world as a slightly later poet with much in common with Homer, the "Homeric Question" has generated in turn its Hesiodic corollary (but cf. West 1966: 40–8; see Nagy 1996b on Hesiod's identity). The meter and language shared by the poems in question point to a common oral tradition. If, then, "Homer" is to be regarded as the product rather than the producer of this tradition, it seems natural to apply the same reasoning to Hesiod. At its most extreme this approach, perhaps ironically, comes to resemble a depersonalized version of an older way of viewing the Hesiodic poems. That approach, which centered on different "schools" of epic poetry, distinguished a narrative "Ionic" tradition which found its greatest practitioner in Homer, from another "Boeotian" tradition which was primarily didactic. It was the latter tradition which produced the Hesiodic works. Modern criticism is more likely to find the roots of this tradition in the Near East than in Boeotia, and is far less likely to point to one individual poet, the "genius" of the tradition, as the author of the *Theogony* and *Works and Days*. It agrees with the older school of criticism nonetheless, in seeing the genre rather than the individual voice of the poet as defining the poetry.

This basic question: not who, but whether, Hesiod was, may be the first place where Hesiodic criticism has suffered from its assimilation into the study of Homer. The two questions probably do have a single answer. What matters here, however, is less the answer than the influence that the question has had upon the way critics read Hesiod. The two most important poems taken to be "Hesiodic," the *Works and Days* and the *Theogony*, mark themselves off by insisting on a personal author. The *Theogony* is every bit as particular in identifying its author as a shepherd of Mount Helicon as the *Works and Days* is to identify itself as the work of a small landholder in Ascra, in Mount Helicon's shadow. This does not, of course, prove anything about the poems' authorship. An invented persona is as effective as autobiography as a centralizing device, and as effective for either a single poet or for a tradition. The identification is, however, important to our understanding of the poem.

In contrast to the Hesiodic poems the *moi* of Homer's "Tell *to me* O goddess . . . " (*Od.* 1.1; *Il.* 2.484) does not claim for itself any individuality. The unifying principle of these poems lies in the narrative itself, not in the personality of the poet. As a result, the unity of the poet can be challenged, as it has been, without finally threatening the unity of the poem. After many excellent works of post-Parry Homeric criticism we are left with a new understanding of the way in which the Homeric poems were composed, but, finally, with essentially the same poems. The unity of the *Iliad* and the *Odyssey* lies, for the most recent criticism, where it always lay: in the narrative of the poems themselves (see Chapter 21, by Edwards and Chapter 22, by Slatkin). Nor is this surprising. As intriguing as we may find characterizations of Phemius, Demodokus, and even Achilles as poets, the poems exist independently of their portrayal of the poets. In fact, to the extent that the voice of the Homeric narratives is intended to be taken as both impersonal and universal, that is, to the extent that it is to be taken as the voice of the Muses themselves, the poems themselves ask to be taken as the products more of a tradition than of a particular poetic voice.

The same is not true of the *Works and Days* in particular, and, to a lesser degree, the *Theogony*. Here the persona of the author is the major unifying element of the poem. As a result, when the author is problematized, so also is the unity of the poem. Although there is no necessary connection here, the result occurs nonetheless. What is affected first is the assumption that the poems have any unity at all. A prejudice remains that a tradition cannot create a unified work of art in the way that an individual poet can. The Homeric poems are able to weather this prejudice because their unity lies precisely where we are accustomed to find it, in the narrative. In the Hesiodic case, however, where the unity is one of theme rather than of narrative, the less familiar form makes the unity of the poem less apparent to the modern reader. The poems are therefore more susceptible: when the identity of the poet is shaken, with it tends to go the unity of the poem.

What is affected next is the kind of questions we tend to ask of the poems. *Kleos* ("renown"), for example, is a central interest of the Homeric poems, and with it comes a corresponding interest in poetry, precisely as a tradition, as the communicator and creator of fame (see further Chapter 21, by Edwards and Chapter 22, by Slatkin). *Kleos* plays a far less important role within the Hesiodic poems. As a result, when a critic interested in the question of orality comes to the Homeric poems he or she finds immediately a corresponding interest in the poems themselves. But not in Hesiod. Similarly, to the extent that an interest in orality, and so in *kleos*, leads back to an interest in the nature of heroism, the critic finds an echoing interest in Homer. But not in Hesiod. And finally, the discovery of an oral tradition has raised questions in the minds of scholars about the complex relation of an individual and his culture (see further Chapter 21, by

Edwards). Again the interest is reflected in Homer far more than in Hesiod. In a nutshell, a critic whose interest lies in the oral tradition will find a study of the Homeric poems richly rewarding because the poems themselves are interested in this tradition (see further Chapter 13, by J. Foley). Hesiod is far more doubtful. His Muses, famously, are as able to tell lies that seem like truth as they are to tell the truth (*Th.* 27–8). Within the Hesiodic tradition the poet's task seems to be to tell one from the other.

The evidence for and against authorship by a single poet of the two great "Hesiodic" poems is in itself not very different from the evidence in the case of Homer. As we will see below, the *Works and Days* and the *Theogony* are no less unified works of art than the *Iliad* or the *Odyssey*, and the language they employ is sufficiently close to argue against a great separation between the two traditions. Nor, as will be apparent in our consideration of the entire Hesiodic cycle, are the Hesiodic poems any less embedded in the overall epic tradition than the Homeric narratives. The impact of the question, however, is as different in the two cases as are the poems themselves. To come to the "Hesiodic question" from the Homeric one does no harm. But to come to the Hesiodic poems with a focus on the distinction between the persona of the poet and the composition of the poem is to undermine precisely the trope that the poem itself is attempting to establish. To lose the poet in this sense is also, in large measure, to lose the poem itself.

A simple factual "biography" can, and in classical times quite universally was, derived from the details introduced into the *Works and Days* and *Theogony*. From the *Theogony* we learn that Hesiod, so named, was watching over his sheep on Mount Helicon when the Muses came to him and inspired him with song. The *Works and Days* fits this gem of information into a greater overall setting. Hesiod's father was an unsuccessful sailor who had moved from Aeolian Cyme to Ascra, where he acquired a small holding in the shade of Mount Helicon. Hesiod himself, presumably having perfected his poetic voice while tending the family flocks, once crossed over to Euboea to compete in a poetic competition for Amphidamus, whose participation in the Lelantine wars would date the contest to around 730–700 (see West 1966: 43–4 and 1978: 30–40 for a "biography" of the poet and his brother). Having won the contest Hesiod dedicated his prize, a tripod, to "the Muses of Helicon," deliberately recalling the opening of the *Theogony*. After the death of their father Hesiod and his brother Perses (whose name may or may not reflect an origin in Asia Minor) divided his property. Perses, however, took more than his due share and bribed the local officials or "kings" to support his side of the dispute, prompting Hesiod to compose the *Works and Days* in protest. An aside in the poem informs us that Perses has in fact, as Hesiod warned, proved unable to prosper with his ill-gotten gains, and has been reduced finally to begging from his brother.

This is explicitly the persona given us for the author of the *Works and Days* and, if the *Theogony*'s reference to "Hesiod" is taken as referring to the author of the poem, it is the expanded form of the persona of that poet as well. The "biography" itself is quite clear. What is not clear is what we are intended to do with it. The simplest explanation of why Hesiod portrays himself in this way may be the one which is currently the least fashionable, that Hesiod portrays himself as a modest, but not impoverished peasant landholder because this is what he was. But while such an explanation may seem satisfying, it is not sufficient. A poet may choose to include autobiographical material in his poem, but even in a poem of the seventh century there still must be a reason for including it. To understand why Hesiod, or the Hesiodic tradition, might consider it important to point to a particular social position it is necessary to look at the social position itself.

The great constant of Hesiod's "biography" is his marginalization. The Muses come to Hesiod not as a poet, but as a shepherd. Their first words are abusive, and their description of their powers ambivalent. Hesiod's father, as has often been noted, had made a backward migration, not from mainland Greece to Asia Minor, but from Aeolia in Asia Minor to mainland Greece. Hesiod's social position is similarly liminal. He is neither one of the "kings," nor, as his praise of the kings in the *Theogony* makes clear, is his division from them in the Thersites mold. Hesiod is neither king nor beggar; he is neither purely a farmer or purely a shepherd; and, I would argue, he correspondingly locates his own poetry as neither simply part of a greater poetic tradition, nor as simply opposed to it. The issue is not whether this biography is true. It is rather what the biography contributes to the poem. Whether we see the biography as invented to fit the poem, or the poem as a reflection of an actual poet upon his experience, the detail that has been selected emphasizes the marginality of the poet's own position. In order to understand the poems, therefore, it will prove necessary to understand this marginality as well.

The Hesiodic Cycle

Another factor which distinguishes Hesiodic from Homeric poetry is its interconnectedness. In the case of the *Works and Days* and the *Theogony* for example, the "biographies" of the two poems are quite deliberately connected, first in the *Theogony's* explicit reference to Hesiod, and then by the *Works and Days'* reference to the Muses of Mount Helicon. Nor are these the only ties between the poems. The appearance of the Prometheus story in both poems and both poems' focus on Zeus, alongside the presence in both of a personal narrator, suggests an almost deliberate cross-referencing to a common worldview. Most famously, and apparently most pointedly, the author of the *Works and Days* begins the poem proper with a particle *ara* ("then/after all"), which points backward: "There is not then, after all, only one Strife . . . " The point of the particle seems a reference to the single Strife of *Th.* 225. The point of the reference appears to be a desire to make explicit that this poem forms one element of a greater whole.

The two major Hesiodic poems are not only connected to each other, they are also connected to the minor Hesiodic works, although by rather less definite ties (see further Chapter 24, by Burgess). Although both poems begin, as the Homeric poems do, with a direct invocation, neither poem comes to a clear ending. There is no burial of Hektor, or final settlement of Odysseus' battle with the suitors. Instead the *Theogony* trails off into a history of great women and the *Works and Days*, in the very last line, brings up the entirely new subject of divination by bird-signs. It is impossible to know whether the fragments of the cycle that seem to be being introduced here, the *Catalogue of Women* and the *Divination by Birds*, led to the addition of these connections, or whether the references spawned a new collection to be attributed to Hesiod. It may not matter. What does seem significant is the importance of the cycle to the poems.

A reason for that importance has already become apparent. By virtue of its self-inclusion within a cycle, Hesiodic poetry proclaims itself as part of a greater whole. This same sense of composition appears to a small degree in the two major Hesiodic poems. The *Theogony*, as we will see below, is composed of a patchwork of genealogies and stories which, placed together, create a single overall vision of the divine order. In other words, the poem's very nature reveals its interest in viewing each of its separate elements as also parts of a whole. The same is true of the *Works and Days*. Here, although the components are different – a description of the farmer's year, an account of sailing and trade, a fable, some myths, a study of neighborly relations, a list of lucky and unlucky days – the aim is much the same: to show the single thread of meaning that underlies all the varied phenomena which make up human life. The composition may well reflect a tradition in which sections of a poem would be recited separately (see Chapter 4, by Jensen). It is not at all difficult to imagine a poet, or a poetic tradition, putting together elements of various lengths, any combination of which might make up a particular performance. Nor is it difficult, conversely, to see how the individual components of such a poem might maintain their character by being recited independently. The proem to the *Theogony,* for example, is often seen as a "Hymn" on its own, and in the *Contest of Homer and Hesiod*, Hesiod is portrayed as performing on his own the segment of the *Works and Days* which opens "The Farmer's Year," while Homer, challenged to a similar recital, is forced (one might imagine) to resort to a generic battle scene.

The structure of the *Works and Days* and *Theogony* thus reflects, in small, what might have been the overall structure of a greater cycle. Connecting passages in the two major poems, for example, often serve simultaneously as the end of one section and the beginning of the next, and so are able to be used as either. It is a collection, moreover, whose parts are related more as they are in a bunch of flowers than as they are in a watch. There is very little "clock-like" about Hesiod. Within this relatively fluid structure then, there seems no reason why the *Works and Days* should not include the *Divination by Birds* or even the *Astronomy,* just as one could easily imagine the poem including only one of the two myths which illustrate the hardship of human life, or as leaving out the section on sailing, or as omitting any number of the general precepts governing human life which Hesiod includes. Similarly, the *Catalogue of Women*, which appears at the end of the *Theogony,* simply continues the movement of the poem as a whole, from the primeval gods, to the Titans, to the more fully anthropomorphic Olympians, through to the end of purely divine generation that occurs with the completion of Zeus' order, and the consequent movement to the goddesses who bore children to the great men of old, and from there to the women of that generation. The connection of the *Shield of Herakles* to the *Catalogue* is evident in the poem's opening phrase "Or like her . . ." (*É oiê*, from whence the other name of the *Catalogue*, "The Eoiae") as well as in the Argument to the *Shield*. If it is true, moreover, as the Argument claims, that only the first 56 lines of the *Shield* formed part of the *Catalogue* it seems that the *Shield* itself, and the battle of Herakles which introduces it, were also added as an expansion of the text (see Chapter 24, by Burgess).

In the case of the *Catalogue*, however, what remains is mostly only the names, cited as genealogical evidence by later authors. What we do not have, as we do in the case of the *Theogony* or the *Works and Days* is any idea of the theme which these stories might have been intended to illustrate. Had we such a theme it might become evident that the addition of the *Shield*, if it was an addition, did, or did not, further the overall theme of the poem. As the poem stands we cannot know, any more than we can know definitely that the *Catalogue* itself did have such a theme, and was not, as has often been assumed, merely a list of essentially unconnected stories. This is equally true of the rest of the cycle. Given the fragments we possess we cannot know how, or whether, these poems contributed to a "Hesiodic" vision of the world. What we can see, however, is the implications of the cycle itself, and in this, as in so many ways, the great difference between Homer and Hesiod.

The tendency of Hesiodic poetry to operate as a montage almost literally invites additions. Given the poetry's structure, moreover, these additions may simply expand, rather than violate, the integrity of the work. It is not so with Homer. It is difficult, if not impossible, to imagine a book of the *Iliad* subsequent to the burial of Hektor. It is nearly as difficult (despite critics of *Od.* 24) to imagine an addition to the *Odyssey* which would not ruin the carefully balanced structure of the poem (see Chapter 23, by Slatkin). Given this particular kind of integrity, the tendency to disregard the fact of the Homeric Cycle in interpreting the *Iliad* or *Odyssey* is only natural. The case is very different with the *Theogony* and *Works and Days*. Here, where, like a fractal, each individual section both mirrors the theme of the whole and goes into making it up, the fact of the Hesiodic Cycle, even in its absence, may provide a crucial clue to the unity of the poems that remain. To ignore the implications of the Cycle in this case would then be to ignore exactly the key to Hesiodic poetry.

The distinctive mark of the Hesiodic tradition seems to be its inclusiveness, both within the individual poems and within the Cycle altogether. It is an inclusiveness, moreover, which branches off into many fields other than epic poetry. The *Theogony*, for example, is notable for the similarity of its myth cycle to that of Near Eastern texts such as the *Enuma Elish*, where a cycle of three generations of gods, characterized by a struggle between the male and female, leads finally, after the challenge of a final god of disorder, to the divine kingship of Marduk (see Mondi 1984, 1990; Walcot 1966; West 1966; 18–31). Similarly, the *Works and Days*, which has, in particular, been distinguished as an example of didactic poetry, is notable for its similarity to "Wisdom Literature," another Near Eastern tradition (see Chapter 20, by Burkert). It is particularly notable here, moreover, that a particular persona and a particular situation is often taken as the connecting theme of a given poem's advice (see West 1978: 25–30). In the case of the *Works and Days* other, more anthropologically inclined scholars have noted the poem's links to peasant traditions, many of which continue in the Mediterranean. In this light, Hesiod's overall vision of human wealth as a "zero-sum" proposition, his inclination towards a "superstitious" and even numinal sense of the divine, the delicate balance he maintains between a sense of the importance of cooperation and a jealous maintenance of his own independence, and even his distrust of women and sailing, are not so much individual peculiarities as they are the reflection of a long peasant tradition (see Detienne 1963; Walcott 1970; Millet 1984).

The tradition is epic nonetheless. Structurally, in the employment of ring composition, and conceptually, in their focus on a single theme, the *Theogony* and *Works and Days* remain essentially Greek and essentially epic (on definitions of epic, see Chapter 1, by Martin). Structurally, the *Theogony* opens and closes with the Muses (1, 915, 1022), in precisely the way, for example, that the Prometheus episode opens and closes with Zeus rendering Prometheus immobile (517–22; 613–16), or the way in which Hesiod marks off Zeus' consolidation of his order through his children by beginning and ending the episode with the birth of Athena. In each case, as well, the structural device points out the thematic connection, in the Muses' dependence upon Zeus, in the lesson that Prometheus learns that one cannot escape the will of Zeus (613), and in Hesiod's pointed description of Athena as the goddess who, like her father, combines power and wisdom (896). Similarly, in the *Works and Days*, Hesiod takes care to open and close the poem with Zeus (1, 765) just as he opens and closes the Farmer's Year with the Pleiades (383, 615), Zeus' markers, or the "Days" with the importance of noting and understanding the ways of the gods (765–9, 824–8).

One other major difference between the Hesiodic and Homeric traditions should be mentioned. The world of the Homeric poems is a world in which "one man could lift a stone such that it takes two men to lift now." It is a world distinct and closed off from the contemporary world of Homer's audience, a quality which fascinates the poet, most particularly of the *Odyssey* (see Grene 1969). Hesiod's interests are very different. They lie completely in the here and now. The *Works and Days* is all but combative in its use of the contemporary world as the world of the poem. The same, despite appearances, is true of the *Theogony*. Here the past becomes, essentially, "pre-history," the time before the current reign of Zeus. As such it is told, as "pre-history" most commonly is, in order to illustrate the nature of the cosmos that has emerged from it.

The *Theogony*

If the Hesiodic tradition works as a fractal, the *Theogony* might have been designed as its model. The poem combines, as if they were a web and woof, two quite distinct ways of telling a single story. The first set of strands consists of genealogies, from the first appearance of Chaos to the final births of the heroes. The second is the series of myths which chart the narrative progress of the poem. The story told independently by either is of the gradual development of the cosmos from a primeval collection of independent elements into a unified order whose epicenter is Zeus.

Both strands are mythological. Within the Hesiodic tradition this implies that the material in one sense is the poet's own invention, and in another sense not. Hesiod, or the tradition, clearly felt comfortable tailoring a myth to suit a particular context, as with the story of Prometheus, which appears in quite different versions in the *Theogony* and the *Works and Days*. Similarly, as has been noted, many of the names of Hesiod's genealogies come transparently from his own descriptions (Solmsen 1949; thus the Nereids of *Th.* 243–64, or the names of the Muses, *Th.* 77–9 from *Th.* 65–9). Nor is the poet limited to a single tradition. As in the paralleling of the Prometheus story with the myth of the Five Ages, two very different myths, "another account" as Hesiod puts it, can be used to point out a single, basic truth about human life.

On the other hand it also seems clear that the poet, in his own mind at any rate, is not simply inventing his material. His description of Aphrodite is telling:

> And she, Aphrodite
> [Foam-born goddess and well-crowned Cytheria]
> Is called by the gods and by men, because in the foam [*aphros*]
> She was raised. But also Cytheria, as she touched upon Cythera,
> And Cyprus-born, for she was born in famed Cyprus,
> And genital-loving [*philommeides*], as from genitals she came to the light.

> (*Th.* 195–200)

The passage is a justification of the myth. According to Homer, Aphrodite is simply the child of Zeus and Dione. As Hesiod points out, however, Aphrodite's traditional epithets, "Cytherean" and "Cyprian," her name itself, and the wonderful reinterpretation of Homer's *philommêdes*, "laughter-loving", all confirm an alternate account of her birth, the one which he has adopted. There are, after all, many stories for the poet to choose among. His job, as the Muses imply, is to find the true one.

Hesiod's is thus a double task. On the one hand he must discover the essential truth that the traditions available to him convey. On the other he must, in the light of that truth, choose between those traditions. The challenge, of course, is circular. But then Hesiod, who is deeply aware of the ambivalence of human life, would be the first to acknowledge that.

The narrative side of the *Theogony* describes the coming to power of Zeus as a series of confrontations and victories. The genealogies of the poem tell the same story, seen now as a spontaneous evolution. As the original beings, Chaos (or "Gap"), Earth (Gaia), Tartarus, and Eros (the driving principle of all which is to come) begin to produce new generations, divinity differentiates itself into three major lines. From Chaos, through Night, come the descendants primarily catalogued in *Th.* 211–32, the negative abstractions whose positive counterparts will be born to Zeus at the end of the poem. From Sea (Pontos), the child of Earth and Heaven, come the monsters who will be largely overcome by the heroic sons of Zeus (*Th.* 233–336). And in the third, central line, Earth herself gives rise first to Heaven (Ouranos) and the features of nature, the Sea and Hills, and then with Heaven to the Titans, and finally to the Olympians and Zeus (see Nelson 1998). A divinity immanent in the cosmos thus develops into an order whose center is Zeus, the focal point of the central line.

The narrative of the *Theogony* tells the same story, only in more detail. Here we see the ratification of this order as Zeus distributes their *timai* ("honors" or "privileges") to the gods, confirming, denying, or renewing the *timai* of gods of the earlier generations, locating the *timai* of the gods of his own generation in relation to himself, and essentially begetting into existence a new kind of *timé*, that of the gods who are his children. The older gods come first. In a series of asides on Hecate, Styx, and the Hundred-Handers, we are shown Zeus determining the honors of the generation which came before him. The theme is made explicit in Zeus' conquests over the Titans, Atlas, and Prometheus, in the Titanomachy and in what is essentially a defeat of Earth and Tartarus in the person of their son Typhoeus.

Zeus' leadership in relation to the gods of his own generation is established first in the trick played on Kronos, through which Zeus, the youngest son, is enabled (like the stone which replaced him) to become the first child to emerge from his parents (*Th.* 488–97). This primacy is confirmed in Zeus' leadership of the battles against the Titans and Typhoeus. Finally we see Zeus' predominance, both among the gods of his generation and among the gods of the future, in his assumption of the power of generation itself. With the swallowing of Metis the possibility of genuine generation among the gods virtually ceases. The gods of the next generation are almost entirely the children of Zeus, and are all, essentially, simply aspects of Zeus' new order. The exceptions, Triton, the son of Poseidon, and Panic, Fear, and Harmonia, children of Ares and Aphrodite, are simply dim reflections of their fathers' divine *timé*. In the final, mini-narrative of the poem, Hera's attempt to match Zeus' generation of Athena is able to produce only the crippled god, Hephaistos. The narrative, essentially, thus shows us where the other strand of the poem, the tale of divine generation, has come to an end.

The narrative elements of the *Theogony* serve another function as well; they reveal the essential nature of Zeus' order. This lies in the coming together of force and intelligence within Zeus. Throughout the poem, force and intelligence, remaining separate, have rendered both each other and the overall order unstable. In the three episodes which portray first Heaven, then Kronos, and finally Zeus as threatened with overthrow, the female element originates a "cunning plan" violently executed by the son. Earth thus supplies Kronos with the cunning needed to castrate his father, and then supplies Rhea with the trick needed to overthrow Kronos. This pattern is ended by Zeus.

Heaven suppressed his children within their mother; Kronos swallowed them himself. Zeus finds the correct solution by swallowing not the child but the mother, ensuring that the female element is not left behind to plot against him. By so doing, moreover, Zeus incorporates the female element of cunning within himself. Hesiod underlines the point by naming Zeus' consort "Metis," or Intelligence (for Hesiod's combination of myths see West 1966: 401–2), and by pointing out the combination of power and wisdom which makes Athena, the only child of this union, so resemble her father.

The narrative episodes that have led up to this point have brought out the same theme. In the challenge of Prometheus Zeus counters cunning with cunning. In the challenge of the Titans he counters force with force. And in the final challenge, the challenge of Typhoeus, Zeus uses both, employing first "his sharp mind" and then his thunder (*Th.* 836–41).

The result of this combination of force and intelligence within Zeus is, quite simply, the emergence of order itself. Zeus' ability to first perceive and then overcome the threat of disorder personified in Typhoeus marks the final step in the establishment of his reign (see Mondi 1984). Zeus' winds, the well-ordered Notus and Boreas and Zephyr, exist in contrast to the unordered destructive winds that stem from Typhoeus, but now as elements locked within Tartarus, his own father (*Th.* 868–80). Hesiod concludes:

> But when the blessed gods had finally accomplished their labor
> And with the Titans decided their honors by force,
> Then it was that they urged, all through the counsels of Earth,

Zeus to be king and to rule, far-seeing Olympian Zeus,
Over the immortals. And he divided their honors amongst them.

(*Th.* 881–5)

After the last challenge of her final son, Typhoeus, Earth with her paradigmatic cunning has joined the force of the male gods. The result is a new distribution of divine *timê* and a new order, personified in a new generation sprung from Zeus and characterized by order and harmony. The poem has come full circle, back to the Muses of the invocation and the world of the poet. In other words we have returned to the world of ordinary life. As such it is the world, informed by the divine order of Zeus, which will appear again in the *Works and Days*.

The deepest connection between the *Theogony* and the *Works and Days* lies in their sense of a divine order which informs human life (see Clay 2003). We see this, for example, in Hesiod's focus on peace. Whether one sees Hesiod as a peasant farmer unimpressed by the aristocracy's obsession with war, or whether one sees a tradition interested in essentially non-Homeric values creating a poetic persona to fit, the message is unmistakable. The Homeric tradition focuses on war. In the Hesiodic tradition *aretê* is achieved by the sweat of one's brow (*WD* 289), and the sweat is not from bearing one's shield against the enemy.

In the *Contest of Homer and Hesiod* Hesiod is given his backhanded victory because he sings of peace and productivity while Homer sings of war. Although the *Theogony* could challenge a dozen *Iliads* for violence, and violence of a grotesquerie very alien to Homer, the characterization is a fair one (see Otto 1954). The violence of the *Theogony* is the violence of prehistory. The same vision reappears in the *Works and Days* in the myth of the Five Ages, a mini-history of the human race, where men move from the Golden Age and the protracted adolescence of the Silver Age, through two generations of warriors, the Bronze Age and the Heroes, to our current position, where not violence, but injustice, is the primary problem in human life.

Precisely the same contrast appears in Hesiod's depiction of the gods. The world of the Homeric gods is the world of the Homeric kings, both of whom occupy themselves in feasting, competition, patronage, and jealously guarding their *timê*, their personal honor, against all challenges. Hesiod's is a radically different sense of the divine, marked by a very different sense of *timê*. *Timê* in the *Theogony* is not a mark of a god's individual power. It is a prerogative distributed by Zeus, and so the mark of each god's particular place within a greater divine order. As such the gods' *timai* are marked by their names (as the Muses, *Th.* 75–80), their attendants (as Aphrodite, *Th.* 201–6), or their children (as Styx, *Th.* 383–5, or Ares, *Th.* 933–6). Nowhere, in either the *Theogony* or the *Works and Days*, do the gods feast. Nowhere do they come to earth to inspire a favorite. After the establishment of Zeus' reign they do not even compete among themselves. Instead they attend to business, and in the *Works and Days* just as in the *Theogony*: Poseidon at sea, Demeter on land, Justice in the law-courts, and Zeus supervising it all.

This compartmentalization, however, does not imply that man's relation to the gods is any easier or more predictable in Hesiod than it is in Homer. A peculiarity of Hesiod's conception of peace will illustrate. The myth of the Five Ages, which describes mankind's movement away from war, is a myth not of progress but of degeneration. Evil has not been eliminated from human life; violence has only been replaced by injustice. The sense, moreover, in which injustice might be considered the worse evil, appears in Hesiod's characterization of the diseases which escaped from Pandora's jar: "On their own they wander among mortals, bringing evil / In silence – since the counselor Zeus took out their voices" (*WD* 104–5). The reason why it is so hard to guard against injustice is similar: because its threat is not an open one. This, it will turn out, is the nature of Zeus' new order when it is seen, as it is in the *Works and Days*, from the human perspective.

The *Works and Days*

The *Works and Days* covers a dazzling array of materials: "autobiography," myth, fable, proverbs, practical observation, nature-writing, economic description, and astrology. Even the briefest glance at the various "sections" that the poem is commonly divided into –

Proem to Zeus (1–10)
Autobiography (11–41)
The Prometheus myth (42–105)
The myth of the Five Ages (106–201)
The fable of the hawk and the nightingale (201–11)
Justice and reciprocity (212–383)
The farmer's year (384–617)
Sailing and trading by sea (618–94)
Marriage and religious precepts (695–764)
The "Days" (765–828)

reveals why scholars have found it difficult to discover unity in the poem. The problem, however, is often that scholars are looking in the wrong place.

Like the *Theogony*, the unity of the *Works and Days* lies not in particular connections, or in any particular arrangement of its sections, but in its theme. Hesiod is not coy about what that theme is. It appears immediately, in the warning that Hesiod gives to Perses through his picture of the two kinds of Strife. The evil Strife, which Perses is following, encourages violence and cheating and brings disaster. The good Strife, Hesiod's patroness, leads men to competition and hard work, but brings wealth. The message is a simple one: human beings never get something for nothing.

Hesiod's argument, essentially, is that human life is not hard by accident; it is hard because Zeus has willed it to be so. We can see this, for example, in the simple fact that the earth does not yield men food without work. If Zeus did not want men to have hardship, Hesiod argues, a single day's work could yield us food enough for a year (*WD* 42–6). And this lesson, observable all around us, turns out to be precisely the same as that contained by tradition, in the personal picture of Zeus bringing hardship to human life in the Prometheus myth, and in the impersonal depiction of the growing difficulty of human life in the myth of the Five Ages.

From here Hesiod will go on to observe the same lesson, that for human beings good is always blended with evil, in all the disparate aspects of human life that he covers. It will appear in the fable, which depicts (as in the Proem) the strong suddenly shown to be weak; it will appear in the punishment which follows ill-gotten wealth, in the human tendency to give only after having gotten something oneself, in the drawbacks and benefits of lending one's goods, in the fact that there is no harvest without a plowing and no spring without a winter to precede it. The smallest details of life show the same pattern: the balance of risk against profit in trading by sea, or in loading a wagon, the risks and benefits inherent in marriage, the hidden bonuses and dangers of entertaining neighbors, of gossip, of pot-luck feasts, and finally of lucky and unlucky days. Perses, it turns out, simply fits into this pattern. The evil Strife encourages a man to gain wealth without hardship. But, as no human good comes without evil, unearned wealth can only be followed by retribution. The better way is the good Strife, which faces its evil, hard work, and then enjoys its consequent wealth in safety. As Hesiod points out, a secure half is much better than a precarious whole (*WD* 40–1).

The idea that human good is never unmixed with evil is a commonplace of Greek thought. What is new is Hesiod's application of the idea to the punishment which follows injustice. What is even more new is Hesiod's sense of how good and evil are related. For the two kinds of Strife, within Hesiod's vision, are not only opposites, they are also twins, and the difficulty of telling them apart is apparent in the very discovery that they were not one, but two.

This idea appears in the *Theogony* as well. The Hesiodic world as it emerges in the course of the *Theogony* is one of doubles: the twinning of Sleep and Death, of Heaven and Tartarus, of the dark abstractions born from Night, including the Fates, with their positive counterparts born from Zeus, again including the Fates (on Hesiod's sense of ambiguity see Vernant 1983: 240, 1988: 199–201; Nagler 1990). The *Works and Days*, similarly, views good and evil as often difficult to distinguish: neighbors, wives, children, the kings, plowing late (which may also succeed), or thrift (which can be harmful), or even idle gossip, who is herself a goddess, can all be good or evil. This also is the nature of women, and the way in which they have introduced evil into the world, in the *Works and Days* in the jar which carries both Hope and Diseases, and in the *Theogony* in the new parameters: that a man must marry, and so have the evil of a wife, or not marry, and see his life's work descend to his useless relatives (*Th.* 602–12).

Even more importantly, however, women are a paradigm for evil because they are deceptive: they are an evil which looks like a good (see Arthur 1982, 1983). Like the portions in Prometheus' sacrifice, good, among human beings, is concealed inside evil, and evil lies within apparent good. This is also true of the two Strifes; work, which looks evil, is in fact good, while cheating, which seems an attractive alternative, is evil. Zeus' divine order, from the point of view of the Muses, is settled. From the human point of view, however, the point of view of the poet, it is deeply ambiguous. This is why the quality men need, for Hesiod, is not a good will, but a good intelligence (*WD* 293–4). Where good and evil are twins the crucial task in human life is to tell the one from the other.

This is not, however, the end of the story. Zeus' order, for Hesiod, is not a corporation, impersonally and mechanically slotting each request into its appropriate department. Nor is it simply a malevolent hall of mirrors. It is rather a dynamic world, where good and evil are twinned, most significantly, as they develop over time. What is critical, Hesiod points out, is to know what will be better "afterwards, and in the end" (*WD* 294). This obsession with time is apparent from the very opening of the *Works and Days*, where Hesiod reworks yet another Homeric value by undermining the stability of *kleos* (*WD* 1–4). It continues in the poem's focus on cause and effect, and in the surprising revelations about Perses (*WD* 394–97). It appears most deeply however, in Hesiod's depiction of the Farmer's Year.

Viewed as a teaching manual Hesiod's account of farming is woefully inadequate. Seen as an evocation of the experience of farming, however, the reason for Hesiod's vagaries, repetitions, omissions, and extended description becomes clear (see Nelson 1998). So also does the section's place within the poem as a whole. For it is in the world of the Seasons, who are, in the great double-identification of the *Theogony*, both the natural Seasons which govern man's fields (*erga*), and the social forces, Dike (both "Justice" and "Penalty"), Good Order, and Peace which govern his "works" (also *erga*) (*Th.* 901–2), that Hesiod finds his greatest image for both the structure and the ambiguity of human life. In describing farming Hesiod describes what it is like to live within a regular order which is constantly shifting and which demands constant watchfulness. In the great order of the Seasons good and evil, winter and summer, drought and rain, heat and cold, scarcity and plenty, succeed one another. But within that order any individual drought, storm, or harvest may bring salvation or disaster. As Hesiod says about a spring rainfall: "One way at one time, and another at another is Zeus' mind who holds the aegis; / it is hard for mortal men to know" (*WD* 483–4).

Hesiod, as he is depicted by the tradition, is not only a farmer; he is also a poet, and as such operates within a similarly ambiguous world. The most famous declaration of

Hesiod's Muses may be that they can speak truth, and they can also speak lies that seem like truth. The declaration creates a new kind of liminality (see, e.g., Vernant 1983; Detienne 1986; Bowie 1993). The poet of the Homeric tradition mediates between those who do great deeds and those who hear about them. Among the Phaeacians he sets the rhythm for a dance he cannot see. In Ithaca he is the teller of a tale whose completion he himself will be part of. In the *Iliad* the only singer is Achilles – at the moment when he ceases to be a part of the war being sung (*Il.* 9.185–91). Hesiod's liminality is rather different. He is caught not between actors and audience, but between lies and the truth.

Hesiod is (or is made to be) a poet of strong opinions. He approves of plowing early, of diligence and thrift, and of kings who do their job. He dislikes women, sailing, his brother Perses, kings who take bribes, and idle chatter. And yet each of these elements of human life end up, finally, as ambiguous. Although the persona may seem to imply a world of black and white, a world within which choices are simply right or wrong, the world, in short, of didactic poetry in its implicitly derogatory sense, the Hesiodic world is far more complex than this, and less easy to operate within. In this way Hesiod's liminality reflects more than just his "in-between" position. It also reflects the ambivalence inherent in his vision of reality. The poet, whose task is to find the true figure among the deceptive ones, cannot stand simply in one camp or the other.

The final reason that Hesiod gives for his belief in justice follows an admission of uncertainty:

> Now indeed would I not myself be just among men
> Nor have my son just – since it's bad for a man to be just
> If the greater right is held by the less righteous man.
> But these things I don't yet expect counselor Zeus to accomplish.

(*WD* 270–3)

The reason for the expectation reveals also what, to Hesiod, it means to be human:

> Now Perses, you cast these things into your heart,
> And listen to Justice, and forget about force altogether.
> For this is the *nomos* ["law, way"] for men, assigned by Cronos' son,
> That for fish and for beasts and for birds that are winged,
> They eat one another, since there is no justice among them.
> But to man he gave justice, which by far is the best
> As it turns out.

(*WD* 274–80)

The "as it turns out" is Hesiod's special ambivalent touch.

Achilles' description of the two jars upon Zeus' threshold (*Il.* 24.525–33) sees human life, as Hesiod does, as at best a blend of good and of evil. Similarly Homer, like Hesiod, locates the meaning of human life as between animals on the one hand, and gods on the other (see, e.g. Redfield 1975; Schein 1984). What is different is the measuring rod. For Homer mortality is the essential feature of human life. If human life is a balance of evil and good it is because we are both mortal, unlike the gods, and aware of our mortality, unlike the animals, and in this lies both the bitterness and the ever-fleeting sweetness of human life. This is not Hesiod's vision. For him the essential mark of humanity, and the basis of the balance of good and evil, is not mortality but work. The limitation on human life that maintains this balance is not death, but *diké* ("justice"). It may be a less grand vision than Homer's, but it is a far more immediate one, and this, for Hesiod, appears to be precisely its validation.

The seamlessness of Homeric narrative, a seamlessness created largely through distancing, is one of its great beauties. Hesiod's cragginess, in contrast, jams together fable and myth, the common observation that men must work to eat, the "superstitious" prescriptions of days and actions, and the feel of the plow in a farmer's hands. It is a cragginess, however, that has its own beauty, and a poetry that, in its own rough way, knows itself. If the immediacy of the discourse allows the seams to show, it also teaches us to regard the seams as part of the discourse.

What we see in Hesiod is an involvement with the physical world, and a mutual inter-involvement of the ethical and the physical, that will not finally compartmentalize human life – even under a divine system whose hallmark is precisely a compartmentalized order. Hesiod, in his new vision of what constitutes divine *timé*, and his correspondingly new vision of human *areté*, may seem to present us with a flat new world, with all the vivid colors of the heroes drained out. One glance at the farmer's calendar, if done with a genuine desire to see, dissipates any such impression. The beauty of Hesiod's world lies in the tiny things, in the snail who crawls up the branch in springtime, in the leaves falling from the trees in the autumn cool, in the fleeting luxury of the life of a young girl not yet learned in the ways of golden Aphrodite. As a fractal, each of these moments captures the same message that was learned by Prometheus, that Perses is on his way towards, that is embodied in the ship broken up in a sudden spring squall, and that is held in the constant mind of Zeus. Within the Hesiodic tradition this message was a stark one: that there is no good without suffering, no wealth without work, no harvest without planting. But the poem, not so much in its message as in its way of conveying that message, has something else to say to us as well: that there is a great whole; that within that whole the smallest and the greatest have finally the same meaning; and that not everything can be judged by the standard of Homer.

FURTHER READING

Translations

Of current translations of Hesiod M. L. West's (repr., 1999) prose translation may be the most literal but is also (largely in accordance with West's attitude towards Hesiod) rather plodding and a bit dull. Both Dorothea Wender's translation (1973) and Richmond Lattimore's (1959) read well, but are light on notes and additional information. Stanley Lombardo (1993) renders Hesiod in a colloquial idiom which may be a bit exaggerated. The translation of *Works and Days* by David Tandy and Walter Neale (1996), done with an eye to the social sciences, contains abundant additional material, as does Richard Caldwell's text of the *Theogony* (1987), which takes a largely psychological approach.

Commentaries

The two standard, and comprehensive, commentaries on the main Hesiodic poems are both by M. L. West (*Theogony*, 1966; *Works and Days*, 1978). Both have very useful introductions as well, largely focusing on the Near Eastern ties of Hesiod's work. In the case of the *Works and Days*, however, West is in general unimpressed with Hesiod's level of poetic ability, and his commentary reflects this attitude. W. J. Verdenius also has a more limited but interesting and informative commentary on the first half of the *Works and Days* (1985).

Other works

The following include the major and most accessible of the discussions of Hesiod in, as should be clear from the various titles, his various aspects.

Jenny Strauss Clay, *Hesiod's Cosmos* (2003).

Marcel Detienne, *Crise agraire et attitude religieuse chez Hèsiode* (1963).

David Grene, "Hesiod: religion and poetry in the *Works and Days*," in Jeanrond and Rike (1991).

B. A. van Groningen, *La Composition littéraire archaïque grecque* (1958).

Minna Skafte Jensen, "Tradition and individuality in Hesiod's *Works and Days*," *Classica et Mediaevalia* 27 (1966).

Paul Millet, "Hesiod and his world," *Proceedings of the Cambridge Philological Society* 209 (1984).

Robert Mondi, "The ascension of Zeus and the composition of Hesiod's *Theogony*," *Greek, Roman, and Byzantine Studies* 25 (1984).

—— "Greek mythic thought in the light of the Near East," in Edmunds (1990).

Stephanie Nelson, *God and the Land: The Metaphysics of Farming in Hesiod and Vergil* (1998).

Friedrich Solmsen, *Hesiod and Aeschylus* (1949).

Peter Walcot, *Hesiod and the Near East* (1966).

—— *Greek Peasants, Ancient and Modern: A Comparison of Social and Moral Values* (1970).

CHAPTER TWENTY-FOUR

The Epic Cycle and Fragments

Jonathan S. Burgess

Introduction

There were many early Greek epics besides the canonical *Iliad*, *Odyssey*, *Theogony*, and *Works and Days*. Often they were also attributed to Homer and Hesiod, who seemed to have been legendary representatives of heroic and didactic composition respectively. There were other legendary singers of epic, like Musaeus and Orpheus, but most early epic poets were rather obscure, and unfortunately we know little about most early poems as well. Countless traditional compositions in oral traditions of early epic were never recorded. A number were recorded only not to survive. Some fragments have been preserved, and ancient sources often provide further information about the contents of lost poems. Especially notable is the Epic Cycle, a collection of early epics that spanned the mythological past from theogonic beginnings to the death of Odysseus. Our knowledge about non-canonical early Greek epic, limited though it is, is valuable because it gives us a more comprehensive sense of the mythological range and narrative strategies of the genre.

It is clear that different types of epic traditions flourished from the eighth century to the fifth century BCE, and that the singers of early hexameter compositions knew of more than the Trojan War. The Theban wars (e.g., in the Epic Cycle) and Herakles (e.g., the *Capture of Oechalia*, more than one *Heraclea*) were certainly popular topics, but much other heroic material could be worked into epic (e.g., Argonautic material in the *Corinthiaca* by Eumelos, *Theseids* featuring Theseus). Early epic was not always heroic narrative; often verse was organized by genealogy (e.g., the Hesiodic *Catalogue*, the *Phoronis*) or by traditional lore, similarly to the didactic *Works and Days* by Hesiod (e.g., the Hesiodic *Precepts of Chiron*). Religious and philosophical speculation could also be expressed in epic verse (e.g., Orphic epic, the verse of Empedocles). The surviving *Homeric Hymns*, hexameter compositions that were usually comparably brief and which served as prefaces to performance of epic narrative, contained much mythic and cultic information on divinities. Many epics are admixtures of different types of material and not easily classified (see Chapter 1, by Martin, Chapter 23, by Nelson, and Chapter 28, by Garner).

There are many difficulties in reconstructing these early epics. Sometimes we know little more than the title of a poem or the name of a poet. Often poems were ascribed to multiple authors. Many were ascribed implausibly to Homer or Hesiod, and some remained anonymous. Different poems could be labeled with the same title (which were probably not original to the epics but applied to them at a later date), and the same poem could be known by more than one title. Some epics became attached to longer works, and parts of epics became known as independent works (e.g., the Hesiodic *Catalogue* continues the *Theogony*, and the Hesiodic *Shield of Herakles* is itself a part of the *Catalogue*). Added to these difficulties is the probability that many of these epics existed as fluid oral traditions that were performed over long periods of time; textual recordings may represent a late version, or one manifestation of several versions.

It appears that no early epic matched the *Iliad* and *Odyssey* in length, but many were reportedly of considerable length, often 6,000 to 7,000 lines (the Theban epics in the Cycle, the *Danais*), possibly more (Panyassis' *Heraclea* was about 9,000). The *Cypria* is said to have had eleven books, though others may have been as short as a couple of books (*Iliou Persis*, *Telegony*). Early epic is usually seen as coming to a close by the fifth century. Certainly epic did not end then, but hexameter compositions in the classical age began to stray from standard boundaries of the genre. Epic poets could describe the recent past (Choerilus of Samos), or display a scholarly perspective (Antimachus of Colophon). Oral traditions of earlier epic composition were dying out, and certain fixed texts, such as those in the Epic Cycle, became well known as exemplars of what was no longer being performed. Attic tragedians featured the narratives contained in non-Homeric epic and may have been influenced by these texts; later composers of epic (e.g. Apollonius of Rhodes, Virgil, and Quintus of Smyrna) probably knew surviving examples of Cyclic and other non-canonical epic.

Nature of the Epic Cycle

Early epics were part of a mythological system of great scope and depth. Though the poems commonly had the purpose of providing mythical foundations for specific locations, they could encompass large chunks of the divine and heroic past. Local myth was embedded within a Panhellenic sense of the Greek heroic age and often reached back to the origins of the gods as well. Our modern sense of mythological "cycles" is often an artificial construct (Foley 1999a), but in antiquity a coherent yet flexible account of the mythological past was assumed as the background for epic verse. In this sense the Epic Cycle represents a literary manifestation of a longstanding notional arrangement of early Greek myth. But the Epic Cycle is far from comprehensive, and by no means should the Cycle poems be considered the sole or most authoritative narratives of their myth.

It is not clear exactly how many poems were part of the Epic Cycle (see Davies 1986: 96–7). It certainly began with early history of the divinities. The *Titanomachy*, besides telling of divine strife (cf. Hesiod's *Theogony*), reached back to divine origins (or possibly was preceded by a Cyclic *Theogony*). The second major section of the Cycle featured poems about the Theban wars. The *Oedipodia* narrated the defeat of the Sphinx by Oedipus and his subsequent marriage to the queen of Thebes. The *Thebais* focused on the later quarrel between his two sons, Eteocles and Polynices, over the rule of Thebes; the result was a failed attack on the city by an expedition from Argos. The *Epigoni* featured a second, successful attack by the sons of the original expedition. A fourth epic, the *Alcmaeonis*, is often thought to follow; it narrated the adventures of the son of Amphiaraus, one of the main attackers in the first Theban war. The last major section of the Epic Cycle told the story of the Trojan War and its aftermath. The *Cypria* narrated the early years in the war, the *Aethiopis* featured important events in the last year of the war, the *Little Iliad* and *Iliou Persis* focused on the fall of Troy, the *Nosti* narrated the return home of various Greek heroes, and the *Telegony* told of the final events in the life of Odysseus after his return. A greater amount of information has survived for the Trojan War section of the Cycle, apparently because it served as background material for the increasingly dominant *Iliad* and *Odyssey*. Besides fragments, we possess a concise prose summary from antiquity of this section of the Epic Cycle.

Manifestations of the Cycle

The Epic Cycle existed in different manifestations at various points in its development and transmission. Since the origins of Cyclic epics are very uncertain, it may be best to start with our firmest evidence and move backwards in time. Most informative is the prose summary of the Trojan War section of the Cycle. This is preserved in a single manuscript of the *Iliad* (the famous Venetus A); the section of the summary that covers the *Cypria* is preserved by itself in additional manuscripts. We can tell from information provided by a ninth-century CE scholar named Photius (in his discussion of books entitled *Bibliothêkê*, "Library") that the summaries are excerpts from an account of the whole Epic Cycle in the *Chrestomatheia Grammatikê* ("Useful literary knowledge") by Proclus. Photius indicates the scope of Proclus' summary of the Cycle and reports his comments, but Photius does not himself preserve the Proclus summary, as is sometimes mistakenly claimed. In antiquity this Proclus was understood to be the well-known Neoplatonist from the fifth century CE, but it is often suspected that the author was a different Proclus of the second century CE. The issue hinges on the duration of survival for the Cycle poems themselves. John Philoponos claimed in the sixth century CE that the Epic Cycle could no longer be found because it had become eclipsed by a verse compendium of myth composed by Pisander of Laranda in the third century CE. This may suggest that a fifth-century Proclus would have had trouble finding a manuscript of the Cycle to summarize, but it is not impossible that stray copies survived until his time.

The Proclus summary briefly indicates the author and number of books for each poem before concisely summarizing it. The sequence of the poems is indicated ("next comes," "following is"), including where the *Iliad* and *Odyssey* fit into the story. On the whole the summary provides a clear and comprehensive account of the narrative of the Trojan War. But when the summary is examined closely, it becomes obvious that it is not always consistent with the surviving fragments. The content of the Cycle poems is not usually at issue, though it can be; for instance, Herodotus (2.117) famously contradicts the Proclus summary on the return voyage of Paris in the *Cypria*. But it is the scope of the Cycle poems that is more commonly at issue, for several fragments and *testimonia* indicate a greater span of narrative for the poems than what the Proclus summary allows. For instance, in Proclus the *Little Iliad* ends before the sack of Troy, but numerous *testimonia* indicate that the poem covered the fall of the city.

As well, the beginnings and endings of the poems in the summary can be abrupt, and frequently overlap in material. The division between the *Aethiopis* and the *Little Iliad* indicated by Proclus is odd; one poem ends with the dispute over Achilles' arms and the next begins with the judgment on them. Other divisions in the Proclus summary suggest reduplication of material. The *Little Iliad* ends with the Trojans holding a victory feast after having hauled the wooden horse into the city, whereas the *Iliou Persis* begins with this same victory feast. The *Iliou Persis* ends with the Greeks sailing off from Troy, whereas the *Nosti* begins with the Greeks still there. And the *Telegony* seems to overlap with the *Odyssey*. The Cyclic poem opens with the burial of the suitors, though a burial of the suitors occurs in Book 24 of the Homeric poem.

The peculiarities of the summary, especially discrepancies between Proclus and fragments, have been explained in various ways. Perhaps Proclus based his summary not on the poems themselves, but rather on a pre-existing summary or summary tradition. There are other possibilities: the summary by Proclus could have been changed or curtailed when it was used in the *Iliad* manuscript tradition, or Proclus could have selectively summarized the verse he found in the Epic Cycle, or the Cycle poems themselves could have been curtailed when the Epic Cycle was created, with Proclus subsequently and faithfully summarizing their shortened forms as he found them. The old view that suspected Proclus of wrongly claiming to know the Epic Cycle, or of extensively misrepresenting it, is probably over-skeptical. Whatever its origin, the summary still seems to be a very precious source of authentic information, though very misleading impressions would be acquired of the Cycle poems if one accepted Proclus uncritically.

"Epic Cycle" is the standard translation of *epikos kuklos*, which literally means "epic circle." The word *kuklos* denoted artifacts of a circular shape but was used metaphorically in various ways, including in reference to compilations of literary or mythological material. There is no direct use of the phrase "Epic Cycle" until the time of the Roman empire, and even then most quotations of verse refer to individual poems of the Cycle, not the Epic Cycle (this may suggest the continuing existence of some Cycle epics independently of the Epic Cycle, even after it was formed). However, the scholia tradition that has its roots in the Hellenistic period mentions "cyclic" poetry, as does the Hellenistic poet Callimachus (Epigram 28, in Pfeiffer 1953). And Aristotle intriguingly mentions an Eristic syllogism about the *kuklos* of Homeric poetry (*Anal. Post.* 77b32). This probably associates Homer with the genre of epic in general, a popular equation until the narrowing of the Homeric canon in the Hellenistic age. It also suggests some concept of a gathering of epic poems. The Aristotle *testimonium* does not necessarily refer to our Epic Cycle, and perhaps nothing more is meant than a notional sense of epic coherence, or ephemeral rhapsodic performances of material from different epics.

In any event it is likely that the Epic Cycle was constructed as a textual edition of related epics sometime in the Hellenistic period. The evidence for this is admittedly slight, but suggestive in its totality. A shortened prologue of the *Iliad* surfaced in the fourth century BCE and may have been used to abbreviate a textual joining of the *Cypria* to the *Iliad*. The manipulation of the last line of the *Iliad* so as to lead directly into the *Aethiopis* could have had the same function. There are also references in the scholia to "Cyclic" editions of the *Iliad* and *Odyssey*. Though the Proclus summary does not describe the contents of the Homeric poems, it does point out their place in the sequence of poems, and so presumably the *Iliad* and *Odyssey* in some form (perhaps with their beginnings and endings smoothed over) were part of the Epic Cycle in its Hellenistic verse manifestation. The organization of the Epic Cycle in the Hellenistic period is also reflected or paralleled by certain artifacts. "Homeric" bowls of Hellenistic date (see Sinn 1979) frequently illustrated a few scenes identified as being from Cycle poems, as did later plaques of the Roman period ("*Iliacae tabulae*"; see Sadurska 1964). Prose summaries of literature became common in the Hellenistic period, and undoubtedly such summaries existed of the Cycle long before Proclus. The epitome of the ending of the mythological handbook of Apollodorus is indeed similar to Proclus in its treatment of the Trojan War, although with a bit more detail that can be used cautiously to fill in the gaps of the Proclus summary.

A fifth-century inscription from the northern Black Sea quite remarkably records what is otherwise identified as the first line of the *Little Iliad*. But manuscripts of the Epic Cycle poems do not seem to have been widespread in later antiquity, judging from the lack of certain papyri fragments. Most surviving fragments are quotations from the Roman empire. All early references to the Cycle epics refer to them as individual poems, not as part of a gathering of epics. The earliest is Herodotus, who discusses the *Cypria* and *Epigoni* (2.117, 4.32). Aristotle in the *Poetics* mentions the *Cypria* and *Little Iliad*, as well as *Theseids* and *Heracleids* (in chs. 8, 23). Some indirect reports suggest that Cycle poems were known even earlier. Pindar, for instance, is said to have known an anecdote about the *Cypria* being given to Stasinus by Homer (Aelian *VH* 9.15), and the elegiac poet

Callinus, dated to the seventh century, is said to have known the *Thebais* (as a Homeric poem; Pausanias 9.9.5). Such reports may stem from scholarly confusion or guesswork, however.

From the above it will be clear that the Epic Cycle does not seem to have existed as a unit before the Hellenistic period, though the poems that later were gathered into it stem at least from the Archaic age. It is not necessary to suppose, in fact, that any of the Cycle poems were composed with knowledge of other Cycle poems. The summary by Proclus may make it appear to us that different sections of the story of the Trojan War have been "assigned" to certain epic poets, but this is most likely illusory. Most probably the Cycle epics happened to have been recorded in the Archaic age, and then survived long enough to be used in a compilation of epics at a later date.

It may also seem that the Cycle poems were designed to fit around the *Iliad* and *Odyssey*, but even here caution is necessary. Some in antiquity thought the Epic Cycle a circle because it "encircled" the Homeric poems, and this view seems to be widely shared today. But in fact the theogonic and Theban parts of the Cycle do not suggest the *Iliad* and *Odyssey* as centerpieces. And it is worth stressing again that the Proclus summary may not represent the boundaries of independent manifestations of the poems. The *Aethiopis* fragment that joins directly to the *Iliad* could not have originated with the poem, since no performable epic could begin in such a way. It is true that the Cycle poems contain many plot elements that are surprisingly similar to those of the Homeric poems. Many of these correspondences can be attributed to the thematic typology of oral traditions, but the school of thought in Homeric studies known as neoanalysis has plausibly argued that some shared motifs originated in Cyclic traditions. This does not necessitate the conclusion that the *Iliad* and *Odyssey* were influenced by the Cycle poems specifically. It is very probable, though, that the Homeric poems were composed within the context of oral traditions that led to the Epic Cycle. And even if the poems in the Epic Cycle were composed with knowledge of the *Iliad* and *Odyssey*, it would be mistaken to view them as solely derived from Homeric poetry.

Date and Authorship of the Cycle Poems

The issue of motif priority raises the question of the date of the Cycle poems. Ancient chronologies provide general dates for several of the poets believed to have composed non-Homeric epic, and these start in the eighth century (e.g. Eumelus, author of Corinthian epic; Arctinus, reputed author of the *Titanomachia*, the *Aethiopis*, and *Iliou Persis*). However , the ancient chronologies are vague and inconsistent, and many scholars have put no faith in them. In addition the authorial ascriptions themselves are dubious. Early direct references to the poems either do not name an author, or indicate that "Homer" was thought to have composed them. It would be nice to believe that later scholars recovered the true authors, but even then several candidates are often offered for the same poem. It should be kept in mind that arguments about the date or locality of the Cycle poems are often directly linked with these weak authorial ascriptions.

Other external evidence has been thought to point to the date of the Cycle poems. Early Greek art often represents myth that is narrated in the Epic Cycle, but this need not reflect the Cycle poems specifically (though it does reveal the early importance of "Cyclic" myth, thereby encouraging faith in the antiquity of Cyclic traditions). It has often been asserted that beliefs or practices implied by the Cyclic poems (such as a hero cult) are "post-Homeric," but this is a problematic line of reasoning. Not only are the cultural practices difficult to date, but it is clear that the Homeric poems suppress much that is not in line with its poetic and cultural strategies. Occasionally possible connections have been established between the Cycle poems and external factors. The *Telegony* is ascribed to the

Cyrenean poet Eugammon, and a testimony reports that in the poem a son of Penelope was named Arcesilaus. A number of kings named Arkesilas ruled Cyrene during the reign of the Battiads in the early history of Cyrene, and the *Telegony* probably specified that Arcesilaus was their mythical forebear. In this case ancient chronology, which placed Eugammon in the first half of the sixth century, seems very plausible, and the poem can with some confidence be linked to sixth-century Cyrene. The *Aethiopis* specified the island Leuke as the afterlife location of Achilles and was ascribed to a Milesian poet, Arctinus. Milesians dominated colonization of the Black Sea, where an island central to cult worship of Achilles was called "Leuke." Since colonization of the Black Sea began in the second half of the seventh century, it would seem that the Cycle poem is a Milesian poem dating from some period after this.

The summary by Proclus certainly suggests a post-Homeric Cycle, since the poems seem to serve as introductions and sequels for the *Iliad* and *Odyssey.* But it is not certain whether early manifestations of the Cycle poems had these parameters. Dating of the Cycle poems on the basis of fragments is hampered by the scarcity of evidence (only about 130 lines of verse for the whole Epic Cycle). It has been proposed that the fragments contain formulaic elements that are indicative of oral composition (Notopoulos 1964: 18–45; Burkert 1981; cf. McLeod 1966 for Panyassis), but others see here only clumsy imitation of Homeric features (Kirk 1976: 183–200; Curti 1993). Though the fragments consist for the most part of the same epic language as Homeric poetry, linguistic analyses can place some Cyclic verse as late as the second half of the sixth century (Wackernagel 1970: 181–3; Davies 1989a; cf. Schmitt 1990). Methodological problems hamper firm conclusions about these issues. There is disagreement about what constitutes formulaic elements, which in any event are not immediately indicative of date. It may be misleading that the two long Homeric poems necessarily form the bulk of the database with which to judge what is early or normal in lexical and formulaic matters. Critics can be inconsistent in their faulting Cyclic verse as too non-Homeric (innovative) yet at the same time too Homeric (imitative). It is not always certain that the ancient quotations of Cyclic verse are accurate. It would also be valid to suppose that the fragments represent only a late manifestation of a fluid poetic tradition that began much earlier.

Some apparently close connections between the Cycle poems and the Homeric poems have been considered revealing evidence for Cyclic dependence on the *Iliad* and *Odyssey.* For instance, the *Iliou Persis* contained the recovery of Aethra, mother of Theseus, by her grandsons. It has been thought that this episode was inventively spun out of a reference to an aged handmaiden of Helen's named Aethra in the *Iliad* (3.144), but this may be one of multiple examples where Homeric poetry alludes to an extensive web of pre-Homeric myth (Jenkins 1999). To give another example, the *Telegony* ends with Telegonus unwittingly killing his own father with a spear made from a stingray. This might look as if it was based on the prophecy of Teiresias in the *Odyssey* (11.134–5) that death will come to Odysseus "from the sea." Or rather, it looks as if it was based on a misunderstanding of the *Odyssey* prophecy, since the prophecy is usually understood to denote a death "away from the sea," a meaning which modern folklore *comparanda* seem to confirm. On the other hand, the *Odyssey* passages would seem to be based on some pre-existing story, and oracles in Greek myth are typically open to different interpretations.

If one decides in these cases that Cyclic epic has inventively built episodes out of minor Homeric passages, then it must be concluded that Cyclic poetry is not only dependent on the *Iliad* and *Odyssey,* but that it has a detailed and apparently textual knowledge of them. That is a common opinion, and it seems to be supported by first impressions of apparent instances of intertextuality between Homeric and Cyclic epic. But it has become increasingly difficult to view epic in the Archaic age as resulting from a few poets incompetently imitating texts of the *Iliad* and *Odyssey*. Not only is it doubtful that texts could be used in such a way at this early date, it is not at all clear that the Homeric poems were initially that influential (Burgess 2001: 47–131).

Critical Assessments of the Cycle

Cyclic epic has long suffered in comparison to the *Iliad* and the *Odyssey*. In antiquity Aristotle in the *Poetics* criticized the lack of unity in non-Homeric epic (ch. 23), and Callimachus, echoed by Horace, stated that he hated the "Cyclic" poet (Epigram 28 in Pfeiffer 1953). It is clear that as the Homeric poems became more celebrated other, non-Homeric, epic was neglected. The *Iliad* and *Odyssey* were featured at the Panathenaic festival and later became canonical texts at the very center of educational and booktrade circles. The very creation of the Epic Cycle resulted from marginalization of non-Homeric epic, as did the later epitomizing of it by Proclus and others. The Epic Cycle apparently organized epic in terms of mythological chronology for ease of reading; the summary of Proclus removed the need to read the verse itself by providing just the bare facts of their content. Early hexameter poems remained of interest to scholars of antiquity, but their disagreements and confusion about non-Homeric epic is itself indicative of a general lack of knowledge of them. The failure of early epics to survive is the result of this marginalization of non-canonical epic.

Modern scholarship has usually been heavily influenced by the negative view of the Cycle in the ancient world. But the criteria for criticism of Cyclic epic by Aristotle, which focuses on unity of form, is open to reconsideration (Scaife 1995). No longer valid are the fundamental assumptions of Hellenistic scholars such as Aristarchus, who celebrated Homeric poetry by contrasting it to Cyclic verse (Severyns 1928). A textual focus devoid of accurate historical knowledge or any understanding of oral traditions led to the portrayal of Homer as the fountainhead of all epic, and for the Archaic age this picture is very misleading and in a sense inverts the situation. Today an oralist approach has demonstrated conclusively that Homeric poetry is derived from long traditions of oral composition; it is most probable that the mythological traditions that led to the Cycle poems are also pre-Homeric. Certainly the *Iliad* and *Odyssey* display extensive knowledge of the material that was narrated in the Cycle (see Chapter 21, by Edwards and Chapter 22, by Slatkin). In fundamental ways non-Homeric epic and the Homeric poems share the same language, compositional techniques, typological scenes, and mythological traditions.

Yet it is still valid to see an essential distinction between the Homeric and the Cyclic (stressed in Griffin 1977), just as there is a difference of style between Homeric and Hesiodic verse (see Chapter 23, by Nelson). Fragments of early Greek epic seem to display an entirely different pace from the Homeric norm. An example can be seen by comparing the brief account of the death of Astyanax in the *Little Iliad* (fr. 21.3–4 in Bernabé 1987; fr. 20.3–4 in Davies 1988) with the meditative foreboding of his coming fate in Books 6, 22, and 24 of the *Iliad*. The difference cannot just be attributed to the aesthetic failings of Cyclic verse, however. It appears that the Cycle poems relied on third-person narrative, whereas direct speech by characters is prominent in the Homeric poems. The Cycle poems covered multiple episodes; in contrast the *Iliad* and *Odyssey* expansively focused on a limited amount of narrative. Aristotle (*Poetics*, ch. 23) complained that the non-Homeric epic covered too vast a span of narrative material, but epic must have often needed to do this in order to give a comprehensive sense of a story in its entirety. As a result the Cyclic and Homeric styles are necessarily dissimilar (though portions of Homeric verse may have been quite Cyclic in nature). Even as we celebrate the felicities of poetic expression in the *Iliad* and *Odyssey*, it is necessary to recognize and accept the existence of very different narrative strategies. It is probable that Cyclic poetry, which could quickly cover many action-packed adventures, was very satisfying to an early audience.

It is also apparent that the Cycle epics had cultural functions that went beyond the expression of narrative. Greek myth can be too fantastic for the taste of some, but it obviously served the needs of the ancient Greeks in a variety of ways. To the extent that early epic narrated such myth in verse form, it must have been of great value in its time. There are many indications that the Cycle poems served the interests of contained geographical areas. Many of the differences between Cyclic and Homeric epic can be explained by their status as local and Panhellenic poetry respectively (Nagy 1990c: 70–9). Details of great local relevance in Cyclic epic would have been suppressed by the *Iliad* and *Odyssey* in their attempt to appeal to a wider audience of the Greek world.

Since the early 1990s, it has been increasingly felt that the Cycle epics, whatever their date and literary value, result from authentic oral traditions. There has been a growing appreciation of the rich resources of the Cyclic and non-Homeric epic traditions, and a greater willingness to appreciate their poetic strategies and cultural functions. Certainly much of this interest has been spurred by new editions of early epic, which have provided scholars with informative and accurate tools with which to do research in the area. But scholars have also abandoned a schematic approach that portrayed the Cycle poems as simply the derivative satellites of the *Iliad* and *Odyssey* (see Scaife 1995 and Holmberg 1998). The question of how Cyclic epic relates to local concerns is often explored (e.g., Aloni 1986: 51–67; Burgess 2002), as is how Cyclic poetry is intertextually connected with other poetic traditions (e.g., Burgess 1996; J. Marks 2002 and 2003; West 2002). Neoanalyst arguments about the influence of Cyclic traditions on the Homeric poems continue to be made (e.g., Dowden 1996; West 2003b). For speculation on the performance of Cyclic poetry, see Burgess 2004. In general the Cycle poems are usually seen less as isolated fixed texts and more like fluid traditions, and accordingly the relative extent of multiformity for Cyclic and Homeric poetry can be a topic of intense speculation (cf. Finkelberg 2000; Nagy 2001b).

The Epic Cycle and fragments of early non-Homeric epic have always had a certain antiquarian importance, in the sense that they often constitute the earliest evidence for mythological material. Beyond appreciating their testimony for myth, however, we can through them better comprehend the variety of narrative and cultural functions of early Greek epic. The *Iliad* and *Odyssey* came from oral poetic and mythological traditions, and early non-Homeric poetry may help us comprehend these traditions in a more sophisticated manner. Because so many poems were lost and surviving information about them is often incomplete or conflicting, the conclusions to reach are not always clear. But what we know is of great value, and investigation of non-canonical early Greek epic should continue to be profitable.

FURTHER READING

The most recent editions of fragments of early Greek epic, including the Epic Cycle, are Bernabé 1987 and Davies 1988; the former is more complete but some may find the latter easier to use. These replace older editions, including Allen 1912, the fifth volume of the Oxford Classical Text edition of Homer.

A new Loeb edition of early epic, with useful translations of fragments and testimonia, is West 2003a, replacing Evelyn-White 1914. For the Theban cycle, see also Torres Guerra 1995.

The standard edition of Hesiodic fragments is Merkelbach and West 1967.

For surveys of Epic Cycle issues see Rzach 1922, West 1996, and Latacz 1997. The major general studies of the Cycle in English are Monro 1901: 340–8, Murray 1934: 339–45, Huxley 1969, Griffin 1977, Davies 1986 and 1989b, and Burgess 2001. See further Debiasi 2005.

The most thorough studies of Photius and Proclus on the Cycle are Severyns 1938 and 1953; Severyns 1963 is the standard edition of the Proclus summary.

For further bibliography, see Bernabé 1987: xx–xxxiv, with *addenda* at 284–8 in the 1996 corrected edition (already out of date).

CHAPTER TWENTY-FIVE

Apollonius of Rhodes

D. P. Nelis

Long considered to be a literary failure, a would-be Homer who dared to imitate the *Iliad* and *Odyssey* by writing a version of the ancient, pre-Homeric story of Jason and the Argonauts and their quest for the Golden Fleece, Apollonius Rhodius has only since the 1960s or 1970s begun to be recognized as an epic poet of great merit and considerable influence. His *Argonautica*, a poem of 5,835 verses arranged in four books, the only epic poem to survive in its entirety from the long period between Homer and Virgil, quickly became the canonical version of this most ubiquitous of Greek myths. Numerous papyri and frequent imitations and adaptations by both Greek and Roman writers (Theocritus, Catullus, Varro Atacinus, Virgil, Valerius Flaccus, Dionysius Periegetes, the author of the *Orphic Argonautica*) testify to its impact and popularity. Apollonius was also the author of scholarly treatises devoted to the study of Homer, Hesiod, and Archilochus, as well as a number of other hexameter poems that related the foundations of cities, including Caunus, Alexandria, Naucratis, Rhodes, and Cnidus. In all, he was one of the leading lights of one of the most brilliant periods in Greek literary history, the third century BCE in Ptolemaic Alexandria.

Author and Date

Our sources for the life of Apollonius are few in number and of disputable value (Hunter 1989: 1–12; Rengakos 1992; Lefkowitz 2001). They provide us with "a labyrinth of self-contradictory statements" (Pfeiffer 1968: 141), but some details seem to emerge. He was probably from Alexandria, probably spent part of his life in Rhodes and, most importantly for the understanding of his literary career, was the Librarian of the great Library of Alexandria (on which institution see Fraser 1972:1, 312–19), between about 270 and 245 BCE. It is during this period that he will have composed the *Argonautica*.

For a long time, one of the single most influential "facts" about Apollonius' career (confusedly transmitted by the two *Lives* which accompany the manuscripts of the *Argonautica*) was that he quarreled with his former "teacher," Callimachus, over the composition of his epic and went into exile in Rhodes, before eventually returning to Alexandria with a second, successful version of the poem. As a result of this story, Apollonius was identified as one of the Telchines attacked by Callimachus in the prologue to his *Aetia*. This famous text (on which see Stephens and Acosta-Hughes 2002) is an important statement of poetic principle and is of vital importance for our understanding of the reception of Homeric and post-Homeric epic poetry in third-century Alexandria. It is therefore necessarily a passage of key importance for any attempt to understand the development of the epic tradition and the literary context in which Apollonius' *Argonau-tica* was written (though for a very different view see Cameron 1995); but it should not be used to fill gaps in the life of Apollonius, and today, rightly, the biographical reconstruc-tion of a bitter literary dispute between Apollonius, the archaizing epic poet, and Callimachus, the anti-epic modernist, is rejected by most scholars (Lefkowitz 2001; see, however, Green 1997a: 8–13, 1997b). Its origin can probably best be explained by the attempt of an over-zealous biographer to combine knowledge of the Rhodian period of the poet's life with the existence of an alternative version of at least the first book of the *Argonautica* (the so-called *proekdosis*; see Schade and Eleuteri 2001: 29–33), mention of which is made several times in the ancient scholia on the poem. Instead, it is now generally agreed that the *Argonautica* is in an important sense an epic that is in step with Calli-machean poetic theories and practice and, more generally, in fine tune with the literary trends prevalent in Hellenistic Alexandria (see Margolies DeForest 1994), even if he does not go quite as far as some of his contemporaries in experimenting with Homeric metrical, lingustic and stylistic norms.

In this context, it is difficult to overemphasize the importance of the fact that Apollo-nius was Librarian of the great center of scholarship founded and promoted by Ptolemy I. Not only does tenure of this position place him right at the heart of the vibrant literary world of the mid-third century BCE, it also sees him holding the most influential position of royal patronage open to a poet. The foundation of such a great library was in no way a sign of intellectual withdrawal into an ivory tower cut off from the realities of contem-porary politics and society. It was instead a gesture of considerable political and cultural importance. To be at the head of such an institution was to occupy a post not only of great intellectual prestige, but also one of considerable cultural influence (Cameron 1995: 1–70). That a man in such a position wrote an *Argonautica*, an ancient saga about Greeks involved in a journey overseas and their encounters with non-Greek civilizations all around the fringes of the Mediterranean world, should be an essential detail for readers of this quintessentially Hellenistic epic. It would, however, be a mistake to underestimate the other key fact arising from Apollonius' tenure of the post of Librarian: that he had access to a great collection of books. The *Argonautica* is the highly learned, bookish product of a bookish age (see Bing 1988 and Cameron 1995, who emphasizes continuities with the traditional oral culture, and appreciation of this fact must be central to any interpretation of the work. In particular, Apollonius was a student of Homer, and his epic poem is based on long and detailed study of the *Iliad* and *Odyssey*. Both on the level of large-scale narrative patterns and of detailed verbal interaction, the ideal reader of the *Argonautica* should be engaged in deciphering the traces of a fascinating dialogue between the texts of the *Argonautica* and of the *Iliad* and *Odyssey*. Apollonius was in fact a Homeric scholar in his own right (Rengakos 1994), and the elaboration of his epic style may be read as a kind of commentary on Homeric epic as it was studied in third-century Alexandria. To a greater or lesser extent of course, all Hellenistic poets are involved in this process (Rengakos 1993), and in interpreting the work of such writers as Apollonius, Callimachus, Theocri-tus, Aratus, and Nicander, appreciation of a constant and complex intertextual engage-ment with Homer must be a key element.

Unfortunately, full access to the complexities of this process of rereading and rewriting is denied us by our ignorance about relative chronology. It is generally believed that the *Argonautica* post-dates the *Aetia* (or at least its first two books) and the *Hecale* of Callimachus, and that it predates Theocritus' *Idylls* 13 and 22, two poems that deal with episodes from the story of the Argonauts. But it would be unwise to base too much critical weight on this chronology, and there are heavyweight counter-arguments (Köhnken 1965 and 2001; Cameron 1995: 247–62). In any case, the *Argonautica* stands out as one of the most fascinating creations of the Hellenistic age.

The Poem

The *Argonautica* recounts the mythical voyage of the Argonauts who, on the order of King Pelias, undertake a long and dangerous voyage to Colchis, located on the southeast corner of the Black Sea (modern Georgia), in search of the Golden Fleece and, eventually, succeed in returning with it to Greece (for an overview of the myth see Gantz 1993: 340–73). They are led by Jason, a young hero who succeeds in winning the Fleece from Aeetes, king of Colchis, with the help of Medea, the Colchian princess expert in magic powers with whom he gets involved in a love affair, and who accompanies him back to Greece, thus providing the setting for Euripides' great tragic play of betrayal and infanticide, *Medea*.

In length the poem may be said to fit perfectly Aristotle's prescription that an epic should be "about as long as the number of tragedies presented at one sitting" (*Poet.* 1459b 21f.). It is without question meticulously structured. Books 1 and 2 give the reasons for the voyage, describe the gathering of the crew and relate the voyage to Colchis. They include the encounter with Hypsipyle and the Lemnian women (*Arg.* 1.609–914); the crew's loss of Hylas and Herakles (1.1207–357); the boxing match between Polydeuces and Amycus (2.1–97); the encounter with the Harpies and Phineus, and his prophecy (2.178–447); the passage through the Clashing Rocks, or Symplegades (2.549–606); and the long voyage along the southern coast of the Black Sea (2.619–1261). Book 3 is dedicated to the story of Jason and Medea and the completion of the hero's trials. It includes a memorable depiction of Aeetes, father of Medea and tyrannical ruler of Colchis (3.302–438; also 4.212–40); a dramatic account of the young princess falling in love with the foreign hero (3.275–98, 439–824); and the *aristeia* of Jason when he yokes the bulls and defeats the earthborn men (3.1246–407). Book 4 relates the actual taking of the Fleece (99–182) and the return journey, which follows a quite different route from the outward voyage, bringing the Argonauts home to Greece via the Danube, the Rhone, the western coast of Italy, Corfu, North Africa, and Crete. It includes the murder of Apsyrtus (410–81), the encounter with Circe in Italy (659–752), Orpheus' singing match with the Sirens (885–922), the stay in the land of the Phaeacians (982–1223), the beaching of the "Argo" on the Libyan shore and the subsequent carrying of the ship back to the sea (1232–587), and eventually the return to Greece via Crete, where the giant Talos is defeated by Medea's magical powers (1638–688). The poem ends with the Argonauts setting foot safely back in Greece, and the poet looking forward to future recitations of his work (1773–774). In the final line he addresses his heroes: "and happily did you step out onto the beach of Pagasae" (4.1781). The reader is thus offered both easy, natural closure and the possibility of endless repetition of the poem and its story. Apollonius here draws attention to issues such as the relationship between his poem and the Argonautic myth as a whole and the very difficulty of deciding on a beginning and an end in order to mark out his poem within that whole.

The structure of the work as a whole is on the one hand straightforward, recounting the events of the voyage in chronological order. But it is also elaborately and intricately worked out, with numerous subtle thematic patterns offering the reader several ways of finding cohesion within the events actually narrated in the poem (see Hurst 1967; Pietsch 1999; Clare 2002). At the same time, Apollonius also creates connections between his poem and those events that form part of the myth as a whole but that he decides not to relate (e.g., How did a Golden Fleece end up in Colchis? What happened to Medea when she arrived in Greece?). And so by the way in which he draws attention to this process of selectivity he is able to emphasize both the arbitrary nature of his chosen beginnings and ends and his control over the many versions of story he has inherited (see Hunter 1993b: 122–4; Wray 2000; Clare 2002: 9–32; Goldhill 1991).

In dealing with these questions, Apollonius' technique suggests both a familiarity with Homeric book divisions and a close engagement with literary criticism concerning narrative form and poetic unity (Hunter 2001). Apollonius offers subtle play on his readers' expectations concerning the poetics of narrative, combining Homeric form, characterized by a strong sense of epic scale and comprehensiveness, with modernist techniques favoring a more selective or discontinuous approach. Similarly, as a narrator he subtly reworks Homeric norms, moving away from the essentially univocal and distanced Homeric mode to a more uneven and intrusive narratorial role. A good example of both Apollonius' reliance on and deviation from Homeric style may be seen in the use of the Muses. Strikingly, they do not appear in the opening line of the poem, as they do in the Homeric epics, but are first mentioned only in line 1.22, where the poet says, "Let the Muses be the *hypophêtores* of my song." The term *hypophêtores* is difficult, and debate has raged over whether it means "producers" or "interpreters." The latter seems more likely, since it suggests that initially the voice of the poet assumes responsibility for the story and, subsequently, allows us to see a subtle development in the handling of the Muses (Feeney 1991: 90–3). By the opening of Book 3, Erato is asked to "stand beside" the poet and tell the love story of Medea and Jason. By the opening of Book 4 the poet admits his inability to continue the narrative and transfers full responsability for knowledge and recounting of human motivations to a Muse, probably Erato again. When the Muses appear for the final time in the poem, the poet sings in obedience to them (4.1381f.). These changes in the relationship with a Muse or the Muses chart an intense engagement with such key issues as the fictionality of the narrative, its status as truth, and the very act of narration itself; such experimental variation is a feature of Apollonius' technique on all levels. And here, as everywhere else in the *Argonautica*, Homer is the starting point for gauging the nature and extent of Apollonian experimentation.

Apollonius and Homer

In the absence of the Muse, Apollonius' *Argonautica* opens with a strong declaration of its generic status: "Beginning with you, Apollo, I will recount the deeds of the heroes of old." The words "deeds of heroes" (*klea phôtôn*, *Arg.* 1.1), allude to the Homeric formula *klea andrôn*, the subject of epic song in Homer (*Il.* 9.189, 9.524; *Od.* 8.73). At the same time, Apollonius "begins from Apollo," just as does the *Iliad* (*Il.* 1.8), before filling in, again in Iliadic fashion (*Il.* 1.12–42), enough of the relevant background detail necessary to bring the story up to his chosen starting point, the catalogue of the heroes who gathered to set sail on the "Argo." But even as the *Iliad* seems to provide the dominant frame of reference, Odyssean elements also appear, with the emphasis on voyaging and suffering (*Arg.* 1.15–17) clearly inviting the reader to compare the Argonauts' journey with the wanderings of Odysseus. (On the Homeric poems generally, see Chapter 21, by Edwards and Chapter 22, by Slatkin.)

Subsequently, it is in fact the *Odyssey* that functions as the key model, and Apollonius uses it in a number of ways (Dufner 1988; Knight 1995). On one level, the *Argonautica*, like the *Odyssey*, recounts a journey in which the hero's ultimate aim is the completion of a safe return to Greece; each is in fact engaged in a hazardous *nostos* ("homecoming"). On another level, Apollonius reworks the *Odyssey* in Books 1 and 2 for the outward voyage and then again, but this time much more obviously, for the return journey of Book 4, when his heroes sail past Calypso, encounter the Sirens, Scylla and Charybdis, Circe, and Alkinoos and Arete. In doing so he locates the wanderings of Odysseus on the map of the Mediterranean and indulges in a learned commentary on the efforts of Homeric geographers to locate the story on a map of the known world (Delage 1930; Meyer 2001). On yet another level, the *nekuia* of *Od.* 11 turns out to be a key model as Apollonius casts the whole voyage of the "Argo" as a *katabasis*, a journey to Hades, setting up Colchian Aia, the goal of the expedition, as the land of the dead, and the winning of the Golden Fleece as a safe return from Hades (Hunter 1993b: 182–8; Dräger 2001: 80–4; Nelis 2001: 228–55). Even as he indulges in displaying the relevance of Homeric precedent, Apollonius also takes care to emphasize that Jason's voyage predates that of Odysseus and the Trojan War as a whole when, at 1.558f., the baby Achilles watches his father Peleus, one of the Argonauts, sail away. Overall, Apollonius is clearly interested in combining key aspects of both the *Iliad* and the *Odyssey* in a single poem, even if the very nature of the story as a tale of voyaging privileges the role of the latter.

In addition, Apollonius' exploration of the nature and value of heroism and his complicated and allusive depiction of Jason both involve a turning away from the *Iliad*'s picture of warriors obsessed with *kleos* ("renown") won on the battlefield. Nevertheless, key Iliadic moments and themes are very carefully reworked. The poem contains a number of battle scenes that, while few in number, represent a remarkable concentration of Iliadic moments, culminating in the almost hyper-Iliadic description of Jason's struggle with the fire-breathing bulls of Aeetes and the earthborn men at the end of Book 3. The conflation of Homeric type-scenes into a single representative example is a cornerstone of Apollonian technique. A clear example is provided by the sacrifice described at *Arg.* 1.402–49, a scene that contains close imitation of the Homeric language of sacrifice and reveals traces of the influence of a number of different Iliadic and Odyssean passages, but resonates particularly with *Od.* 3.430–63 (in Nestor's palace) and *Il.* 1.446–66 (the sacrifice to Apollo on Chryse; see Knight 1995: 49–62).

Many scenes in the *Argonautica* show similar fusion of Homeric precedents: Olympus scenes, shipwrecks and storms, descriptions of sailing, arrivals and departures, scenes of welcome and hospitality, similes, assemblies and exchanges of speeches – all show Apollonius' desire to adapt Homer's use of type-scenes but to avoid excessive repetition. At the same time, the *Argonautica* contains a number of detailed and brilliantly inventive imitations of particularly famous Homeric passages: to take two examples, a catalogue modeled on the catalogue of ships in *Il.* 2 and an *ecphrasis* of Jason's cloak, which reworks Achilles' shield in *Il.* 18. By the same token, Apollonius also enjoys setting up the expectation of large-scale Homeric borrowings only to disappoint, as when the games the Argonauts play on Circe's island manage to compress the games of *Il.* 23 into one line (*Arg.* 4.851), and when descriptions of a River Acheron and an entrance to Hades seem to set up an actual descent into the Underworld, only for the Argonauts to do no such thing (2.727–51). At all times, therefore, the *Argonautica* declares itself to be a complex reworking of both *Odyssey* and *Iliad*, and Apollonius in so doing shows himself to be an insightful interpreter of many aspects of Homeric poetic technique.

Attention to Homeric detail can be taken to surprising extremes, placing enormous demands on the attention and learning of the audience, thus highlighting the highly bookish quality of the *Argonautica*, as of so much Hellenistic poetry. For example, Apollonius, whose scholarly work on Homer included a work entitled *Against Zenodotus* (an important redactor of the Homeric poems), works into the *Argonautica* allusions to Homeric *hapax legomena* and many other highly arcane aspects of Homeric language and style (Rengakos 1994; Kyriakou 1995a). At *Arg.* 3.942, the parallel suggested between Aphrodite's help for Jason, in the form of Medea, and Athena's support for Nausikaa, another princess, is supported by the use of *sunerithos*, a *hapax* (a word said once) at *Od.*

6.32, where the goddess assures the girl of her help. Unsurprisingly, therefore, readers of the *Argonautica* are also expected to be aware of trends in Homeric scholarship. A remarkable example of this technique occurs early in Book 1 in the song of Orpheus. Both the narrative context in which his performance is set and the content of his song are modelled on elements in *Od.* 8 (Nelis 1992). There, Demodocus sings for the entertainment of Odysseus and the Phaeacians a song about the adulterous love affair between Ares and Aphrodite, a scandalous subject which was later allegorized as a precursor of Empedoclean theory concerning the cosmic forces of Love and Strife. Apollonius shows his awareness of this allegorical interpretation when his Orpheus, in a context full of allusion to Demodocus and *Od.* 8, sings a song of cosmogony in which *neikos*, strife, is responsible for the creation of the world. The self-conscious nature of the work is nowhere more visible than in this song of Orpheus, which provides guidance, on a number of levels, on how to interpret the work as a whole. Orpheus is a figure of the ideal poet, possessor of scientific knowledge and producer of enchanting song. On the simplest level, that of narrative time, the subject of Orpheus' song, the creation of the cosmos, provides the temporal and physical setting within which the Argonautic adventures take place. It therefore situates them in time and makes the process of history a key theme in the work. As such, the *Argonautica* becomes bound up in a complex way with the past, the narrative present (that is, the world in whch the Argonauts live) and the narrative future (the contemporary world of the reader, for whom the Argonautic saga becomes a crucial part of his or her past as a Greek).

This relationship helps to explain the aetiological nature of the work, the numerous individual *aetia* (on which see Valverde Sanchez 1989) providing illustrations of the links between the reader's present and her or his past and adding up to an explanation of the relationship between present and past. It is thus not so remarkable that the Hellenistic period saw a remarkable interest in the myth of the Argonauts, with a number of authors such as Theocritus, Callimachus, Dionysius Scytobrachion, Euphorion, and Nicander all adapting the story or parts of it – and all this following the numerous references to the myth in the many local histories produced during the fourth and third centuries BCE. Apollonius himself wrote works about the foundations of cities and local history (Krevans 2000). In this context, Apollonius' role as head of the Library and the very nature of the Argonaut myth, a story of Greeks overseas, suggests that the tale has enormous historical and cultural relevance for the contemporary audience in third-century Alexandria. In the hands of Apollonius the tale becomes for third-century Greeks a culture history, an exploration of the nature of Hellenism and of the very presence of Greeks in Egypt.

This historical dimension of the poem was for a long time ignored in readings of Hellenistic poetry, when it was seen as a product of the ivory tower and as *l'art pour l'art*, divorced from conetmporary realities. But towards the end of the twentieth century the emphasis has swung towards historicizing interpretations and our reading of the *Argonautica* has been correspondingly enriched (Hunter 1993b: 152–69; Stephens 2002: 171–237). As a result, readers must face the possibility that Apollonius' epic recounts not an obscure archaic myth but rather a tale of contemporary historical and cultural significance. To a great extent this is due to the profound and pervasive cultural values that were attached to the Homeric epics, and so due attention must be paid to the fact that Apollonius, both as poet and librarian, chose to write an epic at all.

In the Hellenistic age Homer was thought of as a figure of divine authority, the author of canonical texts that preserved information about Greek history and who in important ways could be used to define what it was to be Greek. He was also seen as the founder of literature itself, an idea illustrated through the image of him as primal Ocean, from which all other literary forms flow down to the present day. The whole issue of the post-Homeric epic tradition is fraught with difficulties, and uncertainty hovers over much of what we would like to know about the epic poems composed between Homer and Apollonius. The fragments of the Epic Cycle (on which see Chapter 24, by Burgess) are notoriously difficult to date, both in terms of the original date of composition of individual works and of the combination of these works into a Cyclic format aimed at completing the set of stories of early Greek "history" by including all those Homer had chosen not to relate. To this extent the Cycle may be considered Homeric in spirit and intention, but Aristotle's *Poetics* 59a–b contains searching criticism of the Epic Cycle, which by his day obviously had a reputation as poetry of low quality, far inferior to that of Homer. Similar views of Cyclic inferiority are found in Callimachus, and the inimitabilty of Homer becomes a strikingly common topos.

Apollonius writes his poem, then, at a time when the status of epic as a genre is in some sense problematic, at the very least to the extent that the very existence of the model of excellence and the perceived inferiority of subsequent efforts means that Apollonius had to confront the idea that his poem might be received as another Cyclic failure. There are indeed some who see the *Argonautica* as a genuinely conservative attempt to recreate an archaic worldview, but it seems much more likely that Apollonius takes up the challenge of trying to create an epic poem which would be meaningful both as an attempt to invite comparison with Homer (by choosing to write about an ancient Greek myth), while at the same time speaking to the social and cultural concerns of his contemporary readers. Controversy exists over his originality in doing so. Some scholars believe that the Hellenistic period saw an enormous outpouring of large epic poems, especially on historical subjects (Ziegler 1966), but others argue that hardly any epic of any kind can be proven to have been written in the century before Apollonius (Cameron 1995: 263–302; for discussion see Kerkhecker 2001). On either view, Apollonius' 'mythological' epic looks like an original experiment aimed at producing a new epic for Hellenistic Alexandria, and the ambition involved in attempting to do so must not be underestimated.

Apollonius and Other Sources

While Homer is the key model throughout the *Argonautica*, we must not underestimate the depth and breadth of Apollonius' reading. In origin, the myth lends itself easily to analysis in terms of folktale patterns. It conforms to the story-type in which a young hero undergoes a series of trials assisted by a number of helpers with magical gifts of various kinds (cf. Lynceus and his fabulous eyesight, Orpheus the singer, the winged Boreads, and others). An early version of the story was well known to Homer (*Od.* 12.69–72, *Argo pasimelousa*; cf. *Il.* 7.468f., 21.41, 23.748) and may have even provided the model for a number of episodes of the *Odyssey*, most probably Circe, but also perhaps also the Sirens, the Planctae ("Wandering Rocks") and the voyage to Hades (see Meuli 1921; for discussion see Scherer 2002: 10f.). No such early versions of the story will have survived as texts for Apollonius. He will, however, have consulted both references to and fuller versions of the Argonautic saga by Hesiod, Eumelus, Mimnermus, Simonides, Pindar, Aeschylus, Sophocles, Euripides, Antimachus, and Callimachus; and the ancient scholia also name a series of more or less obscure prose writers who also transmitted the tale, for example, Hecataeus, Acusilaus, Pherecydes, and Timaeus.

Pindar's fourth Pythian ode, the earliest surviving complete work that treats the myth, is certainly a key model (Scherer 2002: 22–5), but tragic sources also form a crucial element in Apollonius' revamping of the story (Nishimura-Jensen 1996). The poem as a whole can be read as the prelude to Euripides' *Medea* even as it is profoundly influenced by it, especially in its depiction of the key figures of Jason and Medea. We also have some access to fascinating, but unfortunately fragmentary, glimpses of Apollonius' reworking of Aeschylus and Sophocles. Book 3 of the *Argonautica* may well be particularly rich in allusion to lost tragedies. Aeschylus, for example, at *Arg.* 3.851–53, looks like a possible source for the description of the "drug of Prometheus," while at 3.845, 858, and 865 (see Hunter 1989: 187f.) Sophocles' *Colchian Women* and *Rhizotomoi* both seem to provide models for the help given to Jason by Medea in order to enable him to survive the trials set by Aeetes. That said, Aeschylus wrote plays called *Argo*, *Hypsipyle*, *Cabeiroi* and *Lemnian Women*, a possible tetralogy, while Sophocles, in addition to his *Colchian Women* and *Rhizotomoi* also composed plays entitled *Phrixus*, *Lemnian Women*, and *Amycus*, plus two more on *Athamas* and *Phineus*. Tragic influence on the *Argonautica* in general must have been more pervasive than we can now directly establish, and its influence is certainly felt not only in the use of particular plays for individual scenes or episodes, of course. The relatively un-Homeric nature of Book 3 as a whole may be explained by much of its subject matter, particularly the erotic elements, but Apollonius adopts tragic techniques in the confrontations between Medea and Chalciope and between Jason and Medea, while throughout the book knowledge of the events described in Euripides' *Medea* creates a highly tragic atmosphere. The resultant fusion of epic and tragic elements may reflect the influence of Aristotelian criticism, which saw the *Iliad* as a tragic epic. The generic experimentation was certainly to prove influential, since *Argonautica* 3 provides the key model for the tragedy of Dido in the fourth book of Virgil's *Aeneid* (Nelis 2001: 125–80).

Excessive emphasis on imitation and allusion, however, may lead to a failure to appreciate innovation and invention. These are also important aspects of Apollonius' art. Given our relatively patchy knowledge of earlier versions of the myth and of the individual episodes and themes within it, this is an area in which it is difficult to offer definite conclusions. Overall, though, the impression gained from study of the relevant sources is one of superb control of the material on the part of the poet and of significant freedom in the reworking of the myth, and that the *Argonautica* is indeed a highly original and innovative version of an old story. At the beginning of the poem, Apollonius highlights his relationship to his forerunners when he says, "The ship is sung in the songs of earlier poets, who tell how it was constructed by Argos, on the orders of Athena" (*Arg.* 1.18f.). It is not by chance that these words come immediately before the catalogue of Argonauts (1.23–233). Lists of those who sailed on the "Argo" were numerous in antiquity, and while certain names were fixed by Apollonius' day, there was also considerable room for variation, and it is certainly the case that anyone who studied the tradition could easily draw up a list of many more than the fifty Argonauts required to fill the fifty-oared ship the "Argo" was assumed to be. Opening the *Argonautica* with the catalogue thus gives Apollonius an immediate opportunity to stamp his authority on the tradition by stating who has been included and excluded, marking himself both as faithful transmitter of culturally important knowledge and as an original, learned scholar-poet. Following the catalogue, the entire episode of the "Argo"'s departure shows clear traces of both traditional scenes (the launching of the ship) and Apollonian invention, as the poet highlights crucial themes and characters. The short, intriguing scene in which Iphias, an old priestess of Artemis, kisses Jason's hand and tries to speak to him, but fails to do so as he is carried along by the excited crowd, looks like an Apollonian invention (Nelis 1991). Similarly, the quarrel involving Idas, Idmon, and Jason leading to the song of Orpheus contains traditional aspects (cf. the epic quarrels between Hektor and Polydamas, Tydeus and Amphiaraus, Odysseus and Euryalus, and, in the song of Demodocus, Achilles and Odysseus (see Vian 1976: 72 n. 3)) combined with the striking content of the song itself, a cosmogony and theogony in strikingly Hesiodic and Empedoclean mode.

In a number of other key areas, Apollonius confidently adapts standard elements of the epic genre in new ways. The role of the gods, for example, is deeply complex (see Feeney 1991: 57–98, Hunter 1993b: 75–100). On the one hand, the poem lends itself to interpretation as a realistic narrative of historical events that, despite happening in the distant past, are inextricably related to the contemporary world of the reader. The way in which the poem contains fragments of a history of the divine by incorporating different aspects of traditional succession myths firmly links this realistic narrative to the divine action in the poem. By this process the story may be read as an aetiological account of the coming to power of Zeus and of the divine dispensation in place in the world "today." Read thus, the poem can be seen, despite his absence from the actual narrative of the poem, to privilege the role of Zeus, and his anger has been seen as the key motor of the action in response to the role of Achilles' anger in the *Iliad* (Dräger 2001). On the other hand, Apollonius was only too aware of the vast amount of scholarship devoted to investigating the Homeric gods, and so his text consistently alludes to the different ways of reading divine forces in an epic narrative, whether as real deities like those of religious cult, as symbols, or as moral or physical allegories (e.g., Eros = the human sensation of erotic infatuation, Zeus = wisdom and knowledge, Hera = air, Apollo = the sun, and so on).

Furthermore, the poet is often deliberately ambiguous as far as divine motivations are concerned, and in the opening sections of the poem he flaunts the absence of Zeus, whose will had been highlighted at *Il.* 1.5. Instead, it is the human Pelias who first motivates the action (*Arg.* 1.15 f.), until Hera's anger is revealed as a key organizing principle behind events (hinted at in 1.14; cf. 3.1133–6). Similarly, the idiosyncratic handling of Zeus and his absence from the narrative of the poem may be seen not as acknowledging his untouchable majesty, but rather as drawing attention to the problematic nature of a supremely inscrutable authority based on the possession of force and the threat of violence. On this reading the poem may be read metatextually as a commentary on the nature of narrative fictions involving the divine and as an extended meditation on the role of the gods in the Homeric epics, indeed on the very nature of traditional Greek epic and on the very feasability of composing an epic narrative in which the gods play a central role. Yet such a highly literary approach to the text does not of course preclude any sense of its promoting a moral or philosophical seriousness in its handling of the nature of the relationship between the human and the divine. The world depicted by Apollonius is one in which divine power and human ignorance combine to suggest a bleak and pessimistic view of the human condition.

Like his handling of the gods, Apollonius' depiction of his hero, Jason, has long perplexed scholars. He has been seen as a failed attempt at the portrayal of a traditional Homeric hero (whatever that may be thought to be), as an anti-hero, as a "love" hero, or as an ordinary man. To some extent, each of these categorizations is in some way useful and true, but as before, any overall interpretation based on an overly realistic or naturalizing reading must fail to do justice to the complexities of the text. There is no doubt that Apollonius is intent on exploring the very concept of heroism, but the frame of reference within which he attempts to do so is intensely literary. From one point of view, Jason is the hero of the *Argonautica* in the same way that Achilles is the hero of the *Iliad* and Odysseus of the *Odyssey*. But we must be wary of assuming that an epic must have a single hero who dominates the action (Feeney 1986a). Apollonius also allows his reader to see the whole crew of the "Argo" as embodying the virtues necessary for heroic status, and it seems clear that he thus raises the question of the value of individual action in comparison with communal action. It is not irrelevant that the Argonauts build (2.717–19) an altar to *Homonoia* (Concord), a powerful symbol of their functioning as a team. Similarly, when faced with meeting Aeetes, Jason prefers to adopt the power of words and diplomacy instead of outright force, and in a key scene set up to resemble a typical epic *aristeia*, it is his words which help seduce Medea (3.976; see Goldhill 1991: 301–5). This scene in Book 3 is directly related to another example of variation on Homer in Book 1 (1.721–67), where Jason, before going to meet Hypsipyle, shoulders a cloak that resembles in many ways the shield of Achilles in *Iliad* 18. Whereas the Homeric hero required the shield to return to war in order to kill Hektor and avenge Patroklos, his Apollonian counterpart ends up under a cloak in bed with Hypsipyle (on the symbolism of the cloak see Scheid and Svenbro 1996). The rewriting of the Iliadic shield in the *ecphrasis* of the cloak acts as a symbol for Apollonius' composition of a new kind of epic, one in which the depiction of love and erotic motivations plays a key role.

The crucial importance of love as a central theme of the poem becomes particularly clear when Jason eventually faces the bulls and the earthborn giants at the end of Book 3. He does so under the protection of magic spells acquired from Medea because of her love for him and her desire to protect him from supernatural dangers. The confrontation with such monstrous enemies can hardly be described as a traditonal *aristeia*, yet it is described in such a way as to recall Iliadic battle scenes, and the whole episode has an intensity that sets it apart from the rest of the poem. That said, Jason here clearly does show traditional heroic virtues of bravery and skill as a fighter in this scene, and any attempt to deny him martial heroism founders on this passage. Certain characters within the epic resent their presence in this new kind of poem, particularly Idas (Fränkel 1960, with the comments of Glei 2001: 6f.) and Herakles (Feeney 1991: 95–8, Hunter 1993b: 25–36). While it is simplistic to say that they are meant to be seen as adherents of a traditional heroic code, their presence does help to highlight the originality of Jason as an epic hero, and their words and actions throughout the poem provide a frame of reference within which Jason's behavior may be judged.

Another important aspect of Jason – and of almost all the Argonauts – is their youth. Their adventure is obviously to be seen a kind of traditional tale about the initiation of young warriors. Jason represents the type of the young man on the edge of manhood who must prove himself in order to assume his rightful place in adult society. Telemachus, Orestes, and Theseus are comparable figures from within the same mythical tradition (Vidal-Naquet 1996). This background also provides a setting for Jason's relationship with Medea, as their story becomes one of sexual initation for both man and woman (cf. Hylas and the nymph at *Arg.* 1.1221–40 and Beye's suggestion (1982: 155–7) that the Fleece represents Medea's virginity).

Just as the character of Jason has perplexed readers and critics, so has that of Medea. It has often been remarked that when she first enters the poem she is a shy young girl, but that soon after she is depicted as an experienced magician, her final act in the poem being the destruction of the giant Talos. She loves Jason and is speechless in her innocence when she meets him, but at the same time she is capable of cleverly deceiving both her sister Chalciope and her brother Apsyrtus. Medea may be seen in the light of a number of epic paradigms: she is a lover, like Helen; a magician, like Circe; a nubile princess, like Nausikaa and Ariadne; and a plotter of the murder of Apsyrtus, like the deadly Clytemnestra. And, overall, she is the Medea of Euripides, whose earlier play all Apollonius' readers presumably have already read, but which the Hellenistic poet turns into a sequel to his own work. Apollonius may partly be reacting here against the Aristotelian idea that a character should be "whole" and consistent, but Medea is also thus depicted in order to enable Apollonius to link her to a number of models and to explore a number of key issues in the poem. Medea is of course the focus of the erotic, and Apollonius provides a famous description of her nascent passion for Jason, detailing both her physical sensations and mental torments.

The power of love has been a key theme in the poem since the Lemnos episode in Book 1, but in Book 3 it comes to dominate the narrative, leading to the murder of Apsyrtus and culminating in the narrator's bleak comment following that character's death: "Frightful Eros, great curse, hated by all, source of deadly strife, sadness and troubles, and many other pains in addition" (*Arg.* 4.445–7). These words may suitably be thought typical of Apollonius' whole epic, a subtle, brilliantly complex and troubling work that has at last come into its own and is receiving the kind of detailed scholarly interpretation it deserves. Strikingly, its status in the view of some scholars seems finally to reflect the reputation the poem enjoyed in antiquity. The *Nachleben* of the *Argonautica* is a topic whose surface has barely been scratched, but to judge from the evidence of its reception in second- and first-century BCE. Rome it was considered something of a classic. The profound debt owed by Virgil to Apollonius in the writing of the *Aeneid* (the subject of Nelis 2001) testifies to the central role of the *Argonautica* in the reception of the Greek epic tradition at Rome and to its pivotal importance in the elaboration and development of the later Roman epic tradition.

FURTHER READING

The standard text of the *Argonautica* is that of Vian and Delage in the French Budé series (1976–96). It contains a translation and abundant notes on all aspects of the poem. Fränkel's Oxford Classical Text (1961) must still be consulted by all those who read the poem in Greek.

More recently, a number of excellent translations have appeared in several languages. For anglophone readers the versions by Hunter (prose, 1993a) and Green (verse, 1997a) provide reliable translations and useful introductions to the major aspects of the work.

Important background studies of Alexandrian society and literature are Fraser 1972, Hutchinson 1988, Goldhill 1991, Cameron 1995, and Fantuzzi and Hunter 2002.

There are now many book-length studies, for example Hurst 1967, Beye 1982, Fusillo 1985, Clauss 1993, Hunter 1993b, Rengakos 1994, Albis 1996, Pietsch 1999, Dräger 2001, Clare 2002, and at least two major commentaries are in progress, by Cuypers on Book 2 (1997) and Campbell on Book 3 (1994). Two more recent collections provide useful surveys of the state of current scholarship and will no doubt serve as platforms for further study: Harder, Wakker, and Regtuit 2000, and Papanghelis and Rengakos 2001.

CHAPTER TWENTY-SIX

Quintus of Smyrna

Alan James

Students who read the Homeric epics for the first time are understandably surprised that most of the familiar story of the Trojan War is not included in their narratives. The *Iliad* is focused on the story of Achilles' anger and its consequences over just a few weeks, although by poetic sleight of hand it incorporates some earlier episodes (see Chapter 21, by Edwards), whilst the *Odyssey* narrates Odysseus' adventures after the war with just occasional recollections of the war itself (see Chapter 22, by Slatkin). Consequently, when these two epics achieved the status of unrivaled classics, at least by the fifth century BCE, other early Greek epics that covered the Trojan legend, later known collectively as part of the Epic Cycle, were adapted to form a sequence: the *Cypria* covering the war before the *Iliad*, the *Aithiopis*, the *Little Iliad*, and the *Sack of Ilion* the rest of the war from the *Iliad's* end, and the *Returns* and *Telegony*, with the *Odyssey* between, the war's aftermath (see Chapter 24, by Burgess). Despite Aristotle's assessment of these Cyclic epics as inferior to the Homeric for lack of dramatic coherence, or unity (*Poet.* 1459b1ff.), they remained influential for centuries. The only positive evidence for the time of their final loss is the statement in John Philoponos' commentary on Aristotle's *Posterior Analytics* (Wallies 1909: 13.3.156–7), written in the early sixth century CE, that it was caused by preference for the version of the same subject matter in a Greek epic written by Peisandros of Laranda in the reign of Alexander Severus (222–35 CE), which covered the whole range of Greek mythology, not just the Trojan War. The *coup de grâce* could well have been delivered at what is now the favored date for the destruction of the great library at Alexandria, 272, during civil disorder associated with Zenobia's resistance to the emperor Aurelian.

As we shall see, evidence for the floruit of Quintus of Smyrna points to the late third century CE, and the obvious purpose of his epic was to provide a replacement, in the language and style of the Homeric epics, of just that part of the Epic Cycle which had covered the Trojan War between the end of the *Iliad* and the beginning of the *Odyssey*. This his work does in fourteen books totalling nearly 8,800 lines, rather more than half the length of the *Iliad*. The success with which it met an obvious need led to its circulation with the Homeric epics through late antiquity and the Byzantine Middle Ages, its influence being attested by Eustathios and John Tzetzes in the twelfth century, and it survives as the only full-scale poetic narrative in Greek of the war's main events.

Quintus' epic has usually been known by the Latin title *Posthomerica*, a translation of the Greek *Ta meth' Homeron* used in some of its manuscripts, which is more likely to reflect copyists' arrangement of texts than to be the author's choice. The English equivalent would be *The Sequel to Homer*, like the French *La Suite d'Homère* used for Vian's Budé edition (Vian 1963, 1966, 1969). However, readers may well prefer one of the titles used for the three English translations: *The Fall of Troy, The War at Troy, The Trojan Epic*; I shall use the last. Until recently there was no external evidence for Quintus' date, and because of the success with which he imitates Homer and avoids obvious anachronisms there is very little internal indication. The only ostensibly autobiographical information is in an invocation of the Muses introducing a catalogue of the heroes who entered the wooden horse (12.306–13):

> Muses, I ask you to tell me precisely, one by one,
> The names of all who went inside the capacious horse.
> You were the ones who filled my mind with poetry,
> Even before the down was spread across my cheeks,
> When I was tending my noble sheep in the land of Smyrna,
> Three times as far as shouting distance from the Hermos,
> Near Artemis' temple, in the Garden of Liberty,
> On a hill that is not particularly high or low.

This contains echoes of two early-epic invocations of the Muses, one at *Il.* 2.484–92, which introduces another catalogue, and one at Hes. *Th.* 1–34. The latter accounts for the image of shepherding, but that may also be symbolically applicable to Quintus, perhaps as a teacher. The fact that Smyrna famously claimed Homer as one of its sons is no reason to doubt that it was really Quintus' home (*pace* Hopkinson 1996). The detailed description cannot be verified, but it is consistent with numerous passages that show his familiarity with western Asia Minor (Vian 1959b: 114–44). The circumstance of an educated Greek of Smyrna having a Latin personal name indicates that he lived within the long period of Roman rule, and the same is suggested by two passages in the *Trojan Epic*: one is a simile describing the use of wild beasts for public executions in an amphitheatre (6.532–6), and the other is a prophecy of the founding of Rome and of the Roman empire in terms that would have been less appropriate after the inauguration of Constantinople as a seat of government in 330 (13.336–41). Its indebtedness and its influence in the tradition of late Greek epic show that Quintus' work was written within a period just a little longer than the third century CE.

The first external evidence for Quintus' date was provided by a papyrus codex published in 1984 (Hurst et al. 1984; Kessels and Van der Horst 1987; James and Lee 2000: 7–9). It contains a poem in the language and meter of Greek epic titled *The Vision of Dorotheos*, purporting to be an autobiographical record of a Christian's vision in "the house of God." At line 300 the author names himself "Dorotheos the son of Quintus," and at the end of the text there is a colophon: "the end of the vision of Dorotheos son of the poet Quintus." The latter's identification with our poet is corroborated by some evidence of his epic's influence on *The Vision*, and the generally accepted identification of this Dorotheos with one mentioned several times in Eusebios' *Ecclesiastical History* (7.32.2–4, 8.1.4, 8.6.1–5) – he was made priest at Antioch about 290 and martyred during the persecution of Diocletian – would place Quintus' floruit firmly in the second half of the third century CE.

The *Trojan Epic* was given to the modern world by the discovery of its manuscript text in the Greek monastery of San Niccolò di Casoli near Otranto in the Heel of Italy, no more than a few years after the fall of Constantinople in 1453, by Cardinal Bessarion, a Greek émigré patron of learning who presented his Greek manuscripts to the senate of Venice in 1468. The record of this discovery, made by another émigré scholar, Konstantine Laskaris, had the curious consequence that in all printed editions of the *Trojan Epic* down to the eighteenth century its author is misnamed "Quintus of Calabria," because in antiquity Calabria denoted the Heel of Italy. Bessarion's manuscript is lost, but numerous copies, direct and indirect, survive. The one complete manuscript text not derived from it, the so-called *Parrhasianus* preserved at Naples (*Neapolitanus graecus II F 10*), has been used to reconstruct a common ancestor, which was probably not earlier than the thirteenth century (Vian 1959a). Considering the lateness of all surviving manuscripts, the text is in remarkably good condition. Of its modest total of lacunae only one is more than a few lines long – probably 48 lines after 4.524 due to the loss of one page of a codex. The first printed edition was the Aldine of 1505, but it was L. Rhodomann, in his edition of 1604, who first put the text into a tolerable state through a great number of convincing emendations. Substantial improvements were made to the text in two nineteenth-century editions (Koechly 1850; Zimmermann 1891), but at the same time it was marred by unnecessary emendation and conjectured lacunae. Most of these excesses were undone (Giangrande 1986) and the text was finally established on the basis of a thorough recension of the manuscripts in Vian's edition. This remains the standard, the later complete critical edition of Pompella, obscurely published in Italy (Pompella 1979, 1987, 1993), having been largely ignored. The latter certainly errs on the side of conservatism, but occasionally its text is superior to Vian's. It has now been published in one volume by Olms-Weidmann (Pompella 2002).

After Koechly's still useful commentary on the whole *Trojan Epic* (Koechly 1850) only two have been published. That of Kakridis (1962) accompanies a general study. Its appearance shortly before volume 1 of Vian's edition was unfortunate, because for most matters it was superseded by the latter's accompanying commentary, despite its brevity. Since then two full-scale commentaries on individual books have been published, Campbell's on Book 12 (1981a) and James and Lee's on Book 5 (2000), and a briefer one on parts of Book 10 by Hopkinson (1994c: 105–20), the episode of Paris and Oinone, which has the unique distinction among Quintus' work of having inspired a well-known English poem, Tennyson's *The Death of Oenone*. It is extraordinary that the first ever English translation was A. S. Way's of 1913, which remains in print and is the only, highly unsatisfactory, form in which the work is available to the English-reading public. Though not without merit, it is based on the long-superseded Greek text that accompanies it and it is often excessively free. Also, because it is in blank verse it has many more lines than the original. The only subsequently published English translation, the very literal prose one of F. M. Combellack (1968), has long been out of print. It is accurate, but it has the disadvantages of being based on a superseded text, though with some account taken of volume 1 of Vian's edition, and of providing only occasional scanty notes. In view of this unsatisfactory state of affairs I have completed an English translation based on assessment of both Vian's and Pompella's texts, which is used here for all my quotations. It is in a meter of five or six stressed syllables per line separated by either one or two unstressed syllables. This gives a rhythm comparable with that of the Greek hexameters and is sufficiently flexible to permit an unforced line-for-line rendering. I have provided it with a full introduction to all aspects of the work and a commentary dealing with textual problems and sources in a manner suitable for non-specialist readers.

The contents of the *Trojan Epic* were largely dictated by its undertaking to cover the same part of the Trojan War as the *Aithiopis*, the *Little Iliad* and the *Sack of Ilion*. Their contents are known to us in some detail from surviving summaries and they were certainly known to Quintus, although the fact that he follows sequences for some episodes that differ from theirs makes it more likely that their texts were not available to him. Consequently most critics have dismissed the *Trojan Epic* as merely episodic (Appel 1994) simply because Aristotle did the same for the Cyclic epics. Recently, however, there have been attempts at unprejudiced appraisal (Schmiel 1986; Schenk 1997; Schmidt 1999) and that is the spirit of what follows. The time span of its narrative is not greatly different from those of the *Iliad* and the *Odyssey*, the focus being on twenty-two days out of about twice that number. Far more important for the dramatic unity of the Homeric epics is the extent to which they are dominated by a single hero (see Chapter 6, by Nagy), respectively Achilles and Odysseus, and it is clear that Quintus constructed his poem with an eye to the dominance of first Achilles and then his son Neoptolemos.

Achilles dominates the first five books, with his last two victories over the would-be saviors of Troy, Penthesileia (Book 1) and Memnon (Book 2), his death and funeral (Book 3), the funeral games in his honor (Book 4), and the contest between Telamonian Ajax and Odysseus for the prize of his armor, which causes the death of Ajax, Achilles' nearest rival as champion of the Greeks (Book 5). Books 6, 7, and 8 are a closely knit narrative unit: after their decision to send for Neoptolemos the Greeks are defeated by Eurypylos, Troy's last great ally (Book 6); they are rescued from further defeat by the arrival of Neoptolemos (Book 7), who finally kills Eurypylos (Book 8). By preferring the version of the story that places Neoptolemos' arrival before Philoktetes' (unlike the *Little Iliad*) Quintus maximizes the dominance of Neoptolemos: though the focus shifts to Philoktetes and the death of Paris in the second half of Book 9 and through Book 10, his role is prominent up to the Greeks' departure. The last four books, 11–14, form another closely knit narrative: unsuccessful in their assault on the walls of Troy (Book 11), the Greeks resort to the trick of the wooden horse (Book 12) and sack the city overnight (Book 13), only to suffer the wreck of their fleet after their triumphal departure (Book 14), an ironic coda to the story that encroaches on the subject matter of the Cyclic *Returns*. One device making for unity that the *Trojan Epic* shares with the *Iliad* and the *Odyssey* is foreshadowing of later events (Duckworth 1936), not so much definite prediction as vague foreshadowing, which heightens suspense most notably in the final build-up to the sack in Books 12 and 13.

Use of sources is the aspect of Quintus' work that has received far more exhaustive treatment than any other, with particular interest in the question of whether he was directly influenced by Latin poetry (Mondino 1958; Vian 1959b: 17–109; Keydell 1963). There is no clear evidence for the source or sources followed for his version of the Trojan War, given the probable absence of the Cyclic epics. Despite the overwhelmingly important general influence of the Homeric epics, he does not consistently follow the little information they provide about events that belong to his narrative. Only two surviving works contain a narrative of relevant events sufficiently extensive for helpful comparison: Apollodoros' *Library*, a compendium of Greek heroic mythology, the relevant part of which survives in an abbreviated form similar to the summaries of the Cyclic epics, and the prose *Diary of the Trojan War*, purporting to be an eyewitness account by the fictional Dictys of Crete, which survives in a Latin translation probably later than the *Trojan Epic*. Both works contain substantial correspondences with Quintus' narrative, and it has been conjectured that he was indebted for its main features to some such handbook as the *Library*. But the likelihood of this is diminished by the impressive evidence for his literary culture, the wide range of extant works exploited by him for occasional elaboration of his narrative, apart from three that exert a pervasive influence: the *Iliad*, the *Odyssey* and the *Argonautica* of Apollonius of Rhodes (Vian 2001).

The involvement of the Amazon queen Penthesileia in the exploits of Achilles was already an episode of the *Aithiopis*, but Quintus' version in Book 1 differs from the latter's in some details. The same is true of the story of Memnon as told in the *Aithiopis* and Book 2. The metamorphosis of the Aithiopian army into birds is shared by Quintus and only relatively late sources. Quintus had to choose, in Book 3, between two versions of how Achilles was killed: by Paris with Apollo's help, as in the *Aithiopis*, or by Apollo alone. In opting for the latter he emphasizes Achilles' unique status. The mourning for, and funeral of, Achilles are modelled largely on those of Patroklos in the *Iliad*, as the funeral games in Book 4 are on those of Patroklos in *Iliad* 23, though with much less focus on the chariot race and addition of some events taken from later games. The contest between Ajax and Odysseus for the armor of Achilles in Book 5 is introduced by description of the armor, especially the scenes on the shield, which owe much to those in *Iliad* 18, but with noteworthy innovation (Byre 1982). The contest itself combines elements from three earlier versions: on Nestor's advice Agamemnon compels Trojan prisoners to decide after listening to the rival speeches, as in a court of law. Ovid's version (*Met.* 13.1–381) is so similar in parts, most strikingly in Ajax's main speech, that direct influence is the only plausible explanation (James and Lee 2000: 80–106). The following madness and suicide of Ajax owe something to Sophocles' *Ajax*.

The sequence of events in Books 6 and 7, with the decision to send for Neoptolemos followed by Eurypylos' arrival and initial success, from which the Greeks are saved by Neoptolemos, is dramatically effective and different from other known versions. No mention is made of Priam's resort to bribery to obtain Eurypylos' help. This is typical of Quintus' general avoidance of material discreditable to his heroes; he tends to idealize them, emphasizing their virtues and minimizing their faults (Mansur 1940). The only event in Book 8 that belongs certainly to the traditional story is the killing of Eurypylos by Neoptolemos.

Deiphobos' rallying of the Trojans in Book 9 gives prominence to the patriotic theme of saving one's homeland, of which Hektor is the main vehicle in the *Iliad*. The subsequent bringing of Philoktetes owes some details to Sophocles' *Philoktetes* and to the encounter between the Argonauts and Phineus (Ap. Rhod. *Arg.* 2.178–306). The version of the death of Paris in Book 10 is different from those in the *Little Iliad* and Dictys: mortally wounded in battle, he survives long enough to seek healing from his deserted wife Oinone. It also departs from Parthenios' summary of her story in having Paris visit her in person and Oinone immolate herself on his pyre. The unsuccessful assault on the walls of Troy in Book 11 owes something both to Euripides' *Phoinician Women* and to Virgil's *Aeneid*: the whole of Aeneas' action in using rocks to repel first a Greek testudo and then an ascent by scaling ladder recalls his dislodging of a turret from Priam's palace onto the Greeks as they attack with a testudo and scaling ladders (Virg. *Aen.* 2.438–68). The story of the wooden horse, which occupies Book 12, is prominent in all the ancient sources. Scholars have reached opposite conclusions (notably Keydell 1963: 1286–9; Vian 1959b: 95–101, 1969: 78–84; Campbell 1981a: *passim*) as to whether Quintus' version was influenced by Virgil's (*Aen.* 2.13–249). What is undeniable is that Virgil's sequence of events is substantially closer to Quintus' than is that of the early Greek epics, the main difference being that Quintus has Laocoön blinded by Athena before the horse's entry into Troy and then his sons, not himself, killed by the snakes after it. The role of Sinon is essentially the same in both versions, though Virgil alone highlights it at overwhelming length. In my judgment, whilst Quintus clearly distanced himself from Virgil's version, it is hardly credible that he was not influenced by it. The narrative of the sack of Troy in Book 13 is closer to Apollodoros' summary than to that of the Cyclic *Sack of Ilion*. Its most important departure from both is the placing of Astyanax's killing immediately after that of his grandfather Priam instead of at the division of spoils the next day.

The first half of Book 14, events preceding the Greeks' departure, largely accords with earlier sources, except that the long speech of Achilles to Neoptolemos in a dream seems to be a novel adaptation of two different appearances of Achilles' ghost in the *Little Iliad* and the *Returns*. The consequent sacrifice of Polyxena is indebted to Euripides' *Hekabe*. Concerning the circumstances of the departure, Quintus follows not the Cycle but a simplified version favored by the tragedians: departure as a single fleet and its partial destruction by Athena's storm. The narrative of the storm largely follows the Cyclic version and is too different from that in Seneca's *Agamemnon* (421–578) for its influence to be plausible. Undeniable influence, however, was exerted by the storm with which Juno wrecks the fleet of Aeneas (*Aen.* 1.34–123), particularly her visit to Aeolus and the cave of the winds, which contributes an otherwise novel feature of Quintus' narrative.

Quintus' use of the dactylic hexameter (Koechly 1850: xxxii–xlviii; Wifstrand 1933: *passim*; Vian 1959b: 212–49; James and Lee 2000: 30–31) is similar to that of the Homeric epics, except that he has a much greater preponderance of dactylic over spondaic feet, which produces an unparalleled frequency of wholly dactylic lines. No other extant poem on a comparable scale reproduces the language and style of its models as closely as does the *Trojan Epic* those of the *Iliad* and the *Odyssey* (Koechly 1850: xlix–c; James and Lee 2000: 21–4). It has been calculated (Vian 1959b: 182–92) that of its 940 different adjectives 720 are Homeric, of which 149 are used ten or more times, a measure of Quintus' tendency to exaggerate the typically Homeric heavy use of ornamental adjectives. On the other hand he avoids the Hellenistic vice of using rare or unique words of disputed meaning. Occasionally his linguistic usage differs from that of early epic, showing the influence of classical Attic and later prose, but this is very much the exception that proves the rule. The extent to which Quintus imitates the Homeric use of formulae, at least those involving a name with an epithet, prompted the observation (Hoekstra 1965: 17) that the generally held belief that the complexity and efficiency of Homer's formulaic systems could only belong to poetry composed orally by illiterate bards was challenged by Quintus' example. This was recently demonstrated (James and Lee 2000: 27–30) by analysis of name-epithet systems involving six heroes mentioned frequently enough by both Homer and Quintus – Agamemnon, Achilles, Aeneas, Ajax, Odysseus, Priam – plus one frequent common noun, the usual word for "ship," *naus*. In five of these seven examples Quintus' system is not greatly inferior to its Homeric counterpart in elaboration, i.e. in the number of different combinations. The Homeric systems differ from those of Quintus most consistently in having a greater proportion of combinations used with significant frequency. Very much less marked is the superior economy, or efficiency, of the Homeric systems, i.e. their freedom from doublets, equivalent expressions identical in grammatical and metrical function. A very striking observation is that for all the general similarity of Quintus' systems to the Homeric, the proportion of combinations taken with little or no modification from Homer is consistently small.

Quintus' narrative technique also resembles the Homeric in the use of sense units repeated with variation, especially in battle sequences, but unlike Homer he mostly avoids precisely repeated lines. The dramatic character of the Homeric epics is reflected in the *Trojan Epic*, where speeches are rather less frequent but of similar average length. In another stylistic feature, the use of extended similes (Niemeyer 1883–4; Vian 1954; Roberts 1986: *passim*), Quintus follows the *Iliad* rather than the *Odyssey*, and actually outdoes his model in their frequency, probably being influenced by the comparable practice of Oppian in his didactic epic the *Halieutika* (late second century CE), which was certainly familiar to him. The subject matter of his similes is drawn very largely from recurrent themes in the *Iliad's* similes, with occasional supplement from the similes of later epics. Usually he conflates elements from two or more thematically related similes; the process tends to become more complex as his work progresses, and he produces variations on his own earlier imitations. Though relatively few of his similes seem to be thematically original, many have touches that strongly suggest personal observation and a feel for nature.

Quintus' undertaking to narrate the Trojan War in the Homeric manner inevitably entailed some maintenance of the Homeric divine machinery. As regards the frequency of divine intervention in human action there is no great difference between the *Iliad* and the

Trojan Epic. Mostly the same Olympian deities feature in both, but a significant difference is that some agents of repeated intervention in the *Trojan Epic* – personified Fate and personifications of aspects of warfare – are relatively inconspicuous in the *Iliad*. Many interventions simply affect human decision or initiative, but others have undeniably miraculous effects – physical rescue or the guiding of weapons – and these provide the best means of measuring the difference between the two epics. The *Iliad*, despite its prevailing realistic presentation of events, has at least seven such miraculous interventions in combats of major importance. The *Trojan Epic* has only the following three: Apollo fatally wounds Achilles with an arrow (3.30–138); Apollo removes Deiphobos in a mist (9.256–63); Aphrodite removes Aeneas in a mist (11.288–97). All the other major combats, involving the deaths of Penthesileia, Memnon, Eurypylos, and Paris, are entirely without divine intervention. That is one feature of the Homeric epics kept to a minimum by Quintus. His moral awareness and the probable influence on it of Stoic philosophy has been the object of considerable comment (Kakridis 1962: 178–81; Vian 1963: xvi–xviii, xxxv–xxxvii). The many moral maxims in the *Trojan Epic* (about ninety) have been criticized as exhibiting an uncomfortable mix of traditional paganism with Stoic doctrine, detracting from the poem's Homeric character. Certainly it amounts to some degree of modernization of Homeric epic. About two-thirds of the maxims are spoken by characters, with a heavy concentration in the speeches of Nestor and Odysseus, part of the general idealization of heroes mentioned above, a way of making them morally edifying. Stoic beliefs are apparent in the omnipotence of Fate, more or less identified with the will of Zeus, and in the way human souls survive after death. A memorable expression of the latter occurs at 7.87–89:

> There is, moreover, a saying among us
> That to an eternal home in heaven go the souls
> Of the good, but those of the bad to darkness.

This has been thought to show the influence of Christian belief, but there is nothing that is not attributable to Greek philosophy, even though it is tempting to see some link with the Christianity of Quintus' son Dorotheos.

The following passages are among the *Trojan Epic's* best.

1.716–81 Achilles' grief after killing Penthesileia prompts Thersites to insult him grossly for giving way to lust for a female enemy, hinting that he is no better than Paris (733–5):

> Scoundrel, where now is your strength of body and mind?
> Where is the might of the noble king? Surely you know
> How great has been the cost to Troy of lust for women.

Enraged, Achilles strikes him dead with his fist, which produces approving comment from the Greeks. Achilles justifies his action in view of Thersites' habitual abusiveness. Diomedes alone, as a kinsman of Thersites, is ready to challenge Achilles to combat, but both are persuaded to bury their anger. One might have expected Quintus to play down the sexual aspect of the Amazon legend, given his general euphemistic tendency. But here it is given prominence and is made to serve a moral lesson by being put in the mouth of a disreputable character who is promptly punished. The killing of Thersites by Achilles in response to his accusation was part of the traditional story at least since the *Aithiopis*. Its present rhetorical elaboration owes much to *Il.* 2.211–77, where Thersites accuses Agamemnon of greed and lust, and is reprimanded and struck by Odysseus, referred to explicitly at 759–60, much to the army's satisfaction as here. This is a case of Homeric influence producing divergence from the Cyclic version, which had the whole army divided over the killing and Achilles obliged to go to Lesbos for expiation.

5.317–32 The prize of Achilles' armor is awarded by the jury of Trojan prisoners to Odysseus, whose joy is not shared by the army. Ajax is numbed by the shock of disappointment and has to be led away (323–8):

> Pain and confusion overwhelmed him. All through his body
> His crimson blood was boiling, and bitter bile came flooding
> Over into his liver. Dreadful anguish gripped
> His heart, and through the base of his brain sharp pain
> Came shooting up and totally enveloped the membranes,
> Making his mind confused.

The remarkable physiological detail with which Ajax's condition is described may well be an original touch on the part of Quintus, whose interest in medical matters is indicated by several passages, notably 1.76–82, a simile of partial recovery from blindness, and 12.400–15, the blinding of Laocoön described accurately as an attack of congestive glaucoma. Here two matters of medical theory are reflected. The first is that of the four humors that determine human temperament. Preponderance of yellow bile produces a choleric temperament, and in this case it affects the liver. Secondly, since the third century BCE there had been some understanding of the brain's function, in particular of its occipital lobes. Precise mention of this is included in Apollonius' description of Medea's emotional condition at Ap. Rhod. *Arg.* 3.761–5, which clearly influenced the present passage. A taste for anatomical precision is shown by some of the *Iliad's* descriptions of wounds, but Quintus could draw on diverse sources to give it a modern flavor.

9.68–144 The Trojans are appalled at the sight of the Greek army streaming out across the plain, but Deiphobos is inspired to address them. He reminds them that they are fighting not just for Paris and Helen but for their families and homeland; Achilles is not alive, and the hard work of war will be rewarded by a natural change to peace (104–09):

> Are you not aware that for the suffering race
> Of men hard work is followed by joy and prosperity;
> That after the devastating winds of a dreadful storm
> Zeus brings on a day of cloudless skies for mortals;
> That deadly sickness is followed by health and strength, and war
> By peace?

It is hardly necessary to look for a particular source for this likening of human fortune to weather, but one is reminded of the terms in which Ajax acknowledges universal change (Soph. *Aj.* 669–77). The Trojan men are thus encouraged to arm for battle, helped by wives, children and fathers, and to march out. The picture of an aged father showing the scars of past battles on his chest (120–4) could have been influenced by some such source as Livy 2.23.4. The opposed armies engage in intense combat, watched from Troy's walls by anguished women and elders (138–43). The similarity of this picture to that at *Aen.* 12.131–3 could be fortuitous. Quintus' two descriptions, of arming and fighting, effectively reflect the appeal to family duty in Deiphobos' speech and give the whole passage a pleasing balance.

12.500–85   After the wooden horse has been brought into Troy and Laocoön's sons have been devoured by snakes, the Trojans' sacrifices, made in the hope of peace, fail to burn and the altars collapse. Other sinister omens include weeping statues, bloodstained temples, moving walls, opening gates, mournful bird cries, hidden stars, sacred laurels withered, and wild beasts in the city. The detailing of no fewer than fifteen portents presaging Troy's destruction may be considered more in the style of ancient historians than of poets. Among earlier Greek poets we find sacrifices that will not burn (Soph. *Ant.* 1006–11), statues sweating blood, and strange sounds in temples (Ap. Rhod. *Arg.* 4.1284–5). It is the accumulation of so many items that is most remarkable here. The only comparable passage is Virgil's description, at slightly greater length, of sixteen portents associated with the death of Julius Caesar (Virg. *Geo.* 1.466–88), which became the prototype of similar passages in later Roman epics. Most of the portents are different from Quintus', but two are the same: weeping statues of gods and wolves howling inside cities. The most compelling reason for believing that Quintus was influenced by that passage is that it is followed by a reference to the collective guilt inherited by Rome from Troy (*Geo.* 1.501–2). The likelihood of a tradition of such portents in this particular context is indicated by their occurrence at a slightly earlier point in the narrative of Diktys (5.7). Virgil records portents following the theft of the Palladion (*Aen.* 2.171–5), including the statue's sweating.

As the Trojans remain unimpressed by all this, Kassandra appears from the palace looking as wild as a lioness (535–8):

> Her hair was streaming out
> Over her silvery shoulders all the way down her back.
> Her eyes were flashing fearlessly. Under her head her neck,
> Like the stem of a tree in a gale, kept writhing this way and that.

In response to her warning that the portents indicate disaster and that the Trojans' feast will be their last she is rebuked for shamelessness and madness, and is turned away from the horse, which she has approached with an axe and a burning brand. As the feast begins, the Greeks inside the horse are relieved at her removal. According to the Cyclic epics Kassandra and Laocoön both argued for the horse's destruction after its entry. Her separate and later intervention here tallies with its brief mention at *Aen.* 2.246–7, where her never being believed by the Trojans is noted, as it is by Quintus at 526–8. Book 12 ends with dramatic tension heightened by a complex interaction of the human and the divine.

FURTHER READING

Quintus' epic is still most easily available to the English-reading public in Way's Loeb edition originally published in 1913, which is unsatisfactory because its Greek text has been superseded and its verse translation is often very loose. Combellack's prose translation (1968) is accurate, but it is partly based on a superseded text and is long out of print. My own verse translation, based on the latest editions and accompanied by an introduction and a commentary suited to non-specialist readers, was published in 2004.

The best critical edition of the Greek, accompanied by a French translation and commentary, is Vian's Budé edition (3 vols., 1963–9). But a more recent edition, with a more conservative text than Vian's, is that of Pompella, which is now more easily available (Pompella 2002). There are two commentaries on the whole epic in addition to Vian's: Koechly's in Latin (1850, reprinted 1968), with prolegomena that are valuable for language and meter; and Kakridis's in modern Greek (1962), with a general study. Of the three detailed commentaries on individual books,

Campbell's on Book 12 (1981a), Hopkinson's on parts of Book 10 (1994c), and James and Lee's on Book 5 (2000), the last has an introduction dealing particularly with the poet's date, language, and formulaic expression. The best general studies are those by Vian (1959b) and Keydell (1963), both especially valuable for questions of the epic's sources.

Journal articles most likely to interest the non-specialist reader are the following: Appel 1994, Byre 1982, Duckworth 1936, Schenk 1997, Schmidt 1999, Schmiel 1986, and Vian 1954.

CHAPTER TWENTY-SEVEN

Nonnus

Robert Shorrock

There is little that can be said with certainty about the author of the longest surviving poem from the whole of antiquity. It appears that Nonnus came from the town of Panopolis in Upper Egypt, and by his own testimony seems to have lived and worked in the literary metropolis of Alexandria (*Dion.* 1.13). Allusions to Nonnus by other writers suggest that the *Dionysiaca* was in the public domain by 470 CE (Vian 1976: xv–xviii), whilst an allusion by Nonnus to the poet Cyrus of Panopolis reveals that he must have been writing after 441 CE (Shorrock 2001: 144–6).

Late antiquity was a time of great mobility, especially for poets (Cameron 1965), and it would not be surprising to discover that Nonnus had indeed traveled widely, whether for education or employment. The details that Nonnus supplies about the cities of Tyre, Beirut, and Athens might suggest personal experience; it is, however, equally possible that Nonnus never left Egypt and knew about these places from written sources. Curiously, perhaps, Egypt features hardly at all in Nonnus' epic.

It has often been asserted that, since the *Dionysiaca* is full of alcoholic and sexual excess and astrological lore, its author must have been pagan in his outlook. This view is complicated by the attribution to Nonnus of a hexameter *Paraphrase of St John's Gospel*. One response has been to imagine that Nonnus abandoned his 48-book "pagan" epic after a conversion to Christianity and that he channeled his creative energies into a more respectable activity: turning the unadorned prose of St John's Gospel into a poem in the grand meter of Homer. To say nothing of the over-rigid distinction between pagan and Christian discourses that this implies, comparative metrical analysis of the two poems renders this hypothesis highly implausible: the *Paraphrase* is the less technically accomplished of the two, suggesting that it was in fact composed at an earlier date than the *Dionysiaca*. (On theological grounds the *Paraphrase* best suits a date after the Council of Ephesus in 431 CE.)

The following chapter is divided into four main sections. The first section considers the form and content of Nonnus' vast epic. The second is concerned with allusion and intertextuality, with the way that Nonnus engages with the Greek literary and mythological tradition in order to give a universalizing texture to his work. The third section focuses on metapoetry and examines some of the ways in which the narrative of the *Dionysiaca* draws attention to the process and practice of writing an epic poem. The chapter concludes with a discussion of the various afterlives of the *Dionysiaca*.

1 Form and Content

The story of Dionysus

The *Dionysiaca* is narrated in 48 books (equivalent to the *Iliad* and the *Odyssey* combined) and comprises more than 21,000 lines. It tells the long and eventful story of Dionysus, the hero who grows up to become a god.

The action begins several generations before the birth of Dionysus with the abduction of his great-aunt, Europa, and the fruitless attempts of his grandfather, Cadmus, to find her. But Cadmus' voyaging is not a total failure: he helps Zeus to defeat Typhon, the hundred-handed monster who has launched a chaotic takeover bid for Olympus, and receives Harmonia (the love-child of Ares and Aphrodite) as a reward for his efforts. There follows an account of the various offspring of Cadmus and Harmonia that culminates in Book 8 with the rescue of Dionysus from the smoldering corpse of his mother Semele.

After a second period of gestation, in the thigh of Zeus, Dionysus is eventually transported to the mountain court of Rhea in Asia Minor. It is here that he grows up amidst bears and lions, in company with a band of playful satyrs. Here too he falls in love for the first time, with the young satyr Ampelus. Such is Dionysus' love for Ampelus that he would gladly renounce his destined place in heaven in order to remain with him. Their relationship is not to last, however, as Ampelus falls awkwardly from the back of a bull, is gored by its horns, and is decapitated. Yet Ampelus is not to have died in vain: he is resurrected as a vine at the end of Book 12. It is thus that wine is invented, a liquid that gives comfort and pleasure; and something that Dionysus will keep constantly by his side.

No sooner has wine been discovered than Dionysus is given opportunity to try out its power. Zeus sends him instructions that he is to drive the impious race of Indians out of Asia and to teach the entire world about the benefits of viticulture. Through these labors Dionysus will earn for himself a place in heaven at the side of his father Zeus. A vast army from both Europe and Asia is now mustered, and Dionysus begins his long advance towards the heart of enemy territory and the (unnamed) city of the Indian chieftain Deriades. An early skirmish with the enemy at Lake Astacis in Book 14 proves the superiority of the Dionysiac force and the effectiveness of wine as a weapon, capable of incapacitating all that drink it. The power of wine is further demonstrated by Dionysus' conquest of the virgin huntress Nicaea, the first of many such erotic encounters. Where the oxherd Hymnus fails in his "pastoral" attempt to seduce Nicaea, Dionysus is successful. His superior charm consists of nothing more nor less than wine. By chance, the mountain spring from which Nicaea drinks is polluted with the wine that had been used to drug Lake Astacis. In her incapacitated state, he rapes her and leaves her pregnant.

Dionysus continues his advance towards the city of Deriades, overcoming numerous waves of enemy resistance and taking every opportunity to introduce the vine to those that he meets along the way, such as the shepherd Brongus and the family of King Staphylus. At last, Dionysus crosses the river Hydaspes and enters the territory of Deriades. Here in Book 25, at the halfway point of the *Dionysiaca*, the Indian War proper can be said to begin. It is a conflict on an epic scale that lasts for seven years.

In the seventh and final year of the war Dionysus receives a set of divinely crafted armor and the Olympian gods descend to earth to help out favorites on either side. When the fighting inclines in favor of the Dionysiac force, Hera deceives Zeus, drives Dionysus mad and thus gives ascendancy to the besieged Indians. The deception does not last for long, however: Dionysus regains his sanity and returns to the battlefield in Book 36. After one inconclusive encounter with Deriades, in which the Indian is defeated but allowed to go free, Dionysus makes a temporary truce and celebrates funeral games for his dead friend Opheltes. Battle is then resumed for a short period by sea, after which Dionysus closes in single combat with Deriades for a second and final time. The Indian leader attempts to flee, but is deceived by Athena into standing his ground and is killed by the faintest touch of Dionysus' *thyrsus*.

After the death of Deriades and the surrender of the Indian city in Book 40, Dionysus establishes a client king, divides up the spoils and sets off on his journey "homewards." His journey takes him first to the home of his grandfather Cadmus in Tyre, where he meets Herakles and partakes for the first time of ambrosia and nectar, the food and drink of the gods. He then moves on to Beroe, where he competes with Poseidon for the girl who gives her name to that same city. Although he is unsuccessful, he proves himself to be a worthy competitor against Zeus's brother, and is encouraged by the promise of future amorous conquests.

Dionysus next revisits the home of his mother Semele and his own earthly place of birth, Thebes, in Books 44–6. Here he encounters a hostile Pentheus, whose death he causes at the hands of his mother Agave. Out of pity for Agave and her surviving sister Autonoe, Dionysus gives them wine to soothe their cares. After Thebes, Dionysus journeys to Athens where he teaches the art of viticulture to Icarius, who is then killed by neighbors who think that the new drink of powerful, mind-altering wine must be a kind of poison. Naxos is Dionysus' next port of call. He arrives on the island just after Theseus has departed, in time to offer comfort to an abandoned Ariadne. With Ariadne in tow, Dionysus pays a visit to Argos, the city of his implacable enemy, Hera. Here he enters battle with Perseus. Although Perseus petrifies Ariadne with his Gorgon's head, he is no match for Dionysus, who does not need winged sandals to fly through the air, even to touch Olympus. But for the timely intervention of Hermes, Dionysus would have wreaked destruction on Argos, Mycenae, and Perseus, and would even have wounded Hera.

After making peace with his stepbrother Perseus, Dionysus continues on his journey into the final book of the epic. In Thrace he is attacked by an army of giants, stirred up by their mother Earth at the instigation of Hera. Zeus had needed the help of Cadmus to defeat the giant Typhon; Dionysus almost effortlessly defeats this younger band of Typhons. He takes a break from fighting only to wrestle an athletic maiden into submission and kill her murderous father. From Thrace Dionysus makes his way back to his childhood home, the court of Rhea. Here he faces his final erotic challenge: the seduction of the virgin Aura who has dedicated herself to Artemis. Conventional techniques of seduction induce only scorn on the part of Aura, and Dionysus resorts to the method that worked so effectively (and serendipitously) with Nicaea: wine. In this familiarly deceptive manner, Dionysus rapes Aura. She gives birth to twin boys. One son she kills, the other, Iacchus, is snatched away by Dionysus and transported to Athens and the care of Athena and the Bacchants of Eleusis.

In this way Dionysus' earthly labors are brought to an end. In the final lines of the poem, having proved himself to be worthy of a place at his father's table on Olympus, the hero at last becomes a god.

Style and meter

The *Dionysiaca* has a verbal energy and a capacity for prolific growth that makes it look like a literary version of the vine itself. Nonnus' style is characterized by linguistic exuberance, a constant striving for variation and antithesis, and a fondness for mythological *exempla*. Most striking are the compound epithets, many of them coined by the poet himself, that appear in abundance throughout the poem (see Hopkinson 1994a: 14–16).

Nonnus' text is also highly episodic and discursive, so much so that it often appears that the aim of the poet "is not the coherence of the whole, but the effect of individual scenes, not clarity of line, but intensity of color" (Keydell 1936: 910.14–28). These are qualities that are shared by much contemporary poetry. Although Michael Roberts's work on late antique poetics focuses exclusively on the Latin poetic tradition, his observations on the "jeweled style" with its emphasis on fragmentation, polished juxtaposition, and glittering display represent an equally apt description of Nonnus' style (Roberts 1989). Striking parallels can also be adduced with late antique material culture, specifically mosaics, tapestries, and portraiture (Riemschneider 1957).

From a metrical point of view, Nonnus' hexameter lines represent something of a gold standard, marking a return to, even an improvement on, the tightly controlled form of the Callimachean hexameter (see further Whitby 1994). In addition to the adherence to Callimachean "rules" on, for example, the position and form of the caesura and the placement of monosyllables, Nonnus reduced the combination of dactyls and spondees permitted in any line from twenty in Callimachus to only nine. Within this limited metrical range, the purely dactylic line predominates. Nonnus' capacity to produce exact and exacting quantitative verse seems especially impressive when one considers an important linguistic change that had taken place by this time: little distinction was now made between long and short vowels in ordinary speech, and word accent, not vowel length, began to be used to determine the quantity of syllables. Nonnus' response to this change can be seen in his adoption of a rigorous system for the regulation of accent at different positions in the hexameter line. At line ends, for example, words are accented on the ultimate or penultimate syllable (with no such words accented on their antepenultimate syllables). Nonnus' high metrical standards are only compromised on rare occasions when quotations from Homer or some other author are introduced directly into the text. The strict discipline of Nonnus' hexameters forms a striking counterpoint to the rhetorical luxuriance of the poetry itself.

Structure

Despite its many digressions and embellishments, Nonnus' narrative follows closely the orthodox life-story of Dionysus as described, for example, by Apollodorus in his compendium of mythology, the *Bibliotheca*. This loose narrative framework is, however, only one of a number of different structural systems used by Nonnus in an attempt to underpin and shore up the vast edifice of the *Dionysiaca*. One such structure is that of the "Royal Encomium." Along the lines of the model laid down by Menander Rhetor, the *Dionysiaca* can be divided into encomiastic sections: introduction (Books 1–2), ancestry and homeland (3–7), birth, upbringing and education (8–12), followed by achievements both in war and in peace (13–40) and concluding with an epilogue (48). Another system of organization is supplied by the technique of ring-composition. Around the hub of the Indian War is arranged a series of episodes in mirror image. In the opening two books of the epic, Zeus rapes Europa and struggles to defeat the monster Typhon; in the final book Dionysus effortlessly defeats the Thracian giants and concludes his activities on earth by raping Aura. Similarly, Cadmus' marriage and meandering attempt to establish a home for himself in Books 3–5 are paralleled by Dionysus' own homeward journeying and marriage with Ariadne in Books 40–8.

A further contribution to the structure of the epic is made by astrology. There can be no doubting the significant role played by astral lore and planetary wanderings in the *Dionysiaca*. The enigmatic tablets of Harmonia in Book 12 constitute a set of horoscopes for a cosmic year (each of the six tablets covers two star signs) that begins at the beginning of Greek mythology and moves down to the end of the age of heroes. It has been argued that, in an analogous manner, the *Dionysiaca* constitutes its own cosmic year, with its 48 books divisible into four seasons each consisting of the twelve signs of the zodiac.

The systems of astrology, ring-composition and encomium come persuasively into view at different times over the course of the epic. Yet not one of these structures is able to bear the entire weight of the 48-book narrative. It is in vain that one looks for a single, unifying superstructure: the narrative of the *Dionysiaca* refuses to be contained within the rigid bonds of any one system. Conventional approaches to Nonnus' narrative have seen this overlapping web of structures as a sign of poetic incompetence and degeneracy from the classical Golden Age, suggesting that Nonnus has failed to develop and sustain a coherent narrative structure. Our postmodern age can afford to be more sympathetic to the multiple structures and narratives contained within the *Dionysiaca*. We have already seen how from a stylistic point of view Nonnus was the product of an age when surface display and the juxtaposition of individual scenes came to dominate over wider narrative concerns. In one important respect, however, Nonnus' epic ran counter to the spirit of the age: scale. In fifth-century CE Egypt epyllia, encomia, and *patria* – works of small scale and modest ambition – were the prevalent literary modes of expression. The appearance of a 48-book epic must have been nothing short of astonishing. Nonnus attempted what no other poet from the whole of late antiquity was ever to attempt: the combination of an ornate and episodic style with the demands of a grand, unifying narrative. Nonnus' multiplex narrative is the result of that attempt, and from our knowledge of the epic's early reception, it was a spectacular success.

Allusion and Intertextuality

The universe of epic

It is hardly an exaggeration to say that the world of late antiquity was obsessed by hidden meanings and allegorical interpretation, and was adept at reading allusively in order to penetrate beneath the surface of the text. In this regard, Nonnus' epic provided his audience with the ultimate allusive reading experience. The *Dionysiaca* encompasses a breath-taking sweep of Greek literature, actively engaging with over one thousand years of literary tradition. Every conceivable genre appears to be represented: Homeric epic, Hellenistic epyllion, pastoral, encomium, Greek tragedy, the Greek novel, hymns, foundation stories, cosmogonies, astrology and epigram, veering at times into the territory of philosophy and history (see, e.g., Harries 1994: 64; also Chapter 28, by Garner). This inclusivity is not merely fortuitous. By transplanting the entirety of Greek literature into his *Dionysiaca*, Nonnus has created a universal poetic experience. The all-embracing nature of this Dionysiac epic can be profitably compared with the potation of wine, whose invention is described in Book 12:

> ὅττι πολυτρίπτοιο νέαις λιβάδεσσιν ὀπώρης
> σὸν ποτὸν ἄνθεα πάντα δεδέξεται · ἓν ποτὸν ἔσται
> μιγνύμενον πάντεσσι, καὶ εἰς μίαν ἵξεται ὀδμήν
> ἄνθεσι παντοίοις κεκερασμένον

(12.240-3)

With the new pools of well-trodden fruit, your drink will contain all of the flowering plants. One drink will be suffused with everything; and in one scent will be contained a blend of every kind of flower.

Just as Dionysus' wine blends together all flowering plants, so Nonnus' epic blends together all of the flowers that are contained within the garden of Greek literature (on the garden of poetry see the introductions to the "Garlands" of Meleager and Philip preserved at *AP* 4.1.1–2; 4.2.1–4). The astrological tablets of Harmonia that exist to provide an inclusive history of the whole cosmos, "containing everything in one": *ein heni panta pherousan* (12.44), further encourage this inclusive view of Nonnian epic. An alternative, though complementary, way of considering the all-encompassing nature of the *Dionysiaca* is to be found in the proem, where Nonnus makes a suggestive connection between himself and Proteus, the slippery shape-shifter who makes his earliest appearance in Homer's *Odyssey.* Just as Proteus exists in one and many forms, so the single form of the narrative will embrace any number of different forms, narratives, and genres.

Epic cycle

The imagery of wine considered above suggests an indiscriminate mixture of ingredients, yet Nonnus' arrangement is far from random. At the heart of the *Dionysiaca* stands the poet's direct engagement with Homer's *Iliad* (see Chapter 21, by Edwards). Nonnus' imitation is not a piecemeal appropriation of selected Iliadic "highlights," but a sustained attempt to appropriate the whole of Homer's narrative and recast it in a new Dionysiac form (Shorrock 2001: 67–90). The resulting *Indiad* extends from Book 25 to Book 40 and deals inventively with various narrative challenges along the way: when faced, for example, with an immortal "Achilles" who has no cause to sulk, Homeric *mênis* is neatly transformed into Dionysiac *mania*.

In Greek literary tradition, Homer's *Iliad* did not stand in isolation but was integrated into the wider assemblage of the Epic Cycle, a formal collection of texts dating from the seventh and sixth centuries BCE that provided a systematized arrangement of Greek mythology, from the marriage of Uranus and Gaia down to the end of the age of the heroes (see Chapter 24, by Burgess). This Cycle established a chronological framework that became canonical for all subsequent mythological handbooks. A work such as Apollodorus' *Bibliotheca* is certainly more compendious than the original Cycle would have been, but although it incorporates much new material, it adheres closely to the same essential framework. In Apollodorus, therefore, Greek mythology begins with a divine union followed by Gigantomachy; the voyage of the "Argo" then leads into the cycle of Theban stories. The cycle of mythology concludes with the narratives of the Trojan War, which extend from the birth and upbringing of Achilles, Zeus's decision to initiate war, the assembly of the troops, through to the final year of the war, the sack of Troy, and the homecomings of the heroes.

Nonnus, aware of this Greek literary tradition, does not simply engage with Homer's *Iliad* in isolation, but ambitiously recasts the whole of the mythological cycle that surrounded it, in an attempt to create a mythological cycle of his own, predicated on the narrative of Dionysus. Zeus's union with Europa (Book 1) is followed immediately by a Gigantomachy, in which Typhon wrestles for world domination (1–2). There follows a re-scripted version of Apollonius Rhodius' *Argonautica* that narrates the voyages of Cadmus and his efforts to found the city of Thebes (3–5). After a lengthy description of Theban affairs there begin the narratives of the Indian War, extending from the birth and upbringing of Dionysus (8–12), through the preliminary stages of the war (including Zeus' decision to initiate the war and the assembly of the troops) (13–24), to the last year of the war and the sack of the Indian city (25–40), and, finally, the homecoming of the hero (40–8).

Nonnus' attempt to create a mythological cycle suggests important connections with the work of the third-century CE poet Pisander of Laranda. Although only the scantest fragments now remain of Pisander's 60-book epic, *Heroikai Theogamiai*, it is clear that this poem represented an attempt to update the Epic Cycle, narrating the history of the world from the union of Zeus and Hera down to the time of Alexander the Great. According to a sixth-century CE source, Pisander's poem was so successful that it doomed the Epic Cycle to extinction. It is possible that Nonnus' own updated version of the cycle of Greek mythology did the same for Pisander.

Latin culture and language

Nonnus' mythological ambitions accord well with his project to contain the whole of
Greek literature within the pages of his epic. The *Dionysiaca* represents both a mythological and a literary cosmos. In this respect Nonnus' epic finds an obvious analogue in
Ovid's *Metamorphoses*, a text whose universalizing ambitions have been clearly documented (see Chapter 34, by Newlands). Although this similarity would seem to support the
idea that Nonnus was conversant with Latin literature, it is by no means apparent that this
was actually the case. Nonnus would no doubt have learned the rudiments of Latin at
school, and may even have been introduced to a "classic" such as Virgil by means of an
interlinear Greek-Latin text, but the *Dionysiaca* provides no evidence to suggest that
Nonnus extended his reading of Latin literature beyond the schoolroom. Although the
poet makes an open reference to the benefits of Roman *imperium* (*Dion.* 41.389–93), he
appears to make no allusion, explicit or implicit, to Roman literature. Where similarities do
occur it is likely that a shared Hellenistic source is involved (Hollis 1994: 60 n. 16).
Whether Nonnus was genuinely ignorant of Latin literature or whether he consciously
chose to suppress his knowledge, the important point is that Nonnus acts as if the entire
Latin literary tradition had never existed. It is on Athens, not Rome, that his gaze is
symbolically fixed, and it is Homer, not Ovid or Virgil, whom he addresses as "father."

Metapoetry

Poetry and wine

In recent years, critics have become increasingly interested in the self-conscious manner in
which the epic poet participates in the world of his poem. Ecphrastic descriptions alert the
reader to the artful construction of the text, characters present themselves as potential
doublets for the figure of the poet, while the journey of the hero functions as a suggestive
metaphor for the poet's own journey from the inception of the text to its conclusion. Such
an approach, pioneered by critics of Latin poetry, can be fruitfully applied to the later
Greek tradition (e.g., Harries 1994). Nonnus acknowledges his own place in the "self-
conscious" tradition of epic at the very beginning of the *Dionysiaca*. Before commencing
his narrative about Dionysus, Nonnus first undergoes initiatory rites that will turn him
into a Dionysiac poet:

ἄξατέ μοι νάρθηκα, τινάξατε κύμβαλα, Μοῦσαι,
καὶ παλάμῃ δότε θύρσον ἀειδομένου Διονύσου.
(1.11–12)

Bring me the fennel-stalk, clash the cymbals, Muses,
and hand me the *thyrsus* of Dionysus, subject of my song.

Armed with the *thyrsus* and, a few lines later, with a fawn-skin tied around his shoulders,
Nonnus begins his journey through the pages of the *Dionysiaca* in tandem with his
subject. The boundaries that traditionally separate a poet from his song have here been
blurred, inviting consideration – right from the start of the epic – of the parallels that exist
between the god of wine and his inspired poet.

Clear connections between wine and song/poetry are pointed up through the epic. In
addition to the frequent use of words that describe "pouring" and "mixing," Nonnus
draws an explicit connection between his poetry and drink when he announces his
attention to "blend a song": *keraso melos* (25.11). The wine of Dionysus and the poetry
of Nonnus are to be understood as analogous substances: both products are sweet,

deceptive, and liable to have an intoxicating, potentially fatal, effect on the mind of the recipient.

Poetry and wine are not just analogous products, but are similar in the way in which they are produced and distributed. It is important to remember that wine is not invented until Book 12, and that it is only then that Dionysus begins his mission to subdue the peoples of India and carry the gift of wine to all the races of the world. Up until this point the narrative has been concerned with Dionysus' ancestry, his birth and adolescence. In a similar way, the first twelve books can be seen to represent Nonnus' own emergence into the literary tradition, and his first faltering attempts to discover and articulate his own poetic voice. For Nonnus, it is wine, or rather the vine from which wine derives, that equates with his own newly discovered approach to writing poetry, his own Dionysiac poetic. Dionysus himself provides a description of the vine and its powerful nature that is wholly applicable to Nonnus' emergent poetic:

> ἀμφὶ δὲ δένδρεα πάντα κάτω νεύοντα καρήνῳ
> εἴκελα λισσομένῳ κυρτούμενον αὐχένα κάμπτει,
> ὑψιτενῆ δὲ πέτηλα γέρων ἐκλίνατο φοῖνιξ·
> ἀμφὶ δὲ μηλείῃ τανύεις πόδας, ἀμφὶ δὲ συκῇ
> χεῖρας ἐφαπλώσας ἐπερείδεαι· ὑμετέρην δέ,
> δμωίδες ὡς δέσποιναν, ἐλαφρίζουσιν ὀπώρην,
> εὖτε τιταινομένων πετάλων ἑλικώδεϊ παλμῷ
> ἀμφιπόλων ὑπὲρ ὦμον ἀνέρχεαι·

(12.272–84)

On all sides the trees bow down their nodding heads, like a man at prayer with bended neck. The old palm-tree dips its lofty leaves. You [namely, the vine] stretch your feet around the apple tree, around the fig you spread your hands and hold on tight. They support your fruit as slaves support their mistress, while you advance over the shoulders of your servants with a darting twist of spreading greenery.

Just like the vine, then, the Dionysiac poetic has the capacity to insinuate itself into the forest of Greek literature. It does not aim to create a radically new landscape, but seeks instead to transform an existing one. It wraps its tendrils tightly around established genres, forcing them to play the part of servants to their own domineering mistress. No sooner has Nonnus discovered his new poetic gift than he has an opportunity to use it. In Book 13, Dionysus is instructed to destroy the Indian race and spread the gift of wine to all the nations of the earth, thereby earning a place in heaven; Nonnus now embarks on his own analogous mission to transform the established literary landscape, dominated by such landmarks as Callimachus' *Hecale*, Homer's *Iliad* and Euripides' *Bacchae*. He will turn Callimachean water into wine, transform Homeric *ménis* into Dionysiac *mania*, and inject a new element of pity into the end of Euripides' merciless tragedy. Everywhere will, in addition, be suffused with an atmosphere of eroticism. For not only is Aphrodite a natural companion of Dionysus, but the vine is none other than a metamorphosed version of the young satyr Ampelus, Dionysus' former lover. It is in this way that Nonnus will attempt to earn a place for himself in the literary pantheon.

Fathers and sons

A crucial factor in understanding Dionysus and his mission is his relationship with his father Zeus. From his earliest childhood, when he first fixes his gaze on Olympus, until his apotheosis, when he finally earns a seat at Zeus's table, Dionysus remains obsessively focused on the attempt to live up to, imitate, and even surpass his father. For Nonnus too, paternity is a dominant and explicit concern. After a break from the narrative of the Indian War, he calls on the Muse to transport him back to the battlefield, asking that he be armed with the spear and shield of "father Homer": *patros Homérou* (25.265). The hexameter *Dionysiaca*, replete with "stock" epithets, epic catalogues, and Homeric allusions, clearly betrays Nonnus' genealogy as a son of Homer. Nonnus strives to emulate his father and relies on his protection when venturing onto the battlefield of epic.

Nonnus' relationship with Homer, like that of Dionysus with Zeus, strays beyond the bounds of filial piety, however. During an interlude from fighting in Book 18, the friendly king Staphylus urges Dionysus to return to war and imitate the deeds of his father in battle. The words of encouragement have a positive effect but reveal for the first time that Dionysus has ambitions not merely to imitate but to surpass his father: Κρονίδην νείκεσσε, καὶ ἤθελε μείζονα νίκην ... ζῆλον ἔχων Κρονίδαο (He vied with the son of Cronus, and wanted a greater victory (i.e. than his father's) ... to rival the son of Cronus) (18.311–13). These words offer a valuable insight into Nonnus' epic ambitions. His engagement with Homer, especially his attempt to rewrite the *Iliad* as a Dionysiac narrative, represents a steel-tipped poetic homage; it is an attempt not merely to rival Homer, but to surpass him. (On the anxious relationship between poetic fathers and their sons see Bloom 1973.)

Imitation and usurpation

The dangers of imitation and usurpation are given prominence throughout the epic by a suggestive sequence of figures: Marsyas, Typhon, Aphrodite, and Phaethon. The skin-stripped body of Marsyas, the satyr who dared to take on Apollo in a musical contest, stands at the intersection between proem and narrative (Book 1.41–4), as a disquieting warning to all those who would challenge figures of authority. It is a warning that Typhon would have done well to heed before embarking on his own disastrous attempt to usurp the role of Zeus and establish a new world order (1–2). Typhon's attempt at world domination ends in catastrophic failure: having thrown the world into chaos he is finally defeated by the combined forces of Zeus and Cadmus (Dionysus' maternal grandfather) and safely entombed under the mountains of Sicily. His fate is enough to give any imitator pause for thought. Prominently positioned at the start of the epic, the story of Typhon raises profound doubts and fears about Nonnus' own mimetic undertaking. Will Nonnus, the novice epic poet with global ambitions, have any more success controlling the hexameters of Homer than Typhon did in controlling the thunderbolts of Zeus?

The debate about imitation and usurpation is continued by Aphrodite in Book 24 and Phaethon in Book 38. Unlike Typhon, both figures are safely contained within Nonnus' narrative, presented as stories that have no capacity to impact *directly* on the course of the *Dionysiaca*. It is clearly significant for the development of Nonnus as an epic poet that the narrative chaos of the first two books is never again to be repeated. In Book 24, after crossing the river Hydaspes, Dionysus is entertained by a bard who tells of how Aphrodite falls in love with the loom and abandons her magic girdle for the spindle of Athena. Her neglect of the affairs of love soon begins to disturb the order of the cosmos. What is more, her attempts at weaving are disastrous: the fruit of her loom is not fine and well spun but "coarse" and "monstrous." Her attempts at imitation, like Typhon's, result in the most grotesque of parodies. Unlike Typhon, however, she does not suffer extreme punishment. The laughter of the gods is enough to shame Aphrodite into returning to her traditional domain, abandoning her textile while it is only half-finished: *hemiteleston* (24.322). The failure of Aphrodite's project provokes further consideration of Nonnus' enterprise. Do we join with the gods in their mocking response to the efforts of an artist whose talents lie elsewhere? And is it the reader or the poet who contemplates abandoning the text of the *Dionysiaca* at its mid-way point?

In Book 38, the story of Phaethon, the son of a god who strives, above all else, to imitate his father, is obviously and directly relevant to the experiences of Nonnus and Dionysus. The young boy, longing for his absent father, constructs an imitation version of the chariot of the sun, with rams in the place of horses. As he grows older, he abandons his toy cart and begins to covet the real thing. At length his father gives way to his pleas and he is allowed to drive his father's chariot for a single day. Clothed in Helios' own cloak, he steps into the chariot and receives instructions about how he must keep the horses on their familiar course. But even before Phaethon has begun his journey, his efforts are doomed to failure. He is incapable of controlling the spirited horses, veers off course and thereby throws the cosmos into confusion. At this point, Zeus intervenes to restore order, dashing Phaethon from his chariot with a lethal thunderbolt. In a manner analogous to that of Phaethon, Nonnus has progressed from "play-acting" – small-scale attempts to imitate Homer in the early books of his epic – to the real thing: a chance to ride the chariot of Homer through Books 25–40 in his own replay of the *Iliad*. Unlike Phaethon, Nonnus proves himself capable of keeping the chariot of Homeric epic firmly on course.

Dangers still remain for Nonnus in the books ahead. As an appropriate conclusion to his grand mythological cycle, it might reasonably be expected that Nonnus would follow his *Iliad* with a similar replay of the *Odyssey*. Books 40–8 provide something quite different. Although they do supply a narrative of wandering and return that offers general parallels with the *Odyssey*, the direct relationship with Homer that characterized Books 25–40 has entirely disappeared. It is a predictable though misguided response to see Nonnus' movement away from Homer in these final books as a poetic failure, an abandonment of a clear model in favor of an ununified medley of episodes. In fact, Nonnus' movement away from Homer in Books 40–8 is a sign of his poetic power. After demonstrating his ability to control his father's chariot, Nonnus strikes out alone, on a course of his own making, deliberately flouting the advice given by Helios to his son to keep to the familiar track. The final books of the epic represent Nonnus' audacious attempt to break free from the influence of his father, risking both poetic confusion and literary death in order to become a strong poet in his own right.

Literary Afterlives

The emergence of the *Dionysiaca* in the fifth century CE had an immediate and profound effect on the literary climate of late antiquity. Though no late antique poet was ever again to attempt a work of such monumental ambition, successive generations of poets (Colluthus and Christodorus, Pamprepius, Dioscorus and Musaeus, and others) show marked signs of Nonnian influence in terms of language and meter.

Corroborating evidence for Nonnus' early popularity is a sixth-century CE papyrus fragment excavated in Egypt that preserves several books of the *Dionysiaca* (P. Berol. 10567). The breadth of his influence is suggested by the sixth-century CE poet and historian Agathias from Myrina, on the coast of Asia Minor, who quotes part of the proem of the *Dionysiaca* from memory (*Histories* 4.23.5). "The most influential Greek poet since Callimachus" (Cameron 1982: 227) continued to be read at Constantinople throughout the Middle Ages (see Lind 1978). A copy of the *Dionysiaca* was commissioned there by the thirteenth-century polymath and scholar Maximus Planudes. In January 1423 this manuscript (the celebrated *Laurentianus*) was acquired by the young Italian humanist, Francesco Filelfo, and transported to Florence, where it remains to this day. It was from a derivative version of this same manuscript that the first printed edition of the *Dionysiaca* was produced in Antwerp in 1569 by G. Falkenburg. Once established in the West, Nonnus continued to exercise an important creative influence on a long line of writers. Although the influence of the *Dionysiaca* on Milton's *Paradise Lost* remains open to speculation, in the eighteenth century Nonnus was read and admired by Goethe and found an enthusiastic "patron" in the Italian Giovan Batista Marino, whose works of erotic mythology owe much to Nonnus' epic. In nineteenth-century England, the *Dionysiaca* was championed by the eccentric novelist Thomas Love Peacock. His attempts to convert his friend Shelley to the charms of Nonnian poetry were not obviously successful, though it has recently been suggested that the *Dionysiaca* did indeed have a direct influence on Shelley's *Prometheus Unbound* (see Shorrock 2001: 1–2 for details and further bibliography).

In 1903, the editor of Peacock's novels, Richard Garnett, published a fictional account of the life of Nonnus that attempted to reconcile the poet's supposed authorship of the "pagan" *Dionysiaca* and the "Christian" paraphrase of St John's Gospel. In this amusing narrative Apollo encounters Nonnus within a week of his conversion to Christianity. When put to the test Nonnus reveals his true pagan spirit by refusing to destroy his copy of the *Dionysiaca*. In his contrite state he then decides to destroy his *Paraphrase*, but Apollo forbids it: "Thou shalt publish it. That shall be thy penance." Just over a decade later, Nonnus' influence is to be noted on one of the most famous of all modern Greek poets: C. P. Cavafy. His poem, "Refugees," written in October 1914, enthuses about the language and imagery in the work of a fellow Alexandrian writer.

In the late twentieth century, Nonnus found his way into two different works of fiction. He appears in dramatized and unforgettable form in Theodore Zeldin's 1988 novel *Happiness* and earns high praise in Roberto Calasso's *The Marriage of Cadmus and Harmony*, published in the same year. Even higher praise is accorded by the fact that Calasso's fictive reworking of Greek mythology owes a large debt to the narrative of the *Dionysiaca*. His successful imitation must count as the sincerest form of flattery (Shorrock 2003).

The enthusiastic "amateur" reception of Nonnus' *Dionysiaca* contrasts sharply with the epic's reception by "professional" critics. One critic has suggested that "the loss of Nonnus' *Dionysiaca* would be no great cause for lamentation." Although this view is extreme, it can hardly be regarded as heretical. The majority of critics who do engage with the *Dionysiaca* do not consider the text in its own right, but use it rather as a means to more "edifying" ends: it provides an extensive and invaluable mine of mythological detail, often unattested elsewhere; at the same time it serves as an important resource in the search for fragments of lost Hellenistic texts, rare specimens trapped in the plentiful amber of Nonnus' poetry.

There are, however, signs of an emerging critical interest in the *Dionysiaca* as a literary and cultural artifact. Attempts are starting to be made to unpack the social, political, and cultural implications of Nonnus' text (Chuvin 1990, 1991; Bowersock 1990, 1994), although much work remains to be done in this regard. An important collection of essays appeared in 1994 (Hopkinson 1994b), while 2001 saw the publication of the first English monograph devoted to the epic as a literary text (Shorrock 2001). A series of essays on Nonnus can also now be accessed via the World Wide Web (R. Newbold at www.nonnus. adelaide.edu.au). Such increased interest has been facilitated and encouraged by the groundbreaking work of Vian and his indefatigable team of Budé editors, whose thirty-year project to provide a text, translation, and detailed commentary is now moving towards its magisterial conclusion.

FURTHER READING

Nonnus' *Dionysiaca* is a *mega biblion* with a surprisingly slender bibliography. It is most readily accessible through the three volumes of W. H. D. Rouse's exuberant, but dated, Loeb translation (1940).

For a general introduction to the social and cultural milieu of the fifth century CE see Bowersock 1990; Cameron 1965, 2004; Chuvin 1990. Lindsay (1965) paints a highly impressionistic, though stimulating picture of Nonnus as a Graeco-Egyptian poet. An excellent general introduction to the linguistic, literary, cultural and political dimensions of the epic is provided by a volume of essays, *Studies in the Dionysiaca of Nonnus* edited by Neil Hopkinson (1994b).

A series of articles exploring Nonnus' work from a psychoanalytical perspective can now be accessed via the World Wide Web (www.nonnus.adelaide.ed.au). For a detailed study of the *Dionysiaca* as a literary work, and the first and only English monograph on the subject, see Shorrock 2001.

The Budé Nonnus (1974–) was inaugurated under the editorship of Francis Vian with the aim of providing a text, translation, and detailed commentary for the *Dionysiaca*. This colossal work of scholarship, now almost complete, represents an indispensable resource for all those with a serious interest in Nonnian studies. For the later reception of Nonnus' epic see Lind 1978 and Shorrock 2003.

CHAPTER TWENTY-EIGHT

Epic and Other Genres in the Ancient Greek World

R. Scott Garner

Introduction

The title of this essay is perhaps deceiving since on the surface it assumes (1) the existence of some monolithic category of poetry that was understood as "epic" throughout the Greek world and (2) genres of verbal art other than epic that were equally well defined throughout this entire period. In truth, however, neither of these statements brings us close to the actualities of ancient Greece. Indeed, Richard Martin has demonstrated in Chapter 1 of this volume that the definition of "epic" was ever-changing in the Greek world, encompassing early on the entire body of traditional hexameter poetry that was recited orally and then gradually narrowing its limits to Homeric and heroic sagas that achieved a greater sense of fixity as writing eventually made its full influence known. (Cf. Chapter 41, by Jenkyns. See also Ford 1997 on the various aspects of defining "epic," especially in terms of an archaic performance context.)

Non-epic genres also had a large range of flexibility throughout the history of Greek literature, and here it is necessary to distinguish between genres as understood by their practitioners and genres as delimited by outside theorizers. As Depew and Obbink have noted, metadiscourse among the ancients concerning genre distinctions often took place at some distance from the actual genres themselves and sometimes even included falsification or fictionalizing of the involved "performative matrix" (2000a: 3). Additionally, much ancient theorizing about genres "arose quite apart from conceptualizations of genre that were production-and-performance-based" (p. 3). The resulting normative and static categories that developed were therefore often formalistic creations – sometimes produced centuries after the artistic works themselves – useful for little more than drawing up literary canons or grouping together works sharing a small set of characteristics that could be analyzed in detail.

On the other hand, ancient Greek writers and performers would have had very different views on the proper limitations upon their art forms. Several studies such as those by Havelock (1963, 1982) and Thomas (1989) have made clear the degree to which oral communicative processes affected the literature and society of the archaic and early classical periods, and the composer of an elegy, tragedy, or philosophical treatise during these times necessarily had to take into account the dominant oral context into which a current work of verbal art was to be sent forth, even if its presentation was to occur in a written form. Such a context presented a traditional framework within which the composer fashioned his or her words in order to make them meaningful to an audience and produce any desired effects. However, since audiences and their previous experiences with the various types of verbal art were continually changing, so too were their expectations, and the result was a constant negotiation between artists and audiences concerning the proper form, content, and arena for specific types of composition (cf. Day 2000; Depew 2000). The formal structures and thematic conventions that gradually emerged were thus usually unwritten (especially in the archaic period (Rossi 1971)), occasionally even unrecognized (Bauman 1977: 27), and always subject to alteration, but the social force that they exerted in directing a composer's efforts within a specific cultural setting, institution, or event was the closest thing to a prescriptive effect of genre that most ancient authors would have experienced. (Cf. Bauman 1977: 25–35.) Consequently, the degree to which an author and audience felt enabled or constrained by traditional expectations is the extent to which genre can be understood as an active consideration in the composition of early Greek literature, a situation that remained the norm even for those literary forms such as historiography that were conceived as written texts but nevertheless often felt the need to distinguish themselves or establish authority in terms of their oral surroundings. (Cf. Boedeker 2000.)

Unfortunately for our purposes here, however, such socially aware and performance-based genre distinctions did not always necessitate having epic itself (in whatever way it was understood at that particular time) as a standard reference point, even though many types of Greek literature did invite generic comparisons of either form or content with the epic poetry that was always omnipresent – with the result that Aristotle compared tragedy with epic in their metrical, thematic, evolutional, and formalistic aspects while Herodotus continually strove to distinguish his *Histories* from epic, especially in terms of plausibility but also with respect to an overall purpose in narrating the events selected for inclusion (Lateiner 1989: 99–100; Boedeker 2000: 103–5). Such analyses of genre thus bring to light only a small number of the complex interactions that Greek literature experienced in connection with epic, and we must therefore shift our focus away from actual generic qualifications and look instead at the relationships maintained between epic and other literary types in several different areas, whether on the level of compositional technique, textual allusion, or philosophical reaction.

In what follows, then, there has been an attempt to organize the material not in accordance with Greek distinctions of genre but with regard for the kinds of interaction that different works had with the ever-evolving category of epic poetry. An initial emphasis has been placed on archaic poetic works because of their large number of affinities with epic; the essay then proceeds to take into account several prose genres as well as tragedy, with discussion centering primarily on developments through the classical period but also including a brief glance at works from the Hellenistic period.

The Homeric Hymns

The Homeric Hymns, a collection of 33 poems of varying length dedicated to Greek divinities, provide an excellent starting point for our investigation since they demonstrate many of the difficulties involved in trying to determine precise relationships between a given set of Greek literary works and epic poetry. In some respects the Hymns are very similar to Homeric and Hesiodic epic, employing the same dactylic hexameter as well as the epic *Kunstsprache* with its attendant formulaic phrases, and at least some ancient authors even attributed various Hymns to Homer himself (e.g., Thucydides 3.104.4 names Homer as the author of our *Hymn to Apollo*). However, by the time of the Alexandrians the Hymns seem to have become disassociated somewhat from

Homer – though on what grounds is unknown – and the relative obscurity into which the poems eventually fell is indicated by their transmission in manuscripts that often include them with Hellenistic and other late poetry rather than alongside the rest of the Homeric corpus (Clay 1997: 489; cf. Allen et al. 1936: xi–lviii).

Any attempt at understanding the relationship between the Homeric Hymns and epic involves at least three important issues: the date of the Hymns, the Hymns' historical position within an Ionian epic or parallel poetic tradition, and their performance context within that tradition. Because both sufficient internal evidence and external testimonia are lacking, dating of the Hymns has been performed mainly on the basis of linguistic and stylistic features found in the four longest Hymns. Building upon and reacting to earlier studies by Zumbach (based on isolated linguistic forms and supposed later innovations (1955)), Allen et al. (based on digamma employment patterns (1936: xcvi–cix)), and Hoekstra (based on modifications in the Hymns' formulaic phraseology (1969)), Richard Janko (1982) has undertaken a most detailed examination of diachronic linguistic developments within the Hymns. And although objections have been raised concerning the overall methodology employed (see, e.g., Hoekstra 1986), his chronological ordering of the major Hymns (*Aphrodite*: 675 BCE, Delian portion of the *Apollo*: 660 BCE, *Demeter*: 640 BCE, Pythian portion of the *Apollo*: 585 BCE, *Hermes*: end of the sixth century BCE (all dates approximate)) has become more or less the standard that must be argued against. When the shorter poems are included, a range of dates for the corpus extends into at least the fifth century (West 2003b: 5) and possibly much further even into the second century or beyond (Clay 1997: 489). As a comparison, the approximate dates given by Janko for the *Iliad*, *Odyssey*, *Theogony*, and *Works and Days* are 740, 725, 675, and 660 BCE respectively.

Janko's analysis of the Hymns also provides a scheme for the poems' historical positions within the poetic traditions of early Greece. Previously, C. O. Pavese had suggested that the Hymns (with the exception of the Delian portion of the *Hymn to Apollo*) and poems of Hesiod formed a continental branch of rhapsodic poetry separate from, though parallel to, an Ionic branch of epic that gave rise to the epics of Homer (1972: 111–65; 1974; a summary and redefinition of terms is found in 1998: 73–84). Janko's stemma for the poetic traditions, however, is somewhat more complex. He similarly posits an Ionic branch including the *Iliad*, *Odyssey*, and the Delian portion of the *Hymn to Apollo*, but he places the *Hymn to Aphrodite* (along with the *Cypria*) in a Northern Aeolic branch of poetry and the rest of the Hymns and the works of Hesiod in a mainland tradition accepting of cross-influences from both the Ionic and Northern Aeolic branches (1982: 196–200). If nothing else, the existence of such divergent and complex theories on the development of the early Greek poetic traditions indicates just how difficult the precise relationships among these early texts are to define.

Even less well understood is the original compositional context surrounding the Hymns: were the poems composed orally or through the use of writing, and what function did the Hymns perform among their earliest audiences? Studies concerning the first of these issues – the degree to which writing influenced the composition of the Hymns – have usually involved quantitative approaches based on formulaic density (Notopoulos 1962; Pavese 1972: 199–230; Cantilena 1982; Janko 1982: 18–30), enjambement (Richardson 1974: 331–3; Clayman and van Nortwick 1977; Barnes 1979; Janko 1982: 30–3), or metrical irregularities (Janko 1982: 33–40). Such analyses have been able to show that the Hymns have a tendency toward the same characteristics as those found in poems produced through oral-formulaic composition; however, the small sample size of the Hymnic corpus makes any investigations of this type less reliable. Additionally, since about the 1980s, comparisons with other poetic traditions have made clear the difficulty in categorizing a work of verbal art as either oral or written, with many different levels of textual influence being possible, especially for works such as the Hymns that have ultimately been preserved only in written form, however they were first conceived. (See, for example, Foley 1990: ch. 1 (esp. pp. 5–8) on the concept of an "oral-derived text" or Lord 1995: 212–37 on the possibilities of a "transitional text.") Most scholars, though, are now willing to concede that the Hymns at least have their roots in oral traditional processes, even if it is uncertain how far removed from those beginnings the texts actually are.

But this tradition-based derivation for the Hymns also implies an oral performance context at some point in early Greece as well, and two sets of information concerning these poems are usually brought forward in this regard. First, we have the internal evidence of the poems, which often close with a request for favor from the divinity. These requests can be general in nature – asking for general prosperity or other vague favors – but they sometimes seem to refer to the specific performance venue at a contest or possibly a festival (e.g., Hymns 6 and 26 respectively). Twelve of the Hymns also close with formulaic variants of "I will take heed both for you and other singing," three conclude with "After beginning from you, I will pass over to another *hymnos*," and two (Hymns 31 and 32) refer specifically to a following song that will involve heroes and their famous deeds (see Clay 1997: 493). In 1795, F. A. Wolf paired these indications of subsequent singing related to the Hymns with two namings by Pindar (*Nemean* 2.3) and Thucydides (3.104, with specific reference to the *Apollo*) of such hymns as *prooimia* in order to theorize that the Hymns were originally preludes to recitations of Homeric epic performed during formal contests and festivals (Wolf 1795: 112–13), and this line of reasoning has dominated modern scholarship and remained the mainstream view on the matter. (Cf. West 2003b: 3–4, where this view is adopted without question.) However, Clay (1997: 495–8) has reasonably expressed caution concerning the prevailing view, since (1) Pindar's reference to *prooimia* was used to describe songs sung in honor of Zeus, and of our surviving corpus only one brief Hymn (23) is actually addressed to Zeus; (2) most Hymns referring to a subsequent song to be sung appear on linguistic and stylistic grounds to be rather late in composition; (3) *prooimion* can refer to prose texts as well as poetry and can be meant either as a prelude or a separate introductory composition; and (4) the existence of both long and short Hymns seems to indicate that there may have been different practical needs for performing such poems, and there may have therefore been several different types of occasions on which these Hymns were sung.

Obviously, much debate surrounds the relationship that existed between the Homeric Hymns and other epic, and accordingly a degree of subjectivity will always be involved in any investigations into the Hymns' stylistic or oral-formulaic qualities. One can argue that the preserved poems should "be conceived of as orally composed" (Pavese 1998: 73) and independent from works in the Homeric and Ionian tradition (pp. 73–86); or that the Hymns reflect a greater amount of written fixity, with poets being able to include specific textual allusions and editing techniques among poems (e.g., West 2003b: *passim*, esp. pp. 11–12 on *Apollo*); or that the Hymns are oral-derived texts dependent upon traditional techniques of signification and reception (e.g., J. Foley 1995: 136–80; Garner 1996: 370–1). However, as we shall see, such uncertainty concerning the exact interactions of epic and non-epic forms is the rule rather than the exception in ancient Greece.

Other Archaic Non-epic Poetry

In general, the scholars who have attempted to analyze the relationships that archaic lyric, iambic, and elegiac poetry maintained with epic have developed three main lines of inquiry, each of which has its own advantages and shortcomings. Two of these method-ologies involve direct comparisons of the non-epic poems with Homeric and other Greek hexametric poetry, with the first approach focusing on metrical developments in the different branches of poetry and the second examining non-epic poetic texts by means of intertextual parallels with Homer and Hesiod. One important result of the metrical analyses, which normally compare the various non-epic meters with the dactylic hexameter in terms of diachronic development, has been the variety of hypotheses that derive the hexameter from either a pherecratic prototype (Nagy 1974; with further refinements and responses to criticism in 1979b, 1990c: 439–64, 1996a, 1998) or a combination of other verse types (e.g., hemiepes and paroemiac (West 1973a and Haslam 1976) or the chori-ambic dimeter B plus pherecratean (Berg 1978)), with meter itself often seen as a by-product of traditional diction (Bowie 1981). However, even though adherents of these theories have used isolated formulaic phrases and regular dialectal variation to support the link between epic and non-epic forms during diachronic development processes, relatively little attention has been focused on the synchronic nature of the relationships between the different types of poetry.

The second method of analyzing the relationship between epic and non-epic poetries – that of exploring intertextuality between the different poetic types – assumes a fixed form for the Homeric (and with lesser importance Hesiodic) poems that was drawn upon by other authors in order to infuse their own poems with more meaning. From this perspec-tive, a Homeric phrase appearing in a lyric poem is said to be relying upon the lofty nature of epic to create a noble aesthetic within the isolated lyric poem as well, or to go even further, a scene in a lyric poem showing parallels with a particular Homeric episode is described as making direct reference to the fixed epic in an attempt to create a thematic link available to an audience steeped in the knowledge of the *Iliad* or *Odyssey*, even to the extent of knowing the content of individual lines. (Both types of analysis are exemplified in Rissman 1983 as they relate to Sappho; cf. Svenbro 1975.) Although such studies have been quite useful in compiling phrases and scenes common to epic and other poetic forms, the assumptions on which the method is based are difficult, as a fixed text of Homer (particularly with respect to individual lines) is quite unlikely for at least the earlier archaic poets, even if scenes and story lines are allowed as canonical at an early date. (Cf. S. West 1988; Janko 1992: 20–38, which include the further complications of regional variation and rhapsodic re-performance.)

The third method of investigating the relationship between early Greek epic and non-epic poetry has not relied directly upon a comparison between different poetic forms but has instead concentrated on the degree to which orality pervaded early Greek society in general. As was pointed out above, the dominant cultural mindset of the early Greeks was very much an oral one and the literacy that led to the eventual writing down of early poetic texts was a late-arriving phenomenon, especially in terms of dissemination among the general population of archaic Greece. Consequently, several scholars have realized the importance of oral performance for lyric, iambic, and elegiac poems that have reached us in textualized form, either by concentrating on the intent and themes of the works within the cultural context of pre-classical Greece (e.g., Nagy 1990a and 1990c) or by investi-gating the specific performance contexts for individual authors and poems (e.g., Gentili 1988). Through analyses of these sorts, an understanding of early non-epic poetry has developed that places it in an oral traditional context similar to that underlying the composition of the Homeric and other early Greek epics, and, accordingly, great strides have been made in determining the meaning of individual poems as received by their original audiences. Nevertheless, such studies have not usually gone so far as to consider the specific expressive means by which these poems achieved their full effects within such traditional arenas, and several scholars have even accepted the ramifications of a predom-inantly oral cultural outlook but persist in defining non-epic poems as consciously derivative of the epics in terms of phraseology or message (e.g., Page 1964a; Giannini 1973; Gentili 1988).

There is, however, a fourth possible approach toward archaic lyric, iambic, and elegiac poetry that builds upon each of the above methodologies but requires neither a hierarchical positioning of the different poetic branches in relation to epic nor a static, textualized status for any of the poems involved. Instead, investigations into the syntactic structuring, metrical irregularities, and repeating phraseology within the various types of non-epic poetry all seem to indicate that many of these poetic forms were greatly immersed in oral-formulaic traditions of their own, which paralleled and sometimes intersected with – though without ever becoming subordinate to – early Greek epic traditions. For example, just as the epic hexameter has been shown to have a dominant four-part structuring system that enables the poet to regularly employ traditional phraseology (Fränkel 1926, 1955; see further Foley 1990: 73–80; Russo 1997), so too can similar systems (consisting of either three or four phraseological units per line, depending on the metrical type) be seen at work in archaic elegiac, iambo-trochaic, and even Lesbian stanzaic verse (Garner 2003: 22–66). And in the same way that Parry showed that the modification and juxtaposition of epic formulae gave rise to metrical irregularities such as *brevis in longo* and *brevis in hiatu* (1971: 191–239), it can likewise be shown that epic correption involving short vowels occurs not only in epic but also within elegy for precisely the same reasons of formulaic composition (Garner 2003: 26–36, 61–4). Additional evidence for the traditional (and possibly oral) nature of non-epic composition can also be gleaned from recent studies of enjambement practices in such works (e.g., H. R. Barnes 1995 specifically on elegy).

Of course, no specific archaic Greek poem can ever be said definitively to have been composed orally, but investigations such as those listed above are making it increasingly more difficult to ignore the possibility of non-epic oral traditions enabling the production of works by authors such as Archilochus, Solon, and even Sappho. Hierarchical models of Greek poetry must therefore be adjusted, and similarities between epic and non-epic poems – either on a phraseological or thematic level – are probably better seen not as the result of intertextual allusion but as a manifestation of a much larger traditional and oral-formulaic phenomenon embedded within early Greek poetic culture.

Interestingly, however, by the end of the archaic period, a discernible change begins to takes place in this established setting for artistic composition, as many of the oral traditional features common in earlier poetry suddenly find little place in works by authors such as Pindar or Bacchylides and are instead replaced by a greater awareness of the artist's position within the historical context engendered by his poetic predecessors. At this point, it becomes possible not only to refer to Homer and Hesiod as the idealized personifications of the epic tradition they helped create in the past (cf. Nagy 1990c: 202) but also to agree with or react against specific messages they had conveyed. Thus, Pindar is able to refer to Homer by name three times and to the Homerids once: three of these four mentionings portray the earlier tradition in a positive light; however, the fourth instance (at *Nemean* 7.20–30) occurs as Pindar takes Homer to task for giving Odysseus more fame than he likely deserved, a feat that was possible because of the earlier poet's ability to deceive and seduce by means of "sweet words" and "cleverness." (Cf. also Stesichorus' rejection of the epic accounts of Helen's conveyance to Troy (frr. 192–3 PMG).) Such references require only a small degree of fixity (textualized or otherwise) for the Homeric corpus at this time, but it is clear that Pindar is using traditional material in order "to absorb it and supersede it" (Lamberton 1997: 40). Homer, Hesiod, and the epic tradition that they represent have become by the late sixth century the proponents of an established worldview and cultural outlook against which any new poetic idea must first be tested or compared (see Chapters 21–3, by Edwards, Slatkin, and Nelson).

Philosophy

A parallel development occurs in the Greek philosophical thought that was beginning to develop at about this same time in Ionia. Xenophanes of Colophon, a poet writing in the mid-sixth century, provides our earliest preserved references to Homer and Hesiod as representatives of their poetic tradition, and these mentionings occur only so that he can denounce the theological systems that these early poets had helped develop. According to Xenophanes, "Homer and Hesiod attributed to gods all the things which are shameless and worthy of blame among men, and they voiced aloud many of the gods' unjust deeds – stealing, adultery, and deception of each other" (fr. 11 DK). A half century later, the comments of Heraclitus are perhaps even harsher: although he was the wisest of the Greeks, Homer himself made mistakes concerning the knowledge of manifest things (fr. 56 DK) and was to be "thrown out of the contests and whipped" (fr. 42 DK), presumably because of the influence that traditional ideas held through performances in such arenas.

In his own time, Plato – a seeming admirer of Homer if his 150 or so quotes of the author are any indication (Richardson 1992: 34–5; cf. Howes 1895 and pseudo-Longinus *On the Sublime* 13.3–4) – also wished to do away with Homer and the hold that his poetic tradition had on people's minds. With specific references to the *Iliad* and the *Odyssey*, Plato describes Homer's works as dangerous because of their representation of death as an evil and of important characters as being able to be overcome by emotions; such depictions would be ineffective in shaping defenders of the city (*Rep.* 376e–383a; cf. Lamberton 1997: 36). Further, the mimetic nature of epic required a certain separation from the realities of life, and this removal caused such poetry to be useless as a tool for perceiving actual truth and (even worse) misleading in its claims (*Rep.* 595a–601b). Nowhere are Plato's views on the worthlessness of epic put forth more clearly than in his *Ion*, where a rhapsode skilled in performing Homer – who is represented as the best of all poets (530b, 531d) – professes himself to be an expert in the matters of which he sings, only to have Socrates show that in fact he knows nothing but to sing in an aesthetically pleasing and divinely inspired way. For Plato, then, as well as for Xenophanes and Heraclitus before him, epic poetry has become the traditional standard against which new claims to truth must be argued, and Homer himself has become the most common personification of this worldview.

However, this philosophical antagonism toward epic begins to fade even by the time of the next generation, and in Aristotle there is little trace of Plato's direct attacks against Homer. Aristotle does conclude in his *Poetics* that epic is inferior to tragedy, but nevertheless his admiration for Homer in particular is made clear not only by the more than 100 times he quotes the poet in his extant works (Richardson 1992: 36) but also by the fact that he attempted to rescue Homer from the toughest charges of his critics through a collection of *Homeric Problems*. Though the preserved remains of the collection cannot be trusted as the authentic work of Aristotle himself, it is clear that this collection set a precedent for later criticism by actually systematizing the methods that could be used to make sense of the details of the Homeric texts on historical, moral, or political grounds (Richardson 1992: 36–7; Lamberton 1997: 37). Additionally, as Lamberton (1997: 37) has pointed out, Aristotle often looked to the poetry of the past in order to find the seeds of philosophical thought that would be developed by later thinkers. Therefore, when Aristotle (*De an.* 427a) quotes Empedocles' statements on thought and perception and equates them to a similar statement from the *Iliad*, it seems as if Homer has become as much of a proto-philosopher as he was a poet. (Cf. also Cherniss 1935: 80.)

In turn, if ancient testimonia from authors such as Cicero and Plutarch can be believed, the early Stoics also took up this practice of attempting to find hidden philosophical truths in the works of early Greek poets, especially Homer and Hesiod. According to the usual understanding of Stoic practice, early poets were taken as having a correct understanding of the world, its physics, and its gods but then deliberately disguising this knowledge within epic narratives about unrelated topics. Stoics found it necessary to allegorically interpret these works – often with the help of etymologies – in order to demonstrate that Homer and his ilk were indeed proponents of Stoic thought. This traditional conception of how the Stoics proceeded has recently been called into question, as the Stoics may have been interested in understanding myths in general as allegories to be interpreted more than they were concerned with a single poet's treatment of them in a specific text (Long 1992). However, for most Stoics, epic undoubtedly constituted an invaluable source of information to be searched for hidden meanings and underlying truths concerning the world and its workings (see Lamberton 1997: 38). Clearly, epic poetry had been fully transformed from an early traditional model to be argued against into a representation of truth that must be searched carefully for the authoritative knowledge it embodied.

Historiography

The search for truth was also central to Greek historians, and epic poetry made itself felt in this arena as well (see Chapter 5, by Raaflaub). In the most general sense, epic provided several general traits that proved instrumental in the depiction of historical events: a focus on sources of causality, the mimetic representation of important events, large-scale character development for decision-making personalities, and even type-scene structures for the patterning of recurring actions such as dramatic speeches (Strasburger 1972). However, the precise relationship between epic and historiography varied greatly from writer to writer. With Herodotus, the debt owed to epic is especially clear in terms of his imagery, diction, and narrative structuring (Lateiner 1989: 19), with the result that even ancient critics noticed the similarities between Herodotus and Homer (e.g., [Long.] *On the Sublime* 13.3). (Cf. Aly 1921: 263–77, however, on the idea that such similarities may have been part of a larger cultural influence of epic rather than of direct influence from a single author or text.) Additionally, even Herodotus' cultural outlook and conceptual frame can be seen as inspired greatly by the conflicts of the *Iliad* and the *Odyssey*'s tightly constructed plot and interwoven travel tales (Lateiner 1989: 214).

Looking at specific passages that show the reliance of Herodotus on Homer, we can see that Herodotus' description at 2.148 of the Egyptian labyrinth takes its details from the depiction of Priam's palace in the *Iliad* and of Odysseus' palace in the *Odyssey*, and the nearby artificial Lake Moeris has as its model the Acheron as described at *Odyssey* 10.508ff. (Armayor 1978b). Similarly, Herodotus' catalogue of Xerxes' invading force (7.59ff.) seems to derive specifics of costuming, weaponry, and perhaps even numbers of the contingents involved from the catalogues given by Homer for the Greeks and Trojans in Book 2 of the *Iliad* (Armayor 1978a). But of course the passage that sets the stage for comparisons between epic and Herodotus is that which appears at the very beginning of the *Histories*. Herodotus' proem is essentially a prose imitation of epic proems in both form and substance; in it he names as his theme the great deeds of men and declares his goals of keeping these deeds and the men who performed them from losing their glory while also searching out the causes of the war that rose among them (Lateiner 1989: 41). The affinities with epic openings, especially the *Iliad*'s, are obvious.

However, even though Herodotus openly used Homer and other epic as a model for his own efforts, his stated views toward the historical claims of the early poets are actually quite antagonistic. Herodotus refers to Homer, Hesiod, and other early poets 21 times within his *Histories*, but he never endorses the truth behind their testimony and only once (4.29) quotes Homer to support a claim of his own (Lateiner 1989: 99). According to

Herodotus, poets fabricate details for their own purposes – inventing rather than research-ing – and they prefer what is suitable to what is accurate (2.23, 2.116–7, 3.115), and on some occasions their stories are unbelievable at their roots (e.g., 2.120 where he discusses the absurdity of risking an entire city's welfare over the case of a single woman Helen). (See further Neville 1977: 4–7.) Just as within the realm of philosophy, then, the first attitudes expressed toward epic in historiography are for the most part critical and reactionary in nature.

However, historiography's views toward the early poets also seem to soften somewhat quickly, and Thucydides is much less harsh toward epic than was Herodotus. Thucydides' linguistic debt to epic has been detailed by Smith (1900) and reminiscences of Homer can be found in specific passages (see, e.g., Frangoulidis 1993 and Mackie 1996 on the Sicilian narrative in Thuc. Book 6), but once again the most important relationship for Thucydi-des with the poets is in terms of their value as historical sources. Just as was Herodotus, Thucydides is always skeptical about the information provided in early poetry (e.g., 1.9.4, 1.10.3, 6.2.1) and believes that poets distort things in the name of art (1.21.1); however, as long as one applies critical tests concerning believability (1.20.1), the evidence of the poets can indeed be used as the foundation for a probable historical hypothesis (cf. Lateiner 1989: 99–100). The authority of epic has now been rescued from its detractors in yet another literary arena.

Tragedy

The issue of epic authority was also important on the tragic stage, with the topics found in epic constituting a large percentage of tragic composition as well. Estimates vary, but we will not be too far wrong if we suggest that approximately one-third of the plays put on by Aeschylus, Sophocles, and Euripides dealt with subjects figuring prominently within epic. (Cf. Gould 1983: 32–3; Farmer 1998: 24.) Nevertheless, playwrights seem to have avoided competing directly with the *Iliad* and *Odyssey* themselves, as many fewer plays are devoted to the specific topics covered by these poems as they exist today (Lamberton 1997: 41). Such reluctance to treat Homeric themes did little, however, to keep ancient critics from noticing what affinities of content still surfaced between the tragedians and Homer: Athenaeus provides the anecdotal claim that Aeschylus declared his tragedies to be "cuts taken from Homer's mighty dinners" (8.347e), and Diogenes Laertius judges Homer as the epic Sophocles and Sophocles as the tragic Homer (4.20), probably because of Sophocles' great interest in heroic behavior and Homeric character. (Cf. Easterling 1984: 1; Farmer 1998: 24.)

Further borrowing from epic may have been involved in the actual diction of the tragic poets (see, e.g., Sideras 1971; Garson 1985), but for modern scholars the primary focus of tragedy's relationship with epic material has been in the area of allusion. An ever-increas-ing number of studies have been directed at determining how the tragedians incorporated indirect references to epic texts within their own works in order to allow audience members to better interpret the action playing out in front of them, with one especially thoroughgoing analysis being that of Richard Garner (1990), who enumerates dozens of tragic passages that seem to involve reference to Homer. The range of subtlety involved in the allusions varies, but of special interest are the discovered patterns that (1) the *Iliad* is alluded to twice as often as the *Odyssey*, (2) the most common location for allusions is within dramatic speech, and (3) the epic passages most often referenced are Homeric similes (1990: 22–4).

Of course, the loss of much epic material as well as the changes that even Homer's epics have undergone since the classical period make it impossible to determine with certainty what constitutes an epic allusion that an average audience member would have been able to understand. Indeed, it is difficult to know even how classical playwrights and their audiences experienced epic in general. In his *Iphigenia at Aulis* Euripides refers to stories found "in the writing-tablets of the Pierian Muses" (*en deltois Pierisin*, 798), and it therefore seems likely that tragedians had texts of Homer and perhaps other poets at their disposal. Additionally, as Lamberton points out (1997: 42), it is likely that by this time elementary education in reading and writing had become reasonably widespread in Athens among the wealthy, and Plato makes it clear that such education was expected to include hexameter poetry (*Laws* 809e–810a); therefore, it is probable that not only playwrights but also many members of their audiences would have been well versed in at least Homer, probably Hesiod, and maybe many other poets, having an understanding of their poetry even beyond what would be gained simply by listening to contemporary rhapsodes perform. However, it is difficult to know what the exact contents of such educational texts might have been, and though they seem to have corresponded well with our received texts in terms of length and episode arrangement, there can be no doubt that individual lines still varied greatly from text to text at this time (Lamberton 1997: 33, 39).

Novel

Finally, at least a brief mention should be made of the Greek novel and the relationship that such post-classical works had with epic. B. P. Reardon has stated that "the *Odyssey* itself is the fountainhead of Greek romance" (1991: 6), and when one looks at the story-patterns of the Greek novels with their love interests, problematic journeys, and climactic reunions, it is hard not to see the resemblance between these Hellenistic works and their epic predecessor. Additionally, similar first-person narrative techniques can be seen within Odysseus' tale to the Phaeacians and sections of Achilles Tatius' work (Hägg 1971: 318); and Heliodorus' technique of beginning his work *in medias res* with an accompanying flashback also seems to have its model in the *Odyssey* (Reardon 1991: 40).

But because Greek novels were probably intended as lighter reading for the well educated (Bowie 1985: 128; Reardon 1989: 11), their authors also found it advantageous to interface with Homeric and Hesiodic material by means of epic quotations, allusions, and imitations. On one hand, Chariton represents a somewhat simplistic approach in his usage of epic material, with the majority of his approximately thirty quotations of Homer embedded organically into his narration as uncited substitutions for words that he might otherwise have written himself (Hägg 1971: 95). Nearly all of Chariton's quotations represent gnomic statements or other well-known selections from Homer's texts that any educated Greek would understand immediately. As a contrast, Heliodorus represents an author using epic material in a much more refined manner. Heliodorus also includes embedded quotations alongside cited references to epic within his novel, but he often further adapts epic material for his own purposes, for instance at 2.19 reversing an insulting Homeric verse concerning beggars (*Od.* 17.222) so that it instead praises the noble heroes of the romance (noted by Morgan (1989: 391 n. 43); see Garson 1975 for further examples). Both authors gain stylistic ornamentation and associative value from their epic usages, but Heliodorus' epic adaptations create a much richer text for learned interpretation.

Conclusion

Several other Greek literary types – for instance, comedy, oratory, or Hellenistic lyric – could also have found places in this discussion, but the above survey seems sufficient to provide a clear overall picture of the general sorts of relationships that developed among epic and various kinds of literature at different points in Greek history. In the archaic period, epic was but one of many competing forms of poetry that were performed orally, and the interactions among epic, hymnic, lyric, elegiac, and iambo-trochaic verse forms were likely to have been of a dynamic nature with parallel poetic traditions occasionally intersecting and reinforcing each other. By the end of the archaic period, however, the idea of a static epic tradition that represented an older view of the world was beginning to become entrenched, with the result that philosophers, historians, and even poets themselves started to react strongly against epic in terms of poetics, content, truth-value, or ideals. Gradually the antagonism toward Homer and Hesiod – the two poets most consistently chosen as embodiments of the fuller epic tradition – faded, and epic ultimately became used as a source that fed heightened intellectual activity throughout Greek society, whether it be on an aesthetic, historical, or hermeneutical level.

FURTHER READING

For further investigation of the issues involved in defining ancient genres, see the various essays in Depew and Obbink 2000b. An important study discussing the relationship between epic and the Homeric Hymns is Janko 1982, but see further the introductory remarks in the new edition of the Hymns by M. L. West 2003b as well as the discussions in Clay 1997 and J. Foley 1995: 136–80.

Outlines of the performative nature of archaic non-epic poetry can be found especially in Nagy 1990c and Gentili 1988, while examinations of the formulaic qualities of these poems are provided in Page 1964a and Giannini 1973.

For a brief but informative introduction to the reception of Homer in antiquity and its role in shaping philosophy and education throughout the Greek period, see Chapter 11, by Lamberton; also Lamberton 1997 and the bibliography therein. The debt of tragedy to Homeric epic – especially in terms of allusion – has been well illustrated by Richard Garner (1990).

Though historiography and the novel tend to be studied in more piecemeal fashion, as they relate to Greek epic, many editions and commentaries address concerns such as Homeric allusions in the later texts or differences between epic and later narrative techniques. Additionally, Hägg 1971, Lateiner 1989, and Reardon 1991 all contain several important insights pertinent to the study of these later genres as they look back at early Greek epic practices.

CHAPTER TWENTY-NINE

Homer's Post-classical Legacy

Casey Dué

Is it more reasonable to suppose that there was one supreme genius who created two such similar and stupendous works of art, or that there were many such poets, each master of the same grand style, and all having the same poetic purposes and all in control of the same poetic powers?

(John Scott, *Homer and his Influence*, p. 10)

Homeric Questions

I would like to begin my discussion of Homer's post-classical legacy by calling attention to the inherent difficulties in the very idea of Homer's post-classical legacy (see Chapter 42, by Kallendorf). Who or what is Homer? The quotation that I have chosen to lead off this chapter hints at the complexity of this question by proposing two equally plausible answers; which supposition is correct, and whether the question is even a valid one, depends on which scholar you ask. "Homer" is the traditional name assigned since antiquity to the author of the *Iliad* and *Odyssey*, and "author" is indeed one of the many personas attributed to Homer over the past 2,500 years. And while it is not the purpose of this chapter to address the so-called "Homeric Question" – that is, the questions surrounding the origin and authorship of the *Iliad* and *Odyssey* (see Chapter 21, by Edwards and Chapter 22, by Slatkin) – we must understand that "Homer" has over the years been many different things to many different people. Many scholars now equate Homer with an oral tradition, in which there were generations of singers who, using traditional techniques and language, could compose vast stretches of poetry in performance (see, e.g., Nagy 1996c and Foley 1999b). In the Middle Ages, Homer was not only the primal poet, the forerunner and teacher of Virgil, but also a sage who had access to divine wisdom, and who was believed to reveal sacred truths to those who could properly interpret his texts (Lamberton 1992). In antiquity, it was believed that a divinely inspired blind poet named Homer composed not only the *Iliad* and *Odyssey*, but all of the epic poetry in existence. He was, in essence, a culture hero, like Palamedes, who according to Greek tradition invented writing. Many different cities claimed to be the birthplace of Homer, and no one knew where he died. In fact, all of the biographical information that survives from antiquity about the figure of Homer conforms to known patterns of Greek folklore, mythology, and poetics, and has no basis in any reliable information preserved from the lifetime of such a man. In short, from the earliest references to Homer in antiquity this figure is already a mystery and a source of controversy, laid claim to by many groups, revered by all, but belonging to none (Graziosi 2002: 125).

The Transmission of Homer to the Middle Ages and Beyond

With such controversy surrounding the figure of Homer, about whom, if he ever existed, there is no certain information, the *Iliad* and *Odyssey* themselves must take center stage when we consider the topic of Homer's post-classical legacy. To be comprehensive, we should also consider the many other works attributed to Homer in antiquity, including all of the epic traditions encompassed by the Epic Cycle (such as the *Cypria* and the *Aethiopis*; see Chapter 24, by Burgess), the Homeric Hymns (see Chapter 28, by Garner), and even a comic poem entitled the *Margites* and a parody of the *Iliad* known as the *Battle of Frogs and Mice*. These works are all included in scholarly modern editions of Homeric poetry, such as the Oxford Classical Text edited by Monro and Allen, even though conventionally when we refer to "Homer," we usually mean the *Iliad* and *Odyssey*. In the earliest documented phases of the ancient Greek reception of Homer it was believed that Homer was a historical person, and that he invented and composed all of Greek heroic epic and the Homeric Hymns. (The didactic hexameter poetry of Hesiod was never attributed to Homer; two additional hexameter poets, often cited in antiquity in conjunction with Homer and Hesiod, are Orpheus and Musaeus; see Chapter 23, by Nelson.) At some point, however, the question arose whether one person could have composed all of the epics in existence, and the poems began to be separated into those thought to be composed by Homer – the *Iliad* and *Odyssey* – and those that were not. The fifth century BCE historian Herodotus, for example, tells us that Homer lived roughly 400 years before his own time, which would be about 825 BCE (Hdt. 2.53). At one point in his history he mentions the lost epic poem called the *Cypria* and notes that he does not think that it was composed by Homer (Hdt. 2.117).

Such debates did nothing to detract from Homer's status as the first and greatest of all poets: in antiquity Homer was often referred to as simply "the poet," without further qualification or specification, the inspiration of all subsequent poets (see Chapter 11, by Lamberton; also Harmon 1923). The performance of Homeric poetry was a central feature of one of the most important religious festivals of the ancient world, the Panathenaia in honor of Athena in Athens. The interpretation of Homeric poetry became one of the principal occupations of scholars and philosophers. At the great centers of learning in the Hellenistic world, Alexandria in Ptolemaic Egypt and Pergamum in Asia Minor, scholars and poets and philosophers such as Zenodotus, Aristophanes of Byzantium, Aristarchus, and Crates of Mallos devoted their lives to textual and literary criticism and composed scholarly commentaries on countless literary works. As Robert Browning has noted: "the impressive textual, grammatical, metrical, and lexigraphic studies of the great Alexandrian scholars laid the foundation on which all European literary and philological studies have been built" (1992: 134).

Homeric poetry was known to the ancient world primarily in performance. Most scholars would agree that in their earliest incarnations the poems that came to be our *Iliad* and *Odyssey* were composed orally and in the context of performance (see Chapter 13, by J. Foley and Chapter 4, by Jensen). Even after this tradition died out, the primary access to the poems for most people would have been in the performances of professional rhapsodes. How the poems came to be fixed in the form that we now have them and written down is still a matter of great controversy. But at some point the texts of the *Iliad* and *Odyssey* did become fixed, recorded, copied, and copied again and again for centuries (see Chapter 10, by Haslam). With the exception of a few ancient quotations that survive in other texts, Homeric papyri are the oldest surviving witnesses to the text of Homer. These papyrus documents are all fragmentary, and range in date from as early as the third century BCE to the seventh century CE. The vast majority of the fragments were discovered in Egypt, and now reside in collections located all over the world. The earliest quotations and papyrus fragments of Homeric poetry reveal that the texts of the *Iliad* and *Odyssey* were still somewhat fluid in antiquity. It is only in about 150 BCE that the texts became fixed in the form that we find in the medieval period. It is thought that the work of the Alexandrian scholars that was taking place at this time played an important role in establishing the relatively standardized text of Homer that is found in the medieval manuscripts of the *Iliad* and *Odyssey.*

After papyrus ceased to be used, the *Iliad* and *Odyssey* were copied onto parchment codices, which resemble modern books in their shape and construction (see Chapter 10, by Haslam). These manuscripts often contained not only the texts of the poems but also excerpts from the scholarly commentaries of antiquity, which were copied into their margins. These writings in the margins, known as "scholia," contain notes on the text that explain points of grammar, usage, the meaning of words, interpretation, and disputes about the authenticity of verses. The earliest extant and complete medieval manuscript of Homer, hand copied and assembled by Byzantine Greek scholars, is the tenth century CE manuscript of the *Iliad* known as the Venetus A (Marcianus Graecus 454, now located in Venice), and it is the one on which modern texts are primarily based. When Jean Baptiste Gaspard d'Ansse de Villoison first published the Venetus A codex in 1788, the wealth of ancient scholarship contained in the scholia sparked a revolution in Homeric studies, about which I will have more to say below. (For images of medieval manuscripts of Homer and more information about the Venetus A, ancient scholarship, and Homeric papyri, visit the Center for Hellenic Studies Multitext of Homer web site at www.stoa.org./chs.)

The first printed edition of the Greek text of the *Iliad* and *Odyssey* was made in Milan in 1488. Over the course of this more than 2000-year period of transmission, the figure of Homer and the texts of the *Iliad* and *Odyssey* were constantly reinterpreted. Already in the classical period many aspects of Homeric poetry needed explanation or could be found objectionable. The language of the poems is an artificial poetic dialect that spans centuries of time and immense geographical distances. Similarly the myths that the poems narrate are an accumulation of traditions from a vast array of times and places (see Chapter 3, by Edmunds). The representation of heroes and gods in Homeric epic troubled some thinkers and seemed at odds with contemporary values at various points in antiquity (see Chapter 7, by Louden). The figure of Socrates in the dialogues of the philosopher Plato, for example, attacks poetry and even bans it from his ideal state in Plato's *Republic.* The later Neoplatonic philosophers, however, embraced poetry and invoked Homer as a voice of authority from the past, a revealer of wisdom and truth (Lamberton 1992). One of the ways that this could be done was by reading Homer allegorically, a practice that can be documented as far back as the sixth century BCE and that would continue into the Middle Ages. In an allegorical reading, heroes and their adventures, gods, monsters, natural phenomena, and physical objects – in short, anything at all – can be read as symbols of deeper truths, available to those with the skills to interpret them. For Neoplatonists such as Porphyry, for example, the *Odyssey* came to be an allegory for the fate of souls and the struggle of one soul in particular through the realm of matter (Lamberton 1992: 127). Christian scholars were able to interpret the *Odyssey* along similar lines. In the notes to his 1615 translation, George Chapman captures both Neoplatonic and the Christian interpretations in his own articulation of what he saw to be the central allegory of the *Odyssey.*

Deciphering the intangling of the wisest in his affections and the torments that breed in every
pious mind; to be thereby hindered to arrive; so directly as he desires, at the proper and only
true natural country of every worthy man, whose haven is heaven and the next life, to which
this life is but a sea in continual aesture and vexation. (Underwood 1998: 23).

The Greek East and the Latin West

Homer was transmitted from antiquity to the Middle Ages and beyond not only through
the work of literary scholars and philosophers, but also through education. The *Iliad* and
Odyssey remained the centerpieces of Greek education from classical times through the
Byzantine empire (Browning 1992: 146). Allegorical interpretation of Homeric poetry
continued to be an important tool for reading the texts in the Christian Byzantine culture.
But even beyond allegory, Homer was cited as an authority alongside scripture in both
secular and Christian rhetoric (Browning 1992). As Christianity gained ascendancy in late
antiquity, pagan scholars had attempted to establish the Homeric texts as a kind of
authoritative scripture akin to the Christian texts. Such early influential figures as Augustine disapproved of most of pagan literature, but some early Christian scholars saw Homer
as a kind of visionary who had anticipated Christianity, and claimed that Homer had read
Moses and the prophets (Lamberton 1986: 242). As Robert Browning (1992) explains,
Byzantine Greeks saw Homeric poetry and Christianity as two important and interlocking
sides of their heritage, and for this reason no attempt was made to replace the *Iliad* and
Odyssey as the central school texts in the Greek East.

But while Homer's centrality remained constant in the Greek culture of the Byzantine
empire in the East, the Greek language and Greek literature along with it were slowly
disappearing in the Latin West. Augustine in the fourth century CE barely knew Greek,
and eventually the Greek texts could not be read at all in western Europe. The *Iliad* and
Odyssey would not be translated into Latin or English until the late fifteenth and sixteenth
centuries. Instead, Virgil's *Aeneid* (see Chapter 33, by Putnam), in which the Trojan hero
Aeneas narrates the fall of Troy in extensive flashbacks while on his journey to found
Rome, would be read and revered. A short verse summary of the Trojan War known as the
Ilias Latina was also well known. Virgil, however, knew not only the *Iliad* and *Odyssey*, but
also the poems of the Epic Cycle, and the *Aeneid* is infused with the myths and images of
Greek epic. In this way Virgil became an important transmitter of Greek epic traditions to
the Middle Ages. Other Latin poets, such as Catullus, Ovid (see Chapter 34, by Newlands), Propertius, and Seneca were likewise well versed in Greek epic and tragedy, and
through them the legend of Troy and the reputation of Homer was passed on.

Two Latin prose accounts of the Trojan War, both of which were translations of Greek
originals, also became important transmitters of the Trojan War myths. These texts,
known as the *Journal of the Trojan War* by Dictys of Crete (*Ephemeris belli Troiani*) and
the *History of the Destruction of Troy* by Dares the Phrygian (*Daretis Phrygii de excidio
Troiae historia*), are the products of an era in the Greek world known as the Second
Sophistic. In the literature of this period (around 60 to 230 CE), ancient readers were
treated to claims of a truer and more accurate account of the Trojan War – truer even than
the version they were used to reading in the epic poetry of the Homeric *Iliad* and *Odyssey*
(Dué and Nagy 2003: xv). Dictys of Crete and Dares the Phrygian both claimed to offer
eyewitness accounts of the Trojan War. The *Journal of the Trojan War*, attributed to Dictys
of Crete, purports to be a journal kept by a companion of the Cretan hero Idomeneus
during the Trojan War; Dares' account claims to be told by a Trojan priest (mentioned in
Iliad 5.9). These accounts not only directly contradict Homer in many places, but they
also include narratives that are not featured in the Homeric tradition. The dry, chronicle-
like style of these narratives, together with the absence of any divine intervention or

causality, made Dictys and Dares appear more factual and historical to the readers of late antiquity and the Middle Ages. The account attributed to Dares was particularly influential because of its Trojan perspective. (One of Rome's central myths was that their founding hero, Aeneas, was a Trojan. Later, the Goths, Franks, and English would all claim descent from Trojan heroes.) And so while the name of Homer remained attached to the legend of Troy as its premier poet, Virgil's *Aeneid* and the vastly divergent prose accounts attributed to Dares and Dictys became the primary means of transmitting the story of Troy after the disappearance of the Greek language in western Europe.

The Trojan War in Medieval Literature

Thus, in the Middle Ages and into the Renaissance, the tale of Troy is a very different one from that of the Homeric *Iliad*. The plight of the Trojans and the adventures of Aeneas after the war is over, as well as Aeneas' romance with the Carthaginian queen Dido, take center stage, as in Marlowe's *Dido, Queen of Carthage* (1593). (For more examples, see Chapter 42, by Kallendorf.) Just as influential as Virgil, however, would be the accounts of Dares and Dictys, which were the ultimate inspiration for the Trojan War romances of the Middle Ages. Around 1160 a Frenchman, Benoît de Ste Maure, composed his *Roman de Troie*, which tells the story of Troy in verse, basing it primarily on Dares and Dictys. Benoît's account transforms the Trojan warriors into chivalrous Christian knights and introduces for the first time the romance of Troilus and Briseida (later known as Cressida). In the *Iliad*, Troilus is mentioned as one of the sons of Priam and Hecuba; in another well-known myth, narrated in the Epic Cycle and depicted frequently in vase paintings, the Greek hero Achilles kills Troilus in an ambush. Briseis in the *Iliad* is the prize and concubine of Achilles. When Agamemnon takes Briseis for himself after being forced to give up his own prize Chryseis in Book 1 of the *Iliad*, Achilles' anger leads him to withdraw from battle and sets in motion the plot of the epic. In Benoît's account, however, Briseis is in no way connected with Achilles. Rather, she is the daughter of a Trojan priest living in the Greek camp. Although she is the lover of Troilus, she soon deserts him for the Greek warrior Diomedes. Her treachery becomes the nucleus of many subsequent adaptations in countless other medieval versions of the tale, including Boccaccio's *Il Filostrato* (where her name is changed to Criseida), Chaucer's *Troilus and Criseyde*, and Shakespeare's *Troilus and Cressida* (Shakespeare's only play on a Trojan theme).

Equally influential was the prose translation of Benoît into Latin, the *Historia Destructionis Troiae*, made by the Sicilian Guido delle Colonne (*ca.*1287). Other popular translations and adaptations of Benoît's romance and Colonne's prose translation of it include John Lydgate's English *Troy Book* (*ca.*1420) and Raoul Lefèvre's French *Recueil des Histoires de Troie* (1464). (For a more comprehensive list, see Appendix A in Scherer 1964.) William Caxton's translation of Lefèvre's work became the first book printed in English in 1474. It was reprinted many times and was an important source for Shakespeare. Finally, Boiardo's *Orlando Innamorato* (left unfinished in 1494) and Ariosto's *Orlando Furioso* (a continuation of Boiardo) blended several cycles of romance, including those of Charlemagne, Arthur, and Troy. Such romances, together with Virgil's *Aeneid*, in turn inspired much of Troy-themed music, opera, and art in the coming centuries. (See Chapter 42, by Kallendorf, and further below.)

These works all depart dramatically from the plot of the *Iliad*, and reveal a fundamental disconnect between the Latin and Greek worlds at this time. But although the *Iliad* and *Odyssey* were no longer known in Europe, the name of Homer lived on, indelibly associated with poetry and the genre of epic (see Chapter 1, by Martin). It was known that Homer was Virgil's teacher, so to speak, with the result that, as in antiquity, Homer was imagined as the primordial poet, the first in a long chain of inspired artists. Even more than that, Homer became, as we have seen, a sage and prophetic visionary, capable of concealing fundamental truths beneath the surface of his poetry. Because the texts of the *Iliad* and *Odyssey* were lost to western Europe, the Homer of the Middle Ages was that which could be gleaned through Plato, as transmitted by the writings of Neoplatonic philosophers and scholars. The scholars of the Middle Ages of course could not read Plato in the original Greek either. Instead they read the commentaries of previous scholars and the meager amount of Plato that was translated into Latin. The understanding of poetry, especially Homeric epic, that was transmitted through the Middle Ages was that poetry had many levels of meaning and required explication. The poet was a philosopher and a sage who cloaked wisdom and truth beneath a superficial veneer.

This is the Homer of Dante, who, as Robert Lamberton has pointed out, composed his *Divine Comedy* only a generation before the recovery of Greek in Europe and the first translations of Homer into Latin (Lamberton 1986: 283). Virgil is Dante's guide through hell and purgatory in the *Inferno* and *Purgatorio*, leaving him only as Dante ascends to heaven in the *Paradiso*, where, as a pagan, Virgil cannot go. For Dante, Homer is the "poeta sovrano" ("the sovereign poet," in canto 4 of the *Inferno*), even though Dante cannot have known the *Iliad* or *Odyssey* (and in fact he often departs from them when narrating the myths of the various Greek heroes). Dante sets himself up as the inheritor of the poetic craft from Virgil, who in turn inherited it from Homer. (See especially the narrator's words to Virgil in canto 2 of the *Inferno*, "you are my teacher, my master, and my guide," in the translation of Pinsky (1994).) In keeping with the Neoplatonic and Christian allegorical readings of Homer and Virgil that were standard in late antiquity and the Middle Ages, Dante's work is full of complex allegory and layers of meaning that go far beyond the surface narrative. The *Divine Comedy* is set up as the journey of a man who has strayed from the correct path into woods populated by savage beasts. Virgil saves this man (who is generally equated with Dante himself) by showing him the way out. The way is difficult and requires a descent, like those of Odysseus and Aeneas, through the Under-world before enlightenment can be achieved.

The Recovery of Homer

The dramatic date of Dante's *Divine Comedy* is 1300, and it was composed some years after that. Within a few years of this composition Italy would be the focal point for a renewed interest in Greek and Greek literature and the movement now known as the Renaissance. The fourteenth century Italian humanists Petrarch and Boccaccio were two early scholars interested in the recovery of the Greek language and the Homeric poems. Petrarch obtained Greek manuscripts of the poems from Byzantium and commissioned a word-by-word Latin translation from Leo Pilatus. This was followed by the translations into Latin by P. C. Decembrio and Lorenzo Valla in the fifteenth century. Within about a century of the first Greek printed editions of the *Iliad* and the *Odyssey* in 1488, the Homeric texts were beginning to regain their privileged place in the history of European literature; they would have a profound impact on visual and musical traditions as well.

By the middle of the sixteenth century, both prose and verse translations of the poems existed in French and Latin, and these were followed at the end of the century with translations into English. Although Shakespeare's *Troilus and Cressida* takes as its theme the medieval romance, Shakespeare also incorporates Homeric scenes that he may well have read in English, French, or Latin translations of the *Iliad*. In 1581, Arthur Hall published his *Ten Books of Homer's Iliads* in England, which were based on the French version of Hugues Salel. In 1598 George Chapman published the first of his enormously influential poetic translations, entitled *Seven Books of the Iliads of Homer, Prince of Poets* (books 1, 2, 7–11). This was followed by *Achilles' Shield*, also in 1598, *Twelve Books* in 1608, a complete translation of the *Iliad* in 1611, and *Homer's Odysses* (*ca.* 1615).

More than two centuries later Keats articulates the profound impact of Chapman's translations in his poem "On first looking into Chapman's Homer" (1820):

> Much have I travell'd in the realms of gold,
> And many goodly states and kingdoms seen;
> Round many western islands have I been
> Which bards in fealty to Apollo hold.
> Oft of one wide expanse had I been told
> That deep-brow'd Homer ruled as his demesne;
> Yet did I never breathe its pure serene
> Till I heard Chapman speak out loud and bold:
> Then felt I like some watcher of the skies
> When a new planet swims into his ken;
> Or like stout Cortez when with eagle eyes
> He star'd at the Pacific – and all his men
> Look'd at each other with a wild surmise –
> Silent, upon a peak in Darien.

In this poem knowledge of the Homeric texts by way of the translations of Chapman opens up an entirely new poetic world. Although by Keats's time the *Iliad* and *Odyssey* were available in many translations and Greek was being studied throughout Europe, Keats's poem could be interpreted as capturing the precise moment when, for England at least, Homer ceased to be the shadowy poet of the past, venerated but not familiar, and became instead a body of poetry that could be absorbed and understood.

Chapman was criticized by some for his often free translations of the Homeric texts, as would be Alexander Pope in the early eighteenth century. Both poets were attempting to capture what they saw to be the spirit of the original. Chapman believed that he had a special connection to Homer, which he articulated in Neoplatonist terms, that allowed him to surpass all other translators that had come before him in revealing the true meaning of the Homeric texts (Underwood 1998: 20–1). For Pope, translating Homer was a means of furthering his poetic career. His *Iliad* and *Odyssey*, like Chapman's, were attuned to the poetics of his day, and in the early eighteenth century it was Augustan Rome, not archaic Greece, that evoked admiration and emulation. Pope's challenge was to elevate the Homeric epics to the reputation of Virgil's *Aeneid*, which continued to be the standard by which epic was measured in Neoclassicist England. The result was two poems that are very different from their Greek originals. The renowned classicist Richard Bentley famously commented: "It is a pretty poem, Mr. Pope, but you must not call it Homer" (Underwood 1998: 32–3). Translation is necessarily an act of interpretation (see Chapter 12, by Armstrong), and interpretation is necessarily grounded in the aesthetics and cultural norms of one's age. Every generation since the Renaissance has produced new translations of Homer and commentaries that reflect both advancements in scholarship and current conceptions about poets and poetry.

Homer in Early English Literature

Whether in translation or in the original Greek, Homeric epic now became once again a model for poetic inspiration, particularly on an epic scale. Even when Greek could not be read in western Europe, Homer had always been associated with the idea of epic, and with its origins. When the *Iliad* and *Odyssey* were once again accessible, they in turn inspired new epics, some of which can only be said to be influenced by Homer in their ambitious epic scale, and others that more directly engage the Homeric texts. Spenser's unfinished *Faerie Queene* (1590–6) is a heavily allegorical epic that tells the adventures of knights in the court of the mythical Faerie Queene. Allusions to Troy are abundant, and its allegorical foundation owes a great deal to Neoplatonic readings of Homer and Virgil, but the poem is not directly dependent on Homer in any way.

The connection between Homeric epic and Milton's *Paradise Lost* (1667), which narrates the story of Adam and Eve, is not obvious at first glance, but the relationship is worth exploring. Milton signals a debt to Homer in his opening verses, which echo those of the *Iliad*. Milton studied Latin, Greek, and many other languages, and, influenced by his extensive knowledge of Homer and Virgil, is said to have conceived a desire to compose a great national epic very early in life. He fulfilled this plan only in retirement, by which point he was blind. Milton may well have perceived a bond between himself and Homer, who in antiquity was consistently portrayed as blind (Graziosi 2002: 125ff.). The belief in a blind Homer derives at least partially from the Homeric texts themselves, most notably the Homeric *Hymn to Apollo*, in which the narrator proclaims that he is a blind man from Chios, and *Odyssey*, Book 8, in which the blind poet Demodokos entertains the feasting Phaeacians: "him the muse had dearly loved, but she had given to him both good and evil, for though she had endowed him with a divine gift of song, she had robbed him of his eyesight" (*Od.* 8.63–4). But an equally important blind figure in Homer is Teiresias, the "seer" and prophet of Apollo whose ability to know the past and future and to interpret the will of the gods was directly linked to his blindness. The frontispiece to Chapman's translation of the *Odyssey* equates the blind Homer with the visionary Teiresias (see Lamberton 1986: 8–9). It is reasonable to suppose that Milton, whose *Paradise Lost* is both epic in form and scale and religious in content, thought that his blindness gave him special access to both poetic inspiration and divine knowledge. Indeed, Andrew Marvell, a close associate of Milton, explicitly associates Milton's blindness with Teiresias' prophetic abilities in his introductory poem, "On Paradise Lost."

Homer in Art

The representation of scenes from Homeric epic in European art began as early as the Middle Ages, in the form of wall paintings, illuminated manuscripts, tapestries, carved chests, and stained glass. Most of these works of art were not directly inspired by the *Iliad* or *Odyssey*, however. As in the case of European literature and music, lack of knowledge of the Greek language ensured that Virgil, Ovid, and the medieval romances were far more influential than the *Iliad* or *Odyssey* in medieval and early Renaissance art. It has often been observed that in the earliest Greek art that depicts scenes recognizable from Greek epic traditions, scenes from the Epic Cycle are far more common than those of the *Iliad* and *Odyssey* (see Snodgrass 1998). The same phenomenon can be observed in medieval and early Renaissance art. The most popular episodes are those that derive from the traditions of the Epic Cycle, known from Latin sources like Virgil and Ovid, and the adventures of the Trojan hero Aeneas, narrated in Virgil's *Aeneid*. The most frequently depicted were the myths that narrated the cause of the Trojan War, especially the Judgment of Paris and the love of Paris and Helen, and, after the Trojan War, the tragic love affair of Aeneas and Dido. As in literature, the popularity of Virgil's *Aeneid* and the central place of the Trojans in many European foundation myths led to an emphasis on Trojan heroes, not Greek. In the early fourteenth century, a Frenchman by the name of Jean de Longuyon wrote his enormously influential *Voeux du Paon* (*Vows of the Peacock*), in which he narrated the adventures and virtues of nine pagan, biblical, and Christian heroes, which he called the "Nine Worthies" (*neuf preux*). Among these was the Trojan prince Hektor. Hektor and the Nine Worthies were subsequently depicted in frescoes, painted ceilings, statues, tapestries, stained glass, and manuscripts throughout the fourteenth and fifteenth centuries.

By the sixteenth century, however, the *Iliad* and *Odyssey* were known in several languages, and works of art inspired by these two epics began to appear with more frequency. Francesco Primaticcio and his students carried out a series of fifty-eight scenes from the *Odyssey* (now lost) for the Galerie d'Ulysse in the palace of Fontainebleau; these scenes were later engraved and published by the Flemish artist Theodorus van Thulden in 1632. Nevertheless, the Epic Cycle (by way of Ovid and Virgil) and Virgil's *Aeneid* continued to be significant literary influences throughout the Renaissance and beyond. The works of Raphael (1483–1520) and Peter Paul Rubens (1577–1640) are good illustrations of this trend. Raphael painted a *Young Man Rescuing an Old* (detail of the *Fire in the Borgo*), thought to be inspired by the story of Aeneas and Anchises. Also attributed to Raphael are designs (now lost) for tapestries and ceramics, including a *Judgment of Paris* and an *Abduction of Helen*. Rubens worked approximately a century later. Drawing on Greek epic traditions, he painted his *Judgment of Paris*, *Odysseus and Nausicaa*, *Marriage of Peleus and Thetis*, and *Polyphemus*, and indebted to Virgil's *Aeneid* are his *Dido and Aeneas* and *Death of Dido*. In addition to these paintings Rubens produced eight oil sketches for tapestry cartoons of the life of Achilles. The eight episodes spanned the full range of known ancient literary sources for Achilles' life, and included *Achilles Dipped in the Styx*, *The Education of Achilles*, *Achilles in Scyros*, *The Anger of Achilles*, *Thetis Receiving the Armor of Achilles from Hephaestus*, *The Death of Hector*, *Briseis Returned to Achilles*, and *The Death of Achilles*.

Of course art is rarely a simple illustration of a literary work, and often no one source can be pinpointed as the source of an artist's inspiration. The Renaissance, however, was a time in which the works of classical antiquity were being held up as models for painters, sculptors, and poets. Even two centuries later, European art was still profoundly influenced by neoclassicism. Jacques-Louis David (1748–1825) rose to prominence with such neoclassical paintings as the *Funeral of Patroclus* (1778), *Hector* (1778), and *Patroclus* (1780), which he presented upon his arrival in Paris in 1781 for membership in the French Academy. Two years later David became a full member of the Academy when he exhibited his renowned *Andromache Mourning Hector* (1783, Figure 29.1). In this painting the corpse of Hektor, wreathed in laurel, is laid out on his bed. Andromache sits at his side stretching out her arm in a gesture of lament, while the young Astyanax reaches up to her as if attempting to comfort her. On a candelabrum there is written in Greek verses 725–7 of *Iliad* 24: "Husband, you have perished, cut off from your life-force, and you leave me a widow in the halls. And our son is still very much a child, the one whom you and I, ill-fated, bore . . . " Carved in relief on the bed are famous scenes from the *Iliad*: the farewell of Hektor and Andromache (narrated in *Iliad* 6) and the killing of Hektor by Achilles (narrated in *Iliad* 22). David's painting therefore alludes directly to the *Iliad* in a variety of ways. In 1788 David completed another classically themed painting, *The Loves of Paris and Helen*. This painting may likewise depict a scene from the *Iliad*. Paris and Helen are painted in brilliant colors alone together on a couch. At first glance we might assume that this is the moment in Sparta before the war when Helen and Paris fall in love. Helen's downcast gaze, however, seems to indicate reluctance to be with Paris. If this is the case, the painting could represent a scene from *Iliad* 3, in which Aphrodite compels Helen to join Paris in their bedroom after Paris' unsuccessful duel against Menelaos.

By the time of David's death in 1825 the neoclassicist fervor in Europe had diminished considerably and the Romantic movement had gained ascendancy in art and literature. Whereas the neoclassicists promoted the timeless and universal standards of classical literature and art, the Romantics, decrying the rigid constraints of rationalism, emphasized

Figure 29.1   Jaccques-Louis David, *Andromache Mourning Hector* (1783). Photo: Erich Lessing/Art
Resource, NY.

the power of emotion and argued that each generation must find its own, original forms of
expression. Nevertheless, many of David's students defended neoclassicism against the
Romantics, and for this reason David's influence continued to be felt for another half
century (Lee 2002: 321). Jean-Auguste-Dominique Ingres (1780–1867) was one of
David's students at the turn of the century. Early in his career he won the prestigious
Prix de Rome with *The Ambassadors of Agamemnon at the Tent of Achilles* (1801).
Like David's *Andromache Mourning Hector*, this painting is intertextual with the *Iliad*
in that it depicts a scene known primarily from the *Iliad* and not the Latin or medieval
romance traditions. And although the taking of Briseis by Agamemnon was related in
Ovid's *Heroides*, other works point to the primacy of Homer in the literary influences on
Ingres. In the *Iliad*, Achilles withdraws from battle, outraged and dishonored by the
taking of Briseis, his prize of war. Achilles then asks his mother Thetis, who is a goddess, to
convince Zeus to honor him by giving aid to the Trojans in his absence. Ingres's *Thetis
Imploring Jupiter to Honor Achilles* (1811) depicts Thetis in abject supplication of an all-
powerful Zeus. In addition to these Iliadic scenes (both of which allude to Book 1 of the
Iliad), Ingres also painted an *Aphrodite Wounded by Diomedes* (1805), an event narrated in
Iliad 5.

But perhaps the best known and most programmatic of Ingres's neoclassical paintings is the monumental *Apotheosis of Homer* (1827, Figure 29.2), commissioned for the ceiling of the Egyptian antiquities room in the Louvre, and later taken down and displayed vertically. In this painting, a blind Homer sits enthroned on high before a temple as a winged Victory crowns him with laurel. At his feet are allegorical representations of the *Iliad* (identified by her sword) and *Odyssey* (identified by her oar). Homer is surrounded and worshipped by forty-six figures of poets, musicians, artists, philosophers, lawgivers, and statesmen from antiquity up to the Renaissance. Among the figures are Orpheus, Hesiod, Sappho, Pindar, Aeschylus, Euripides, Sophocles, Pisistratus, Phidias, Pericles, Alcibiades, Herodotus, Demosthenes, Socrates, Plato, Aristotle, Aesop, Alexander the Great, Aristarchus, Virgil, Dante, Michaelangelo, Raphael, Shakespeare, and Mozart. The structural composition of the *Apotheosis of Homer* pays homage to Raphael by combining two of Raphael's most celebrated frescoes in the Vatican palace, *The School of Athens* (1509), which depicts Plato and Aristotle surrounded by the great philosophers of antiquity, and *Parnassus* (1509–10), in which Apollo is the central figure, surrounded by poets ranging from Homer and Sappho to Dante and Petrarch. (Ingres is also likely to have known the ancient relief sculpture by Archelaos of Priene, in which Homer is seated on a throne and holds a sceptre; this relief was published in 1683 by Gisbert Cuper. On Raphael, Ingres, and Cuper, see Clay 2004: 1–2.) The arrangement of the figures in both Raphael's *Parnassus* and Ingres's *Apotheosis of Homer* suggests an unbroken continuum from archaic Greece to the present day, while at the same time asserting the primacy of the classical models. In both paintings, moreover, the blind figure of Homer reigns supreme

Figure 29.2   Jean-Auguste-Dominique Ingres, *Apotheosis of Homer* (1827). Photo: Erich Lessing/Art Resource, NY.

among poets. Homer's position is elevated above the others, and in Raphael's painting, Homer turns his head up to the sky in a pose that suggests divine inspiration. A strikingly similar image of Homer would later appear as the frontispiece to Chapman's translation of the *Odyssey*. This Homer is the sage and visionary of Neoplatonism, whose special connection with the gods elevates him above all other poets, philosophers, and artists and confers on him his own kind of divinity by way of the immortality of his poetry.

Although the Romantic movement brought an end to the supremacy of classical literature and art in European culture, Homeric poetry never lost its privileged place as the cornerstone of western civilization. Artists of every era of the nineteenth and twentieth centuries have drawn inspiration from the *Iliad*, *Odyssey*, and the larger classical tradition. Auguste Rodin (1840–1917) sculpted in several versions and sizes *Polyphemus* (the one-eyed Cyclops who terrorizes Odysseus and his men in the *Odyssey*), *Hecuba*, and *The Education of Achilles*. Pierre-Auguste Renoir (1841–1919) painted and sculpted several versions of *The Judgment of Paris*, and Pablo Picasso (1881–1973) painted an *Ulysses and the Sirens* (1946).

One of the most interesting of modern attempts to engage Homeric poetry in art can be found in the work of Giorgio de Chirico (1888–1978). Chirico is considered to be an influential forerunner of the Surrealists and co-inventor of "metaphysical" painting, a kind of painting that, while rendered with topographic and perspective detail, is full of dream-like symbols and which replaces the human form with an image that resembles a tailor's dummy, the *manichino* (Gimferrer 1988). One of Chirico's earliest metaphysical paintings, *The Enigma of the Oracle* (1909), depicts a cloaked figure standing in a high location that, reminiscent of Delphi, overlooks a town and, in the distance, the sea. The cloaked figure, in the far left of the painting, turns away from the viewer. The right side of the painting is taken up by a statue, whose head is just visible over a black curtain. The painting's most immediate subject is the Delphic oracle of Apollo, but we know from the artist's own writings that *The Enigma of the Oracle* was inspired by Arnold Böcklin's *Ulysses and Calypso* (1883), and by reading Homer: "I was reading. A few lines of Homer captivated me. Odysseus on Calypso's island. I read some of the descriptions, and then the picture stood there in my mind's eye. I felt that I had found something at last" (Schmeid 2002: 15).

The Enigma of the Oracle was one of three paintings that Chirico presented in the first public showing of his work, at the Salon d'Automne in Paris, 1912. Chirico went on to paint over the course of the next seven years the series of works that he termed "metaphysical." In 1919 Chirico's work took on a controversial new direction that harkened back to the classical forms of the Renaissance, but throughout his career and up until his death in 1978 he often returned to the *manichino* and the themes of his metaphysical paintings. Among these are several different versions of a painting that Chirico first produced in 1917, *Hector and Andromache* (Figure 29.3). Chirico, moreover, continued to be influenced by Böcklin; he painted two versions of a *Ulysses* in 1922 and 1924 that recall Böcklin's 1869 work, *Ulysses on the Seashore*. More than 40 years later, Chirico painted a vastly different, far more youthful version of Odysseus in his *The Return of Ulysses* (1968). In his recent book on Chirico, Wieland Schmeid describes *The Return of Ulysses* in this way:

> Ulysses [= Odysseus] is depicted rowing a small boat through restless waves. But these are not the waves of the sea; they are ripples on a pond that has somehow found its way into a living room. Has he returned home from an ocean voyage, to relive in memory the dangers he has faced and mastered? Or were his adventures nothing but a dream, and he has never left the home of his yearnings? We do not know. (Schmeid 2002: 111)

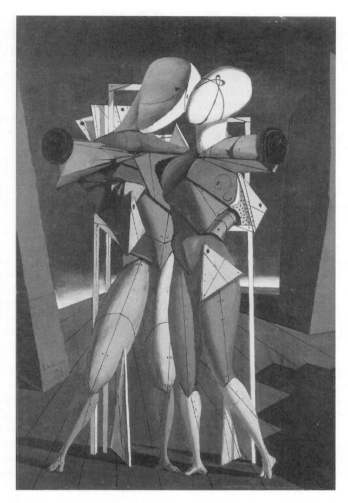

Figure 29.3   Giorgio de Chirico, *Hector and Andromache* (1917). Photo: Scala/Art Resource, NY.

Before leaving the topic of Homer in European art, mention must be made of the artist John Flaxman (1775–1826), who, as Richard Armstrong has noted, singlehandedly established an iconographic tradition for the *Iliad* and *Odyssey* (see Armstrong 2000b). Flaxman's illustrations, which have been subsequently printed in countless translations of Homer, are thought to have been conceived of as drawings prepatory to a larger sculptural work. They were engraved and published by Tommaso Piroli in 1793, and a second 1805 edition contained further engravings by William Blake. In his own day Flaxman's drawings were extremely influential; such painters as David, Ingres, and Francisco Goya are all indebted in various ways to Flaxman. More recently the drawings have been appreciated primarily for their illustrative value, and continue to be the archetype for most modern illustrations of the *Iliad* and *Odyssey* (Armstrong 2000b: 34–5).

The Tale of Troy in Opera

In addition to the revival of classical forms of literature and art the Renaissance also saw the birth of opera, which from its beginnings drew heavily on classical myth for its plots. As in art, the medieval romances and the Greek epic traditions that were transmitted through the work of Virgil and other Roman poets were far more influential than the *Iliad* or *Odyssey*. The work that is generally considered the first opera is the *Euridice* (1600) by Jacopo Peri (and set to verse by Ottavio Rinuccini). Peri, who also composed a *Dafne* three years earlier, was most likely indebted to the Latin hexameter poetry of Virgil's *Georgics* and Ovid's *Metamorphoses* and not any Greek version of the tale. Other dramas had been sung to music before the *Eurydice*, including Lodovico Dolce's tragedy *The Trojans*, which was sung to music composed by Claudio Merulo in 1566. Dolce was an Italian who had edited a new edition of Dante in 1555; his knowledge of the story of the Trojan War was probably heavily indebted to Dante and ultimately Virgil. Drawing on the traditions of the Epic Cycle, Carlo Caproli's *The Wedding of Peleus and Thetis* was the first opera heard in Paris in 1654. Other popular opera themes that derive from the Epic Cycle are the love of Paris and Helen and the sacrifice of Iphigeneia. Purcell's *Dido and Aeneas* (produced *ca.*1689) was the earlist English opera on a Trojan theme. Berlioz's *The Trojans* (composed 1853–9) was likewise heavily influenced by Virgil's *Aeneid*, as Berlioz recalls in his memoirs. And as recently as 1955, William Walton debuted his *Troilus and Cressida* (based primarily on Chaucer). The *Iliad* and *Odyssey* were not without impact in music, however. Several operas have been based on the *Odyssey*, including *The Return of Ulysses to his Homeland* (1640) by Claudio Monteverdi (1567–1643), *Ulysses* (1703) by François Rebel (1701–75), *Penelope* (1785) by Niccolo Piccinni (1728–1800), *Penelope* (1795) by Domenico Cimarosa (1749–1801), and *Penelope* (1913) by Gabriel Fauré (1845–1924).

It would be far beyond the scope of this essay to trace the many manifestations of Homeric influence in modern European culture and I refer the reader to the more comprehensive treatments in, for example, Stanford 1963, Scherer 1964, Finsler 1973, and Burrow 1993. Needless to say, from the Renaissance onwards the presence of Homer is felt in all aspects of literature, music, and art. Increasingly, the idea of Homer as a visionary sage, the universally praised and yet shadowy first and best poet on whom all future poets depend, came to be replaced by a familiarity with the *Iliad* and *Odyssey* themselves that allowed for imitation, allusion, and intertextuality. But familiarity with the texts raised many difficult questions for poets and scholars whose previous understanding of epic was firmly rooted in Virgil's *Aeneid*. The more one got to know Homer, the more alien he became.

Homeric Scholarship and the Question of Genius

The reappearance of the Greek epics in western Europe and the revival of interest in Greek language and literature that this sparked ushered in an age of marked neoclassicism, in which Greek literature was venerated as the premier form of literary expression. In the seventeenth and eighteenth centuries, however, Homeric poetry became the focus of debates concerning originality and genius, the nature of poets and poetry, and the relationship of the poet to his or her culture. Homeric poetry played a central role in the *querelle des anciens et des modernes* ("quarrel between Ancients and Moderns") in the late seventeenth century, in which literary scholars in France and England debated the current debt to antiquity and the extent to which contemporary poets should imitate classical models. Translation became a polemical act, by which one argued for one side or the other. As we have seen, both Chapman's and Pope's translations are as much their own poetic expression as they are "Homer's." Pope explicitly discussed his translations in terms of "fire" and "invention," which were concepts that pervaded discussions of poetry and genius at the time (Simonsuuri 1979).

In this context an interest in vernacular literature began to develop and early theories about the orality of the Homeric poems were formulated, together with the so-called "Homeric Question." Homer was now thought to be a genius, but one who was born and who composed in a primitive culture. Or alternatively, Homer was the genius who had collected the songs of a primitive people and joined them into a whole. Bentley objected that Pope's *Iliad* was not "Homer" largely because it was too sophisticated and too much like Virgil (Underwood 1998: 33). Bentley was among a group of scholars who had begun to question traditional views about Homer as poet and to argue that the Homeric poems were composed orally and transmitted over the course of many generations by reciters known as rhapsodes. The culture that had given birth to the Homeric epics soon became the center of intense inquiry. In 1730, Giambattista Vico published his massive work, *La scienza nuova seconda*, which contained within it a book-long discussion entitled "Della discoverta del vero Omero" ("On the discovery of the true Homer"). Vico argued that poetry is the expression of the culture that produces the poet and that the Homeric epics represent the collective mind of the Greeks. Vico was also arguing against an understanding of Homer, prevalent since antiquity, that made him a theologian and philosopher, a revealer of sacred truths. Vico claimed that poets do not possess esoteric wisdom, but are a product of their culture, and that Homer was a man of the people who had inherited an oral tradition based on historical events in the distant past.

Vico's views were enormously influential, and coincided with a growing interest in folk poetry, particularly English and Scottish ballads, which were being collected and circulated by scholars interested in these questions. In 1760 James Macpherson published *Fragments of Ancient Poetry Collected in the Highlands of Scotland, and Translated from the Gallic or Erse Language*, followed by *Fingal, An Ancient Epic* in 1761 and *Temora, An Epic Poem* in 1763. Macpherson attributed this body of poetry to a third-century Gaelic warrior turned bard named Ossian. The poems enchanted England and Europe and had a significant impact on subsequent literature, ushering in almost single-handedly the Romantic movement. It was later discovered that Macpherson's "translations" were largely poems of his own creation, based on songs and tales that he had collected in trips to the Highlands in 1760 and 1761. Macpherson was born and raised in the Scottish Highlands and was well versed in the Gaelic mythological traditions that were still vibrant during his lifetime, even as the English were vigorously attempting to suppress Highland culture. It had been Macpherson's goal when he set out in 1760 to collect and translate a Highland epic akin to the Homeric *Iliad*. He soon came to believe, however, that the poetry he was able to collect had been corrupted over the many centuries since the lifetime of Ossian, and he therefore felt compelled to reconstruct this epic on the basis of the sum total of his knowledge of the tradition (Stafford 1996). The similarities between the legendary figure of Ossian and the conception of Homer at this time are striking. Both were seen to be primitive folk poets of "original genius" whose poems were transmitted orally for centuries and became corrupted through time, and both were thought to embody the creativity of a primitive culture.

In Germany, the philosopher and critic Johann Gottfried von Herder developed ideas similar to Vico's, and, inspired by the Ossianic poems of Macpherson, published his own collection of *Volkslieder* in 1778–9, which contained German, Nordic, and English songs. (Herder then in turn inspired the Grimm brothers in the collection of German folktales.) Herder is well known for his theories about the close relationship between thought and language and the ties between language and culture, theories which inspired scholarly interest in a variety of folk traditions, including dance, music, and art. He became close friends with the German poet Goethe, and it is under Herder's influence that Goethe and others composed the works that came to be known as the *Sturm und Drang* (storm and stress), the predecessor of the German Romantic movement. These poets rejected the formal constraints of neoclassicism in favor of natural enthusiasm, which they saw to be exemplified by Homeric poetry.

Thus between the early Renaissance and the late eighteenth century the figure of Homer had been transformed into a variety of incarnations in both academic and literary circles, and was consistently the focal point of poetic controversy. The Homeric Question was now in the process of being formulated, and it was in this context that Villoison published the tenth-century Venetus A codex manuscript of the *Iliad* of Homer (codex Marcianus Graecus 454) in 1788. As I have noted above, this manuscript contains a wealth of scholia, those marginal and interlinear notes that accompany the text of Homer in a wide variety of manuscripts and that derive ultimately from the Alexandrian scholars of antiquity. With the publication of the Venetus A, Homeric scholars of the late eighteenth century suddenly found themselves blessed with a treasure trove of information about what scholars of the second century BCE knew about Homer. It seemed that it would now be possible to reconstruct Homer and Homer's original text, and all of the Homeric questions could be solved (Nagy 1997: 106).

This was the hope and belief of Villoison, the editor of the *editio princeps* of the Venetus A, who viewed the scholia as an authoritative witness to an authoritative edition of Homer, constructed by the premier textual critic of Homer in antiquity, Aristarchus. But the views of Friedrich August Wolf, published in 1795 in his *Prolegomena ad Homerum*, proved to be more influential. Wolf questioned the authoritativeness of the scholia and the work of the Alexandrian critics. Wolf argued, moreover, that the Homeric poems had been transmitted by rhapsodes in an oral tradition that had corrupted the texts irreparably over time. For these reasons, the true and genuine text of Homer could never be recovered. Wolf produced his own editions of the Greek texts of the *Iliad* and *Odyssey*, relying heavily on the medieval transmission of the two poems and disregarding much of the textual work of the Alexandrians. Wolf's editions established a kind of medieval vulgate that continues to be followed to this day in modern printed editions: the line numbers in use by all modern editors are those of the highly conservative "Wolfian vulgate."

The debates associated with the Homeric Question only intensified after publication of the Venetus A and continued to dominate scholarly discussions of Homer in the nineteenth century. The "question" (which was, in reality, many questions) became increasingly concerned with authorship. Did the *Iliad* and *Odyssey* have the same author? If so, when did he live? If not, how did the poems come to be in the form that we now have them? Fierce opposition arose between scholars who believed in Homer, a single genius and creator of the two foundational epics of western civilization, and those who saw the Homeric texts as the products of potentially many poets composing over many generations. These Unitarians on the one hand and Analysts on the other, armed with all of the tools of philology, scrutinized the poems and produced learned readings in defense of variations on these two positions. Analysts further debated among themselves about the age and authenticity of various portions of the poems, as they searched for the oldest and "most Homeric" segments.

Another important branch of the Homeric Question in the nineteenth century was a concern with the relationship between myth, epic, and history (see Chapter 5, by Raaflaub). Did the Trojan War take place? If so, how closely does the *Iliad* reflect what actually happened? In the late nineteenth century a wealthy businessman, Heinrich Schliemann, astonished the world when he uncovered the remains of a Bronze Age Troy in a mound known as Hisarlik in northwestern Turkey, and soon after, the wealthy Bronze

Age citadel in Mycenae in mainland Greece, where Agamemnon was said to have ruled (see Chapter 9, by Sherratt). Schliemann had set out from the beginning to find the Troy of the Homeric poems, and quite literally bulldozed his way towards that goal, destroying most of what would turn out to be Bronze Age Troy. Later, when he uncovered human remains covered in gold and wearing a gold mask in a Mycenaean tomb, he sent a telegram to the king of Greece, proclaiming that he had looked upon the face of Agamemnon. Schliemann's methodology and naiveté have been fiercely criticized by modern archaeologists and historians, but his accomplishment, namely the discovery of a previously unknown Bronze Age world not unlike that depicted in the Homeric epics – the world now known as Mycenaean Greece – had a lasting and profound impact on our understanding of the *Iliad* and *Odyssey* and the historical context in which they were generated.

Old and New Questions

Homeric scholarship over the past century has in many ways advanced our understanding of the Homeric poems. Schliemann's excavations gave rise to modern archaeology, which has demonstrated the many connections between material culture and the objects described in the poems (see Chapter 9, by Sherratt). Linguists have analyzed the dialect layers present in the language of the poems, and have shown that some phrases and poetic concepts have traveled across geographical boundaries and go back at least as far as the Bronze Age. In the 1930s an American classicist named Milman Parry and his assistant, Albert Lord, went to Yugoslavia, where they collected 12,544 songs, stories, and conversations from 169 singers of the still flourishing South Slavic epic song tradition. These singers composed extremely long epic poems *in performance*. To do this they drew on a vast storehouse of traditional themes and phrases that worked within the meter or rhythm of the poetry. They used what are called formulae, instead of individual words, to build each verse as they went along. Parry and Lord applied this discovery to the Homeric epics, and formulated the thesis that the language of the Homeric poems had evolved over time within an oral epic song tradition, and that the *Iliad* and *Odyssey* were generated in performance. (For more on Parry and Lord and the South Slavic heroic song tradition, see Chapters 13, by J. Foley and Chapter 4, by Jensen.)

The developments of archaeology, linguistics, philology, comparative literature, anthropology, and literary theory have not solved the Homeric questions, however (see Nagy 1996b). Debates about the historicity of the Trojan War persist as excavations at the site of Troy continue to take place, and eminent Homerists still debate whether or not a man named Homer ever existed, and if he did, what his role was in the creation of the *Iliad* and *Odyssey*. Nevertheless, the centrality of the poems in western literature remains unquestioned. The Trojan War is an archetypal conflict that in greater and lesser degrees infuses modern war epics, tales of betrayed love, and depictions of wartime suffering, while the *Odyssey* provides a paradigm for physical and spiritual journeys and tales of homecoming. James Joyce's *Ulysses* (1922), set in Dublin in 1904 and regarded as one of the greatest novels of all time, is constructed around powerful thematic and structural allusions to the *Odyssey*; other important literary adaptations and transformations include Derek Walcott's *Omeros* and Nikos Kazantzakis's *The Odyssey: A Modern Sequel*. In addition to these works, many works of modern popular fiction explore the story of Troy from new angles. A good example is Charles Frazier's *Cold Mountain*, which chronicles a soldier's long and tumultuous journey home after being injured in the Civil War. Increasingly, the tale of Troy is being told from the point of view of women in such novels as *Cassandra*, by Christa Wolf, *Daughter of Troy*, by Sarah Franklin, and *According to Helen* by Florence Wallin. These developments in fiction reflect as well the feminist scholarship of the last three decades of the twentieth century, which focuses on such characters as Penelope, Helen, Andromache, and Briseis as well as the song traditions of women that are featured in the poems (Dué 2002 and Chapter 8, by H. Foley). Finally, ever since the invention of cinema the *Iliad*, *Odyssey*, and other tales from Greek myth have been adapted for the big screen, including most recently the Coen brothers' striking adaptation of the *Odyssey*, *O Brother, Where Art Thou?* (2000), and the epic blockbuster *Troy* (2004), which narrates the Trojan War from the theft of Helen to the sack of Troy.

FURTHER READING

For a general introduction to the transmission of Greek literature from antiquity to the Renaissance, see Reynolds and Wilson's *Scribes and Scholars: A Guide to the Transmission of Greek and Latin Literature* (1991).

On the reception of Homeric poetry in antiquity and beyond, see Howard Clarke's *Homer's Readers: A Historical Introduction to the Iliad and Odyssey* (1981), Robert Lamberton and John J. Keaney's *Homer's Ancient Readers: The Hermeneutics of Greek Epic's Earliest Exegetes* (1992), and Barbara Graziosi's *Inventing Homer: The Early Reception of Epic* (2002).

For more on the legacy of Homeric poetry in European literature, music, and art see Margaret Scherer's *The Legends of Troy in Art and Literature* (1964), Georg Finsler's *Homer in der Neuzeit von Dante bis Goethe* (1973) and Diane Thompson's *The Trojan War: Literature and Legends from the Bronze Age to the Present* (2003).

On the "Homeric Question," see Gregory Nagy's *Homeric Questions* (1996b) and Frank Turner's "The Homeric Question," in Morris and Powell 1997: 123–45.

PART IV

Roman Epic

CHAPTER THIRTY

The Origins and Essence
of Roman Epic

Joseph Farrell

Questions about the origins of Roman epic are inseparable from a number of much larger problems. These include debates about the nature of all literary and artistic activity at Rome, and about the role of foreign and particularly Greek influence in the formation and development of Roman culture. Confronting these problems is made difficult not only by the complexity of the issues involved, but by a paucity of evidence for the early period. In such a situation, there is merit simply in asking the proper questions, in determining what answers might be at least possible, and in clearly distinguishing reasonable inference from willful speculation. In this essay, I shall sketch the main lines of discussion and indicate what I believe have been the most productive contributions. But I should like to stress at the outset that this is an area in which one deals, even when on more solid ground, in probabilities or possibilities rather than certainties.

According to one view, the Roman people had no literature to speak of until 240 BCE (see Chapter 31, by Goldberg). In that year, as Cicero tells us (*Brut.* 72–3), the Senate commissioned Livius Andronicus, a Greek freedman originally from Tarentum, to compose a drama. Livius subsequently wrote other dramas that were, to judge from their titles and scanty remains, based on Greek originals; and, according to Livy (27.37.7), he was in 207 commissioned by the state a second time to compose a hymn in honor of Juno Regina. Other writers began to follow his lead, mainly producing tragedies and comedies modeled on Greek originals. For the purposes of this essay, however, Livius' most important work was an epic poem in the form of a translation of Homer's *Odyssey*. Unfortunately, we cannot say when he composed it, or indeed why: unlike his dramatic and choral works, the epic is linked to no state occasion, and it seems possible that it was conceived as a school text, which it was at least in Horace's boyhood (*Ep.* 2.1.69–71). Gnaeus Naevius and then Quintus Ennius succeeded Livius, devoting the bulk of their effort to writing for the stage, but each of them also producing an epic, though these were as different from Livius' epic as they were from each other.

Livius' epic *Odusia*, as a translation of an original Greek text, resembles his dramatic compositions rather closely. Accordingly, those who stress Livius' role as an innovator regard not only epic but poetry in general as a Greek import that arrived in Rome along with a rapidly expanding overseas empire. The idea that Livius introduced something quite new at Rome receives support from the fact that we have no earlier examples of poetry like his, nor can we name a single Roman poet before his time. In addition, this idea is one that the Romans themselves espoused. Around 100 BCE, for instance, the poet Porcius Licinus declared that the Muse had arrived in Rome during the Second Punic War (fr. 1, Courtney 1993: 83–6). This is essentially the same attitude expressed years later by Horace that, when the Romans captured Greece, the captive turned the tables on her uncouth conqueror and taught him something about the fine arts (*Ep.* 2.1.156–63). Some version of this account appears in practically all histories of Latin literature. Its basic message is that Rome before the mid-third century BCE was a rude and uncultured place, politically and militarily powerful but not yet Hellenized and so deficient in aesthetics. When diplomacy and warfare brought members of the Roman elite into contact with the Greek world (the story goes), some of these men became receptive to what this alien but sophisticated and highly attractive culture had to offer. The existence of such a potential audience enabled a few individual geniuses such as Livius to launch a cultural revolution that completely overwhelmed whatever native artistic traditions there had been. In what follows, I will refer to this line of argument as the *protos heuretes* (first discoverer) approach.

On a different view, Roman interest in literature begins much earlier. Again it is Livy (7.2) who mentions dramatic performances more than a century before Livius Andronicus. And again, the occasion is a national emergency – a plague in 364 BCE – and on this occasion as well plays (*ludi scaenici*) are performed, this time by players summoned from Etruria. As for heroic narrative, Cicero (*Brut.* 75; cf. *Tusc.* 4.2.3) and Varro (apud Nonium s.v. *assa voce*, Lindsay 1913: 76) cite the testimony of Cato the Elder concerning an ancient custom of singing songs about the virtues of great men. Quintilian (*Inst.* 1.10.20) and Valerius Maximus (*Mem.* 2.1.10) make general statements in the same vein. The setting of these songs was the banquet, and the performers were, according to Cato, members of the aristocracy. We have no actual example of these *carmina convivalia* (as they have come to be called), but by invoking parallels from other cultures, some scholars have imagined this institution as analogous to an oral tradition of heroic poetry. This theory was developed by and has traditionally been more popular among historians and historiographers (some of whom also count among its most committed opponents) to explain how later Roman historians got their information about the earliest phases of Roman history – particularly before the sack of the city by the Gauls in 390, when it is presumed that any written records would have been destroyed. But if such a tradition did exist, it is reasonable to hypothesize that its influence was also felt by Livius and later epic poets, and that we might detect such influence in the scraps of archaic epic that do survive. The custom of singing at banquets might conceivably provide a performance context for some at least of the early epics, and one might even ask how long the custom of poetic performances at private or public banquets continued, and what the existence of such institutions could tell us about Roman cultural and social life. It is seldom imagined that these *carmina* would stand comparison by traditional literary criteria with the products of later periods, but by losing them we would also have lost access to evidence about the literary and cultural values that obtained in Rome before the mid-third century BCE. The loss of this material might have caused scholars to misconstrue certain aspects of cultural life in the later Republican period as well. In what follows, I will refer to this line of argument as the "bardic culture" approach.

These are on the surface two very different views on the origins of Roman epic. It is worth noting, however, that they are actually incompatible only in an extreme form. When one says that there was "no literature to speak of" before Livius, this can hardly mean that there was none whatsoever, and few would take this position. The question rather is whether any trace of pre-Livian literary traditions survives in the literature that has come down to us. Specifically, if there was an archaic tradition of heroic song, is the character of this tradition reflected to any extent in the literary productions of Livius, Naevius, and later epic poets? It is on this point that scholars remain divided, both on methodological and ideological grounds and on more basic historical issues.

Ideological Issues (1): The "Bardic Culture" Approach

Interpretation is an inescapably circular process, since interpreters always start from assumptions that may themselves be subject to interrogation and contestation. Where there is less evidence to work with, these unspoken assumptions tend to take on even greater importance than usual. This has certainly been true in the study of archaic Roman culture, particularly where the question of literature is concerned.

In general, the "bardic culture" approach has received more criticism on the grounds of its methodological and cultural assumptions than has the *protos heuretes* approach. In some sense this is because those assumptions are rooted in Romantic attitudes towards the past from which Classical Studies as a discipline has been at pains to distance itself. The remarkable success achieved in the study of early Greek epic has played a role here as well. From both internal and comparative evidence, we have learned a enormous amount about the compositional techniques, the performance culture, the social role, and even the literary antecedents of early Greek epic and other genres. Both as an example of what can be done, and also as a specific comparandum, this Greek material stands as a challenge to students of early Roman epic. But of course the evidentiary situations are entirely different. Where students of Greek epic begin with the complete texts of two monumental epics, our earliest Roman examples survive only in fragments. These fragments are individually quite brief, collectively few in absolute terms, and in the case of Livius and Naevius insufficient even to give us a clear picture of how much has been lost. This scanty pattern of survival is bound up with the fact that the reception of these works in antiquity did not accord them a very high status – again in sharp contrast to Homer, who at all periods of Greek cultural history enjoys the highest possible prestige. Thus the wealth of ancillary material available to the student of early Greek epic in the form of textual studies, commentary, and other forms of criticism does not exist for pre-Virgilian epic except in a very attenuated form.

This disparity between the Greek and Roman contexts creates a second difficulty. Having so little evidence to illustrate early Roman epic, but an abundance for early Greek epic, the temptation is strong to fill in some of the gaps on the basis of what we know about Homer. The Romans, like the Greeks, were speakers of an Indo-European language. Comparative evidence suggests that the archaic poetry of several Indo-European languages inherited features from a common tradition, just as the languages themselves inherited features of the parent speech (see Chapter 2, by Katz). It is then at least possible that the Romans inherited such poetic institutions as well. If we know anything about early Roman culture, we know that it valued military prowess. So, when we hear of Cato describing a tradition of songs having to do with the deeds of bygone days, it becomes very tempting to see this as attesting a pre-Livian tradition of Roman heroic poetry.

Here the situation becomes very much more complex. Scholarly opinions about the value of Cato's testimony vary widely. My summary to this point represents perhaps the most optimistic reception of Cato. Although Cato had previously been cited by others, it was B. G. Niebuhr (1776–1831) who effectively introduced these passages into modern historiographical discussion (Momigliano 1957). The context of this intervention is decisive. Niebuhr's theory of archaic Roman *Heldenlieder,* which he directly compared to material such as the *Nibelungenlied,* was formulated within a culture inclined to think in terms of the nineteenth-century nation-state and to understand the essential character of such states from what were supposed to be the primitive characteristics of their ancestors.

It is obvious that in such a climate, Romanists were in difficulties since our evidence about the origins of Roman society is relatively poor (and it was much worse in Niebuhr's time). Cato's *carmina convivalia* thus answered both a perceived historical and a real historiographical problem: by explaining how later witnesses got access to the originary phase of Roman cultural history, it became possible to provide the modern historian with information about the character of the Roman people in the all-important primitive phase of their existence. Not only scholars, but the educated public provided a plentiful audience both for the theory itself and for new cultural productions based thereon. The citation in this context of Macaulay's *Lays of Ancient Rome* (1842) is so apposite that it has become de rigueur. But there was opposition as well: in fact, no less a personage than Mommsen dedicated a portion of his limitless energies to denouncing Niebuhr, and for many years the prevailing view on the fully-developed theory was one of skepticism (Momigliano 1957: 113).

Ideological Issues (2): The *Protos Heuretes* Approach

Objections to the "bardic culture" approach are based in part on the perceived desire of its proponents to assimilate archaic Roman culture to other cultures, especially Greek culture, about which we are better informed. These objections are perhaps more readily visible to critics than are comparable objections to the *protos heuretes* approach, which appears to involve a more modest interpretation of the available evidence and, as I have said, is endorsed in very clear terms by several ancient authorities as well. But the *protos heuretes* approach is not without its hidden biases. In the first place, we know that the ancients tended to posit the existence of a *protos heuretes* even in areas where modern scholars are absolutely sure that there was none, and to exaggerate the importance of the earliest known practitioners in any given field. It is perfectly possible that Livius Andronicus did play a crucially important role in the development of Latin literature (hardly a daring proposition), but that he did not start everything in motion by bringing the very first literature to what had been a cultural wasteland. More specifically, if we ask why a witness such as Horace might prefer a narrative that stresses the role of an individual genius in bringing Latin versions of Greek poetry to a public needing to be convinced of the value of literature, two reasons come immediately to mind. First, since Horace too was a purveyor of Latinate versions of Greek poetic genres to Roman audiences (as he boasts at *Carm.* 3.30.10–14, *Ep.* 1.19.23–34), he will have regarded Livius as establishing a pattern of behavior in which he himself was much involved. If Livius in Horace's judgment was not much of a poet, then he at least inaugurated a process that would be brought to perfection in Horace's own time, in part by Horace himself. The second reason why this model may have appealed to Horace is that in Rome literature never achieved the status that it had traditionally enjoyed in Greek culture. There is thus a sense in which Livius' battle to make a case for literature within the Roman system of values was never finished, but had to be waged continuously by all those who succeeded him, Horace included.

Thus at least Horace's interest in the *protos heuretes* approach is not utterly innocent or transparent. If we turn to modern scholars, the situation is much the same. As Alessandro Barchiesi has well noted, the great German Latinist Friedrich Leo began his *Geschichte der römischen Literatur* with the statement that "Western civilization depends on Graeco-Roman culture, and so does the spread of Christianity through Roman and German peoples ... Roman culture is the spiritual link between the ancient and the modern worlds ... The dynamics of civilization was from East to West" (Leo 1913: 1). On this view, the crucial fact about Roman literature is that it is "the first literature dependent on the Greeks, the first secondary, non home-grown literature" (p. 3). Accordingly, Leo emphasized Livius' role precisely as that of a translator and thus as "the beginner of the first derivative literature of our cultural universe" (p. 59). Leo's approach is so familiar from constant repetition in literary histories down to the present day that it is easy to lose sight of the fact that he, like Horace, uses this conception of Livius to support an effort of self-justification. But, as Barchiesi shrewdly observes, "One could argue that Latin studies have been focusing on translation and transference, not on appropriation and reuse, because the discipline was trying to (re)establish itself (through many an inferiority complex) as the missing link between German Hellenophilia and European national identities" (Barchiesi 2002b). One might extend this argument, *mutatis mutandis*, to the United States, where a sense that "the dynamics of civilization moves from East to West" is taken as an article of faith in American national mythology, but where the measurement of cultural attainments against Old World standards is always fraught with anxiety. And while I have not yet seen a history of Latin literature that takes this line, one can imagine without too much trouble how a version of the *protos heuretes* approach might be updated in terms of postcolonial theory.

It is clear then that neither of our two approaches offers access to evidence that is unmediated by ancient or modern desires and ambitions. Of course, congruency with one or another set of transcultural agendas does not in itself undermine a particular line of interpretation. Nevertheless anyone who approaches this material would do well to bear these issues in mind.

Historical Issues (1): The *Protos Heuretes* Approach

Quite apart from the various filters of cultural desire through which interpreters view the primary and comparative evidence, there are issues of historical interpretation that do not always receive full consideration.

Here I begin with the *protos heuretes* approach. Supporters of this theory tend to exaggerate the poverty of Roman cultural life before the mid-third century. In fact, the dossier of Roman accomplishments in the early period, familiar as it is, remains impressive. By the end of the sixth century, Rome boasted, among other important structures, the largest temple in Italy, that of Jupiter on the Capitoline. Perhaps also in the sixth century but at all events by the early fourth, when the Republican city walls were completed, Rome was by far the largest fortified urban area in Italy. By the end of fourth century, construction had begun on a system of roads that became the most extensive and most technically advanced in the world, and on a system of aqueducts that went well beyond the need to provide the city with water, being clearly intended to accomplish this task in the most conspicuous and impressive way possible. On this evidence, Rome was obviously not backward in terms of material culture. Of course, it is a cliché to say that the Romans were engineers and soldiers, not artists and poets, but none of the monuments just listed was without an important aesthetic dimension. Finally, even if the city had been a backwater, it would be difficult to imagine that the Romans had no literature of any kind; and, as a matter of fact, we can say with certainty that they did in the archaic period have a religious, legal, and annalistic literature. So the conditions necessary to support an imaginative literature of some importance would seem to have been in place.

Beyond this, there is nothing intrisically unlikely about Cato's testimony concerning the *carmina convivalia*, which would fit very easily into such a milieu. Therefore, the idea that Rome was completely uncultivated and unlettered prior to the time when Livius wrote his *Odusia* is a tendentious caricature.

However, if we conceive of our task as combing through the surviving literature for native Roman characteristics inherited from the archaic period, we may be on the wrong track. If the archaic Romans were not uncultivated philistines, neither were they completely un-Hellenized. Almost everything we know about the sociopolitical structure of archaic Rome suggests the influence of Greek institutions, particularly that of the polis itself. The transition from a regal period to one of Republican government parallels the Greek phenomenon that produced first tyrannies and then different forms of oligarchic, democratic, or mixed governments in Greek cities. More generally, Hellenization begins throughout most of the Italian peninsula during the period of Greek colonization, that is, as early as the eighth century (Malkin 1998). New analyses of settlement patterns, foundation narratives of individual cities, mythographic evidence, and archaeological finds and the social practices associated with them all suggest that characteristic elements of Hellenism were part of a common culture familiar to the elite of practically all Italian cities. Among those Greek cultural institutions of literary character that were widely dispersed in archaic Italy we find, specifically, the theater, the symposium, and Homer.

These points are stressed by critics of the *protos heuretes* approach, who have developed updated theories of the relationship between pre- and post-Livian culture. Some continue to argue, in the manner of Niebuhr, for a continuous performance tradition concerned with the heroic deeds of earlier times; they focus either on theatrical performance (Gentili 1977; Zorzetti 1980; Wiseman 1994, 1995, 1998) or on symposiastic settings (Zorzetti 1990; Rüpke 2001b). A full discussion of the origins of the Roman theater is beyond the scope of this essay, but it is a topic that is obviously related to the history of Roman epic. Rome's first epic poets, as I have mentioned, were primarily dramatists who turned out tragedies and comedies year after year, but produced just one epic each. It is therefore necessary to see third- and second-century epic as having taken shape within a literary context dominated by drama. But in a very important sense, the history of theater is bedeviled by the very same questions and paucity of evidence that complicates the study of epic. And, while there have been learned and imaginative efforts to establish the existence and estimate the character of a theatrical culture at Rome from the earliest times, Nicholas Horsfall's objection to these efforts has never, so far as I can see, been answered convincingly:

> Scholars have realized for over a century now that the suviving accounts of the origins of drama in central Italy are substantially of Varronian origin and that behind Varro there stands above all the account of Eratosthenes of the origins of Greek comedy... Our standard texts on the origin of the Roman theatre repeat, then, what remains a first-century BC reconstruction, heavily influenced by the research undertaken a couple of centuries previously on the origins of Attic drama. (Horsfall 1994: 66–8)

At any rate, the history of theater does not provide an independent point of comparison from which one might draw inferences about the history of epic. Rather the two phenomena are subject to exactly the same methodological and evidentiary problems.

Besides the theater, the symposium has recently been suggested as a setting for Roman literary performance in connection with ambitiously revisionist arguments about Roman literary culture. On this view, a "musical culture" of recitation and performance flourished at Rome at least to the time of the first epic poets and perhaps to the end of the first century BCE, when writing and reading began to supplant singing, reciting, and listening as the principal ways of experiencing poetry (Zorzetti 1990; Dupont 1999). Of course the *carmina convivalia* have been adduced in support of this line of argument. But the chronology and perhaps the existence of this tradition are uncertain. As I have mentioned, very few scholars are willing to deny its existence, but just when and for how long did it flourish? This question turns on a point of elementary interpretation of the Latin text that says that these performances took place, according to Cicero's paraphrase of Cato, "multis saeculis ante suam aetatem" (*Brut.* 75). The normal translation of this phrase would be "many generations before his [Cato's] own time," and would mean that

Cato had never witnessed such a performance, but was reporting on the tradition as a matter of hearsay, if not indeed making the whole thing up. However, Niebuhr took the phrase as evidence that these performances took place "*for* many generations *down to* Cato's own time" – a most unlikely interpretation, in my view, but others have followed his lead.

There is another point, however, that is crucial for our interests. Even the most ambitious of recent efforts to build on Cato's testimony regarding the *carmina convivalia* agree about one thing: these poems were not epics. Both Cato and modern proponents emphasize the Greek-style symposia as the relevant settings for these *carmina*. If the comparison is exact, then it is more likely that the *carmina convivalia* were not epic, but rather lyric or other melic poetry, not unlike the *skolia* that are familiar as Greek banquet songs (Zorzetti 1991). If this is true, then Cato's report concerning the *carmina convivalia*, even if it could be taken as evidence of a tradition that flourished right down to Cato's own day, would be only indirectly relevant to our interest in specifically epic poetry.

The case of Homer presents a different aspect. Here we can say with certainty that Homer was known in Italy from a very early period (Malkin 1998), and one expert has written about the adoption of a "Homeric life-style" in central Italy by the eighth century BCE (Ridgway 1988). Even without taking into consideration the individual scenes that may be viewed as part of a Homeric or a theatrical tradition (if this distinction is indeed to be observed in such cases), cycles of wall paintings that allude to the structure of the *Iliad* and *Odyssey*, and that in some cases even draw comparisons between epic literature and events from archaic history, point unmistakably to the central place of Homer in elite Italian culture (Farrell 2004). Indeed, the institutions of Homeric poetry and the symposium seem to converge in some places. We know that Etruscan aristocratic tombs were venues for ritual banqueting, and that some of them were decorated with scenes from Homer and the Epic Cycle (Brilliant 1984). It happens of course that we are much better informed about funeral customs than we are about how people actually lived in the archaic period, and it is an open question how far we can go in drawing inferences from the one sphere about the other. But in the Latin city of Ficana the same implements that characterize the symposium, and that have been found in burials, have also turned up in habitation sites (Rathje 1983, 1990). We can then imagine residents of archaic Latium taking part in Greek-style symposia, and it is not unreasonable to suppose that these occasions would have involved songs of some sort. We do not know whether these occasions took place in rooms decorated with the same sort of Homeric scenes that we find in some of the tombs, but the pattern of inference between burial and habitation sites makes this seem at least possible. It is difficult to imagine that banquets held in the presence of such paintings would not have featured some comment on the scenes represented. But even if existing evidence does not permit us confidently to reconstruct actual performances of the Homeric epics in Roman symposia, Homer is plentifully represented in the material culture of central Italy in the archaic period. For these reasons, the idea that Livius Andronicus introduced Roman readers to Homer and so introduced Hellenic literary culture to Rome has come to seem hopelessly simplistic and badly in need of correction.

Historical Issues (2): The "Bardic Culture" Approach

When we turn to a critique of the "bardic culture" approach, however, we find a comparable set of historical issues. Some of these are simply the converse of problems attached to the *protos heuretes* model. Thus, while our sources depict archaic Rome as a city of culture where Greek influence was very much a factor, the literary tradition, which is by far our most articulate record of political and social life in this period, consists of sources who wrote long after the events that they describe and that are obviously contaminated by Greek narrative traditions. It is certain that Roman historians from time to time assimilated their own accounts to those in their Greek models, both in unimportant details but perhaps in fundamental respects as well. It is therefore impossible to trust the literary tradition alone, since it may anachronistically project a late and more completely Hellenized perspective back on to the early period.

The material record, though less articulate than our literary sources and less focused on Rome itself, does tend to support the idea of early, decisively important Greek influence. Such evidence cuts in two directions, since it indicates on the one hand that Livius' translation will not have found many Roman readers who were unacquainted with Greek culture or indeed with Homer, while on the other hand it greatly compromises the idea of a pristine tradition of heroic poetry in Latin. There are in addition very large gaps in what this record has to tell us. We know for instance, as I have just noted, that the Etruscans painted Homeric cycles on some of their more impressive tombs, and that the tombs themselves were equipped as banqueting spaces. We also know that essentially similar cycles of wall painting appear in (especially) the dining rooms of Roman houses centuries later than the Etruscan tombs (Andreae 1962). It seems reasonable and economical to assume that the Etruscan tombs and the Roman houses belong to a continuous tradition, but we cannot be sure that this is the case.

Finally, there is the material evidence concerning symposiums at Ficana, which creates a strong temptation to assume that if such things took place at a relatively small and unimportant town such as this, they would certainly have been found in Rome, the leading city of the area. But this assumption is far from secure. In the first place, the symposium itself is a malleable institution that the Greeks imported from the Near East before exporting it in turn to Italy (Murray 1990). In Etruria, it appears that well-born women reclined at table along with men, a custom that would have seemed barbarous to the Greeks. About any other adaptations that may have been made we know almost nothing. It is tempting to assume that the Homeric decorations of some rooms reflects the literary element of Italian symposia with some accuracy, but a similar assumption would have eighteenth-century Frenchmen reciting classical Chinese poetry in their drawing rooms. So caution is certainly needed. As for drawing inferences between Ficana and Rome, we know very well that in the late second and early first centuries some of the "hill towns" of Latium, celebrated by Roman writers as repositories of old-fashioned virtue, were more visibly and spectacularly Hellenized than the capital. One thinks in particular of the astonishing sanctuaries at places like Praeneste, Tibur, and Anxur, which eventually served as models for projects that only later began to be built at Rome (Hanson 1959). Evidence such as this suggests that the process of "Hellenization" in Rome was far from linear, and that we would be in error to assume that Rome was always in the vanguard rather than following the lead of other Italian towns.

In addition to these issues, there are more specific problems that bear on our subject but that cannot be solved with confidence. This is not the place to discuss them in full, but it is worthwhile at least to list them for the reader's convenience:

Position of epic in the system of genres. Advocates of the *protos heuretes* approach tend to conflate two facts. One is that Livius is supposed to have founded Roman literature. The other is that he wrote a translation of the *Odyssey*. These are very different things. Livius' first work was a play, and the bulk of his oeuvre is theatrical. He was later recognized for composing a hymn, which was performed, like his plays, in public on a state occasion. We do not know, as I have noted above, when he wrote his epic, or why. Naevius too was a prolific dramatist, and Ennius not only wrote plays but introduced several other genres to Latin literature. In other words, it is far from obvious that epic poetry was the most important genre in archaic Roman literature. It is only with Ennius that we begin to see the idea emerge that the composition of an epic might become the culmination of a poet's career (Farrell 2002). Ennius in effect introduces a system of literary evaluation that places epic poetry at the top. He may have been anticipated in this regard by Livius and Naevius, but it is impossible to measure the contemporary impact of the *Odusia* and the *Bellum Poenicum* against that of Livius' and Naevius' dramas.

We do not know whether Livius composed his Odusia *in a native Italic or in an adapted Greek meter.* About this meter, which is called "Saturnian," we fundamentally know very little. If it is Italic, then we could point to at least one native element of the earliest surviving Latin epics. There are, however, scholars who see the Saturnian as a pre-Livian adaptation of Greek metrical patterns to the very different conventions of the Latin language.

We have no evidence that the Saturnian was an epic meter before Livius. Ennius – who has a very big axe to grind – comments on the Saturnian as a medium for epic poetry as he boasts of his own accomplishment in Latinizing the hexameter, and explains his decision not to include the First Punic War in his universal Roman history. "Others," he says with lordly disdain, "have written historical poetry, in the meter that fauns and satyrs used to sing" (*Ann.* 7.1, fr. 206–7, Skutsch 1985). The plural "others" masks the singular achievement of Naevius, the only poet we can name who wrote historical epic in Latin before Ennius. Naevius did indeed follow Livius in using Saturnians. But Ennius does not say that it had been traditional to write epic poetry in this verse. Rather, he observes that the form was more appropriate to the songs of "fauns and satyrs." Now, this is certainly an insult intended to suggest that the metrical form of the *Bellum Poenicum* is rough and unattractive compared to Ennius' hexameters, but it may also imply that Saturnians were suited not to heroic narrative but to other genres altogether. If so, fauns and satyrs could indicate oracles, and it is possible that (Livius and) Naevius – unsuccessfully, in Ennius' self-interested view – adapted a meter previously used for brief prophetic utterances to the more demanding requirements of epic narrative.

Class and professionalism. Most histories of Latin literature, in keeping with the *protos heuretes* approach, emphasize the fact that all archaic Roman poets were neither Roman nor well-born. Gaius Lucilius, who wrote satires during the late second century BCE, is remembered as the first member of the upper orders of society (he was an equestrian, and his brother a senator) to devote himself to poetry as his principal occupation. It is thus a practically unchallenged article of faith that the old Roman elite would never have taken an interest in poetry for its own sake or composed any themselves, but that when a need for institutional poetry manifested itself in the mid-third century they did the usual thing and hired foreigners to produce it for them. The testimony of Cato instead looks back to a time when members of the aristocracy, and not hired professionals, sang their own songs at banquets. Zorzetti (1990, 1991) treats the evolution from amateur elite to hired professional performance as natural and unproblematic, but in fact Cato does not regard it in this light; and if we can trust his testimony that makes the *carmina convivalia* subjects of performance by the well-born, this would substantially alter our understanding of the cultural change that took place in the mid-third century.

Latin versus Greek. As I have already noted, the material culture of Italy in all periods attests a familiarity with Homer and the Epic Cycle as well as with representations of Greek mythology on stage. We do not have the evidence to match this visual material with the performance or recitation of Greek texts, or with the telling of stories related to the scenes represented, in prose or poetry, in Greek or in Italian languages, by aristocratic amateurs or by professionals. But what seems most impressive is that the Greek stories themselves circulated widely throughout Italy, in such a way that we hear of no competition at all from native Italian literary traditions. This is not to say that such traditions did not exist, but they may have failed to develop very significantly, not because these were uncouth societies that did not appreciate high literature, but rather because Greek literature itself circulated widely among the Italian aristocracy and was so well appreciated that it smothered whatever national literatures there were. If this is so, then what needs explaining is not the near-total absence of evidence about Roman literature before Livius, but rather the fact that so much literary activity *in Latin* suddenly comes into being.

Conclusion

As I noted at the outset, this is a field in which questions are much more plentiful than definite answers, but there is some merit in stating the questions clearly and in the proper terms. I hope to have done this. In any case, it seems only fair to conclude by declaring my own views on the matter, if only in the interest of full disclosure.

In general I agree with those who regard Rome together with virtually all other urban settlements in Italy as "Hellenized" more or less from the beginning. I would limit this statement only by saying that the process of organizing a city along the lines of a Greek polis or of adopting social institutions such as the symposium might not involve conscious choices about whether to "go Greek" or leave behind any explicit memories of such a decision. We have to assume that many Greek borrowings found in archaic Italian culture were in some sense no longer marked as Greek, having been thoroughly assimilated.

Alongside these borrowings, however, are those that become crucial elements of Roman culture, but that remained marked as Greek. The best example is the Roman habit of sacrificing *Graeco ritu*, which was absorbed into the state religion and coexisted with sacrifice *Romano ritu*, but was always understood as a Greek custom. Homer's epics and the Epic Cycle seem to occupy a position analogous to such religious institutions. On the one hand, the Greekness of these myths and of the poems based on them seems never to have been effaced. On the other hand, Odysseus and his son Telegonus were understood to be the founders of Italian cities, just as were other heroes of the Trojan War – eventually including, of course, Aeneas. Thus Homer and his heroes, while never losing their Greek (or Trojan) identity, circulated freely within Italian cultures from a very early date in such a way that (I believe we have to assume) made them an integral part of those cultures, particularly where elite audiences are concerned.

It seems clear, then, that Roman culture in the archaic period was already being shaped by Greek culture, and that such influence was in some cases taken for granted, its Greekness all but forgotten, and in others clearly remembered as a traditional element of difference within Roman culture. At the end of the archaic period, however, political expansion beyond the Italian peninsula creates at Rome itself a considerable anxiety about nativism and foreign influences. One index of this anxiety is, precisely, the creation of a literature in Latin that is based on Greek models. It is not clear, however, that "expansion" and "anxiety" are all that we need to explain the sudden appearance of this phenomenon; or rather, it is obvious that they are not. In particular, it has become clear towards the end of the twentieth century that received accounts about the culture wars that supposedly took place at Rome between "philhellenes" and "traditionalists" are much too schematic and reductive (Gruen 1992). Rather, this is an area in which a lot of work remains to be done.

We can, however, draw one further distinction between the "Hellenization" of the third and second centuries and that of previous epochs. In speaking of Rome as a "Hellenized" city even from the beginning, and of Greek institutions like the symposium and Homeric poetry being thoroughly at home on Italian soil, we are talking about traditional Panhellenic institutions that had their roots in classical Greek culture and that came to Italy in the period of Greek colonization of the West. The reception and understanding of these institutions will have changed over time; some, like polis-style political and social organization, will have come to be understood as, for all intents and purposes, not Greek at all. Others, like Homeric poetry, will have remained Greek, even if Greekness as a point of reference will have changed over time with Italian experience of contemporary Greeks. But by the third century, Romans and other Italians, like the Greeks themselves, will have had to reckon not just with Hellenic but with Hellenistic culture. Even bastions of traditional Hellenic culture such as Athens were in this period challenged and, in certain ways, surpassed by new centers of a more cosmopolitan Hellenistic culture, such as Alexandria and Pergamum; and, under such circumstances, it is only natural to assume that a politically and culturally ambitious city such as Rome, poised to transform itself from a Greek-style polis into the capital of a Hellenistic empire, would have felt the pressures of this cultural shift especially keenly. In literature, and in the transformation of the polis-based institutions that had once supported literary culture into institutions of a very different kind – museums, libraries, and the like staffed with professional scholars who collected, edited, and explicated with great learning the literature of the past, and created a new literature based on their collective scholarship – the distinctive traits of Hellenistic culture are especially marked. One factor that might help explain the sudden developments at Rome in the mid-third century is just this, that poets like Livius, Naevius, and Ennius, and of course their patrons as well, were not just familiar with traditional Hellenic culture, but were responding specifically to contemporary Hellenistic receptions of and interpretations of that culture.

In short, the cultural history of archaic Italy is powerfully conditioned by native receptions of and negotiations first with traditional Greek culture, then with the hybridized culture of the Hellenistic world. There is evidence that the Italic peoples were familiar from of old with the Homeric epics and with such collateral material as the Epic Cycle and tragic representations of episodes from the Trojan saga long before 240 BCE. But while there is some evidence at Rome for sacral songs and perhaps for symposiastic celebration of ancestors, there is no evidence for narrative poetry either parallel to or deriving from the Greek epic tradition. Livius' translation of the *Odyssey* very obviously draws on native traditions in some respects (converting Muses into Camenae, and so forth). As an import, it is hardly unprecedented, since Homer had been a ubiquitous presence in Italic culture since the seventh or eighth century. As an epic poem in Latin, however, as a written text rather than as a song, and possibly as a composition by a professional man of letters rather than a member of the political and social elite, it seems to represent, even if it did not literally start, a revolution in Roman cultural life. The early stages of this revolution are perhaps better represented by the more plentiful compositions for the stage that Livius and his successors produced. But with Livius' literary approach to Homer and the epic came access to a vast store of exegetical material, which had recently begun to be collected and systematized by Hellenistic scholars. Interest in and use of this material by Livius and his successors can be demonstrated (Mariotti 1952); and while it would be a mistake to put Livius, Naevius, or Ennius on the same level as an Aristarchus (Goldberg 1995), it is difficult to deny that they started a process whereby the Roman reception of Homer began to develop in an explicitly scholarly and literary way. This, too, is part of the professionalization of literature at Rome, in which members of the elite would eventually take part, but which in the mid-third century and for some years thereafter may have been viewed by some as an unwelcome novelty. But there was no turning back.

Our knowledge of how Roman poets began to write epic poetry, then, must remain very incomplete. Paradoxically, perhaps, ackowledgment that Rome was a Hellenized city from a very early date compels us to admit that we have next to no evidence for a native tradition of Roman epic in the archaic period. Artistic evidence suggests that the Homeric poems and the Epic Cycle were well known throughout archaic Italy, but may also suggest that Homer himself took the place of any native Italic epic tradition that there may have been. When Roman poets do begin to write epic, they do so not as strangers to Greek literary culture, but as participants in a cultural tranformation that had been shaping the entire Mediterranean world since the death of Alexander the Great. The fact that they begin to write poetry, and not to recite; the fact that they do so in Latin, and not in Greek; and the fact that they do so as professionals, and not as aristocratic amateurs; all of these facts *may* be important components of a cultural revolution parallel to the political one that saw Rome evolve from a Greek-style polis to a Hellenistic empire. But we cannot be sure how much truth there is in these suppositions, and we have seen how strong is the tendency, among ancient as well as modern scholars, to supply Rome with a detailed cultural history in the archaic period on the basis of Greek comparanda. What does seem reasonably clear is that the work of Livius, Naevius, and Ennius directs Roman epic, and poetry in general, along specifically literary lines and puts it in dialogue with the kind of political and cultural issues that dominate Hellenistic literature as well, and that these concerns remain overwhelmingly important in the work of virtually all their successors.

FURTHER READING

The early history of Roman epic and of Roman literature in general is a contested subject. On the basic methodological problems, Momigliano 1957 and Horsfall 1994 offer useful perspectives. What may be called the standard view among scholars, according to which literature on the Greek model began to be imported to Rome quite suddenly by specific individuals (such as Livius Andronicus), was best articulated by Leo 1913 and has been repeated in any number of subsequent reference works (e.g., Conte 1994b).

The contrasting view, which may, despite certain important differences, be said to derive ultimately from Niebuhr 1811, is represented most forcefully by Zorzetti 1990 and 1991. The entire *status quaestionis* is succinctly analyzed by Barchiesi 2002b (a review of Rüpke 2001b).

The problem of the origins of Roman literature is closely related to that of Roman Hellenization in general. The idea that Hellenization can be regarded as a relatively late phenomenon has been effectively dismantled by advances in research and analysis on several fronts. Excellent starting points for further reading in this area are Gruen 1992 and Malkin 1998.

CHAPTER THIRTY-ONE

Early Republican Epic

Sander M. Goldberg

That exercise in false modesty which modern scholars call the *recusatio* became a familiar trope among Augustan poets. Virgil, Horace, Propertius, and Ovid all, at one time or another, profess an inability to celebrate in suitably grand style the heroic deeds of one or another distinguished contemporary. They had good reasons for demurral, though fear of disappointing their *princeps* or his agents was probably not among them. The poets' elaborate diffidence was itself a kind of compliment, not an indication of heavy hints reaching Horace from Agrippa (Hor. *Carm.* 1.6) or Propertius from Maecenas (Prop. 2.1). A more credible motive for the refusal to contemplate epic is suggested by Virgil's own famous *recusatio* in the sixth *Eclogue*:

> Cum canerem reges et proelia, Cynthius aurem
> vellit et admonuit: "pastorem, Tityre, pinguis
> pascere oportet ovis, deductum dicere carmen."
> nunc ego (namque super tibi erunt qui dicere laudes,
> Vare, tuas cupiant et tristia condere bella)
> agrestem tenui meditabor harundine Musam:
> non iniussa cano.

> As I considered singing of kings and battles, the Cynthian
> tweaked my ear and warned: "The shepherd, Tityrus, needs
> to raise fat sheep but to sing a fine-spun song."
> Thus (since there will be others, Varus, eager to sing
> your praises and to record your grim campaigns)
> I will exercise a rustic Muse on a slender pipe.
> I only sing as bidden.

> (*Ecl.* 6.3–9)

Virgil here deliberately recalls the Alexandrian poet Callimachus, who had introduced his famous collection of aetiological poems (*Aitia*) with a similar conceit:

> βροντᾶν οὐκ ἐμόν, ἀλλὰ Διός.
> καὶ γὰρ ὅτε πρώτιστον ἐμοῖς ἐπὶ δέλτον ἔθηκαν
> γούνασιν, Ἀπόλλων εἶπεν ὅ μοι Λύκιος·
> ...] ἀοιδέ, τὸ μὲν θύος ὅττι πάχιστον
> θρέψαι, τὴν Μοῦσαν δ' ὠγαθὲ λεπταλέην·

> Thunder is not for me but for Zeus.
> For when I first set a tablet on my knees,
>   Lykian Apollo said to me,
> " . . .] poet, raise the sacrificial victim to be fat
>   as possible but the Muse, my friend, to be slender"
>   (fr. 1.20–4)

Callimachus' manifesto clearly gave the Augustans their aesthetic catchwords, but something important changed in the process of translation.

Callimachus' quarrel was not specifically with epic. His target was pompous, rambling, and self-important poetry of all kinds, and very little such poetry in the Alexandrian world involved those long hexameter poems on mythological or historic themes we call "epic" (Cameron 1995: 263–302). In contrast, Romans of the first century BCE were surrounded by epics, and most of them were, or were soon thought to be, social embarrassments and artistic failures. The key question for the early history of Roman epic is therefore not how the genre arose but how, after quite promising beginnings, epic fell into such disrepute that by the end of the Republic hardly any poet of stature would risk his reputation by dabbling in it.

Roman epic as we know it began with writing. Whatever bardic tradition the Romans may once have had – the kind of folk poetry Macaulay evokes so vividly in his *Lays of Ancient Rome* – vanished quite early in the history of Latium and left no discernible mark on the later, distinctly literary phenomenon we call "Roman epic" (see Chapter 30, by Farrell). Though the elder Cato, at some point in the early second century BCE, claimed that Romans of still earlier generations praised the deeds of *their* ancestors at banquets (Cic. *Brut.* 75, cf. *Leg.* 2.24.62, *Tusc.* 1.2.3), those *carmina* left no trace for later antiquarians to recover (Goldberg 1995: 43–6). Nothing unequivocally "oral" or "folk" stands behind the earliest attested Roman epic, nor is there very much that is explicitly "Roman" about it. The Roman tradition began instead with a Greek book, Homer's *Odyssey*, and a talented Greek freedman named Livius Andronicus.

This Andronicus was said to have come from Tarentum, one of the great cultural centers of Magna Graecia, probably after the city came under Roman control in 272 BCE. His name suggests a freedman of the Livii Salinatores, one of the most influential aristocratic families of the third century, and he evidently won significant public commissions. He is credited with producing the first formal Latin plays at the *ludi Romani* of 240, and as an old man in 207, he composed a state hymn to Juno at a time of crisis in the second war against Carthage. A formal guild of poets and actors was subsequently established in his honor (Gruen 1990: 80–92). At some (unknown) time and for some (unknown) reason, this same Andronicus also retold the story of Odysseus' return from Troy in Latin verse, an endeavor with far-reaching consequences for Roman literature.

His choice of subject is not in itself surprising. The story of Odysseus' return had strong Italian associations and was of immediate interest to Romans of the time. Many of its episodes were traditionally located in the world Italians knew. Travelers could visit memorials to Odysseus' companions Elpenor on the coast of Latium and Drakon in Leucania. Post-Homeric tradition identified the promontories on the Bay of Naples at Misenum and Baiae with Odysseus' men Misenos and Baios, and sons of Odysseus and Circe named Ardeias, Antias, and Romos were claimed as the eponymous founders of Ardea, Antium, and Rome. Their better-known son Telegonus, hero of the epic *Telegonia* by Eugammon of Cyrene, had strong associations with Tusculum and Praeneste. Nor was Odysseus himself entirely outside the Roman story. According to the fifth-century mythographer Hellanicus of Lesbos, Aeneas came to Italy along with Odysseus, and the Greek hero was linked to the founding of the city (Gruen 1992: 17–21). Andronicus was thus giving Romans their own version of a story engaging in itself and ideologically useful for locating the Roman world within the context of the Greek heroic age.

Andronicus' choice of meter for his new epic, however, was not so obvious. His technical skill must have been considerable, for the dramatic fragments show a marked ease in adapting the quantitative meters of Greek drama, lyric cadences as well as the iambs and trochees of speech, to the stress accents of Latin. Yet he did not bring that skill to bear on the characteristic meter of Greek epic, the dactylic hexameter. Andronicus' new *Odyssey* employed no Greek meter at all but a verse attested only for Latin, the so-called Saturnian. Its name hints at the hoary antiquity of Saturn's reign, and its characteristic cadence appears as early as the Hymn of the Arval Brethren, a ritual chant old enough to predate the phonetic shift of intervocalic *s* to *r* (rhotacism) established in Latin by the fourth century, e.g. "e nos Lases iuvate" ("Help us, Lares"). It was a meter associated with hymns, epitaphs, and official utterances, and its elevation to literary use presented new opportunities and new challenges.

Ancient grammarians did not understand the Saturnian, and we remain uncertain whether the meter was Italic or Greek in origin, or whether its governing principles were quantitative or accentual (Cole 1969). Some formal features, however, and their aesthetic consequences are clear (Goldberg 1995: 58–82). As used by the professional poets of the third century, the Saturnian was a stichic verse of about thirteen syllables divided by a caesura into two unequal parts, the first usually one to three syllables longer than the second. This pattern produces series of layered cola, often featuring stronger breaks at caesura than line end. Repetitions of sound and sense may bridge these boundaries, binding small units into larger ones, such as "ibidemque vir summus | adprimus Patroclus" ("whereupon the finest of men, Patroclus, by far the best," fr. 10), or glossing one phrase with another, as "sancta puer Saturni | filia regina" ("blessed child of Saturn, daughter, queen," fr. 12). Such effects are clear in our longest fragment, describing the destructive power of the sea (fr. 18, cf. Hom. *Od.* 8.138–9):

> namque nullum peius   macerat humanum
> quamde mare saevom: vires cui sunt magnae,
> topper confringent   inportunae undae
>
> for nothing wounds a mortal man worse than
> a savage sea: he whose strength is great,
> the remorseless billows quickly shatter.

These lines survive only because the archaic adverb *topper* ("quickly") caught the eye of the Augustan grammarian Verrius Flaccus. Andronicus' poem had lost its primary readership by the first century; it was only a hoary relic for Cicero (*Brut.* 71) and an unhappy school-memory for Horace (*Ep.* 2.1.69). Yet Saturnian epic as developed by Andronicus and his successor Naevius constituted a powerful opening move in the complex negotiation between Greek poetic models and Roman requirements that dominates Republican literary history. The very opening of Andronicus' poem defines the issue.

> Virum mihi, Camena,   insece versutum
>
> Tell me, Camena, of the clever man

This is, at first glance, simply an astute, rather clever rendering of its famous model, Ἄνδρα μοι ἔννεπε, Μοῦσα, πολύτροπον, ὃς μάλα πολλά ("Tell, me, Muse, of the clever man who many things . . . ," *Od.* 1.1). Its word order specifically evokes the original.

With *insece* Andronicus offers a rare Latin word of similar meaning, sound, and accent to Homer's own uncommon ἔννεπε; *versutum*, built on *verto*, renders πολύτροπον with a Latin version of the same metaphor. Metrical necessities serve the needs of sense: Homer's vocative and verb are reversed to accommodate both the Saturnian caesura and the naturally enclitic vocative, while alliteration of *virum … versutum* links the cola across that divide. Andronicus, educated Greek and skillful poet, nevertheless abandons the Muse. He calls upon one of the Camenae, nymphs associated with a spring outside Rome's Porta Capena, to play that role. Whether or not that spring deliberately substitutes for Hippocrene and "Camena" is meant to suggest "carmen," the promotion certainly declares that the Romans' poet, who can follow Greek models as a matter of choice, has an Italian inspiration behind this epic venture. He is himself *versutus*, perhaps even playing on the sense "adapt" or "translate" already established for *vortere* on the stage (e.g. Plaut. *Asin.* 11, *Trin.* 19), and, of course, he makes this declaration in a meter that is itself Italic rather than Greek (Hinds 1998: 58–63).

Andronicus' program for developing epic conventions in Roman terms was pursued even more aggressively by his successor Gnaeus Naevius in a poem on an explicitly Roman topic, the First Punic War of 264–241 BCE. This work was on a significantly grander scale. Andronicus' version of the *Odyssey* apparently filled only a single book roll. At some point in the later second century, Naevius' *Bellum Poenicum* was divided into seven (Suet. *Gram.* 2.4). Though he too was a successful dramatist with much practical skill in adapting Greek meters to the demands of Latin, Naevius continued Andronicus' experiment with the Saturnian. His poem's stylistic effects were thus similar. Here, for example, is Naevius describing Aeneas' wife and mother as they flee the destruction of Troy (fr. 5):

> amborum uxores
> noctu Troiad exibant   capitibus opertis
> flentes ambae, abeuntes,   lacrimis cum multis

> Their two wives
> fled Troy by night, heads covered,
> both weeping, leaving with many tears

Each colon, shaped as so often by alliteration and homoioteleuton, contains a discrete idea, while the nearly parallel ablative phrases link successive verses. A combination of participles and finite verbs paces the action, revealing itself piece by piece to dramatic and poignant effect.

But why does the fall of Troy appear at all in a poem about Romans and Carthaginians fighting over Sicily? The answer is quite remarkable. Naevius included in his account the story of the Roman people – from Troy to Aeneas' stop in Carthage, and on to his eventual landing in Italy – and he did so not in simple chronological order but in some kind of elaborate flashback. Book One included the consul Valerius Messala's landing in Sicily in 263 (fr. 3):

> Manius Valerius
> consul partem exerciti   in expeditionem
> ducit

> Manius Valerius
> the consul leads part of his army
> on a foray

Something there – various explanations have been offered – must have recalled the Trojan fugitives, whose story then continued through Books Two (the visit to Carthage, fr. 20) and Three (the arrival in Italy, fr. 26) before the historical narrative resumed by Book Four, which mentions a Roman invasion of Malta in the early 250s (fr. 37). This structure may owe something to the complexity of the *Odyssey*'s narrative. It certainly established Naevius as a pioneer in the tendency, later so famously developed by Virgil, to see the Roman present in the context of its legendary past, and Virgil's own epic would in fact owe much to Naevius (Wigodsky 1972: 22–39).

By some reckonings, the *Bellum Poenicum* marked the beginning of serious, i.e. non-dramatic, poetry in Latin. That at least is what a verse chronicler named Porcius Licinus claimed around the end of the second century (Courtney 1993: 83–6):

> Poenico bello secundo Musa pinnato gradu
> intulit se bellicosam in Romuli gentem feram.

> At the time of the Second Punic War the Muse with winged step
> introduced her warlike self to Romulus' fierce race.

Naevius' primacy, however, was short-lived. So was the Saturnian style with which he and Andronicus had accomplished so much. The instigator of their eclipse was another south-Italian immigrant to Rome, Quintus Ennius.

Ennius was a Calabrian by birth, served in the war against Hannibal, and came to Rome toward the end of the third century. His social standing was probably higher than that of his predecessors. Where Andronicus had been a freedman client of the Livii and Naevius a Campanian outsider to the halls of power, Ennius – who claimed descent from the legendary King Messapus (Sil. *Pun.* 12.393–7) and equal fluency in Latin, Oscan, and Greek (Gell. *NA* 17.17.1) – mixed easily with Rome's elite. Although he too wrote plays for the public stage (several of his tragedies became classics) and taught grammar privately, he also enjoyed the company of an impressive array of Roman nobles. Cato, it was said, brought him to Rome. There were stories of him visiting, strolling, and traveling with the great Fulvii, Sulpicii, and Cornelii of his day. His portrait was believed to adorn the tomb of the Scipios (Gruen 1990: 106–22). Such was the man who blazed a new path for Roman epic and, in the glamour of his success, not just surpassed his predecessors but reduced them at a stroke from innovators to archaisms.

The instrument of this revolution was a verse chronicle of Roman history from the city's origins to what was then the present day. Originally conceived in fifteen books ending with events of the late 180s, Ennius soon added three more to his *Annales* to bring the story into the 170s. It was not just the vast scope of the project, however, that overshadowed its predecessors. Ennius brought deep changes to the epic enterprise. Most obvious of these was his use of Homer's meter, the dactylic hexameter, freshly adapted to Latin requirements. This was itself a significant achievement, and when Ennius invokes the Muses, "who strike great Olympus with their feet" (1), it is hard not to hear his pride in substituting the "Muses' foot," i.e. the hexameter, for what he would famously dismiss as "the verses of fauns and soothsayers" (206–7).

The hexameter offered real advantages, for its longer line gave the poet a broader canvas on which to create more extensive, ambitious, and even dazzling effects. These are evident in a fragment describing the famous augury of Romulus and Remus:

> Curantes magna cum cura tum cupientes
> regni dant operam simul auspicio augurioque.
> in †monte Remus auspicio sedet atque secundam
> solus avem servat. at Romulus pulcer in alto   75
> quaerit Aventino, servat genus altivolantum.
> certabant urbem Romam Remoramne vocarent.

omnibus cura viris uter esset induperator.
expectant veluti consul quom mittere signum
volt, omnes avidi spectant ad carceris oras   80
quam mox emittat pictos e faucibus currus:
sic expectabat populus atque ore timebat
rebus utri magni victoria sit data regni.
interea sol albus recessit in infera noctis.
exin candida se radiis dedit icta foras lux   85
et simul ex alto longe pulcerrima praepes
laeva volavit avis. simul aureus exoritur sol
cedunt de caelo ter quattuor corpora sancta
avium, praepetibus sese pulcrisque locis dant.
conspicit inde sibi data Romulus esse propritim   90
auspicio regni stabilita scamna solumque.

Carefully then, taking great care, desiring
a kingdom, they together take the auspices and augury.
On the Murcus (?) Remus sits in wait and watches
for a favorable flight alone. Noble Romulus on high   75
Aventine seeks and watches for the high-soaring race.
They vied to call the city either Rome or Remora.
All men cared which one became their ruler.
They wait as when the consul is about to give
the signal, all watching anxiously the starting gates   80
to see how soon he sends the painted chariots from the barrier:
so the people wait, worry on each face for their
affairs, for which should be given the victory of highest rule.
Meanwhile the sun had set into the depth of night.
Then struck by rays a shining light showed itself openly   85
and at once on high from far away a beautifully winged
left-moving flight advanced. Just as the golden sun arises,
there came from heaven a dozen blessed bodies
of birds, settling on the place with noble wings.
Thus Romulus saw that given to himself alone,   90
confirmed by auspices, were the base and bulwark of a kingdom.

Much in this extraordinary passage reflects poetic values and preoccupations already characteristic of early Latin poetry, including the deliberate alliterations (e.g. *pulcerrima praepes*) and redundancies (e.g. *auspicio augurioque, scamna solumque*). There is quite a lot of word play, not just the so-called *figura etymologica* of *curantes… cum cura* but the serious association of the *altus Aventinus* with *avis* (the *genus altivolantum*) and the striking succession of syllables in *laeva volavit avis*. Other effects are directly created by the hexameter form, as in 86–7, where caesurae after the fifth element (much more natural to Latin than to Greek hexameters) breaks the revelation into small units (*ex alto, longe, pulcerrima praepes, laeva,* and at last *avis*) as the omen gradually comes into view and is recognized.

Still more striking is the simile at 79–83, which casts the witnesses to this legendary augury in the image of their descendants, the crowd gathered for the chariot races at historical Rome's greatest festival, the *ludi Romani*. Romulus and Remus are themselves in a kind of race, with the slower Remus the inevitable loser (cf. Remora, suggesting *mora*, "delay"), and the crowd gathered to watch their vigil on the peaks of the Aventine would have assembled in precisely the place, eventually the site of the Circus Maximus, where the chariot races were held. The augury thus offers a window on Rome's future as Ennius, like Naevius before him, smoothes the joints between past and present, fact and myth.

Such technical innovations forever eclipsed the Saturnian as an epic meter, yet it was not simply a casualty of Hellenization at Rome. Greek learning, the knowledge not just of Greek texts but of how Greeks studied their texts, was always a force in Roman epic. When Andronicus described two dancers as "weaving rapidly between themselves" (*nexebant multa inter se*, fr. 20), he was translating not Homer, whose Halios and Laodamas were "rapidly exchanging steps" (ταρφε' ἀμειβομένω, *Od.* 8.379) but a Hellenistic gloss on Homer's image (πυκνῶς πλέκοντες, Schol.V *ad* 379). Andronicus evidently read his Homer with a schoolmaster's notes. When Naevius, still loyal to Andronicus' Camenae, nevertheless called them "nine like-minded daughters of Jupiter" (fr. 1), he shows awareness of the Greek tradition and acknowledges, if only tacitly, what Ennius would make explicit: "know that we, whom they call Muses, are the Camenae" ("Musas quas memorant nosce nos esse Camenas," 487). The Ennian context was probably an event of 179, when Fulvius Nobilior transferred a shrine of the Camenae to the Temple of Hercules of the Muses. The civic institution thus aligned itself with poetic practice: "Camenae" became synonymous in Latin poetry with "Musae."

The new meter inevitably brought Ennius' poem closer to a Greek sense of epic style. Where his Saturnian predecessors were limited to allusions and calques, Ennius could create direct equivalents of characteristic Homeric mannerisms. Line ends like "divomque hominumque pater, rex" (591) and "patrem divomque hominumque" (592) are clearly modeled on the common epithet for Zeus, πατὴρ ἀνδρῶν τε θεῶν τε ("father of men and gods"), down to the repetition, less natural in Latin than in Greek, of the enclitic connective. Homeric similes could be reproduced with their characteristic elaboration, such as the warrior rushing to battle like a high-spirited horse who has slipped his tether (535–9; cf. *Il.* 6.506–11, 15.263–8). Latin epic thus acquired the weight of its Greek predecessor.

This gain also made possible, perhaps demanded, a new relationship between the poet and his subject. Likening a charging Roman to Homer's thoroughbred imports the Homeric context into the Roman setting, in effect establishing that soldier as the equivalent of Paris or Hektor. So most strikingly in Book 15, a Roman tribune making his stand before the Greek city of Ambracia in 189 BCE is described like Ajax defending the Achaean ships (391–8; cf. Hom. *Il.* 16.102–11). In such a context, the ostensibly ornamental device acquires ideological significance, for the allusion claims for the historic figure the stature of the legendary figure. The tribune's valor becomes "epic." Such an elevation was a powerful, but potentially problematic device. Glorifying contemporary deeds brings epic to the edge of panegyric, and not every successor would know how to avoid the precipice. Ennius himself had no doubt about his own position. The poet who elevated his Romans to Homeric status himself became Homer. Literally. Book 1 of the *Annales* began with a vision in which the spirit of Homer appeared to the poet and explained how, by a process of transmigration, his soul was living on in Ennius (Skutsch 1985: 147–53). This passage, which Horace (not without irony) would call Ennius' "Pythagorean dream" (*Ep.* 2.1.52), became a famous symbol of Ennius' dominance, but the very success of his *Annales* as both record and glorification of the Roman achievement set a not-entirely-happy standard for coming generations. The *Annales* could not be equaled, much less replaced. It could only be extended with new poems recording new achievements, and that is what happened.

Nearly two dozen epics on historical subjects are ascribed to authors of the late Republic or early empire. None survived to become a literary landmark. Varro of Atax, who won some renown for his translation of Apollonius' *Argonautica,* also wrote an epic on Caesar's Sequanian War of 58 BCE that proved much less successful. Works such as Hostius' *Istrian War,* on a campaign of 129 BCE, and *The Gallic War* of Furius Bibaculus, also dedicated to Caesar's exploits, have left even less trace in the record. When Quintilian, at the end of the first century CE, scanned Latin epic for useful stylistic models, he found almost nothing worth mentioning from this period (*Inst.* 10.1.85–92; White 1993: 78–84). The artistic dilemma facing late Republican epicists is well illustrated by Cicero, who in 54 wrote, but wisely shelved, an epic on Caesar's campaigns (*Q. fr.* 3.7.6) but eventually circulated a poem on his own consulship – and paid a high price for that indulgence. His bad fortune would be, as Tacitus dryly remarked, not that he wrote such poetry but that it was remembered (*Dial.* 21).

Cicero was not, technically, a bad poet. A youthful astronomical poem translating the Hellenistic poet Aratus' *Phaenomena* was read with interest. Lucretius borrowed from it. So did Virgil, who also culled phrases from Cicero's poem celebrating his fellow-townsman, Marius. Virgil's debt to Cicero may in fact be seriously underrated, the casualty of a reputation so low that ancient scholars were reluctant to gather the evidence (Wigodsky 1972: 109–14). What caused the problem for Cicero? It was not simply the egotism of the consular poem, at least not for contemporaries. Its most notorious surviving line, "o fortunatam natam me consule Romam" ("fortunate Rome, born in my consulship," fr. 12) was not obviously or at once offensive. Cicero was in fact hailed as *pater patriae* for saving the state from Catiline's conspiracy of 63 BCE, and he himself later, and without provoking ridicule, hailed the day on which the leading conspirators were condemned as "the city's birthday" (*Flac.* 102).

The serious flaw lay in its subject, specifically in Cicero's conviction that Catiline was thwarted not by the eventual battle that destroyed his army in Etruria but by the consul's steadfast eloquence at home: "cedant arma togae, concedat laurea laudi" ("let arms yield to the toga, the laurel defer to praise," fr. 11). That was a bold sentiment to express in a society where military prowess was the main source of civic authority and an unusual one to find in a genre increasingly focused on military achievement. Unfortunately for its author, whatever claim it had to truth was already wearing thin by the 50s, when the line was first turned against Cicero by political enemies (*Pis.* 73). By the late 40s, as we easily infer from his reduced role in Sallust's *Bellum Catilinae* (the title itself repudiates Cicero's priorities), his claim to dominance was beyond salvage. When a parodist eventually changed *laudi* to *linguae*, the alteration quickly displaced the original. *De consulatu suo* was thus an ideological failure before it became an artistic one (Goldberg 1995: 148–54). Epic's fixation on claims of contemporary success turned the genre into a laughingstock. Or a bore. Small wonder that Virgil in the early 30s would shun *reges et proelia*, especially when we recall that *rex* was Latin slang for "bigshot."

An alternative was already emerging, however, from a renewed attention to Greek poetry by young, well-educated aristocrats of the late Republic. Though Romans had long been reading Callimachus and Aratus, a taste for the more arcane aspects of Greek learning and the aesthetic that modern critics call "Alexandrian" became increasingly pronounced at Rome around the time that the poet-scholar Parthenius of Nicaea arrived, probably in the 60s, and Helvius Cinna brought the famously erudite poet Euphorion into vogue (Courtney 1993: 212–14; Lightfoot 1999: 50–76). One result of these developments was the new interest in mythological narrative attested by Cinna's lost *Zmyrna* on the incestuous love of the Cyprian Zmyrna for her father and by Catullus' sixty-fourth poem, on the marriage of Peleus and Thetis.

The new aesthetic shows clearly in Catullus 64, which used the readers' familiarity with its mythological subject to license a learned obscurity in detail and a marked complexity in structure. This tendency is clear from the outset:

> Peliaco quondam prognatae vertice pinus
> dicuntur liquidas Neptuni nasse per undas
> Phasidos ad fluctus et fines Aeeteos,

cum lecti iuvenes, Argivae robora pubis,
auratam optantes Colchis avertere pellem...

Pines once nurtured on the Pelian height
are said to have swum across Neptune's fluid billows
to the eddies of Phasis and Aeetian borders,
when hand-picked young men, the flower of Argive youth,
seeking to appropriate the golden pelt of Colchis...

(64.1–5)

The "Argo" is introduced without being named, and Peleus will soon appear without being identified as a member of its crew (19). The spondaic cadence that ends line 3 would have struck conservative readers like Cicero as a Hellenistic affectation (cf. *Att.* 7.2.1), and they would soon have been struggling with the kind of learned kenning that turns "Athena" into the "the resident of blessed Itonus" ("sancti incola Itoni," 228) because the Boeotian town of Itonus had a famous sanctuary of the goddess. Catullus' structure also challenges his readers. A coverlet on Thetis' marriage bed interrupts the wedding narrative with an ecphrasis describing Ariadne's misery on Naxos (50–264), after which the opening story slips quickly into a song by the Fates (323–81) and then a lament, almost Hesiodic in tone, for the passing of that heroic age when gods and men could dine together (384–408).

The learning and generic play, however, are not exclusively Greek. While avoiding echoes of earlier hexameter poetry, Catullus makes extensive, occasionally sly use of other Roman precedents (Thomas 1999: 12–29). Phrases such as "Peliaco vertice," "lecti iuvenes, Argivae robora pubis," and "auratam pellem," for example, recall a standard school text of his generation, Ennius' tragedy *Medea exul*:

utinam ne in nemore Pelio securibus
caesa accidisset abiegna ad terram trabes,
neve inde navis inchoandi exordium
cepisset, quae nunc nominatur nomine
Argo, quia Argivi in ea delecti viri
vecti petebant pellem inauratam arietis
Colchis...

Would that fir timber in the Pelian grove, though
struck by axes had not fallen to earth
nor then undertaken the beginning of a ship
which now is known by the name
Argo, since on it the chosen Argive men
were carried in quest of the golden pelt of the ram
of Colchis...

(253–9 W)

Catullus' readers thus come to the wedding celebration via tragedy, and the echoes return, with more thematic than narrative relevance, when Ariadne in the embedded tale recalls the tragic opening of the frame.

Iuppiter omnipotens, utinam ne tempore primo
Cnosia Cecropiae tetigissent litora puppes

Omnipotent Jupiter, would that in early times
the Cecropian sterns had not touched the Knossian shores

(64.171–2)

The rejected Ariadne then immediately begins to speak in the voice of Ennius' rejected Medea:

> nam quo me referam? quali spe perdita nitor?
> Idaeosne petam montes? at gurgite lato
> discernens ponti truculentum dividit aequor.
> an patris auxilium sperem? [etc.]

> Where shall I turn? With what hope shall I endure, ruined?
> Shall I seek the Idaean peaks? The ocean intervenes,
> interposing the seas' billows with a great gulf
> Shall I seek my father's help? [etc.]   (177–80)

> quo nunc me vortam? quod iter incipiam ingredi?
> domum paternamne? anne ad Peliae filias?

> Where shall I now turn? What path shall I begin to tread?
> To my father's house? To the daughters of Pelias? (284–5 W)

This relentless recollection of tragic Ennius turns the Catullan hexameters conspicuously away from echoes of epic Ennius.

Generic play of another kind may be at work in the Fates' prophecy (64.323–81), which Catullus shaped into stanzas of irregular length with the refrain, "currite ducentes subtegmina, currite, fusi" ("run, spindles, drawing out the threads, run"). The device is overtly Hellenistic. He would have found it in Theocritus' first two *Idylls,* and it was then taken up by Virgil in *Eclogue* 8 (cf. *Ecl.* 4.46 echoing Catullus). Yet the Fates' celebration of the marriage soon centers on the *aristeia* of Peleus' future son, Achilles, and their praise of his "extraordinary virtues and brilliant deeds" ("egregias virtutes claraque facta," 64. 348) also recalls the traditional panegyric of Greek *skolia* praising heroes like Harmodius and Aristogeiton and, perhaps, those other *carmina* in which first-century Romans thought their ancestors praised the "clarorum virorum laudes atque virtutes" (cf. Cic. *Tusc.* 4.2.3). Catullus sometimes experimented with archaic models: his hymn to Diana recalls Saturnian rhythms (34). Here he gives a Hellenistic gloss to another archaic form and in doing so again calls attention to something his poem is not.

The final thing that poem 64 lacks is length, although brevity was not in itself an Alexandrian requirement. Callimachus' *Aitia* eventually filled four books, each running to over a thousand elegiac verses. His *Hecale*, the story of Theseus and the bull of Marathon, was perhaps a thousand hexameters. For the Romans, however, a "fine-spun song" soon came to mean a short one: Cinna's *Zmyrna*, which Catullus compared so pointedly to the traditional *Annales* of Volusius in poem 95, was barely 30 lines long. Catullus 64 required only 408 lines. Virgil would take less than 250 to tell his interlocking stories of Aristaeus and Orpheus (*Geo.* 4.315–558). A compact, learned narrative on a mythological subject – what modern scholars call an epyllion ("little epic") – promised escape from the bombast and obsequiousness to which longer hexameter narratives were increasingly prone.

That solution, however, left little opportunity for traditional epic, which by the Republic's end could claim only a checkered past and a dubious future. Thus the rise of the Augustan *recusatio*. The gradual realization in the early 20s that a poet of superior skill and – as many must surely have thought – superior sense was actually writing such an epic must have created a sensation. The shock and surprise of it are palpable in Propertius' famous announcement.

> Actia Vergilium custodis litora Phoebi,
>   Caesaris et fortis dicere posse ratis,

qui nunc Aeneae Troiani suscitat arma
    iactaque Lavinis moenia litoribus.
cedite Romani scriptores, cedite Grai!
    nescio quid maius nascitur Iliade.

(2.34.61–6)

Phoebus' protection of the Actian shore and Caesar's
    Brave fleet – Virgil's glad to tell of these.
He now summons up the arms of Trojan Aeneas
    And the walls built on Lavinian shores.
Make way, Roman writers, and you Greeks, make way!
    Something greater than the *Iliad* is being born.

The evocation of Trojan arms and Lavinian shores suggests that he had heard a recitation of *Aeneid* 1, but Virgil would, as we now know, actually have little to say about Actium or about any contemporary event. Propertius is caught here in his own expectation, able to imagine not what Virgil was actually writing, but only what he himself refused to write at the beginning of Book 2, where he admitted that amorous wrestling was *his* idea of an *Iliad* (Prop. 2.1.13–14). Yet we should not fault his failure of vision. How Virgil confounded contemporary expectations and restored the genre to respectability was truly beyond imagining and represents in every sense a new chapter in the history of Roman epic.

FURTHER READING

The fragmentary epic poets are, with the exception of Ennius, commonly cited from the collection *Fragmenta poetarum latinorum,* originally edited by Willy Morel. Its third instantiation (Blänsdorf 1995) does not entirely escape the editorial problems of its predecessors, but combines elegant presentation with updated bibliographies. These features are especially valuable for Anglophone readers approaching this material through Warmington 1961, first published 1936, an edition whose convenience is its main virtue. Ennius' *Annales* is masterfully served by Skutsch 1985. Courtney 1993 is also indispensible.

The social and biographical testimony for early epic, long the province of rather narrowly focused literary and social histories of the genre, has been receiving renewed attention from scholars with much broader horizons: Suerbaum 1968, Gruen 1990, and Rüpke 2000, 2001a are particularly significant examples. For the Saturnian meter see Cole 1969, with new suggestions by Freeman 1998 and Parsons 1999. Literary discussion, including matters of patronage, aesthetics, and influence is provided by Goldberg 1995 and Hinds 1998: 52–83.

How we read the fragmentary literature of the Republic is deeply, though sometimes imperceptibly, influenced by the Augustan reception of it. Wigodsky 1972 is fundamental; White 1993 is excellent on Roman attitudes toward poets and poetry. The essays gathered in Thomas 1999 represent some of the best current thinking on the Augustans' reception of their Alexandrian and Republican predecessors, although Cameron 1995 provides a bracing challenge to current orthodoxy. Lightfoot 1999 contains much of relevance to Latin studies.

CHAPTER THIRTY-TWO

Lucretius

Monica R. Gale

Lucretius and Epicureanism

Lucretius' *De rerum natura* (*On the Nature of Things* or *On the Nature of the Universe*), usually dated to approximately 55 BCE, is a work of great ambition. Though it is normally classified by modern scholars as a didactic rather than an epic poem, its scale (six books of hexameters, a total of more than 7,000 lines) and its global aspirations (it purports to teach the reader about the nature of everything that exists) are anomalous in the context of earlier didactic. Like Hesiod's *Works and Days*, Lucretius' poem is addressed to a named recipient, Memmius (almost certainly to be identified with the politically prominent Gaius Memmius, praetor in 58 BCE), and combines technical subject matter with a strong moralizing undercurrent. On the other hand, Hesiod and his successors had usually confined their work within a much smaller compass (Greek didactic poems known to us are generally limited to a single book, of a few hundred lines) and dealt with far less grandiose themes. Although the philosophical poems of Parmenides and Empedocles are a partial exception to the latter rule, the scope and scale of the *De rerum natura* (*DRN*) point rather to a strong affinity with the "totalizing impulse" (Hardie 1993: 1) of heroic epic. In what follows, I will suggest that Lucretius invites us in a number of more concrete and specific ways to read his work against the background of Homeric and Ennian epic rather than (or in addition to) the didactic tradition of Hesiod. Some of the implications of this generic affiliation will be discussed below. First, however, it may be useful to look briefly at the main tenets of the philosophical system expounded in the poem.

Lucretius tells us explicitly (*DRN* 3.1–8) that he follows in the footsteps of Epicurus (341–270 BCE; the philosopher is identified by name in 3.1042), whose monumental prose treatise *On Nature* – or possibly a shorter summary of the main doctrines – seems to have served the poet as a direct source (Clay 1983: 26–35 and 111–68; Sedley 1998, esp. 134–65). Lucretius' main focus is on the physical nature of the world and its human (and animal) inhabitants; but Epicurus had declared physics subordinate to ethics, and it can be argued that for the poet too physics is essentially a means to an end. The goal of life, for Epicurus and his followers, is pleasure, defined as the removal of physical pain and mental disturbance: while sensual pleasure is not thereby excluded, its ultimate end is the attainment of tranquillity (*ataraxia*). Epicurus held that the two greatest threats to our peace of mind are unfounded fears and insatiable desires, and it is here that physics and ethics are connected. The two central planks of Epicurus' physical doctrine are rationalism and materialism: the universe consists exclusively of matter (reducible ultimately to indestructible atoms) and empty space (or void). There is no supernatural or non-physical realm, and everything that happens in the world is susceptible of a scientific explanation. The gods do exist, but do not intervene in human life in any way; the soul – like everything else in the universe – is a material entity, which simply disintegrates and ceases to exist when we die. Hence, we should limit our desires to those which can be physically satisfied (desire for abstract qualities such as fame or love is futile because inherently insatiable, and therefore to be avoided). Fear, on the other hand, can be eliminated by the study of nature: once we realize that we are not in the hands of arbitrary gods, and that we need have no apprehensions about the fate of the soul after death, the two most powerful sources of human anxiety will, in Epicurus' view, have been eradicated. Lucretius makes it clear throughout his poem – particularly in the "syllabuses" which introduce the topics for discussion at the beginning of each of the six books – that the elimination of such fears is his underlying purpose.

The *DRN* aims to encompass all the essential elements of Epicurus' physical theory, while repeatedly reminding us of the ethical implications of the doctrine. The poem is structured as a persuasive argument, rather than an impersonal exposition; Memmius' role is in this respect an important one, offering the reader a model of active engagement with the poet's teaching (the didactic speaker repeatedly anticipates and deals with possible objections to his argument, often placing these counter-arguments in the mouth of his addressee (Classen 1968: 15–16, Clay 1983: 212–25, Mitsis 1994)). Lucretius frequently draws attention – both explicitly and implicitly – to broader repercussions which follow from the various stages of his argument: the opening proposition that "nothing can come into being out of nothing," for instance, is given an anti-theological slant by the addition of the word *divinitus*, "by divine agency," while the extended discussion of the nature of the soul in Book 3 culminates in an impassioned diatribe against the fear of death.

The poem is ordered in such a way as to emphasize the all-embracing scope of Lucretius' teaching: we begin on the microscopic level (Books 1 and 2 deal with the atomic structure of matter, the formation of compounds, and atomic motion), and move "outwards" to human and animal life (Books 3 and 4 are devoted respectively to the nature of the mind and soul – or life force – and to sensation, thought, sex, and heredity), and finally to the cosmos (Book 5 covers cosmogony, cosmology, and human prehistory, Book 6 a looser assortment of meteorological and other phenomena, including thunder and lightning, earthquakes, plagues, and magnetism). This movement from the minimal to the maximal level appears designed to reflect the assurance (stated more explicitly at 6.527–34) that Epicurus' teaching is absolutely comprehensive: there is nothing that it cannot account for (Kennedy 2000).

Epic or Didactic?

Lucretius' decision to embody his philosophical message in the form of an epic/didactic poem is an inherently paradoxical one. Though the idea that poetry might deal with such an abstruse and highly technical subject as atomic physics would not have seemed alien to an ancient audience (the didactic poets of the Hellenistic period seem to have relished the challenge of versifying apparently intractable material, while the philosopher-poets of the sixth and fifth centuries BCE offered a precedent for the combination of verse-form and philosophical subject matter), Lucretius had to confront a problem which arose specifically from the combination of *Epicurean* philosophy with this particular literary form. A number of ancient authorities (see especially Epicurus frr. 117 and 163; Diog. Laert. 10.120; Cic. *Fin.* 1.71–2 and 2.12; Plut. *Mor.* 1087a, 1094d–e) suggest that

Epicurus himself maintained a dismissive and hostile attitude towards poetry and the liberal arts in general. There is some controversy about the precise details of Epicurus' views on the subject (almost nothing survives of the philosopher's own writings on this topic, and the treatises on poetics and rhetoric composed by the Epicurean Philodemus – a contemporary of Lucretius – are also very fragmentary and often difficult to interpret). It can be argued with some plausibility, however, that his objections were twofold: first, poetry was strongly associated in the ancient world with mythology; and, secondly, Epicurus' linguistic theory seems to have involved the idea that words should be employed in their "proper" sense (Epicurus, *Ep. Hdt.* 37–8; Diog. Laert. 10.31), an attitude which would seem to preclude the use of the stylized and figurative language characteristic of poetic discourse. Homeric epic, in particular, had been subject to philosophical criticism from at least the sixth century BCE for its depiction of amoral and frivolous gods; given Epicurus' rationalist and anti-theological worldview, as well as the centrality of the epics in the Greek (and Roman) educational system, it is easy to see how they might have become a particular target for attack (Gale 1994: 10–18; Asmis 1995; on ancient critical responses to the "divine apparatus" of epic, see also Feeney 1991: 5–56; on the importance of epic poetry in the ancient educational system, see Keith 2000: 8–18).

On the other hand, the prestige attached to epic as the most authoritative and highly respected of the literary genres made it in some respects a very appropriate and desirable vehicle for a poet seeking to insist on the sublimity and supreme importance of Epicurus' teachings (Conte 1994a; cf. Schrijvers 1970, esp. 27–50). Lucretius does not attempt to gloss over the tension between rationalist doctrine and poetic form; rather, he can be seen to justify his appropriation of the epic form by a process of implicit negotiation which continues throughout the poem.

Lucretius' most explicit comments on his relationship with the epic tradition fall in the proem to Book 1. Following the opening invocation of Venus (discussed below) and a brief "syllabus" for the poem (1.50–61), the poet acclaims Epicurus as a hero who defeated the "monster," *religio* ("religion" or "piety"); the sacrifice of Iphigenia is then described at some length to exemplify the evils prompted by traditional belief in interventionist gods. The reader is warned not to be deterred from philosophical study by the "terrifying words" of the *vates* ("soothsayers," a word later adopted by the Augustans to designate poets writing in an inspired or elevated manner, but at this date still, apparently, somewhat derogatory); as a representative of these *vates*, Lucretius singles out Ennius (on whom see Chapter 31, by Goldberg), whose ideas about the afterlife are held up to ridicule. Ennius and Homer – whose reincarnation the Roman poet had claimed to be – are handled here with a characteristic combination of admiration and derision. The former is praised in 1.117–18 as "the first to bring down from lovely Helicon a garland of everlasting leaves," and the admiring epithet "ever-flourishing" is applied to the latter (1.124); Homer's ghost is represented (probably in allusion to Ennius' own proem) as teaching his successor about – significantly – "the nature of the universe" (*rerum natura*, 1.126). Lucretius, then, follows in the critical tradition of reading the Homeric poems as bearers of philosophical and theological meaning, but emphatically rejects the message they convey (indeed, he goes on to make the errors promulgated by Homer and his successors the *grounds* for his own engagement with theological and eschatological questions, 1.127–35). Also striking, from a programmatic point of view, is the juxtaposition of Epicurus as hero (note especially the imagery of conquest and victory in 1.72–9 (West 1969: 57–60; Hardie 1986: 194–5; Gale 1994: 118–19)) with the Trojan War heroes sardonically referred to in line 86 as "foremost of men":

Humana ante oculos foede cum vita iaceret
in terris oppressa gravi sub religione

. . .

primum Graius homo mortalis tollere contra
est oculos ausus *primus*que obsistere contra

. . .

ergo vivida vis animi pervicit, et extra
processit longe flammantia moenia mundi
atque omne immensum peragravit mente animoque,
unde refert nobis victor quid possit oriri,
quid nequeat, finita potestas denique cuique
quanam sit ratione atque alte terminus haerens.
quare religio pedibus subiecta vicissim
obteritur, nos exaequat victoria caelo.
   Illud in his rebus vereor, ne forte rearis
impia te rationis inire elementa viamque
indugredi sceleris. quod contra saepius illa
religio peperit scelerosa atque impia facta.
Aulide quo pacto Triviai virginis aram
Iphianassai turparunt sanguine foede
ductores Danaum delecti, *prima virorum*.

(DRN 1.62–3, 66–7, 72–86)

When human life lay shamefully grovelling on the earth for all to see, weighed down beneath the oppressive weight of Religion . . . *a man of Greece* [namely Epicurus] was *first* who dared to raise his mortal eyes and *first* to stand against her . . . And so the lively force of his mind prevailed, and he advanced far beyond the flaming walls of the world and ranged through the unbounded universe in his mind and thought; from there, in victory, he brought back to us knowledge of what can come to be and what cannot, what limits are placed on the power of each thing as a deep-set boundary-stone. And so Religion in turn is trampled underfoot, and we – by his victory – are raised to heaven.

In dealing with these matters, I am anxious about one thing: that you might perhaps think you are embarking on the study of an impious philosophy and setting foot on a path of wickedness. On the contrary, religion itself has more often inspired wicked and impious deeds – just as at Aulis, the chosen leaders of the Greeks, *foremost of men*, foully polluted the altar of the Virgin Diana with the blood of Iphianassa [Iphigenia].

Lucretius, by implication, sets up a line of generic succession stretching from Homer through Ennius to his own poem; but at the same time, there is a hint that the *DRN* will surpass or even supersede its predecessors. Homer and Ennius are lauded as the producers of "everlasting" poetry; but the kind of heroism they celebrated is implicitly called into question, and Epicurus' philosophical "conquest" held up as an alternative to the military exploits with which epic is most strongly associated. Earlier epic poetry is criticized for its propagation of false stories about the afterlife (and, presumably, about the gods); Lucretius' poem, by contrast, offers us the Truth.

The combination of rejection and appropriation programmatically displayed at this early stage in the poem is reflected in various ways throughout the rest of the work. Homer is once again referred to by name at the end of Book 3, in the course of the diatribe against the fear of death. Lucretius recommends that his readers dispel any lingering reluctance to confront their own mortality by employing the conventional topos "even the greatest of men must die." The point is expanded into a catalogue of Greek and Roman "heroes" (3.1025–44), the ordering of which is rhetorically significant. The poet begins conventionally enough with kings and warriors, but the climactic position at the end of the list is reserved for Democritus and – of course – Epicurus. The poets (*unus Homerus*, "the one and only Homer," is specifically singled out here) come after the generals, but before the philosophers: the implication is, once again, that poetic artistry, though admirable, is ultimately less important than philosophical truth (Segal 1990: 171–80).

Metapoetic subtexts can be detected in a number of other passages. In 1.471–82, for example, the Trojan War is pointedly selected as an example of an historical event, something which – Lucretius is arguing – does not exist in its own right, but as an epiphenomenon of the interaction of atoms in space. Strikingly, the void is referred to both at the beginning and at the end of this passage as "the space in which all things come about" ("res in quo quaeque geruntur/gerantur"), a phrase evocative of the Latin expression *res gestae*, "exploits." The implication once again seems to be that the meta-phorical "exploits" of Epicurean atoms are far more fundamentally important than the literal exploits of the Trojan War heroes. Similarly, in 3.832–42 the Punic Wars are dismissed, in strikingly Ennian language (compare Enn. *Ann.* fr. 309, Skutsch 1985), as matters of little importance to us *now*, given that we were not yet born when they occurred. A more extensive quotation – this time from the *Odyssey* – is incorporated into the proem of the same book: here, Lucretius describes in terms of a mystical revelation the power of Epicurus' philosophy to uncover all the secrets of the universe, including the abodes of the gods. Lines 3.18–22 are a close translation of *Odyssey* 6.42–6, where Athena is returning to Olympus after bringing aid to her favorite, Odysseus: she leaves behind the mortal world and ascends to the peaceful dwellings of the gods. But Lucretius adds two lines which again seem to offer a pointed commentary on the errors of Homer's world-view: "nature supplies them with all their needs, and nothing detracts at any time from their peace of mind" (3.23–4). It is easy to see here an implicit critique directed at the original Homeric context of the lines: for Lucretius, the gods could never interfere in human affairs as Athena does, because this would very emphatically "detract from their peace of mind" (see further Gale 1994: 107–14).

In addition to passages of implicit programmatic engagement, Lucretius seeks through-out the poem to "neutralize" the dangerous mythological content of his epic intertexts (Hardie 1986: 176–93; Gale 1994: esp. 26–50 and 111–14, and 2000: 113–15). On a number of occasions (e.g. 2.600–60, 4.580–94, 5.396–415), a brief mythological narrative is juxtaposed with a scientific explanation for the phenomenon in question. The process of demythologization effected by this combination of traditional myth and Epicurean truth can be seen to operate on a more subtle level in several of the (relatively numerous) passages where Lucretius echoes Homeric language or imagery. Particularly characteristic is the cooption of Homeric similes in descriptions of natural phenomena. Whereas Homer compares a warrior's prowess, or an army advancing into battle, to a storm or flood, Lucretius describes the storm or flood itself in Homeric language. Often, though not always, tenor and vehicle are reversed (that is, Lucretius implicitly or explicitly compares his storms and floods to warriors, as in 6.96–8, where the "battling winds" recall a simile applied in *Il.* 16.765–9 to Greeks and Trojans clashing in battle). In all these instances, the poet is careful to emphasize the fact that these are natural and impersonal processes: personification is acceptable as a poetic ornament (a point explicitly stated with reference to the use of metonymy in 2.655–60), so long as we keep clear in our minds the fact that the elements of the natural world are neither animate nor controlled by gods. Lucretius seeks to appropriate the grandeur and glamour of Homeric narrative for his epic of nature, while rigorously excluding the conventional divine machinery.

We have seen that this exclusion is programmatically announced in the proem to Book 3; on a more subtle level, a similar element of polemic can be detected in the very first simile of the poem, at 1.280–9. By way of introduction to the concept of invisible particles, the poet reminds us that we already accept the existence of unseen forces in nature, such as wind; and winds must be corporeal because they have a similar impact on their surroundings to that of flooding rivers. The comparison of wind and flood is based, again, on a Homeric simile (*Il.* 5.87–92: Diomedes attacks like a river in spate); but where Homer attributes the flood to "Zeus' rain," Lucretius pointedly substitutes *natura* as the agent of destruction (more specifically, *mollis aquae...natura*, "the soft substance of water," 1.281; but in this marked context the periphrasis seems more than just an equivalent to the simple noun *aqua*).

Though, as I have argued, Lucretius invites the reader to consider his poem primarily in the tradition of Homeric/Ennian epic, occasional allusions to didactic predecessors suggest that the poet is *also* keen to offer a corrective to this branch of the tradition, insofar as it too has contributed to erroneous conceptions of the relationship between human beings and the gods. The most sustained example is the history of civilization at the end of Book 5, which repeatedly evokes the Hesiodic Myth of Ages (Hes. *WD* 109–201; cf. also 42–105 (Prometheus and Pandora) and 225–37 (the just city)), particularly in describing the life of the very first human beings (5.925–1010). Lucretius accepts certain features of Hesiod's picture of the Golden Age (spontaneous production of food, 5.937–8; no agriculture, 5.933–6; absence of disease, 5.929–30), but – once again – denies any role to the gods, and severely rationalizes the details of the Hesiodic account (the absence of disease is attributed to the greater toughness of early humans' physique and the milder climate they enjoyed; the earth's spontaneous production of food is not miraculous, rather the primitive humans simply live on wild fruits and acorns similar to those which can still be found today). Hesiod's four "metallic" ages are similarly demythologized and integrated into Lucretius' account of early developments in metalworking (5.1241–96: note especially the Hesiodic echo in 1289, which recalls *WD* 150–1); and the Prometheus myth is implicitly dismissed in 5.1091–1104, where Lucretius explains how a thunderbolt first brought fire down from heaven and "distributed" it amongst human beings (see further Gale 1994: 164–74 and 177–8).

The philosophical poet Empedocles is handled somewhat more gently, and in fact receives warmer praise than any other writer apart from Epicurus. Lucretius expresses admiration, it appears, for both the style and the content of Empedocles' work: in contrast to the ambiguous, riddling language of Heraclitus (1.638–44), his "surpassingly bright discoveries" (*praeclara reperta*, 1.732) are, it seems, clarified rather than obscured by the use of poetic form.

The imagery of light and darkness employed in the poet's critique of Heraclitus and Empedocles is picked up in 1.921–50 (repeated, with the omission of the first five lines, as the proem to Book 4), where Lucretius comments on his own employment of poetic form. Poetry, he suggests, is like the honey which doctors smear round the rim of a cup in order to fool a sick child into taking unpleasant-tasting medicine: like honey, his poetry is bright and sweet, while Epicurus' teaching seems at first glance "rather grim" (*tristior*, 1.944 = 4.19). The apologia embodied in these lines constitutes Lucretius' most explicit response to Epicurus' critique of poetry, and offers a theoretical justification for the opportunistic exploitation of Homeric and Ennian intertexts which I have outlined in this section. Poetic form, Lucretius suggests, has a unique power to attract and "enchant" the reader (just as the honey "captivates" the sick child). This is, of course, just what makes it so dangerous; but it also renders it a powerful tool if used as a vehicle for philosophical truth (the child would not drink the medicine at all if not lured by the sweet honey). Poetic imagery and language can help to shed light on the sometimes difficult and superficially unattractive truths of Epicurean philosophy; but such poetry will only be *beneficial* if the content (the medicine in the cup) accords with (Epicurean) truth.

Lucretius' admiring but antagonistic relationship with his poetic predecessors is easily explicable in purely literary terms: the literary principles inherited by late Republican and Augustan writers from the enormously influential Alexandrian poet and scholar

Callimachus (fl. *ca.* 285–246 BCE) set a premium on originality and avoidance of trite and hackneyed themes. A partial allegiance to Callimachean poetics is implied by the metaphors of untrodden path, untouched spring, and garland of fresh flowers at the beginning of the passage under discussion (1.926–30 = 4.1–5). It is important, however, that Lucretius also offers us a philosophical justification of his poetic practice: ultimately, poetic form is subordinated to philosophical content in this work, and the poet's ramble through "the pathless haunts of the Muses" (1.926 = 4.1) is, paradoxically, already mapped out by the footprints left by Epicurus (3.3–4). (On Lucretius and Callimachus, see further Kenney 1970; Brown 1982; on Lucretius' poetics in general, see Schrijvers 1970: 27–50 and 325–40; Clay 1976; Gale 1994: 138–55; Kat. Volk 2002b: 94–118.)

Philosophy as poetry

One of the most immediately striking characteristics of Lucretius' poetry is the vivid and minutely observed detail with which both natural phenomena and the familiar sights, sounds, and smells of the human world are described. The concrete, sensuous precision of these descriptive passages is perhaps the most obvious tool employed by the poet in order to bridge the opposition between philosophical content and poetic form discussed at the end of the previous section. The use of analogies drawn from the everyday world is licensed by Epicurus' insistence on the importance and reliability of sensory evidence (see e.g. Diog. Laert. 10.31–2); and the Homeric simile offered precedents for the poetic evocation both of sublime and awe-inspiring natural phenomena (storms, floods, the night sky) and of humble domestic scenes (cheese-making, blacksmithing, the behavior of small children or domestic animals).

Formally, too, the extended comparisons traditional in narrative epic (and, to a lesser extent, in earlier didactic) proved both poetically and philosophically advantageous for the Epicurean poet. In Lucretius' hands, the extended simile is transformed into an instrument of didactic instruction, serving particularly to illustrate processes which are necessarily unfamiliar or inaccessible (because invisible, or remote in time or space). At the same time, the use of imagery serves to "poeticize" the abstract theoretical propositions of atomic physics (West 1969; Schiesaro 1990; Dalzell 1996: 59–65).

The Lucretian simile is notable for the precision with which the two things being compared are matched. Where Homeric similes often rely for their effect on the *contrast* between, for example, the tumult of battle and the peaceful agricultural or domestic scene to which it is compared, Lucretius tends to compare processes or phenomena which are essentially similar (West 1970: 272–5; Hardie 1986: 219–23; Gale 1994: 63–5 and 114-16). The comparison of wind and river in 1.280–9 (discussed above) exemplifies this propensity particularly clearly: water and wind are in fact *both* composed of invisible particles, and operate in exactly the same way; the similar effect they have on their environment (emphasized by verbal echoes between the simile and its context) is *more* than just superficial analogy. Examples could easily be multiplied: the heap of poppy seeds described in 2.453–5, or the morning mist in 5.460–6, or the sound of clothes on a line snapping in the wind, 6.114-15, are closely similar to, or even instances of, the processes they are introduced to illustrate (the smooth, round atoms of liquids; the rising of light particles which caused the formation of aether at the beginning of the world; the production of thunder through collision of clouds blown by high winds). In these instances, the simile not only serves an illustrative function, but also acts as a heuristic device: we can tell that the atoms of liquids must be smooth and round *because* they behave like poppy seeds.

The impact of the formal similes is deepened and reinforced by the densely metaphorical texture of the expository passages. Lucretius avoids the use of technical terminology as far as possible (Dalzell 1996: 72–103; Sedley 1998: 35–49; Kennedy 2000), preferring to take advantage of the connotative potential of metaphorical expressions (such as *semina*, "seeds," or *exordia*, "first beginnings" or more literally the "warp-threads" laid on a loom; contrast Epicurus' technical term *atomos*, "the indivisible"). Metaphors of this kind may interact with similes to form complexes of imagery which recur through the poem. The metaphorical connection between the formation of atomic compounds and plant or animal reproduction implied by the term *semina*, for instance, anticipates the more explicit analogy between the earth and an animal or human mother employed extensively in the cosmogony and zoogony of Book 5 (see especially 5.783–836). The metaphorical link between atoms and warp-threads, too, recurs in different ways throughout the poem (West 1969: 80–2; Snyder 1983): compounds are "woven" of atoms like a garment, and, also like a garment, can be pulled apart again (the rays of the sun "unweave" the sea, like Penelope with Laertes' shroud, 5.267 and 389; the image works particularly well in Latin, because the word for "ray," *radius*, is also the technical term for the shuttle used in weaving). Perhaps most prominent of all is a third complex of metaphors, relating to warfare: the atoms are like warriors, and Nature is their commanding officer. (See especially 2.118–20 and 323–32, where atomic motion is compared to skirmishing troops or military maneuvers; the image of Nature as general is suggested especially by such recurring phrases as *foedera naturae*, "nature's treaties," and *natura gerit res*, "nature conducts her affairs/wages war" (discussed above in connection with the Trojan War *exemplum* in 1.471–82); for further examples and discussion, see Mayer 1990; Gale 2000: 232–40.)

All these systems of imagery help to bring the impersonal cosmos of Epicurus to life, and to give it, so to speak, human interest; yet for that very reason they also have the potential to mislead the reader (Kennedy 2000; Gale 2004). Unlike a warrior, an atom has no volition of its own, nor is it, like a warp-thread, the instrument of some purposeful agent; the earth, unlike a human or animal mother, is not alive, nor can it feel anything for its "offspring." The poet cannot afford to allow us to take his metaphors too literally, or they might open the door for creative and controlling deities to creep back into his system. Lucretius seeks to pre-empt this danger by undercutting his own metaphors, employing a technique similar to the juxtaposition of myth and scientific explanation discussed on p. 444 above. At 2.600–60, most obviously, a lengthy digression is devoted to the cult of the earth-goddess Cybele, leading to the conclusion that the earth is neither a goddess nor a living being; this prominent passage helps to "defuse" the risk entailed by metaphorical references to Mother Earth in Book 5 and elsewhere. Similarly prominent are the two somewhat surreal passages (1.915–20 and 2.973–90) in which the notion that the atoms are animate is subjected to *reductio ad absurdum* (if they are alive, are we to assume that they also laugh, cry, engage in philosophical debate?); the poet also denies explicitly at 1.1021–34 (cf. 5.419–31) that the confluence of atoms which brought about the formation of our world was a conscious or purposeful action.

Two further systems of imagery may be mentioned briefly here: these relate not only to the movements and interaction of the atoms, but also to the reader's gradually increasing apprehension of the truths of Epicurean philosophy. Metaphors of light and darkness are prominent throughout the poem, particularly in the proems; they frequently serve to point a contrast between the blissful pleasure enjoyed by the Epicurean disciple and the stormy passions of the unenlightened, or to convey the intellectually "illuminating" effect of Epicurean philosophy or Lucretius' poetry. Alongside the recurrent image of understanding as illumination, and sometimes combined with it, we find the portrayal of the poem as a journey (Schrijvers 1970: 16–26; Fowler 2000): teacher/poet and pupil/reader are imagined as traveling together towards the truth, following the traces of Epicurus' footprints. (Light and dark: e.g. 1.136–7, 3.1–2, 5.10–12, and the repeated passage 1.146–8 = 2.59–61 = 3.91–3 = 6.39–41; poem as journey: e.g. 1.80–2, 1.331–3,

2.82, 3.3–4, 5.55–6, 6.27–8, 6.92–3; note also the closing lines of Book 1, 1114–17, where the image of philosophical study as a torch-lit path combines the two metaphors.)

Lucretius' depiction of the atoms as warriors, and of the philosopher and his disciple as engaged in a "quest" for the truth, bring us back to the relationship between the *DRN* and narrative or heroic epic. It can be argued that this imagery not only serves to enliven Lucretius' presentation of atomic physics, but also contributes to the working out of the poet's claim to rival the epics of Homer and Ennius. The metaphors of travel, in particular, help to convey a sense of narrative progression: the didactic speaker is not simply *describing* the world around us, but – as it were – guiding us on a journey through it, a journey already mapped out by Epicurus (note, in this connection, that the relatively unusual verb *peragrare*, initially applied to Epicurus' intellectual "expedition" beyond the walls of the world in 1.74, is used again with reference to the composition of the poem, 1.926 = 4.1, and to the pupil's increasingly independent progress in 2.677: "cetera consimili mentis ratione peragrans/invenies…," "ranging through everything by a similar process of thought, you will discover…"). From another point of view, the "plot" of the poem centers on the personified atoms: in addition to fighting metaphorical wars under the leadership of Nature, they come together in "assemblies" (*concilia* or *congressus*, e.g. 1.484, 2.120, 2.1065, 5.67; Gale 1994: 122–4) and lay the foundations of the world (implicitly depicted as a city, especially by the repeated use of the phrase *moenia mundi*, "the walls of the world," through the "gates" of which Epicurus bursts out in 1.71). These systems of imagery, taken together, suggest parallels with the different branches of the narrative epic tradition: the heroic quest, the epic of war, the foundation epic.

It is worth pointing out that the characterization of both Epicurus and *Natura* makes them somewhat unconventional heroes, from the perspective of Roman Republican ideology as well as epic tradition. The very Roman opening of the poem, in which Venus is appealed to as *Aeneadum genetrix*, "mother of Aeneas' line" (1.1), to grant peace to her people as well as bestow her "charm" (*lepos*, 28) on the poet's work, gives way abruptly to the praise of a *Greek* hero (*Graius homo*, 66), whose triumphs are not military but intellectual. The near-juxtaposition of Roman Venus and Greek Epicurus seems a deliberately provocative gesture on the poet's part. Despite his apparently conventional praise of Memmius in 26–7 and 42–3 as the scion of a splendid aristocratic line, on whom the security and good government (*communis salus*, 1.43) of his country depends, Lucretius will soon make it clear that Epicurean doctrine comes into direct conflict with traditional Roman values (Fowler 1989). Service to one's country is a mirage: it is better to be a subject than a ruler (5.1129–30), and the desire for political power is merely a misguided reaction to the fear of death (2.14–61, 3.59–93). The futile struggle for wealth and glory results only in cutthroat competitiveness and ultimately civil war; true triumphs are won with words, not weapons (5.50). Lucretius' other hero, *Natura*, occupies an even more anomalous role, as a female general. The substitution of an abstract entity personified as feminine for that most virile of literary stereotypes, the epic hero, implies a inversion of conventional gender roles comparable to the *militia amoris*, the "warfare of love," idealized by the Roman elegists. By elevating their beloved to the status of a *domina*, a "mistress" in the social as well as the erotic sense, and by suggesting that their sexual tussles are comparable with military engagements, the elegists underline their subversion of conventional Roman values; much the same could be said, *mutatis mutandis*, of Lucretius. (On female figures in the *DRN*, see especially Fowler 1996; for a different interpretation, see Nugent 1994 and Keith 2000: 36–40, 107–11.)

Part of Venus' role in the proem, then, is to lull the reader into a temporary sense of security: initially, this seems like a conventional epic exordium, though Venus – by didactic convention (compare Hesiod and Aratus, who appeal to Zeus, and the prayer to twelve rural deities at the opening of Virgil's *Georgics*) – stands in for the Muse or Muses more commonly addressed by epic poets. From an Epicurean perspective, however, the prayer, like the poet's use of personification elsewhere in the poem, is distinctly problematic, and has for this reason been one of the most controversial parts of the work. Given that the poet will argue (perhaps as early as 1.44–9, though the authenticity of the lines at this point in the poem is disputed) that the gods do not intervene in any way in the human world, it seems perverse in the extreme to begin by asking Venus both to bestow *lepos* ("charm," "attractiveness") on the poem, and to petition her lover Mars on behalf of the Roman people. Most critics agree that the goddess is to be understood (retrospectively, in the case of the first-time reader) as a symbol or personification; amongst the numerous interpretations, she has been held to represent Epicurean pleasure (Bignone 1945: 136–44; cf. Elder 1954; Schrijvers 1970: 272–9), especially by contrast with the stern authority of Stoic Zeus (Asmis 1982); natural creativity, and/or the reproductive instinct (e.g. Giancotti 1959: 201–17; cf. Clay 1983: 87–95); or a kind of Epicurean version of the Empedoclean force of Love, held by the Presocratic philosopher to govern the universe alternately with the opposing force of Strife (represented here by Mars; see Furley 1970; Sedley 1998: 15–17, 23–7). Another possibility is to regard her as a complex, composite symbol, simultaneously representing *all* these positive forces (Gale 1994: 208–23). In any case, it is clear that, as the poem progresses, Venus is "eclipsed" (Clay 1983: 226–34) or demythologized (Gale 1994: 211–14). Once she has served her function as the honey on the cup of philosophy – the *captatio benevolentiae* designed to secure the attention and good will of a possibly hostile audience – the sense of familiarity and security which she provides is rapidly eroded. Already in 1.56 Venus' role as creative, nurturing deity has been taken over by impersonal *natura*; significantly, too, her epithets *genetrix* ("mother", 1.1) and *alma* ("nourisher" or "life-giver", 1.2) are reallocated to Mother Earth in 2.599 and 992 respectively. Still more striking is the poet's reply to anonymous objectors at 2.167–74:

> at quidam contra haec, ignari materiai,
> naturam non posse deum sine numine credunt
> tanto opere humanis rationibus admoderate
> tempora mutare annorum frugesque creare,
> et iam cetera, mortalis quae suadet adire
> *ipsaque deducit dux vitae dia voluptas*
> *et res per Veneris blanditur saecla propagent,*
> ne genus occidat humanum.

Some, however, knowing nothing of the nature of matter, believe that Nature unaided by the power of the gods could not bring about the changes of the seasons or the growth of crops so conveniently for human purposes, nor all those other things which *divine pleasure, the guide of life, urges and leads us mortals to enjoy, tempting us to reproduce our kind through the work of Venus*, lest the human race die out.

The language here strongly recalls the picture of Venus in the proem to Book 1, but impersonal forces (*natura* and *voluptas*, or pleasure) now take over the role played by the goddess at the beginning of the poem. Venus herself – both here and more strikingly in the finale to Book 4 – is now demoted to the status of metonym for sexual reproduction ("res per Veneris . . . saecla propagent," "to reproduce our kind through the work of Venus", 2.173; cf. "haec Venus est nobis," "this [namely the emission of semen brought on by sexual desire] is our Venus", 4.1058).

Almost equally controversial is the poem's surprise ending. The lengthy and gruesome account of the Athenian plague (based on Thuc. 2.47–53) which concludes Book 6 has seemed to many readers an oddly disturbing finale for a poem designed to recommend peace of mind and freedom from anxiety. Again, a number of different interpretations have been put forward; constraints of space preclude a full discussion here, though it seems worth drawing attention in the present context to the fact that abrupt endings are not unusual in ancient epic (the *Aeneid* is the most obvious example, but we might also compare the problematic ending of the *Odyssey*, and note too that closure at the end of the *Iliad* is somewhat undercut by Priam's reminder that the fighting must continue after the burial of Hektor, 24.667). It seems significant, moreover, that Lucretius' plague is intertextually related to both the beginning and the end of the *Iliad* as well as to Thucydides (Gale 1994: 112–14, P. G. Fowler 1997: 126–9). Like the proem, the poem's finale can be read in a variety of ways, which need not be regarded as mutually exclusive (see especially Commager 1957; Schrijvers 1970: 312–24; Clay 1983: 257–66; Segal 1990: 228–37; P. G. Fowler 1997), and its very abruptness might be thought to offer an effective "shock-treatment" for any reader still unmoved at this late stage by the poet's Epicurean message. Some critics (notably David Sedley (1998: 160–5)) continue to believe, however, that the work is unfinished and that Lucretius – had he lived to complete his poem – would have added a comforting coda or a concluding exhortation to counteract the bleak images with which the text, as we have it, breaks off.

In the course of this chapter, I have pointed out a number of ways in which the poetry and the philosophy of the *DRN* seem to be in tension with each other. Criticism of the poem for much of the last century revolved around these tensions, though the tendency in recent decades has been to suggest – as I have done here – that the poet finds ways of successfully resolving them. More recently still, certain critics (notably Duncan Kennedy and the late Don Fowler) have begun to draw attention once again to the stresses and strains imposed by the sometimes contradictory demands of poetic and philosophical discourse and to the problematic nature of Lucretius' claim to represent a world which is completely impersonal and demythologized. As the Fowlers note in their *Oxford Classical Dictionary* article (D. P. and P. G. Fowler 1996a: 890), Lucretius can be seen to construct his own "myths": the anthropomorphic treatment of Nature and Mother Earth, and the personification of atomic matter, certainly create their own problems for the poet. We should beware of implying that in adapting the epic form to the presentation of Epicurean philosophy Lucretius ties up all the loose ends and smoothes over all the rough edges; and of course the fact that *not* all readers of the *DRN* have been convinced by its didactic message offers an indication that writers cannot control the response of actual, historical readers of their texts as fully as they might wish to do. Nevertheless, it seems fair to say that modern criticism of the poem has successfully dispelled the long-maintained view that the *DRN* consists of "oases of poetry" amid long stretches of dry philosophy; on the contrary, Lucretius offers his reader not simply versified prose, but a genuine fusion of closely reasoned argument and persuasive rhetoric, with the grandeur and monumentality of Homeric and Ennian epic.

FURTHER READING

The standard text of the *De rerum natura* is Cyril Bailey's Oxford Classical Text (2nd edn., 1922). Several serviceable translations of the poem are now available: Esolen 1995 (verse) and M.F. Smith 2001 (prose) are particularly recommended; Latham 1994 (prose) and Melville 1997 (verse) include good introductions and notes (by J. Godwin and D. P. and P. G. Fowler respectively). A new verse translation, by Alicia Stallings, is forthcoming from Penguin Books.

Bailey's three-volume commentary (1947) remains an invaluable resource. There are also commentaries on individual books or parts of books by P. M. Brown (1984 and 1997), D. P. Fowler

(2002), E. J. Kenney (1971), J. Godwin (1986 and 1991), R. D. Brown (1987), C. D. N. Costa (1984) and G. Campbell (2003).

In addition to the works cited above, see W. R. Johnson 2000 for a lively general introduction to the poem and a fascinating account of its modern reception; also useful is Kenney 1995. Toohey 1996 includes a chapter on Lucretius. A number of points touched on above are developed in more detail in Gale 2001.

CHAPTER THIRTY-THREE

Virgil's *Aeneid*

Michael C. J. Putnam

Virgil's *Aeneid* is the single most widely read and discussed work of poetry by a Roman author, with a deep and continuing influence on western letters that has endured for more than two millennia (see Chapter 42, by Kallendorf). While Virgil was still at work on its composition it was hailed as a rival of Homer's *Iliad* by the contemporary poet Propertius (Prop. 2.34.61–6), and its status as a masterpiece has been assured from the time of its publication, shortly after its author's death in 19 BCE. Commentary upon the poem began immediately. This took the form of emulation by Virgil's younger contemporary Ovid and by a host of later writers whose number is by no means limited to producers of epic. Publication also initiated the practice of intense exegesis, which approached the epic from a variety of angles. This tradition reached its antique culmination in the fourth and fifth centuries, in the work of Macrobius, for whom Virgil was a philosopher and abundant source of knowledge, and of Servius, whose detailed analysis of all Virgil's poetry summarized past criticism and anticipated the rich, ongoing vein of allegorical explanation soon to be first fully tapped in the *Expositio* of Fulgentius.

The author of this masterpiece was born in Mantua, in the Po valley, in 70 BCE. Educated at Cremona and Milan, he soon became part of the Epicurean community at Naples, the city with which he remained most closely associated and where he lies buried. Although the patron of his first major work, the *Eclogues*, published probably in 37 BCE, seems to be the statesman and author Gaius Asinius Pollio, he soon entered the circle of Maecenas, confidante of the future emperor Augustus and patron as well of the poets Horace and Propertius. It was to Maecenas that Virgil dedicated his next work, the *Georgics*; it was completed at Naples probably in 30 BCE and read to Augustus in 29. The remaining dozen years of the poet's life were devoted to the *Aeneid*. At his death, if we can trust the ancient *vitae*, he would have wished to spend still three more years polishing his epic and then to devote the remainder of his life to the study of philosophy.

This progress, from *Eclogues*, then *Georgics*, to *Aeneid* was richly cumulative and in due course came to serve as a model poetic career. Though Virgil employs the same meter (dactylic hexameter) for all his poetry, as we move from work to work we gradually climb a hierarchical ladder of genres, already established in the poetry of the Greeks, which grow in importance. This takes us, first, from pastoral poetry, nominally the entertaining but slender songs of Arcadian shepherds, to didactic with, in Virgil's case, its realistic association of anonymous, agricultural man with the nature that he must tame and live with for survival. The *Aeneid*, in place of climax, takes us into epic, which is to say into a world of named heroes and their noteworthy deeds, specifically locatable in space and accomplished over a particular span of time.

But for all the upward thrust of this literary development that peaks in the genre of epic, Virgil never loses sight of his previous poetry. The first of the ten *Eclogues* deals with the effects of Roman civil war on the bucolic world, with one shepherd, his land saved from proscription, living on in a leisured realm of creativity, while the other is relegated by "an impious, barbarous soldier" to lands as distant as they are lacking in civilization. Likewise the concluding book of the *Aeneid* in large measure treats what happens when two rival chieftains, who, at least on the surface, are rivals for the hand of the same woman and the same ruling power, fight to the death. Mention of shade and its ambiguities open and close the initial *eclogue* and is prominent in the epic's final line. This last also suggests the implicit idea of unwonted exile, so prominent in Virgil's programmatic first pastoral (see Putnam 2001b, esp. 331–3).

We will see this same combination of a linear teleology, here represented by the evolution from lesser to grander genre, with a type of circularity, one that here turns in on itself to embrace and enclose the whole in a manner that transcends literary type, operative in the *Aeneid* itself. Here we will find the various trajectories, achieved or projected in the poem, that take us from the demise of Troy to the rise of Rome, from Aeneas to Augustus, from civil battling and enemies abased to a golden time of empire assured and confirmed. These linear leaps are complemented and challenged, as the plot moves forward, by a pervasive emotionality in both the divine and human spheres of the poem that, from the beginning of the narrative to its grim conclusion, continually pits rational with irrational, restraint with the violent uses of power. Virgil uses much the same language, at the poem's start, to describe the anger of Juno, that unleashes a savage sea storm against the Trojans, as he does to limn the sudden bout of rage that incites Aeneas to kill his suppliant antagonist praying for compassion (*misericordia*) as the poem ends.

Two factors of importance mark the formation of Virgil's genius, which is to say serve as background for the creation of the *Aeneid*. One is the figure of Augustus and the Rome that we associate with his name. The future emperor, who only received the title by which history knows him in 27 BCE, was born in 63, seven years after the birth of his greatest poet. His rise to supreme eminence began dramatically in the year 44 when, at the age of 19, he succeeded to the name and to the legions of his great-uncle and adoptive father, Julius Caesar, after the latter's murder. The next years of his life, which are not without abuses of power found refracted in some of Aeneas' less uplifting moments where vengeance rules his thinking, led to an inevitable showdown with Augustus' arch rival, Marcus Antonius. This confrontation occurred in a sea battle off Actium, on the west coast of Greece, in September 31, when Antony and his Egyptian consort Cleopatra were decisively vanquished. Both committed suicide as Augustus entered Alexandria in August of the subsequent year.

Though Rome's citizens would not have known this outcome then and there to be certain, the defeat of Antony nevertheless signals two things. First it represents the end of the civil warring that had plagued the Roman republic for a century. Though his propaganda would have had his people believe otherwise, Augustus's victory also initiates the Roman empire, with political authority essentially consolidated in the hands of one man. In the case of Rome's first emperor this meant the beginning of an extraordinary rule that extended some forty-five years until his death in 14 CE. We duly entitle his span of dominion the Augustan age and rank it, along with Periclean Athens, Florence under the Medici, and the England of Elizabeth I, as one of the moments in western history when the arts particularly flourished. Augustus, for instance, boasted that he found Rome a city of brick and left it a city of marble, and already within three years of Actium he had dedicated three major architectural monuments. The momentum would continue scarcely unabated over the next decades.

But we should also bear in mind that the outstanding poets and the major writer of prose that we associate with the Augustan era were, in four out of five cases, born well before peace became assured at Actium, and even Ovid, whose career reached into the reign of Tiberius, Augustus' successor, was already 12 years of age in 31, the year Augustus came to power. Moreover, although Virgil, Horace, Propertius, and Tibullus as well as the historian Livy were all at work on their masterpieces in the 20s, the first two poets at least had already produced extraordinary writing in the preceding decade, writing that in the case of Virgil reflects the contemporary ugliness of ongoing civil war. We must also remember that, even when penning the *Aeneid* in the years after Actium, Virgil places in the foreground, as the gist of his narrative, only the rise to omnipotence of one man and his allies. He ends at the moment of ambiguous victory that results from such a movement, not with some glorious aftermath with peace confirmed, an appropriate marriage celebrated, a new city established and the titular hero undergoing apotheosis – all events that by various means the poem predicts in a future beyond its conclusion.

Likewise, in moments of prophecy and through the ekphrasis of Aeneas' shield Virgil has us attend to a still more distant time to come, to the brilliant age of Augustus. But he is carefully writing not an *Augustiad* but the saga of Aeneas, hypothetical ancestor of the emperor who both is, and is not, marked as his allegorical representative. Moreover Virgil chooses to end his poem with his hero's problematical act of killing and with the disturbing lack of conclusiveness this leaves in its wake, not with a comedic set of plot resolutions that might bring felicity to his characters and satisfaction to his readers. The *Aeneid* is a far tougher poem, with a message about the employment of absolute power that remains ever worthy of contemplation.

A further factor of importance for students of Virgil's intellectual heritage as he wrote the *Aeneid* is the past history of epic. This consists of a Greek tradition, comprising primarily Homer's *Iliad* and *Odyssey* along with the Hellenistic epic of Apollonius of Rhodes, with its focus on matters erotic and artistic, which melded into Rome's late-blooming contributions to the form. Epic at Rome began over again, as it were, with Livius Andronicus' translation of the *Odyssey*, but then set out in an essentially novel direction, with the writing of historical epic that focused on the challenges and accomplishments of Rome building its Mediterranean domain. Naevius initiates this new departure in the late third century with his monographic account of Rome's first war against Carthage (264–241 BCE), the *Bellum Poenicum*. This new tradition reached its climax in the *Annales* of Ennius who, representing himself as Homer and therefore as the incarnation of the epic poet and representative of the epic past, followed Rome's march year by year from its foundation until near his death in 169 BCE (see Chapter 31, by Goldberg).

Virgil is indebted to many aspects of this multifaceted heritage. Honoring both Homer and Ennius, the *Aeneid* chronicles events in Rome's early past which happen also to follow soon upon those that end the *Iliad* and be contemporary with the story of the *Odyssey*, while in a series of flashes forward we also watch the course of Roman history as it evolves toward the world of Augustus, the poet's present. But Virgil's allegiance to, and brilliant expansion on, Homer is more complex. We have another *Odyssey*, a sea voyage documented in the epic's first six books which leads in the second and final sextet to reaching, and laying claim, to the promised land. The parallel to Odysseus's regaining of his Ithacan fiefdom and of his wife is, for Aeneas, to establish a basis of power in a new land with a new mission. The beginnings of Roman history seem to supersede the search for any close approximation of Greek myth.

For all its correspondences to the *Odyssey*, it is the *Iliad*, the story of Greeks fighting Trojans, that, documented in a series of ironic reversals, most affected Virgil's tale of one of Troy's remnants moving on to Italy. We find ourselves in the initial books of the *Aeneid* watching a long-suffering hero for the most part passively enduring his fated destiny. His vaunted piety is symbolized not in acts of heroic gallantry but in shouldering his father and leading his son out of the flames of Troy while, in the emblematic opening scene of the poem, this ability to withstand life's crises is tested by a storm set in motion by the resentful goddess Juno's savagery. The hero's self seems largely sublimated in favor of allegiance to a higher, impersonal goal. By the time we reach the epic's final three books and Aeneas has followed his inexorable course toward victory over his rival Turnus, not only has the enduring hero turned to active implementation of his fate but Virgil more and more draws not on some Trojan equivalent for Aeneas' march forward but on the figure of Achilles. It is to the *Iliad* that Virgil turns, and to its grandest hero on the Greek side, the best of the Achaeans. In particular it is to the moment when he kills his Trojan opponent Hector, in the *Iliad*'s twenty-second book, that Virgil most richly and intensely alludes as his epic reaches its close. It is as if once again, as we saw in the case of Virgil's structuring of the *Aeneid* as well as in the development of his own poetic production, the circling back on beginnings was as important to Virgil as any teleology based on Roman historical evolution from Aeneas to Augustus. Virgil poises his reader, his hero, and his poem at its conclusion not at a moment of overriding nobility for all concerned, at a magnificent juncture on the way to Augustan magnificence, but back where western epic began, with Achilles' vengeful killing of Hector.

But there is a major difference between the two episodes which makes the similarity all the more striking. This stems from what is perhaps Virgil's most original contribution to the development of epic, namely what we might call an ethical dimension to heroic action, based not on the inherited etiquette of behavior during one-on-one clashes in battle but on a grander, more overarching scheme of human conduct whereby the victorious use their strength with restraint to spare their humiliated antagonist and make the stability of peace, not ongoing vengeance, of paramount importance as war nears an end. It is a more social form of heroism than Homer's that the poem adumbrates in the abstract, one where individual acts of heroism share in responsibility for attaining and securing larger social goals. The notion is very Roman, and in a moment we will look in detail at the passage where Virgil spells it out for his hero as well as his audience to ponder. Suffice it to say here that Virgil's return, at his epic's close, to the *Iliad* with his hero's emulation of Achilles, calls into question the possibility of implementing, in Rome and elsewhere, this higher morality of what we might call the heroism of *imperium*, the heroism of administering supreme power morally, and of those stalwart champions who share in its realization. The sublimation of selfhood and its private emotional responses does not remain with him at the end as vengeance drives him to kill in a paroxysm of fury.

A word is in order here on our inherited text of the poem. From time to time it has been suggested that the ending of the poem as we have it is unfinished and that Virgil, had he lived longer, would have modified or even extended it, to mitigate or dissipate Aeneas's rage and bring about some of the plot satisfactions that the reader might feel led to expect. The *Aeneid* would find a parallel in the tenth, and last, book of Lucan's *Pharsalia*, which clearly is incomplete. But unlike Lucan's final book, which is less than half the length of its predecessor and ends *in mediis rebus*, Virgil's twelfth not only completes exactly half the canonical number of books that Alexandrian scholars set for Homer and therefore for future epicists, it is also the longest in the *Aeneid*. Its structure is masterfully crafted, moving from a figurative wounding of Turnus at the start to the literal, deadly sword-thrust of Aeneas at the conclusion.

It therefore closely follows the pattern of Book 4 where the metaphorical hurt that Dido is suffering yields place to the actual wound she inflicts upon herself as suicide with the sword of Aeneas. But, as we have seen, the ending in particular performs several functions.

By having the language applied to Aeneas at the conclusion of the book recall that associated with Juno at the beginning of the poem, Virgil not only rounds his poem carefully off; he also schools his reader in a repetitiveness and cyclicity that characterizes the entire poem. References in Book 12 to the first *Eclogue* also serve the same purpose for Virgil's oeuvre as a whole, reminding the reader that tensions between ideal and real, happiness and suffering, civilized behavior and barbarity that surface regularly in the epic are operative in Virgil's imagination long before he began the composition of his epic.

The polarities that distinguish the poem are also to be found in the major strands of Virgilian criticism. Foremost and longest enduring is the interpretation of the poem as in praise of Aeneas, which is also to see Aeneas as the pious, magnanimous hero whose conduct stands as prototype for all Roman political and military heroes culminating in Augustus, and whose epic story sets the tone for Rome's own rise to greatness. In such a view the essence of the poem is the glorification of the Roman empire, and therefore of imperial power in general, as incorporated in Aeneas and his latter-day epigone, Rome's first emperor. Such political power, as we have seen and as such a reading of the poem supports, brings with it a new responsibility not to strive, in Homeric fashion, for celebrity as an individual displaying unique prowess but to put self at the service of state. This means for Aeneas that he become the incorporation of piety symbolized in carrying his father out of the ruins of Troy. He must stoically bear whatever burdens fate puts in his way during this progress toward a grand destiny and then practice restraint once that authority has been won. This in essence is the view of Richard Heinze in his influential *Vergils epische Technik* (1903). The complementary view of Aeneas as Stoic, proto-Christian hero is given its most well-known expression toward the end of the Second World War by T. S. Eliot (1945).

Five years later Viktor Pöschl's *Die Dichtkunst Vergils* heightened the reader's awareness of the richness of Virgil's symbolism as a way of showing how the dark and light aspects of the poem are ever pitted against each other, with the positive aspects only winning the day as the poem reaches its finale. Over the course of the subsequent decades a deepened awareness of Virgil's bleak side drew the attention of critics (see, e.g. Putnam 1965; Johnson 1976). A compromise interpretation of the poem, aware both of the glory and of the price of Aeneas's positive qualities as a hero – and of the greatness of Augustan Rome – and of the violence which peppered his, and Rome's, rise to authority, would seem to do the poem most justice (cf. Hardie 1986; Feeney 1991: 129–87; Quint 1993: 50–96).

The *Aeneid* reaches its major crisis only twelve lines before its conclusion. It is a climax different from anything with which Homer presents us in the *Iliad* and the *Odyssey*, and it leaves little room for a denouement that eases us away from the poem's climactic act of heroism which has occurred immediately before. We don't find ourselves wondering, in anticipation, whether, at the end of the *Iliad*, Achilles will ransom the body of Hector, whom he has killed two books earlier, to the dead hero's aged father and take a meal with him, in semblance of a return to humanity. Nor do we ponder whether Odysseus will finally make it home to Penelope and limit his violence against the predatory suitors. Nor, if we think of the *Argonautica* of Apollonius Rhodius, do we worry for the *Argo*'s picaresque heroes as their adventures lead them duly back to the beach at Pagasae. Virgil's crisis arises from a concentrated focus, on the part of the hero, as well as of the poem's reader, on a question of ethics. Aeneas has vanquished his arch enemy Turnus who, on his knees, begs his opponent for forbearance. Spare him, prays the suppliant, or if his conqueror opts to kill, send his body back to his family. The choice is Aeneas', and he hesitates.

Virgil has formulated the moral dilemma of this moment with the help of Homer. Throughout Book 12, but especially as its ending draws near, Virgil, by constant allusion, asks his reader to keep in the foreground of his thinking the action of the twenty-second book of the *Iliad*, as Achilles' chase of Hector ends in the latter's fatal wounding in the throat and his death. Aeneas possesses the Homeric hero's omnipotence, but Virgil has imagined him, at the beginning of the final scene, into a different ethical situation. The spear thrust, that leads to the first wound Aeneas inflicts on Turnus, is not mortal, like that inflicted by Achilles on Hector. By having him merely pierce his opponent's thigh, and by allowing the victim a chance to appeal for clemency, Virgil sets up, for hero and reader alike, an ethical quandary of different dimensions from anything to be found, as far as we know, in earlier ancient epic.

It might have been otherwise. Virgil could have emulated Homer's pattern closely and made the spear wound fatal. He could have given an accompanying speech to his hero, paralleling Achilles' ugly curse on Hector "for what you have done to me" (*Il.* 22.347). Knowledge of Homer leads us to expect some similar words of invective on Aeneas' part, listing the reasons why Turnus' death is deserved. His breaking of the treaty and attempt to take for his own Aeneas' fated bride are the usual indictments marshaled by critics from Virgil's fourth-century commentators up to the present. When Aeneas does speak at the end, before he kills, his reasoning is different, but after the initial wounding, Virgil gives words not to the victor but to the vanquished, to Turnus. The words are a petition that provokes the crisis of Aeneas' hesitation.

I will return later to the ending and to further aspects of Homer's role in its generation. I would like first to turn to an examination of a moment earlier in the *Aeneid* where Virgil puts into the mouth of Aeneas' father, Anchises, words addressed to his son which we expect to have special validity within the narrative of the poem, and for the future of Rome beyond the poem's present. (On Anchises in the Underworld see Feeney 1986b and Zetzel 1989.) With the Sibyl's guidance Aeneas has hazarded the journey into the Underworld, which is the subject of the epic's sixth book. There son meets father who, at the conclusion of their visit, displays for him a parade of the ghosts of Roman heroes to come, from Aeneas' own immediate descendants to the wraiths of Caesar and Pompey. At the end, by way of summary contrast between the accomplishments of Greece and Rome, he projects to his son a model for the behavior of his descendants. The passage comes at the conclusion of the poem's first half and in notable ways serves to balance, as well as to anticipate, its finale (6.847–53):

> "excudent alii spirantia mollius aera
> (credo equidem), vivos ducent de marmore vultus,
> orabunt causas melius, caelique meatus
> describent radio et surgentia sidera dicent:
> tu regere imperio populos, Romane, memento
> (hae tibi erunt artes), pacique imponere morem,
> parcere subiectis et debellare superbos."

"Others will hammer out breathing bronzes more softly (indeed I believe it), and will draw living features from marble, will plead cases better, will outline with a rod the pathways of the heavens and tell of the rising stars: do you, Roman, remember to rule peoples with commanding might (these will be your arts), to impose a custom for peace, to spare the defeated and war down the proud."

Romanists have often found puzzling the initial four lines, which clearly offer an idiosyncratic but highly effective précis of Greek achievement in the fine arts, in rhetoric, and in astronomy. Doesn't late Republican portrait sculpture rival that of the Greeks, and isn't Cicero the equal of Demosthenes? Whatever his reasoning, Virgil would have us feel otherwise here, as he takes us on a chronological tour beginning with the sixth century when the first bronze statues were in fact made from sheets of that metal beaten into shape against a wooden model (the sculptor would also use a hammer to polish bronze statues made from metal poured around a mould). We move next to the fifth century, the presumed high point of the art of marble sculpture in Greece with the work of Polycleitos and Phidias. The fourth century embraced the acme of the rhetor's skill in Isocrates, Aeschines, and Demosthenes. And we progress from the fourth into the third in watching a noble procession of astronomers from Eudoxus to Callippus to Conon.

There is another evolutionary process as well in these lines, for as Virgil links sculptors with orators and astronomers we also move from under-earth to earth to heavens. The products of the inner earth, marble and bronze ore, take quasi-human shape through the sculptor's metamorphic skill. The etymological pun by which *excudent* anticipates and complements *causas* takes us from the shaping of inanimate nature into man's living image, to man himself, to the particular features, the face (*os*) of the orator, as he crafts words into the spoken form at which his audience focuses its attention. Humans, literally and in Virgil's words, are ranged between earth and sky, where we locate the many and various movements of the celestial bodies, to the understanding of which astronomers bring the exactitude of their science. They impose an order on the heavens that parallels what sculptors bring to the unworked products of the earth and what speakers apply to language's chaotic jumble in order to lend conviction to their ingenuity.

These two developmental aspects of lines 847–50 find counterpoise in the concentrated artistry by which Virgil blends together his intellectual summary of Greek artistic and scientific accomplishment into an aesthetic whole. The poet makes us look at changes taking place over four hundred years of historical time and at placement in space that guides us from what we do with primal matter beneath our feet to what influences us, and how we control it for our own good, from a realm in the distance above us. But his deployment of words and his intense use of figuration has the effect of unifying these linear outlines into a brilliant entity. Assonance, alliteration, and rhyme take us from *mollius* to *melius*, uniting the "softness" of the sculptor's artistry with the quality of the rhetor's presentation. The aural and grammatical echoes of *spirantia aera* and *surgentia sidera* not only help frame the four lines but help us see bronze and stars, life-giving breath and the energy of constellations on the rise, in terms of each other.

The end rhyme of *vultus* and *meatus* has the same effect for the quartet's inner lines, again connecting the features that workers in stone give to their raw material with the regular paths that heavenly bodies trace in the sky. The same is true of the sonic echo of *ducent* and *dicent*, conjoining the artisan's Orphic gift to "lead" with the astronomer's power, which he shares with the orator, to "tell," and to tell is likewise to bring to the sky the regulating potential of words.

The balances which we have traced between lines 847 and 850, the verses' framing lines, and 848–9, its central duo, are given final imprint as we follow out the implications of Virgil's chain of verbs. Our movement is from the first word, *excudent*, to the last, *dicent*, and in between we have the rhyming reflection of two other verbs, *orabunt* (849) and *describent* (850), which initiate adjacent lines. The whole forms a grand chiasmus that builds on itself, as satisfying to the eye of the reader as it is pleasing to the ear of the hearer. Nouns, participles and verbs all conspire to emphasize ABBA order which, in Virgil's own brilliant aesthetic presentation, rhetorically reflects and conjoins the varied artistries of which it tells. Virgil breathes with his sculptors and speaks with his astronomers. His art about art makes every detail matter within an extraordinarily taut, holistic design.

As we advance from Greece to Rome and follow what may be Virgil's intended chronology from a golden age of Greek science to the rise of Roman imperial ambitions in the fourth century, Virgil eases the transition for us. Though we abandon the highly concrete, palpable world of statuary and stars for an abstract look at the application of

Roman power, still both eye and ear readily make the jump from *radio* to *imperio* – both words are in the same metrical position in adjacent lines – from the astronomer's didactic rod to the might by which Rome exerts its rule. *Populos* thus follows in the sequence that links bronze with marble, court cases, and constellations, against which varied types of artistry are applied to give them shape and order. It is the Roman genius to take the raw material of nations and teach them civilization and proper patterns of governance.

In particular it is the duty of the Romans "to establish a custom for peace." The phrase has been interpreted in two ways, as meaning either to make peace such a constant in society that war becomes a thing of the past, or to civilize the usage of peace so that it, too, becomes regular. The two are in fact all but the same. Peace and civilization should be complementary entities, and it is Roman might, the strength to impose the continuity of tested custom documenting a race's larger morality, that will make this equivalence possible. Society, societies, and their political well-being are the subjects of Roman artistry.

But, this said, the rhetoric of the second segment of Anchises' formulation is remarkably different from the first. Though we move in terms of ideas from concrete to abstract, in presentation something opposite also occurs. Via apostrophe we are vividly present as Anchises, through one word of address, metamorphoses his son into the incorporation of all Romans to come, a symbol of the variety of Rome's future illustrious nobles whose ghosts Aeneas has just seen through his father's eyes. The magic of Anchises' apostrophe forces mutation on his son and at the same time brings before us a figure of all Romans to come, one standing for many, one learning to behave for many.

Just as Roman power and its usage is the subject of Anchises' lines, so the idea of power permeates its rhetoric, which serves, therefore, as a metaphor of what it presents. Anchises' apostrophe is an imperative, "remember," and this imperative, which anticipates a series of dependent infinitives (*regere, imponere, parcere, debellare*), develops a verbal hierarchy, a grammar of subordination delineating commanding authority and submission to it. This will take palpable shape in the matter of which it tells, the might of Rome, which, in Anchises' idealizing vision, will make peace usual, once those haughty enough to oppose her have been defeated and – the vision continues – have been spared and presumably reincorporated into society. Anchises suggests an ethics of forbearance for those in power in order to secure that very power, of self-mastery in order morally to master others.

Likewise *imperium* and *imponere* are linguistically and sonically related, confirming by etymology and alliteration that the assurance of ruling power depends on the strength to impose peace, an apparently unnatural event in human affairs which needs the presence of force to bring it about. Further there is the visual interplay of *superbos* and *subiectis*, based on the Latin differentiation of *super* and *sub*, of high and low, above and beneath, contrasting physical postures that slide easily into moral metaphor through the distinction between the powerful and the powerless, the victorious and the vanquished, rulers and slaves. Finally there is the contrast between *alii* and *tu*, a plurality of "others" and a singular "you" with its implications of autocracy.

But there are puzzling elements about these final hexameters, especially by comparison to the preceding quartet of lines. For one thing we turn from four verses to three, from an even number of lines, in whose deployment symmetry and equipoise are conspicuous, to an odd number which by juxtaposition suggests that balance and a fulfilling completion, at least at the moment when Anchises casts his overarching glance on Rome and Romans to the end of their Republic, are missing elements in this history. Other complementary figures are operative too. As we follow out the ideological continuum which Anchises would have us contemplate we find that Virgil is making dramatic use of hysteron proteron, the trope that puts the first in last place and reverses the expected natural or rational order of what is presented. We expect Anchises to tell a tale that takes us from the prideful battled down, to the humiliated spared, to peace at last made customary in a world civilized and managed by the proper use of Roman regulatory *imperium*. We expect a movement from war to compassion to ordered harmony. We find the opposite. From Anchises' words we take with us into the second half of the poem not a portrait of peace and civilized morality following on a time of strife but of the triumphant conclusion of warring down the proud.

And here another figure comes into play, a figure to which we have been carefully schooled in the preceding verses, namely chiasmus. The look at the intellectual achievement of the Greeks that Virgil gives to Anchises is deeply reliant on this patterning to bring the satisfactions that it does. We expect nothing less from Virgil's outline of future Roman experience – a political ordering of the world perhaps even more valuable than the spiritual and intellectual exploits of the Greeks because it would presumably include and subsume them in this grander, all-embracing dispensation. The absence of chiasmus and its perfecting concinnity in the portrait of Rome abets the negative implications of the use of hysteron proteron. This double figuration puts before the reader interrelated questions. First, will the process from peace to war be reversed by the end of the poem? Second, will that reversal bring about the fulfillment of Anchises' words through chiasmus, so that we will in fact find at work in the performative ethics behind Roman might something as artistic, as proportional, as the intellectual feats of Greece, as seen in Virgil's intense portrayal?

It is only in the last dozen lines of the poem that we realize that Virgil has no intention of giving us the pleasure of a happy rounding out of Roman history, at least as allegorized in the prototypical behavior of Aeneas. The *Aeneid*'s last six books give substance to the phrase *debellare superbos* as Aeneas does battle with Turnus and his followers. According to the narrator, Turnus' haughtiness immediately after his killing of Pallas in Book 10 is worthy of exclamation (10.502) and shortly later, in one of Virgil's rare uses of apostrophe within the third-person story line, he addresses him as "you, Turnus the proud" (*te, Turne, superbum*, 10.514). The adjective confirms a previous reference to Turnus' "proud orders" (*iussa superba*, 10.445) and anticipates the description of the hero as again *superbus* in the final book (12.326) as he embarks on a spate of slaughter.

What happens at the poem's conclusion is therefore crucial to the evolution of Anchises' rhetoric. Turnus has indeed been "warred down" by Aeneas's initial wounding, with his earlier pride now replaced by humility. Virgil speaks of his "humbled eyes" (*humilis... oculos*, 12.930). And we do for a moment edge backward, structurally and linguistically, into the previous segment of Anchises' command, that Romans in their martial affairs "spare the subjected" (*parcere subiectis*). Turnus is now a *supplex*, on his knees in prayer or, to rephrase so as to bring out the play on the prefix *sub* with its reminder of *subiectis*, with his knees folded up beneath him. But at this point Virgil's reconstruction of Anchises' rhetoric comes to a stop. There is no sparing, and the epic ends, first with the humbling, then with the indignation of someone deprived by death of all his power. Whatever the reader may wish or imagine, there is no *elogium* of the victorious champion at the end nor any pronouncement that peace has been reached and its continuity assured as custom. The incompletions of Rome and of Virgil's rhetoric remain to complete the poem.

Anchises gives us several hints in his previous description of Roman greats, to which his magnificent words about artistry form the climax, that there are more realistic continua at work in Roman history than his apophthegmatic exhortation by itself is meant to suggest. That his summary overview deals with the actual operations of *imperium* in the implementation of Rome's political ambitions is clear from its fourfold repetition within a 40-line stretch of his speech (there are no parallels elsewhere in Virgil to this concentrated use of the word). And we find accompanying this repetition another form of iteration where language complements the tale it tells. According to Anchises, Brutus may do away with the last of Rome's kings, Tarquin the Proud, and initiate the era of the Republic, but the adjective history allots to Tarquin (and the poem to Turnus before his humbling), *superbus*, is transferred by Anchises to the mind of Brutus, the deposer (*animam...* *superbam*, 6.817), and Brutus' "harsh axes" (*saevas...securis*, 819), symbols of a magistrate's authority but here used without restraint, are soon passed to a later warrior-statesman, T. Manlius Torquatus, "fierce with his axe" (*saevum...securi*, 824).

As he nears the end of his list Anchises turns to Caesar and Pompey, the famous father-in-law, son-in-law combination whose fighting brought Rome's century of civil war to its penultimate climax in the battle of Pharsalus in 48 BCE. The lines have particular stress as apostrophe, the figure's first appearance in Anchises' address, leads to exclamation in a line whose incompletion leaves it impressive (6.832–5):

> "ne pueri, ne tanta animis adsuescite bella
> neu patriae validas in viscera vertite viris;
> tuque prior, tu parce, genus qui ducis Olympo,
> proice tela manu, sanguis meus!"

"Do not, my children, grow used in your minds to such battles or turn the power of your strength against the innards of your fatherland; do you first, you spare, who draw your lineage from Olympus. Throw away the spears from your hand, my blood!"

The powerful implication of the final words, that Anchises' "blood," his descendant, according to Julian myth, Julius Caesar, is also a shedder of blood, takes on special significance in a context where close relatives, at arms against each other, epitomize the horrors of civil war at its worst. It is also disquieting that his particular command to Caesar – *tu prior, tu parce* – comes so few lines before Anchises' generalized exhortation to Aeneas as epitome of all Romans, *memento...parcere subiectis*. It is as if to say that the effectiveness of such a global order for the sweep of Roman *imperium* was valueless without the necessity of a reminder of it on individual occasions, even to those who should by now live it as second nature, and that even then there was no guarantee that the mandate would be obeyed.

I would like now to turn to the specific word of command that Anchises uses, *memento* (remember), and to follow out its implications for the poem as a whole. There are many themes which serve to unify the *Aeneid* and to connect the epic with Virgil's early work. For the latter, Virgil's references to shade and to exile, that serve to mesh the first *Eclogue* together, occur throughout the *Aeneid*, to make cumulative appearances in the poem's final line. As far as the epic itself is concerned, there is no more important unifying factor than the idea of memory which is regularly represented by the verb *meminisse* (to remember, which is to say to keep in one's mind) or the causative form it takes in verbs such as *memorare* or *monere* (to remind, to recall to one's attention) (see Most 2001 for an insightful interpretation of Virgil on memory).

Virgil makes this clear with great energy and particularity at the start of the poem (*Aen.* 1.1–7):

> Arma virumque cano, Troiae qui primus ab oris
> Italiam fato profugus Laviniaque venit
> litora, multum ille et terris iactatus et alto
> vi superum, saevae memorem Iunonis ob iram,
> multa quoque et bello passus, dum conderet urbem
> inferretque deos Latio; genus unde Latinum
> Albanique patres atque altae moenia Romae.

I sing of arms and a man who, exiled by fate, first came to Italy and the Lavinian shores from the coast of Troy, much tossed about on land and on sea by the violence of the gods, from the

remembering wrath of savage Juno, and suffering much in war also until he should found a
city and bring his gods to Latium, whence came the Latin race, and the Alban fathers and the
walls of lofty Rome.

We first hear of memory at line 4 where the narrator tells of harsh Juno's "remembering
wrath" which forces the epic's hero to endure so much hardship on water and land in the
process of founding the city that leads to Rome. The reader has to wait until eight
lines after the beginning to find Virgil's appeal to the Muse, something that we find
already in the opening lines of Homer's epics ("O goddess," in the *Iliad*; "O Muse," in
the *Odyssey*). The emphasis that this hiatus brings, playing as it does on the reader's
expectations, makes the appeal, when it comes, all the more striking: *Musa, mihi causas
memora* . . . ("Muse, recall to my mind the reasons . . ."). What the narrator asks to be
reminded of by the Muse are the sources of Juno's resentment, what she holds against so
upright a hero and so worthy a task as the foundation of Rome in order to put so many
troublesome barriers in his way. Fifteen lines later we hear further not of Juno's personified anger, going about its harsh business, but of the goddess herself, *memor Saturnia*
(23). The daughter of Saturn is in the process of recollecting now in detail the causes of
her hurt as she rouses up a violent storm against the Trojans. The request to the Muse to
tell of the reasons for Juno's hostility is surrounded by two direct references to the
goddess, first to her wrath, then to the reasons why she harbors it.

Virgil thus builds up a symbiosis between the narrator's storytelling and the story he
tells, through the intimacy each story has with Juno, and anger is the focal emotion. This
in turn puts into relief a major difference between Homer's initiating apostrophes to the
goddess-muse and Virgil's address in line 8 of his epic. The poet of the *Odyssey* asks for
inspiration to tell of his wily hero and his deeds. The author of the *Iliad* commands her to
sing of the wrath of Achilles, son of Peleus. By deliberately recalling Achilles' anger Virgil
would have us most directly remember the opening of the *Iliad*, but he would also have us
note the change from Achilles to Juno. The "I" of the narrator may sing of arms and of
the man who wields them, Aeneas, but the Muse must prompt him, where Juno's
animosity is concerned.

It is this combination that rules the poem and that comes to the fore most strikingly at
its finale as Virgil polishes his poem to completion by remembering, and by reminding his
reader of, the abstracts that ruled its start. When, as the epic concludes, Aeneas passes
beyond hesitation and decides to kill instead of to spare, it is because of a surge of
recollections, *monimenta* (12.945, eight lines before the end, balancing *memora* at 1.8).
The tangible object that jars Aeneas' memory is the sword belt of the youth Pallas whom
Turnus had killed during the action of the tenth book. This baldric, which he was now
wearing, had depicted on it the Danaids' murders of their husbands, sons of Aegyptus,
brother of Danaus, on their wedding night. Kin were killing kin. Here is the context
(12.945–7):

> ille, oculis postquam saevi monimenta doloris
> exuviasque hausit, furiis accensus et ira
> terribilis . . .

(Aeneas), after he had drunk in the remembrance of his savage resentment and the spoils, set
aflame by furies and terrifying in his wrath . . .

If *monimenta* helps define for Aeneas his memory of Pallas' death, the linguistic context
that Virgil gives the word takes the reader back to the opening of the poem where the
three acts of memory which we traced are associated with parallel descriptions of Juno. At
line 4, as we saw, we hear of *saevae memorem Iunonis . . . iram*. Line 9 finds her *dolens*, filled

with resentment, and at 25 she, and we, are reminded of "the causes of her angers and her savage resentments" (*causae irarum saevique dolores*). The satisfactions that come to the reader at the poem's conclusion lie not so much in what Aeneas does as in the poem's extraordinary structure. We do not complete the chiasmus suggested by Anchises' language that might have led to temperateness and peace. Instead we turn back on ourselves and return to the beginning of the epic. This movement brings the realization that we have been involved in a poem driven at its poles by memory which in turn arouses anger, ferocity, and rancor. The song of Aeneas and his weapons abides complicitly in the memory, and the remembering, of Juno and her hatreds.

Sight is a crucial sense at the moment of Aeneas' metamorphosis. He has heard, and pondered, the words of Turnus when suddenly the sword belt of Pallas, which Turnus had been wearing all along, "appeared" (*apparuit*, 12.941), as if it were a sudden omen. This manifestation triggers Aeneas' anger, the palpable baldric before him by a type of metonymy standing in for the dead youth with body despoiled. Aeneas sees Pallas in his mind's eye and takes his place, as his final words tell us, in claiming vengeance from Turnus.

The reader also remembers Book 10 and sees the belt itself and its contents (10.497–8):

> . . . una sub nocte iugali
> caesa manus iuvenum foede thalamique cruento.

> . . . the throng of youths foully slain on one marriage night and the bloodied chambers.

At both points where the belt is mentioned, but especially at the poem's conclusion, a reader contemporary with Virgil could do with ease what a modern student can only accomplish in his imagination. He must visualize the portico which Augustus built adjacent to his temple to Apollo on the Palatine and which was certainly open by 25 BCE while Virgil was at work on his masterpiece. It harbored in the spaces between its columns statues of the Danaids murdering their husbands, to implement their father's hatred of his brother. He would also see nearby, on the doors of the temple itself, further examples of the emperor's penchant for monumentalizing vengeance. They depicted two examples of vendetta on the part of Apollo, first against Brennus, who had sacked the god's sanctuary at Delphi, second against Niobe, who boasted of her equality with Leto, his mother. That the emperor continued to take with utmost seriousness this tangible memorialization of vendetta for all to see and contemplate was reaffirmed in 2 BCE when he dedicated the still unfinished temple to Mars Ultor, Mars the Avenger, as the centerpiece of his new forum, a temple vowed forty years earlier at the battle of Philippi.

But just as Horace, in a brilliant ode (*Carm.* 3.11), glorifies the *clementia* of Hypermestra, the one Danaid who spares her husband, so Virgil makes clear his own prejudice against the Danaids' vendetta by the word *turpe*. Their sly act of slaughter was ugly and immoral. By taking this stance Virgil pits one patriarch against another, the present ruler of Rome against Anchises, the dispenser of crucial wisdom to his son. Augustus wins the day, but not without the poet's commentary. The *Aeneid* stands out among ancient epics for having unrelenting rage the focus of its conclusion, but this conclusion gains particular prominence because the epic's main father figure preaches, at the center of the poem, the opposite of what Augustan monumentality would seem to maintain, namely to spare a suppliant rather than to kill in vengeance, an act which only spawns further acts of revenge. We can distinguish Anchises from the Old Testament's almighty God not through what the father sayeth but from what he sayeth not. Anchises proclaims not that vengeance is sweet but that it should never be the final motivation for action, especially if that action takes a life or lives. At the conclusion of the *Aeneid* the opting for vengeance is the emotion-driven decision of the son, which flouts the reasoned commandment of the father.

The *sermo* (speech) that Turnus utters which causes Aeneas to hesitate brings another father-figure, as well as Anchises, into our picture (12.931–8):

> "...equidem merui nec deprecor" inquit;
> "utere sorte tua. miseri te si qua parentis
> tangere cura potest, oro (fuit et tibi talis
> Anchises genitor) Dauni miserere senectae
> et me, seu corpus spoliatum lumine mavis,
> redde meis. vicisti et victum tendere palmas
> Ausonii videre; tua est Lavinia coniunx,
> ulterius ne tende odiis."

"Indeed I have deserved it nor do I pray it away," he says. "Use your opportunity. If any care for a pitiable parent can touch you, I beseech you (for such also was your father Anchises), take pity on the old age of Daunus and give me back, or, if you prefer, my body despoiled of light, to my people. You have conquered and the Ausonians have seen me, vanquished, stretch forth my hands; Lavinia is your wife. Do not continue further in your hatred."

In coming to grips with the problematics of Turnus' words, which is to say with the ethical dilemma which they force Aeneas to face, Virgil asks the reader to perform several acts of memory. The most obvious, in terms of the epic's plot, is the remembrance of Anchises and of his last and most significant moment in the poem where, as we have seen, he gives Roman Aeneas the mandate to remember to have compassion on the humbled foe. Aeneas' noteworthy *pietas*, which took him into the world of the dead to learn of his and Rome's future, could now be activated again, as is the reader's recollection of it, by Turnus' reminder. The result would be the sudden awareness that Turnus' situation exactly particularizes what Anchises leaves in generalities. Should he have wanted, Virgil could have perfected his poem by having the outcome of its concluding crisis complement the ethical dicta with which Anchises commissions his son at the end of its first half.

As abstract becomes concrete, Aeneas' sparing of the vanquished could have served as the first example of putting into effect a moral decision that, when imitated and repeated, becomes a custom, or, to follow Anchises' exact focus, makes customary the resulting peace. The outcome would be the initiation, at least in ancient epic, of a heroism of non-action where the final triumph rests not with some glorious deed of valor that results from physical prowess – this Aeneas has already accomplished – but with a highly spiritual decision on the hero's part to yield to Turnus' prayer and to renounce hatred, which Cicero defines as wrath that has become habitual, and the use of palpable force it regularly engenders. Anger and the bouts of revenge it often stimulates come naturally to mankind. Forbearance, by contrast, asks us to rise heroically above ourselves and embrace a morality of moderation. Virgil fails to grant his very human Aeneas this privilege, nor does he ask his reader to accept a form of heroism for which he has not been schooled by the Greco-Roman epic tradition. Whatever gratification the reader gleans from the end of the *Aeneid* lies elsewhere.

A new father enters the picture when we turn to the second act of memory which Virgil asks of us as we contemplate the implications of Turnus' words for Aeneas, and for us as readers. He expects us to think of Priam's prayer to Achilles at *Iliad* 24.485–7:

But now Priam spoke to him in the words of a suppliant: "Achilleus like the gods, remember your father, one who is of years like mine, and on the door-sill of sorrowful old age." (trans. Lattimore 1961)

By means of this echo Virgil's magic changes Turnus into the aged king Priam, likewise a suppliant, but, in terms of the allusion, asking not for his own life but for the opportunity to buy back the body of Hector, his son. We thus make a quantum leap, through the refiguration of Turnus, seen against the background of the *Iliad*'s evolution, from Book 22 to Book 24 and to the epic's final moments. We move from Turnus, as a Hector vainly appealing for his life, to Turnus as Priam, pleading for his son's corpse, with the critical difference that Turnus is still alive.

By this powerful act of compression Virgil for a moment teases us into the belief that there is the possibility of another type of summation for the poem, not dissimilar to that which Anchises suggested in Book 6 (and Turnus has just carefully reminded son of father). The end of the *Aeneid* would then satisfy the reader by its parallelism to the end of the *Iliad*, Virgil's foremost model and the initiating masterpiece of western literature. Achilles foregoes his anger against Hector and, at least for a time, against the Trojans. He responds positively to the Trojan king's request that he be allowed to take Hector's body back to Troy where the dead hero can be mourned, burned, and buried. Funerary rites and poetry's ritual join in bringing the poem to a fulfilled conclusion. The parallel that Turnus' words adumbrate proposes a similar ending for the *Aeneid* with, of course, the essential difference. We think, for a moment at least, that we may not be dealing solely with a corpse to be ransomed but possibly instead with a conquered hero whose sparing would completely alter the death-driven mode of *Iliad* 22 through 24 – and of *Aeneid* 10 through 12 – and lead us into a different tonal as well as ethical realm. To spare would be to actuate one of the implications of Anchises' monition, namely that sufficient vengeance is exacted from a defeated foe by the act of humiliation, that death need not be demanded when the prideful have been made to supplicate.

Instead of these alternative endings Virgil remains with *Iliad* 22 as the multiple allusions to it in the epic's final book had led us to expect. There is no compassion for the humbled hero in what follows. The language of the epic's end, as we have seen, takes us back relentlessly to its start as Aeneas' rearoused anger and finalizing vendetta return us to where we began, with Juno's vengeful hatred against the Trojans. Virgil leaves us with the ominous sense that this circularity is his pessimistic way of candidly depicting the continuity not only of Aeneas' career but of Roman, and human, history as it evolves. What remains constant is our natural propensity for hatred and its consequences, however changed or changing the circumstances might be.

The finale of the *Aeneid* suggests that the open-ended rhetoric of Anchises' grand pronouncement on the ethical use of power in Rome's future is metaphoric for the poem's plot. No custom for peace is established because Aeneas' emotional response to a reminder of his grief at Pallas' death forestalls any remembrance of Anchises' exhortation. Virgil has prepared his reader for this outcome from the beginning of the poem, but Book 7 also forms a major part of his design. When linked with the final book it makes of the second half of the poem a smaller whole, complementing the circularity of the epic itself. Continuity rests in the renewed presence of Juno and in the negative energy she fosters.

There is a series of links between the end of Book 6 and the story line of Book 7, as Anchises' heady generalities yield to the particularities of war. The friction in this sequence puts the patriarch's lofty sentiments in ironic light. First, once more, is the idea of memory. Anchises' command, *memento*, finds its counterpart at line 41 of the subsequent book as the narrator directs the Muse "do you, goddess, do you enliven the poet-seer's memory" (*tu vatem, tu, diva, mone*). What is to be restored to the singer's memory is not a sequence of bellicose events that leads to peace but a peaceful world upset by war (7.41–2):

> . . . dicam horrida bella,
> dicam acies actosque animis in funera reges, . . .

I will tell of dreadful warring, of battle-lines and of kings driven to their deaths by animosity…

If the opening of the poem linked Juno's memory with the poet's necessary recollection, here the beginnings (*exordia*, 40) of the first battle, that the poet will recall to mind, are juxtaposed to the *maior ordo* (44), the grander narrative thread of the epic's second half. This, as the word's rich lexicon posits for us, will also consist of ranks of troops and their disposition for conflict. Lines of battle and lines of verse will soon be interwoven and complementary.

This initial act of memory finds its counterpart as the book draws to a close in a further apostrophe, this time not to a singular muse but to the goddesses as a group (7.641, 645):

> Pandite nunc Helicona, deae, cantusque movete,…
> et meministis enim, divae, et memorare potestis…

O goddesses, open Helicon wide and give voice to your song,… for you, divine ones, both remember and have the ability to bring matters to mind;…

The book's initial apostrophe asked for the speaker's aid in telling of battles and kings. Now he needs to recall "kings roused to war" (*bello exciti reges*, 642) and battle-lines, men, and arms. What follows from here to the end of the book is a detailed catalogue of those regal warriors and their weaponry. If in the first prayer there is agreement between the arrangement of soldiery and the demands of patterned verse, here the link between poetry and plot lies in the idea of opening out which, often in Virgil, beginning with Aeolus' unpenning of his destructive winds in Book 1, betokens a release of negative energy. In Book 7 what immediately precedes the second apostrophe to the Muses is Juno's descent from heaven to bash open the twin gates of the temple of Bellum (607, 622). Here turning war loose on the land is paralleled in the narrator's careful, detailed recollection of a selected group of Latin warriors. War's temple and the slopes of Helicon are conspirators in Virgil's creative enterprise.

The second way in which Virgil applies irony to Anchises' words, as the so-called Iliadic half of the *Aeneid* begins, is through the idea of art. Aeneas' father has told us of what Roman political and military *artes* will consist, by comparison to Greek aesthetic, rhetorical, and scientific accomplishment. Roman artistry will take shape through figurative, not literal means, through the application of abstractions to the raw material of real people performing real actions. It is an artistry of ethos, Anchises suggests, metaphoric for a way of life to which the reasoned, ultimately dispassionate use of power is central and essential.

What we find, as we enter the world of Latium and the immediacy of war, is a display of artistry that is largely martial and therefore disruptive, not creative, in nature. The word *ars* itself is applied directly twice to the work of Allecto, the Fury that Juno conjures up from the Underworld to ignite the flames of fighting in Italy. We hear first, in the words of the goddess, of her dread assistant's "thousand arts of harming" (*mille nocendi artes*, 7.338) as she sets out to perform her task. Then, as she brings her endeavors to a conclusion, Virgil speaks of the "new art" (*arte nova*, 477) by which she stimulates the hounds of Ascanius, son of Aeneas, to attack Silvia's tamed stag while at the same time their master "is set afire by a love of extraordinary praise" (*eximiae laudis succensus amore*, 496).

This art of war-making has a particular slant toward Virgil's contemporary Rome because, as the goddess's words of exhortation to the Fury continue, we learn that "you are able to arm brothers, once of one mind, to do battle, and overturn houses with hatred" ("tu potes unanimos armare in proelia fratres / atque odiis versare domos," *Aen.* 7. 335–6). It is a civil war that the Fury is setting out to ignite.

But the responsibility for the artistry that crafts war into being lies primarily with Juno herself. Allecto can boast, her duties done (7.545):

> "en, perfecta tibi bello discordia tristi; ..."

"Behold, for you, discord burnished into being with the sadness of war; ..."

It is the creation of war that the aptitudes of Allecto have perfected for Juno. After Allecto returns to her infernal abode, the finishing touch to the manufacture of war is added by the goddess herself. The image is that of an artisan giving his work its last polish (572–3):

> nec minus interea extremam Saturnia bello
> imponit regina manum.

No less in the meantime does the queen, Saturn's daughter, put her final hand to the war.

The first "artifact" of the Trojan presence in Italy is, in the tradition of Anchises, an abstraction, but it serves as an accessory of war, not peace. Virgil may want us to associate the two details by responding to the aural connection between *paci ... imponere morem* (6.852) and *bello imponit regina manum*. The restraint that Anchises asks of Aeneas, and of his successors Caesar and Pompey, and the resultant imposition of custom upon peace that he urges on Rome suffers metamorphosis into the hand that crafting Juno places upon war, consummated into effective form.

That final gesture is the opening of the *geminae Belli portae* (7.607). Virgil gives the moment particular stress by treating it an as an ekphrasis: "there was a custom ..." (*mos erat*). The figure in turn lends force to one of the rare moments in the *Aeneid* where the poet takes us directly into the Rome of Augustus (601–6):

> mos erat Hesperio in Latio, quem protinus urbes
> Albanae coluere sacrum, nunc maxima rerum
> Roma colit, cum prima movent in proelia Martem,
> sive Getis inferre manu lacrimabilem bellum
> Hyrcanisve Arabisve parant, seu tendere ad Indos
> Auroramque sequi Parthosque reposcere signa ...

There was a custom in Hesperian Latium, which from then the cities of Alba cherished as sacred, now Rome, mightiest of things, cherishes, when they first rouse Mars to war or prepare with their hand to bring tearful war either to the Getae or the Hyrcani or the Arabes, or to make their way to the Indi or to pursue the East and demand the standards back from the Parthians.

The tradition that the temple of Janus Geminus, on the north side of the Forum Romanum, was closed in times of peace but open when the Romans were at war is as old as king Numa Pompilius under whom it was first closed (Platner and Ashby 1965: 278–80; Richardson 1992: 207–8; Steinby 1996: 92–3). It remained open, and Rome remained at war, until a second closing after the First Punic War. After that it was not closed again until the reign of Augustus who boasted that he had shut the gates on three occasions, the first, in 30 BCE, after the victories at Actium and Alexandria.

Virgil's point here is understated but clear. During the Augustan era the doors of War were regularly unclosed because Rome was engaged in battle against foreign enemies. The century of civil strife was now over and Rome could deflect its extensive martial propensities, visualized by Virgil in the fighting between Caesar and Pompey, away from its own guts and on to its enemies abroad.

Rome now uses the skill of its own hand (*manu*) to bring tearful war elsewhere. But the *manus* that Juno applies to Allecto's handiwork to bring it to completion and that she now puts to use to unbolt the gates of War's temple (7.620–2) –

> tum regina deum caelo delapsa morantis
> impulit ipsa manu portas, et cardine verso
> Belli ferratos rumpit Saturnia postis.

Then the queen of the gods herself, daughter of Saturn, slipping down from heaven, pushed against the delaying doors with her hand, and broke open War's jambs of iron as they turned on their hinge

– looks to something nearer to hand. Juno takes on a task which the old king Latinus refuses because he knows that in this case to unclose the gates is tantamount to declaring a civil war, which is to say, to setting a pattern for the internecine strife that gripped Rome for the several decades that preceded the victories over Antony and Cleopatra. The artistry of Juno and the hoary tradition connected with Janus Geminus merge to portend not the permanent realization of Anchises' custom for peace but instead, as the Aeneadae proceed to assure their domination in Italy, the implementation of war's customariness and in particular of fighting where kin slaughter kin. Juno wins the day as we plunge into the general conflict that leads inevitably to the single combat between Aeneas and Turnus, and to the latter's violent end. It is no accident on Virgil's part that it is the sight of a sword belt, which has somehow depicted upon it forty-nine murders of cousins by cousins, that causes Aeneas to bring that death about. Once more art and destructiveness, not art and peace, seem to complement each other.

A more enigmatic, less immediate difference between the ethical grounding of Anchises' command and the impulses behind the events of Book 7, especially as they anticipate the epic's final reaches, lies in the idea of emotionality itself. A key figure in this regard for Virgil's exposition is the particular Muse that he apostrophizes at 7.37, namely Erato. As critics have long noted, Virgil is here making a clear bow, as he begins the second half of his epic, to the opening line of the third book, which likewise initiates its poem's second half, of Apollonius Rhodius' *Argonautica*: "Come now, Erato, stand nearby and tell me . . ." (Εἰ δ᾽ ἄγε νῦν, Ἐρατώ, παρά θ᾽ ἵστασο, καί μοι ἔνισπε . . .). Apollonius' etymological wordplay in the subsequent lines makes clear why he has chosen her for his addressee. His plot can only evolve, and Jason gain possession of the golden fleece, if he is aided "by the love of Medea" (Μηδείης ὑπ᾽ ἔρωτι, *Arg.* 3.3). As sharer in the power of Aphrodite, it is appropriate that Erato bear "a name associated with love" (ἐπήρατον οὔνομ᾽, 5). What follows in Apollonius' tale is a meeting between Athena and Hera where the two divinities conspire to approach the goddess of love and to enlist her aid in making Medea become enamored of Jason. She agrees, and hastens to procure the services of her child, the boy Eros, whose wounding arrow brings about the desired result.

Virgil's careful variation on this event elaborates its complexity. If we look at the most simple level of eroticism in the second half of the poem, it concerns the love between Turnus and Lavinia to whom the hero considers himself betrothed though the Fates pronounce otherwise. Turnus' involvement is deep. At 12.70, for instance, we hear that "love put him in turmoil" (*illum turbat amor*), and at the end, in his final gesture of submission, he names Lavinia as Aeneas': "yours is Lavinia for wife" (*tua est Lavinia coniunx*, 12.937).

Turnus may be in love with Lavinia but he is also the subject of adoration on the part of Latinus' wife Amata who, we learn at the beginning of the story of events in Latium, wishes Turnus to be her son-in-law "with an astonishing love" (*miro amore*, 7.57). Her name, meaning "beloved," may imply that, to whatever degree, the passion was reciprocated (she takes her own life in Book 12 when she thinks that Turnus has been killed). There is no need in either case for Venus or Cupid to intervene and set hearts aflame. As for Aeneas, we never hear that any mutual affection exists between him and Lavinia or that passion for her serves in any way as a driving force for him as he enters into conflict with the Latins. Unlike Jason and Medea, whom Aphrodite and her son bring together, Virgil never allows Aeneas and his fated wife even to meet.

Virgil's major alteration to Apollonius is to remain with Juno (Apollonius' Hera), who initiates the epic's second half as she had the first. There is no need to resort to Venus' intervention. And instead of claiming Eros as her ally, as she stirs up renewed violence that parallels the storm scene of Book 1, it is the Fury Allecto whom we have seen her summon from the Underworld to aid and abet her designs. Eros, though by no means eliminated, is subsumed into a more universal madness that grips Trojans as well as Latins as Juno and her minion go about their work. The "fury's evil" (*furiale malum*, 7.375) strikes Amata. "She rages in wild madness" (*sine more furit lymphata*, 377) and "assays a greater madness" (*maiorem . . . orsa furorem*, 386) as in Bacchic revelry she drives her daughter and fellow mothers from their city into the forest. The "love" that now strikes Turnus, Allecto's second victim, as a result of the Fury's interference, is for battle (7.461–2):

> saevit amor ferri et scelerata insania belli,
> ira super . . .

His love of the sword rages and the criminal madness of war and, on top of that, anger . . .

And, as we observed earlier, her final victim, Ascanius, is "inflamed by a love of outstanding praise" (496) as his dogs chase, and he wounds, Silvia's tamed stag. But, in all this generalized passion, in the multivalent manifestations of negative emotion that Juno and her Fury arouse, the notion of sexuality and its driving force lie ever just beneath the surface, from here until the epic's conclusion. Whatever the varied emotions that Virgil's Erato may animate her poet to tell, the particular inspiration of Apollonius' Ἐρατώ is never far distant. For instance one of the phrases that Virgil uses to describe the maddened mothers, at 7.392, is *furiis accensas* ("set aflame by furies"). It is more than coincidental that the only other occasion on which Virgil utilizes the phrase is in his description, during the epic's final lines, of Aeneas' response to seeing the sword belt of Pallas that Turnus is wearing. He, too, is "set aflame by furies and terrifying in his anger" (*furiis accensus et ira / terribilis*, 12.946–7).

To follow out the suggestiveness of this parallelism and seek to elicit implications from these words so pointedly placed, let us expand our study of emotionality in the poem and turn to the figure of Dido. If any character in the *Aeneid*, aside from the titular hero, remains etched in the reader's mind from the poem as a whole it is that of the Carthaginian queen, lured into a passionate liaison with Aeneas through the machinations of Venus and Juno. She is then driven to suicide when her lover, following the dictates of fate and the commands of Jupiter and Mercury, abandons her for Italy and the initiation of the Roman future. There is no question of the truth of her affection or of the depth of Aeneas' response. We hear, for example, at 4.395, that he "tottered in his mind with a mighty love" (*magno . . . animum labefactus amore*). Her tragedy, which has caught the imagination of so many later artists, lies not only in Virgil's graphic delineation of her downfall and death but in the insolvable moral challenges that each protagonist confronts: for Aeneas, between heart and head, affection and duty, individual fulfillment and the dictates of destiny; for Dido, between loyalty to her late husband and a bond of love, that she considers tantamount to marriage, for her handsome visitor, which is to say also on her part between a sense of abstract duty and the tugs of emotion.

Virgil keeps Dido before us for the remainder of the epic with a series of reminders that themselves often act to trigger the memory. The Carthaginian queen enters the plot in Book 1 when she receives the shipwrecked Trojans and their leader into her hospitality. She stays before the reader in the second and third books as she bears witness to the epic's single greatest act of memory, Aeneas' tale of his adventures from the final collapse of Troy to his arrival at Carthage. (We know from the subject of the artwork on her new temple to Juno that Dido knows in detail about the penultimate moments of Troy's demise. This establishes an immediate bond of empathy between hero and host.) And her craving for his story's repetition near the start of Book 4 only deepens her emotional involvement with her guest.

As the epic continues in Book 5, we first watch her funeral pyre glisten as the Trojans sail away, and then remember an earlier, happier Dido during the conclusion of the funeral games for Anchises when Iulus/Ascanius, performing the *lusus Troiae* (5.571–2)

> Sidonio est invectus equo, quem candida Dido
> esse sui dederat monimentum et pignus amoris.

is carried on a Sidonian horse which shining Dido had given him as a reminder of herself and as a pledge of love.

Dido's palpable reminder to Iulus of her affection for him is also Virgil's recollection of her for us.

We meet Dido next in her extraordinary appearance in Book 6 where Aeneas sees her among the suicides in the company of her husband (6.450–76). He addresses an apology to her but receives no response. We next meet her directly in Book 9 where once again Ascanius is involved. Among other prizes that he offers Nisus and Euryalus, if they reach Aeneas at Pallanteum, is (9.266)

> ...cratera antiquum quem dat Sidonia Dido.

...an ancient mixing bowl which Sidonian Dido gives him.

Here the extraordinary use of the present tense has an effect parallel to that of the figure apostrophe, and to the employment of *monimentum* at 5.572, in enlivening Dido directly before the reader.

The last direct mention of Dido comes in Book 11 at the moment Aeneas is preparing the body of Pallas for the funeral pyre (11.72–5):

> tum geminas vestis auroque ostroque rigentis
> extulit Aeneas, quas illi laeta laborum
> ipsa suis quondam manibus Sidonia Dido
> fecerat et tenui telas discreverat auro.

Then Aeneas took out twin clothes, stiff with gold and purple, which some time ago Sidonian Dido herself, happy in her efforts, had made with her own hands and varied the texture with slender gold.

Virgil asks us here to perform two acts of memory at this, one of the most intensely personal occasions for Aeneas in the poem. The first is to recall the two cloaks that Priam brought with him from Troy with which to wrap the corpse of Hector, should his request to Achilles to ransom his son succeed (*Il.* 24.580). The second is to note that line 75, along with the name Dido that brings the preceding hexameter to an end, is repeated exactly from *Aen.* 4.264 where we find Aeneas, during the period when he is most smitten with the Carthaginian queen, wearing a cloak (*laena*) that she had woven for him. Remembrance, therefore, of two emotionally charged moments, in the Homeric background and in Aeneas' past, lends special force to the last time that Aeneas, and we, see Pallas directly. More than any of the other preceding reminders of Dido, this reference brings implicit eroticism to the surface. It prepares us for, and helps explain, the virulence of Aeneas' reaction upon sighting Pallas' baldric on Turnus as the epic ends.

Dido may here leave the poem in name, but Virgil uses the potential of allusion to keep her strongly in the reader's mind as well at both the beginning and end of his epic's last book. Book 12 begins with one of the most powerful similes in ancient epic, because instead of reinforcing actual events through extended metaphor, it uses literal description to figure the inner workings of a character's mind. The particular focus here is the *violentia* of Turnus and the reasons behind it (12.4–8):

> Poenorum qualis in arvis
> saucius ille gravi venantum vulnere pectus
> tum demum movet arma leo, gaudetque comantis
> excutiens cervice toros fixumque latronis
> impavidus frangit telum et fremit ore cruento.

Just as in Punic fields a lion, when he has been stricken in the chest by hunters with a grievous wound; then at last he moves forward into battle and, joyfully tossing his flowing mane from his neck, fearlessly breaks the marauder's piercing arrow and roars with bloody mouth.

We are dealing not with two heroes fighting it out on the battlefield but with the psychic hurt and ensuing violence of one of the epic's main characters, recast as a lion wounded by a plurality of hunters who become, in the course of the simile, a single robber. So we are presumably meant to visualize the theft of Lavinia by the Trojans, under the leadership of Aeneas, from Turnus, and the latter's impassioned response.

But the setting "in Punic fields" has the effect of recalling Dido, and the recollection is confirmed by the allusion of line 5 to the opening two verses of Book 4:

> At regina gravi iamdudum saucia cura
> vulnus alit venis et caeco carpitur igni.

But the queen, long stricken by grievous yearning, fosters the wound with her blood and is caught in the grasp of dark fire.

As the epic begins its bleak final course, the Carthaginian queen, stricken metaphorically with a wound soon to take a literal, deadly form, re-enters the epic as Turnus, suffering the wound of his love for Lavinia. On this occasion, as figurative turns to actual, the final wound will not be inflicted by a woman driven to self-slaughter by an absconding Aeneas, whose sword she uses for the mortal blow, but will be the result of Aeneas himself plunging his sword into the enemy's chest.

Virgil complicates, and deepens, the meaning of the opening simile by having its final phrase, *fremit ore cruento*, look back to the concluding words of Jupiter's reassuring speech to Venus in Book 1, after the Trojans, largely in safety, have braved Juno's elemental storm and reached the shore of Carthage. The king of the gods anticipates a future moment when, under Augustus, civil wars will come to an end and *impius Furor*, madness coupled with impiety because it fosters fraternal strife, will at last be imprisoned and "Dreadful to behold will roar with bloody mouth" (*fremet horridus ore cruento*, 1.296).

Shortly afterwords, in Book 12, king Latinus will admit that he took up "impious arms" (*arma impia*, 12.31) when siding with Turnus against Aeneas. We thus find Aeneas' primary opponent, whom Virgil's narrator has already projected as an embodiment of pride, now not only motivated by a destructive passion worthy of Dido, with all that such a proclivity implies for future events, but also the incorporation of civil war and its ugly form of destructiveness. Both of these aspects of Turnus stay with us to the epic's final scene as Virgil offers Aeneas and us a chance to ponder for a final, crucial time the words of Anchises which are at the center of this chapter. The prideful has been battled into submission. The forbearance that should follow, as we have seen, could take two forms: the generalized sparing of the humbled (*parcere subiectis*) and the particular sparing of Pompey by Caesar that Aeneas' father commands (*parce*). At the end of the poem Aeneas has a chance to show compassion not only to the epitome of pride brought low but also the opportunity to play the role of Caesar with a symbol of civil warring now at his mercy.

We can begin to illustrate some reasons why matters take a different turn by looking at the last appearance of Dido in the poem, once more accomplished by allusion. Here is Aeneas' reaction upon seeing the belt of Pallas on Turnus the suppliant (12.945–8):

> ille, oculis postquam saevi monimenta doloris
> exuviasque hausit, furiis accensus et ira
> terribilis: "tune hinc spoliis indute meorum
> eripiare mihi?"

> He, after he had drunk in with his eyes the remembrances of his fierce grief and the armor [of Pallas which Turnus wore], set aflame by furies and terrifying in his wrath: "Are you, clothed in the spoils of what belongs to me, to be snatched hence from me?"

Virgil's etymological wordplay, moving from *exuvias*, what someone takes off or is relieved of, to *indute*, the act of donning, brings home the fact that Turnus, the killer of Pallas and wearer of his baldric, has also to some degree become Pallas himself (The first is based on *ex-*uo*, the second from *indo- + *uo*.). It is this duplex vision that rouses Aeneas's fury and drives him to kill without mercy. But Virgil's language would also have us think of a moment in Book 4 where Dido, readying herself for suicide, asks her unwitting sister to prepare a pyre (4. 495–8)

> "...et arma viri thalamo quae fixa reliquit
> impius exuviasque omnis lectumque iugalem
> quo perii, super impones: abolere nefandi
> cuncta viri monimenta iuvat monstratque sacerdos."

> "...and place upon it the impious man's weapons, which he left affixed in our bedroom, and all his clothing and the marriage couch where I met my doom: it gives me pleasure to obliterate all the reminders of the wicked man, and the priestess shows the way."

Something that had been worn, and the memories it brings, figure prominently in each passage, and lead in each instance to impetuous action. For Dido suicide is in store, the only way for the tragic queen to rid herself of a desire no longer requited. For Aeneas it means a burst of terrifying anger in which Pallas gains retribution over his killer. The deep emotionality of each moment is beyond question. As far as Aeneas is concerned such a vehement response is not unexpected. For instance, Virgil describes at length in Book 10 the horrors that Aeneas perpetrates at Pallas' death when, among other exploits, he takes eight captives to be offered as human sacrifice on Pallas' funeral pyre, dispatches a suppliant, asking for mercy in the name of his killer's father and son, as well as a priest of Apollo and Diana. But the final fury to which sight of Pallas' baldric drives Aeneas is the more ethically dubious because it specifically goes against the dictates of Anchises to practice moderation and have peace as an aim when an enemy has been laid low. Aeneas fosters ongoing revenge, not restraint, as the epic ends, with the soul of Turnus being exiled from his body, and Virgil offers us no relief from his dark vision.

Emotionality in the *Aeneid*, especially emotionality with a sexual component however latent, is always suspect, often subversive. Dido, mad with love, attempts to lure Aeneas away from the fulfillment of his Roman mission and fails in her effort. The killing to which remembrance of Pallas drives Aeneas can be viewed as even more undercutting of the standards which Anchises sets for Roman imposition of its might. To see the full extent of the change in Aeneas over time from this perspective we must return again to the epic's opening. We have seen how the language Virgil gives Juno at the epic's opening is paralleled in his description of Aeneas' final burst of fury. Virgil never allows Aeneas any such fervid expression of emotion as the epic begins. In fact his very suppression of deep feeling during the larger course of his epic is one of the characteristics that has commended him to earlier critics as an emblem of Stoic virtue, hoisting the burden of his father and leading his son by hand out of the ruins of Troy.

This unquestioning endurance of a grand destiny beyond his control, of the responsibilities consequent to the journey toward Rome and Augustus, is one way to distinguish Aeneas from the existential paradoxes that are the lot of Achilles or from Odysseus' picaresque absorption of knowledge. He begins his journey battered by the storm of Juno's fury and, even after he and his companions have withstood its onslaught and his words seek to reassure them, still, the narrator tells us, "he suppresses his grief deep in his heart" (*premit altum corde dolorem*, 1.209). Virgil does allow his hero a vehement outburst of anger in Book 2 against Helen, a passage so striking, and no doubt so troubling to the poem's ancient readers, that, according to Servius, Virgil's executors attempted to suppress it. But when his siege of emotion has passed, Venus makes an appearance to chide her son (2.594–5):

> "nate, quis indomitas tantus dolor excitat iras?
> quid furis?"

"My child, what is the enormous resentment that rouses your uncontrollable anger? Why this rage?"

At his mother's intervention, he is soon again on course, peering beyond his own sufferings into a vision of the gods at work destroying Troy. In Book 4 he again yields to his own inner feelings by accepting Dido as lover. Once more an emissary from heaven sets him back on the path of duty and prevents his calm ears from hearing her complaints: "his mind remains unmoved" (*mens immota manet*, 4.449). Sense of duty complemented by piety urges him on to pluck the golden bough of life-in-death. He can then enter the Underworld to learn from his father the future glory of Rome and to observe its heroes one by one. Once again in Book 7 there is the fury of Juno to withstand, as the poem's second half begins its course, but Book 8 brings with it not only a tour of the site of future Rome but, by means of the ekphrasis of Aeneas' shield, another look at her incipient eminence, culminating in a description of the battle of Actium and the emperor's subsequent triumph. The future has something in which Rome can glory.

But by the time we reach Aeneas' extraordinary spate of vengeance in Book 10, after the death of Pallas, and the uncontrolled savagery of the epic's concluding lines, we find the hero now allowing himself to give full expression to the *dolor* that has previously been suppressed or deflected. There is no divine intervention before or after the killing, and the furies that beset Aeneas are part of his own inner being, not imposed from without. Another careful bow from the ending back to the beginning will help to clarify this development. Among the symptoms which the hero displays, as he confronts the deadly possibilities of Juno's storm, is that (1.92) extemplo Aeneae solvuntur frigore membra

suddenly his limbs were undone with cold.

This is the same response that Virgil allots Turnus in the epic's penultimate line (12. 951):

. . . ast illi solvuntur frigore membra

. . . but his limbs were undone with cold.

Turnus has now replaced the earlier Aeneas, but what he confronts is not a symbolic representation of Juno's wrath but a manifestation of fury in the person of the hero who has already vanquished him. Aeneas, the passive hero in Book 1, can escape the death at sea which he senses might be imminent. At the end of Book 12, as matters come full circle, the hero, who earlier must endure his frightening destiny, now inflicts death on his victim. As passive hero becomes active and the exile achieves a position of total dominance, the *dolor* that at the beginning of the epic he was not allowed to express finds public release in one final manifestation of rage.

But within the changes that this circularity brings there is also an ironic repetitiveness. Aeneas may slay his suppliant antagonist in a final display of heroism, but he, too, is still passive as well as active, a victim, not of physical force but of inner emotions that for this moment at least direct his destiny. As someone who is *furiis accensus* he is not only parallel to the mothers in Book 7, maddened by Allecto, he is like Juno at 1.29, "aflamed" (*accensa*) by the many angers and resentments (*dolores*, 25) in her life that cause her hatred of the Trojans.

One final manifestation of ring-composition brings with it one last irony. As scholars now often note, Virgil uses the same verb, *condere*, to describe the founding of Rome, in the fifth line from the start of his epic, as he does for the burial of Aeneas' sword in the chest of Turnus three lines before its conclusion. Turnus may thus be viewed as a necessary sacrifice for the establishment of Rome, the last in a long line of victims that dot Aeneas' progress, from the helmsman Orontes, lost during the opening tempest, to the many deaths that the war brings as the epic draws to a close. But the manner of Turnus' death is one last reminder of Anchises' prescriptive warning about the moderate uses of power, especially absolute power.

There will be nothing easy in Virgil's vision of Rome and its future, or about human history in general, for that matter. Real and ideal, nature and culture, emotionality and restraint unremittingly confront each other throughout his brilliant poem. The distinction between the line that takes us through history from Troy to Rome, from Aeneas to Augustus and to a moment, in the "now" of the poet's writing, when one can speak of a renewed golden age, and the circle, by which the poet's rhetoric ever and again draws us back from end to beginning, which is to say, into the constancy of destructive human emotionality, is never, perhaps could never be, resolved.

The hesitation of Aeneas before killing Turnus betrays a poem, and a poet, in crisis. We have had evocative examples of such pauses before. Dido hesitates before leaving her chamber to depart with Aeneas on the hunt, and toward suicide. The golden bough hesitates, even though we are told that it will come easily or not at all, before Aeneas plucks it, and foresees, which is to say readies himself to initiate, the Roman future through the guidance of his father. Vulcan delays before agreeing to make the armor of Aeneas, for to do so means assurance both of the immediate battling soon to come and of the more general "triumphs of the Romans . . . and wars fought one after another" displayed on Aeneas' shield that constitute the core of Rome's unremittingly martial history as it evolves (*Romanorum…triumphos…pugnataque in ordine bella*, 8.626, 629). This final crisis and the poem's deliberate incompletions feed on each other, at the end leaving the reader with a series of challenges but with no doubt about the profound honesty of both poet and masterful poem.

FURTHER READING

Biographical details are well set forth in the entry for "Virgil (Publius Vergilius Maro)" by D. and P. Fowler in the *OCD*: 1602–7.

The bibliography for Virgil is vast and spans centuries. For reviews of scholarship on the *Aeneid*, both as elegant as they are magisterial, see Williams 1967, Hardie 1998. Equally exhaustive and authoritative is the bibliography for the *Aeneid* by Suerbaum 1980: 2. 31. 1. 3–358, updated and condensed in 1999: 385–410.

Among valuable *ancillae* and collections devoted, in whole or part, to the *Aeneid* are Horsfall 1995a; Martindale 1997; Stahl 1998; Perkell 1999; Spence 2001; Anderson and Quartarone 2002.

For import recent collections of hitherto published essays see Commager 1966; Bloom 1986 and 1987; Harrison 1990; and Quinn 2000.

Influential book-length studies of the Aeneid include Heinze 1903 (trans. 1993); V. Pöschl *Die Dichtkunst Virgils* (Innsbruck, 1950), trans. as *The Art of Vergil* by G. Seligson (Ann Arbor, 1962); Otis 1963; Putnam 1965; Johnson 1976; Conte 1986. Hardie 1986 redresses the balance against darker readings of the poem.

For a survey of Virgil's views of art see Putnam 2001a, and for analysis of the poet's use of ekphrasis, and in particular his descriptions of works of art, see Putnam 1998. For a more detailed discussion of the implicit eroticism of the ending of the *Aeneid*, see Putnam 1995.

CHAPTER THIRTY-FOUR

Ovid

Carole E. Newlands

From the very start of his poetic career, Ovid was obsessed with the idea of writing an epic poem. In the first of his earliest love poems, the *Amores*, Ovid claims that he had embarked upon writing an epic poem when Cupid interrupted the enterprise by mischievously stealing a foot from a line of verse, thereby turning hexameter into pentameter and creating an elegiac couplet (*Am.* 1.1.1–4):

> Arma gravi numero violentaque bella parabam
> edere, materia conveniente modis.
> Par erat inferior versus: risisse Cupido
> dicitur atque unum surripuisse pedem.

> I was preparing to write of weaponry and violent war in solemn metre, with theme suiting the rhythm. The second line of verse was equal to the first: Cupid seems to have smiled and snatched away one foot.

Epic poetry is reductively defined in the first line here as "weaponry and violent wars in solemn metre." Like Virgil's *Aeneid*, Ovid's first elegiac poem begins with *arma*, which are then, however, wittily rejected for the metaphorical weaponry of love that will preoccupy his elegiac poetry. Indeed, Ovid's amatory poetry is consistently defined against epic poetry, while epic themes and heroes are subsumed by an erotic perspective. Thus in *Amores* 1.9, where Ovid develops most consistently the metaphor of love as warfare, Achilles, Agamemnon and Hector all appear as lovers; Mars too, we are reminded, was ensnared in bed with Venus (33–40).

Yet Homeric epic was, as Quintilian was to say, the highest art form (*Inst.* 10. 1. 46), and Ovid was an extremely ambitious poet. Ovid met the challenge of epic with a tour de force, the *Metamorphoses*, a lengthy poem of some 12,000 hexameter lines in fifteen books that accommodates to the sweep of epic the elegiac strategies derived from the neoteric and Hellenistic poets: the exploration of erotic, psychologically complex, and bizarre themes; the elevation of the small-scale, intricately structured narrative; the cultivation of a sophisticated, witty, and allusive style. Within a chronological framework that greatly exceeds the epic norm in scale by extending from Creation to the author's own times, the poet encompasses a vast number of mostly Greek myths linked under the general rubric of metamorphosis, change of human form. (See Feeney 1999 for the argument that Ovid challenges authoritative and canonical patterns of time.)

Ovid eschews the social and cultural dimension of Greek myth for human and psychological drama. His myths are ostensibly aetiological in that they attempt to account for the present shape of the world by explaining the origins of its natural and cultural phenomena, yet as Niklas Holzberg points out, the aetiology of natural phenomena allows for the exploration of human psychology (1977: 151). Indeed, with his elevation of complex passions as a serious subject for poetry, Ovid expands the emotional range of epic. In particular, since metamorphosis involves the change of the human body into something alien to it, often by a punitive deity, in Ovid's poem metamorphosis provides the pretext for psychological and ethical exploration of the instability of selfhood in a world of drastically unequal power relations. Ovid thus took the kind of unusual and recondite topic popular in Hellenistic poetry as inspiration for his exploration of human identity and the powerful forces that can influence, alter, and even destroy it.

The generic status of the *Metamorphoses* has been a major preoccupation of twentieth-century scholarship. Readers have by no means been agreed on whether the *Metamorphoses* can properly be termed an epic poem. For many critics, who agree with the attack by John Dryden on Ovidian wit, the poem fatally lacks appropriate seriousness or epic dignity (Dryden 1700; see discussion in Tissol 1997: 11–18). In 1945, and again in 1955, critics Hermann Fränkel and L. P. Wilkinson respectively initiated a change in scholarly attitudes towards the poet that would progressively reclaim his important place in literary history. Yet as recently as 1997 the poet Ted Hughes, in his introduction to his *Tales from Ovid*, denied epic status to the *Metamorphoses*, claiming it "resembles an epic" only in its length and metre (see also Due 1974: 164; Knox 1986). Certainly, the *Metamorphoses* lacks a unified plot; it has no guiding hero or set of heroes; the most intense fighting takes place not on a battlefield but at weddings. The precedent for works on myths of metamorphosis lies in Hellenistic, not epic poetry, with poems such as Nicander's *Heteroioumena* ("Things changed") and Boeus' *Ornithogonia* ("Origins of birds"); in addition, an older contemporary of Ovid, Aemilius Macer, wrote (or translated) a work on transformations of birds, and Parthenius likewise wrote a *Metamorphoses* (see Myers 1994: 21–6 for Hellenistic precedents). But it is unlikely that any of these works were as ambitious in scale as Ovid's *Metamorphoses*. The *Metamorphoses* is not an anthology of myth (although often, even today, it is treated as such), for Ovid audaciously and ingeniously connects the myths to one another in a variety of ways to create a smooth, if artificial temporal progression (cf. Due 1974).

In addition to the influence of Hellenistic poetry, Ovid's *Metamorphoses* is also profoundly shaped by his predecessors in Roman epic tradition. In addition to the important precedent of Virgil's *Aeneid*, Ennius' *Annales* provided in its first edition a model for a fifteen-book poem covering an extensive period of time (see, e.g., Hardie 1993: 13; Wheeler 1999: 23–4). But the *Metamorphoses* resists the nationalistic, teleological focus of these works. Although it encompasses the subjects of several epics, in particular the Theban cycle in Books 3–4, the *Iliad*, the *Odyssey*, and the *Aeneid* in Books 12–15, the text has its own idiosyncratic approach to epic themes, often emphasizing the marginal character and marginal event, and the erotic and the pathetic over the martial and heroic. For instance, Ovid takes the story of Thebes from the rape of Europa and Cadmus' foundation of the city to the dismemberment of Pentheus and the madness of Athamas and Ino (2.836–4.603). But as with the Homeric, and the Virgilian epics later, Ovid's treatment focuses on lesser-known characters and incidents; we hear of the doomed love of Narcissus and Echo (3.339–510), rather than of Oedipus and Jocasta, Polynices and Eteocles.

Likewise, as Niklas Holzberg observes, in Ovid's version of the *Aeneid* (*Met.* 13.623–14.580) only 200 of these 926 lines actually retell Virgil's poem; the rest is devoted to erotic and marvellous tales that omit anything of national significance (Holzberg 1997: 41). The deferral or subordination of tales of patriotic import to erotic tales is itself a political gesture. Garth Tissol and Stephen Hinds have shown in different ways how Ovid, rather than being oppressed by the authority of Virgil's epic, here appropriates the *Aeneid* to produce all the more emphatically his own version of epic and indeed of Roman history (Tissol 1997: 177–91; Hinds 1998: 99–122). With his bold appropriation of earlier epic poetry, Ovid rewrote the rules for Roman epic.

The *Fasti*, the poem on which Ovid was working at the same time as the *Metamorphoses*, has proved a useful foil in marking out the generic terrain of the *Metamorphoses*. As an elegiac poem on the Roman calendar that, in six books, covers the events worthy of commemoration – religious, political, historical, as well as astronomical – in the first six months of the Roman year, the *Fasti* forms a Roman counterpart to the *Metamorphoses*. Indeed, there are self-conscious parallels between the two poems, the most overt being the lengthy myth of Proserpina narrated in both *Met.* 5 and in *Fast.* 4. Modifying the early comparative study of these two versions of the myth by Richard Heinze, Stephen Hinds suggests that, while generic conventions are important markers of difference, as Heinze argued, they also provide a set of limitations that both the *Metamorphoses* and the *Fasti* challenge and transgress in different ways (Heinze 1919; Hinds 1987b, 1992). Denis Feeney has argued that the *Metamorphoses* is "imperial in its totalising ambition" (1998: 70). Yet it is self-consciously poised against the *Fasti*, a poem that overtly resists single explanations for the various phenomena of Roman religion, history, and cult that it commemorates. The *Metamorphoses* remains an open-ended work as it exists in dialogue with Ovid's own poetry and earlier epic.

Indeed, in addition to challenging epic norms, the poem also ambitiously encompasses a wide variety of genres – tragedy, pastoral, elegy, for instance – within a broad epic compass. As Stephen Harrison comments, fundamental to the poem is "generic multiplicity within a formally epic framework" (2002: 89). The power struggles of the poem are not confined to those between gods and humans but include that of the poet with his literary predecessors as he strives to mark out his own epic terrain.

The tension in Ovid's poem between its non-traditional themes and its epic form is expressed in the proem, a conventional landmark of Ovidian criticism, for the proem is teasingly ambiguous (1.1–4):

> In nova fert animus mutatas dicere formas
> corpora: di, coeptis (nam vos mutastis et illa)
> adspirate meis primaque ab origine mundi
> ad mea perpetuum deducite tempora carmen.

My mind impels me to sing of forms changed into new bodies: gods, inspire my enterprise (since you have changed that too), and spin out a continuous song from the first beginnings of the world to my own times. (text, Anderson 1988)

The proem is audaciously short for an epic poem, a mere four lines. Yet despite the initial brevity, Ovid announces here that he will write a *perpetuum carmen* (4), a continuous poem from the beginning of time to his present age. Yet the verb he uses to describe the process of composition, *deducite* (4), "spin out," recalls the *deductum carmen*, the sophisticated, refined song, that Virgil's Callimachean Apollo commands the poet to sing in *Eclogue* 6.5 in lieu of epic arms and heroes. The poem thus embraces both epic and Callimachean ideals of poetic form. Yet *deducite* itself contains a further ambiguity, for, as

Gianpiero Rosati points out, the metaphor of spinning out thread suggests "the idea of continuity and extension"; the word thus encapsulates both Callimachean refinement and the continuous sequencing of epic (Rosati 1999: 247). The originality of this proem, and of the following work, is boldly expressed with the initial phrase, *in nova*, a seemingly autonomous manifesto of originality, for at first the reader does not encounter the qualifying noun *corpora* until the second line; the proem thus unfolds from the opening gambit that stresses the originality of Ovid's new poem.

These four lines lack any reference to heroes or to warfare; instead they emphasize change (*mutatas, mutastis*), and the role of the gods in metamorphosis not only of the human body but also of Ovid's body of poetry (see Farrell 1999a and Theodorakopoulos 1999). Thus the proem suggests that this poem will be a very different kind of epic, far more ambitious in temporal scope than Homeric epic or the *Aeneid* and encompassing many different genres, yet with the sophistication, the attention to psychological detail, literary self-reflexivity and the wit that his readers have come to expect from Ovid's elegiac poetry. In addition, the experience of reading the poem, with the surprising syntactic shift in the opening two lines, embodies change itself within the style and structure as well as the theme of the poem.

How then does Ovid achieve the effect of a "continuous poem" when he is dealing with a vast complex of myths and a vast stretch of time? The continuity of the poem exists in constant tension with its narrative fluidity as connections between myths and indeed books are created in a variety of ways. Rarely is there closure at the end of books of the poem. For instance, Book 1 begins an audacious trend by ending at the beginning of the story of Phaethon, so that movement between books is interconnected. Sometimes individual myths are linked by a kind of natural chronology; for instance in Book 1 the Flood (253–415) follows the story of Lycaon's impiety against the gods (163–252). At other times the transitions are much more contrived, a facet of the poem to which Quintilian objected (4.1.77), but which gives the impression of continuity for the whole poem. For example, again in Book 1, when the river-gods come to Daphne's father after her metamorphosis into a laurel, we are told that one river-god, Inachus, is absent, because he has lost his daughter (1.568–87). The text then launches into the story of Jupiter's seduction of Io and her metamorphosis into a cow (1.588–746). Sometimes too a storyteller, for instance Orpheus, takes up most of Book 10 (148–739) with his tales of "unnatural" or unlucky love.

As Stephen Wheeler has pointed out, more than a third of the poem is narrated by character-narrators other than Ovid (1999: 162–3). The device of storytelling creates a further vital tension between the seamless flow of the poem and its multiplicity of voices. Indeed, sometimes more than one narrator will participate in a storytelling session, as when Theseus' men are guests in the cave of the river-god Achelous while his waters are in spate (8.547–9.97) (see Barchiesi 1989: 57–64 on Archelous as storyteller; Barchiesi 2002a and Wheeler 1999 on the many storytelling voices). Such sessions can create their own internal dramas and ironic juxtapositions. When Pirithous, one of Theseus' men, forgets that he is the guest of an immensely powerful river-god and questions the gods' power of metamorphosis, the elderly Lelex hastily intervenes with his story of two pious worshipers of the gods, Philemon and Baucis, who are metamorphosed at the end of their virtuous lives into sacred trees (8.611–724). Achelous follows with a story further intended to demonstrate the ability of the gods to change the shape of humans (8.725–878). Yet since his story concerns how a wicked king, Erysichthon, cut down a sacred tree, it sheds ironic light on the outcome of the story of Philemon and Baucis. The gods' power of metamorphosis, it seems, is circumscribed, for it cannot guarantee perpetuity of form or indeed ultimately resist the various forces of change that dominate the world.

The poem thus is characterized by multiple narrators, whose stories reflect their various biases and ideologies; in addition, their stories are shaped by the needs of their particular situations. Thus, as Frederick Ahl has pointed out, Cephalus, telling the tragic story of his marriage to Procris on the island of Aegina, does not tell his audience of his wife's sexual affair with Minos, for the king is their bitter enemy (7.472, 690–865) (1985:211). Correspondingly their stories are affected by their different audiences and by the exigencies of specific circumstances (see Wheeler 1999). As the storytelling session in Achelous' cave suggests, audiences are usually mixed; the disbelief of Pirithous is matched with the hasty piety of the elderly Lelex. After Daphne has been transformed into a laurel and a symbol of Augustan victory, the river-gods who gather at the home of Daphne's father, the river Peneus, are uncertain whether to console him or to congratulate him (*Met.* 1. 577–8). The flexible responses of the internal audience have suggestive implications for the poem's readership, which has generated multiple points of view. We should indeed resist the idea that there is one correct reading of this poem (Due 1974; Feldherr 2002: 178).

The swift shifts in tone, subject, and points of view within and between tales justly characterize this poem as, in Calvino's terms, "a poem of rapidity" (1991: 43). The meter too gives the impression of swiftness, as Ovid prefers dactyls much more than Virgil in the *Aeneid* (Anderson 1997: 354–5). Critics, however, have sought to impose an overall, coherent narrative structure on the poem. Brooks Otis treated the poem as a symphony in four movements, leading towards an Augustan climax (1970). Holzberg has persuasively argued for a tripartite structure to the poem, which moves in pentads (thematic sections of five books) from the affairs of the gods to those of humans and then of heroes in "historical time" (1997). But this way of reading the poem militates against what Neil Hopkinson calls its "proliferating diversity" (2000: 9). There is a good deal of overlap between these "sections," as the gods, for instance, are important in varying degrees throughout the poem, gaining center stage again, for instance, in the final book. Separating the poem in this way ignores the blurred confines between humans and gods that preoccupies the poem and undermines the epic hierarchy of separate spheres.

Thus, while the small-scale narratives of individual metamorphoses are linked in a purportedly chronological framework, the structure of the poem is itself metamorphic, shifting in style, location, narrator, tone, and audience. As Calvino comments, "the passion which dominates his compositional skills is not systematic organisation but accumulation" (1991: 43). Or, as W. R. Johnson put it in a landmark essay of 1970, the style of the poem is "counter-classical" in that it challenges the primacy of hierarchical notions of stability and unity.

With its focus on sexuality and psychological drama, its critique of unequal power relations, and its dazzlingly fluid, often paradoxical style and structure, the *Metamorphoses* pushes Roman epic in a new direction. Although historical and national themes emerge only in the final three books and are in muted form at the very end, the poem, I argue, remains deeply political in its orientation. Since the poem was written between 2 and 8 CE, shortly before Ovid was banished to Tomis on the Black Sea by the emperor Augustus, it is tempting to connect the poem's obsession with crime and punishment to Ovid's own experiences of an increasingly autocratic dynasty seeking, indeed, in divinization legitimacy for its rule (see Syme 1978: 205–14). Myths of metamorphosis provided him with a rich and complex field for exploration of the uses and abuses of power.

For Ovid's immediate followers in epic tradition, particularly Lucan and Statius, the world in which their heroes move is filled with narrative delays and divagations, and is fatally corrupted by the demystification of the divine and heroic apparatus initiated in Ovid's *Metamorphoses*. Indeed, metamorphosis itself is for the most part an anti-heroic concept in that, with only a few exceptions, human beings change to a lesser form of life. Thus Ovid's poem offers new perspectives on the staples of heroic epic: the battle, the hero, and the gods. Keeping in mind Feeney's observation that "scarcely an area of epic technique is left unscathed by Ovid's powerful experiments," let me now deal with each of these three features in turn (Feeney 1991: 239). I shall suggest that by destabilizing epic norms, the *Metamorphoses* opens the genre up to more fluid reinvention.

The Battlefield

The traditional site for violence in epic is the battlefield, and that site is characterized by face-to-face combat among men who are in general equally matched. In the *Metamorphoses*, however, violence for the most part is enacted *outside* the battlefield and is directed against those who lack adequate defence, whether because of their gender, their age, their profession, or their sheer mortality. On the few occasions when heroes do fight one another, the circumstances or their actions are often ridiculous or grotesque. The most violent fighting in the *Metamorphoses* takes place at weddings. Thus when the *Metamorphoses* comes in time to the Trojan War and the subject matter of the *Iliad*, long-winded Nestor, though encamped outside Troy, tells not of the present combat but instead of the battle between the Lapiths and the Centaurs at the wedding of Hippodamia (12.168–535). Moreover, much of the fighting he describes is crudely comic and hardly heroic; mixing bowls serve as weapons along with swords. It is important to recognize, as Holzberg cautions, that the grotesque nature of such scenes calls into question not Homeric poetry but rather hero worship (1997: 141). We are invited to see traditional heroes in a new, less flattering light.

The battle among heroes that takes place at the wedding of Perseus and Andromeda (5.3–249), is an episode that, as Alison Keith argues "constitutes a sustained meditation on the action of heroic epic," for the brutality of Homer and the sentimentality of Virgil are intensified within the brief compass of 250 lines (2002: 241; cf. Otis 1970: 57). Perseus, with only a few companions but with the assistance of Minerva, fights for his wife against a greater number of armed rivals, headed by Phineus, the spurned fiancé; thus the parallels with *Odyssey* 22 are particularly striking, along with details from Virgil's Italian war in the *Aeneid*.

Most critics have treated this episode as a parody of heroic battle (cf. Keith 2002: 245 and Due 1974: 78). Yet the episode implicitly attacks as false the premise that the hero must be defined and proved through martial prowess, for the entire fight is unnecessary. In the end, after a good deal of bloodshed, all Perseus has to do is to swing round Medusa's head and turn his enemies into statues, and we have to wonder why he did not do this earlier. Indeed, this unnecessary fight provides the occasion for the deconstruction of heroic norms of miltary prowess, ancestral pride, and immortality. The heroes appear as inept, cruel, and pathetically pretentious. For instance, Perseus is presented as an opportunist, killing Athis with a log (55–7) and swinging a mixing bowl instead of a sword (79–84); Phineus kills Idas by mistake (89–96); so slippery with blood does the floor of the banquet hall become that several heroes slip and fall, meeting their deaths as they struggle to get up (74–8); the venerable seer Aethion, once "sagacious" (146), has been deceived by a lying portent (146); Astyages thinks a petrified soldier is alive and strikes the figure with his sword, making a metallic sound (200–6). Heroic genealogy too here is flawed. Not only are most of the ancestors mentioned quite obscure, but also the parentage of Astreus, we are told, is in doubt (144–5), Agyrtes is *infamis*, disgraced (148), because he killed his father, and Nileus, who bears a lavish representation in silver and gold of the River Nile on his shield, has lyingly claimed (*ementitus*, 188) that his father is the Nile (187–9). The episode ends with a bitter play upon the heroic goal of immortality on the battlefield. Perseus promises his enemy Phineus that in the future he will never be violated by the sword but rather will be an eternal monument, *mansura ... monimenta per aevum* (227). Playing off the double meaning of *monimentum* as literary memorial and monument, Perseus literalizes his promise by turning Phineus into a statue to be placed in the palace of the fiancée who jilted him (224–35). The episode ends with a bad joke that makes fun of the hero's traditional desire for immortal glory; Phineus will always, we are told, be looked at by his former fiancée (228–9); always he will keep his craven expression (234–5). The hero is memorialized as a perpetual emblem of unheroic fear and the object of a woman's scorn.

Glenn Most noted the influence that the *Metamorphoses* had on the development of grotesque forms of death in Neronian literature (1992: 393–4; see also Due 1974: 77). Indeed, for Karl Galinsky Ovid panders to the tastes of his Roman public, debased by the contemporary, savage pleasures of the amphitheater rather than the battlefield (1975: 110–57). But the violence of the nuptial battles is, paradoxically, pointedly gratuitous. In these often ridiculous and exaggerated scenes of violence, the poem is ironic about epic conventions, undermining the heroic ethos and inviting critical scrutiny of traditional heroic values, in particular the prowess that rests on pride of birth and martial skill, and on the elevation of glory through killing. With characteristic humor, irony, and grotesquerie, the poem provides an alternative look at the battlefield, revealing the mistakes, the mess, the vain pretensions, the false motives and claims that often fuel combat. As a product of a state vested in military success, yet haunted by the specter of past civil wars, the poem challenges Rome's most cherished values and ideals.

Writers from Aristophanes to the present day have, like Ovid, employed humor, along with the grotesque and the absurd, to critique prevailing social and political beliefs and norms. George Bernard Shaw in his 1894 play *Arms and the Man*, for instance, invites his audience to scrutinize their assumptions about the motives underpinning the state's exaltation of martial valor and patriotism. When his heroine Raina, starstruck with romantic ideas of military glory culled from books and trips to the opera, asks her "chocolate cream soldier" to describe a cavalry charge, he puts a severe dent in her fantasy by describing it as a handful of peas thrown against a window pane. Indeed, what Leonard Barkan calls "the anti heroic thrust of metamorphosis" is well captured by Ted Hughes in *Tales from Ovid* when, in the fight between Achilles and Cygnus, he uses an absurdly domestic, comic image to describe how "the flaring helmet flew off in shards/Like the shell of a boiled egg" (Barkan 1986: 85; Hughes 1997: 171). Metamorphosis often involves the absurd and the grotesque; above all, change in human form reminds the reader of the fragility of the human body and the instability, rather than immortality, of human identity.

The Hero

Not surprisingly, conventional epic heroes (on whom see Chapter 6, by Nagy) are given unconventional treatment in Ovid's poem. Thus, when Theseus, slayer of the Minotaur, makes an extensive appearance in the poem (8.172–9. 94), his chief role is as guest of the river god Achelous, his job to listen to stories, not recount his own heroic exploits. Although Achilles does appear on the battlefield, he is introduced in the poem not as the killer of Hector, but as the "victor over Cygnus" (*Met.* 12.150), a non-Iliadic character. Since Cygnus has divine protection from death by weaponry, Achilles finds he cannot kill him until he resorts to throttling him, a shameful manner of death that is associated with women, not with heroes (12.138–43). Alison Keith argues that Achilles' reputation is unharmed by Cygnus' shameful death (1999: 232). Yet surely the failure of heroic weaponry here and Achilles' resort to a non-traditional means of killing does impugn his masculinity, particularly since Cygnus' bird-like associations are confirmed by his rebirth into a swan and, indeed, escape from the battlefield (12.143–5). Achilles in fact fails to put an end to Cygnus, and in the confrontation with him, Achilles' high-minded pursuit of honor is seriously put in question. Indeed, as the bird particularly associated with Apollo and poetry, the final escape of the swan acts as a metaphor for this poem's resistance through metamorphosis to the ethos of conventional heroism (see Ahl 1982, esp. 373–7 on the association of the swan with poetry; Keith 1992: 137–46).

In the *Metamorphoses*, as Keith argues, Ovid develops the scrutiny of gender difference that is only implicit in earlier epic (1999: 216). Indeed, the battlefield is an important site where epic heroes find their masculinity challenged, often against the feminine or the transsexual. Since Achilles kills Cygnus in a womanly manner, by suffocation, it is fitting that his own death is described as unmanly, not heroic; rather, he dies in womanish war, *femineo . . . Marte* (12.610), at the hands of an effeminate Paris assisted by Apollo. Paris is described as the "timid abductor of a Greek wife" (12.609) and, until Apollo comes on the scene, he is taking rare and easy potshots at nondescript Greeks on the battlefield (12.599–601).

Even Nestor's long account of the battle of Lapiths and Centaurs, an important myth commonly interpreted as the contest between civilization and barbarism, has as its structural fulcrum the indeterminate gender identity of Caeneus (*Met.* 12. 168–209, 459–535), a hero who had been born a woman (173–5), and who, like Cygnus, escapes death on the battlefield by apparently becoming a bird (see Keith 1999: 233–8 for more on the myth). The putative femininity of Caeneus is directly challenged in the fight by the Centaur Latreus, who taunts the bisexual hero to return to carding wool (*Met.* 12. 470–6). On the battlefield, the traditional site of heroic self-definition, the masculinity of both challenger and challenged is put in question. Although Latreus is described as aggressively masculine ("the greatest of the Centaurs in body and limb . . . and toting a long Macedonian pike," *Met.* 12.463–6), all his verbal bluster and physical blows come to nought, while Caeneus easily dispatches him (*Met.* 12.478–93). The traditional prowess of the epic hero is thus tested in circumstances that challenge conventional perceptions of heroic virtue and manliness. Indeed, more often than not, heroes appear as lovers or sexual predators; desire for Atalanta makes Meleager champion her right to the spoils of the boar hunt and inspires him to a greater effort in the chase (8.324–28; 433–6); the fighting at the weddings takes place over the brides. The emotional range of epic is thus expanded, even as its traditional values are put in question.

Moreover, the epic hero is measured against the new, prominent presence of women within the epic. Indeed, in the *Metamorphoses* women impinge on traditionally masculine, heroic spheres. A classic test case for the display of heroic prowess, the Calydonian boar hunt (8.260–444), degenerates in the *Metamorphoses* into farce, as the venerable Nestor pole-vaults into a tree (365–8), Telamon trips over a tree root (378–9), and the first successful shot to the boar is delivered by a woman (380–3) (see Horsfall 1979 on the boar hunt as parody; Keith 1999 on the undermining of epic masculinity). The hunt pits male against female and in the process the men are found wanting (Keith 1999: 230). For although Atalanta is the first to wound the boar, the men, apart from Meleager, are ashamed and begrudge her any honor in the outcome of the hunt (380–90, 425–44).

When they transgress onto traditional male territory, the women of the poem challenge conventional notions of epic femininity as passive, modest, and domestic. Indeed, Ovid's poem gives extraordinary play to female experience and to the female voice. Although male sexual desire is a prominent motif of the poem, not all women are sexual victims. Indeed, the instances of female sexual desire explored in the poem are particularly complex; Byblis (9.450–665) and Myrrha (10.298–502), for instance, pursue incestuous relationships. Words rather than weapons are generally the female instrument of choice;

some of the poem's most eloquent speakers are women. Drawing on tragedy and his own *Heroides*, where he impersonated the voices of various mythical heroines, Ovid produces in the *Metamorphoses* powerfully articulate women such as Medea, Scylla, Byblis, and Myrrha. Self-reflecting, self-doubting, but always audacious, these women exemplify a new kind of heroism in that they challenge in their dramatic monologues conventional morality and directly pursue the fulfillment of their own sexual desire against terrible odds. The results of such transgression of normative female roles is inevitably disastrous, however, resulting in silence, death, or metamorphosis (see Keith 1992 and Sharrock 2002: 99–101).

But, as Alison Sharrock points out, the poem also strikingly gives voice to the type of intimate female experience not normally documented in epic (2002: 104–6). For instance, Alcmena provides another model of heroism by describing the pain of giving birth to Hercules (9.275–323), and Dryope describes in vivid detail the gradual process of metamorphosis into a tree and her agonized loss of her nursing infant (9. 371–91). Through a variety of female experiences then, the poem questions conventional masculine ideas of heroism.

Amy Richlin has argued that the *Metamorphoses* encodes a strong male bias that is particularly evident in scenes of sexual violence, where the reader becomes a complicit voyeur (1992). In response, critics have pointed out that Ovid's text characteristically offers shifting perspectives on the action and its characters, including scenes of sexual violence; moreover, readers, male or female, can be resistant as well as complicit (see Johnson 1996: 22 on Apollo and Daphne; Lively 1990 on resisting readers). As Sharrock claims, more than any previous epic, "Ovid's work gives space to a female voice, in however problematic a manner, and to both male and female voices which reflect explicitly on their own gendered identity" (2002: 95). Indeed, the important role that Ovid gives the female voice in his epic influences later epic, in particular the personified Rome and the anguished wives of Rome's political leaders in Lucan, and the storytelling Hypsipyle in the *Thebaid* (see further Chapter 8, by H. Foley).

In addition to women, the poem also introduces to epic an entirely new type of hero, the artist, who can be male or female (see, e.g., Leach 1974; Lateiner 1984; Solodow 1988: 203–31; Harries 1990). While gods, kings, and heroes are often cruel and inept, it is the artist in this poem who demonstrates higher ambitions and indeed challenges conventional structures of power, though often failing (see Leach 1974 on the theme of the failed artist). In particular, artists who challenge the gods are cruelly punished for their audacity. The Minyeids, who prefer to weave and tell stories rather than worship Bacchus, are turned into bats (4.1–415). Apollo strips the skin from his rival in music, the satyr Marsyas (6.382–400). When Arachne and Minerva compete in weaving and the judges can find no fault in either tapestry, the goddess strikes Arachne in a rage and turns her into a spider (6.1–145). As Rosati points out, while the contest reveals the partiality and the ideology of producers of texts, such obvious partiality works against Arachne. Though she and Minerva are judged equally matched in skill, she is drastically unequal in power and hence falls an easy prey to the goddess. Thus the story of Arachne, like those of the Minyeids and Apollo and Marsyas, is a fable about the problematic relations between the artist and power (Rosati 1999: 251). This theme too underpins the story of Daedalus and Icarus (8.183–235). True, Daedalus challenges nature itself by building wings for himself and his son, wings that tragically fail because he has not taken into account human fallibility. Yet Daedalus would not have made the wings in the first place were it not for his vexed relationship with his king and employer, Minos of Crete, who keeps him prisoner on the island in order to preserve the secret of the labyrinth. The legendary Orpheus ignores the power of the Bacchantes to his peril (11.1–66).

An exception to the motif of the failed artist might seem to be Pygmalion, who creates the perfect woman in sculpture and, thanks to the intervention of a deity, Venus, sees his dream wife come alive at his touch (10.238–97) (see, e.g. Otis 1970: 57). But as a result, he no longer has his perfect work of art; moreover, as "father" and husband of this living work of art, he is the progenitor of the incestuous Myrrha and Cinyras, his great granddaughter and grandson (10.298–518) (see Janan 1988).

Critics have variously tried to identify Ovid as poet with these individual artists. But Ovid reveals the flaws in them all. Indeed, these myths problematize the status of the artist and of the work of art. Nonetheless, in these myths he translates the *aristeia* of the hero into that of the artist or the poet who, despite failure, achieves something great in defiance of the powerful forces that attempt to constrain and censor artistic autonomy, often with shocking brutality. The only artist to emerge unscathed at the end of the poem is Ovid himself, who announces in the poem's epilogue that he alone, through his work, will survive the wrath of Jupiter and the forces of nature to gain poetic immortality (15. 871–9). But this of course is placed in the future.

Through these myths of the artist as hero the poem also reflects on its own status as a deeply ambiguous work, inevitably corrupted by the violence it describes, often so seductively. Book 6 in particular is framed by stories in which weaving as a form of writing comes under critical scrutiny as an especially dangerous and daring form of artistic communication (see Rosati 2002 on the literary metaphor of weaving). The tapestries of Arachne and Minerva have been commonly interpreted as metapoetic paradigms for Ovid's own work (see Feeney 1991). Likewise, Philomela's tapestry provides a self-reflexive critique of Ovid's own poetry (6.424–674). Deprived of her tongue and voice through brutal rape by her brother-in-law Tereus, Philomela bravely finds a way to communicate her story through writing in woven thread a pitiable poem, a *carmen miserabile* (6.582) (see McKeown on *Am.* 2.4.27; cf. *Met.* 5.339). Her new textual language, however, does not solve the problem of violence and provide a peaceful solution; rather, it sparks a terrible revenge for, as a written document sent to be read, Philomela's tapestry departs from her control. Indeed, she and her sister Procne, the recipient of the tapestry, lose virtually all moral ground when they become as violent as Tereus and slay and cook his son (*Met.* 6.424–674). Philomela's cloth, white with purple signs metaphorically representing speech and blood stains (577), reflects the ambiguous status of writing as a potentially dangerous form of communication that can both express and engender violence in an aesthetically pleasing form. Yet the often violent paradoxes of Ovid's work, the horror and the wit, the beauty and the suffering, resist any kind of passive reception. Indeed, the departure of Philomela's text from her hands also shifts the responsibility of the text's interpretation on to the reader; thus too written works, through circulation and the possibility of endless reproduction, can escape the jealous, authoritarian powers that threaten to destroy them.

The Gods

The gods are by no means "creatures of mythological fantasy" as has often been thought (see Feeney 1991: 188–249 and Due 1974: 88). In an era when Rome was creating its own gods through the imperial cult of apotheosis, Ovid's anthropomorphic gods raise topical ethical and political problems from the poem's start.

Sexual violence is particularly the province of the gods, and it is here that unequal relations of power are most graphically displayed as the gods follow their own pleasure without apparent concern for the consequences. The poem begins with a myth of Creation that separates the gods from humans, and humans from nature (*Met.* 1.5–88). These distinctions collapse as the poem itself is characterized by the often disastrous interpenetration of these three spheres. The gods in love are reduced to often comically human dimensions, yet pursue their lusts with Olympian abandon and disregard for the consequences. Yet the gods are not always successful. Apollo's first love, and the first love story of the poem, represents the god's failure to seduce (1.452–567). Despite his traditional powers of poetry and healing, Apollo can neither charm Daphne with his speeches nor heal his own wounds of unrequited love. Although Jupiter seduces Io, he cannot withstand the scrutiny of his wife Juno, and turns Io into a cow to evade, unsuccessfully, her prying eyes (1.583–746). The sometimes comic ineptitude of the gods in sexual affairs, their obsession with lust rather than with justice or with war, draws the gods down misleadingly, as it turns out, to a human level, for in the end they always have their tremendous, incontestable power at hand. As Ovid notes of Jupiter's transformation into a bull to seduce Europa, with a side-glance at his own paradoxical poetics, "political authority and love do not sit well together" (*Met.* 2. 846–7). All the same, the anthropomorphic behavior of the gods invites the reader to judge them by human standards.

The gods' seductions generally take place outdoors, in an idyllic natural setting. Such landscapes are a special feature of the *Metamorphoses*, which sets it apart from other epics; they occur particularly in the first five books, forming the special, amatory playground of the gods (Hinds 2002: 122). Indeed, landscape is the special care of Jupiter who after the disastrous fire of Phaethon comes down to earth to check that the groves and springs of Arcadia are in working order, and immediately falls for the nymph Callisto (2.405–8). He thereby acts, as Stephen Hinds points out, like the rhetorical poet, creating his own ideal landscape (2002: 129). Yet, as Hugh Parry first argued (1964), these beautiful landscapes, the inspiration of so many wonderful paintings in western art, are also dangerous for those who are not gods (see also Segal 1969; Feldherr 1997). Although they seem to harmonize with the beauty of the gods' youthful victims, they inevitably fail to protect their innocence. Lured into a sense of safety by the peaceful, beautiful surroundings, these victims find their trust in the protection of the landscape misplaced as they are pursued, raped, or transformed by gods. Sometimes, in addition to their fatal, deceptive allure, these landscapes help provide the means for the victim's destruction; the water of Diana's attractive pool, for instance, transforms Actaeon into a stag (3.289–90). The idyllic landscapes prove sympathetic with divine lust. Disturbingly, readers too are seduced by the beauty of these landscapes and become complicit with the gods' desire.

Yet since further punishment often follows seduction, the reversal of the landscape from place of safety to site of suffering is particularly stark. Indeed, often the victims, particularly the women, become through metamorphosis part of the landscape (see Keith 2000). As plants, pools, or animals, they thus become even more vulnerable to processes of change, decay, and aggression. Yet the violent disjunction between appearance and reality also keeps an insistent focus upon the pressing problem of divine justice and authority. Sometimes this problem is openly expressed by the Ovidian narrator himself as when, in a possibly self-referential comment at the start of the story of Actaeon, he guides the reader's response by asking, "What crime was there in a mistake?" (*quod enim scelus error habebat?*, 3.142) To be sure, the aestheticization of violence is an attractive and troubling aspect of the poem, yet it is also integral to the poem's view of the gods as connoisseurs of human flesh rather than of human virtue.

The first appearance of the gods in the poem, however, presents them in their traditional function as the guardians of justice and human morality. As in the *Iliad*, the first book involves an important council of the gods. Jupiter has been appalled by his treatment at the court of king Lycaon, where he was served human flesh; the other gods concur with his wish that for this terrible impiety all humankind should be destroyed (1.163–261). However, as Frederick Ahl and others have pointed out, this Ovidian Jupiter is a figure of excessive anger (see Ahl 1985: 68–99; Segal 1999: 401–7). Lycaon has already been punished by metamorphosis into a wolf for his impiety (232–9). And although the rest of Lycaon's populace dutifully worshiped Jupiter (220–1), and the palace contained household gods, like any proper Roman home (231), nonetheless they too are to be destroyed. As in the story of Diana and Actaeon, the crime seems completely out of proportion to the punishment, human annihilation. The other gods moreover are represented as selfish and sycophantic, caring only that their sacrificial offerings are not lost (244–52).

Strikingly, Jupiter is compared to the emperor Augustus at two key points in this narrative. First, when Jupiter summons the other gods to council, he is described as living in the heavenly equivalent of the emperor's Palatine (1.168–76). Secondly, the gods' shock and concern at the attack on their leader is described as comparable to that of the Roman world at the assassination of Julius Caesar, a concern that is equally gratifying to Jupiter as to Augustus (199–208). There are no further explicit political comparisons or references in the poem until the final book when, in a concluding encomiastic prayer to the emperor, Augustus is again compared to Jupiter (15.858–60). Yet the depiction of Jupiter in the myth of Lycaon establishes an important paradigm for this poem, defining it as a work that is intimately concerned with crime and punishment and that invites its readers to evaluate the justice of its protagonists – gods, heroes, rulers – as they exercise power and mete out punishment. Notably Jupiter, the first storyteller of the *Metamorphoses*, controls the narrative here (see Segal 1999: 404). From the start then, the poem suggests that the biases and ideologies of individual storytellers have political as well as aesthetic import.

With its treatment of the Golden Age, moreover, Book 1 further establishes the importance of punishment as well as metamorphosis to this poem. Whereas in Book 1 of Virgil's *Aeneid* (1.286–96) Jupiter prophesies a future Golden Age to be established under Augustus, in Book 1 of the *Metamorphoses* the Golden Age is long in the past and will not be renewed. Indeed, the opening description of the Golden Age suggests that the present age of Iron belongs to Rome:

> Aurea prima sata est aetas, quae vindice nullo
> sponte sua, sine lege fidem rectumque colebat.
> Poena metusque aberant nec verba minantia fixo
> aere legebantur nec supplex turba timebat
> iudicis ora sui, sed erant sine vindice tuti.
> (1.89–93)

The first age created was golden and it cultivated trust and justice of its own accord, without prosecutor or law. Punishment and fear were absent; no threatening words were inscribed on bronze and read, no suppliant crowd feared the faces of its judge, but all were safe without a prosecutor.

The opening lines of this description, framed by *vindice* (prosecutor) in the same metrical position in the line, strikingly depict the Golden Age in terms not of its abundance but of its lack of negatives – negatives that are in fact central to the Roman state and its system of justice. The description is oriented towards the Iron Age and Rome itself, with its bronze tablets of law, the Twelve Tables, here seen as "threatening," not equitable or just (91–2). Indeed, law here is disturbingly represented as a system of punishment that inspires fear and endangers citizens rather than protecting them (93). Thus a continuum is established between the punitive, threatening Jupiter and the mortal lawgivers of Rome; in divine and human society alike justice is drastically skewed, the imbalance exacerbated by the troubling contiguity of humans and gods. Although the majority of the myths in the poem are Greek, this poem, then, is marked out from its beginning as a very Roman poem.

The only deity who can be called unreservedly beneficent and compassionate to humans is, perhaps not surprisingly in a work that gives so much play to the female voice, the goddess Isis, who brings about a necessary change of sex in the youthful Iphis (*Met*. 9. 666–797). The story of her sufferings as Io, a sexual victim who is metamorphosed into a cow as a result of Jupiter's philandering and becomes the prey of his jealous wife, is told at length in the poem's opening book (1. 583–746). As someone who has experienced both human and animal form she is particularly qualified to understand the sufferings of humans and to preside over a story of transsexuality. Moreover, as an Egyptian goddess, she lies outside the classical pantheon with all its political implications for Rome.

Through Isis, Ovid comes into fundamental conflict with perhaps the most overtly propagandistic part of Virgil's *Aeneid*, the polarization of the Egyptian and Graeco-Roman gods on the shield of Aeneas. By contrast to Aeneas' anthropomorphic deities, the Egyptian gods on Cleopatra's side are depicted as monstrous examples of decadent barbarity (*Aen*. 8.698–700). At first, Ovid's text seems to follow Virgil's line by emphasizing the foreignness of Isis. When she appears to the pregnant Telethusa she is accompanied by the animal gods Anubis, Bubastis, and Apis along with her son Harpo-crates-Horus and spouse Osiris, and she holds her cultic rattle, the sistrum, and snakes (690–4). Anubis, described as *latrator*, "barker," overtly recalls *Aeneid* 8.698 where the same rare noun characterizes the canine-headed god, the only god there named. Yet Isis describes herself here as *dea auxiliaris* (699), a goddess come to help, as she will prove to be by assenting later to Telethusa's prayer that her daughter become a son. The rarity of the adjective *auxiliaris* suggests that divine succour is an unusual phenomenon. With his compassionate Isis, Ovid here corrects the bias of Virgil's epic against Egyptian deities. Although in an earlier, Hellenistic version of this story, the goddess was Leto, Ovid provocatively dissociates his deity from his roguish Graeco-Roman pantheon (see Bömer 1969–86: vol. 4, 469). Indeed, he grants virtue to Isis alone, a goddess whose cult in Augustan Rome remained controversial; Augustus, it seems, tolerated the cult as long as Isis was worshiped outside the Pomerium. Given the general conduct of the gods throughout the *Metamorphoses*, it is not surprising that Ovid should look outside the Olympian pantheon for one truly compassionate deity.

Those who achieve apotheosis in the poem, particularly in its second half, by contrast have close connections with Roman state cult: Hercules (9.229–72), Aeneas (14.581–608), Romulus (14.772–851), and Julius Caesar (15.745–851), with a prospective glance at Augustus' future deification (15.852–70). The apotheoses of the first three prepare the way for the official institution of imperial cult under Augustus. Since apotheosis involves upwards metamorphosis, not downwards, as is usual, is a new stable order created with the establishment of the Caesarean dynasty at the poem's end? Are these gods exceptions to the selfish, violent deities of the rest of Ovid's poem? The final celebration of Julius Caesar's apotheosis with its concluding encomium of Augustus (15. 852–70) has particularly incited much controversy, and characteristically there can be no one "correct" reading of this passage, as with any other in the *Metamorphoses*.

It is important, however, not to dismiss the poem's final, Caesarean section as empty flattery but rather to understand it within the context of contemporary dynastic politics. Hinds has pointed out that the notion of virtue or heroism is not a major concern of Julius Caesar's apotheosis; the military exploits of Julius Caesar are presented as less important than his "fathering" of Augustus by adoption (15.750–78). Ovid thus acknowledges, perhaps with irony, the new integration of apotheosis with dynastic politics (Hinds 1987a: 24–6; see also Feeney 1991: 210–24 on Ovid and the imperial cult). Julius Caesar's apotheosis, moreover, prepares the way for that of Augustus, for deification was seen as essential both for giving legitimacy to Augustus' reign and also for ensuring continuity of rule through his chosen heirs (see *Met*. 15.750–61).

Part of the particular discomfort of the concluding encomium, however, comes from the confrontation of Ovidian myth with contemporary political realities and the aspirations of Augustus himself towards divinity. Here virtue does become an issue. While apotheosis of Rome's citizens removes metamorphosis from the realm of myth to that of contemporary reality, it also confronts the readers of the poem directly with what it means to become a god. Ovid draws attention to the disjunction between official ideology and his own poetic practice in the *Metamorphoses* when in his encomiastic prayer to Augustus he compares the emperor directly to Jupiter (15.858–60):

> Iuppiter arces
> temperat aetherias et mundi regna triformis,
> terra sub Augusto est; pater est et rector uterque.

Jupiter governs the citadels of heaven and the kingdom of the tripartite world, the earth is under the rule of Augustus; each is father and guide.

With this divine analogy, Ovid honors Augustus as a world ruler; he also stresses his well-ordered and caring guidance of his subjects. Both Augustus and Jupiter are described as father-figures who guide their subjects in a well-ordered world. But, as Feeney remarks, the divine–human analogy is always slippery terrain, particularly with Ovid's gods (1991: 220). The word *temperat* associates Jupiter with temperance and moderation, not a characteristic he has displayed up to this point in the poem. Indeed, we are directly reminded of a contrasting view of Jupiter shortly thereafter, when Ovid in his epilogue claims that his work will escape the "anger of Jupiter" (*Iovis ira*, 15.871). He thus evokes the angry Jupiter of the paradigmatic myth of Lycaon; indeed, the poem is framed by these two references to the anger of Jove. The contrasting views of Jupiter presented at the end of Book 15 mark the disjunction between the official rhetoric of imperial encomium and the mythical construction of the gods within Ovid's poem.

Encomium, in any event, is often protreptic, praising the emperor for qualities one hopes to see develop or be maintained; it is often underpinned by anxiety (see Whitby 1998: 1–13). Since the gods have been so closely implicated in the exercise of unjust, disproportionate punishment, the concluding section of the poem, as it grapples with the language of official encomium, at the very least reveals deep unease and anxiety about the emperor's new arrogation of authority through the imperial cult of divinity. Which kind of Jupiter will Augustus prove to be? While the addition of more deities to the Olympian pantheon visibly demonstrates Rome's supremacy in the western world, it may be a mixed blessing for the empire's citizens. In an age of increasingly autocratic measures on the part of Augustus, the poem's exploration of the uses and abuses of power in the hands of gods, kings, and heroes, is at any rate surely relevant and timely. And probably not without relevance to Ovid himself, the ultimate victim of the anger of his Jupiter, Augustus (see Feeney 1991: 222 on the Jupiter/Augustus analogy).

It is important, then, that the final apotheosis of Julius Caesar and the encomium of Augustus should not be read in isolation from the rest of the poem and its depiction of the conduct of the divine denizens of Olympus. The opening book of the *Metamorphoses* linked metamorphosis with the contemporary world and established unequal power relations as a major theme of the poem. Correspondingly, in the final book of the poem, when Rome's new gods are presented for scrutiny, the official rhetoric of praise strains against the poem's demonstrations of divine cruelty and arrogance. And it strains too against the principle of constant change and flux, expounded in the long speech of Pythagoras at the start of this final book (15.60–478) (see Myers 1994: 133–66 and Hopkinson 2000: 3–4). Pythagoras argues that the idea of constant flux has political relevance that contradicts Augustan ideas of stable world order. For other great cities and empires have risen and fallen; so too, it is implied, will Rome (15.431–52) (see Hardie 1993: 95). Indeed, as Tissol remarks, Augustan propaganda at the end cannot cancel out fifteen books of metamorphosis; the poem's ending emphasizes "the ubiquity of change" (1997: 190–1). And, I may add, the ubiquity of punishment, acknowledged in Ovid's defiant epilogue (15.871–9). Metamorphosis generally involves punishment as well as change of human body and identity. Only the disembodied text, however, being endlessly reproducible, will escape both the anger and the laws of men, nature, and the gods.

Although the poet was crushed by exile under Augustus, the *Metamorphoses* has proved resilient and epic in its influence. Ovid changed the myths he inherited from Graeco-Roman tradition. His idealistic artist Pygmalion was, in an earlier version, a king who had sex with a statue of Venus, his Actaeon was a peeping Tom (see Otis 1970: 396–400, 418–19). So too his *Metamorphoses* have encouraged their own proliferation of new versions of myths in new forms. Much attention has been given to the relationship of Ovid's epic to its predecessors, in particular the *Aeneid*. Yet the *Metamorphoses* profoundly influenced subsequent Roman epic poetry. The debt of later epic such as Lucan's *Bellum civile*, Valerius Flaccus' *Argonautica*, and Statius' *Thebaid* to Ovid's poem extends beyond theme and narrative structure to the idea of epic itself; after Ovid Roman epic, which had developed as national poetry, became an important vehicle for political critique as well as creating a new forum for female subjectivity. But the reception of this poem is a topic that is epic in scope and has been well discussed by others. Although the epic poem itself is no longer a vital literary genre, Ovid's poem has metamorphosed into other forms in art, music, drama, as well as other types of literature. Indeed, the last decades of the twentieth century have shown an extraordinary flowering of Ovidian transformations outside academia in the novel, drama, and poetry.

Let me conclude with one small example that demonstrates how profoundly and intimately this poem has influenced western culture, extending even to the intimacies of daily life. The Courtauld Gallery in London displays a sixteenth-century Italian wedding chest designed to stand at the foot of a marriage bed. It is painted by Jacopo Tintoretto with two scenes from Book 6 of the *Metamorphoses*. In one, Latona with the infants Diana and Apollo in her arms, is turning the Lycian peasants into frogs; in the other Apollo and Diana avenge Latona by firing their fatal arrows against the children of Niobe against the backdrop of a contemporary Italian town and pleasing river landscape. By focusing on female experience, the paintings emphasize the importance of female subjectivity and of female readers and female viewers in the interpretation of the poem. How are we today to respond to these two myths, which a young bride over 400 years ago would see each morning and evening from the marriage bed? The chest embodies powerful contradictions. A precious cultural artifact, it is designed nonetheless to be used. The theme of punishment in the paintings seems at odds with the beauty and preciousness of the design and materials. The Courtauld description of the paintings claims, however, that they promote maternal virtue. But they can also be seen as a warning against maternal pride; or of the importance of upholding a rigid social hierarchy; or again as a horrific reminder of child mortality. A view of the world as both hierarchical and violent, ordered and unpredictable, is at any rate at the heart of these depictions of Ovidian myth, whatever other interpretations we may wish to subscribe to. Such powerful contradictions are themselves endemic to Ovid's poem and surely in large part explain the resilience of the *Metamorphoses* and the epic nature of its influence.

FURTHER READING

A starting point should be three collections of essays on Ovid, *Transformations*, ed. P. Hardie, A. Barchiesi, and S. Hinds (1999); *The Cambridge Companion to Ovid*, ed. P. Hardie (2002); and *Brill's Companion to Ovid*, ed. B. Boyd (2002), along with the excellent introductory pamphlet on Ovid by J. Barsby, *Ovid* (1978).

S. Hinds, "Essential epic: genre and gender from Macer to Statius," in the important collection of essays, *Matrices of Genre: Authors, Canons and Society*, ed. M. Depew and D. Obbink (2000b): 221–44, explores in formal, ideological, and epistemological terms the tension between Roman generic theory and Roman generic practice.

G. Rosati's essay, "Narrative techniques and narrative structures," in *Brill's Companion to Ovid* (2002): pp. 271–304, provides a sophisticated analysis of complex problems of narrative technique, in particular the multiplication of narrative voices in the *Metamorphoses*.

For those with Latin, R. J. Tarrant's Oxford text of the *Metamorphoses* (2004) will now probably supersede the Teubner text of W. S. Anderson (1988). Anderson himself provides fine commentaries on Books 1–5 and Books 6–10 (1997 and 1972 respectively); for the entire poem there is the seven-volume German commentary of F. Bömer (1969–86).

A. Mandelbaum's translation (1993) has proved very popular. Opinions are divided about the merits of D. R. Slavitt's translation (1994). He takes liberties with Ovid's text through his own poetic embellishments. To my mind these work and make the translation vivid, fast-paced, and in the Ovidian spirit, but not everyone agrees.

There have been several recent works on the reception of Ovid. C. Martindale (ed.) *Ovid Renewed* (1988) examines Ovidian influences on literature and art from the Middle Ages to the twentieth century; S. A. Brown, *The Metamorphosis of Ovid: From Chaucer to Ted Hughes* (1999) provides a broad survey of Ovidianism in English literature. R. Lyne, *Ovid's Changing Worlds* (2001) explores the important role played by Golding and Sandys, the first English translators of the *Metamorphoses*, in the complex, troubled process of the assertion of national identity. J. Bate, *Shakespeare and Ovid* (1993), examines Shakespeare's transformation of Ovidian materials throughout his career.

But an initial, immediate sense of the transformative power of the *Metamorphoses* can be gained from Petrarch's *Canzoniere* and Shakespeare's *A Midsummer Night's Dream*. C. W. Bynum, *Metamorphosis and Identity* (2001), while focused on the twelfth and thirteenth centuries, provides a rich meditation on different intellectual paradigms for understanding the complex meanings of metamorphosis.

Examples of Ovidian transformations in other literary genres are: in poetry, Ted Hughes, *Tales from Ovid* (1997); M. Hofmann and J. Lasdun (eds.) *After Ovid: New Metamorphoses* (1994); in the novel, C. Ransmayer, *The Last World: With an Ovidian Repertory*, trans. J. Woods (1990); David Malouf, *An Imaginary Life* (1978); Jane Alison, *The Love-artist* (2001); in drama, Mary Zimmerman, *Metamorphoses* (2002).

CHAPTER THIRTY-FIVE

Lucan

Shadi Bartsch

Of the several works of the Neronian poet Marcus Annaeus Lucanus (39–65 CE), only his political epic has come down to us; of the rest, both poetry and prose (including an *Iliacon*, the *Laudes Neronis, Catacthonion, Orpheus, Adlocutio ad Pollam, Medea, Silvae, De incendio urbis*, and the *Epistulae ex Campania*) only fragments remain. His surviving epic, *Pharsalia* or *Bellum civile*, may also be incomplete; we have ten books of a work which seems to have remained unfinished at the time of the poet's death. From the main sources on his life – the historians Tacitus and Dio, the poet Statius, and three ancient *Vitae* – we can surmise with some certainty that the poet, like his uncle Lucius Annaeus Seneca, was born in Corduba, Spain, on November 3, 39 CE, into a family of equestrian rank, and brought to Rome before the age of one. After the recall of his uncle from exile to be Nero's tutor in 49 CE, and after his own education – first, probably, under the Stoic Cornutus and then at Athens – Lucan seems to have enjoyed some prominence at the court of Nero, who was only two years older and shared his literary interests. Their relationship was good: Lucan praised the emperor with the *Laudes Neronis* at the Neronia of 60 CE, and at some period in the early 60s he was advanced to senatorial rank, appointed quaestor, and granted membership in the college of augurs.

At this point – after Seneca's retirement in 62 CE – the sources uniformly point to a quarrel between the poet and the young emperor (for details, see Ahl 1976: 333–53 and the bibliography in Bartsch 1997: 181–2 n. 46) which led to a ban in 64 CE on public recitals by Lucan. For literary or political reasons, Lucan then joined the Pisonian conspiracy, and, after the betrayal of the plot, was forced to commit suicide on April 15, 65 CE. His father and uncle followed a year later. (For Lucan's life and death in the classical sources, see [Suetonius] *Vita Lucani*, Tacitus *Annals* 15.48–70, Statius *Silvae* 2.7, Vacca *Vita Lucani*, and the anonymous Vita of the *Codex Vossianus*.)

Contents of the *Bellum civile*

Lucan's epic treats years 49–47 BCE of the civil war between Julius Caesar and Gnaeus Pompey (and his successors). After a proem which praises Nero in terms that some have found ambiguous (including the ancient commentators), Lucan goes on to narrate the causes of the conflict, Caesar's crossing of the Rubicon (despite the pleas of a personified Roma), and his capture of Arminium. After an address to his troops, Caesar begins his march on Rome; the city is thrown into terror by this new development and the seers Arruns and Figulus both foretell ruin. At the start of the second book, older citizens recall the gruesome happenings of the previous civil war between Sulla and Marius, while the Stoic hero Cato informs Brutus of his decision to support Pompey, "lest he think he has triumphed on his own behalf" (2.324). The brave Domitius, an ancestor of Nero's, resists the Caesarian troops at Corfinium as they overrun Italy, but to no avail, and Pompey is forced to flee the peninsula at Brundisium. He successfully eludes Caesar's blockade to get to Epirus.

In the next two books, we follow Caesar's military campaigns in Italy, Gaul, Spain, Illyricum, and Africa: he plunders Rome and moves on to besiege Massilia, where he defeats Pompey's forces in a horrific naval battle. His troops are similarly successful against the Republican forces of Afranius and Petreius near Ilerda in Spain, though in Illyricum one of his soldiers, Vulteius, commits suicide with a raftful of men rather than fall into Pompeian hands, and in Africa his deputy Curio is defeated and killed in a battle against the African king Iuba.

In Book 5, the narrative turns back to the exiled Senate in Epirus, which meets to legitimize Pompey's leadership in the struggle against Caesar. Appius goes to consult the oracle of Apollo at Delphi, where the Pythia prophesies his death in terms he fails to understand. Meanwhile, Caesar subdues a mutiny in his army and sails across the stormy Adriatic, intending to do battle with the Pompeian forces in Epirus when all his own forces finally arrive. An abortive attempt to sail back to Brindisium on his own to muster these troops fails when a storm almost sinks his little boat. Worried about the outcome of the coming battle, Pompey sends his wife Cornelia to Lesbos for safety. In the subsequent book, Caesar tries but fails to surround Pompey's army at Dyrrachium, and then moves his forces to Thessaly instead. In a famous scene of necromancy, Pompey's cowardly son Sextus consults a Thessalian witch, Erictho, who can disrupt the course of nature, knows the mysteries of Hades, and returns the dead to life (unless she has nibbled off their faces first). Erictho duly resuscitates a dead soldier and forces him to foretell the course of future events: Pompey will be defeated, but Caesar too will be assassinated in the years to come.

Book 7 treats the battle itself. Although Pompey is reluctant to engage, he is persuaded to do so by the restless soldiers and by Cicero's oratory (although Cicero was not historically present at this battle). Carnage ensues, Pompey's forces are routed, and Caesar has a happy picnic overlooking the battlefield and its unburied corpses. In the next book, Pompey flees to Lesbos to collect Cornelia, and decides, after consultation with his allies, to seek assistance from the young Pharaoh of Egypt. The treacherous Pharaoh sends a small boat to meet him offshore and has him murdered in it while Cornelia watches in horror; her husband is decapitated and the headless corpse is tossed overboard to wash up on the Egyptian coast, where a stray Roman soldier buries it.

Book 9 starts with the catasterism of Pompey: his soul ascends to heaven and then flutters down to take up residence in the hearts of Brutus and Cato. Cato assumes control of Pompey's forces and leads them to North Africa, where they are beset by thirst, despair, and an assortment of lethal snakes. They finally reach Leptis, where they spend the winter. In the meantime, Caesar is on a tour of the ruined site of Troy, a city once as great as Rome is in his own time. In the last book, he continues on to Egypt, where he and Cleopatra have an affair and he pledges his support to her. Pothinus, Ptolemy's minister, tries to assassinate Caesar, fails, and is killed himself (the point at which Caesar's *Bellum civile* ends), and in some 15 additional lines we end with Caesar fighting off the forces of another Egyptian, one Ganymede. (Lucan's epic concludes at a point in time covered near the beginning of the pseudo-Caesarian *Bellum Alexandrinum*.) (On the question of whether the epic is complete as it stands, see the comprehensive discussion, with bibliography, in Masters 1992: 216–57).

Reception of the *Bellum civile*

The *Bellum civile* has generated through the ages an astonishing variety of critical responses. Lucan's closest contemporary Petronius seems to be taking a swipe at the epic when his mad poet Eumolpus deplores the choice of historical events as a topic for epic, since such a topic is marked by the absence of mythology and divine agency (Petr. 118.6). A few decades after Lucan's death, Statius may not have had much choice but to praise him in an occasional poem addressed to Lucan's widow Polla, *Silvae* 2.7, on the occasion of Lucan's birthday; here the *Aeneid* itself is said to pay homage to Lucan as he sings among the Romans ("ipsa te Latinis / Aeneis venerabitur canentem," 2.7.79–80) and the poet's early death at the hands of the "rabid tyrant" (100) is lamented as a tragic and untimely loss. Quintilian, in his assessment of Roman epic writers, is more dismissive: Lucan is "fiery and passionate and brilliant in his maxims, and, in my opinion, more to be imitated by orators than by poets" (*Inst.* 10.1.90: "Lucanus ardens et concitatus et sententiis clarissimus et, ut dicam quod sentio, magis oratoribus quam poetis imitandus"). And this criticism in turn may find an answer in a short epigram put into Lucan's mouth by Martial: "Some people say I'm not a poet: but the book dealer who sells me sure thinks I am" (14.194: "Sunt quidam, qui me dicant non esse poetam:/Sed qui me vendit bybliopola putat"). Taking this as praise, however, should perhaps give us pause: Ahl (1976: 74) points out that this lugubrious sequence of spondees may itself be a comment on Lucan's metrification, which was criticized for its monotony. Martial's evidence does show the poem was being read; indeed, the Suetonian *Vita* of the poet tells us that his work was used as a school-text, and put up for sale by careless dealers as well as conscientious ones. ("Poemata eius etiam praelegi memini, confici vero ac proponi venalia non tantum operose et diligenter sed inepte quoque.") The grammarian Fronto thought Lucan's style excessive (Fr. *Ep.* A 344); the first seven lines, he complained, are just a repetition of same theme over and over. In the early fifth century Jerome, in defending the role of literary commentaries, lists Lucan as an author studied in this way, along with Virgil, Sallust, Cicero, Terence, Plautus, Lucretius, Horace, and Persius (*Adv. Ruf.* 1.16), while remaining manuscripts from the fifth and sixth centuries to the late Middle Ages almost rival in number those of Virgil, and generally rank with Juvenal, Persius, and Terence.

However popular the poem, Roman readers continued to find fault with it, especially with its "historical" features (no divine machinery, no beginning *in medias res* but rather a chronological sequence of events, and even excessive historical accuracy). Isidore of Seville criticized Lucan for having written a history, not a poem (*Etym.* 8.7.10) as did before him Servius (*ad Aen.* 1.382: "Lucanus namque ideo in numero poetarum esse non meruit, quia videtur historiam composuisse, non poema"). Nonetheless, the poem was popular in the medieval period, when its rhetorical style and scientific excursuses were admired by its readers. In the first circle of Dante's hell, Lucan is one of the *quattro grand'ombre* (*Inferno* 4.83) in Limbo, the four great poets of antiquity who come to greet Virgil (as the fifth) and Dante and to enroll the latter among their number. Lucan thus stands with Homer, Horace, Ovid, and Virgil in Dante's estimation; Chaucer too would honor the poet in the *House of Fame* (line 1499), and he was quoted or imitated in later medieval commentaries and romances.

Despite the criticism of J. C. Scaliger in his commentary on Manilius (where Lucan is denounced for his lack of astronomical expertise) and in the *Poetics* (where he is deemed irrational), Lucan's fortunes did not wane during the Renaissance. The *editio princeps* of

Lucan was issued at Rome by Sweynheym and Pannartz in 1469. In 1493 his commentator Joannes Sulpitius tells us it is impossible to choose between Lucan and Virgil. Christopher Marlowe translated the first book of the *Bellum civile* into English in 1600, while Thomas May's popular 1627 translation and 1630 supplement continued the story to the death of Julius Caesar. It has long been acknowledged that Milton's Lucifer in *Paradise Lost* (1667) shares a marked similarity with Lucan's demonic Caesar, and Petrarch and Tasso owed him a debt as well. In the seventeenth and eighteenth centuries the French classical dramatists such as Corneille were much influenced by Lucan's style and subject matter, while writers of operatic libretti mined the *Bellum civile* for operas – an example is Handel's *Guilio Cesare in Egitto* – and "whole cohorts of Whigs, radicals, revolutionaries and Romantics" (Martindale 1993: 65) found Lucan republican zeal *au gout*. The eighteenth century saw yet another new translation of the poem into English, by Nicholas Rowe in 1718.

Nonetheless, Lucan's fortunes were now on the wane. Despite Shelley's confession that he preferred Lucan to Virgil, the tides of taste had turned, and our author, with his "warts projecting from Herculean veins" (so quoth an admirer of his content, William Hayley, in 1782; cf. Martindale 1993: 66) had ceased to excite admiration. Voltaire had already dubbed the author of the *Bellum civile* a "declamatory gazetteer" and his work incoherent in his *Essay on Epic Poetry* (1727). In 1825 Joel Barlow complains of Lucan's rambling style, which destroys, he claims, the interest of its "great national subject," and while Macaulay admired the poem's vigor and declamatory passages, he detested Lucan's interest in the grotesque and his "furious partiality" (quoted in Duff 1928: xiv–xc). Both German and English scholarship since the mid-nineteenth century continued to be largely disparaging until the second half of the twentieth century. These critics often reiterated forms of criticism that had come before, decrying Lucan's reliance on "rhetoric" (understood as the use of paradox, hyperbole, and *sententiae*), his frothing denunciations of the Julio-Claudian regime, his sluggish versification, and his elevation of ethical commentary to the level of epic action. As late as 1967, M. P. O. Morford's study of Lucan's "rhetorical epic," while usefully showing the techniques and themes Lucan borrowed from declamation and prior epic, contends that this segmented, prosodically monotonous, and macabre piece of work can hardly be hailed a masterpiece.

Fortunately, in more recent work these stylistic qualities have been understood as part of the message rather than as a veil drawn in front of it. Publications by Ahl, Brisset, Gagliardi, and Martindale between 1960 and 1980 stimulated new critical interest in the poem and sought to show it was worthy of serious attention. W. R. Johnson's influential study, *Momentary Monsters*, opened up a whole new way of appraising the poem: not as epic, but as anti-epic, an exercise in nihilism, a depiction of a world whose machinery had gone mad, where the Stoic Cato can only seem a caricature of the figure of the sage, and where the witch Erictho is Lucan's crazy, grotesque version of Virgil's Sybil. The poem's center is the "witty skepticism that devotes itself to demolishing the structures it erects as fast as it erects them" (Johnson 1987: x). Just before the publication of this book, Henderson had published a long article whose anti-articulacy was itself a commentary on the difficulties of reading the poet; his difficult discussion of the linguistic war within the text and his treatment of the narrator's dual desire tell the story and to protest its telling seemed, like Johnson's work, to lay a new path for criticism. It may be fair to say that these works, combined with Martindale's 1976 study of Lucanian paradox and hyperbole, helped to shape a school that includes the late twentieth-century work of Bartsch, Leigh, Masters, Roller, and other scholars. In particular, what Henderson and Johnson enabled was a way of reading Lucan *without* respect for what one might call the "organic fallacy": in other words, passages which suggested that the poet or the narrator was mired in self-contradiction, confusion, or even in his own lack of literary ability could now be read as part of the poem's message, part of its effort to rip apart the structures of intelligibility on which it was expected to stand.

This deconstructionist approach (for so it has been called, not entirely fairly: reading Lucan this way still requires complicity with that most old-fashioned of critical assumptions, authorial intention) has not won universal unanimity. Lucan's poem can still provoke vastly different responses, with a rift opening up between the prominent Anglo-American school of interpretation described above and an incredulous critical audience centered in Italy. Perhaps the strongest elucidation of this rift is to be found in Narducci's broadside in Esposito and Nicastri 1999, which charges that these "postmodern" scholars' work (Leigh is excepted) is marred by personal biases, bizarre associations, and metaliterary fallacies: in short, that the envelope of interpretation has been pushed far too far and has deteriorated into sheer critical self-indulgence. With less justification, perhaps, Narducci also deplores readings that suggest a lack of unity in either the narrator or in the trajectory of his poem, even though scholars have found in both these approaches a way to make rich sense of aspects of the epic difficult to explain otherwise, such as inconsistencies in the narratorial voice, the shifting portrayal of Pompey, or the curious nature of Lucan's "stoicism." It remains to be seen whether this quarrel will prove a productive one, but this author's essential sympathy with the non-unitary model of reading will be obvious in the body of this essay. (Let us not, with Brutus at *BC* 2.244ff., contend that selecting neither side is the path of virtue!)

Stylistic texture of the *Bellum civile*

Civil war: a country turns violently against itself, and, in Lucan's opening image – a reverse mirror image of the final act of the *Aeneid* (on which see Chapter 33, by Putnam) – plunges its sword into its *own* viscera, signaling the onset of an epic in which agent and recipient of violence will be the same people. Fronto may have complained of the monotony of these initial lines, but in them is contained *in nuce* the major themes of the *Bellum civile:* a war that is (paradoxically) more internecine than even civil war; a criminal act on which (paradoxically) legality has been conferred, a pollution that affects the entire world, kindred soldiers pitted against kindred soldiers, and – as the language takes on the shape of its content – words pitted against themselves (*signa/signis, pila/pilis*). The boundaries of the state-as-body have been breached; as the narrative proper moves into action after the praise of Nero, Caesar ceases to hesitate at the most significant boundary of them all, the narrow banks of the Rubicon, and crosses over into Italy, permanently leaving behind (by his own account) the laws he has scorned and voicing the cynical prerogative of those in power: the guilt shall (after the war) belong to the other side.

Lucan's language strains to express conceptually and grammatically the outrage of these themes. As Henderson notes, this language is "caught up in the 'civil war' of Lucan's text, where opposed senses tear themselves up and rip the signifiers from signification" (1987: 128; for further discussion, see Hübner 1972, 1975; Martindale 1976; Bramble 1982; Henderson 1987; and Bartsch 1997). The poem is marked by a constant usage of paradox, catachresis, subject–object reversal, the inversion of ethical terminology, and the use of negatives to confound epic expectation ("negation antithesis," Bramble 1982: 46–61). And so we see Lucan using antonyms to set common concepts on their head: against expectation, his warriors *flee* to war (*in bellum fugitur*, 1.404) only the *exiled* senators gather at Rome; Cornelia's punishment for surviving Pompey is – *to survive* Pompey; and, of course, Scaeva's great valor on the battlefield is now a criminal act, *scelus*. Normal oppositions fall apart, as has, already, the normative opposition between two sides of a battlefield, where friend and foe should be clearly delineated. Reversal rules the day: cowards do not seek flight, the brave do not seek battle (4.749); even Cato's remarriage to Marcia is a string of negatives denoting what was not there and what did not happen.

The sense of confusion is enhanced by other atypical usages of language: in particular, the strange way in which the agency associated with human intervention in the world is canceled out, to be replaced by a world in which the animate becomes inanimate, the inanimate animate. Swords are struck by humans, bodies are the protection for shields, chests pass through spears, and, as Clytemnestra might cry, the dead are killing the living. Darkness does not come of its own accord, but depends on the agency of the dead ("modo luce fugata/descendentem animam," 6.713–4), which Henderson (1987) translates as "a soul on its way down, having just put the light of day to flight." Lucan's syntactic choices here seem to resonate with the larger sentiments of the narrator, who laments the passivity and paralysis of his own position and those of his peers: as he exclaims in despair over the battle of Pharsalus, Fortuna stripped his generation of the chance to fight against their master (7.645–6: "post proelia natis / si dominum, Fortuna, dabas, et bella dedisses") And when agency is reversed, teleology must follow: the reverse trajectory of this epic is from freedom to slavery, and from the existence of Rome to its undoing. Unlike the relentless forward movement of the *Aeneid*, the *Bellum civile* presents us with a deformed and fragmented narrative (Quint 1993: 131–209). No heroism indeed, here, at least not ethically unperverted heroism: Caesar's whirlwind agency, or the *aristeia* of Scaeva, are forms of *virtus* that must be counted as *nefas*. And Lucan's prosaic vocabulary works still further to undo the stylistic register of epic. His use of such words as *mors*, *aqua*, *caelum* jolts us back into the tawdry world of non-heroic action, while his unmusical and monotonous prosody, with its dreary spondees, works in strange contrast to the frantic interventions of the narrator into his own story. His extensive use of enjambment only adds to the non-poetic effect. (On the sameness of both sides in civil war, see Jal 1963: 322–6, 415–16. On the ethics of civil war, Roller 1996.)

The Body in Pieces

The *Bellum civile*'s bodies are notoriously prone to fragmentation, like the poem's epic narrative itself and like the formal structures and rhetorical figures it disdains to leave unwracked. Men shed limbs and organs and scarcely notice, like the anonymous twin in the naval battle at Massilia who in leaning over to grip an enemy ship loses first one hand, then the other, before tossing his torso itself on to the boat (3.609 ff.). The destruction of the body is the fleshy enactment of the raging attack on normative boundaries that civil war itself enacts. Precedent was offered by the struggle between Marius and Sulla, brought to life in an old man's laments in Book 2: there had been no one to lament Baebius, ripped apart and lying in his own guts, or Antonius, whose head was carried by its white hair; the mutilated trunks of the Crassi, or Marius Gratidianus, whose arms were pulled off his body, his tongue severed, his ears and nose cut off, and last off all, his unbelieving eyeballs plucked from their sockets.

How to read this assault on the human form? Lucan himself gives us the answer, if one well supplemented by recent scholarship on his treatment of narrative form, the influence of Stoicism, and the influence of the arena. For this mutilation is repeated in Sulla's surgery on Rome as he seizes power once again: "While he is cutting back the limbs that are now too rotten to survive, his medicine transgresses the bounds, and his hand pursued too far where the disease led it" ("dumque nimis iam putria membra recidit / excessit medicina modum, nimiumqe secuta est, / qua morbi duxere, manus," *BC* 2.141–3). The human body and the body of the state suffer the same fate, and the violated boundaries of the physical form are echoed over and over in the transgressed political boundaries of the state and its institutions: Caesar's impious crossing of the Rubicon, an army in the forum, the plebs mixing with the *potentes*; the lurking possibility of an Egyptian woman as a leader of Rome, the former Senate now meeting in Epirus; a leader who revels in, rather than laments, the death of Roman citizens; and of course, in one of the poem's most famous passages, the traditional *aristeia* transformed into an act of evil.

Quint too suggests that "the narrative disunity of the *Pharsalia* corresponds to a body in pieces, mutilated until it is beyond recognition" (1993b: 141) – a reaction to the stress on unity in ancient literary criticism from Aristotle to Cicero. Moreover, "the epic narrative, which classical literary theory describes with the metaphor of the whole, well-knit body, is deliberately fragmented by Lucan to depict a world out of joint" (p. 147). Glenn Most, in pointing out that Lucan has a greater percentage of amputation wounds than his epic predecessors and than Statius and Silius both, suggests that "one way to interpret the Neronian obsession with the dismemberment of the human body, then, is to see in it the symptom of an anguished reflection upon the nature of human identity and upon the uneasy border between men and animals" (1992: 405; animals were regularly torn apart in the amphitheater).

Lucan here may be reflecting Roman Stoic attitudes towards the human body, which is discussed in Seneca and Epictetus in terms of its expendability and relative non-importance where the sage's happiness is concerned. Among these writers, to disdain bodily pain as an indifferent becomes now the highest trophy of *virtus*, or, as Lucan's uncle Seneca put it, "the wise man is vulnerable to no injury: therefore it does not matter how many spears are hurled at him, since he is penetrable (*penetrabilis*) by none" (Sen. *Const. Sap.* 3.5). Read against this background, the lack of interest in suffering or pain (or its elision in favor of the merely grotesque) might be taken itself as a form of grotesque commentary on the dehumanizing Stoic emphasis on mind over matter, and Lucan's Scaeva now becomes a twisted metaphor for the Stoic sage (even as the narrator condemns him for a *virtus* used only in the service of evil). Pierced by so many weapons that nothing can protect his innards except the spears that have made of him a human hedgehog, Scaeva is now inured to further harm; his ultra-penetrability has become ultra-impenetrability. In metaphorical terms, his willingness to completely relinquish his body to abuse has made him immune to that abuse, just like the good Stoic sage.

The Narrator's Voice

The narrator's intrusion into his own story to comment on the unfolding action or to apostrophize a character is not a frequent feature of traditional epic; used sparingly, as in Virgil's famous apostrophe of Nisus and Euryalus in *Aen.* 9 (*fortunati ambo*) it can draw the reader still further into sympathy with the fate of the protagonists, or alternatively set up an interplay of "further voices" (the term is R. O. A. M. Lyne's) to illustrate the conflicting loyalties of the author himself. In the *Bellum civile*, however, narratorial apostrophe occurs with such regularity as to merit the designation of "master-trope" (Martindale 1993). As Mayer notes,

> Nothing is so typical of Lucan's epic technique, nothing sets him so far apart from all other poets in this genre, as his tendency to abandon narrative for an editorial reflection upon events. So he appeals to characters in the poem, or in his own person denounces peoples and places, in a manner both jarring and strident. (Lucanus 1981: 148)

The epic devotes so much attention to the narrator's reaction to the events he unfolds that he astonishingly claims in Book 9 to be Caesar's match in also producing an account of the civil war:

If it is right for Latin Muses to promise anything, future generations shall read (of) me and you both, as long as the honors of the Homeric poet will last: our *Pharsalia* will live, and we will be condemned to obscurity in no period ("siquid Latiis fas est promittere Musis, / quantum Zmyrnaei durabunt uatis honores, / uenturi me teque legent; Pharsalia nostra / uiuet, et a nullo tenebris damnabimur aeuo," 9.983–6).

The regularity and the vehemence of the narrator's apostrophes are further complicated by the apparent shift in their political allegiances. At first he condemns any attempt to justify either Caesar or Pompey ("quis iustius induit arma scire nefas," 1.126–7), and indeed, Caesar emerges as the less culpable: he cannot endure a superior, but Pompey not even an equal (1.125–6). The Stoic spokesperson Cato makes it clear that he is only choosing the latter over the former to make Pompey's victory a benefit for the Republic, not for Pompey himself ("nec, si fortuna fauebit, / hunc quoque totius sibi ius promittere mundi / non bene conpertum est: ideo me milite uincat / ne sibi se uicisse putet," 2.320–2). And yet Pompey's status seems to improve as the narratives winds on, so that, say, his botched follow-up to the victory at Brundisium is put down to piety by the narrator. Despite the narrator's prediction in Book 7 – that we readers *will* favor Pompey in this war (7.207–13) – Cato still considers the dead general a potential *rex* and *dominus* in his funeral "elegy," and calls his death a "gift" to his troops. Indeed, the image of him fleeing the battlefield in Book 7, or skulking in the underbrush in Book 8, make it hard for us to obey the narrator's command in Book 9 to side with him, breath bated.

Attenuated from the beginning in comparison to the dynamic energy of the Caesarian lightning-bolt, described as just a shadow of a great name, Pompey does not quite manage to be rescued by readings of him as a *proficiens* struggling despite himself to give up his attachment to his reputation and to glory, and finally (almost) settling into his catasterism at the beginning of Book 9 (Marti 1945). Masters (1994) would take Pompey's mediocrity (and Lucan's affectionate excesses) as evidence that the whole epic is an exercise in parody; Bartsch (1997) notes that while Cato calls it *furor* to participate in civil war, and *furor* not to participate (2.292, 295), he chooses to participate anyhow. Given that a passionate and engaged response is sought from us, too, by the narrator – especially in contrast to the general apathy of the gods, who, when they are mentioned, are content to watch and not intervene – she suggests that our position is meant to parallel that of Cato, and our best option, however flawed it might be, is to believe in an impossible future. The issue of the reader's (or spectator's) political engagement or detachment from the events unfolding in the poem also forms the core of Leigh's 1997 study on spectacle and audience in the epic.

In earlier work, both Masters (1992) and Henderson (1987) have offered the alternative possibility that we should read the narrator as "schizophrenic," torn between the aggressive forward-moving energy of a Caesar and the reluctance and hesitation of a Pompey, with a corresponding reflection in Lucan's narrative style:

Lucan's *Bellum Civile* is a deliberate counterpoise to Caesar's commentary of the same name; that, in short, just as Lucan opposes and confronts Virgil in the domain of literary epic, so does he oppose and confront Caesar in the domain of history. (Masters 1992: 17–18)

For Lucan too has shown himself to be practiced in violating traditions, crossing boundaries, and twisting language to his ends. In other words, "the new poet standing at the end of a tradition must be a Caesar" (p. 10).

Lucan's Virgil

However ambivalent we may find Virgil's depiction of the Julio-Claudian teleology that provided his poem with its forward thrust and that paralleled, in its coming to power, the triumph of Aeneas a millennium before, it is unquestionable that Lucan fastens on the most relentlessly ideological aspects of the poem only to set them on their head. As Hardie has well pointed out, *this* poem abjures the idea of the "one man" whose concern for his countrymen and whose sense of *pietas* will lead him to found (eventually) Rome: the *Bellum civile* is a poem in which, as Hardie notes, "the Republic is destroyed by the struggle between Caesar and Pompey to become that one man" (1993: 7). In Lucan's frequent gladiatorial imagery, the two men are *pares*, their ambitions depraved, and the success of one of them is the state's (and the poet's) undoing. Lucan's world contains no acts of commendable bravery on the battlefield, nor does his Underworld give us hope: just the depiction of an equally corrupt set of dead names, described by a rotting no-name of a soldier who is given voice in turn by no divine seer but a female witch who likes to masticate on faces. Indeed, world and Underworld seem reversed: while Pompey is an *umbra* and walks the earth, Lucan's Underworld stands in sharp contrast to the parade of not-yet-living *umbrae* that Anchises points out to his son in Book 6 of the *Aeneid*. The glorious predictions of Anchises about the future of Rome find no parallel in the glum pronouncements of the Pythia to Appius Claudius and of Erictho's corpse to Sextus Pompey.

And there are no gods – or rather, no portrayal of gods in action. The poet's Olympus is uninhabited by recognizable gods, and although Lucan apostrophizes the *rector Olympi* at *BC* 2.4, he goes on to doubt both his existence and his agency in the lines that follow. The poem, in fact, is notably devoid of divine action. Even the origin of the story's events is not the consequence of a divine anger, but the madness of the Romans themselves, a race who plunge their victorious sword into themselves rather than the Rutulian enemy; if Juno's rage, or Allecto's, is echoed anywhere, it is in the filthy Erictho, who may stand above them. The absence of divine intervention and divine will is all the more stark in comparison to Virgil's *Aeneid*, with its myth of Augustan descent from Venus, and its tussle of wills between the supporters and opponents of our Trojan hero. *Fatum* and *fortuna*, virtual synonyms here, take their place. And here, obviously, one more reason to read Lucan: *because* he does not conform to the standards of versification, narrative, decorum, and ideology associated with his great predecessor Virgil. To fail along these lines was, for him, a failure that carried its own biting commentary on the imperial rhetoric of his own day. (On Lucan and Virgil see further Thompson and Bruère 1968; Narducci 1979; Hardie 1993; Martindale 1993.)

Stoicism in the Epic

Lucan's epic is just Stoic enough to drive home to us the inversion of any Stoic universe in this poem. This was not always the most common reading of his relationship to Stoic orthodoxy: Marti, who saw Pompey as a Stoic *proficiens*, also saw the epic in its entirety as expressing the theme of "the tribulations of humanity in its struggle toward the Stoic ideal of wisdom and harmony with the divine principle" (1945: 355). If Pompey is Man, and Caesar all that is evil in the human soul, Cato is the perfect sage; he follows the divine law of the universe, hosts god inside his breast, and cultivates austerity. Yet such an account leaves unresolved the startlingly unstoic nature of Lucan's outlook. Like the Stoics, he too may privilege fate and *fortuna* as the historical movers of worldly events; he may refer to the final destruction of the universe in his description of a world gone awry; and his cosmology may be thoroughly orthodox; but the failure of a benevolent providence provides the pessimistic spine of the story and cannot be reconciled with Stoicism's more hopeful view (Feeney 1991: 269–301). One could see the clash of Stoic and non-Stoic elements as itself a reflection of the poem's incessant dualities: an uncertainty between them that Feeney (p. 280) dubs "a confrontation between the Stoic dispensation and a non-teleological randomness."

Even Lucan's Cato does not fit well into any kind of normative framework for a Stoic sage. His horror at feeling no fear during the collapse of his world reads oddly against Horace's "iustus et tenax propositi vir" of *Carm.* 3.3, who lets the ruins of the shattered world strike him without fear. Equally oddly, when he explains his participation in the war to Brutus at *BC* 2.287 by telling him that "where the fates drag virtue, it will follow unwilling" ("quo fata trahunt, virtus secura sequetur"), we should remember that the distinction between following and being dragged is often the pivot by which a Stoic worldview can be distinguished from others. Seneca writes in *Ep.* 107.11 that "The fates lead the willing and drag the unwilling," and by this criterion Cato is both *nolens* and *volens* at the same time: he is being dragged and follows simultaneously (Bartsch 1997: 120). In a world where the gods are guilty of making even Cato guilty, Stoicism cannot make sense, and Cato's self-contradictory stances sharply underline this. (On Stoic elements in the poem, see Schotes 1969; Due 1970; Gagliardi 1970; Lapidge 1989; Loupiac 1998. On Lucan's use of *fatum* and *fortuna*, see Dick 1967; Le Bonniec 1970; Ahl 1974; Liebeschutz 1979b; Feeney 1991.)

Political Engagement

Biographical criticism is out of fashion these days, but in the case of a poet who joined a conspiracy to end the life of the representative of the political system he most railed against, it seems almost unjust to ignore the facts of his life: this would be to criticize the poet for the ideological excesses of his writing yet ignore the fact that he risked his life in the Pisonian conspiracy against Nero. It could fairly be argued that his death makes it that much less likely that Lucan was engaging in nothing more than (as various accounts have claimed) a rhetorical exercise, an elaborate joke, or a criticism of Julius Caesar with no bearing upon his descendant in power. The main reason to forswear from any use of the lives in interpretation would be Tacitus' comment that the conspirators intended to set up another emperor in Nero's place rather than restore the Republican constitution, or the suggestion in Suetonius' *Vita* that what was driving Lucan was poetic pique. Some ancient gossip, too, might give us pause: Ahl (1976: 343–4) reminds us of Tacitus' report of a rumor that Lucan had incriminated his mother Acilia to save his own life: "Whether the rumour is true or not is, at this stage, irrelevant. That Tacitus thought it was true meant that he could not take Lucan's political ideals seriously."

Although one would think Lucan's hostility to the Julio-Claudian dynasty emerges in sharp relief from the fabric of this poem, there have been critics to deny even this hostility. Many of these point to the flattery of Nero at the beginning of the first book (1.33–66) as an example of Lucan's fondness, or at least neutrality, towards his own emperor and erstwhile friend, and the positive portrayal of Domitius Ahenobarbus at Corfinium in Book 2 (and Domitius' comportment in Book 7) is similarly taken as a mark of approval of Nero's ancestry. The issue of the Stoic belief in the possibility of a just kingship may also be brought to bear here (for such arguments, see, e.g., Brisset 1964). But it is difficult to reconcile such arguments with passages in the narrator's own voice such as 7.432 ff., in which Liberty has fled, never to return, while "our lot is the worst of all the peoples who bear tyranny, we whom it shames to be slaves" ("ex populis qui regna ferunt sors ultima nostra est / quos servire pudet," 7.444–5). That Lucan calls himself and his contemporaries slaves *in the present* seems to undermine any possibility of reading Nero's kingship as just.

Let us return to the preface for the final lines of this essay. As early as the scholiasts on Lucan, doubt about its intentions was raised not so much by the fulsome nature of the narrator's praise but by the odd terminology in which it is expressed: the *Adnotationes super Lucanum* and the *Commenta Bernensia* both take lines 55 and 57 to refer to Nero's supposed obesity and bad eyesight. Some modern readers have sought confirmation of these facts in Nero's life, but it is now the *communis opinio* that this physiognomical interpretation constitutes a unlikely misreading of traditional astronomical terminology. A more interesting question is why these commentators felt they had to subvert the praise in the first place. (Even Virgil is fulsome in praise of Augustus in Book 2 of the *Georgics*, and in much the same language.) Perhaps in the end the best way of reading the beginning is to apply to it the poet's reminders that we must lie to power: like the Roman matrons, who lament at *BC* 2.37–42 that the victory of one man will bring with it (simulated) rejoicing, the narrator too condemns his own preface when he reminds us of "all the words with which, for so long now, we have been lying to our masters" ("omnes voces, per quas iam tempore tanto / mentimur dominis," *BC* 5.385–6). (Further on the preface: see the extensive bibliography at Bartsch 1997: 173–4. On the question of whether Lucan's hostility to Nero only begins after Book 3, see Ahl 1976: 333–53.)

FURTHER READING

Two important studies of Lucan that helped to revive critical interest in the poem are Morford's *The Poet Lucan* (1967) and Ahl's introductory *Lucan* (1976); Morford is particularly sensitive to the rhetorical sensibility of the poem, while Ahl offers a comprehensive discussion of the entire work and its major characters. Readers interested in the notion that the *Civil War* is a Stoic work should start with Marti's early article, "The meaning of the *Pharsalia*" (1945). Other important articles from this era of scholarship include Bramble's excellent discussion in *The Cambridge History of Classical Literature* (1982) and Martindale's perceptive 1976 essay on Lucanian paradox; Martindale reads this figure as itself a trope for civil war. The latter surely paved the way for Johnson's *Momentary Monsters* (1987), the first book to find critical value in the very excesses which other readers saw as flaws. Two books from the 1990s explore the idea of epic at war with itself: Masters's 1992 *Poetry and Civil War in Lucan's Bellum civile* and Bartsch's 1997 *Ideology in Cold Blood: A Reading of Lucan's Civil War*, while Leigh's *Lucan: Spectacle and Engagement* (1997) discusses the poem in terms of spectatorship, arguing that its amphitheatrical elements oblige readers to find themselves complicit in or indifferent to the events of the war.

Editions and translations into modern English

Lucanus, Marcus Annaeus, *Bellum civile*, ed. A. E. Housman (1970).
Lucanus, Marcus Annaeus, *Pharsalia*, ed. C. E. Haskins (1971).
Lucanus, Marcus Annaeus, *De bello civili libri X*, ed. D. R. Shackleton Bailey (1988).
Susan H. Braund, *Lucan: Civil War* (1992).
J. D. Duff, *Lucan: The Civil War*, Loeb Classical Library (1928).
Jane W. Joyce, *Lucan: Pharsalia* (1993).
P. F. Widdows, *Lucan: Civil War* (1988).

Internet resources

Helpful bibliographies: http://www.let.kun.nl/V.Hunink/documents/lucanbciii bibliography.htm
http://www.unibas.ch/klaphil/fs/lucan_bibl1.html
http://uts.cc.utexas.edu/cgi-bin/cgiwrap/silver/frame.cgi?lucan:.metrics
 The full Latin text: http://www.thelatinlibrary.com/lucan.html
 A full English translation (by Ridley): http://sunsite.berkeley.edu/OMACL/Pharsalia/

CHAPTER THIRTY-SIX

Valerius Flaccus

Andrew Zissos

The Poet

Valerius Flaccus is one of the most elusive literary figures of the Roman imperial period. Virtually nothing certain is known about him, beyond the fact that he wrote his epic *Argonautica* – no other works are attested – in the Flavian era (69–96 CE). For his life and career, there is no external evidence beyond a brief obituary notice by the rhetorician Quintilian: "We have lost a good deal recently in [the death of] Valerius Flaccus" (*Inst.* 10.1.90). This has enabled scholars to fix the death of Valerius at some point before 96 CE (the latest possible date for publication of Quintilian). Regarding his date of birth there is no indication whatsoever. Because of the paucity of external evidence, scholars have sought autobiographical clues from the *Argonautica* itself. Of such internal clues, most compelling are a reference in the proem to the Sibyl (the "Cymaean prophetess") and the mention of a sacred tripod residing in the poet's own house (1.5–7). These lines have led to a widespread assumption that Valerius was a member of the college of priests in charge of the Sibylline books, the *quindecimviri sacris faciundis*. This hypothesis gains some marginal support from the allusion to the Bath of Cybele at *Arg.* 8.239–41, a rite that was supervised by the *quindecimviri*. If Valerius was a *quindecimvir*, then he was a Roman citizen of considerable means and social standing, almost certainly of the senatorial order. A number of scholars have rightly sounded a note of caution, however, pointing out the dangers of taking these lines as literal autobiography. It is conceivable that the narrating persona is presented as a member of a prestigious and notably "bookish" Roman priesthood for reasons of literary "authority" – much like the use of the *vates* (prophet) figure in earlier Augustan poetry (Barchiesi 2001b).

Valerius' epic has been transmitted to our time unfinished. It breaks off abruptly 467 lines into the eighth book, as the Argonauts, having acquired the golden fleece, attempt to evade their Colchian pursuers. It is possible that the *Argonautica* was completed and subsequently lost its ending through the vagaries of textual transmission; more likely, though, is that Valerius died before finishing it. Whatever the case, an issue of some importance is the intended length of the epic. Until well into the twentieth century most critics believed that it would have run to ten or twelve books, the latter matching the book total of Virgil's *Aeneid*, which exerted a strong influence on Valerius. The critical tide has turned, however, since the important analysis advanced by Schetter (1959), which provides persuasive structural arguments (on which more below) in favor of a total of eight books. Since Book 8 breaks off at line 467 and none of the others exceeds 850-odd lines, it follows that less than 400 verses would have been added to complete the opus. How much more of the myth would have been covered in those additional lines is an open question, though anything beyond the return journey seems unlikely.

Thematics

I sing of seas first traversed by mighty sons of gods, and of the fate-speaking ship that, having dared to seek the shores of Scythian Phasis and to burst a course through the Clashing Rocks, finally came to rest on fiery Olympus. (*Arg.* 1.1–4)

Although Valerius' subject is myth rather than history, he ascribes immense historical importance to the Argonauts' expedition. In Roman poetry the "Argo" was generally the first ship, and hence a potent symbol of the rise of technology and the human conquest of nature. Ancient constructions of cultural history were virtually unanimous in regarding the invention of navigation as a pivotal moment (for better or worse) in early human development. Apollonius Rhodius had rejected this aspect of the myth: for him the voyage of the "Argo" was merely an extraordinary application of existing technology rather than an essential innovation. As Valerius' opening verse makes clear, his poem follows the dominant Roman tradition in making the Argonauts the world's first sailors. Their voyage inaugurates the first properly international phase of human affairs by enabling ready interchange between far-flung terrestrial regions. The birth of *commercium* and the end of the Saturnian Golden Age are alluded to (1.246–7, 1.500), but without unambiguously signaling a moral decline. The "Argo" will be rewarded with catasterism (i.e. a placement in the heavens as a new constellation) (1.4), and some members of its crew will achieve apotheosis (1.561–7). Sailing will result in intercourse between nations and the rise of great empires, as the Jovian prophecy at 1.531–60 makes clear. That Jupiter is presiding over a global transformation is given powerful symbolic expression through the dramatic account of the liberation of Prometheus in Books 4 and 5 (discussed below). The resolution of the Titan's suffering at the supreme god's behest signals final Olympian acceptance of Prometheus' technological benefaction to humankind, of which sailing is the latest and most consequential offshoot.

For Valerius, then, the Argonautic expedition is an event of transcendent geopolitical importance, inaugurating a new world order based on international competition. It results in a "Darwinian" struggle between nations that may (or may not) culminate in Rome. The idea of a succession of world empires was well known to ancient historiography, probably coming to the Greeks from Asiatic sources. To the original sequence of Assyrian, Median, and Persian monarchies, the Greek and Roman empires were added in due course. Valerius' historical plan deviates from these schemes only in consolidating the initial Asiatic series of monarchies into a single unit, so as to make the Trojan War, an event which his epic frequently anticipates, the first significant transfer of power from one nation to the next. Moreover, Valerius follows the lead of a small number of earlier writers, including the Greek historian Herodotus, who had treated the Argonautic expedition as a direct cause of the Trojan War. These adaptations result in the superimposition of a schema of universal history upon the inherited mythopoetic tradition.

As with the *Aeneid*, a central concern of the *Argonautica* is to account for the combination of providential and aleatory forces that govern human affairs. The Virgilian "world system" that Valerius (partially) resurrects involves an overarching principle of theodicy. This is based on the teleological notion of Jovian *fata* which dictate – at least in broad outline – the unfolding of a providentially guaranteed human destiny, preordaining such crucial historical events as the fall of Troy and the rise of Rome. At the same time, the parallelism between divine will and Roman destiny that pervades the *Aeneid* – and Augustan culture generally – is not unambiguously asserted in the *Argonautica* (Schönberger 1965: 125).

As the foregoing might suggest, the gods play a far more prominent role in the Flavian *Argonautica* than in its Hellenistic predecessor. One of Valerius' habitual procedures for reworking an episode from Apollonius is to motivate it on the divine level, in other words, to provide an explicit supernatural causation that is wanting in the earlier epic (Hershkowitz 1998b: 220–1). Some notable examples of this transformative strategy include the episodes of Hylas' abduction (engineered by Juno), the Lemnian massacre (incited by Venus), and the demise of Cyzicus (brought about by Cybele). In short, there is a pervasive management of important narrative events on the divine level: the uncertainties and causal obscurities of Apollonius' epic are largely resolved into explicit narrative articulations of divine will (Feeney 1991: 317). As in Virgilian epic, the heroes themselves often seem constrained to carry through a course of action whose outcome is essentially predetermined (Burck 1979). This treatment is all the more notable in that Valerius was writing in the wake of Lucan's radical experimentation with exclusion of the divine machinery in the *Bellum civile*. Where Lucan presented a cosmos in which the gods were either non-existent, uninterested, or merely powerless and irrelevant, Valerius re-entrenches the Olympian divinities of the *Aeneid* as major characters in their own right as well as decisive determinants of events on the human level. A slight divergence is the assignment of prominent roles to lesser deities, for example, that of Boreas in witnessing the sailing of the "Argo" and inciting a violent storm in response (*Arg.* 1.574–607).

Working against an overarching principle of theodicy are the personal – often petty and vindictive – agendas of the gods under Jupiter. This divine behavior, an essentially Homeric feature, imparts a sense of chaos and contingency on the level of individual events, undermining the smooth and untroubled master-narrative of Jovian *fata*. Here a strong note of pessimism is sounded, for individual deities, often demonstrating flaws that are all too human, have considerable scope to degrade or pervert the precise manner in which individual historical strands are enacted without negating the final outcome decreed by Jupiter. The result of this contradiction in divine agency is frequently – perhaps even programmatically – tragic, and reflects an "irreducible moral ambiguity" in Valerius' epic universe (Barich 1982: 133). This disquieting aspect becomes increasingly prominent as the narrative progresses, and seems to dominate the action of the second half of the poem (see the section "Structure," below.)

On the human level, Valerius moves away from the composite focus of Apollonius' epic, in which the Argonauts as a group serve as something like a "collective hero" in the context of a noticeably democratic undertaking. While collective depictions of the Argonauts are not lacking in Valerius' epic, the focus is for the most part on a small number of prominent individuals: Jason and Hercules in the first half of the poem, and Jason and Medea in the second. In attributing motivations to Jason and other Argonauts, Valerius effects a re-evaluation of epic heroism, emphasizing personal glory as a central heroic preoccupation. Throughout the poem, *gloria* is the counterpart to and compensation for the labors and perils faced by the epic hero (Ripoll 1998: 207). This ideological nexus – an essentially Homeric construct, supplemented with notions of apotheosis – is largely absent from the Greek *Argonautica*, where Jason expresses only a fatalistic acceptance of the troubles the gods have in store for him (Ap. Rhod. *Arg.* 1.298–300). It is also a fundamental departure from the *Aeneid*: one of Virgil's important ideological innovations was to relegate the pursuit of personal glory to a position of secondary importance, enshrining *pietas* rather than *gloria* as the proper heroic motivation.

Style, Sources, Models

The myth of the Argonauts was among the most popular subjects in ancient literature and the visual arts from the archaic period onwards. Writing in the Flavian era, Valerius stands late in a long and rich tradition. His reworking of the myth is an ambitious undertaking that exploits a wide spectrum of Argonautic and non-Argonautic sources – not only epic, but tragedy and lyric; not only poetry, but prose (Hershkowitz 1998b: 38–66 provides a helpful overview). This complex literary genealogy notwithstanding, it is widely recognized that Valerius' principal artistic debts are to Apollonius and Virgil, that he grafts on to the narrative body of the former the poetic language and thematic concerns of the latter. It will be useful to elaborate upon, as well as explore the limits of, this popular critical formulation.

Apollonius Rhodius

In shaping the overall plot of his epic, Valerius conforms closely to Apollonius' *Argonautica* (see Chapter 25, by Nelis). The basic story line includes much of the familiar Apollonian material, and generally adheres to the order of events in the Hellenistic epic. From Apollonius Valerius takes the gathering of heroes, the Hylas subplot (by which Hercules is lost to the expedition), the stopover on Lemnos (complete with a flashback to the massacre of Lemnian males), the hospitality and inadvertent death of Cyzicus, Pollux's boxing match with Amycus, Phineus and the Harpies, the perilous passage through the Clashing Rocks, Jason's trials in Colchis (yoking bronze bulls, slaying earth-born men), Juno's plot to have Medea fall in love with Jason (achieved with the help of Venus), Medea's magical assistance of Jason both in the trials and the acquisition of the fleece, her desperate flight to Greece with the Argonauts, the pursuit of a Colchian fleet led by her brother Absyrtus, and the hasty marriage of Jason and Medea en route. At the same time, Valerius adds a number of new episodes. In Book 1, for example, nothing after the catalog (350–483) is derived from Apollonius. The storm at sea (1.574–658) is perhaps a somewhat predictable post-Virgilian supplement to the Apollonian narrative, but the necromancy (730–51, indebted to Lucan's Erichtho episode) and the suicide of Jason's parents (771–850, discussed below) represent more significant departures from the Hellenistic poem, in which neither parent comes to any harm. In later books the rescue of Hesione from a sea-monster (2.431–539, perhaps inspired by Diod. Sic. 4.42), the deliverance of Prometheus by Hercules (4.58–81, 5.154–76), and above all the Colchian civil war (6.1–760) do not occur in Apollonius. Conversely, a number of Apollonian episodes are omitted, including the battle with the Giants (Ap. Rhod. *Arg.* 1.942–1011), the attack of the Stymphalian birds (2.1030–92) and the encounter with the sons of Phrixus (2.1093–1230). It also seems likely that Valerius had in mind to omit much of Apollonius' account of the return voyage.

While his debt to Apollonius is clearly substantial, Valerius operates principally on a schematic level: his treatment of the episodes themselves is invariably innovative. The Greek *Argonautica* is often brilliant in its treatment of individual scenes, but is generally considered to suffer from "episodicity": it does not provide particularly strong thematic or structural links between the different parts of the narrative. The Hellenistic poem unfolds according to a guiding aesthetic that privileges miniaturization, fragmentation, digression, and episodic juxtaposition. Valerius, by contrast, consistently strives to create strong causal, thematic, and symbolic connections between different episodes (Venini 1971: 606).

The reshaping of Apollonius' narrative to create intricately interrelated episodes is perhaps most compellingly seen in Valerius' handling of Prometheus, the Titan enduring repetitive torture by Jupiter for his technological assistance to humankind. The Hellenistic

Argonautica includes an account of the Argonauts passing by the site of the Titan's captivity (Ap. Rhod. *Arg.* 2.1246–50) and witnessing a round of his grim torture by Jupiter's liver-pecking bird, but this is a stand-alone episode that has no vital connection to the enclosing narrative. Apollonius' account of Prometheus is cyclical in its implications, with no hint of remission: the suffering Titan is merely a part of the scenery viewed by the Argonauts en route to Colchis. In the Roman epic, by contrast, Prometheus is freed from his bondage and torture, and the scene of deliverance is the climactic event of the outward voyage. The episode serves as the culmination of a elaborate narrative sequence that starts in the first book of the poem with Juno's diatribe against her hated stepson Hercules (1.113–19). After being separated from his comrades through that goddess's machinations, Hercules is ordered by Jupiter to liberate Prometheus (4.58–81). Somewhat later in the narrative, the mighty ex-Argonaut arrives, simultaneously with but separately from the "Argo" itself, at the Caucasus, site of the Titan's captivity, and sets about ripping away his adamantine fetters (5.154–76).

Valerius' inclusion of Prometheus' deliverance within the framework of the Argonautic legend is a bold innovation, unattested elsewhere in ancient literature. Although less than fifty lines are devoted to the liberation scene, it is of immense thematic importance. Prometheus was for the ancients both the source and symbol of human technology, and hence a figure of obvious significance in an epic on the inception of navigation. Moreover, his deliverance is the last and most important *aristeia* of Hercules, the greatest of the Argonauts. In structural terms, a crucial aspect of the Prometheus narrative is its division into two parts (4.58–81, 5.154–76). This is significant because the two sections enclose a series of episodes – the boxing match between Pollux and Amycus (4.99–343), the inset tale of Io (4.344–421), the encounter with the prophet Phineus (4.422–646), and the traversal of the Clashing Rocks (4.637–710) – all of which resonate with the Promethean frame, contributing to the issues of civilizing progress and theodicy that the Titan inevitably evokes. The result is an intricately crafted narrative sequence that illustrates Valerius' ability to adapt the mythological and literary tradition to produce complex thematic movements unexampled in Apollonius.

In transforming the Apollonian episode, Valerius establishes various points of contact with the sympathetic treatment of the Titan in Aeschylus' *Prometheus Bound*. In this respect, the most telling enclosure of the Promethean framing narrative is the tale of Io, an Argive princess who suffers the jealous wrath of Juno because of Jupiter's amorous attention. This is the only enclosed passage without an exemplar in Apollonius; it creates a suggestive structural correspondence with the *Prometheus Bound*, of which the extended Io episode (561–886) is the most important section. The mythologically arbitrary but thematically powerful connection of Io to the plight of Prometheus was almost certainly an Aeschylean invention. Valerius' Io narrative not only provides a structural mirroring of the *Prometheus Bound*, but also replays the Aeschylean investigation of theodicy in a nascent Jovian cosmos. Unlike the tragedy, however, stress is placed on the suffering heroine's final ascension to godhead from the outset (*Arg.* 4.346), and there is a marked improvement in the presentation of Jupiter, who emerges as a more sublime and equitable figure.

Another enclosed episode that reflects directly upon the "Promethean" frame is that of the blind prophet Phineus, whom the Argonauts deliver from the tormenting Harpies (4.422–636). Although largely based on the corresponding episode in Apollonius, it deviates from its model in one important respect by symbolically casting Phineus as a second Prometheus figure (Mehmel 1934: 30). Like Prometheus, Phineus has been punished by Jupiter for trying to improve mortal existence: for attempting to "shed light" on the future through prophecy. The attribution of the seer's actions to compassion for humankind (4.479–81) elaborates the motif of the suffering culture hero, signaling his status as a symbolic double of Prometheus. In addition, Valerius deftly exploits the similar plight of the two figures, both of whom Jupiter afflicts with winged tormentors: Prometheus' liver-devouring vulture is matched by the Harpies, who descend from the air to disrupt Phineus' meals by stealing and polluting his food. The assimilation of Phineus to Prometheus allows the poet indirectly to mitigate the notorious belligerence that traditionally marked the relationship between the Titan and Jupiter. Jovian compassion is matched by Phineus' contrition, thereby introducing a strong note of reconciliation into the Promethean equation. All of this, of course, is far removed from Apollonius' account, attesting to Valerius' impressive ability radically to transform the narrative material of his Hellenistic predecessor.

Virgil

If Apollonius is the primary source on the level of plot, Valerius makes Virgil his principal model on the linguistic, conceptual, and thematic levels. In general terms the Roman *Argonautica* eschews the "epic objectivity" often said to be characteristic of the Homeric poems, opting instead for a more Virgilian exploration of the subjective experiences of his characters – their feelings, emotions, and moral judgments. The Flavian epic manifests a heightened interest in private thoughts and the workings of the human psyche under stressful or perilous circumstances. It tends to focus as much on the psychological impact of narrative action as on the action itself (Mehmel 1934: 22), and its persistent striving for pathos goes somewhat beyond the *Aeneid*.

The language of the *Argonautica* is classicizing, elevated – and for the most part noticeably Virgilian. Valerius inherited from his Augustan predecessor an epic diction that was fully elaborated on the technical level, and to a large extent resolved into quasi-formulaic phrases that could be appropriated as the need arose (Nordera 1969: 1). It is with Flavian epic, and Valerius in particular, that the tendency of Latin epic to reproduce Virgilian language and modes of expression first emerges (Summers 1894: 24; Nordera 1969: 6–7). In addition, Valerius shuns rhetorical exuberance and an uninhibited "aesthetic of the gruesome", two notorious hallmarks of "Silver" Latin literature. But while these aspects attest to something like a Virgilian "generic ethos," this is by no means the whole story. As scholars have long recognized, the *Argonautica* exhibits a number of decidedly un-Virgilian features, such as pervasive irony, brevity of expression, referential obscurity, and a certain artificiality of conceit. It takes more than a glance, for example, to grasp that "Alcides has long since enclosed his brow in the gaping jaws of Cleone" ("Cleonaeo iam tempora clausus hiatu/Alcides," *Arg.* 1.34–5) means that Hercules has slain the Nemean lion (i.e. by virtue of the fact that he is wearing its hide). Such touches have led some critics to characterize Valerius as a "mannerist" or "baroque" poet reacting – like Lucan and Statius – to the classicism of Virgilian epic (Nordera 1969: 84–6; Burck 1971: 5–23). It follows from the above that Valerius' poetic style is considerably more difficult than Virgil's. Unlike the *Aeneid*, which privileges immediacy and clarity, the *Argonautica* often lapses into an aesthetically distanced and "anti-popular" style, full of deliberate obscurities and formal refinements that impose a daunting hermeneutic burden on the reader.

Valerius' debt to Virgil is nowhere more clearly seen than in the tendency to opt for large-scale episodic mirroring of the *Aeneid*. One of the earliest examples of such imitation is found in the storm scene at *Arg.* 1.574–658. While drawing inspiration from Diod. Sic. 4.43, and perhaps owing something to Hom. *Od.* 5.282–450, Valerius' sea storm is primarily modeled on Virg. *Aen.* 1.50–156, with which it maintains an overt and sustained parallelism. A more complex and suggestive practice is the large-scale mirroring of a model passage in a substantially different narrative domain. This intertextual stratagem first occurs in the account of the Argonauts' departure in Book 1, which systematically "replays" Virgil's treatment of Aeneas' leave-taking of Dido in the second half of *Aeneid* 4. Jason's words at *Arg.* 1.198, *non sponte feror*, have long been recognized as an echo of Aeneas' *Italiam non sponte sequor* (*Aen.* 4.361). The statement invokes the context of the model passage and initiates a sustained intertextual engagement with the narrative in *Aeneid* 4. The imitation continues with a dream visitation (1.302–8) in which the tutelary spirit of the *Argo* urges immediate departure, clearly modeled on *Aen.* 4.553–83. Shortly afterwards, Jason's parents decide, like Dido, to commit suicide (albeit for very different reasons). They perform a necromancy and then, just prior to taking his own life, Aeson utters a curse against Pelias (*Arg.* 1.788–815), corresponding structurally to Dido's prophetic curse against Aeneas at *Aen.* 4.607–29. These parallels are strengthened by careful reworking of the language and formulations of the Virgilian model (*Arg.* 1.795–810 contains numerous reminiscences of *Aen.* 4.607–17). Finally, it is worth noting that both textual sequences conclude with a suicide at the end of a book, and that the opening passage of the subsequent book describes the hero sailing off in blissful ignorance.

The precise effects of such large-scale engagements vary from case to case, but they are rarely mere formal recapitulations devoid of thematic or figural force. In the present instance, the echo of Virgil's Dido episode has broader significance as the early connotation of a tragic destiny that will become increasingly prominent in the second half of the epic. In Valerius' final books, the union of Jason and Medea will be narrated through dense allusion to Virgilian models of sexual and marital negativity, Aeneas and Dido in particular (Hardie 1993: 91). On the intertextual level, Jason thus follows a trajectory that replays the tragedy of Dido not as an isolated misstep in an otherwise exemplary heroic career, but rather as an all-encompassing paradigm that adumbrates an irrevocably grim destiny.

As profound as Valerius' debt to Apollonius and Virgil undoubtedly is, it has sometimes been overemphasized in modern criticism, often at the expense of other aspects of Valerius' intertextual program. Additional influences, especially Homeric (Fuà 1988; Zissos 2002), but also of poets such as Pindar, Catullus, Ovid, Seneca, and Lucan, and historians such as Herodotus and Diodorus Siculus, are more significant than is generally recognized. Indeed, the *Argonautica* is insistently hypertextual in nature: dense, multi-level allusivity is a defining and constitutive feature of the poem. In contemplating almost any passage in the poem, the reader's awareness of Valerius' reception and reworking of a wide spectrum of earlier literature is a crucial determinant of the aesthetic effect. The *Argonautica* is also shot through with self-consciousness, demonstrating a particular predilection for referring to its own belated status that owes more to Ovidian epic technique than to either Apollonius or Virgil. Valerius repeatedly draws attention to his own status as a poetic "recycler," or to his mediating role as a selector of variants within the tradition (Malamud and McGuire 1993; Zissos 1999). Such metaliterary strategies depend upon a rich and diverse intertextual program.

Structure

Apollonius' four-book epic is essentially bipartite in structure, employing the formal device of a "proem in the middle" placed at the precise center of his narrative (Ap. Rhod. *Arg.* 3.1–4), and combined with the closural motif of the completion of a journey (i.e. the Argonauts' arrival in Colchis). The medial proem features an invocation to the Muse Erato, and signals a quasi-generic shift from the adventures of the outward voyage to Medea's love for Jason. This bipartite organization with its strongly marked physical "center" clearly influenced Valerius: like Apollonius, he provides a medial proem immediately following completion of the outward voyage. Moreover, Valerius' second proem follows its model in signaling a thematic redirection via the "introduction" of Medea, the crucial figure in the second half of both epics. But while evincing a clear formal indebtedness it makes an important departure on the programmatic level by announcing a switch to depravity and horror rather than erotics:

> Begin now, goddess, another song and tell of the wars of the Thessalian chief, which you have seen. My mind, my voice do not suffice. We have come to the madness and the abominable compact of the [king's] daughter, and the vessel frightened beneath the dreadful maiden. The accursed battles on the portent-bearing fields arise before me. (*Arg.* 5.217–21)

Before Valerius, of course, Apollonius' bipartite narrative structure had been creatively adapted by Virgil: in this as in other matters, the *Aeneid* stands as a crucial mediating term between the two Argonautic epics. Virgilian influence can be seen in Valerius' displacement of his second proem some 216 lines from the start of Book 5, which appears deliberately to "outdo" the more modest postponement of 36 lines in *Aeneid* 7. Valerius also follows Virgil in dividing his poem into "Odyssean" and "Iliadic" halves, though he goes beyond his model in the disjunctive effects of this type of narrative structure.

One of Valerius' more significant innovations within the epic *Argonautica* tradition is the inclusion of a lengthy battle narrative at Colchis, in which Jason and his companions provide decisive aid to the Colchian king Aeetes in his conflict with his brother Perses (6.1–760). As a result, the Flavian epic involves a perilous sea voyage followed by war and other trials on land, with the two thematic movements separated by a "proem in the middle" – a quintessentially Virgilian arrangement (Schetter 1959). Valerius, however, inverts the relative valences of the two halves of his poem. The *Aeneid* makes the second half its *maius opus* ("greater work" *Aen.* 7.45), maintaining a more epic register in the later books, which offer a series of martial narratives whose consequence is nothing less than the founding of Roman civilization. For the *Argonautica* the situation is rather different: with respect to the providential staging of a larger human destiny, the poem is clearly weighted towards the first half, which opens with the inauguration of navigation and closes with Hercules' liberation of Prometheus. Despite some notable Homeric touches, the martial activity of the second half unfolds in the context of a particularly degraded form of civil war that, unlike Aeneas' conflict with the Latins, is historically inconsequential, and serves as little more than a convenient expedient for inciting Medea's destructive sexual passion. As a mildly paradoxical result, the debased "Iliadic" violence contributes to the "hypertrophy of the epic apparatus" in the later books (Feeney 1991: 326).

Valerius' bifurcated approach to his narrative gives structural expression to a fundamental tension in the developed mythographic tradition, which had arisen centuries earlier when Attic dramatists grafted on to the earlier legendary heroic material a tragedy of guilt and retribution. According to the canonical version of Euripides, Jason and Medea meet with calamity years after the expedition while living as exiles in Corinth. At that time Jason forsakes Medea in favor of the Corinthian princess Creusa, and Medea consequently murders both Creusa and her own children by Jason. In Valerius' fifth book, shortly after the medial proem, an ecphrastic description of the prophetic scenes engraved upon the doors of the Colchian temple of the Sun offers a detailed prolepsis of this tragic aftermath:

> his former spouse he abandons: avenging Furies watch from the palace roof. His wife, sore distressed in her chamber and moved to anger by her rival, prepares a robe and the deadly gift of a jewelled crown, first bewailing all her sufferings. With this gift the unhappy rival is adorned before her country's altars; and already, in the grip of the flaming poison, wraps all the palace in fire. These marvels had the Fire-god wrought for the Colchians, though as yet they knew not what enterprise was that, or who it is that with winged serpents cleaves the air, dripping

with murder; they hate them nevertheless, and turn away their gaze. (*Arg.* 5.444–54; trans. Mozley 1934)

The sequence amounts to something like a résumé of Euripides' or Seneca's *Medea* (Davis 1990: 61), signaling an emergent poetics of guilt and retribution, of tragic *nefas*. This is borne out in the second half of the poem, which contains a great many further anticipations of the tragic fallout of the expedition. As Garson (1965: 108–9) observes, "the leitmotif of [Valerius' later narrative] is the final tragedy. [The poet] wants his readers to know that what is happening now is leading inevitably up to it ... only the Roman narrative is wholly colored by allusions to the final outcome."

The "proem in the middle" thus inaugurates a profound transformation of the narrative, a radical tragic contamination of Valerius' epic. The initial, teleologically focused account of heroic striving and technological triumph gives way to an essentially regressive narrative pattern of tragic dénouement constructed around the anguished figure of Medea. In the epic's second half, tragedy provides a narrative telos as well as a conceptual domain and an allusive background against which Valerius' thematic treatment emerges. The narrative shifts from a pattern of purposive and providentially guaranteed development to a more fitful and aleatory mode characterized by narrative delays, faltering repetition, and a heightened sense of moral indeterminacy. This is perhaps most evident in the account of the laborious attempts by Juno and Venus to bend Medea to their purpose through erotic engulfment. This extended sequence, which takes up much of Books 6 and 7, is marked by repeated narrative regressions, by disruptions of linear narrative flow. Notable here is the disproportionate effort expended by the goddesses, the fitful and convulsive straining of the divine machinery, in comparison with the model passage in Apollonius (Fucecchi 1996: 129). Throughout this protracted (and at times exasperating) account, what is being highlighted is Medea's anguished resistance to the dictates of Juno's master-plan. It is largely through the ethical and metaliterary posture of the ill-fated Colchian princess that Valerius gives expression to the complexities of his darkly tragic mythographic sensibility in the later books of the poem.

Historical Context

At first glance, Valerius' decision to take his theme from Greek myth rather than Roman history (note the *recusatio* or foreswearing of the latter at 1.12–14) seems to indicate an escape from contemporary realities. But even a cursory examination of Valerius' narrative suffices to convey the extent to which the poem is embedded in its cultural and historical moment. As numerous critics have pointed out, the mythical world in which Jason and his comrades move has been thoroughly "Romanized." Despite the obviously Greek background of the myth, Valerius' poem manifests a preoccupation with Roman culture and history (Summers 1894: 56–7; Pollini 1984: 51–61; Boyle 1991: 272–5). On a straightforward narrative level, the Flavian poet can be seen to alter details of his subject matter in order to provide links to the Roman world. In the first book, for example, Jupiter is made to prophesy a succession of world empires that will lead to Rome (1.531–60, discussed above). Other allusions to Roman history or culture in the poem include the conquest of Jerusalem (1.12–14); the *Fasti*, or lists of Roman magistrates (2.245); the god Janus (2.620); a Roman purification ceremony (3.417–58); the eruption of Vesuvius (4.507–9); Roman civil war (6.402–6); the Italian hero Picus (7.232–4); the festival of Bellona (7.635–6); and a Roman wedding custom (8.243–6). Equally notable are the numerous Roman geographical references, which are often substituted for Greek references in Apollonius.

The "politics" of the poem are a rather more complex matter. A flattering analogy between the Argonauts and the emperor Vespasian is asserted in the proem (1.7–21); such gestures were virtually compulsory in this period though, and this one is not sustained in the subsequent narrative. So much for overt political content; elsewhere the anxieties and preoccupations of the non-imperial Roman aristocracy seem to inflect Valerius' treatment of the myth. The view of history traditionally inscribed in Roman epic, that of a heroic aristocracy, is subjected to increasing ideological pressure in the Flavian period. One of the central conflicts within elite Roman culture at this time was the incompatibility between Roman aristocratic ambition and desire for public distinction on the one hand and the increasing restrictions imposed by the political configurations of the principate on the other. This contemporary tension surfaces almost immediately in Valerius' narrative, when Jason's heroism and popular esteem are presented as problematic for Pelias: "the renown of [Jason] weighed upon him, as did his valor, which is never pleasing to a tyrant" (1.30). This is a striking divergence from the traditional version of the myth, in which the quest for the golden fleece was Jason's first notable deed. The deviation creates a telling correspondence with contemporary Rome, where aristocratic exercise of authority or pursuit of military glory was likewise decidedly double-edged; indeed, it was a commonplace of the first century that too much renown would draw the hostile attention of the emperor. Thus, at its very outset, the Flavian *Argonautica* signals a reprocessing of the traditional mythic material in ways that resonate with the concerns of the Roman nobility.

A little later, the poem establishes an even stronger symbolic equivalence between its hero and the contemporary Roman aristocrat, as latent political tensions in Flavian Rome rise to the narrative surface. This occurs when Jason, ordered by Pelias to retrieve the golden fleece, carefully considers his options. Upon realizing that the tyrant is craftily engineering his destruction, Jason's first impulse is to raise a rebellion: "What is he to do? Should he call to his aid the fickle populace that hates the old tyrant, and the *patres* who for a long time now have pitied Aeson?" (1.71–3). The stratification of a fictive Thessalian society into distinct segments or power blocs – *populus, tyrannus, patres* – serves to transform the mythic picture by evoking contemporary political realities. Indeed, the use of the term *patres* ("senators") in this mythological context invests the scene with an unmistakably Roman flavor. More precisely, the existence of senators as a specific political body, and a potential source of support against a single monarch succinctly reproduces the political configuration of the early principate. Intriguingly, the thought of leading the *patres* in rebellion is a fleeting one, which fades from consciousness altogether before it can be seriously entertained. In this way, Valerius offers a disconcertingly accurate picture of an atrophied senatorial class, no longer in possession of a stable power-base and thus ultimately impotent in its anger and resentment against a despotic ruler. The brief scene thus provides a trenchant reflection of the enduring tensions between emperor and non-imperial elite in the late first century, along with the familiar pattern of mingled accommodation and resistance on the part of the latter.

The concluding episode of the first book, featuring the "political suicide" of Jason's parents, is another scene rich in contemporary resonance, evoking the suicides of the senatorial opposition under the early principate. In this passage, already mentioned above, Pelias orders the execution of Jason's father shortly after the "Argo" has set sail (1.700–29). Upon hearing the news, Aeson and his wife Alcimede decide to pre-empt the death sentence by ending their lives together before the arrival of the imperial executioners (1.730–73). Once again, the passage bears an unmistakable contemporary stamp. The poet has created a death scene all too familiar to the nobles of the early principate, a scene repeatedly recorded in the historian Tacitus' scathing chronicle of the period (e.g., Tac. *Ann.* 11.3, 15.61–4, 16.18–9, 16.33–5). The suicide of Aeson and Alcimede reproduces many of the details found in the historical accounts: the tyrant's death sentence, the choice of the wife to die with her husband, the arrival of troops or magistrates at the home of the condemned, and the striking disjunction between the private circumstances of the suicide and the public status of the executioners (McGuire 1997: 192–3).

FURTHER READING

Latin texts of the *Argonautica* have been published in Teubner editions by E. Courtney (1970) and W. W. Ehlers (1980). The most up-to-date text is the two-volume bilingual French edition by G. Liberman (1997, 2002). Anglophone readers of Valerius Flaccus have been at a disadvantage for centuries. The first full English translation of the poem was produced for the Loeb Classical Library by J. H. Mozley in 1934 (with the usual facing Latin text); it remains to the present day the only complete and reliable translation in English. The recent translation of D. Slavitt (1999) is both arbitrarily lacunose and, at times, grossly inaccurate. H. G. Blomfield's excellent translation of Book 1 (1916) comes complete with helpful notes, but copies of this highly readable volume may be hard to come by. A. J. Boyle and J. P. Sullivan's *Roman Poets of the Early Empire* (1991) includes an elegant translation of Book 7.

Perhaps the best introductions to the poem in English are the relevant sections of Feeney 1991 and Hardie 1993, both seminal works. A brief but dense and informative thematic overview is found in Boyle 1991. Hershkowitz 1998b is a rare book-length study which offers a useful distillation of the state of scholarship on Valerius, particularly with respect to poetics, as well as an exhaustive bibliography. The classic study on self-consciousness in the poem is Malamud and McGuire 1993, updated in certain respects in Zissos 1999. McGuire 1997 well situates the poem in its sociopolitical context. Detailed commentaries in English are available for Book 2 by H. M. Poortvliet (1991) and for Books 5 and 6 by H. J. W. Wijsman (1996 and 2000); both commentators are readable, but Poortvliet is the more reliable of the two. A commentary on Book 1 by A. Zissos will be available shortly after publication of this volume.

CHAPTER THIRTY-SEVEN

Statius

William J. Dominik

> Stazio la gente ancor di là mi noma:
>> cantai di Tebe, e poi del grande Achille;
>> ma caddi in via con la seconda soma.
>>> (Dante, *Purgatorio* 21.85–7)

> Statius is what people on earth still call me:
>> I sang of Thebes and then of mighty Achilles,
>> but I fell by the wayside with the second burden.

Thus speaks Statius when Dante and his guide Virgil encounter him in the *Purgatorio*. In these few lines Dante Alighieri refers to the *Thebaid* and *Achilleid*, the epics for which Publius Papinius Statius (*ca.* 45–*ca.* 96 CE) was widely known and admired in the Middle Ages. The *Thebaid* is unique for a Roman epic in that it survives in a completed and polished form, whereas only a little over a book of the *Achilleid* was written before the poet died. Although the *Thebaid* and *Achilleid* are very different types of epics, they both adopt a theme from Greek mythology and contain a *recusatio* to the emperor Domitian for not writing an epic on the emperor and his deeds (*Theb.* 1.14–19, *Achil.* 1.14–19). Statius did write a historical poem, *On the German War*, which dealt with Domitian's German campaign (see *Sil.* 4.2.63–7). Since only four lines are extant, however, it is impossible to know if this was the poem about his exploits promised to Domitian (*Theb.* 1.32–3, *Achil.* 1.18–19). The *Silvae*, a collection of Statius' occasional poems rediscovered in the early fifteenth century, refers frequently not only to his life and his circumstances but also to the composition of his epics. It is here we learn that Statius was guided by his father, an accomplished poet who died around 79 CE, when he undertook to compose the *Thebaid* (*Sil.* 5.3.234–8). This is significant since its themes seem to have been anticipated in an epic by the elder Statius on the civil war of 69 (*Sil.* 5.3.195–208), which unfortunately does not survive.

Subject and Background of the *Thebaid*

The subject of Statius' *Thebaid* is the attempt of Polynices, son of Oedipus and Jocasta, to gain control of the throne from his brother Eteocles. The brothers agree to alternate rule in Thebes on an annual basis, but Eteocles declines to step down from the throne after his first year of rule. Polynices then seeks the aid of neighboring monarchs in an attempt to regain power. The subject of the *Thebaid* formed part of a long literary tradition that seems to have commenced with the Epic Cycle, a collection of Greek poems written in the seventh and sixth centuries BCE (see Chapter 24, by Burgess). Although the *Thebaid* of the Epic Cycle has not survived, its subject seems to have provided an important stimulus to later poets, including Antimachus, whose *Thebaid* of the fifth century BCE consisted of twenty-four books in the Homeric fashion. While Antimachus' epic and numerous Greek tragedies of roughly the same period are lost to us today, a number of Greek tragedies dealing with the Theban saga do survive, namely Aeschylus' *Seven Against Thebes*, Euripides' *Suppliant Women* and *Phoenician Women*, and Sophocles' *Oedipus Tyrannus*, *Oedipus at Colonus*, and *Antigone*, as do the Roman tragedies of Seneca, notably *Oedipus* and the incomplete *Phoenician Women*. From these and other sources it is apparent that Statius derived aspects of the plot and treatment of his themes and characters in his own *Thebaid*, which was completed after a dozen years in the early 90s CE.

Narrative Structure of the *Thebaid*

In addition to the programmatic prologue (*Theb.* 1.1–45) and the highly allusive epilogue (12.810–19), three broad movements or divisions to Statius' *Thebaid* can be identified: (1) the initial impetus of the narrative toward war (1.46–4.645), (2) the delay in Nemea (4.646–6.946), and (3) the reactuation of the narrative toward war followed by the actual fighting (7.1–12.809). Statius indicates his intent of altering the direction or impetus of the narrative by inserting within each of these broad narrative divisions an invocation to the Muses (1.1–45, 7.628–31) or Apollo (4.649–51) for divine inspiration in relating the subsequent events of the movement. On a more basic level the narrative structure (or plot) of the work is divided into twelve books, each with its own internal structure and unity. Significantly, eight of these books (1, 2, 4, 7–11) open with a scene highlighting the causative and destructive role of the gods in the forward movement of the narrative. Four consecutive books (7–10) in the third movement commence with a scene stressing the harmful nature of supernatural intervention and culminate in the death of one of the Seven, the demise in each case serving as an illustration of the supreme manifestation of divine interference in human affairs. Thus the structure itself of these books becomes a reflection of the supernatural cause–human effect relationship in which divine intervention precipitates human death and suffering. Elsewhere in the narrative Statius frequently juxtaposes scenes showing the harmful effects of divine intervention in human affairs with passages highlighting this disastrous interference of the higher powers. This juxtapositional technique is effective in suggesting the destructive nature of the divine cause-human effect relationship that defines the rest of the poem.

Prologue and invocation (Thebaid 1.1–45): setting the theme

The major function of the opening book is to draw immediate attention to the role of the supernatural powers in contriving to effect widespread human destruction and suffering. The prologue and invocation to the Muses (*Theb.* 1.1–45) is consistent with this purpose. This introductory section allows Statius to provide essential background information relevant to his theme of *fraternas acies* ("fraternal strife," 1.1): the description of the immense suffering that the gods have inflicted upon Thebes in the past and the suffering that her citizens are yet to endure immediately establishes an atmosphere of despair and hopelessness by pointing forward to the inevitability of tragic events.

First movement *(*Thebaid *1.46–4.645): preparations for war*

The first movement of the epic narrates Polynices' recruitment of an army led by the Seven against Thebes, including Adrastus, king of Argos, who is the only leader among the Seven to survive the war. After the motivating speech of Jupiter, in which he declares that he will set the brothers against each other (*Theb.* 1.214–47, esp. 224–5, 241–6), there is the arrival of Polynices at Argos and his clash with Tydeus (*Theb.* 1); the marriages of Polynices and Tydeus to Adrastus' daughters, Antigone and Ismene; Tydeus' mission to Eteocles and his slaying of the ambushers sent against him by Eteocles (*Theb.* 2); the account and suicide of Maeon, the lone survivor from the ambush; the return of Tydeus to Argos and his exhortation to war; the taking of the auspices for war (*Theb.* 3); the catalogue of the Argive armies; the necromancy to find out the result of the ensuing conflict; and the arrival of the troops at Nemea (*Theb.* 4).

Second movement: delay in Nemea *(*Thebaid *4.646–6.946)*

The second movement includes the story of Hypsipyle (*Theb.* 5.49–498), former Queen of Lemnos, which involves the Lemnian massacre and her enslavement at the court of King Lycurgus as the nurse of Opheltes (*Theb.* 5), and the funeral games held in honor of Opheltes, who is slain by a serpent as Hypsipyle tells her tale to Adrastus and the Argives (*Theb.* 6). The insertion of this metadiegetic narrative so arrests the flow of the chronological narrative that the impression of a long delay in the progress of the Argive army toward Thebes is created. Hypsipyle's tale parallels the themes and events treated in the main narrative. The fluctuating fortunes of the Lemnian women resemble the frequent change in circumstances of the Argives and Thebans in the main narrative. As with the scheme of Jupiter, the plan of Venus to exact retribution sets family members against one another and involves the guiltless in its fulfillment. This episode features one of the most gruesome examples of supernaturally inspired violence and bloodshed in the poem. Venus instigates the women's human sacrifice (5.157–65) and massacre of their Lemnian husbands, fathers, and children with the assistance of the Furies (190–240; cf. 85–169). The massacre related by Hypsipyle, a scene of total desolation and bizarre morbidity, is horrific and pathetic (212–61). The focus of the entire episode is on the heroic action of Hypsipyle in rescuing her father from the frenzied Lemnian women (240–95).

Third movement *(*Thebaid *7.1–12.809): war between Thebes and Argos*

The second half of the epic commences with Jupiter's motivating speech in which he commands Mars to stir up war (*Theb.* 7.6–33, esp. 27–32). The narrative accelerates with a series of battles between the Argive and Theban sides as it moves toward the inevitable duel between Polynices and Eteocles. These deaths include nearly all of the rest of the Seven: Amphiaraus, an Argive prophet, who is engulfed by the earth and plunges to his doom in the Underworld (*Theb.* 7); Tydeus, king of Calydon, who gnaws on the skull of his victim at the point of his own death (*Theb.* 8); the Argive Hippomedon, who is weakened by the onslaught of the river Ismenus and falls to the Thebans' projectiles; Parthenopaeus, the son of Atalanta, who falls mysteriously in battle and entreats his mother for a proper burial (*Theb.* 9); and the Argive Capaneus, who challenges the gods and is struck down by Jupiter (*Theb.* 10). These deaths build up to the mutual fratricide of Polynices and Eteocles and to Creon's banishment of Oedipus from Thebes (*Theb.* 11). The rest of the action in the epic is taken up with the lamentations of the widows, the funeral rites of the Thebans, the cremation of the brothers, the military intervention of

Theseus at Thebes on behalf of the unburied Seven, and his rout of Creon on the battlefield (*Theb.* 12).

Epilogue (Thebaid *12.810–19): literary predecessors*

Statius mentions Virgil's *Aeneid* in his epilogue and declares that his *Thebaid* is not to rival it but to follow its path reverently: "uiue, precor; nec tu diuinam Aeneida tempta, / sed longe sequere et uestigia semper adora" ("Live, I pray; nor challenge the divine *Aeneid*, but follow from afar and always venerate its tracks," *Theb.* 12.816–17). These lines are significant for their acknowledgment of poetic indebtedness to Virgil, for their self-conscious, self-referential acknowledgment of the *Thebaid*'s own belatedness in the poetic and epic traditions, and for their self-positioning, self-memorializing statement regarding the *Thebaid*'s own contribution to these traditions. The reference to the *Aeneid* in this *envoi* clarifies the role of the *Thebaid* and its intellectual focus in relation to the *Aeneid* and other texts, especially its relation to earlier poetry and epic and its role within these traditions. The *Thebaid* pointedly follows the lead of Virgil's epic in its construction of a mythical framework with contemporary meaning and relevance. Statius stresses his debt directly to the *Aeneid* and through various intertexual allusions to this and other works of such precursory poets as Homer, Pindar, Callimachus, Apollonius Rhodius, Ennius, Lucretius, Catullus, Livy, Propertius, Horace, Virgil, Ovid, Lucan, Valerius Flaccus, and Martial.

Thebaid 12.817 ("sed *longe* sequere et *uestigia* semper adora", "but follow from afar and always venerate its tracks") recalls *Aeneid* 2.711 ("et *longe* seruet *uestigia* coniunx", "and from afar let my wife [Creusa] stay in my footsteps"), an intertextual reference that suggests the relationship between the *Thebaid* and the *Aeneid* should be viewed not so much as one of master and epigone but rather in cultural terms of husband and wife (Nugent 1996: 70–1), that is, as different and later in the tradition. *Thebaid* 12.817 also recalls the story of Eurydice in the narratives of Virgil's *Georgics* (4.453–527, esp. 485–502) and Ovid's *Metamorphoses* (10.1–85, esp. 48–63), where she follows her husband with the same result as Creusa in the *Aeneid*. Furthermore, *Theb.* 12.816–17 brings to mind examples in Greek lyric and elegy where a poet refers to his groundbreaking role in the poetic craft, for instance in *Pyth.* 4, where Pindar mentions that he is a guide to others in the poetic art and can set an example of the short path, that is, concise narrative (247–8), and in the prologue to Callimachus' *Aetia*, where Apollo bids Callimachus *not* to follow the common paths of other poets but to tread an unworn path (*Aet.* fr. 1.25–8). Unlike these poets, however, Statius bids his epic to follow in the tracks of a precursor, even if it is at a distance.

The *ratis* of Statius (*Theb.* 12.809), a "ship" of poetry, which recalls others such as those of Pindar (e.g., *Nem.* 3.26–7, *Ol.* 6.101, *Pyth.* 10.51–2), Apollonius (*Arg.* 4.1773–5), Propertius (3.3.22–3, 3.9.3–4), Horace (*Carm.* 2.10.1–24, 4.15.1–4), Virgil (*Geo.* 2.39–46, 4.116–17), Ovid (*Tr.* 3.329–30, *AA* 3.26), and Valerius Flaccus (*Arg.* 1.1–4), is described by the poet as being deserving of a haven (*portum*, "harbor," *Theb.* 12.809; cf. *Sil.* 4.4.88–9), ostensibly from the apparently endless tale of epic grief, despair, and ruination it describes. While Statius' employment of the nautical metaphor to refer to the end of the *Thebaid*'s journey is reminiscent of Pindar's use of the anchor to indicate the end of an ode (*Ol.* 6.101), it also recalls Ennius' self-conscious statement (possibly) at or towards the end of his *Annals*' original epilogue to the fifteenth book (*Ann.* sed. inc. fr. 69), where he likens a distinguished *poeta* finishing a demanding literary task to a champion racing steed in retirement (Dominik 1993: 44–5).

The sentiments in the *Thebaid*'s epilogue regarding the epic's immortality ("iam certe praesens tibi Fama benignum / strauit iter coepitque nouam monstrare futuris" ("Indeed, already present Fame has laid a kindly path for you and begun to parade you as a new creation before the future") 12.812–13) and especially its popularity among Italian youth ("Itala iam studio discit memoratque iuuentus" ("and Italian youth avidly learn and remember you") 815) bring to mind similar statements of epic poets preceding Statius, including the bold prediction of Ennius that his subject and poem would win renown among peoples far and wide (*Ann.* 1 fr. 11 (Skutsch 1985)), Apollonius' expression of hope that his *Argonautica* would grow in poetic appeal through the years (*Arg.* 4.1773–5), and Lucan's bold prediction on the future immortality of his epic (*BC* 9.986). This didactic aspect of the *Thebaid*'s epilogue also recalls Lucretius' *De rerum natura*, especially 3.1–30 and 5.55–90, and verbal reminiscences emphasize the thematic link (Malamud 1995: 26–7).

But the epilogue also recalls similar pronouncements in non-epic texts, including Pindar, *Ol.* 6, where he appeals to Poseidon to prosper his poems (105); Catullus 1.1, where the poet expresses the hope that his *libellus* ("little book") would live and last for more than one century (9–10); Horace, *Carm.* 2.20 and 3.30, especially the line where he declares confidently that through the composition of his poetry he has erected a monument more lasting than bronze (3.30.1); and Martial 1.1, where he states his name and observes that his readers have given him more fame throughout the world while he is alive than many poets have after their deaths (1–6). The strongest allusion to poetic immortality in the *Thebaid*'s epilogue is to Statius' precursor Ovid, whose reference to a poem's *dominus* ("master") in the opening lines of the *Tristia* (1.1.1–2) is echoed in *Theb.* 12.810: "Durabisne procul dominoque legere superstes" ("Will you long endure and survive your master to be read?"). Ovid predicts in the epilogue to the *Metamorphoses* (15.871–9, esp. 875–9) and in the last poem of *Amores* 1 (1.15.41–2; cf. *Am.* 1.15.7–9, 3.15.19–20; *Tr.* 3.7.49–54) that his name will be immortalized in the memory of future generations. Like the epic of Ovid (*Met.* 15.874–9), the already well-known work of Statius will continue to grow in fame (*Theb.* 12.812–19); like the envy that afflicts the poetry of Ovid (*Am.* 1.15.39–42, *Pont.* 4.16) and Callimachus (*Ap.* 105–13), the envy obscuring the *Thebaid* will pass away (or be spurned) and the epic will receive its due honors (*Theb.* 12.818–19).

Virgilian and Lucanian Reminiscences in the *Thebaid*

As the epilogue emphasizes, the *Thebaid* does follow directly in the footsteps of the *Aeneid*, as many scenes from the *Aeneid* are rewritten into the *Thebaid*. Statius also stresses his poetic debt to Virgil in the prologue through an intertextual reference to the *Aeneid* in his use of *arma* ("arms," *Theb.* 1.33), an image-symbol of internecine war (cf. 1.33–40). It recalls the *Aeneid*'s opening words, *arma uirumque* ("arms and the man [Aeneas]"), which are themselves pointed allusions to the *Iliad* (the Trojan War) and the *Odyssey* (the hero Odysseus) respectively. In the narrative between the proemial and concluding acknowledgments of poetic indebtedness to Virgil, resemblances between the *Thebaid* and *Aeneid* abound.

Statius' narration of the origins of the war (*Theb.* 1.390–400) is reminiscent of Virgil's account of the cause of the war in Latium (*Aen.* 7.45–106); Adrastus' banquet (*Theb.* 1.515–56) and telling of the tale of Coroebus (557–668) resemble Dido's banquet (*Aen.* 1.695–756) and Evander's account of the Cacus myth (8.185–279) respectively; the appearance of the shade of Laius (*Theb.* 2.1–25) recalls the appearances of the ghosts of Hector (*Aen.* 2.268–97) and Anchises (5.719–45); the presentation of the irreverent Capaneus (*Theb.* 3.602) is similar to Mezentius (*Aen.* 7.648); the serpent that slays Archemorus (*Theb.* 5.538–54) recalls the snake that kills Laocoon and his two sons (*Aen.* 2.201–24); the funeral games for Opheltes (*Theb.* 6.296–946) evoke the memory of those held in honor of Anchises (*Aen.* 5.104–544); Jupiter's dispatching of Mars to incite the Argives to a furious war-lust against Thebes (*Theb.* 7.22–33) corresponds to Juno's incitement of Allecto (*Aen.* 7.330–40); the incident featuring Bacchus' tigers (*Theb.* 7.564–607) resembles the episode of Iulus' hounds (*Aen.* 7.475–510); the mission of Hopleus and Dymas (*Theb.* 10.347–448) emulates the Nisus and Euryalus episode (*Aen.* 9.176–449); the fate of Parthenopaeus, slain by the Theban warrior Dryas (*Theb.* 9.856–907), brings to mind the similar fates of Eurylaus (*Aen.* 9.420–7) and Pallas (10.479–99), while the solicitude of Atalanta, Parthenopaeus' mother (*Theb.* 9.570–635) resembles the similar states of Euryalus' mother (*Aen.* 9.284–90; cf. 12.805–7) and Evander, Pallas' father (8.558–84); and the duel between Theseus and Creon (*Theb.* 11.768–81) recalls the duel between Aeneas and Turnus (*Aen.* 12.928–52). Through this rewriting of these and other scenes from the *Aeneid*, Statius suggests that the histories of Thebes and Argos have important parallels in the history of the Roman nation.

The *Thebaid* sings too, as the prologue pronounces (*Theb.* 1.33–4), in the Lucanian fashion of the *sceptrum* ("scepter"; cf., e.g., Luc. *BC* 8.489–90, 558–60, 692–9; 10.87–9, 138–40), which is transmuted by Statius into a symbol of manic, irreverent power (*Theb.* 11.655–6; cf. 1.33–40, 11.654–5). Statius is inspired to relate *fraternas acies* ("fraternal strife," *Theb.* 1.1) between Eteocles and Polynices, which specifically recalls Lucan's *cognatas acies* ("familial strife," 1.4) between Pompey and Caesar. There is much of Lucan elsewhere in the *Thebaid*, including its apostrophes, especially the one condemning Eteocles and Polynices to Tartarus after the description of their mutual fratricide (*Theb.* 11.574–9; cf. *BC* 7.552–6), which is just one of a number of passages in the *Thebaid* containing an implicit reference to the responsibilities of a monarch and a subtle warning against failing to heed them. The influence of Lucan is palpably evident in the *Thebaid*'s numerous descriptions of human violence featuring dismemberment and the rending of human flesh (e.g., 7.760–70, 9.259–65, 10.515–18), internecine images that are anticipated in the *Thebaid*'s prologue (1.33–40).

Themes of the *Thebaid*

The *Thebaid* is a meditation primarily on the theme of power. The subject chosen by Statius was an ideal vehicle for an exploration on this topic. Virtually every event in the epic is related in some way to the unfavorable aspects of the exercise of power on the supernatural and monarchal levels. Prominent is the issue of its pursuit and abuse, the consequent suffering and impotence of its victims. Scholars in the twentieth century tended to shape their view of the *Thebaid* according to the Judeo-Christian concept of retribution and guilt, which is usually based on Jupiter's opening, programmatic speech asserting that human criminality demands divine retribution (*Theb.* 1.214–47). But there is little evidence to sustain such an interpretation since the crimes cited by him (esp. in 227–47) were either committed unintentionally, or were motivated primarily by the supernatural powers, or had already been avenged.

Use and abuse of supernatural power

The *Thebaid* is a tale of the supernaturally engineered annihilation of humanity. The divine apparatus of the *Thebaid* underpins its thematic structure, as the destructive impact upon mankind of its relationship with the gods is the focus of the entire epic. Abuse of supernatural power is the predominant, pervasive motif in the *Thebaid*. The numerous cruel and unjust actions of the higher powers bear testimony, as does their frequent lack of compassion and concern for humanity. Although the gods occasionally take a fleeting interest in the misfortune of a favorite person or express a selfish – if mostly justifiable – concern over the fate of a special city, their attitude toward the human race is generally one of hostility or indifference. Through their actions the various supernatural powers are instrumental in inciting humanity to violence and bloodshed. Without their frequent harmful interventions, especially those of Jupiter, Pluto, and the Furies, the motivation for much of the human action in the *Thebaid* would be lacking. Jupiter plays the critical motivating role in the epic since his stated purpose in instigating the conflict between the Thebans and Argives is the destruction of the Theban and Argive races and almost every major incident of the poem works toward this end. The fulfillment of his decrees (*Theb.* 1.214–47, 3.229–52, 7.6–33) and those of his brother Pluto (8.34–79) demands the death and suffering of countless innocent victims, who are caught up in a tragic war incited primarily by malevolent supernatural forces. Mankind's subsequent irrational and impious conduct is often shown to be inspired by divine powers who are essentially antagonistic to the human race and are shown propelling it headlong toward destruction.

Olympians such as Juno (e.g., *Theb.* 10.131), Venus (e.g., 5.157–8), Apollo (e.g., 1.596–604, 627–33), Diana (e.g., 9.665–7), and Bacchus (cf., e.g., 7.211–14) are shown on many occasions inspiring various human figures to commit hideous crimes or contriving to create a situation favorable to the perpetration of inhuman deeds. Mars, one of the most frightening deities in the *Thebaid*, is shown on numerous occasions destroying nations or inflaming people to violence (e.g., 3.577–93, 7.131–9, 8.383–7), but Tisiphone and Megaera are portrayed directly as imposing their will on various human figures more frequently than any of the other supernatural powers in the main narrative. These incidents include conspiring to prompt Oedipus' curse on his sons (cf. 1.51–2), setting upon Eteocles and Polynices and infusing them with jealousy and hatred of each other and an insatiable lust for power (1.123–30, 7.466–7), and bringing about the fratricide of Polynices and Eteocles by influencing their actions (11.150–4, 197–209, 383–92). These and other scenes attest to the general powerlessness of mankind and its lack of free will in a world dominated by malevolent and uncaring deities. The concentration of Statius in the battle narrative (7.632–11.572) upon the Seven, whose destructive behavior is divinely motivated and whose deaths – with the exception of those of Tydeus and of course Adrastus, who survives the war – can be attributed to the harmful intervention of the gods, bears testimony to the ultimate futility of human life in the face of overwhelming supernatural opposition. The *Thebaid* depicts a hostile universe in which the innocent are likely to become the victims of supernatural vindictiveness just as much as the flagitious.

Use and abuse of monarchal power

The attitude of Statius toward the institution of monarchy is unequivocal even though the motivation for the actions of monarchs in the *Thebaid* is usually attributable to the harmful intervention of supernatural powers. The picture of monarchy that emerges from the *Thebaid* is predominantly negative despite the generally favorable portrait of Adrastus and the ambiguous presentation of Theseus. This negative impression is based mostly upon the conduct of Eteocles and Creon, with occasional references to actions of previous monarchs such as Oedipus and Laius. A cruel and oppressive institution, monarchy inflicts widespread and long-standing suffering upon subjects who are largely innocent of any wrongdoing. Major episodes (*Theb.* 1.164–95, 2.384–3.113, 10.268–314, 11.648–761) – the first two accompanied by a suitable apostrophe or editorial comment (1.165–8, 3.99–113) – exemplify his hostile attitude toward the inevitable tyranny of monarchy. In each scene words of reproach directed at the reigning monarch by one of his subjects represent the hostility of the populace toward their ruler. A vivid picture of the lust for *nuda potestas* ("raw power," 1.150) and its destructive consequences is framed around the claim of Polynices to the throne and determination of Eteocles to maintain sovereignty over Thebes. The debasement of the brothers results from Polynices' insatiable quest for monarchal power (see 1.314–23, 2.307–21, 4.88–9) and Eteocles' abuse of his position and desire to retain the throne (cf. 2.399). This picture of a corrupt monarchy extends to Eteocles' predecessors and successor. The actions of Oedipus, Laius, and Creon are consistent with the pattern of monarchal cruelty established over successive generations of rule in Thebes.

The actions of Adrastus and Theseus do not on the surface conform to this pattern of tyrannical monarchy. But the monarchs are not immune from destructive influences. Statius occasionally emphasizes the benevolence, piety, and self-restraint of Adrastus as well as the civilizing role of Theseus, but overall this plays a relatively minor part in the presentation of institutional monarchy in the poem. In fact Statius extends his despairing picture of institutional monarchy to include the actions of these seemingly just and benevolent regents; for not even they are untainted by the madness that afflicts participants in war. Adrastus ignores omens that portend disaster for Argos by warring against Thebes (cf. *Theb.* 3.456–8, 499–551, 619–47) and enthusiastically sanctions the cowardly nocturnal attack on the Theban camp in which the victims are mercilessly slain while sleeping (10.227–44, esp. 236–44, 266–8). Theseus shows a similar eagerness for the slaughter of war (12.595). When the Athenians mow down the helpless Thebans on the battlefield, Theseus is at the forefront of the conflict and wreaks destruction among the Thebans on the battlefield. The Athenian monarch easily slays a multitude of Theban warriors (741–51), including Creon, whom he dispatches quickly without showing even a trace of mercy (768–82). The question of whether Theseus' alleged purpose of ensuring the burial of the Argive corpses justifies the violent means of its attainment raises questions similar to those on the necessity of Aeneas' slaying of Turnus at the end of the *Aeneid*. Perhaps Theseus' action is justified (cf. 12.711–14, esp. 714), but his conduct compares unfavorably with the behavior of Virgil's Aeneas, who at least pauses briefly and gives some thought to sparing Turnus before dispatching him in a blind rage (*Aen.* 12.928–52, esp. 946, 951).

Consequences of the abuse of power

The *Thebaid* is a compelling statement of the horrifying and sorrowful consequences of the imprudent pursuit and exercise of power. Its opening words – *fraternas acies* ("fraternal strife", *Theb.* 1.1) – allude to what is to Statius the worst kind of human violence: that which is directed against one's own flesh and blood. Statius moves in reaction to warfare and its horrors; his abhorrence of war is suggested in the violent atmosphere, gory descriptions, and tragic results of the fighting. The mass destruction and suffering caused by the fighting that takes place in the poem is evidence of the futility of war, since virtually no one emerges unscathed from its devastating effects and little seems to be achieved. The pathetic effect of the lament scenes contributes greatly to the overall impression of despair and ruination that pervades the narrative. The tragic consequences of war are evident in the deaths of men of all ages and from every walk of life; the women, children, elderly, and infirm are left only to vent their grief and bear their losses. Fittingly, the epic narrative ends with the depiction of the intense grief of war's survivors (788–807), thus giving final emphasis to the ultimate futility of human violence and bloodshed.

Statius goes to considerable lengths to establish a consistent picture of the weakness and suffering of the human race in an oppressive universe. The Thebans and Argives are largely portrayed as the helpless victims of a war instigated by Jupiter (e.g., *Theb.* 1.241–6; cf. 1.224–5, 3.248–51) to destroy their races. The imposition of divine will upon humanity is seen consistently to be the major factor behind the weak and helpless state of mankind and the inability of mankind to control its own destiny. Dante, who valued the companionship of Statius on his spiritual journey and admired his moral framework, believed him to have been a Christian (*Purgatorio* 22.73, 89–90), perhaps because the *Thebaid* reveals an obvious sympathy for the lot of mankind and sensitivity to human suffering. The persecution, suffering, lamentation, and fear attributed to the emperor Domitian in the *Purgatorio* (22.83–4, 90) reflects the climate of terror, death, destruction, and grief at Thebes, which foreshadows Dante's city of Dis, a metaphoric model for Hell. An air of guarded hope and optimism for the future of mankind does emerge midway through the final book (*Theb.* 12.481–518) in the description of the altar of Clementia ("Clemency"), which in its presentation of the ideal of humanity and compassion constitutes a solemn entreaty to a ruler to adopt a conciliatory approach to his subjects, but the appearance of this benevolent goddess is not enough to dispel the pall of gloom and despair that overhangs the epic.

Characterization in the *Thebaid*

Perhaps because there is no central figure in the *Thebaid*, none of the figures in the epic undergoes the type of sustained development of character that Aeneas experiences in the *Aeneid*. Polynices is perhaps the most memorable figure. He has a great many unique personal qualities but is also portrayed as a typically corrupt aspirant to the throne; his character ranges from an affectionate concern for his wife Argia (*Theb.* 2.352–62) to extreme cruelty and vindictiveness (cf., e.g., 1.316–23; 2.313–32; 3.365–82; 6.316–26; 11.97–112, 497–573). There is often a dramatic change in the personalities of humans when they are made subject to the influence of supernatural powers or released from their control. In general a certain pattern of behavior and attitude emerges among the various human characters in the speeches and narrative, which is then undermined by the later speeches and actions of these figures in reaction to the harmful influences of the supernatural powers or the absence of these forces, and this phenomenon finally is perceived as a pattern of the entire characterizing process in the epic. Oedipus is portrayed as bitter and vindictive when he is under the control of the Furies (cf. 1.51–2, 7.466–9, 11.617–19), but is an entirely different person when these powers leave him alone (cf. 11.599–633, esp. 617–21). Amphiaraus is depicted as a pious and peace-loving priest (e.g., 3.620–47, 5.731–52) until he is filled with a desire for war and an insatiable bloodlust under the influence and watchful gaze of the higher powers (7.703–12, 695–704, 736–59; cf. 779–80). This transition in the personalities of the various characters occurs at many different points in the progression of the narrative. While Oedipus and Amphiaraus undergo a radical transformation of character just prior to their final appearances, characters such as Polynices and his brother are barely allowed to show even a hint of their real nature before they are set against each other by supernatural forces and their personalities are transmuted (1.123–43).

Contemporary Relevance of the *Thebaid*

Statius creates in the *Thebaid* a mythic cosmos that reflects his contemporary Rome. The despairing portrait of the divine powers, institutional monarchy, the great war, and the human condition evidenced in the *Thebaid* necessarily invites a comparison with events and personalities in Rome during the turbulent reigns of the Julio-Claudian and Flavian emperors, most of whom were portrayed as inflicting long-standing suffering upon the citizenry during and after the civil wars. The *Zeitgeist* of the Julio-Claudian and Flavian periods, which were alleged by ancient writers to be gloomy and violent, pervades and infects the *Thebaid*. In the *Thebaid* the abuse of power on the supernatural and human levels and the condemnation of the violation of justice are applicable to the contemporary political situation under the Julio-Claudians and Flavians. The *Thebaid* reflects not only the heart of Statius' pessimistic world view but also his concern and that of his contemporaries about the harsh and oppressive atmosphere and terrible political uncertainties of his age.

Since the *Thebaid* was not pure allegory, correspondences between contemporary personalities and events in Rome and the characters and incidents in the *Thebaid* are not clear-cut. In his composition Statius set about expressing the concerns of his age through general rather than specific reminiscences of events and characters. Nevertheless numerous scenes and figures in the *Thebaid* invite a comparison with the contemporary political situation at Rome and to specific historical figures under the Principate. During the Middle Ages commentators and glossators frequently commented on the contemporary relevance of the *Thebaid* from a sociopolitical perspective. One of the most compelling identifications made in medieval *accessus* (introductions to the poets and their works) was between the sons of Oedipus and those of Vespasian. In the eyes of these medieval scholars, the *Thebaid* was a serious study on kingship and its responsibilities. Accordingly, Statius was viewed as providing a message and a lesson on the pursuit and abuse of power for the Roman public and emperors through the theme of *fraternas acies* ("fraternal strife").

Attention is directed immediately toward this theme and comparison between the Theban and imperial brothers in the opening line of the *Thebaid* (cf. *Theb.* 1.184). This analogy is based mainly on the antipathy between the Theban brothers and their mutual fratricide, which not only recall the rumored hostility between the sons of Vespasian and the alleged poisoning of Titus by Domitian (Suet. *Dom.* 2.3; cf. *Tit.* 9.3) but also the long-standing feud between Jupiter and his brothers (cf. *Theb.* 8.34–79). The similarity in circumstances between all three sets of brothers (Theban, imperial, and Olympian) serves to identify Domitian all the more closely with his Theban and Olympian counterparts. The suggested parallel between Eteocles and Domitian, who is described in an *accessus* (Bern, cod. 528, and London, BL, Burney 258) to the *Thebaid* as *nequissimus imperator* ("a most wicked emperor"), is strengthened by the reference to Eteocles as *princeps* ("first citizen," *Theb.* 1.169). Indeed the theme of *fraternas acies* in the imperial house was a political *locus communis* in the first century CE. Although represented as flesh and blood characters in the *Thebaid*, Eteocles and Polynices exemplify the type of leaders who have driven Rome to political ruin and intellectual despair. The enmity and fratricide of the brothers could easily invite a comparison with any number of other examples of familial discord and bloodshed among the Julio-Claudians.

Other links between the Theban and imperial courts are suggested in the speech of the anonymous Theban (*Theb.* 1.173–96), the exile of Polynices (1.312–89), and the treacherous ambush of Tydeus and its aftermath (2.482–3.217). Numerous scenes of terror and brutality in the *Thebaid* reflect the atmosphere of despair, fear, and violence that marked the anarchy of 68–9 CE. The sentiments of the anonymous Theban concerning the political uncertainties and vagaries of quickly changing rulers surely would have struck a sympathetic chord with Statius' audience (cf. Tac. *Hist.* 1.85). Many in it would have suffered through the quick succession of five emperors – Nero, Galba, Otho, Vitellius, and Vespasian – during this chaotic period and experienced the reigns of three emperors – Vespasian, Titus, and Domitian – from 79 to 81. Especially compelling to an audience of the late first century would have been Statius' suggestion that the destruction arising from the sowing of the serpent's teeth by Cadmus had destined Thebes to endure civil discord forever (*Theb.* 1.180–5). In mythological terms the obvious Roman parallel is Romulus and Remus, for the founding of Rome upon Romulus' slaying of Remus seemed to later Romans to foredoom her to eternal civil strife (cf. Liv. 1.6.4–2.7.3, Hor. *Epod.* 7.17–20,

Luc. *BC* 1.95–7). The recent civil wars would only have served to confirm this political parallel between Thebes and Rome. The exile of Polynices and instigation of the ambush by Eteocles naturally bring to mind the many cases involving exile or violent elimination of imagined, potential, or actual political opposition under the Julio-Claudian and Flavian emperors. This connection between the Theban and imperial courts is further stressed when Maeon, the sole Theban survivor of the ambush, takes his own life in the presence of the Theban monarch (*Theb.* 3.81–91). The reaction can be said reasonably to reflect the type of response one would expect of an imperial audience under similar circumstances: the leading citizens are unnerved (92) and the shaken councilors can only raise a murmur (92–3).

The *Achilleid*

In the prologue to the *Achilleid*, Statius recuses himself from writing an epic on Domitian's life and instead begs the emperor's indulgence to write an epic on Achilles (*Achil.* 1.14–19). Unfortunately Statius completed only 1,100 lines before he died, probably earlier in the same year (96 CE) as the emperor Domitian's death. The *accessus* to the *Achilleid* in the *Liber Catonianus*, a medieval schoolbook, maintains that the poem had an ethical purpose, which was shown in Thetis' concern for her son and Achilles' obedience to his mother.

Outline of the Achilleid

Statius declares that the subject matter and scope of the *Achilleid* is the whole life of Achilles from his upbringing in Scyros, whereas Homer had told only of Achilles' confrontation with Hector in the *Iliad* (*Achil.* 1.3–7). In the narrative Thetis, Achilles' divine mother, fearing that Achilles will be persuaded to join the expedition to Troy, hides Achilles at the house of Lycomedes in Scyros (1.198–282). She persuades him to wear feminine clothing and instructs him how to impersonate a maiden to avoid detection (318–48). As the Greeks prepare for war, Calchas divulges where Thetis has concealed Achilles, whereupon Ulysses and Diomedes depart for Scyros to find him (397–559). Achilles, who has fallen in love with Deidamia, forces himself upon her (560–674). Achilles is discovered when he selects armor from an array of gifts offered to the maidens of the court by Ulysses and Diomedes (841–84). After Deidamia bemoans Achilles' impending departure (1.927–60), he leaves with Ulysses and Diomedes for Troy (2.1–22). Ulysses diverts Achilles' thoughts from Deidamia by reciting the origins of the Trojan War (2.23–85), after which Achilles relates the story of his youth (2.86–167). The manuscript breaks off at this point.

Themes and allusions in the Achilleid

The *Achilleid* seems to be an attempt at a new type of epic. In comparison with the dark and somber mood of the *Thebaid*, the *Achilleid* is lighthearted, even romantic in tone. The hero Achilles is portrayed in an untraditional manner by Statius, who in contrast to the Homeric presentation of Achilles as an intrepid, warlike, and pitiless hero, depicts him as a complex and subtle figure. Statius combines the idyllic-pathetic and sexual elements of elegy with traditional heroic elements in a subtle play of ambiguity and sentimental *chiaroscuro*. The epic has erotic and clearly Ovidian overtones in the sexual ambiguity of Achilles. The tension between the masculine and feminine is evident in an emergent masculinity that struggles to be kept under control by the androgynous qualities of boyhood (e.g., *Achil.* 1.335–7). Thetis shows both the foreknowledge of a goddess and the love and solicitude of a human mother for her son. While the youthful appearance of Achilles makes it possible for him to impersonate a daughter of King Lycomedes, his underlying masculinity constantly threatens to expose his real identity, as shown by the maidens' attraction to him (*Achil.* 1.366–78, 566–7), his love for and rape of Deidamia (1.560–636), and his instinctive longing to pursue his heroic destiny on the battlefield of Troy (1.852–66). In the end Achilles' discovery and departure for Troy proves inevitable. Deidamia is portrayed as a pathetic and tragic victim of fate (1.929–55, 2.23–6), reminiscent of the tragic circumstances of Dido in Virgil's *Aeneid*. Although he loves Deidamia and regrets his departure, these feelings are not enough to override his impulsive desire to meet his destiny on the battlefields of Troy.

As in the *Thebaid*, Statius frequently alludes in the *Achilleid* to numerous other poetic predecessors, including Homer, Euripides, Horace, Propertius, Catullus, Virgil, and especially Ovid. Possible allusions in the *Achilleid* to the contemporary political situation at Rome are not as easy to establish as they are for the *Thebaid*. Benker (1987: 87–9) has attempted to draw a connection between Achilles and Domitian by suggesting, for example, that Achilles' concealment in female dress among the daughters of King Lycomedes is reminiscent of Domitian's flight from the Capitol in 69 CE when he disguised himself as a priestess of Isis in order to escape from the fighting against the Vitellians. Given the unfinished state and the very different nature of the *Achilleid*, however, a case for its political allusiveness cannot be made with the same degree of plausibility as for the *Thebaid*. Medieval commentators themselves did not suggest it.

Reception of the *Thebaid* and *Achilleid*

As is evident from the epilogue to the *Thebaid* (12.812–15) and Juvenal's fourth Satire (4.82–7), Statius was a popular epic poet in his own lifetime and was already being read in the schools. During the second century CE it appears that archaizing influences contributed to a decline in his popularity. The appearance of the *Thebaid* and *Achilleid* in late fourth-century glosses and commentaries suggests that he had regained his popularity as an epic poet by this time. Statius greatly influenced the style and language of Ausonius, Prudentius, Paulinus of Nola, and especially Claudian, who modeled aspects of his incomplete epic *Rape of Proserpina* on the *Achilleid* (see Chapters 39 and 40, by Barnes and Trout). During the fifth century this popularity was maintained, as is evident in the figure of Sidonius Apollinaris, who preferred Statius to Virgil, and in the important commentary of Lactantius Placidus on the *Thebaid*. After the fifth century the popularity of Statius seems to have waned until the late eighth century, when during the Carolingian renaissance his epics were frequently copied. Although a small number of manuscripts of the *Thebaid* and *Achilleid* survive from the eighth to eleventh centuries, which indicate that they were almost certainly read in the schools during this time, it was not until the twelfth century that his epics became extremely popular as standard school texts alongside the works of Virgil, Ovid, and Juvenal. Thus the survival of the *Thebaid* and *Achilleid*, which have been copied and commented upon in some 112 and 95 manuscripts respectively, was assured.

There were two different general approaches (moral and historiographical) to the epics of Statius in the Middle Ages, which reflected to some extent their different audiences in the schoolroom and scholarly circles. Throughout this period Statius was regarded as a *poeta doctus* ("learned poet"), the standard epithet for a poet who was thought capable of imparting wisdom in his verse. The *Achilleid* was more popular than the *Thebaid* in the classroom and featured as one of the six elementary texts in the *Liber Catonianus*. One of the reasons for the popularity of the *Achilleid* had to do with its moral didacticism. Statius, who had written about the education of Achilles at the end of the *Achilleid* (2.96–167), was regarded in medieval *accessus* as a *poeta doctor* ("poet-teacher") not only of stories but also on the education of children; the *Achilleid* was considered to provide examples to Romans of how to rear their children and to behave toward their mothers and teachers. This didactic element to the *Achilleid* is also evident in *accessus* to the *Thebaid*. As a *poeta doctor* Statius was thought to provide many lessons in the *Thebaid*, including the need for children to avoid anger.

Statius was also regarded in medieval *accessus* as a *poeta historiographus* ("historiograph-ical poet"), which reflected the prevailing view of the *Thebaid* as a history with moral overtones. The *Thebaid* especially encouraged a scholarly approach and sociopolitical interpretations because of the issues it raised; accordingly, the epic was viewed as a lesson to teach emperors to avoid fraternal war. Although the poem was regarded as having an application to the imperial era, it was not specific enough to teach its readers about the period. Notwithstanding any possible allegorical meaning that may be ascribed to the poem, scholarly interpretation of the poem in the Middle Ages did not seem to involve allegory, perhaps because of the anthropomorphic corporeality of supernatural powers such as Mars and Venus and abstract forces such as *furor* ("Madness") and *pietas* ("Piety") (cf. Dominik 1994a: 3, 18–19, 39, 74).

The influences of the fragmentary *Achilleid* and intact *Thebaid* upon European litera-ture have been widespread and enduring, especially during the Middle Ages, when they were adapted by various writers. The Middle Irish *Togail na Tebe* (*Destruction of Thebes*) perhaps originated around the turn of the millennium, while there are Middle Irish versions of the *Achilleid*. The *Super Thebaiden* of pseudo-Fulgentius, which may be from the twelfth or thirteenth century, offers an allegorical version of the *Thebaid*. The *Achilleid* was influential upon European writers such as Dante, who accompanies Statius in the *Purgatorio* (21–33). Until the sixteenth century Statius' *Thebaid* served as the main inspiration for various adaptations of the Oedipus myth, including the twelfth-century versions known as *Roman de Thèbes*, which relate the fratricide of Eteocles and Polynices. Giovanni Boccaccio was similarly inspired by the *Thebaid* in the composition of his *Teseide*.

Among English poets Chaucer uses the *Thebaid* in *Troilus and Criseyde*, especially in 2.82–112 and 5.1478–1519, while his depiction of Troilus recalls Statius' Oedipus. Chaucer also mentions Statius by name in *The Knight's Tale* (1.2294), in *House of Fame* (2.1460), and in *Troilus and Criseyde* at the end of an apostrophe (5.1786–92, esp. 5.1791–2), which is reminiscent of the epilogue to the *Thebaid* (12.810–19, esp. 811–12). In *Anelida and Arcite* Chaucer depicts the superficially positive attributes of Statius' Theseus. John Lydgate draws on the theme of the *Thebaid* for his *Siege of Thebes*. After the Middle Ages the *Achilleid* and *Thebaid* continued to play an important role in European literature, scholarship, and in the schools. English poets and scholars of the neoclassical period, notably Alexander Pope and Thomas Gray, translated parts of the *Thebaid* into English verse. Although the popularity of the *Thebaid* and *Achilleid* declined after the eighteenth century, they have remained a subject of interest among scholars. At the beginning of the twenty-first century the epics have regained some of the popularity they held in eighteenth-century scholarship.

FURTHER READING

For critical bibliographies on the *Thebaid*, see Dominik 1996, who discusses the critical reception of the *Thebaid* in the twentieth century up until the mid-1990s, followed by the survey of Coleman 2003, who also discusses recent scholarship on the *Achilleid*. The most recent editions and transla-tions of these epics are by Shackleton Bailey (2003). The standard texts of the *Thebaid* and *Achilleid* are by Hill (1983) and Dilke (1954) respectively.

The major critical studies in English on the *Thebaid* are by Vessey (1973), who makes considerable claims for its stature after a couple of centuries of scholarly neglect in the Anglophone world; Ahl (1986), who deals with a wide range of thematic issues and argues for a political reading; Dominik (1994a), who treats the theme of power and its political implications; Dominik (1994b), who examines the role of the speeches; and McGuire (1997), who discusses the themes of civil war, tyranny, and suicide in Flavian epic.

Important studies of the *Thebaid* in languages other than English in the past quarter century are those of Schubert (1984), who studies the role of Jupiter in the Flavian epics; Frings (1991), who analyzes aspects of Statius' narrative technique; Frings (1992), who explores the themes of fraternal hatred and murder in comparison with Seneca's *Thyestes*; Ripoll (1998), who investigates the nature of the heroic code found in Flavian epic; Franchet d'Espèrey (1999), who treats the themes of war, violence, and peace in the *Thebaid*; and Criado (2000), who examines non-Virgilian elements of Statius' theological conception in the epic.

There are no book-length critical studies in English on the *Achilleid*, although Clogan (1968) provides an informative discussion of the medieval *Achilleid*. In other languages Rosati (1994) furnishes an illuminating introduction to his text and translation, while Benker (1987) argues that aspects of Achilles' portrayal draw attention to various flaws in the emperor Domitian.

A number of modern studies in languages other than English deal with the *Thebaid* and *Achilleid*. Taisne (1994) explores the images and allusions in the works of Statius and attempts to locate their sources. Delarue (2000) discusses how Statius alludes to and adapts the works of his predecessors and examines the thematic and structural unity of his epics. The *Epicedion* of Delarue et al. (1996) contains individual essays by modern scholars of Statius from a variety of critical perspectives in different languages.

CHAPTER THIRTY-EIGHT

Silius Italicus

Raymond D. Marks

The *Punica* of Silius Italicus was in its day an anomaly. Taking as its subject an event from Roman history, the Second Punic War, it hearkened back to the late Republic, when historical epic flourished, and defied the trend among epic poets in the first century CE to write on mythological themes; one thinks, in particular, of the epics of Silius' contemporaries, the *Argonautica* of Valerius Flaccus and the *Thebaid* and *Achilleid* of Statius (see Chapters 36 and 37, by Zissos and Dominik). From the perspective of epic's subsequent development, the *Punica* is doubly anomalous in that mythological epic not only continues to predominate after Silius, but epics on a grand scale – and the *Punica*, at 17 books, is the longest to have come down to us from Roman antiquity – do not really resurface until the Christian epics of the fifth century CE; here one may compare Silius' successor Claudian, whose epics are comparatively short (see Chapters 40 and 39, by Trout and Barnes). Traditionally, the *Punica* has benefited little from this place in Roman literary history: for recalling an older tradition of historical epic composition, it is considered old-fashioned and, for being the last of the large-scale epics, it is looked upon as the final specimen of a dying breed. Yet however out-of-step or belated the *Punica* may seem to some today, its poet certainly did not see it as such. It embraces unapologetically the vast expanse of the epic tradition, both Roman and Greek, over which it gazes, and although its theme is drawn from the distant, historical past, it strives to speak to its times. Moreover, for rejecting the retreat of his contemporaries and successors into the world of Greek mythology, Silius appears all the less resigned to the marginalization of epic within the literary landscape of his day; to the contrary, it bespeaks of an earnest attempt to assert the abiding value and relevance of the genre to Rome's cultural heritage.

The author of the *Punica*, whose full name is Tiberius Catius Asconius Silius Italicus, was born during the reign of Tiberius, probably in 28 CE. He was an advocate in his early years, an informer (*delator*) under Nero, and consul in 68 CE. During the civil wars of 69, he allied himself with Vitellius against the Flavian faction, but does not appear to have suffered for this choice: under the first Flavian emperor, Vespasian, he served as proconsul in Asia in 77–8, and one of his sons was suffect consul under the third, Domitian, in 94 (McDermott and Orentzel 1977: 24–7). Shortly after his proconsulship, it seems, Silius retired from public life to Naples and there began the *Punica*, which he worked on from about 80 to 98, composing at a rate of roughly one book per year (Wistrand 1956). Suffering from an incurable disease, he starved himself to death by 102.

Silius was a devoted admirer of the poet Virgil; he bought the land around his tomb (Mart. 11.48–9) and celebrated his birthday more dutifully than his own (Plin. *Ep.* 3.7.8). Such admiration is no less evident in his poetry than in his personal life. Virgil is, by far, Silius' most significant epic model in the *Punica*, and it is an affiliation revealed straightaway in the opening verses of its proem. "Ordior arma, quibus caelo se gloria tollit / Aeneadum patiturque ferox Oenotria iura / Carthago" (1.1–3: "I begin with arms, by which the glory of the Aeneadae raises itself up to heaven and ferocious Carthage suffers Oenotrian laws."). The second word of the *Punica*, *arma*, recalls the first word of the *Aeneid* ("arma uirumque cano," 1.1), the rhythm of the first verse imitates that of the *Aeneid*'s, and the Romans are pointedly called *Aeneadum* at the beginning of the second. The prominence with which Silius here acknowledges Virgil is consistent with the central importance of the *Aeneid* to his epic as a whole. Virgil's guiding hand can be seen everywhere in the *Punica*, from its diction, phrasing, and meter to its choice of motifs, descriptive touches, and rhetorical tropes. Allusions to the *Aeneid* abound, and many of Silius' characters and episodes are drawn, in whole or in part, from its pages. The war between Rome and Carthage is even conceived as a continuation of the *Aeneid*, not only in that Dido's curse provides its cause, but in that a Virgilian teleology defines its end (von Albrecht 1964: 144–84; Ahl et al. 1986: 2493–501; Hardie 1993: *passim*; Pomeroy 2000).

There are, nevertheless, some notable differences between the two epics, and Silius, no less subtly and allusively, calls our attention to them in his proem. Virgil's opening formula, "arma uirumque cano", outlines, in Homeric terms, the two-fold theme of the *Aeneid*: it will be, in part, about war (*arma*), like the *Iliad*, and, in part, about a hero's journey (*uirum*), like the *Odyssey*; these parts correspond, to the epic's second and first halves, respectively. Turning to Silius' *arma* and the allusion to Virgil it evokes, we are struck by the absence of a corresponding *uirumque* in his opening formula and acknowledge a difference in the *Punica*'s scope: unlike the *Aeneid*, it will recount an Iliadic war throughout (*arma*) rather than an Odyssean journey (*uirumque*) in part. Silius keeps this promise not only by his choice of theme – the *Punica* is, after all, about a war – but by the consistent manner in which he deploys it over the course of the epic. A considerable portion of the poem is devoted to military matters; according to one estimate, battle scenes and troop catalogues account for about 5,000 (around 40 percent) of its 12,202 verses (Matier 1989b: 5). Furthermore, many of its seventeen books are structured around major conflicts and campaigns: Hannibal's siege of Saguntum (1–2), Hannibal's march to Italy (3), the battles at the Ticinus and Trebia (4), the battle at Lake Trasimene (5), Fabius' dictatorship (7), the battle at Cannae (9–10), Hannibal's defeats in Italy (12), Marcellus' siege of Syracuse (14), Scipio's Spanish campaign (15–16), and Scipio's African campaign (17).

As *uirumque* in the *Aeneid*'s proem also identifies its hero, its absence in the *Punica*'s proem points to another difference between the two epics: whereas Virgil's epic is unified by the deeds of one man (*uir*), namely Aeneas, Silius' is not. The force of this disavowal has not always hit home with readers of the *Punica*, many of whom have insisted, despite it, that the epic should conform to the *Aeneid*'s example (Matier 1989a: 3–4). The *Punica*, however, simply does not have an Aeneas, someone who is a hero both in the narratological sense, i.e. "hero" defined as the character around whom the action of the epic principally revolves, and in what we may call the ethico-cultural sense, i.e. "hero" defined as the character who best represents the ethical and cultural ideals of his society. The Carthaginian leader Hannibal comes close to satisfying the first definition but, as he is the perfidious enemy of Rome, hardly satisfies the second. Conversely, Romans such as Fabius, Paulus, or Scipio represent certain Roman ideals, but, as they are many, clearly cannot be, each, the hero of the epic in the narratological sense. What Silius offers, instead, is an alternative to the Virgilian model or, better yet, an adaptation of it. On this his identification of the Romans in the proem is illuminating: they are *Aeneadum* at the beginning of the second verse and *uiros*, Virgil's *uir* in the plural, a few verses later: "da, Musa, decus memorare laborum / antiquae Hesperiae, quantosque ad bella crearit / et quot Roma uiros" (1.3–5: "Muse, allow me to recall the glorious labors of ancient Hesperia, and how great and how many men Rome bred for battles"). The hero of the *Punica*, so it is revealed, is not one, but many, the Roman many; these will be the "Aeneas" or "Aeneases", around whom the epic's action revolves and in whom its heroic ideals are embodied (von Albrecht 1964: 20–3).

Silius' failure to acknowledge Lucan in the proem is no less revealing. Indeed, it is curious that Silius, facing the challenge of composing an historical epic, prefers to bridge the gulf that separates his work from the *Aeneid*, as we have just seen, than to identify it with the *Bellum civile*, an epic, by all appearances, better suited for the task; its subject, after all, is historical, its theme war, its heroes many. Silius' view of epic and vision of Rome clashed too radically with Lucan's, however. Whereas Lucan grimly describes a Rome polluted by civil strife, Silius taps into the commemorative tradition of epic poetry; he observes the ancient dictate of the genre, to sing of *klea andrôn*, a phrase echoed in *gloria Aeneadum* (1.1–2). Lucan also offers a pessimistic view of war; for him ambition in arms is crooked, martial valor an oxymoron. Silius, on the other hand, celebrates Rome's quest for military glory; the immortal glory obtained by arms, he says, will be his theme ("arma, quibus caelo se gloria tollit," 1.1). The moralizing tone of the *Punica* as a whole confirms this initial impression. That the Romans follow the just and divinely sanctioned cause and in doing so exhibit their *fides* or trustworthiness, in particular, is emphasized repeatedly and with little equivocation (von Albrecht 1964: 55–86). In Lucan, by contrast, it is difficult to identify anyone who is not, in some measure, implicated in crimes against his fellow citizens and thus guilty of the very opposite of *fides*, namely *perfidia* or perfidy. While this difference in approach reflects, to some degree, a difference in historical subject – for Lucan civil war, for Silius a war against a foreign foe – the fact, nevertheless, remains that they could have selected different themes for their epics, but did not. These poets are making choices, and Silius' choice, at least, is to sing of Rome's glorious rise rather than her ignominious decline, and to that end he found Virgil's *arma* better suited than Lucan's *bella*.

Notwithstanding his expressed allegiance to Virgil, Silius draws extensively from other epic poets, Lucan included. Many of his episodes and characters, especially Hannibal, have models in the *Bellum civile*, and his grotesque desciptions of death and fondness for geographical and ethnographical detail appear to show Lucan's influence as well (Brouwers 1982; Ahl et al. 1986: 2501–4, 2511–19). Another historical epic that may have influenced Silius is Ennius' *Annales*, which, in fact, covered the Second Punic War in Books 8 and 9 (see Chapter 31, by Goldberg). Unfortunately, the *Annales* is preserved in such a fragmentary state that little can be definitively said about Silius' familiarity with the work; a few scattered allusions to it, though, have been identified, and there is the possibility that the *Punica* was originally planned to comprise eighteen books in imitation of Ennius' (Häussler 1978: 148–61; Matier 1991). Silius avails himself of still other, non-historical epics, chief among which are Homer's *Iliad* and *Odyssey* (Juhnke 1972: 13–24, 185–226; Ripoll 2001). Sometimes, he follows Homer quite closely, as in the battle between Scipio the Elder and the river Trebia in Book 4, which is modeled after Achilles' battle with the Scamander in *Iliad* 21. More often, however, allusions to Homer work in tandem with allusions to others; the Nekyia of Book 13 and the funeral games of Book 16, for example, show the influence of *Odyssey* 11 and *Iliad* 23, but have much in common with similar episodes in *Aeneid* 6 and 5 as well. The influence of Ovid's *Metamorphoses* (Bruère 1958, 1959) is also evident at points, and to a lesser extent that of Valerius Flaccus (Ripoll 1999) and perhaps Statius (Venini 1969).

The other major font from which the *Punica* draws is prose history, especially Livy's account of the Second Punic War in the third decade of his *Ab urbe condita*. This affiliation too is announced in the proem. Touching on the general theme of his epic in 1.3–11, Silius says that the fortunes of both sides, Roman and Carthaginian, varied considerably in all three Punic wars: "quaesitum diu, qua tandem poneret arce / terrarum Fortuna caput" (1.7–8: "it was a long time in question on which citadel Fortune would finally place the head of the world"). After explaining that the Carthaginians three times (i.e. before each war) broke their treaties with Rome (1.8–11), he then clarifies in 1.12–14 what made the second war different from the others: "sed medio finem bello excidiumque uicissim / molitae gentes, propiusque fuere periclo, / quis superare datum" ("But in the middle war the peoples strove, in turn, to finish off and extinguish each other, and those to whom it was given to prevail were closer to danger"). Between these two statements Silius echoes what was one sentence in Livy's preface to his account of the Second Punic War (Liv. 21.1.2): "adeo uaria fortuna belli ancepsque Mars fuit ut proprius periculum fuerint qui uicerunt" ("so shifting was the fortune of war and so indeterminate its warfare that those who conquered were closer to danger"). Just as at the beginning of its proem the *Punica* identifies itself by allusion with the Virgilian epic, so, later, it identifies itself by allusion with Livian historiography.

That Livy is a privileged historical source for Silius is demonstrated by numerous correspondences between the two in both details of historical fact and interpretation (Nicol 1936: 96–125). Although Silius surely must have drawn on other sources, especially in the second half of the *Punica*, where Livy's influence is less conspicuous, none appears to have been used as extensively as Livy. As for the once fashionable view that Silius relies on earlier annalists when he departs from Livy, this has been discredited not least of all because so little of those annalists remains that we cannot reliably assess the extent to which he might have used them (Nesselrath 1986). It would be wrong, however, to think of the *Punica* simply as a versified history or an epic translation of Livy. It is, at its core, a poem, which, as such, does not strive to be comprehensive, scholarly, or accurate in its use of historical sources, but aims at telling its own epic truths and its own epic story. To this end, Silius strips down Livy's account to basic elements, such as prominent persons and major events, draws from them a coherent dramatic story centered on certain guiding themes, and then casts that story in an epic idiom, replete with heroic *aristeiai*, supernatural events, and divine interventions.

The resultant "epicization" of history has not always been well received by readers of the *Punica*, some of whom have faulted it for being too "epic," others for being too "historical" (von Albrecht 1964: 9–14). It is granted, of course, that achieving such a synthesis can be difficult; the historical subject and the vehicle of its exposition, the epic genre, may carry incompatible or competing expectations, and Silius' application of divine machinery to his historical theme has, for one, evoked vociferous criticism from scholars (Feeney 1991: 301–12). Yet we must not forget that composing epic and composing history were not mutually exclusive activities, as the tradition of historical epic poetry in Rome, of which Silius himself is a part, amply attests. Second, the very fact that readers of the *Punica* have arrived at such contradictory, critical judgments suggests that the fault lies less with Silius' compositional strategy or his execution thereof than with the failure of critics to accept the epic on its own terms, as a work that sincerely aims to reconcile its epic form and historical content, as far as possible, to their mutual benefit.

Consider Livy's view of the war, to which Silius alludes in the proem, that those who won it were the closer to defeat. This interpretation so deeply influences Silius' account of events that he deploys it on an epic-wide scale: Rome's defeats comprise seven books of the *Punica*, beginning in Book 4 and ending with her most humiliating defeat at Cannae in Books 9 and 10, while in Book 11 her fortunes begin to improve and continue to do so until she wins the war in Book 17, another seven-book group. Livy's interpretation, as we can see, gives Silius the theme around which to structure his narrative: the two extremes of Roman fortune, which are balanced out, as are the terms of the paradox itself. To bring the paradox into such bold relief, however, Silius must subordinate chronological to thematic concerns and must, therefore, abandon Livy's annalistic method of composition, which requires a thorough account of a year's events to be followed by those of the next. Expanding upon or condensing events achieves the desired effect; seven books (4–10) are devoted to Rome's defeats early in the war, though these events cover only three years, 218–216 BCE, and another seven (11–17) to Rome's recovery and victory, though these events cover, disproportionately, fifteen years, 215–201 BCE (cf. Wallace 1968). In the end, history not only serves epic, but epic serves history, and one might even say that the *Punica* turns out to be a better vehicle for conveying Livy's paradoxical interpretation of the war than Livy himself.

Such interplay between epic and history is no less crucial to the *Punica*'s conception than to its overall design. Early on, for example, the two work together through Juno to set the war in motion. This goddess, picking up where she left off in the *Aeneid*, continues to harbor anger and resentment toward the Romans, those descendants of ancient Troy and of Trojan Aeneas (1.21–8). A more recent event, though, galls her too, the First Punic War; by it she wished to check Rome, which was rising at the expense of Carthage, but failed when her beloved city bowed in defeat (1.29–37). Since then she has found a new agent by which to settle the old score, the Carthaginian Hannibal, who takes on the full force of the goddess's wrath ("iamque deae cunctas sibi belliger induit iras / Hannibal," 1.38–9) and, with that, becomes the heir to her two-fold legacy of hostility toward Rome. Silius underlines this very point shortly thereafter in the retrospective digression of 1.81–139; there, Hannibal, as a boy, vows to destroy Rome both in the presence of his father Hamilcar, who would be defeated in the First Punic War, and before a statue of Dido in a temple dedicated to her in Carthage (Küppers 1986: 61–92). Later, in the ekphrasis of Hannibal's shield in Book 2 Silius ties together these two pasts once again; the shield's engraved images reveal a chain of cause-and-effect, leading from the story of Dido and Aeneas to Hannibal's vow, the First Punic War, and the beginning of the present war (2.406–452) (Vessey 1975; Küppers 1986: 154–164). In sum, for Silius Hannibal is both the avenger of Carthage's, and his father's, defeat in the First Punic War and the executor of Dido's ancient curse against Aeneas' descendants. Epic and history, converging in the Carthaginian, thus give rise to a war and a poem about war.

Epic and history continue to work together in shaping the course of the war, and we witness this especially through the figure of Hannibal, whose changing fortunes in the war are complemented by changes to his epic models. As he enjoys success early on, the ancient enemies of Troy and Aeneas, as we know them from Homer and Virgil, appear to live again through him and join in his victories. His swift, deadly wrath evokes comparison with Achilles (*Pun.* 7.120–2), as does his ornately decorated shield in Book 2, which is modeled after the Greek's in *Iliad* 18. At Cannae, Diomedes is reborn in Hannibal, whose encounter with Scipio in *Punica* 9 (411–69) is in many respects a replay of his own with Ares in *Iliad* 5. Avenging Asbyte's death at Saguntum in *Punica* 2 (188–263), Hannibal mirrors Turnus, who avenges Camilla's in *Aeneid* 11, and elsewhere is regularly aided and protected by Juno, the same goddess who helps the Rutulian in the *Aeneid*. But as Hannibal's fortunes change after Cannae, so do his epic models. This new Achilles, invading the land of Troy's descendants, wreaks havoc until a Roman Achilles emerges, Scipio, who, invading Africa in Book 17, transforms him into a vanquished Hector. Whereas in his victory at Cannae Hannibal played the role of Diomedes, that legendary enemy of the gods, in Book 12, when he faces off against Jupiter at Rome (605–728), he more closely resembles the ill-fated Patroclous in defeat. The most ironic epic twist in Hannibal's story, however, is his transformation into the object of Dido's curse, Aeneas: when leaving Italy in Book 17, he recalls Aeneas abandoning Troy (17.211–217), and soon after, when caught in a sea-storm on his way to Carthage (17.236–89), he again recalls Aeneas, who was likewise caught in a sea-storm before reaching Carthage in *Aeneid* 1. Hannibal, who led Carthage into the war, is thus transformed, on the eve of her defeat, into the original cause of her woes (R. D. Marks 2003: 138–43).

Hannibal's story may be written in and by the pasts of epic and history, but there is a divine plan for Rome's future that guides and determines the course of the war as well. In Book 3, as Hannibal crosses the Alps, the goddess Venus questions Jupiter about Rome's fate. The god explains to her that he himself has brought about the war because the Romans have become restive and idle in recent years and have ceased to thirst for fame and glory, as their forefathers once did. The war, he says, will compel them to change their ways and, further, will set them on a path toward world rule: "magnae molis opus multoque labore parandum / tot populos inter soli sibi poscere regnum" (3.582–3: "a great effort is required of Rome, and with much toil she must prepare to demand for herself alone hegemony among so many peoples"). On the one hand, this teleological move represents yet another gesture of reconciliation between the *Punica*'s historical theme and its epic medium; by subjecting the events of the Second Punic War to the mechanisms of fate and divine governance, it brings the war in line with a Virgilian, epic vision of history, such as one finds in Jupiter's speech to Venus in *Aeneid* 1, where a similar teleology ties the epic past of Aeneas to Rome's historical future. On the other hand, this move entails a bold and original reworking of the epic's historical subject. For one, it distances from the war the very figure who is most closely associated with it, Hannibal. Indeed, despite his central role in its conception and his sustained presence in the *Punica*, the war is, in the final analysis, not about him – he merely facilitates a much grander design – but about Rome (Vessey 1982: 333–4). Likewise, it draws our attention away from the ostensible theme of the epic, the Second Punic War itself. For that "external" conflict between Rome and Carthage turns out to be a framing story within which a more important story plays itself out, namely, Rome's "internal" struggle to break out of her malaise and to transform herself into a city worthy of her imperial destiny.

Silius sets the stage for this story within the story in Books 1–2, where he recounts the siege and fall of Rome's Spanish ally Saguntum. This city's demise is itself a significant historical event in that it marks the traditional starting point of the war between Rome and Carthage (cf. Polyb. 3.6; Liv. 21.5–6). In Silius' hands, however, it also becomes a critical point of reference for his treatment of Rome's early struggles in the war (von Albrecht 1964: 55–62; Vessey 1974b). Telling, for one, is his moralizing view of the Saguntines' resistance, which testifies to their *fides* or trustworthiness. This point is most conspicuously made in Book 2, where the god Hercules, pitying the city and despairing of her chances, calls upon the goddess Fides herself to inspire the Saguntines to stay true to Rome and to resist (2.475–525). Rome's moral character and, above all, her *fides* will be likewise put to the test under trying circumstances, during her series of defeats in Books 4–10. Of particular note, however, is Saguntum's fall and the manner in which it is achieved. In response to Hercules' intervention, the goddess Juno orders the Fury Tisiphone to compel Saguntum to fall by her own hand (2.526–91), which the city does as her citizens, thereupon, commit collective suicide (2.592–680). Through this innovative account – the emphasis on suicide is largely unhistorical – Silius introduces a paradox that will prove to be crucial for our understanding of Rome's story in the epic, that out of defeat there comes victory. By this is meant not simply that one may achieve a kind of moral victory by defeat, though the Saguntines and Romans both do, each winning immortal glory for facing adversity with *fides* (2.696–707; 9.340–53). Rather, defeat may lead, in still more concrete terms, to victory on the battlefield. Indeed, it is no accident that Saguntum, throughout the account of her siege, reminds us of her ally Rome (Dominik 2003: 474–80); for she is, as it were, Rome's Doppelgänger and, by her self-sacrifice, becomes a surrogate victim, which allows the real Rome to be spared and, in the end, to win the war (McGuire 1997: 209–10).

That one city's loss should be another's gain is a notion familiar to readers of Virgil's *Aeneid*, where the destruction of Troy is seen as the compensatory sacrifice for the future rise of Rome. Yet while Silius accomplishes much the same by the fall of Saguntum in *Punica* 2, he does not stop there. Saguntum, it turns out, is not only a sacrifical substitute for Rome, but a prefiguration (cf. von Albrecht 1964: 24–7): before Rome may rise, she too must fall and, in doing so, even follows her predecessor's suicidal example. We see this in the very first Roman death in the war, that of Catus, who before the battle at the Ticinus rides headlong into a spear that never should have hit him (4.134–42). We also see it in the self-destructive acts of Rome's leaders thereafter: Scipio the Elder, who rushes out to oppose Hannibal at the Ticinus and the Trebia in Book 4, but is twice defeated and almost perishes in each battle; Flaminius, who marches into Hannibal's trap at Lake Trasimene and is defeated and killed there in Book 5; and Minucius, who in Book 7 rashly challenges Hannibal, though he is saved at the last minute by Fabius. Fabius, in fact, is the only Roman to get the better of Hannibal in these books; as dictator in Book 7, he turns the tables on the Carthaginian, who, impatiently pressing for battle, is repeatedly frustrated and worn down by his adversary's delaying tactics.

Although Fabius successfully staves off defeat and for doing so wins the praise of his fellow Romans (7.730–50) and of the poet himself (6.619–40; 7.1–9), even he cannot prevent the disaster to come in Books 9–10; there, the consul Varro leads Rome into the battle at Cannae and to her worst defeat of the war. This battle represents the low point of Rome's fortunes as well as the climax in the story of her self-destruction, and Silius innovates widely to impress this fact upon us. He introduces, for example, the themes of familial strife and suicide through the fictional tale of Solymus, a Roman who on the eve of battle mistakenly kills his father, Satricus, and then in despair kills himself (9.66–177). In connection with the battle we encounter several allusions to Rome's future civil wars. At the end of Book 8, a Roman soldier, who rattles on about the coming defeat (656–76), recalls Lucan's bacchant, who similarly foretells events from the civil war between Caesar and Pompey at the end of *Bellum civile* 1 (673–95). In the catalogue of Roman forces in Book 8 and in the battle narrative of Books 9 and 10 Silius also includes several Romans who, according to our historical sources, never were at Cannae, but whose names, tellingly, evoke those of participants in Rome's civil wars in the first century BCE and in 69 CE (McGuire 1997: 136–44). Silius' strategy throughout Books 4–10 and, especially, at Cannae in Books 9–10 is clear: what appear to be a string of Hannibalic victories turn out to be, in fact, a series of *devotiones* or suicidal sacrifices. Rome has been killing herself. As pitiable as this fate may be, however, we must not forget the lesson of Saguntum's demise, that faithful acts of self-sacrifice, though they may bring defeat, may also bring victory. Rome's story after Cannae exposes the truth of this paradox; for her collective self-immolation has allowed a new, stronger Rome to be born, like a phoenix, out of the ashes of the old.

In Books 11–17 the war takes on an entirely different look. Roman victories now come in bunches, and the Carthaginians fail to win another major conflict for the rest of the war. While it is, in part, a stroke of good fortune, Hannibal's decline, that changes the tide (Fucecchi 1990), Rome undergoes some significant changes herself. Whereas before she was unified for her self-destruction, she is now unified for her self-preservation and, ultimately, victory: shortly after Cannae, for example, we see Scipio compelling a band of deserters to stand by Rome (10.415–48) and, later, those at Rome pulling together and acting as one (12.295–319). Rome is also revitalized and rejuvenated after Cannae, a change observable especially in her leadership. Generals emerge who take the war to the Carthaginians: Fulvius takes Capua in Book 13 and Marcellus Syracuse in Book 14. A new-found vitality is seen in leaders such as Nero, who in Book 15 rushes to head off Hasdrubal at the Metaurus, and the aged Livius, who, joining Nero there, becomes young again in the victory. Of Rome's leaders in the post-Cannae era, however, it is Scipio who most embodies the qualities of his reborn city: young, swift, energetic, he makes short work of the Carthaginians in Spain (Books 15–16) and then invades Africa, where his victory over Hannibal at Zama brings the war to a triumphant conclusion (Book 17). As we can see, in the post-Cannae years Rome is transformed into a new, reinvigorated city. No doubt, this is the city Jupiter hoped and planned for in Book 3, a Rome preparing herself for world rule.

The *Punica* evolves in significant ways up to its very end, and it is necessary, therefore, that one's reading evolves with it. In particular, the notion of collective heroism must be reconsidered in light of Scipio's emergence on the scene in Books 15–17. Certain individuals, to be sure, have already stood out from the Roman many; Fabius, Marcellus, and Paulus come to mind. Yet in Scipio we encounter the most heroic and "epic" Roman of them all. No other is the subject of so many omens and prophecies or is attended by so many miraculous events (e.g., *Pun.* 4.101–30, 7.487–91, 9.543–6, 13.503–15, 15.180–99, 16.580–91; Fucecchi 1993). Lengthy episodes of traditional, epic character are designed for him, such as the funeral games in Book 16 (275–591) and the Nekyia of Book 13, in which he encounters shades of the dead (381–895). He is also figured as a new Hercules, particularly early in Book 15, where he is visited by the goddesses Virtus and Voluptas (18–128), just as Hercules was said to have been visited by the goddesses Arete and Kakia (Bassett 1966). Furthermore, Scipio stands in closer relation to the gods than any other. He often enjoys their favor and support (e.g., 4.417–79, 9.428–59, 15.138–48, 17.48–58) and is even the son of the god Jupiter, a pedigree confidently asserted by the poet himself in the epic's final two verses (17.653–4). Although Silius has not written, as Virgil did, an epic about arms and a man – there are in the *Punica*, as we have seen, many men – it might be said, nevertheless, that he has written an epic that begins with arms (*ordior arma*, 1.1), but ends with a man.

Scipio's story, so considered, has important consequences for political interpretations of the epic. For years scholars were reluctant to read the *Punica* in any significant relation to the Flavian context in which it was composed. The epic, so it was thought, is the work of a nostalgic, escapist poet and reveals itself as such through infrequent allusions to contemporary figures and events, its heroization of Rome's distant past, and plaintive references to subsequent moral decline. This interpretation holds up reasonably well for much of the epic, but fails to take into proper account Scipio's rise to power in the Roman leadership in its final books; therein, as Rome's gods, people, and Senate throw their support behind him (15.138–48, 16.580–99, 16.698–700), the war effort becomes, essentially, his personal charge and their collective fate his personal responsibility. If we see in this development the prospect of a new political reality in Rome, that of one-man rule, and, as such, a sign of things to come, we would be right. In Book 3, after Jupiter explains the purpose of the war (571–83), a passage discussed above, he goes on to prophesy events from the war itself, ending with Scipio's victory at Zama (584–92), and from that point catapults us into the first century CE with a prophecy about the reigns of the Flavian emperors, Vespasian, Titus, and Domitian (593–629). In a move reminiscent of Jupiter's teleology in *Aeneid* 1, whereby Virgil ties the past of Aeneas to the future of Augustus, Silius here links the past of the Second Punic War to the future of the Flavian emperors and, thereby, suggests that in the war Rome not only starts on her path toward world rule, as we have seen, but takes her first, critical steps toward her more distant, imperial future (cf. McGuire 1997: 98–103; Ripoll 1998: 492–5).

In recent years scholars have shown a greater awareness of the *Punica*'s potential to speak to the political realities of its day. There is, though, considerable difference of opinion on how the epic is to be read as such. According to some, the epic advocates a return to the old ways of the Republic and in doing so expresses opposition to the Flavian regime, more narrowly, or to the institution of the Principate, more broadly (Mendell 1924: 100–2; Ahl et al. 1986: 2556–8; McGuire 1997: *passim*). Others believe that the epic's view of the past is consistent with the Flavians' and especially Domitian's call for a return to traditional values and thus does not reflect Silius' opposition to the contemporary regime, but his complicity with it or, at least, with its policy of moral restoration (McDermott and Orentzel 1977; Liebeschuetz 1979a: 167–79; Mezzanotte 1995). There is some truth to both of these interpretations, but neither, on its own, satisfactorily describes the complex picture of Rome that Silius paints through his epic. It is true, on the one hand, that he praises Rome during the Second Punic War for her moral character and contrasts her with Rome in later days when her morals would decline and she would become embroiled in civil conflict (*Pun.* 3.588–90, 9.346–53, 10.657–8, 14.684–8; cf. 13.850–67). On the other hand, the Rome we witness in the epic has to change and, in fact, does over the course of the war; had she not, she would have been destroyed by Hannibal and would have failed to live up to the destiny of world rule, which Jupiter imposed on her in Book 3. It cannot be said, therefore, that Silius subscribes to a uniformly positive or negative opinion of the old Republic he describes in his epic or of the imperial future that would follow and in which he himself lived; he offers a more balanced, even-handed view of both, acknowledging their respective advantages and disadvantages (Cf. Laudizi 1989: 155–8; Ripoll 1998: 526–8).

Silius does not spell out in the *Punica* what his ideal Rome might look like, but one may suppose that it would combine the best of both Romes, the old-time morality of the Republic and the military strength of the Empire, and it might even be said that Rome, as she is under Scipio in the epic's final books, comes quite close to this vision. While it may still be disputed whether Silius viewed the city in his own day, Domitian's Rome, as such, it is, nevertheless, clear that with the *Punica* he gave the emperor and his fellow Romans an instructive lesson, drawn from their own past, about how they might fight through times of adversity with *fides* and fortitude and might reinvent themselves without losing, in the process, those core values that had been commonly held among them and would continue to hold them together. If there is one lesson to draw from the epic, then, it may be this, that striking a balance between tradition and innovation is critical to Rome's survival and success. And coming from Silius, a survivor himself, such a message is indeed fitting; having lived under no less than twelve emperors and through a year of bloody civil war, he saw Rome reinvent herself many times, yet persevere nonetheless.

Although the poet Martial speaks quite highly of Silius' poetry in several of his epigrams, modern critics have been less charitable, preferring to reiterate the negative judgment of Pliny the Younger in support of their own: Silius "would write with greater care than talent" ("scribebat carmina maiore cura quam ingenio," *Ep.* 3.7.5) (Vessey 1974a; Matier 1989b: 2–5). In recent years, though, this judgment has come under serious scrutiny (Laudizi 1989: 19–26), and an appreciation of Silius' sophisticated, literary artistry has begun to emerge (Pomeroy 1989). Even so, Silius' influence on western literature has never been considerable. There is very meager evidence that he was read or known before the fourteenth century, and even after the discovery of a manuscript of the *Punica* introduced the epic to the modern world in 1417, it has never had a wide readership; it does appear, however, to have enjoyed some popularity in England through the end of the eighteenth century (Bassett 1953). Today, the *Punica* is in search of readers, who may look to Delz (1987) for the Latin text, to Duff (1934) for an English translation, and to Spaltenstein (1986, 1990) for a commentary covering all seventeen books.

FURTHER READING

Although the *Punica* has received much more scholarly attention in Germany and Italy than in England and America, there are several fine studies of the epic in English. Chief among them is Ahl, Davis, and Pomeroy 1986, which offers a helpful overview of the poem and addresses many of its major themes, characters, and literary influences. As for studies of a more narrow scope, there are a number of good works on Silius' models and sources.

Nicol 1936 remains an indispensable work on his use of historical materials, and his relation to epic predecessors has been discussed by Matier 1991 (Ennius), Hardie 1993, and Pomeroy 2000 (Virgil), and Bruère 1958 and 1959 (Ovid). Also, the influence of philosophy is not inconsiderable, as Billerbeck 1985 and Matier 1990 have demonstrated. Important studies of individual characters include Vessey 1982 on Hannibal and Bassett 1966 on Scipio, while the role of the gods in the poem has been treated by Feeney 1991.

Among late twentieth-century trends in Silian scholarship, one may note, in particular, the equally compelling, though very different political readings of McDermott and Orentzel 1977 and McGuire 1997 and the gendered readings of Augoustakis 2003a and 2003b. Silius' place within the literary culture of his times is the subject of two excellent studies, Vessey 1974a and Pomeroy 1989. For an English translation, there is Duff 1934, which also includes the Latin text.

CHAPTER THIRTY-NINE

Claudian

Michael H. Barnes

1   Life and Career

Claudius Claudianus, like many of the greatest Latin poets, came from the provinces of the empire. He was born in Alexandria, Egypt sometime around 370 CE, and died a young man, probably in 404. One of Claudian's last works, a panegyric celebrating the sixth consulship of the emperor Honorius, is confidently dated to that year, and we possess nothing else that would give us reason to think that he survived much longer. He lived in an age of great social and political ferment. Throughout the third century the Roman empire was beset by a grinding succession of emperors with short reigns and short fuses, by debilitating outbreaks of plague, and by ceaseless troubles along its vast frontiers. The solution of the emperor Diocletian in 285 was to divide the realm into western and eastern halves, thus creating two political entities that would, in time, meet two separate fates. The eastern, predominantly Greek-speaking half would continue, in various shapes, for well over a millennium, its capital at Constantinople finally falling to the Ottoman Turks in 1453. The western half, by contrast, succumbed early on to invasions by Germanic and other peoples, and in 476 the German general Odoacer deposed its young, feeble emperor, the ironically named Romulus Augustulus. The reign of Odoacer, who was proclaimed the king – not, significantly, the emperor – of Italy, still marks in the public consciousness the end of the Roman empire in the west.

Socially, the demographics of the empire had undergone near-revolutionary changes since the days of the Flavians in the late first century. Although the empire fought constantly to stem the tide of barbarian invasions on its borders, much of the imperial administrative corps was in fact already of barbarian stock, and the same can be said of the military. Stilicho, the most powerful man in the western empire between 395 and 408, was himself half-Vandal. In addition, a flourishing Christianity had reached the highest levels of imperial government and maintained an uneasy relationship with traditional religions throughout both halves of the empire. This tension required of the ambitious Roman citizen careful social and political navigation. In the West, for example, the city of Rome was still strongly pagan at the end of the fourth century, but the new capital at Milan was "the home of uncompromising Christian orthodoxy" (Cameron 1970: 228; see Matthews 1975: 183ff.). A successful politician would have to be competent in the religious and political languages of each city. There is some evidence, mainly a short Easter hymn entitled *De Salvatore* ("On the Savior"), that Claudian was at least nominally a Christian – the poem may have been just another commission – but he was characterized as a pagan by other ancient writers, including his contemporaries Augustine and Orosius. Augustine refers to Claudian as "a stranger to the name of Christ" ("a Christi nomine alienus," *De civ. Dei* 5.26), while the Christian apologist and historian Orosius, perhaps merely taking his cue from Augustine, describes him as "an exceptional poet, certainly, but an awfully stubborn pagan" ("poeta quidem eximius sed paganus pervicacissimus," *Adv. Pag.* 7.35.21). It is possible that both men were misinformed, and that Claudian was a quiet Christian, but the result is the same in either case: by no test can his poetry be called "Christian." (See the full discussion in Cameron 1970: 189ff., who cites Fargues's assertion (p. 195) that if we depended solely on Claudian's poetry for our knowledge of the period, we would never guess that Christianity existed at the time.)

Sometime in his early twenties Claudian left Alexandria to make his fortune in the West. His brilliant debut on the western political and literary scene came on January 1 of 395, an important year in the political history of the Roman empire. The powerful Catholic emperor Theodosius I ("the Great") died that same month, leaving the reins of power to his two young sons. The 18-year-old Arcadius now held the eastern throne at Constantinople, the 10-year-old Honorius the western seat at Milan. It is clear enough that Theodosius, while campaigning with his eastern armies in the West, had in the months before he died appointed Stilicho, a supremely ambitious and cunning general, to be the regent of young Honorius. Upon Theodosius' death, however, Stilicho quickly made his power play, asserting that the emperor had secretly made him regent not only of Honorius in the West, but also of Arcadius in the East. To make good this improbable, legally dubious claim on Arcadius – and thus against a succession of Arcadius' ministers, themselves not slow to grasp the political opportunities surrounding the rule of a young and, from all indications, dull-witted emperor – Stilicho needed not just his own military strength and political savvy, but a superb propagandist. To control the entire empire, he needed someone to do his talking for him, someone to make his claims, attack his enemies, and assert his influence as eloquently and as forcefully as the occasion demanded. Enter Claudian.

The Alexandrian poet's first published work in Latin was a celebration of the incoming consuls for 395, two young and inexperienced members of the wealthy and influential Anicii clan, named Probinus and Olybrius. Delivered publicly at Rome, during a ceremony of high pomp and visibility, the *Panegyricus dictus Olybrio et Probino consulibus* ("Panegyric for the Consuls Probinus and Olybrius") garnered immediate praise among the well-connected and well-educated at Rome for its liveliness, respect for tradition, and eloquence. Claudian's performance must go down as one of the more remarkable events in the literary world of the fourth century; heretofore he had published nothing in Latin, and his success immediately set his star high in the literary constellation, where it would not wane during his brief but prolific career. Indeed, only a few years later, in 400 or so, the Roman Senate expressed its admiration for Claudian by setting up, under the auspices of the emperors, a bronze statue of the poet in the Forum of Trajan (Cl. *Get. praef.* 7–10), the inscription on which has come down to us (*CIL* 6.1710). Claudian's meteoric rise, in its brevity and intensity, calls to mind the similar career of Lucan (on whom see Chapter 35, by Bartsch), who also moved in the highest imperial circles and who has likewise been condemned for his "rhetorical" style and for being less an epic poet than a historical one. Not for Claudian, however, Lucan's barely disguised contempt for his powerful patron, much less any real-world involvement in political conspiracy. Claudian was nothing if not loyal to Stilicho.

The *Panegyricus*, then, won the admiration of certain aristocrats at Rome, who brought him in turn to the court at Milan. There he attracted the attention of Stilicho, and when one year later (January 396) Claudian delivered another important panegyric, it is clear that the poet had aligned himself with the general. In his celebration of Honorius' third consulship (*Panegyricus dictus honorio Augusto tertium consuli*), Claudian goes out of his way to vouchsafe the arrangement that Stilicho claimed to have had with Theodosius (*III Cons.* 142–62). In the climax of the work, the dying Theodosius privately addresses Stilicho (151–53):

> ergo age, me quoniam caelestis regia poscit,
> tu curis succede meis, tu pignora solus
> nostra foue: geminos dextra tu protege fratres.

> Therefore come, since the heavens demand me:
> you take up my charge; you alone watch over
> my children: let your right hand protect my two sons.

Here, barely a year after his public debut, Claudian is not only delivering the official speech inaugurating the consulship of the reigning western emperor, but, by buttressing Stilicho's controversial claim to rule as regent over *both* emperors, he is also clearly indicating where his true allegiance lies. This will hardly be the last time Claudian redefines crucial events in Stilicho's favor.

This allegiance would define his career. Most of the rest of Claudian's major works are, in one way or another, vehicles to promote the achievements, claims, and political designs of his patron Stilicho. Even works that do not take Stilicho directly as their subject typically manage to reflect much of the glory of the occasion onto him: two other panegyrics celebrating Honorius' fourth and sixth consulships (in 398 and 404), for example, feature lengthy tributes to Stilicho that rather obscure the emperor himself. The few exceptions are the poem celebrating the consulship of Manlius Theodorus in 399, the majority of Claudian's sizable body of short poems and fragments, and the *De raptu Proserpinae* ("The abduction of Proserpina"), the mythological epic on which he seems to have worked intermittently for many years.

The panegyrics of 395 and 396 were followed in 397 by the two-book *In Rufinum* ("Against Rufinus"), a blistering postmortem of Flavius Rufinus, Stilicho's rival for control of Arcadius and, owing to his own close connection to Theodosius, the one-time regent of the eastern empire. Rufinus had been killed by the returning eastern army in November of 395, but Claudian's no-holds-barred attack on the memory of the dead man served a larger purpose of extolling Stilicho, presented throughout as the noble foil of a greedy, depraved Rufinus. Stilicho now found himself in need of such public propaganda, for he had lately been proclaimed a *hostis publicus* ("public enemy") by Rufinus' more dynamic and ambitious successor, the eunuch Eutropius. The charge was the result of Stilicho's recent indecisive battle with the Visigothic potentate Alaric (one of four such clashes; see below). Stilicho's precarious position was exacerbated by Eutropius' intrigue in North Africa with a powerful native prince named Gildo, who, since his appointment in 386 by Theodosius, had overseen the western empire's vital economic interests there, most importantly the grain supply on which Rome at this time was utterly dependent (Cl. *Get.* 17ff.; Cameron 1970: 93). Eutropius had induced Gildo to abandon the West and bring his wealthy territory under the control and protection of the East; thus would Eutropius augment his own power throughout the empire by crippling Rome with food shortages and economic stasis – and he would bleed Stilicho's authority in the bargain.

Stilicho's task was thus to get out of a potentially fatal political bind without embroiling himself personally in an open conflict with the other half of the empire. How to eliminate Gildo and wrest Africa and its grain away from the East and back to the West? His solution was Gildo's exiled brother Mascezel, who had lately arrived at Milan. The brothers were embroiled in a bloody feud, and so Stilicho outfitted Mascezel, shipped him off to war against Gildo, and kept a low profile. Mascezel quickly destroyed his brother, and an open breach between the two imperial courts was averted. (Mascezel, afterwards no longer useful to Stilicho, was killed in Italy not long after; our sources are rightly suspicious of Stilicho's role.) Claudian's *De bello Gildonico* ("The war against Gildo"), composed and recited right on the heels of Gildo's defeat, will be considered in detail in Section 3. For the moment it is enough to say that in the *De bello Gildonico* Claudian minimizes the obviously crucial role of Mascezel, playing up instead his status as victim of the cruel and lascivious Gildo, and foregrounds the timely decisiveness not, as usual, of Stilicho (here just the wise and loyal adviser) but of Honorius, since Stilicho had too much at stake to be portrayed as the prime mover against the East's profitable new acquisition. In addition to this up-to-the-minute historical epic – a *rara avis* in extant Greco-Roman literature – Claudian in 398 also composed a panegyric in honor of Honorius' fourth consulship and an epithalamium for the wedding of Honorius and Maria, Stilicho's daughter. Both texts afford opportunities to depart from the main subject and praise Stilicho in suitably lavish fashion, thereby reminding the audience who really wields the power at court.

Stilicho's root problem, the powerful Eutropius, remained. If anything, the eunuch's power, despite the setback with Gildo, had only increased. For in 398 Eutropius personally led the army in a successful campaign against the Huns in Armenia, and was rewarded with no less than the consulship for the year 399. This promotion was met, at Stilicho's bidding, by the savage (and savagely funny) invective of Claudian, who with the first book of his *In Eutropium* ("Against Eutropius") elevates the depravity of Eutropius to world-historical proportions and makes a case for the title of the greatest polemicist in the Latin language. But external events in the East soon brought about the eunuch's fall. In the summer of 399, before his consulship was over, Eutropius was deposed and exiled to Cyprus after the defeat of his troops by Gothic armies. Claudian celebrates Eutropius' defeat – styled, naturally, as Stilicho's victory – in a second book of *In Eutropium*. In addition to these two books of invective, Claudian in 399 also delivered, as an obvious counterpoint to Eutropius' consulship in the East, a panegyric celebrating the consulship of the esteemed Manlius Theodorus in the West.

In 400 Stilicho finally achieved the consulship. Claudian celebrated his patron's ascendancy with no less than three books of panegyric (*De consulatu Stilichonis I, II,* and *III*) that trace Stilicho's accomplishments in war – among them a truncated account of the war against Gildo that now entirely omits Mascezel – and illuminate his many virtues, with a heavy emphasis, especially in the mythologically inflected third book, on his transcendence of natural limitations. It is the capstone of Claudian's career as a panegyrist. Around this time Claudian married a bride handpicked by Serena, Stilicho's wife, and vacationed in Libya.

The following year, Alaric led an army of his countrymen over the Alps into Italy, overrunning the underprepared Roman units that lay in his way on the other side. He besieged Milan in early 402, sowing fear and panic throughout the city, and prompting Honorius to make plans to flee to Gaul. The city was eventually relieved by Stilicho, who forced Alaric to move southwest. Nevertheless, the relative ease with which Milan had been attacked led to the immediate decision to move the western capital further down into the Italian peninsula, to Ravenna. On Easter Sunday of that year the armies of Stilicho and Alaric met at Pollentia. The battle itself was little more than a draw, but the end result – a Gothic retreat and the conclusion of a formal treaty – earned Stilicho the credit for a victory. Yet by no means was it a decisive one: Alaric escaped, his forces checked and harried but, for all their disorganization, still potent. (He would lead his army back to Italy and famously sack Rome in 410.) Nevertheless Claudian celebrated Stilicho's achievement in the *De bello Getico* ("The Gothic War"), a masterpiece of epic propaganda delivered in Rome very soon after Pollentia, perhaps even in that very month.

Alaric's knack for survival led to claims by later writers that Stilicho had made a traitorous pact with him. That this was the third time (a decisive Roman victory at Verona some months later would be the fourth) that Alaric had eluded Stilicho in battle was no doubt evidence enough, for some, of a conspiracy; but such a view, in addition to being the product of hindsight, takes Alaric, a resourceful and opportunistic leader, too lightly. In the end, it is true that Stilicho's victory at Pollentia was partial and short-lived – so much so that, in light of the events of the next decade and despite the ringing claims of a thorough victory by Claudian and Prudentius, later writers, including Cassiodorus, could with little trouble portray it instead as a Gothic victory (Dewar 1996: xxxiv). The *De bello Getico*, then, affords us yet another opportunity to weigh the propagandist's immediate response against the slower verdict of history.

The last securely datable work we possess is the *Panegyricus dictus Honorio Augusto sextum consuli* ("Panegyric on the sixth consulship of the Emperor Honorius"), delivered in Rome at the beginning of 404. A healthy portion (127–330) of the poem is taken up by a narrative of the battles at Pollentia and, now, Verona, with its more advantageous outcome. Stilicho is in fact the dominant presence throughout the entire poem, and this presentation reflects the political reality in the western empire, where Stilicho's power over a weak emperor had been complete for some time. Stilicho was elected consul again in 405, and since Claudian did not write a panegyric on this occasion, or on the occasion of Stilicho's impressive victory at Faesulae in 406, we can only assume that he died sometime in 404. That Claudian left Stilicho as a result of the rapidly escalating political risks associated with his service is not out of the question; Stilicho had acquired a sizeable body of enemies over the years. Less likely is the theory that he fell out of favor with Stilicho and simply ceased production, for a poet of Claudian's caliber would not have remained long without a patron, at least in the West. (His merciless attacks on the eastern court over the years would seem to preclude any favorable reception in the East.) Yet however uncertain the circumstances of Claudian's fate, we do know that sometime before 408, and perhaps as early as 404–5, Stilicho gathered together Claudian's major political works and published them in a posthumous edition that presumably doubled as an omnibus propaganda pamphlet. Coupled with the unfinished state of several of Claudian's works – including an incomplete encomium of Serena – Stilicho's deed argues for Claudian's death, not his relocation.

Stilicho himself survived his propagandist by only a few years. His plan to control the eastern empire, by force where necessary, resulted in an alliance with Alaric that never yielded fruit. The combination of an invasion of Italy by the barbarian Radagaisus in 405, which occupied Stilicho for two years, and the challenge posed by the usurper Constantine III, declared emperor by the troops in Britain, proved too much for even this hardened political survivor to overcome. Other men caught Honorius' ear, and Stilicho was brought down in a palace coup and beheaded in August of 408.

One more work remains to be mentioned. Throughout his career, Claudian labored on a mythological epic, the unfinished *De raptu Proserpinae*. Its date of publication is a matter of some controversy, and the difficulties surrounding it highlight the comparative ease with which his political poetry may be dated. It is likely enough that the three books of the *De raptu* were recited and circulated separately over a period of several years, but this period might have been 395–7 (Gruzelier 1993: xvii–xxi), making the poem a product of his youthful leisure, one abandoned as he became ever more burdened by the rapid-fire commissions dictated by Stilicho's fortunes; or it may have been the pet work of a much longer time, from the summer of 397 to the end of his life, and so remaining unfinished for rather more natural reasons (Cameron 1970: 452–66). As it stands, the *De raptu* is three books long. Its subject is an old myth, familiar in its outlines from the *Homeric Hymn to Demeter* (see Connor 1993): Pluto's abduction of Proserpina, daughter of Ceres, for his bride. Book 1 introduces the principals, Book 2 describes the abduction, and Book 3 presents the agricultural aetiology that underlies the myth and sees the beginning of Ceres' search for Proserpina. It is Claudian's most famous work.

The *De raptu* is both highly traditional, its timeworn subject adorned by allusions to a cornucopia of Claudian's poetic forebears, and radically different from anything those earlier poets might have written. It is an extraordinarily visual poem, a testament to Claudian's tremendous gift for ecphrasis and the elaboration of fine detail. Brightness and color are leitmotifs, and the highly polished pageantry of the poem make it eminently readable. In the company of this epic are the remains of a pair of Gigantomachies, one in Greek and one in Latin. The Greek version is an early piece, written before Claudian left the East for Rome in the early 390s, and exists only in fragments; the Latin one, clearly unfinished, may well have suffered the same fate as the *De raptu* and been interrupted by his death. Cameron (1970: 467–73) at least thinks so, and there are no serious obstacles to this view.

Claudian's major works may be divided conveniently into four categories: (1) his panegyrics (eight in all: one for Probinus and Olybrius, three for Honorius, one for Manlius Theodorus, one for Stilicho, and the Fescennine verses and epithalamium for Honorius and Maria), (2) his invectives (*In Rufinum* and *In Eutropium*), (3) his epics (*De bello Gildonico, De bello Getico, De raptu Proserpinae*, and the two incomplete Gigantomachies), and (4) the so-called *carmina minora*, a body of shorter poems that range in scope from the political, including verses in honor of Stilicho's wife, to the inquisitive and playful. Claudian the high-powered propagandist also wrote light, ornamental verse on the wonders of the magnet, the lobster, Gallic mules, the phoenix, and the electric ray, and on the plight of poor lovers.

2 Considerations of Genre and Style

The reader who comes to this chapter having perused a few of Claudian's works – one of the invectives, say, or the *De raptu Proserpinae* – may be forgiven for wondering why Claudian merits a place in a volume devoted to ancient epic poetry. Such a reaction is in fact useful if it prompts readers to think about the generic requirements, as it were, of epic. Notwithstanding a generous, inclusive definition of epic poetry and an awareness of the potentially limiting artificiality of generic taxonomies, it must be admitted that the works of Claudian that are by consensus labeled his epics bear little superficial resemblance to the epics of Homer, Virgil, and Statius. They are, to start with, comparatively brief. The *De bello Gildonico* is 526 and the *De bello Getico* 647 lines long, each considerably shorter than any single book of the *Aeneid* or *Thebaid*. Moreover, while the contents of Claudian's epics are traditional enough – generals and wars, gods and giants, virgins and quests – the poetic style in which they are rendered differs from that of his predecessors in the genre. Claudian's is not a classical style, though he is regularly praised for the technical felicity of his hexameters; he places no premium on a unified, balanced structure, much less on a controlled narrative pace, but rather on elaborate imagery and set speeches. This has led, and not only in the twentieth century, to accusations of rhetorical decadence and denunciations of an aesthetic that values a baroque, soulless visuality and a high, mannered eloquence at the expense of emotional and narrative depth, and even of narrative itself. Claudian's most insightful critic of recent times, Alan Cameron, has gone so far as to say,

> To put it bluntly, Claudian is almost incapable of writing true narrative. It is hardly an exaggeration to say that all Claudian's major poems, epics no less than panegyrics and invectives, consist of little but a succession of speeches and descriptions. (1970: 262–3)

This is true, as far as it goes, and Claudian's imagistic, highly rhetorical (in the neutral sense) style can leave the reader groomed on Homeric and Virgilian epic wondering just what has become of the genre, or even whether, to restate the question, Claudian's epics are really epics at all. Is it true, as Cameron goes on to claim, that in the end Claudian "is not really writing epic at all" (1970: 264)?

These two claims are easily countered. First, length is no determinant of generic status, as Hesiod's works bear out. The modern invention of the category "epyllion" ("miniature epic") to account for the briefer epics of the Hellenistic age (when epic proved able to absorb even the vogue for miniaturism) reflects an understanding that such factors as content, meter, and the use of traditional poetic conventions (the extended simile, the catalogue, the *concilium deorum*, and so on) trump matters of bare form (see further Crump 1931; Gutzwiller 1981). These conventions are certainly present in Claudian's epics, which are written in the standard epic hexameter and, as we have noted, have as their subjects the typical concerns of epic. More crucial for our understanding of Claudian is the realization that the very brevity of Claudian's political poetry, including the *De bello Gildonico* and the *De bello Getico*, is a direct function of its performance arena. As a court poet, Claudian was writing topical poetry for the senatorial aristocracy, an exclusive circle of wealthy, well-educated elites at Rome, Milan, and Ravenna. His immediate reputation depended upon the favor of his patron and of these men – whom his verse was often trying to persuade, mollify, or cajole – and we must understand that Claudian's major works were composed to be delivered before their audience. His style is in part a reflection of the prevailing taste among this class, an "audience . . . with whom [Claudian was] more intimately involved than ever Vergil or Ovid were in their day" (Gruzelier 1990: 302). Claudian knows, as Gruzelier further observes (1990: 302), these aristocrats'

> appreciation of the grandeur of rhetoric and wide-ranging literary references to the great tradition of earlier poets, their satisfaction in trite moral platitudes, their love of the brightness and glitter of gorgeous embroidered fabrics and rich jewels, their insecurity in the face of the Germanic tribes forever threatening the outskirts of their vast empire, their interest in the back-biting and intrigues of their own narrow court, and their curiosity about those of the Eastern one.

It is Claudian's attention to these desires and his ability to adapt his style accordingly that largely account for the qualities of his poetry and his tremendous success.

As for Claudian's style, scholars now recognize that the appreciation of late antique poetry – both Latin and Greek – has long been stifled by biases arising from the study of the canonical poetry of classical Greece and, especially, of Augustan Rome. Michael Roberts, responding to Cameron's charge that Claudian's work suffers from too much elaborate description and speechifying and not enough narrative, gets straight to the point (1989: 2–3):

> [Cameron's] criticism of [Claudian's] descriptive purple passages depends on the classical aesthetic of unity of the whole, the proportion of the parts, and the careful articulation of an apparently seamless composition. Late antique poetry is not like this. The seams not only show, they are positively advertised – nonclassical certainly, but not necessarily evidence of deficient technique. These are precisely the qualities the poets aim for. Taste has changed. To

appreciate late antique poetry properly, it is necessary to view it on its own terms rather than from the perspective, conscious or not, of classical aesthetics.

As the master-genre of the ancient world (see the Introduction by J. Foley), epic is, furthermore, an omnivorous species: it incorporates into itself the voices, tropes, and themes of other genres as it evolves (as it must) over the centuries. A bare summary of this dynamic would include Hesiod's recasting of Near Eastern "wisdom-literature"; Apollonius Rhodius' infusion of ethnography, aetiology, and the erotic; the echo of pastoral and the interlacing of myth and political panegyric in Virgil; Lucan's rhetorical *sententiae* and bloodsoaked ironies; and so on. The opening up of epic to new generic elements contributes to greater variations of convention and theme, thereby creating an ever larger palette for the epic poet: thus we see, to take only a few examples, Apollonius' revision of traditional heroic characterization alongside Nonnus' substitution of a god in place of the mortal hero; and Lucan's abandonment of the gods in his historical epic against Silius Italicus' reintroduction of them into his. In Claudian's case this means primarily a fusion between epic conventions and the techniques and motifs of panegyric and invective, Claudian's court staples. The result is a vibrant epic poetry that, yes, sacrifices the narrative momentum one associates with Homer to achieve instead what we might call rhetorical momentum, an almost cinematic sequentiality of inventive images and well wrought speeches that carries the reader along from one set piece to the next (cf. Gruzelier 1990: 311f.). In more ways than one, in this age of the all-powerful, all-pervasive political image, breathlessly plied and manipulated by competing spin doctors, Claudian is a poet for our times.

Amid all this variation and innovation, we must recognize in the end that the meaning of epic is, finally, whatever the culture in which it is embedded decides it is. Or, as Richard Martin observes in the opening chapter of this volume, any attempt to define epic must "begin with the assumption that 'epic' is a contingent and culture-bound category." If we hold Claudian's epics to the generic expectations founded upon Homer (expectations that eventually slide into limitations), they are likely to be denied such status, and, in ways subtle and not, accordingly judged inferior. Moreover, a radical difference in style does not preclude serious engagement with epic voices of the past; allusion and a deep intertextuality are among the hallmarks of Claudian's poetry.

If, despite these arguments, Claudian's major works are still infrequently read – excepting perhaps the *De raptu Proserpinae*, which continues to be peeked at by students and scholars, especially those seeking familiar mythological harbors in their ventures into the Late Imperial period – this is due in some part to the modern impatience with, if not outright distaste for, patronage poetry (Apollonius Rhodius has suffered the same fate: see Hunter 1993b: 2–3), and especially imperial propaganda. Claudian is easily the most political poet in this volume, the achievements of his career directly shaped, as we have seen, by the shifting political fortunes of Stilicho. These prejudices are, it is hoped, ebbing, as innovative scholarly work on late antiquity since the 1970s has succeeded in bringing the rich complexities of the period into the mainstream of classics. As a witness to important events at a crucial time in Roman history, Claudian is an important historical source for the western empire at the close of the fourth century CE. His work must, as will become clear below, be used very carefully, for as a historical source Claudian is full of distortions, omissions, and revisions of the contemporary record; he is, after all, a professional propagandist. But this is what, on one level, makes him interesting. His work is, as we have seen, something of a primer in the strategy and techniques of the propagandist (Cameron 1970: 46ff.), and the study of such techniques is no less relevant now than it was at the close of the fourth century.

Still, the value of Claudian's work lies not just in the opportunities it provides to study ancient political propaganda. In the history of ancient literature, the *De bello Gildonico* and the *De bello Getico* are distinguished as the only surviving epics on *contemporary* subjects. (I consider the sixth-century *Iohannes* of Corippus a work of the early medieval period, though of course that distinction is contestable.) Of the historical epics that we possess, Ennius treated the events of his lifetime in the second half of the *Annales*, but precious little of this has come down to us; as for extant epics, Lucan was writing around a hundred years after the events of his *Bellum civile*, and Silius Italicus almost three full centuries after the events of the *Punica*. The remains of Claudian's two Gigantomachies are, as well, among our best surviving examples of that most durable of epic themes. The Greek version may well have had a influence on the gigantomachy in the opening books of the *Dionysiaca* of Nonnus, Claudian's native countryman (Cameron 1970: 14–18; on Nonnus see Chapter 27, by Shorrock).

3   The *De bello Gildonico*: Epic and Politics

In light, then, of the uniqueness of Claudian's war epics, let us focus in what remains not on the more popular *De raptu Proserpinae* but on the *De bello Gildonico*. Despite its greater familiarity to readers, the *De raptu Proserpinae* is something of a footnote to Claudian's career; it may well be, as von Albrecht claims, that "Claudian's picture of the world and society [in the *De raptu*] reflects the hierarchical structure of the late Roman Empire" (1999: 326), but on the whole it reads rather more like a luxurious escape from the pressures of the imperial court than an attempt to engage it in mythological guise. In any case, fine introductions to the *De raptu Proserpinae* may be found elsewhere (see, e.g., Connor 1993; Gruzelier 1993: xvii–xxxi; von Albrecht 1999: 317–27). The *De bello Gildonico*, on the other hand, affords the reader many opportunities to examine the intersections between Claudian's poetic and political techniques, the tools most responsible for his fame in antiquity.

The *De bello Gildonico* supports Cameron's assertion above that Claudian's poetry consists mainly in speeches and descriptions at the expense of narrative (see esp. 1970: 263–4). The poem opens with the poet's elation at the restoration of harmony between the western and eastern empires in the wake of Gildo's astonishingly rapid defeat. The scene then shifts to the run-up to war, and in the first speech, a vividly personified Rome comes before Jove and the rest of the Olympian gods to lament her hunger and mistreatment at Gildo's hands. She is followed by a personified Africa, who continues the complaint against Gildo, portrayed as a monster of competing appetites and vices. Jove breathes new life into Rome and decides to send Theodosius I and his father, Theodosius the Elder, to the two sleeping emperors. The former visits Arcadius in the East and upbraids the young ruler for preferring the utility and profit of an alliance with Gildo to what is right and best for the entire empire ("ergo fas pretio cedet? mercede placebit / seditio," 260–1: "and so will what is right yield to profit? is rebellion for sale?"), and advises him to heed the wise counsel of Stilicho. Arcadius wakes and immediately resolves to heed his father's words. In the West, the shade of the elder Theodosius, invoking his earlier triumphs in North Africa, rouses Honorius to arms. Honorius promptly summons Stilicho, who tells him not to dignify Gildo's defeat with his presence, but rather to make use of Mascezel, who deserves vengeance for the inhuman crimes that Gildo has perpetrated on his family. Stilicho prepares the troops, and Honorius delivers an inspiring speech to his men in which he derides the worth of Gildo's troops and Gildo himself, described as a drunken, overly perfumed wretch, enfeebled by old age and incest. An omen bolsters Honorius' confident rhetoric, and the ships are launched. They face dangerous weather before reaching various harbors. The poem ends there, well before the army (presumably including Mascezel, though Claudian does not say so) is ready to engage Gildo.

The *De bello Gildonico* challenges our comfortable notions of the boundaries between genres – or, seen another way, demonstrates epic's capacity to subsume the techniques and motifs of other genres, in this case panegyric and invective. On a formal level, the traditional epic panoply is on conspicuous display: the *concilium deorum*; the personification of Rome (found in Lucan, for example); the cast of exempla from Rome's heroic past (e.g., Regulus, 79; Fabius and Marcellus, 89; Cincinnatus and Curius, 111; Tullus Hostilius, 254); the catalogue (415–23); the simile (the departing fleet, for instance, is compared to the one that embarked at Aulis against Troy, 484–5); and a hoary twin bill: the omen of the eagle and serpent (467–71), and the reference to the war of the cranes and pygmies (474–8), each of which is found in Homer (*Il.* 12.200–7 and 3.2–7, respectively). Alongside these are panegyrical elements: the portrayal of the emperors, so quick to heed the commands of the august Theodosii, as properly deferential to their elders; Theodosius I's fulsome praise of Stilicho (288–320); the flattering representation of Honorius, rousing the troops with spirited oratory (427–66; we must remember that Honorius was only thirteen years old at this time); and the brave Roman sailors damning the storms and cliffs that hinder their desire to carry out the emperor's will (486–515). Invective also has its place, as we have seen: the depiction of Gildo's army as undisciplined and timid (432–43), and of their leader as on the one hand murderous, greedy, and expert in the criminal arts ("instat terribilis uiuis, morientibus heres", 165: "he looms as a terror to the living and heir to the dying") and on the other as effeminate, diseased, and cowardly (444–50), recalls the verbal carpet-bombing practiced in the *In Rufinum* and *In Eutropium*.

Claudian's first political epic is also a remarkable example of this poet's ability to marshal epic themes and motifs into the service of political authority, each reinforcing the other. It is significant, for example, that Claudian presses the Theodosii, sources of unimpeachable authority after their death, into service as messengers of Jove. On a generic level, they play the traditional epic role of the authoritative divine messenger (Mercury, typically, but other gods as well) whose words must perforce be heeded by the dutiful hero; one might think, among a number of examples, of Mercury's admonition to Aeneas at *Aen.* 4. 265–76. Thus the content of their advice (in a word, trust Stilicho), which according to the norms of the epic genre can hardly be disobeyed, may acquire, on a real-world political level, a greater potency and greater weight in the aristocratic circles of Claudian's audience. Moreover, like Aeneas, Honorius and Arcadius are approvingly figured as dutiful sons, fit continuators of their forebears' virtues and wardens of the future of Roman empire. Claudian's representation of political figures in an epic landscape flatters all involved and reinforces the rightness of their actions. A modern public relations firm could hardly do better.

A thorough account of the political tact and guile on display in the *De bello Gildonico* would include Claudian's diminishment of Mascezel; his representation of Stilicho as the rightful regent of both emperors; his subtle reminder of Stilicho's position as father-in-law to Honorius, a position that acquires greater authority in light of the emphasis, as we have just seen, on filial duty; and the way in which Claudian suggests that Gildo is but another in a long line of African rebels, when, in fact, he had rendered invaluable aid to the Romans in the elder Theodosius' war against Firmus in Mauretania in 373–5. (On all these matters the reader is referred to the fundamental analysis of Cameron 1970: 93–123.) We might wonder, too, why the poem ends where it does. A sequel describing the victory was either never written or destroyed (Cameron 1970: 115–16). An account of the actual battle, in which even Claudian would have been hard pressed to avoid celebrating Mascezel, would have won Stilicho little political capital and even proved embarrassing if not handled just right. Stilicho could gain only so much credit for a war in which he did not fight. Plus, why antagonize the eastern court, which no doubt saw the outcome as a blow to its designs? And why remind the western court of the good service of Mascezel, when Stilicho (probably) had just had him assassinated? Best to emphasize a restoration of the concord between the two halves of the empire, as Claudian does in the opening lines, and keep silent about all the uncomfortable details.

The present discussion may end with a brief word on another representation of the Gildonic war, one fashioned by Claudian a year and a half later. It serves as a revealing commentary both on the demands of Claudian's job as court propagandist and on Claudian's own powers of generic manipulation. When Claudian delivered the first book of his panegyric of Stilicho's consulship in January of 400, he briefly recapitulated the war against Gildo. But whereas in the earlier epic we saw that he had portrayed Gildo as a pathetic, drunken sybarite and his troops as cowardly skirmishers, at *Stil.* 1.246–69 the same man and army are represented as menacing, even terrifying opponents. To signal the measure of the threat, Claudian employs a characteristically epic technique, the catalogue, to describe the exotic and gruesomely outfitted array of Nubians, Garamantians, and Nasamonians that threaten to overrun North Africa. They are now a formidable, awesome lot. The skies over Carthage are darkened by their arrows (258). Gildo is nothing less than a second Memnon or Porus (264–7). But all this epic furniture is of course to the greater glory of Stilicho, who opposes Gildo as another Alexander and Achilles (268–9). Here we may see clearly the essence of Claudian's political and poetic art: though his patron demands a rewriting of the history of the Gildonic war, one in which he, not Mascezel, assumes the chief role, Claudian's technique remains the same. To achieve so brazen a political goal – the re-presentation of Stilicho's role in the entire war, and even of the nature of the war itself – requires a deft manipulation of the vocabulary and the conventions of epic.

FURTHER READING

Still far the best introduction to Claudian, and the touchstone for modern scholarship, is Alan Cameron's seminal work, *Claudian: Poetry and Propaganda at the Court of Honorius* (1970). Authoritative, inexhaustibly informative, and highly readable, it is one of the twentieth century's best works on any ancient author, and the present chapter owes much to it. I have been influenced by Cameron's readings of the major poems and by his interpretations of Claudian's poetic techniques at virtually every turn. My chronology in section 1 follows his, which is conveniently summarized at 1970: xv–xvi.

The standard Latin text is Hall 1985; the titles of Claudian's works and all citations in this chapter come from this magisterial edition. Translations of all of Claudian's works may be found in Platnauer's Loeb editions (2 vols., 1922), but these are in need of updating in light of Hall's better text and the outmoded English style. There are several translations of the *De raptu Proserpinae*: the most faithful is now the one in Gruzelier's first-rate edition and commentary (1993). The poet David Slavitt's rendering of the poem (1997) is livelier but comparatively unreliable as a guide to the Latin.

Claudian is well served by a number of single-volume commentaries on his major works. We have already mentioned Gruzelier 1993. On the *Panegyricus dictus Honorio Augusto quartum consuli*, see Barr 1981; on the *In Rufinum*, Levy 1971; on the *Panegyricus dictus Honorio Augusto sextum consuli*, Dewar 1996. Long 1996, while not a formal commentary, is an excellent study of the *In Eutropium*; her bibliography is also a good starting place for those who want to pursue the study of Claudian further.

Binns 1974 contains good introductions to the literary world and major authors of the fourth century CE, including a fine chapter on Claudian by Cameron. The best introduction to late antique poetic style is Roberts 1989. Excellent introductions to the historical and political background of Claudian's career at the imperial court may be found in Matthews's classic *Western Aristocracies and Imperial Court AD 364–425* (1975) and in Cameron 1970; for the eastern court, see Cameron and Long 1993. On the history of Alaric and the Goths, see *inter alia* the relevant parts of Wolfram 1988.

CHAPTER FORTY

Latin Christian Epics
of Late Antiquity

Dennis E. Trout

Late Latin Christian epic, with the exception perhaps of Prudentius' *Psychomachia*, remains one of antiquity's better-kept secrets. Yet, Latin epics and *epyllia*, which virtually disappear from view in the second century, proliferated in later antiquity. Thereafter appeal and serviceability preserved their fortunes and encouraged imitation throughout (and beyond) the Middle Ages. Although some late antique epics, like Claudian's *De raptu Proserpinae* or the fifth-century *epyllia* of Dracontius (Bright 1987; Connor 1993; Chapter 39, by Barnes) creatively engaged with well-known mythological episodes, while others, like Claudian's *De bello Getico* ("The Gothic War") or Corippus' sixth-century *Iohannis*, restaged recent historical events (Cameron 1983), much of the Latin epic poetry surviving from the centuries separating Constantine (306–37) from Gregory the Great (590–604) more overtly proclaimed Christian content and aims. These latter efforts are the subject of this chapter, but even they, ranging from Juvencus' early fourth-century Gospel epic to Venantius Fortunatus' sixth-century *Vita Martini*, form a remarkably diverse lot. Such span and scope present interpretative challenges whose resolution must begin with recognition of the intimate connections between this poetry and the dynamic and occasionally confrontational times and circumstances in which they were composed.

The three centuries that followed Constantine's conversion to Christianity witnessed the gradual eclipse of many old ways of thinking, the rise of new modes of political, social, and religious life, and a slow but commensurate re-forging of Roman identity around the tenets, precepts, and values of late ancient Christianity (Markus 1990). Initially the Christianization of society and the consolidation of religious authority within the institutions of an imperially sanctioned Church ran parallel to such phenomena as the decline of traditional civic cult, the evolution of an ideology of divine rulership, the expansion of the imperial bureaucracy, and the subtle renegotiation of the social hierarchy (MacMullen 1997; Garnsey and Humfress 2001; Swain and Edwards 2004). But eventually Roman rule in the West dissolved and a poet such as Venantius Fortunatus in sixth-century Gaul would find his patrons in the courts of Merovingian kings, the monasteries of their queens, and the churches of influential bishops (George 1992; Brown 2003). Inevitably, then, the epic poetry of this period, with its blend of Christian themes and classically derived forms, its manifold aesthetic and rhetorical aims, and its diverse audiences, must be viewed against this shifting background.

Similarly the literary qualities of the Christian epics cannot be isolated from trends more broadly evident in the artistic and intellectual history of the age. Poets, like architects, sculptors, and even philosophers, were all engaged to some extent in reconciling the legacy of the classical past with contemporary tastes and realities. Virgil, of course, remained the touchstone of late Latin poets, soundly seconded by Horace, Ovid, Lucan, and Statius; but late Latin poetry is distinguished by innovation as well as imitation. The backward looking "neoclassicism" of much late Latin poetry, secular and Christian alike, lies in creative tension with a startling "neo-Alexandrian" mannerism (Charlet 1988). If late antique epicists echo and borrow from their classical predecessors, often adopting their ideology of imperial destiny as well as their rhetorical and literary principles, their works also reveal an accentuated taste for miniaturization and description, a preference for episodic structure at the expense of narrative flow, and a delight in sophisticated verbal patterning that yields dense textures of repetition and variation. Drawn to images of gems and flowers and to metaphors of color and light, for example, the late antique poet is, in Michael Roberts' formulation, like a jeweler carefully setting individual words and phrases into endless arrangements of subtle variation (Roberts 1989). Though both the neoclassical and "baroque" qualities of this poetry have at times provoked charges of decadence and irrelevance, these features must rather be seen as the poetic expression of aesthetic values that also energize the sculptural program of the Arch of Constantine, late antique ivories, and sarcophagi (Cameron 2004).

So, too, the noteworthy generic realignments of this period of renaissance and reformation, of conservatism and Christianization, should be read as signs of cultural vitality. Literary genres are by nature unstable and late antiquity was a period of fertile mutations, especially in poetry's *mélange des genres* (Fontaine 1975 and 1988). Thus readers who view late Latin epic from an early imperial perspective meet the unexpected as well as the familiar. Late antique epics still center their attention upon the *gesta* of "heroes," though these are now Christ, the patriarchs, apostles, and saints (or personified virtues). Moreover, they continue to employ such conventions as invocations, direct speech, epithets, and epic diction, preferring, for example, *nuntius* to *angelus* and styling God *Tonans*, the Thunderer. Yet, the boundaries that might distinguish epic from other discursive modes become increasingly blurry. In part, this is because poetic diction and style are now quite at home in such prose genres as historiography and panegyric. Yet at the same time epic also absorbs the proclivity of panegyric and, in the case of the Christian epics, hagiography, to subordinate narrative development to serialized tableaux and conventional scenes. Furthermore, the tendency of poets to sacrifice narrative thrust to episodic elaboration and exegetical commentary, especially in the case of the biblical epics, lends this poetry an epigrammatic feel as rhetorical and interpretive passages intrude more heavily upon the "story." Late Latin epic, therefore, is the unruly heir not only of its classical forbears but also of such genres, often in their Christian guise, as the commentary and biography. One result of this hybridization is a taxonomic fluidity. Late Latin epics are routinely subcategorized, as they are below, but not always in the same manner (e.g., Kirsch 1989; Pollmann 2001a, 2001b). The following is a sample of Latin Christian epic and the reactions of its modern readers.

Fourth-century Renewal

Latin epic poetry benefited from the spirit of renewal that revitalized the intellectual and artistic life of the Latin world in the century after Constantine. The general restoration of confidence in the military capacity and political authority of the empire coupled with the emergence of an imperially sponsored Christianity to create conditions that encouraged the creation of the first truly public programs of Christian art, architecture, and literature.

Virtually every such experiment sifted more or less self-consciously through the inherited legacy to identify those components of the past that could or simply had to be appropriated. Inevitably Christian poets quickly turned to epic, so long recognized as the most sublime form of poetry. Epic, which had served to vocalize other versions of Roman identity, imperial destiny, and cosmic order, was the sole poetic form suitable for expressing the grand historical, ideological, and theological claims at the core of Christian thought. Yet it was not necessarily clear how epic, so closely associated with the heroes, gods, legends, and myths of the pre-Christian age could be bent to Christian ends. The Christian poet would somehow have to reconcile or distinguish between the narrative content of classical epic (largely fiction and lies from the Christian point of view) and the lexical and stylistic sources of its literary power and cultural sway. Allegorical or philosophical *interpretationes christianae* might salvage parts of the *Aeneid* (Courcell 1984: 726–46), for example, but composing new poems for Christian audiences presented Christian poets with different challenges. What were the appropriate themes of such poetry? How could the language and devices of epic be tailored to express those themes? The solutions offered by fourth-century poets (and here we consider three examples) anticipate the major trends that characterize the Christian epics of later antiquity.

The acknowledged fountainhead of Christian Latin epic is the *Evangeliorum libri quattuor* of the Hispano-Roman aristocrat and presbyter C. Vettius Aquilinus Juvencus (Fontaine 1981; Roberts 1985: 67–76; Herzog 1993b). Setting out the "life-sustaining deeds (*vitalia gesta*) of Christ" (*praef. Evang.* 19) in four books (the number of the Gospels) totaling 3,184 hexameters, Juvencus (fl. 330) both initiated a long-running series of biblical epics and directly engaged the classical epic heritage in ways that would influence not only later Christian epicists but directly or indirectly most late antique Christian poets. Juvencus' narrative, based primarily upon the Gospel of Matthew, begins with the annunciation and concludes with the risen Christ's appearance in Galilee. Within its starkly episodic presentation of the life of its hero, Juvencus' narrative is especially attentive to the revelation of Christ's *virtus* through miracles. The narrative itself is framed by a 27-line prologue and a final address (4.802–12) that announce and recall the poet's apologetic and aesthetic aims.

At the outset, in his elegantly structured prologue, Juvencus declares both his affinity for and his distance from his epic forbearers (Kirsch 1989: 85–92; Carruba 1993; Deproost 1998). If the *carmina* of Homer and Virgil, relating through fictions (*mendacia*) the *gesta* of ancient men, could win such long-lasting fame for subject and poet alike, his faith, Juvencus declares, will surely bestow upon him immortal glory (*immortale decus*). For his *carmen* will celebrate the true deeds of Christ (*praef. Evang.* 6–20). But beyond this innate superiority of Christian truth over pagan fiction, eschatology, too, favors the Christian epicist: Juvencus can imagine (in lofty neologisms) that his "work" (*opus*), by ensuring his own salvation, will also survive the final conflagration destined to unfold when Christ the Judge, "glory of the high-throned father" (*altithroni genitoris gloria*), descends in flame-throwing cloud (*flammivoma nube*) (*praef. Evang.* 21–4). Embracing this cosmic perspective, the Christian epicist summons not the Muse but the "sanctifying Spirit" (*sanctificus Spiritus*) to inspire his song and sprinkle his mind with the pure waters of the sweet Jordan (*praef. Evang.* 25–7). Yet at the end of his work, like Virgil in the *Georgics* (4.559–66), Juvencus also sets his poetic act amid mundane events. It is the "peace of Christ" fostered in the world by a Constantine eager for "eternal life," that has encouraged the poet to proclaim "the glory of the divine law" (*divinae gloria legis*) with the "earthly adornments of language" (*ornamenta terrestria linguae*) (4.802–12). So Juvencus at once claims and transforms such familiar epic themes as poetic rivalry, divine inspiration, literary immortality (on multiple levels), and historical self-consciousness. The effect will be long-lived.

Juvencus' final lines remind us that the composition of the *Evangeliorum libri quattuor* is as firmly linked to the remarkable opportunities of Constantine's later years as is the *Aeneid* to the times of Augustus. Juvencus' poem is an epic for a new age, protreptic and catechetic, intended to enhance the Bible's appeal for educated readers (e.g., Aug. *Conf.* 3.5.9), while also offering insight into some of the religion's central claims. The language and images of venerated poets, Lucretius, Ovid, Lucan, and Statius, as well as Virgil, are recalled throughout, while Juvencus otherwise imports into the epic lexicon *profeta* and *daemon*. The poet's paraphrase of the biblical text favors the extended passages of direct speech expected by epic's audience. And adhering to a durable line of Christian apologetics aimed at reassuring others of Christianity's social respectability, Juvencus seems determined to sever Christianity cleanly from its Jewish background. Not only does the poet present Christ as the fulfillment of Old Testament prophecy, but he also refigures Israel as bucolic Italian countryside (e.g., 1.364; 3.459–61) while Romanizing the poem's hero. Finally, elaborating the core of the poem's *exordium*, Juvencus persistently extends his epic's reach beyond human history to the cosmic and soteriological design revealed by the Gospel story. Christ is the *vitae spes unica*, "life's only hope," in fact, the very *auctor vitae* (3.521; 3.503). In sum, Juvencus, the Christian poet, works simultaneously within and against the literary traditions he has inherited.

The fourth century witnessed two further notable contributions to the evolution of late Latin epic, Proba's *Cento Vergilianus de laudibus Christi* and Paulinus of Nola's *epyllion* on John the Baptist. The *Cento*'s author is traditionally identified as Faltonia Betitia Proba (*ca.* 322–70), wife of the urban prefect Clodius Celsinus Adelphius (Matthews 1992; Herzog 1993a; Green 1995; but cf. Shanzer 1986 and 1994). Exact dating of the poem is difficult, but both Proba's claim to have written a more conventional epic on the theme of civil war, echoing Lucan and presumably treating the struggle between Constantius II and Magnentius (1–8; cf. 47–9 with *arma virum pugnasque canebam*), as well as her choice of the cento form have led some scholars to favor the early 360s and to posit a relationship between her *Cento* and Julian's legislation restricting Christian teachers (e.g., Clark and Hatch 1981; Green 1995). *Centones* were "patchworks" composed by sampling early poets and Proba constructed her *Cento* (almost) entirely by stitching together lines and half-lines taken from the works of Virgil. The cento was a well-established type by the fourth century, but presented the Christian epicist with special problems, for the biblical proper names were obviously not to be found in Virgil's verses and the form imposed severe limits upon the poet's freedom of expression. But Virgil's works were also saturated with familiar language and religious images that might, with some ingenuity, be turned to a new purpose (Clark and Hatch 1981). Indeed, one of Proba's stated goals was to show that Virgil had, in fact, "sang of Christ's sacred gifts (*pia munera*)" (line 23, cf. Green 1997: 556). Proba's *Cento*, then, rearranging Virgil's own words, is a further manifestation of the popular notion that Virgil was (somehow) a proto-Christian (Courcelle 1957).

At 694 lines, 55 of which are prefatory (with the cento proper beginning at l. 24), Proba's poem is considerably shorter than Juvencus' but her *Cento*, a remarkable survival from the pen of a woman, can claim marks of distinction. Proba, who styles herself *vatis* (12), also rejects traditional sources of poetic inspiration in favor of God (*deus omnipotens*) and the Spirit (9–12) and anticipates her poetic immortality (18–22). But her *Cento* is also the earliest Christian epic to present Old Testament episodes. She elaborates on the actions of the Father (*Pater*) in accounts of Creation, the Fall, and the Flood, adding non-biblical material, before engaging with the *maius opus* (334): the story of the Son (*progenies*), who came as man, "*virtus* mixed with God" (338–9). Proba's narrative is inevitably more abbreviated than Juvencus' but her *heros* (518) is sharply (and idiosyncratically) defined. The *Cento*'s Christ, for example, flashes in anger (not forgiveness) from the Cross (621–3) and is a decidedly apocalyptic messenger (e.g., 497–504). Proba herself, however, is a conservative spokeswoman, showing little interest in the ascetic trends about to break over western Christianity (Clark and Hatch 1981). But for all its dexterity and apparent popularity, Proba's *Cento* was not uncontroversial even in late antiquity. Jerome, who approved of Juvencus' submission of the Gospel story to the laws of meter (*Ep.* 70.5), ridiculed Proba's efforts as puerile (*Ep.* 53.7). And though other Christian *centones* do survive (*CSEL* 16), none are on the scale of Proba's. The future of biblical epic lay in the wider horizons opened up by Juvencus.

As the fourth century was drawing to a close Paulinus of Nola (*ca.* 352–431) blended the poetic principles announced by Juvencus with the hagiographic impulses by then so prominent in Latin Christianity to produce his *Laus sancti Iohannis*. Totaling only 330 lines, Paulinus' *epyllion* on John the Baptist (*Carm.* 6) is both a miniature epic and an *encomium* (or panegyric), and as such foreshadows later hagiographic epic (Prete 1974). The aristocratic Paulinus, then in the throes of his own decision to renounce his secular past and its poetry (Trout 1999: 79–89), quickly acknowledged his debts to the fourth century's new wave. His opening line, "Highest Father, eternal power of things and heaven" (*Summe pater rerum caelique aeterna potestas*) probably signaled his appreciation of Proba (*Cento* 29) as well as his affection for Virgil (*Aen.* 10.18), while Juvencus echoes throughout the work (Flury 1973; Duval 1989). Moreover, Paulinus' *Laus Iohannis* is similarly episodic in structure, classical in its layered allusions, and Romanizing in its effect. But the inventiveness displayed by Paulinus in the *Laus Iohannis* is perhaps more brazen even than that displayed by Proba.

Although it is a work of biblical paraphrase, Paulinus far outstrips the sketch of John's *vita* in the Gospel of Luke, his primary source. Paulinus' additions are an index of both his own poetic and apologetic strategies and the ascetic tendencies then so prominent in western aristocratic circles (Herzog 1975: 214–23; Trout 1999: 98–100). Paulinus invented a precocious childhood for John (205–18) and transformed John's desert wilderness into an image of the classical Golden Age (240–6). He endowed John with semi-divine status, styling him (as Statius had the Argonauts) a demi-god (252: *semideus vir*; cf. Stat. *Theb.* 3.518). And under Paulinus' pen John's baptism acquired a redemptive force other Christian writers carefully reserved for Christ (258–67). The poet of the *Laus Iohannis* was not only determined to unroll sacred history in melodious verse (18–19) but also to set up an ascetic *exemplum* for his readers to emulate (249–54). Epic's paedeutic role has forcefully resurfaced.

The decades separating Juvencus from Paulinus witnessed remarkable advances in the Christianization of the Roman empire. Imperial patronage, ecclesiastical consolidation, elite conversions, and the rise of orthodoxy as well as asceticism changed the face of Roman society. These political, social, and religious developments were accompanied by pioneering efforts to express Christian history, anthropology, and cosmology in the meter, lexicon, and conventions of epic poetry. Fourth-century poets did not shy away from Virgil and his successors even if they might seek to sanitize them. The grandeur of epic poetry might be retained and its cultural capital usurped while its assumptions about Roman destiny, history, and the gods were interrogated and sublimated. But as the fourth century drew to a more troubled close, as imperial legislation increased the pressure upon paganism and "heresy," and as the fifth century opened with the Germanic incursions into Italy that led to the Visigothic sack of Rome (410 CE), a new stridency began to animate relations between Rome's pagans and Christians.

Prudentius and the *Psychomachia*

Prudentius has known a more consistent readership than any other late Latin poet. Literary theory and current fascination with the late antique cult of the saints have brought him a new generation of readers (especially of the *Peristephanon*), while his allegorical epic, the *Psychomachia* ("Battle in/for the Soul"), widely read and imitated in the Middle Ages and Renaissance, is again an object of close scrutiny and provocative assessment (e.g., Smith 1976; Nugent 1985; James 1999; Gnilka 2000, 2001). After serving in the imperial civil service, Aurelius Prudentius Clemens (348 – after 405), a native of Roman Spain, devoted himself to Christian poetry. He visited Rome, probably between 400 and 405, and in the latter year, at age 57, wrote the preface to an edition of his works that provides our limited biographical information. Like Paulinus of Nola, Prudentius composed in a variety of meters to produce a richly textured body of Christian poetry. Yet hexametrical verse occupies a central position in Prudentius' oeuvre, while Virgil's influence has infiltrated virtually every cranny of his lyrical verse (e.g., Mahoney 1934; Roberts 1989: 92–9; Castelli 1996; Lükhen 2002: 90–104). Both of Prudentius' book-long didactic (or dogmatic) poems, the *Apotheosis*, on the nature of Christ's divinity, and *Hamartigenia*, on the origins of sin, employ hexameters (and recall Lucretian didactic (Fontaine 1981: 195–206)), as do his two polemical books *Contra Symmachum*. But Prudentius' epic *tour de force* was the *Psychomachia*, which, though perhaps composed shortly after 405, in the manuscripts falls between his didactic poems and the *Contra Symmachum* (Fontaine 1981: 195–209; Bastiaensen 1993: 108–13). As the first "fully-fledged allegorical poem" in western literature (Lewis 1938), as well as for reasons that should become obvious, the *Psychomachia* has had an abiding influence upon art and literature and has ineluctably attracted literary scholars.

The *Psychomachia* extends to 915 hexameters and is prefaced by 68 iambic lines, a formal innovation of continuing popularity. This *Praefatio*, echoing Ambrose and initiating the poem's catena of Pauline allusions (Hanna 1977), introduces the *Psychomachia*'s subject matter and interpretive strategies by presenting the tale of Abraham's faith, victory over wickedness, and reward as a "form" (*figura*) of the Christian's combat against enslaving desire (*libido*) waged in preparation for Christ's entry into the heart (*cor*) and the fruitful marriage of Spirit and soul (*anima*). Prudentius' opening hexameters (1–20) then call upon Christ to "tell" (*dissere*) how the soul (*mens*) is equipped with mighty Virtues (*virtutes*) capable of driving the Vices (*vitia, culpae*) from the "hollow of our breast" (*nostri de pectoris antro*). This inner space, stark and bereft of physical description, is the field (*campus*) upon which Prudentius' personified (female) Vices and Virtues swagger, vaunt, and pursue their deadly struggles. The body of the poem is structured as a series of discreet episodes. Particular Virtues step out to vanquish their natural enemies in bloody combat: Fides, first, overcomes "Worship of the Gods of Old" (*veterum cultura deorum*); then Pudicitia (Chastity) defeats Libido (Lust); and so on for a total of six set pieces before Pax (Peace) takes the stage (631). But the lull is only momentary, for as the Thunderer (*Tonans*) smiles down from above, treacherous Discord (known also as Heresy) unexpectedly steps from the throng to wound Concord. Only when Heresy has been pinioned with a javelin through the tongue by Faith and torn limb from limb by countless hands is order truly established. Now the poem can draw to a close with the construction of a great jewel-encrusted temple (of the heart) fit to receive the Son of Man (*hominis Filius*), a new city of God. Prudentius' final prayer-like address to Christ (888–915) both recalls the opening invocation and once more draws the poem's allegory back into the present time of the reader: the soul is indeed such a battlefield as that depicted in these verses, where the battle lines will inevitably waver to and fro until *Christus Deus* arrives to set in order all the "jewels of the Virtues" (*virtutum gemmae*).

Prudentius' theme was eminently suited to engage Virgilian epic at multiple levels (Mahoney 1934: 47–80). The poet's very first hexameter line, "Christe, graves hominum semper miserate labores" ("O Christ, who has ever had pity upon men's deep sufferings") boldly echoes Aeneas' invocation of Apollo in the Sibyl's cave (*Aen.* 6.56): "Phoebe, gravis Troiae semper miserate labores" ("O Phoebus, who has ever had pity upon Troy's deep sufferings"). Virgil's well-known line had prefaced the revelation of personal and Roman destiny that awaited Aeneas in Book 6 of the *Aeneid*; Prudentius' usurpation challenged not only Apollo as the source of poetic inspiration but also Virgilian-derived conceptions of the relationship between man, history, and god (Smith 1976: 271–6; Lükhen 2002: 45–6). Similarly the *Psychomachia*'s combat scenes draw heavily and often subversively on epic battle imagery, not to portray the manliness of narrowly self-interested heroes but rather to demonstrate the capacity of *Virtus* to vanquish Vice, a victory with universal implications for salvation history as well as for the ultimate deserts of every soul. Consider, for example, Fides' early dispatch of "Worship of the Gods of Old" (*veterum cultura deorum*)

> Illa hostile caput falerataque *tempora vittis*
> *altior insurgens* labefactat, et ora cruore
> de pecudum satiata *solo adplicat* et pede calcat
> *elisos* in morte *oculos* animamque malignam
> fracta intercepti commercia *gutturis* artant,
> *difficilemque obitum* suspiria longa fatigant.
>   (30–5)

But she [Fides], rising higher, smites her foe's head down, with its fillet-decked brows, lays in the dust that mouth that was sated with the blood of beasts, and tramples the eyes underfoot, squeezing them out in death. The throat is choked and the scant breath confined by the stopping of its passage, and long gasps make a hard and agonizing death. (trans. Thomson 1949)

Each of these six lines contains a Virgilian quote or echo (in italic), producing a web of ironies that, though hardly unambiguous, encourages the knowing reader to participate in the construction of meaning, in part, by recalling the words' original context (Smith 1976: 282–5; Nugent 1985: 17–25; Lükhen 2002: 57–8). For example, with the expression *veterum cultura deorum* (which appears in the line preceding those just quoted), Prudentius points to a speech of Evander in Book 8 of the *Aeneid*. Evander's words, appropriately, appear in the context of the ritual scene, a sacrifice to Hercules, that greets Aeneas upon his arrival at the (future site) of Rome. But the full force of Prudentius' allusion to this speech is generated by Evander's particular use of the words, for the Arcadian king, prefacing his story of Hercules and Cacus, informed Aeneas that the rites he was witnessing had not been imposed upon the Arcadians by any "empty superstition, unmindful of the gods of old" (8.187: "vana superstitio veterumque ignara deorum"). Of course, many of Prudentius' Christian contemporaries had come to see such pagan *cultura* and animal sacrifice as, at best, nothing more than *vana superstitio*. This ironic reversal prepares for the elision, several lines later, of paganism and the mindless brutality exemplified by the monster Cacus himself, for Prudentius' "pede calcat / elisos in morte oculos" (32–3), describing Fides' dispatch of "Worship of the Gods of Old," echoes Evander's (etiological) account of Hercules slaying Cacus (*Aen.* 8.261; cf. Courcelle 1984: 572–7).

Woven through the *Psychomachia* in this manner, Virgilian allusions fashion the soul into an epic battlefield, where Christian Virtues and pagan Vices harangue and duel in an eerily familiar manner, but whereupon any superficially "Virgilian" worldview rooted in pagan sacrifice, false gods, and the alleged sins of Lust, Anger, Pride, and Greed is also challenged and rejected. Such blows surely resonated deeply for Prudentius' educated contemporaries; read against the background of recent and ongoing imperial initiatives to eviscerate paganism, a program explicitly paralleled by Prudentius' own *Contra Symmachum*, they impart distinct "historical" overtones to an epic that initially seems to float free from temporal entanglement (Smolak 2001). Yet in the opening years of the fifth century, with the increasing "breakdown of civility" between pagans and Christians and with Augustine soon to publish the first books of the *City of God* and Orosius his *History against the Pagans,* Virgil's language and ideas were too deeply embedded in contemporary minds ever to be simply a neutral medium (MacCormack 1998: quote 139).

Prudentius now seems the Latin Christian poet *par excellence,* master of creative reception and brilliant composition. Widely read in classical, biblical, and Christian literature and committed to honoring God through his poetry, Prudentius expressed his ideas with a depth of feeling, a command of media, and a flair for the dramatic as well as the grotesque that set him apart. And yet Prudentius' aims and achievements remain controversial. Some have seen the *Psychomachia* as a radical and sophisticated assault upon the *Aeneid,* using Virgil to subvert Virgil and banish all potential sympathy for the Augustan poet's historical and transcendental vision (Smith 1976). Others emphasize the tensions and ambiguities that seem to signal the poet's own intellectual uncertainties or the fondness for wordplay and verbal manipulation that firmly align him with the poetic tradition (Nugent 1985; Malamud 1989). If the heroic posturing, graphic violence, and bloodletting perpetrated by Prudentius' feminine Christian *Virtutes* have dismayed some readers (e.g., Lewis 1938: 68–70), others have found ways to salvage the poet's aesthetic sensibility and Christian credentials (e.g., Nugent 1985: 19–20; James 1999). Such ongoing debates signal not Prudentius' failure but his poem's engagement with issues of historical moment and universal scope. His popularity in the Middle Ages speaks for itself.

Biblical Epic in the Fifth and Sixth Centuries

Juvencus introduced biblical epic in the early fourth century but only in the fifth, amid the changed circumstances brought by Germanic settlement and the diffusion of monastic piety, did his successors step forward. Five major works composed between the early fifth and the mid-sixth century exemplify the genre, its diversity and its history (Roberts 1985: 76–106; cf. Fontaine 1981: 245–64; Witke 1971: 145–232). Two of these works represented New Testament material: Sedulius' *Paschale Carmen* (second quarter of the fifth century), which begins with a prefatory book glossing select Old Testament episodes before treating the Gospels in four more books, and Arator's two-book *Acts of the Apostles* (or *Historia Apostolica*), recited at Rome in the spring of 544. The other three take up Old Testament episodes: the so-called *Heptateuchos,* attributed to Cyprianus (Gallus), dating (probably) to the early fifth century and reworking material from the first seven books of the Bible; the three-book *Alethia* of the rhetor Claudius Marius Victorius, composed at Marseilles in the second quarter of the fifth century and devoted to Genesis 1–19; and Avitus of Vienne's late-fifth-century *De spiritalis historiae gestis* in five (short) books, recasting Genesis 1–9 and the Exodus from Egypt. Though distinct in theme, style, and proportion of exegetical intrusion, these works are united by their hexametrical re-presentation of Christian scripture and their self-conscious allusions to their epic forebears.

Stylistic enhancement, audience appeal, educational aims, and moral edification are explicitly cited by biblical epicists as reasons for composition. Sedulius, for example, recorded his desire to offer his discerning readers a Gospel story "honeyed-up with the charm of verse" (*CSEL* 10, p. 5: *versuum...blandimento mellitum*) while Claudius Marius Victorius announced his aim to shape young minds and hearts to the true path of virtue (*Precatio* 104–5). How these poets conceived of their activity and how they worked, transforming scriptural texts into hexameter poetry, has provoked discussion. Some scholars have emphasized the paraphrastic aspects of these literary projects. The skills of rhetorical paraphrase had long been a part of every educated person's repertoire and continued to be taught in the schools of late antiquity. The paraphrast was expected to abbreviate, expand, or reorder his model, changing its form without adulterating its content, perhaps to clarify meaning but more often to add ornament to a balder text. Thus poetic paraphrase, beyond application of the rules of meter, entailed the use of figures and tropes, lexical variation, and stylistic amplification through, for example, ecphrases and digressions.

All of this has now been amply demonstrated (Roberts 1985). So, too, the correlative engagement of these poets with the poetry of the epic tradition. The late antique biblical epicists signaled their epic pretensions not only by choosing to narrate *gesta*, by celebrating heroes, by invoking sources of divine inspiration, or by deploying metaphor and allegory, but also by frequent direct recall and creative imitation of their classical predecessors, Ovid, Lucan, and others, but especially Virgil. Sedulius' *Paschale Carmen* is so replete with Virgilian allusions and echoes, his Christ rendered in such rich Virgilian hues, his theme so bound up with notions of *pietas* and destiny, that it has been (almost) possible to think of the poem as an "*Enéide* chrétienne" (Springer 1988: 76–95; van der Laan 1993). In a similar vein, Ovid's treatment of creation at the beginning of the *Metamorphoses* offered the Christian poet Victorius both language for enhancing and a foil for highlighting the biblical version of creation (Roberts 2002). Avitus' *De spiritalis historiae gestis* displays his control and manipulation of Lucan, Lucretius, Ovid, Statius, and Virgil (as well as Christian poets), while his Adam, Noah, and Moses typologically adumbrate a Christ who resonates both in harmony and dissonance with Virgil's Aeneas (Arweiler 1999: 221–346; Hecquet-Noti 1999: 38–47, 65–73). In Arator's mid-sixth-century *Acts of the Apostles* God as Christ is Lucan's *rector Olympi* (1.37; Luc. *BC* 2.4, cf. *Aen.* 2.799); Peter and Paul are, like Virgil's Bacchus and Ceres, the "lights of the world" (2.1219; *Geo.* 1.5–6); and nearly every episode is reconstructed on a substratum of classical as well as scriptural allusions (Schrader et al. 1987 with McKinlay's apparatus).

It seems undeniable, then, that both the practice of rhetorical paraphrase and the abiding allure of classical epic, as the highest form of poetic expression, influenced the self-understanding and work habits of the biblical epicists. Yet, at the same time, the formal claims of paraphrase and the weight of the epic legacy were neither serious breaks upon creativity nor impediments to individual interpretive designs (Roberts 1985: 161–218). Sedulius, for example, organizing his material in respect to his soteriological interests, privileged Christ's miracles (1.26: *clara salutiferi miracula Christi*) over his speeches and parables. Avitus, concerned in his *De spiritalis historiae gestis* to explicate salvation history, took considerable liberty in typologically and allegorically recasting Old Testament episodes so that they spoke to contemporary theological and ecclesiological debates. In fact, the independence of mind often shown by the biblical epicists challenges the boundary between "paraphrase" (even in the most generous sense) and "originality." Some scholars, therefore, prefer to locate the more immediate impulses towards the composition and form of the biblical epics in the example set by Juvencus and, especially, in the models and inspiration provided by contemporary scriptural exegesis and commentary in prose, which often included paraphrase (Springer 1988: 9–22; Hillier 1993; Nodes 1993).

Indeed, as scholars identify more closely the particular didactic and polemic agenda that animated the biblical epics, their status as thoughtful and original works on multiple levels becomes ever clearer. Sedulius' animosity towards the heretical doctrines he associated with Sabellianism and Arianism, for example, fundamentally shaped his Gospel narrative and set the tone and terms of his amplifications and exegetical intrusions (Springer 1988: 33–70). Arator's *Historia Apostolica* alternates passages of literal and mystical interpretation of the Book of Acts while affirming papal primacy in Byzantine Italy and offering its audience baptismal catechesis (Fontaine 1981: 260–4; Hillier 1993).

Avitus' arrangement and interpretations of his material from Genesis and Exodus in his *De spiritalis historiae gestis*, a virtual study in sin and redemption, are deeply indebted to his reading of Augustine and, in turn, further promoted Augustinian views on original sin, grace, and baptism, whose rigor had been openly resisted in fifth-century Gaul (Nodes 1985, 1993: 55–73; Weaver 1996; Wood 2001).

Like Virgil or Lucan, then, the biblical epicists engaged with issues of the day in narratives about the past but their manifest didactic aims also push these works towards a category of exegetical epic or verse commentary. This didactic or epigrammatic quality, as much as any respect it commanded as literature, for example, ensured that Sedulius' *Paschale Carmen* was widely read in the Middle Ages. But the development of biblical epic also reveals something about the evolution of ancient epic more generally (and the future of medieval epic). By the time Avitus of Vienne composed his *De spiritalis historiae gestis* in the late 490s he could call upon not only an astoundingly wide range of classical authors but also some two centuries of Christian literature and poetry, summoning Lactantius, Ambrose, and Augustine as well as Juvencus, Prudentius, Paulinus of Nola, Sedulius, Marius Victor, and Sidonius (see, e.g., Hecquet-Noti 1999: 323–7). A half-century later Arator's *Historia Apostolica*, referencing Virgil, Lucan, and Statius while unearthing the baptismal symbolism of Acts, and performed before an appreciative audience in the basilica of S. Pietro in Vincoli, defies our categories. Biblical epic has established itself as a vital and organic mode of expression notable on its own terms, creatively overrunning the boundaries of scriptural exegesis and Christian doctrine, of classical epic and rhetoric, capable of fulfilling didactic as well as pleasurable ends (Witke 1971; Malsbary 1985).

Hagiographic Epic

The literary self-consciousness of sixth-century Christian poets is immediately evident in the "genealogy" with which Venantius Fortunatus introduced his epic celebrating Martin of Tours (Ven. Fort. *VM* 1.15–25):

> Primus enim, docili distinguens ordine carmen,
> maiestatis opus metri canit arte Juvencus.
> Hinc quoque conspicui radiavit lingua Seduli
> paucaque perstrinxit florente Orientius ore
> martyribusque piis sacra haec donaria mittens,
> prudens prudenter Prudentius immolat actus.
> Stemmate, corde, fide pollens Paulinus et arte
> versibus explicuit Martini dogma magistri.
> Sortis apostolicae quae gesta vocantur et actus,
> facundo eloquio sulcavit vates Arator.
> Quod sacra explicuit serie genealogus olim,
> Alcimus egregio digessit acumine praesul.

> First of all, marking off his poem in skillful measure,
> Juvencus sang of the work of the Divine Majesty with metrical art.
> Then too the speech of illustrious Sedulius shone forth
> and Orientius touched briefly upon a few matters in ornate words.
> And sending his sacred gifts to the holy martyrs,
> prudent Prudentius prudently offered accounts of their deeds.
> Paulinus, mighty in family, heart, faith, and skill,
> unfurled in verses the doctrines of Martin the teacher.
> What are called the deeds and acts of the apostolic community
> Arator the poet ploughed through with effortless eloquence.
> That which the genealogist [Moses] once unfolded in sacred order,
> Alcimus the bishop disposed with distinguished subtlety.

To this lineage of holy poet-prophets (*sanctorum culmina vatum*) Fortunatus, conventionally proclaiming his inadequacy, added his own work, an account of the deeds (*gesta*) of the blessed Martin (1.45). Born in northern Italy about 540 and educated at Ravenna, Fortunatus made his career as poet, courtier, and bishop within the aristocratic and ecclesiastic circles of Merovingian Gaul (Brennan 1985; George 1992). Therein Fortunatus compiled the extensive corpus of occasional verse, panegyrics, and *vitae* that included his hexametrical *Vita Sancti Martini*, composed between 573 and 576 and presented to Tours' (now famous) bishop, Gregory. In this opening section Fortunatus tactfully proclaimed himself the heir of the biblical epicists, of Prudentius (here as author of the *Peristephanon*), and of Paulinus of Périgueux (Petrocorium), who a century earlier had already composed a six-book *Vita Martini* based, like Fortunatus', upon Sulpicius Severus' late-fourth-century prose *Life of Martin* and *Dialogues*. With less overt fanfare Fortunatus also displayed throughout his four-book poem adroit command of the classical epicists, especially Virgil and Ovid, as well as Claudian (Labarre 1998: 161–210; Roberts 2001: 267–75). By the 570s, as Fortunatus knew, a diverse body of Christian and classical prose and poetry loomed up like a mountain behind any poet who would fashion a Christian holy man into an "epic hero."

Hagiographic epic, like biblical epic, was rooted in the fourth century. Paulinus of Nola's *epyllion* on John the Baptist had already blurred the boundaries between Gospel paraphrase and hagiography while two of his annual "birthday" poems (*natalicia*) honoring St Felix blended panegyric, hagiography, and epic overtones to represent the "life" of Nola's guardian saint (Trout 1999: 166–9). It is hardly surprising that holy men should join Christ, the patriarchs, and the apostles to become heroes in epic verse. Hagiography was deeply rooted in Christian literary practice and Sulpicius Severus' *Vita Martini*, composed in the final years of the fourth century while Martin was still living (and supplemented after Martin's death by the *Dialogues*), was the first Latin classic of the field. When Severus wrote it was still necessary to defend Martin, Tours' controversial bishop, for asceticism was socially suspect and monasticism not yet assimilated. By the time Paulinus and Fortunatus wrote, however, the cult of St Martin was prominent well beyond Gaul.

But the Martinian epics of Paulinus of Périgueux and Venantius Fortunatus are not easily qualified. They are at once expressions in poetry of the popularity of saints' lives in late Roman and Merovingian Gaul; of the continuing demand for sophisticated verse that, like the biblical epics, echoed classical poetry while expounding Christian themes; and a further example of the art of rhetorical paraphrase. Yet a century of change as well as individual aims and dispositions separate Paulinus and Fortunatus (Van Dam 1993). Both poets may have drawn upon the same textual resources (though Paulinus' sixth book did adapt a miracle ledger not used by Fortunatus, and Fortunatus had the example of Paulinus before him) and carefully preserved the order of the Severan narrative, but their choices for omission, abbreviation, and rhetorical amplification, their manipulation of individual episodes, and the aesthetic values they signaled by their stylistic choices conspired to yield two distinct poetic projects and two different images of the heroic Martin. Paulinus expanded and commented upon episodes, often sententiously, in a quest for the moral and spiritual meaning behind Martin's actions, while his emphasis upon divine love gives his poem an overarching unity. Moreover, his Martin's heroic qualities most immediately serve the saint's image as an ideal patronal bishop. Fortunatus' hero is, by contrast, the celestial guardian of the developed sixth-century cult center at Tours; his poem is a series of discreet medallions; and his elaborately descriptive verse a premier representative of the jeweled style (Roberts 1994 and 1995; Labarre 1998). That neither Paulinus nor Fortunatus grants their hero psychological complexity or moral growth should, perhaps, be credited to the conventions of contemporary panegyric. But, as Fortunatus revealed in his opening credits, the epigrammatic and exegetical qualities of his "last epic of antiquity" owe just as much to the manner in which the earlier biblical epicists had already transformed generic expectations (Roberts 2001).

From Juvencus, who heads Fortunatus' list of *vates* who set out God's work in poetic measure, to Fortunatus himself, the range of Christian epic defies most generalizations. Christian epicists engaged with their classical predecessors, especially Virgil, with admiration and rivalry. They deployed the conventions of epic poetry in different degree but, as time passed, they also had at their disposal an ever-deepening reservoir of Christian models. Christian epics, too, celebrated deeds, those of God, Christ, the Patriarchs, the apostles, and the saints, and to do so they drew not only upon Christian scripture and prose hagiography, but also upon the rhetorical principles of panegyric and the exegetical modes of scriptural commentary. Tending towards the discursive and episodic, Christian epic more often found its momentum in epigrammatic reflection, reversal, and antithesis than in narrative integrity or psychological complexity. Simply put, the aesthetics and the aims of Christian epicists reflect and express the dynamic evolution of late ancient culture and its literature over a period of three remarkable centuries.

FURTHER READING

Further reading might best begin with the poems themselves. The list below is meant to offer initial guidance to those seeking out texts and translations. Unfortunately many of these works, even in Latin, remain difficult to obtain. Moreover, some still lack complete English translations. Readers interested in the critical history of specific Latin texts can start with the entries of the *Clavis Patrum Latinorum* (*CPL*). Otherwise, the chapter's citations point to many important studies of individual authors, works, and themes.

Roberts 1989 will initiate the interested reader into broader matters of style and aesthetics, while Brown 2003 vigorously surveys the panoramic background. Each provides a sure foothold within a vast terrain still inviting exploration.

Alcimus Avitus, *De spiritalis historiae gestis* (*CPL* 995). *MGH AA* 6 (Peiper); *SC* 444. Hecquet-Noti 1999, books 1–3; Nodes 1985, books 1–3. Shea 1997, English translation.

Arator, *De actibus apostolorum / Historica apostolica* (*CPL* 1504). *CSEL* 72 (McKinlay). Schrader, Roberts, and Makowski 1987, English translation.

Claudius Marius Victorius, *Alethia* (*CPL* 1455). *CSEL* 16 (Schenkl), *CCSL* 128 (Hovingh). English selections at White 2000.

Cyprianus Gallus, *Heptateuchos* (*CPL* 1423). *CSEL* 23 (Peiper). English selection at White 2000.

Juvencus, *Evangeliorum libri quattuor* (*CPL* 1385). *CSEL* 24 (Huemer). English selections at White 2000.

Paulinus of Nola, *Carmina* (*CPL* 203). *CSEL* 30 (De Hartel / Kamptner). P. G. Walsh, *ACW* 40 (1975).

Paulinus of Périgueux, *Vita Martini* (*CPL* 1474). *CSEL* 16 (Petschenig).

Proba, *Cento Vergilianus* (*CPL* 1480). *CSEL* 16 (Schenkl). Clark and Hatch 1981, text and English translation.

Prudentius, *Opera* (*CPL* 1437–45). *CSEL* 61 (Bergman); *CCSL* 126 (Cunningham). Thomson 1949, text and English translation; Lavarenne 1955–63, text and French translation; Eagan 1962, 1965, English translation.

Sedulius, *Paschale Carmen* (*CPL* 1447). *CSEL* 10 (Huemer). English selections at Sigerson 1922; Swanson 1957; and White 2000.

Venantius Fortunatus, *Vita Martini* (*CPL* 1033). *MGH AA* 4.1 (Leo); Quesnel 1996, text and French translation.

CHAPTER FORTY-ONE

Epic and Other Genres in the Roman World

R. Jenkyns

The relationship between epic and other genres can be seen in terms of two processes: the incorporation into epic poetry of themes and colors drawn from literature of different kinds; and the influence of epic poems upon writers whose own work was not of epic character. This chapter will discuss both these streams of influence. However, we shall not be able fully to understand the relationship between Latin epic poetry and other genres without some thought about the nature of genre and of epic. So this issue must be briefly revisited. A first consideration is this. We need to maintain a balance between two propositions: on the one hand, classical poets and their readers had a stronger sense of genre and its conventions than do most writers and readers today; on the other, classical poets and readers probably did not have as clear-cut and tight a sense of genre and its expectations as some modern scholars have supposed. The practice of writers is always likely to run far ahead of the ability of critics and theorists to categorize or describe it. (The fundamental study of the interplay of genres is Kroll 1924; see too the critique of Kroll by Barchiesi 2001a.)

We should also note that generic labels are not all of the same kind: some are much looser and more inclusive than others. "Pastoral," for example, denotes a restricted type of literature, one that demands adherence to certain conventions and allusion to an inherited tradition. By contrast, "novel" is a large, baggy category: almost any work of prose fiction above a certain length falls into it. "Epic" comes somewhere in between these two, more exact than "novel," less bound to convention than "pastoral." To us "epic" suggests first and foremost a certain elevation of theme and tone (which is why the term can be intelligibly applied to a novel or film, and even to music or painting); to the ancients the necessary condition, rather, was the use of a particular meter. Their sense of what an epic might contain, in terms of style and subject, was therefore likely to be more accommodating than is ours. Some modern discussions of the nature of epic have the unintended effect of excluding the *Odyssey*, but when our eye turns to Greece and Rome, any definition that leaves that poem out is obviously a non-starter.

Let us consider a genre belonging to our own time: the epic film. The "Hollywood epic" obeys a number of conventions. It must be long. It must be set in the past, probably no later than the sixteenth century, and preferably much earlier. It should be in wide-screen format. There must be a handsome, well-muscled hero, and probably a busty heroine too. There must be grandiose sets, representing the wealth and splendor of an imposing civilization. There must be heroic combat, and scenes requiring huge numbers of extras. And so on. A movie need not have every one of these characteristics to qualify as an epic, but it must have a fair number of them.

We all know what a Hollywood epic is; we recognize it at once when we see it. We also know that the category is fuzzy at the edges (is *Lawrence of Arabia* an epic, for example?) and that this fuzziness is entirely unproblematic, because the term carries no prescriptive authority and because terms with no determinate origin tend to have uncertain boundaries anyway (compare geographical terms like "East Anglia" or "the Midwest"). The attitude of ancient readers and writers to epic forms may have been more like this than is commonly recognized. It was not so much that there were "rules" of epic to be followed, or alternatively challenged, but rather that admired and attractive models existed which would naturally influence the composition of any large narrative poem. If an epic poet diverges from his predecessors, it need not mean that he is defying convention; this may rather be a matter of natural evolution, a healthy combination of tradition and the individual talent.

When we ask what the Greeks themselves meant by *epos*, much of the answer turns out to be disconcertingly bald and simple. Epos was verse in hexameters, and the terms *epopoios* and *epôn poiêtês* ("writer of epos") indicated a poet who used this meter (Cameron 1995: 268f.). Aristotle defines epic, as he does other genres, in metrical terms, though he also indicates that size and grandeur are characteristics of epos. He seems to allow that an epos could in theory be in a meter other than hexameter, but experience has shown hexameter to be the best, because it is the most dignified and stately (*Poetics* 1449b, 1456a, 1459b). The question thus arises whether epos is helpful or expressive as a generic term. To put the issue in other words: does the fact that the Greeks defined epos in terms of meter suggest that there were strong and clear expectations of what poetry composed in that meter ought to contain? The answer is probably no: from the start, the hexameter was used for a wide range of poetic purposes. It has been suggested that in using the hexameter for bucolic verse Theocritus was consciously creating a dissonance between the form of the verse and its content. But there is no good reason to believe this, and Theocritus indeed uses the hexameter for poems of widely differing type. The same argument has been applied to Latin verse satire. But this genre uses no meter other than the hexameter, throughout its history from Lucilius to Juvenal. The hexameter is indeed so superbly flexible a tool that we should not be surprised to find the poets exploiting its versatility. Didactic poetry, likewise, was always written in hexameters: when Ovid composes his *Ars Amatoria* in elegiac couplets, his choice of meter announces that this will be a parody of didactic verse, not the real thing.

The key is to be found not in the language of literary taxonomists but in the practice of the poets themselves. And when we look at the Latin poets, it seems clear that they could distinguish without difficulty between one stream of tradition descending from Homer (a tradition of heroic narrative – what we call epic) and a tradition descending from Hesiod (what we call didactic). In the first line of the *Aeneid* Virgil signals that Homer is the *prôtos heuretês* (original inventor) of the genre in which he is composing. "*Arma virumque cano*" ("I sing of arms and the man...") – *arma* alludes to the epic of war, such as the *Iliad* and the second half of the *Aeneid*, *virum* to the *Odyssey*. Both the Homeric epics begin, like the *Aeneid*, with a noun in the accusative. Virgil's *Arma* corresponds to the *Iliad*'s *Mênin* (wrath). In the case of Virgil's second noun the correspondence is even closer, as *virum* is an exact translation of *Andra*, the first word of the *Odyssey*.

Virgil's generic manifesto at the start of his heroic poem, not explicit and yet plain to see, is both like and distinct from the way in which he had opened the *Georgics*, at the start of which he had laid out the subjects of each of its four books, one by one. He begins, "Quid faciat laetas segetes, quo sidere terram / vertere..." ("What makes the crops flourish, under what star to turn the earth . . . ''). As the fourth-century commentator Servius noted, this is an allusion to Hesiod. Whereas Virgil summarizes the contents of the second, third and fourth books in a single phrase, he divides the subject of the first book into two, corresponding to the division of subject matter in Hesiod's *Works and Days*.

Virgil's generic indicator here is especially subtle, for he acknowledges Hesiod as his pattern, but only for the first book. And indeed the *Georgics* is remarkable, perhaps unique, in the way in which it develops and modifies its character as it proceeds. In the final book it modulates into mythological narrative, with the story of Orpheus and Eurydice enclosed within the story of Aristaeus. Here Virgil's model, for form and tone, is Catullus' *Peleus and Thetis* (poem 64). The story of Orpheus and Eurydice, first found here in extant literature, may draw upon a lost Hellenistic source; the story of Aristaeus borrows elements from Menelaus' account of his adventures on the return from Troy in the fourth book of the *Odyssey*. Here we may feel the inadequacy of our critical language to do justice to the grace and fluidity of Virgil's procedures. To say that Virgil becomes epic here would be too ponderous. For one thing, a writer may borrow from a predecessor without necessarily adopting that predecessor's genre; for another, the Aristaeus story is the outer case containing the inner story of Orpheus, that exquisite *spätlese* of the neoteric aesthetic, and it is the inner story which forms the emotional heart of the *Georgics*' last pages. And anyway, Menelaus' adventures are a diversion within the *Odyssey* itself, a kind of folktale told in an unemphatic part of the poem. What Virgil's practice does show is that poetic kinds (and we might remember that "genre" is merely the French for "kind") were not straitjackets but forms which the poet could mold and develop.

Virgil's use of Hesiod and Homer as separate generic indicators may help to clarify Lucretius' purposes. In this present volume, devoted to epic poetry, Lucretius is included (see Chapter 32, by Gale), but no other didactic verse in Latin, and this is indeed defensible. For Lucretius' enterprise was, among other things, an attempt to infuse into the didactic genre the grandeur, scale and romance of epic. To begin with, there is the simple matter of length: at about 7,000 lines *De rerum natura* is vastly longer than any Greek didactic poem known to us, and roughly the same size as the *Aeneid*. The introduction to the poem – perhaps one should say, series of introductions – is the longest in classical literature. The poets named in it are not Hesiod or Aratus, the chief didactic poet of the Hellenistic age, neither of whom Lucretius ever mentions, but Homer and the man who had claimed to be Homer's heir in Latin, Ennius. The list of the great men who have died, which comes at the climax of the third book, culminates in Epicurus, preceded by Democritus, the John the Baptist of the Epicurean story; but immediately before them is, again, Homer. Among didactic poets Lucretius does indeed acknowledge Empedocles, who receives an extended tribute in the middle of the first book, but it is significant that Empedocles' verse was marked by a vehemence and energy which foreshadow Lucretius' own, and which distinguish him from other didactic poets in Greek.

Lucretius opens his poem with a magnificent hymn to Venus. The incorporation of hymn into his work is in itself an indication of his ambition to reach out beyond the conventional limits of the didactic form to embrace other genres or modes. His style, with its heavy alliterations, compound adjectives and occasionally archaizing forms of meter, vocabulary, and morphology, is another generic indicator. This style is not the product of romantic nostalgia or a wistful longing for a nobler past. On the contrary, he is strikingly free of that veneration for the good old days that marks (and sometimes mars) so many Latin writers. As a small but telling instance of this, he never uses the word *antiquus* as a term of praise; contrast, for example, Cicero and Virgil. Rather, his language asserts the grandeur of his theme by evoking Ennius and the tradition of Latin epic. Epicureanism was easily portrayed as an ignoble philosophy, setting pleasure, rather than virtue, as the proper object of human choice; as a purely materialist doctrine, it might also seem to remove romance, mystery, and splendor from the world. Lucretius' medium becomes part of his message: it declares that Epicurus' teaching, rightly understood, possesses excitement and majesty.

He also conveys this idea through occasional allusion to epic poems. Thus he takes a description of the gods' blessed life on Olympus out of the *Odyssey*, and turns it, by means of a paraphrase that is not far from direct translation, into an expression of Epicurus' theory that the gods are indifferent to human concerns and play no part in the government of the world (3.18–22; cf. Hom. *Od.* 6.42–6). That allusion is unusually direct; elsewhere, Lucretius' allusions to epic are likely to be implicit or more generalized. Praising Epicurus himself, he presents this retiring quietist as a kind of epic hero. He is (we are told) a man whose spirit conquered and journeyed beyond the blazing walls of the cosmos and through the infinite, from where he returned victorious, bringing us the knowledge of nature's laws:

> unde refert nobis victor quid possit oriri,
> quid nequeat, finita potestas denique cuique
> quanam sit ratione atque alte terminus haerens.
> quare religio pedibus subiecta vicissim
> obteritur, nos exaequat victoria caelo.

(1.75–9)

> Whence, victorious, he brings back to us the knowledge of what can come to be and what cannot, and the principle by which each thing has its capacity delimited and its deep-set boundary-stone, how religion is now trampled underfoot, his victory makes us equal to the heavens.

The idea of Epicurus as a traveller in the spirit to vastly distant regions does seem to evoke Odysseus, whose voyages took him beyond the known world, the man who "saw the cities of many men and knew their mind" (*Od.* 1. 3). Then we see religion brought low and trampled upon. Taken with the repeated stress on victory (*victor*... *victoria*, with *pervicit*, "conquered," coming shortly before the lines quoted) and the idea that Epicurus "brings back to us" spoils – not slaves or precious objects but the greatest good, philosophical truth – we are coaxed into seeing the great man as a figure out of heroic verse, an Achilles of the spirit or a Roman general returning in triumph to his city. When Lucretius describes the spring rains, in superbly vehement language, as father sky penetrating mother earth, we might feel that he is referring to fertility cult rather than to literature (1.250f.). Yet the sacred marriage of sky and earth lies behind the coupling of Zeus and Hera in the fourteenth book of the *Iliad* (see especially lines 347–51). Aeschylus used the theme magnificently in his *Danaids* (fr. 44), and was to be echoed in turn by Euripides (fr. 898.7ff.). Lucretius' metaphor lifts didactic verse simultaneously into high literature and into the sphere of the sacred.

So we need to feel the distinction between didactic epos and high epic in order to appreciate how Lucretius is enlarging the generic scope of didactic poetry. But that enlarging ambition carries him downwards as well as up. Oddly entwined with his search for sublimity is a movement in the opposite direction: he rams deliberately prosaic and even clumsy language into the texture of his verse. One instance of this is his use of ponderous connectives, like *quapropter* or the ostentatiously cumbrous *quare etiam atque etiam* (not only lumpish in expression, but requiring three elisions in consecutive words). Another is his fondness for the word *ratio*. Perhaps a philosophical poet could not have avoided this word altogether, even if he had wished to, but Lucretius multiplies its appearances by using it in phrases like *qua ratione* (and compare 1.77, cited above). On the larger scale, he ends his two middle books with a quasi-popular form of vigorous argumentation, the diatribe: his great diatribe on death forms the climax to the third book, and the diatribe on love to the fourth (Wallach 1976: 1–10; Brown 1987: 137–9). In the first of these diatribes he evokes another genre, forensic oratory. Lucretius here draws a series of metaphors from the law-courts, echoing legal phraseology and presenting Nature as an advocate, attacking the man who complains about death. And some of the language is rough-and-tumble: "Aufer abhinc lacrimas, baratro," Nature declares ("Away with those tears, greedy-guts") (3.955).

In the diatribe on love Lucretius goes a good deal further. Here, with rough sarcasm, he mocks the besotted lover, unable to see the object of his passion as she really is:

> nigra melichrus est, immunda et fetida acosmos,
> caesia Palladium, nervosa et lignea dorcas,
> parvula, pumilio, chariton mia, tota merum sal,
> magna atque immanis cataplexis plenaque honoris.
> balba loqui non quit, traulizi, muta pudens est:
> at flagrans odiosa loquacula Lampadium fit.
>
> (4.1160–5)

A swarthy girl is "honey-hued," a dirty, smelly one is "a gypsy," a grey-eyed one is "the image of Athena," a stringy, gawky one "a gazelle." A little midget is "one of the graces," "just pure wit," a great big lump is "simply amazing," and "so dignified". If she stammers and cannot speak, "she lisps," if she is dumb, she is "modest," while a ghastly spiteful chatterbox is "a little firework."

The mass of Greek words in these lines takes us towards colloquial speech (compare Cicero's letters, in contrast to his more formal works). But Lucretius does not only use many individual loan-words from the Greek: in a couple of places the text cannot be construed as Latin at all. *Chariton mia*, "one of the graces," and *traulizi*, "she lisps," are merely chunks of raw Greek transliterated, and the fact that they do not appear in Greek script may be only an accident of transmission. Such mixing of languages is alien to formal verse style. Lucilius had done it in his satires, but even he was to be reproached by Horace for the licence (*Sat.* 1.10.20–30). Horace himself will translate a snatch of Homer rather than quoting him directly, even at the cost of losing punch (e.g. *Sat.* 1.9.78). Yet here is Lucretius in the grandest of all didactic poems breaching the convention. He not only soars higher than all previous didactic poets, but drops lower as well.

In the diatribe on death especially he finds a new tone, satiric and grandly declamatory at the same time, which we shall not meet again in Latin verse until it is rediscovered by Juvenal a century and a half later. It seems impossible to say whether Juvenal owed a direct debt to Lucretius or came upon this tone by another route, but from his echoes of Virgil we can at least see that he was aware of bringing a kind of epic resonance into a genre that might seem extremely different.

Lucretius' greatest transformation of the didactic genre was to create a fusion of aesthetic splendor and moral energy. *De rerum natura* is a work of evangelism, offering salvation. Only believe, it says, and you too can be secure and happy. This transformation had a profound influence on Virgil's two greatest works. The *Georgics* does not preach a particular doctrine but, inspired by Lucretius, it is pervaded by moral seriousness and a moral vision (though we should not forget that it contains lightness and sparkle too). Lucretius' influence on the *Aeneid* in this respect is less obvious, but as important. For the *Aeneid* too is a poem about salvation. The hero is introduced in the opening lines as a man on a quest, "dum conderet urbem / inferretque deos Latio" ("until he should establish a city and bring his gods to Latium") (*Aen.* 1.5f.). We have good reason to believe the story that Virgil was an Epicurean in his youth, but to judge from the *Aeneid*, his own thought became less individualist as he grew older. Lucretius' idea of salvation is inward and spiritual, whereas Virgil finds human security in social and political institutions – in city and governance, in established cult and custom. Milton, introducing his own epic, declares it to be a didactic poem, his purpose being "That to the heighth of this great Argument / I may assert Eternal Providence, / And justify the ways of God to men" (*Paradise Lost* 1. 24–6). But he is only making explicit what had been implicit in Virgil's epic long before. If we define the didactic genre in terms of Hesiod or Aratus, we shall probably not be tempted to regard the *Aeneid* as didactic in any degree at all. But if we define didactic in terms of *De rerum natura*, we can see that one of Virgil's innovations was to suffuse epic with the moral drive of Lucretian didactic. Lucretius wrote a didactic poem colored by epic tone, and Virgil, in some degree, inverts this pattern. He also incorporates didactic elements into the *Aeneid* more directly, and on a smaller scale. Anchises' account of the nature of the universe in the sixth book, a blend of theology, cosmology, and philosophy, is strongly and deliberately Lucretian in style and language (*Aen.* 6.724 ff.).

Virgil's annexation of Lucretius is part of his universalizing ambition. When Sibelius praised the symphony for its severity of form and the logic making an inner connection between all its motifs, Mahler disagreed: "No," he said, "the symphony must be like the world. It must be all-embracing." The *Aeneid* can be seen as a symphony in words that attempts to fulfill both ideals at the same time: Virgil wants, as it were, to be both Mahler and Sibelius. The *Aeneid* is more tautly constructed, its parts more carefully related to one another, than in any previous epic poem, yet it also seeks to embrace past and present, myth and history, both the *Iliad* and the *Odyssey*, and much more besides. To understand the relationship between Virgil's epic and other genres, we need to appreciate how strange and original his ambition was. We tend to assume that the "great poem" will take a subject of universal scope and importance, as do the *Aeneid*, *The Divine Comedy*, and *Paradise Lost*. Critics have taken immensity of theme and a massive moral weight to be general characteristics of "secondary epic," whereas in reality they are distinctively Virgilian. Our idea of classical epic is inevitably dominated by Homer and Virgil, partly because of their greatness, partly because the *Aeneid* is so closely related to the *Iliad* and *Odyssey*, and partly perhaps because Aristotle's brief remarks on epic may seem to prescribe something on the Homeric and Virgilian pattern.

But there were never any other epics much like the *Iliad* and *Odyssey* – or at least not until Virgil. The Epic Cycle was quite different in scale and character; the *Argonautica* of Apollonius was quite unlike; Ennius' *Annales* is hugely unlike, spreading as it does across the centuries, even though he presents himself as the Homer of the Latin language. Virgil's decisions – to rework the two Homeric epics and to "embrace the world" – were both radically innovative. That all-embracing ambition included the will to embrace other genres within the overall epic structure. One example of this is the fourth book of the *Aeneid*, which assumes the character of a tragic drama, with Dido as the protagonist. Dido's story conforms very well to Aristotle's description of tragedy as a drama centred upon an individual who is essentially virtuous but imperfect and who falls through an error or mistake (*Poetics* 1453a). At one point Virgil even makes the likeness to the theater explicit. The tormented queen is harried by Aeneas in her dreams:

> Eumenidum veluti demens videt agmina Pentheus
> et solem geminum et duplices se ostendere Thebas,
> aut Agamemnonius scaenis agitatus Orestes,
> armatam facibus matrem et serpentibus atris
> cum fugit ultricesque sedent in limine Dirae.
>
> (*Aen.* 4.469–73)

As Pentheus in his madness sees appear the ranks of Furies and a double sun and Thebes twice over, or like the haunted Orestes, Agamemnon's son, on stage, when he flees from his mother, armed with brands and black torches, and the avenging Fiends sit upon the threshold.

The first part of this simile alludes to Euripides' *Bacchae*, the latter part to the *Oresteia* of Aeschylus. So Dido's story is not tragic only in the looser sense that it grandly depicts the suffering of a noble hero; its shape and plot have the character of a stage spectacle. We naturally think of fifth-century Athens; but if early Latin tragedy had survived, we should probably pick up things which, as it is, we miss. There was a cost to putting a tragedy inside the larger story: casting Dido as a tragic protagonist, Virgil had to demote Aeneas, for a while, to a secondary role, and this creates difficulties for him, in narrative and in the disposition of the reader's sympathies. Whether he fully succeeded in overcoming those difficulties will probably go on being debated as long as the *Aeneid* is read.

Virgil also brought humbler tones into his epic. These may be brief. When Aeneas and his company eat an alfresco meal of fruits piled on to wheaten pastry, they eat the fruit first before turning upon the cereal substructure. This provokes a childish joke from Aeneas' son (*Aen.* 7. 116f):

"heus, etiam mensas consumimus?" inquit Iulus,
nec plura, adludens.

"Hey, are we eating our tables too?" asked Iulus – only that, as a joke.

To match the casual, silly innocence of this, Virgil's style becomes for a moment quite un-epic: *heus* is colloquial, and the two tiny phrases hung on to the sentence's end are alien to the grand style. But Iulus' little joke has in fact a portentous significance, and the style instantly switches back to epic amplitude as the narrative returns from son to father, and Aeneas picks up the happy omen.

But Virgil's most original and inventive use of material from another genre is on a much larger scale. The eighth book of the *Aeneid* sees the hero on the site of the future Rome, and these scenes import into the poem topography, antiquarianism, and the origins of later Roman beliefs and customs. Etiology – the account of the origins of cults, customs, or monuments – could in principle appear in any genre: it is found in some of Euripides' plays, for example. But it is especially associated with the Alexandrian poetry of the third century, and is part of that age's fascination with what is sometimes called scholarship but which is better understood as a spirit of intellectual inquiry that embraces history, literary study, and science alike. Apollonius of Rhodes wrote *Ktiseis*, "Foundations," about the origins of cities; above all, Callimachus' largest work, *Aetia*, "Origins" or "Causes," used etiology as its principle of organization. The narrative in this book of the *Aeneid* is remarkably leisurely: war has broken out and Aeneas is in urgent need of allies, but although King Evander, his host, can provide little support, he seems neither hurried nor anxious, but content to be taken on an extended ramble around the local sights. It is as though Virgil wants us to feel that Aeneas is enjoying a short holiday before the grim business of battle begins, and matching form to content, he enjoys a holiday from the usual themes of epic. The hero takes a trip to the site of Rome, and the poet takes a trip to Alexandria.

This could easily have been an arid exercise, but Virgil's extraordinary achievement is to infuse this generic play with emotional color, and indeed to use it to develop a new style of sensibility, an original way of blending patriotism and history. What he does is to evoke a very distant past, the prehistory of Rome, centuries before Romulus, and through Evander's narration a past vastly more distant even than that. He combines this with a subtle and complex tone which is both tender and ironic, mingling a humorous feeling for the quaintness and simplicity of an early world with an affectionate warmth. The influence of this on his contemporaries was powerful and immediate. We can almost see the moment at which it hits some of them: Propertius in his fourth book, not in the previous three; Tibullus in his second book, not the first. Ovid's homage to this part of Virgil will come much later, in his own etiological poem, the *Fasti*, but it is probably significant that the Virgilian themes cluster in its first book, such is the force of their impact on other poets' imaginations.

One moment in the *Aeneid* had an especial appeal:

> talibus inter se dictis ad tecta subibant
> pauperis Euandri, passimque armenta videbant
> Romanoque Foro et lautis mugire Carinis.
> (Aen. 8.359–61)

Conversing thus together, they reached humble Evander's house, and saw all around cattle lowing in the Roman Forum and the smart Carinae.

Lautus, "smart" or "chic," is a nicely chosen word, showing Virgil's generic sensitivity, for it belongs to the prose of everyday life, and is nowhere else found in lyric or epic verse: a soupçon of tart modernity is dropped into the epic idyll.

Virgil's cows were irresistible. At any rate, they were not resisted by Propertius:

> Hoc quodcumque vides, hospes, qua maxima Roma est,
>   ante Phrygem Aenean collis et herba fuit;
> atque ubi Navali stant sacra Palatia Phoebo,
>   Euandri profugae procubuere boves.
> (Prop. 4. 1. 1–4)

All this that you see, stranger, where mighty Rome is now, before Aeneas the Phrygian was hill and grass, and where the Palatine stands, hallowed to Apollo of the Ships, the cattle of exiled Evander lay.

Or by Tibullus:

> Romulus aeternae nondum formaverat urbis
>   moenia, consorti non habitanda Remo;
> sed tunc pascebant herbosa Palatia vaccae
>   et stabant humiles in Iovis arce casae.
> (Tib. 2.5.23–6)

Romulus had not yet laid out the walls of the eternal city, where his brother Remus was not to dwell, but cows then grazed the grassy Palatine and lowly huts stood on Jupiter's citadel.

Or by Ovid:

> hic, ubi nunc Roma est, incaedua silva virebat,
>   tantaque res paucis pascua bubus erat.
> (Fast. 1.243–4)

Here, where Rome is now, green woodland grew unfilled, and so great a city was pasturage for a few cattle.

Comparing these passages, we might notice how much wittier and more economical Virgil is than his imitators. Humorously sliding two ages together, he has historic cows mooing in the modern city; the others spell out the distinction between past and present (and do not allow the cattle to moo). Modern discussion of allusion and intertextuality in Latin poets is commonly in terms of emulation and the use of older poetry as a spring-board for innovation and originality; that, indeed, is how Virgil used Theocritus, Hesiod, and Homer. But such an account hardly fits what is going on here. We should probably envisage something more like the impact of Beethoven and Wagner on the composers who came after them: Virgil opens up such enticing new areas of imaginative possibility that it is difficult not to follow him, and unnatural to go on writing as though he had not happened. The current of influence is fascinating: Virgil lets the material of another genre into his epic and transforms it in the process, and then the current flows out of epic into the elegiac poets.

There has been much debate over whether Ovid's *Metamorphoses* is an epic or not. If the argument of this chapter is valid, the question is too anxious. If we recast the question in terms of the ancient world – "Is the *Metamorphoses* an epos?" – the answer is easy but trivial: as a long narrative poem in dactylic hexameters, clearly it is. If the question is interpreted as one about character – "Is this a heroic poem?" or "Is it like Virgil?" – then it is not different in kind from other questions about literary tone and intent, and a subjective or ambivalent answer may be entirely reasonable. The debate is too anxious for another reason also. Part of Ovid's stock in trade is his insouciance, and that includes an engagingly casual attitude towards literary conventions. He starts the *Metamorphoses* by speaking about his own inclinations, remembers that he ought to be calling upon divine assistance, begins an invocation to the gods, interrupts it with a cheeky parenthesis, and then gives it up in order to get on with the story – all in four lines. If this is a generic indicator, it is one that says, "See how little I'm bothered about generic boundaries."

Aristotle noted with approval that Homer's epics handled a single story. In those terms Ovid's poem, with its more than two hundred stories, is the very opposite of what an epic ought to be. This multiplying of tales is fundamental to the nature of the *Metamorphoses* and a subject which belongs in another chapter. What concerns us here is how far these tales are generically diverse.

Ovid tells stories of quite different type, sometimes setting them side by side with the effect of deliberate discontinuity. A good example comes in the eighth book. The tale of Daedalus and Icarus is touching, a piece of romantic mythology subtly and delicately told (*Met.* 8.183–235). It is immediately followed by the story of how Daedalus out of jealousy had killed his nephew, who was then turned into a partridge (*Met.* 8.236–59). This has, by contrast, the character of a folktale; it is a "Just So" story ("why the partridge flies so near the ground"), with a folktale's comic irrationality. Meanwhile, Daedalus has changed without warning from a loving father to a monster murdering out of petty envy. A much less talented poet could have found a way to join the two tales more smoothly: Daedalus, bereaved of his son, might have looked back upon the crime of his youth and lamented that he was justly punished. Ovid prefers the link to be preposterous: Daedalus' victim happens, for no reason, to be roosting by the spot where he is burying his son.

In the course of his poem Ovid draws on history as well as myth; his stories may be farcical, humorous, moving, slippery, grisly. This is plain to any reader; a less easy question is how far it is helpful to describe this evident diversity in terms of genre. Several of the tormented heroines in the middle books of the poem, torn between love and moral duty, do recall the damsels in distress who were so prominent in the narrative poems of the neoterics (Catullus' Ariadne, Calvus' Io, Cinna's Zmyrna); the neoteric allusion is most marked in the story of Scylla which opens the eighth book. Later in the same book the hunting of the Calydonian boar, part of the story of Meleager, is thick with Homeric echoes, though here the intention is at least partly burlesque (*Met.* 8.273–444) (Hollis 1970; Horsfall, 1979). When Ovid describes the creation of the world, he admits one or two Lucretian touches: the phrase *semina rerum*, "seeds of matter," a couple of lines of heavy alliteration (*Met.* 1.9, 55 f.), but these are slight compared to the absorption of Lucretian tone into Anchises' cosmology in the *Aeneid*. In the ghastly story of Tereus, Procne, and Philomela, an echo of the tragedian Accius has been detected; in the story of Io – previously Calvus' theme – we find one line end with the mimicking of a couple of neoteric mannerisms (*Met.* 6.645 f., 1.732; Hollis 1970: xxivf.).

These are only momentary dashes of Lucretian or neoteric color. The surprise with the *Metamorphoses* is not that there is stylistic variation but that it is so limited. Virgil's command of large-scale structure and mastery of verse technique allowed him a huge range of stylistic expression within his tightly disciplined framework. Ovid's poem, much more diffuse, is held together by a continuity of style and tone, above all by the sense, even at the most serious, sensuous or poignant moments, that humor is not very far away. For the most part, the *Metamorphoses* makes its bow to other genres and goes on its own way rather than absorbing them into its substance.

None of the epics written in the following century shows that ambition to be universal which is displayed, in quite different ways, by both the *Aeneid* and the *Metamorphoses*. And none of the epicists of the Flavian period – Statius, Silius Italicus, and Valerius Flaccus – develops epic poetry much beyond the possibilities already known to the Augustan age. The one exception, perhaps, is Statius' *Achilleid*, in which the account of Achilles' childhood and youth comes closer to the *Bildungsroman* or novel of development than anything in epic narrative before (the nearest likeness would be the story of the young Telemachus in the early books of the *Odyssey*). The child as hero is a new and sometimes charming conception, but the *Achilleid* is only a fragment, and it is a little melancholy to reflect that it would probably have become much more conventional had Statius lived to carry it further.

But a generation earlier one poet had discovered a new way of writing epic: Lucan. His *Bellum civile* imports into epic elements of a prose genre: the techniques of oratory and declamation. Quintilian's judgment (*Inst.* 10.1.90), that he was a better model for orators than poets, might not wholly have displeased him, for his poem is, in part, a philippic in verse. Eight lines into the *Bellum civile* he addresses the citizenry with a rhetorical question, "quis furor, o cives, quae tanta licentia ferri?" ("What is this madness, fellow citizens, what is all this liberty given to the sword?"). It is as though he were a statesman addressing a *contio*, a public gathering of the Roman people. Constantly he harangues one part of an imagined audience or another. We have just heard him demanding the citizens' attention in line 8 of his first book. In line 21 he addresses Rome, in line 30 Pyrrhus, in line 37 the gods, in line 41 Caesar. Traditionally the epic poet maintained an air of objectivity and impersonality; in contrast, Lucan boasts that he is a partisan (7.205–13). His hope, he explains, is that future generations will be influenced by him to come down on Pompey's side. Characteristically, his way of saying this is to buttonhole an individual: "legent et adhuc tibi, Magne, favebunt" ("They will read and still they will favor you, Magnus [i.e. Pompey]") (7.213).

If the *Iliad* and the *Odyssey* represent primary epic and the *Aeneid* secondary epic, the next stage might be called tertiary epic. Once the possibilities of heroic verse seem to have been exhausted, the time comes, or so the ambitious and original poet may feel, for anti-heroic epic or parody of epic. Byron's *Don Juan* has been called the second epic in English, after *Paradise Lost*; the poet himself calls it an "epic Satire" and sends up epic conventions, "After the style of Virgil and of Homer, / So that my name of epic's no misnomer." Something similar seems to happen in the development of Latin literature. After Virgil, the truly creative poet could only "admire and do otherwise," to borrow the words of

Gerard Manley Hopkins. The *Metamorphoses* is already moving towards the character of tertiary epic, being essentially designed to entertain rather than edify, and turning at moments into outright parody. The *Bellum civile*, for its part, is radically anti-heroic, a poem without a hero, without gods, in which the centerpiece is a battle that is not ennobled by any of the individual feats of valor that had been the staple of epic warfare. This poem is not perhaps an "epic satire," like *Don Juan*, but a satiric epic. The first flash of sardonic wit comes in the very first line: "Bella per Emathios plus quam civilia campos..." ("Wars more than civil on the plains of Thessaly..."). The wars are "more than civil" – the usual translation, "worse than civil," makes more natural English, but loses the irony – because Pompey had been Caesar's son-in-law: they are an intimate, family affair. And thus the high epic note (*bella* as the first word, just as Virgil had begun with *arma*) and the wittily bitter note sound together from the very start. The *sententia*, the pointed, pithy, or epigrammatic sentence or saying, pervades every page of Lucan. It is equally pervasive in both the prose and the tragedies of his uncle Seneca, and so it might be said to characterize the age as much as the individual poet. But together with Lucan's oratorical pose, its effect is to import the tones of satire and diatribe into the epic genre.

If Lucan made the epic poem satiric, Juvenal, half a century later, at moments comes close to inverting that pattern, importing into satire a kind of epic grandeur. In some of his poems he finds a high, sardonic tone, bleak and yet spacious, that is distinctively his own. On occasion, though, we catch an echo of Virgil. In his tenth satire he surveys the vanity of the supposed blessings for which people pray. Long life, for example, brings the humiliations of old age, impotence among them:

> nam coitus iam longa oblivio, vel si
> coneris, iacet exiguus cum ramice nervus
> et, quamvis tota palpetur nocte, iacebit.
>   (10.204–6)

For sex has now long been forgotten, or if you should try, your little organ with its swollen veins just lies there, and even if poked all night long, will lie there still.

In "iacet...iacebit" ("lies...and will lie") there is an echo of Virgil's Theseus in Tartarus: "sedet aeternumque sedebit" ("he sits there and will sit for ever") (*Aen*. 6. 617). The word parody does not quite do justice to Juvenal's effect: through the epic resonance he blends pity and contempt.

Another of Juvenal's examples, a little later in the poem, is Priam, who had he lived less long, would have avoided his miserable end. First he describes the grand funeral that Priam might have had, in a sonorous and majestic seven-line sentence that any epic poet might be pleased to have written. Then the tone shifts:

> longa dies igitur quid contulit? omnia vidit
> eversa et flammis Asiam ferroque cadentem.
> tunc miles tremulus posita tulit arma tiara
> et ruit ante aram summi Iovis ut vetulus bos,
> qui domini cultris tenue et miserabile collum
> praebet ab ingrato iam fastiditus aratro.
>   (10.265–70)

So what benefit did long life bring him? He saw everything in ruins and Asia falling to fire and the sword. Then, laying aside his headdress he took up his weapons, a tremulous soldier, and fell before the altar of almighty Jupiter like a poor old ox which offers its scrawny, pitiable neck to its master's knife, scorned now by the ungrateful plough.

These lines are saturated in memories of the *Aeneid*. The picture of Priam's death recalls the second book, the idea of Asia itself falling in ruin comes from the beginning of the third, and the crumpling ox echoes a passage in the fifth book where an ox is slaughtered and the monosyllable *bos* at the line's end mimics the suddenness of the animal's collapse (*Aen.* 5.481). But the adjective *vetulus*, "poor old," colloquial and contemptuous, modifies the epic overtones. The blending of two generic characters produces a bitter, declamatory grandeur, pitying and mocking at once.

Juvenal's great contemporary, the historian Tacitus, differs from him in many obvious ways, yet each in his fashion fuses the grand and the sardonic. The very first sentence of Tacitus' *Annals* forms an unorthodox hexameter. A speaker in Tacitus' early work, the *Dialogus*, advises orators to make use of poets and names Virgil and Lucan (*Dial.* 20). Virgilian color and vocabulary are common in him (Syme 1958: 357–8). He may seem to be turning away from the heroic when he writes dourly of the contrast between his work and the splendid material available to historians of earlier epochs: "nobis in arto et inglorius labor" ("My work is on narrow matter and inglorious") (*Ann.* 4. 32). Yet he echoes Virgil, who preparing to write about bees, had declared,

> in tenui labor; at tenuis non gloria, si quem
> numina laeva sinunt auditque vocatus Apollo.
> (*Geo.* 4.6–7)

My work is on small matter, but not small the glory, if the adverse powers let one be and Apollo hears my prayer.

Though recalling Virgil, Tacitus' echo has a darker tone, but somewhat like Juvenal he achieves through his sardonic relentlessness, his very narrowness indeed, a kind of black grandeur. History-writing performed in antiquity some of the functions that the literary novel has performed in more recent centuries: in prose it was the most ambitious medium for narrative art and for the serious representation and analysis of human motive and action. Longinus called Herodotus *Homerikótatos*, most Homeric, and Tacitus similarly might be called the most Virgilian of Latin prose writers. By the second century CE epic itself might seem to be exhausted as a genre, but it could still fertilize a literary imagination that was quite differently made.

FURTHER READING

Kroll's study (1924) remains fundamental to the understanding of the relationship between epic and other genres; Barchiesi's essay (2001a) is an interesting analysis of it.

The title of D. R. Dudley's essay, "The satiric element in Lucretius" (1965), explains itself, as does that of Edward Vincent George, *Aeneid VIII and the Aitia of Callimachus* (1974). Wider in scope is Walter Wimmel's *Kallimachos in Rom* (1960). Relevant too is ch. 2 of Brooks Otis's *Virgil: A Study in Civilized Poetry* (1963) (on the supposed "obsolescence of epic").

The influence of the *Aeneid* on Virgil's younger contemporaries is considered in ch. 14 of Richard Jenkyns's *Virgil's Experience* (1998) and in Matthew Robinson's "Augustan Responses to Virgil" in Clarke, Currie, and Lyne, *Epic Interactions*.

The generic status of Ovid's *Metamorphoses* has been much debated. See, for example, Brooks Otis, *Ovid as an Epic Poet* (1970), and Stephen Hinds, *The Metamorphosis of Persephone: Ovid and the Self-conscious Muse* (1987b), chs. 5 and 6 (on the relationship between elegy and epic).

For discussion of particular places where epic relates to other genres, see especially, among the works cited in the main text, Wallach 1976 and Horsfall 1979.

CHAPTER FORTY-TWO

Virgil's Post-classical Legacy

Craig Kallendorf

> The figure of the poet may be used as a kind of constant by which to measure the progress of human thought. Every age has tended to fashion a Vergil after its own image, as it were.
> (D. R. Stuart, quoted in Ziolkowski 1993: 27)

There is no question that Virgil's *Aeneid* has played a significant role in the construction of western culture over the past two millennia. Roman schoolmasters began teaching the poem almost as soon as it was published, and it has remained in the canon of "great books" through to the present day, at least in translation. To state the obvious, however, immediately raises a series of questions. Who read the *Aeneid*? Why did they read this poem? To what uses did they put what they found there? Finally, how did the *Aeneid* stimulate literary, artistic, and musical creativity to help generate the succession of post-classical cultures that connect Virgil's time to ours? The essay that follows is designed to answer these questions.

Reading Virgil

From the time of its composition through the end of the twentieth century, the number of people who could read the *Aeneid* comfortably in the original seldom rose much above 10 per cent of the total population, but this minority included the wealthy, influential aristocrats and churchmen who shaped the society in which they lived. Indeed for centuries this educated elite also accounted for most of the people who could afford to own a copy of the text. For fifteen of the twenty centuries that followed the publication of the poem, the only choice for anyone who wanted to own a copy of the *Aeneid* was to make one himself or to pay someone to do it for him. Neither of these options was open to the poor: even the former required a substantial investment of time and access to a base text in someone else's library, and those who took the latter option often used the manuscript they commissioned to advertise their wealth and social standing by having it beautifully illustrated and bound. Once it was finished, such a manuscript became a treasured cultural commodity, passed from hand to hand in a series of exchanges that conferred prestige once again on each new owner. Among the seven earliest manuscripts copied by the sixth century, for example, is the "codex Romanus" (Rome, Vatican Library, Vat. Lat. 3867), prepared for a wealthy patron in Rome at the end of the fifth century, present in the royal abbey of St Denis for much of the Middle Ages, then listed in the first inventory of the Vatican Library in 1475 (Reynolds 1983: 433–4; Wright 2001: 68). The same pattern prevailed for the thousand or so manuscripts of the *Aeneid* copied over the next millennium (Alessio 1984: 432–43). The manuscript at Paris, Bibliothèque Nationale, Latin 7939A, for example, was copied by the Venetian nobleman Leonardo Sanudo, after which it entered the French royal library in 1669. Similarly London, British Library, Kings MS 24 was executed for Lodovico Agnelli, apostolic protonotary for Pope Sixtus IV and secretary to Cardinal Francesco Gonzaga; it then passed to Joseph Smith, the English consul in Venice, and entered the library of King George III in 1765 (Alexander 1994: 109–11, items 42 and 43).

In theory the invention of printing in the fifteenth century lowered the cost of books, increasing correspondingly the number of possible readers, but it is important not to overstate the potential for change at the beginning, at least: a small pocket-sized book initially cost 5 to 10 percent of a month's wages for a schoolteacher, who would still be able to afford only a handful of such commodities (Kallendorf 1999: 157). Thus while books indeed gradually became more affordable over the following centuries, Virgil nevertheless retained a privileged place in the libraries of the rich and powerful. For example a copy of the first printed edition of the *Aeneid*, by the famous Venetian printer Aldus Manutius, went into the libraries of two English noblemen, Sir John H. Thorold (1734–1815) and James L. Lindsay, the Earl of Crawford and Balcarres (1847–1913), before ending up in the collection of the American financier John Pierpont Morgan (1837–1913) (Kallendorf and Wells 1998: 78–9, no. 36). And another famous edition of Virgil, printed by the Birmingham printer John Baskerville in 1757, was actually financed by a subscription in which nobles such as the Earl of Leicester, influential individuals from the church or state establishment such as the Rev. William George, Provost of King's College, Cambridge, and members of the commercial or cultural elite like "Ben. Franklin Esq. of Philadelphia, FRS" put up the publication costs of the book. Even as late as the beginning of the twentieth century, wealthy individuals such as Junius S. Morgan (1867–1932), the nephew of the financier, devoted considerable time and expense to collecting editions of Virgil – in this case, several hundred of them, now at the Princeton University Library.

Obviously there is a variety of reasons why the rich and powerful were drawn to the *Aeneid*, ranging from personal taste to a peer-induced consensus about what was fashionable, but in the end Virgil's poetry occupied a more central place in western culture than other classical texts at least in part because the story it told was widely interpreted as the archetypal pattern for the very establishment and diffusion of that culture. Aeneas left his homeland and traveled westward, taking possession of a new land and bringing civilization to it as he merged his countrymen with the indigenous inhabitants. This is part of what makes western culture distinctive – most other civilizations do not trace their beginnings to a journey – and since educated people for two millennia knew the story of the *Aeneid*, they naturally returned to it again and again as one great power succeeded another, anchoring the rise and fall of new empires in the same Trojan myth. Thus by the thirteenth century, the English could claim that their more direct descent from Aeneas should give them authority over the Franks; among the Franks, however, the noble rulers of Boulogne, Flanders, and Orléans and the cities of Paris, Rheims, Tours, Metz, Nîmes, Narbonne, Troyes, Toulouse, and Clermont all claimed Trojan origins. When the Europeans exported their empires abroad, they glorified their successes in poems such as Luis de Camoens's *Os Lusiados*, a modern epic that was clearly constructed in imitation of the *Aeneid* (Waswo 1997: 1–11, 60–1, 82–4). The early American settlers envisioned their experience in the same terms, so that Benjamin Tompson's *New Englands* [sic] *Crisis*, Cotton Mather's *Magnalia Christi Americana*, and Joel Barlow's *Columbiad* present this westward cultural movement as well in reference to the *Aeneid* (Shields 2001: 30–7, 56–71, 255–8). During this period, advances in scholarship led eventually to the recognition that the Trojan legend was myth, not fact, but the archetype retained its appeal so long as it remained at the center of the educational experience of the elite (Waswo 1997: 119–26).

Indeed, as cultural power moved from one center to the next, political authority continued to rest on explicitly Virgilian foundations. When the empire in Rome, for example, was transformed into the Holy Roman Empire in Aachen, Charlemagne took for himself Aeneas' epithet of *pius* ("pious"), Alcuin described the emperor's goals with a Virgilian phrase, *parcere subiectis* ("to spare the conquered"; *Aen.* 6.853), and Einhard wrote a biography of Charlemagne in which he described the emperor as a new Aeneas. Several centuries later, when Dante dreamed of an imperial power that would bring peace to the warring city-states of Italy, he turned to Henry VII as the legitimate heir of Aeneas and argued his position with Virgilian rhetoric. When the Holy Roman emperorship passed to the Hapsburgs, its Virgilian iconography was transferred as well. Leone Leoni's bronze statue of Charles V, for example, depicts him as a second Aeneas, victorious over a conquered Fury, and the imperial palace in Genoa was decorated with a series of tapestries illustrating the *Aeneid*, woven to the designs of Perino del Vaga. Philip II in turn associated the lion in the Spanish royal arms with the insignia of the Trojan kings, so that the Hapsburgs assumed Aeneas' piety when they took up his lion shield; and Philip had the phrase from the *Aeneid* in which Jupiter prophesies an all-powerful empire in Rome, *imperium sine fine dedi* ("I have established an empire without end," *Aen.* 1.279), inscribed on his funeral catafalque in Seville (Tanner 1993: 61–2, 92–3, 113, 115–16, 198–202, 204).

This imperial iconography rested on Christian foundations as well, with the emperor being associated with both priest and king in Old Testament terms. Here, too, the *Aeneid* provided supporting material, for early on, Virgil was baptized into the new Christian faith. In the fourth century CE, the emperor Constantine gave an address to an ecclesiastical assembly in which he associated the *nova progenies* ("new seed of man") in Virgil's *Fourth Eclogue* with Christ, Virgil's *virgo* ("virgin") with Mary, the establishment of a new Golden Age on earth with the resurrection of Christ and the institution of baptism, and so forth. In some form this interpretation was accepted by Proba, Ambrose, Prudentius, Augustine, Abelard, and Dante, who wrote in *Purgatory* 22.64–73 that the *Fourth Eclogue* caused the pagan poet Statius to convert secretly to Christianity. Virgil, in other words, was a *poeta theologus*, a prophet of sorts who, as poet, attained some measure of theological understanding through inspiration. Different writers saw this process working in somewhat different ways. Cristoforo Landino, for example, cited passages from Job, the Psalms, and the Gospel of John as parallels to lines from Book 6 of the *Aeneid*, which told of Aeneas' descent to the Underworld, but in the end he concluded that the "old theology" of the ancients was not precisely the same as the "new theology" of Christianity (Kallendorf 1999: 95–115). Landino's commentary, however, was folded into a commentary by Giovanni Fabrini (first published in 1575–6) which went even further than his source in uniting the two streams of theology. As late as the middle of the twentieth century, especially in Germany, one could occasionally still read that spiritual affinities between Virgil and Christianity bring "us back to the old view that Virgil, like Isaiah, was a real prophet of Christ" (Kallendorf 1999: 103 n. 35; Ziolkowski 1993: 77–88).

Virgil's place at the center of the educational curriculum for almost two thousand years also in the end reinforced the dominant political and social values of those who read his poetry. For one thing, from the early Middle Ages through the end of the Renaissance and beyond, the language of international affairs and the church was Latin, so that a major educational goal for the upper classes was to be able to attain the facility in Latin on which professional advancement rested. If we examine what students wrote in the copies of the

Aeneid that they used as school texts during this period, we can clearly see them struggling to learn basic Latin vocabulary and grammar, clarifying nuances of correct usage, unraveling syntax, building their vocabulary through study of etymologies, and identifying the rhetorical figures of speech so they could write an elegant Latin of their own. Other marginal notes sometimes reflect the effort to move beyond learning the language to scrutinizing the text for its insight into behavior and morality. In most cases individual passages such as "discite iustitiam moniti et non temnere divos" ("be warned, learn justice and not to scorn the gods," *Aen.* 6.620) are underlined, in preparation for transfer to a commonplace book in which similar sentiments can be retrieved upon suitable occasions in the future. The lessons behind such underlinings and references are clear: work hard for God, country, and what is right, then accept what cannot be changed as part of divine justice (Kallendorf 1999: 31–61). These passages in turn became the subjects of emblems, in which phrases from Virgil like "pietas filiorum in parentes" ("the piety of children toward their parents"; *Aen.* 2.706) and "audentes fortuna iuvat" ("fortune assists the bold," *Aen.* 10.284) are accompanied by appropriate pictures (Fagiolo 1981: 253–4). Both content and pedagogy might seem deliberately calculated to instill passivity into generations of students, who among other things learned to sit still for hours on end through tedious line-by-line commentary and banal moralizing, but this, in the end, also served the interests of the state. As Robert Graves has noted, it was precisely these qualities that "first commended him [Virgil] to government circles, and have kept him in favour ever since" (quoted in Ziolkowski 1993: 99).

The *Aeneid*, in short, served for almost two thousand years as a vehicle through which the powerful elites of Europe visualized the culture they wanted and brought that culture into being. That is not to say that the poem had no impact on the other 90 percent of the population, but we must be careful how we define that impact. Beginning from a romantic premise about the separateness and purity of popular culture, Domenico Comparetti wrote a classic study of Virgil in the Middle Ages in which he claimed that medieval Naples preserved popular legends about Virgil, who was associated with magic, talismans, and supernatural events. Modern research has largely discredited this claim, showing instead that here, as elsewhere, much of popular culture is derived from learned sources, once (or more) removed (Pasquali 1981: xv–xxxiv). Thus there is evidence that the common people indeed knew something about the *Aeneid*, but the poem actually served as a bridge of sorts between rich and poor. In some cases a Latin text served this function. For example, one of the most famous of the early editions of Virgil, edited by Sebastian Brant and printed by Johannes Grüninger in 1502, contains a short poem at the end that suggests that the illustrations in the book were added to make it accessible to those who lacked fluency in Latin (Patterson 1987: 104–5). In other cases, a translation linked the world of Latin learning to those who could read, but in the vernacular only, for from the Renaissance on, the *Aeneid* was also available in good translations, a number of which were prepared by poets who were well regarded in their own right: Annibal Caro in Italy; Clément Marot and Joachim Du Bellay in France; Enrique de Villena, Fray Luis de León, and Gregorio Hernández de Velasco in Spain; and Gavin Douglas, Henry Howard (Earl of Surrey), and John Dryden in England. And when Philip II traveled throughout the Hapsburg territories in pursuit of the title of Holy Roman Emperor, his courtiers prepared a series of triumphal arches in Antwerp that presented him as the heir of Aeneas. This series may well have been pitched initially to the city's ruling elite, but the main point would hardly have been lost on the crowds (Tanner 1993: 135–7). Similarly both Shakespeare's *The Tempest* and Alonso de Ercilla's *La Araucana* present arguments in the vernacular about whether Dido remained chaste after the death of her husband Sychaeus, suggesting once again that while the details would presumably resonate with the learned, something of Virgil's story nevertheless must have been known to those with only a rudimentary education, indeed even to the illiterate who visited the Globe Theatre and listened to chivalric romances read aloud by others.

To say that the *Aeneid* served as a bridge between those at the center of power and those on the peripheries, however, is not to claim that the rich and powerful simply used the poem to silence all ideological opposition to the status quo. Indeed, while most reactions to the poem confirm the assertion that the *Aeneid* reinforced the educational, religious, and political values that its elite readers found reflected there, there is significant evidence that Virgil's poem also helped a handful of readers and imitators articulate their opposition to the power structures of their day. Today such readers follow in the footsteps of the so-called "Harvard School," an influential group of critics who hear Virgil speaking in two voices, those of personal loss as well as public achievement. That is, when we listen to Dido and Turnus as well as Aeneas, we hear failures as well as successes – of Aeneas, of the Augustan order, and of human nature in general and its ability to reach its goals. Readers like this, however, can be found as far back as Augustan Rome, when Ovid produced a notoriously irreverent version of the *Aeneid* that dissolves Virgil's ideological pretensions in irony and indetermination (Thomas 2001: 74–83).

In the fourteenth century, Petrarch rebuked Aeneas first for being a traitor, then a worshiper of false gods, and finally for not actually being *pius* ("pious") as he should have been, thereby challenging Virgil's poem as a proper authority for religious and political activity (Kallendorf 1999: 394–5). At the beginning of the fifteenth century, Christine de Pizan used the figure of Dido to articulate a female voice that suggests that from her perspective, male values and priorities look very different indeed (Desmond 1994: 195–224). In the next century, Alonso de Ercilla wrote an epic in imitation of the *Aeneid*, *La Araucana*, which ostensibly casts the Spanish invaders of Chile as the victorious Trojans but which also, like its model, shows great sympathy for the indigenous warriors defending their land, thereby calling into question both the Spanish imperial enterprise and the Roman one on which it was based (Kallendorf 2003). Similarly, *The Tempest* repeats the Virgilian pattern of westward colonization, but again, Shakespeare's play uses its Virgilian subtext to raise disturbing questions about exactly what gives an invader the right to displace Caliban, or Turnus, for that matter (Tudeau-Clayton 1998: 194–244).

It is important to acknowledge that the *Aeneid* raised doubts about the legitimacy of the cultural and political order in the minds of some of its readers over the centuries. More often, however, it was appropriated by churchmen, educators, and rulers, who found in it a pattern for the civilization they spent their lives constructing.

The *Aeneid* in Art, Music, and Literature

As we have seen, on the ideological level Virgil's readers looked into his poem and saw themselves reflected there. On the artistic level, the same thing happened. Two initial examples taken from early illustrated editions of the *Aeneid* will show how this process works. First, let us turn again to the 1502 Brant-Grüninger edition mentioned above (Figure 42.1). The characters in this illustration are dressed in costumes from the turn of the sixteenth century, not from ancient Rome, and the wooden ring within which the heroes fight, along with the armor and weapons stacked behind it, suggest that Aeneas and Turnus have just finished a battle according to the conventions of medieval warfare. What is more, the cities in the background look like the northern European cities of Brant and Grüninger's day, not the Roman ruins that were still visible in much of southern Europe. In short, this picture blends the Roman world of the *Aeneid* with the late medieval world of the illustrator. A similar blending occurs in our next illustration, an engraving that accompanied John Dryden's influential English translation in an edition of 1716 (Figure 42.2). Here again, the artist has visualized a key moment from the *Aeneid* in terms of the

Figure 42.1 *Publii Virgilii Maronis opera* (Strasbourg: Johannes Gruninger, 1502), fo. 407v. Princeton University Library.

prevailing aesthetic of his day. The subject of the engraving is the death of Dido, but the scene is dominated not by Dido, but by Iris, who is depicted at the very moment of descent, which demands the greatest technical skill to execute. The foreshortening is not so severe as in, for example, Tintoretto's *Miracle of St Mark*, but here, too, we are encouraged to admire the skill of the artist in controlling a difficult composition. The scene unfolds on a city square that was clearly constructed on the model of, say, Il Gesù in Rome, showing the dissociation of form from function that characterizes the architecture of this period. In other words, the engraving is typically baroque, and once again, the *Aeneid* serves as a mirror in which the observers, intentionally or not, see themselves (Kallendorf 2001: 124–8).

The same thing happens when we turn from the early editions of the *Aeneid* to works of art derived from it. For example, wealthy families in Renaissance Italy often commissioned for their children a special wedding gift, a *cassone*, or large chest, into which clothing,

Figure 42.2 *Aeneid* 4.690-5, from *The Works of Virgil ... Translated into English Verse, by Mr. Dryden* (London: Jacob Tonson, 1716), vol. 2, following p. 454. Princeton University Library.

linens, and the like could be stored. These *cassoni* were decorated with pictures, often derived from literary sources. One of the most famous painters of such pictures was Apollonio di Giovanni, whose workshop in Florence produced a number of wedding chests with scenes derived from the *Aeneid*. On one of them, a *cassone* now in the Yale

University Art Gallery, we can see a scene in which Aeneas founds Rome, the city to which the young couple who received the wedding chest ultimately traced their ancestry. Apollonio di Giovanni also painted the miniatures in a manuscript of Virgil's works now in the Biblioteca Riccardiana in Florence (MS. 492). The scene (fol. 62r) where Juno visits Aeolus to ask him to release the winds and cause a storm (*Aen.* 1.65–75) is also found on the Yale wedding chest, where the gods wear clothing from the fifteenth century CE, not the first century BCE. In other words, the painter who looked for inspiration in the *Aeneid* saw the poem through the lens of his own culture, producing luxury objects which celebrated the power and lineage of the family that commissioned them (Fagiolo 1981: 224–7).

The *Aeneid* also served as inspiration for decorative items in other domestic spheres. For example, in the sophisticated court culture of northern and central Italian cities including Mantua, Ferrara, and Urbino, artists – among them Benvenuto Cellini and Michelangelo – designed objects such as gold saltcellars and silver inkwells that could be used as impressive gifts to advance diplomatic ends. With this goal in mind, Duke Guidobaldo II of Urbino ordered two sets of ceramic plates to be prepared from designs by Battista Franco as gifts for the Emperor Charles V and Cardinal Alessandro Farnese. Included among these plates were scenes from the Trojan War as depicted in Book 2 of the *Aeneid*, including the Trojan horse (*Aen.* 2.255), the flame that touches Ascanius' head (*Aen.* 2.683), and Aeneas leading his family away from Troy (*Aen.* 2.1130–83). These scenes show a close alliance among artist, patron, and scholar. The depiction of Aeneas leading his family away from Troy (Figure 42.3), for example, depends not only on Virgil's text but also on Servius' commentary to it, suggesting that a humanist such as Annibal Caro or Pietro Aretino, known to be at Guidobaldo's court when the designs for these plates were made in the middle of the sixteenth century, must have had a hand in their production. And it is certainly no accident that the humanist duke turned for his subject to the *Aeneid*, given Charles V's well-known interest in tracing his descent from the Trojan prince. The clothing in these scenes looks more Roman than that in Apollonio di Giovanni's wedding chest, but the scenes are surrounded by borders in which armed putti and embracing couples entwine themselves in a typical mannerist fantasy (Fagiolo 1981: 245–8), showing that once again, the subject matter of the past is seen through the stylistic lens of the present.

Not all appropriations of the *Aeneid*, however, enter into the machinations of the high and mighty. Plaquettes, for example, could be made in silver, but they were commonly made of bronze and could be made even more cheaply in lead, allowing their diffusion to all social classes as ornaments for everything from boxes to mirrors. Hercules and Cacus, for example, appear on the famous silver inkwell made by Cristoforo Foppa (called Caradosso) for Giovanni d'Aragona, but there is a version in lead as well as the original one in silver. Prints, too, were cheap enough to be widely diffused, such that Andrea Briosco (called Il Riccio) found it easy to obtain a copy of Marcantonio Raimondi's engraving of Raphael's death of Dido and make a bronze plaquette from it. These plaquettes range in quality from high to low, often showing mastery of the latest artistic techniques, but as Peter Flötner's illustration of Dido shows, it remained difficult to envision Virgil's world consistently in its own terms, for the Carthaginian queen is placed in the square of a German city with towered circular buildings, balconied houses, and a square fountain typical of sixteenth-century northern European architecture (Fagiolo 1981: 234–44).

Passages from the *Aeneid* also guided the artistry of a number of popular spectacles through the ages. Each year, for example, the King of Naples presented to the Pope a white horse as a recognition of his obligations to his feudal lord. This presentation was generally accompanied by a big celebration, in which a temporary structure with a relevant

Figure 42.3   Ceramic plate depicting the flight of Aeneas from Troy. Museo Civico, Pesaro.

theme was constructed, then blown apart in a fireworks display. The neoclassical structure that was exploded on September 9, 1730 in Piazza SS. Apostoli in Rome during the presentation to Pope Clement XII alludes specifically to the fall of Troy and to Aeneas, and the motto that accompanies the structure is taken directly from the *Aeneid:* "Tantae molis erat Romanam condere gentem imperiumque" ("so great an effort it was to found the Roman people and their empire," *Aen.* 1.33–4). A similar structure was exploded in Piazza Farnese on June 29, 1744, when the white horse from Naples was presented to Pope Benedict XIV. An engraving of this structure shows a scene from Book 6 of the *Aeneid*, in full-blown neoclassical style, in which Aeneas descends to the Underworld (Fagiolo 1981: 255–61). What is more, the tournaments that remained so popular in the chivalric culture of the Middle Ages and the Renaissance traced their origins to the *Troiae lusus*, the equestrian exercises of Ascanius and the other young Trojans at the funeral games for Anchises in *Aen.* 5.838–44. The choreography of these exercises, which parallels certain types of dancing popular in this period, was associated with the labyrinth of Crete (*Aen.* 5.831–3). This association provides a deeper significance to these events, which took on overtones of a sacred cosmological dance: that is, the tournaments were generally held in the spring, when the general return to life recalled the descent to the Underworld and the return to the world of light (Fagiolo 1981: 261; Greene 2001: 408–15).

When we move to the so-called "major arts" (i.e., painting and sculpture), we find that works derived from the *Aeneid* are grouped around the points of greatest emotional tension in Virgil's text, visualized in accordance with a succession of stylistic and cultural norms. The first group focuses on Book 2, the fall of Troy. Early on, the invading Greek army suddenly disappeared and a mysterious wooden horse was found outside the walls of Troy. A Trojan priest, Laocoön, warned against taking the horse into the city; two serpents promptly swam ashore and wrapped themselves around Laocoön and his sons, crushing them to death in a mass of agonized screams and writhing limbs. This group of figures was the subject of a famous sculpture from the Hellenistic era, which was discovered in Rome in 1506. The mannered style of the sculpture resonated immediately with the mannerism of the early sixteenth century, such that Laocoön's death became the subject of a print by Marcantonio Raimondi, a fresco in the Palazzo Ducale in Mantua by Rinaldo Mantovano, and other works. Thanks largely to the deception of Sinon, Laocoön's warnings were ignored and the horse was brought into Troy, where it disgorged a group of hidden Greek warriors, who opened the gates to the Greek army and began the final destruction of the city. This final battle appealed in particular to the same mannerist aesthetic, as seen in an anonymous sixteenth-century print (Figure 42.4), where the invaders and defenders prove almost indistinguishable from one another amidst the jumbled confusion of falling buildings and muscled torsos. In the midst of this confusion, Aeneas took the household gods and his family members out of the city in one of the most famous scenes in the *Aeneid*. This scene was freely absorbed into any context in which Virgilian *pietas* ("piety") might

Figure 42.4 Anonymous sixteenth-century woodcut depicting the fall of Troy.

be appropriate, such as Raphael's *Fire in the Borgo*, a fresco in the Vatican palace in which, while Pope Leo IV made the sign of the cross and extinguished a fire that had broken out in ninth-century Rome, a man leads his son away from the flames with his aged father on his back. Again, however, the emotional content of the scene and its focus on movement and physical effort made it especially attractive to mannerist and baroque artists such as Gian Lorenzo Bernini, whose famous sculpture of these figures still stands in the villa of the Roman family that commissioned it.

Other artistic works were inspired by Aeneas's encounter with Dido in Carthage. Among an important group of Virgilian landscapes by the seventeenth-century French painter Claude Lorrain is one in which Aeneas surveys the city of Carthage with Dido. This painting, like the others in the series, places a small group of people into a landscape in which they are dwarfed by the natural features, and by the classical buildings, some of them half-ruined, that encroach upon it. These paintings powerfully capture a moment of delicate balance, between a disappearing countryside and rapid urbanization, between the optimism of renewing a culture based on antiquity and the pessimism of knowing that its decay will inevitably follow. Claude's scenes in turn influenced the series that J. M. W. Turner painted in the middle of the nineteenth century to illustrate Book 4 of the *Aeneid*. Turner drew from Claude his ability to place heroic figures into an ominous, brooding landscape, but as his *Dido Building Carthage* shows, he was able to infuse the scene with a new monumentality that drives home its power as a warning against the moral threats posed by the wealth of a rapidly industrializing age. As Aeneas' relationship with Dido ends, the tragedy that results has proven especially susceptible to changes in taste and cultural norms. Andrea Mantegna's grisaille, for example, shows a restrained suffering in accordance with Renaissance norms; in the seventeenth-century painting by G. Coli and F. Gherardi, Dido expires in a flurry of emotion and movement at the base of a structure that closely resembles Bernini's tabernacle at the main altar in St Peter's in Rome; while the Dido of Pompeo Batoni (1708–87) looks up at the departing Aeneas with a full measure of neoclassical restraint (Fagiolo 1981: 105–9, 194–217; Llewellyn 1984: 117–40; McKay 1993: 351–64).

These works inspired by the emotional high points of the *Aeneid* come together in more than a dozen cycles, painted between the sixteenth and eighteenth centuries to decorate palaces in central and northern Italy. These cycles project the power and prestige of the men who commissioned them, men such as Andrea Doria, the Genoese admiral who arranged a depiction of the shipwreck of Aeneas in which Jupiter was identified with the Emperor Charles V and Doria himself appeared as Neptune, positioned on the same plane as the imperial deity because mastery of the sea had been granted to him. As we would expect, each of these powerful patrons saw the *Aeneid* through the prism of his own culture. Giulio Boiardo, for example, commissioned a cycle of frescoes around 1540 for his ancestral home at La Rocca Di Scandiano in which the painter Nicolò dell'Abate made Virgil's poem compatible with the chivalric world of the *Orlando innamorato*, written by Giulio's ancestor, Matteo Maria Boiardo. The contemporaneous Sala dell'Eneide in the Palazzo Spada in Rome in turn relies on the Virgilian exegesis of the Neoplatonist Cristoforo Landino, in which the obstacles that Aeneas overcame parallel the purificatory process by which the Christian soul returns to its heavenly father. This synthesis reflects the interests and beliefs of the man who commissioned it, Gerolamo Capodiferro (1502–59), who received his humanist education in Sadoleto's circle and occupied a series of important positions in the Papal court of Paul III. This Christian Neoplatonism was raised to an even higher level in the Galleria di Enea in Rome's Palazzo Doria Pamphili in Piazza Navona, where Pietro da Cortona used the *Aeneid* to prefigure the transfer of the true religion from east to west; here Juno and Venus, the lily and the dove, the active and contemplative lives of Neoplatonism, are reconciled in the heraldic emblem of the Pamphili, the family of Pope Innocent X, who owned the palace. When allegorical interpret-ations like these fell out of favor in the eighteenth century, the *Aeneid* was seen once again in literal terms, so that a group of martial scenes from Book I were chosen to decorate the walls of the royal armory in Turin. These scenes are suffused with the heroic dignity of neoclassicism, while the slightly later cycle in the Sala di Enea e Didone in the Villa Borghese in Rome passes from allegory to neoclassical heroism to the first traces of a new preromantic sensibility (Fagiolo 1981: 120–93).

In music, the fourth book of the *Aeneid* (containing the tragedy of Dido) was the most influential, followed by the second book (on the fall of Troy), demonstrating again the tendency to engage the text at its points of greatest emotional tension. As early as the ninth and tenth centuries, manuscripts of the *Aeneid* were marked with neumes, or guidance for singing verses from these two books. At the beginning of the sixteenth century, the musicians Josquin des Prez, Orlando di Lasso, and Adrian Willaert began composing settings of *dulces exuviae*, Dido's farewell to Aeneas (*Aen.* 4.651ff.), but settings of Virgil's own words have proved less important than works inspired by them. Once again, Book 4 provided the inspiration for Henry Purcell's *Dido and Aeneas*, which has become the most famous of a group of operas based on Dido's story, but Pietro Metastasio wrote a libretto, *Didone abbandonata*, that was set to music almost once a year between 1724 and 1824, and individual arias for this libretto were also composed by such major figures as Mozart and Schubert. By the nineteenth century, themes from classical literature were becoming less common on stage, which makes the appearance of Hector Berlioz's monumental opera, *Les Troyens*, all the more striking. The work's length also delayed its production, but finally in 1969, a hundred years after the composer's death, a complete performance of the entire four-hour production was mounted (Draheim 1993: 317–44).

Virgil's impact on western literature is quite literally incalculable, ranging from Chaucer and Shakespeare to Forster and Conrad, but his impact has been most significant on those post-classical poets who also wrote epic. Dante's *Divine Comedy* is not, strictly speaking, an epic, but it is clear from his choice of Virgil as his initial guide in the poem and as the master of *lo bello stilo* ("the pleasing style," *Inf.* 1.87) that has brought him honor, that Dante envisioned his poem as part of this tradition. On the most basic level, the relation-ship is verbal: Dante quotes Virgil's poetry more than two hundred times, more than any sources other than the Bible and Aristotle; the phrase *selva antica* ("ancient wood," *Purg.* 28.23) comes directly from *Aen.* 6.179. Other references involve details of plot, as when Dante-pilgrim tries three times to embrace the shade of a musician named Casella (*Purg.* 2.80–1) in the same way as Aeneas had tried to embrace Anchises (*Aen.* 6.700–2). As any reader of the *Divine Comedy* knows, however, Virgil occupies a greater, and ultimately more ambiguous, role in Dante's poem. By selecting Virgil rather than, say, Aristotle as his guide, Dante clearly intended to honor him as the foremost representative of ancient culture. Modern scholarship, however, emphasizes Virgil's shortcomings in the poem. In *Inferno* 20, for example, Dante has Virgil correct his own text by putting into his mouth an account of the founding of Mantua that contradicts the one in the *Aeneid*. Even as a character in the poem, Virgil is a flawed guide, faltering at the Gate of Dis in *Inferno* 8–9 and reacting foolishly to the demons in *Inferno* 21–3. Finally, in *Purgatorio* 30, Virgil withdraws from the poem, first by quoting a line from his *Aeneid* (6.883), then by translating another line (*Aen.* 4.23), and finally by echoing a passage from his *Georgics* (4.525–7). Indeed Virgil had to withdraw from the *Divine Comedy*, for he remained a pagan even though his poetry should have led him, like Statius in *Purgatorio* 22.40–1, to repentance and conversion to Christianity. Thus, as the author of the *Aeneid*, Virgil occupies for Dante the same ambivalent position he occupies in medieval culture in general: an author whose work represents the best that the classical past can offer, while remaining suspect for its pagan underpinnings (Hollander 1993: 253–69; Kallendorf 2000: 7–8).

Unlike the *Divine Comedy*, there is no confusion about the genre of Petrarch's *Africa*: it is clearly an epic, written in the language and form of the *Aeneid*. The poem follows one of the major figures of Roman republican history, Scipio Africanus, from his invasion of Africa through his victory over the Carthaginians at the battle of Zama to a triumphal celebration in Rome. The *Africa* draws on other sources, to be sure, but it is also an imitation of Virgilian epic. Scipio's dream at the beginning, for example, is obviously modelled on Cicero's *Somnium Scipionis* and the commentary to it written by Macrobius, but it also takes from Virgil a parade of Roman heroes, a Platonizing discourse on why suicide is wrong, and a view of history played out against the backdrop of a moral universe. And while the battles of the last four books recount information from Livy, they also draw from the last six books of the *Aeneid*, as Petrarch understood them. For Petrarch, Virgil's epic sought to praise the virtues of its hero Aeneas and condemn the vices of those like Turnus and Dido who opposed him. Petrarch therefore describes the warring armies in black and white terms, assigning *pietas* ("piety") to Scipio and *furor* ("fury"), *dolus* ("fraud"), and *rabies* ("madness") to Hannibal. And lest the moral lines blur, the dalliance with Dido is rewritten so that the Dido figure, Sophonisba, consorts not with Scipio but with Massinissa, his chief lieutenant. The resulting poem strikes modern readers as less than successful. Its main problem, its relentless moralizing, results directly from how the *Aeneid* itself was understood by Petrarch, which was matched by those who followed him in the Renaissance revival of learning (Kallendorf 1989: 19–57).

Spenser's *The Faerie Queene* in turn shows what happens when Virgil's poem is incorporated into the Protestant culture of Elizabeth I's England. The medieval and Renaissance commentators to the *Aeneid* had stressed the roles of reason, labor, and merited reward in the poem: that is, Aeneas worked hard to understand how he should act and grew into a heroism that reaps the rewards that are due to hard work and self-denial. To a Protestant like Spenser, however, this interpretation smacked of works righteousness. The Reformation emphasized that salvation comes by faith alone, so that in Book I of *The Faerie Queene*, Spenser rewrites the Polydorus episode as a parable on grace and Aeneas' departure from Carthage, previously allegorized as a triumph of the will, as the infusion of grace into a reformed Redcrosse through the supernatural agency of Una and Arthur. Duessa's descent into Aesculapius' lair parodies Aeneas' descent to the Underworld, but Redcrosse's instruction in the House of Holinesse corrects the parody, emphasizing the need to trust in the mercy of God. In Book 2, Spenser rewrites the Dido story repeatedly, making Phaedria and Acrasia into concupiscent Didos based on *Aeneid* 4 and Alma, Medina, and Belphoebe into chaste Didos of the non-Virgilian historical tradition, surrogates for Elizabeth I. In Book 3, however, Spenser returns to the chaste Dido and suggests, through Britomart, that married love can and should reconcile public and private, so that Spenser can express his anxieties about Elizabeth's failure to produce an heir by referring to the Protestant preference for chastity within marriage (Watkins 1995: 90–178).

Like Spenser, Milton turned to the *Aeneid* in writing a religious epic with an argument "Not less but more heroic" (*Paradise Lost* 9.14) than the pagan literature on which it was based. In recounting the Fall from Paradise, Milton tells how evil, aroused by Satan, is converted by God to good. The structure of his poem rewrites the *Aeneid*, where Juno, like Satan, is motivated by a sense of injured merit (*Aen.* 1.27; *PL* 1.98) and tormented by the thought of lasting pain that results from an unfavorable judgment (*Aen.* 1.36; *PL* 1.55), then stirs up war by releasing a monster, Allecto in the model (*Aen.* 7), Sin in the imitation (*PL 2*). Milton's twelve-book division echoes Virgil's, as does his distinctive high style, noticeably coordinate and marked by verbal repetition, enjambement, theme and variation, and repetition of phrase to clarify meaning. In terms of both language and thought, Milton's characteristic procedure is to transcend his source while leaving deliberate evidence of it. For example, Michael's prophecy of Israel's royal house, which will lead to Christ, ends like this:

> he shall ascend
> The throne hereditary, and bound his reign
> With earth's wide bounds, his glory with the heavens.
> (*PL* 12.369–71)

This recalls Jupiter's prophecy about Augustus, "imperium Oceano, famam qui terminet astris" ("whose power will extend to the sea, and fame to the stars," *Aen.* 1.287), but it also recalls Anchises' prophecy in Book 6, "illa incluta Roma, imperium terris, animos aequabit Olympo" ("that famous Rome will make her empire equal to the earth, and her spirit to heaven," *Aen.* 6.781–2). These two allusions guide us in turning from the city of man to the city of God, in a process which works the same way throughout the poem: we recognize the allusion at the same time as we correct it, so that we are tempted by the beauty of the past just as Christ was tempted by Satan in *Paradise Regained*, but like Christ, we have the means for distinguishing true from false and are expected to judge accordingly (Gransden 1984). The poem that results cannot help but bring the epic tradition per se to a close, in that the new Christian heroism surpasses the pagan heroism of old but cannot itself be surpassed in turn.

As Ernst Robert Curtius has eloquently argued, the unity of European culture that extends from Homer (see the chapters by Edwards and Slatkin) to Goethe, in which Virgil plays such a significant role, has been irrevocably shattered in the twentieth century (Curtius 1953: 3–16). Part of this is undoubtedly due to changes in education, for Virgil's role in modern culture has inevitably declined along with the study of Latin in the schools. Thus in music, for example, there simply have not been very many references to the *Aeneid* in the twentieth century (Draheim 1993: 334–5), and the author of the most significant modern literary adaptation, Hermann Broch, actually knew very little about either Virgil himself or his *Aeneid*. When there are more precise references, they are increasingly filtered through a "pessimistic" perspective that sees Virgil not as the supporter of Rome and her imperial vision, but as an author whose sympathies really lay with the victims of wealth and power, a veiled critic of the status quo who merited appropriation by, for example, the opponents of the Vietnam war (Thomas 2001: xi). Imitations of Virgil, therefore, tend toward irony (Cyril Connolly's *The Unquiet Grave*) and parody (Anthony Burgess's *A Vision of Battlements*) (Ziolkowski 1993: 134–45, 203–22).

The basic pattern that prevailed in preceding centuries, however, continues to shape this modified Virgilian reception. Between the two world wars, for example, different local situations produced different Virgils: in Italy, as a nationalist countryman with traditional views on government and work; in France, as a protofascist shaped by Parisian student life; in Germany, as a spirit almost Christian by nature who could stand against the emergence of National Socialism; and in Latin America, as a prophet of peace sent providentially to prepare the way for Christ (Ziolkowski 1993: 56). Thus while the number of Virgil's readers gradually declined through the twentieth century, the variety of perspectives brought to the text rose. It is impossible to say what the twenty-first century will bring, but in one way or another, the *Aeneid* will undoubtedly remain a mirror into which new generations of readers will look and see themselves.

FURTHER READING

Marilynn Desmond, *Reading Dido: Gender, Textuality, and the Mediaeval Aeneid* (1990).

Craig W. Kallendorf, *In Praise of Aeneas: Virgil and Epideictic Rhetoric in the Early Italian Renaissance* (1989).

—— (ed.) *Vergil* (1993).

—— *Virgil and the Myth of Venice: Books and Readers in the Italian Renaissance* (1999).

Charles Martindale (ed.) *Virgil and His Influence: Bimillennial Studies* (1984b).

Annabel Patterson, *Pastoral and Ideology, Virgil to Valéry* (1987).

John C. Shields, *The American Aeneas: Classical Origins of the American Self* (2001).

Marie Tanner, *The Last Descendant of Aeneas: The Hapsburgs and the Mythic Image of the Emperor* (1993).

Richard F. Thomas, *Virgil and the Augustan Reception* (2001).

Margaret Tudeau-Clayton, *Jonson, Shakespeare and Early Modern Virgil* (1998).

Richard Waswo, *The Founding Legend of Western Civilization: From Virgil to Vietnam* (1997).

John Watkins, *The Specter of Dido: Spenser and Virgilian Epic* (1995).

Theodore Ziolkowski, *Virgil and the Moderns* (1993).

Bibliography

Aarne, A., and S. Thompson. 1981. *The Types of the Folktale: A Classification and Bibliography*, 2nd edn. FF Communications 184. Helsinki. First edn., 1964, by Aarne.

Abusch, T. 1986. "Ishtar's proposal and Gilgamesh's refusal: an interpretation of *The Gilgamesh Epic*, Tablet 6, Lines 1–79," *History of Religions* 26: 143–87.

—— 1993a. "Gilgamesh's request and Siduri's denial, Part I: The meaning of the dialogue and its implications for the history of epic," in M. Cohen, D. Snell, and D. Weisberg (eds.), *The Tablet and the Scroll: Near Eastern Studies in Honor of William W. Hallo*, pp. 1–14. Bethesda, MD.

—— 1993b. "Gilgamesh's request and Siduri's denial, Part II: An analysis and interpretation of an old Babylonian fragment about mourning and celebration," *Journal of the Ancient Near Eastern Society of Columbia University* 22: 3–17.

—— 1999. "The epic of Gilgamesh and the Homeric epics," in *Mythologies: Methodological Approaches to Intercultural Influences*. Proceedings of the Second Annual Symposium of the Assyrian and Babylonian Intellectual Heritage Project, pp. 1–6. Paris, October 4–7, 1999.

—— 2001a. "The development and meaning of the Epic of Gilgamesh: an interpretive essay," *Journal of the American Oriental Society* 121: 614–22.

—— 2001b. "The Epic of Gilgamesh and the Homeric epics," in Whiting 2001: 1–6.

Abusch, T., J. Huehnergard, and P. Steinkeller (eds.) 1990. *Lingering Over Words: Studies in Ancient Near Eastern Literature in Honor of William L. Moran*. Harvard Semitic Studies 37. Atlanta.

Adamietz, J. 1976. *Zur Komposition der Argonautica des Valerius Flaccus*. Munich.

Afanasjeva, V. K. 1974. "Mündlich überlieferte Dichtung ('Oral Poetry') und schriftliche Literatur in Mesopotamien," *Acta Antiqua Academiae Scientiarum Hungaricae* 22: 121–35.

Ahl, F. M. 1974. "The shadows of a divine presence in the *Pharsalia*," *Hermes* 102: 567–90.

—— 1976. *Lucan: An Introduction*. Cornell Studies in Classical Philology 39. Ithaca, NY.

—— 1982. "Amber, Avalon, and Apollo's singing swan," *American Journal of Philology* 103: 373–411.

—— 1985. *Metaformations*. Ithaca, NY.

—— 1986. "Statius' 'Thebaid': a reconsideration," *Aufstieg und Niedergang der Römischen Welt*, II.32.5: 2803–912.

—— 1993. "Form empowered: Lucan's Pharsalia," in A. J. Boyle (ed.), *Roman Epic*, pp. 125–42. London and New York.

Ahl, F. M., M. A. Davis, and A. Pomeroy. 1986. "Silius Italicus," *Aufstieg und Niedergang der römischen Welt*, II.32.4: 2492–561.

Akmajian, A., R. A. Demers, A. K. Farmer, and R. M. Harnish. 2001. *Linguistics: An Introduction to Language and Communication*, 5th edn. Cambridge, MA.

Akurgal, E. 1976. *Die Kunst der Hethiter*, 2nd edn. Munich.

Albis, R. V. 1996. *Poet and Audience in the Argonautica of Apollonius.* Lanham, MD.

Albright, W. F. 1942. "The creation of the composite bow in Canaanite mythology," *Journal of Near Eastern Studies* 1: 227–9.

Alcock, L. 1972: *'By South Cadbury is that Camelot...': the Excavation of Cadbury Castle 1966–1970.* London.

Alessio, G. C. 1984. "Medioevo: tradizione manoscritta," in Francesco della Corte (ed.) *Enciclopedia virgiliana,* vol. 4, pp. 432–43. Rome.

Alexander, J. J. G. 1994. *The Painted Page: Italian Renaissance Book Illumination 1450–1550.* Munich.

Alexander, R. 1998. "South Slavic traditions," in J. Foley 1998d: 273–9.

Alexiou, M. 1974. *The Ritual Lament in Greek Tradition.* Cambridge.

Allen, N. J. 1993. "Arjuna and Odysseus: a comparative approach," *South Asia Library Group Newsletter* 40: 39–43.

Allen, S. H. 1999. *Finding the Walls of Troy: Frank Calvert and Heinrich Schliemann at Hissarlik.* Berkeley.

Allen, T. W. (ed.) 1912. *Homeri opera V, Hymnos Cyclum fragmenta Margiten Batrachomyomachiam Vitas continens.* Oxford.

——— 1921. *The Homeric Catalogue of Ships.* Oxford.

Allen, T. W., W. R. Halliday, and E. E. Sikes (eds.) 1936. *The Homeric Hymns,* 2nd edn. Oxford.

Aloni, A. 1986. *Tradizioni arcaiche della Troade e composizione dell' Iliade.* Milan.

——— 1998. *Cantare glorie di eroi: Comunicazione e performance poetica nella Grecia arcaica.* Turin.

Al-Rawi, F. N. H., and A. R. George. 1990. "Tablets from the Sippar library II. Tablet II of the Babylonian Creation Epic," *Iraq* 52: 147–90.

——— and ——— 1995. "Tablets from the Sippar library IV. An Incantation from *Mis pî" Iraq,* 57: 199–220.

Alster, B. 1973. "An aspect of 'Enmerkar and the Lord of Aratta'," *Revue d'assyriologie* 67: 101–10.

——— 1974. "The paradigmatic character of Mesopotamian heroes," *Revue d'assyriologie* 68: 49–60.

——— 1976. "Early patterns in Mesopotamian literature," in B. L. Eichler (ed.) *Kramer Anniversary Volume: Cuneiform Studies in Honor of Samuel Noah Kramer,* pp. 13–24. Altes Orient und Altes Testament 25. Kevelaer.

——— 1987. "A note on the Uriah letter in the Sumerian sargon legend," *Zeitschrift für Assyriologie* 77: 169–73.

——— 1990. "Lugalbanda and the early epic tradition in Mesopotamia," in Abusch et al. 1990: 59–72.

——— 1992. "Interaction of oral and written poetry in early Mesopotamian literature," in Vogelzang and Vanstiphout 1992: 23–69.

——— 1995. "Epic tales from ancient Sumer: Enmerkar, Lugalbanda, and other cunning heroes," in J. Sasson 1995: vol. 4. 2315–26.

Aly, W. 1921. *Volksmärchen, Sage und Novelle bei Herodot und seinen Zeitgenossen: Eine Untersuchung über die volkstümlichen Elemente der altgriechischen Prosaerzählung.* Göttingen. Repr: 1969.

Amiet, P. 1977. *Die Kunst des Alten Orients.* Freiburg.

Anderson, M. J. 1997. *The Fall of Troy in Early Greek Poetry and Art.* Oxford.

Anderson, W. S. 1972. *Ovid: Metamorphoses 6–10.* Norman, OK.

——— 1988. [1977] *P. Ovidii Nasonis Metamorphoses.* Stuttgart and Leipzig.

——— 1997. *Ovid: Metamorphoses 1–5.* Norman, OK.

Anderson, W. S., and L. N. Quartarone (eds.) 2002. *Approaches to Teaching Vergil's Aeneid.* New York.

Andreae, B. 1962. "Der Zyklus der Odysseefresken im Vatikan," *Rheinisches Museum* 69: 106–17.

André-Salvini, M. 1996. "Niobe," in *Collectanea Orientalia: Etudes offerts à A. Spycket.* Winona Lake, IN.

Annus, Amar. 2001. "Ninurta and the Son of Man," in R. M. Whiting (ed.) *Mythology and Mythologies: Methodological Approaches to Intercultural Influences.* Melammu Symposia 2, pp. 7–17. Helsinki.

Antonaccio, C. 1995. *An Archaeology of Ancestors: Tomb Cult and Hero Cult in Early Greece.* Lanham, MD.

Anttila, R. 1989. *Historical and Comparative Linguistics,* 2nd edn. Amsterdam.

Appel, W. 1994. "Grundsaetzliche Bemerkungen zu den *Posthomerica* und Quintus Smyrnaeus," *Prometheus* 20: 1–13.

Archi, A. 1979. "L'Humanité des Hittites," in *Florilegium anatolicum: Mélanges offerts à Emmanuel Laroche*, pp. 37–48. Paris.

—— 2002. "Ea and the Beast: a song related to the Kumarpi Cycle," in P. Taracha (ed.) *Silva Anatolica: Festschrift für Maciej Popko*, pp. 1–10. Warsaw.

Armayor, O. K. 1978a. "Herodotus' catalogues of the Persian empire," *Transactions of the American Philological Association* 108: 1–9.

—— 1978b. "The Homeric influence on Herodotus' story of the labyrinth," *Classical Bulletin* 54: 68–72.

Armstrong, R. 2000a. "Penelope's challenge to her translators," *Classical and Modern Literature* 20/1: 37–76.

—— 2000b. "A picture waiting to happen: Penelope's agency and illustrations to the *Odyssey*," *Classical and Modern Literature* 20/4: 19–57.

—— 2000c. Review of Venuti 1998. *Classical and Modern Literature* 20/2: 73–80.

Arnold, M. 1960 [1861]. "On translating Homer," In R. H. Super (ed.) *The Complete Prose Works of Matthew Arnold*, 1: *On the Classical Tradition*, pp. 97–216. Ann Arbor, MI.

Aro, S., and R. M. Whiting (eds.) 2000. *The Heirs of Assyria: Proceedings of the Opening Symposium of the Assyrian and Babylonian Intellectual Heritage Project Held in Tvärminne, Finland, October 8–11, 1998.* Melammu Symposia 1. Helsinki.

Arthur, M. B. 1981. "The divided world of *Iliad VI*," in H. P. Foley (ed.) *Reflections of Women in Antiquity*, pp. 19–44. London and New York.

—— 1982. "Cultural strategies in Hesiod's *Theogony*: law, family, society," *Arethusa* 15: 63–82.

—— 1983. "The dream of a world without women," *Arethusa* 16: 97–116.

Arweiler, A. 1999. *Die Imitation antiker und spätantiker Literatur in der Dichtung "De spiritalis historiae gestis" des Alcimus Avitus.* Berlin and New York.

Ascherson, N. 2002. *Stone Voices. The Search for Scotland.* London.

Asmis, E. 1982. "Lucretius' Venus and Stoic Zeus," *Hermes* 110: 458–70.

—— 1995. "Epicurean poetics," in D. Obbink (ed.) *Philodemus and Poetry: Poetic Theory and Practice in Lucretius, Philodemus, and Horace*, pp. 15–34. New York and Oxford.

Astour, M. C. 1967. *Hellenosemitica*, 2nd edn. Leiden.

Aubet, M. E. 1993. *The Phoenicians and the West.* Cambridge. 2nd edn., 2001.

Auerbach, E. 1968. *Mimesis: The Representation of Reality in Western Literature*, trans. W. Trask. Princeton, NJ. Trans. from *Mimesis: dargestellte Wirklichkeit in der abendländischen Literatur*, 1946. Bern.

Augoustakis, A. 2003a. "*Lugendam formae sine virginitate reliquit*: reading Pyrene and the transformation of landscape in Silius' *Punica* 3," *American Journal of Philology* 124: 235–57.

—— 2003b. "*Rapit infidum victor caput*: ekphrasis and gender-role reversal in Silius Italicus' *Punica*, in P. Thibodeau and H. Haskell (eds.) *Being There Together: Essays in Honor of Michael C. J. Putnam on the Occasion of his Seventieth Birthday*, pp. 110–27. Afton.

Augusti, J. C. W. 1827. *Grundriss einer historisch-kritischen Einleitung in's Alte Testament.* Leipzig.

Austen, R. 1999. *In Search of Sunjata: The Mande Oral Epic as History, Literature and Performance.* Bloomington, IN.

Austin, M. M., and P. Vidal-Naquet. 1977. *Economic and Social History of Ancient Greece*, trans. M. M. Austin. Berkeley.

Autenrieth, G. 1877. *An Homeric Dictionary*, trans. R. P. Keep. London.

Badalkhan, S. 2004. " 'Lord of the Iron Bow': the return motif in fifteenth-century Balochi epic," *Oral Tradition* 19: 253–98.

Bader, F. 1989. *La Langue des dieux, ou l'hermétisme des poètes indo-européens.* Pisa.

Bailey, C. (ed.) 1922. *De rerum natura: Libri sex*, 2nd edn. Oxford.

—— (ed.) 1947. *Lucretius: De rerum natura*, 3 vols. Oxford.

Bailey, J., and T. Ivanova (trans.) 1998. *An Anthology of Russian Folk Epics.* Armonk, NY.

Baker, M. (ed.) 1998. *Routledge Encyclopedia of Translation Studies.* London.

Bakker, E. 1997. *Poetry in Speech: Orality and Homeric Discourse.* Ithaca, NY and London.

Baldick, J. 1994. *Homer and the Indo-Europeans: Comparing Mythologies.* London and New York.

Barchiesi, A. 1989. "Voci e istanze narrative nelle Metamorfosi di Ovidio," *Materiali e Discussioni* 23: 55–97.

—— 1993. "L'Epos,' in G. Cavallo, P. Fedeli, and A. Giardina (eds.) *Lo spazio letterario di Roma antica*, vol. 1, pp. 115–41. Rome.

—— 2001a. "The crossing," in S. J. Harrison (ed.), *Texts, Ideas, and the Classics*, pp. 142–63. Oxford.

—— 2001b. "Genealogie letterararie nell' epica imperiale: fondamentalismo e ironia," *Fondation Hardt: Entretiens sur l'antiquité classique* 47: 315–54.

—— 2002a. "Narrative technique and narratology in the *Metamorphoses*," in P. Hardie (ed.) *The Cambridge Companion to Ovid*, pp. 180–99. Cambridge.

—— 2002b. Review of Rüpke 2001a. *Bryn Mawn Classical Review*, 2002.06.26.

Barich, M. J. 1982. "Aspects of the poetic technique of Valerius Flaccus." Dissertation, Yale University.

Barkan, L. 1986. *The Gods Made Flesh: Metamorphosis and the Pursuit of Paganism*. New Haven, CT.

Barnes, H. R. 1979. "Enjambement and oral composition," *Transactions of the American Philological Association* 109: 1–10.

—— 1995. "The structure of the elegiac hexameter: a comparison of the structure of elegiac and stichic hexameter verse," In M. Fantuzzi and R. Pretagostini (eds.) *Struttura e storia dell'esametro greco*, vol. 1, pp. 135–61. Rome.

Barnes, W. R. 1995. "Virgil: the literary impact" in Horsfall 1995a: 257–92.

Barr, W. 1981. *Claudian's Panegyric on the Fourth Consulate of Honorius*. Liverpool Latin Texts. Liverpool.

Barsby, J. 1978. *Ovid*. Oxford.

Bartonek, A. 1997. "Le iscrizioni greche arcaiche dei secoli VIII e VII da Ischia," *Annali dell'Istituto Universitario Orientale di Napoli, Sezione Filologico-Letteraria* 19: 109–27.

Bartsch, S. 1997. *Ideology in Cold Blood: A Reading of Lucan's Civil War*. Cambridge, MA.

Bassett, E. L. 1953. "Silius Italicus in England," *Classical Philology* 48: 155–68.

—— 1966. "Hercules and the hero of the *Punica*," in L. Wallach (ed.) *The Classical Tradition: Literary and Historical Studies in Honor of H. Caplan*, pp. 258–73. Ithaca, NY.

Bastiaensen, A. A. R. 1993. "Prudentius in recent literary criticism," in J. Den Boeft and A. Hilhorst (eds.) *Early Christian Poetry: A Collection of Essays*, pp. 101–34. Leiden.

Bate, J. 1993: *Shakespeare and Ovid*. Oxford.

Bauman, R. 1977. *Verbal Art as Performance*. Prospect Heights, IL.

—— 1992. *Folklore, Cultural Performances, and Popular Entertainments*. Oxford.

Bauman, R., and P. Ritch. 1994. "Informing performance: producing the *Coloquio* in Tierra Blanca," *Oral Tradition* 9: 255–80.

Bauman, R., and J. Sherzer (eds.) 1989. *Explorations in the Ethnography of Speaking*, 2nd edn. Cambridge.

Baumgarten, A. I. 1981. *The Phoenician History of Philo of Byblos: A Commentary*. Leiden.

Beaulieu, P.-A. 1993. "Hymns as Royal Inscriptions," *NABU (Nouvelles Assyriologiques Brèves et Utilitaires)* 84: 69–71.

—— 2000. "The descendants of Sin-l'qi-unninni," in J. Marzahn and H. Neumann (eds.) *Assyriologica et Semitica: Festschrift für Joachim Oelsner anlässlich seines 65. Geburtstages am 18. Februar 1997*. Alter Orient und Altes Testament 252, pp. 1–16. Münster.

Beck, B. E. F. 1982. *The Three Twins: The Telling of a South Indian Folk Epic*. Bloomington, IN.

Beckman, G. 1982. "The Anatolian myth of Illuyanka," *Journal of the Ancient Near Eastern Society* 14: 11–25.

—— 1983. "Mesopotamians and Mesopotamian learning at Ḫattuša," *Journal of Cuneiform Studies* 35: 97–114.

—— 1995a. "Royal ideology and state administration in Hittite Anatolia," in J. Sasson 1995: 529–43.

—— 1995b. "The siege of Uršu text (*CTH* 7) and Old Hittite historiography," *Journal of Cuneiform Studies* 47: 23–34.

—— 1997a. "Excerpt from the Hurro-Hittite bilingual wisdom text," in W. W. Hallo (ed.) *The Context of Scripture*, vol. 1, pp. 216–17. Leiden.

—— 1997b. "Mythologie (hethitisch)," *Reallexikon der Assyriologie und vorderasiatischen Archäologie* 8: 564–72.

—— 2001a. "The Hittite Gilgamesh," in B. R. Foster, *The Epic of Gilgamesh*, pp. 157–65. New York.

—— 2001b. "Sargon and Naram-Sin in Ḫatti: reflections of Mesopotamian antiquity among the Hittites," in D. Kuhn and H. Stahl (eds.) *Die Gegenwart des Altertums: Formen und Funktionen des Altertumsbezugs in den Hochkulturen der Alten Welt*, pp. 85–91. Heidelberg.

—— 2003. "Gilgamesh in Ḫatti," in G. Beckman, R. Beal, and G. McMahon (eds.) *Hittite Studies in Honor of Harry A. Hoffner, Jr. on the Occasion of His 65th Birthday*, pp. 37–57. Winona Lake, IN.

—— Forthcoming. *The Hittite Gilgamesh: Edition, Translation and Commentary.*

Behr, H.-J., G. Biegel, and H. Castritius (eds.) 2003. *Troia – Traum und Wirklichkeit: Ein Mythos in Geschichte und Rezeption*. Braunschweig.

Beissinger, M., J. Tylus, and S. Wofford (eds.) 1999. *Epic Traditions in the Contemporary World: The Poetics of Community*. Berkeley and Los Angeles.

Belcher, S. 1999. *Epic Traditions of Africa*. Bloomington, IN.

Ben-Amos, D. 1976. "Analytical categories and ethnic genres," in D. Ben-Amos (ed.) *Folklore Genres*, pp. 215–42. Austin. First published 1969 in *Genre* 2: 265–301.

Benjamin, W. 1969 [1923]. "The task of the translator," in H. Arendt (ed.) *Illuminations*, trans. H. Zohn, pp. 69–82. New York.

Benker, M. 1987. *Achill und Domitian: Herrscherkritik in der Achilleis des Statius*. Erlangen-Nürnberg.

Benveniste, E. 1930. "Le texte du *Drakht asûrîg* et la versification pehlevie," *Journal Asiatique* 217: 193–225.

—— 1932a. "Une apocalypse pehlevie: le *Zâmasp Nâmak*," *Revue de l'Histoire des Religions* 196: 337–80.

—— 1932b. "Le Mémorial de Zarêr," *Journal Asiatique* 221: 245–93.

—— 1966, 1974. *Problèmes de linguistique générale*, vols. I and II. Paris.

Benzi, M. 2002. "Anatolia and the eastern Aegean at the time of the Trojan War," in Montanari 2002: 343–405.

Berg, N. 1978. "Parergon metricum: Der Ursprung des griechischen Hexameters," *Münchener Studien zur Sprachwissenschaft* 37: 11–36.

Bergin, O. 1970. *Irish Bardic Poetry*. Dublin.

Bergren, A. L. T. 1983. "Odyssean temporality: many (re)turns," in C. A. Rubino and C. W. Shelmerdine (eds.) *Approaches to Homer*, pp. 38–71. Austin.

Berlin, A. 1979. *Enmerkar and Ensukhesdanna: A Sumerian Narrative Poem*. Occasional Publications of the Babylonian Fund. Philadelphia.

—— 1983. "Ethnopoetry and the Enmerkar epics," *Journal of the American Oriental Society* 103: 17–24.

Bernal, M. 1987: *Black Athena: The Afroasiatic Roots of Classical Civilization*, 1: *The Fabrication of Ancient Greece 1785–1985*. London.

Bernabé, A. (ed.) 1987. *Poetae epici Graeci: Testimonia et fragmenta*, vol. 1. Leipzig. Corrected edn., 1996.

Bertels, Y. E. et al. (eds.) 1960–71. *Ferdowsi: Shâhnâma* I–IX. Moscow.

Beye, C. R. 1969. "Jason as love-hero in Apollonius' *Argonautika*," *Greek, Roman, and Byzantine Studies* 10: 31–55.

—— 1982. *Epic and Romance in the Argonautica of Apollonius*. Carbondale, IL.

—— 1993. *Ancient Epic Poetry: Homer, Apollonius, Virgil*. Ithaca, NY.

Biebuyck, D. P. 1972. "The epic as a genre in Congo oral literature," in R. M. Dorson (ed.) *African Folklore*, pp. 257–73. Bloomington, IL and London.

—— 1976. "The African heroic epic," *Journal of the Folklore Institute* 13: 5–36.

Biebuyck, D. P., and K. Mateene (eds. and trans.) 1969. *The Mwindo Epic from the Banyanga (Congo Republic)*. Berkeley.

Bietak, M., and N. Marinatos. 1995. "The Minoan wall paintings from Avaris," *Egypt and the Levant* 5: 49–62.

Biggs, R. 1974. *Inscriptions from Tell Abu Ṣalābīkh*. Oriental Institute Publications 99. Chicago.

Bignone, E. 1945. *Storia della letteratura latina*, vol. 2. Florence.

Billerbeck, M. 1985. "Aspects of Stoicism in Flavian epic," *Papers of the Liverpool Latin Seminar* 5: 341–56.

Bing, J. D. 1977. "Gilgamesh and Lugalbanda in the Fara period," *Journal of the Ancient Near Eastern Society of Columbia University* 9: 1–4.

Bing, P. 1988. *The Well-Read Muse: Past and Present in Callimachus and the Hellenistic Poets.* Hypomnemata 90. Göttingen.

Binns, J. W. (ed.) 1974. *Latin Literature of the Fourth Century.* Greek and Latin Studies: Classical Literature and its Influence. London and Boston.

Bird, C. 1972. "Heroic songs of the Mande hunters," in R. M. Dorson (ed.) *African Folklore*, pp. 275–93. Bloomington, IN and London.

Bischoff, B. 1990. *Latin Palaeography, Antiquity and the Middle Ages.* Cambridge.

Black, J. A. 1992. "Some structural features of Sumerian narrative poetry," in Vogelzang and Vanstiphout 1992: 71–101.

—— 1998. *Reading Sumerian Poetry.* Ithaca, NY.

Blackburn, S. H. 1989. "Patterns of development for Indian oral epics," in Blackburn et al. 1989: 15–32.

Blackburn, S. H., and J. B. Flueckiger. 1989. "Introduction," in Blackburn et al. 1989: 1–11.

Blackburn, S. H., P. J. Claus, J. B. Flueckiger, S. S. Wadley (eds.) 1989. *Oral Epics in India.* Berkeley, Los Angeles, and London.

Blänsdorf, J. (ed.) 1995. *Fragmenta poetarum latinorum epicorum et lyricorum praeter Ennium et Lucilium.* Stuttgart.

Blegen, C. W. 1962. *The Mycenaean Age: The Trojan War, the Dorian Invasion, and Other Problems.* Cincinnati.

—— 1975. "Troy VII," in *The Cambridge Ancient History*, 3rd rev. edn. Vol. II, Part 2, ch. xxi (c), pp. 161–4. Cambridge.

Blegen, C. W., J. L. Caskey, M. Rawson, and J. Sperling. 1958. *Troy IV: Settlements VIIa, VIIb and VIII.* Princeton, NJ.

Blomfield, H. G. (trans.) 1916. *The Argonautica of Gaius Valerius Flaccus Setinus Balbus. Book 1.* With notes by the author. Oxford.

Bloom, H. 1973. *The Anxiety of Influence: A Theory of Poetry.* New York.

—— (ed.) 1986. *Virgil: Modern Critical Views.* New York.

—— (ed.) 1987. *Modern Critical Interpretations: Virgil's* Aeneid. New York.

Blümer, W. 2001. *Interpretation archaischer Dichtung: Die mythologischen Parten des Erga Hesiods.* Münster.

Blumberg, K. 1931. "Untersuchungen zur epischen Technik des Apollonios von Rhodos." Dissertation, Leipzig.

Blusch, J. 1970. *Formen und Inhalt von Hesiods individuellen Denken.* Bonn.

Boardman, J. 1999. *The Greeks Overseas*, 4th edn. London.

Boedeker, D. 2000. "Herodotus' genres," in Depew and Obbink 2000b: 97–114.

Bogatyrev, P., and R. Jakobson. 1929. "Die Folklore als eine besondere Form des Schaffens," in *Donum Natalicium Schrijnen*, pp. 900–13. Nijmegen-Utrecht.

Boling, R. G. 1975. *Judges: Introduction, Translation, and Commentary.* Anchor Bible. Garden City, NY.

Bömer, F. 1969–86. *P. Ovidius Naso Metamorphosen: Kommentar*, 7 vols. Heidelberg.

Bona Quaglia, L. 1973. *Gli "Erga" di Esiodo.* Turin.

Bonner, S. Z. (1966) "Lucan and the Declamation Schools," *American Journal of Philology* 87: 257–89.

Børdahl, V. 1996. *The Oral Tradition of Yangzhou Storytelling.* Richmond, Surrey.

Børdahl, V., and J. Ross (eds.) 2002. *Chinese Storytellers: Life and Art in the Yangzhou Tradition.* Boston.

Borsetto, L. 1989. *L'Eneida Tradotta: Riscritture poetiche del testo di Virgilio nel XVI secolo.* Milan.

Bottéro, J. 1977. "Les noms de Marduk, l'écriture et la 'logique' en Mésopotamie ancienne," in M. de J. Ellis (ed.) *Essays on the Ancient Near East in Memory of Jacob Joel Finkelstein.* Memoirs of the Connecticut Academy of Arts and Sciences 19, pp. 5–28. Hamden, CT.

—— 1992a. *L'Épopée de Gilgameš*. Paris.

—— 1992b. *Mesopotamia: Writing, Reasoning and the Gods*. Chicago.

—— 1995. "Akkadian literature: an overview," in J. Sasson 1995: 2293–303.

Bottéro, J., and S. N. Kramer. 1989. *Lorsque les dieux faisaient l'homme*. Paris.

Bowersock, G. W. 1990. *Hellenism in Late Antiquity*. Cambridge.

—— 1994. "Dionysus as an epic hero," in Hopkinson 1994b: 156–66.

Bowie, A. M. 1981. *The Poetic Dialect of Sappho and Alcaeus*. New York.

Bowie, E. L. 1985. "The Greek novel," in P. E. Easterling and B. M. W. Knox (eds.) *The Cambridge History of Classical Literature*, vol. 1, pp. 123–39. Cambridge.

—— 1993. "Lies and fiction and slander in early Greek poetry," in C. Gill and T. P. Wiseman (eds.) *Lies and Fiction in the Ancient World*, pp. 1–37. Austin.

Bowman, A. K., and J. D. Thomas. 1983. *Vindolanda: The Latin Writing-tablets*. London.

Bowra, C. M. 1952. *Heroic Poetry*. London.

—— 1972. *Homer*. London.

Boyce, M. 1954. "Some remarks on the transmission of the Kayanian Heroic Cycle," in F. Steiner (ed.) *Serta Cantabrigiensia* (Studies presented to the 23rd Congress of Orientalists), pp. 45–52. Wiesbaden.

—— 1955. "Zariadrês and Zarêr," *Bulletin of the School of Oriental and African Studies* 17: 463–77.

—— 1957. "The Parthian Gôsân and the Iranian minstrel tradition," *Journal of the Royal Asiatic Society* 18: 10–45.

Boyd, B. (ed.) 2002. *Brill's Companion to Ovid*. Leiden.

Boyd, T. W. 1995. "A poet on the Achaean wall," *Oral Tradition* 10: 181–206.

Boyle, A. J. 1991. "Valerius Flaccus," in A. J. Boyle and J. P. Sullivan (eds.) *Roman Poets of the Early Empire*, pp. 270–7. London.

—— (ed.) 1993. *Roman Epic*. London.

Bradbury, N. M. 1998. "Traditional referentiality: the aesthetic power of oral traditional structures," in J. Foley 1998d: 136–45.

Bramble, J. C. 1982. "Lucan," in E. J. Kenney and W. V. Clausen (eds.) *The Cambridge History of Classical Literature*, vol. II: *Latin Literature*, pp. 533–57. New York.

Branch, M. 1994. "The invention of a national epic," in M. Branch and C. Hawkesworth (eds.) *The Uses of Tradition: A Comparative Enquiry into the Nature, Uses and Functions of Oral Poetry in the Balkans, the Baltic, and Africa*, pp. 195–212. London and Helsinki.

Brault, G. J. 1978. "The French chansons de geste," in Oinas 1978: 193–215.

Braund, D. 1994. *Georgia in Antiquity: A History of Colchis and Transcaucasian Iberia, 550 BC–AD 562*. Oxford.

Braund, S. M. 1996. "Ending epic: Statius, Theseus and a merciful release," *Proceedings of the Cambridge Philological Society* 42: 1–23.

—— (trans.) 1999. *Lucan: Civil War*. Oxford.

Brelich, A. 1958. *Gli eroi greci*. Rome.

Bremmer, J. N. 1998. "Near Eastern and native traditions in Apollodorus' account of the Flood," in F. Garcia Martínez and G. P. Luttikhuizen (eds.), *Interpretations of the Flood*, pp. 39–55. Leiden.

Brennan, B. 1985. "The career of Venantius Fortunatus," *Traditio* 41: 49–78.

Bright, D. 1987. *The Miniature Epic in Vandal Africa*. Norman, OK.

Brilliant, R. 1984. *Visual Narratives: Storytelling in Etruscan and Roman Art*. Ithaca, NY.

Brisset, J. 1964. *Les Idées politiques de Lucain*. Paris.

Brouwers, J. H. 1982. "Zur Lucan-Imitation bei Silius Italicus," in J. Den Boeft and A. H. M. Kessels (eds.) *Actus: Studies in Honour of H. L. W. Nelson*, pp. 73–87. Utrecht.

Brown, P. M. 1984. *Lucretius: De rerum natura I*. Bristol.

—— 1997. *Lucretius: De rerum natura III*. Warminster.

Brown, P. R. 2003. *The Rise of Western Christendom*, 2nd edn. Oxford.

Brown, R. D. 1982. "Lucretius and Callimachus," *Illinois Classical Studies* 7: 77–97.

—— 1987. *Lucretius on Love and Sex: A Commentary on* De rerum natura *IV, 1030–1287*. Leiden.

Brown, S. A. 1999. *The Metamorphosis of Ovid: From Chaucer to Ted Hughes*. London.

Browne, E. G. 1902–24. *A Literary History of Persia*, 4 vols. Cambridge.

Browning, R. 1992. "The Byzantines and Homer," in Lamberton and Keaney 1992: 134–48.

Bruère, R. T. 1958. "*Color Ovidianus* in Silius' *Punica* I–VII," in N. I. Herescu (ed.) *Ovidiana*, pp. 475–99. Paris.
—— 1959. "*Color Ovidianus* in Silius' *Punica* VIII–XVII," *Classical Philology* 54: 228–45.
Bryce, T. 1998. *The Kingdom of the Hittites.* Oxford.
Buccellati, G. 1990. "On poetry – theirs and ours," in Abusch et al. 1990: 105–34.
Bühler, C. F. 1960. *The Fifteenth-Century Book: The Scribes, the Printers, the Decorators.* Philadelphia.
Buitenen, J. A. B. van (trans.) 1973, 1975, 1978. *The Mahâbhârata: 1 The Book of the Beginning; 2 The Book of the Assembly Hall* and *3 The Book of the Forest; 4 The Book of Virâta* and *5 The Book of the Effort.* Chicago.
Burck, E. 1971. *Vom römischen Manierismus: Von der Dichtung der frühen römischen Kaiserzeit.* Darmstadt.
—— 1979. "Die *Argonautica* des Valerius Flaccus." in E. Burck (ed.) *Das Römische Epos*, pp. 208–53. Darmstadt.
Burgess, J. S. 1996. "The non-Homeric *Cypria*," *Transactions of the American Philological Association* 126: 77–99.
—— 2001. *The Tradition of the Trojan War in Homer and the Epic Cycle.* Baltimore.
—— 2002. "Kyprias, the *Kypria*, and multiformity," *Phoenix* 56: 234–45.
—— 2004. "Performance and the Epic Cycle," *Classical Journal* 100: 1–23.
Burkert, W. 1973. "Von Amenophis II zur Bogenprobe des Odysseus," *Grazer Beiträge* 1: 69–78.
—— 1979. *Structure and History in Greek Mythology and Ritual.* Berkeley.
—— 1981. "Seven against Thebes: an oral tradition between Babylonian and Greek literature," in C. Brillante, M. Cantilena, and C. O. Pavese (eds.) *I poemi epici rapsodici non Omerici e la tradizione orale*, pp. 29–51. Padua.
—— 1982. "Literarische Texte und funktionaler Mythos: Ištar und Atrahasis," in J. Assman, W. Burkert, and F. Stolz (eds.) *Funktionen und Leistungen der Mythos: Drei altorientalische Beispiele.* Orbis Biblicus et Orientalis 48, pp. 63–82. Göttingen.
—— 1983. "Oriental myth and literature in the Iliad," in Robin Hägg (ed.) *The Greek Renaissance of the Eighth Century B.C.: Tradition and Innovation*, pp. 51–6. Stockholm.
—— 1984. *Die orientalisierende Epoche in der griechischen Religion und Literatur.* Heidelberg.
—— 1985. *Greek Religion*, trans. John Raffan. Cambridge, MA.
—— 1987. "The making of Homer in the sixth century B.C.: Rhapsodes versus Stesichoros," in *Papers on the Amasis Painter and his World.* Colloquium Sponsored by the Getty Center for the History of Art and the Humanities and Symposium Sponsored by the J. Paul Getty Museum, pp. 43–62. Malibu, CA.
—— 1992. *The Orientalizing Revolution: Near Eastern Influence on Greek Culture in the Early Archaic Age*, trans. of Burkert 1984 by M. E. Pinder and W. Burkert. Cambridge, MA.
—— 1995. "Lydia between East and West or how to date the Trojan War: a study in Herodotus," in Carter and Morris 1995: 139–48.
—— 2001. "La religione greca all'ombra dell'Oriente: I livelli dei contatti e degli influssi," in Ribichini et al. 2001: 21–30.
—— 2003a. *Die Griechen und der Orient.* Munich.
—— 2003b. *Kleine Schriften II: Orientalia.* Göttingen.
Burrow, C. 1993. *Epic Romance: Homer to Milton.* Oxford.
Busch, S. 1993. "Orpheus bei Apollonios Rhodios," *Hermes* 121: 301–24.
Butcher, S. H., and A. Lang (trans.) 1929 [1879]. *The Odyssey of Homer Done into English Prose.* London.
Butler, S. (trans.) 1968 [1900]. *The Odyssey of Homer.* New York.
B-W 2001. *Die frühen römischen Historiker*, vol. 1 (Von Fabius Pictor bis Cn. Gellius), ed. H. Beck and U. Walter. Texte zur Forschung 76. Darmstadt.
Bynum, C. W. 2001. *Metamorphosis and identity.* New York.
Bynum, D. 1976. "The generic nature of oral epic poetry," in D. Ben-Amos (ed.) *Folklore Genres*, pp. 35–58. Austin, TX.
Byre, C. S. 1982. "Per aspera (et arborem) ad astra: ramifications of the Allegory of Arete in Quintus Smyrnaeus, *Posthomerica* 5.49–68," *Hermes* 110: 184–95.
Caduff, G. 1986. *Antike Sintflutsagen.* Göttingen.
Caldwell, R. S. (trans.) 1987. *Hesiod's* Theogony. Cambridge, MA.

Calvino, I. 1991. *Perché leggere i Classici*. Milan.

Cambiatore, T. (trans.) 1532. *La Eneide di Virgilio Tradotta in terza rima*. Venice.

Cameron, A., and J. Long, with a contribution by L. Sherry. 1993. *Barbarians and Politics at the Court of Arcadius*. Berkeley.

Cameron, A. 1965. "Wandering poets: a literary movement in Byzantine Egypt," *Historia* 14: 470–509.

—— 1970. *Claudian: Poetry and Propaganda at the Court of Honorius*. Oxford.

—— 1982. "The empress and the poet: paganism and politics at the court of Theodosius II," *Yale Classical Studies* 27: 217–89.

—— 1983. "Corippus' *Iohannis*: epic of Byzantine Africa," in F. Cairns, (ed.) *Papers of the Liverpool Latin Seminar*, vol. 4, 1983, pp. 167–80. Liverpool.

—— 1995. *Callimachus and His Critics*. Princeton, NJ.

—— 2004. "Poetry and literary culture in late antiquity," in S. Swain and M. Edwards (eds.) *Approaching Late Antiquity*, pp. 327–54. Oxford.

Caminos, R. A. 1977. *A Tale of Woe, from a Hieratic Papyrus in the A. S. Pushkin Museum of Fine Arts in Moscow*. Oxford.

Campanile, E. 1970–3 (publ. 1980). "L'étymologie du celtique *bard(h)os," *Ogam* 22–5: 235–6.

—— 1977. *Ricerche di cultura poetica indoeuropea*. Pisa.

—— 1990. *La ricostruzione della cultura indoeuropea*. Pisa.

Campbell, G. 2003. *Lucretius on Creation and Evolution: A Commentary on* De rerum natura *5.772–1104*. Oxford.

Campbell, L. 1999. *Historical Linguistics: An Introduction*. Cambridge, MA.

Campbell, M. 1981a. *A Commentary on Quintus Smyrnaeus, Posthomerica XII*. Mnemosyne Supplements 71. Leiden.

—— 1981b. *Echoes and Imitations of Early Epic in Apollonius Rhodius*. Mnemosyne Supplements 72. Leiden.

—— 1983. *Studies in the Third Book of Apollonius Rhodius' Argonautica*. Altertumswissenschaftliche Texte und Studien 9. Hildesheim.

—— 1994. *A Commentary on Apollonius Rhodius Argonautica 1–471*. Mnemosyne Supplements 141. Leiden.

Campbell-Thompson, R. 1930. *The Epic of Gilgamesh: Text, Transliteration, and Notes*. Oxford.

Canciani, F. 1981. "Aineias," in John Boardman et al. (eds.) *Lexicon Iconographicum Mythologiae Classicae*, vol. I.1, pp. 381–96. Zurich.

Canitz, A. E. C. 1996. "'In our awyn langage': the nationalist agenda of Gavin Douglas's *Eneados*," *Vergilius* 42: 25–37.

Cannon, G. 1990. *The Life and Mind of Oriental Jones: Sir William Jones, the Father of Modern Linguistics*. Cambridge.

Cantilena, M. 1982. *Ricerche sulla dizione epica, I: Per uno studio della formularità degli Inni omerici*. Rome.

Capomacchia, A. M. G. 2001. "Heroic dimension and historical perspective in the ancient Near East," in T. Abusch, P.-A. Beaulieu, et al. (eds.), *Historiography in the Cuneiform World*, Part 1. Proceedings of the XLVe Rencontre Assyriologique Internationale, pp. 91–7. Bethesda, MD.

Caquot, A., M. Sznycer, and A. Herdner (eds.) 1974. *Textes Ougaritiques*, vol. 1. Littératures du Proche-Orient Ancien 7. Paris.

Cardauns, B. 1976. *M. Terentius Varro: Antiquitates rerum divinarum*, 2 vols. Abhandlungen der Geistes- und Sozialwissenschaftlichen Klasse. Einzelveröffentlichung 1. Mainz.

Carpenter, R. 1946. *Folktale, Fiction and Saga in the Homeric Epics*. Berkeley.

Carruba, O. 1998. "Hethitische und anatolische Dichtung," in J. Prosecky (ed.) *Intellectual Life of the Ancient Near East*, pp. 67–89. Prague.

Carrubba, R. W. 1993. "The Preface to Juvencus' biblical epic: a structural study," *American Journal of Philology* 114: 303–12.

Carsprecken, J. F. 1952. "Apollonius Rhodius and the Homeric epic," *Yale Classical Studies* 13: 33–143.

Carter, J. B., and S. P. Morris (eds.) 1995. *The Ages of Homer: A Tribute to Emily Townsend Vermeule*. Austin.

Cartledge, P. 2001. *Spartan Reflections*. London and Berkeley.

Cartledge, T. W. 1992. *Vows in the Hebrew Bible and the Ancient Near East.* Journal for the Study of the Old Testament Supplement 147. Sheffield.

Cassuto, U. 1971. *The Goddess Anat*, trans. Israel Abrahams. Jerusalem.

—— 1955. "The Israelite epic," in *Biblical and Oriental Studies*, vol. 2, trans. Israel Abrahams, pp. 69–109. Jerusalem.

Castelli, E. 1996. "Imperial reimaginings of Christian origins: epic in Prudentius's poem for the martyr Eulalia," in E. Castelli and H. Taussig (eds.) *Reimagining Christian Origins: A Colloquium Honoring Burton L. Mack*, pp. 173–84. Valley Forge, PA.

Cavigneaux, A. 1999. "A scholar's library in Meturan? With an edition of the Tablet H 72 (Textes de Tell Haddad VII)," in T. Abusch and K. van der Toorn (eds.) *Mesopotamian Magic: Textual, Historical, and Interpretative Perspectives*, pp. 251–73. Groningen.

Cavigneaux, A., and J. Renger. 2000. "Ein altbabylonischer Gilgameš-Text aus Nippur," in A. R. George and I. L. Finkel (eds.) *Wisdom, Gods, and Literature: Studies in Assyriology in Honor of W. G. Lambert*, pp. 91–103. Winona Lake, MN.

Caxton, W. (trans.) 1962 [1490]. *Caxton's* Eneydos (1490), *Englished from the French* Liure des Eneydes (1483). Early English Text Society 57. Oxford.

Center for Hellenic Studies, Washington DC. Forthcoming. *Iliad* translation for Multitext Homer Project, trans. C. Dué, M. Ebbott, D. Frame, L. Muellner, and G. Nagy. www.stoa.org/chs/

Chadwick, H. M. 1912. *The Heroic Age.* Cambridge.

Chadwick, J. 1976. *The Mycenaean World.* Cambridge.

Chao G. 2001a. "Chinese oral traditions," a special issue of *Oral Tradition* 16/ii.

—— 2001b. "The Oirat epic cycle of *Jangar*," in Chao 2001a: 402–35.

Chapman, G. (trans.) 1967. *Chapman's Homer: The Iliad, The Odyssey, and the Lesser Homerica*, 2 vols., 2nd edn., ed. A. Nicoll. Bollingen Series 41. Princeton, NJ.

Charlet, J.-L. 1988. "Aesthetic trends in late Latin poetry (325–410)," *Philologus* 132: 74–85.

Charpin, D. 1997. "La version mariote de l'insurrection générale contre Naram-Sin," in D. Charpin and J.-M. Durand (eds.) *Florilegium marianum*, 3: *Recueil d'études à la mémoire de Marie-Thérèse Barrelet*, pp. 9–18. Paris.

—— 2003. "Esquisse d'une diplomatique des documents mésopotamiens," *Bibliothèque de l'Ecole des Chartes* 160: 487–511.

Charpin, D. and J.-M. Durand. 1985. "La prise du pouvoir par Zimri-Lim," *Mari: Annales de Recherches interdisciplinaires* 4: 293–343.

Cherniss, H. 1935. *Aristotle's Criticism of Presocratic Philosophy.* Baltimore.

Christensen, A. 1932. *Les Keyânides.* Copenhagen.

Chuvin, P. 1990. *A Chronicle of the Last Pagans*, trans. B. A. Archer. Cambridge, MA.

—— 1991. *Mythologie et géographie dionysiaques: Recherches sur l'œuvre de Nonnos de Panopolis.* Clermont-Ferrand.

Civil, M. 2003. "Reading Gilgameš II: Gilgameš and Huwawa," in W. Sallaberger, K. Volk, and A. Zgoll (eds.) *Literatur, Politik und Recht in Mesopotamien: Festchrift für Claus Wilcke.* Orientalia Biblica et Christiana 14, pp. 77–86. Wiesbaden.

Cizek, E. 1972. *L'Époque de Néron et ses controverses idéologiques.* Roma Aeterna 4. Leiden.

Clanchy, M. T. 1993. *From Memory to Written Record.* Oxford.

Clare, R. J. 2002. *The Path of the Argo: Language, Imagery and Narrative in the Argonautica of Apollonius Rhodius.* Cambridge.

Clark, E., and D. Hatch. 1981. *The Golden Bough, the Oaken Cross: The Virgilian Cento of Faltonia Betitia Proba.* Chico, CA.

Clark, J. (ed.) 1977. *The Ozidi Saga. Collected and Translated from the Ijo of Okabou Ojobolo.* Ibadan, Nigeria.

Clarke, H. 1981. *Homer's Readers: A Historical Introduction to the* Iliad *and* Odyssey. Newark, NJ.

Classen, C. J. 1968. "Poetry and rhetoric in Lucretius," *Transactions of the American Philological Association* 99: 77–118. Repr. in Classen 1986: 331–73.

—— (ed.) 1986. *Probleme der Lukrezforschung.* Hildesheim.

Claus, P. J. 1989. "Behind the text: performance and ideology in a Tulu oral tradition," in Blackburn et al. 1989: 55–74.

Clauss, J. J. 1993. *The Best of the Argonauts: The Redefinition of the Epic Hero in Book 1 of Apollonius's Argonautica.* Berkeley.

Clay, D. 1976. "The sources of Lucretius' inspiration," in J. Bollack and A. Laks (eds.) *Etudes sur l'épicurisme antique*, pp. 205–27. Lille. Repr. in Clay 1998: 138–60.

—— 1983. *Lucretius and Epicurus*. Ithaca, NY.

—— 1998. *Paradosis and Survival: Three Chapters in the History of Epicurean Philosophy*. Ann Arbor, MI.

—— 2004. *Archilochos Heros: The Cult of Poets in the Greek Polis*. Cambridge, MA.

Clay, J. S. 1983. *The Wrath of Athena: Gods and Men in the* Odyssey. Princeton, NJ.

—— 1989. *The Politics of Olympus: Form and Meaning in the Major Homeric Hymns*. Princeton, NJ.

—— 1997. "The Homeric hymns," in Morris and Powell 1997: 489–507.

—— 2003. *Hesiod's Cosmos*. Cambridge.

Clayman, D. L., and T. van Nortwick. 1977. "Enjambement in Greek hexameter poetry," *Transactions of the American Philological Association* 107: 85–92.

Clogan, P. M. 1968. *The Medieval Achilleid of Statius*, edited with introduction, variant readings, and glosses. Leiden.

Clover, C. J. 1986. "The long prose form," *Arkiv för nordisk filologi* 101: 10–39.

Cobet, J. 2003. "Vom Text zur Ruine: Die Geschichte der Troia-Diskussion," in Ulf 2003a: 19–38.

Cobet, J., and H.-J. Gehrke. 2002. "Warum um Troia immer wieder streiten?," *Geschichte in Wissenschaft und Unterricht* 53: 290–325.

Cohen, B. (ed.) 1995. *The Distaff Side: Representing the Female in Homer's Odyssey*. Oxford.

Cohen, S. 1973. "Enmerkar and the Lord of Aratta." Dissertation, University of Pennsylvania.

Colarusso, J. (ed.) 2002. *Nart Sagas from the Caucasus: Myths and Legends from the Circassians, Abazas, Abkhaz, and Ubykhs*. Princeton, NJ.

Cole, T. 1969. "The Saturnian verse," *Yale Classical Studies* 21: 3–73.

Coleman, K. M. 2003. "Recent scholarship on the *Thebaid* and *Achilleid*: an overview," in D. R. Shackleton Bailey (ed. and trans.) *Statius: Thebaid, Books 1–7*, pp. 9–37. Cambridge, MA.

Collins, D. 2001. "Homer and rhapsodic competition in performance," *Oral Tradition* 16: 129–67.

Collins, W. A. 1998. *The Guritan of Radin Suane: A Study of the Besemah Oral Epic from South Sumatra*. Bibliotheca Indonesica 28. Leiden.

Collombert, P., and L. Coulon. 2000. "Les dieux contre la mer: Le début du 'papyrus d'Astarté' (pBN 202)," *Institut français d'archéologie orientale du Caire* 100: 193–242.

Combellack, F. M. 1968. *The War at Troy: What Homer Didn't Tell, by Quintus of Smyrna*. Norman, OK.

Commager, H. S. 1957. "Lucretius' interpretation of the plague," *Harvard Studies in Classical Philology* 62: 105–18.

—— (ed.) 1966. *Virgil: A Collection of Critical Essays*. Englewood Cliffs, NJ.

Connelly, B. 1986. *Arab Folk Epic and Identity*. Berkeley.

Connor, P. 1993. "Epic in mind: Claudian's *De raptu Proserpinae*," in A. J. Boyle (ed.) *Roman Epic*, pp. 237–60. London and New York.

Conroy, C. 1980. "Hebrew epic: historical notes and critical reflections," *Biblica* 61: 1–30.

Conte, G. B. 1966. "Il proemio della Pharsalia," *Maia* 18: 42–53.

—— 1974. *Saggio di commento a Lucano. Pharsalia VI 118–260: l'Aristia di Sceva*, Università degli Studi di Pisa, Istituto per le Scienze dell'Antichità, Biblioteca degli studi classici e orientali 2. Pisa.

—— 1986. *The Rhetoric of Imitation: Genre and Poetic Memory in Virgil and Other Latin Poets*. Ithaca, NY.

—— 1994a. "Instructions for a sublime reader: form of the text and form of the addressee in Lucretius' *De rerum natura*," trans. G. W. Most, in *Genres and Readers: Lucretius, Love Elegy, Pliny's Encyclopedia*, pp. 1–34. Baltimore.

—— 1994b. *Latin Literature: A History*, trans. J. Solodow. Baltimore.

Conway, J. K., K. Keniston, and L. Marx (eds.) 1999. *Earth, Air, Fire, Water: Humanistic Studies of the Environment*. Amherst, MA.

Conybeare, F. C., J. R. Harris, and A. S. Lewis. 1913. *The Story of Ahikar from the Aramaic, Syriac, Arabic, Armenian, Ethiopic, Old Turkish, Greek and Slavonic Versions*, 2nd edn. Cambridge.

Coogan, M. D. (ed.) 1998. *The Oxford History of the Biblical World*. Oxford and New York.

Cook, E. 1995. *The Odyssey in Athens: Myths of Cultural Origins*. Ithaca, NY.

—— 2004. "Near Eastern sources for the palace of Alkinoos," *American Journal of Archaeology* 108: 43–77.

Cook, J. M. 1973. *The Troad: An Archaeological and Topographical Study.* Oxford.

Cooper, J. S. 1992. "Babbling on: recovering Mesopotamian orality," in M. E. Vogelzang and H. L. J. Vanstiphout (eds.) *Mesopotamian Epic Literature: Oral or Aural?*, pp. 103–22. Lewiston, NY.

—— 2001. "Literature and history: the historical and political referents of Sumerian literary texts," in T. Abusch, P.-A. Beaulieu, J. Huehnergard et al. (eds.) *Historiography in the Cuneiform World*, Part 1. Proceedings of the XLVe Rencontre Assyriologique Internationale, pp. 131–47. Bethesda, MD.

—— 2002. "Buddies in Babylonia: Gilgamesh, Enkidu, and Mesopotamian homosexuality," in T. Abusch (ed.) *Riches Hidden in Secret Places: Ancient Near Eastern Studies in Memory of Thorkild Jacobsen*, pp. 73–85. Winona Lake, MN.

Cooper, J. S., and Wolfgang Heimpel. 1983. "The Sumerian Sargon legend," *Journal of the American Oriental Society* 103: 67–82.

Coote, M. P. 1978. "Serbo-Croatian heroic songs," in Oinas 1978: 257–85.

Costa, C. D. N. 1984. *Lucretius: De rerum natura V.* Oxford.

Cotterill, H. B. (trans.) 1911. *Homer's Odyssey.* London.

Cottrell, L. 1984. *The Bull of Minos. The Discoveries of Schliemann and Evans*, rev. edn., with intro. by P. Levi. London.

Courbin, P. 1957. "Une tombe géométrique," *Bulletin de Correspondance Hellénique* 81: 322–86.

Courcelle, P. 1984. *Lecteurs païens et lecteurs chrétiens de l'Enéide. I. Les témoinages littéraires.* Paris.

—— 1957. "Les Exégèses chrétiennes de la quatrième églogue," *Revue des Etudes Anciennes* 59: 294–319.

Courtney, E. (ed.) 1993. *The Fragmentary Latin Poets.* Oxford.

—— (ed.) 1970. *C. Valeri Flacci Argonauticon libri octo.* Leipzig.

Cowell, F. R. 1948. *Cicero and the Roman Republic.* London.

Crane, G. 1988. *Calypso: Backgrounds and Conventions of the Odyssey.* Frankfurt.

Creed, R. P. 1992. "Sutton Hoo and the recording of *Beowulf*," in C. B. Kendall and P. S. Wells (eds.) *Voyage to the Outer World: The Legacy of Sutton Hoo.* Medieval Studies at Minnesota 5, pp. 65–75. Minneapolis.

Cremona-Casoli, A. 1931. *Tommaso Cambiatori Reggiano (1370?–1444), primo traduttore del l'Eneide in terza rima.* Reggio Emilia.

Criado, C. 2000. *La teología de la Tebaida Estaciana: El anti-virgilianismo de un clasicista.* Hildesheim.

Cribiore, R. 2001. *Gymnastics of the Mind: Greek Education in Hellenistic and Roman Egypt.* Princeton, NJ.

Cross, F. M. 1973. *Canaanite Myth and Hebrew Epic.* Cambridge, MA.

—— 1998. *From Epic to Canon: History and Literature in Ancient Israel.* Baltimore.

Crump, M. 1931. *The Epyllion from Theocritus to Ovid.* Oxford.

—— 1998. *From Epic to Canon.* Baltimore.

Curti, M. 1993. "L'officina dei cicli," *Studi Classici e Orientali* 43: 33–47.

Curtius, E. R. 1953. *European Literature and the Latin Middle Ages*, trans. Willard R. Trask. Princeton, NJ.

Cuypers, M. P. 1997. "Apollonius Rhodius Argonautica 2.1–310: a commentary." Dissertation, Leiden.

Daddi, F. P. 2003. "From Akkad to Ḫattuša: the history of Gurparanzaḫ and the river that gave him its name," in *Semitic and Assyriological Studies presented to Pelio Fronzaroli*, pp. 476–94. Wiesbaden.

Dalley, S. 1989. *Myths from Mesopotamia.* Oxford. Repr. 1991, 1998.

—— 1991. "Gilgamesh in the Arabian Nights," *Journal of the Royal Asiatic Society* 1: 1–17.

—— (ed.) 1998. *The Legacy of Mesopotamia.* Oxford.

Dalzell, A. 1996. *The Criticism of Didactic Poetry: Essays on Lucretius, Virgil, and Ovid.* Toronto.

Davidson, O. M. 1980. "Indo-European dimensions of Herakles in *Iliad* 19.95–133," *Arethusa*, 13: 197–202.

—— 1988. "Formulaic analysis of samples taken from the *Shâhnâma* of Ferdowsi," *Oral Tradition* 3: 88–105.

—— 1994. *Poet and Hero in the Persian Book of Kings.* Ithaca, NY.

—— 1998a. "Epic as a frame for speech-acts: ritual boasting in the *Shâhnâma* of Ferdowsi," in H. Tristram (ed.) *New Methods in the Research of Epic*, pp. 271–85. Tübingen.

—— 1998b. "The text of Ferdowsi's *Shâhnâma* and the burden of the past," *Journal of the American Oriental Society* 118: 63–68.

—— (ed.) 2000. *Comparative Literature and Classical Persian Poetics: Seven Essays.* Bibliotheca Iranica: Intellectual Traditions Series 4. Costa Mesa, CA.

—— 2001. "Some Iranian poetic tropes as reflected in the 'Life of Ferdowsi' traditions," in M. G. Schmidt and W. Bisang (eds.) *Philologica et Linguistica: Festschrift für Helmut Humbach.* Supplement, pp. 1–12. Trier.

Davies, M. 1986. "*Prolegomena* and *Paralegomena* to a new edition (with commentary) of the fragments of early Greek epic," *Nachrichten der Akademie der Wissenschaften in Göttingen* 1 phil. hist. Kl., 2: 91–111.

—— (ed.) 1988. *Epicorum Graecorum fragmenta.* Göttingen.

—— 1989a. "The date of the Epic Cycle," *Glotta* 67: 89–100.

—— 1989b. *The Epic Cycle.* Bristol.

Davis, D. 1992. *Epic and Sedition: The Case of Ferdowsi's Shâhnâmeh.* Fayetteville, AR.

Davis, M. 1990. "*Ratis audax*: Valerius Flaccus' bold ship," in A. J. Boyle (ed.) *The Imperial Muse: Ramus Essays on Roman Literature of the Empire: Flavian Epicist to Claudian*, pp. 46–73. Bendigo, Australia.

Day, J. W. 1985. *God's Conflict with the Dragon and the Sea.* Cambridge.

—— 2000. "Epigram and reader: generic force as (re-)activation of ritual," in Depew and Obbink 2000b: 37–57.

Debiasi, A. 2003. "L'epica perduta. Eumelo, il Ciclo, l'occidente." Dissertation, Università degli Studi di Roma "La Sapienza."

—— 2005. *L'epica perduta. Eumelo, il Ciclo, l'occidente. Hesperìa* 20. Rome.

De Boer, C. 1966 [1915–38]. "*Ovide moralisé*": *Poème du commencement du quatorzième siècle*, 5 vols. Wiesbaden.

de Hamel, C. 1992. *Scribes and Illuminators.* Toronto.

DeJong, I. 2001. *A Narratological Commentary on the Odyssey.* Cambridge.

de Jong, J. W. 1985. "The over-burdened Earth in India and Greece," *Journal of the American Oriental Society* 105: 397–400.

Delage, E. 1930. *La Géographie dans les Argonautiques d'Apollonios de Rhodes.* Bordeaux and Paris.

Delarue, F. 2000. *Stace, poète épique: originalité et cohérence.* Louvain.

Delarue, F. S. Georgacopoulou, P. Laurens, and A.-M. Taisne (eds.) 1996. *Epicedion: Hommage à P. Papinius Statius, 96–1996.* Poitiers.

Del Olmo Lete, G. 1981. *Mitos y leyendas de Canaón según la tradición de Ugarit.* Madrid.

Delz, J. (ed.) 1987. *Sili Italici Punica.* Stuttgart.

de Martino, S. 1995. "Music, dance, and processions in Hittite Anatolia," in J. Sasson 1995: 2661–9.

de Moor, J. C. 1971. *The Seasonal Pattern in the Ugaritic Poem of Baᶜlu according to the Version of Ilimilku.* Alter Orient und Altes Testament 16. Neukirchen-Vluyn and Kevelaer.

—— 1987. *An Anthology of Religious Texts from Ugarit.* Nisaba 16. Leiden.

—— 1988. "The seasonal pattern in the legend of Aqhatu," *Studi Epigrafici e Linguistici* 5: 61–78.

—— 1997. *The Rise of Yahwism*, 2nd edn. Leuven.

Depew, M. 2000. "Enacted and represented dedications: genre and Greek hymn," in Depew and Obbink 2000a: 59–79.

Depew, M., and D. Obbink 2000a. "Introduction," in Depew and Obbink 2000b: 1–14.

—— (eds.) 2000b. *Matrices of Genre: Authors, Canons, and Society.* Cambridge, MA.

Deproost, P.-A. 1998. "*Ficta et facta*: la condemnation du 'mensonge des poètes' dans la poésie latine chrétienne," *Revue des Etudes Augustiniennes* 44: 101–21.

Desmond, M. 1994. *Reading Dido: Gender, Textuality, and the Medieval Aeneid.* Minneapolis.

Detienne, M. 1963. *Crise agraire et attitude religieuse chez Hésiode.* Collection Latomus, Revue des Études Latines 68. Brussels.

—— 1973. *Les maîtres de vérité dans la Grèce archaïque*, 2nd edn. Paris.

de Vries, B. 1967. "The style of Hittite epic and mythology." Dissertation, Brandeis University.

Dewar, M. 1994. "Laying it on with a trowel: the proem to Lucan and related texts," *Classical Quarterly* 44: 199–211.

—— 1996. *Panegyricus de Sexto Consolatu Honorii Augusti.* Oxford.

Diakonoff, I. M., and N. B. Jankowska. 1990. "An Elamite Gilgamesh text from Argištihenele, Urartu (Armavi-blur, 8th century B.C.)," *Zeitschrift für Assyriologie* 80: 102–23.

Dick, B. F. 1967. "Fatum and fortuna in Lucan's *Bellum civile*," *Classical Philology* 62: 235–42.

Dickinson, O. T. P. K. 1986. "Homer, the poet of the Dark Age," *Greece and Rome*, n.s. 33/1: 20–37.

Dietrich, J. 1999. "*Thebaid*'s feminine ending," *Ramus* 28: 41–53.

Dietrich, M., O. Loretz, and J. Sanmartín. 1976. *Die Keilalphabetischen Texte aus Ugarit*. Alter Orient und Altes Testament, 24/1, Neukirchen-Vluyn and Kevelaer, 2nd edn. 1995. Repr. as *The Cuneiform Alphabetic Texts from Ugarit, Ras Ibn Hani and Other Places*. Abhandlungen zur Literatur Alt-Syrien-Palästinas 8. Münster.

Dilke, O. A. W. 1954. *Statius, Achilleid: Edited with Introduction, Apparatus Criticus and Notes.* Cambridge.

—— 1972. "Lucan's political views and the Caesars," in D. R. Dudley (ed.) *Neronians and Flavians: Silver Latin I*, pp. 62–82. London and Boston.

Diller, H. 1962. "Die dichterische Form von Hesiods *Erga*," in E. Heitsch (ed.) *Hesiod*, pp. 239–74. Darmstadt.

Djilas, M. 1958. *Land without Justice: An Autobiography of His Youth.* New York.

Dodds, E. 1951. *The Greeks and the Irrational.* Berkeley.

Doherty, L. 1995. *Siren Songs. Gender, Audiences, and Narrators in the Odyssey.* Ann Arbor, MI.

Döhl, H. 1980. "Mykenische Kampfdarstellungen Bild und Deutung im prähistorischen Griechenland," *Materialhefte zur Ur- und Frühgeschichte Niedersachsens* 16: 21–32.

Dolce, L. 1568. *L'Enea di M. Lodovico Dolce tratto dall'Eneida di Virgilio.* Venice.

Dominik, W. J. 1993. "From Greece to Rome: Ennius' *Annals*," in Boyle 1993: 37–58.

—— 1994a. *The Mythic Voice of Statius: Power and Politics in the Thebaid.* Leiden.

—— 1994b. *Speech and Rhetoric in Statius' Thebaid.* Hildesheim.

—— 1996. "Statius' *Thebaid* in the twentieth century," in R. Faber and B. Seidensticker (eds.) *Worte, Bilder, Töne: Studien zur Antike und Antikerezeption Bernhard Kytzler zu ehren.* Würzburg.

—— 2003. "Hannibal at the gates: programmatising Rome and *Romanitas* in Silius Italicus' *Punica* 1 and 2," in A. J. Boyle and W. J. Dominik (eds.) *Flavian Rome: Culture, Image, Text*, pp. 469–97. Leiden.

Doniger O'Flaherty, W. 1976. *The Origin of Evil in Hindu Mythology.* Berkeley.

—— (trans.) 1981. *The Rig Veda: An Anthology.* Harmondsworth.

Donlan, W. 1999. *The Aristocratic Ideal and Selected Papers.* Wauconda, IL.

Donner, H., and W. Röllig (eds.) 1964. *Kanaanäische und Aramäische Inschriften.* Wiesbaden.

Dornseiff, F. 1934. "Hesiods Werke und Tage und das Alte Morgenland," *Philologus* 89: 397–415. Repr. 1956 as *Kleine Schriften I. Antike und alter Orient.* Leipzig, pp. 72–95. 2nd edn. 1959.

Dorson, R. M. 1978. "Introduction," in Oinas 1978: 1–6.

Dothan, T., and M. Dothan. 1992. *People of the Sea: The Search for the Philistines.* New York.

Dougherty, R. P. 1928. "Writing upon parchment and papyrus among the Babylonians and the Assyrians," *Journal of the American Oriental Society* 48: 109–35.

Dova, S. 2000. "Who is *makartatos* in the *Odyssey*?," *Harvard Studies in Classical Philology* 100: 53–65.

Dowden, K. 1996. "Homer's sense of text," *Journal of Hellenic Studies* 116: 47–61.

Dräger, P. 1993. *Argo Pasimelousa: Der Argonautenmythos in der griechischen und römischen Literatur.* Palingenesia 43. Stuttgart.

—— 2001. *Die Argonautika des Apollonios Rhodios: Das zweite Zorn-Epos der griechischen Literatur.* Beiträge zur Altertumskunde Band 158. Munich.

Draheim, J. 1993. "Vergil in music," in C. W. Kallendorf (ed.) *Vergil*, pp. 317–44. New York.

Dresden, M. J. 1971. "Middle Iranian," in C. A. Ferguson, C. T. Hodge, and H. H. Paper (eds.) *Linguistics in South West Asia and North Africa*, pp. 26–63. Current Trends in Linguistics 6. The Hague.

Driver, G. R. 1956. *Canaanite Myths and Legends.* Edinburgh.

Dryden, John (trans.) 1944 [1697]. *Virgil's Aeneid.* New York.

—— 1700. Preface to *Fables Ancient and Modern.*

DuBois, T. A. 1995. *Finnish Folk Poetry and the* Kalevala. New York.

Duchêne, H. 1996. *Golden Treasures of Troy: The Dream of Heinrich Schliemann*, trans. J. Leggatt. New York.

Duckworth, G. E. 1936. "Foreshadowing and suspense in the *Posthomerica* of Quintus of Smyrna," *American Journal of Philology* 57: 58–86.

Dudley, D. R. 1965. "The satiric element in Lucretius," in D. R. Dudley (ed.) *Lucretius.* London.

Dué, C. 2000. "Poetry and the Dêmos: state regulation of a civic possession," in R. Scaife (ed.) Stoa Consortium. http://www.stoa.org/demos/camws-casey.html.

—— 2001. "Achilles' golden amphora in Aeschines' *Against Timarchus* and the afterlife of oral tradition," *Classical Philology* 96: 33–47.

—— 2002. *Homeric Variations on a Lament by Briseis.* Lanham, MD.

Dué, C., and G. Nagy. 2003. "Preliminaries to Philostratus's *On Heroes*," in Maclean and Aitken 2003: xv–xli.

Due, O. S. 1962. "An essay on Lucan," *Classica et Medievalia* 22: 68–132.

—— 1970. "Lucain et la philosophie," in *Lucain: Fondation Hardt, Entretiens sur l'antiquité classique* 15: 201–32.

—— 1974. *Changing Forms: Studies in the Metamorphoses of Ovid.* Copenhagen.

Duff, J. D. (trans.) 1928. *Lucan: The Civil War.* Loeb Classics Library. Cambridge, MA.

—— (ed.) 1934. *Silius Italicus: Punica*, 2 vols. Loeb Classical Library. Cambridge, MA.

Dufner, C. M. 1988. "The *Odyssey* in the *Argonautica*: reminiscence, revision, reconstruction." Dissertation, Princeton University.

Dumézil, G. 1968. *Mythe et épopée*, I: *L'Idéologie des trois fonctions dans les épopées des peuples indo-européennes.* Paris. 2nd edn. 1986.

—— 1971. *Mythe et épopée*, II: *Types épiques indo-européens: Un héros, un sorcier, un roi.* Paris. 2nd edn., 1986. English trans. 1973, A. Hiltebeitel, *The Destiny of a King.*

—— 1973. *Mythe et épopée*, III: *Histoires romaines.* Paris. 2nd edn., 1978; 3rd edn., 1981.

—— 1975. *Fêtes romaines d'été et d'automne, suivi de dix questions romaines.* Paris.

—— 1980. *Camillus: A Study of Indo-European Religion as Roman History*, trans. A. Aranowicz and J. Bryson, ed. with intro. by U. Strutynski. Berkeley and Los Angeles (= Part 2 of *Mythe et épopée* III = Dumézil 1973, plus Appendices 1 and 2 of Dumézil 1973, plus Appendices 3 and 4 of Dumézil 1975).

—— 1983. *The Stakes of the Warrior*, trans. D. Weeks, ed. with intro. by J. Puhvel. Berkeley. (= Part 1 of *Mythe et épopée* II = Dumézil 1971).

—— 1986. *The Plight of the Sorcerer*, trans. D. Weeks et al., ed. J. Puhvel and D. Weeks, intro. by D. Weeks. (= Part 2 of *Mythe et épopée* II = Dumézil 1971).

—— 1995. *Mythe et épopée* I, II, III. New corrected edn., with original pagination retained in the inner margins. Preface by J. Grisward. Paris.

Dumont, A. M. 1986. "L'Eloge de Néron," *Bulletin de l'Association Guillaume Budé* 16: 22–40.

Dumont, L. 1991. *Homo aequalis II, L'idéologie allemande: France-Allemagne et retour.* Paris.

Dupont, F. 1999. *The Invention of Literature: From Greek Intoxication to the Latin Book*, trans. J. Lloyd. Baltimore.

Durand, J.-M. 1993. "Le mythologème du combat entre le dieu de l'orage et la mer en Mésopotamie," *Mari: Annales des Recherches Interdisciplinaires* 7: 41–61.

Durante, M. 1976. *Sulla preistoria della tradizione poetica greca, Parte seconda: Risultanze della comparazione indoeuropea.* Rome.

Durnford, S. P. B. 1971. "Some evidence for syntactic stress in Hittite," *Anatolian Studies* 21: 69–75.

Duval, Y.-M. 1989. "Les premiers rapports de Paulin de Nole avec Jérôme: moine et philosophe? Poète ou exégète?," *Studi Tardoantichi* 7: 177–216.

Eagan, M. C. 1962, 1965. *Fathers of the Church: The Poems of Prudentius*, 2 vols. Washington, DC.

Easterling, P. E. 1984. "The tragic Homer," *Bulletin of the Institute of Classical Studies* 31: 1–8.

Easton, D. F., J. D. Hawkins, A. G. Sherratt, and E. S. Sherratt. 2002. "Troy in recent perspective," *Anatolian Studies* 52: 75–109.

Ebbott, M. 2003. *Imagining Illegitimacy in Classical Greek Literature.* Lanham, MD.

Edel, E. 1966. *Die Ortsnamenliste aus dem Totentempel Amenophis III.* Bonn.

Edmunds, L. (ed.) 1990. *Approaches to Greek Myth.* Baltimore.

—— 1993. *Myth in Homer: A Handbook.* Highland Park, NJ.

—— 1997. "Myth in Homer," in Morris and Powell 1997: 415–41.

Edwards, G. P. 1971. *The Language of Hesiod in its Traditional Context*. Oxford.

Edwards, I. E. S., C. J. Gadd, and N. G. L. Hammond (eds.) 1970. *The Cambridge Ancient History*, 3rd edn., vol. 1. Cambridge.

Edwards, M. W. 1987. *Homer: Poet of the Iliad*. Baltimore.

—— 1991. *The Iliad: A Commentary*, vol. V: *Books 17–20*. Cambridge.

Edzard, D. O. 1976–80. "Keilschrift," *Reallexikon der Assyriologie und vorderasiatischen Archäologie* 5: 544–68.

—— 1991. "Gilgameš and Huwawa," *Zeitschrift für Assyriologie* 81: 165–233.

—— 1994. "Sumerian epic: epic or fairy tale?," *Bulletin of the Canadian Society for Mesopotamian Studies* 27: 7–14.

Ehlers, W. W. (ed.) 1980. *Gai Valeri Flacci Argonauticon libri octo*. Stuttgart.

Ehrismann, O. 1987. *Nibelungen Lied: Epoche-Werk-Wirkung*. Munich.

Eichgrün, E. 1961. *Kallimachos und Apollonios Rhodios*. Berlin.

Eichner, H. 1993. "Probleme von Vers und Metrum in epichorischer Dichtung Altkleinasiens," in G. Dobesch and G. Rehrenböck (eds.) *Hundert Jahre Kleinasiatische Kommission*, pp. 97–169. Vienna.

Eickhoff, R. L. (trans.) 2001. *The Odyssey: A Modern Translation of Homer's Classic Tale*, New York.

Eisenstein, E. L. 1979. *The Printing Press as an Agent of Change*. Cambridge.

Elder, J. P. 1954. "Lucretius 1.1–49," *Transactions of the American Philological Association* 85: 88–120.

Elderkin, G. W. 1913. "Repetition in the *Argonautica* of Apollonius," *American Journal of Philology* 34: 198–201.

Eliot, T. S. 1945. *What is a Classic?* London. Repr. 1951, in *On Poetry and Poets*, pp. 52–74. London.

—— 1967 [1920]. "Euripides and Professor Murray," in *The Sacred Wood*, pp. 71–7. London.

Ellis, M. de J. 1982. "Gilgamesh's approach to Ḥuwawa: a new text," *Zeitschrift für Orientforschung* 28: 123–31.

Elsner, J. and J. Masters (eds.) 1994. *Reflections of Nero: Culture, History, and Representation*. London.

Elwell-Sutton, L. P. 1976. *The Persian Metres*. Cambridge.

Emmert, T. 1990. *Serbian Golgotha: Kosovo, 1989*. East European Monographs 278. New York.

Enterline, L. 2000. *The Rhetoric of the Body: From Ovid to Shakespeare*. Cambridge.

Erbse, Hartmut. 1953. "Homerscholien und hellenistische Glossare bei Apollonius Rhodius," *Hermes* 81: 163–96.

—— 1993. "Die Funktion des Rechtsgedankens in Hesiods 'Erga'," *Hermes* 121: 19–30.

Erskine, A. 1995. "Culture and power in Ptolemaic Egypt: the museum and library of Alexandria," *Greece and Rome* 42: 38–48.

—— 2001. *Troy between Greece and Rome: Local Tradition and Imperial Power*. Oxford.

Esolen, A. (trans.) 1995. *Lucretius: On the Nature of Things: De rerum natura*. Baltimore.

Esposito, P., and Nicastri, L. (eds.) 1999. *Interpretare Lucano*. Miscellanea di studi, Università degli studi di Salerno, Quaderni del dipartimento di scienze dell'antichità, 22. Naples.

Evans, A. J. 1921–35. *The Palace of Minos at Knossos* I–IV. London.

Evelyn-White, H. G. (ed. and trans.), 1914. *Hesiod, the Homeric Hymns and Homerica*. Cambridge, MA.

Fagiolo, M. 1981. *Virgilio nell'arte e nella cultura europea*. Rome.

Fagles, R. (trans.) 1996. *Homer, The Odyssey*. New York.

Falkenstein, A. 1951. "Zur Chronologie der sumerischen Literatur," in F. Thureau-Dangin (ed.) *Compte rendu de la IIme Rencontre Assyriologique internationale, organisée à Paris du 2 au 6 juillet 1951*, pp. 13–30. Paris.

Falkowitz, R. S. 1983. "Notes on Lugalbanda and Enmerkar," *Journal of the American Oriental Society* 103: 103–14.

Fanfani, P. (ed.) 1851. "Compilazione della Eneide di Virgilio fatta volgare per Ser Andrea Lancia Notaro Fiorentino," *Etruria* 1: 162–88, 221–52, 296–318, 497–508, 625–32, 745–60.

Fantham, E. 1985. "Caesar and the mutiny: Lucan's reshaping of the historical tradition in *De bello civili* 5, 237–373," *Classical Philology* 80: 119–31.

—— 1992. "Lucan's Medusa-excursus: its design and purpose," *Materiali e Discussione* 28: 95–119.

—— 1999. "The role of lament in the growth and eclipse of Roman epic," in Beissinger et al. 1999: 221–35.

Fantuzzi, M. 1988. *Ricerche zu Apollonio Rodio: Diacronie della dizione epica*. Filologia e Critica 58. Rome.

——, and R. Hunter 2002. *Muse e modelli: la poesia ellenistica da Alessandro Magno ad Augusto*. Rome-Bari.

Farmer, M. S. 1998. "Sophocles' Ajax and Homer's Hector: two soliloquies," *Illinois Classical Studies* 23: 19–45.

Farrell, J. 1999a. "The Ovidian *corpus*: poetic body and poetic text," in Hardie et al. 1999:127–41.

—— 1999b. "Walcott's *Omeros*: the classical epic in a postmodern world," in Beissinger et al. 1999: 270–96.

—— 2002. "Greek lives and Roman careers in the classical vita tradition," in P. Cheney and F. A. de Armas (eds.) *European Literary Careers: The Author from Antiquity to the Renaissance*, pp. 24–46. Toronto.

—— 2004. "Roman Homer," in R. Fowler (ed.) *The Cambridge Companion to Homer*, pp. 254–71. Cambridge.

Faure, P. 1980: *Ulysse le Crétois (XIIIe s. av. J-C)*. Paris.

Febvre, L., and H.-J. Martin. 1976. *The Coming of the Book: The Impact of Printing, 1450–1800*. London.

Feeney, D. C. 1986a. "Epic hero and epic fable," *Comparative Literature* 38: 137–58.

—— 1986b. "History and revelation in Vergil's underworld," *Proceedings of the Cambridge Philological Society* 212 (n.s. 32): 1–24.

—— 1986c. " 'Stat magni nominis umbra': Lucan on the greatness of Pompeius Magnus," *Classical Quarterly* 36: 239–43.

—— 1991. *The Gods in Epic: Poets and Critics of the Classical Tradition*. Oxford.

—— 1998. *Literature and Religion at Rome*. Cambridge.

—— 1999. "*Mea tempora*: patterning of time in the *Metamorphoses*," in Hardie et al. 1999: 13–30.

Fehling, D. 1984. "Die alten Literaturen als Quelle der neuzeitlichen Märchen," in S. Wolfdietrich (ed.) *Antiker Mythos in unseren Marchen*. Veröffentlichungen der Europaischen Märchengesellschaft, 6, pp. 52–63. Kassel.

Feldherr, A. 1997. "Metamorphosis and sacrifice in Ovid's Theban narrative," *Materiali e Discussioni*, 38: 25–55.

—— 2002. "Metamorphosis in the *Metamorphoses*," In Hardie 2002: 163–79.

Felson-Rubin, N. 1993. *Regarding Penelope: From Character to Poetics*. Princeton, NJ.

Felson-Rubin, N. and L. Slatkin. 2004. "Gender and Homeric epic," in R. Fowler (ed.) *The Cambridge Companion to Homer*, pp. 91–114. Cambridge.

Fenik, B. 1968. *Typical Battle Scenes in the Iliad: Studies in the Narrative Techniques of Homeric Battle Description*. Hermes Einzelschriften 21. Wiesbaden.

—— 1986. *Homer and the Nibelungenlied: Comparative Studies in Epic Style*. Cambridge, MA.

Ferrari, L. 1963. *Osservazioni su Quinto Smirneo*. Palermo.

Ferry, D. (trans.) 1992. *Gilgamesh: A New Rendering in English Verse*. New York.

Fetten, F. 2000. "Archaeology and anthropology in Germany before 1945," in H. Härke (ed.) *Archaeology, Ideology and Society: The German Experience*. Gesellschaften und Staaten im Epochenwandel 7, pp. 140–79. Frankfurt am Main.

FGrH. 1923–. *Die Fragmente der griechischen Historiker*, 3 vols. in 15, ed. F. Jacoby. Leiden.

Fine, E. 1984. *The Folklore Text: From Performance to Print*. Bloomington, IN.

Finkelberg, M. 2000. "The *Cypria*, the *Iliad*, and the problem of multiformity in oral and written tradition," *Classical Philology* 95: 1–11.

Finley, J. H., Jr. 1978. *Homer's Odyssey*. Cambridge, MA.

Finley, M. I. 1957. "Homer and Mycenae: property and tenure," *Historia* 6: 133–59.

—— 1962 [1954]. *The World of Odysseus: Homer and His Age in Archaeology, Literature and History*. Cleveland.

—— 1964. "The Trojan War," *Journal of Hellenic Studies* 84: 1–9.

—— 1977. *The World of Odysseus*, 2nd edn. New York and London.

—— 1982. *Economy and Society in Ancient Greece*, ed. B. D. Shaw and R. P. Saller. New York.

Finnegan, R. 1970. *Oral Literature in Africa*. Oxford.

—— 1977. *Oral Poetry: Its Nature, Significance and Social Context*. Cambridge. Repr. 1992, Bloomington, IN.

—— 1988. *Literacy and Orality: Studies in the Technology of Communication*. Oxford.

—— 1995. "Introduction; or, Why the comparativist should take account of the South Pacific," in R. Finnegan and M. Orbell (eds.) *South Pacific Oral Traditions*, pp. 6–29. Bloomington, IN and Indianapolis.

Finsler, G. 1973. *Homer in der Neuzeit von Dante bis Goethe*. Hildesheim.

Fitton, J. L. 1995. *The Discovery of the Greek Bronze Age*. London.

Fittschen, K. 1969. *Untersuchungen zum Beginn der Sagendarstellungen bei den Griechen*. Berlin.

Fitzgerald, J. L. (trans.) 2004. *The Mahâbhârata: 11. The Book of the Women and 12. The Book of Peace, Part One*. Chicago.

Flueckiger, J. B. 1986. *Gender and Genre in the Folklore of Middle India*. Ithaca, NY.

—— 1989. "Caste and regional variants in an oral epic tradition," in Blackburn et al. 1989: 33–54.

—— 1999. "Appropriating the epic: gender, caste, and regional identity in Middle India," in Beissinger et al. 1999: 131–51.

Flueckiger, J. B., and L. Sears (eds.) 1991. *Boundaries of the Text: Epic Performances in South and Southeast Asia*. Ann Arbor, MI.

Flury, P. 1973. "Das sechaste Gedicht des Paulinus von Nola," *Vigiliae Christianae* 27: 129–45.

Folena, G. (ed.) 1956. *la istoria di Eneas vulgarizata per Angilu di Capua*. Collezione di testi siciliani dei secoli XIV e XV, 7. Palermo.

Foley, H. P. 1978. "Reverse similes and sex roles in the *Odyssey*," *Arethusa* 11: 7–26. Repr. 1984 in J. Peradotto and J. P. Sullivan (eds.), *Women in the Ancient World: The Arethusa Papers*, pp. 59–78. Albany, NY: and 1988 in H. Bloom (ed.) *Homer's The Odyssey*, pp. 87–101, New York.

—— 1995. "Penelope as moral agent," in Cohen 1995: 93–116.

Foley, J. M. 1985. *Oral-Formulaic Theory and Research: An Introduction and Annotated Bibliography*. New York. Updated online version at www.oraltradition.org.

—— 1988. *The Theory of Oral Composition: History and Methodology*. Bloomington, IN. Repr. 1992.

—— 1990. *Traditional Oral Epic: The* Odyssey, Beowulf, *and the Serbo-Croatian Return Song*. Berkeley. Repr. 1993.

—— 1991. *Immanent Art: From Structure to Meaning in Traditional Oral Epic*. Bloomington, IN.

—— 1995. *The Singer of Tales in Performance*. Bloomington, IN.

—— 1996. "*Guslar* and *Aoidos*: traditional register in South Slavic and Homeric epic," *Transactions of the American Philological Association* 126: 11–41.

—— 1997. "Oral tradition and its implications," in Morris and Powell 1997: 146–73.

—— 1998a. "The impossibility of canon," in J. Foley 1998d: 13–33.

—— 1998b. "Individual poet and epic tradition: the legendary singer," *Arethusa* 31: 149–78.

—— 1998c. "The rhetorical persistence of traditional forms in oral epic texts," in L. Honko, J. Handoo, and J. M. Foley (eds.) *The Epic: Oral and Written*, pp. 80–93. Mysore.

—— (ed.) 1998d. *Teaching Oral Traditions*. New York.

—— 1999a. "Epic cycles and epic traditions," in J. N. Kazaziz and A. Rengakos (eds.) *Euphrosyne: Studies in Ancient Epic and Its Legacy in Honor of Dimitris N. Maronitis*, pp. 99–108. Stuttgart.

—— 1999b. *Homer's Traditional Art*. University Park, PA.

—— 1999c. "Experiencing the *Siri Epic*," *Folklore Fellows Network* 17 (June): 13–23. Repr. 2000 in *Indian Folklife* 1 / ii: 22–32.

—— 2002. *How to Read an Oral Poem*. Urbana, IL. With E-companion at www.oraltradition.org.

—— 2003. "How genres leak in traditional verse," in M. C. Amodio and K. O'B. O'Keeffe (eds.) *Unlocking the Wordhord: Anglo-Saxon Studies in Memory of Edward B. Irving, Jr.*, pp. 76–108. Toronto.

—— 2004a. "Epic as Genre," in R. Fowler (ed.) *The Cambridge Companion to Homer*, pp. 171–87. Cambridge.

—— 2004b. "Textualization as mediation: the case of traditional oral epic," in R. Modiano, L. Searle, and P. Shillingsburg (eds.) *Voice, Text, Hypertext: Emerging Practices in Textual Studies*, pp. 101–20. Seattle.

—— (ed. and trans.) 2004c. *The Wedding of Mustajbey's Son Bećirbey as Performed by Halil Bajgorić*. Folklore Fellows Communications 283. Helsinki. With E-edition at www.oraltradition.org.

Fontaine, J. 1975. "Le mélange des genres dans la poésie de Prudence," in *Etudes sur la poésie latine tardive d'Ausone à Prudence: Recueil de travaux de Jacques Fontaine.* pp. 1–24. Paris.

—— 1981. *Naissance de la poésie dans l'occident chrétien.* Paris.

—— 1988. "Comment doit-on appliquer la notion de genre littéraire à la littérature latine chrétienne du IVe siècle?," *Philologus* 132: 53–73.

Ford, A. 1988. "The classical definition of *rhapsodia*," *Classical Philology* 83: 300–7.

—— 1992. *Homer: The Poetry of the Past.* Ithaca, NY.

—— 1997. "Epic as genre," in Morris and Powell 1997: 396–414.

—— 1999. "Performing interpretation: early allegorical exegesis of Homer," in Beissinger et al. 1999: 33–53.

Ford, P. K. 1974. "The well of Nechtan and 'La Gloire lumineuse'," in G. I. Larson (ed.) *Myth in Indo-European Antiquity*, pp. 67–74. Berkeley.

Fortson, B. W. 2004. *Indo-European Language and Culture: An Introduction.* Malden, MA.

Foster, B. R. 1987. "Gilgamesh: sex, love, and the ascent of knowledge," in J. H. Marks and R. M. Good (eds.) *Love and Death in the Ancient Near East: Essays in Honor of Marvin Pope*, pp. 21–42. Guilford, CT.

—— 1991. "On authorship in Akkadian literature," *Annali: Rivista del Dipartimento di Studi Asiatici e del Dipartimento di Studi e Ricerche su Africa e Paesia Arabi* 51: 17–32.

—— (ed.) 1993. *Before the Muses: An Anthology of Akkadian Literature*, 2 vols. Bethesda, MD. Repr. 1996.

—— (ed.) 1995. *From Distant Days: Myths, Tales, and Poetry of Ancient Mesopotamia.* Bethesda, MD.

—— (ed.) 2001. *The Epic of Gilgamesh.* Norton Critical Edition. New York.

Foster, H. W. 2004. "The role of music," in J. Foley 2004c: 223–60.

Fowler, D. P. 1989. "Lucretius and politics," in M. T. Griffin and J. Barnes (eds.) *Philosophia Togata: Essays on Philosophy and Roman Society*, pp. 120–50. Oxford.

—— 1996. "The feminine principle: gender in the *De rerum natura*," in G. Giannantoni and M. Gigante (eds.) *Epicureismo greco e romano: Atti del Congresso Internazionale, Napoli, 19–26 Maggio, 1993*, pp. 813–22. Naples. Repr. in D. P. Fowler 2002: 444–52.

—— 2000. "The didactic plot," in Depew and Obbink 2000b: 205–19.

—— 2002. *Lucretius on Atomic Motion: A Commentary on* De rerum natura, *Book 2, Lines 1–332.* Oxford.

Fowler, D. P., and P. G. Fowler. 1996a. "Lucretius," in *The Oxford Classical Dictionary*, 3rd edn., pp. 888–90. Oxford.

—— and —— 1996b. "Virgil (Publius Vergilius Maro)," in *The Oxford Classical Dictionary*, 3rd edn., pp. 1602–7. Oxford.

Fowler, P. G. 1997. "Lucretian conclusions," in D. H. Roberts, F. M. Dunn, and D. P. Fowler (eds.) *Classical Closure: Reading the End in Greek and Latin Literature*, pp. 112–38. Princeton.

Fraenkel, E. 1927. "Lucan als Mittler des antiken Pathos," in *Vorträge der Bibliothek Warburg 1924–1925*, pp. 229–57. Leipzig and Berlin.

Frahm, E. 1999. "Nabû-zuqup-kenu, das Gilgames-Epos und der Tod Sargons II," *Journal of Cuneiform Studies* 51: 73–90.

Frame, D. 1978. *The Myth of Return in Early Greek Epic.* New Haven, CT.

Franchet d'Espèrey, S. 1999. *Conflit, violence et non-violence dans la Thébaïde de Stace.* Paris.

Frangoulidis, S. 1993. "A pattern from Homer's *Odyssey* in the Sicilian narrative of Thucydides," *Quaderni Urbinati di Cultura Classica* 44: 95–102.

Frank, R. 1992. "*Beowulf* and Sutton Hoo: the odd couple," in C. B. Kendall and P. S. Wells (eds.) *Voyage to the Outer World: The Legacy of Sutton Hoo.* Medieval Studies at Minnesota 5, pp. 47–64. Minneapolis.

Franke, S. 1995. "Kings of Akkad: Sargon and Naram Sin," in J. Sasson 1995: 831–42.

Fränkel, H. 1926. "Der kallimachische und der homerische Hexameter," *Nachrichten von der Gesellschaft der Wissenschaften zu Göttingen* (phil.-hist. Klasse): 197–229.

—— 1945. *Ovid: A Poet between Two Worlds.* Berkeley.

—— 1955. *Wege und Formen frühgriechischen Denkens: Literarische und philosophiegeschichtliche Studien*, ed. Franz Tietze. Munich.

—— 1960. "Ein Don Quijote unter den Argonauten des Apollonios," *Museum Helveticum* 14: 1–19.

—— (ed.) 1961. *Apollonii Rhodii Argonautica.* Oxford.

Fraser, P. M. 1972. *Ptolemaic Alexandria*, 3 vols. Oxford.

Frazer, J. G. (trans.) 1921. *Apollodorus: The Library*, 2 vols. Loeb Classical Library. Cambridge, MA.

Frazer, J. G. 1923. *Folk-lore in the Old Testament*, abridged edn. New York.

Freeman, P. M. 1998. "Saturnian verse and early Latin poetics," *Journal of Indo-European Studies* 26: 61–90.

Friedrich, J. 1950. "Churritische Märchen und Sagen in hethitischer Sprache," *Zeitschrift für Assyriologie* 49: 213–55.

Friedrich, R. 1991. "The hybris of Odysseus," *Journal of Hellenic Studies* 111: 16–28.

Frings, I. 1991. *Gespräch und Handlung in der Thebais des Statius*. Stuttgart.

—— 1992. *Odia fraterna als manieristiches Motiv: Betrachtungen zu Senecas Thyest und Statius' Thebais*. Stuttgart.

Friþriksson, A. 1994. *Sagas and Popular Antiquarianism in Icelandic Archaeology*. Aldershot.

Fromkin, V. A. et al. 2000. *Linguistics: An Introduction to Linguistic Theory*. Malden, MA.

Frymer-Kensky, T. 1992. *In the Wake of the Goddesses: Women, Culture and the Biblical Transformation of Pagan Myth*. New York.

Fuà, O. 1988. "La presenza di Omero in Valerio Flacco," *Atti della Accadèmia delle Scienze di Torino* 122: 23–53.

Fucecchi, M. 1990. "Il declino di Annibale nei *Punica*," *Maia* 42: 151–66.

—— 1993. "Lo spettacolo delle virtù nel giovane eroe predestinato: annalisi della figura di Scipione in Silio Italico," *Maia* 45: 17–48.

—— 1996. "Il restauro dei modelli antichi: tradizione epica e tecnica manieristica in Valerio Flacco," *Materiali e Discussione* 36: 101–65.

Furley, D. J. 1970. "Variations on themes from Empedocles in Lucretius' proem," *Bulletin of the Institute of Classical Studies* 17: 55–64.

Furumark, A. 1941. *The Chronology of Mycenaean Pottery*. Stockholm.

Fusillo, M. 1985. *Il Tempo delle Argonautiche*. Filologia e Critica 49. Rome.

Fusillo, M., and G. Paduano. 1986. *Apollonio Rhodio, Le Argonautiche*. Milan.

Gabba, E. 1991. *Dionysius and the History of Archaic Rome*. Berkeley.

Gadd, C. J. 1966. "Some contributions to the Gilgamesh epic," *Iraq* 28: 105–21.

Gagliardi, D. 1970. *Lucano poèta della libertà*. Collana di studi classici 8; Studi e testi dell'antichità 5. Naples.

Gale, M. R. 1994. *Myth and Poetry in Lucretius*. Cambridge.

—— 2000. *Virgil on the Nature of Things: The Georgics, Lucretius and the Didactic Tradition*. Cambridge.

—— 2001. *Lucretius and the Didactic Epic*. London.

—— 2004. "The story of us: a narratological analysis of Lucretius' *De rerum natura*," in M. R. Gale (ed.) *Latin Epic and Didactic Poetry: Genre, Tradition and Individuality*, pp. 49–71. Swansea.

Galinsky, K. 1975. *Ovid's Metamorphoses: An Introduction to its Basic Aspects*. Oxford.

Gantz, T. 1993. *Early Greek Myth: A Guide to Literary and Artistic Sources*. Baltimore.

García Yebra, V. 1994. *Traducción: Historia y Teoría*. Biblioteca Románica Hispánica II. Estudios y Ensayos 387. Madrid.

Gardiner, J., and J. Maier. (eds. and trans.) 1984. *Gilgamesh*. New York: Knopf.

Garner, R. 1990. *From Homer to Tragedy: The Art of Allusion in Greek Poetry*. London and New York.

Garner, R. S. 1996. "*Ei pote*: a note on Homeric phraseology," *Oral Tradition* 11: 363–73.

—— 2003. "Studies in early Greek colometry: traditional techniques of composition and word placement in Archaic epic and other verse forms." Dissertation, Princeton University.

Garnsey, P., and C. Humfress. 2001. *The Evolution of the Late Antique World*. Cambridge.

Garriga, C. 1996. "The Muses in Apollonius of Rhodes: the term UPOFHTORES," *Prometheus* 22: 105–14.

Garson, R. W. 1965. "Some critical observations on Valerius Flaccus' *Argonautica*. II," *Classical Quarterly* 15: 104–20.

—— 1975. "Notes on some Homeric echoes in Heliodorus' *Aethiopica*," *Acta Classica* 18: 137–40.

—— 1985. "Aspects of Aeschylus' Homeric usages," *Phoenix* 39: 1–5.

Gaskill, H. (ed.) 1996. *The Poems of Ossian and Related Works*. Edinburgh.

Gasparov, M. L. 1996. *A History of European Versification*, trans. G. S. Smith and M. Tarlinskaja; ed. G. S. Smith with L. Holford-Strevens. Oxford. (Russian original 1989.)

Gaster, T. H. 1950. *Thespis.* New York.

—— 1969. *Myth, Legend, and Custom in the Old Testament: A Comparative Study with Chapters from Sir James G. Frazer's Folklore in the Old Testament.* New York.

Gentili, B. 1977. *Lo spettacolo nel mondo antico.* Bari.

—— 1988. *Poetry and its Public in Ancient Greece.* Baltimore. Trans. 1984 by A. Thomas Cole from *Poesia e pubblico nella Grecia antica da Omero al V secolo.* Rome.

Gentry, F. G. 1998. "Key concepts in the *Nibelungenlied*," in McConnell 1998: 66–78.

George, A. R. (trans.) 1999. *The Epic of Gilgamesh: The Babylonian Epic Poem and Other Texts in Akkadian and Sumerian.* London and New York.

—— (ed.) 2003. *The Babylonian Gilgamesh Epic.* Oxford.

George, A. R., and F. N. H. Al-Rawi. 1996. "Tablets from the Sippar Library VI: Atra-hasis," *Iraq* 58: 147–90.

George, D. B. 1988. "Lucan's Caesar and Stoic *oikeiosis*: the Stoic fool," *Transactions of the American Philological Association* 118: 331–41.

—— 1991. "Lucan's Cato and Stoic attitudes to the Republic," *Classical Antiquity* 10: 237–58.

George, E. V. 1974. *Aeneid VIII and the Aitia of Callimachus.* Leiden.

George, J. 1992. *Venantius Fortunatus: A Latin Poet in Merovingian Gaul.* Oxford.

Giancotti, F. 1959. *Il preludio di Lucrezio.* Messina and Florence.

Giangrande, G. 1986. "Osservazioni sul testo e sulla lingua di Quinto Smirneo," *Siculorum Gymnasium* 39: 41–50.

Giannini, P. 1973. "Espressioni formulari nell'elegia greca arcaica," *Quaderni Urbinati di Cultura Classica* 16: 7–78.

Gibson, J. C. L. 1975. "Myth, legend and folklore in the Ugaritic Keret and Aqhat Texts," in L. A. Schökel (ed.) *Congress Volume.* Supplements to Vetus Testamentum 25, pp. 60–8. Leiden.

Giesecke, M. 1991. *Der Buchdruck in der frühen Neuzeit.* Frankfurt.

Gimferrer, P. 1988. *Giorgio de Chirico.* New York.

Ginsberg, H. L. 1945a. "The North-Canaanite myth of Anath and Aqhat i," *Bulletin of the American Schools of Oriental Research* 97: 3–10.

—— 1945b. "The North-Canaanite myth of Anath and Aqhat ii," *Bulletin of the American Schools of Oriental Research* 98: 15–23.

—— 1946. *The Legend of King Keret,* Bulletin of the American Schools of Oriental Research Supplements 23. New Haven, CT.

Giorgieri, M. 2001. "Die hurritische Fassung des Ullikummi-Lieds und ihre hethitische Parallele," in G. Wilhelm (ed.) *Akten des IV. Internationalen Kongresses für Hethitologie Würzburg, 4.–8. Oktober 1999,* pp. 134–55. Wiesbaden.

Gjerstad, E. 1944. "The colonization of Cyprus in Greek legend," *Opuscula Archaeologica* 3: 107–23.

Glei, R. F. 2001. "Outlines of Apollonian scholarship 1955–1999," In T. D. Papanghelis and A. Rengakos (eds.) *A Companion to Apollonius Rhodius,* pp. 1–26. Leiden.

Glenisson, L. (ed.) 1988. *Le Livre au Moyen Age.* Paris.

Gnilka, C. 2000. *Prudentiana I: Critica.* Munich and Leipzig.

—— 2001. *Prudentiana II: Exegetica.* Munich and Leipzig.

Gnoli, G. 1965a. "La sede orientale del fuoco Farnbag," *Rivista degli Studi Orientali* 2: 301–11.

—— 1965b. "Lo stato di 'maga'," *Annali: Istituto Orientale di Napoli* 15: 105–17.

—— 1967. *Ricerche storiche sul Sistan antico.* Rome.

—— 1980. *Zoroaster's Time and Homeland: A Study on the Origins of Mazdeism and Related Problems.* Naples.

Godley, A. D. (trans.) 1926. *Herodotus with an English Translation,* 4 vols. Cambridge, MA.

Godwin, J. 1986. *Lucretius: De rerum natura IV.* Warminster.

—— 1991. *Lucretius: De rerum natura VI.* Warminster.

Goedicke, H. 1975. *The Report of Wenamun.* Baltimore.

Goldberg, S. 1993. "Saturnian epic: Livius and Naevius," in Boyle: 19–36.

—— 1995. *Epic in Republican Rome.* New York and Oxford.

Goldhill, S. 1991. *The Poet's Voice: Essays on Poetics and Greek Literature.* Cambridge.

Gordon, C. (trans.) 1949. *Ugaritic Literature: A Comprehensive Translation of the Poetic and Prose Texts.* Rome.

Gordon, C. 1962. *Before the Bible: The Common Background of Greek and Hebrew Civilization*. London.

—— 1966. *Ugarit and Minoan Crete: The Bearing of their Texts on the Origins of Western Culture*. New York.

Gorman, V. B. 2001. *Miletos, the Ornament of Ionia*. Ann Arbor, MI.

Gould, J. 1983. "Homeric epic and the tragic moment," in T. Winnifrith, P. Murray, and K. W. Gransden (eds.) *Aspects of the Epic*, pp. 32–45. London.

Grafton, A. 1992. "Renaissance readers of Homer's ancient readers," in Lamberton and Keaney 1992: 149–72.

Gransden, K. W. 1984 "The *Aeneid* and *Paradise Lost*," in C. Martindale (ed.) *Virgil and his Influence: Bimillennial Studies*, pp. 95–116. Bristol.

Gray, D. 1947. "Homeric epithets for things," *Classical Quarterly* 61: 109–21.

—— 1954. "Metal-working in Homer," *Journal of Hellenic Studies* 74: 1–15.

—— 1955. "Houses in the *Odyssey*," *Classical Quarterly* n.s. 5: 1–12.

—— 1968. "Homer and the archaeologists," in M. Platnauer (ed.) *Fifty Years (and Twelve) of Classical Scholarship*, pp. 24–31. Oxford.

Gray, J. 1964. *The KRT Text in the Literature of Ras Shamra*, 2nd edn. Leiden.

—— 1965. *The Legacy of Canaan*. Supplements to Vetus Testamentum 5, 2nd edn. Leiden.

Grayson, A. K. 1975. *Babylonian Historical-Literary Texts*. Toronto.

Graziosi, B. 2002. *Inventing Homer: The Early Reception of Epic*. Cambridge.

Green, P. (trans.) 1997a. *The Argonautika by Apollonius Rhodius*. Berkeley.

—— 1997b. " 'These fragments I have shored against my ruin': Apollonius Rhodius and the social revalidation of myth for a new age," in P. Cartledge, P. Garnsey, and E. Gruen (eds.) *Hellenistic Constructs, Essays in Culture, History and Historiography*, pp. 35–71. Berkeley.

Green, R. P. H. 1995. "Proba's Cento: its date, purpose, and reception," *Classical Quarterly* 45: 551–63.

—— 1997. "Proba's Introduction to her Cento," *Classical Quarterly* 47: 548–59.

Greene, T. M. 1963. *The Descent from Heaven: A Study in Epic Continuity*. New Haven, CT.

Greene, T. 2001. "Labyrinth dances in the French and English Renaissance," *Renaissance Quarterly* 44: 1403–66.

Greenstein, E. L. 1998. "The retelling of the flood story in the Gilgamesh epic," in J. Magness and S. Gitin (eds.) *Hesed Ve-Emet: Studies in Honor of Ernest S. Frerichs*. Brown Judaic Studies 320, pp. 197–204. Atlanta.

Grene, D. 1969. "The *Odyssey*: an approach," *Midway* 9: 47–68.

—— 1991. "Hesiod: religion and poetry in the Works and Days," in W. G. Jeanrond and J. L. Rike (eds.) *Radical Pluralism and Truth: David Tracy and the Hermeneutics of Religion*, pp. 142–58. New York.

Gresseth, G. K. 1957. "The quarrel between Lucan and Nero," *Classical Philology* 52: 24–7.

—— 1975. "The Gilgamesh Epic and Homer," *Classical Journal*, 70: 1–18.

—— 1979. "The *Odyssey* and the *Nalopâkhyâna*," *Transactions of the American Philological Association* 109: 63–85.

Griffin, J. 1977. "The Epic Cycle and the uniqueness of Homer," *Journal of Hellenic Studies* 97: 39–53.

—— 1980. *Homer on Life and Death*. Oxford.

Griffiths, A. 1985. "Patroklos the ram," *Bulletin of the Institute for Classical Studies* 32: 49–50.

—— 1989. "Patroklos the ram (again)," *Bulletin of the Institute for Classical Studies* 36: 139.

Grimal, P. 1960. "L'Eloge de Néron au début de la *Pharsale*," *Revue des Etudes Latines* 38: 296–305.

—— 1983. "Quelques aspects du stoïcisme de Lucain dans la *Pharsale*," *Bulletin de l'Association Guillaume Budé* 69: 401–16.

Grimm, W. 1857. "Die Sage von Polyphem," *Abhandlungen der königlichen Akademie der Wissenschaften zu Berlin*, phil.-hist. Klasse, 1–30. Repr. 1887 in G. Hinrichs (ed.) *Kleinere Schriften*, vol. 4, pp. 428–62. Gütersloh.

Groddek, D. 2000–2. " '[Diese Angelegenheit] höre Ištar von Nineve nicht!' Eine neue Episode einer Erzählung des Kumarbi-Kreises," *Welt des Orients* 31: 23–30.

Groningen, B. A. van. 1958. *La Composition littéraire archaïque grecque*. Amsterdam.

Grottanelli, C, 1989. "The roles of the guest in the epic banquet," in C. Zaccagnini (ed.) *Production and Consumption in the Ancient Near East*, pp. 272–332. Budapest.

Gruen, E. S. 1990. *Studies in Greek Culture and Roman Policy*. Leiden.

—— 1992. *Culture and National Identity in Republican Rome*. Ithaca, NY.

Gruzelier, C. 1990. "Claudian: court poet as artist," in A. J. Boyle (ed.) *The Imperial Muse: Flavian Epicist to Claudian*. Victoria, Australia.

—— 1993. *De raptu Proserpinae*. Oxford.

Gumpert, M. 2001. *Grafting Helen: The Abduction of the Classical Past*. Madison, WI.

Gunkel, H. 1910. *Genesis*. HKAT 1/1, 3rd edn. Göttingen.

Gurney, O. R. 1955. "The Sultantepe tablets: IV. the Cuthean legend of Naram-Sin," *Anatolian Studies* 5: 93–113.

Gusmani, R., M. Salvini, and P. Vannicelli (eds.) 1997. *Frigi e frigio*. Rome.

Güterbock, H. G. 1938. "Die historische Tradition und ihre literarische Gestaltung bei Babyloniern und Hethitern, II. Teil," *Zeitschrift für Assyriologie* 44: 45–149.

—— 1946. *Kumarbi: Mythen vom churritischen Kronos aus den hethitischen Fragmenten zusammengestellt, übersetzt, und erklärt*. Zurich.

—— 1951. "The Song of Ullikummi – revised text of the Hittite version of a Hurrian Myth," *Journal of Cuneiform Studies* 5: 135–61.

—— 1952a. "The Song of Ullikummi – revised text of the Hittite version of a Hurrian myth (continued)," *Journal of Cuneiform Studies* 6: 8–42.

—— 1952b. *The Song of Ullikummi*. New Haven.

—— 1961. "Hittite mythology," in S. N. Kramer (ed.) *Mythologies of the Ancient World*, pp. 139–79. Garden City, NY. Repr. in Güterbock 1997: 49–62.

—— 1969. "Ein neues Bruchstück der Sargon-Erzählung, 'König der Schlacht'," *Mitteilungen der deutschen Orientgesellschaft* 101: 14–26.

—— 1978. "Hethitische Literatur," in W. Röllig (ed.) *Neues Handbuch der Literatur-Wissenschaft*, vol. 1, pp. 211–53. Wiesbaden.

—— 1986. "Troy in Hittite texts? Wilusa, Ahhiyawa, and Hittite history," in Mellink 1986: 33–44. Repr. in Güterbock 1997: 223–8.

—— 1997. *Perspectives on Hittite Civilization: Selected Writings of Hans Gustav Güterbock*, ed. H. A. Hoffner, Jr. Assyriological Studies 26. Chicago.

Gutzwiller, K. 1981. *Studies in the Hellenistic Epyllion*. Königstein.

Gyaltsho, Z. 2001. "*Bab Sgrung*: Tibetan epic singers," *Oral Tradition* 16: 280–93.

Haas, V. 1994. *Geschichte der hethitischen Religion*. Leiden.

Habinek, T. N. 1998. *The Politics of Latin Literature: Writing, Identity, and Empire in Ancient Rome*. Princeton, NJ.

Hackman, O. 1904. *Die Polyphemsage in der Volksüberlieferung*. Helsingfors.

Hägg, T. 1971. *Narrative Technique in Ancient Greek Romances: Studies of Chariton, Xenophon Ephesius, and Achilles Tatius*. Instituti Atheniensis Regni Sueciae 80, 8. Stockholm.

Haider, P. W. 1996. "Griechen im Vorderen Orient und in Ägypten bis ca. 590 v. Chr." in Ulf 1996: 59–115.

Haidu, P. 1993. *The Subject of Violence: The "Song of Roland" and the Birth of the State*. Bloomington, IN.

Hainsworth, J. B. 1991. *The Idea of Epic*. Berkeley.

—— 1993. *The Iliad: A Commentary*, vol. III: *Books 9–12*. Cambridge.

Hale, T. A. 1998. *Griots and Griottes: Masters of Words and Music*. Bloomington, IN.

Hall, J. B. 1985. *Claudii Claudiani Carmina*. Bibliotheca Scriptorum Graecorum et Romanorum Teubneriana. Leipzig.

Halliwell, S. 1986. *Aristotle's Poetics*. London.

Hallo, W. W. 1983. "Lugalbanda excavated," *Journal of the American Oriental Society* 103: 165–80.

—— 1990. "Proverbs quoted in epic," in Abusch et al. 1990: 203–17.

Hallo, W. W., and K. L. Younger, Jr. (eds.) 1997, 2002. *The Context of Scripture*: vol. 1, *Canonical Compositions from the Biblical World*; vol. 2, *Monumental Inscriptions from the Biblical World*. Leiden.

Hammer, D. 1998. "The politics of the *Iliad*," *Classical Journal* 94: 1–30.

Hammer, D. 2002. *The Iliad as Politics: The Performance of Political Thought*. Norman, OK.

Hampl, F. 1975. "Die Ilias ist kein Geschichtsbuch," in F. Hampl, *Geschichte als kritische Wissenschaft*, vol. 2, pp. 51–99. Darmstadt.

Händel, P. 1954. *Beobachtungen zur epischen Technik des Apollonios Rhodios*. Munich.

Hanna, R. 1977. "The sources and the art of Prudentius' *Psychomachia*," *Classical Philology* 72: 108–15.

Hansen, K. H. 1954. *Das Iranische Königsbuch: Aufbau und Gestalt des Schahname von Firdosi*. Wiesbaden.

Hansen, O. 1994. "A Mycenaean sword from Bogazköy-Hattusa found in 1991," *The Annual of the British School at Athens* 89: 213–15.

Hansen, W. 1972. *The Conference Sequence: Patterned Narration and Narrative Inconsistency in the Odyssey*. Berkeley.

—— 1983. "Greek mythology and the study of the ancient Greek oral story," *Journal of Folklore Research* 20: 101–12.

—— 1990. "Odysseus and the oar: a folkloric approach," in L. Edmunds (ed.) *Approaches to Greek Myth*, pp. 241–72. Baltimore.

—— 1997. "Homer and the folktale." in Morris and Powell 1997: 442–62.

—— 2002. *Ariadne's Thread: A Guide to International Tales Found in Classical Literature*. Ithaca, NY.

Hanson, J. A. 1959. *Roman Theater Temples*. Princeton Monographs in Art and Archaeology 33. Princeton, NJ.

Harder, M. A., R. F. Regtuit, and G. C. Wakker (eds.) 2000. *Apollonius Rhodius*. Louvain.

Hardie, P. R. 1986. *Virgil's Aeneid: Cosmos and Imperium*. Oxford.

—— 1993. *The Epic Successors of Virgil: A Study in the Dynamics of a Tradition*. Roman Literature and its Contexts. Cambridge.

—— 1998. *Virgil*. Greece and Rome: New Surveys in the Classics 28. Oxford.

—— (ed.) 2002. *The Cambridge Companion to Ovid*. Cambridge.

Hardie, P. R., A. Barchiesi, and S. Hinds (eds.) 1999. *Ovidian Transformations: Essays on Ovid's Metamorphoses and its Reception*. Cambridge.

Hardwick, L. 2000. *Translating Words, Translating Cultures*. London.

Harlan, L. 2003. *The Goddesses' Henchmen: Gender in Indian Hero Worship*. New York.

Harmon, A. 1923. "The Poet KAT' EΞOXHN," *Classical Philology* 18: 35–47.

Harpham, G. G. 1987. *The Ascetic Imperative in Culture and Criticism*. Chicago.

Harries, B. 1990. "The spinner and the poet: Arachne in Ovid's *Metamorphoses*, *Proceedings of the Cambridge Philological Society* 36: 64–82.

—— 1994. "The pastoral mode in the *Dionysiaca*," in Hopkinson 1994b: 63–79.

Harris, J., and K. Reichl (eds.) 1997. *Prosimetrum: Crosscultural Perspectives on Narrative in Prose and Verse*. Cambridge.

Harris, R. 1990. "Images of women in the Gilgamesh epic," in Abusch et al. 1990: 219–30.

Harrison, S. (ed.) 1990. *Oxford Readings in Virgil's Aeneid*. Oxford.

—— 2002. "Ovid and genre: evolutions of an elegist," in P. Hardie 2002: 79–94.

Harvilahti, L. 2000. "Altai oral epic," *Oral Tradition* 15: 215–29.

—— 2003. *The Holy Mountain: Studies on Upper Altay Oral Poetry*. Folklore Fellows Communications 282. Helsinki.

Haslam, M. W. 1976. Review of G. Nagy 1974. *Journal of Hellenic Studies* 96: 202.

—— 1997. "Homeric papyri and the transmission of the text," in Morris and Powell 1997: 55–100.

Hatto, A. T. 1980. "General Introduction," in Hatto and Hainsworth 1980: vol. 1, 1–7.

—— 1991. *Eine allgemeine Theorie der Heldenepik*. Opladen.

—— 2000. "Textology and epic texts from Siberia and beyond," in Honko 2000b: 129–60.

Hatto, A. T., and J. B. Hainsworth (eds.) 1980, 1989. *Traditions of Heroic and Epic Poetry*, 2 vols. London.

Haubold, J. 2000. *Homer's People: Epic Poetry and Social Formation*. Cambridge.

—— 2002a. "Greek epic: a Near Eastern genre?," *Proceedings of the Cambridge Philological Society* 48: 1–19.

—— 2002b. "Wars of *Wissenschaft*: the new quest for Troy," *International Journal of the Classical Tradition* 8: 564–79.

Häussler, R. 1976. *Das historische Epos der Griechen und Römer bis Vergil.* Studien zum historischen Epos der Antike 1. Heidelberg.

—— 1978. *Das historische Epos von Lucan bis Silius und seine Theorie,* Studien zum historischen Epos der Antike II. Teil: Geschichtliche Epik nach Vergil. Heidelberg.

Havelock, E. A. 1963. *Preface to Plato.* Cambridge, MA.

—— 1978. *The Greek Concept of Justice from its Shadow in Homer to its Substance in Plato.* Cambridge, MA.

—— 1982. *The Literate Revolution in Greece and its Cultural Consequences.* Princeton, NJ.

Hawkins, J. D. 1998. "Tarkasnawa King of Mira," *Anatolian Studies* 48: 1–31.

—— 2000. *Corpus of Hieroglyphic Luwian Inscriptions.* Berlin.

Hawkins, J. D., and D. F. Easton. 1996. "A hieroglyphic seal from Troia," *Studia Troica* 6: 111–18.

Haymes, E. R. 1977. *Das mündliche Epos: Eine Einführung in die 'Oral Poetry' Forschung.* Stuttgart.

—— 1998. "Heroic, chivalric, and aristocratic ethos in the *Nibelungenlied,*" in McConnell 1998: 94–104.

Haymes, E. R., and S. T. Samples. 1996. *Heroic Legends of the North: An Introduction to the Nibelung and Dietrich Cycles.* New York.

Healey, J. F. 1990. "The early alphabet," in Hooker 1990: 197–257.

Heath, M. 1985. "Hesiod's didactic poetry," *Classical Quarterly* n.s. 35: 245–63.

—— 1989. *Unity in Greek Poetics.* Oxford.

Hecker, K. 1974. *Untersuchungen zur akkadischen Epik.* Altes Orient und Altes Testament 8. Kevelaer.

Hecquet-Noti, N. 1999. *Avit de Vienne: Histoire Spirituelle, Tome I (Chants I–III).* Paris.

Heidel, A. 1946. *The Gilgamesh Epic and Old Testament Parallels.* Chicago. Repr. 1949.

Heimlich, R. 2002. "The new Trojan Wars," *Archaeology Odyssey,* July/August: 16–35, 53, 55.

Heinze, R. 1903. *Vergils epische Technik.* Leipzig. Trans. 1993 as *Virgil's Epic Technique* by D. and H. Harvey and F. Robertson. Berkeley.

—— 1919. *Ovids elegische Dichtung.* Leipzig.

Heitsch, E. 1966. *Hesiod.* Darmstadt.

Helck, W. 1979. *Die Beziehungen Ägyptens und Vorderasiens zur Aegäis bis ins 7. Jahrhundert vor Chr.* Darmstadt.

—— 1983. "Zur ältesten Geschichte des Hatti-Reiches," in R. Boehmer and H. Hauptmann (eds.) *Beiträge zur Altertumskunde Kleinasiens: Festschrift für Kurt Bittel,* pp. 271–81. Mainz.

Hendel, R. S. 1987a. "Of demigods and the deluge: toward an interpretation of *Genesis* 6: 1–4," *Journal of Biblical Literature* 106: 13–26.

—— 1987b. *The Epic of the Patriarch: The Jacob Cycle and the Narrative Traditions of Canaan and Israel.* Harvard Semitic Monographs 42. Atlanta.

Henderson, J. G. W. 1987. "Lucan: the word at war," *Ramus* 16: 122–64.

—— 1997. "The name of the tree: recounting Odyssey xxiv 340–2," *Journal of Hellenic Studies* 117: 87–116.

Henige, D. 1974. *The Chronology of Oral Tradition: Quest for a Chimera.* Oxford.

Henry, P. L. 1982. "Furor heroicus," *Zeitschrift für celtische Philologie* 39: 235–42.

Hershkowitz, D. 1998a. *The Madness of Epic: Reading Insanity from Homer to Statius.* Oxford.

—— 1998b. *Valerius Flaccus' Argonautica: Abbreviated Voyages in Silver Latin Epic.* Oxford.

Hertel, D. 2001. *Troia: Archäologie, Geschichte, Mythos.* Munich.

—— 2003. *Die Mauern von Troia: Mythos und Geschichte im antiken Ilion.* Munich.

Herter, H. 1955. "Bericht über die Literatur zur hellenistichen Dichtung seit dem Jahre 1921. II: Teil: Apollonios von Rhodos," *Bursians Jahresberichte* 285: 213–410.

Herzog, R. 1975. *Die Bibelepik der lateinischen Spätantike,* vol. 1. Munich.

—— 1993a. "Faltonia Betitia Proba," in R. Herzog (ed.) *Restauration et renouveau: La littérature latine de 284 à 374 après J.-C.,* pp. 384–8. Turnhout.

—— 1993b. "Juvencus (C. Vettius Aquilinus Iuvencus)," in R. Herzog (ed.) *Restauration et renouveau: La littérature latine de 284 à 374 après J.-C.,* pp. 378–84. Turnhout.

Heubeck, A. 1955. "Mythologische Vorstellungen des Alten Orients im archaischen Griechentum," *Gymnasium,* 62: 508–25. Repr. in Heitsch 1966: 545–70.

—— 1979. *Schrift.* Göttingen.

Heubeck, A., and A. Hoekstra. 1989. *A Commentary on Homer's* Odyssey, *Vol. II (Books IX–XVI).* Oxford.

Heubeck, A., S. West, and J. B. Hainsworth (eds.) 1988–90. *A Commentary on Homer's* Odyssey, 3 vols. Oxford.

Hill, D. E. (ed.) 1983. *P. Papinii Statii Thebaidos Libri XII.* Leiden.

Hillier, R. 1993. *Arator on the Acts of the Apostles: A Baptismal Commentary.* Oxford.

Hillen, H. J. 2003. *Von Aeneas zu Romulus. Die Legenden von der Gründung Roms.* Düsseldorf.

Hiltebeitel, A. 1976. *The Ritual of Battle: Krishna in the Mahâbhârata.* Albany. Repr. 1990.

Hinds, S. 1987a. "Generalising about Ovid," *Ramus* 16: 4–31.

—— 1987b. *The Metamorphosis of Persephone: Ovid and the Self-conscious Muse.* Cambridge.

—— 1992. " 'Arma' in Ovid's *Fasti*," *Arethusa* 25: 81–153.

—— 1998. *Allusion and Intertext: Dynamics of Appropriation in Roman Poetry.* Roman Literature and its Contexts. Cambridge.

—— 2000. "Essential epic: genre and gender from Macer to Statius," in Depew and Obbink 2000c: 221–44.

—— 2002. "Landscapes with figures: aesthetics of place in the *Metamorphoses* and its tradition," in Hardie 2002: 122–49.

Hobsbawm, E. 1969. *Bandits.* New York.

Hock, H. H., and B. D. Joseph. 1996. *Language History, Language Change, and Language Relationship: An Introduction to Historical and Comparative Linguistics.* Berlin.

Hoekstra, A. 1965. *Homeric Modifications of Formulaic Prototypes.* Amsterdam.

—— 1967. "Hésiode et la tradition orale," *Mnemosyne,* 4th ser., 10: 193–225.

—— 1969. *The Sub-Epic Stage of the Formulaic Tradition: Studies in the Homeric Hymns to Apollo, to Aphrodite, and to Demeter.* Amsterdam.

—— 1986. Review of Janko 1982. *Mnemosyne* 39: 158–64.

Hoffner, H. A., Jr. 1968. "Birth and namegiving in Hittite texts," *Journal of Near Eastern Studies* 27: 198–203.

—— 1970. "Remarks on the Hittite version of the Naram-Sin legend," *Journal of Cuneiform Studies* 23: 17–22.

—— 1976. "Enki's command to Atrahasis," in B. L. Eichler (ed.) *Kramer Anniversary Volume: Cuneiform Studies in Honor of Samuel Noah Kramer.* Altes Orient und Altes Testament 25, pp. 241–5. Kevelaer.

—— 1988. "The Song of Silver – a member of the Kumarbi cycle of 'Songs'," in E. Neu and C. Rüster (eds.) *Documentum Asiae Minoris Antiquae: Festschrift für Heinrich Otten zum 75. Geburtstag,* pp. 143–66. Wiesbaden.

—— 1991. *Hittite Myths.* Society of Biblical Literature Writings from the Ancient World 2. Atlanta.

—— 1997. "Crossing of the Taurus," in W. W. Hallo (ed.) *The Context of Scripture,* vol. 1, pp. 184–5. Leiden.

—— 1998a. *Hittite Myths,* 2nd edn., ed. G. M. Beckman. Atlanta.

—— 1998b. "Hurrian civilization from a Hittite perspective," in G. Buccellati and M. Kelly-Buccellati (eds.) *Urkesh and the Hurrians: Studies in Honor of Lloyd Cotsen,* pp. 167–200. Malibu, CA.

Hollander, R. 1993. "Tragedy in Dante's *Comedy*," in C. W. Kallendorf (ed.) *Vergil,* pp. 253–69. New York.

Hollis, A. S. (ed.) 1970. *Ovid Metamorphoses Book VIII.* Oxford.

—— 1994. "Nonnus and Hellenistic poetry," in Hopkinson 1994b: 43–59.

Hollis, S. T. 1990. *The Ancient Egyptian "Tale of Two Brothers": The Oldest Fairy Tale in the World.* Norman, OK.

Holmberg, I. 1995. "The *Odyssey* and female subjectivity," *Helios* 22: 103–22.

—— 1998. "The creation of the ancient Greek Epic Cycle," *Oral Tradition* 13: 456–78.

Holmes, J. S. 1988. *Translated! Papers on Literary Translation and Translation Studies.* Amsterdam.

Holton, M., and V. D. Mihailovich (trans.) 1997. *Songs of the Serbian People: From the Collections of Vuk Karadžić.* Pittsburgh.

Holzapel, O. 1990. "Heimkehr des Gatten," in K. Ranke (ed.) *Enzyklopädie des Märchens: Handwörterbuch zur historischen und vergleichenden Erzählforschung,* vol. 6. Cols. 702–7. Berlin.

Holzberg, N. 1997. *Ovid. Dichter und Werk.* Munich. Trans. 2002 as *Ovid, the Poet and His Work* by G. M. Goshgarian. Ithaca, NY.

Honko, L. (ed.) 1998a. *The Siri Epic as Performed by Gopala Naika*. In collaboration with C. Gowda, A. Honko, and V. Rai, 2 vols. Folklore Fellows Communications 265–6. Helsinki.
—— 1998b. *Textualising the Siri Epic*. Folklore Fellows Communications 264. Helsinki.
—— 2000a. "Text as process and practice: the textualization of oral epics," in Honko 2000b; 3–54.
—— (ed.) 2000b. *Textualization of Oral Epics*. Berlin and New York.
—— (ed.) 2002a. *The Kalevala and the World's Traditional Epics*. Helsinki.
—— 2002b. "The Kalevala as performance," in Honko 2002a: 13–25.
Hooker, J. T. 1990. *Reading the Past: Ancient Writing from Cuneiform to the Alphabet*. Berkeley and Los Angeles.
Hope Simpson, R., and O. T. P. K. Dickinson. 1979. *A Gazetteer of Aegean Civilisation in the Bronze Age*, vol. I: *The Mainland and Islands*. Studies in Mediterranean Archaeology 52. Göteborg.
Hope Simpson, R., and J. F. Lazenby. 1970. *The Catalogue of the Ships in Homer's Iliad*. Oxford.
Hopkinson, N. 1994a. "Nonnus and Homer," in Hopkinson 1994b: 9–42.
—— (ed.) 1994b. *Studies in the Dionysiaca of Nonnus: Proceedings of the Cambridge Philological Society*. Supplementary volume 17. Cambridge.
—— 1994c. *Greek Poetry of the Imperial Period: IV Quintus Smyrnaeus*. Cambridge.
—— 1996. "Quintus Smyrnaeus," in S. Hornblower and A. Spawforth (eds.) *The Oxford Classical Dictionary*, 3rd edn. Oxford.
—— (ed.) 2000. *Metamorphoses XIII*. Cambridge.
Horkheimer, M., and T. W. Adorno. 1999. "Odysseus, or myth and enlightenment," in M. Horkheimer et al., *Dialectic of Enlightenment*, trans. John Cumming, pp. 43–80. New York.
Hornblower, S. 1991. *A Commentary on Thucydides*, vol. I. Oxford.
Hornblower, S. and A. Spawforth (eds.) *The Oxford Classical Dictionary*, 3rd edn. Oxford.
Horsfall, N. M. 1979. "Epic and burlesque in Ovid, *Metamorphoses* 8. 260 ff," *Classical Journal* 74: 319–32.
—— 1984. "Aspects of Virgilian influence in Roman life," in *Atti del Convegno mondiale scientifico di studi su Virgilio 1981*, vol. 2, pp. 47–63. Milan.
—— 1987. "The Aeneas legend from Homer to Virgil," in J. N. Bremmer and N. M. Horsfall (eds.) *Roman Myth and Mythography*, pp. 12–24. London.
—— 1991. *Virgilio: L'epopea in alambicco*. Naples.
—— 1994. "The prehistory of Latin poetry: some problems of method," *Rivista di Filologia* 122: 50–75.
—— (ed.) 1995a. *A Companion to the Study of Virgil*. Mnemosyne Supplements 151. Leiden.
—— 1995b. "Virgil's impact at Rome: the non-literary evidence," in Horsfall 1995a: 249–55.
—— 2000. *Virgil, Aeneid 7: A Commentary*. Mnemosyne Supplements 198. Leiden.
Howard, M. 1955. "Technical description of the ivory writing-boards from Nimrud," *Iraq* 17: 14–20.
Howes, G. E. 1895. "Homeric quotations in Plato and Aristotle," *Harvard Studies in Classical Philology* 6: 153–237.
"H. P." (trans.) 1847. *The Iliad of Homer Translated into English Prose as Literally as the Different Idioms of the Greek and English Languages Will Allow*. "By a Graduate of the University of Oxford." First American edition. Princeton, NJ.
Hruška, B. 1974. "Zur letzen Bearbeitung des Lugalbandaepos," *Archiv für Orientalforschung* 42: 62–65.
Huart, C., and H. Massé (eds. and trans.) 1926. *Asadi Tôsi, Garshâspnâma*. Paris. 2nd edn. 1951.
Hubbard, T. 1995. "Hesiod's fable of the hawk and the nightingale reconsidered," *Greek, Roman, and Byzantine Studies* 36: 161–71.
Hübscher, P. A. 1940. "Die Charakteristik der Personen in Apollonios' Argonautika." Dissertation, Freiburg.
Hübner, U. 1972. "Hypallage in Lucans *Pharsalia*," *Hermes* 100: 577–600.
—— 1975. "Studien zur Pointentechnik in Lucans *Pharsalia*," *Hermes* 103: 200–11.
Hughes, Ted. 1997. *Tales from Ovid*. New York.
Humphries, R. 1969. *Lucretius: The Way Things Are*. Bloomington, IN.
Hunink, V. 1993. "Lucan's praise of Nero," in F. Cairns and M. Heath (eds.) *Papers of the Leeds International Latin Seminar 7: Roman Poetry and Prose, Greek Rhetoric and Poetry*. Arca 32, pp. 135–40. Leeds.

Hunter, R. L. 1987. "Medea's flight: the fourth book of the *Argonautica*," *Classical Quarterly* 37: 129–39.

—— (ed.) 1989. *Apollonius of Rhodes, Argonautica 3*. Cambridge.

—— 1991. "Greek and non-Greek in the *Argonautica* of Apollonius," in S. Said (ed.) *Hellenismos: Quelques jalons pour une histoire de l'identité grecque*, pp. 81–99. Leiden.

—— (trans.) 1993a. *Apollonius of Rhodes: Jason and the Golden Fleece (The Argonautica)*. Oxford.

—— 1993b. *The Argonautica of Apollonius: Literary Studies*. Cambridge.

—— 1995. "The divine and human map of the *Argonautica*," *Syllecta Classica* 6: 13–27.

—— 2001. "The poetics of narrative in the *Argonautica*," in T. D. Papanghelis and A. Rengakos (eds.) *A Companion to Apollonius Rhodius*, pp. 93–125. Leiden.

Hurst, A. 1967. *Apollonios de Rhodes: Manière et cohérence*. Biblioteca Helvetica Romana 8. Rome.

Hurst, A., O. Reverdin, and J. Rudhart. 1984. *Vision de Dorothéos, Papyrus Bodmer 29*. Cologny-Geneva.

Hutchinson, G. 1988. *Hellenistic Poetry*. Oxford.

Huxley, G. L. 1969. *Greek Epic Poetry from Eumelos to Panyassis*. London.

Irvin, D. 1978. *Mytharion: The Comparison of Tales from the Old Testament and the Ancient Near East*. Alter Orient und altes Testament 32. Neukirchen-Vluyn.

Ivantchik, A. I. 1993. *Les Cimmériens au Proche Orient*. Göttingen.

Izre'el, S. 1997. *The Amarna Scholarly Tablets*. Groningen.

Jackson, P. 1999. "The extended voice: instances of myth in the Indo-European corpus." Dissertation, Uppsala University.

—— 2002. Verbis pingendis: *Contributions to the Study of Ritual Speech and Mythopoeia*. Innsbruck.

Jackson, S. 1993. *Creative Selectivity in Apollonius' Argonautica*. Amsterdam.

Jacob, C. 1996. "Lire pour écrire: navigations alexandrines," in M. Baratin and C. Jacob (eds.) *Le Pouvoir des bibliothèques: la mémoire des livres en Occident*, pp. 47–82. Paris.

Jacobsen, T. 1939. *The Sumerian King List*. Assyriological Studies 11. Chicago.

—— 1943. "Primitive democracy in ancient Mesopotamia," *Journal of Near Eastern Studies* 2: 159–72. Repr. 1970 in T. Jacobsen, *Toward the Image of Tammuz*, pp. 157–70. Cambridge.

—— 1976. *The Treasures of Darkness: A History of Mesopotamian Religion*. New Haven, CT.

—— (ed.) 1987. *The Harps That Once…: Sumerian Poetry in Translation*. New Haven, CT.

—— 1989. "Lugalbanda and Ninsuna," *Journal of Cuneiform Studies* 41: 69–86.

—— 1990. "The Gilgamesh epic: tragic and romantic vision," in Abusch et al. 1990: 231–49.

Jacoby, F. (ed.) 1923–. *Die Fragmente der griechischen Historiker*, 3 vols in 15. Leiden.

Jacopin, P.-Y. 1988. "Anthropological dialectics: Yukuna ritual as defensive strategy," *Schweizerische Amerikanisten-Gesellschaft*, Bulletin, 52: 35–46.

Jakobson, R. 1931. "Über die phonologischen Sprachbünde," in Jakobson 1971: 137–43.

—— 1949. "On the theory of phonological affinities between languages," in Jakobson 1990: 202–13.

—— 1952. "Studies in comparative Slavic metrics," *Oxford Slavonic Papers* 3: 21–66. Repr. in Jakobson 1966: 414–63.

—— 1960. "Closing statement: linguistics and poetics," in T. A. Sebeok (ed.) *Style in Language*, pp. 350–77. New York and London.

—— 1966. *Selected Writings*, vol. IV. The Hague.

—— 1971. *Selected Writings*, vol. I, 2nd edn. Berlin, New York, and Amsterdam.

—— 1990. *On Language*, ed. L. R. Waugh and M. Monville-Burston. Cambridge, MA.

Jal, P. 1963. *La Guerre civile à Rome: Etude littéraire et morale*. Paris.

—— 1982. "La Place de Lucain dans la littérature antique des guerres civiles," in J.-M. Croisille and P.-M. Fauchère (eds.) *Neronia 1977: Actes du 2e Colloque de la Société internationale des études néroniennes (Clermont-Ferrand, 27–28 mai 1977)*, pp. 83–91. Clermont-Ferrand.

James, A. (trans.) 2004. *The Trojan Epic: Posthomerica, by Quintus of Smyrna*. Baltimore.

James, A., and K. Lee. 2000. *A Commentary on Quintus of Smyrna, Posthomerica V*. Mnemosyne Supplements 208. Leiden.

James, P. 1999. "Prudentius' *Psychomachia*: the Christian arena and the politics of display," in R. Miles (ed.) *Constructing Identities in Late Antiquity*, pp. 70–94. London and New York.

Jamison, S. W. 1994. "Draupadî on the walls of Troy: *Iliad* 3 from an Indic perspective," *Classical Antiquity* 13: 5–16.

—— 1996. *Sacrificed Wife/Sacrificer's Wife: Women, Ritual, and Hospitality in Ancient India.* New York.

—— 1997. "A Gândharva marriage in the *Odyssey*: Nausicaa and her imaginary husband," in J. Greppin and E. C. Polomé (eds.) *Studies in Honor of Jaan Puhvel, Part Two: Mythology and Religion*, pp. 151–60. Washington, DC.

—— 1999. "Penelope and the pigs: Indic perspectives on the *Odyssey*," *Classical Antiquity* 18: 227–72.

Janan, M. 1988. "The Book of Good Love: design versus desire in *Met.* 10," *Ramus* 17: 110–37.

Janda, M. 1997. *Über "Stock und Stein": Die indogermanischen Variationen eines universalen Phraseologismus.* Dettelbach.

—— 2000. *Eleusis: Das indogermanische Erbe der Mysterien.* Innsbruck.

Janko, R. 1982. *Homer, Hesiod and the Hymns: Diachronic Development in Epic Diction.* Cambridge.

—— 1990. "The *Iliad* and its editors: dictation and redaction," *Classical Antiquity* 9: 326–34.

—— 1992. *The Iliad: A Commentary, vol. IV: Books 13–16.* Cambridge.

Janowski, B., K. Koch, and G. Wilhelm (eds.) 1993. *Religionsgeschichtliche Beziehungen zwischen Kleinasien, Nordsyrien und dem Alten Testament.* Göttingen.

Jasanoff, J., H. C. Melchert, and L. Oliver (eds.) 1998. *Mír curad: Studies in Honor of Calvert Watkins.* Innsbruck.

Jason, H. 1969. "A multidimensional approach to oral literature," *Current Anthropology* 10: 413–26.

—— 1977. *Ethnopoetry: Form, Content, Function.* Forum Theologiae Linguisticae 11. Bonn.

Jeffery, L. H. 1990. *The Local Scripts of Archaic Greece*, rev. edn. by A. W. Johnston. Oxford.

Jeffreys, E. (ed. and trans.) 1998. *Digenis Akritis: The Grottaferrata and Escorial Versions.* Cambridge.

Jeffreys, E., and M. Jeffreys. 1986. "The oral background of Byzantine popular poetry," *Oral Tradition* 1: 504–47.

Jenkins, T. E. 1999. "Homēros ekainopoiēse: Theseus, Aithra, and variation in Homeric myth-making," in M. Carlisle and O. Levaniouk (eds.) *Nine Essays on Homer*, pp. 207–26. Lanham, MD.

Jenkyns, R. 1998. *Virgil's Experience.* Oxford.

Jensen, M. S. 1966. "Tradition and individuality in Hesiod's *Works and Days*," *Classica et Mediaevalia* 27: 1–27.

—— 1980. *The Homeric Question and the Oral-Formulaic Theory.* Copenhagen.

—— 1999. "Dividing Homer: when and how were the *Iliad* and the *Odyssey* divided into songs?," *Symbolae Osloenses* 74: 5–35, 73–91.

Jensen, P. 1906–1929. *Das Gilgamesch-Epos in der Weltliteratur*, 2 vols. Strassburg.

Johnson, J. W. 1980. "Yes, Virginia, there is an epic in Africa," *Review of African Literatures* 11: 308–26.

—— 1986. *The Epic of Son-Jara: A West African Tradition.* Bloomington, IN.

—— 2000. "Authenticity and oral performance: textualizing the epics of Africa for Western audiences," in Honko 2000b: 237–46.

—— (ed. and trans.) 2003. *Son-Jara: The Mande Epic*, text by Fa-Digi Sisòkò, 3rd edn. Bloomington, IN.

Johnson, J. W., T. A. Hale, and S. Belcher (eds.) 1997. *Oral Epics from Africa: Vibrant Voices from a Vast Continent.* Bloomington, IN.

Johnson, R. R. 1970. "Ancient and medieval accounts of the 'invention' of parchment," *California Studies in Classical Antiquity* 3: 115–22.

Johnson, W. A. 1993. "Pliny the Elder and standardized roll heights in the manufacture of papyrus," *Classical Philology* 88: 46–50.

Johnson, W. R. 1970. "The problem of the counter-classical sensibility and its critics," *California Studies in Classical Antiquity* 3: 123–51.

—— 1976. *Darkness Visible.* Berkeley.

—— 1987. *Momentary Monsters: Lucan and His Heroes.* Cornell Studies in Classical Philology 47. Ithaca, NY.

—— 1996. "The rapes of Callisto," *Classical Journal* 92: 9–24.

—— 2000. *Lucretius and the Modern World.* London.

Jones, J. W., Jr. 1961. "Allegorical interpretation in Servius," *Classical Journal* 56: 217–26.

Jones, N. F. 1984. "Perses, work 'in season,' and the purpose of the *Works and Days*," *Classical Journal* 79: 307–23.

Jones, W. 1993. *The Collected Works of Sir William Jones*, 13 vols, ed. G. Cannon. New York. (Lightly rev. repr. of *The Works of Sir William Jones*. London, 1807.) Original publication of "The Third Anniversary Discourse" in *Asiatick Researches* 1 (1788): 415–31.

Joplin, P. K. 1984. "The voice of the shuttle is ours," *Stanford Literary Review* 1: 25–53.

Joyce, J. W. (trans.) 1993. *Lucan: Pharsalia*. Ithaca, NY.

Juhnke, H. 1972. *Homerisches in römischer Epik flavischer Zeit: Untersuchungen zu Szenennachbildungen und Strukturentsprechungen in Statius' Thebais und Achilleis und in Silius' Punica*. Munich.

Kakridis, P. I. 1962. (in Modern Greek). *Quintus of Smyrna: A General Study of the Posthomerica and its Poet*. Athens.

Kallendorf, C. W. 1989. *In Praise of Aeneas: Virgil and Epideictic Rhetoric in the Early Italian Renaissance*. Hanover.

—— (ed.) 1993. *Vergil*. New York.

—— 1994. *A Bibliography of Renaissance Italian Translations of Virgil*. Biblioteca di bibliografia italiana 136. Florence.

—— 1999. *Virgil and the Myth of Venice: Books and Readers in the Italian Renaissance*. Oxford.

—— 2000. "*Aeneid*," in R. Lansing (ed.) *The Dante Encyclopedia*, pp. 7–8. New York.

—— 2001. "The *Aeneid* transformed: illustration as interpretation from the Renaissance to the present," in S. Spence (ed.) *Poets and Critics Read Virgil*, pp. 121–48. New Haven, CT.

—— 2003. "Representing the other: Ercilla's *La Araucana*, Virgil's *Aeneid*, and the 'New' World encounter," *Comparative Literature Studies* 40: 394–414.

Kallendorf, C. W., and M. X. Wells. 1998. *Aldine Press Books at the Harry Ransom Humanities Research Center: A Descriptive Catalogue*. Austin.

Karageorghis, V. 1969. *Salamis: Recent Discoveries in Cyprus*. New York.

—— 1976. *Kition, Mycenaean and Phoenician Discoveries*. London.

Katz, D. 1987. "Gilgamesh and Akka: Was Uruk ruled by two assemblies?," *Revue d'Assyriologie et d'Archéologie Orientale* 81: 105–14.

—— 1993. *Gilgamesh and Akka*. Groningen and Broomall, PA.

Katz, J. T. 1998. "How to be a dragon in Indo-European: Hittite *illuyankaš* and its linguistic and cultural congeners in Latin, Greek, and Germanic," in Jasanoff et al. 1998: 317–34.

—— Forthcoming. "The Indo-European background of Homeric formula." To appear in the Proceedings of the Colloquium "Les Enjeux théoriques des débats sur la formule homérique" (Lille, April 2000), ed. P. Rousseau and G.-J. Pinault.

Katz, M. A. 1991. *Penelope's Renown: Meaning and Indeterminacy in the Odyssey*. Princeton, NJ.

Kay, M. W. 1995. *The Index of the Milman Parry Collection, 1933–1935: Heroic Songs, Conversations, and Stories*. New York.

Keaney, J. J., and R. Lamberton (eds.) 1996. [Plutarch] *Essay on the Life and Poetry of Homer*. American Philological Association American Classical Studies 40. Atlanta.

Keith, A. M. 1992. *The Play of Fictions: Studies in Ovid's Metamorphoses Book 2*. Ann Arbor, MI.

—— 1999. 'Epic masculinity in Ovid's *Metamorphoses*," in Hardie et al. 1999: 214–39.

—— 2000. *Engendering Rome: Women in Roman Epic*. Roman Literature and its Contexts. Cambridge.

—— 2002. "Sources and genres in Ovid's *Metamorphoses*," in B. Boyd (ed.) *Brill's Companion to Ovid*, pp. 235–69. Leiden, Boston, and Cologne.

Kemball-Cook, B. (trans.) 1993. *The Odyssey of Homer*. London.

Kennedy, D. 2000. "Making a text of the Universe: perspectives on discursive order in the *De rerum natura* of Lucretius," in A. R. Sharrock and H. Morales (eds.) *Intratextuality: Greek and Roman Textual Relations*, pp. 205–25. Oxford.

Kenney, E. J. 1970. "*Doctus Lucretius*," *Mnemosyne* 23: 366–92. Repr. in Classen 1986: 239–65.

—— 1971. *Lucretius: De rerum natura Book III*. Cambridge.

—— 1976. "Ovidius Prooemians," *Proceedings of the Cambridge Philological Society* 22: 46–53.

—— 1995. *Lucretius*. Greece and Rome New Surveys in the Classics 11, 2nd edn. Oxford.

Ker, J. C., K. Keniston, and L. Marx (eds.) 1999. *Earth, Air, Fire, Water: Humanistic Studies of the Environment*. Amherst, MA.

Ker, W. P. 1897. *Epic and Romance: Essays on Mediaeval Literature*. London.

Kerkhecker, A. 2001. "Zur internen Gattungsgeschichte der römischen Epik: Das Beispiel Ennius," in E. A. Schmidt (ed.) *L'Histoire littéraire immanente dans la poésie latine. Fondation Hardt: Entretiens sur l'Antiquité Classique* 47, pp. 39–88.

Kessels, A. H. M. 1982. "Dreams in Apollonius' *Argonautica*," in J. den Boeft and A. H. M. Kessels (eds.) *Actus: Studies in Honour of H. L. W. Nelson*, pp. 155–73. Utrecht.

Kessels, A. H. M., and P. W. Van der Horst. 1987. "The vision of Dorotheus," *Vigiliae Christianae* 41: 313–59.

Keydell, R. 1936. "Nonnos," in *Paulys Real-Encyclopädie der classischen Altertumswissenschaft* 17, 1: 904–20.

—— 1963. "Quintus von Smyrna," in *Paulys Real-Encyclopaedie der classischen Altertumswissenschaft* 47: 1271–96.

Khaleghi-Motlagh, D. (ed.) 1988–. *Ferdowsi: The Shahnameh*. New York.

Kilian-Dirlmeier, I. 1985. "Fremde Weihungen in griechischen Heiligtümern vom 8. bis zum Beginn des 7. Jahrhunderts v. Chr," *Jahrbuch des Römisch-germanischen Zentralmuseums* 32: 215–54.

Kilmer, A. D. 1996. "Fugal features of Atra-Hasis: the birth theme," in Vogelzang and Vanstiphout 1996: 127–39.

King, P. J., and L. E. Stager. 2001. *Life in Biblical Israel*. Louisville, KY.

Kinsella, T. (trans.) 1969. *The Tain*. Dublin.

Kirk, G. S. 1970. *Myth: Its Meaning and Function in Ancient and Other Cultures*. Cambridge and Berkeley.

—— 1976. *Homer and the Oral Tradition*. Cambridge.

—— 1985. *The Iliad: A Commentary*, vol. I: *Books 1–4*. Cambridge.

—— 1990. *The Iliad: A Commentary*, vol. II: *Books 5–8*. Cambridge.

Kirsch, W. 1989. *Die lateinische Versepik des 4. Jahrhunderts*. Berlin.

Klein, J. 1976. "Šulgi and Gilameš: two brother peers (Šulgi O)," in B. L. Eichler (ed.) *Kramer Anniversary Volume: Cuneiform Studies in Honor of Samuel Noah Kramer*. Altes Orient und Altes Testament 25, pp. 271–92. Kevelaer.

—— 1983. "The capture of Agga by Gilgameš (GA 81 and 99)," *Journal of the American Oriental Society* 103: 201–4.

—— 2002. "A new look at the 'Oppression of Uruk' episode in the Gilgameš epic," in T. Abusch (ed.) *Riches Hidden in Secret Places: Ancient Near Eastern Studies in Memory of Thorkild Jacobsen*, pp. 187–201. Winona Lake, MN.

Klein, L. 1931. "Die Göttertechnik in den *Argonautika* des Apollonius Rhodius," *Philologus* 86: 18–51, 215–57.

Klinger, J. 1996. *Untersuchungen zur Rekonstruktion der hattischen Kultschicht*. Wiesbaden.

Klinkott, H. (ed.) 2001. *Anatolien im Lichte kultureller Wechselwirkungen: Akkulturationsphänomene in Kleinasien und seinen Nachbarregionen während des 2. und 1. Jahrtausends v. Chr.* Tübingen.

Knight, V. 1995. *The Renewal of Epic: Responses to Homer in the Argonautica of Apollonius*. Mnemosyne Supplements 152. Leiden.

Knox, P. 1986. *Ovid's Metamorphoses and the Traditions of Augustan Poetry*. Cambridge.

Koechly, A. 1850. *Quinti Smyrnaei Posthomericorum libri XIV... prolegomenis et adnotatione critica ... Leipzig*. Repr. 1968, Amsterdam.

Koenen, L. 1994. "Cyclic destruction in Hesiod and the catalogue of women," *Transactions of the American Philological Association* 124: 1–34.

Köhnken, A. 1965. *Apollonios Rhodios und Theokrit*. Hypomnemata 12. Göttingen.

—— 2001. "Hellenistic chronology: Theocritus, Callimachus and Apollonius Rhodius," in T. D. Papanghelis and A. Rengakos (eds.) *A Companion to Apollonius Rhodius*, pp. 73–92. Leiden.

Koitabiashi, M. 1998. "Music in the texts from Ugarit," *Ugarit-Forschungen* 30: 363–96.

Kolsti, J. 1990. *The Bilingual Singer: A Study in Albanian and Serbo-Croatian Oral Epic Traditions*. New York.

Komoróczy, G. 1974. " 'Folklore,' Literatur, 'Folkloristik' in der sumerischen Überlieferung," *Acta Antiqua Academiae Scientiarum Hungaricae* 22: 113–20.

Komoróczy, G. 1975. "Akkadian epic poetry and its Sumerian sources," *Acta Antiqua Academiae Scientiarum Hungaricae* 23: 41–63.

Kopcke, G., and I. Tokumaru (eds.) 1992. *Greece Between East and West: 10th–8th Centuries BC*. Mainz.

Korfmann, M. (ed.) 1991–2004. *Studia Troica*, vols. 1–14. Mainz am Rhein.

—— 1998. "Troia, an ancient Anatolian palatial and trading center: archaeological evidence for the period of Troia VI/VII," *Classical World* 91: 369–85.

—— 2002. "Ilios, ca. 1200 BC – Ilion, ca. 700 BC: report on findings from archaeology," in Montanari 2002: 209–26.

Korfmann, M. et al. 2001. *Troia. Traum und Wirklichkeit*. Stuttgart.

Korpel, M. 1997. "Exegesis in the work of Ilimilku of Ugarit," *Oudtestamentische Studien* 40: 86–111.

Koster, S. 1970. *Antike Epostheorien*. Wiesbaden.

Kovacs, D. 1987. "Ovid's *Metamorphoses* 1. 2." *Classical Quarterly* n.s. 37: 458–65.

Kovacs, M. G. (trans.) 1989 [1985]. *The Epic of Gilgamesh*. Stanford, CA.

Kramer, S. N. 1938. *Gilgamesh and the Huluppu-Tree: A Reconstructed Sumerian Text*. Chicago.

—— 1944a. "The death of Gilgamesh," *Bulletin of the American Schools of Oriental Research* 94: 2–12.

—— 1944b. "The Epic of Gilgamesh and its Sumerian sources," *Journal of the American Oriental Society* 64: 7–23.

—— 1946. "Heroes of Sumer," *Proceedings of the American Philosophical Society* 90: 120–30.

—— 1949. "Gilgameš and Agga," *American Journal of Archaeology* 53: 1–18.

—— 1952. *Enmerkar and the Lord of Aratta: A Sumerian Epic Tale of Iraq and Iran*. Philadelphia.

Kramer, S. N., and T. Jacobsen. 1954. "Enmerkar and Ensukušširanna," *Orientalia* 23: 232–34.

Krevans, N. 2000. "On the margins of epic: the Ktisis poems of Apollonius," in A. Harder, G. Wakker, R. Regtuit (eds.) *Apollonius Rhodius*. Hellenistica Groningana 4, pp. 69–84. Groningen.

Kroll, W. 1924. *Studien zum Verständnis der römischen Literatur*. Stuttgart.

Kugel, J. A. 1981. *The Idea of Biblical Poetry: Parallelism and its History*. New Haven, CT.

Kuhrt, A. 1995. *The Ancient Near East, c.3000–330 BC*, 2 vols. London.

Kupper, J.-R. 1998. *Lettres royales du temps de Zimri-Lim*. Archives royales de Mari 28. Paris.

Küppers, J. 1986. *Tantarum causas irarum. Untersuchungen zur einleitenden Bücherdyade der Punica des Silius Italicus*. Berlin and New York.

Kyrieleis, H., and W. Röllig. 1988. "Ein altorientalischer Pferdeschmuck aus dem Heraion von Samos," *Mitteilungen des deutschen archäologischen Instituts, Athenische Abteilung* 103: 37–75.

Kyriakou, P. 1994. "Empedoclean echoes in Apollonius Rhodius' *Argonautica*," *Hermes* 122: 309–19.

—— 1995a. *Homeric Hapax Legomena in the Argonautica of Apollonius Rhodius: A Literary Study*. Palingenesia 54. Stuttgart.

—— 1995b. "Katabasis and the Underworld in the *Argonautica* of Apollonius Rhodius," *Philologus* 139: 256–64.

Labarre, S. 1998. *Le Manteau partagé: Deux métamorphoses poétiques de la Vie de saint Martin chez Paulin de Périgueux et Venance Fortunat*. Paris.

Laessøe, J. 1953. "Literacy and oral tradition in ancient Mesopotamia," in F. F. Hvidberg (ed.) *Studia Orientalia: Ioanni Pedersen septuagenario A.D. VII ID. Nov. anno 1953 a collegis discipulis amicis dicata*, pp. 205–18. Copenhagen.

Lamberg-Karlovsky, C. C. 1996. *Beyond the Tigris and Euphrates: Bronze Age Civilizations*. Beer-Sheva 9. Beer-Sheva.

Lambert, W. G. 1957. "Ancestors, authors, and canonicity," *Journal of Cuneiform Studies* 11: 1–14.

—— 1962. "A catalogue of texts and authors," *Journal of Cuneiform Studies* 16: 59–77.

—— 1997. "Gilgamesh in literature and art in the second and first millennia," in J. Maier (ed.) *Gilgamesh: A Reader*, pp. 50–62. Wauconda, IL.

Lambert, W. G., and A. R. Millard. 1969. *Atra-ḥasīs: The Babylonian Story of the Flood*. Oxford.

Lamberterie, C. de. 1997. "Milman Parry et Antoine Meillet," in Létoublon 1997: 9–22. Trans. as "Milman Parry and Antoine Meillet" in Loraux et al. 2001: 409–21.

Lamberton, R. 1986. *Homer the Theologian*. The Transformation of the Classical Heritage 9. Berkeley.

—— 1988. *Hesiod*. New Haven, CT.

—— 1992. "The Neoplatonists and the spiritualization of Homer," in Lamberton and Keaney 1992: 115–33.

—— 1997. "Homer in antiquity," in Morris and Powell 1997: 33–54.

Lamberton, R., and J. J. Keaney (eds.) 1992. *Homer's Ancient Readers: The Hermeneutics of Greek Epic's Earliest Exegetes*. Princeton, NJ.

Lana, I. 1971. "Il proemio di Lucano," in *Studi di storiografia antica in memoria di L. Ferrero*, pp. 131–47. Turin.

Landsberger, B. 1960. "Einleitung in das Gilgameš-Epos," in P. Garelli (ed.) *Gilgameš et sa légende*. Proceedings of the VIIme Rencontre Assyriologique Internationale, pp. 1–30. Paris.

—— 1968. "Zu vierten und siebenten Tafel des Gilgamesch-Epos," *Revue d'assyriologie* 62: 97–135.

Lang Y. 2001. "The bard Jusup Mamay," *Oral Tradition* 16: 222–39.

Lapidge, M. 1989. "Stoic cosmology and Roman literature, first to third century AD," *Aufstieg und Niedergang der römischen Welt*, II.36.3: 1379–429.

Laroche, E. 1971. *Catalogue des textes hittites*. Paris.

Larsen, T. M. 1995. "The Babel/Bible" controversy and its aftermath," in Sasson 1995: 95–106.

Larson, J. 1995. *Greek Heroine Cults*. Madison, WI.

Latacz, J. (ed.) 1991. *Zweihundert Jahre Homer-Forschung*. Stuttgart.

—— 1997. "Epischer Zyklus (ἐπικὸς κύκλος)," in H. Cancik and H. Schneider (eds.) *Der Neue Pauly*, vol. 3, cols. 1154–6. Stuttgart.

—— 2001. *Troia und Homer: Der Weg zur Lösung eines alten Rätsels*, 2nd edn. Munich.

Lateiner, D. 1984. "Mythic and non-mythic artists in Ovid's *Metamorphoses*," *Ramus* 13: 1–30.

—— 1989. *The Historical Method of Herodotus*. Toronto.

Latham, R. E. (trans.) 1994. *Lucretius: On the Nature of the Universe*, rev. J. Godwin. Harmondsworth.

Lattimore, R. (trans.) 1959. *Hesiod*. Ann Arbor, MI. Repr. 1991.

—— (trans.) 1961 [1951]. *The Iliad of Homer*. Chicago.

—— (trans.) 1967. *The Odyssey of Homer*. New York. Repr. 1991.

Laudizi, G. 1989. *Silio Italico: Il passato tra mito e restaurazione etica*. Galatina.

Lavarenne, M. 1955–63. *Prudence*, 4 vols. Paris.

Lawall, G. 1966. "Apollonius' *Argonautica*: Jason as anti-hero," *Yale Classical Studies* 19: 121–69.

Lazard, G. (ed. and trans.) 1964. *Les premiers poètes persans (IXe–Xe siècles)*, 2 vols. Tehran and Paris.

—— 1971. "Pahlavi, Parsi, and Dari: les langues de l'Iran d'après Ibn al-Muqaffa," in C. E. Bosworth (ed.) *Iran and Islam (In Memory of V. Minorsky)*, pp. 361–91. Edinburgh.

—— 1975. "The rise of the new Persian language," in *Cambridge History of Iran*, vol. 4, pp. 595–657. Cambridge.

Leach, E. W. 1974. "Ekphrasis and the theme of artistic failure in Ovid's *Metamorphoses*," *Ramus* 3: 102–42.

Lebek, W. D. 1976. *Lucans Pharsalia: Dichtungsstruktur und Zeitbezug*. Göttingen.

Le Bonniec, H. 1970. "Lucain et la religion," in *Lucain. Fondation Hardt, Entretiens sur l'antiquité classique* 15: 159–200.

Lebrun, R. 1995. "From Hittite mythology: the Kumarbi cycle," in J. Sasson 1995: 1971–80.

Lee, S. 1999. *David*. London.

Lefevere, A. 1992. *Translation, Rewriting, and the Manipulation of Literary Fame*. London.

Lefkowitz, M. 2001. "Myth and history in the biography of Apollonius Rhodius," in T. D. Papanghelis and A. Rengakos (eds.) *A Companion to Apollonius Rhodius*, pp. 51–71. Leiden.

Leigh, M. 1997. *Lucan: Spectacle and Engagement*. Oxford.

—— 2000. "Lucan and the Libyan tale," *Journal of Roman Studies* 90: 95–109.

Lemaire, A. 1992. "Writing and writing materials," in *Anchor Bible Dictionary*, vol. 6, pp. 999–1008.

Leo, F. 1913. *Geschichte der römischen Literatur*. Berlin.

Lesko, L. 1990. "Some comments on ancient Egyptian literacy and literari," in S. Israelit-Groll (ed.) *Studies in Egyptology Presented to Miriam Lichtheim*, pp. 656–67. Jerusalem.

Létoublon, F. (ed.) 1997. *Hommage à Milman Parry: le style formulaire de l'épopée et la théorie de l'oralité poétique*. Amsterdam.

Levet, P. 2003. "L'expression du vrai et de la verité dans les Posthomerica de Quintus de Smyrne," in D. Accorinti and P. Chuvin (eds.) *Des Géants à Dionysos: Mélanges de mythologie et de poésie grecques offerts à Francis Vian*, pp. 357–83. Alexandria.

Levi, M. A. 1949. "Il prologo della 'Pharsalia'," *Rivista di Filologia e di Istruzione Classica* 27: 71–8.

Levin, D. N. 1971. *Apollonius' Argonautica Re-Examined: The Neglected First and Second Books.* Leiden.

Levy, H. 1971. *Claudian's In Rufinum: An Exegetical Commentary.* Cleveland.

Lewis, C. S. 1938. *The Allegory of Love: A Study in Medieval Tradition.* Repr. of 1936 edn. Oxford.

Lewis, N. 1974. *Papyrus in Classical Antiquity.* Oxford.

—— 1989. *Papyrus in Classical Antiquity: A Supplement.* Brussels.

Lewis, P. E. 2000. "The measure of translation effects," in Venuti 2000: 264–83.

Liberman, G. (ed. and trans.) 1997. *Valerius Flaccus. Argonautiques I. Chantes I–IV.* Paris.

—— (ed. and trans.) 2002. *Valerius Flaccus. Argonautiques II. Chantes V–VIII.* Paris.

Lichtheim, M. 1973–84. *Ancient Egyptian Literature,* 3 vols. 1976, vol. 2: *The New Kingdom*; 1984, vol. 3: *The Late Period.* Berkeley.

Lieberman, S. 1990. "Canonical official cuneiform texts: towards an understanding of Assurbanipal's personal tablet collection," in Abusch et al. 1990: 305–36.

Liebeschuetz, J. H. W. G. 1979a. *Continuity and Change in Roman Religion.* Oxford.

—— 1979b. "The system rejected: Lucan's *Pharsalia*," in Liebeschuetz 1979a: 140–55.

Lightfoot, J. L. 1999. *Parthenius of Nicaea.* Oxford.

Limet, H. 1972. "Les Chants épiques sumériens," *Revue belge de philologie et d'histoire* 50: 3–24.

Lincoln, B. 1975. "Homeric Lyssa: wolfish rage," *Indogermanische Forschungen* 80: 98–105.

—— 1981a. "On the imagery of Paradise," *Indogermanische Forschungen* 85: 151–64.

—— 1981b. *Priests, Warriors, and Cattle: A Study in the Ecology of Religions.* Berkeley.

—— 1999. *Theorizing Myth: Narrative, Ideology, and Scholarship.* Chicago.

Lind, L. R. 1978. "Nonnos and his readers," *Res Publica Litterarum* 1: 159–70.

Lindsay, J. 1965. *Leisure and Pleasure in Roman Egypt.* London.

Lindsay, W. M. (ed.) 1913. *Sexti Pompei Festi De verborum significatu quae supersunt cum Pauli epitome.* Leipzig.

Lively, G. 1999. "Reading resistance in Ovid's *Metamorphoses*," in Hardie et al. 1999: 197–213.

Liverani, M. 1993. "Model and actualization: the kings of Akkad in the historical tradition," in M. Liverani (ed.) *Akkad: The First World Empire,* pp. 41–67. Padua.

—— 1995. "The deeds of ancient Mesopotamian kings," in J. Sasson 1995: 2353–66.

Livrea, E. 1973. *Apollonii Rhodii Argonauticon Liber Quartus.* Florence.

Llewellyn, N. 1984. "Virgil and the visual arts," in C. Martindale (ed.) *Virgil and his Influence: Bimillennial Studies,* pp. 117–40. Bristol.

Lloyd, J. B. 1996. "Anat and the 'double' massacre of KTU 1.3 ii," in Wyatt et al. 1996: 151–65.

Lloyd, S. 1978. *The Archaeology of Mesopotamia from the Old Stone Age to the Persian Conquest.* London.

Logue, C. 1981. *War Music: An Account of Books 16–19 of Homer's Iliad.* Harmondsworth.

Lombardo, S. (trans.) 1993. *Hesiod.* Indianopolis.

—— (trans.) 1997. *Homer Iliad.* Indianapolis.

—— (trans.) 2000. *Homer Odyssey.* Indianapolis.

Long, A. 1992. "Stoic readings in Homer," in Lamberton and Keaney 1992: 44–66.

Long, J. 1996. *Claudian's In Eutropium, Or How, When, and Why to Slander a Eunuch.* Chapel Hill, NC.

Longman, T., III. 1990. *Fictional Akkadian Autobiography: A Generic and Comparative Study.* Winona Lake, MN.

Loprieno, A. (ed.) 1996. *Ancient Egyptian Literature: History and Forms.* Leiden.

—— 2003. "Travel and fiction in Egyptian literature," in D. O'Connor and S. Quirke (eds.) *Mysterious Lands,* pp. 31–51. London.

Loraux, N., G. Nagy, and L. Slatkin. (eds.) 2001. *Antiquities.* Postwar French Thought 3. New York.

Lord, A. B. 1953. "Homer's originality: oral dictated texts," *Transactions of the American Philological Association* 84: 124–34.

—— 1960. *The Singer of Tales.* Cambridge, MA. Repr. 2000, with new intro. by S. Mitchell and G. Nagy.

—— 1990. "Gilgamesh and other epics," in Abusch et al. 1990: 371–80.

—— 1991. *Epic Singers and Oral Tradition.* Ithaca, NY.

—— 1995. *The Singer Resumes the Tale,* ed. M. L. Lord. Ithaca, NY.

Lord, G. 1956. *Homeric Renaissance: The Odyssey of George Chapman.* New Haven, CT.

Lord, M. L. 1967. "Withdrawal and return: an epic story pattern in the Homeric Hymn to Demeter and in the Homeric poems," *Classical Journal* 62: 241–8.

Lorimer, H. L. 1947. "The hoplite phalanx with special reference to the poems of Archilochus and Tyrtaeus," *Annual of the British School at Athens* 42: 76–138.

—— 1950. *Homer and the Monuments.* London.

Louden, B. 1999. *The Odyssey: Structure, Narration, and Meaning.* Baltimore and London.

Loupiac, A. 1998. *La Poétique des éléments dans la Pharsale de Lucain.* Collection Latomus 241. Brussels.

Lovatt, H. 1999. "Competing endings: re-reading the end of the *Thebaid* through Lucan," *Ramus* 28: 126–51.

Lowenstam, S. 1981. *The Death of Patroklos: A Study in Typology.* Beiträge zur Klassischen Philologie 133. Königstein.

—— 1997. "Talking vases: the relationship between the Homeric poems and archaic representations of epic myth," *Transactions of the American Philological Association* 127: 21–76.

Lucanus, M. A. 1970. *Bellum civile,* ed. A. E. Housman. Oxford.

—— 1971. *Pharsalia,* ed. C.E. Haskins, with intro. by W. E. Heitland. Hildesheim.

—— 1981. *Civil War VIII,* ed. with commentary by R. Mayer. Warminster, Wilts.

—— 1988. *De bello civili libri X,* ed. D. R. Shackleton Bailey. Bibliotheca Scriptorum Graecorum et Romanorum Teubneriana. Stuttgart.

Luce, J. V. 1975. *Homer and the Heroic Age.* London.

—— 2003. "The case for historical significance in Homer's landmarks at Troia," in G. A. Wagner, E. Pernicka, and H.-P. Uerpmann (eds.) *Troia and the Troad: Scientific Approaches,* pp. 9–30. Berlin.

Luckenbill, D. D. 1927. *Ancient Records of Assyria and Babylonia,* vol. 2. Chicago.

Ludwig, E. 1931. *Schliemann of Troy: The Story of a Goldseeker,* trans. D. F. Tait. London.

Lühken, M. 2002. *Christianorum Maro et Flaccus: Zur Vergil- und Horazrezeption des Prudentius.* Göttingen.

Lutgendorf, P. 1991. *The Life of a Text: Performing the Ramcaritmanas of Tulsidas.* Berkeley.

Lyne, R. O. A. M. 1983. "Lavinia's blush: Vergil, *Aeneid* 12.64–70," *Greece and Rome* 30: 55–64.

—— 2001. *Ovid's Changing Worlds.* Oxford.

Macan, T. (ed.) 1829. *The Shah Namah.* Calcutta.

Macaulay, T. B. 1997 [1842]. *Lays of Ancient Rome.* Gateway Editions. Washington, DC.

McCarter, P. K. 1980. *I Samuel: A New Translation with Introduction, Notes, and Commentary.* Anchor Bible. Garden City, NY.

—— 1984. *II Samuel. A New Translation with Introduction, Notes, and Commentary.* Anchor Bible. Garden City, NY.

McCarthy, W. B. 2001. "Oral theory and epic studies," *Choice* 39/i (September): 61–75.

Machinist, P. 1978. "The epic of Tukulti-Ninurta I: a study in Middle Assyrian literature," Dissertation, Yale University.

McConnell, W. (ed.) 1998. *A Companion to the* Nibelungenlied. Columbia, SC.

MacCormack, S. 1998. *The Shadows of Poetry: Vergil in the Mind of Augustine.* Berkeley.

McDermott, W. C. and A. E. Orentzel. 1977. "Silius Italicus and Domitian," *American Journal of Philology* 98: 24–34.

McDonald, W. A., and C. G. Thomas. 1990. *Progress into the Past: The Rediscovery of Mycenaean Civilization,* 2nd edn. Bloomington.

MacDougall, H. A. 1982. *Racial Myth in English History: Trojans, Teutons, and Anglo-Saxons.* Montreal.

McGrath, K. 2004. *The Sanskrit Hero: Karna in Epic Mahabharata.* Leiden.

McGuire, D. T. 1997. *Acts of Silence: Civil War, Tyranny, and Suicide in the Flavian Epics.* Hildesheim.

McKay, A. 1993. "Vergil translated into European art," in C. W. Kallendorf (ed.) *Vergil,* pp. 345–64. New York.

McKeown, J. 1998. *Ovid: Amores III: A Commentary on Book Two.* Leeds.

Mackie, C. J. 1996. "Homer and Thucydides: Corcyra and Sicily," *Classical Quarterly* 46: 103–13.

McKitterick, R. 1989. *The Carolingians and the Written Word.* Cambridge.

Maclean, J. K. B., and E. B. Aitken (trans. and eds.) 2003. *Flavius Philostratus: On Heroes*. Atlanta.

McLeod, W. 1966. "Studies on Panyassis – an heroic poet of the fifth century," *Phoenix* 20: 95–110.

—— 1984. "The bow and the axes," in A. L. Boegehold et al. (eds.) *Studies Presented to Sterling Dow on his Eightieth Birthday*. Greek, Roman and Byzantine Studies Monograph, pp. 203–10. Durham.

MacMullen, R. 1997. *Christianity and Paganism in the Fourth to Eighth Centuries*. New Haven, CT.

Maginn, W. 1850. *Homeric Ballads*. London.

McNeill, I. 1963. "The metre of the Hittite epic," *Anatolian Studies* 13: 237–42.

Mahoney, A. 1934. *Vergil in the Works of Prudentius*. Washington, DC.

Maier, J. 1983. "Charles Olson and the poetic uses of Mesopotamian scholarship," *Journal of the American Oriental Society*, 103 Repr. in J. M. Sasson (ed.) *Studies in Literature from the Ancient Near East Dedicated to Samuel Noah Kramer by Members of the American Oriental Studies*. American Oriental Series 65, pp. 227–35. New Haven, CT.

—— (ed.) 1997. *Gilgamesh: A Reader*. Wauconda, IL.

Majidzadeh, Y. 1976. "The Land of Aratta," *Journal of Near Eastern Studies* 35: 105–14.

Malamud, M. 1989. *A Poetics of Transformation: Prudentius and Classical Mythology*. Ithaca, NY.

—— 1995. "Happy birthday, dead Lucan: (p)raising the dead in *Silvae* 2.7," *Ramus* 24: 1–31.

Malamud, M., and D. T. McGuire. 1993. "Flavian variant: myth. Valerius' *Argonautica*," in Boyle 1993: 192–217.

Malcolm, N. 1998. *Kosovo: A Short History*. New York.

Malkin, I. 1998. *The Returns of Odysseus: Colonization and Ethnicity*. Berkeley.

Mallory, J. P. 1989. *In Search of the Indo-Europeans: Language, Archaeology and Myth*. London.

—— 1997. "Indo-European homeland," in J. P. Mallory and D. Q. Adams (eds.) *Encyclopedia of Indo-European Culture*, pp. 290–9. London.

Mallowan, M. E. L. 1964. "Noah's Flood reconsidered," *Iraq* 26: 62–82.

Malsbary, G. 1985. "Epic exegesis and the use of Vergil in the early biblical poets," *Florilegium* 7: 55–83.

Mandelbaum, A. (trans.) 1995. *The Metamorphoses of Ovid*. New York.

Manning, S. 1992. "Archaeology and the world of Homer: introduction to a past and present discipline," in C. Emlyn-Jones, L. Hardwick, and J. Purkis (eds.) *Homer: Readings and Images*, pp. 117–42. London.

Mansur, M. W. 1940. *The Treatment of Homeric Characters by Quintus of Smyrna*. New York.

Margalit, B. 1989. *The Ugaritic Poem of Aqht*. Beihefte zur Zeitschrift für die Alttestamentliche Wissenschaft 182. Berlin.

—— 1999. "The legend of Keret," in Watson and Wyatt 1999: 203–33.

Margolies DeForest, M. J. 1994. *Apollonius' Argonautica: A Callimachean Epic*. Mnemosyne Supplements 142. Leiden.

Marinatos, N. 1990. "Celebrations of death and the symbolism of the lion hunt," in R. Hägg and G. C. Nordquist (eds.) *Celebrations of Death and Divinity in the Bronze Age Argolid*, pp. 143–8. Stockholm.

—— 1993. *Minoan Religion*. Columbus, SC.

—— 1998. "The Tell el Dab'a paintings: a study in pictorial tradition," *Egypt and the Levant* 8: 83–100.

Marinatos, S. 1973. *Kreta, Thera und das mykenische Hellas*, 2nd edn. München.

Mariotti, S. 1952. *Livio Andronico e la traduzione artistica. Saggio critico ed edizione dei frammenti dell'* Odyssea. Pubblicazioni dell'Università di Urbino. Serie di lettere e filosofia 1. Milan.

Markoe, G. 2000. *Phoenicians*. London.

Marks, J. 2002. "The junction between the *Kypria* and the *Iliad*," *Phoenix* 56: 1–24.

—— 2003. "Alternative Odysseys: the case of Thoas and Odysseus," *Transactions of the American Philological Association* 133: 209–26.

Marks, R. D. 2003. "Hannibal in Liternum," in P. Thibodeau and H. Haskell (eds.) *Being There Together: Essays in Honor of Michael C. J. Putnam on the Occasion of his Seventieth Birthday*, pp. 128–44. Afton, MN.

Markus, R. 1990. *The End of Ancient Christianity*. Cambridge.

Marti, B. M. 1945. "The meaning of the *Pharsalia*," *American Journal of Philology* 66: 352–76.

—— 1964. "Tragic history and Lucan's *Pharsalia*," in C. Henderson, Jr. (ed.) *Classical, Medieval, and Renaissance Studies in Honor of Berthold Louis Ullman*, vol. 1, pp. 165–204. Rome.

—— 1970. "La Structure de la Pharsale," *Lucain. Fondation Hardt, Entretiens sur l'antiquité classique.* 15: 1–50.

Martin, H.-J. 1997. *Histoire et pouvoirs de l'écrit.* Paris.

Martin, R. P. 1984. "Hesiod, Odysseus, and the instruction of princes," *Transactions of the American Philological Association* 114: 29–48.

—— 1989. *The Language of Heroes: Speech and Performance in the Iliad.* Ithaca, NY.

—— 1993. "Telemachus and the last hero song," *Colby Quarterly* 29: 222–40.

—— 1997. "Similes and performance," in E. Bakker and A. Kahane (eds.) *Written Voices, Spoken Signs: Tradition, Performance, and the Epic Text*, pp. 138–66. Cambridge, MA.

—— 2000. "Synchronic aspects of Homeric performance: the evidence of the Hymn to Apollo," in M. González de Tobia (ed.) *Una nueva visión de la cultura griega antigua hacia el fin del milenio*, pp. 403–24. La Plata, Argentina.

—— 2001. "Rhapsodizing Orpheus," *Kernos* 14: 23–33.

Martindale, C. A. 1976. "Paradox, hyperbole and literary novelty in Lucan's *De bello civili*," *Bulletin of the Institute of Classical Studies* 23: 45–54.

—— 1984a. "The Politician Lucan," *Greece & Rome* 31: 64–79.

—— 1984b. *Virgil and his influence.* Bristol.

—— (ed.) 1988. *Ovid Renewed.* Cambridge.

—— 1993. *Redeeming the Text: Latin Poetry and the Hermeneutics of Reception.* Cambridge.

—— (ed.) 1997. *The Cambridge Companion to Virgil.* Cambridge.

Marzolph, U. 2002. "The Persian national epic in between tradition and ideology," in Honko 2002a: 276–93.

Mason, Herbert (trans.) 2003 [1970]. *Gilgamesh: A Verse Narrative.* Boston.

Masson, E. 1974. *Cyprominoica.* Göteborg.

Masson, O. 1983. *Les Inscriptions chypriotes syllabiques*, 2nd edn. Paris.

Masters, J. 1992. *Poetry and Civil War in Lucan's* Bellum civile. Cambridge.

—— 1994. "Deceiving the reader: the political mission of Lucan's *Bellum civile 7*," in J. Elsner and J. Masters, *Reflections of Nero: Culture, History, and Representation*, pp. 151–77. Chapel Hill.

Matasović, R. 1996. *A Theory of Textual Reconstruction in Indo-European Linguistics.* Frankfurt am Main.

Matier, K. O. 1989a. "Hannibal: the real hero of the *Punica*?," *Acta Classica* 32: 3–17.

—— 1989b. *Silius Italicus at Bay: Pliny, Prejudice and the Punica.* Durban.

—— 1990. "Stoic philosophy in Silius Italicus," *Akroterion* 35: 68–72.

—— 1991. "The influence of Ennius on Silius Italicus," *Akroterion* 36: 153–8.

Matthews, J. 1975. *Western Aristocracies and Imperial Court AD 364–425.* Oxford.

—— 1992. "The poetess Proba and fourth-century Rome: questions of interpretation," in M. Christol et al. (eds.) *Institutions, société, et vie politique dans l'empire Romain au IVe siècle ap. J.-C.*, pp. 277–304. Paris and Rome.

Mayer, K. 1996. "Helen and the Dios Boulê," *American Journal of Philology* 117: 1–15.

Mayer, R. 1990. "The epic of Lucretius," *Papers of the Leeds International Latin Seminar* 6: 35–43.

Mehmel, F. 1934. *Valerius Flaccus.* Hamburg.

Meid, W. 1978. *Dichter und Dichtkunst in indogermanischer Zeit: Einige allgemeine Gedanken zum Problem der indogermanischen Dichtersprache und der sprachlichen Tradition überhaupt.* Innsbruck.

Meier, S. A. 1986. "Baal's fight with Yam (KTU 1.2.I, IV). A part of the Baal myth as known in KTU 1.1, 3–6?," *Ugarit-Forschungen* 18: 241–54.

Meier-Brügger, M. 2003. *Indo-European Linguistics*, trans. C. Gertmenian. Berlin. (German original 2002, 8th edn.)

Meillet, A. 1921, 1936. *Linguistique historique et linguistique générale*, vols. I, II. Paris.

—— 1923. *Les Origines indo-européennes des mètres grecs.* Paris.

—— 1925. *La Méthode comparative en linguistique historique.* Oslo.

Meillet, A. 1967. *The Comparative Method in Historical Linguistics*, trans. G. B. Ford, Jr. Paris.

Melchert, H. C. 1995. "Indo-European languages of Anatolia," in J. Sasson 1995: 2151–9.

—— 1998. "Poetic meter and phrasal stress in Hittite," in Jasanoff et al. 1998: 483–94.

—— 2003. "Prehistory," in H. C. Melchert (ed.) *The Luwians*, pp. 8–26. Leiden.

Mellink, M. J. (ed.) 1986. *Troy and the Trojan War: A Symposium held at Bryn Mawr College, October 1984.* Bryn Mawr.

—— 1995. "Homer, Lycia, and Lukka," in Carter and Morris 1995: 33–43.

Melville, R. (trans.) 1997. *Lucretius: On the Nature of the Universe.* Oxford.

Mendell, C. W. 1924. "Silius the reactionary," *Philological Quarterly* 3: 92–106.

Merkelbach, R. 1952. "Die pisistratische Redaktion der homerischen Gedichte," *Rheinisches Museum*, n.s. 95: 23–47.

Merkelbach, R., and M. L. West. (eds.) 1967. *Fragmenta Hesiodea.* Oxford.

Merrill, A. L. 1968. "The House of Keret: a study of the Keret legend," *Svensk Exegetisk Årsbok* 33: 5–17.

Merrill, R. (trans.) 2002. *The Odyssey of Homer.* Ann Arbor, MI.

Meuli, K. 1921. *Odyssee und Argonautica.* Berlin.

Meyer, D. 2001. "Apollonius as a Hellenistic geographer," in T. D. Papanghelis and A. Rengakos (eds.) *A Companion to Apollonius Rhodius*, pp. 217–35. Leiden.

Meyer, E. 1969. *Heinrich Schliemann: Kaufmann und Forscher.* Göttingen.

Meyers, E. M. (ed.) 1997. *Oxford Encyclopedia of Archaeology of the Near East.* Oxford.

Mezzanotte, A. 1995. "Echi del mondo contemporaneo in Silio Italico," *Rendiconti dell'Istituto Lombardo* 129: 357–88.

Michalowski, P. 1983. "History as charter: more observations on the Sumerian king list," *Journal of the American Oriental Society* 103: 237–48.

—— 1988. "Divine heroes and historical self-representation: from Gilgamesh to Shulgi," *Bulletin of the Society of Mesopotamian Studies* 16: 19–23.

—— 1989. *The Lamentation over the Destruction of Sumer and Ur.* Winona Lake, MN.

—— 1992. "Orality, literacy and early Mesopotamian literature," in Vogelzang and Vanstiphout 1992: 227–45.

—— 1995. "Sumerian literature: an overview," in J. Sasson 1995: 2279–91.

—— 1996. "Ancient poetics," in Vogelzang and Vanstiphout 1996: 141–53.

—— 2003. "A man called Enmebaragesi," in W. Sallaberger, K. Volk, and A. Zgoll (eds.) *Literatur, Politik und Recht in Mesopotamien: Festschrift für Claus Wilcke.* Orientalia Biblica et Christiana 14, pp. 195–208. Wiesbaden.

Milik, J. T. 1976. *The Books of Enoch.* Oxford.

Miller, P. D. 1973. *The Divine Warrior in Early Israel.* Cambridge, MA.

—— 2000. *The Religion of Ancient Israel.* Louisville, KY.

Millett, P. 1984. "Hesiod and his world," *Proceedings of the Cambridge Philological Society* 210 (n.s. 30): 84–115.

Mills, D. H. 2002. *The Hero and the Sea: Patterns of Chaos in Ancient Myth.* Wauconda, IL.

Milne, P. J. 1988. *Vladimir Propp and the Study of Structure in the Hebrew Bible.* Bible and Literature Studies 13. Sheffield.

Minavi, M. (ed.) 1932. *The Letter of Tansar.* Tehran.

Minchin, E. 1996. "The performance of lists and catalogues in the Homeric epics," in I. Worthington (ed.) *Voice into Text: Orality and Literacy in Ancient Greece*, pp. 3–20. Leiden, New York, and Cologne.

—— 2001. *Homer and the Resources of Memory: Some Applications of Cognitive Theory to the* Iliad *and the* Odyssey. Oxford.

—— 2002. "Speech acts in the everyday world and in Homer: the rebuke as a case study," in I. Worthington and J. M. Foley (eds.) *Epea and Grammata: Oral and Written Communication in Ancient Greece*, pp. 71–97. Leiden, Boston, and Cologne.

Minorsky, V. 1964. "The older preface to the Shāh-nāma," in *Iranica: Twenty Articles.* Publications of the University of Tehran 755, pp. 260–74.

Mitchell, S. 1991. *Heroic Sagas and Ballads.* Ithaca, NY.

Mitchell, S., and G. Nagy (eds.) 2000. New Introduction to Lord 1960, in Lord 2000: vii–xxix.

Mitsis, P. 1994. "Committing philosophy to the reader: didactic coercion and reader autonomy in *De rerum natura*," in A. Schiesaro, P. Mitsis, and J. S. Clay (eds.) *Mega Nepios: The Addressee in Didactic Epic*, pp. 111–28. Pisa.

Mohl, J. (ed.) 1838–78. *Le Livre des rois*, 7 vols. Paris.

Molé, M. 1951. "Garshāsp et les Sagsār," *La Nouvelle Clio* 3: 128–38.

—— 1952, 1953. "Le partage du monde dans la tradition iranienne," *Journal Asiatique* 240: 455–63; "Note complémentaire," *Journal Asiatique* 241: 271–3.

—— 1953. "L'epopée iranienne après Firdosi," *La Nouvelle Clio* 5: 377–93.

—— 1960. "Deux notes sur le Rāmāyaṇa. I: L'initiation guerrière de Rāma et celle de Rustam," *Collection Latomus* 45 (*Hommages à Georges Dumézil*): 140–50.

—— 1963. *Le Problème zoroastrien*. Paris.

—— 1967. *La Légende de Zoroastre*. Paris.

Momigliano, A. 1957. "Perizonius, Niebuhr and the character of early Roman tradition," *Journal of Roman Studies* 47: 104–14.

—— 1974. *Quinto contributo alla storia degli studi classici e del mondo antico*. Rome.

—— 1984. "Reconcile Greeks and Trojans," in *Settimo contributo alla storia degli studi classici e del mondo antico*, pp. 437–62. Rome.

Mondi, R. 1984. "The ascension of Zeus and the composition of Hesiod's *Theogony*," *Greek, Roman, and Byzantine Studies* 25: 325–44.

—— 1990. "Greek mythic thought in the light of the Near East," in L. Edmunds (ed.) *Approaches to Greek Myth*, pp. 142–98. Baltimore.

Mondino, M. 1958. *Su alcune fonti di Quinto Smirneo*. Turin.

Monro, D. B. (ed.) 1901. *Homer's Odyssey: XIII–XXIV*. Oxford.

Monro, D. B., and T. W. Allen. (eds.) 1920. *Homeri Opera* I–V, 3rd edn. Oxford.

Montanari, F. (ed.) 2002. *Omero tremila anni dopo*. Rome.

Moon, W. G. (ed.) 1983. *Ancient Greek Art and Iconography*. Madison, WI.

Mooney, G. W. 1912. *The Argonautica of Apollonius Rhodius*. Dublin.

Moran, W. L. 1987. "Some considerations of form and interpretation in *Atra-Hasis*," in F. Rochberg-Halton (ed.) *Language, Literature, and History: Philological and Historical Studies Presented to Erica Reiner*, pp. 245–55. New Haven, CT.

—— 1991. "The Epic of Gilgamesh: a document of ancient humanism," *Canadian Society for Mesopotamian Studies* 22: 15–22.

—— 1995. "The Gilgamesh epic: a masterpiece from ancient Mesopotamia," in J. Sasson 1995: 2327–36.

Moreau, A. 1994. *Le Mythe de Jason et Médée: Le va-nu-pied et la sorcière*. Collection Verité des Mythes. Paris.

Morford, M. P. O. 1967. *The Poet Lucan: Studies in Rhetorical Epic*. Oxford.

Morgan, J. R. (trans.) 1989. "Heliodorus: an Ethiopian story," In B. P. Reardon (ed.) *Collected Ancient Greek Novels*, pp. 349–588. Berkeley.

Morgan, T. J. 1998. *Literate Education in the Hellenistic and Roman Worlds*. Cambridge.

Morpurgo Davies, A. 1998. *History of Linguistics*, ed. G. Lepschy, vol. 4: *Nineteenth-century Linguistics*. London.

Morris, I. 1986. "The use and abuse of Homer," *Classical Antiquity*, 5: 81–138.

—— 1988. "Tomb cult and the Greek Renaissance: the past in the present in the eighth century BC," *Antiquity* 62: 750–61.

Morris, I., and B. Powell (eds.) 1997. *A New Companion to Homer*. Leiden and New York.

Morris, S. P. 1989. "A tale of two cities: the miniature frescoes from Thera and the origins of Greek poetry," *American Journal of Archaeology* 93: 511–35.

—— 1992. *Daidalos and the Origins of Greek Art*. Princeton, NJ.

—— 1997. "Homer and the Near East," in Morris and Powell 1997: 599–623.

Most, G. W. 1989. "Cornutus and Stoic allegoresis: a preliminary report," in *Aufstieg und Niedergang der römischen Welt*, 2.36.3, pp. 2014–65. Berlin.

—— 1992. "*Disiecti membra poetae*: the rhetoric of dismemberment in Neronian poetry," in R. Hexter and D. Selden (eds.) *Innovations of Antiquity*, pp. 391–419. New York.

—— 2001. "Memory and forgetting in the *Aeneid*," *Vergilius* 47: 148–70.

Moulton, R. G. 1896. *The Literary Study of the Bible: An Account of the Leading Forms of Literature Represented in the Sacred Writings.* Boston.

Mowinckel, S. 1935. "Hat es ein israelitisches Nationalepos gegeben?," *Zeitschrift für die alttestamentliche Wissenschaft* 53: 130–52.

Mozley, J. H. (ed. and trans.) 1934. *Valerius Flaccus.* London and Cambridge, MA.

Muecke, F. 1983. "Foreshadowing and dramatic irony in the story of Dido," *American Journal of Philology* 104: 134–55.

Muellner, L. 1996. *The Anger of Achilles: Mēnis in Early Greek Epic.* Ithaca, NY.

Mullen, E. T. 1980. *The Divine Council in Canaanite and Early Hebrew Literature.* Chico, CA.

Munday, J. 2001. *Introducing Translation Studies: Theories and Applications.* London.

Murko, M. 1929. *La Poésie populaire épique en Yougoslavie au début du XXe siècle.* Paris.

—— 1978. "Die Volksepik der bosnischen Mohammedaner," in von See 1978a: 385–98. Originally published in *Zeitschrift des Vereins für Volkskunde* 19 (1909): 13–30.

Murnaghan, S, 1987. *Disguise and Recognition in the* Odyssey. Princeton, NJ.

Murray, A. T. (trans.) 1995. *The Odyssey,* 2 vols., 2nd edn., rev. by G. E. Dimock. Loeb Classical Library. Cambridge, MA.

—— (trans.) 1999. *Iliad,* 2 vols., 2nd edn., rev. by W. F. Wyatt. Loeb Classical Library. Cambridge, MA.

Murray, G. 1934. *The Rise of the Greek Epic,* 4th edn. Oxford.

Murray, O. (ed.) 1990. *Sympotica: A Symposium on the Symposium.* Oxford.

M-W. 1967. *Fragmenta Hesiodea,* ed. R. Merkelbach and M. L. West. Oxford.

Myers, K. S. 1994. *Ovid's Causes.* Ann Arbor, MI.

Mylonas, G. E. 1966. *Mycenae and the Mycenaean Age.* Princeton, NJ.

Myres, J. 1958. *Homer and His Critics.* London.

Naddaf, G. 1986. "Hésiode, précurseur des cosmogonies grecques de type 'évolutionniste'," *Revue de l'Histoire des Religions* 203: 339–64.

Nadaï, J.-C. de. 2000. *Rhétorique et poétique dans la Pharsale de Lucain: La crise de la représentation dans la poésie antique.* Bibliothèque d'études classiques 19. Leuven.

Nafisi, S., and A. Vullers (eds.) 1934–6. *Shahnama,* 10 vols. Tehran.

Nagler, M. N. 1974. *Spontaneity and Tradition: A Study in the Oral Art of Homer.* Berkeley.

—— 1990. "Discourse and conflict in Hesiod," *Ramus* 21: 88–90.

Nagy, G. 1974. *Comparative Studies in Greek and Indic Meter.* Cambridge, MA.

—— 1979a. *The Best of the Achaeans: Concepts of the Hero in Archaic Greek Poetry.* Baltimore. 2nd edn., 1999.

—— 1979b. "On the origins of the Greek hexameter: synchronic and diachronic perspectives," in B. Brogyanyi (ed.) *Studies in Diachronic, Synchronic, and Typological Linguistics: Festschrift for Oswald Szemerényi on the Occasion of his 65th Birthday,* pp. 611–31. Amsterdam.

—— 1989. "Early Greek views of poets and poetry," in G. Kennedy (ed.) *The Cambridge History of Literary Criticism,* vol. 1: *Classical Criticism,* pp. 1–77. Cambridge.

—— 1990a. *Greek Mythology and Poetics.* Ithaca, NY.

—— 1990b. "Hesiod and the poetics of pan-Hellenism," in Nagy 1990a: 36–82.

—— 1990c. *Pindar's Homer: The Lyric Possession of an Epic Past.* Baltimore.

—— 1992. Introduction to Homer, *The Iliad,* trans. R. Fitzgerald. Everyman's Library no. 60, pp. v–xxi. New York.

—— 1994. "The name of Apollo: etymology and essence," in Solomon 1994: 3–7.

—— 1996a. "Homeric convergences and divergences in early Greek poetry and song," in M. Fantuzzi and R. Pretagostini (eds.) *Struttura e storia dell'esametro greco,* vol. 2, pp. 63–110. Rome.

—— 1996b. *Homeric Questions.* Austin.

—— 1996c. *Poetry as Performance: Homer and Beyond.* Cambridge.

—— 1997. "Homeric scholia," in Morris and Powell 1997: 101–22.

—— 1998. "Is there an etymology for the dactylic hexameter?," in Jasanoff et al. 1998: 495–508.

—— 1999a. "As the world runs out of breath: metaphorical perspectives on the heavens and the atmosphere in the ancient world," in Ker et al. 1999: 37–50.

—— 1999b. "Epic as genre," in Beissinger et al. 1999: 21–32.

—— 1999c. Review of Vielle 1996, *Classical Review* 49: 279–80.

—— 2001a. "Eléments orphiques chez Homère," *Kernos* 14: 1–9.

—— 2001b. "Homeric poetry and problems of multiformity: the 'panathenaic bottleneck'," *Classical Philology* 96: 109–19.

—— 2001c. "The sign of the hero: a prologue," in Maclean and Aitken 2001: xv–xxxv.

—— 2002. *Plato's Rhapsody and Homer's Music: The Poetics of the Panathenaic Festival in Classical Athens.* Cambridge, MA.

—— 2003. *Homeric Responses.* Austin.

Nagy, J. F. 1985. *The Wisdom of the Outlaw: The Boyhood Deeds of Finn in Gaelic Narrative Tradition.* Los Angeles and Berkeley.

—— 1986. "Orality in medieval Irish literature: an overview," *Oral Tradition* 1: 272–301.

Narducci, E. 1979. *La provvidenza crudele: Lucano e la distruzione dei miti augustei.* Pisa.

—— 1985. "Ideologia e tecnica allusiva nella *Pharsalia*," in *Aufsteig und Niedergang der römischen Welt* II.32.3: 1538–64.

—— 1999. "Deconstructing Lucan, ovvero le nozze (coi fichi secchi) di Ermete Trismegisto e di Filologia," in Esposito and Nicastri 1999: 349–87.

Natzel, S. 1992. *Klea Gunaikon: Frauen in der Argonautika des Apollonios Rhodios.* Trier.

Nelis, D. P. 1991. "Iphias: Apollonius Rhodius, *Argonautica* 1.311–16," *Classical Quarterly* 41: 96–105

—— 1992. "Demodocus and the song of Orpheus: Ap. Rhod. *Arg.* 1.496–511," *Museum Helveticum* 49: 153–70.

—— 2000. "Apollonius Rhodius and the traditions of Latin epic poetry," in M. A. Herder, G. Wakker, and R. Regtuit (eds.) *Apollonius Rhodius.* Hellenistica Groningana 4, pp. 85–103. Leuven.

Nelson, S. 1997. "The justice of Zeus in Hesiod's fable of the hawk and the nightingale," *Classical Journal* 92: 235–47.

—— 1998. *God and the Land: The Metaphysics of Farming in Hesiod and Vergil.* Oxford.

Nesselrath, H.-G. 1986. "Zu den Quellen des Silius Italicus," *Hermes* 114: 203–30.

Neu, E. 1988. "Varia Hurritica: Sprachliche Beobachtungen an der hurritisch-hethitischen Bilingue aus Ḫattuša," in E. Neu and C. Rüster (eds.) *Documentum Asiae Minoris Antiquae: Festschrift für Heinrich Otten zum 75. Geburtstag*, pp. 235–54. Wiesbaden.

—— 1996. *Das hurritische Epos der Freilassung I. Untersuchungen zu einem hurritisch-hethitischen Textensemble aus Ḫattuša.* Wiesbaden.

Neumann, G. 1999. "Wie haben die Troer im 13. Jahrhundert gesprochen?," *Würzburger Jahrbücher für die Altertumswissenschaft* 23: 15–23.

Neville, J. 1977. "Herodotus on the Trojan War," *Greece and Rome* 24: 3–12.

Newman, F. W. 1905 [1861]. "Homeric translation in theory and practice: a reply to Matthew Arnold," in *On Translating Homer by Matthew Arnold, with F. W. Newman's "Homeric Translation" and Arnold's "Last Words,"* pp. 112–216. London.

Newman, J. K. 1986. *The Classical Epic Tradition.* Madison, WI.

Nicol, J. 1936. *The Historical and Geographical Sources Used by Silius Italicus.* Oxford.

Niditch, S. 1987. *Underdogs and Tricksters. A Prelude to Biblical Folklore.* San Francisco.

—— 1989. "Eroticism and death in the tale of Jael," in P. L. Day (ed.) *Gender and Difference in Ancient Israel*, pp. 43–57. Minneapolis.

—— 1990. "Samson as culture hero, trickster, and bandit: the empowerment of the weak," *Catholic Biblical Quarterly* 52: 608–24.

—— 1993a. *Folklore and the Hebrew Bible.* Minneapolis.

—— 1993b. *War in the Hebrew Bible: A Study in the Ethics of Violence.* New York.

—— 1996. *Oral World and Written Word: Ancient Israelite Literature.* Louisville, KY.

—— 1997. *Ancient Israelite Religion.* Oxford and New York.

Niebuhr, B. G. 1811. *Römische Geschichte.* Vol. 1. Berlin.

Niemeier, W.-D. 1999. "Mycenaeans and Hittites in war in western Asia Minor," in R. Laffineur (ed.) *Polemos: Le contexte guerrier en Egée à l'Age du Bronze*, Aegaeum 19, pp. 141–55. Liège and Austin.

Niemeyer, H. G. 1984. "Die Phönizier und die Mittelmeerwelt im Zeitalter Homers," *Jahrbuch des Römisch-Germanischen Zentralmuseums* 31: 1–94.

Niemeyer, K. A. E. 1883–4. *Ueber die Gleichnisse bei Quintus Smyrnaeus.* Programm Zwickau.

Nilsson, M. P. 1933. *Homer and Mycenae.* London.

Nishimura-Jensen, J. M. 1996. "Tragic epic or epic tragedy? Narrative and genre in Apollonius' *Argonautica.*" Dissertation, University of Wisconsin.

Nodes, D. 1984. "Avitus of Vienne's spiritual history and the semipelagian controversy," *Vigiliae Christianae* 38: 185–95.

—— 1985. *Avitus: The Fall of Man. De spiritalis historiae gestis libri I–III. Edited from Laon, Bibliothèque Municipale, Ms. 273.* Toronto.

—— 1993. *Doctrine and Exegesis in Biblical Latin Poetry.* Leeds.

Noegel, S. B. 1991. "A Janus parallelism in the Gilgamesh flood story," *Acta Sumerologica* 13: 419–21.

—— 1993. "Fictional Sumerian autobiographies," *Journal of the Association of Graduates in Near Eastern Studies* 4: 46–53.

—— 1994. "An asymmetrical Janus parallelism in the Gilgamesh flood story," *Acta Sumerologica* 16: 306–08.

—— 1995. "Another Janus parallelism in the Atra-Hasis epic," *Acta Sumerologica* 17: 342–4.

—— 1997. "Raining terror: another wordplay cluster in Gilgamesh tablet XI (Assyrian Version, ll. 45–7)," *Nouvelles Assyriologiques Brèves et Utilitaires,* 75: 39–40.

Nöldeke, T. 1894–1904. "Das iranische Nationalepos," *Grundriss der iranischen Philologie,* 2: 130–211. Repr. in C. Bartholomae et al. (eds.) *The Iranian National Epic,* trans. L. Bogdanov. Cama Oriental Institute 7. Bombay, 1930.

—— (ed.) 1879. *Geschichte der Perser und Araber: aṭ-Ṭabarî.* Leiden.

—— 1944. "Ein Beitrag zur Schahname-Forschung," In *Hazâra-ye Ferdowsi,* pp. 58–63. Tehran.

Norden, Eduard. 1966. "Virgil's Aeneis im Lichte ihrer Zeit," in B. Kytzler (ed.) *Kleine Schriften zum klassischen Altertum,* pp. 358–421. Berlin. Originally published 1901 in *Neue Jahrbücher für das klassische Altertum* 7: 249–82, 313–34.

Nordera, R. 1969. "I virgilianismi in Valerio Flacco," in A. Traina (ed.) *Contributi a tre poeti latini,* pp. 1–92. Bologna.

Notopoulos, J. A. 1962. "The Homeric hymns as oral poetry: a study of the post-Homeric oral tradition," *American Journal of Philology* 83: 337–68.

—— 1964. "Studies in early Greek oral poetry," *Harvard Studies in Classical Philology* 68: 1–77.

Noy, D. 1963. "Riddles in the wedding meal," *Maḥanayim* 83: 64–71 (in Hebrew).

Nugent, S. G. 1985. *Allegory and Poetics: The Structure and Imagery of Prudentius' Psychomachia.* Frankfurt.

—— 1992. "Vergil's 'Voice of Women' in *Aeneid V,*" *Arethusa* 25: 255–92.

—— 1994. "*Mater* matters: the female in Lucretius' *De rerum natura,*" *Colby Quarterly* 30: 179–205.

—— 1996. "Statius' Hypsipyle: following in the footsteps of the *Aeneid,*" *Scholia* 5: 46–71.

Nyberg, H. S. 1938. *Die Religion des alten Iran,* trans. H. H. Schaeder. Leipzig.

O'Brien, J. V. 1993. *The Transformation of Hera: A Study of Ritual, Hero, and the Goddess in the Iliad.* Lanham, MD.

Ó Cathasaigh, T. 1977. *The Heroic Biography of Cormac mac Airt.* Dublin.

O'Donnell, J. J. 1998. *Avatars of the Word: From Papyrus to Cyberspace.* Cambridge, MA.

Ogilvie, R. M. 1965. *A Commentary on Livy, Books 1–5.* Oxford.

O'Gorman, E. 1995. "Shifting ground: Lucan, Tacitus and the landscape of civil war," *Hermathena* 158: 117–31.

O'Higgins, D. 1988. "Lucan as *Vates,*" *Classical Antiquity* 7: 208–26.

Oinas, F. (ed.) 1978. *Heroic Epic and Saga.* Bloomington, IN.

Okpewho, I. 1975. *The Epic in Africa: Toward a Poetics of the Oral Performance.* New York. Repr. 1979.

—— 1992. *African Oral Literature: Backgrounds, Character, and Continuity.* Bloomington, IN.

Olearius, A. 1656. *Vermehrte Neue Beschreibung der Muscowitischen und Persischen Reyse.* Schleswig. Repr. 1971, Tübingen.

Oliensis, E. 1999. "Sons and lovers: sexuality and gender in Virgil's poetry," in C. Martindale (ed.) *The Cambridge Companion to Virgil*, pp. 294–311. Cambridge.

Opie, I. and P. 1974. *The Classic Fairy Tales*. London.

Opland, J. 1983. *Xhosa Oral Poetry: Aspects of a Black South African Tradition*. Cambridge.

Oppenheim, A. L. 1964. *Ancient Mesopotamia: Portrait of a Dead Civilization*. Chicago and London. 2nd edn. 1977.

—— 1969. "The Story of Idrimi, King of Alalakh," in J. B. Pritchard, (ed.) *Ancient Near Eastern Texts Relating to the Old Testament*, 3rd edn., pp. 557–8. Princeton.

Orlin, L. 1970. *Assyrian Colonies in Cappadocia*. The Hague.

Ormand, K. 1994. "Lucan's *auctor vix fidelis*," *Classical Antiquity* 13: 38–55.

Osborne, R. 1996. *Greece in the Making, 1200–479 BC*. London and New York.

Otis, B. 1963. *Virgil: A Study in Civilized Poetry*. Oxford.

—— 1970. *Ovid as an Epic Poet*, 2nd edn. Cambridge.

Otten, H. 1958. "Die erste Tafel des hethitischen Gilgamesch-Epos," *Istanbuler Mitteilungen* 8: 93–125.

—— 1973. *Eine althethitische Erzählung um die Stadt Zalpa*. Wiesbaden.

Otto, W. F. 1954. *The Homeric Gods: The Scriptural Significance of Greek Religion*, trans. M. Hadas. New York.

Pache, C. O. 2004. *Baby and Child Heroes in Ancient Greece*. Urbana, IL.

Paduano, G. 1972. *Studi su Apollonio Rodio*. Rome.

Paduano, G., and M. Fusillo. 1986. *Apollonio Rhodio: Le Argonautiche*. Milan.

Pagán, V. 2000. "The mourning after: Statius' *Thebaid* 12," *American Journal of Philology* 121: 423–52.

Page, D. L. 1959. *History and the Homeric Iliad*. Sather Classical Lectures 31. Berkeley.

—— (ed.) 1962. *Poetae Melici Graecae*. Oxford.

—— 1964a. "Archilochus and the oral tradition," *Archiloque: Entretiens sur l'Antiquité Classique* 10: 117–79.

—— 1964b. "Homer and the Trojan War," *Journal of Hellenic Studies* 84: 17–20.

—— 1973. *Folktales in Homer's "Odyssey."* Cambridge, MA.

—— 1977. "Naqqâli and Ferdowsi: creativity in the Iranian national tradition," Dissertation, University of Pennsylvania.

Page, M. E. 1979. "Professional story telling in Iran: transmission and practice," *Iranian Studies* 12: 195–215.

Pagliaro, A. 1940. "Lo zoroastrismo e la formazione dell'epopea iranica," *Annali, Istituto Univers. Orientale di Napoli*, n.s. 1: 241–51.

Palaima, T. G. 2004. "Sacrificial feasting in the Linear B documents," *Hesperia* 73: 217–46.

Papanghelis, T. D. and A. Rengakos (eds.) 2001. *A Companion to Apollonius Rhodius*. Leiden.

Papathomopoulos, M. 2002. *Concordantia in Quinti Smyrnaei Posthomerica*. Hildesheim.

Paratore, E. 1966. *Seneca e Lucano (nel diciannovesimo centenario della morte): Conferenza tenuta nella seduta pubblica a classi riunite del 16 aprile 1966*, Problemi attuali di scienza e di cultura, Quaderni 88. Rome.

—— 1982. "Néron et Lucain dans l'exorde de la *Pharsale*," in J.-M. Croisille and P.-M. Fauchère (eds.) *Neronia 1977: Actes du 2e Colloque de la Société internationale des études néroniennes, Clermont-Ferrand, 27–8 mai 1977*, pp. 93–101. Clermont-Ferrand.

Pardee, D. 1997a. "The 'Aqhatu legend," in Hallo and Younger 1997: vol. 1, 343–56.

—— 1997b. "The Ba'lu myth," in Hallo and Younger 1997: vol. 1, 241–74.

—— 1997c. "The Kirta Epic," in Hallo and Younger 1997: vol. 1, 333–43.

Parker, S. B. 1977. "The historical composition of *KRT* and the cult of El," *Zeitschrift für die Alttestamentliche Wissenschaft* 89: 161–75.

—— 1989. *The Pre-Biblical Narrative Tradition: Essays on the Ugaritic Poems* Keret *and* Aqhat," Society of Biblical Literature, Resources for Biblical Study 24. Atlanta.

—— (ed.) 1997. *Ugaritic Narrative Poetry*. trans. M. S. Smith, S. B. Parker, E. L. Greenstein, T. J. Lewis, and D. Marcus. Society of Biblical Literature, Writings from the Ancient World 9. Atlanta.

Parkes, M. B. 1992. *Pause and Effect*. Berkeley.

Parkinson, R. B. 1997. *The Tale of Sinuhe and other Ancient Egyptian Poems, 1940–1640 BC*. Oxford.

—— 2002. *Poetry and Culture in Middle Kingdom Egypt: A Dark Side to Perfection*. London.

Parpola, S. 1983. "Assyrian library records," *Journal of Near Eastern Studies* 42: 1–29.
—— 1997a. "The man without a scribe," in B. Pongratz-Leisten, H. Kühne, and P. Xella (eds.) *Anašadî Labnani lu allik, Beiträge zu altorientalischen und mittelmeerischen Kulturen. Festschrift für Wolfgang Röllig*, pp. 315–23. Neukirchen-Vluyn.
—— 1997b. *The Standard Babylonian Epic of Gilgamesh*. State Archives of Assyria Cuneiform Texts 1. Helsinki.
—— 1998. "The esoteric meaning of the name Gilgamesh," in J. Prosecky (ed.) *Intellectual Life in the Ancient Near East: Papers Presented at the 43rd Rencontre assyriologique internationale, Prague, July 1–5, 1996*, pp. 315–29. Prague.
Parry, A. (trans.) 1971. "Homeric formulae and Homeric metre" (from *Les Formules et la métrique d'Homère*, Paris, 1928), in M. Parry 1971: 191–239.
Parry, H. 1964. "Violence in a pastoral setting," *Transactions and Proceedings of the American Philological Society* 95: 268–82.
Parry, M. 1971. *The Making of Homeric Verse: The Collected Works of Milman Parry*, ed. A. Parry. Oxford.
Parsons, J. 1999. "A new approach to the Saturnian verse and its relation to Latin prosody," *Transactions of the American Philological Association* 129: 117–37.
Paschal, G. W. 1904. *A Study of Quintus of Smyrna*. Chicago.
Pasquali, G. 1981. "Prefazione dell'editore," in D. Comparetti, *Virgilio nel Medioevo*, pp. xv–xxxiv. Florence.
Patterson, A. 1987. *Pastoral and Ideology, Virgil to Valéry*. Berkeley.
Patzek, B. 1992. *Homer und Mykene: Mündliche Dichtung und Geschichtsschreibung*. Munich.
—— 1996. "Homer und der Orient," in U. Magen and M. Rashad (eds.) *Vom Halys zum Euphrat: Thomas Beran zu Ehren*, pp. 215–25. Münster.
Patzer, H. 1952. "Rhapsoidos," *Hermes* 80: 314–24.
Pavese, C. O. 1972. *Tradizioni e generi poetici della Grecia arcaica*. Istituto di Filologia Classica, Filologia e Critica 12. Rome.
—— 1974. *Studi sulla tradizione epica rapsodica*. Rome.
—— 1998. "The rhapsodic epic poems as oral and independent poems," *Harvard Studies in Philology* 98: 63–90.
Payton, R. 1991. "The Ulu Burun writing-board set," *Anatolian Studies* 41: 99–106.
Pedersen, J. 1941. "Die KRT Legende," *Berytus* 6: 63–105.
Pedersén, O. 1998. *Archives and Libraries in the Ancient Near East 1500–300 B.C.* Bethesda, MD.
Penglase, C. 1994. *Greek Myths and Mesopotamia: Parallels and Influence in the Homeric Hymns and Hesiod*. London.
Peradotto, J. 1990. *Man in the Middle Voice: Name and Narration in the* Odyssey. Princeton, NJ.
Perkell, C. G. 1981. "On Creusa, Dido, and the quality of victory in Virgil's *Aeneid*," in H. P. Foley (ed.) *Reflections of Women in Antiquity*, pp. 355–78. New York and London.
—— (ed.) 1999. *Reading Vergil's* Aeneid: *An Interpretive Guide*. Norman, OK.
Peruzzi, E. 1998. *Civiltà greca nel Lazio preromano*. Florence.
Pertusi, A. 1964. *Leonzio Pilato fra Petrarca e Boccaccio: Le sue versioni omeriche negli autografi di Venezia e la cultura greca del primo umanesimo*. Civiltà Veneziana Studi 16. Venice.
Peter, H. (ed.) 1993 [1914]. *Historicorum Romanorum Fragmenta*, vol. 1, 2nd edn. by H. Peter. Repr. with bibliographical addenda. Leipzig.
Petersen, D., and M. Woodward. 1977. "Northwest Semitic religion, a study in relational structures," *Ugarit-Forschungen* 9: 233–48.
Petrarca, Francesco. 1985. *Letters on Familiar Matters / Rerum familiarium libri XVII–XXIV*, trans. A. S. Bernardo. Baltimore.
Petrosyan, A. Y. 2002. *The Indo-European and Ancient Near Eastern Sources of the Armenian Epic: Myth and History*. Washington, DC.
Pettinato, G. 1981. *The Archives of Ebla: An Empire Inscribed in Clay*. New York.
Pfeiffer, R. 1953. *Callimachus*, vol. II: *Hymni et Epigrammata*. Oxford.
—— 1968. *A History of Classical Scholarship from the Beginnings to the End of the Hellenistic Age*. Oxford.
—— 1976. *A History of Classical Scholarship 1300–1850*. Oxford.

Pfeiffer, R. H., and W. G. Pollard. 1957. *The Hebrew Iliad: The History of the Rise of Israel under Saul and David: Written during the Reign of Solomon probably by the Priest Ahimaz.* New York.

Pfister, F. 1909, 1912. *Der Reliquienkult im Altertum*, vols. I, II. Giessen.

Phillips, N. 1981. *Sijobang: Sung Narrative Poetry of West Sumatra.* Cambridge.

Pichon, R. 1912. *Les Sources de Lucain.* Paris.

Piemontese, A. 1980. "Nuova luce su Firdawsi: Uno Shâhnâma datato 614H./1217 a Firenze," *Istituto Orientale di Napoli, Annali* 40: 1–38, 189–242.

Pietsch, C. 1999. *Die Argonautika des Apollonios von Rhodos: Untersuchungen zum Problem der einheitlichen Konzeption des Inhalts.* Hermes Einzelschriften 80. Stuttgart.

Pinney, G. F. 1983. "Achilles Lord of Scythia," in Moon 1983: 127–46.

Pinsky, R. (trans.) 1994. *The Inferno of Dante.* New York.

Platnauer, M. 1922. *Claudian*, 2 vols. Loeb Classical Library. Cambridge, MA.

Platner, S. B., and T. Ashby. 1965. *A Topographical Dictionary of Ancient Rome.* Rome.

Pöschl, V. 1950. *Die Dichtkunst Vergils.* Innsbruck. English trans. 1962 by G. Seligson, *The Art of Vergil.* Ann Arbor, MI.

Poliziano, A. 1976 [1867]. *Prose volgari inedite e poesie latine e greche edite e inedite*, ed. I. del Lungo. Hildesheim.

Pollini, E. 1984. "Il motivo della *visendi cupido* nel Giasone di Valerio Flacco," *Maia* 36: 51–61.

Pollmann, K. 2001a. "The transformation of the epic genre in Christian late antiquity," *Studia Patristica* 36: 61–75.

—— 2001b. "Das lateinische Epos in der Spätantike," in J. Rüpke (ed.) *Von Göttern und Menschen erzählen*, pp. 93–129. Stuttgart.

Polvani, A. M. 2003. "Hittite fragments of the Atraḥasīs myth," in *Semitic and Assyriological Studies Presented to Pelio Fronzaroli*, pp. 532–9. Wiesbaden.

Pomeroy, A. J. 1989. "Silius Italicus as 'Doctus Poeta'," *Ramus* 18: 119–40.

—— 2000. "Silius' Rome: the rewriting of Vergil's vision," *Ramus* 29: 149–68.

Pompella, G. 1979. *Quinto Smirneo, Le Postomeriche, libri I–II.* Naples.

—— 1981. *Index in Quintum Smyrnaeum.* Hildesheim.

—— 1987. *Quinto Smirneo, Le Postomeriche, libri III–VII.* Cassino.

—— 1993. *Quinto Smirneo, Le Postomeriche, libri VIII–XIV.* Cassino.

—— 2002. *Quinti Smyrnaei Posthomerica.* Hildesheim.

Pongratz-Leisten, B. 2001: "Überlegungen zum Epos in Mesopotamien am Beispiel der Kutha-Legende," in J. Rüpke (ed.) *Von Göttern und Menschen erzählen: Formkonstanzen und Funktionswandel vormoderner Epik.* Potsdamer altertumswissenschaftliche Beiträge 4, pp. 12–41. Stuttgart.

Poortvliet, H. M. (ed.) 1991. *C. Valerius Flaccus Argonautica Book II.* Amsterdam.

Pope, A. 1943 [1715–20]. *The Iliad of Homer in the English Verse Translation by Alexander Pope, Illustrated with the Classical Designs of John Flaxman.* New York.

Poppe, E. 1995. Introduction, *Imtheachta Aeniasa: The Irish Aeneid.* Irish Texts Society 6. London.

Porada, E. 1981. "The cylinder seals found at Thebes in Boeotia," *Archiv für Orientforschung* 28: 1–70.

Poucet, J. 1985. *Les Origines de Rome: Tradition et histoire.* Brussels.

Pound, E. 1954. *Literary Essays of Ezra Pound*, ed. with intro. T. S. Eliot. Norfolk, CT.

Powell, B. B. 1991. *Homer and the Origin of the Greek Alphabet.* Cambridge.

—— 2002. *Writing and the Origins of Greek Literature.* Cambridge.

Pratt, L. 1993. *Lying and Poetry from Homer to Pindar: Falsehood and Deception in Archaic Greek Poetics.* Ann Arbor, MI.

Preminger, A. (ed.) 1965. *Encyclopedia of Poetry and Poetics.* Princeton, NJ.

Prete, S. 1974. "Paolino di Nola: La parafrasi biblica della *laus Iohannis* (carm. 6)," *Augustinianum* 14: 625–35.

Prins, Y. forthcoming. "Metrical translation: nineteenth-century Homers and the hexameter mania," in S. Bermann and M. Wood (eds.) *Nation, Language, and the Ethics of Translation.* Princeton, NJ.

Pritchard, J. B. (ed.) 1955 [1950]. *Ancient Near Eastern Texts Relating to the Old Testament*, 2nd corrected and enlarged edn. Princeton, NJ. 3rd edn. 1969. 4th edn. 1974.

Psychoundakis, G. (trans.) 1995. *Omêrou Iliada.* Heraklion.

—— (trans.) 1996. *Omêrou Odusseia.* Heraklion.

Pucci, P. 1977. *Hesiod and the Language of Poetry.* Baltimore.
—— 1987. *Odysseus Polytropos: Intertextual Readings in the* Odyssey *and* Iliad. Ithaca, NY.
Puhvel, J. 1984–. *Hittite Etymological Dictionary.* Berlin.
—— 1987. *Comparative Mythology.* Baltimore.
—— 1991. *Homer and Hittite.* Innsbruck.
Putnam, M. 1965. *The Poetry of the Aeneid.* Cambridge. Repr. 1988, Ithaca, NY.
—— 1995. "Possessiveness, sexuality, and heroism in the *Aeneid*," in his *Virgil's Aeneid: Interpretation and Influence*, pp. 27–49. Chapel Hill, NC.
—— 1998. *Virgil's Epic Designs.* New Haven, CT.
—— 2001a. "The ambiguity of art in Virgil's *Aeneid*," *Proceedings of the American Philosophical Society* 145: 162–83.
—— 2001b. "The loom of Latin," *Transactions of the American Philological Association* 131: 329–39.
Qazvini, M. 1944. "Muqaddama-ye qadim-e Shâhnâma," in *Hazâra-ye Ferdowsi*, pp. 123–48. Tehran.
Qazvini, M., and M. Mo'in (eds.) 1953. *Chahâr Maqâla.* Tehran.
Quain, B. H. 1942. *The Flight of the Chiefs: Epic Poetry of Fiji*, Foreword by W. E. Leonard. New York.
Quesnel, S. 1996. *Venance Fortunat. Oeuvres Tome IV: Vie de Saint Martin.* Paris.
Quinn, S. (ed.) 2000. *Why Vergil?* Wauconda, IL.
Quint, D. 1993a. *Epic and Empire. Politics and Generic Form from Virgil to Milton.* Princeton, NJ.
—— 1993b. "Epics of the defeated: the other tradition of Lucan, Ercilla, and D'Aubigné," in Quint 1993a: 131–209.
Raaflaub, K. A. (ed.) 1986. *Social Struggles in Archaic Rome: New Perspectives on the Conflict of the Orders.* Berkeley. 2nd edn. 2005. Oxford.
—— 1987. "Herodotus, political thought, and the meaning of history," in D. Boedeker and J. Peradotto (eds.) *Herodotus and the Invention of History, Arethusa* 20: 221–48.
—— 1991. "Homer und die Geschichte des 8. Jh.s v. Chr," in J. Latacz (ed.) *Zweihundert Jahre Homer-Forschung* pp. 205–56. Stuttgart.
—— 1993. "Homer to Solon: the rise of the polis. The written sources," in M. H. Hansen (ed.) *The Ancient Greek City-State*, pp. 41–105. Copenhagen.
—— 1997a. "Homeric society," in Morris and Powell 1997: 624–48.
—— 1997b. "Soldiers, citizens and the evolution of the early Greek polis," In L. G. Mitchell and P. J. Rhodes (eds.) *The Development of the Polis in Archaic Greece*, pp. 49–59. London.
—— 1998a. "A historian's headache: how to read 'Homeric Society'?," in N. Fisher and H. van Wees (eds.) *Archaic Greece: New Approaches and New Evidence*, pp. 169–93. London.
—— 1998b. "Homer, the Trojan War, and history," *Classical World* 91: 386–403.
—— 2000. "Poets, lawgivers, and the beginnings of political reflection in archaic Greece," in C. Rowe and M. Schofield (eds.) *The Cambridge History of Greek and Roman Political Thought*, pp. 23–59. Cambridge.
—— 2002. "Philosophy, science, politics: Herodotus and the intellectual trends of his time," in E. Bakker, I. de Jong, and H. van Wees (eds.) *Brill's Companion to Herodotus*, pp. 149–86. Leiden.
—— Forthcoming. "Historical approaches to Homer," in S. Deger-Jalkotzy and I. Lemos (eds.) *Ancient Greece from the Mycenaean Palaces to the Age of Homer.* Edinburgh.
Rabel, R. A. 1985. "The Harpies in the *Aeneid*," *Classical Journal* 80: 317–25.
Rathje, A. 1983. "A banquet service from the Latin city of Ficana," *Analecta Romana* 12: 7–29.
—— 1990. "The adoption of the Homeric banquet in central Italy in the orientalizing period," in Murray 1990: 279–88.
Reardon, B. P. 1989. "General Introduction," in B. P. Reardon (ed.) *Collected Ancient Greek Novels*, pp. 1–16. Berkeley.
—— 1991. *The Form Of Greek Romance.* Princeton, NJ.
Redfield, J. 1975. *Nature and Culture in the* Iliad. Chicago.
Reed, J. D. 1998. "The death of Osiris in *Aeneid* 12. 458," *American Journal of Philology* 119: 399–418.
Reed, R. 1972. *Ancient Skins Parchments and Leathers.* London and New York.

Rees, A., and B. Rees. 1961. *Celtic Heritage: Ancient Tradition in Ireland and Wales.* London.

Reichelt, H. (ed.) 1928–31. *Die soghdischen Handschriftenreste des Britischen Museums in Umschrift und mit Übersetzung herausgegeben*, 2 vols. Heidelberg.

Reichl, K. 1992. *Turkic Oral Epic Poetry.* New York.

—— 2000a. *The Oral Epic: Performance and Music.* Berlin.

—— 2000b. *Singing the Past: Turkic and Medieval Poetry.* Ithaca, NY.

—— 2001. *Das usbekische Heldenepos Alpomish. Einführung, Text, Übersetzung.* Wiesbaden.

Reitz, C. 1996. *Zur Gleichnistechnik des Apollonios von Rhodos.* Studien zur klassischen Philologie 99. Frankfurt.

Rengakos, A. 1992. "Zur Biographie des Apollonios von Rhodos," *Wiener Studien* 105: 39–67.

—— 1993. *Der Homertext und die hellenistischen Dichter.* Hermes Einzelschriften 64. Stuttgart.

—— 1994. *Apollonios Rhodios und die antike Homererklärung.* Zetemata 92. Munich.

Renger, J. M. 1978. "Mesopotamian epic literature," in Oinas 1978: 27–48.

Reuss, E. 1881. *Der Geschichte der Heiligen Schriften Alten Testaments.* Braunschweig.

Reusser, C. 1996. "Mars Ultor: Capitolium," in E. M. Steinby (ed.) *Lexicon Topographicum Urbis Romae* vol. 3, pp. 230–1. Rome.

Revard, S. P., and J. K. Newman 1993. "Epic. I. History (Revard) and II. Theory (Newman)," in A. Preminger and T. V. F. Brogan (eds.) *The New Princeton Encyclopedia of Poetry and Poetics*, pp. 361–75. Princeton, NJ.

Reynolds, D. F. 1995. *Heroic Poets, Poetic Heroes: The Ethnography of Performance in an Arabic Oral Epic Tradition.* Ithaca, NY.

—— 1999. "Problematic performances: overlapping genres and levels of participation in Arabic oral epic-singing," in Beissinger et al. 1999: 155–68.

—— 2000. "Creating an epic: from apprenticeship to publication," in Honko 2000b: 263–78.

Reynolds, L. D. 1983. "Virgil," in L. D. Reynolds (ed.) *Texts and Transmission: A Survey of the Latin Classics*, pp. 433–6. Oxford.

Reynolds, L. D., and N. G. Wilson. 1991. *Scribes and Scholars: A Guide to the Transmission of Greek and Latin Literature*, 3rd edn. Oxford.

Rhousopoulos, A. 1855. *Encheiridion tes Hellenikes Arkhaiologias.* Athens.

Ribichini, S., M. Rocchi, and P. Xella (eds.) 2001. *La questione delle influenze vicino-orientali sulla religione greca.* Rome.

Richardson, L., Jr. 1992. *A New Topographical Dictionary of Ancient Rome.* Baltimore.

Richardson, N. J. 1974. *The Homeric Hymn to Demeter.* Oxford.

—— 1992. "Aristotle's reading of Homer and its background," in R. Lamberton and J. J. Keaney (eds.) *Homer's Ancient Readers: The Hermeneutics of Greek Epic's Earliest Exegetes*, pp. 30–40. Princeton, NJ.

—— 1993. *The Iliad: A Commentary, vol. VI: Books 21–24.* Cambridge.

Richlin, A. 1992. "Reading Ovid's rapes," in A. Richlin (ed.) *Pornography and Representation in Greece and Rome*, pp. 158–79. Oxford.

Richter, W. 1960. *Das Epos des Naevius.* Göttingen.

Ridgway, D. 1988. "The Etruscans," in J. Boardman, N. G. L. Hammond, D. M. Lewis, M. Ostwald (eds.) *The Cambridge Ancient History*, 2nd edn, vol. 4. pp. 634–75. Cambridge.

Riemschneider, M. 1957. "Der Stil des Nonnos," *Berliner byzantinische Arbeiten* 5: 46–70.

Rinchindorji. 2001. "Mongolian-Turkic epics: typological formation and development," in Chao 2001a: 381–401.

Ripoll, F. 1998. *La Morale héroïque dans les épopées latines d'époque flavienne: Tradition et innovation.* Louvain.

—— 1999. "Silius Italicus et Valerius Flaccus," *Revue des Études Anciennes* 101: 499–521.

—— 2001. "Le Monde homérique dans les *Punica* de Silius Italicus," *Latomus* 60: 87–107.

Rissman, L. 1983. *Love as War: Homeric Allusion in the Poetry of Sappho.* Königstein.

Riyâhi, M. A. (ed.) 1993. *Sar-Chashma-hâ-ye Ferdowsi Shenâsi.* Tehran.

Roberts, C. H., and T. C. Skeat. 1983. *The Birth of the Codex.* London.

Roberts, M. 1985. *Biblical Epic and Rhetorical Paraphrase in Late Antiquity.* Liverpool.

—— 1989. *The Jeweled Style: Poetry and Poetics in Late Antiquity.* Ithaca, NY.

—— 1993. *Poetry and the Cult of the Martyrs: The Liber Peristephanon of Prudentius.* Ann Arbor, MI.

Roberts, M. 1994. "St. Martin and the leper: narrative variation in the Martin poems of Venantius Fortunatus," *Journal of Medieval Latin* 4: 82–100.

—— 1995. "Martin meets Maximus: the meaning of a late Roman banquet," *Revue des Etudes Augustiniennes* 41: 91–111.

—— 2001. "The last epic of antiquity: generic continuity and innovation in the *Vita Sancti Martini* of Venantius Fortunatus," *Transactions of the American Philological Association* 131: 257–85.

—— 2002. "Creation in Ovid's *Metamorphoses* and the Latin poets of late antiquity," *Arethusa* 35: 403–15.

Roberts, T. 1986. "A study of the similes in late Greek epic." MA thesis, University of Sydney.

Robinson, M. Forthcoming. "Augustan responses to Virgil," in M. J. Clarke, B. G. F. Currie, and R. O. A. M. Lyne (eds.) *The Interactions of Epic*. Oxford.

Rochberg-Halton, F. 1984. "Canonicity in cuneiform texts," *Journal of Cuneiform Studies* 36: 127–44.

Roghair, G. H. (ed.) 1982. *The Epic of Palnadu: A Study and Translation of Palnati Virula Katha, a Telugu Oral Tradition from Andhra Pradesh, India*. New York.

Roller, M. B. 1996. "Ethical contradiction and the fractured community in Lucan's *Bellum civile*," *Classical Antiquity* 15: 319–47.

Röllig, W. (ed.) 1978. *Altorientalische Literaturen*. Neues Handbuch der Literaturwissenschaft 1. Wiesbaden.

—— 1978–90. "Literatur," *Reallexikon der Assyriologie und vorderasiatischen Archäologie* 7: 48–66.

Rollinger, R. 1996. "Altorientalische Motivik in der frühgriechischen Literatur am Beispiel der homerischen Epen," in Ulf 1996: 156–210.

—— 2001. "The ancient Greeks and the impact of the ancient Near East: textual evidence and historical perspective (ca.750–650 B.C.)," in Whiting 2001: 233–64.

Römer, W. H. P. 1980. *Das sumerische Kurzepos "Bilgamesh und Akka": Versuch einer Neubearbeitung*. Kevelaer.

—— 1999. *Die Sumerologie: Einführung in die Forschung und Bibliographie in Auswahl*, 2nd edn. Münster.

Rosati, G. 1994. *Stazio, Achilleid: Introduzione, traduzione e note*. Milan.

—— 1999. "Form in motion: weaving the text in the *Metamorphoses*," in Hardie et al. 1999: 241–53.

—— 2002. "Narrative techniques and narrative structures," in B. Boyd (ed.) *Brill's Companion to Ovid*, pp. 271–30. Leiden.

Rossi, L. E. 1971. "I generi letterari e le loro leggi scritte e non scritte nelle letterature classiche," *Bulletin of the Institute of Classical Studies* 19: 69–94.

Rouse, W. H. D. (trans.) 1937. *Homer: The Story of Odysseus*. New York.

—— (trans.) 1938. *Homer: The Story of Achilles*. New York. Repr. 1966.

—— 1940. *Nonnus: Dionysiaca*. Loeb Classical Library. Cambridge, MA.

Rousseau, P. 1996. *"Dios d' eteleieto boulé*: Destin des héros et dessein de Zeus dans l'intrigue de l'*Iliade*," Dissertation, University Charles de Gaulle, Lille III.

Roux, G. 1949. *Le Problème des Argonautes: Recherches sur les aspects religieux de la légende*. Paris.

Royston, B. 1991. *Politics and Painting: Murals and Conflict in Northern Ireland*. Rutherford.

Rudich, V. 1997. *Dissidence and Literature under Nero: The Price of Rhetoricization*. London.

Ruijgh, C. 1957. *L'élément achéen dans la langue épique*. Assen.

—— 1989. "La langue et l'écriture," in R. Treuil, P. Darcque, J.-C. Poursat, and G. Touchais (eds.) *Les Civilisations égéennes du Néolithique et de l'Age de Bronze*, pp. 569–84. Paris.

—— 1995. "D'Homère aux traditions proto-mycéniennes de la tradition épique," in J. P. Crielaard (ed.) *Homeric Questions*, pp. 1–92. Amsterdam.

—— 1997. "La date de la création de l'alphabet grec et celle de l'épopée homérique," *Bibliotheca Orientalis* 54: 533–603.

Rüpke, J. 2000. "Räume literarischer Kommunikation in der Formierungsphase römischer Literatur," in M. Braun et al. (eds.) *Moribus antiquis res stat Romana: Römische Werte und römische Literatur im 3. und 2. Jh. v. Chr.* Beiträge zur Altertumskunde, 134, pp. 31–52. Leipzig.

—— 2001a. "Kulturtransfer als Rekodierung: Zum literarturgeschichtlichen und sozialen Ort der frühen römischen Epik," in Rüpke 2001b: 42–64.

—— (ed.) 2001b. *Von Göttern und Menschen erzählen: Formkonstanzen und Funktionswandel vormoderner Epik.* Stuttgart.

Russo, J. 1997. "The formula," in Morris and Powell 1997: 238–60.

Rutherford, I. 2001. "The Song of the Sea (ŠA A.AB.BA SÌR): thoughts on KUB 45.63," in G. Wilhelm (ed.) *Akten des IV. Internationalen Kongresses für Hethitologie Würzburg, 4.-8. Oktober 1999*, pp. 598–609. Wiesbaden.

Rutz, W. 1960. "*Amor Mortis* bei Lucan," *Hermes* 88: 462–73.

—— (ed.) 1970a. *Lucan.* Darmstadt.

—— 1970b. "Lucan und die Rhetorik," in *Lucain. Fondation Hardt, Entretiens sur l'antiquité classique* 15: 233–66.

—— 1985. "Lucans Pharsalia im Lichte der neuesten Forschung (mit einem bibliographischen Nachtrag 1980 bis 1985 von H. Tuitje [Göttingen])," *Aufstieg und Niedergang der römischen Welt* II.32.3, 1457–537.

Rzach, A. 1922. "Kyklos," in G. Wissowa, W. Kroll, K. Mittelhaus, and K. Ziegler (eds.) *Paulys Real-Encyclopädie der classischen Altertumswissenschaft*, vol. 11.2, cols. 2347–435. Stuttgart.

Saada, L. (ed.) 1985. *La Geste hilalienne.* Version de Bou Thadi (Tunisie), recueillie, établie, et traduite de l'arabe par L. Saada, récitation de Mohammed Hsini, préface de Jean Grosjean. Paris.

Sacks, K. 1981. *Polybius on the Writing of History.* Berkeley.

Sadurska, A. 1964. *Les Tables Iliaques.* Warsaw.

Saenger, P. 1997. *Space between Words: The Origins of Silent Reading.* Stanford.

Ṣafâ, D. 1944. *Ḥamâsa sarâ'i dar Irân.* Tehran.

Saggs, H. W. F. 1963. "The Nimrud letters, 1952," *Iraq* 25: 70–80.

Sale, M. 1999. "Virgil's formularity and *Pius Aeneas*," in E. A. Mackay (ed.) *Signs of Orality: The Oral Tradition and its Influence in the Greek and Roman World*, pp. 199–220. Leiden.

Salverda de Grave, J.-J. (ed.) 1964 [1925–9]. *Eneas, roman du XIIe siècle*, 2 vols. Paris.

Salvini, M. 1988. "Die hurritischen Überlieferungen des Gilgameš-Epos und der Kešši-Erzählung," in V. Haas (ed.) *Hurriter und Hurritisch*, pp. 157–72. Constance.

Sandars N. K. (trans.) 1972 [1960]. *The Epic of Gilgamesh.* London.

Sandys, G. 1970 [1632]. *Ovid's Metamorphosis, Englished, Mythologized, and Represented in Figures.* Lincoln, NE.

Sanford, E. M. 1931. "Lucan and his Roman critics," *Classical Philology* 26: 233–57.

Sarkârâti, B. 1975. "Gorz-e niyâ-ye Rostam," in *Nashriya-ye dâneshkada-ye adabiyât o ulum-e ensâni*, pp. 323–38. Tabriz.

—— 1979 [1357]. "Bonyân-e asâtiri hamâsa-ye melli-ye Irân," in *Nashriya-ye dâneshkada-ye adabiyât o ulum-e ensâni*, pp. 1–61. Tabriz.

Sasson, Jack M. 1984. "The biographic mode in Hebrew historiography," in W. B. Barrick and J. R. Spencer (eds.) *In the Shelter of Elyon: Essays on Ancient Palestinian Life and Literature in Honor of G. W. Ahlström* (*Journal for the Study of the Old Testament*, Supplement Series 31), pp. 305–12. Sheffield.

—— 1992. "Gilgamesh epic," in *The Anchor Bible Dictionary*, vol. 2: 1024–7.

—— (ed.) 1995. *Civilizations of the Ancient Near East*, 4 vols. New York. Repr. 2000 in 2 vols., Peabody, MA.

—— 1998. "About 'Mari and the Bible'," *Revue d'Assyriologie* 92: 97–123.

—— 2000. "'The Mother of All etiologies," in S. M. Olyan and R. C. Culley (eds.) *"A Wise and Discerning Mind": Essays in Honor of Burke O. Long.* Brown Judaic Studies 325, pp. 205–20. Providence, RI.

—— 2001. "On reading the diplomatic letters in the Mari archives," *Amurru* 2: 329–38.

Sasson, V. 2001. "The waw consecutive/waw contrastive and the perfect: verb tense, context, and texture," *Zeitschrift für die alttestamentliche Wissenschaft* 113: 602–17.

Saussure, F. de. 1916. *Cours de linguistique générale.* Critical edn. 1972 by T. de Mauro. Paris.

Sax, W. S. 1999. "Worshipping epic villains: a Kaurava cult in the central Himalayas," in Beissinger et al. 1999: 169–86.

—— 2002. *Dancing the Self: Personhood and Performance in the Pândav Lîlâ of Garhwal.* New York.

Saylor, C. 1978. "*Belli spes inproba*: the theme of walls in Lucan, *Pharsalia* VI," *Transactions of the American Philological Association* 108: 243–57.

638

Bibliography

Saylor, C. 1986. "Wine, blood, and water: the imagery of Lucan *Pharsalia* IV.148–401," *Eranos* 84: 149–56.

Scaife, R. 1995. "The *Kypria* and its early reception," *Classical Antiquity* 14: 164–97.

Schachermeyr, F. 1935. *Hethiter und Achäer*. Mitteilungen der Altorientalische Gesellschaft 9. Leipzig.

Schade, G., and P. Eleuteri 2001. "The textual tradition of the Argonautica," in T. D. Papanghelis and A. Rengakos (eds.) *A Companion to Apollonius Rhodius*, pp. 27–49. Leiden.

Schedl, C. 1965. "Das sind die Zeugungen." *Forschungen und Furtschritte* 39: 239–41.

Schefold, K. 1993. *Götter- und Heldensagen der Griechen in der früh- und hocharchaischen Kunst*. München.

Scheid, J., and J. Svenbro 1996. *The Craft of Zeus: Myths of Weaving and Fabric*, trans. C. Volk. Revealing Antiquity 9. Cambridge, MA.

Schein, S. 1984. *The Mortal Hero*. Berkeley.

—— (ed.) 1996. *Reading the Odyssey: Selected Interpretive Essays*. Princeton, NJ.

Schenk, P. 1997. "Handlungsstruktur und Komposition in den *Posthomerica* des Quintus Smyrnaeus," *Rheinisches Museum* 140: 363–85.

Scherer, B. 2002. "Mythos, Katalog und Prophezeiung. Studien zu den Argonautika des Apollonios Rhodios." Dissertation, Leiden.

Scherer, M. 1964. *The Legends of Troy in Art and Literature*. New York.

Schetter, W. 1959. "Die Buchzahl der *Argonautica* des Valerius Flaccus," *Philologus* 103: 297–308.

Scheub, H. 1977. "Body and image in oral narrative performance," *New Literary Criticism* 8: 345–67.

Schiesaro, A. 1990. *Simulacrum et imago: Gli argomenti analogici nel* De rerum natura. Pisa.

Schliemann, H. 1880: *Ilios: The City and Country of the Trojans*. London.

Schmeid, W. 2002. *Giorgio de Chirico: The Endless Journey*. New York.

Schmidt, B. B. 1994. *Israel's Beneficent Dead*. Forschungen zum Alten Testament 11. Tübingen.

—— 1995. "Flood narratives of ancient Western Asia," in J. Sasson 1995: 2337–51.

Schmidt, E. G. 1999. "Quintus von Smyrna – der schlechteste Dichter des Altertums?," *Phasis* 1: 139–50.

Schmidt, M. 2000: "Archaeology and the German public," in H. Härke (ed.) *Archaeology, Ideology and Society: The German Experience*. Gesellschaften und Staaten im Epochenwandel 7, pp. 240–70. Frankfurt am Main.

Schmiel, R. 1986. "The Amazon Queen: Quintus of Smyrna, Book 1," *Phoenix* 40: 185–94.

Schmitt, R. 1967. *Dichtung und Dichtersprache in indogermanischer Zeit*. Wiesbaden.

—— (ed.) 1968. *Indogermanische Dichtersprache*. Darmstadt.

—— 1990. "Zur Sprache der kyklischen *Kypria*," in W. Görler and S. Koster (eds.) *Pratum Saraviense*, pp. 11–24. Stuttgart.

Schnapp, A. 1993. *La Conquête du passé: Aux origines de l'archéologie*. Paris.

Schönberger, O. 1965. "Zum Weltbild der drei Epiker nach Lucan," *Helikon* 5: 123–45.

—— 1970. "Ein Dichter römischer Freiheit: M. Annaeus Lucanus," in *Lucan*, ed. W. Rutz. Wege der Forschung 235, pp. 525–45. Darmstadt.

Schotes, H. A. 1969. *Stoische Physik, Psychologie und Theologie bei Lucan*. Bonn.

Schrader, R., J. Roberts, and J. Makowski. 1987. *Arator's On the Acts of the Apostles (De actibus apostolorum)*. Atlanta.

Schrijvers, P. H. 1970. *Horror ac divina voluptas: Etudes sur la poétique et la poésie de Lucrèce*. Amsterdam.

—— 1989. "Interpréter Lucain par Lucain, *La Pharsale* I, 1–8, II, 234–325," *Mnemosyne* 42: 62–75.

Schröder, W. A. 1971. *M. Porcius Cato, das erste Buch der Origines: Ausgabe und Erklärung der Fragmente*. Meisenheim am Glan.

Schröter, R. 1973. "Die Krise der römischen Republik im Epos Lukans über den Bürgerkrieg," in *Krisen in der Antike: Bewusstsein und Bewältigung, Geschichte und Gesellschaft*, vol. 13, pp. 99ff. Düsseldorf.

SCHS. 1953–. *Serbo-Croatian Heroic Songs* (*Srpskohrvatske junačke pjesme*), vols. 1–2, 3–4, 6, 14. Belgrade and Cambridge, MA.

Schubert, W. 1984. *Jupiter in den Epen der Flavierzeit*. Frankfurt.

—— (ed.) 1999. *Ovid: Werk und Wirkung*. Frankfurt.

Schuchhardt, C. 1891. *Schliemann's Excavations: An Archaeological and Historical Study*, trans. E. Sellers. London.

Scodel, R. 1982. "The Achaean wall and the myth of destruction," *Harvard Studies in Classical Philology* 86: 33–50.

—— 2002. *Listening to Homer: Tradition, Narrative, and Audience*. Ann Arbor, MI.

Scott, J. 1963. *Homer and His Influence*. New York.

Sealey, R. 1957. "From Phemios to Ion," *Revue des Études Grecques* 70: 312–51.

Sedley, D. N. 1998. *Lucretius and the Transformation of Greek Wisdom*. Cambridge.

Seele, Astrid. 1995. *Römische Übersetzer, Nöte, Freiheiten, Absichten: Verfahren des literarischen Übersetzens in der griechisch-römischen Antike*. Darmstadt.

Segal, C. P. 1969. *Landscape in Ovid's Metamorphoses: A Study in the Transformation of a Literary Symbol*. Hermes Einzelschriften 23. Wiesbaden.

—— 1990. *Lucretius on Death and Anxiety: Poetry and Philosophy in* De rerum natura. Princeton, N.J.

—— 1992. "Bard and audience in Homer," in Lamberton and Keaney 1992: 3–29.

—— 1994. *Singers, Heroes, and Gods in the* Odyssey. Ithaca, NY.

—— 1999. "Ovid's Arcadia and the characterization of Jupiter in the *Metamorphoses*," in W. Schubert (ed.) *Ovid: Werk und Wirkung*, pp. 401–12. Frankfurt.

Segre, C. (ed.) 1953. *Volgarizzamenti del Due e Trecento*. Turin.

Serés, G. 1997. *La traducción en Italia y España durante el siglo XV: La* "Ilíada *en romance*" *y su contexto cultural*. Salamanca.

Severyns, A. 1928. *Le Cycle épique dans l'école d'Aristarque*. Liège and Paris.

—— 1938. *Le Codex 239 de Photius*, vols. 1–2 of *Recherches sur la Chrestomathie de Proclos*. Paris.

—— 1953. *La Vita Homeri et les sommaires du Cycle: Etude paléographique et critique*, vol. 3 of *Recherches sur la Chrestomathie de Proclos*. Paris.

—— (ed.) 1963. *La Vita Homeri et les sommaires du Cycle: Texte et traduction*, vol. 4 of *Recherches sur la Chrestomathie de Proclos*. Paris.

Seydou, C. 1983. "Réflexions sur les structures narratives du texte épique: l'exemple des épopées peule et bambara," *L'Homme* 23/3: 41–54.

—— 1990. "Identity and epics: African examples," in L. Honko (ed.) *Religion, Myth, and Folklore in the World's Epics: The Kalevala and its Predecessors*, pp. 403–23. Berlin and New York.

Shackleton Bailey, D. R. (ed. and trans.) 2003. *Statius: Thebaid, Books 1–7*. Cambridge, MA.

Shaffer, A. 1983. "Gilgamesh, the cedar forest, and Mesopotamian history," *Journal of the American Oriental Society* 103: 307–13.

Shahbazi, A. S. 1991. *Ferdowsí: A Critical Biography*. Costa Mesa, CA.

Shåked, S. 1970. "Specimens of Middle Persian verse," in M. Boyce and I. Gerschevitch (eds.) *W. B. Henning Memorial Volume*, pp. 395–405. London.

Shanzer, D. 1986. "The anonymous *Carmen contra paganos* and the date and identity of the Centonist Proba," *Revue des Etudes Augustiniennes* 32: 232–48.

—— 1994. "The date and identity of the Centonist Proba," *Recherches Augustiniennes* 27: 75–96.

Shapiro, A. 1994. *Myth into Art: Poet and Painter in Classical Greece*. London and New York.

Sharrock, A. 2002. "Gender and sexuality," in P. Hardie (ed.) *The Cambridge Companion to Ovid*, pp. 95–107. Cambridge.

Shea, G. W. 1997. *The Poems of Alcimus Ecdicius Avitus: Translation and Introduction*. Tempe, AZ.

Sherratt, A., and S. Sherratt. 1998. "Small worlds: interaction and identity in the ancient Mediterranean," in E. H. Cline and D. H. Cline (eds.) *The Aegean and the Orient in the Second Millennium*. Aegaeum 18, pp. 329–42. Liège and Austin.

Sherratt, S. 1990. " 'Reading the texts': archaeology and the Homeric question," *Antiquity* 64: 807–24.

—— 1996. "With us but not of us: the role of Crete in Homeric epic," in D. Evely, I. S. Lemos, and S. Sherratt (eds.) *Minotaur and Centaur: Studies in the Archaeology of Crete and Euboea Presented to Mervyn Popham*. British Archaeological Reports, International Series 638, pp. 87–99. Oxford.

—— 2003. "Visible writing: questions of script and identity in early Iron Age Greece and Cyprus," *Oxford Journal of Archaeology* 22: 225–42.

Sherratt, S., and A. Sherratt. 1993. "The growth of the Mediterranean economy in the early first millennium BC," *World Archaeology* 24/3: 361–78.

Shields, J. C. 2001. *The American Aeneas: Classical Origins of the American Self.* Knoxville, TN.

Shorrock, R. E. C. 2001. *The Challenge of Epic: Allusive Engagement in the Dionysiaca of Nonnus.* Mnemosyne Supplements 210. Leiden.

—— 2003. "The artful mythographer: Roberto Calasso and *The Marriage of Cadmus and Harmony*," *Arion* 11/2: 83–99.

Shulman, D. D. 1986. "Battle as metaphor in Tamil folk and classical tradition," in S. H. Blackburn and A. K. Ramanujan (eds.) *Another Harmony: New Essays on the Folklore of India*, pp. 105–30. Berkeley.

Sideras, A. 1971. *Aeschylus Homericus.* Göttingen.

Siegelová, J. 1971. *Appu-Märchen und Ḥedammu-Mythus.* Wiesbaden.

Sigerson, G. 1922. *The Easter Song Being the First Epic of Christendom.* Dublin.

Sihvola, J. 1989. *Decay, Progress, the Good Life?: Hesiod and Protagoras on the Development of Culture.* Helsinki.

Siikala, A.-L. 2000. "Generic models, entextualization, and creativity: epic tradition on the southern Cook Islands," in Honko 2000b: 343–69.

Silberman, N. A. 1982. *Digging for God and Country: Exploration, Archaeology and the Secret Struggle for the Holy Land, 1799–1917.* New York.

Simonsuuri, K. 1979. *Homer's Original Genius: Eighteenth-Century Notions of the Early Greek Epic (1688–1798).* Cambridge.

Sims-Williams, N. 1976. "The Sogdian fragments of the British Library," *Indo-Iranian Journal* 18: 43–82.

Singer, I. 1999. "A political history of Ugarit," In Watson and Wyatt 1999: 603–733.

—— 2002. *Hittite Prayers.* Atlanta.

—— 2003. "The Great Scribe Taki-Šarruma," in G. Beckman, R. Beal, and G. McMahon (eds.) *Hittite Studies in Honor of Harry A. Hoffner, Jr. on the Occasion of His 65th Birthday*, pp. 341–48. Winona Lake, IN.

Singerman, J. E. 1986. *Under Clouds of Poesy: Poetry and Truth in French and English Reworkings of the* Aeneid, *1160–1513.* New York.

Sinn, U. 1979. *Die Homerischen Becher.* Berlin.

Sinos, D. S. 1980. *Achilles, Patroklos, and the Meaning of Philos.* Innsbrucker Beiträge zur Sprachwissenschaft 29. Innsbruck.

Sjoestedt, M.-L. 1940. *Dieux et héros des Celtes.* Paris.

Skendi, S. 1954. *Albanian and South Slavic Oral Epic Poetry.* Philadelphia. Repr. 1969, New York.

—— 1980. *Balkan Cultural Studies.* East European Monographs 72. New York.

Skjærvø, P. O. 1998a. "Eastern Iranian epic traditions I: Siyâvaš and Kunâla," in Jasanoff et al. 1998: 645–58.

—— 1998b. "Eastern Iranian epic traditions II: Rostam and Bhîṣma," *Acta Orientalia Academiae Scientiarum Hungaricae* 51: 159–70.

Sklenar, R. J. 2003. *The Taste for Nothingness: A Study of Virtus and Related Themes in Lucan's Bellum civile.* Ann Arbor, MI.

Skutsch, O. (ed.) 1972. *Ennius.* Entretiens sur l'antiquité classique 17. Vandoeuvres-Geneva.

—— (ed.) 1985. *The Annals of Quintus Ennius.* Oxford.

Slatkin, L. M. 1987. "Genre and generation in the *Odyssey*," METIS: *Revue d'anthropologie du monde grec ancien* 2: 259–68.

—— 1991. *The Power of Thetis: Allusion and Interpretation in the Iliad.* Berkeley and Los Angeles.

—— 1996. "Composition by theme and the *mêtis* of the *Odyssey*," in S. L. Schein (ed.) *Reading the Odyssey*, pp. 223–37. Princeton, NJ.

Slavitt, D. R. (trans.) 1994. *The Metamorphoses of Ovid.* Baltimore.

—— (trans.) 1997. *Broken Columns: Two Roman Epic Fragments.* Philadelphia.

—— (trans.) 1999. *The Voyage of the Argo. The Argonautica of Gaius Valerius Flaccus.* Baltimore and London.

Slyomovics, S. 1987. *The Merchant of Art: An Egyptian Hilali Oral Epic Poet in Performance.* Berkeley.

Smith, C. F. 1900. "Traces of epic usage in Thucydides," *Transactions of the American Philological Association* 31: 69–81.

Smith, J. D. 1977. "The singer or the song? A reassessment of Lord's 'Oral Theory'," *Man*, n.s. 12: 141–53.

——— 1979. "Metre and text in Western India," *Bulletin of the School of Oriental and African Studies* 62: 347–57.

——— 1980. "Old Indian: the two Sanskrit epics," in Hatto and Hainsworth 1980: vol. 1, 48–78.

——— 1989. "Scapegoats of the gods: the ideology of the Indian epics," in Blackburn et al. 1989: 176–94.

——— 1990. "Worlds apart: orality, literacy, and the Rajasthani folk-*Mahâbhârata*," *Oral Tradition* 5: 3–19.

——— 1991. *The Epic of Pabuji: A Study, Transcription, and Translation.* Cambridge.

Smith, M. 1976. *Prudentius' Psychomachia: A Reexamination.* Princeton, NJ.

Smith, M. F. (trans.) 2001. *Lucretius: On the Nature of Things.* Indianapolis and Cambridge.

Smith, M. S. 1986. "Interpreting the Baal cycle," *Ugarit-Forschungen* 18: 313–39.

——— 1994. *The Ugaritic Baal Cycle*, vol. 1: *Introduction with Text, Translation and Commentary of KTU 1.1–1.2.* Supplements to *Vetus Testamentum* 55. Leiden.

——— 2001. *The Origins of Biblical Monotheism.* Oxford.

Smith, W. B., and W. Miller (trans.) 1944. *The Iliad of Homer: A Line for Line Translation in Dactylic Hexameters.* New York.

Smolak, K. 2001. "Die *Psychomachie* des Prudentius als historisches Epos," in M. Salvadore (ed.) *La poesia tardoantica e medievale*, pp. 125–48. Alessandria.

Snodgrass, A. 1971. *The Dark Age of Greece.* Edinburgh.

——— 1974. "An historical Homeric society?", *Journal of Hellenic Studies* 94: 114–25.

——— 1980. *Archaic Greece: The Age of Experiment.* London.

——— 1987. *An Archaeology of Greece: The Present State and Future Scope of a Discipline.* Sather Classical Lectures 53. Berkeley.

——— 1998. *Homer and the Artists: Text and Picture in Early Greek Art.* Cambridge.

Snyder, J. M. 1983. "The warp and woof of the universe in Lucretius' *De rerum natura*," *Illinois Classical Studies* 8: 37–43.

Solmsen, F. 1949. *Hesiod and Aeschylus.* Cornell Studies in Classical Philology. Ithaca, NY.

Solodow, J. B. 1988. *The World of Ovid's Metamorphoses.* Chapel Hill, NC.

Solomon, J. (ed.) 1994. *Apollo: Origins and Influences.* Tucson, AZ.

Sommer, M. 2000. *Europas Ahnen: Ursprünge des Politischen bei den Phönikern.* Darmstadt.

Soysal, O. 1987. "KUB XXXI 4 + KBo III 41 und 40 (Die Puḫanu-Chronik): Zum Thronstreit Ḫattušilis I," *Hethitica* 7: 173–253.

——— 1988. "Einige Überlegungen zu KBo III 60," *Vicino Oriente* 7: 107–28.

——— 1999. "Beiträge zur althethitischen Geschichte: Ergänzende Bemerkungen zur Puhanu-Chronik und zum Menschenfresser-text," *Hethitica* 14: 109–45.

Spalinger, A. J. 2002. *The Transformation of an Ancient Egyptian Narrative: P. Sallier III and the Battle of Kadesh.* Göttinger Orientforschungen 4; Ägypten 40. Wiesbaden.

Spaltenstein, F. 1986. *Commentaire de Punica de Silius Italicus: Livres 1 à 8.* Geneva.

——— 1990. *Commentaire de Punica de Silius Italicus: Livres 9 à 17.* Geneva.

Speiser, E. A. 1950. "The Epic of Gilgamesh," in J. B. Pritchard (ed.) *Ancient Near Eastern Texts Relating to the Old Testament*, pp. 72–99. Princeton, NJ.

Spence, S. (ed.) 2001. *Poets and Critics Read Vergil.* New Haven, CT.

Springer, C. 1988. *The Gospel as Epic in Late Antiquity: The Paschale Carmen of Sedulius.* Leiden.

Stafford, F. 1996. "Introduction: the Ossianic poems of James Macpherson," in Gaskill 1996: v–xxi.

Stahl, H.-P. (ed.) 1998. *Vergil's Aeneid: Augustan Epic and Political Context.* London.

Stanford, W. B. (ed.) 1963 [1954]. *The Ulysses Theme: A Study in the Adaptability of a Traditional Hero.* Oxford. Repr. 1991.

——— (ed.) 1967. *The Odyssey of Homer*, 2nd edn. New York and London.

Starke, F. 1997. "Troia im Kontext des historisch-politischen und sprachlichen Umfeldes Kleinasiens im 2. Jahrtausend," *Studia Troica* 7: 447–87.

Starr, R. J. 1991. "Explaining Dido to your son: Tiberius Claudius Donatus on Vergil's Dido," *Classical Journal* 87: 25–34.

Steinby, E. M. 1996. *Lexicon Topographicum Urbis Romae*, vol. 3. Rome.

Steiner, G. 1992 [1975]. *After Babel: Aspects of Language and Translation*, 2nd edn. Oxford.

Steiner, R. C., and C. F. Nims. 1985. "Ashurbanipal and Shamash-shum-ukin: a tale of two brothers from the Aramaic text in demotic script," *Revue biblique* 92: 60–81.

Stephens, S. 2002. *Seeing Double: Intercultural Poetics in Ptolemaic Alexandria*. Berkeley.

Stephens, S., and B. Acosta-Hughes. 2002. "Rereading Callimachus' *Aetia* Fragment 1," *Classical Philology* 97: 238–55.

Stock, B. 1983. *The Implications of Literacy*. Princeton, NJ.

Stone, R. M. 1988. *Dried Millet Breaking: Time, Words, and Song in the Woi Epic of the Kpelle*. Bloomington, IN.

Strasburger, H. 1972. *Homer und die Geschichtsschreibung*. Sitzungsberichte der Heidelberger Akademie der Wissenschaften, Jahrgang 1972, 1. Heidelberg. Repr. 1982 in W. Schmitthenner and R. Zoepffel (eds.) *Studien zur Alten Geschichte*. Collectanea 42, vol. 2, pp. 1057–97. Hildesheim.

Strunk, K. 1982. "'Vater Himmel' – Tradition und Wandel einer sakralsprachlichen Formel," in J. Tischler (ed.) *Serta Indogermanica: Festschrift für Günter Neumann zum 60. Geburtstag*, pp. 427–38. Innsbruck.

Suerbaum, W. 1968. *Untersuchungen zur Selbstdarstellung älterer römischer Dichter*. Spudasmata 19. Hildesheim.

—— 1980. "Hundert Jahre Vergil-Forschung: Eine systematische Arbeitsbibliographie mit besonderer Berücksichtigung der 'Aeneis'," in *Aufstieg und Niedergang der römischen Welt*, II.31.1: 3–358; updated and condensed 1999 in *Vergils Aeneis: Epos zwischen Geschichte und Gegenwart*, pp. 385–410. Stuttgart.

—— (ed.) 2002. *Die archaische Literatur von den Anfängen bis Sullas Tod*. Handbuch der lateinischen Literatur der Antike, vol. 1. Munich.

Sullivan, J. P. 1982. "Petronius' *Bellum civile* and *Lucan's Pharsalia*: a political reconsideration," in J.-M. Croisille and P.-M. Fauchère (eds.) *Neronia 1977: Actes du 2e Colloque de la Société internationale des études néroniennes (Clermont-Ferrand, 27–28 mai 1977)*, pp. 151–5. Clermont-Ferrand.

—— 1985. *Literature and Politics in the Age of Nero*. Ithaca, NY.

Summers, W. C. 1894. *A Study of the Argonautica of Valerius Flaccus*. Cambridge.

Suzuki, M. 1989. *Metamorphoses of Helen: Authority, Difference, and the Epic*. Ithaca, NY.

Svenbro, J. 1975. "Sappho and Diomedes: some notes on Sappho 1 LP and the epic," *Museum Philologum Londiniense* 1: 37–46.

Swain, S., and M. Edwards (eds.) 2004. *Approaching Late Antiquity: The Transformation from Early to Late Empire*. Oxford.

Swanson, R. A. 1957. "Easter poem," *Classical Journal* 52: 289–97.

Syme, R. 1958. *Tacitus*. Oxford.

—— 1978. *History in Ovid*. Oxford.

Symington, D. 1991. "Late Bronze Age writing-boards and their uses: textual evidence from Anatolia and Syria," *Anatolian Studies* 41: 111–23.

Taisne, A.-M. 1994. *L'Esthétique de Stace: La peinture des correspondences*. Paris.

Talmon, S. 1981. "Did there exist a biblical national epic?," in *Proceedings of the Seventh World Congress of Jewish Studies*, vol. 2: *Studies in the Bible and the Ancient Near East*, pp. 41B61. Jerusalem.

Tandy, D. W., and W. C. Neale. 1996. *Hesiod's* Works and Days: *A Translation and Commentary for the Social Sciences*. Berkeley.

Tanner, M. 1993. *The Last Descendant of Aeneas: The Hapsburgs and the Mythic Image of the Emperor*. New Haven, CT.

Taplin, O. 1992. *Homeric Soundings: The Shaping of the Iliad*. Oxford.

Taqizâda, S. H. 1944. "Shâhnâma o Ferdowsi," in *Hazâra-ye Ferdowsi*, pp. 17–107. Tehran.

Tarrant, R. J. 1982. "Editing Ovid's *Metamorphoses*: problems and possibilities," *Classical Philology* 77: 342–60.

—— 1995. "Classical Latin literature," in D. C. Greetham (ed.) *Scholarly Editing: A Guide to Research*, pp. 95–148. New York.

—— 2004. *P. Ovidi Nasonis Metamorphoses*. Oxford.

Tarzia, W. 1989. "The hoarding ritual in Germanic epic tradition," *Journal of Folklore Research* 26/2: 99–121.

Tavadia, J. C. 1950. "A didactic poem in Zoroastrian Pahlavi," *Indo-Iranian Studies* 1: 86–95.

—— 1955. "A rhymed ballad in Pahlavi," *Journal of the Royal Asiatic Society* (for 1955): 29–36.

Taylor, L. R. 1931. *The Divinity of the Roman Emperor.* Philological Monographs 1. Middletown.

Tedlock, D. 1983. *The Spoken Word and the Work of Interpretation.* Philadelphia.

Thalmann, W. G. 1984. *Conventions of Form and Thought in Early Greek Epic Poetry.* Baltimore.

—— 1992. *The Odyssey: An Epic of Return.* Boston.

—— 1998. *The Swineherd and the Bow: Representations of Class in the* Odyssey. Ithaca, NY.

Theodorakopoulos, E. 1999. "Closure and transformation in Ovid's *Metamorphoses*," in Hardie et al. 1999: 142–61.

Thiel, K. 1993. *Erzählung und Beschreibung in den 'Argonautika' des Apollonios Rhodios: Ein Beitrag zur Poetik des hellenistischen Epos.* Palingenesia 45. Stuttgart.

Thomas, R. 1989. *Oral Tradition and Written Record in Classical Athens.* Cambridge.

Thomas, R. F. 1982. "The Stoic landscape of Lucan 9," in R. F. Thomas, *Lands and Peoples in Roman Poetry: The Ethnographical Tradition*, Proceedings of the Cambridge Philosophical Society, Supplementary vol. 7, pp. 108–23. Cambridge.

—— 1999. *Reading Virgil and His Texts.* Ann Arbor, MI.

—— 2001. *Virgil and the Augustan Reception.* Cambridge, MA.

Thompson, D. P. 2003. *The Trojan War: Literature and Legends from the Bronze Age to the Present.* Jefferson, NC.

Thompson, L., and R. T. Bruère. 1968. "Lucan's use of Vergilian reminiscence," *Classical Philology* 63: 1–21.

Thompson, S. 1955–8. *Motif-index of Folk-literature: A Classification of Narrative Elements in Folktales, Ballads, Myths, Fables, Mediaeval Romances, Exempla, Fabliaux, Jest-books, and Local Legends*, 6 vols, rev. edn. Bloomington, IN.

Thomson, H. J. 1949. *Prudentius*, vol. 1. Cambridge, MA.

Tigay, J. H. 1982. *The Evolution of the Gilgamesh Epic.* Philadelphia. Repr. 2002, Wauconda, IL.

Tinney, S, 1995. "A new look at Naram-Sin and the 'Great Rebellion'," *Journal of Cuneiform Studies* 47: 1–14.

Tissol, G. 1997. *The Face of Nature.* Princeton, NJ.

Todorov, T. 1990. *Genres in Discourse*, trans. C. Porter. Cambridge.

Toohey, P. 1996. *Epic Lessons: An Introduction to Ancient Didactic Poetry.* London and New York.

Torres Guerra, José B. 1995. *La Tebaida homérica como fuente de Ilíada y Odisea.* Madrid.

Tortorici, E. 1996. "Ianus Geminus, Aedes" and "Ianus, Imus, Medius, Summus," in E. M. Steinby (ed.), *Lexicon Topographicum Urbis Romae*, vol. 3, pp. 92–4. Rome.

Tournay, R. J., and A. Shaffer. 1994. *L'Épopée de Gilgamesh.* Littératures anciennes du Proche-Orient 15. Paris.

Toury, G. 1995. *Descriptive Translation Studies and Beyond.* Amsterdam.

Traill, D. 1995. *Schliemann of Troy: Treasure and Deceit.* London.

Trevelyan, H. 1942. *Goethe and the Greeks.* Cambridge.

Troia 2001. *Troia: Traum und Wirklichkeit.* Exhibition catalogue. Stuttgart.

Trout, D. 1999. *Paulinus of Nola: Life, Letters, and Poems.* Berkeley.

TUAT. Kaiser, O. (ed.) 1982–2001. *Texte aus der Umwelt des Alten Testaments.* Gütersloh.

Tudeau-Clayton, M. 1998. *Jonson, Shakespeare and Early Modern Virgil.* Cambridge.

Turner, E. G. 1968. *Greek Papyri.* Oxford. 2nd edn. 1980.

—— 1971. *Greek Manuscripts of the Ancient World.* Oxford. 2nd edn. 1987.

—— 1977. *The Typology of the Early Codex.* Philadelphia.

Uchitel, A. 1999. "Local versus general history in Old Hittite historiography," in C. S. Kraus (ed.), *The Limits of Historiography: Genre and Narrative in Ancient Historical Texts*, pp. 55–67. Leiden.

Ulf, C. 1990. *Die homerische Gesellschaft.* Munich.

—— (ed.) 1996. *Wege zur Genese griechischer Identität.* Berlin.

—— (ed.) 2003a. *Der neue Streit um Troia: Eine Bilanz.* Munich.

—— 2003b. "Was ist und was will 'Heldenepik': Bewahrung der Vergangenheit oder Orientierung für Gegenwart und Zukunft?", in Ulf 2003a: 262–84.

Ünal, Ahmet. 1986. "Das Motiv der Kindesaussetzung in den altanatolischen Literaturen," in K. Hecker and W. Sommefeld (eds.), *Keilschriftliche Literaturen: Ausgewählte Vorträge der XXXII. Rencontre Assyriologique Internationale*, pp. 129–36. Berlin.

Underwood, S. 1998. *English Translators of Homer from George Chapman to Christopher Logue*. Plymouth.

Ungern-Sternberg, J. von. 1988. "Überlegungen zur frühen römischen Überlieferung im Lichte der Oral-Tradition-Forschung," in Ungern-Sternberg and Reinau 1988: 237–65.

Ungern-Sternberg, J. von, and H. Reinau (eds.), 1988. *Vergangenheit in mündlicher Überlieferung*. Stuttgart.

Unvala, J. M. (ed.) 1923. "*Drakht i Asurik*," *Bulletin of the School of Oriental and African Studies* 2: 637–78.

Valverde Sánchez, M. 1989. *El aition en las Argonáuticas de Apolonio de Rodas*. Murcia.

Van Brock, N. 1959. "Substitution rituelle," *Revue Hittite et Asianique* 65: 117–46.

Vance, E. 1970. *Reading the Song of Roland*. Englewood Cliffs, NJ.

Van Dam, R. 1993. *Saints and Their Miracles in Late Antique Gaul*. Princeton, NJ.

van den Hout, T. 1995. "Khattushili, King of the Hittites," in J. Sasson 1995: 1107–20.

—— 2002. "Another view of Hittite literature," in S. de Martino and F. P. Daddi (eds.), *Anatolia Antica: Studi in memoria di Fiorella Imparati*, pp. 857–78. Florence.

van der Laan, P. W. A. T. 1993. "Imitation créative dans le *Carmen Paschale* de Sédulius," in J. Den Boeft and A. Hilhorst (eds.), *Early Christian Poetry: A Collection of Essays*, pp. 135–66. Leiden.

van der Merwe, C. H. J. 1999. "The elusive biblical Hebrew term WYHY: a perspective in terms of its syntax, semantics, and pragmatics in 1 Samuel," *Hebrew Studies* 40: 83–114.

van der Mieroop, M. 2000. "Sargon of Agade and his successors in Anatolia," *Studi micenei ed egeo-anatolici* 42: 133–59.

van der Toorn, K., B. Becking, and P. W. van der Horst (eds.) 1995. *Dictionary of Deities and Demons in the Bible*. Leiden.

van Nortwick, T. 1992. *Somewhere I Have Never Traveled: The Second Self and the Hero's Journey in Ancient Epic*. New York.

Vansina, J. 1985. *Oral Tradition as History*. London and Madison, WI.

Vanstiphout, H. L. J. 1992. "Repetition and structure in the Aratta cycle: their relevance for the orality debate," in Vogelzang and Vanstiphout 1992: 247–64.

—— 1995. "Memory and literacy in ancient western Asia," in J. Sasson 1995: 2181–96.

—— 1998. "Reflections on the dream of Lugalbanda: a typological and interpretive analysis of LH 322–365," in J. Prosecky (ed.), *Intellectual Life in the Ancient Near East: Papers Presented at the 43rd Rencontre assyriologique internationale, Prague, July 1–5, 1996*, pp. 397–412. Prague.

—— 2002. "*Sanctus* Lugalbanda," in T. Abusch (ed.), *Riches Hidden in Secret Places: Ancient Near Eastern Studies in Memory of Thorkild Jacobsen*, pp. 259–89. Winona Lake, MN.

—— 2003: *Epics of the Sumerian Kings: The Matter of Aratta*. Writings from the Ancient World 20. Atlanta. Repr. 2004, Leiden.

Van Wees, H. 1992. *Status Warriors: War, Violence and Society in Homer and History*. Amsterdam.

Veenhof, R. (ed.) 1986. *Cuneiform Archives and Libraries*. Leiden.

Vendryes, J. 1937. "Antoine Meillet," *Bulletin de la Société de Linguistique de Paris* 38: 1–42.

Venini, P. 1969. "Silio Italico e il mito Tebano," *Rendiconti dell'Istituto Lombardo* 103: 778–83.

—— 1971. "Sulla struttura delle *Argonautiche* di Valerio Flacco," *Rivista di Istituto Lombardo* 105: 597–620.

Venuti, L. (ed.) 1992. *Rethinking Translation: Discourse, Subjectivity, Ideology*. New York.

—— 1995. *The Translator's Invisibility: A History of Translation*. New York.

—— 1998. *The Scandals of Translation: Towards an Ethics of Difference*. New York.

—— (ed.) 2000. *The Translation Studies Reader*. London.

Verdenius, W. J. 1962. "Aufbau und Absicht der Erga," in *Hésiode et son influence, Entretiens sur l'antiquité classique* 7: 111–59.

—— 1985. *A Commentary on Hesiod: "Works and Days," vv. 1–382*. Mnemosyne Supplements 86. Leiden.

Vermeule, E. 1979. *Aspects of Death in Early Greek Art and Pottery*. Sather Classical Lectures 46. Berkeley.

—— 1986. "Priam's castle blazing," in M. Mellink (ed.) *Troy and the Trojan War*, pp. 77–92. Bryn Mawr, PA.

—— 1987. "Baby Aigisthos and the Bronze Age," *Proceedings of the Cambridge Philological Society* 213: 122–152.

Vernant, J.-P. 1971. "Mètis et les mythes de souveraineté," *Revue de l'Histoire des Religions* 180: 29–76.

—— 1983. *Myth and Thought Among the Greeks*. London.

—— 1988. *Myth and Society in Ancient Greece*, trans. J. Lloyd. New York.

—— 1991. *Mortals and Immortals: Collected Essays*, ed. F. Zeitlin, trans. A. Szegedy-Maszak. Princeton, NJ.

Vessey, D. W. T. C. 1973. *Statius and the Thebaid*. Cambridge.

—— 1974a. "Pliny, Martial and Silius Italicus," *Hermes* 102: 109–16.

—— 1974b. "Silius Italicus on the fall of Saguntum," *Classical Philology* 69: 28–36.

—— 1975. "Silius Italicus: the shield of Hannibal," *American Journal of Philology* 96: 391–405.

—— 1982. "The dupe of destiny: Hannibal in Silius, *Punica* III," *Classical Journal* 77: 320–35.

Vian, F. 1954. "Les comparaisons de Quintus de Smyrne," *Revue de Philologie* 28: 30–51, 235–43.

—— 1959a. *Histoire de la tradition manuscrite de Quintus de Smyrne*. Paris.

—— 1959b. *Recherches sur les Posthomerica de Quintus de Smyrne*. Paris.

—— 1963. *Quintus de Smyrne, la Suite d'Homère, livres I–IV*. Paris.

—— 1966. *Quintus de Smyrne, la Suite d'Homère, livres V–IX*. Paris.

—— 1969. *Quintus de Smyrne, la Suite d'Homère, livres X–XIV*. Paris.

—— 1976. *Nonnos de Panopolis, Les Dionysiaques: Tome I. Chants I–II*. Paris.

—— 2001. "Echoes and imitations of Apollonius Rhodius in late Greek epic," in T. D. Papanghelis and A. Rengakos (eds.) *A Companion to Apollonius Rhodius*. Mnemosyne Supplements 217, pp. 285–308. Leiden.

Vian, F., and E. Battegay. 1984. *Lexique de Quintus de Smyrne*. Paris.

Vian, F., and E. Delage. 1976–96. *Apollonios de Rhodes, Argonautiques*. Paris.

Vico, G. 1730. *Principi d'una scienza nuova d'intorno alla comune natura della nazioni in questa seconda impressione con più propia maniera condotti, e di molto accresciuti*. Naples.

Vidal-Naquet, P. 1986. *The Black Hunter: Forms of Thought and Forms of Society in the Greek World*. Baltimore.

—— 1996. "Land and sacrifice in the *Odyssey*," in S. L. Schein (ed.) *Reading the Odyssey*. Princeton, NJ.

Vielle, C. 1996. *Le Mytho-cycle héroïque dans l'aire indo-européenne: Correspondances et transformations helléno-aryennes*. Louvain.

Villena, Enrique de. 1994. *Obras completas*, vol. 2: *Traducción y glosas de la Eneida, libros 1–3*. Biblioteca Castro. Madrid.

Villoison, J. B. G., de (ed.) 1788. *Homeri Ilias ad veteris codicis Veneti fidem recensita*. Venice.

Virolleaud, C. 1936. *La Légende Phénicienne de Danel: Texte Cunéiforme Alphabétique avec Transcription et Commentaire*. Bibliothèque Archéologique et Historique 21. Mission de Ras Shamra, 1. Paris.

Visicato, G. 2000. *The Power of Writing: The Early Scribes of Mesopotamia*. Bethesda, MD.

Vleeming, S. P., and J. W. Wesselius. 1985. *Studies in Papyrus Amherst 63*. Amsterdam.

Vogelzang, M. E., and H. L. J. Vanstiphout (eds.) 1992. *Mesopotamian Epic Literature: Oral or Aural?* Lewiston, NY.

—— and —— (eds.) 1996. *Mesopotamian Poetic Language: Sumerian and Akkadian*. Cuneiform Monographs 6. Proceedings of the Groningen Group for the Study of Mesopotamian Literature 2. Groningen.

Vogt-Spira, G. (ed.) 1990. *Strukturen der Mündlichkeit in der römischen Literatur*. Tübingen.

Volk, Katharina. 2002a. "*Kléos áphthiton* revisited," *Classical Philology* 97: 61–8.

—— 2002b. *The Poetics of Latin Didactic: Lucretius, Vergil, Ovid, Manilius*. Oxford.

Volk, Konrad. 1995. *Inanna und Šukaletuda: zur historisch-politischen Deutung eines sumerischen Literaturwerkes*. Wiesbaden.

von Albrecht, M. 1964. *Silius Italicus: Freiheit und Gebundenheit römischer Epik*. Amsterdam.

—— 1970. "Der Dichter Lucan und die epische Tradition," *Lucain: Fondation Hardt, Entretiens sur l'antiquité classique* 15: 267–308.

—— 1999. *Roman Epic: An Interpretive Introduction*. Leiden.

von Albrecht, M. 2000. *Das Buch der Verwandlungen.* Dusseldorf.

von Haehling, R. 1989. *Zeitbezüge des T. Livius in der ersten Dekade seines Geschichtswerkes.* Stuttgart.

von See, K. 1978. "Was ist Heldendichtung?," in *Europäische Heldendichtung,* pp. 1–38. Darmstadt.

von Soden, W. 1953. "Das Problem der zeitlichen Einordnung akkadischer Literaturwerke," *Mitteilungen der Deutschen Orient-Gesellschaft* 85: 14–26.

von Veldeke, H. 1986. *Eneasroman.* Stuttgart.

von Weiher, E. 1980. "Ein Fragment der 5. Tafel des Gilgameš-Epos aus Uruk," *Baghdader Mitteilungen* 11: 106–19.

—— 1983. *Spätbabylonische Texte aus Uruk.* Part II, Ausgrabungen der deutschen Forschungsgemeinschaft in Uruk-Warka, 10, no. 3. Berlin.

Vullers, A. 1855, 1864. *Lexicon Persico-Latinum,* 2 vols. Bonn.

Vulpe, N. 1994. "Irony and the unity of the Gilgamesh epic," *Journal of Near Eastern Studies* 53: 275–83.

Wace, A. J. B., and F. H. Stubbings (eds.) 1962. *A Companion to Homer.* London.

Wackernagel, J. 1970. *Sprachliche Untersuchungen zu Homer.* Göttingen.

Wadley, S. S. 1989. "Choosing a path: performance strategies in a North Indian epic," in Blackburn et al. 1989: 79–101.

—— 1998. "Creating a modern epic: oral and written versions of the Hindi epic Dhola," in L. Honko, J. Handoo, and J. M. Foley (eds.) *The Epic: Oral and Written,* pp. 151–60. Mysore.

Walcot, P. 1958. "Hesiod's hymns to the Muses, Aphrodite, Styx and Hecate," *Symbolae Osloensis* 34: 5–14.

—— 1966. *Hesiod and the Near East.* Cardiff.

—— 1970. *Greek Peasants, Ancient and Modern: A Comparison of Social and Moral Values.* Manchester.

Walker, C. B. F. 1987. *Cuneiform.* London.

Wallace, M. V. T. 1968. "Some aspects of time in the *Punica* of Silius Italicus," *Classical World* 62: 83–93.

Wallach, B. P. 1976. *Lucretius and the Diatribe against the Fear of Death.* Leiden.

Wallies, M. 1909. *Commentaria in Aristotelem Graeca.* Berlin.

Waltz, P. 1906. *Hésiode et son poème moral.* Bibliothèque des Universités du Midi 12. Bordeaux.

Wang, C. H. 1988. *From Ritual to Allegory: Seven Essays in Early Chinese Poetry.* Hong Kong.

Warmington, E. H. (ed.) 1961. *Remains of Old Latin,* vol. 1 (Ennius and Caecilius), vol. 2 (Livius, Naevius, Pacuvius, Accius). Cambridge, MA. First edn. 1936, Loeb Classical Library.

Warner, A. G., and E. Warner (trans.) 1905–25. *The Shahnama of Firdausí I–X.* London.

Wasserman, N. 2003. *Style and Form in Old-Babylonian Literary Texts.* Cuneiform Monographs 27. Leiden.

Waswo, R. 1997. *The Founding Legend of Western Civilization: From Virgil to Vietnam.* Hanover.

Watkins, C. 1986. "The language of the Trojans," in M. J. Mellink (ed.) *Troy and the Trojan War,* pp. 45–68. Bryn Mawr.

—— 1987. "Linguistic and archaeological light on some Homeric formulas," in S. N. Skomal and E. C. Polomé (eds.) *Proto-Indo-European: The Archaeology of a Linguistic Problem. Studies in Honor of Marija Gimbutas,* pp. 286–98. Washington, DC.

—— 1992. "Le Dragon hittite Illuyankas et le géant grec Typhôeus," *Comptes Rendus de l'Académie des Inscriptions et Belles-Lettres* [for 1992]: 319–30.

—— 1994. *Selected Writings,* 2 vols., ed. L. Oliver. Innsbruck. Originally published 1986.

—— 1995. *How to Kill a Dragon: Aspects of Indo-European Poetics.* New York.

—— 1998. "Homer and Hittite revisited," in P. Knox and C. Foss (eds.) *Style and Tradition: Studies in Honor of Wendell Clausen,* pp. 201–11. Stuttgart.

—— 2000a. *The American Heritage Dictionary of Indo-European Roots,* 2nd edn. Boston.

—— 2000b. "L'Anatolie et la Grèce: résonances culturelles, linguistiques et poétiques," *Comptes Rendus de l'Académie des Inscriptions et Belles-Lettres* [2000]: 1143–58.

—— 2000c [publ. 2001]. "A distant Anatolian echo in Pindar: the origin of the aegis again," *Harvard Studies in Classical Philology* 100: 1–14.

—— 2002a. "ΕΠΕΩΝ ΘΕΣΙΣ. Poetic grammar: word order and metrical structure in the Odes of Pindar," in H. Hettrich (ed.) *Indogermanische Syntax: Fragen und Perspektiven*, pp. 319–37. Wiesbaden.

—— 2002b. "Homer and Hittite revisited II," in K. A. Yener and H. A. Hoffner, Jr. (eds.) *Recent Developments in Hittite Archaeology and History: Papers in Memory of Hans G. Güterbock*, pp. 167–76. Winona Lake, IN.

Watkins, J. 1995. *The Specter of Dido: Spenser and Virgilian Epic.* New Haven, CT.

Watson, W. G. E., and N. Wyatt (eds.) 1999. *Handbook of Ugaritic Studies.* Handbuch der Orientalistik 39. Leiden.

Watts, J. W. 1989. "Hnt: an Ugaritic formula of intercession," *Ugarit-Forschungen* 21: 443–9.

Way, A. S. [pseud. "Avia"] (trans.) 1904 [1880]. *The Odyssey of Homer in English Verse*, 3rd edn. London.

—— 1913. *Quintus Smyrnaeus, The Fall of Troy, with an English Translation.* Loeb Classical Library. Cambridge, MA. Repr. 2000.

Weaver, R. 1996. *Divine Grace and Human Agency: A Study of the Semi-Pelagian Controversy.* Macon.

Weidner, E. F. 1939/41. "Studien zur Zeitgeschichte Tukulti-Ninurta I," *Archiv für Orientalforschung* 13: 109–24.

Weinstock, S. 1971. *Divus Julius.* Oxford.

Wendel, C. 1935. *Scholia in Apollonium Rhodium.* Berlin.

—— 1949. *Die griechisch-römische Buchbeschreibung verglichen mit der Vorderen Orients.* Halle.

Wender, D. (trans.) 1973. Theogony *and* Works and Days, *by Hesiod; and Elegies of Theognis.* Harmondsworth.

—— 1978. *The Last Scenes of the Odyssey.* Leiden.

Wente, E. 1995. "The scribes of ancient Egypt," in J. Sasson 1995: 2211–22.

West, D. A. 1969. *The Imagery and Poetry of Lucretius.* Edinburgh.

—— 1970. "Virgilian multiple-correspondence similes and their antecedents," *Philologus* 114: 262–75.

West, M. L. 1966. *Hesiod: "Theogony."* Oxford.

—— 1973a. "Greek Poetry 2000–700 B.C," *Classical Quarterly* 23: 179–92.

—— 1973b. *Textual Criticism and Editorial Technique.* Stuttgart.

—— 1978. *Hesiod: "Works and Days."* Oxford.

—— 1983. *The Orphic Poems.* Oxford.

—— 1985. *The Hesiodic Catalogue of Women: Its Nature, Structure, and Origins.* Oxford.

—— 1988. "The rise of the Greek epic," *Journal of Hellenic Studies* 108: 151–72.

—— 1996. "The Epic Cycle," in S. Hornblower and A. Spawforth (eds.) *Oxford Classical Dictionary*, 3rd edn., p. 531. Oxford.

—— 1997a. "Akkadian poetry: metre and performance," *Iraq* 59: 175–87.

—— 1997b. *The East Face of Helicon: West Asiatic Elements in Greek Poetry and Myth.* Oxford. Repr. 2000.

—— (trans.) 1999. *Hesiod,* Theogony *and* Works and Days. Oxford.

—— 2001. *Studies in the Text and Transmission of the Iliad.* Munich and Leipzig.

—— 2002. " 'Eumelos': a Corinthian epic cycle?," *Journal of Hellenic Studies* 122: 109–33.

—— (ed.) 2003a. *Greek Epic Fragments.* Loeb Classical Library. Cambridge, MA.

—— (ed. and trans.) 2003b. *Homeric Hymns, Homeric Apocrypha, Lives of Homer.* Loeb Classical Library 496. Cambridge, MA.

—— 2003c. "Iliad and Aethiopis," *Classical Quarterly* 53: 1–14.

West, S. 1988. "The transmission of the text," in A. Heubeck, S. West, and J. B. Hainsworth (eds.) *A Commentary on Homer's Odyssey*, vol. 1: *Introduction and Books i–viii*, pp. 33–48. Oxford.

Westenholz, J. G. 1983. "Heroes of Akkad," *Journal of the American Oriental Society* 103: 327–36.

—— 1997. *Legends of the Kings of Akkade.* Winona Lake, IN.

Westenholz, U., and A. Westenholz. 1997. *Gilgamesh. Enuma Elish. Guder og mennesker i oldtidens Babylon.* Illustreret af babylonske kunstnere. Copenhagen.

Wheeler, S. 1999. *A Discourse of Wonders.* Philadelphia.

Whitby, M. 1994. "From Moschus to Nonnus: the evolution of the Nonnian style," in Hopkinson 1994b: 99–155.

Whitby, M. (ed.) 1998. *The Propaganda of Power: The Role of Panegyric in Late Antiquity.* Mnemosyne Supplements 183. Leiden.

White, C. 2000. *Early Christian Latin Poets.* London and New York.

White, P. 1993. *Promised Verse: Poets in the Society of Augustan Rome.* Cambridge.

Whiting, R. M. (ed.) 2001. *Mythology and Mythologies. Methodological Approaches to Intercultural Influences.* Proceedings of the Second Annual Symposium of the Assyrian and Babylonian Intellectual Heritage Project, Paris, France, October 4–7, 1999. Helsinki.

Whitley, J. 1988. "Early states and hero cults: a reappraisal," *Journal of Hellenic Studies* 108: 173–82.

Widdows, P. F. (trans.) 1998. *Lucan: Civil War.* Bloomington, IN.

Wifstrand, A. 1933. *Von Kallimachos zu Nonnos: Metrisch-stilistische Untersuchungen.* Lund.

Wigodsky, M. 1972. *Vergil and Early Latin Poetry.* Hermes Einzelschriften 24. Wiesbaden.

Wijsman, H. J. W. (ed.) 1996. *Valerius Flaccus Argonautica Book V: A Commentary.* Leiden.

—— (ed.) 2000. *Valerius Flaccus, Argonautica, Book VI: A Commentary.* Leiden.

Wikander, S. 1938. *Der arische Männerbund: Studien zur indo-iranischen Sprach und Religionsgeschichte.* Lund.

—— 1950. "Sur le fonds commun indo-iranien des épopées de la Perse et de l'Inde," *La Nouvelle Clio* 1/2: 310–29.

—— 1957. "Nakula et Sahadeva," *Orientalia Suecana* 6: 66–96.

Wilamowitz-Moellendorff, U. von. 1924. *Hellenistische Dichtung in der Zeit des Kallimachos.* Berlin.

Wilcke, C. 1969. *Das Lugalbandaepos.* Wiesbaden.

—— 1971. "Sumerischen Epen," in W. von Einsiedel, G. Woerner, V. Bompiani (eds.) *Kindlers Literaturlexikon*, vol. 6, pp. 2111–15. Zurich.

—— 1975. "Formale Gesichtspunkte in der sumerischen Literatur," in S. J. Lieberman (ed.) *Sumerological Studies in Honor of Thorkild Jacobsen*, pp. 205–316. Chicago.

—— 1977. "Die Anfänge der akkadischen Epen," *Zeitschrift für Assyriologie* 67: 153–216.

—— 1987. "Lugalbanda," *Reallexikon der Assyriologie und vorderasiatischen Archäologie* 7: 117–31.

—— 2000. *Wer Las und Schrieb in Babylonien und Assyrien: Überlegungen zur Literalität im alten Zweistromland.* Bayerischen Akademie der Wissenschaften, philosophische-historischer Klasse, Sitzungsberichte, Jahrgang 2000, Heft 6. Munich.

Wilhelm, G. 1988. "Neue Gilgameš-Fragmente aus Ḫattuša," *Zeitschrift für Assyriologie* 78: 99–121.

—— 1989. *The Hurrians.* Warminster.

Wilkinson, L. P. 1955. *Ovid Recalled.* Cambridge.

Williams, G. 1978. *Change and Decline.* Berkeley.

Williams, R. D. 1967. *Virgil.* Greece and Rome: New Surveys in the Classics 1. Oxford. Repr. with addenda, 1978 and 1988.

—— 1972. *The Aeneid of Virgil: Books 1–6.* Basingstoke and London.

Wimmel, W. 1960. *Kallimachus in Rom.* Wiesbaden.

Winckelmann, J. 1764. *Geschichte der Kunst des Altertums.* Dresden.

Winkler, J. 1990. "Penelope's cunning and Homer's," in *Constraints of Desire: The Anthropology of Sex and Gender in Ancient Greece*, pp. 129–62. New York.

Winter, U. 1983. *Frau und Göttin.* Göttingen.

Wiseman, D. J. 1955. "Assyrian writing-boards," *Iraq* 17: 3–13.

Wiseman, T. P. 1994. *Historiography and Imagination: Eight Essays on Roman Culture.* Exeter.

—— 1995. *Remus: A Roman Myth.* Cambridge.

—— 1998. *Roman Drama and Roman History.* Exeter.

Wistrand, E. K. H. 1956. *Die Chronologie der Punica des Silius Italicus.* Göteborg.

Witke, C. 1971. *Numen Litterarum: The Old and the New in Latin Poetry from Constantine to Gregory the Great.* Leiden.

Wolf, F. A. 1795. *Prolegomena ad Homerum, sive de operum Homericorum prisca et genuina forma variisque mutationibus et probabili ratione emendandi.* Halle.

—— 1985 [1795]. *Prolegomena to Homer*, trans. A. Grafton, G. Most, and J. Zetzel. Princeton, NJ.

Wolff, F. 1935. *Glossar zu Firdousis Schahname.* Berlin.

Wolfram, H. 1988. *A History of the Goths.* Berkeley.

Wood, I. 2001. "Avitus of Vienne, the Augustinian poet," in R. Mathisen and D. Shanzer (eds.) *Society and Culture in Late Antique Gaul: Revisiting the Sources*, pp. 263–77. Aldershot.

Wood, M. 1985. *In Search of the Trojan War*. London.

Wood, R. 1769. *An Essay on the Original Genius of Homer*. London.

Woodard, R. D. 1997. *Greek Writing from Knossos to Homer*. Oxford.

Wray, D. 2000. "Apollonius' masterplot: narrative strategy in 1," in A. Harder, G. Wakker, R. Regtuit (eds.) *Apollonius Rhodius*. Hellenistica Gröningana 4, pp. 239–65. Gröningen.

Wright, D. H. 2001. *The Roman Vergil and the Origins of Medieval Book Design*. Toronto.

Wright, D. P. 2001. *Ritual in Narrative: The Dynamic of Feasting, Mourning and Retaliation in the Ugaritic Tale of Aqhat*. Winona Lake, MN.

Wüstenfeld, F. (ed.) 1858, 1860. *Das Leben Muhammeds nach Muhammed Ibn Ishâk bearbeitet von Abd el-Malik Ibn Hischâm*, 2 vols. Göttingen.

Wyatt, N. 1985. "Killing and cosmogony in Canaanite and biblical thought," *Ugarit-Forschungen* 17: 375–81.

—— 1996. *Myths of Power: A Study of Royal Myth and Ideology in Ugaritic and Biblical Tradition*. Ugaritisch-Biblische Literatur 13. Münster.

—— 1997. "Ilimilku's ideological programme: Ugaritic royal propaganda, and a biblical post-script," *Ugarit-Forschungen* 29: 775–96.

—— 1998. "Arms and the King: the earliest allusions to the *Chaoskampf* motif and their implica-tions for the interpretation of the Ugaritic and biblical traditions," in M. Dietrich and I. Kottsie-per (eds.) *"Und Mose schrieb dieses Lied auf...": Studien zum Alten Testament und zum Alten Orient: Festschrift für O. Loretz zur Vollendung seines 70. Lebensjahres mit Beiträgen von Freunden, Schülern und Kollegen*. Alter Orient und Altes Testament 250, pp. 833–82. Münster.

—— 1999a. "The Aqhat story (KTU 1.17–19)," in Watson and Wyatt 1999: 234–58.

—— 1999b. "Degrees of divinity: mythical and ritual aspects of West Semitic kingship," *Ugarit-Forschungen* 31: 853–87.

—— 2001. "The mythic mind," *Scandinavian Journal of the Old Testament* 15: 3–56.

—— 2002a. "Ilimilku the theologian: the ideological roles of Athtar and Baal in KTU 1.1 and 1.6," in O. Loretz, K. Metzler, and H. Schaudig (eds.) *Ex Mesopotamia et Syria Lux: Festschrift für Manfried Dietrich zu seinem 65. Geburtstag am 6.11.2000*. Alter Orient und Altes Testament, 281, pp. 845–56. Münster. With additional postscript as ch. 14 in N. Wyatt (ed.) *"There's such divinity doth hedge a king": Essays on Royal Ideology in Ugaritic and Old Testament Literature*. SOTS Monograph Series. London. 2005.

—— 2002b. *Religious Texts from Ugarit*, 2nd edn. The Biblical Seminar 53. Sheffield.

—— 2004. " 'Water, water everywhere...': musings on the aqueous myths of the Near East," in D. A. González Blanco and J. P. Vita, eds., *De la tablilla a la inteligencia artificial: Homenaje al Prof. Jesús Luis Cunchillos en su 65 aniversario*, pp. 211–59. Zaragoza.

Wyatt, N., W. G. E. Watson, and Jeffery B. Lloyd. (eds.) 1996. *Ugarit, Religion and Culture: Proceedings of the International Colloquium on Ugarit, Religion and Culture. Edinburgh, July 1994. A Festschrift for J. C. L. Gibson*. Ugaritisch-Biblische Literatur 12. Münster.

Ying, L. 2001. "The bard Jusup Mamay," *Oral Tradition* 16: 222–39.

Young, P. H. 2003. *The Printed Homer: A 3,000 Year Publishing and Translation History of the* Iliad *and* Odyssey. Jefferson, NC and London.

Zanker, G. 1979. "The love theme in Apollonius' *Argonautica*," *Wiener Studien* 13: 52–75.

—— 1988. *The Power of Images in the Age of Augustus*, trans. A. Shapiro. Ann Arbor, MI.

Zeitlin, F. 1996. "Figuring fidelity," in *Playing the Other: Gender and Society in Classical Greek Literature*, pp. 19–52. Chicago.

Zetzel, J. E. G. 1989. "*Romane memento*: justice and judgement in *Aeneid* 6," *Transactions of the American Philological Association* 119: 263–84.

Zhambei G. 2001. "*Bab sgrung*: Tibetan epic singers," in Chao 2001a: 280–93.

Zhirmunsky, V. 1967. "The epic of 'Alpamysh' and the return of Odysseus," *Proceedings of the British Academy* 52: 267–86.

Ziegler, K. 1966. *Das hellenistische Epos: Ein vergessenes Kapitel griechischer Dichtung*. 2, Auflage, mit einem Anhang: Ennius als hellenistischer Epiker. Leipzig. Trans. into Italian and supplemented 1988 by M. Fantuzzi as *L'epos ellenistico: un capitolo dimenticato della poesia greca, con appendice Ennio poeta epico ellenistica*. Bari.

Zimmermann, A. 1891. *Quinti Smyrnaei Posthomericorum libri XIV.* Leipzig. Repr. 1969, Stuttgart.

Ziolkowski, T. 1993. *Virgil and the Moderns.* Princeton, NJ.

Zissos, A. 1999. "Allusion and narrative possibility in the *Argonautica* of Valerius Flaccus," *Classical Philology* 94: 289–301.

—— 2002. "Reading models and the Homeric program in Valerius Flaccus's *Argonautica*," *Helios* 29: 69–96.

Zissos, A., and I. Gildenhard. 1999. "Problems of time in *Metamorphoses* 2," in Hardie et al. 1999: 31–47.

Zorzetti, N. 1980. *La pretesta e il teatro latino arcaico.* Forme materiali e ideologie del mondo antico 14. Naples.

—— 1990. "The *Carmina Convivalia*," in Murray 1990: 289–307.

—— 1991. "Poetry and the ancient city: the case of Rome," *Classical Journal* 86: 311–29.

Zumbach, O. 1955. *Neuerungen in der Sprache der homerischen Hymnen.* Zurich.

Zumthor, P. 1983. *Introduction à la poésie orale.* Paris.

Index